the SEARCH for racial EQUALITY through LAW

FIFTH EDITION, revised printing

William
SHIRLEY

Kendall Hunt
publishing company

These documents are for use of BLR 222 students. These documents have been edited. Omitted material is indicated by an ellipsis (…), although citations, references, and footnotes in the original are ordinarily omitted without indication

Cover image © Shutterstock, Inc.

Kendall Hunt
publishing company

www.kendallhunt.com
Send all inquiries to:
4050 Westmark Drive
Dubuque, IA 52004-1840

CONTENTS

CHAPTER ONE

CHAPTER THREE

Slavery

Themes

- The primacy of positive law and the inability of courts to find a principled basis for ending slavery
- The embedding of slavery in the Constitution and the results thereof
- The authority of states to individually decide for slavery or freedom
- The meaning and effect of slaves as property
- The dilemma of judges caught between law and morality

- Identifying a slave: presumptions and burdens of proof
- Escape from slavery: sojourn, manumission, fugitive—the development of these doctrines and comity
- *Dred Scott*: the ultimate failure of law to solve the conflict between property and humanity, and between slave and free states

---

SOMERSET v. STEWART
Court of King's Bench (1772)
1 Lofft 1; 12 Geo. 3

Easter Term, May 14, 1772

LORD MANSFIELD.—The question is, if the owner had a right to detain the slave, for the sending of him over to be sold in Jamaica. In five or six cases of this nature, I have known it to be accommodated by agreement between the parties: on its first coming before me, I strongly recommended it here. But if the parties will have it decided, we must give our opinion. Compassion will not, on the one hand, nor inconvenience on the other, be to decide; but the law: in which the difficulty will be principally from the inconvenience on both sides. Contract for sale of a slave is good here; the sale is a matter to which the law properly and readily attaches, and will maintain the price according to the agreement. But here the person of the slave himself is immediately the object of enquiry; which makes a very material difference. The now question is, whether any dominion, authority or coercion can be exercised in this country, on a slave according to the American laws? The difficulty of adopting the relation, without adopting it in all its consequences, is indeed extreme; and yet, many of those consequences are absolutely contrary to the municipal law of England. We have no authority to regulate the conditions in which law shall operate. On the other hand, should we think the coercive power cannot be exercised. ... The setting 14,000 or 15,000 men at once free loose by a solemn opinion, is much disagreeable in the effects it threatens. ... Mr. Stewart advances no claim on contract; he rests his whole demand on a right to the negro as slave, and mentions the purpose of detainure to be the sending of him over to be sold in Jamaica. If the parties will have judgment, fiat justitia, ruat coelum, let justice be done whatever the consequence. 50£ a head may not be a high price; then a loss follows to the proprietors of above 700,000£ sterling. How would the law stand with respect to their settlement; their wages? How many actions for any slight coercion by the master? We cannot in any of these points direct; the law must rule us. In these particulars, it may be matter of weighty consideration, what provisions are made or set by law. Mr. Steward may end the question, by discharging or giving freedom to the negro. I did think at first to put the matter to a more solemn way of argument: but ... I do not imagine, after the point has been discussed on both sides so extremely well, any new light could be thrown on the subject. If the parties chuse to refer it to the Common Pleas, they can give them that satisfaction whenever they think fit. An application to Parliament, if the merchants think the question of great commercial concern, is the best, and perhaps the only method of settling the point for the future. The Court is greatly obliged to the gentlemen of the Bar who have spoke on the subject; and by whose care and abilities so much has been effected, that the rule of decision will be reduced to a very easy compass. ... I think it right the matter should stand over. ...

Trinity Term, June 22, 1772.

LORD MANSFIELD.—On the part of Somerset ... I shall recite the return to the writ of habeas corpus, as the ground of our determination; omitting only words of form. The captain of the ship on board of which the negro was taken, makes his return to the writ in terms signifying that there have been, and still are, slaves to a great number in Africa; and that the trade in them is authorized by the laws and opinions of Virginia and Jamaica; that they are goods and chattels; and, as such, saleable and sold. That James Somerset, is a negro of Africa, and long before the return of the

King's writ ... was sold to Charles Steward, Esq. then in Jamaica, and has not been manumitted since; that Mr. Steward, having occasion to transact business, came over hither, with an intention to return; and brought Somerset, to attend and abide with him, and to carry him back as soon as the business should be transacted. That such intention has been, and still continues, and that the negro did remain till the time of his departure, in the service of his master Mr. Steward, and quitted it without his consent; and thereupon, before the return of the King's writ, the said Charles Stewart did commit the slave on board the "Ann and Mary," ... to be kept till he should set sail and then to be taken with him to Jamaica, and sold there as a slave. And this is the cause why he, Captain Knowles ... commander of the above vessel ... did the said negro ... detain; and on which he now renders him to the order of the Court. We pay all due attention to the opinion of Sir Philip Yorke, and Lord Chief Justice Talbot, whereby they pledged themselves to the British planters, for all the legal consequences of slaves coming over to this kingdom or being baptized ... [because] a notion had prevailed, if a negro came over, or became a Christian, he was emancipated, but [this had] no ground in law; that he and Lord Talbot, when Attorney and Solicitor-General, were of opinion, that no such claim for freedom was valid. ... We are so well agreed, that we think there is no occasion of having it argued ... [and] the only question before us is, whether the cause on the return is sufficient? If it is, the negro must be remanded; if it is not, he must be discharged. Accordingly, the return states, that the slave departed and refused to serve; whereupon he was kept, to be sold abroad. So high an act of dominion must be recognized by the law of the country where it is used. The power of a master over his slave has been extremely different, in different countries. The state of slavery is of such a nature, that it is incapable of being introduced on any reasons, moral or political; but only positive law, which preserves its force long after the reasons, occasion, and time itself from whence it was created, is erased from memory: it's so odious, that nothing can be suffered to support it, but positive law. Whatever inconveniences, therefore, may follow from a decision, I cannot say this case is allowed or approved by the law of England; and therefore the black must be discharged.

PATTINSON v. WHITAKER
Michigan Territorial Supreme Court (1807)
1 Blume 414

AUGUSTUS B. WOODWARD, J. At a Session of the Supreme Court Continued and held on friday the twenty third day of October one thousand eight hundred Seven at the house of the Marshall, pursuant to adjournment was present Augustus B. Woodward Chief judge of the territory of Michigan.

The motion of Elijah Brush, Counsel for Richard Pattinson, that a warrant issue to apprehend the bodies of *Jane*, a Mulatto Woman, of about twenty years of age, and *Joseph*, a boy of about eighteen years who are now within this territory, and the lawfull property of the Said Richard Pattinson, was Considered by the Court and was Over ruled. ...

"In the Matter of Richard Pattinson, a Subject of his Britanick Majesty, residing in the town of Sandwich, in the County of Essex, in his Britannic Majesty's province of upper Canada, who moves the Court for a Warrant to apprehend Joseph Quinn, and Jane. ... his Slaves now within this territory."

"This motion has been Supported by the advocates for the applicant on three different grounds: on the principles of the law of nations: on the principles of the Common law, and on the domestic regulations of this Country.

First it is Contended that by the principles of the law of nations where the property of a Subject or Citizen of one, are accidentally found within the territories of the other, that they are on being reclaimed, to be restored to the lawfull proprietor.

Secondly: it is Contended that on the principles of the Common law, it is an injury to the lawfull proprietor of any article to deprive him of, and to withhold from him his property; that an alien equally with a Subject may hold personal property, and is therefore equally injured by the deprivation. ...

Thirdly: it is Contended that both the United States of American and Great Britain recognize Slaves as *property*, and as *personal property* on this Continent, that by the treaty we are bound to respect and protect the Subjects of his Britannic Majesty in the full enjoyment and use of their lawfull property. ...

The first position relative to the law of nations may be, and probably is both Correct and just. ...

Such nations for instance are France and Spain. They are Coterminous nations; and their boundary is a land boundary. They are Separated by the Pyrenean Mountains. If a horse, an ox, a mule, a goat, a Sheep, or other animal, the property of a farmer, or peasant, dwelling on one Side of the boundary Should Stray across the boundary, and be found on the farm or possession of another, dwelling on the other Side of the boundary, they would in all probability be reciprocally restored, and it is Certainly perfectly just that they Should be.

The case of articles of property is however very different from that of *persons*. Those nations, and all the nations of Europe, deny an *obligation* of restoring *persons*. It is not a part of the law of nations. The Murderer, the traitor, the thief, the deserter from Military Service, are all received by other Nations, and they do not hold themselves bound to restore them when they are demanded. If it has been Sometimes done, it has been as a matter of Curtesy from one nation to another. It is regarded as a matter of *favor* not as a matter of *right*.

The principles of the Common law are equally inapplicable to the Cases of *persons*. By the Common law persons cannot be the Subject of property. They can only become So by particular Statute, and every Such Statute is itself unjust, and in Contravention of the rights of human nature. If the right of property can only exist by Statute, the manner of protecting and Sustaining it as a right of property, must be regulated by Statute also, and neither the principles of the law of nations, or of the Common law are Strictly applicable to Cases of this Kind.

On the third position the fact must be admitted, that both the United States of America and Great Britain recognize a *right of property in persons* on this Continent, or in other Words *a State of Slavery*. Great Britain however does not recognize this right within her European dominions, and the United States of America do not recognize it in all parts of their dominions. In two of the american States, those of Massachusetts and Ohio, and in this territory of Michigan, with the exception of the rights of british Setlers, Slavery is not permitted.

Great Britain also does not extend her Curtesy So far as to admit a right of *property* in *persons*, or in other words a *right of Slavery*, even where the right is established by law by other nations and Countries. On the Contrary if a person is by the laws of any other Country a Slave, and Can find his way into her European dominions, She refuses to restore him to the master, and liberates him. The Case of James Somerset decided by Lord Mansfield, and which was the Case of a Slave who had abandoned the Service of a Virginian Master, fully Settles this principles. It has been ever Since Supported, and is Uniformly Considered the law of that Country.

… It Would Seem therefore extremely Singular that She Should ask of others what She is not Willing to give them.

Admitting it then as unquestionable that the principle of the english law, as decided by Lord Mansfield, is *that a right of property cannot exist in the human Species*, it only remains to enquire whether the Same principle is to be received here. …

But I am Compelled here to ask has not my Country, by permitting and Sanctioning a State of internal domestic Slavery, effectually denied me the privilege of Saying what Lord Mansfield did Say in England in the Case of James Somerset, *that a right of property Cannot exist in the human Species*?

In Some parts of the United States, as in Some parts also of the British Dominions, a judicial Character Could not lay down this position. …

But in this part of her dominions my Country does enable me to lay down this position, and to act upon it, with a very Slight exception, and that entirely in favor of british Setlers, by virtue of a Special treaty. In other respects her will is THERE SHALL BE NEITHER SLAVERY, NOR INVOLUNTARY SERVITUDES IN THIS TERRITORY. *I am therefore bound to Say, and do Say, that a right of property in the human Species Cannot exist in this territory, excepting as to persons in the actual possession of british Setlers within this territory on the eleventh day of July one thousand Seven hundred Ninety Six, and that every other man coming into this territory is by the law of the land a freeman, unless he be a fugitive from lawfull labor & Service in Some other american State or territory, and then he must be restored.* …

In this instance it is Sufficient to over rule the present Motion, and the motion is overruled.

DENISON v. TUCKER
Michigan Territorial Supreme Court (1807)
1 Blume 385

AUGUSTUS B. WOODWARD, J. In the matter of Elizabeth Denison, James Denison, Scipio Denison, and Peter Denison Jun against Catherine Tucker, on a writ of habeas Corpus.

The Court Considered the return to the writ of Habeas Corpus awarded in this case Sufficient, and ordered Elizabeth Denison, James Denison, Scipio Denison and Peter Denison jun to be restored into the possession of Catherine Tucker. ...

The return to the writ of Habeas Corpus applied for and granted in this case brings out the question of Slavery in general, as it applies to the territory of Michigan.

Slavery is not at this day permitted in England. ...

In this territory Slavery is absolutely and peremptorily forbidden.

The question necessary to be decided is the Sufficiency of the return. It reposes the right to hold the applicants in a State of Servitude on a provision in the treaty of London of the nineteenth day of November one thousand Seven hundred ninety four negotiated betwen Lord Grenville on the part of the British government, and by the honorable John Jay on the part of the American. ...

The provision in the treaty of one thousand Seven hundred ninety four is in the following words. "All Setlers and traders Shall Continue to enjoy unmolested all their property of every Kind. It shall be free to them to Sell their lands, houses, or effects, or to retain the property thereof at their discretion."

It has been denied that the term *property*, as here used, includes Slaves. That term, it is Said, does not apply to the human Species in England, and by the laws of the United States of America, made previously to the existence of this treaty, the term *property* Cannot apply to the human Species in this territory. ...

Property is the Creature of Civilized Society. In a State of nature, unprotected by law, it is both the Child of Caprice, and the Victim of force. Its rights Created & protected by Civilized Society, the tenure of them can be regulated by its laws alone. Different Civilized Societies may render that a Subject of property which others refuse to Consider as Such; and Some may regulate the nature & tenure of property in a manner that Contravenes the just and inalienable rights of human Nature. In these latter Cases it is a Species of hostility Carried on by that Society on particular Members of it. The State of Nature is as it were again introduced, and force Can alone redress an evil, which, where *it* is incompetent, must be Submitted to as irremediable.

So Magistrates and public officers are the creatures of Civilized Society. Their rights, their powers, their duties, as individual Members of the great family of the human Species, are totally distinct from their rights, their powers, their duties as Servants and trustees of the particular civilized Society which creates them. Deriving their powers and rights from this Source they must necessarily be regulated by the obvious Condition of the trust, an implicit obedience to the Known will of the nation or Society delegating it.

The term property is here used with a latitude the most extensive of which it can possibly be made Susceptible. It is *lands, houses, effects, and property of every Kind*. If the words had been added, *Slaves only excepted*, doubt Could not have existed; but in the general, and unqualified Stipulation which is made, every thing which can become the Subject of property is included.

The Spanish nation has made the *human Species* a Subject of property. It first Subjected to this humiliation the people of America; It afterwards extended it to the People of africa. A principle which forms no part of the law of nations, or of any other law, was made the pretext of this oppression. It was that those who enslaved were believers in the religion of Jesus Christ, and those who were thus enslaved were not believers in that religion. A Similar principle has been adopted by the disciples of Mohammed. The true believers were not Subject to be made Slaves, while infidels were Subjected to that degradation. ...

The french nation followed in the Same Steps. The Slavery of the people of America and of the people of Africa is recognized by Spain & by France both as it relates to the Islands and to the Continent. The Slavery of the people of America and of the people of africa was recognized by France in Louisiana & Canada previous to the Cession of those Countries to other powers. ...

Great Britain has uniformly claimed the foremost rank among the nations of Europe in the Cause of the liberties of mankind. Her Conduct however has not always been Conformable to the true Spirit of these high pretentions. She has recognized the Slavery of the people of Africa both in the islands, and on the Continent, and her Refusal to abolish the Slave trade was made a Subject of Complaint, by the united States while they yet remained in the State of Colonies. She recognizes the Slavery of both Americans & Africans in Canada, and did So at the time of her Cession of this part of them to the United States of America.

The United States of America Claim the foremost rank of all the nations of the World in protecting and maintaining the liberties of Mankind. This nation however has long recognized the Slavery of the people of Africa, She Still Recognizes that Slavery, and the Slave trade itself has not yet reached its expiring moment.

The *human species* therefore can be *the Subject of property* in various Countries, and among others in our own; and in an expression where *property* is Spoken of in terms So ample and So absolutely unqualified as those of the treaty now in consideration, *Slaves* must be considered to be included if at the time of the use of them Slavery had a legal existence in the Country in relation to which they have been used.

The principles of the law of nations on the Subject of Slavery as well as the operation of local laws, and the particular time of their Commencement and expiration have been much discussed. Some general positions Seem to be Susceptible of the most precise ascertainment. Some of those which are deemed applicable will be here enumerated. ...

Third. The inhabitants of a conquered or ceded Country remain Subject to their own laws until they have been changed by the laws of the conquering or acquiring power. ...

Fifth. The operation of the former laws Continues until the actual possession has been received. A *Contract to Cede* is not *a cession in fact*. Though this Country was *contracted* to be ceded by the treaty of one thousand Seven hundred eighty three, it was not *ceded in fact*. The possession was not transferred. The Congressional Ordinance of one thousand Seven hundred eighty Seven did not at the

time of its passage reach here for want of this actual Cession. A Second *Contract* to Cede was made in one thousand Seven hundred Ninety four. The actual Cession was *contracted* to be made on the first day of July one thousand Seven hundred Ninety Six. It was not however made in fact, and the possession actually transferred until the eleventh day of July one thousand Seven hundred Ninety Six. On the morning of that day the British officers and troops abandoned the Country, the flag of their nation was lowered, and that of the United States of America waved over this modern Bosphorus. Up to this last day the laws of the province of upper Canada were those by which the inhabitants were governed. The erection of the County of Wayne, and the establishment of the american System of jurisprudence in it immediately followed, and effected the first political alterations.

From these preliminary data I am ready to admit it as a principle, *that if the Subjection of the human Species, or any part of them as the people of America or of Africa, and their respective descendants, to a State of Slavery, has been Sanctioned by law in this Country, the present territory of Michigan, by France, while that nation possessed the Country, and has not been Since Contradicted, by the laws of Great Britain, to whom She Ceded it, or if it has been in any manner Sanctioned by Great Britain, and not Contradicted by the laws of the United States of America, to whom the Country was ceded by Great Britain, Since the eleventh day of July on thousand Seven hundred Ninety Six, that the right to retain the human species in Subjection [*] to a State of Slavery, Still Subsists, according to the tenor and operation of the laws in force in the Same, previous to the eleventh day of July one thousand Seven hundred Ninety Six.*

This leads to the question as to what the laws of the Country were prior to that day. A law of france, and a law of Great Britain are both noticed in the return. ...

The ordinance of the french government of the fifteenth of april one thousand seven hundred nine, on the Subject of Slavery, is very explicit. It is in these words. ...

"Ordinance of Mr. Raudot, Intendant, of the 15th of april 1709, register No 3. folio 32. VO

"Who, under the good pleasure of his Majesty, ordains that all Panis and Negroes, who have been, or Shall hereafter be bought, Shall belong, in full property, to those who have acquired them, or Shall acquire them, in quality of Slaves."

This ordinance may be considered as brought to a termination by the Statute of the province of upper Canada of the thirty first day of May one thousand Seven hundred Ninety three. This wise & humane Statute is in the following Words.

"*AN ACT to prevent the further introduction of Slaves, and to limit the term of Contracts for Servitude within this province.* ... Be it enacted ... that from and after the passing of this act, it Shall not be lawfull for ... any Negro, or other person who Shall Come or be brought into this province after the passing of this act, be Subject to the Condition of a Slave. ...

II. *Provided always* that nothing herein Contained Shall ... liberate any Negroe ... from the ... possession of the Owner thereof. ...

III. And in order to prevent the Continuation of Slavery within this province, *Be it enacted by the authority aforesaid* that immediately from and after the passing of this act, every Child that Shall be born of a Negro mother or other woman Subjected to Such Service as aforesaid, Shall abide & remain with the master or Mistress, in whose Service the mother Shall be living at the time of Such Child's birth, ... and Such master or Mistress ... may retain him or her in their Service until every Such Child Shall have attained the age of twenty five years, at which time they and each of them shall be entitled to demand his or her discharge from, and Shall be discharged by Such Master or Mistress from any further Service. ... always, that in case any issue Shall be born of Such Children during their infant Servitude, or after, Such issue Shall be entitled to all the rights & privileges of free born Subjects. ...

Some New and distinct inquiries however here burst into attention. Is the law of Canada or the provision of one thousand Seven hundred eight Seven to operate after the actual possession of the Country by the american government? Are those born after that period to remain in Servitude until they attain the age of twenty five years, or are they to be free from their birth? Are those born in the interval betwen the date of the Canadian Statute and the introduction of the american laws to be Considered as Slaves or free persons? And are they, or not, to remain in Servitude for twenty five years?

From the date of the actual acquisition the American government has promptly, Steadily and uniformly manifested its disposition to introduce its own forms of government, and to apply its own laws. In this Country it has recognized, even in a temporary point of view, neither the previous laws of France, nor those of Great Britain, in any one, even the Smallest degree. *I am therefore bound to Say that from and after the eleventh day of June one thousand Seven hundred Ninety Six the french ordinance and the Canadian Statute ceased to have effect, and that every human being born in this territory after that day, or at most a day not far distant from it, was born a free person, and is not Subject to the twenty five years Servitude provided for in other Cases.*

But a person born in the interval, while the Statute of upper Canada was in operation, that is to Say after the thirty-first day of May one thousand Seven hundred ninety three, and before the eleventh day of june one thousand Seven hundred Ninety Six, might lawfully be detained during that interval as part of the twenty five years allowed by that Statute. So after the application of the american laws Such persons do not become absolutely free. There may be a State of *qualified Slavery*, as well as a State of absolute and unqualified Slavery; and the right of the master, though less in degree, is Still *a right of property*. A property in the Servitude of these persons existed at the date of the cession, and this property is by the treaty to remain *unmolested*. ...

This Statute of the province of upper Canada brings the existence of Slavery in the territory of Michigan to as early and to as favorable a Close as perhaps the imperfections necessarily attached to all human measures will allow to be expected. All Slaves living on the thirty first day of May one thousand Seven hundred Ninety three, and in the possession of Settlers in this territory on the eleventh day of July one thousand Seven hundred Ninety Six Continue Such for life. The Children of the females of them born after the thirty first day of May one thousand Seven hundred Ninety three and previous to the erection of the County of Wayne, and the establishment of the american System of jurisprudence, Continue in Servitude for twenty five years. After this period they are absolutely free. Their Children born before or after this period are absolutely free from their birth. All persons other that those who have been described are free by the Congressional provision of one thousand Seven hundred eighty Seven, excepting only where they are refugees from Service or labor in another State, and then they must be restored to those lawfully entitled to Claim Such labor or Service. The interests of humanity are probably therefore as much protected for the present as can reasonably be expected and their future Sacrifice and abandonment at the Shrine of avarice and Cupidity remain perhaps alone to be guarded against.

I Consider the return to the Writ of HABEAS CORPUS *Sufficient*; and it is *ordered* that Elizabeth Denison, James Denison, Scipio Denison, *and* Peter Denison junior, *be restored to the possession of* Catherine Tucker."

NEAL v. FARMER
Supreme Court of Georgia (1851)
9 Georgia 555

... This was an action brought by Nancy Farmer against William Neal to recover damages for the killing of a Negro slave, the property of Mrs. Farmer. On the trial, the plaintiff proved the killing and closed. The defendant introduced no testimony. The Jury found a verdict for plaintiff for $825.

The defendant then moved for a new trial, [asserting]. ...

1. That the Jury found for the plaintiff, when there was no evidence that the plaintiff had prosecuted the defendant either to conviction or acquittal for the killing.

NISBET, J. The [motion] for a new trial ... [is] based upon the grounds that the killing of a slave is a felony at Common Law, and that in all cases of felonies, the civil remedy is suspended until the offender is prosecuted to conviction or acquittal. The reply of the plaintiff was, that it is not a felony at Common Law to kill a slave. ...

1. ... [I]n Georgia, in cases of treason and of such crimes as are felonies by the Common Law, the person injured is not entitled to his action, until the offender is prosecuted to a conviction or acquittal. ... It is assumed by the plaintiff in error, that the settlers of the Colony of Georgia brought with them the Common Law of Great Britain, so far as it was applicable to their condition, and that by that law, as it stood in England in 1732, when the Colony of Georgia was settled, and as it was held throughout our entire colonial history, and is still held in Georgia, it is felony for a white man to kill a slave. The first of these assumptions is not controverted. It is not at all questionable that the Common Law, so far as it was applicable to the condition of such a community, was of force in the Colony of Georgia, and so continued until modified by the Acts of the Colonial Legislature, after that was organized in 1751. ... Is it a felony at Common Law to kill a slave? ...

Common Law recognizes but one species of slavery as having existed in England under its sanction at any time, and that is *villenage*. It was stated by Mr. Hargrave, in his learned argument in the Sommersett case, that there was no provision in the laws of England to regulate any slavery, but that of *villenage*, and, therefore, he insisted that no slavery could be lawful in England, except such as would consistently fall under that denomination. ...

3. ... [A]nd if it be true, that the *status* of the African slave be the same with that of the feudal villein, and the Law of Villenage was of force, at the settlement of the Colony of Georgia, in England, one of the strongest positions in his argument is gained; because, if the same, it comes under the Law of Villenage, and by that law it was felony to kill a villein—consequently a felony to kill an African slave. ... [But] were the laws which recognized the institution of villenage, and protected the life of the villein, a part of the Common Law, when this Colony was settled in 1732?

Lord Coke says, that the law favors life, liberty and dower. This favoritism to liberty seems gradually to have operated in the destruction of the bondage of the villein. ... According to Lord Mansfield, the last confession of villenage in Court, (which was one of the ways in which men became villeins,) occurred in the time of the sixth Henry.

The institution, very much to the satisfaction of British lawyers, and judges, and statesmen, (although the latter were at the time fostering, by parliamentary enactments, the slave trade to Africa,) became substantially extinct in the latter years of the reign of Elizabeth.

Thus it is clear, that the Law of Villenage had gone into disuse in England, one hundred and fifteen years before the settlement of Georgia, and that the subjects of it had notoriously ceased to be in 1617. It was, I am constrained to believe, no part of the Common Law in 1732. ... Common law has no application to the condition of slavery in England, or in Georgia. This is the question ... and such is our judgment. ...

8. It is theoretically every where, and in Georgia experimentally true, that two races of men living together, one in the character of masters and the other in the character of slaves, cannot be governed by the same laws. Whatever rights humanity, or religion, or policy, may concede to the slave, they must, in the nature of the relation, be often different from those of the master. The forms of proceeding, and the rules of evidence for their protection, as well as the penalties for their violation, must necessarily, in many instances, be different. The civil rights of the master do not appertain to the slave. Of these, he can have none whatever. The rights personal, if they might be so designated, of the slave, are, some of them, essentially different from those of the master, and cannot, therefore, be the subject of a common system of laws. *They must be defined by positive enactments, which, whilst they protect the slave, guard the rights of the master.* If the Common law be applicable to a state of slavery, it would seem to be applicable as much in one as another particular. If it protects the life of the slave, why not his liberty? and if it protects his liberty, then it breaks down, at once, the *status* of the slave. The Colonies received the Common Law, as applicable to their condition, that being in numerous particulars different from that of the parent State. They received it as *slave*-holding communities, and as applicable to them as slave-holders. It is absurd to talk about the Common Law being applicable to an institution which it would destroy. It came to our fathers as the law of the white man, a subject of the British Crown, so far as his circumstances made it desirable to him to appeal to its protection. It recognized slavery only in one point of view, and that is, as an interest to be protected for the benefit of the masters. It may be said, that the Common Law, in protecting the life of the slave, interferes with no right of the master, inasmuch as the master has no right to take the life of his slave. The title to a slave in Georgia now, and under the Colonial Government, is not and was not derived from positive law. The faculty of holding slaves was derived from the Trustees of the Colony, acting under authority of the British Crown, as a *civil* right, in 1751, by an ordinance of that board. Before that time, their introduction was prohibited. The regulation of slave property is as much the province of municipal law, as the regulation of any other property, and its protection equally its obligation; but we deny that property in slaves, and the title by which they are held, are the creations of statutory law. To view this question fairly, let the inquiry go back to a period subsequent to the ordinance of the Trustees, in 1751, and anterior to any legislation upon the subject of slavery. Licensed to hold slave property, the Georgia planter held the slave as a chattel; and whence did he derive title? Either directly from the slave-trader, or from those who held under him, and he from the slave-captor in Africa. The property in the slave in the planter, became thus just the property of the original captor. In the absence of any statutory limitation upon that property, he holds it as unqualifiedly as the first proprietor held it; and his title, and the extent of his property were sanctioned by the usage of nations, which had grown into a law. Property thus acquired in slaves, was *confirmed* by Statute in Georgia, ... and recognized by the State Constitution, ... and by the compromises of the Federal Constitution. ...

9. Moreover, the Act of 1770, which is the first Colonial Act providing for the punishment of white men for killing slaves, is perfectly conclusive, that prior to that time it was not an offence against the law—of course the Common Law—to kill a slave, and that there was no limitation of the power of the master over him, except that which religion, or humanity, or interest may be presumed to have imposed. ...

Let the judgment be affirmed.

Who Is a Slave?

GOBU v. GOBU
Supreme Court of North Carolina (1802)
1 N.C. 188

Trespass and false imprisonment; plea that the plaintiff is a slave. …

It appeared … that the plaintiff, when … about eight days old, was placed in a barn by some person unknown; that the defendant, then a girl of about twelve years of age, found him there, conveyed him home, and has kept possession of him ever since; treating him with humanity, but claiming him as her slave. The plaintiff was of an olive colour, between black and yellow, had long hair and a prominent nose. …

BY THE COURT. I acquiesce … to the presumption of every black person being a slave. It is so because the negroes originally brought to this country were slaves, and their descendants must continue slaves until manumitted by proper authority. If therefore a person of that description claims his freedom, he must establish his right to it by such evidence as will destroy the force of the presumption arising from his color.

But I am not aware that the doctrine of presuming against liberty has been urged in relation to persons of mixed blood, or to those of any color between the two extremes of black and white; and I do not think it reasonable that such a doctrine should receive the least contenance. Such persons may have descended from Indians … at least in the maternal; they may have descended from a white parent in the maternal line or from mulatto parents originally free, in all which cases the offspring, following the condition of the mother, is entitled to freedom. Considering how many probabilities there are in favor of the liberty of these persons, they ought not to be deprived of it upon mere presumption. …

Verdict that the plaintiff is free.

ADELLE v. BEAUREGARD
Supreme Court of Louisiana (1810)
1 Mart.La. 183

The plaintiff, a woman of colour, claimed her freedom.

Paillette for the defendant. The plaintiff must prove that she was born free, or has been emancipated.

Ellery for the plaintiff. Even if the defendant could prove his possession of the plaintiff as his slave, still the Spanish law would require him to produce some written title, or at least that he acquired possession of her without fraud.

BY THE COURT. ... The law cited by the plaintiff is certainly applicable to the present case. We do not say that it would be so if the plaintiff were a negro, who perhaps would be required to establish his right by such evidence as would destroy the force of the presumption arising from colour; negroes brought to this country being generally slaves, their descendants may perhaps fairly be presumed to have continued so, till they show the contrary. Persons of colour may have descended from Indians on both sides, from a white parent, or mulatto parents in possession of their freedom. Considering how much probability there is in favor of the liberty of those persons, they ought not to be deprived of it upon mere presumption, more especially as the right of holding them in slavery, if it exists, is in most instances of being satisfactorily proved. Gobu vs. Gobu, Taylor 115.

The defendant then proved he had brought the plaintiff from the West-Indies; had placed her in a boarding school in New-York and in a few years after sent her to New-Orleans where ... she brought the present suit.

Judgment for Plaintiff.

ALFRED NICHOLS v. WILLIAM F. BELL
Supreme Court of North Carolina
46 N.C. 32; 1853 N.C. LEXIS 68; 1 Jones Law 32

December, 1853, Decided

NASH, C. J. This action is upon a guaranty, and two questions arose upon the trial below. We will consider them in the order in which the case presents them. The first is, upon the introduction of parol evidence to prove the consideration, upon which the guaranty arose. It was insisted on behalf of the defendant, that the case upon which the action is founded, was within the act 1826, and that the consideration ought to appear upon the face of the instrument. This objection is answered by the cases of MILLER v. IRWIN, 1st Dev. and Bat. 103. COOPER v. [**2] CHAMBERS, 4 Dev. 281. ADCOCK v. FLEMING, 2 Dev. & Bat. 223. *ASHFORD v. ROBINSON, 8 Ired. 116.* 3 Kent's Com. 122. These authorities show that a guaranty is not within the Statute. They also show that where the contract is in parol, evidence may be resorted to, to establish the consideration. The second objection is, that the Court erred in refusing the instructions required. The plaintiff is a man of color; the case states, "that he was neither black nor white," but that he was of a brown "color, between that of an African and a mulatto," and that "neither of his parents could have been a white person." The plaintiff then proved, that, "in Onslow, where the con tract was made, he was reputed to be a free person, was "called and known as free Alfred Nichols." The defendant requested the Court to instruct the jury, that, in the case of persons of a *shade* of color darker than that of a mulatto, the law presumed they were slaves. The Court *could* not give such instructions. We know of no law or decision, which authorises such presumption. In 1802, in the case GOBU v. GOBU, Taylor Rep. 16, the Court for the first time recognised, as a presumption of law, that a man's right to freedom depended upon his color. It was decided, that, if he was black, he was by law presumed to be a slave. This case was followed by that of *SCOTT v. WILLIAMS, 1 Dev. 376,* and it has gradually grown up into a principle, which cannot now be controverted. But both these cases confine the presumption to a black color. In the latter case, Judge DANIEL, before whom the case was tried below, in instructing the jury as to the right to freedom of Jane Scott, the mother of defendant, stated to them, if she was of a *black African complexion, they* might presume from that fact that she was a slave; if she was of a *yellow complexion, no presumption* of slavery arose. Judge HALL, in delivering the opinion of this Court, recognised the distinction made below, between a black and yellow complexion. How it was thought possible, that the Judge could give the instructions required we cannot well see. It would have been in direct conflict with the only cases on the subject, contained in our reports. Here the plaintiff is described, as being neither black nor white, but of a brown color, between that of an African and a mulatto. The Court was asked to tell the jury, as a matter of law, that if the plaintiff was a shade darker than a mulatto, he was to be presumed to be a slave. If we had the power, we certainly have not the disposition to extend the principle further, than as recognised in the cases cited. Let the presumption rest upon the African color; that is a decided mark: but to carry it into shades, would lead us into darkness, doubt and uncertainty, for they are as various as the admixture of blood between the races, and against the rule that presumptions are always in favor of liberty.

Judgment affirmed.

HUDGINS v. WRIGHTS
Supreme Court of Virginia (1806)
1 Hen. & M. (Va.) 134

The appellees ... asserted this right [to freedom] as having been descended, in the maternal line, from a free Indian woman; but their genealogy was very imperfectly stated. ... [T]he youngest ... [had] the characteristic features, the complexion, the hair and eyes ... the same with those of whites. ... [The grandmother] had long black hair, was of the right Indian copper colour, and was generally called an Indian by the neighbours, who said she might recover her freedom, if she would sue for it.

... [T]he late chancellor, perceiving from his own view, that the youngest of the appellees was perfectly white, and that there were gradual shades of difference in colour between the grandmother, mother, and grand-daughter, (all of whom were before the Court,) ... determined that the appellees were entitled to their freedom; and, moreover, on the ground that freedom is the birthright of every human being, which sentiment is strongly inculcated by the first article of our "political catechism," the bill of rights— he laid it down as a general position, that whenever one person claims to hold another in slavery, the *onus probandi* lies on the claimant.

JUDGE TUCKER. ... From the first settlement of the colony of Virginia to the year 1778, (Oct. Sess.) all negroes, ... brought into this country by sea, or by land, were slaves. And by the uniform declarations of our laws, the descendants of the females remain slaves to this day, unless they can prove a right to freedom, by actual emancipation, or by descent in the maternal line from an emancipated female.

... [A]ll American Indians brought into this country since the year 1705, and their descendants in the maternal line, are free. ...

All white persons are and ever have been free in this country. If one evidently white, be notwithstanding claimed as a slave, the proof lies on the party claiming to make the other his slave.

Nature has stampt upon the African and his descendants two characteristic marks, besides the difference of complexion, which often remain visible long after the characteristic of colour either disappears or becomes doubtful; a flat nose and wooly head of hair. The latter of these characteristics disappears the last of all; and ... predominates uniformly where the party is in equal degree descended from parents of different complexions, whether white or Indians; giving to the jet black hair of the Indian a degree of flexure. ... Its operation is still more powerful [in] ... persons descended equally from European and African parents. So pointed is this distinction between the natives of Africa and the aborigines of America, that a man might as easily mistake the glossy, jetty cloathing of an American bear for the wool of a black sheep, as the hair of an American Indian for that of an African. ... Upon these distinctions as connected with our laws, the burthen of proof depends. ...

Suppose three persons, a black or mulatto man or woman with a flat nose and woolly head; a copper-coloured person with long jetty black, straight hair; and one with a fair complexion, brown hair, not woolly nor inclining thereto, with a prominent Roman nose, were brought together before a Judge upon a writ of Habeas Corpus, on the ground of false imprisonment and detention in slavery: that the only evidence with the person detaining them in his custody could produce was an authenticated bill of sale from another person, and that the parties themselves were unable to produce any evidence concerning themselves. ... How must a Judge act in such a case? ... He must discharge the white person and the Indian out of custody, ... [until] the holder ... [proves] them to be lineally descended in the maternal line from a female African slave; and he must redeliver the black or mulatto person, with the flat nose and woolly hair ... unless the black person or mulatto could ... produce proof of his descent, in the maternal line, from a free female ancestor. ... This case shews my interpretation of how far the *onus probandi* may be shifted from one *party* to the other: and is, I trust, a sufficient comment upon the case to shew that I do not concur with the Chancellor in his reasoning on the operation of the first clause of the Bill of Rights, which was notoriously framed with a cautious eye to this subject, and was meant to embrace the case of free citizens, or aliens only; and not by a side wind to overturn the rights of property, and give freedom to those very people whom we have been compelled from imperious circumstances to retain, generally, in the same state of bondage that they were in at the revolution, in which they had no concern, agency or interest. But ... I heartily concur with him [the chancellor] in pronouncing the appellees absolutely free; and am therefore of the opinion that the decree be affirmed. ...

This Court, not approving of the Chancellor's principles and reasoning in his decree made in this cause, except so far as and the same relates to white persons and native American Indians, but entirely disapproving thereof, so far as the same relates to native Africans and their descendants, who have been and are now held as slaves by the citizens of this state, and discovering no other error in the said decree, affirms the same.

STATE v. HARDEN
Supreme Court of South Carolina (1832)
2 Spears 151n

... All natural Persons who, by law, are entitled to protection, may be the subject of assault and battery. Slaves are chattels, and their right to protection belongs to their master. ... Free Negroes, without any of the political rights which belong to a citizen, are still, to some extent, regarded by the law as possessing both natural and civil rights. The rights of life, liberty and property, belong to them, and must be protected by the community in which they are suffered to live. ...

The second ground [of Harden's appeal] supposes that to prove the freedom of a Negro, general reputation of being a free man, and living accordingly, will not be sufficient. But I apprehend there is no such rule. By law, every Negro is presumed to be a slave, the onus of proving his freedom ... is cast upon him. But the manner in which it shall ... be proved, is not, and cannot be defined. The proof must ... vary according to circumstances. In some, it might be necessary to produce a deed of manumission, in others, no such necessity could exist. ... Proof that a negro has been suffered to live in a community for years, as a free man, would *prima facie*, establish the fact of freedom. Like all other *prima facie* showing it may be repelled, and shown that, notwithstanding it, he is a slave, not legally manumitted, or set free. But until this is done, the general reputation of freedom would ... establish it. ...

The Meaning of Slavery

BULLOCH v. THE LAMAR
Circuit Court, District of Georgia
4 F. Cas. 654 (1844)

WAYNE, J. The libellant seeks to recover compensation for two negroes, who were his property, and who were drowned, the canoe in which they were, having been run under by the steamer Lamar ... in the Savannah river.

The point ... in the case is, was the canoe run down, by such negligence, want of skill, or carelessness in the navigation and management of the Lamar, as to entitle the libellant to recover compensation from her owners, for the loss which he has sustained. In all cases of collision ..., the essential enquiry is, whether proper measures of precaution have been taken by the vessel which runs down another.

It was in the evening, after or about six o'clock, in October. When the Lamar reached McGilvry's bar, between two and three miles from Savannah, the steam "was checked down," that the boat might go slow, as the water was shallow on the bar. * * * When the Lamar, following the channel, had crossed the bar, the captain called for headway. * * * In two minutes, after the order was given for headway, the canoe was run under. [At] the point where the accident occurred ... there was a thick verdure of trees ... It is considered a very bad part of the river on account of the trees, which throw a shade out and make the river dark.

Can that ... be considered a judicious and careful order ... which directs a steamer to be put under headway, under her usual pressure of steam, just at the moment she is entering such a pass at night, without moon enough to give her light, with a towboat on each side, covering more than half the width of the channel?

[T]he order for headway caused the disaster, and ... it amounted to gross neglect. ...

"Every boat navigating the river is bound to make use of all reasonable precautions to avoid injuring others, which precautions may vary with circumstances. In a fog, for example, a steamboat ought not to run at her full speed, if by so doing she increases the danger to other craft; for she must regard their safety as well as her own." Lawrence v. Jones, 1 West. Law J. 28. If responsible in such a case, why not in a case of running at night, under the usual press of steam, in a narrow and difficult channel, close in shore darkened by the shade of trees; so much so, that objects cannot be seen at the same distance that they may be of a clear night on the water.

I shall direct a decree to be entered ... directing that the libellant shall recover one thousand dollars, and that the respondents shall pay all costs.

GORMAN v. CAMPBELL
Supreme Court of Georgia, 1853
14 Ga. 137

This was an action to recover the value of a Negro man named London, whom the plaintiff Gorman had hired to Campbell, the defendant, as a steamboat hand, on the Ocmulgee and Altamaha rivers, and who had been drowned while so hired.

The testimony exhibited the following state of facts: The Negro was employed on board the steamboat Sam Jones. It is not customary, on the river, to employ Negroes in the labor of clearing out obstructions, or cutting new passages in the river, unless under circumstances of urgent necessity. On this occasion, the Captain and the white hands were employed in cutting away logs in the rivers, to clear a passage for the boat, when this Negro engaged in the work of his own accord, and worked for about half an hour, in the presence and sight of the Captain, without any thing being said to him. At length, when the log on which he was cutting was about to give way, the Captain called to him to quit and get off the log. The Negro then jumped on another log, which proved to be loose, and floated down the stream with him on it. Soon his hat fell off, in endeavoring to recover which, he fell into the water and was drowned.

The charge of the Court to the jury was, that in the case of a bale or box of goods, it would be the Captain's duty to place in safety; but it was different with the kind of property in dispute; that it was sentient being, capable of volition and locomotion; and if they believed the boy London was engaged in the work by the express command or permission the Captain, the defendant was liable: but if they believed the Negro engaged in work of his own free will, and the Captain forbid him to do it, the defendant was not liable, because the owner of the boat and its officers, are not required to keep the Negro in chains, which he must do if he were responsible for any act of his, however trivial, while on the boat, if it should end disastrously.

Under this charge, the jury found for defendant, and plaintiff excepted to the same.

LUMPKIN, J. ... Did the Court charge the jury correctly as to the law of this case? ...

... [T]he charge of the Court ... is defective, as many charges are, in laying down correctly a general principle without applying it to the facts of the case before the jury, and which is not true, as restricted to these facts. Our brother ruled rightly in instructing the jury that if the boy acted by the command or even permission of the Captain and officers of the boat, that the owners were liable for his loss.

But he failed to state to the jury, as he should have done, that if they believed the testimony of Bishop, that London was engaged for one-half hour in the presence of the Captain, in cutting a log, before he interfered to stop him, and that he only interposed when he saw the peril impending, by the giving way of the sundered log, that then his permission should be implied. For to neglect to exercise authority to forbid a thing, is to permit it.

But this error is one of omission. His Honor next charged the jury that if the boy engaged in this hazardous employment of his own accord, and the Captain commanded him to desist, that the defendant is not liable. And that coercion was not necessary to be used with this species of property: otherwise, resort must be had to chains.

Now the first clause of these instructions is a generality: but it is not the law of this case, as made out by the proof. This Negro did engage in this work of his own accord; and the Captain did order him to desist; and yet the defendant should be made liable, because the Captain did not arrest the work *immediately*, and before it was too late. What signifies it that he hallooed to him to get away when the timber was sliding from beneath his feet, after standing by for a half hour previously, and seeing him cutting the log? Nothing is more dangerous than to lay down general propositions, which, instead of aiding, scarcely ever fail to mislead juries. Courts should apply the principles of law to the facts in evidence in each particular case; stating those facts hypothetically.

Hiring is a contract of bailment; and the hirer is bound to exercise ordinary diligence in taking care of the property. And not only is the hirer liable, if the slave be put to a different service from that for which he was employed, whereby injury accrues to the owner.

But even in following the calling for which he was engaged, it is still the duty of the hirer to exercise proper care in the supervision of the slave. And he not only *may* use coercion even to chains, if necessary, for the protection of the property from peril, but it is his duty to do so. And he will make himself responsible, if neglecting his obligations in this respect the property is destroyed, or its value impaired. This portion of the charge, therefore, was fundamentally erroneous.

And humanity to the slave, as well as a proper regard for the interest of the owner, alike demand that the rules of law, regulating this contract, should not be relaxed. We must enforce the obligations which this contract imposes, by making it the interest of all who employ slaves, to watch over, their lives and safety. Their improvidence demands it. They are incapable of self-preservation, either in danger or in disease.—This office devolves upon those who are entrusted, for the time being, with their custody and control. And if they fail faithfully to perform it, it becomes a high and solemn duty of all Courts to enforce the trust by the only means in their power—a direct appeal to the pocket of the delinquent party. ...

Had London been killed while employed as one of the boat-hands, for which service he was hired, the defendant would not have been liable unless the loss had been occasioned by his wilful misconduct or culpable neglect.

But having engaged, in the presence of the Captain of the boat, in a different and more dangerous business from that which was stipulated and intended by the parties, the hirer is responsible for the loss of life which occurred, although, by inevitable casualty. And it is no protection that the loss arose from the voluntary act of the slave.

The judgment of the Circuit Court must be reversed, and the cause remanded for a new trial.

PONTON v. WILMINGTON & WELDON RR. CO.
Supreme Court of North Carolina (1858)
51 N.C. 246

The action was brought for the negligence of one of the servants of the company in permitting a switch to be out of place, whereby a collision took place between two trains, which caused the injury and death of the plaintiff's slave. The injury took place at a place called Joyner's station. A freight train, in the night time, ha passed from the main track upon the *turnout* without readjusting the switches, in consequence of which the next passenger train took the turnout and ran in upon the freight train. The slave in question was a brakeman on the freight train, hired from the plaintiff for that service; he was at his proper place when the collision happened and was crushed to death between the trains. The company had in their employment at Joyner's station a person whose duty it was to adjust the switches.

RUFFIN, J. The question in this case is not new to the profession, though it is raised now for the first time in the Courts of this State. It is indeed of recent occurrence anywhere and owes its origin, or rather prevalence, probably to the great number of servants needed and employed on the steamboats and railroads, which have come so much into use in our times, and on which so many casualties or injuries from negligence happen. The leading case upon the subject is that of *Priestly v. Fowler*, 3 Mees. & Wells., 1, in which, after an *advisari*, the opinion of the Court of Exchecquer was delivered by *Lord Abinger*, C. B., who presented several strong reasons, founded on policy and social necessity, why a master ought not to be liable to one servant for damages arising from the negligence of a fellow-servant for damages arising from the negligence of a fellow-servant engaged in the same employment. The point was again made in *Hutchison v. R. R.*, 5 Exch., 343, when, after another *advisari, Baron Alderson* delivered the opinion of the Court, approving of *Priestly v. Fowler*, and laying down the same doctrine and applying it to persons in the same service on a railroad, with the qualification that the employer must take due care not to expose the servant to unreasonable risks. He states the principle to be that the servant when he engages to serve undertakes, as between him and his master, to run all the ordinary risks of the service, which includes the risk of the negligence of a fellow-servant, acting in the discharge of his duty as servant of the common master; but while the servant undertakes those risks he has a right to require that the master shall take reasonable care to protect him by associating him only with persons of ordinary skill and care. ...

Indeed, the counsel for the plaintiff admitted that the rule was so thoroughly settled that it could not be shaken unless upon the distinction that the injury complained of in this case was to the person of a slave. The distinction was put upon the difference between a hired freeman and a slave, the former being competent to make what terms he chooses in his contract and to leave the service, if dangerous, at his will, while the latter, by the hiring, becomes the property, temporarily, of the hirer, with no will of his own and is beyond the control of the owner. But the distinction does not seem sound. It might be if the slave were the person to be benefited by the recovery. But the action is by the owner for his benefit, and it is obvious that it is in his power also, by stipulations in the contract, to provide for the responsibility of the bailee for exposing the slave to extraordinary risks, or for his liability to the owner for all losses arising from any cause. It is sufficient protection to his property as owner when it is put on the same footing with the protection to a freeman, as the Court thinks it ought to be. In the cases in the Courts of the Southern States, already alluded to, the injury was generally to slaves, and both in those in which the decisions were for or against the employers such a distinction was disregarded, or rather, not noticed. It would be singular "if the owner of a slave could recover for damages sustained (248) by a slave," when upon the same state of facts the slave, if he had been a freeman, could not have recovered. ...

It results form the principles thus established that the present action cannot be maintained, as there was no want of ordinary care on the part of the company to provide a competent number of persons, fit, or supposed to be fit, to discharge the duties, by the neglect of which the injury arose. There was a man at the switch, or rather for it, who failed of due diligence and caused the damage. But it does not appear that he had ever failed of his duty before, or if he had, that it ever came to the knowledge of the company or any of its officers who had the direction in that department, or had been suggested to them. The same is to be said of the engineers and conductors, in the selection of whom and keeping them in the employment of the company there does not appear to have been any blame. It may be remarked that among the first cases on this point in this country was that of *Farwell v. R. R.*, 4 Metc., 49, which arose from laches of the same sort that caused the damage here, the displacement of a switch, which threw off the train, and the engineer, the plaintiff, was injured, but was not allowed to maintain an action against the employer.

STATE v. MANN
Supreme Court of North Carolina (1829)
2 Devereux Law Rep. 263

The Defendant was indicted for an assault and battery upon *Lydia*, the slave of one *Elizabeth Jones*.

On the trial it appeared that the Defendant had hired the slave for a year;—that during the term, the slave had committed some small offence, for which the Defendant undertook to chastise her—that while in the act of so doing, the slave ran off, whereupon the Defendant called upon her to stop, which being refused, he shot at and wounded her.

His Honor, Judge DANIEL, charged the Jury, that if they believed the punishment inflicted by the Defendant was cruel and unwarrantable, and disproportionate to the offence committed by the slave, that in law the Defendant was guilty, as he had only a special property in the slave.

A verdict was returned for the State, and the defendant appealed.

No Counsel appeared for the Defendant.

RUFFIN, Judge.—A Judge cannot but lament, when such cases as the present are brought into judgment. It is impossible that the reasons on which they go can be appreciated, but where institutions similar to our own, exist and are thoroughly understood. The struggle, too, in the Judge's own breast between the feelings of the man, and the duty of the magistrate is a severe one, presenting strong temptation to put aside such questions, if it be possible. It is useless however, to complain of things inherent in our political state. And it is criminal in a Court to avoid any responsibility which the laws impose. With whatever reluctance therefore it is done, the Court is compelled to express an opinion upon the extent of the dominion of the master over the slave in North-Carolina.

The indictment charges a battery on *Lydia*, a slave of *Elizabeth Jones*. Upon the face of the indictment, the case is the same as [*State v. Hale*]. ... No fault is found with the rule then adopted; nor would be, if it were now open. But it is not open; for the question, as it relates to a battery on a slave by a stranger, is considered as settled by that case. But the evidence makes this a different case. Here the slave had been hired by the Defendant, and was in his possession; and the battery was committed during the period of hiring. With the liabilities of the hirer to the general owner for an injury permanently impairing the value of the slave, no rule now laid down is intended to interfere. That is left upon the general doctrine of bailment. The enquiry here is, whether a cruel and unreasonable battery on a slave, by the hirer, is indictable ... Our laws uniformly treat the master or other person having the possession and command of the slave, as entitled to the same extent of authority. The object is the same—the services of the slave; and the same powers must be confided. In a criminal proceeding, and indeed in reference to all other persons but the general owner, the hirer and possessor of a slave, in relation to both rights and duties, is, for the time being, the owner. ... [U]pon the general question, whether the owner is answerable *criminaliter*, for a battery upon his own slave or other exercise of authority or force, not forbidden by statute, the Court entertains but little doubt.—That he is so liable, has never yet been decided, nor, as far as is known, been hitherto contended. There have been no prosecutions of the sort. The established habits and uniform practice of the country in this respect, is the best evidence of the portion of power, deemed by the whole community, requisite to the preservation of the master's dominion. If we thought differently, we could not set our notions in array against the judgment of everybody else, and say that this, or that authority, may be safely lopped off. This has indeed been assimilated at the bar to the other domestic relations; and arguments drawn from the well established principles, which confer and restrain the authority of the parent over the child, the tutor over the pupil, the master over the apprentice, have been pressed on us. The Court does not recognize their application. There is no likeness between the cases. They are in opposition to each other, and there is an impassable gulf between them.— The difference is that which exists between freedom and slavery—and a greater cannot be imagined. In the one, the end in view is the happiness of the youth, born to equal rights with that governor, on whom the duty devolves of training the young to usefulness, in a station which he is afterwards to assume among freemen. To such an end, and with such a subject, moral and intellectual instruction seem the natural means; and for the most part, they are found to suffice. Moderate force is superadded, only to make the others effectual. If that fail, it is better to leave the party to his own headstrong passions, and the ultimate correction of the law, than to allow it to be immoderately inflicted by a private person. With slavery it is far otherwise. The end is the profit of the master, his security and the public safety; the subject, one doomed in his own person, and his posterity, to live without knowledge, and without the capacity to make anything his own, and to toil that another may reap the fruits. What moral considerations shall be addressed to such a being, to convince him what, it is impossible but that the most stupid must feel and know can never be true—that he is thus to labor upon a principle of natural duty, or for the sake of his own personal happiness, such services can only be expected from one who has no will of his own; who surrenders his will in implicit obedience to that of another. Such obedience is the consequence only of uncontrolled authority over the body. There is nothing else which can operate to produce the effect. The power of the master must be absolute, to render the submission of the slave perfect. I most freely confess my sense of the harshness of this proposition, I feel it as deeply as any man can. And as a principle of moral right, every person in his retirement must repudiate it. But in the actual condition of things, it must be so. There is no remedy. This discipline belongs to the state of slavery. They cannot be disunited, without abrogating at once the rights of the master, and absolving the slave from his subjection. It constitutes the curse of slavery to both the bond and free portions of our population. But it is inherent in the relation of master and slave.

That there may be particular instances of cruelty and deliberate barbarity, where, in conscience the law might properly interfere, is most probable. The difficulty is to determine, where *a Court* may properly begin. Merely in the abstract it may well be asked, which power of the master accords with right. The answer will probably sweep away all of them. But we cannot look at the matter in that light. The truth is, that we are forbidden to enter upon a train of general reasoning on the subject. We cannot allow the right of the master to be brought into discussion in the Courts of Justice. The slave, to remain a slave, must be made sensible, that there is no appeal from his master; that his power is in no instance, usurped; but is conferred by the laws of man at least, if not by the law of God. The danger would be great indeed, if the tribunals of justice should be called on to graduate the punishment appropriate to every temper, and every dereliction of menial duty. No man can anticipate the many and aggravated provocations of the master, which the slave would be constantly stimulated by his own passions, or the instigation of others to give; or the consequent wrath of the master, prompting him to bloody vengeance, upon the turbulent traitor—a vengeance generally practiced with impunity, by reason of its privacy. The Court therefore disclaims the power of changing the relation, in which these parts of our people stand to each other.

We are happy to see, that there is daily less and less occasion for the interposition of the Courts. The protection already afforded by several statutes, that all-powerful motive, the private interest of the owner, the benevolences towards each other, seated in the hearts of those who have been born and bred together, the frowns and deep execrations of the community upon the barbarian, who is guilty of excessive and brutal cruelty to his unprotected slave, all combined, have produced a mildness of treatment, and attention to the comforts of the unfortunate class of slaves, greatly mitigating the rigors of servitude, and ameliorating the condition of the slaves. The same causes are operating, and will continue to operate with increased action, until the disparity in numbers between the whites and blacks, shall have rendered the latter in no degree dangerous to the former, when the police [sic] now existing may be further relaxed. This result, greatly to be desired, may be much more rationally expected from the events above alluded to, and now in progress, than from any rash expositions of abstract truths, by a Judiciary tainted with a false and fanatical philanthropy, seeking to redress an acknowledged evil, by means still more wicked and appalling than even that evil.

I repeat, that I would gladly have avoided this ungrateful question. But being brought to it, the Court is compelled to declare, that while slavery exists amongst us in its present state, or until it shall seem fit to the Legislature to interpose express enactments to the contrary, it will be the imperative duty of the Judges to recognize the full dominion of the owner over the slave, except where the exercise of it is forbidden by statute. And this we do upon the ground, that this dominion is essential to the value of slaves as property, to the security of the master, and the public tranquility, greatly dependent upon their subordination; and in fine, as most effectually securing the general protection and comfort of the slaves themselves.

PER CURIAM.—Let the judgment below be reversed, and judgment entered for the Defendant.

UNITED STATES v. AMY
Circuit Court, District of Virginia
24 F. Cas. 792 (1859)

TANEY, J. The prisoner (Amy) in this case was indicted for stealing a letter from the post-office, containing articles of value. ... [S]he was at the time the offence was committed, and at the time of trial, a slave. ... [T]he prisoner ... was found guilty by the jury. ... The act of March 3, 1825 (section 22), under which the prisoner is indicted, provides that, if any person shall steal or take a letter from the mail, or any post-office, the offender shall, upon conviction thereof, be imprisoned not less than two, nor more than ten, years.

It has been argued ... that a slave, in the eye of the law, is regarded as property; and, as the act of congress speaks only of persons, ... it was not intended, and does not operate, upon slaves.

It is true that a slave is the property of the master ... ; and it is equally true that he is not a citizen, and would not be embraced in a law operating only upon that class of persons. Yet, he is a person, and is always spoken of and described as such in the state papers and public acts of the United States.

The offences were as likely to be committed by slaves as by freemen, and the mischief is equally great whether committed by the one or the other. ... And if the slave himself is not within the law, the crime might be committed daily, and with perfect impunity, and all of the safeguards which congress intended to provide for the protection of its mails

and post-offices would be of no value. Such a construction would defeat the whole evident object and policy of the law, and would rather tempt to the commission of these offences by the certainty of impunity, than to prevent them by the fear of punishment.

It is true, that some of the offences created by this act of congress subject the party to both fine and imprisonment, and it is evident that the incapacity and disabilities of a slave were not in the mind and contemplation of congress when it inflicted a pecuniary punishment; for he can have no property, and is also incapable of making a contract, and consequently could not borrow the amount of the fine. ... And we think it must be admitted that, in imposing these pecuniary penalties, congress could not have intended to embrace persons who were slaves, and we greatly doubt whether a court of justice could lawfully imprison a party for not doing an act, which, by the law of his condition, it was impossible for him to perform; and to imprison him, to compel the master to pay the fine, would be equally objectionable, as that would be punishing an innocent man for the crime of another.

The case before us, however, does not involve this question ... The offence of which the prisoner has been found guilty is punished by the law by imprisonment only. ...

[W]e see no ground for setting aside the verdict or suspending the sentence.

Sojourn

THE SLAVE, GRACE
Admiralty Court (Great Britain) (1827)
2 Hagg. Admir. 94

In 1822, Mrs. *Allan* of *Antigua* came to *England*, bringing with her ... a domestic slave, named *Grace*. She resided with her mistress in this country until 1823, and accompanied her voluntarily on her return to *Antigua*. Mr. *Wyke*, collector of the customs at *Antigua* and the original prosecutor of the present suit, was a passenger on board the same ship. On their arrival at *Port St. John*, in the island of *Antigua, Grace*, with whose character and situation Mr. *Wyke* was well acquainted, landed with her mistress, without any exception made to her condition, and without any formalities at the custom-house observed or required. She continued with Mrs. *Allan*, [as] ... a domestic slave, till *August* 8th, 1825, when she was seized by ... customs at *Antigua*, "as forfeited to the king, on suggestion of having been illegally imported in 1823." The information was filed in *June*, 1826. Mr. *Allan* then made an affidavit of claim, as sole owner and proprietor of Grace, as his slave; and Mr. *Wyke*, a single witness, was examined on interrogatories. On *August* 5, 1826, the judge of the Vice Admiralty Court of *Antigua* decreed, after argument, "that the woman *Grace* be restored to the claimant, with costs and damages for her detention."

From this sentence an appeal was prosecuted on the part of the crown, and the principal question made, was—whether ... slavery was so divested by landing in *England* that it would not revive on a return to the place of birth and servitude?

LORD STOWELL, J. ... I have looked with the utmost attention to discover, if possible, the foundation of her complaint—that she being a free person is treated as a slave. The truth of that complaint depends upon the nature of that freedom, if any, which she enjoyed before the institution of this suit; and I can find nothing that warrants any such assertion of a freedom so conferred. The sole ground upon which it appears to have been asserted is that she had been resident in *England* some time as a servant ... but without the enjoyment of any manumission that could alone deliver her from the character of a slave which she carried with her when she left *Antigua*; for I think it demonstrable that she could derive no character of freedom ... merely by having been in *England*, without manumission; for a manumission is a title against all the world. The mode of treatment applied to such persons is a strong illustration between the effect produced by a residence in *England* and that conferred by a manumission; for manumissions are not uncommon in *England* and always granted where there is an intention of giving the party an absolute title to freedom. This suit, therefore, fails in its foundation: she was not a free person; no injury is done her by her continuance in a state of slavery, and she has no pretensions to any other station than that which was enjoyed by every slave of the family. If she depends upon such a freedom, conveyed by a mere residence in *England*, she complains of a violation of right which she possessed no longer than whilst she resided in *England*, but which had totally expired when that residence ceased and she was imported into *Antigua*. ...

The real and sole question which the case of *Sommersett* brought before Lord *Mansfield*, ... was, whether a slave could be taken from this country in irons and carried back to the *West Indies*, to be restored to the dominion of his master? And all the answer ... required was, that the party who was a slave could not be sent out of *England* in such a manner and for such a purpose. ...

It is very observable, that Lord *Mansfield* ... confines that question ... expressly to *this country*, for he says, "the *now* question is, Whether any dominion, authority, or coercion can be exercised on a slave in this country according to the *American laws, meaning thereby the laws of the West Indies? ...*" In the final judgment he delivers himself thus: "The state of slavery is so odious that nothing can be suffered to support it but positive law": that is, the slavery as it existed in the *West Indies*; for it is to that he looks, considering that many of the adjuncts that belonged to it there were not admissible under the law of *England.* ...

The public inconvenience that might follow from an established opinion that negroes became totally free in consequence of a voyage to *England*, without any express act that declared them to be so, is not altogether to be overlooked. It is by no means improbable that, with such a temptation presented to them, many slaves might be induced to try the success of various combinations to procure a conveyance to *England* for such purpose; and, by returning to the colony in their newly-acquired state of freedom, if permitted, might establish a numerous population of free persons, not only extremely burthensome to the colony, but, from their sudden transition from slavery to freedom, highly dangerous to its peace and security. ...

It has been observed, that the sovereign state has declared, that all laws made in the colonies, contradicting its own law, shall be null and void, and cannot be put in execution; but is that the character of the laws in the colonies for the encouragement of the proprietors of slaves? Has it not, since the declaration of its judgment against slavery, declared, in the most explicit and authentic manner, its encouragement of slavery in its colonial establishments? Have not innumerable acts

passed which regulate the condition of slaves, and which tend to consider them, as the colonists themselves do, ... as mere goods and chattels, as subject to mortgages, as constituting part of the value of estates, as liable to be taken in execution for debt—to be publicly sold for such purposes; and has it not established courts of the highest jurisdiction for the carrying into execution provisions for all these purposes; and these its most eminent courts of justice—its these regulations are carried into effect with most scrupulous attention and under the authority of acts of parliament? Can any man doubt that at this time of day slaves in the colonies may be transferred by sale made in *England*, and which would be affirmed without reference to the Court so empowered; for the acts of Parliament, including the recent Consolidation Act, prescribe and regulate the manner in which these transfers of slaves are to be securely made in this kingdom, and the mode to be adopted where money is lent on mortgage upon the security of slaves; and how, under the guarantee of such protection, can it be asserted that the law of *England* does not support, and in a high degree favour, the law of slavery in its *West India* colonies, however it may discourage it in the mother country? Is it not most certain that this trade of the colonies has been the very favourite trade of this country, and so continues, so far as can be judged from encouragement given in various forms—the making of treaties, the institution of trading companies, the devolution of property from one company to another, the compulsion of the colonies to accept this traffic, and the recognition of it in a great variety of its laws? If it be a sin, it is a sin in which this country has had its full share of the guilt, and ought to bear its proportion of the redemption. How this country can decline to perform the act of justice, in performing the act of charity, men of great wisdom and integrity have not been able to discover. ... Sentence affirmed.

HARRY v. DECKER & HOPKINS
Supreme Court of Mississippi (1818)
Walker (Mississippi) 36

OPINION OF THE COURT. ... The facts in this case are not controverted; that the three negroes were slaves in Virginia; that in seventeen hundred and eighty four they were taken by John Decker to the neighbourhood of Vincennes [, Indiana]; that they remained there from that time until the month of July, 1816; that the ordinance of Congress, passed in the month of July in the year 1787, and that the constitution of the state of Indiana was adopted on the 29th June, 1816. ... We will now come to the [Northwest] ordinance, and the sixth article of the compact, which declares, "there shall be neither slavery nor involuntary servitude in said territory otherwise than for the punishment of crimes, whereof the party shall be duly convicted." Preceding the sixth article, it is ordained and declared, that the six articles shall be considered as articles of compact, between the original states, and the people and states in said territory, and forever remain unalterable, unless by common consent. ... That the sovereign may contract with the people, is an acknowledged principle, and the only question is, whether the compact shall be obligatory on the parties. That the people of the territory were parties is evident, that their condition was changed from absolute subjection, to the condition of free men, is equally clear. ... But according to the construction of the defendants' counsel, those who were slaves at the passing of the ordinance, must continue in the same situation[.] Can this construction be correct? Would it not defeat the great object of the general government[?] It is obvious it would, and it is inadmissible upon every principle of legal construction. Considering the six articles of compact equally obligatory and binding, made upon sufficient consideration, all the objection as to the want of power in congress to make the compact with the people of the said territory must vanish. Another point in this case was relied on, namely, that if the petitioners were not freed by the 6th article of the ordinance, they became so by the adoption of the constitution of Indiana. Even the power of the people, in their sovereign capacity, is denied, to effect a general emancipation. ... The question then resolves itself into this. What were the rights delegated by the people to the convention, or what was the trust or power of that convention? ... Freedom was extended to the slaves in Massachusetts by their constitution—I have it from high authority, and I have examined their statutes, and can find no general statute of emancipation; and so guarded was our convention upon this subject, that they inhibited the legislature from the exercise of the power. Pennsylvania, Delaware, New-Jersey, New-York, and the New England States, Massachusetts excepted, have legislated on this subject, and that it is a proper subject of legislative interference, when not restrained by the constitution, is evident by the caution of our convention and the exercise of the power by the several legislatures before mentioned. ... If old Decker was not a party to the articles of compact, it cannot be denied but that he was, or those who claim under him were parties to the constitution of Indiana; if he was, how can he claim a particular exemption from the operation of the constitution, according to the principles of the social compact before laid down, and if inequality was to exempt, would it not tend to destroy it? Does not the first article of the constitution declare the condition of the people of Indiana free, ... and by the ... [Indiana] constitution, the sixth section of the ordinance is adopted, and ... all laws conflicting with the provision of the constitution are repealed. Can it be that slavery exists in Indiana? If it does, language loses its force, and a constitution intended to protect rights, would be illusory and insecure, indeed. If the language is plain, saying there shall be neither slavery nor involuntary servitude, does it comport with the constitution to say *there shall* be slavery? This dilemma cannot be got over, by those who give it a construction, that would make the petitioners slaves. Why resort to construction in a case so plain? Do the rules of construing statutes apply to a constitution? Where does the power reside of restraining the people in their sovereign capacity? Is there any such power recognized? ... But it is contended that the provisions of the constitution admit of a different construction—that it is prospective, and to give it the meaning its language imports, would violate vested rights. What are these vested rights, are they derived from nature, or from the municipal law? Slavery is condemned by reason and the laws of nature. It exists and can only exist, through municipal regulations, and in matters of doubt, is it not an unquestioned rule, that courts must lean "in favorem vitae et libertatis." Admitting it was a doubtful point, whether the constitution was to be considered prospective in its operation or not, the defendants say, you take from us a vested right arising from municipal law. The petitioners say you would deprive us of a natural right guaranteed by the ordinance and constitution. How should the Court decide, if construction was really to determine it? I presume it would be in favour of liberty. ...

COMMONWEALTH v. THOMAS AVES
Supreme Judicial Court of Massachusetts (1836)
18 Pick. (Mass.) 193

Habeas corpus. On the 17th of August, 1833, upon the petition of Levin H. Harris, of Boston, representing that a colored female child, named Med, of New Orleans, was unlawfully restrained of her liberty by Thomas Aves of Boston; a writ of *habeas corpus* was granted. ...

Aves states ... he has the child in his custody; that in 1833, Samuel Slater, a citizen of ... Louisiana ... purchased the child and its mother as ... slaves by the laws of that State; that from the time of the purchase until about the first day of May, 1836, the mother and child remained the slaves of Slater in New Orleans ... ; that on or about that day Mary Slater, the wife of S. Slater and the daughter of Aves, left New Orleans for the purpose of coming to Boston and visiting her father, intending to return to New Orleans and to her husband, (who remained in that city,) after an absence of four or five months ... ; that the mother of the child remained in New Orleans, in slavery ... the property of S. Slater by the laws of Louisiana; that Mary Slater brought the child with her from New Orleans to Boston, having and retaining the child in her custody as the agent and representative of her husband, her object, intent, and purpose being to have the child accompany her and remain in her custody and under her care during her temporary absence from New Orleans, and that the child should return with her to New Orleans, their legal domicil; that the child was confided to the custody and care of Aves by Mary Slater, to be by him kept and nurtured during the absence of Mary Slater from Boston for a few days on account of ill health; that by the laws of Louisiana the marriage of a slave is void; that this child is the daughter of a slave, born in a state of slavery, and ... by force of the laws of Louisiana ... [the] right of guardianship over the infant children of a slave, where such children are not themselves slaves, devolves upon

the owner of their mother; that if this child is, by force of the laws of Massachusetts, now emancipated and a free person, S. Slater, as the owner of the mother ... is entitled to the custody of the person of the child as its legal guardian, ... that the child is about six years of age and wholly incapable of taking care of itself; that it is absolutely necessary that some person should have the custody of the person of the child and the right to restrain it of its liberty; that no private person nor magistrate has, by the laws of Massachusetts, any right to take the child out of the possession of Aves while he continues to use that possession and custody only for the purpose of benefiting the child, and only restraining it of its liberty so far as is necessary for its safety and health. ...

SHAW C. J. ... The case presents an extremely interesting question, not so much on account of any doubt or difficulty attending it, as on account of its important consequences. ...

The precise question presented ... is, whether a citizen of any one of the United States, where negro slavery is established by law, coming into this State, for any temporary purpose of business or pleasure, staying some time, but not acquiring a domicil here, who brings a slave with him as a personal attendant, may restrain such slave ... during his continuance here, and convey him out of this State on his return, against his consent. It is not contended that a master can exercise here any other of the rights of a slave owner, than such as may be necessary to retain the custody of the slave during his residence, and to remove him on his return. ...

Without pursuing this inquiry farther, it is sufficient for the purposes of the case before us, that by the constitution adopted in 1780, slavery was abolished in Massachusetts, upon the ground that it is contrary to natural right and the plain principles of justice. ...

Such being the general rule of law, it becomes necessary to inquire how far it is modified or controlled in its operation; either,

1. By the law of other nations and states, as admitted by the comity of nations to have a limited operation within a particular state; or
2. By the constitution and laws of the United States.

In considering the first, we may assume that the law of this State is analogous to the law of England, in this respect; that while slavery is considered as unlawful and inadmissible in both, and this because contrary to natural right and to laws designed for the security of personal liberty, yet in both, the existence of slavery in other countries is recognized, and the claims of foreigners, growing out of that condition, are, to a certain extent, respected. ...

Sommersett's case, ... decides that slavery, being odious and against natural right, cannot exist, except by force of positive law. But it clearly admits, that it may exist by force of positive law. And it may be remarked, that by positive law, in this connection, may be as well understood customary law as the enactment of a statute. ...

The same doctrine is recognized in Louisiana. In the case of *Lunsford v. Coquillion*, ... it is thus stated:—"The relation of owner and slave is, in the States of this Union in which it has a legal existence, a creature of the municipal law." ...

The conclusion to which we come from this view of the law is this:

That by the general and now well established law of this Commonwealth, bond slavery cannot exist, because it is contrary to natural right, and repugnant to ... [our] constitution and laws, designed to secure the liberty and personal rights of all persons within its limits. ...

That, as a general rule, all persons coming within the limits of a state, become subject to all its municipal laws, civil and criminal, and entitled to the privileges which those laws confer; that this rule applies as well to black as whites, except in the case of fugitives, ... that if such persons have been slaves, they become free, not so much because any alteration is made in their *status*, or condition, as because there is no law which will warrant, but there are laws, if they choose to avail themselves of them, which prohibit, their forcible detention or forcible removal.

That the law arising from the comity of nations cannot apply; because if it did, it would follow as a necessary consequence, that all those persons, who, by force of local laws, ... have acquired slaves as property, might bring their slaves here, and exercise over them the rights and power which an owner of property might exercise, and for any length of time short of acquiring a domicil; that such an application of the law would be wholly repugnant to our laws, entirely inconsistent with our policy and our fundamental principles, and is therefore inadmissible. ...

The constitution and laws of the United States, then, are confined to cases of slaves escaping from other States and coming within the limits of this State without the consent and against the will of their masters, and cannot ... extend to a case where the slave does not escape ... [but comes] within the limits of this State ... [by the master's] own act and permission. ... It is upon these grounds we are of opinion, that an owner of a slave in another State where slavery is warranted by law, voluntarily bringing such slave into this State, has no authority to detain him against his will, or to carry him out of the State against his consent. ...

This opinion is not to be considered as extending to a case where the owner of a fugitive slave, having produced a certificate according to the law of the United States, is *bona fide* removing such slave to his own domicil, and in so doing passes through a free State. ...

The child ... being of too tender years to have any will or give any consent to be removed, and her mother being a slave and having no will of her own and no power to act for her child, she is necessarily left in the custody of the law. The respondent having claimed the custody of the child, in behalf of Mr. and Mrs. Slater, who claim the right to carry her back to Louisiana, to be held in a state of slavery, we are of opinion that his custody is not ... a proper and lawful custody.

Under a suggestion made in the outset of this inquiry, that a probate guardian would probably be appointed, we shall for the present order the child into temporary custody, to give time for an application to be made to the judge of probate.

SCOTT v. EMERSON
Supreme Court of Missouri (1852)
15 Mo. 576

SCOTT, J. This was an action instituted by Dred Scott against Irene Emerson, the wife and administratrix of Dr. John Emerson, to try his right to freedom. His claim is based upon the fact that his late master held him in servitude in the State of Illinois, and also in that territory ceded by France to the United States, under the name of Louisiana, which lies north of 36 degrees 30 minutes, north latitude, not included within the limits of the State of Missouri.

It appears that his late master was a surgeon in the army of the United States, ... stationed at Rock Island, a military post in the State of Illinois, and at Fort Snelling, ... in the territory of the United States, above described, at both of which places Scott was detained in servitude ... [from] 1834 until ... 1838. The jury was instructed, in effect, that if such were the facts, they would find for Scott. He accordingly obtained a verdict. The defendant ... sued out this writ of error.

Cases of this kind are not strangers in our courts. Persons have been frequently here adjudged to be entitled to their freedom on the ground that their masters held them in slavery in territories or States in which the institution was prohibited. From the first case decided in our courts, it might be inferred that this result was brought about by a presumed assent of the master, from the fact of having voluntarily taken his slave to a place where the relation of master and slave did not exist. But subsequent cases base the right "to exact the forfeiture of emancipation," as they term it, on the ground it would seem, that it is the duty of the courts of this State to carry into effect the Constitution and laws of other States and territories, regardless of the rights, the policy or the institutions of the people of this State. ...

... It is a humiliating spectacle, to see the courts of a State confiscating the property of her own citizens by the command of a foreign law. If Scott is freed, by what means will it be effected, but by the Constitution of the

State of Illinois, or the territorial laws of the United States? Now, what principle requires the interference of this court? Are not those governments capable of enforcing their own laws; and if they are not, are we concerned that such laws should be enforced, and that, too, at the cost of our own citizens? States, in which an absolute prohibition of slavery prevails, maintain that if a slave, with the consent of his master, touch their soil he thereby becomes free. The prohibition in the act, commonly called the Missouri Compromise, is absolute. ...

Now are we prepared to say, that we shall suffer these laws to be enforced in our courts? On almost three sides the State of Missouri is surrounded by free soil. If one of our slaves touch that soil with his master's assent, he becomes entitled to his freedom. Considering the numberless instances in which those living along an extreme frontier would have occasion to occupy their slaves beyond our boundary, how hard would it be if our courts should liberate all the slaves who should thus be employed. How unreasonable to ask it. If a master sends his slave to hunt his horses or cattle beyond the boundary, shall he thereby be liberated? But our courts, it is said, will not go so far. If not go the entire length, why go at all? The obligation to enforce to the proper degree, is as obligatory as to enforce any degree. Slavery is introduced by a continuance in the territory for six hours as well as for twelve months, and so far as our laws are concerned, the offense is as great in the one case as the other. Laws operate only within the territory of the State for which they are made, and by enforcing them here, we, contrary to all principle, give them an extra-territorial effect. ...

It is conceived, that there is no ground to presume or to impute any volition to Dr. Emerson, that his slave should have his freedom. He was ordered by superior authority to posts where his slave was detained in servitude, and in obedience to that authority he repaired to them with his servant, as he very naturally supposed he had a right to do. To construe this into an assent to his slave's freedom would be doing violence to his acts. …

Times are not now as they were when the former decisions on this subject were made. Since then not only individuals but States have been possessed with a dark and fell spirit in relation to slavery, whose gratification is sought in the pursuit of measures, whose inevitable consequences must be the overthrow and destruction of our government. Under such circumstances it does not behoove the State of Missouri to show the least countenance to any measure which might gratify this spirit. She is willing to assume her full responsibility for the existence of slavery within her limits, nor does she seek to share or divide it with others. Although we may, for our own sakes, regret that the avarice and hard-heartedness of the progenitors of those who are now so sensitive on the subject, ever introduced the institution among us, yet we will not go to them to learn law, morality or religion on the subject.

As to the consequences of slavery, they are much more hurtful to the master than the slave. There is no comparison between the slave in the United States and the cruel, uncivilized negro in Africa. When the condition of our slaves is contrasted with the state of their miserable race in Africa; when their civilization, intelligence and instruction in religious truths are considered, and the means now employed to restore them to the country from which they have been torn, bearing with them the blessings of civilized life, we are almost persuaded, that the introduction of slavery amongst us was, in the providence of God, who makes the evil passions of men subservient to His own glory, a means of placing that unhappy race within the pale of civilized nations.

GAMBLE J., dissenting opinion. … It is, undoubtedly, a matter to be deeply regretted, that men who have no concern with the institution of slavery, should have claimed the right to interfere with the domestic relations of their neighbors, and have insisted that their ideas of philanthropy and morality should be adopted by people who are certainly capable of deciding upon their own duties and obligations. That the present owners of slaves, when denounced, in terms that would be appropriate, if they had actually kidnaped the slaves from the coast of Africa, or had inherited the fortunes accumulated by such iniquitous traffic, should feel exasperated by such wanton and unfounded attacks, is but natural. That, alienation of feeling and, finally, settled hostility will be produced by this course of conduct, is greatly to be apprehended. But, in the midst of all such excitement, it is proper that the judicial mind, calm and self balanced, should adhere to principles established when there was no feeling to disturb the view of the legal question upon which the rights of parties depend.

In this State, it has been recognized, from the beginning of the government, as a correct position in law, that a master who takes his slave to reside in a State or Territory where slavery is prohibited, thereby emancipates his slave; [Here Gamble cited eight Missouri cases decided between 1822 and 1837.] … These decisions, which come down to the year 1837 seem to have so fully settled the question, that since that time there has been no case bringing it before the court for any reconsideration until the present. …

The principle thus settled, runs through all the cases subsequently decided, for they were all cases in which the right to freedom was claimed in our courts, under a residence in a free State or territory, and where there had been no adjudication upon the right to freedom in such State or territory.

But the supreme court of Missouri, so far from standing alone on this question, is supported by the decisions of the other slave States, including those in which it may be supposed there was the least disposition to favor emancipation. In Lunsford vs. Coquillon … the supreme court of Louisiana held, that the removal of a slave by his master from Kentucky to Ohio, with intention to reside there, *ipso facto* emancipates the slave. The same court, in Marie Louise vs. Marot … and in Smith vs. Smith … holds "that the fact of a slave being taken by the owners to the kingdom of France or others country, where slavery is not tolerated, operates upon the condition of the slave and produces immediate emancipation." …

The cases here referred to, are cases decided when the public mind was tranquil, and when the tribunals maintained in their decisions, the principles which had always received the approbation of an enlightened public opinion. Times may have changed, public feeling may have changed, but principles have not and do not change; and, in my judgment, there can be no safe basis for judicial decisions, but in those principles, which are immutable.

It may be observed, that the principle is either expressly declared or tacitly admitted in all these cases, that where a right to freedom has been acquired, under the law of another State or community, it may be enforced by action, in the courts of a slaveholding State; for, in every one of these cases, the party claiming freedom had not procured any adjudication upon his right in the country where it accrued.

... I hold it to be my duty to declare, that the voluntary removal of a slave, by his master, to a State, territory or country in which slavery is prohibited, with a view to a residence there, entitles the slave to his freedom, and that that right may be asserted by action in our courts under our laws.

So far as it may be claimed in this case, that there is anything peculiar in the manner in which the slave was held in the free country, by reason of his master being an officer of the United States army, it is sufficient to answer, that this court, in Rachael vs. Walker, 4 Mo. Reports 350, considered the effect of that circumstance, and decided that such officers were not authorized, any more than private individuals, to hold slaves, either in the north-west territory or in the territory west of the Mississippi and north of thirty-six degrees thirty minutes, north latitude. The act of Congress, called the Missouri Compromise, was, in that case, held as operative as the ordinance of 1787.

PLEASANTS v. PLEASANTS
Supreme Court of Virginia (1799)
2 Call (Virginia) 319

This was an appeal from a decree of the High Court of Chancery, ... brought by *John Pleasants* deceased, against *Charles Logan, Samuel Pleasants*, junior, *Isaac Pleasants* and *Jane* his wife, *Thomas Pleasants*, junior, and *Margaret* his wife, *Elizabeth Pleasant, Robert Langley* and *Elizabeth* his wife, *Margaret Langley, Elizabeth Langley* the younger, and *Anne May*. The bill states, that the said *John Pleasants* by his last will devised as follows: "my further desire is, respecting my poor slaves, all of them as I shall die possessed with, shall be free if they chuse it when they arrive at the age of thirty years, and the laws of the land will admit them to be set free without their being transported out of the country. I say all my slaves now born or hereafter to be born, whilst their mothers are in the service of me or my heirs, to be free at the age of thirty years as above mentioned, to be adjudged of by my trustees their age." That the said *John Pleasants*, in a subsequent part of his will, devised to the plaintiff eight of the said slaves upon the same condition, that he should allow them to be free if the laws of the land would admit of it. That the testator then devised [to the various defendants his other slaves] on the same conditions on which he devised the eight slaves to the plaintiff. ... That the several devisees became possessed [of other slaves] under the will [of] ... *Johnathan Pleasants* in the year 1777, [who], by his last will, made the following devise: "And first believing that all mankind have an undoubted right to freedom and commiserating the situation of the negroes which by law I am invested with the property of, and being willing and desirous that they may in a good degree partake of and enjoy that inestimable blessing, do order and direct, as the most likely means to fit them for freedom, that they be instructed to read, at least the young ones as they come of suitable age, and that each individual of them that now are or may here after arrive to the age of thirty years may enjoy the full benefit of their labor in a manner the most likely to answer the intention of relieving from bondage. And, whenever the laws of the country will admit absolute freedom to them, it is my will and desire that all the slaves I am now possessed of, together with their increase, shall immediately on their coming to the age of thirty years as aforesaid become free, or at least such as will accept thereof, or that my trustees hereafter to be named, or a majority or the successors of them may think so fitted for freedom, as that the enjoyment thereof will conduce to their happiness, which I desire they may enjoy in as full and ample a manner as if they had never been in bondage, and on these express conditions and no other do I make the following bequests of them." That the testator then proceeds to dispose of his slaves among the [defendants] ... and the plaintiff; again expressing in almost every particular devise, the same positive condition in favor of their freedom. ... That the plaintiff is heir at law and executor of the said *John Pleasants*, deceased, as well as executor of the said *Jonathan Pleasants*; and in those characters, ... applied to the Legislature for the manumission of the said slaves; but the Legislature were of opinion, that it belonged to the Judiciary. That the plaintiff hath been much embarrassed as to the mode of bringing the question before the Courts, as the slaves could not sue at common law: 1. On account of their not being capable of being manumitted, but upon the terms mentioned in the act of

Assembly. 2. As they claimed their freedom in the nature of a legacy. That the devises to the defendants were only on condition, that they would emancipate them when they arrived at a certain age, and the laws would permit it. ... That there are no debts due from the said *John* and *Jonathan Pleasant*, now unsatisfied. That the plaintiff hath applied to the defendants to emancipate the said slaves; but they refuse. Therefore, the bill prays, that the slaves may be delivered up to the plaintiff, to be holden in trust for the purposes of the wills of the said *John* and *Johnathan Pleasants*; that the Court would direct the manner of their manumission; and for general relief. ...

The Court of Chancery ... declared ... that, in equity, [those slaves] ... who were thirty years old or older, in ... 1782, when the act authorising manumission was enacted [were free at that time. Those born before the testators death, but not yet thirty in 1782, became free when they turned thirty. Those slaves] ... born since the statute was enacted, were at their birth entitled to freedom. [The Court of Chancery referred the case] ... to a commissioner, to ascertain their [the slaves'] ages, and to take an account of their profits since their respective rights to freedom accrued. From which decree the defendants appealed. ...

ROANE, Judge. ... The doctrines of the common law, relative to perpetuities as to estates of inheritance, hold *a fortiori* as to terms, for years and personal chattels. If it be contrary to the policy of that law, to render unalienable, for a long space of time, real estates of inheritance, on reasons of public inconvenience and injury to trade and commerce, these reasons apply, with much more force, as to interests of short duration in lands and personal chattels; not only, because the latter are better adapted to the purposes of trade than the former, but also, because of their transitory and perishable nature. ...

The utmost limits allowed by law for the vesting of an executory devise ... is the term of a life or lives, in being, and twenty-one years after. This limitation, then, has become a fixed canon of property, and ought not to be lightly departed from: And the true distinction is, where the event must happen, if at all, within those limits, the executory devise is good; and on the happening of the contingency, the estate will become absolute, in the remainder-man.

... [In] the case before us, the happening of the contingency here; i.e. the passing a law to authorise emancipation, standing simply, is too remote, as it may not happen within 1,000 years: But, when the testator goes on further, and means the benefit of it to persons *in esse*, (for they are the objects of his bounty, and unless it happened within their lives, it might as well, as to them, not happen at all,) this restrains the happening of the contingency, ... and makes the executory devise good. ...

The construction, in this case, must be, as it would have been at the instant of the testator's death. ... [T]hat is to say, the right of freedom was good, if the contingency happened within the legal limits, in favor of such as might be *in esse* to enjoy it, and void, if it happened beyond those limits.

To come now to the case before us, as it really is. The contingency has happened within the limits. The effect is, that the limitation over has thenceforth become vested, in interest, in all the appellees, then *in esse*, and vested in possession, as to all, then or as they might become thirty years of age. As to all the slaves, then *in esse*, but under thirty years of age, their right to freedom was complete, but they were postponed as to the time of enjoyment. They were in the case of persons bound to service for a term of years, who have a general right to freedom, but there is an exception out of it, by contract or otherwise.

What then, after the passing of the act, is the condition of the children born of mothers; so postponed in the enjoyment of their freedom? Are they, at their birth, entitled to freedom? Or, are they too, to be postponed, until the age of thirty? The condition of the mothers of such children, is, that of free persons, held to service, for a term of years: such children are not the children of slaves. They never were the property of the testator or legatees, and he or they can no more restrain their right to freedom, than they can that of other persons born free. The power of the testator in this respect, has yielded to the great principle of natural law, which is also a principle of our municipal law, that the children of a free mother are themselves also free. The conditions of the will then, as applicable to such children, if indeed it was intended, or can be construed to apply to them, is void, as being contrary to law; it being an attempt to detain in slavery, persons that are born free. ...

The view of the subject I have now taken, (which will sustain the claim of the plaintiff ...) will supersede the necessity of a very delicate and important enquiry: namely, whether the doctrine of perpetuities is applicable to cases in which human liberty is challenged? ...

... There is yet one part of the *Chancellor's* decree, which I could have wished had not been made. I mean the reference to a commissioner to ascertain the profits of the slaves. We have no precedents, either of the

Courts of *England* or this country, to guide us. In the former country, indeed, no such case could occur, because slavery is not there tolerated; and, in this country, I believe no instance can be produced of profits being adjudged to a person held in slavery, on recovering his liberty. Among a thousand cases of palpable violations of freedom, no jury has been found to award, and no Court has yet sanctioned a recovery of the profits of labour, during the time of detention. Yet, it must be admitted, that juries are often excellent *Chancellors*. But, this is not a palpable violation of freedom. To say the least, it is a very nice question, whether these plaintiffs be entitled to freedom or not. And, ought the Court, in such a doubtful case, to award that, which the whole equity of the country, flowing through a thousand channels, has not yet awarded in a single instance? It seems to be a solecism, to award ordinary profits to recompence the privation of liberty; which, if it is to be recompenced, the power of money cannot accomplish.

But what, with me, is decisive [is that] ... all the children born of the female negroes in question, since the passage of the act of 1782, are, and were thenceforth entitled to freedom by birth, the burthen of rearing such persons, during their infancy (which must be borne by the legatees,) will form perhaps not an unreasonable set-off against the profits of those who were capable of gaining profit by their labor.

I have thus endeavored to make known the grounds upon which my opinion is founded. I entirely concur in the result of the *Chancellor's* decree, except in the particulars, in which I have already stated my opinion to be different. As it is the policy of the country to authorize and permit emancipation, I rejoice to be an humble organ of the law in decreeing liberty to the numerous appellees now before the Court. And this, upon grounds, as I suppose, of strict legal right, and not upon such grounds as, if sanctioned by the decision of this Court, might agitate and convulse the Commonwealth to its centre.

This was a bill filed in April 1854 ... [by the] executor of John L. Poindexter, to obtain a construction of the will of Poindexter, and directions for the guidance of the executor. The heirs and devisees of Poindexter, ... were the defendants in the suit. The difficulty in the construction of the will related to the ... following clause:

"The negroes loaned my wife, at her death I wish to have their choice of being emancipated or sold publicly. If they prefer being emancipated, it is my wish that they be hired out until a sufficient sum is raised to defray their expenses to a land where they can enjoy their freedom; and if there should not be enough of the perishable property loaned my wife to pay off the legacies ... they are to be hired until a sufficient sum is raised to pay the deficiency. If they prefer being sold and remaining here in slavery, it is my wish they be sold publicly, and the money arising be equally divided between my sister ... the children or heirs of my brother ... my nephews ... and my niece Nancy Bailey." ...

DANIEL, J. ... The language of the main clause in the will bearing on the subject ... seems to me is a plain and unambiguous tender by the testator to his slaves, of an election, at the death of his wife, to be emancipated or to be sold publicly as slaves. If they prefer to be emancipated, it is his will that after being hired out till the sums mentioned are raised, they shall enjoy their freedom. If, on the other hand, they prefer to remain in slavery, then it is his will that they remain slaves. ...

Is the condition one which the slaves have the legal capacity to perform? ...

[Quoting U.S. Supreme Justice Joseph Story, in *Emerson v. Howland* (1816), the Court noted] "In Virginia slavery is expressly recognized, and the rights founded upon it are incorporated into the whole system of the laws of the state. The owner of the slave has the most complete and perfect property in him. The slave may be sold or devised or pass by descent, in the same manner as other inheritable estate. He has no civil rights or privileges. He is incapable of making or discharging a contract, and the perpetual right to his services belongs exclusively to the master."

Judge Tucker, in his notes to his edition of Blackstone ... [says] "Slaves ... are excluded from social rights. Society deprives them of personal liberty, and abolishes their right to property; and in some countries even annihilates all their other natural rights." ...

When we assent to the general proposition, as I think we must do, that our slaves have no civil or social rights; that they have no legal capacity to make, discharge or assent to contracts; that though a master enter into the form of an agreement with his slave to manumit him, and the slave proceed fully to perform all required of him in the agreement, he is without remedy in case the master refuse to comply with his part of the agreement; and that a slave cannot take any thing under a decree or will except his freedom; we are led necessarily to the conclusion that nothing short of the exhibition of a positive enactment, or of legal decision having equal force, can demonstrate the capacity of a slave to exercise an election in respect to his manumission. ...

A master contemplating the manumission of his slaves might, no doubt, first ascertain their wishes on the subject, and if he pleased, then proceed to shape his course accordingly; and it could form no objection to a deed or will emancipating them, should it appear on the face of the instrument that the act of manumission was in conformity with their choice. ... But in the case before us, the operation of the will, as an instrument of emancipation, is made to depend on the choice of the slaves.

In the case supposed, the *master has fully manumitted his slaves*. In the case before us, the *master has endeavored to clothe his slaves with the uncontrollable and irrevocable power of determining for themselves whether they shall be manumitted*. And in so doing, he has, I think essayed the vain attempt to reconcile obvious and inherent contradictions. ...

On the whole, it seems to me that the provisions of the will respecting the manumission of the slaves, are not such as are authorized by law and are void, and consequently that the Circuit court erred in declaring the slaves and their increase to be free at the death of the life tenant. ...

MONCURE, J. [Dissenting] I think the bequest contained in the will ... that the negroes ... "have their choice of being emancipated or sold publicly," is a valid bequest, and emancipated them *in futuro* upon a condition precedent.

Whether a master should have power to emancipate his slave or not, is a [legislative] question ... and not [judicial]. ... It was answered by the legislature by the act of 1782, giving the right to emancipate by will or by deed. That act, substantially, has ever since remained, and yet remains, in full force; modified only by the act of 1806, requiring slaves thereafter emancipated to leave the state. ...

A master may emancipate his slaves *against* their consent. Why may he not make such consent the condition of emancipation? There seems to be nothing in the policy of the law which forbids his doing so. He may certainly, in his lifetime, consult the wishes of his slaves, and emancipate them or not accordingly. Why may he not direct his executor to consult their wishes, and emancipate them or not accordingly? Is not the one as much opposed to the policy of the law as the other? the consultation by the master, as much as the consultation by the executor? ...

His legatees, certainly, cannot complain of his act or the manner in which he has seen fit to exercise it. They can claim only what he has chosen to give them; and cannot complain that he has given them his slaves only on condition that they prefer to remain in slavery. It was *his* to give them absolutely or conditionally; and it is *theirs* to refuse or accept them as given. There is nothing in the policy of the law which requires them to claim the slaves against his will. ... The intention of the testator, if lawful, must prevail. It is a law to all who claim under his will. ...

It is argued, that slaves have no civil rights or legal capacity, and cannot therefore elect between freedom and slavery, though authorized to do so by their master. The premises of this argument are certainly true, at least as a general rule, but the conclusion is I think unsound. The fallacy of the argument ... consists in supposing that to make such an election would be to exercise a civil right or capacity. It is admitted that slaves are capable of receiving freedom, if conferred in the mode prescribed by law. It must also be admitted that it may be conferred conditionally. It was so conferred in the cases of *Pleasants v. Pleasants, ... Elder v. Elder's ex'or, ...* The right to confer it absolutely, which the law expressly gives, includes the right to confer it conditionally. The only question is, whether such condition may be the willingness of the slave to receive his freedom. Why may it not? Slaves emancipated absolutely, still have an election between freedom and slavery. They may become slaves again ... under the act of February 18, 1856. ... Why may not the master give them such an election directly, instead of giving it to them indirectly, by first making them free? Why should he be compelled to lose his property in such of his slaves as prefer to remain so, in order that he may give freedom to such as prefer it? It is said that a slave emancipated by an election given him by his master, would become free by his own act, and not by the act of his master. But this is not so. A slave can become free only the act of his master; an[d] the act must be done in a certain prescribed mode. When the act has been done in that mode, it may be made to depend on the willingness of the slave as well as upon any other condition. And whether made to depend on that or any other condition, it is the act of the master, and not the happening or performance of the condition which confers the right to freedom. The agency by which the condition is performed, is constituted by the master; and such performance is thus, in effect, his own act. There is nothing in the relation of master and slave, nor in the condition of slavery, which can prevent a master from adopting the agency of his slave for such a purpose. He can do so on the same principle on which it is admitted he may make his slave his agent for other purposes. Certainly nothing is better settled than that a slave cannot make a valid contract, even for his own freedom; and cannot enforce the execution of a promise of his master, even though it be to confer freedom upon him, and though the consideration on which it was made has been fully performed on the part of the slave. But it is equally well settled that a slave may avail himself of an act of emancipation duly executed by his master, whether such emancipation be absolute or conditional. ...

... [T]he testator might have emancipated the slaves absolutely. He was willing to do so, but did not wish to force freedom upon them against their will, and therefore gave them their choice, as that case decided he might lawfully do. Ought we now to frustrate his will, and award the slaves unconditionally to those to whom he gave them only on condition that the slaves reject the boon of freedom which he offers them? I think no. ...

MITCHELL v. WELLS
Supreme Court of Mississippi (1859)
37 Mississippi 235

HARRIS J. The appellee filed her bill ... as a citizen and resident of the State of Ohio. ...

Appellee alleges that she is a free woman of color, and daughter of testator, who died in ... Mississippi, in October, 1848. That by his will, testator bequeathed to complainant a watch, bed, and three thousand dollars, to be raised out of his estate. ... Wells's estate was worth $23,808, and her legacy was a lien on the estate. That complainant was a minor at the date of the will, and the executors were directed to invest the legacy for her. That the defendant retains the legacy on the pretext that complainant is a slave. That in 1846 her father took her to Ohio, and domiciliated her there, and ever afterwards recognized and treated her as a free woman; that her freedom was established by law in Ohio. ...

I think it demonstrable, both upon principle and the weight of authority, that a slave, once domiciliated as such, in this State, can acquire no right, civil or political, within her limits, by manumission elsewhere. That manumission and citizenship, elsewhere conferred, cannot, even upon principles of comity, under our laws and policy, vest any right here. ...

If it be conceded that there is nothing in the public policy of Mississippi opposed to the abolition of slavery, but that her policy only extends to the prevention of abolition *in her limits*, and is not opposed to their removal elsewhere to be set free; and further, that slaves, free negroes, or persons of color, may take and hold property in this State, either directly or through the intervention of a trustee: then their laws of comity entitle them, in the State of Mississippi, to all the rights belonging to them as citizens of the State so recognizing them, not inconsistent with our general policy.

If, on the contrary, our policy is opposed to the whole doctrine of negro emancipation, as at war with the interests and happiness of both races, then, whatever tends to encourage emancipation, or to thwart the cherished policy of our State and people, or to establish the opposite policy, must be void, and should be so declared within the limits of Mississippi. ...

To determine, then, what is the public policy of Mississippi, is the important point in issue. ...

... [O]ur first Constitution authorized the legislature to pass laws to permit the owners of slaves to emancipate them, under certain restrictions, ... but ... as early as 1822, *emancipation*, except for some distinguished service, and even then proven to and sanctioned by the legislature, was prohibited.

... [A]s late as February, 1857, the legislature of this State declared that "It shall not be lawful for any person, either by deed, will, or other conveyance, directly or in trust, either express or secret, or otherwise, to make any disposition of any slave or slaves, for the purpose or with the intent to emancipate such slave or slaves in this State, or to provide that such slaves be removed to be emancipated elsewhere; or by any evasion or indirection so to provide that the Colonization Society, or any donee or grantee, can accomplish the act, intent, or purpose designed to be prohibited by this article. Nor shall it be lawful ... to remove any slave or slaves from this State, with the intent to emancipate such slave or slaves." ...

I cannot therefore doubt, in view of the whole subject, that it *now is* and *ever has been*, the policy of Mississippi to protect, preserve, and perpetuate the institution of slavery as it exists amongst us, and to prevent emancipation generally of Mississippi slaves. ...

A slave once domiciliated here, *during the continuance of that domicile* has no such rights. If the appellee possess them at all, then she must have derived them from the law of her new domicile. That law, *proprio vigore*, has no extraterritorial operation, and could *vest no right* in the appellee *here*, except by the comity or consent of the

State of Mississippi. … [Here Judge Harris cites Thomas R. R. Cobb, Judge Ruffin's opinion in *State v. Mann*, Chief Justice Roger B. Taney's opinion in *Dred Scott v. Sandford* (1857), and the theories of James Kent to support his position that blacks could have no rights in Mississippi unless the state, by comity, gave them such rights.]

But again: I wholly dissent from the application of the doctrine of "comity" to cases like this. …

After all that learned writers have announced on this subject, it may be truly said, that by "comity," among states or nations, is only meant what is understood by courtesy, politeness, good-breeding, among families and neighbors.

Tested by these principles, on what foundation does this claim to the obligations of comity, in the case before us, rest?

The State of Ohio, forgetful of her constitutional obligations to the whole race, and afflicted with a *negro-mania*, which inclines her to *descend*, rather than elevate herself in the scale of humanity, chooses to take to her embrace, as citizens, the neglected race, who by common consent of the States united, were regarded, at the formation of our government, as an inferior caste, incapable of the blessings of free government, and occupying, in the order of nature, an intermediate state between the irrational animal and the white man.

Ohio persists; and not only so introduces slaves into her own political organization, but her citizens extend encouragement and inducement to the removal of slaves from Mississippi into the limits of Ohio; and then, in violation of the laws and policy of Mississippi, and in violation of the laws of the United States in relation to the rendition of fugitive slaves, introduces them into her limits as citizens.

… [I]t seems to me that comity is terminated by Ohio, in the very act of degrading herself and her sister States, by the offensive association, and that the rights of Mississippi are outraged, when Ohio ministers to emancipation and the abolition of our institution of slavery, by such unkind, disrespectful, lawless interference with our local rights.

The obligations of comity being mutual and reciprocal, as well as voluntary, no State in the confederacy may violate that comity towards others, and thereby impose obligations on such others not previously existing.

Ohio, by allowing the manumission of defendant in error in her jurisdiction, and conferring rights of citizenship *there*, contrary to the known policy of Mississippi, can neither confer freedom on a Mississippi slave, nor the right to acquire, hold, sue for, nor enjoy property in Mississippi.

Let the decree be reversed and bill dismissed, at the cost of defendant in error.

HANDY J., dissenting. I cannot concur in the views of this case taken by the majority of the court.

We see that the whole scope of these statutes is to prohibit emancipations of slaves in this State, by deed or will, to take effect here or in other States, and emancipations made in other States to be exercised here; and prohibitions against free negroes of other States coming into this State; and that, so far as the legislature has … not thought fit to interdict the enjoyment of any civil right of a free person of color residing in another State, and manumitted according to the law of that State, except to prohibit such persons from coming to, and remaining in, this State. And when we look at the extent of this policy, as expounded and settled by the decisions of this court, we see that, *in every case in which the question has been presented to this court, emancipations by deed, or other legal act, made in other States, bona fide, and not for the purpose of evading our laws, by the return of the slave here, have been held to be valid, and not in contravention of our laws and policy*; and, accordingly, it has been invariably held, that free persons of color, so manumitted in other States, might sue and maintain their legal rights in our courts.

It seems to me that the doctrine which debars such a person of a remedy in our courts for such rights as are not in contravention of our declared policy, cannot be justified upon principles of justice, humanity, or sound law. The right which he seeks to enforce is not forbidden by any law or declared policy of this State. If this State and that of which he is a subject, were foreign nations under treaty of peace and friendship, the denial of such right here would, upon principles of public law, be just cause of war. … But the States are bound together by much stronger ties than those created by treaty.

Each State is bound to respect and protect, within her limits, the rights to which any person residing in another State of the confederacy may be entitled by the laws of that State, unless clearly interdicted by the laws and policy of the State where they may be sought to be enforced. This results necessarily from the nature of the union, from the remaining sovereignty of the States, and from the high duty of each State to protect the rights of her people against the violence of the other States; and if this principle is denied, this Union is the frailest and most imperfect of human fabrics.

[I dissent] widely from the opinion of the majority of the court. …

WRIGHT v. DEACON
Supreme Court of Pennsylvania, 1819
5 Sergeant and Rawle (Pa.) 62

A hearing before a judge, on a *habeas corpus,* in the case of a fugitive slave from another state, and the judge's certificate of his absconding, delivered to the master claiming him, in order that he remove the slave, are conclusive; and a *homine replegiando* does not lie in such case, to try the right of the fugitive to freedom.

This was a writ *de homine replegiando,* sued out by the plaintiff, a colored man, against the defendant, who was the keeper of the prison of the city and county of *Philadelphia*; and the defendant's counsel now moved to quash, on the ground of its having issued contrary to the constitution and laws of the *United States.* The facts were submitted to the Court, in a case stated, by which it appeared, that the plaintiff, having been claimed by *Rasin Gale,* of *Kent* county, in the State of *Maryland,* as a fugitive from his service, was arrested by him in the county of *Philadelphia,* and carried before *Richard Renshaw,* Esq., justice of the peace, who committed the plaintiff to prison, in order that inquiry might be made into the claim of the said *Gale.* The plaintiff then sued out a *habeas corpus,* returnable before Thomas Armstrong, Esq., an associate Judge of the Court of Common Pleas. Judge Armstrong, having heard the parties, gave a certificate, that it appeared to him, by sufficient testimony, that the plaintiff owed labor or service to the said *Gale,* from whose service in the state of *Maryland* he had absconded, and the said judge, therefore, in pursuance of the act of the Congress of the *United States* in such case made and provided, delivered the said certificate to the said *Gale,* in order that the plaintiff might be removed to the state of *Maryland.*

Browne and *S. Levy,* in support of the motion, contended, that the *homine replegiando* was illegal; that the claim being made according to the act of Congress, the slave must be delivered up; that the decision of Judge Armstrong was conclusive under the constitution and laws of the *United States*; and that the only remedy the plaintiff had, was to claim his freedom, and have it tried in *Maryland,* after his removal thither.

TILGHMAN, C. J. This is a matter of considerable importance, and the Court has therefore held it some days under advisement. Whatever may be our private opinions on the subject of slavery, it is well known that our southern brethren would not have consented to become parties to a constitution under which the *United States* have enjoyed so much prosperity, unless their property in slaves had been secured. This constitution has been adopted by the free consent of the citizens of *Pennsylvania,* and it is the duty of every man, whatever may be his office or station, to give it a fair and candid construction. By the 2d sect. of the 4th art. it is provided, "that no person held to service or labor in one state, under the laws thereof, escaping into another, shall, in consequence of any law or regulation therein, be discharged from such service or labor, *but shall be delivered up, on claim of the party to whom such service or labor may be due.*" Here is the principle: the fugitive is to be delivered up, on *claim* of his master. But it required a law, to regulate the manner in which this principle should be reduced to practice. It was necessary to establish some mode in which the claim should be made and the fugitive be delivered up. Accordingly, it was enacted by the act of Congress "respecting fugitives from justice and persons escaping from the service of their masters," sect.

5, that the person to whom the labor or service of the fugitive was due, his agent or attorney, should be empowered to arrest such fugitive, and carry him before any judge of the Circuit or District Court of the *United States*, residing or being within the state, or before any magistrate of a county, city or town corporate, wherein such arrest should be made, and upon proof to the satisfaction of the said judge or magistrate, either by oral testimony, or affidavit taken before and certified by the magistrate of the state or territory from which the said fugitive had fled, that the person so arrested, did, under the law of the said state or territory from which he had fled, owe service or labor to the person claiming him, it should be the duty of the said judge or magistrate, to give a certificate thereof to such claimant, *which should be sufficient warrant for removal of a fugitive from labor to the state or territory from which he fled*. It plainly appears, from the whole scope and tenor of the constitution and act of Congress, that the fugitive was to be delivered up, on a summary proceeding, without the delay of a formal trial in a court of common law. But, if he had really a right to freedom, that right was not impaired by this proceeding; he was placed just in the situation in which he stood before he fled, and might prosecute his right in the state to which he belonged. Now, in the present instance, the proceeding before Judge Armstrong, and the certificate granted by him, are in exact conformity to the act of Congress. That certificate therefore was a legal warrant to remove the plaintiff to the state of *Maryland*. But if this writ of *homine replegiando* is to issue from a state court, what is its effect, but to arrest the warrant of Judge Armstrong, and thus defeat the constitution and law of the *United States*? The constitution and the law say, that the master may remove his slave by virtue of the judge's certificate: but the state court says, that he shall not remove him. It appears to us, that this is the plain state of the matter, and that the writ has been issued in violation of the constitution of the United States. We are, therefore, of opinion, that it should be quashed.

Writ quashed.

PRIGG v. PENNSYLVANIA
Supreme Court of the United States (1842)
41 U.S. 539

The Fugitive Slave Act of 1793, under the authority of Article IV of the Constitution, authorized the owner to seize a fugitive slave and bring him or her before a federal judge or state magistrate, who, upon satisfactory proof "that the person so seized or arrested doth, under the laws of the state or territory from which he or she fled, owe service or labour to the person claiming him or her, it shall be the duty of such judge or magistrate to give a certificate to such claimant. ..."

Prigg applied to a Pennsylvania magistrate for a certificate of removal of a Maryland escaped slave. When the certificate was refused, Prigg forcibly removed the slave and her children (one of them born more than a year after the mother escaped from Maryland) from Pennsylvania and returned her to Maryland. Prigg thereby violated, and was convicted under, an 1826 Pennsylvania statute specifically intended to prevent forcible removal of fugitive slaves without a court order.

The Supreme Court reversed the conviction and held the state statute unconstitutional on the ground that the Fugitive Slave Clause of the Constitution itself gave exclusive authority to the national government to regulate the handling of fugitive slaves, leaving no authority whatsoever to the states.

MR. JUSTICE STORY. ... [T]he second section of the fourth article [of the U.S. Constitution says] ...

"No person held to service or labour in one state under the laws thereof, escaping into another, shall in consequence of any law or regulation therein, be discharged from such service or labour; but shall be delivered up, on claim of the party to whom such service or labour may be due."

... Historically, it is well known, that the object of this [fugitive slave] clause was to secure to the citizens of the slaveholding states the complete right and title of ownership in their slaves, as property, in every state in the Union into which they might escape from the state where they were held in servitude. The full recognition of this right and title was indispensable to the security of this species of property in all the slaveholding states; and, indeed, was so vital to the preservation of their domestic interests and institutions, that it cannot be doubted that it constituted a fundamental article, without the adoption of which the Union could not have been formed. Its true design was to guard against the doctrines and principles prevalent in the non-slaveholding states, by preventing them from intermeddling with, or obstructing, or abolishing the rights of the owners of slaves. ...

... [I]f the Constitution had not contained this clause, every non-slave-holding state in the Union would have been at liberty to have declared free all runaway slaves coming within its limits, and to have given them entire immunity and protection against the claims of their masters; a course which would have created the most bitter animosities, and engendered perpetual strife between the different states. The clause was, therefore, of the last importance to the safety and security of the southern states; and could not have been surrendered by them without endangering their whole property in slaves. ...

How, then, are we to interpret the language of the clause? ...

The clause manifestly contemplates the existence of a positive, unqualified right on the part of the owner of the slave, which no state law or regulation can in any way qualify, regulate, control, or restrain. The slave is not to be discharged from service or labour, in consequence of any state law or regulation. Now, certainly, without indulging in any nicety of criticism upon words, it may fairly and reasonably be said, that any state law or state regulation, which interrupts, limits, delays, or postpones the right of the owner to the immediate possession of the slave, and the immediate command of his service and labour, operates, *protanto*, a discharge of the slave therefrom. ...

We have ... not the slightest hesitation in holding, that, under and in virtue of the Constitution, the owner of a slave is clothed with entire authority, in every state in the Union, to seize and recapture his slave, whenever he can do it without any breach of the peace, or any illegal violence. In this sense, and to this extent this clause of the Constitution may properly be said to execute itself; and to require no aid from legislation, state or national.

But the clause of the Constitution does not stop here; nor indeed, consistently with its professed objects, could it do so. Many cases must arise in which, if the remedy of the owner were confined to the mere right of seizure and recaption, he would be utterly without any adequate redress. He may not be able to lay his hands upon the slave. He may not be able to enforce his rights against persons who either secrete or conceal, or withhold the slave. He may be restricted by local legislation as to the mode of proofs of his ownership; as to the Courts in which he shall sue, and as to the actions which he may bring; or the process he may use to compel the delivery of the slave. Nay, the local legislation may be utterly inadequate to furnish the appropriate redress, by authorizing no process *in rem*, or no specific mode of repossessing the slave, leaving the owner, at best, not that right which the Constitution designed to secure— a specific delivery and repossession of the slave, but a mere remedy in damages; and that perhaps against persons utterly insolvent or worthless. The state legislation may be entirely silent on the whole subject, and its ordinary remedial process framed with different views and objects; and this may be innocently as well as designedly done, since every state is perfectly competent, and has the exclusive right to prescribe the remedies in its own judicial tribunals, to limit the time as well as the mode of redress, and to deny jurisdiction over cases, which its own policy and its own institutions either prohibit or discountenance. ...

And this leads us to the consideration of the other part of the clause, which implies at once a guaranty and duty. It says, "But he (the slave) shall be delivered up on claim of the party to whom such service or labour may be due." Now, we think it exceedingly difficult, if not impracticable, to read this language and not to feel that it contemplated some farther remedial redress than that

which might be administered at the hands of the owner himself. A claim is to be made. What is a claim? It is, in a just juridical sense, a demand of some matter as of right made by one person upon another, to do or to forbear to do some act or thing as a matter of duty. ... The slave is to be delivered up on the claim. By whom to be delivered up? In what mode to be delivered up? How, if a refusal takes place, is the right of delivery to be enforced? Upon what proofs? What shall be the evidence of a rightful recaption or delivery? When and under what circumstances shall the possession of the owner, after it is obtained, be conclusive of his right, so as to preclude any further inquiry or examination into it by local tribunals or otherwise, while the slave, in possession of the owner, is in transit to the state from which he fled?

These, and many other questions, will readily occur upon the slightest attention to the clause; and it is obvious that they can receive but one satisfactory answer. They require the aid of legislation to protect the right, to enforce the delivery, and to secure the subsequent possession of the slave. If, indeed, the Constitution guarantees the right, and if it requires the delivery upon the claim of the owner, (as cannot well be doubted,) the natural inference certainly is, that the national government is clothed with the appropriate authority and functions to enforce it. ...

It is plain, then, that where a claim is made by the owner, out of possession, for the delivery of a slave, it must be made, if at all, against some other person; and inasmuch as the right is a right of property capable of being recognized and asserted by proceedings before a Court of justice, between parties adverse to each other, it constitutes, in the strictest sense, a controversy between the parties, and a case "arising under the Constitution" of the United States; within the express delegation of judicial power given by that instrument. Congress, then, may call that power into activity for the very purpose of giving effect to that right; and if so, then it may prescribe the mode and extent in which it shall be applied, and how, and under what circumstances the proceedings shall afford a complete protection and guaranty to the right.

Congress has taken this very view of the power and duty of the national government. ... The result of their deliberations, was the passage of the act of 1793, which ... proceeds, in the third section, to provide, that when a person held to labour or service in any of the United States, shall escape into any other of the states or territories, the person to whom such labour or service may be due, his agent or attorney, is hereby empowered to seize or arrest such fugitive from labour, and take him or her before any judge of the Circuit or District Courts of the United States, residing or being within the state, or before any magistrate of a county, city, or town corporate, wherein such seizure or arrest shall be made; and upon proof to the satisfaction of such judge or magistrate, either by oral evidence or affidavit, &c., that the person so seized or arrested, doth, under the laws of the state or territory from which he or she fled, owe service or labour to the person claiming him or her, it shall be the duty of such judge or magistrate, to give a certificate thereof to such claimant, his agent or attorney, which shall be sufficient warrant for removing the said fugitive from labour, to the state or territory from which he or she fled. The fourth section provides a penalty against any person who shall knowingly and willingly obstruct or hinder such claimant, his agent, or attorney, in so seizing or arresting such fugitive from labour, or rescue such fugitive from the claimant, or his agent, or attorney when so arrested, or who shall harbour or conceal such fugitive after notice that he is such; and it also saves to the person claiming such labour or service, his right of action for or on account of such injuries.

In a general sense, this act may be truly said to cover the whole ground of the Constitution ... as to ... fugitive slaves. ... If this be so, then it would seem, upon just principles of construction, that the legislation of Congress, if constitutional, must supersede all state legislation upon the same subject; and by necessary implication prohibit it. For if Congress have a constitutional power to regulate a particular subject, and they do actually regulate it in a given manner, and in a certain form, it cannot be that the state legislatures have a right to interfere; and, as it were, by way of complement to the legislation of Congress, to prescribe additional regulations, and what they may deem auxiliary provisions for the same purpose. ...

The remaining question is, whether the power of legislation upon this subject is exclusive in the national government, or concurrent in the states, until it is exercised by Congress. In our opinion it is exclusive. ...

In the first place, ... the right to seize and retake fugitive slaves, and the duty to deliver them up, in whatever state of the Union they may be found, and of course the corresponding power in Congress to use the appropriate means to enforce the right and duty, derive their whole validity and obligation exclusively from the Constitution of the United States; and are there, for the first time, recognized and established in that peculiar character.

Before the adoption of the Constitution, no state had any power whatsoever over the subject, except within its own territorial limits, and could not bind the sovereignty or the legislation of other states. ...

In the next place, the nature of the provision and the objects to be attained by it, require that it should be controlled by one and the same will, and act uniformly by the same system of regulations throughout the Union. If, then, the states have a right, in the absence of legislation by Congress, to act upon the subject, each state is at liberty to prescribe just such regulations as suit its own policy, local convenience, and local feelings. The legislation of one state may not only be different from, but utterly repugnant to and incompatible with that of another. ...

It is scarcely conceivable that the slaveholding states would have been satisfied with leaving to the legislation of the non-slaveholding states, a power of regulation, in the absence of that of Congress, which would or might practically amount to a power to destroy the rights of the owner. If the argument, therefore, of a concurrent power in the states to act upon the subject-matter in the absence of legislation by Congress, be well founded; then, if Congress had never acted at all; or if the act of Congress should be repealed without providing a substitute, there would be a resulting authority in each of the states to regulate the whole subject at its pleasure; and to dole out its own remedial justice, or withhold it at its pleasure and according to its own views of policy and expediency. Surely such a state of things never could have been intended, under such a solemn guarantee of right and duty. ...

Upon these grounds, we are of opinion that the act of Pennsylvania upon which this indictment is founded, is unconstitutional and void. It purports to punish as a public offence against that state, the very act of seizing and removing a slave by his master, which the Constitution of the United States was designed to justify and uphold. ...

MR. JUSTICE M'LEAN, dissenting. ... In a state where slavery is allowed, every coloured person is presumed to be a slave; and on the same principle, in a non-slaveholding state, every person is presumed to be free without regard to colour. On this principle, the states, both slaveholding and non-slaveholding, legislate. The latter may prohibit, as Pennsylvania has done under a certain penalty, the forcible removal of a coloured person out of the state. Is such law in conflict with the act of 1793?

The act of 1793 authorizes a forcible seizure of the slave by the master, not to take him out of the state, but to take him before some judicial officer within it. The act of Pennsylvania punishes a forcible removal of a coloured person out of the state. Now, here is no conflict between the law of the state and the law of Congress. The execution of neither law can, by any just interpretation, in my opinion, interfere with the execution of the other. ...

No conflict can arise between the act of Congress and this state law. The conflict can only arise between the forcible acts of the master and the law of the state. The master exhibits no proof of right to the services of the slave, but seizes him and is about to remove him by force. I speak only of the force exerted on the slave. The law of the state presumes him to be free, and prohibits his removal. Now, which shall give way, the master or the state? The law of the state does, in no case, discharge, in the language of the Constitution, the slave from the service of his master. ...

The presumption of the state that the coloured person is free may be erroneous in fact; and if so, there can be no difficulty in proving it. But may not the assertion of the master be erroneous also; and if so, how is his act of force to be remedied? The coloured person is taken, and forcibly conveyed beyond the jurisdiction of the state. This force, not being authorized by the act of Congress nor by the Constitution, may be prohibited by the state. ...

It appears, in the case under consideration, that the state magistrate before whom the fugitive was brought refused to act. In my judgment he was bound to perform the duty required of him by a law paramount to any act, on the same subject, in his own state. But this refusal does not justify the subsequent action of the claimant. He should have taken the fugitive before a judge of the United States, two of whom resided within the state. ...

Federal Position

RACE-RELATED CONSTITUTIONAL
PROVISIONS
Pre-Civil War

Article I, Section 2:

3. Representatives and direct taxes shall be apportioned among the several States which may be included within this Union, according to their respective numbers, which shall be determined by adding to the whole number of free persons, including those bound to service for a term of years, and excluding Indians not taxed, three fifths of all other persons. ...

Article I, Section 9:

1. The migration or importation of such persons as any of the States now existing shall think proper to admit, shall not be prohibited by the Congress prior to the year one thousand eight hundred and eight, but a tax or duty may be imposed on such importation, not exceeding ten dollars for each person. ...

4. No capitation, or other direct, tax shall be laid, unless in proportion to the census or enumeration hereinbefore directed to be taken. ...

Article IV, Section 2:

3. No person held to service or labor in one State under the laws thereof, escaping into another, shall in consequence of any law or regulation therein, be discharged from such service or labor, but shall be delivered up on claim of the party to whom such service or labor may be due.

Article V:

The Congress, whenever two thirds of both Houses shall deem it necessary, shall propose amendments to this Constitution, or, on the application of the legislature of two thirds of the several States, shall call a convention for proposing amendments, which in either case, shall be valid to all intents and purposes, as part of this Constitution when ratified by the legislatures of three fourths of the several States, or by conventions in three fourths thereof, as the one or the other mode of ratification may be proposed by the Congress; Provided that no amendment which may be made prior to the year one thousand eight hundred and eight shall in any manner affect the first and fourth clauses in the ninth section of the first article; and that no State, without its consent, shall be deprived of its equal suffrage in the Senate.

THE ANTELOPE
United States Supreme Court (1825)
23 U.S. (10 Wheat.) 66

In 1808 Congress prohibited the importation of slaves into the United States. A series of subsequent federal enactments punished persons engaged in the slave trade, forfeited their ships, and provided that the Negroes be returned to Africa. The ship Antelope, bearing 280 Africans, most of whom had been seized by pirates from slave ships, was apprehended off the coast of Florida by a United States revenue cutter for suspected violation of the slave trade acts. The vice consuls of Spain and Portugal claimed the Africans as the property of citizens of their countries. The United States appealed from the circuit courts decision for the foreign claimants. The issue before the Court was whether the federal statutes applied to forfeit slaves owned by foreign nationals.

MARSHALL, C. J. . . . In prosecuting this appeal, the United States assert no property in themselves. They appear in the character of guardians, or next friends, of these Africans, who are brought, without any act of their own, into the bosom of our country, insist on their right to freedom, and submit their claim to the laws of the land, and to the tribunals of the nation. The consuls of Spain and Portugal, respectively, demand these Africans as slaves, who have, in the regular cause of legitimate commerce, been acquired as property, by the subjects of their respective sovereigns, and claim their restitution under the laws of the United States.

In examining claims of this momentous importance—claims in which the sacred rights of liberty and of property come in conflict with each other—which have drawn from the bar a degree of talent and of eloquence, worthy of the questions that have been discussed, this court must not yield to feelings which might seduce it from the path of duty, and must obey the mandate of the law.

That the course of opinion on the slave-trade should be unsettled, ought to excite no surprise. The Christian and civilized nations of the world, with whom we have most intercourse, have all been engaged in it. However abhorrent this traffic may be to a mind whose original feelings are not blunted by familiarity with the practice, it has been sanctioned, in modern times, by the laws of all nations who possess distant colonies, each of whom has engaged in it as a common commercial business, which no other could rightfully interrupt. It has claimed all the sanction which could be derived from long usage and general acquiescence. That trade could not be considered as contrary to the law of nations which was authorized and protected by the laws of all commercial nations; the right to carry on which was claimed by each, and allowed by each. . . .

The question, whether the slave-trade is prohibited by the law of nations has been seriously propounded, and both the affirmative and negative of the proposition have been maintained with equal earnestness. That it is contrary to the law of nature, will scarcely be denied. That every man has a natural right to the fruits of his own labor, is generally admitted; and that no other person can rightfully deprive him of those fruits, and appropriate them against his will, seems to be the necessary result of this admission. But from the earliest times, war has existed, and war confers rights in which all have acquiesced. Among the most enlightened nations of antiquity, one of these was, that the victor might enslave the vanquished. This, which was the usage of all, could not be pronounced repugnant to the law of nations, which is certainly to be tried by the test of general usage. That which has received the assent of all, must be the law of all. Slavery, then, has its origin in force; but as the world has agreed, that it is a legitimate result of force, the state of things which is thus produced by general consent, cannot be pronounced unlawful.

Throughout Christendom, this harsh rule has been exploded, and war is no longer considered, as giving a right to enslave captives. But this triumph of humanity has not been universal. The parties of the modern law of nations do not propagate their principles by force, and Africa has not yet adopted them. Throughout the whole extent of that immense continent, so far as we know its history, it is still the law of nations, that prisoners are slaves. Can those who have themselves renounced this law, be permitted to participate in its effects, by purchasing the beings who are its victims? Whatever might be the answer of a moralist to this question, a jurist must search for its legal solution, in those principles of action which are sanctioned by the usages, the national acts, and the general assent, of that portion of the world of which he considers himself as a part, and to whose law the appeal is made. If we resort to this standard, as the test of international law, the question, as has already been observed, is decided in favor of the legality of the trade. Both Europe and American embarked in it; and for nearly two centuries, it was carried on, without opposition, and without censure. A jurist could not say, that a practice, thus supported, was illegal, and that those engaged in it might be punished, either personally or by deprivation of property. In this commerce thus sanctioned by universal assent, every nation had an equal right to engage. How is this right to be lost? Each may renounce it for its own people; but can this renunciation effect others?

No principle of general law is more universally acknowledged, than the perfect equality of nations. Russia and Geneva have equal rights. It results from this equality, that no one can rightfully impose a rule on another. Each legislates for itself, but its legislation can operate on itself alone. A right, then, which is vested in all, by the consent of all, can be divested only by consent; and this trade, in which all have participated, must remain lawful to those who cannot be induced to relinquish it. As no nation can prescribe a rule for others, none can make a law of nations; and this traffic remains lawful to those whose governments have not forbidden it. If it be consistent with the law of nations, it cannot in itself be piracy. It can be made so only by statute; and the obligation of the statute cannot transcend the legislative power of the state which may enact it.

If it be neither repugnant to the law of nations, nor piracy, it is almost superfluous to say, in this court, that the right of bringing in for adjudication, in time of peace, even where the vessel belongs to a nation which has prohibited the trade, cannot exist. The courts of no country execute the penal laws of another, and the courts of the American government, on the subject of visitation and search, would decide any case in which that right had been exercised by an American cruiser, on the vessel of a foreign nation, not violating our municipal laws, against the captors. It follows, that a foreign vessel engaged in the African slave-trade, captured on the high seas, in time of peace, by an American cruiser, and brought in for adjudication, would be restored. ...

The general question being disposed of, it remains to examine the circumstances of the particular case. [The Court denied the Portuguese claims, taking judicial notice of the fact that] Americans, and others who cannot use the flag of their own nations, carry on this criminal and inhuman traffic, under the flags of other countries. ... [The real owner of the Africans claimed by Portugal] belongs to some other nation; and feels the necessity of concealment. [Because the Court was evenly divided over the legitimacy of the Spanish claim, it affirmed the lower court's decree, though it reduced the number of Africans to be restored to the Spanish owners.]

THE UNITED STATES, APPELLANTS, v. THE LIBELLANTS AND CLAIMANTS OF THE SCHOONER AMISTAD
Supreme Court of the United States
40 U.S. 518

OPINION

Mr. Justice STORY delivered the opinion of the Court.

This is the case of an appeal from the decree of the Circuit Court of the District of Connecticut, sitting in admiralty. The leading facts, as they appear upon the transcript of the proceedings, are as follows: On the 27th of June, 1839, the schooner L'Amistad, being the property of Spanish subjects, cleared out from the port of Havana, in the island of Cuba, for Puerto Principe, in the same island. On board of the schooner were the captain, Ransom Ferrer, and Jose Ruiz, and Pedro Montez, all Spanish subjects. The former had with him a negro boy, named Antonio, claimed to be his slave. Jose Ruiz had with him forty-nine negroes, claimed by him as his slaves, and stated to be his property, in a certain pass or document, signed by the Governor General of Cuba. Pedro Montez had with him four other negroes, also claimed by him as his slaves, and stated to be his property, in a similar pass or document, also signed by the Governor General of Cuba. On the voyage, and before the arrival of the vessel at her port of destination, the negroes rose, killed the captain, and took possession of her. On the 26th of August, the vessel was discovered by Lieutenant Gedney, of the United States brig Washington, at anchor on the high seas, at the distance of half a mile from the shore of Long Island. A part of the negroes were then on shore at Culloden Point, Long Island; who were seized by Lieutenant Gedney, and brought on board. The vessel, with the negroes and other persons on board, was brought by Lieutenant Gedney into the district of Connecticut, and there libeled for salvage in the District Court of the United States. ****On the 18th of September, Ruiz and Montez filed claims and libels, in which they asserted their ownership of the negroes as their slaves, and of certain parts of the cargo, and prayed that the same might be "delivered to them, or to the representatives of her Catholic majesty, as might be most proper." On the 19th of September, the Attorney of the United states, for the district of Connecticut, filed an information or libel, setting forth, that the Spanish minister had officially presented to the proper department of the government of the United States, a claim for the restoration of the vessel, cargo, and slaves, as the property of Spanish subjects, which had arrived within the jurisdictional limits of the United States, and were taken possession of by the said public armed brig of the United States; under such circumstances as made it the duty of the United States to cause the same to be restored to the true proprietors, pursuant to the treaty between the United States and Spain: and praying the Court, on its being made legally to appear that the claim of the Spanish minister was well founded, to make such order for the disposal of the vessel, cargo, and slaves, as would best enable the United States to comply with their treaty stipulations. But if it should appear, that the negroes were persons transported from Africa, in violation of the laws of the United States, and brought within the United States contrary to the same laws; he then prayed the Court to make such order for their removal to the coast of Africa, pursuant to the laws of the United States, as it should deem fit. ****

On the 7th of January, 1840, the negroes, Cinque and others, with the exception of Antonio, by their counsel, filed an answer, denying that they were slaves, or the property of Ruiz and Montez, or that the Court could, under the Constitution or laws of the United States, or under any treaty, exercise any jurisdiction over their persons, by reason of the premises; and praying that they might be dismissed. They specially set forth and insist in this answer, that they were native born Africans; born free, and still of right ought to be free and not slaves; that they were, on or about the 15th of April, 1839, unlawfully kidnapped, and forcibly and wrongfully carried on board a certain vessel on the coast of Africa, which was unlawfully engaged in the slave trade, and were unlawfully transported in the same vessel to the island of Cuba, for the purpose of being there unlawfully sold as slaves; that Ruiz and Montez, well knowing the premises, made a pretended purchase of them: that afterwards, on or about the 28th of June, 1839, Ruiz and Montez, confederating with Ferrer, (captain of the Amistad,) caused them, without law or right, to be placed on board of the Amistad, to be transported to some place unknown to them, and there to be enslaved for life; that, on the voyage, they rose on the master, and took possession of the vessel, intending to return therewith to their native country, or to seek an asylum in some free state; and the vessel arrived, about the 26th of August, 1839, off Montauk Point, near Long Island; a part of them were sent on shore, and were seized by Lieutenant Gedney, and carried on board; and all of them were afterwards brought by him into the district of Connecticut. ****

The main controversy is, whether these negroes are the property of Ruiz and Montez, and ought to be delivered up; and to this, accordingly, we shall first direct our attention.

It has been argued on behalf of the United States, that the Court are bound to deliver them up, according to the treaty of 1795, with Spain, **** The ninth article provides, "that all ships and merchandise, of what nature soever, which shall be rescued out of the hands of any pirates or robbers, on the high seas, shall be brought into some port of either state, and shall be delivered to the custody of the officers of that port, in order to be taken care of and restored entire to the true proprietor, as soon as due and sufficient proof shall be made concerning the property thereof." This is the article on which the main reliance is placed on behalf of the United States, for the restitution of these negroes. To bring the case within the article, it is essential to establish, First, That these negroes, under all the circumstances, fall within the description of merchandise, in the sense of the treaty. Secondly, That there has been a rescue of them on the high seas, out of the hands of the pirates and robbers; which, in the present case, can only be, by showing that they themselves are pirates and robbers; and, Thirdly, That Ruiz and Montez, the asserted proprietors, are the true proprietors, and have established their title by competent proof.

If these negroes were, at the time, lawfully held as slaves under the laws of Spain, and recognized by those laws as property capable of being lawfully bought and sold; we see no reason why they may not justly be deemed within the intent of the treaty, to be included under the denomination of merchandise, and, as such, ought to be restored to the claimants: for, upon that point, the laws of Spain would seem to furnish the proper rule of interpretation. But, admitting this, it is clear, in our opinion, that neither of the other essential facts and requisites has been established in proof; and the onus probandi of both lies upon the claimants to give rise to the causes foederis. It is plain beyond controversy, if we examine the evidence, that these negroes never were the lawful slaves of Ruiz or Montez, or of any other Spanish subjects. They are natives of Africa, and were kidnapped there, and were unlawfully transported to Cuba, in violation of the laws and treaties of Spain, and the most solemn edicts and declarations of that government. By those laws, and treaties, and edicts, the African slave trade is utterly abolished; the dealing in that trade is deemed a heinous crime; and the negroes thereby introduced into the dominions of Spain, are declared to be free. Ruiz and Montez are proved to have made the pretended purchase of these negroes, with a full knowledge of all the circumstances. And so cogent and irresistible is the evidence in this respect, that the District Attorney has admitted in open Court, upon the record, that these negroes were native Africans, and recently imported into Cuba, as alleged in their answers to the libels in the case. The supposed proprietary interest of Ruiz and Montez, is completely displaced, if we are at liberty to look at the evidence of the admissions of the District Attorney.

If, then, these negroes are not slaves, but are kidnapped Africans, who, by the laws of Spain itself, are entitled to their freedom, and were kidnapped and illegally carried to Cuba, and illegally detained and restrained on board of the Amistad; there is no pretence to say, that they are pirates or robbers. We may lament the dreadful acts, by which they asserted their liberty, and took possession of the Amistad, and endeavoured to regain their native country; but they cannot be deemed pirates or robbers in the sense of the law of nations, or the treaty with Spain, or the laws of Spain itself; at least so far as those laws have been brought to our knowledge. Nor do the libels of Ruiz or Montez assert them to be such.

This posture of the facts would seem, of itself, to put an end to the Whole inquiry upon the merits. But it is argued, on behalf of the United States, that the ship, and cargo, and negroes were duly documented as belonging to Spanish subjects, and this Court have no right to look behind these documents; that full faith and credit is to be given to them; and that they are to be held conclusive evidence in this cause, even although it should be established by the most satisfactory proofs, that they have been obtained by the grossest frauds and impositions upon the constituted authorities of Spain. To this argument we can, in no wise, assent. There is nothing in the treaty which justifies or sustains the argument. We do not here meddle with the point, whether there has been any connivance in this illegal traffic, on the part of any of the colonial authorities or subordinate officers of Cuba; because, in our view, such an examination is unnecessary, and ought not to be pursued, unless it were indispensable to public justice, although it has been strongly pressed at the bar. What we proceed upon is this, that although public documents of the government, accompanying property found on board of the private ships of a foreign nation, certainly are to be deemed prima facie evidence of the facts which they purport to state, yet they are always open to be impugned for fraud; and whether that fraud be in the original obtaining of these documents, or in the subsequent fraudulent and illegal use of them, when once it is satisfactorily established, it overthrows all their sanctity, and destroys them as proof. Fraud will vitiate any, even the most solemn transactions; and an asserted title to property, founded upon it, is utterly void. The very language of the ninth article of the treaty of 1795, requires the proprietor to make due and sufficient proof of his property. And how can that proof be deemed either due or sufficient, which is but a connected, and stained tissue of fraud? This is not a mere rule of municipal jurisprudence. Nothing is more clear in the law of nations, as an established rule to regulate their rights, and duties, and intercourse, than the doctrine, that the ship's papers are but prima facie evidence, and that, if they are shown to be fraudulent, they are not to be held proof of any valid title. This rule is familiarly applied, and, indeed, is of every-days occurrence in cases of prize, in the contests between belligerents and neutrals, as is apparent from numerous cases to be found in the Reports of this Court; and it is just as applicable to the transactions of civil intercourse between nations in times of peace. If a private ship, clothed with Spanish papers, should enter the ports of the United States, claiming the privileges, and immunities, and rights belonging to bona fide subjects of Spain, under our treaties or laws, and she should, in reality,

belong to the subjects of another nation, which was not entitled to any such privileges, immunities, or rights, and the proprietors were seeking, by fraud, to cover their own illegal acts, under the flag of Spain; there can be no doubt, that it would be the duty of our Courts to strip off the disguise, and to look at the case according to its naked realities. In the solemn treaties between nations, it can never be presumed that either state intends to provide the means of perpetrating or protecting frauds; but all the provisions are to be construed as intended to be applied to bona fide transactions. The seventeenth article of the treaty with Spain, which provides for certain passports and certificates, as evidence of property on board of the ships of both states, is, in its terms, applicable only to cases where either of the parties is engaged in a war. This article required a certain form of passport to be agreed upon by the parties, and annexed to the treaty. It never was annexed; and, therefore, in the case of the Amiable Isabella, 6 Wheaton, 1, it was held inoperative.

It is also a most important consideration in the present case, which ought not to be lost sight of, that, supposing these African negroes not to be slaves, but kidnapped, and free negroes, the treaty with Spain cannot be obligatory upon them; and the United States are bound to respect their rights as much as those of Spanish subjects. The conflict of rights between the parties under such circumstances, becomes positive and inevitable, and must be decided upon the eternal principles of justice and international law. If the contest were about any goods on board of this ship, to which American citizens asserted a title, which was denied by the Spanish claimants, there could be no doubt of the right of such American citizens to litigate their claims before any competent American tribunal, notwithstanding the treaty with Spain. A fortiori, the doctrine must apply where human life and human liberty are in issue; and constitute the very essence of the controversy. The treaty with Spain never could have intended to take away the equal rights of all foreigners, who should contest their claims before any of our Courts, to equal justice; or to deprive such foreigners of the protection given them by other treaties, or by the general law of nations. Upon the merits of the case, then, there does not seem to us to be any ground for doubt, that these negroes ought to be deemed free; and that the Spanish treaty interposes no obstacle to the just assertion of their rights. ****

DRED SCOTT v. SANDFORD
United States Supreme Court (1857)
60 U.S. (19 How.) 393

Scott, of Scott v. Emerson, *brought this suit in federal court after being unsuccessful in gaining his freedom through the Missouri courts. The Supreme Court refused to recognize a right in Scott, or in any Negro, to bring a lawsuit in federal court.*

TANEY, C.J. ... The question is simply this: Can a negro, whose ancestors were imported into this country, and sold as slaves, become a member of the political community formed and brought into existence by the Constitution of the United States, and as such become entitled to all the rights, and privileges, and immunities, guarantied by that instrument to the citizen? One of which rights is the privilege of suing in a court of the United States in the cases specified in the Constitution. ...

We think ... not. ... [Negroes] were at [the time of the adoption of the Constitution] considered as a subordinate and inferior class of beings, who had been subjugated by the dominant race, and, whether emancipated or not, yet remained subject to their authority, and had no rights or privileges but such as those who held the power and the Government might choose to grant them. ...

In discussing this question, we must not confound the rights of citizenship which a State may confer within its own limits, and the rights of citizenship as a member of the Union. It does not by any means follow, because he has all the rights and privileges of a citizen of a State, that he must be a citizen of the United States. He may have all of the rights and privileges of the citizen of a State, and yet not be entitled to the rights and privileges of a citizen in any other State. For, previous to the adoption of the Constitution of the United States, every State had the undoubted right to confer on whomsoever it pleased the character of citizen, and to endow him with all its rights. But this character of course was confined to the boundaries of the State, and gave him no rights or privileges in other States beyond those secured to him by the laws of nations and the comity of States. Nor have the several States surrendered the power of conferring these rights and privileges by adopting the Constitution of the United States. Each State may still confer them upon an alien, or any one it thinks proper ... ; yet he would not be a citizen in the sense in which that word is used in the Constitution of the United States, nor entitled to sue as such in one of its courts, nor to the privileges and immunities of a citizen in the other States. The rights which he would acquire would be restricted to the State which gave them.

It is very clear, therefore, that no State can, by any act or law of its own ... introduce a new member into the political community created by the Constitution of tile United States. ...

It becomes necessary, therefore, to determine who were citizens of the several States when the Constitution was adopted. And in order to do this, we must recur to the Governments and institutions of the thirteen colonies, when they separated from Great Britain and formed new sovereignties, and took their places in the family of independent nations. ...

In the opinion of the court, the legislation and histories of the times, and the language used in the Declaration of Independence, show, that neither the class of persons who had been imported as slaves, nor their descendants, whether they had become free or not, were then acknowledged as a part of the people, nor intended to be included in the general words used in that memorable instrument. ...

They had for more than a century before been regarded as beings of an inferior order, and altogether unfit to associate with the white race, either in social or political relations; and so far inferior, that they had no rights which the white man was bound to respect; and that the negro might justly and lawfully be reduced to slavery for his benefit. He was bought and sold, and treated as an ordinary article of merchandise and traffic, whenever a profit could be made by it. ...

And in no nation was this opinion more firmly fixed or more uniformly acted upon than by the English Government and English people. They not only seized them on the coast of Africa, and sold them or held them in slavery for their own use; but they took them as ordinary articles of merchandise to every country where they could make a profit on them, and were far more extensively engaged in this commerce than any other nation in the world.

The opinion thus entertained and acted upon in England was naturally impressed upon the colonies they founded on this side of the Atlantic. And, accordingly, a negro of the African race was regarded by them as an article of property, and held, and bought and sold as such, in every one of the thirteen colonies which united in the Declaration of Independence, and afterwards formed the Constitution of the United States. The slaves were more or less numerous in the different colonies, as slave labor was found more or less profitable. But no one seems to have doubted the correctness of the prevailing opinion of the time.

The legislation of the different colonies furnishes positive and indisputable proof of this fact. ... [Taney quotes Massachusetts and Maryland statutes punishing racial intermarriage.]

These laws show that a perpetual and impassable barrier was intended to be erected between the white race and the one which they had reduced to slavery, and governed as subjects with absolute and despotic power, and which they then looked upon as so far below them in the scale of created beings, that intermarriages between white persons and negroes or mulattoes were regarded as unnatural and immoral, and punished as crimes, not only in the parties, but in the person who joined them in marriage. And no distinction in this respect was made between the free negro or mulatto and the slave, but this stigma, of the deepest degradation, was fixed upon the whole race.

We refer to these historical facts for the purpose of showing the fixed opinions concerning that race, upon which the statesmen of that day spoke and acted. It is necessary to do this, in order to determine whether the general terms used in the Constitution of the United States, as to the rights of man and the rights of the people, was intended to include them, or to give to them or their posterity the benefit of any of its provisions. ...

... [T]here are two clauses in the Constitution which point directly and specifically to the negro race as a separate class of persons, and show clearly that they were not regarded as a portion of the people or citizens of the Government then formed.

One of these clauses reserves to each of the thirteen States the right to import slaves until the year 1808, if it thinks proper. And the importation which it thus sanctions was unquestionably of persons of the race of which we are speaking, as the traffic in slaves in the United States had always been confined to them. And by the other provision the States pledge themselves to each other to maintain the right of property of the master, by delivering up to him any slave who may have escaped from his service, and be found within their respective territories. By the first above-mentioned clause, therefore, the right to purchase and hold this property is directly sanctioned and authorized for twenty years by the people who framed the Constitution. And by the second, they pledge themselves to maintain and uphold the right of the master in the manner specified, as long as the Government they then formed should endure. And these two provisions show, conclusively, that neither the description of persons therein referred to, nor their descendants, were embraced in any of the other provisions of the Constitution; for certainly these two clauses were not intended to confer on them or their posterity the blessings of liberty, or any of the personal rights so carefully provided for the citizen. ...

Indeed, when we look to the condition of this race in the several States at the time, it is impossible to believe that these rights and privileges were intended to be extended to them.

It is very true, that in that portion of the Union where the labor of the negro race was found to be unsuited to the climate and unprofitable to the master, but few slaves were held at the time of the Declaration of Independence; and when the Constitution was adopted, it had entirely worn out in one of them, and measures had been taken for its gradual abolition in several others. But this change had not been produced by any change of opinion in relation to this race; but because it was discovered, from experience, that slave labor was unsuited to the climate and productions of these States: for some of the States, where it had ceased or nearly ceased to exist, were actively engaged in the slave trade, procuring cargoes on the coast of Africa, and transporting them for sale to those parts of the Union where their labor was found to be profitable, and suited to the climate and productions. And this traffic was openly carried on, and fortunes accumulated by it, without reproach from the people of the States where they resided. And it can hardly be supposed that, in the States where it was then countenanced in its worst form C that is, in the seizure and transportation C the people could have regarded those who were emancipated as entitled to equal rights with themselves.

And we may here again refer, in support of this proposition, to the plain and unequivocal language of the laws of the several States, some passed after the Declaration of Independence and before the Constitution was adopted, and some since the Government went into operation.

We need not refer, on this point, particularly to the laws of the present slaveholding States. ... As relates to these States, it is too plain for argument, that they have never been regarded as a part of the people or citizens of the State, nor supposed to possess any political rights which the dominant race might not withhold or grant at their pleasure. ...

And if we turn to the legislation of the States where slavery had worn out, or measures taken for its speedy abolition, we shall find the same opinions and principles equally fixed and equally acted upon. ... [A description of state laws prohibiting racial intermarriage and restricting the liberties of blacks is omitted.]

Chancellor Kent, whose accuracy and research no one will question, states in the sixth edition of his Commentaries ... that in no part of the country except Maine, did the African race, in point of fact, participate equally with the whites in the exercise of civil and political rights.

The legislation of the States therefore shows, in a manner not to be mistaken, the inferior and subject condition of that race at the time the Constitution was adopted, and long afterwards, throughout the thirteen States by which that instrument was framed; and it is hardly consistent with the respect due to these States, to suppose that they regarded at that time, as fellow-citizens and members of the sovereignty, a class of beings whom they had thus stigmatized; whom, as we are bound, out of respect to the State sovereignties, to assume they had deemed it just and necessary thus to stigmatize, and upon whom they had impressed such deep and enduring marks of inferiority and degradation; or, that when they met in convention to form the Constitution, they looked upon them as a portion of their constituents, or designed to include them in the provisions so carefully inserted for the security and protection of the liberties and rights of their citizens.

It cannot be supposed that they intended to secure to them rights, and privileges, and rank, in the new political body throughout the Union, which every one of them denied within the limits of its own dominion. More especially, it cannot be believed that the large slaveholding States regarded them as included in the word citizens, or would have consented to a Constitution which might compel them to receive them in that character from another State. For if they were so received, and entitled to the privileges and immunities of citizens, it would exempt them from the operation of the special laws and from the police regulations which they considered to be necessary for their own safety. It would give to persons of the negro race, who were recognized as citizens in any one State of the Union, the right to enter every other State whenever they pleased, singly or in companies, without pass or passport, and without obstruction, to sojourn there as long as they pleased, to go where they pleased at every hour of the day or night without molestation, unless they committed some violation of law for which a white man would be punished; and it would give them the full liberty of speech in public and in private upon all subjects upon which its own citizens might speak; to hold public meetings upon political affairs, and to keep and carry arms wherever they went. And all of this would be done in the face of the subject race of the same color, both free and slaves, and inevitably producing discontent and insubordination among them, and endangering the peace and safety of the State.

It is impossible, it would seem, to believe that the great men of the slaveholding States, who took so large a share in framing the Constitution of the United States, and exercised so much influence in procuring its adoption, could have been so forgetful or regardless of their own safety and the safety of those who trusted and confided in them.

Besides, this want of foresight and care would have been utterly inconsistent with the caution displayed in providing for the admission of new members into this political family. For, when they gave to the citizens of each State the privileges and immunities of citizens in the several States, they at the same time took from the several States the power of naturalization, and confined that power exclusively to the Federal Government. No State was willing to permit another State to determine who should or should not be admitted as one of its citizens, and entitled to demand equal rights and privileges with their own people, within their own territories. The right of naturalization was therefore, with one accord, surrendered by the States, and confided to the Federal Government. An this power granted to Congress to establish an uniform rule of *naturalization* is, by the well-understood meaning of the word, confined to persons born in a foreign country, under a foreign Government. It is not a power to raise to the rank of a citizen any one born in the United States, who from birth or parentage, by the laws of the country, belongs to an inferior and subordinate class. And when we find the States guarding themselves from the indiscreet or improper admission by other States of emigrants from other countries, by giving the power exclusively to Congress, we cannot fail to see that they could never have left with the States a much more important power C that is, the power of transforming into citizens a numerous class of persons, who in that character would be much more dangerous to the peace and safety of a large portion of the Union, than the few foreigners one of the States might improperly naturalize. ...

The facts with which I shall deal this evening are mainly old and familiar; nor is there anything new in the general use I shall make of them. If there shall be any novelty, it will be in the mode of presenting the facts, and the inferences and observations following that presentation.

In his speech last autumn, at Columbus, Ohio, as reported in "The New-York Times," Senator Douglas said:

"Our fathers, when they framed the Government under which we live, understood this question just as well, and even better, than we do now."

I fully indorse this, and I adopt it as a text for this discourse. I so adopt it because it furnishes a precise and an agreed starting point for a discussion between Republicans and that wing of the Democracy headed by Senator Douglas. It simply leaves the inquiry: "What was the understanding those fathers had of the question mentioned?"

What· is the frame of government under which we live?

The answer must be: "The Constitution of the United States." That Constitution consists of the original, framed in 1787, (and under which the present government first went into operation,) and twelve subsequently framed amendments, the first ten of which were framed in 1789.

Who were our fathers that framed the Constitution? I suppose the "thirty-nine" who signed the original instrument may be fairly called our fathers who framed that part of the present Government. It is almost exactly true to say they framed it, and it is altogether true to say they fairly represented the opinion and sentiment of the whole nation at that time. Their names, being familiar to nearly all, and accessible to quite all, need not now be repeated.

I take these "thirty-nine," for the present, as being "our fathers who framed the Government under which we live."

What is the question which, according to the text, those fathers understood "just as well, and even better than we do now?"

It is this: Does the proper division of local from federal authority, or anything in the Constitution, forbid our *Federal Government* to control as to slavery in *our Federal Territories?*

Upon this, Senator Douglas holds the affirmative, and Republicans the negative. This affirmation and denial form an issue; and this issue - this question - is precisely what the text declares our fathers understood "better than we."

Let us now inquire whether the "thirty-nine," or any of them, ever acted upon this question; and if they did, how they acted upon it - how they expressed that better understanding?

In 1784, three years before the Constitution - the United States then owning the Northwestern Territory, and no other, the Congress of the Confederation had before them the question of prohibiting slavery in that Territory; and four of the "thirty-nine" who afterward framed the Constitution, were in that Congress, and voted on that question. Of these, Roger Sherman, Thomas Mifflin, and Hugh Williamson voted for the prohibition, thus showing that, in their understanding, no line dividing local from federal authority, nor anything else, properly forbade the Federal Government to control as to slavery in federal territory. The other of the four - James M'Henry - voted against the prohibition, showing that, for some cause, he thought it improper to vote for it.

In 1787, still before the Constitution, but while the Convention was in session framing it, and while the Northwestern Territory still was the only territory owned by the United States, the same question of prohibiting slavery in the territory again came before the Congress of the Confederation; and two more of the "thirty-nine" who afterward signed the Constitution, were in that Congress, and voted on the question. They were William Blount and William Few; and they both voted for the prohibition - thus showing that, in their understanding, no line dividing local from federal authority, nor anything else, properly forbids the Federal Government to control as to slavery in Federal territory. This time the prohibition became a law, being part of what is now well known as the Ordinance of '87.

The question of federal control of slavery in the territories, seems not to have been directly before the Convention which framed the original Constitution; and hence it is not recorded that the "thirty-nine," or any of them, while engaged on that instrument, expressed any opinion on that precise question.

In 1789, by the first Congress which sat under the Constitution, an act was passed to enforce the Ordinance of '87, including the prohibition of slavery in the Northwestern Territory. The bill for this act was reported by one of the "thirty-nine," Thomas Fitzsimmons, then a member of the House of Representatives from Pennsylvania. It went through all its stages without a word of opposition, and finally passed both branches without yeas and nays, which is equivalent to a unanimous passage. In this Congress there were sixteen of the thirty-nine fathers who framed the original Constitution. They were John Langdon, Nicholas Gilman, Wm. S. Johnson, Roger Sherman, Robert Morris, Thos. Fitzsimmons, William Few, Abraham Baldwin, Rufus King, William Paterson, George Clymer, Richard Bassett, George Read, Pierce Butler, Daniel Carroll, James Madison.

This shows that, in their understanding, no line dividing local from federal authority, nor anything in the Constitution, properly forbade Congress to prohibit slavery in the federal territory; else both their fidelity to correct principle, and their oath to support the Constitution, would have constrained them to oppose the prohibition.

Again, George Washington, another of the "thirty-nine," was then President of the United States, and, as such approved and signed the bill; thus completing its validity as a law, and thus showing that, in his understanding, no line dividing local from federal authority, nor anything in the Constitution, forbade the Federal Government, to control as to slavery in federal territory.

No great while after the adoption of the original Constitution, North Carolina ceded to the Federal Government the country now constituting the State of Tennessee; and a few years later Georgia ceded that which now constitutes the States of Mississippi and Alabama. In both deeds of cession it was made a condition by the ceding States that the Federal Government should not prohibit slavery in the ceded territory. Besides this, slavery was then actually in the ceded country. Under these circumstances, Congress, on taking charge of these countries, did not absolutely prohibit slavery within them. But they did interfere with it - take control of it - even there, to a certain extent. In 1798, Congress organized the Territory of Mississippi. In the act of organization, they prohibited the bringing of slaves into the Territory, from any place without the United States, by fine, and giving freedom to slaves so bought. This act passed both branches of Congress without yeas and nays. In that Congress were three of the "thirty-nine" who framed the original Constitution. They were John Langdon, George Read and Abraham Baldwin. They all, probably, voted for it. Certainly they would have placed their opposition to it upon record, if, in their understanding, any line dividing local from federal authority, or anything in the Constitution, properly forbade the Federal Government to control as to slavery in federal territory.

In 1803, the Federal Government purchased the Louisiana country. Our former territorial acquisitions came from certain of our own States; but this Louisiana country was acquired from a foreign nation. In 1804, Congress gave a territorial organization to that part of it which now constitutes the State of Louisiana. New Orleans, lying within that part, was an old and comparatively large city. There were other considerable towns and settlements, and slavery was extensively and thoroughly intermingled with the people. Congress did not, in the Territorial Act, prohibit slavery; but they did interfere with it - take control of it - in a more marked and extensive way than they did in the case of Mississippi. The substance of the provision therein made, in relation to slaves, was:

First. That no slave should be imported into the territory from foreign parts.

Second. That no slave should be carried into it who had been imported into the United States since the first day of May, 1798.

Third. That no slave should be carried into it, except by the owner, and for his own use as a settler; the penalty in all the cases being a fine upon the violator of the law, and freedom to the slave.

This act also was passed without yeas and nays. In the Congress which passed it, there were two of the "thirty-nine." They were Abraham Baldwin and Jonathan

Dayton. As stated in the case of Mississippi, it is probable they both voted for it. They would not have allowed it to pass without recording their opposition to it, if, in their understanding, it violated either the line properly dividing local from federal authority, or any provision of the Constitution.

In 1819-20, came and passed the Missouri question. Many votes were taken, by yeas and nays, in both branches of Congress, upon the various phases of the general question. Two of the "thirty-nine" - Rufus King and Charles Pinckney - were members of that Congress. Mr. King steadily voted for slavery prohibition and against all compromises, while Mr. Pinckney as steadily voted against slavery prohibition and against all compromises. By this, Mr. King showed that, in his understanding, no line dividing local from federal authority, nor anything in the Constitution, was violated by Congress prohibiting slavery in federal territory; while Mr. Pinckney, by his votes, showed that, in his understanding, there was some sufficient reason for opposing such prohibition in that case.

The cases I have mentioned are the only acts of the "thirty-nine," or of any of them, upon the direct issue, which I have been able to discover.

To enumerate the persons who thus acted, as being four in 1784, two in 1787, seventeen in 1789, three in 1798, two in 1804, and two in 1819-20 - there would be thirty of them. But this would be counting John Langdon, Roger Sherman, William Few, Rufus King, and George Read each twice, and Abraham Baldwin, three times. The true number of those of the "thirty-nine" whom I have shown to have acted upon the question, which, by the text, they understood better than we, is twenty-three, leaving sixteen not shown to have acted upon it in any way.

Here, then, we have twenty-three out of our thirty-nine fathers "who framed the government under which we live," who have, upon their official responsibility and their corporal oaths, acted upon the very question which the text affirms they "understood just as well, and even better than we do now;" and twenty-one of them - a clear majority of the whole "thirty-nine" - so acting upon it as to make them guilty of gross political impropriety and willful perjury, if, in their understanding, any proper division between local and federal authority, or anything in the Constitution they had made themselves, and sworn to support, forbade the Federal Government to control as to slavery in the federal territories. Thus the twenty-one acted; and, as actions speak louder than words, so actions, under such responsibility, speak still louder.

Two of the twenty-three voted against Congressional prohibition of slavery in the federal territories, in the instances in which they acted upon the question. But for what reasons they so voted is not known. They may have done so because they thought a proper division of local from federal authority, or some provision or principle of the Constitution, stood in the way; or they may, without any such question, have voted against the prohibition, on what appeared to them to be sufficient grounds of expediency. No one who has sworn to support the Constitution can conscientiously vote for what he understands to be an unconstitutional measure, however expedient he may think it; but one may and ought to vote against a measure which he deems constitutional, if, at the same time, he deems it inexpedient. It, therefore, would be unsafe to set down even the two who voted against the prohibition, as having done so because, in their understanding, any proper division of local from federal authority, or anything in the Constitution, forbade the Federal Government to control as to slavery in federal territory.

The remaining sixteen of the "thirty-nine," so far as I have discovered, have left no record of their understanding upon the direct question of federal control of slavery in the federal territories. But there is much reason to believe that their understanding upon that question would not have appeared different from that of their twenty-three compeers, had it been manifested at all.

For the purpose of adhering rigidly to the text, I have purposely omitted whatever understanding may have been manifested by any person, however distinguished, other than the thirty-nine fathers who framed the original Constitution; and, for the same reason, I have also omitted whatever understanding may have been manifested by any of the "thirty-nine" even, on any other phase of the general question of slavery. If we should look into their acts and declarations on those other phases, as the foreign slave trade, and the morality and policy of slavery generally, it would appear to us that on the direct question of federal control of slavery in federal territories, the sixteen, if they had acted at all, would probably have acted just as the twenty-three did. Among that sixteen were several of the most noted anti-slavery men of those times - as Dr. Franklin, Alexander Hamilton and Gouverneur Morris - while there was not one now known to have been otherwise, unless it may be John Rutledge, of South Carolina.

The sum of the whole is, that of our thirty-nine fathers who framed the original Constitution, twenty-one - a clear majority of the whole - certainly understood that no proper division of local from federal authority, nor any part of the Constitution, forbade the Federal Government to control slavery in the federal territories; while all the rest probably had the same understanding. Such, unquestionably, was the understanding of our fathers who framed the original Constitution; and the text affirms that they understood the question "better than we."

But, so far, I have been considering the understanding of the question manifested by the framers of the original Constitution. In and by the original instrument, a mode was provided for amending it; and, as I have already stated, the present frame of "the Government under which we live" consists of that original, and twelve amendatory articles framed and adopted since. Those who now insist that federal control of slavery in federal territories violates the Constitution, point us to the provisions which they suppose it thus violates; and, as I understand, that all fix upon provisions in these amendatory articles, and not in the original instrument. The Supreme Court, in the Dred Scott case, plant themselves upon the fifth amendment, which provides that no person shall be deprived of "life, liberty or property without due process of law;" while Senator Douglas and his peculiar adherents plant themselves upon the tenth amendment, providing that "the powers not delegated to the United States by the Constitution" "are reserved to the States respectively, or to the people."

Now, it so happens that these amendments were framed by the first Congress which sat under the Constitution - the identical Congress which passed the act already mentioned, enforcing the prohibition of slavery in the Northwestern Territory. Not only was it the same Congress, but they were the identical, same individual men who, at the same session, and at the same time within the session, had under consideration, and in progress toward maturity, these Constitutional amendments, and this act prohibiting slavery in all the territory the nation then owned. The Constitutional amendments were introduced before, and passed after the act enforcing the Ordinance of '87; so that, during the whole pendency of the act to enforce the Ordinance, the Constitutional amendments were also pending.

The seventy-six members of that Congress, including sixteen of the framers of the original Constitution, as before stated, were pre- eminently our fathers who framed that part of "the Government under which we live," which is now claimed as forbidding the Federal Government to control slavery in the federal territories.

Is it not a little presumptuous in any one at this day to affirm that the two things which that Congress deliberately framed, and carried to maturity at the same time, are absolutely inconsistent with each other? And does not such affirmation become impudently absurd when coupled with the other affirmation from the same mouth, that those who did the two things, alleged to be inconsistent, understood whether they really were inconsistent better than we - better than he who affirms that they are inconsistent?

It is surely safe to assume that the thirty-nine framers of the original Constitution, and the seventy-six members of the Congress which framed the amendments thereto, taken together, do certainly include those who may be fairly called "our fathers who framed the Government under which we live." And so assuming, I defy any man to show that any one of them ever, in his whole life, declared that, in his understanding, any proper division of local from federal authority, or any part of the Constitution, forbade the Federal Government to control as to slavery in the federal territories. I go a step further. I defy any one to show that any living man in the whole world ever did, prior to the beginning of the present century, (and I might almost say prior to the beginning of the last half of the present century,) declare that, in his understanding, any proper division of local from federal authority, or any part of the Constitution, forbade the Federal Government to control as to slavery in the federal territories. To those who now so declare, I give, not only "our fathers who framed the Government under which we live," but with them all other living men within the century in which it was framed, among whom to search, and they shall not be able to find the evidence of a single man agreeing with them.

Now, and here, let me guard a little against being misunderstood. I do not mean to say we are bound to follow implicitly in whatever our fathers did. To do so, would be to discard all the lights of current experience - to reject all progress - all improvement. What I do say is, that if we would supplant the opinions and policy of our fathers in any case, we should do so upon evidence so conclusive, and argument so clear, that even their great authority, fairly considered and weighed, cannot stand; and most surely not in a case whereof we ourselves declare they understood the question better than we.

If any man at this day sincerely believes that a proper division of local from federal authority, or any part of the Constitution, forbids the Federal Government to control as to slavery in the federal territories, he is right to say so, and to enforce his position by all truthful evidence and fair argument which he can. But he has no right to mislead others, who have less access to history, and less leisure to study it, into the false belief that "our fathers who framed the Government under which we live" were of the same opinion - thus substituting falsehood and deception for truthful evidence and fair argument. If any man at this day sincerely believes "our fathers who framed the Government under which we live," used and applied principles, in other cases, which ought to have led them to understand that a proper division of local from federal authority or some part of the Constitution, forbids the Federal Government to control as to slavery in the federal territories, he is right to say so. But he should, at the same time, brave the responsibility of declaring that, in his opinion, he understands their principles better than they did themselves; and especially should he not shirk that responsibility by asserting that they "understood the question just as well, and even better, than we do now."

But enough! *Let all who believe that "our fathers, who framed the Government under which we live, understood this question just as well, and even better, than we do now," speak as they spoke, and act as they acted upon it. This is all Republicans ask - all Republicans desire - in relation to slavery. As those fathers marked it, so let it be again marked, as an evil not to be extended, but to be tolerated and protected only because of and so far as its actual presence among us makes that toleration and protection a necessity. Let all the guarantees those fathers gave it, be, not grudgingly, but fully and fairly, maintained.* For this Republicans contend, and with this, so far as I know or believe, they will be content.

And now, if they would listen - as I suppose they will not - I would address a few words to the Southern people.

I would say to them: - You consider yourselves a reasonable and a just people; and I consider that in the general qualities of reason and justice you are not inferior to any other people. Still, when you speak of us Republicans, you do so only to denounce us a reptiles, or, at the best, as no better than outlaws. You will grant a hearing to pirates or murderers, but nothing like it to "Black Republicans." In all your contentions with one another, each of you deems an unconditional condemnation of "Black Republicanism" as the first thing to be attended to. Indeed, such condemnation of us seems to be an indispensable prerequisite - license, so to speak - among you to be admitted or permitted to speak at all. Now, can you, or not, be prevailed upon to pause and to

consider whether this is quite just to us, or even to yourselves? Bring forward your charges and specifications, and then be patient long enough to hear us deny or justify.

You say we are sectional. We deny it. That makes an issue; and the burden of proof is upon you. You produce your proof; and what is it? Why, that our party has no existence in your section - gets no votes in your section. The fact is substantially true; but does it prove the issue? If it does, then in case we should, without change of principle, begin to get votes in your section, we should thereby cease to be sectional. You cannot escape this conclusion; and yet, are you willing to abide by it? If you are, you will probably soon find that we have ceased to be sectional, for we shall get votes in your section this very year. You will then begin to discover, as the truth plainly is, that your proof does not touch the issue. The fact that we get no votes in your section, is a fact of your making, and not of ours. And if there be fault in that fact, that fault is primarily yours, and remains until you show that we repel you by some wrong principle or practice. If we do repel you by any wrong principle or practice, the fault is ours; but this brings you to where you ought to have started - to a discussion of the right or wrong of our principle. If our principle, put in practice, would wrong your section for the benefit of ours, or for any other object, then our principle, and we with it, are sectional, and are justly opposed and denounced as such. Meet us, then, on the question of whether our principle, put in practice, would wrong your section; and so meet it as if it were possible that something may be said on our side. Do you accept the challenge? No! Then you really believe that the principle which "our fathers who framed the Government under which we live" thought so clearly right as to adopt it, and indorse it again and again, upon their official oaths, is in fact so clearly wrong as to demand your condemnation without a moment's consideration.

Some of you delight to flaunt in our faces the warning against sectional parties given by Washington in his Farewell Address. Less than eight years before Washington gave that warning, he had, as President of the United States, approved and signed an act of Congress, enforcing the prohibition of slavery in the Northwestern Territory, which act embodied the policy of the Government upon that subject up to and at the very moment he penned that warning; and about one year after he penned it, he wrote LaFayette that he considered that prohibition a wise measure, expressing in the same connection his hope that we should at some time have a confederacy of free States.

Bearing this in mind, and seeing that sectionalism has since arisen upon this same subject, is that warning a weapon in your hands against us, or in our hands against you? Could Washington himself speak, would he cast the blame of that sectionalism upon us, who sustain his policy, or upon you who repudiate it? We respect that warning of Washington, and we commend it to you, together with his example pointing to the right application of it.

But you say you are conservative - eminently conservative - while we are revolutionary, destructive, or something of the sort. What is conservatism? Is it not adherence to the old and tried, against the new and untried? We stick to, contend for, the identical old policy on the point in controversy which was adopted by "our fathers who framed the Government under which we live;" while you with one accord reject, and scout, and spit upon that old policy, and insist upon substituting something new. True, you disagree among yourselves as to what that substitute shall be. You are divided on new propositions and plans, but you are unanimous in rejecting and denouncing the old policy of the fathers. Some of you are for reviving the foreign slave trade; some for a Congressional Slave-Code for the Territories; some for Congress forbidding the Territories to prohibit Slavery within their limits; some for maintaining Slavery in the Territories through the judiciary; some for the "gur-reat pur-rinciple" that "if one man would enslave another, no third man should object," fantastically called "Popular Sovereignty;" but never a man among you is in favor of federal prohibition of slavery in federal territories, according to the practice of "our fathers who framed the Government under which we live." Not one of all your various plans can show a precedent or an advocate in the century within which our Government originated. Consider, then, whether your claim of conservatism for yourselves, and your charge or destructiveness against us, are based on the most clear and stable foundations.

Again, you say we have made the slavery question more prominent than it formerly was. We deny it. We admit that it is more prominent, but we deny that we made it so. It was not we, but you, who discarded the old policy of the fathers. We resisted, and still resist, your innovation; and thence comes the greater prominence of the question. Would you have that question reduced to its former proportions? Go back to that old policy. What has been will be again, under the same

conditions. If you would have the peace of the old times, readopt the precepts and policy of the old times.

You charge that we stir up insurrections among your slaves. We deny it; and what is your proof? Harper's Ferry! John Brown!! John Brown was no Republican; and you have failed to implicate a single Republican in his Harper's Ferry enterprise. If any member of our party is guilty in that matter, you know it or you do not know it. If you do know it, you are inexcusable for not designating the man and proving the fact. If you do not know it, you are inexcusable for asserting it, and especially for persisting in the assertion after you have tried and failed to make the proof. You need to be told that persisting in a charge which one does not know to be true, is simply malicious slander.

Some of you admit that no Republican designedly aided or encouraged the Harper's Ferry affair, but still insist that our doctrines and declarations necessarily lead to such results. We do not believe it. We know we hold to no doctrine, and make no declaration, which were not held to and made by "our fathers who framed the Government under which we live." You never dealt fairly by us in relation to this affair. When it occurred, some important State elections were near at hand, and you were in evident glee with the belief that, by charging the blame upon us, you could get an advantage of us in those elections. The elections came, and your expectations were not quite fulfilled. Every Republican man knew that, as to himself at least, your charge was a slander, and he was not much inclined by it to cast his vote in your favor. Republican doctrines and declarations are accompanied with a continual protest against any interference whatever with your slaves, or with you about your slaves. Surely, this does not encourage them to revolt. True, we do, in common with "our fathers, who framed the Government under which we live," declare our belief that slavery is wrong; but the slaves do not hear us declare even this. For anything we say or do, the slaves would scarcely know there is a Republican party. I believe they would not, in fact, generally know it but for your misrepresentations of us, in their hearing. In your political contests among yourselves, each faction charges the other with sympathy with Black Republicanism; and then, to give point to the charge, defines Black Republicanism to simply be insurrection, blood and thunder among the slaves.

Slave insurrections are no more common now than they were before the Republican party was organized. What induced the Southampton insurrection, twenty-eight years ago, in which, at least three times as many lives were lost as at Harper's Ferry? You can scarcely stretch your very elastic fancy to the conclusion that Southampton was "got up by Black Republicanism." In the present state of things in the United States, I do not think a general, or even a very extensive slave insurrection is possible. The indispensable concert of action cannot be attained. The slaves have no means of rapid communication; nor can incendiary freemen, black or white, supply it. The explosive materials are everywhere in parcels; but there neither are, nor can be supplied, the indispensable connecting trains.

Much is said by Southern people about the affection of slaves for their masters and mistresses; and a part of it, at least, is true. A plot for an uprising could scarcely be devised and communicated to twenty individuals before some one of them, to save the life of a favorite master or mistress, would divulge it. This is the rule; and the slave revolution in Hayti was not an exception to it, but a case occurring under peculiar circumstances. The gunpowder plot of British history, though not connected with slaves, was more in point. In that case, only about twenty were admitted to the secret; and yet one of them, in his anxiety to save a friend, betrayed the plot to that friend, and, by consequence, averted the calamity. Occasional poisonings from the kitchen, and open or stealthy assassinations in the field, and local revolts extending to a score or so, will continue to occur as the natural results of slavery; but no general insurrection of slaves, as I think, can happen in this country for a long time. Whoever much fears, or much hopes for such an event, will be alike disappointed.

In the language of Mr. Jefferson, uttered many years ago, "It is still in our power to direct the process of emancipation, and deportation, peaceably, and in such slow degrees, as that the evil will wear off insensibly; and their places be, *pari passu*, filled up by free white laborers. If, on the contrary, it is left to force itself on, human nature must shudder at the prospect held up."

Mr. Jefferson did not mean to say, nor do I, that the power of emancipation is in the Federal Government. He spoke of Virginia; and, as to the power of emancipation, I speak of the slaveholding States only. The Federal Government, however, as we insist, has the power of restraining the extension of the institution - the power to insure that a slave insurrection shall never occur on any American soil which is now free from slavery.

John Brown's effort was peculiar. It was not a slave insurrection. It was an attempt by white men to get up a revolt among slaves, in which the slaves refused to participate. In fact, it was so absurd that the slaves, with all their ignorance, saw plainly enough it could not succeed. That affair, in its philosophy, corresponds with the many attempts, related in history, at the assassination of kings and emperors. An enthusiast broods over the oppression of a people till he fancies himself commissioned by Heaven to liberate them. He ventures the attempt, which ends in little else than his own execution. Orsini's attempt on Louis Napoleon, and John Brown's attempt at Harper's Ferry were, in their philosophy, precisely the same. The eagerness to cast blame on old England in the one case, and on New England in the other, does not disprove the sameness of the two things.

And how much would it avail you, if you could, by the use of John Brown, Helper's Book, and the like, break up the Republican organization? Human action can be modified to some extent, but human nature cannot be changed. There is a judgment and a feeling against slavery in this nation, which cast at least a million and a half of votes. You cannot destroy that judgment and feeling - that sentiment - by breaking up the political organization which rallies around it. You can scarcely scatter and disperse an army which has been formed into order in the face of your heaviest fire; but if you could, how much would you gain by forcing the sentiment which created it out of the peaceful channel of the ballot-box, into some other channel? What would that other channel probably be? Would the number of John Browns be lessened or enlarged by the operation?

But you will break up the Union rather than submit to a denial of your Constitutional rights.

That has a somewhat reckless sound; but it would be palliated, if not fully justified, were we proposing, by the mere force of numbers, to deprive you of some right, plainly written down in the Constitution. But we are proposing no such thing.

When you make these declarations, you have a specific and well-understood allusion to an assumed Constitutional right of yours, to take slaves into the federal territories, and to hold them there as property. But no such right is specifically written in the Constitution. That instrument is literally silent about any such right. We, on the contrary, deny that such a right has any existence in the Constitution, even by implication.

Your purpose, then, plainly stated, is that you will destroy the Government, unless you be allowed to construe and enforce the Constitution as you please, on all points in dispute between you and us. You will rule or ruin in all events.

This, plainly stated, is your language. Perhaps you will say the Supreme Court has decided the disputed

Constitutional question in your favor. Not quite so. But waiving the lawyer's distinction between dictum and decision, the Court have decided the question for you in a sort of way. The Court have substantially said, it is your Constitutional right to take slaves into the federal territories, and to hold them there as property. When I say the decision was made in a sort of way, I mean it was made in a divided Court, by a bare majority of the Judges, and they not quite agreeing with one another in the reasons for making it; that it is so made as that its avowed supporters disagree with one another about its meaning, and that it was mainly based upon a mistaken statement of fact - the statement in the opinion that "the right of property in a slave is distinctly and expressly affirmed in the Constitution."

An inspection of the Constitution will show that the right of property in a slave is not "*distinctly* and *expressly* affirmed" in it. Bear in mind, the Judges do not pledge their judicial opinion that such right is *impliedly* affirmed in the Constitution; but they pledge their veracity that it is "*distinctly* and *expressly*" affirmed there - "distinctly," that is, not mingled with anything else - "expressly," that is, in words meaning just that, without the aid of any inference, and susceptible of no other meaning.

If they had only pledged their judicial opinion that such right is affirmed in the instrument by implication, it would be open to others to show that neither the word "slave" nor "slavery" is to be found in the Constitution, nor the word "property" even, in any connection with language alluding to the things slave, or slavery; and that wherever in that instrument the slave is alluded to, he is called a "person;" - and wherever his master's legal right in relation to him is alluded to, it is spoken of as "service or labor which may be due," - as a debt payable in service or labor. Also, it would be open to show, by contemporaneous history, that this mode of alluding to slaves and slavery, instead of speaking of them, was employed on purpose to exclude from the Constitution the idea that there could be property in man.

To show all this, is easy and certain.

When this obvious mistake of the Judges shall be brought to their notice, is it not reasonable to expect that they will withdraw the mistaken statement, and reconsider the conclusion based upon it?

And then it is to be remembered that "our fathers, who framed the Government under which we live" - the men who made the Constitution - decided this same Constitutional question in our favor, long ago - decided it without division among themselves, when making the decision; without division among themselves about the meaning of it after it was made, and, so far as any evidence is left, without basing it upon any mistaken statement of facts.

Under all these circumstances, do you really feel yourselves justified to break up this Government unless such a court decision as yours is, shall be at once submitted to as a conclusive and final rule of political action? But you will not abide the election of a Republican president! In that supposed event, you say, you will destroy the Union; and then, you say, the great crime of having destroyed it will be upon us! That is cool. A highwayman holds a pistol to my ear, and mutters through his teeth, "Stand and deliver, or I shall kill you, and then you will be a murderer!"

To be sure, what the robber demanded of me - my money - was my own; and I had a clear right to keep it; but it was no more my own than my vote is my own; and the threat of death to me, to extort my money, and the threat of destruction to the Union, to extort my vote, can scarcely be distinguished in principle.

A few words now to Republicans. *It is exceedingly desirable that all parts of this great Confederacy shall be at peace, and in harmony, one with another. Let us Republicans do our part to have it so. Even though much provoked, let us do nothing through passion and ill temper. Even though the southern people will not so much as listen to us, let us calmly consider their demands, and yield to them if, in our deliberate view of our duty, we possibly can.* Judging by all they say and do, and by the subject and nature of their controversy with us, let us determine, if we can, what will satisfy them.

Will they be satisfied if the Territories be unconditionally surrendered to them? We know they will not. In all their present complaints against us, the Territories are scarcely mentioned. Invasions and insurrections are the rage now. Will it satisfy them, if, in the future, we have nothing to do with invasions and insurrections? We know it will not. We so know, because we know we never had anything to do with invasions and insurrections; and yet this total abstaining does not exempt us from the charge and the denunciation.

The question recurs, what will satisfy them? Simply this: We must not only let them alone, but we must somehow, convince them that we do let them alone. This, we know by experience, is no easy task. We have been so trying to convince them from the very beginning of our organization, but with no success. In all our platforms and speeches we have constantly protested our purpose to let them alone; but this has had no tendency to convince them. Alike unavailing to convince them, is the fact that they have never detected a man of us in any attempt to disturb them.

These natural, and apparently adequate means all failing, what will convince them? This, and this only: cease to call slavery *wrong*, and join them in calling it *right*. And this must be done thoroughly - done in *acts* as well as in *words*. Silence will not be tolerated - we must place ourselves avowedly with them. Senator Douglas' new sedition law must be enacted and enforced, suppressing all declarations that slavery is wrong, whether made in politics, in presses, in pulpits, or in private. We must arrest and return their fugitive slaves with greedy pleasure. We must pull down our Free State constitutions. The whole atmosphere must be disinfected from all taint of opposition to slavery, before they will cease to believe that all their troubles proceed from us.

I am quite aware they do not state their case precisely in this way. Most of them would probably say to us, "Let us alone, do nothing to us, and say what you please about slavery." But we do let them alone - have never disturbed them - so that, after all, it is what we say, which dissatisfies them. They will continue to accuse us of doing, until we cease saying.

I am also aware they have not, as yet, in terms, demanded the overthrow of our Free-State Constitutions. Yet those Constitutions declare the wrong of slavery, with more solemn emphasis, than do all other sayings against it; and when all these other sayings shall have been silenced, the overthrow of these Constitutions will be demanded, and nothing be left to resist the demand. It is nothing to the contrary, that they do not demand the whole of this just now. Demanding what they do, and for the reason they do, they can voluntarily stop nowhere short of this consummation. Holding, as they do, that slavery is morally right, and socially elevating, they cannot cease to demand a full national recognition of it, as a legal right, and a social blessing.

Nor can we justifiably withhold this, on any ground save our conviction that slavery is wrong. If slavery is right, all words, acts, laws, and constitutions against it, are themselves wrong, and should be silenced, and swept away. If it is right, we cannot justly object to its nationality - its universality; if it is wrong, they cannot justly insist upon its extension - its enlargement. All they ask, we could readily grant, if we thought slavery right; all we ask, they could as readily grant, if they thought it wrong. Their thinking it right, and our thinking it wrong, is the precise fact upon which depends the whole controversy. Thinking it right, as they do, they are not to blame for desiring its full recognition, as being right; but, thinking it wrong, as we do, can we yield to them? Can we cast our votes with their view, and against our own? In view of our moral, social, and political responsibilities, can we do this?

Wrong as we think slavery is, we can yet afford to let it alone where it is, because that much is due to the necessity arising from its actual presence in the nation; but can we, while our votes will prevent it, allow it to spread into the National Territories, and to overrun us here in these Free States? If our sense of duty forbids this, then let us stand by our duty, fearlessly and effectively. Let us be diverted by none of those sophistical contrivances wherewith we are so industriously plied and belabored - contrivances such as groping for some middle ground between the right and the wrong, vain as the search for a man who should be neither a living man nor a dead man - such as a policy of "don't care" on a question about which all true men do care - such as Union appeals beseeching true Union men to yield to Disunionists, reversing the divine rule, and calling, not the sinners, but the righteous to repentance - such as invocations to Washington, imploring men to unsay what Washington said, and undo what Washington did.

Neither let us be slandered from our duty by false accusations against us, nor frightened from it by menaces of destruction to the Government nor of dungeons to ourselves. LET US HAVE FAITH THAT RIGHT MAKES MIGHT, AND IN THAT FAITH, LET US, TO THE END, DARE TO DO OUR DUTY AS WE UNDERSTAND IT.

In Re: African-American Slave Descendants Litigation. Appeals of:
DEADRIA FARMER-PAELLMANN, et al., and TIMOTHY HURDLE, et al.
United States Court of Appeals for the Seventh Circuit
471 F.3d 754

December 13, 2006, Decided

OPINION BY:

POSNER

POSNER, *Circuit Judge*. Nine suits were filed in federal district courts around the country seeking monetary relief under both federal and state law for harms stemming from the enslavement of black people in America. A tenth suit, by the Hurdle group of plaintiffs, makes similar claims but was filed in a state court and then removed by the defendants to a federal district court. The Multidistrict Litigation Panel consolidated all the suits in the district court in Chicago for pretrial proceedings. Once there, the plaintiffs (all but the Hurdle plaintiffs, about whom more shortly) filed a consolidated complaint, and since venue in Chicago was proper and in any event not objected to by the parties (other than the Hurdle group, whose objection we consider later in the opinion), the district court was unquestionably authorized, notwithstanding to determine the merits of the suit.

***The suits are a series of mostly identical class actions on behalf of all Americans descended from slaves with whom one or more of the defendants or their corporate predecessors may have been directly or indirectly involved. The consolidated complaint (the Hurdle complaint is similar, so need not be discussed separately) alleges the following facts, for which we do not vouch, but merely summarize, the complaint having been dismissed before the truth or falsity of the allegations was determined.

The defendants are companies or the successors to companies that provided services, such as transportation, finance, and insurance, to slaveowners. At least two of the defendants *were* slaveowners; the predecessor of one of the bank defendants once accepted 13,000 slaves as collateral on loans and ended up owning 1,250 of them when the borrowers defaulted, and

the predecessor of another defendant ended up owning 346 slaves, also as a consequence of a borrower's default. Even before the Thirteenth Amendment, slavery was illegal in the northern states, and the complaint charges that the defendants were violating the laws of those states in transacting with slaveowners. It also claims that there were occasional enslavements long after the passage of the Thirteenth Amendment and that some of the defendants were complicit in those too. By way of relief, the complaint seeks disgorgement to the class members of the profits that the defendants obtained from their dealings with slaveowners.

The legal basis for the plaintiffs' federal claim is 42 U.S.C. § 1982, which provides that "all citizens of the United States shall have the same right, in every State and Territory, as is enjoyed by white citizens thereof to inherit, purchase, lease, sell, hold, and convey real and personal property." A claim based on a federal statute invokes the federal-question jurisdiction of the federal courts. But since most of the conduct of which the plaintiffs complain occurred prior to the passage of the Thirteenth Amendment, and indeed prior to the Civil War, section 1982 does not provide a sturdy basis for the retention of federal jurisdiction over the plaintiffs' nonfederal claims. A frivolous federal law claim cannot successfully invoke federal jurisdiction. So it cannot provide a perch on which to seat nonfederal claims in the name of the federal courts' supplemental jurisdiction. And very few of the plaintiffs *have* a nonfrivolous claim under section 1982.

***The district judge ruled that by virtue of both the political-question doctrine and the requirement of standing to sue derived from Article III of the Constitution, there was no federal jurisdiction over any of the suits and that in any event they had no merit because the applicable statutes of limitations had lapsed and anyway the complaint failed to state a claim. The dismissal was with prejudice. But if the judge was correct that there is no jurisdiction, he should have dismissed the suits without prejudice and thus not decided their merits.

The political-question doctrine bars the federal courts from adjudicating disputes that the Constitution has been interpreted to entrust to other branches of the federal government. The earliest and still the best example is *Luther v. Borden*, (1849). Rhode Island had not adopted a new constitution after the break with England, but instead continued to govern itself under its colonial charter. Restive citizens convened a constitutional convention not authorized by the charter. The convention adopted a new constitution to which the charter government refused to submit, precipitating rebellion and the establishment in 1842 of a rival state government. The Supreme Court refused to decide which of the two competing governments was the legitimate one. It would have been exceedingly difficult to gather and assess, by the methods of litigation, the facts needed for such a decision. It would have been even more difficult to formulate a legal concept of revolutionary legitimacy to guide the decision. Formulating and enforcing a remedy would have presented additional stumbling blocks. The case simply exceeded judicial capabilities. So the Court left the matter to the President, to whom Congress had delegated the duty of resolving it.

A case that sought reparations for the wrong of slavery would encounter similar obstacles, but the plaintiffs have been careful to cast the litigation as a quest for conventional legal relief. All they are asking the federal judiciary to do is to apply state law (plus the one federal statute, 42 U.S.C. § 1982) to the defendants' conduct. They face, of course, formidable obstacles, quite apart from the severely limited applicability of section 1982. To name just one of those obstacles, it is highly unlikely that ante-bellum laws in northern states were intended to confer financial or other benefits on the twenty-first century descendants of slaves. But the obstacles to the vindication of the plaintiffs' legal claims have the form at least of conventional defenses to a lawsuit. If one or more of the defendants violated a state law by transporting slaves in 1850, and the plaintiffs can establish standing to sue, prove the violation despite its antiquity, establish that the law was intended to provide a remedy (either directly or by providing the basis for a common law action for conspiracy, conversion, or restitution) to lawfully enslaved persons or their descendants, identify their ancestors, quantify damages incurred, and persuade the court to

toll the statute of limitations, there would be no further obstacle to the grant of relief.

But we think that the district court was correct, with some exceptions to be noted, in ruling that the plaintiffs lack standing to sue. It would be impossible by the methods of litigation to connect the defendants' alleged misconduct with the financial and emotional harm that the plaintiffs claim to have suffered as a result of that conduct. For example, Aetna is alleged to have written several insurance policies on slaves in the 1850s in violation of state law applicable to the company, and to have obtained premiums from the insureds—the slaveowners—that (we'll assume) exceeded the cost of the insurance to Aetna (its expenses plus the payment of proceeds if the insured event came to pass). The plaintiffs argue that Aetna's net income from this insurance was a wrongful profit that the company should be ordered to restore to the plaintiff classes.

If the insurance business was competitive back then (and the plaintiffs do not argue that it was not), Aetna did not profit in an economic sense from the transactions of which the plaintiffs complain (its "profit" would just be its cost of equity capital), and in any event it would have distributed any profits from the transactions to its share-holders long ago. All that to one side, there is a fatal disconnect between the victims and the plaintiffs. When a person is wronged he can seek redress, and if he wins, his descendants may benefit, but the wrong to the ancestor is not a wrong to the descendants. For if it were, then (problems of proof to one side) statutes of limitations would be toothless. A person whose ancestor had been wronged a thousand years ago could sue on the ground that it was a continuing wrong and he is one of the victims.

The plaintiffs introduce another claim of injury by asserting that had the defendants refused to violate their own states' laws by doing business with slaveowners, there would have been less slavery because the refusal would have been tantamount to subjecting the slaveowners to a partial boycott. That would have raised their costs, and, by making slavery less profitable, might have reduced the amount of it. ("Might," not "would," because the higher costs might simply have depressed the price of a slave.) And had there been less slavery, the argument continues, some of the ancestors of the members of the plaintiff classes would not have been slaves, but instead free laborers, and they would have had some disposable income part of which they might have saved rather than spent, and left to their heirs.

But this causal chain is too long and has too many weak links for a court to be able to find that the defendants' conduct harmed the plaintiffs at all, let alone in an amount that could be estimated without the wildest speculation. It is impossible to determine how much, if any, less slavery there would have been had the defendants not done business with slaveowners, what effect a diminution of slavery would have had on bequests by ancestors of the class members, and how much of the value of those bequests would have trickled down to the class members.

Suppose a class member could prove that he was descended from one of the slaves insured by Aetna or transported by the Union Pacific Railroad (another defendant) or bought with money lent to the buyer by the predecessor of the JPMorgan Chase Bank (still another defendant), and that these transactions were illegal and that the descendants of slaves are among the people whom the laws were intended to protect. Had he not been insured or transported or bought with a bank loan, how would the financial welfare of his remote descendant be affected? Would this ancestor have been freed, or perhaps never enslaved in the first place? As the plaintiffs stress, slavery was profitable; is it conceivable that slave-holders would have been unable to insure, transport, and finance the purchase of slaves if northern companies had been excluded from the provision of these services or had refused to violate their states' laws that sought to keep them from providing the services?

Even if compliance with those laws would have curtailed slavery and even if it could be shown (it could not be) that as a result of that hypothetical curtailment a plaintiff's remote ancestor would not have been a slave but instead a free laborer, how could the wages that the ancestor would have earned as a free laborer be shown to have influenced the wealth of his remote descendant? Economists actually study such issues, under the rubric of "intergenerational mobility," but these are studies of aggregate effects, not of the effects of particular acts, affecting particular individuals, on the wealth of specific remote descendants. There is no way to determine that a given black American today is worse off by a specific, calculable sum of money (or monetized emotional harm) as a result of the conduct of one or more of the defendants.

Nor are the problems of measuring and tracing elided by recasting the relief sought as restitution rather than damages. Restitution—the transfer of the wrongdoer's gain to his victim—is an alternative to damages, the monetization of the victim's loss. It is a sensible remedy for egregious misconduct because it makes the conduct worthless to the defendant by taking away his profit even if it exceeds the loss to the plaintiff. But it presupposes an injury—it is a remedy for a legal wrong—and there is no way in which to determine what if any injury the defendants inflicted on the members of the plaintiff classes.

And again, if there were a legal wrong, it would not be a wrong to any living persons unless they were somehow the authorized representatives to bring suits on behalf of their enslaved ancestors. With some exceptions to be noted, the plaintiffs are suing to redress harms to third parties (their ancestors), without being authorized to sue on behalf of those parties. It is like a suit by a descendant of a Union soldier, killed in battle, against a Civil War era gun manufacturer still in business that sold guns to the Confederacy in violation of federal law. A federal court could not entertain the suit because the plaintiff would be unable to prove a harm to an interest of his (such as his bank account) that the law protects. It is possible that had the ancestor not died when he did he would have become a wealthy person and left bequests so immense that his remote descendant, the plaintiff, would have inherited more money from his parents or grandparents than he actually did. But that is too speculative an inquiry to provide a basis for a federal suit.

The two cases just cited, and others, treat remoteness as a limitation on Article III standing. Still other cases treat it as a nonjurisdictional limitation on who may sue in federal court—but still a limitation. Another group of cases would deem the suit barred by Article III because one function of the Article III standing doctrine is to prevent parties with slight interests in a litigation from crowding those who have the main interests. In our hypothetical case of the Union soldier, the litigant with the paramount interest in the case would be his estate and the damages that the estate could recover would include whatever amount of money he would have wanted his descendant to inherit. If the descendant could sue the tortfeasor directly for that amount (or for the tortfeasor's profit, in a suit for restitution), there would be either double recovery or an impossible task of allocating the monetary recovery between the descendant and the estate.

A few of the plaintiff's claims, however, as we noted at the outset, are claims of subjection to involuntary servitude after it was outlawed by the Thirteenth Amendment, and indeed into the twentieth century.

Cain Wall, Sr. claims that "during the time that [he] was enslaved"—which he contends extended into the 1960s—"one or more of the defendants were doing business in Mississippi or Louisiana. Some of the defendants had reason to know of the enslavement of Cain Wall and yet failed to take steps to eliminate same, while they continued to inure benefits from the illegal, but sanctioned system of servitude post-emancipation." But there is no claim that the defendants subjected Wall (or any other class member) to involuntary servitude or did anything to perpetuate or exacerbate his condition. The claim is that they took no steps to free him. The briefs suggest no basis for thinking that there is any kind of Good Samaritan legal duty to eliminate a violation of the Thirteenth Amendment committed by someone else.

The limitations that Article III places on the right to sue in a federal court require us to affirm, on the basis of lack of standing, the greater part of the district court's judgment. But there are three qualifications. First, although most of the plaintiffs and class members are suing as descendants rather than as representatives of their ancestors' estates authorized to sue on those ancestors' behalf, a few do claim to be suing in such a representative capacity. It is highly unlikely that the estate of anyone who died a century or more ago, or indeed more than half a century ago (for although many former slaves survived into the twentieth century, very few would still have been alive 50 years ago, which is to say in 1956, 91 years after the end of the Civil War), has not yet been closed. But the district judge accepted that the purported representatives had a right to sue on behalf of their ancestors, and the defendants offer only a perfunctory rebuttal. We shall assume without deciding that some of the plaintiffs are legal representatives of their slave ancestors. These plaintiffs not only escape the objection to standing that the suits seek damages for injuries actually suffered by third parties (the ancestors—no longer third parties, but the real parties in interest, merely represented by the plaintiffs), but have less to prove. They just have to prove the injury to the ancestors; the trickle-down question is elided. In all likelihood it would still be impossible for them to prove injury, requiring as that would connecting the particular slavery transactions in which the defendants were involved to harm to particular slaves. But in any event, suits complaining about injuries that occurred more than a century and a half ago have been barred for a long time by the applicable state statutes of limitations. It is true that tolling doctrines can extend the time to sue well beyond the period of limitations—but not to a century and more beyond. Slaves could not sue, and even after the Thirteenth Amendment became effective in 1865 suits such as these, if brought in the South, would not have received a fair hearing. However, some northern courts would have been receptive to such suits, and since the defendants are (and were) northern companies, venue would have been proper in those states. Even in the South, descendants of slaves have had decades of effective access to the courts to seek redress for the wrongs of which they complain. And it's not as if it had been a deep mystery that corporations were involved in the operation of the slave system.

The second qualification concerns a claim, rather buried in the complaint but not forfeited, that in violation of state fraud or consumer protection law members of the plaintiff classes have bought products or services from some of the defendants that they would not have bought had the defendants not concealed their involvement in slavery. This claim has nothing to do with ancient violations and indeed would be unaffected if the defendants' dealings with slaveowners had been entirely legal. It is a complaint of consumers' being deceived because sellers have concealed a material fact. The injury is the loss incurred by buying something that one wouldn't have bought had one known the truth about the product.

It is true that under no consumer protection law known to us, whether a special statute or a doctrine of the common law of contracts or torts, has a seller a general duty to disclose every discreditable fact about himself that might if disclosed deflect a buyer. To fulfill such a duty he would have to know much more about his consumers than he possibly could. But the plaintiffs are charging the defendants with misrepresenting their activities in relation to slavery. A seller who learns that some class of buyers would not buy his product if they knew it contained some component that he would normally have no duty to disclose, but fearing to lose those buyers falsely represents that the product does not contain the component, is guilty of fraud. An example would be a manufacturer who represented that his products were made in the United States by companies that employ only union labor, whereas in fact they were made in Third World sweat-shops.

We do not offer an opinion on the merits of the consumer protection claims, but merely reject the district court's ruling that they are barred at the threshold.

***To summarize, the district court's dismissal, for want of standing, of all but the claims brought by legal representatives of slaves plus the consumer protection claims is modified to be a dismissal without prejudice, and as so modified is affirmed. (Barber's suit is dismissed, also without prejudice, for want of diversity.) The dismissal of the claims brought by the plaintiffs who claim to be legal representatives is affirmed, but on the merits (statute of limitations) and so with prejudice. The dismissal of the consumer protection claims is reversed and the case remanded to the district court for further proceedings on those claims consistent with this opinion. The district court is authorized to retain those claims for the duration of the litigation, except in the case of the Hurdle plaintiffs, as to whom the court is authorized only to conduct pretrial proceedings under 28 U.S.C. § 1407.

To Segregation:
Invidious Discrimination and
Equal Protection

Themes

- Revival of the Declaration's priciple of equality, the post-War Amendments, and the Equal Protection Clause
- The state action doctrine
- States' rights v. federal courts
- "Separate but equal," the various emphases on "separate" and "equal," and the doctrine's ultimate overturning

- The assault on "separate but equal": the education cases
- Constitutional rights as personal rights
- The state, equal protection, and two classes of citizens
- From minimal to strict scrutiny
- Triggering strict scrutiny
- Justifying *Brown*

RACE-RELATED CONSTITUTIONAL PROVISIONS
Post-Civil War

Amendment XIII

Passed by Congress February 1, 1865. Ratified December 18, 1865.

Section 1.—Neither slavery nor involuntary servitude, except as punishment for crime where of the party shall have been duly convicted, shall exist within the United States, or any place subject to their jurisdiction.

Section 2.—Congress shall have power to enforce this article by appropriate legislation.

Amendment XIV

Passed by Congress June 16, 1866. Ratified July 23, 1868.

Section 1.—All persons born or naturalized in the United States, and subject to the jurisdiction thereof, are citizens of the United States and of the State wherein they reside. No State shall make or enforce any law which shall abridge the privileges or immunities of citizens of the United States; nor shall any State deprive any person of life, liberty, or property, without due process of law; nor deny to any person within its jurisdiction the equal protection of the laws. …

Section 5.—The Congress shall have power to enforce, by appropriate legislation, the provisions of this article.

Amendment XV

Passed by Congress February 27, 1869. Ratified March 30, 1870.

Section 1.—The right of citizens of the United States to vote shall not be denied or abridged by the United States or by any State on account of race, color, or previous condition of servitude.

Section 2.—The Congress shall have power to enforce this article by appropriate legislation.

Government (State) Action Requirement

THE CIVIL RIGHTS CASES
(UNITED STATES v. STANLEY.; UNITED STATES v. RYAN.; UNITED STATES v. NICHOLS.; UNITED STATES v. SINGLETON.; ROBINSON & WIFE v. MEMPHIS and CHARLESTON RAILROAD COMPANY)
Supreme Court of the United States
109 U.S. 3

October 15, 1883, Decided

MR. JUSTICE BRADLEY delivered the opinion of the court. After stating the facts in the above language he continued:

It is obvious that the primary and important question in all the cases is the constitutionality of the law: for if the law is unconstitutional none of the prosecutions can stand.

The sections of the law referred to provide as follows:

"SEC. 1. That all persons within the jurisdiction of the United States shall be entitled to the full and equal enjoyment of the accommodations, advantages, facilities, and privileges of inns, public conveyances on land or water, theatres, and other places of public amusement; subject only to the conditions and limitations established by law, and applicable alike to citizens of every race and color, regardless of any previous condition of servitude.

"SEC. 2. That any person who shall violate the foregoing section by denying to any citizen, except for reasons by law applicable to citizens of every race and color, and regardless of any previous condition of servitude, the full enjoyment of any of the accommodations, advantages, facilities, or privileges in said section enumerated, or by aiding or inciting such denial, shall for every such offence forfeit and pay the sum of five hundred dollars to the person aggrieved thereby, to be recovered in an action of debt, with full costs; and shall also, for every such offence, be deemed guilty of a misdemeanor, and, upon conviction thereof, shall be fined not less than five hundred nor more than one thousand dollars, or shall be imprisoned not less than thirty days nor more than one year: Provided, That all persons may elect to sue for the penalty aforesaid, or to proceed under their rights at common law and by State statutes; and having so elected to proceed in the one mode or the other, their right to proceed in the other jurisdiction shall be barred. But this provision shall not apply to criminal proceedings, either under this act or the criminal law of any State: And provided further, That a judgment for the penalty in favor of the party aggrieved, or a judgment upon an indictment, shall be a bar to either prosecution respectively."

Are these sections constitutional? The first section, which is the principal one, cannot be fairly understood without attending to the last clause, which qualifies the preceding part.

The essence of the law is, not to declare broadly that all persons shall be entitled to the full and equal enjoyment of the accommodations, advantages, facilities, and privileges of inns, public conveyances, and theatres; but that such enjoyment shall not be subject to any conditions applicable only to citizens of a particular race or color, or who had been in a previous condition of servitude. In other words, it is the purpose of the law to declare that, in the enjoyment of the accommodations and privileges of inns, public conveyances, theatres, and other places of public amusement, no distinction shall be made between citizens of different race or color, or between those who have, and those who have not, been slaves. Its effect is to declare, that in all inns, public conveyances, and places of amusement, colored citizens, whether formerly slaves or not, and citizens of other races, shall have the same accommodations and privileges in all inns, public conveyances, and places of amusement as are enjoyed by white citizens; and vice versa. The second section makes it a penal offence in any person to deny to any citizen of any race or color, regardless of previous servitude, any of the accommodations or privileges mentioned in the first section.

Has Congress constitutional power to make such a law? Of course, no one will contend that the power to pass it was contained in the Constitution before the adoption of the last three amendments. The power is sought, first, in the Fourteenth Amendment, and the views and arguments of distinguished Senators, advanced whilst the law was under consideration, claiming authority to pass it by virtue of that amendment, are the principal arguments adduced in favor of the power. We have carefully considered those arguments, as was due to the eminent ability of those who put them forward, and have felt, in all its force, the weight of authority which always invests a law that Congress deems itself competent to pass. But the responsibility of an independent judgment is now thrown upon this court; and we are bound to exercise it according to the best lights we have.

The first section of the Fourteenth Amendment (which is the one relied on), after declaring who shall be citizens of the United States, and of the several States, is prohibitory in its character, and prohibitory upon the States. It declares that:

"No State shall make or enforce any law which shall abridge the privileges or immunities of citizens of the United States; nor shall any State deprive any person of life, liberty, or property without due process of law; nor deny to any person within its jurisdiction the equal protection of the laws." ***

An inspection of the law shows that it makes no reference whatever to any supposed or apprehended violation of the Fourteenth Amendment on the part of the States. It is not predicated on any such view. It proceeds ex directo to declare that certain acts committed by individuals shall be deemed offences, and shall be prosecuted and punished by proceedings in the courts of the United States. It does not profess to be corrective of any constitutional wrong committed by the States; it does not make its operation to depend upon any such wrong committed. It applies equally to cases arising in States which have the justest laws respecting the personal rights of citizens, and whose authorities are ever ready to enforce such laws, as to those which arise in States that may have violated the prohibition of the amendment. In other words, it steps into the domain of local jurisprudence, and lays down rules for the conduct of individuals in society towards each other, and imposes sanctions for the enforcement of those rules, without referring in any manner to any supposed action of the State or its authorities.

If this legislation is appropriate for enforcing the prohibitions of the amendment, it is difficult to see where it is to stop. Why may not Congress with equal show of authority enact a code of laws for the enforcement and vindication of all rights of life, liberty, and property? If it is supposable that the States may deprive persons of life, liberty, and property without due process of law (and the amendment itself does suppose this), why should not Congress proceed at once to prescribe due process of law for the protection of every one of these fundamental rights, in every possible case, as well as to prescribe equal privileges in inns, public conveyances, and theatres? The truth is, that the implication of a power to legislate in this manner is based upon the assumption that if the States are forbidden to legislate or act in a particular way on a particular subject, and power is conferred upon n Congress to enforce the prohibition, this gives Congress power to legislate generally upon that subject, and not merely power to provide modes of redress against such State legislation or action. The assumption is certainly unsound. It is repugnant to the Tenth Amendment of the Constitution, which declares that powers not delegated to the United States by the Constitution, nor prohibited by it to the States, are reserved to the States respectively or to the people.

*** In this connection it is proper to state that civil rights, such as are guaranteed by the Constitution against State aggression, cannot be impaired by the wrongful acts of individuals, unsupported by State authority in the shape of laws, customs, or judicial or executive proceedings. The wrongful act of an individual, unsupported by any such authority, is simply a private wrong, or a crime of that individual; an invasion of the rights of the injured party, it is true, whether they affect his person, his property, or his reputation; but if not sanctioned in some way by the State, or not done under State authority, his rights remain in full force, and may presumably be vindicated by resort to the laws of the State for redress. An individual cannot deprive a man of his right to vote, to hold property, to buy and sell, to sue in the courts, or to be a witness or a juror; he may, by force or fraud, interfere with the enjoyment of the right in a particular case; he may commit an assault against the person, or commit murder, or use ruffian violence at the polls, or slander the good name of a fellow citizen; but, unless protected in these wrongful acts by some shield of State law or State authority, he cannot destroy or injure the right; he will only render himself amenable to satisfaction or punishment; and amenable therefor to the laws of the State where the wrongful acts are committed. Hence, in all those cases where the Constitution seeks to protect the rights of the citizen against discriminative and unjust laws of the State by prohibiting such laws, it is not individual offences, but abrogation and denial of rights, which it denounces, and for which it clothes the Congress with power to provide a remedy. This abrogation and denial of rights, for which the States alone were or could be responsible, was the great seminal and fundamental wrong which was intended to be remedied. And the remedy to be provided must necessarily be predicated upon that wrong. It must assume that in the cases provided for, the evil or wrong actually committed rests upon some State law or State authority for its excuse and perpetration.

Of course, these remarks do not apply to those cases in which Congress is clothed with direct and plenary powers of legislation over the whole subject, accompanied with an express or implied denial of such power to the States, as in the regulation of commerce with foreign nations, among the several States, and with the Indian tribes, the coining of money, the establishment of post offices and post reads, the declaring of war, etc. In these cases Congress has power to pass laws for regulating the subjects specified in every detail, and the conduct and transactions of individuals in respect thereof. But where a subject is not submitted to the general legislative power of Congress, but is only submitted thereto for the purpose of rendering effective some prohibition against particular State legislation or State action in reference to that subject, the power given is limited by its object, and any legislation by Congress in the matter must necessarily be corrective in its character, adapted to counteract and redress the operation of such prohibited State laws or proceedings of State officers.

If the principles of interpretation which we have laid down are correct, as we deem them to be (and they are in accord with the principles laid down in the cases before referred to, as well as in the recent case of United States v. Harris, it is clear that the law in question cannot be sustained by any grant of legislative power made to Congress by the Fourteenth Amendment. That amendment prohibits the States from denying to any person the equal protection of the laws, and declares that Congress shall have power to enforce, by appropriate legislation, the provisions of the amendment. The law in question, without any reference to adverse State legislation on the subject, declares that all persons shall be entitled to equal accommodations and privileges of inns, public conveyances, and places of public amusement, and imposes a penalty upon any individual who shall deny to any citizen such equal accommodations and privileges. This is not corrective legislation; it is primary and direct; it

takes immediate and absolute possession of the subject of the right of admission to inns, public conveyances, and places of amusement. It supersedes and displaces State legislation on the same subject, or only allows it permissive force. It ignores such legislation, and assumes that the matter is one that belongs to the domain of national regulation. Whether it would not have been a more effective protection of the rights of citizens to have clothed Congress with plenary power over the whole subject, is not now the question. What we have to decide is, whether such plenary power has been conferred upon Congress by the Fourteenth Amendment; and, in our judgment, it has not.

We have discussed the question presented by the law on the assumption that a right to enjoy equal accommodation and privileges in all inns, public conveyances, and places of public amusement, is one of the essential rights of the citizen which no State can abridge or interfere with. Whether it is such a right, or not, is a different question which, in the view we have taken of the validity of the law on the ground already stated, it is not necessary to examine.

*** But the power of Congress to adopt direct and primary, as distinguished from corrective legislation, on the subject in hand, is sought, in the second place, from the Thirteenth Amendment, which abolishes slavery. This amendment declares "that neither slavery, nor involuntary servitude, except as a punishment for crime, whereof the party shall have been duly convicted, shall exist within the United States, or any place subject to their jurisdiction;" and it gives Congress power to enforce the amendment by appropriate legislation.

This amendment, as well as the Fourteenth, is undoubtedly self-executing without any ancillary legislation, so far as its terms are applicable to any existing state of circumstances. By its own unaided force and effect it abolished slavery, and established universal freedom. Still, legislation may be necessary and proper to meet all the various cases and circumstances to be affected by it, and to prescribe proper modes of redress for its violation in letter or spirit. And such legislation may be primary and direct in its character; for the amendment is not a mere prohibition of State laws establishing or upholding slavery, but an absolute declaration that slavery or involuntary servitude shall not exist in any part of the United States.

It is true, that slavery cannot exist without law, any more than property in lands and goods can exist without law: and, therefore, the Thirteenth Amendment may be regarded as nullifying all State laws which establish or uphold slavery. But it has a reflex character also, establishing and decreeing universal civil and political freedom throughout the United States; and it is assumed, that the power vested in Congress to enforce the article by appropriate legislation, clothes Congress with power to pass all laws necessary and proper for abolishing all badges and incidents of slavery in the United States: and upon this assumption it is claimed, that this is sufficient authority for declaring by law that all persons shall have equal accommodations and privileges in all inns, public conveyances, and places of amusement; the argument being, that the denial of such equal accommodations and privileges is, in itself, a subjection to a species of servitude within the meaning of the amendment. Conceding the major proposition to be true, that Congress has a right to enact all necessary and proper laws for the obliteration and prevention of slavery with all its badges and incidents, is the minor proposition also true, that the denial to any person of admission to the accommodations and privileges of an inn, a public conveyance, or a theatre, does subject that person to any form of servitude, or tend to fasten upon him any badge of slavery? If it does not, then power to pass the law is not found in the Thirteenth Amendment.

In a very able and learned presentation of the cognate question as to the extent of the rights, privileges and immunities of citizens which cannot rightfully be abridged by state laws under the Fourteenth Amendment, made in a former case, a long list of burdens and disabilities of a servile character, incident to feudal vassalage in France, and which were abolished by the decrees of the National Assembly, was presented for the purpose of showing that all inequalities and observances exacted by one man from another were servitudes, or badges of slavery, which a great nation, in its effort to establish universal liberty, made haste to wipe out and destroy. But these were servitudes imposed by the old law, or by long custom, which had the force of law, and exacted by one man from another without the latter's consent. Should any such servitudes be imposed by a state law, there can be no doubt that the law would be repugnant to the Fourteenth, no less than to the Thirteenth Amendment; nor any greater doubt that Congress has adequate power to forbid any such servitude from being exacted.

But is there any similarity between such servitudes and a denial by the owner of an inn, a public conveyance, or a theatre, of its accommodations and privileges to an individual, even though the denial be founded on the race or color of that individual? Where does any slavery or servitude, or badge of either, arise from such an act of denial? Whether it might not be a denial of a right which, if sanctioned by the state law, would be obnoxious to the prohibitions of the Fourteenth Amendment, is another question. But what has it to do with the question of slavery?

***The long existence of African slavery in this country gave us very distinct notions of what it was, and what were its necessary incidents. Compulsory service of the slave for the benefit of the master, restraint of his movements except by the master's will, disability to hold property, to make contracts, to have a standing in court, to be a witness against a white person, and such like burdens and incapacities, were the inseparable incidents of the institution. Severer punishments for crimes were imposed on the slave than on free persons guilty of the same offences. Congress, as we have seen, by the Civil Rights Bill of 1866, passed in view of the Thirteenth Amendment, before the Fourteenth was adopted, undertook to wipe out these burdens and disabilities, the necessary incidents of slavery, constituting its substance and visible form; and to secure to all citizens of every race and color, and without regard to previous servitude, those fundamental rights which are the essence of civil freedom, namely, the same right to make and enforce contracts, to sue, be parties, give evidence, and to inherit, purchase, lease, sell and convey property, as is enjoyed by white citizens. Whether this legislation was fully authorized by the Thirteenth Amendment alone, without the support which it afterward received from the Fourteenth Amendment, after the adoption of which it was reenacted with some additions, it is not necessary to inquire. It is referred to for the purpose of showing that at that time (in 1866) Congress did not assume, under the authority given by the Thirteenth Amendment, to adjust what may be called the social rights of men and races in the community; but only to declare and vindicate those fundamental rights which appertain to the essence of citizenship, and the enjoyment or deprivation of which constitutes the essential distinction between freedom and slavery.

We must not forget that the province and scope of the Thirteenth and Fourteenth amendments are different; the former simply abolished slavery: the latter prohibited the States from abridging the privileges or immunities of citizens of the United States; from depriving them of life, liberty, or property without due process of law, and from denying to any the equal protection of the laws. The amendments are different, and the powers of Congress under them are different. What Congress has power to do under one, it may not have power to do under the other. Under the Thirteenth Amendment, it has only to do with slavery and its incidents. Under the Fourteenth Amendment, it has power to counteract and render nugatory all State laws and proceedings which have the effect to abridge any of the privileges or immunities of citizens of the United States, or to deprive them of life, liberty or property with-out due process of law, or to deny to any of them the equal protection of the laws. Under the Thirteenth Amendment, the legislation, so far as necessary or proper to eradicate all forms and incidents of slavery and involuntary servitude, may be direct and primary, operating upon the acts of individuals, whether sanctioned by State legislation or not; under the Fourteenth, as we have already shown, it must necessarily be, and can only be, corrective in its character, addressed to counteract and afford relief against State regulations or proceedings.

The only question under the present head, therefore, is, whether the refusal to any persons of the accommodations of an inn, or a public conveyance, or a place of public amusement, by an individual, and without any sanction or support from any State law or regulation, does inflict upon such persons any manner of servitude, or form of slavery, as those terms are understood in this country? Many wrongs may be obnoxious to the prohibitions of the Fourteenth Amendment which are not, in any just sense, incidents or elements of slavery. Such, for example, would be the taking of private property without due process of law; or allowing persons who have committed certain crimes (horse stealing, for example) to be seized and hung by the posse comitatus without regular trial; or denying to any person, or class of persons, the right to pursue any peaceful avocations allowed to others. What is called class legislation would belong to this category, and would be obnoxious to the prohibitions of the Fourteenth Amendment, but would not necessarily be so to the Thirteenth, when not involving the idea of any subjection of one man to another. The Thirteenth Amendment has respect, not to distinctions of race, or class, or color, but to slavery. The Fourteenth Amendment extends its protection to races and classes, and prohibits any State legislation which has the effect of denying to any race or class, or to any individual, the equal protection of the laws.

Now, conceding, for the sake of the argument, that the admission to an inn, a public conveyance, or a place of public amusement, on equal terms with all other citizens, is the right of every man and all classes of men, is it any more than one of those rights which the states by the Fourteenth Amendment are forbidden to deny to any person? And is the Constitution violated until the denial of the right has some State sanction or authority? Can the act of a mere individual, the owner of the inn, the public conveyance or place of amusement, refusing the accommodation, be justly regarded as imposing any badge of slavery or servitude upon the applicant, or only as inflicting an ordinary civil injury, properly cognizable by the laws of the State, and presumably subject to redress by those laws until the contrary appears?

After giving to these questions all the consideration which their importance demands, we are forced to the conclusion that such an act of refusal has nothing to do with slavery or involuntary servitude, and that if it is violative of any right of the party, his redress is to be sought under the laws of the State; or if those laws are adverse to his rights and do not protect him, his remedy will be found in the corrective legislation which Congress has adopted, or may adopt, for counteracting the effect of State laws, or State action, prohibited by the Fourteenth Amendment. It would be running the slavery argument into the ground to make it apply to every act of discrimination which a person may see fit to make as to the guests he will entertain, or as to the people he will take into his coach or cab or car, or admit to his concert or theatre, or deal with in other matters of intercourse or business. Innkeepers and public carriers, by the laws of all the States, so far as we are aware, are bound, to the extent of their facilities, to furnish proper accommodation to all unobjectionable persons who in good faith apply for them. If the laws themselves make any unjust discrimination, amenable to the prohibitions of the Fourteenth Amendment, Congress has full power to afford a remedy under that amendment and in accordance with it.

When a man has emerged from slavery, and by the aid of beneficent legislation has shaken off the inseparable concomitants of that state, there must be some stage in the progress of his elevation when he takes the rank of a mere citizen, and ceases to be the special favorite of the laws, and when his rights as a citizen, or a man, are to be protected in the ordinary modes by which other men's rights are protected. There were thousands of free colored people in this country before the abolition of slavery, enjoying all the essential rights of life, liberty and property the same as white citizens; yet no one, at that time, thought that it was any invasion of his personal status as a freeman because he was not admitted to all the privileges enjoyed by white citizens, or because he was subjected to discriminations in the enjoyment of accommodations in inns, public conveyances and places of amusement. Mere discriminations on account of race or color were not regarded as badges of slavery. If, since that time, the enjoyment of equal rights in all these respects has become established by constitutional enactment, it is not by force of the Thirteenth Amendment (which merely abolishes slavery), but by force of the Thirteenth and Fifteenth Amendments.

On the whole we are of opinion, that no countenance of authority for the passage of the law in question can be found in either the Thirteenth or Fourteenth Amendment of the Constitution; and no other ground of authority for its passage being suggested, it must necessarily be declared void, at least so far as its operation in the several States is concerned.

This conclusion disposes of the cases now under consideration.

DISSENT BY:

HARLAN

DISSENT

MR. JUSTICE HARLAN dissenting.

The opinion in these cases proceeds, it seems to me, upon grounds entirely too narrow and artificial. I cannot resist the conclusion that the substance and spirit of the recent amendments of the Constitution have been sacrificed by a subtle and ingenious verbal criticism. "It is not the words of the law but the internal sense of it that makes the law: the letter of the law is the body; the sense and reason of the law is the soul." Constitutional provisions, adopted in the interest of liberty, and for the purpose of securing, through national legislation, if need be, rights inhering in a state of freedom, and belonging to American citizenship, have been so construed as to defeat the ends the people desired to accomplish, which they attempted to accomplish, and which they supposed they had accomplished by changes in their fundamental law. By this I do not mean that the determination of these cases should have been materially controlled by considerations of mere expediency or policy. I mean only, in this form, to express an earnest conviction that the court has departed from the familiar rule requiring, in the interpretation of constitutional provisions, that full effect be given to the intent with which they were adopted.

The purpose of the first section of the act of Congress of March 1, 1875, was to prevent race discrimination in respect of the accommodations and facilities of inns, public conveyances, and places of public amusement. It does not assume to define the general conditions and limitations under which inns, public conveyances, and places of public amusement may be conducted, but only

declares that such conditions and limitations, whatever they may be, shall not be applied so as to work a discrimination solely because of race, color, or previous condition of servitude.

There seems to be no substantial difference between my brethren and myself as to the purpose of Congress; for, they say that the essence of the law is, not to declare broadly that all persons shall be entitled to the full and equal enjoyment of the accommodations, advantages, facilities, and privileges of inns, public conveyances, and theatres; but that such enjoyment shall not be subject to conditions applicable only to citizens of a particular race or color, or who had been in a previous condition of servitude. The effect of the statute, the court says, is, that colored citizens, whether formerly slaves or not, and citizens of other races, shall have the same accommodations and privileges in all inns, public conveyances, and places of amusement as are enjoyed by white persons; and vice versa.

The court adjudges, I think erroneously, that Congress is without power, under either the Thirteenth or Fourteenth Amendment, to establish such regulations, and that the first and second sections of the statute are, in all their parts, unconstitutional and void.

Whether the legislative department of the government has transcended the limits of its constitutional powers, "is at all times,"** "a question of much delicacy, which ought seldom, if ever, to be decided in the affirmative, in a doubtful case. ... *** Every possible presumption is in favor of the validity of a statute, and this continues until the contrary is shown beyond a rational doubt. One branch of the government cannot encroach on the domain of another without danger. The safety of our institutions depends in no small degree on a strict observance of this salutary rule."

Before considering the language and scope of these amendments it will be proper to recall the relations subsisting, prior to their adoption, between the national government and the institution of slavery, as indicated by the provisions of the Constitution, the legislation of Congress, and the decisions of this court. In this mode we may obtain keys with which to open the mind of the people, and discover the thought intended to be expressed.

In section 2 of article IV. of the Constitution it was provided that "no person held to service or labor in one State, under the laws thereof, escaping into another, shall, in consequence of any law or regulation therein, be discharged from such service or labor, but shall be delivered up on claim of the party to whom such service or labor may be due." Under the authority of this clause

Congress passed the Fugitive Slave Law of 1793, establishing a mode for the recovery of fugitive slaves, and prescribing a penalty against any person who should knowingly and willingly obstruct or hinder the master, his agent, or attorney, in seizing, arresting, and recovering the fugitive, or who should rescue the fugitive from him, or who should harbor or conceal the slave after notice that he was a fugitive.

***The first section of the Thirteenth Amendment provides that "neither slavery nor involuntary servitude, except as a punishment for crime, whereof the party shall have been duly convicted, shall exist within the United States, or any place subject to their jurisdiction." Its second section declares that "Congress shall have power to enforce this article by appropriate legislation." This amendment was followed by the Civil Rights Act of April 9, 1866, which, among other things, provided that "all persons born in the United States, and not subject to any foreign power, excluding Indians not taxed, are hereby declared to be citizens of the United States." 14 Stat. 27. The power of Congress, in this mode, to elevate the enfranchised race to national citizenship, was maintained by the supporters of the act of 1866 to be as full and complete as its power, by general statute, to make the children, being of full age, of persons naturalized in this country, citizens of the United States without going through the process of naturalization. The act of 1866, in this respect, was also likened to that of 1843, in which Congress declared "that the Stockbridge tribe of Indians, and each and every one of them, shall be deemed to be and are hereby declared to be, citizens of the United States to all intents and purposes, and shall be entitled to all the rights, privileges, and immunities of such citizens, and shall in all respects be subject to the laws of the United States." If the act of 1866 was valid in conferring national citizenship upon all embraced by its terms, then the colored race, enfranchised by the Thirteenth Amendment, became citizens of the United States prior to the adoption of the Fourteenth Amendment. But, in the view which I take of the present case, it is not necessary to examine this question.

The terms of the Thirteenth Amendment are absolute and universal. They embrace every race which then was, or might thereafter be, within the United States. No race, as such, can be excluded from the benefits or rights thereby conferred. Yet, it is historically true that that amendment was suggested by the condition, in this country, of that race which had

been declared, by this court, to have had—according to the opinion entertained by the most civilized portion of the white race, at the time of the adoption of the Constitution—"no rights which the white man was bound to respect," none of the privileges or immunities secured by that instrument to citizens of the United States. It had reference, in a peculiar sense, to a people which (although the larger part of them were in slavery) had been invited by an act of Congress to aid in saving from overthrow a government which, theretofore, by all of its departments, had treated them as an inferior race, with no legal rights or privileges except such as the white race might choose to grant them.

These are the circumstances under which the Thirteenth Amendment was proposed for adoption. They are now recalled only that we may better understand what was in the minds of the people when that amendment was considered, and what were the mischiefs to be remedied and the grievances to be redressed by its adoption.

We have seen that the power of Congress, by legislation, to enforce the master's right to have his slave delivered up on claim was implied from the recognition of that right in the national Constitution. But the power conferred by the Thirteenth Amendment does not rest upon implication or inference. Those who framed it were not ignorant of the discussion, covering many years of our country's history, as to the constitutional power of Congress to enact the Fugitive Slave Laws of 1793 and 1850. When, therefore, it was determined, by a change in the fundamental law, to uproot the institution of slavery wherever it existed in the land, and to establish universal freedom, there was a fixed purpose to place the authority of Congress in the premises beyond the possibility of a doubt. Therefore, ex industria, power to enforce the Thirteenth Amendment, by appropriate legislation, was expressly granted. Legislation for that purpose, my brethren concede, may be direct and primary. But to what specific ends may it be directed? This court has uniformly held that the national government has the power, whether expressly given or not, to secure and protect rights conferred or guaranteed by the Constitution. United States v. Reese, 92 U.S. 214; Strauder v. West Virginia, 100 U.S. 303. That doctrine ought not now to be abandoned when the inquiry is not as to an implied power to protect the master's rights, but what may Congress, under powers expressly granted, do for the protection of freedom and the rights necessarily inhering in a state of freedom.

The Thirteenth Amendment, it is conceded, did something more than to prohibit slavery as an institution, resting upon distinctions of race, and upheld by positive law. My brethren admit that it established and decreed universal civil freedom throughout the United States. But did the freedom thus established involve nothing more than exemption from actual slavery? Was nothing more intended than to forbid one man from owning another as property? Was it the purpose of the nation simply to destroy the institution, and then remit the race, theretofore held in bondage, to the several States for such protection, in their civil rights, necessarily growing out of freedom, as those States, in their discretion, might choose to provide? Were the States against whose protest the institution was destroyed, to be left free, so far as national interference was concerned, to make or allow discriminations against that race, as such, in the enjoyment of those fundamental rights which by universal concession, inhere in a state of freedom? Had the Thirteenth Amendment stopped with the sweeping declaration, in its first section, against the existence of slavery and involuntary servitude, except for crime, Congress would have had the power, by implication, according to the doctrines of Prigg v. Commonwealth of Pennsylvania, repeated in Strauder v. West Virginia, to protect the freedom established, and consequently, to secure the enjoyment of such civil rights as were fundamental in freedom. That it can exert its authority to that extent is made clear, and was intended to be made clear, by the express grant of power contained in the second section of the Amendment.

That there are burdens and disabilities which constitute badges of slavery and servitude, and that the power to enforce by appropriate legislation the Thirteenth Amendment may be exerted by legislation of a direct and primary character, for the eradication, not simply of the institution, but of its badges and incidents, are propositions which ought to be deemed indisputable. They lie at the foundation of the Civil Rights Act of 1866. Whether that act was authorized by the Thirteenth Amendment alone, without the support which it subsequently received from the Fourteenth Amendment, after the adoption of which it was reenacted with some additions, my brethren do not consider it necessary to inquire. But I submit, with all respect to them, that its constitutionality is conclusively shown by their opinion. They admit, as I have said, that the Thirteenth Amendment established freedom; that there are burdens and disabilities, the necessary incidents of slavery, which constitute its substance and visible form; that Congress, by the act of

1866, passed in view of the Thirteenth Amendment, before the Fourteenth was adopted, undertook to remove certain burdens and disabilities, the necessary incidents of slavery, and to secure to all citizens of every race and color, and without regard to previous servitude, those fundamental rights which are the essence of civil freedom, namely, the same right to make and enforce contracts, to sue, be parties, give evidence, and to inherit, purchase, lease, sell, and convey property as is enjoyed by white citizens; that under the Thirteenth Amendment, Congress has to do with slavery and its incidents; and that legislation, so far as necessary or proper to eradicate all forms and incidents of slavery and involuntary servitude, may be direct and primary, operating upon the acts of individuals, whether sanctioned by State legislation or not. These propositions being conceded, it is impossible, as it seems to me, to question the constitutional validity of the Civil Rights Act of 1866. I do not contend that the Thirteenth Amendment invests Congress with authority, by legislation, to define and regulate the entire body of the civil rights which citizens enjoy, or may enjoy, in the several States. But I hold that since slavery, as the court has repeatedly declared, Slaughterhouse Cases, 16 Wall. 36; Strauder v. West Virginia, 100 U.S. 303, was the moving or principal cause of the adoption of that amendment, and since that institution rested wholly upon the inferiority, as a race, of those held in bondage, their freedom necessarily involved immunity from, and protection against, all discrimination against them, because of their race, in respect of such civil rights as belong to freemen of other races. Congress, therefore, under its express power to enforce that amendment, by appropriate legislation, may enact laws to protect that people against the deprivation, because of their race, of any civil rights granted to other freemen in the same State; and such legislation may be of a direct and primary character, operating upon States, their officers and agents, and, also, upon, at least, such individuals and corporations as exercise public functions and wield power and authority under the State.

***What has been said is sufficient to show that the power of Congress under the Thirteenth Amendment is not necessarily restricted to legislation against slavery as an institution upheld by positive law, but may be exerted to the extent, at least, of protecting the liberated race against discrimination, in respect of legal rights belonging to freemen, where such discrimination is based upon race.

It remains now to inquire what are the legal rights of colored persons in respect of the accommodations, privileges and facilities of public conveyances, inns and places of public amusement?

First, as to public conveyances on land and water. In New Jersey Steam Navigation Co. v. Merchants' Bank, 6 How. 344, this court, speaking by Mr. Justice Nelson, said that a common carrier is "in the exercise of a sort of public office, and has public duties to perform, from which he should not be permitted to exonerate himself without the assent of the parties concerned." To the same effect is Munn v. Illinois, 94 U.S. 113. In Olcott v. Supervisors, 16 Wall. 678, it was ruled that railroads are public highways, established by authority of the State for the public use; that they are none the less public highways, because controlled and owned by private corporations; that it is a part of the function of government to make and maintain highways for the convenience of the public; that no matter who is the agent, or what is the agency, the function performed is that of the State; that although the owners may be private companies, they may be compelled to permit the public to use these works in the manner in which they can be used; that, upon these grounds alone, have the courts sustained the investiture of railroad corporations with the State's right of eminent domain, or the right of municipal corporations, under legislative authority, to assess, levy and collect taxes to aid in the construction of railroads. So in Township of Queensbury v. Culver, 19 Wall. 83, it was said that a municipal subscription of railroad stock was in aid of the construction and maintenance of a public highway, and for the promotion of a public use. Again, in Township of Pine Grove v. Talcott, 19 Wall. 666: "Though the corporation [railroad] was private, its work was public, as much so as if it were to be constructed by the State." To the like effect are numerous adjudications in this and the State courts with which the profession is familiar. The Supreme Judicial Court of Massachusetts in Inhabitants of Worcester v. The Western R.R. Corporation, 4 Met. 564, said in reference to a railroad:

"The establishment of that great thoroughfare is regarded as a public work, established by public authority, intended for the public use and benefit, the use of which is secured to the whole community, and constitutes, therefore, like a canal, turnpike, or highway, a public easement. ... It is true that the real and personal property, necessary to the establishment and management of the railroad, is vested in the corporation; but it is in trust for the public." In Erie, Etc., R.R. Co. v. Casey, 26 Penn. St. 287, the court, referring to an act repealing the charter of a railroad, and under which the

State took possession of the road, said: "It is a public highway, solemnly devoted to public use. When the lands were taken it was for such use, or they could not have been taken at all. ... Railroads established upon land taken by the right of eminent domain by authority of the commonwealth, created by her laws as thoroughfares for commerce, are her highways. No corporation has property in them, though it may have franchises annexed to and exercisable within them."

***Such being the relations these corporations hold to the public, it would seem that the right of a colored person to use an improved public highway, upon the terms accorded to freemen of other races, is as fundamental, in the state of freedom established in this country, as are any of the rights which my brethren concede to be so far fundamental as to be deemed the essence of civil freedom. "Personal liberty consists," says Blackstone, "in the power of locomotion, of changing situation, or removing one's person to whatever places one's own inclination may direct, without restraint, unless by due course of law." But of what value is this right of locomotion, if it may be clogged by such burdens as Congress intended by the act of 1875 to remove? They are burdens which lay at the very foundation of the institution of slavery as it once existed. They are not to be sustained, except upon the assumption that there is, in this land of universal liberty, a class which may still be discriminated against, even in respect of rights of a character so necessary and supreme, that, deprived of their enjoyment in common with others, a freeman is not only branded as one inferior and infected, but, in the competitions of life, is robbed of some of the most essential means of existence; and all this solely because they belong to a particular race which the nation has liberated. The Thirteenth Amendment alone obliterated the race line, so far as all rights fundamental in a state of freedom are concerned.

Second, as to inns. The same general observations which have been made as to railroads are applicable to inns. The word 'inn' has a technical legal signification. It means, in the act of 1875, just what it meant at common law. A mere private boarding-house is not an inn, nor is its keeper subject to the responsibilities, or entitled to the privileges of a common innkeeper. "To constitute one an innkeeper, within the legal force of that term, he must keep a house of entertainment or lodging for all travelers or wayfarers who might choose to accept the same, being of good character or conduct." Says Judge Story:

"An innkeeper may be defined to be the keeper of a common inn for the lodging and entertainment of travelers and passengers, their horses and attendants. An innkeeper is bound to take in all travelers and wayfaring persons, and to entertain them, if he can accommodate them, for a reasonable compensation; and he must guard their goods with proper diligence. ... If an innkeeper improperly refuses to receive or provide for a guest, he is liable to be indicted therefor. ... They (carriers of passengers) are no more at liberty to refuse a passenger, if they have sufficient room and accommodations, than an innkeeper is to refuse suitable room and accommodations to a guest." Story on Bailments, §§ 475–6.

***These authorities are sufficient to show that a keeper of an inn is in the exercise of a quasi public employment. The law gives him special privileges and he is charged with certain duties and responsibilities to the public. The public nature of his employment forbids him from discriminating against any person asking admission as a guest on account of the race or color of that person.

Third. As to places of public amusement. It may be argued that the managers of such places have no duties to perform with which the public are, in any legal sense, concerned, or with which the public have any right to interfere; and, that the exclusion of a black man from a place of public amusement, on account of his race, or the denial to him, on that ground, of equal accommodations at such places, violates no legal right for the vindication of which he may invoke the aid of the courts. My answer is, that places of public amusement, within the meaning of the act of 1875, are such as are established and maintained under direct license of the law. The authority to establish and maintain them comes from the public. The colored race is a part of that public. The local government granting the license represents them as well as all other races within its jurisdiction. A license from the public to establish a place of public amusement, imports, in law, equality of right, at such places, among all the members of that public. This must be so, unless it be—which I deny—that the common municipal government of all the people may, in the exertion of its powers, conferred for the benefit of all, discriminate or authorize discrimination against a particular race, solely because of its former condition of servitude.

***The doctrines of Munn v. Illinois have never been modified by this court, and I am justified, upon the authority of that case, in saying that places of public amusement, conducted under the authority of the law, are clothed with a public interest, because used in a manner to make them of public consequence and to affect the community at large. The law may therefore regulate, to some extent, the mode in which they shall be conducted, and, consequently, the public have rights in respect of such places, which may be vindicated by the law. It is consequently not a matter purely of private concern.

Congress has not, in these matters, entered the domain of State control and supervision. It does not, as I have said, assume to prescribe the general conditions and limitations under which inns, public conveyances, and places of public amusement, shall be conducted or managed. It simply declares, in effect, that since the nation has established universal freedom in this country, for all time, there shall be no discrimination, based merely upon race or color, in respect of the accommodations and advantages of public conveyances, inns, and places of public amusement.

I am of the opinion that such discrimination practiced by corporations and individuals in the exercise of their public or quasipublic functions is a badge of servitude the imposition of which Congress may prevent under its power, by appropriate legislation, to enforce the Thirteenth Amendment; and, consequently, without reference to its enlarged power under the Fourteenth Amendment, the act of March 1, 1875, is not, in my judgment, repugnant to the Constitution.

It remains now to consider these cases with reference to the power Congress has possessed since the adoption of the Fourteenth Amendment. Much that has been said as to the power of Congress under the Thirteenth Amendment is applicable to this branch of the discussion, and will not be repeated.

Before the adoption of the recent amendments, it had become, as we have seen, the established doctrine of this court that negroes, whose ancestors had been imported and sold as slaves, could not become citizens of a State, or even of the United States, with the rights and privileges guaranteed to citizens by the national Constitution; further, that one might have all the rights and privileges of a citizen of a State without being a citizen in the sense in which that word was used in the national Constitution, and without being entitled to the privileges and immunities of citizens of the several States. Still, further, between the adoption of the Thirteenth Amendment and the proposal by Congress of the Fourteenth Amendment, on June 16, 1866, the statute books of several of the States, as we have seen, had become loaded down with enactments which, under the guise of Apprentice, Vagrant, and Contract regulations, sought to keep the colored race in a condition, practically, of servitude. It was openly announced that whatever might be the rights which persons of that race had, as freemen, under the guarantees of the national Constitution, they could not become citizens of a State, with the privileges belonging to citizens, except by the consent of such State; consequently, that their civil rights, as citizens of the State, depended entirely upon State legislation. To meet this new peril to the black race, that the purposes of the nation might not be doubted or defeated, and by way of further enlargement of the power of Congress, the Fourteenth Amendment was proposed for adoption.

Remembering that this court, in the Slaughter-House Cases, declared that the one pervading purpose found in all the recent amendments, lying at the foundation of each, and without which none of them would have been suggested—was "the freedom of the slave race, the security and firm establishment of that freedom, and the protection of the newly-made freeman and citizen from the oppression of those who had formerly exercised unlimited dominion over him"—that each amendment was addressed primarily to the grievances of that race—let us proceed to consider the language of the Fourteenth Amendment.

Its first and fifth sections are in these words:

"SEC. 1. All persons born or naturalized in the United States, and subject to the jurisdiction thereof, are citizens of the United States and of the State wherein they reside. No State shall make or enforce any law which shall abridge the privileges or immunities of citizens of the United States; nor shall any State deprive any person of life, liberty, or property, without due process of law; nor deny to any person within its jurisdiction the equal protection of the laws.

***

"SEC. 5. That Congress shall have power to enforce, by appropriate legislation, the provisions of this article."

It was adjudged in Strauder v. West Virginia, 100 U.S. 303, and Ex parte Virginia, 100 U.S. 339, and my brethren concede, that positive rights and privileges were intended to be secured, and are in fact secured, by the Fourteenth Amendment.

But when, under what circumstances, and to what extent, may Congress, by means of legislation, exert its power to enforce the provisions of this amendment? The theory of the opinion of the majority of the court—the foundation upon which their reasoning seems to rest— is, that the general government cannot, in advance of hostile State laws or hostile State proceedings, actively interfere for the protection of any of the rights, privileges, and immunities secured by the Fourteenth Amendment. It is

said that such rights, privileges, and immunities are secured by way of prohibition against State laws and State proceedings affecting such rights and privileges, and by power given to Congress to legislate for the purpose of carrying such prohibition into effect; also, that congressional legislation must necessarily be predicated upon such supposed State laws or State proceedings, and be directed to the correction of their operation and effect.

In illustration of its position, the court refers to the clause of the Constitution forbidding the passage by a State of any law impairing the obligation of contracts. That clause does not, I submit, furnish a proper illustration of the scope and effect of the fifth section of the Fourteenth Amendment. No express power is given Congress to enforce, by primary direct legislation, the prohibition upon State laws impairing the obligation of contracts. Authority is, indeed, conferred to enact all necessary and proper laws for carrying into execution the enumerated powers of Congress and all other powers vested by the Constitution in the government of the United States or in any department or officer thereof. And, as heretofore shown, there is also, by necessary implication, power in Congress, by legislation, to protect a right derived from the national Constitution. But a prohibition upon a State is not a power in Congress or in the national government. It is simply a denial of power to the State. And the only mode in which the inhibition upon State laws impairing the obligation of contracts can be enforced, is, indirectly, through the courts, in suits where the parties raise some question as to the constitutional validity of such laws. The judicial power of the United States extends to such suits for the reason that they are suits arising under the Constitution. The Fourteenth Amendment presents the First instance in our history of the investiture of Congress with affirmative power, by legislation, to enforce an express prohibition upon the States. It is not said that the judicial power of the nation may be exerted for the enforcement of that amendment. No enlargement of the judicial power was required, for it is clear that had the fifth section of the Fourteenth Amendment been entirely omitted, the judiciary could have stricken down all State laws and nullified all State proceedings in hostility to rights and privileges secured or recognized by that amendment. The power given is, in terms, by congressional legislation, to enforce the provisions of the amendment.

The assumption that this amendment consists wholly of prohibitions upon State laws and State proceedings in hostility to its provisions, is unauthorized by its language. The first clause of the first sectio—"All persons born or naturalized in the United States, and subject to the jurisdiction thereof, are citizens of the United States, and of the State wherein they reside"—is of a distinctly affirmative character. In its application to the colored race, previously liberated, it created and granted, as well citizenship of the United States, as citizenship of the State in which they respectively resided. It introduced all of that race, whose ancestors had been imported and sold as slaves, at once, into the political community known as the "People of the United States." They became, instantly, citizens of the United States, and of their respective States. Further, they were brought, by this supreme act of the nation, within the direct operation of that provision of the Constitution which declares that "the citizens of each State shall be entitled to all privileges and immunities of citizens in the several States." Art. 4, § 2.

The citizenship thus acquired, by that race, in virtue of an affirmative grant from the nation, may be protected, not alone by the judicial branch of the government, but by congressional legislation of a primary direct character; this, because the power of Congress is not restricted to the enforcement of prohibitions upon State laws or State action. It is, in terms distinct and positive, to enforce "the provisions of this article" of amendment; not simply those of a prohibitive character, but the provisions—all of the provisions—affirmative and prohibitive, of the amendment. It is, therefore, a grave misconception to suppose that the fifth section of the amendment has reference exclusively to express prohibitions upon State laws or State action. If any right was created by that amendment, the grant of power, through appropriate legislation, to enforce its provisions, authorizes Congress, by means of legislation, operating throughout the entire Union, to guard, secure, and protect that right.

It is, therefore, an essential inquiry what, if any, right, privilege or immunity was given, by the nation, to colored persons, when they were made citizens of the State in which they reside? Did the constitutional grant of State citizenship to that race, of its own force, invest them with any rights, privileges and immunities whatever? That they became entitled, upon the adoption of the Fourteenth Amendment, "to all privileges and immunities of citizens in the several States," within the meaning of section 2 of article 4 of the Constitution, no one, I suppose, will for a moment question. What are the privileges and immunities to which, by that clause of the Constitution, they became entitled? To this it may be answered, generally, upon the authority of the

adjudged cases, that they are those which are fundamental in citizenship in a free republican government, such as are "common to the citizens in the latter States under their constitutions and laws by virtue of their being citizens." Of that provision it has been said, with the approval of this court, that no other one in the Constitution has tended so strongly to constitute the citizens of the United States one people. Although this court has wisely forborne any attempt, by a comprehensive definition, to indicate all of the privileges and immunities to which the citizen of a State is entitled, of right, when within the jurisdiction of other States, I hazard nothing, in view of former adjudications, in saying that no State can sustain her denial to colored citizens of other States, while within her limits, of privileges or immunities, fundamental in republican citizenship, upon the ground that she accords such privileges and immunities only to her white citizens and withholds them from her colored citizens. The colored citizens of other States, within the jurisdiction of the State, could claim, in virtue of section 2 of article 4 of the Constitution, every privilege and immunity which that State secures to her white citizens. Otherwise, it would be in the power of any State, by discriminating class legislation against its own citizens of a particular race or color, to withhold from citizens of other States, belonging to that proscribed race, when within her limits, privileges and immunities of the character regarded by all courts as fundamental in citizenship; and that, too, when the constitutional guaranty is that the citizens of each State shall be entitled to "all privileges and immunities of citizens of the several States." No State may, by discrimination against a portion of its own citizens of a particular race, in respect of privileges and immunities fundamental in citizenship, impair the constitutional right of citizens of other States, of whatever race, to enjoy in that State all such privileges and immunities as are there accorded to her most favored citizens. A colored citizen of Ohio or Indiana, while in the jurisdiction of Tennessee, is entitled to enjoy any privilege or immunity, fundamental in citizenship, which is given to citizens of the white race in the latter State. It is not to be supposed that any one will controvert this proposition.

But what was secured to colored citizens of the United States—as between them and their respective States—by the national grant to them of State citizenship? With what rights, privileges, or immunities did this grant invest them? There is one, if there be no other—exemption from race discrimination in respect of any civil right belonging to citizens of the white race in the same State. That, surely, is their constitutional privilege when within the jurisdiction of other States. And such must be their constitutional right, in their own State, unless the recent amendments be splendid baubles, thrown out to delude those who deserved fair and generous treatment at the hands of the nation. Citizenship in this country necessarily imports at least equality of civil rights among citizens of every race in the same State. It is fundamental in American citizenship that, in respect of such rights, there shall be no discrimination by the State, or its officers, or by individuals or corporations exercising public functions or authority, against any citizen because of his race or previous condition of servitude. In United States v. Cruikshank, 92 U.S. 542, it was said at page 555, that the rights of life and personal liberty are natural rights of man, and that "the equality of the rights of citizens is a principle of republicanism." And in Ex parte Virginia, 100 U.S. 334, the emphatic language of this court is that "one great purpose of these amendments was to raise the colored race from that condition of inferiority and servitude in which most of them had previously stood, into perfect equality of civil rights with all other persons within the jurisdiction of the States." So, in Strauder v. West Virginia, 100 U.S. 306, the court, alluding to the Fourteenth Amendment, said: "This is one of a series of constitutional provisions having a common purpose, namely, securing to a race recently emancipated, a race that through many generations had been held in slavery, all the civil rights that the superior race enjoy." Again, in Neal v. Delaware, 103 U.S. 386, it was ruled that this amendment was designed, primarily, "to secure to the colored race, thereby invested with the rights, privileges, and responsibilities of citizenship, the enjoyment of all the civil rights that, under the law, are enjoyed by white persons."

The language of this court with reference to the Fifteenth Amendment, adds to the force of this view. In United States v. Cruikshank, it was said: "In United States v. Reese, 92 U.S. 214, we held that the Fifteenth Amendment has invested the citizens of the United States with a new constitutional right, which is exemption from discrimination in the exercise of the elective franchise, on account of race, color, or previous condition of servitude. From this it appears that the right of suffrage is not a necessary attribute of national citizenship, but that exemption from discrimination in the exercise of that right on account of race, &c., is. The right to vote in the States comes from the States; but the right of exemption from the

prohibited discrimination comes from the United States. The first has not been granted or secured by the Constitution of the United States, but the last has been."

Here, in language at once clear and forcible, is stated the principle for which I contend. It can scarcely be claimed that exemption from race discrimination, in respect of civil rights, against those to whom State citizenship was granted by the nation, is any less, for the colored race, a new constitutional right, derived from and secured by the national Constitution, than is exemption from such discrimination in the exercise of the elective franchise. It cannot be that the latter is an attribute of national citizenship, while the other is not essential in national citizenship, or fundamental in State citizenship.

If, then, exemption from discrimination, in respect of civil rights, is a new constitutional right, secured by the grant of State citizenship to colored citizens of the United States—and I do not see how this can now be questioned—why may not the nation, by means of its own legislation of a primary direct character, guard, protect and enforce that right? It is a right and privilege which the nation conferred. It did not come from the States in which those colored citizens reside. It has been the established doctrine of this court during all its history, accepted as essential to the national supremacy, that Congress, in the absence of a positive delegation of power to the State legislatures, may, by its own legislation, enforce and protect any right derived from or created by the national Constitution. It was so declared in Prigg v. Commonwealth of Pennsylvania. It was reiterated in United States v. Reese, 92 U.S. 214, where the court said that "rights and immunities created by and dependent upon the Constitution of the United States can be protected by Congress. The form and manner of the protection may be such as Congress, in the legitimate exercise of its discretion, shall provide. These may be varied to meet the necessities of the particular right to be protected." It was distinctly reaffirmed in Strauder v. West Virginia, 100 U.S. 310, where we said that "a right or immunity created by the Constitution or only guaranteed by it, even without any express delegation of power, may be protected by Congress." How then can it be claimed in view of the declarations of this court in former cases, that exemption of colored citizens, within their States, from race discrimination, in respect of the civil rights of citizens, is not an immunity created or derived from the national Constitution?

This court has always given a broad and liberal construction to the Constitution, so as to enable Congress, by legislation, to enforce rights secured by that instrument. The legislation which Congress may enact, in execution of its power to enforce the provisions of this amendment, is such as may be appropriate to protect the right granted. The word appropriate was undoubtedly used with reference to its meaning, as established by repeated decision of this court. Under given circumstances, that which the court characterizes as corrective legislation might be deemed by Congress appropriate and entirely sufficient. Under other circumstances primary direct legislation may be required. But it is for Congress, not the judiciary, to say that legislation is appropriate—that is—best adapted to the end to be attained. The judiciary may not, with safety to our institutions, enter the domain of legislative discretion, and dictate the means which Congress shall employ in the exercise of its granted powers. That would be sheer usurpation of the functions of a coordinate department, which, if often repeated, and permanently acquiesced in, would work a radical change in our system of government. In United States v. Fisher, 2 Cr. 358, the court said that "Congress must possess the choice of means, and must be empowered to use any means which are in fact conducive to the exercise of a power granted by the Constitution." "The sound construction of the Constitution," said Chief Justice Marshall, "must allow to the national legislature that discretion, with respect to the means by which the powers it confers are to be carried into execution, which will enable that body to perform the high duties assigned to it in the manner most beneficial to the people. Let the end be legitimate, let it be within the scope of the Constitution, and all means which are appropriate, which are plainly adapted to that end, which are not prohibited, but consist with the letter and spirit of the Constitution, are constitutional." McCulloch v. Maryland, 4 Wh. 421.

Must these rules of construction be now abandoned? Are the powers of the national legislature to be restrained in proportion as the rights and privileges, derived from the nation, are valuable? Are constitutional provisions, enacted to secure the dearest rights of freemen and citizens, to be subjected to that rule of construction, applicable to private instruments, which requires that the words to be interpreted must be taken most strongly against those who employ them? Or, shall it be remembered that "a constitution of government, founded by the people for themselves and their posterity, and for objects of the most momentous nature—for perpetual union, for the establishment of justice, for the general welfare, and for a perpetuation of the blessings of liberty—necessarily requires that every interpretation of its powers should have a constant reference to these objects? No interpretation of the words in which those powers are granted can be a sound one, which narrows down their ordinary import so as to defeat those objects." 1 Story Const. § 422.

The opinion of the court, as I have said, proceeds upon the ground that the power of Congress to legislate for the protection of the rights and privileges secured by the Fourteenth Amendment cannot be brought into activity except with the view, and as it may become necessary, to correct and annul State laws and State proceedings in hostility to such rights and privileges. In the absence of State laws or State action adverse to such rights and privileges, the nation may not actively interfere for their protection and security, even against corporations and individuals exercising public or quasi public functions. Such I understand to be the position of my brethren. If the grant to colored citizens of the United States of citizenship in their respective States, imports exemption from race discrimination, in their States, in respect of such civil rights as belong to citizenship, then, to hold that the amendment remits that right to the States for their protection, primarily, and stays the hands of the nation, until it is assailed by State laws or State proceedings, is to adjudge that the amendment, so far from enlarging the powers of Congress—as we have heretofore said it did—not only curtails them, but reverses the policy which the general government has pursued from its very organization. Such an interpretation of the amendment is a denial to Congress of the power, by appropriate legislation, to enforce one of its provisions. In view of the circumstances under which the recent amendments were incorporated into the Constitution, and especially in view of the peculiar character of the new rights they created and secured, it ought not to be presumed that the general government has abdicated its authority, by national legislation, direct and primary in its character, to guard and protect privileges and immunities secured by that instrument. Such an interpretation of the Constitution ought not to be accepted if it be possible to avoid it. Its acceptance would lead to this anomalous result: that whereas, prior to the amendments, Congress, with the sanction of this court, passed the most stringent laws—operating directly and primarily upon States and their officers and agents, as well as upon individuals—in vindication of slavery and the right of the master, it may not now, by legislation of a like primary and direct character, guard, protect, and secure the freedom established, and the most essential right of the citizenship granted, by the constitutional amendments. With all respect for the opinion of others, I insist that the national legislature may, without transcending the limits of the Constitution, do for human liberty and the fundamental rights of American citizenship, what it did, with the sanction of this court, for the protection of slavery and the rights of the masters of fugitive slaves. If fugitive slave laws, providing modes and prescribing penalties, whereby the master could seize and recover his fugitive slave, were legitimate exercises of an implied power to protect and enforce a right recognized by the Constitution, why shall the hands of Congress be tied, so that—under an express power, by appropriate legislation, to enforce a constitutional provision granting citizenship—it may not, by means of direct legislation, bring the whole power of this nation to bear upon States and their officers, and upon such individuals and corporations exercising public functions as assume to abridge, impair, or deny rights confessedly secured by the supreme law of the land?

It does not seem to me that the fact that, by the second clause of the first section of the Fourteenth Amendment, the States are expressly prohibited from making or enforcing laws abridging the privileges and immunities of citizens of the United States, furnishes any sufficient reason for holding or maintaining that the amendment was intended to deny Congress the power, by general, primary, and direct legislation, of protecting citizens of the several States, being also citizens of the United States, against all discrimination, in respect of their rights as citizens, which is founded on race, color, or previous condition of servitude.

Such an interpretation of the amendment is plainly repugnant to its fifth section, conferring upon Congress power, by appropriate legislation, to enforce not merely the provisions containing prohibitions upon the States, but all of the provisions of the amendment, including the provisions, express and implied, in the first clause of the first section of the article granting citizenship. This alone is sufficient for holding that Congress is not restricted to the enactment of laws adapted to counteract and redress the operation of State legislation, or the action of State officers, of the character prohibited by the amendment. It was perfectly well known that the great danger to the equal enjoyment by citizens of their rights, as citizens, was to be apprehended not altogether from unfriendly State legislation, but from the hostile action of corporations and individuals in the States. And it is to be presumed that it was intended, by that section,

to clothe Congress with power and authority to meet that danger. If the rights intended to be secured by the act of 1875 are such as belong to the citizen, in common or equally with other citizens in the same State, then it is not to be denied that such legislation is peculiarly appropriate to the end which Congress is authorized to accomplish, viz., to protect the citizen, in respect of such rights, against discrimination on account of his race. Recurring to the specific prohibition in the Fourteenth Amendment upon the making or enforcing of State laws abridging the privileges of citizens of the United States, I remark that if, as held in the Slaughter-House Cases, the privileges here referred to were those which belonged to citizenship of the United States, as distinguished from those belonging to State citizenship, it was impossible for any State prior to the adoption of that amendment to have enforced laws of that character. The judiciary could have annulled all such legislation under the provision that the Constitution shall be the supreme law of the land, anything in the constitution or laws of any State to the contrary notwithstanding. The States were already under an implied prohibition not to abridge any privilege or immunity belonging to citizens of the United States as such. Consequently, the prohibition upon State laws in hostility to rights belonging to citizens of the United States, was intended—in view of the introduction into the body of citizens of a race formerly denied the essential rights of citizenship—only as an express limitation on the powers of the States, and was not intended to diminish, in the slightest degree, the authority which the nation has always exercised, of protecting, by means of its own direct legislation, rights created or secured by the Constitution. Any purpose to diminish the national authority in respect of privileges derived from the nation is distinctly negatived by the express grant of power, by legislation, to enforce every provision of the amendment, including that which, by the grant of citizenship in the State, secures exemption from race discrimination in respect of the civil rights of citizens.

It is said that any interpretation of the Fourteenth Amendment different from that adopted by the majority of the court, would imply that Congress had authority to enact a municipal code for all the States, covering every matter affecting the life, liberty, and property of the citizens of the several States. Not so. Prior to the adoption of that amendment the constitutions of the several States, without perhaps an exception, secured all persons against deprivation of life, liberty, or property, otherwise than by due process of law, and, in some form, recognized the right of all persons to the equal protection of the laws. Those rights, therefore, existed before that amendment was proposed or adopted, and were not created by it. If, by reason of that fact, it be assumed that protection in these rights of persons still rests primarily with the States, and that Congress may not interfere except to enforce, by means of corrective legislation, the prohibitions upon State laws or State proceedings inconsistent with those rights, it does not at all follow, that privileges which have been granted by the nation, may not be protected by primary legislation upon the part of Congress. The personal rights and immunities recognized in the prohibitive clauses of the amendment were, prior to its adoption, under the protection, primarily, of the States, while rights, created by or derived from the United States, have always been, and, in the nature of things, should always be, primarily, under the protection of the general government. Exemption from race discrimination in respect of the civil rights which are fundamental in citizenship in a republican government, is, as we have seen, a new right, created by the nation, with express power in Congress, by legislation, to enforce the constitutional provision from which it is derived. If, in some sense, such race discrimination is, within the letter of the last clause of the first section, a denial of that equal protection of the laws which is secured against State denial to all persons, whether citizens or not, it cannot be possible that a mere prohibition upon such State denial, or a prohibition upon State laws abridging the privileges and immunities of citizens of the United States, takes from the nation the power which it has uniformly exercised of protecting, by direct primary legislation, those privileges and immunities which existed under the Constitution before the adoption of the Fourteenth Amendment, or have been created by that amendment in behalf of those thereby made citizens of their respective States.

This construction does not in any degree intrench upon the just rights of the States in the control of their domestic affairs. It simply recognizes the enlarged powers conferred by the recent amendments upon the general government. In the view which I take of those amendments, the States possess the same authority which they have always had to define and regulate the civil rights which their own people, in virtue of State citizenship, may enjoy within their respective limits; except that its exercise is now subject to the expressly granted power of Congress, by legislation, to enforce the provisions of such amendments—a power which necessarily carries with it authority, by national legislation, to

protect and secure the privileges and immunities which are created by or are derived from those amendments. That exemption of citizens from discrimination based on race or color, in respect of civil rights, is one of those privileges or immunities, can no longer be deemed an open question in this court.

It was said of the case of Dred Scott v. Sandford, that this court, there overruled the action of two generations, virtually inserted a new clause in the Constitution, changed its character, and made a new departure in the workings of the federal government. I may be permitted to say that if the recent amendments are so construed that Congress may not, in its own discretion, and independently of the action or nonaction of the States, provide, by legislation of a direct character, for the security of rights created by the national Constitution; if it be adjudged that the obligation to protect the fundamental privileges and immunities granted by the Fourteenth Amendment to citizens residing in the several States, rests primarily, not on the nation, but on the States; if it be further adjudged that individuals and corporations, exercising public functions, or wielding power under public authority, may, without liability to direct primary legislation on the part of Congress, make the race of citizens the ground for denying them that equality of civil rights which the Constitution ordains as a principle of republican citizenship; then, not only the foundations upon which the national supremacy has always securely rested will be materially disturbed, but we shall enter upon an era of constitutional law, when the rights of freedom and American citizenship cannot receive from the nation that efficient protection which heretofore was unhesitatingly accorded to slavery and the rights of the master.

But if it were conceded that the power of Congress could not be brought into activity until the rights specified in the act of 1875 had been abridged or denied by some State law or State action, I maintain that the decision of the court is erroneous. There has been adverse State action within the Fourteenth Amendment as heretofore interpreted by this court. I allude to Ex parte Virginia, supra. It appears, in that case, that one Cole, judge of a county court, was charged with the duty, by the laws of Virginia, of selecting grand and petit jurors. The law of the State did not authorize or permit him, in making such selections, to discriminate against colored citizens because of their race. But he was indicted in the federal court, under the act of 1875, for making such discriminations. The attorney-general of Virginia contended before us, that the State had done its duty, and had not authorized or directed that county judge to do what he was charged with having done; that the State had not denied to the colored race the equal protection of the laws; and that consequently the act of Cole must be deemed his individual act, in contravention of the will of the State. Plausible as this argument was, it failed to convince this court, and after saying that the Fourteenth Amendment had reference to the political body denominated a State, "by whatever instruments or in whatever modes that action may be taken," and that a State acts by its legislative, executive, and judicial authorities, and can act in no other way, we proceeded:

"The constitutional provision, therefore, must mean that no agency of the State, or of the officers or agents by whom its powers are exerted, shall deny to any person within its jurisdiction the equal protection of the laws. Whoever, by virtue of public position under a State government, deprives another of property, life, or liberty without due process of law, or denies or takes away the equal protection of the laws, violates the constitutional inhibition; and, as he acts under the name and for the State, and is clothed with the State's power, his act is that of the State. This must be so, or the constitutional prohibition has no meaning. Then the State has clothed one of its agents with power to annul or evade it. But the constitutional amendment was ordained for a purpose. It was to secure equal rights to all persons, and, to insure to all persons the enjoyment of such rights, power was given to Congress to enforce its provisions by appropriate legislation. Such legislation must act upon persons, not upon the abstract thing denominated a State, but upon the persons who are the agents of the State, in the denial of the rights which were intended to be secured." Ex parte Virginia, 100 U.S. 346–7.

In every material sense applicable to the practical enforcement of the Fourteenth Amendment, railroad corporations, keepers of inns, and managers of places of public amusement are agents or instrumentalities of the State, because they are charged with duties to the public, and are amenable, in respect of their duties and functions, to governmental regulation. It seems to me that, within the principle settled in Ex parte Virginia, a denial, by these instrumentalities of the State, to the citizen, because of his race, of that equality of civil rights secured to him by law, is a denial by the State, within the meaning of the Fourteenth Amendment. If it be not, then that race is left, in respect of the civil rights in question, practically at the mercy of corporations and individuals wielding power under the States.

But the court says that Congress did not, in the act of 1866, assume, under the authority given by the Thirteenth Amendment, to adjust what may be called the social rights of men and races in the community. I agree that government has nothing to do with social, as distinguished from technically legal, rights of individuals. No government ever has brought, or ever can bring, its people into social intercourse against their wishes. Whether one person will permit or maintain social relations with another is a matter with which government has no concern. I agree that if one citizen chooses not to hold social intercourse with another, he is not and cannot be made amenable to the law for his conduct in that regard; for even upon grounds of race, no legal right of a citizen is violated by the refusal of others to maintain merely social relations with him. What I affirm is that no State, nor the officers of any State, nor any corporation or individual wielding power under State authority for the public benefit or the public convenience, can, consistently either with the freedom established by the fundamental law, or with that equality of civil rights which now belongs to every citizen, discriminate against freemen or citizens, in those rights, because of their race, or because they once labored under the disabilities of slavery imposed upon them as a race. The rights which Congress, by the act of 1875, endeavored to secure and protect are legal, not social rights. The right, for instance, of a colored citizen to use the accommodations of a public highway, upon the same terms as are permitted to white citizens, is no more a social right than his right, under the law, to use the public streets of a city or a town, or a turnpike road, or a public market, or a post office, or his right to sit in a public building with others, of whatever race, for the purpose of hearing the political questions of the day discussed. Scarcely a day passes without our seeing in this court-room citizens of the white and black races sitting side by side, watching the progress of our business. It would never occur to any one that the presence of a colored citizen in a court-house, or court-room, was an invasion of the social rights of white persons who may frequent such places. And yet, such a suggestion would be quite as sound in law—I say it with all respect—as is the suggestion that the claim of a colored citizen to use, upon the same terms as is permitted to white citizens, the accommodations of public highways, or public inns, or places of public amusement, established under the license of the law, is an invasion of the social rights of the white race.

***My brethren say, that when a man has emerged from slavery, and by the aid of beneficent legislation has shaken off the inseparable concomitants of that state, there must be some stage in the progress of his elevation when he takes the rank of a mere citizen, and ceases to be the special favorite of the laws, and when his rights as a citizen, or a man, are to be protected in the ordinary modes by which other men's rights are protected. It is, I submit, scarcely just to say that the colored race has been the special favorite of the laws. The statute of 1875, now adjudged to be unconstitutional, is for the benefit of citizens of every race and color. What the nation through Congress, has sought to accomplish in reference to that race, is—what had already been done in every State of the Union for the white race—to secure and protect rights belonging to them as freemen and citizens; nothing more. It was not deemed enough "to help the feeble up, but to support him after." The one underlying purpose of congressional legislation has been to enable the black race to take the rank of mere citizens. The difficulty has been to compel a recognition of the legal right of the black race to take the rank of citizens, and to secure the enjoyment of privileges belonging, under the law, to them as a component part of the people for whose welfare and happiness government is ordained. At every step, in this direction, the nation has been confronted with class tyranny, which a contemporary English historian says is, of all tyrannies, the most intolerable, "for it is ubiquitous in its operation, and weighs, perhaps, most heavily on those whose obscurity or distance would withdraw them from the notice of single despot." Today, it is the colored race which is denied, by corporations and individuals wielding public authority, rights fundamental in their freedom and citizenship. At some future time, it may be that some other race will fall under the ban of race discrimination. If the constitutional amendments be enforced, according to the intent with which, as I conceive, they were adopted, there cannot be, in this republic, any class of human beings in practical subjection to another class, with power in the latter to dole out to the former just such privileges as they may choose to grant. The supreme law of the land has decreed that no authority shall be exercised in this country upon the basis of discrimination, in respect of civil rights, against freemen and citizens because of their race, color, or previous condition of servitude. To that decree—for the due enforcement of which, by appropriate legislation, Congress has been invested with express power—every one must bow, whatever may have been, or whatever now are, his individual views as to the wisdom or policy, either of the recent changes in the fundamental law, or of the legislation which has been enacted to give them effect.

For the reasons stated I feel constrained to withhold my assent to the opinion of the court.

The Scrutiny Tests

Minimal Scrutiny: SEPARATE but EQUAL

> # PLESSY v. FERGUSON
> ## Supreme Court of the United States
> ## 163 U.S. 537 (1896)
>
> *May 18, 1896*

MR. JUSTICE BROWN, after stating the case, delivered the opinion of the court.

This case turns upon the constitutionality of an act of the General Assembly of the State of Louisiana, passed in 1890, providing for separate railway carriages for the white and colored races. Acts 1890, No. 111, p. 152.

The first section of the statute enacts "that all railway companies carrying passengers in their coaches in this State, shall provide equal but separate accommodations for the white, and colored races, by providing two or more passenger coaches for each passenger train, or by dividing the passenger coaches by a partition so as to secure separate accommodations: Provided, That this section shall not be construed to apply to street railroads. No person or persons, shall be admitted to occupy seats in coaches, other than, the ones, assigned, to them on account of the race they belong to."

By the second section it was enacted "that the officers of such passenger trains shall have power and are hereby required to assign each passenger to the coach or compartment used for the race to which such passenger belongs; any passenger insisting on going into a coach or compartment to which by race he does not belong, shall be liable to a fine of twenty-five dollars, or in lieu thereof to imprisonment for a period of not more than twenty days in the parish prison, and any officer of any railroad insisting on assigning a passenger to a coach or compartment other than the one set aside for the race to which said passenger belongs, shall be liable to a fine of twenty-five dollars, or in lieu thereof to imprisonment for a period of not more than twenty days in the parish prison; and should any passenger refuse to occupy the coach or compartment to which he or she is assigned by the officer of such railway, said officer shall have power to refuse to carry such passenger on his train, and for such refusal neither he nor the railway company which he represents shall be liable for damages in any of the courts of this State."

The third section provides penalties for the refusal or neglect of the officers, directors, conductors and employees of railway companies to comply with the act, with a proviso that "nothing in this act shall be construed as applying to nurses attending children of the other race." The fourth section is immaterial.

The information filed in the criminal District Court charged in substance that Plessy, being a passenger between two stations within the State of Louisiana, was assigned by officers of the company to the coach used for the race to which he belonged, but he insisted upon going into a coach used by the race to which he did not belong. Neither in the information nor plea was his particular race or color averred.

The petition for the writ of prohibition averred that petitioner was seven eighths Caucasian and one eighth African blood; that the mixture of colored blood was not discernible in him, and that he was entitled to every right, privilege and immunity secured to citizens of the United States of the white race; and that, upon such theory, he took possession of a vacant seat in a coach where passengers of the white race were accommodated, and was ordered by the conductor to vacate said coach and take a seat in another assigned to persons of the colored race, and having refused to comply with such demand he was forcibly ejected with the aid of a police officer, and imprisoned in the parish jail to answer a charge of having violated the above act.

The constitutionality of this act is attacked upon the ground that it conflicts both with the Thirteenth Amendment of the Constitution, abolishing slavery, and the Fourteenth Amendment, which prohibits certain restrictive legislation on the part of the States.

1. That it does not conflict with the Thirteenth Amendment, which abolished slavery and involuntary servitude, except as a punishment for crime, is too clear for argument. Slavery implies involuntary servitude—a state of bondage; the ownership of mankind as a chattel, or at least the control of the labor and services of one man for the benefit of another, and the absence of a legal right to the disposal of his own person, property and services. This amendment was said in the Slaughter-house cases, 16 Wall. 36, to have been intended primarily to abolish slavery, as it had been previously known in this country, and that it equally forbade Mexican peonage or the Chinese coolie trade, when they amounted to slavery or involuntary servitude, and that the use of the word "servitude" was intended to prohibit the use of all forms of involuntary slavery, of whatever class or name. It was intimated, however, in that case that this amendment was regarded by the statesmen of that day as insufficient to protect the colored race from certain laws which had been enacted in the Southern States, imposing upon the colored race onerous disabilities and burdens, and curtailing their rights in the pursuit of life, liberty and property to such an extent that their freedom was of little value; and that the Fourteenth Amendment was devised to meet this exigency.

So too, in the Civil Rights cases, 109 U.S. 3, 24, it was said that the act of a mere individual, the owner of an inn, a public conveyance or place of amusement, refusing accommodations to colored people, cannot be justly regarded as imposing any badge of slavery or servitude upon the applicant, but only as involving an ordinary civil injury, properly cognizable by the laws of the State, and presumably subject to redress by those laws until the contrary appears. "It would be running the slavery argument into the ground," said Mr. Justice Bradley, "to make it apply to every act of discrimination which a person may see fit to make as to the guests he will entertain, or as to the people he will take into his coach or cab or car, or admit to his concert or theatre, or deal with in other matters of intercourse or business."

A statute which implies merely a legal distinction between the white and colored races—a distinction which is founded in the color of the two races, and which must always exist so long as white men are distinguished from the other race by color—has no tendency to destroy the legal equality of the two races, or reestablish a state of involuntary servitude. Indeed, we do not understand that the Thirteenth Amendment is strenuously relied upon by the plaintiff in error in this connection.

2. By the Fourteenth Amendment, all persons born or naturalized in the United States, and subject to the jurisdiction thereof, are made citizens of the United States and of the State wherein they reside; and the States are forbidden from making or enforcing any law which shall abridge the privileges or immunities of citizens of the United States, or shall deprive any person of life, liberty or property without due process of law, or deny to any person within their jurisdiction the equal protection of the laws.

The proper construction of this amendment was first called to the attention of this court in the Slaughterhouse cases, 16 Wall. 36, which involved, however, not a question of race, but one of exclusive privileges. The case did not call for any expression of opinion as to the exact rights it was intended to secure to the colored race, but it was said generally that its main purpose was to establish the citizenship of the negro; to give definitions of citizenship of the United States and of the States, and to protect from the hostile legislation of the States the privileges and immunities of citizens of the United States, as distinguished from those of citizens of the States.

The object of the amendment was undoubtedly to enforce the absolute equality of the two races before the law, but in the nature of things it could not have been intended to abolish distinctions based upon color, or to enforce social, as distinguished from political equality, or a commingling of the two races upon terms unsatisfactory to either. Laws permitting, and even requiring, their separation in places where they are liable to be brought into contact do not necessarily imply the inferiority of either race to the other, and have been generally, if not universally, recognized as within the competency of the state legislatures in the exercise of their police power. The most common instance of this is connected with the establishment of separate schools for white and colored children, which has been held to be a valid exercise of the legislative power even by courts of States where the political rights of the colored race have been longest and most earnestly enforced.

One of the earliest of these cases is that of Roberts v. City of Boston, 5 Cush. 198, in which the Supreme Judicial Court of Massachusetts held that the general school committee of Boston had power to make provision for the instruction of colored children in separate schools established exclusively for them, and to prohibit their attendance upon the other schools. "The great principle," said Chief Justice Shaw, p. 206, "advanced by the learned and eloquent advocate for the plaintiff," (Mr. Charles Sumner,) "is, that by the constitution and laws of Massachusetts, all persons without distinction of age or sex, birth or color, origin or condition, are equal before the law. ... But, when this great principle comes to be applied to the actual and various conditions of persons in society, it will not warrant the assertion, that men and women are legally clothed with the same civil and political powers, and that children and adults are legally to have the same functions and be subject to the same treatment; but only that the rights of all, as they are settled and regulated by law, are equally entitled to the paternal consideration and protection of the law for their maintenance and security." It was held that the powers of the committee extended to the establishment of separate schools for children of different ages, sexes and colors, and that they might also establish special schools for poor and neglected children, who have become too old to attend the primary school, and yet have not acquired the rudiments of learning, to enable them to enter the ordinary schools. Similar laws have been enacted by Congress under its general power of legislation over the District of Columbia, 319, as well as by the legislatures of many of the States, and have been generally, if not uniformly, sustained by the courts.

Laws forbidding the intermarriage of the two races may be said in a technical sense to interfere with the freedom of contract, and yet have been universally recognized as within the police power of the State.

The distinction between laws interfering with the political equality of the negro and those requiring the separation of the two races in schools, theatres and railway carriages has been frequently drawn by this court. Thus in Strauder v. West Virginia, 100 U.S. 303, it was held that a law of West Virginia limiting to white male persons, 21 years of age and citizens of the State, the right to sit upon juries, was a discrimination which implied a legal inferiority in civil society, which lessened the security of the right of the colored race, and was a step toward reducing them to a condition of servility. Indeed, the right of a colored man that, in the selection of jurors to pass upon his life, liberty and property, there

shall be no exclusion of his race, and no discrimination against them because of color, has been asserted in a number of cases. ***So, where the laws of a particular locality or the charter of a particular railway corporation has provided that no person shall be excluded from the cars on account of color, we have held that this meant that persons of color should travel in the same car as white ones, and that the enactment was not satisfied by the company's providing cars assigned exclusively to people of color, though they were as good as those which they assigned exclusively to white persons.

Upon the other hand, where a statute of Louisiana required those engaged in the transportation of passengers among the States to give to all persons travelling within that State, upon vessels employed in that business, equal rights and privileges in all parts of the vessel, without distinction on account of race or color, and subjected to an action for damages the owner of such a vessel, who excluded colored passengers on account of their color from the cabin set aside by him for the use of whites, it was held to be so far as it applied to interstate commerce, unconstitutional and void. Hall v. De Cuir, 95 U.S. 485. The court in this case, however, expressly disclaimed that it had anything whatever to do with the statute as a regulation of internal commerce, or affecting anything else than commerce among the States.

In the Civil Rights case, 109 U.S. 3, it was held that an act of Congress, entitling all persons within the jurisdiction of the United States to the full and equal enjoyment of the accommodations, advantages, facilities and privileges of inns, public conveyances, on land or water, theatres and other places of public amusement, and made applicable to citizens of every race and color, regardless of any previous condition of servitude, was unconstitutional and void, upon the ground that the Fourteenth Amendment was prohibitory upon the States only, and the legislation authorized to be adopted by Congress for enforcing it was not direct legislation on matters respecting which the States were prohibited from making or enforcing certain laws, or doing certain acts, but was corrective legislation, such as might be necessary or proper for counteracting and redressing the effect of such laws or acts. In delivering the opinion of the court Mr. Justice Bradley observed that the Fourteenth Amendment "does not invest Congress with power to legislate upon subjects that are within the domain of state legislation; but to provide modes of relief against state legislation, or state action, of the kind referred to. It does not authorize Congress to create a code of municipal law for the regulation of private rights; but to provide modes of redress against the operation of state laws, and the action of state officers, executive or judicial, when these are subversive of the fundamental rights specified in the amendment. Positive rights and privileges are undoubtedly secured by the Fourteenth Amendment; but they are secured by way of prohibition against state laws and state proceedings affecting those rights and privileges, and by power given to Congress to legislate for the purpose of carrying such prohibition into effect; and such legislation must necessarily be predicated upon such supposed state laws or state proceedings, and be directed to the correction of their operation and effect."

Much nearer, and, indeed, almost directly in point, is the case of the Louisville, New Orleans &c. Railway v. Mississippi, 133 U.S. 587, wherein the railway company was indicted for a violation of a statute of Mississippi, enacting that all railroads carrying passengers should provide equal, but separate, accommodations for the white and colored races, by providing two or more passenger cars for each passenger train, or by dividing the passenger cars by a partition, so as. to secure separate accommodations. The case was presented in a different aspect from the one under consideration, inasmuch as it was an indictment against the railway company for failing to provide the separate accommodations, but the question considered was the constitutionality of the law. In that case, the Supreme Court of Mississippi, 66 Mississippi, 662, had held that the statute applied solely to commerce within the State, and, that being the construction of the state statute by its highest court, was accepted as conclusive. "If it be a matter," said the court, p. 591, "respecting commerce wholly within a State, and not interfering with commerce. between the States, then, obviously, there is no violation of the commerce clause of the Federal Constitution. ... No question arises under this section, as to the power of the State to separate in different compartments interstate passengers, or affect, in any manner, the privileges and rights of such passengers. All that we can consider is, whether the State has the power to require that railroad trains within her limits shall have separate accommodations for the two races; that affecting only commerce within the State is no invasion of the power given to Congress by the commerce clause."

A like course of reasoning applies to the case under consideration, since the Supreme Court of Louisiana in the case of the State ex rel. Abbott v. Hicks, Judge, et al., 44 La. Ann. 770, held that the statute in question did not apply to interstate passengers, but was confined in its application to passengers travelling exclusively within the borders of the State. The case was decided largely upon the authority of Railway Co. v. State, 66 Mississippi, 662, and affirmed by this court in 133 U.S. 587. In the present case no question of interference with interstate commerce can possibly arise, since the East Louisiana Railway appears to have been purely a local line, with both its termini within the State of Louisiana. Similar statutes for the separation of the two races upon public conveyances were held to be constitutional in West Chester &c. Railroad v. Miles, 55 Penn. St. 209; Day v. Owen, 5 Michigan, 520; Chicago &c. Railway v. Williams, 55 Illinois, 185; Chesapeake &c. Railroad v. Wells, 85 Tennessee, 613; Memphis &c. Railroad v. Benson, 85 Tennessee, 627; The Sue, 22 Fed. Rep. 843; Logwood v. Memphis &c. Railroad, 23 Fed. Rep. 318; McGuinn v. Forbes, 37 Fed. Rep. 639; People v. King, 18 N.E. Rep. 245; Houck v. South Pac. Railway, 38 Fed. Rep. 226; Heard v. Georgia Railroad Co., 3 Int. Com. Com'n, 111; S.C., 1 Ibid. 428.

While we think the enforced separation of the races, as applied to the internal commerce of the State, neither abridges the privileges or immunities of the colored man, deprives him of his property without due process of law, nor denies him the equal protection of the laws, within the meaning of the Fourteenth Amendment, we are not prepared to say that the conductor, in assigning passengers to the coaches according to their race, does not act at his peril, or that the provision of the second section of the act, that denies to the passenger compensation in damages for a refusal to receive him into the coach in which he properly belongs, is a valid exercise of the legislative power. Indeed, we understand it to be conceded by the State's attorney, that such part of the act as exempts from liability the railway company and its officers is unconstitutional. The power to assign to a particular coach obviously implies the power to determine to which race the passenger belongs, as well as the power to determine who, under the laws of the particular State, is to be deemed a white, and who a colored person. This question, though indicated in the brief of the plaintiff in error, does not properly arise upon the record in this case, since the only issue made is as to the unconstitutionality of the act, so far as it requires the railway to provide separate accommodations, and the conductor to assign passengers according to their race.

It is claimed by the plaintiff in error that, in any mixed community, the reputation of belonging to the dominant race, in this instance the white race, is property, in the same sense that a right of action, or of inheritance, is property. Conceding this to be so, for the purposes of this case, we are unable to see how this statute deprives him of, or in any way affects his right to, such property. If he be a white man and assigned to a colored coach, he may have his action for damages against the company for being deprived of his so called property. Upon the other hand, if he be a colored man and be so assigned, he has been deprived of no property, since he is not lawfully entitled to the reputation of being a white man.

In this connection, it is also suggested by the learned counsel for the plaintiff in error that the same argument that will justify the state legislature in requiring railways to provide separate accommodations for the two races will also authorize them to require separate cars to be provided for people whose hair is of a certain color, or who are aliens, or who belong to certain nationalities, or to enact laws requiring colored people to walk upon one side of the street, and white people upon the other, or requiring white men's houses to be painted white, and colored men's black, or their vehicles or business signs to be of different colors, upon the theory that one side of the street is as good as the other, or that a house or vehicle of one color is as good as one of another color. The reply to all this is that every exercise of the police power must be reasonable, and extend only to such laws as are enacted in good faith for the promotion for the public good, and not for the annoyance or oppression of a particular class. Thus in Yick Wo v. Hopkins, 118 U.S. 356, it was held by this court that a municipal ordinance of the city of San Francisco, to regulate the carrying on the public laundries within the limits of the municipality, violated the provisions of the Constitution of the United States, if it conferred upon the municipal authorities arbitrary power, at their own will, and without regard to discretion, in the legal sense, of the term, to give or withhold consent as to persons or places, without regard to the competency of the persons applying, or the propriety of the places selected for the carrying on the business. It was held to be a covert attempt on the part of the municipality to make an arbitrary and unjust discrimination against the Chinese race. While this was the case of a municipal ordinance, a like principle has been held to apply to acts of a state legislature passed in the exercise of the police power.

So far, then, as a conflict with the Fourteenth Amendment is concerned, the case reduces itself to the question whether the statute of Louisiana is a reasonable regulation, and with respect to this there must necessarily be a large discretion on the part of the legislature. In determining the question of reasonableness it is at liberty to act with reference to the established usages, customs and traditions of the people, and with a view to the promotion

of their comfort, and the preservation of the public peace and good order. Gauged by this standard, we cannot say that a law which authorizes or even requires the separation of the two races in public conveyances is unreasonable, or more obnoxious to the Fourteenth Amendment than the acts of Congress requiring separate schools for colored children in the District of Columbia, the constitutionality of which does not seem to have been questioned, or the corresponding acts of state legislatures.

We consider the underlying fallacy of the plaintiff's argument to consist in the assumption that the enforced separation of the two races stamps the colored race with a badge of inferiority. If this be so, it is not by reason of anything found in the act, but solely because the colored race chooses to put that construction upon it. The argument necessarily assumes that if, as has been more than once the case, and is not unlikely to be so again, the colored race should become the dominant power in the state legislature, and should enact a law in precisely similar terms, it would thereby relegate the white race to an inferior position. We imagine that the white race, at least, would not acquiesce in this assumption. The argument also assumes that social prejudices may be overcome by legislation, and that equal rights cannot be secured to the negro except by an enforced commingling of the two races. We cannot accept this proposition. If the two races are to meet upon terms of social equality, it must be the result of natural affinities, a mutual appreciation of each other's merits and a voluntary consent of individuals. As was said by the Court of Appeals of New York in People v. Gallagher, 93 N.Y. 438, 448, "this end can neither be accomplished nor promoted by laws which conflict with the general sentiment of the community upon whom they are designed to operate. When the government, therefore, has secured to each of its citizens equal rights before the law and equal opportunities for improvement and progress, it has accomplished the end for which it was organized and performed all of the functions respecting social advantages with which it is endowed." Legislation is powerless to eradicate racial instincts or to abolish distinctions based upon physical differences, and the attempt to do so can only result in accentuating the difficulties of the present situation. If the civil and political rights of both races be equal one cannot be inferior to the other civilly or politically. If one race be inferior to the other socially, the Constitution of the United States cannot put them upon the same plane.

It is true that the question of the proportion of colored blood necessary to constitute a colored person, as distinguished from a white person, is one upon which there is a difference of opinion in the different States, some holding that any visible admixture of black blood stamps the person as belonging to the colored race, (State v. Chavers, 5 Jones, [N.C.] 1, p. 11); others that it depends upon the preponderance of blood, (Gray v. State, 4 Ohio, 353; Monroe v. Collins, 17 Ohio St. 665); and still others that the predominance of white blood must only be in the proportion of three fourths. (People v. Dean, 14 Michigan, 406; Jones v. Commonwealth, 80 Virginia, 538.) But these are question to be determined under the laws of each State and are not properly put in issue in this case. Under the allegations of his petition it may undoubtedly become a question of importance whether, under the laws of Louisiana, the petitioner belongs to the white or colored race.

The judgment of the court below is, therefore,
Affirmed.

MR. JUSTICE HARLAN dissenting.

By the Louisiana statute, the validity of which is here involved, all railway companies (other than street railroad companies) carrying passengers in that State are required to have separate but equal accommodations for white and colored persons, "by providing two or more passenger coaches for each passenger train, or by dividing the passenger coaches by a partition so as to secure separate accommodations." Under this statute, no colored person is permitted to occupy a seat in a coach assigned to white persons; nor any white person, to occupy a seat in a coach assigned to colored persons. The managers of the railroad are not allowed to exercise any discretion in the premises, but are required to assign each passenger to some coach or compartment set apart for the exclusive use of his race. If a passenger insists upon going into a coach or compartment not set apart for persons of his race, he is subject to be fined, or to be imprisoned in the parish jail. Penalties are prescribed for the refusal or neglect of the officers, directors, conductors and employees of railroad companies to comply with the provisions of the act.

Only "nurses attending children of the other race" are excepted from the operation of the statute. No exception is made of colored attendants travelling with adults. A white man is not permitted to have his colored servant with him in the same coach, even if his condition of health requires the constant, personal assistance of such servant. If a colored maid insists upon riding in the same coach with a white woman whom she has been employed to serve, and who may need her personal

attention while travelling, she is subject to be fined or imprisoned for such an exhibition of zeal in the discharge of duty.

While there may be in Louisiana persons of different races who are not citizens of the United States, the words in the act, "white and colored races," necessarily include all citizens of the United States of both races residing in that State. So that we have before us a state enactment that compels, under penalties, the separation of the two races in railroad passenger coaches, and makes it a crime for a citizen of either race to enter a coach that has been assigned to citizens of the other race.

Thus the State regulates the use of a public highway by citizens of the United States solely upon the basis of race.

However apparent the injustice of such legislation may be, we have only to consider whether it is consistent with the Constitution of the United States.

That a railroad is a public highway, and that the corporation which owns or operates it is in the exercise of public functions, is not, at this day, to be disputed. Mr. Justice Nelson, speaking for this court in New Jersey Steam Navigation Co. v. Merchants' Bank, 6 How. 344, 382, said that a common carrier was in the exercise "of a sort of public office, and has public duties to perform, from which he should not be permitted to exonerate himself without the assent of the parties concerned." Mr. Justice Strong, delivering the judgment of this court in Olcott v. The Supervisors, 16 Wall. 678, 694, said: "That railroads, though constructed by private corporations and owned by them, are public highways, has been the doctrine of nearly all the courts ever since such conveniences for passage and transportation have had any existence. Very early the question arose whether a State's right of eminent domain could be exercised by a private corporation created for the purpose of constructing a railroad. Clearly it could not, unless taking land for such a purpose by such an agency is taking land for public use. The right of eminent domain nowhere justifies taking property for a private use. Yet it is a doctrine universally accepted that a state legislature may authorize a private corporation to take land for the construction of such a road, making compensation to the owner. What else does this doctrine mean if not that building a railroad, though it be built by a private corporation, is an act done for a public use?" So, in Township of Pine Grove v. Talcott, 19 Wall. 666, 676; "Though the corporation [a railroad company] was private, its work was public, as much so as if it were to be constructed by the State." So, in Inhabitants of Worcester v. Western Railroad Corporation, 4 Met. 564: "The establishment of that great thoroughfare is regarded as a public work, established by public authority, intended for the public use and benefit, the use of which is secured to the whole community, and constitutes, therefore, like a canal, turnpike or highway, a public easement." It is true that the real and personal property, necessary to the establishment and management of the railroad, is vested in the corporation; but it is in trust for the public."

In respect of civil rights, common to all citizens, the Constitution of the United States does not, I think, permit any public authority to know the race of those entitled to be protected in the enjoyment of such rights. Every true man has pride of race, and under appropriate circumstances when the rights of others, his equals before the law, are not to be affected, it is his privilege to express such pride and to take such action based upon it as to him seems proper. But I deny that any legislative body or judicial tribunal may have regard to the race of citizens when the civil rights of those citizens are involved. Indeed, such legislation, as that here in question, is inconsistent not only with that equality of rights which pertains to citizenship, National and State, but with the personal liberty enjoyed by every one within the United States.

The Thirteenth Amendment does not permit the withholding or the deprivation of any right necessarily inhering in freedom. It not only struck down the institution of slavery as previously existing in the United States, but it prevents the imposition of any burdens or disabilities that constitute badges of slavery or servitude. It decreed universal civil freedom in this country. This court has so adjudged. But that amendment having been found inadequate to the protection of the rights of those who had been in slavery, it was followed by the Fourteenth Amendment, which added greatly to the dignity and glory of American citizenship, and to the security of personal liberty, by declaring that "all persons born or naturalized in the United States, and subject to the jurisdiction thereof, are citizens of the United States and of the State wherein they reside," and that "no State shall make or enforce any law which shall abridge the privileges or immunities of citizens of the United States; nor shall any State deprive any person of life, liberty or property without due process of law, nor deny to any person within its jurisdiction the equal protection of the laws." These two amendments, if enforced according to their true intent and meaning, will protect all the civil rights that pertain to freedom and citizenship. Finally, and to the end that no citizen should be denied, on account of his race, the privilege of participating in the political control of his country, it was declared by the Fifteenth Amendment that "the right of citizens of the United States to vote shall not be denied or abridged by the United States or by any State on account of race, color or previous condition of servitude."

These notable additions to the fundamental law were welcomed by the friends of liberty throughout the world. They removed the race line from our governmental systems. They had, as this court has said, a common purpose, namely, to secure "to a race recently emancipated, a race that through many generations have been held in slavery, all the civil rights that the superior race enjoy." They declared, in legal effect, this court has further said, "that the law in the States shall be the same for the black as for the white; that all persons, whether colored or white, shall stand equal before the laws of the States, and, in regard to the colored race, for whose protection the amendment was primarily designed, that no discrimination shall be made against them by law because of their color." We also said: "The words of the amendment, it is true, are prohibitory, but they contain a necessary implication of a positive immunity, or right, most valuable to the colored race— the right to exemption from unfriendly legislation against them distinctively as colored—exemption from legal discriminations, implying inferiority in civil society, lessening the security of their enjoyment of the rights which others enjoy, and discriminations which are steps towards reducing them to the condition of a subject race." It was, consequently, adjudged that a state law that excluded citizens of the colored race from juries, because of their race and however well qualified in other respects to discharge the duties of jurymen, was repugnant to the Fourteenth Amendment. ***At the present term, referring to the previous adjudications, this court declared that "underlying all of those decisions is the principle that the Constitution of the United States, in its present form, forbids, so far as civil and political rights are concerned, discrimination by the General Government or the States against any citizen because of his race. All citizens are equal before the law." Gibson v. Mississippi, 162 U.S. 565.

The decisions referred to show the scope of the recent amendments of the Constitution. They also show that it is not within the power of a State to prohibit colored citizens, because of their race, from participating as jurors in the administration of justice.

It was said in argument that the statute of Louisiana does not discriminate against either race, but prescribes a rule applicable alike to white and colored citizens. But this argument does not meet the difficulty. Every one knows that the statute in question had its origin in the purpose, not so much to exclude white persons from railroad cars occupied by blacks, as to exclude colored people from coaches occupied by or assigned to white persons. Railroad corporations of Louisiana did not make discrimination among whites in the matter of accommodation for travellers. The thing to accomplish was, under the guise of giving equal accommodation for whites and blacks, to compel the latter to keep to themselves while travelling in railroad passenger coaches. No one would be so wanting in candor as to assert the contrary. The fundamental objection, therefore, to the statute is that it interferes with the personal freedom of citizens. "Personal liberty," it has been well said, "consists in the power of locomotion, of changing situation, or removing one's person to whatsoever places one's own inclination may direct, without imprisonment or restraint, unless by due course of law." 1 Bl. Com. *134. If a white man and a black man choose to occupy the same public conveyance on a public highway, it is their right to do so, and no government, proceeding alone on grounds of race, can prevent it without infringing the personal liberty of each.

It is one thing for railroad carriers to furnish, or to be required by law to furnish, equal accommodations for all whom they are under a legal duty to carry. It is quite another thing for government to forbid citizens of the white and black races from travelling in the same public conveyance, and to punish officers of railroad companies for permitting persons of the two races to occupy the same passenger coach. If a State can prescribe, as a rule of civil conduct, that whites and blacks shall not travel as passengers in the same railroad coach, why may it not so regulate the use of the streets of its cities and towns as to compel white citizens to keep on one side of a street and black citizens to keep on the other? Why may it not, upon like grounds, punish whites and blacks who ride together in street cars or in open vehicles on a public road of street? Why may it not require sheriffs to assign whites to one side of a court-room and blacks to the other? And why may it not also prohibit the commingling of the two races in the galleries of legislative halls or in public assemblages convened for the considerations of the political questions of the day? Further, if this statute of Louisiana is consistent with the personal liberty of citizens, why may not the State require the separation in railroad coaches of native and naturalized citizens of the United States, or of Protestants and Roman Catholics?

The answer given at the argument to these questions was that regulations of the kind they suggest would be unreasonable, and could not, therefore, stand before the law. Is it meant that the determination of questions of legislative power depends upon the inquiry whether the statute whose validity is questioned is, in the judgment of the courts, a reasonable one, taking all the circumstances into consideration? A statute may be unreasonable merely because a sound public policy forbade its enactment. But I do not understand that the courts have anything to do with the policy or expediency of legislation. A statute may be valid, and yet, upon grounds of public policy, may well be characterized as unreasonable. Mr. Sedgwick correctly states the rule when he says that the legislative intention being clearly ascertained, "the courts have no other duty to perform than to execute the legislative will, without any regard to their views as to the wisdom or justice of the particular enactment." Stat. & Const. Constr. 324. There is a dangerous tendency in these latter days to enlarge the functions of the courts, by means of judicial interference with the will of the people as expressed by the legislature. Our institutions have the distinguishing characteristic that the three departments of government are coordinate and separate. Each must keep within the limits defined by the Constitution. And the courts best discharge their duty by executing the will of the law-making power, constitutionally expressed, leaving the results of legislation to be dealt with by the people through their representatives. Statutes must always have a reasonable construction. Sometimes they are to be construed strictly; sometimes, liberally, in order to carry out the legislative will. But however construed, the intent of the legislature is to be respected, if the particular statute in question is valid, although the courts, looking at the public interests, may conceive the statute to be both unreasonable and impolitic. If the power exists to enact a statute, that ends the matter so far as the courts are concerned. The adjudged cases in which statutes have been held to be void, because unreasonable, are those in which the means employed by the legislature were not at all germane to the end to which the legislature was competent.

The white race deems itself to be the dominant race in this country. And so it is, in prestige, in achievements, in education, in wealth and in power. So, I doubt not, it will continue to be for all time, if it remains true to its great heritage and holds fast to the principles of constitutional liberty. But in view of the Constitution, in the eye of the law, there is in this country no superior, dominant, ruling class of citizens. There is no caste here. Our Constitution is color-blind, and neither knows nor tolerates classes among citizens. In respect of civil rights, all citizens are equal before the law. The humblest is the peer of the most powerful. The law regards man as man, and takes no account of his surroundings or of his color when his civil rights as guaranteed by the supreme law of the land are involved. It is, therefore, to be regretted that this high tribunal, the final expositor of the fundamental law of the land, has reached the conclusion that it is competent for a State to regulate the enjoyment by citizens of their civil rights solely upon the basis of race.

In my opinion, the judgment this day rendered will, in time, prove to be quite as pernicious as the decision made by this tribunal in the Dred Scott case. It was adjudged in that case that the descendants of Africans who were imported into this country and sold as slaves were not included nor intended to be included under the word "citizens" in the Constitution, and could not claim any of the rights and privileges which that instrument provided for and secured to citizens of the United States; that at the time of the adoption of the Constitution they were "considered as a subordinate and inferior class of beings, who had been subjugated by the dominant race, and, whether emancipated or not, yet remained subject to their authority, and had no rights or privileges but such as those who held the power and the government might choose to grant them." 19 How. 393, 404. The recent amendments of the Constitution, it was supposed, had eradicated these principles from our institutions. But it seems that we have yet, in some of the States, a dominant race—a superior class of citizens, which assumes to regulate the enjoyment of civil rights, common to all citizens, upon the basis of race. The present decision, it may well be apprehended, will not only stimulate aggressions, more or less brutal and irritating, upon the admitted rights of colored citizens, but will encourage the belief that it is possible, by means of state enactments, to defeat the beneficent purposes which the people of the United States had in view when they adopted the recent amendments of the Constitution, by one of which the blacks of this country were made citizens of the United States and of the States in which they respectively reside, and whose privileges and immunities, as citizens, the States are forbidden to abridge. Sixty millions of whites are in no danger from the presence here of eight millions of blacks. The destinies of the two races, in this country, are indissolubly linked together, and the interests of both require that the common government of all shall not permit the seeds of race hate to be planted under the sanction of law. What can more certainly arouse race hate, what more certainly create and perpetuate a feeling of distrust between these races, than state enactments, which, in fact, proceed on the ground that colored citizens are so inferior and degraded that they cannot be allowed to sit in public coaches occupied by white citizens? That, as all will admit, is the real meaning of such legislation as was enacted in Louisiana.

The sure guarantee of the peace and security of each race is the clear, distinct, unconditional recognition by our governments, National and State, of every right that inheres in civil freedom, and of the equality before the law of all citizens of the United States without regard to race. State enactments, regulating the enjoyment of civil rights, upon the basis of race, and cunningly devised to defeat legitimate results of the war, under the pretence of recognizing equality of rights, can have no other result than to render permanent peace impossible, and to keep alive a conflict of races, the continuance of which must do harm to all concerned. This question is not met by the suggestion that social equality cannot exist between the white and black races in this country. That argument, if it can be properly regarded as one, is scarcely worthy of consideration; for social equality no more exists between two races when travelling in a passenger coach or a public highway than when members of the same races sit by each other in a street car or in the jury box, or stand or sit with each other in a political assembly, or when they use in common the streets of a city or town, or when they are in the same room for the purpose of having their names placed on the registry of voters, or when they approach the ballot-box in order to exercise the high privilege of voting.

There is a race so different from our own that we do not permit those belonging to it to become citizens of the United States. Persons belonging to it are, with few exceptions, absolutely excluded from our country. I allude to the Chinese race. But by the statute in question, a Chinaman can ride in the same passenger coach with white citizens of the United States, while citizens of the black race in Louisiana, many of whom, perhaps, risked their lives for the preservation of the Union, who are entitled, by law, to participate in the political control of the State and nation, who are not excluded, by law or by reason of their race, from public stations of any kind, and who have all the legal rights that belong to white citizens, are yet declared to be criminals, liable to imprisonment, if they ride in a public coach occupied by citizens of the white race. It is scarcely just to say that a colored citizen should not object to occupying a public coach assigned to his own race. He does not object, nor, perhaps, would he object to separate coaches for his race, if his rights under the law were recognized. But he objects, and ought never to cease objecting to the proposition, that citizens of the white and black races can be adjudged criminals because they sit, or claim the right to sit, in the same public coach on a public highway.

The arbitrary separation of citizens, on the basis of race, while they are on a public highway, is a badge of servitude wholly inconsistent with the civil freedom and the equality before the law established by the Constitution. It cannot be justified upon any legal grounds.

If evils will result from the commingling of the two races upon public highways established for the benefit of all, they will be infinitely less than those that will surely come from state legislation regulating the enjoyment of civil rights upon the basis of race. We boast of the freedom enjoyed by our people above all other peoples. But it is difficult to reconcile that boast with a state of the law which, practically, puts the brand of servitude and degradation upon a large class of our fellow-citizens, our equals before the law. The thin disguise of "equal" accommodations for passengers in railroad coaches will not mislead any one, nor atone for the wrong this day done.

The result of the whole matter is, that while this court has frequently adjudged, and at the present term has recognized the doctrine, that a State cannot, consistently with the Constitution of the United States, prevent white and black citizens, having the required qualifications for jury service, from sitting in the same jury box, it is now solemnly held that a State may prohibit white and black citizens from sitting in the same passenger coach on a public highway, or may require that they be separated by a "partition," when in the same passenger coach. May it not now be reasonably expected that astute men of the dominant race, who affect to be disturbed at the possibility that the integrity of the white race may be corrupted, or that its supremacy will be imperilled, by contact on public highways with black people, will endeavor to procure statutes requiring white and black jurors to be separated in the jury box by a "partition," and that, upon retiring from the court room to consult as to their verdict, such partition, if it be a moveable one, shall be taken to their consultation room, and set up in such way as to prevent black jurors from coming too close to their brother jurors of the white race. If the "partition" used in the court room happens to be stationary, provision could be made for screens with openings through which jurors of the two races could confer as to their verdict without coming into personal contact with each other. I cannot see but that, according to the principles this day announced, such state legislation, although conceived in hostility to, and

enacted for the purpose of humiliating citizens of the United States of a particular race, would be held to be consistent with the Constitution.

I do not deem it necessary to review the decisions of state courts to which reference was made in argument. Some, and the most important, of them are wholly inapplicable, because rendered prior to the adoption of the last amendments of the Constitution, when colored people had very few rights which the dominant race felt obliged to respect. Others were made at a time when public opinion, in many localities, was dominated by the institution of slavery; when it would not have been safe to do justice to the black man; and when, so far as the rights of blacks were concerned, race prejudice was, practically, the supreme law of the land. Those decisions cannot be guides in the era introduced by the recent amendments of the supreme law, which established universal civil freedom, gave citizenship to all born or naturalized in the United States and residing her, obliterated the race line from our systems of governments, National and State, and placed our free institutions upon the broad and sure foundation of the equality of all men before the law.

I am of opinion that the statute of Louisiana is inconsistent with the personal liberty of citizens, white and black, in that State, and hostile to both the spirit and letter of the Constitution of the United States. If laws of like character should be enacted in the several States of the Union, the effect would be in the highest degree mischievous. Slavery, as an institution tolerated by law would, it is true, have disappeared from our country, but there would remain a power in the States, by sinister legislation, to interfere with the full enjoyment of the blessings of freedom; to regulate civil rights, common to all citizens, upon the basis of race; and to place in a condition of legal inferiority a large body of American citizens, now constituting a part of the political community called the People of the United States, for whom, and by whom through representatives, our government is administered. Such a system is inconsistent with the guarantee given by the Constitution to each State of a republican form of government, and may be stricken down by Congressional action, or by the courts in the discharge of their solemn duty to maintain the supreme law of the land, anything in the constitution or laws of any State to the contrary notwithstanding.

For the reasons stated, I am constrained to withhold my assent from the opinion and judgment of the majority.

MR. JUSTICE BREWER did not hear the argument or participate in the decision of this case.

BOOKER T. WASHINGTON
Delivers the 1895
Atlanta Compromise Speech

On September 18, 1895, African-American spokesman and leader Booker T. Washington spoke before a predominantly white audience at the Cotton States and International Exposition in Atlanta. His Atlanta Compromise address, as it came to be called, was one of the most important and influential speeches in American history. Although the organizers of the exposition worried that public sentiment was not prepared for such an advanced step, they decided that inviting a black speaker would impress Northern visitors with the evidence of racial progress in the South. Washington soothed his listeners concerns about uppity blacks by claiming that his race would content itself with living by the productions of our hands.

Mr. President and Gentlemen of the Board of Directors and Citizens:

One-third of the population of the South is of the Negro race. No enterprise seeking the material, civil, or moral welfare of this section can disregard this element of our population and reach the highest success. I but convey to you, Mr. President and Directors, the sentiment of the masses of my race when I say that in no way have the value and manhood of the American Negro been more fittingly and generously recognized than by the managers of this magnificent Exposition at every stage of its progress. It is a recognition that will do more to cement the friendship of the two races than any occurrence since the dawn of our freedom.

Not only this, but the opportunity here afforded will awaken among us a new era of industrial progress. Ignorant and inexperienced, it is not strange that in the first years of our new life we began at the top instead of at the bottom; that a seat in Congress or the state legislature was more sought than real estate or industrial skill; that the political convention or stump speaking had more attractions than starting a dairy farm or truck garden.

A ship lost at sea for many days suddenly sighted a friendly vessel. From the mast of the unfortunate vessel was seen a signal, Water, water; we die of thirst! The answer from the friendly vessel at once came back, Cast down your bucket where you are. A second time the signal, Water, water; send us water! ran up from the distressed vessel, and was answered, Cast down your bucket where you are. And a third and fourth signal for water was answered, Cast down your bucket where you are. The captain of the distressed vessel, at last heeding the injunction, cast down his bucket, and it came up full of fresh, sparkling water from the mouth of the Amazon River. To those of my race who depend on bettering their condition in a foreign land or who underestimate the importance of cultivating friendly relations with the Southern white man, who is their next-door neighbor, I would say: Cast down your bucket where you are cast it down in making friends in every manly way of the people of all races by whom we are surrounded.

Cast it down in agriculture, mechanics, in commerce, in domestic service, and in the professions. And in this connection it is well to bear in mind that whatever other sins the South may be called to bear, when it comes to business, pure and simple, it is in the South that the Negro is given a man's chance in the commercial world, and in nothing is this Exposition more eloquent than in emphasizing this chance. Our greatest danger is that in the great leap from slavery to freedom we may overlook the fact that the masses of us are to live by the productions of our hands, and fail to keep in mind that we shall prosper in proportion as we learn to dignify and glorify common labour, and put brains and skill into the common occupations of life; shall prosper in proportion as we learn to draw the line between the superficial and the substantial, the ornamental gewgaws of life and the useful. No race can prosper till it learns that there is as much dignity in tilling a field as in writing a poem. It is at the bottom of life we must begin, and not at the top. Nor should we permit our grievances to overshadow our opportunities.

To those of the white race who look to the incoming of those of foreign birth and strange tongue and habits for the prosperity of the South, were I permitted I would repeat what I say to my own race, Cast down your bucket where you are. Cast it down among the eight millions of Negroes whose habits you know, whose fidelity and love you have tested in days when to have proved treacherous meant the ruin of your firesides. Cast down your bucket among these people who have, without strikes and labour wars, tilled your fields, cleared your forests, builded your railroads and cities, and brought forth treasures from the bowels of the earth, and helped make possible this magnificent representation of the progress of the South. Casting down your bucket among my people, helping and encouraging them as you are doing on these grounds, and to education of head, hand, and heart, you will find that they will buy your surplus land, make blossom the waste places in your fields, and run your factories. While doing this, you can be sure in the future, as in the past, that you and your families will be surrounded by the most patient, faithful, law-abiding, and unresentful people that the world has seen. As we have proved our loyalty to you in the past, in nursing your children, watching by the sick-bed of your mothers and fathers, and often following them with tear-dimmed eyes to their graves, so in the future, in our humble way, we shall stand by you with a devotion that no foreigner can approach, ready to lay down our lives, if need be, in defense of yours, interlacing our industrial, commercial, civil, and religious life with yours in a way that shall make the interests of both races one. In all things that are purely social we can be as separate as the fingers, yet one as the hand in all things essential to mutual progress.

There is no defense or security for any of us except in the highest intelligence and development of all. If anywhere there are efforts tending to curtail the fullest growth of the Negro, let these efforts be turned into stimulating, encouraging, and making him the most useful and intelligent citizen. Effort or means so invested will pay a thousand per cent interest. These efforts will be twice blessed blessing him that gives and him that takes. There is no escape through law of man or God from the inevitable:

The laws of changeless justice bind Oppressor with oppressed;

And close as sin and suffering joined We march to fate abreast. ...

Nearly sixteen millions of hands will aid you in pulling the load upward, or they will pull against you the load downward. We shall constitute one-third and more of the ignorance and crime of the South, or one-third [of] its intelligence and progress; we shall contribute one-third to the business and industrial prosperity of the South, or we shall prove a veritable body of death, stagnating, depressing, retarding every effort to advance the body politic.

Gentlemen of the Exposition, as we present to you our humble effort at an exhibition of our progress, you must not expect overmuch. Starting thirty years ago with ownership here and there in a few quilts and pumpkins and chickens (gathered from miscellaneous sources), remember the path that has led from these to the inventions and production of agricultural implements, buggies, steam-engines, newspapers, books, statuary, carving, paintings, the management of drug stores and banks, has not been trodden without contact with thorns and thistles. While we take pride in what we exhibit as a result of our independent efforts, we do not for a moment forget that our part in this exhibition would fall far short of your expectations but for the constant help that has come to our educational life, not only from the Southern states, but especially from Northern philanthropists, who have made their gifts a constant stream of blessing and encouragement.

The wisest among my race understand that the agitation of questions of social equality is the extremest folly, and that progress in the enjoyment of all the privileges that will come to us must be the result of severe and constant struggle rather than of artificial forcing. No race that has anything to contribute to the markets of the world is long in any degree ostracized. It is important and right that all privileges of the law be ours, but it is vastly more important that we be prepared for the exercise of these privileges. The opportunity to earn a dollar in a factory just now is worth infinitely more than the opportunity to spend a dollar in an opera-house.

In conclusion, may I repeat that nothing in thirty years has given us more hope and encouragement, and drawn us so near to you of the white race, as this opportunity offered by the Exposition; and here bending, as it were, over the altar that represents the results of the struggles of your race and mine, both starting practically empty-handed three decades ago, I pledge that in your effort to work out the great and intricate problem which God has laid at the doors of the South, you shall have at all times the patient, sympathetic help of my race; only let this he constantly in mind, that, while from representations in these buildings of the product of field, of forest, of mine, of factory, letters, and art, much good will come, yet far above and beyond material benefits will be that higher good, that, let us pray God, will come, in a blotting out of sectional differences and racial animosities and suspicions, in a determination to administer absolute justice, in a willing obedience among all classes to the mandates of law. This, coupled with our material prosperity, will bring into our beloved South a new heaven and a new earth.

Source: Louis R. Harlan, ed., *The Booker T. Washington Papers,* Vol. 3, (Urbana: University of Illinois Press, 1974), 583–587.

BOOKER T. WASHINGTON AND OTHERS
(The Souls of Black Folks)
DU BOIS, W.E.B.
1903

Mr. Washington represents in Negro thought the old attitude of adjustment and submission; but adjustment at such a peculiar time as to make his programme unique. This is an age of unusual economic development, and Mr. Washington's programme naturally takes an economic cast, becoming a gospel of Work and Money to such an extent as apparently almost completely to overshadow the higher aims of life. Moreover, this is an age when the more advanced races are coming in closer contact with the less developed races, and the race-feeling is therefore intensified; and Mr. Washington's programme practically accepts the alleged inferiority of the Negro race. Again, in our own land, the reaction from the sentiment of war time has given impetus to race-prejudice against Negroes, and Mr. Washington withdraws many of the high demands of Negroes as men and American citizens. In other periods of intensified prejudice all the Negro's tendency to self-assertion has been called forth; at this period a policy of submission is advocated. In the history of nearly all other races and peoples the doctrine preached at such crises has been that manly self-respect is worth more than lands and houses, and that a people who voluntarily surrender such respect, or cease striving for it, are not worth civilizing.

In answer to this, it has been claimed that the Negro can survive Only through submission. Mr. Washington distinctly asks that black people give up, at least for the present, three things,—

- First, political power,
- Second, insistence on civil rights,
- Third, higher education of Negro youth,

and concentrate all their energies on industrial education, the accumulation of wealth, and the conciliation of the South. This policy has been courageously and insistently advocated for over fifteen years, and has been triumphant for perhaps ten years. As a result of this tender of the palm-branch, what has been the return? In these years there have occurred:

1. The disfranchisement of the Negro.
2. The legal creation of a distant status of civil inferiority for the Negro.
3. The steady withdrawal of aid from institutions for the higher training of the Negro.

These movements are not, to be sure, direct results of Mr. Washington's teachings; but his propaganda has, without a shadow of doubt, helped their speedier accomplishment. The question then comes: Is it possible, and probable, that nine millions of men can make effective progress in economic lines if they are deprived of political rights, made a servile caste, and allowed only the most meagre chance for developing their exceptional men? If history and reason give any distinct answer to these questions, it is an emphatic No. ...

It would be unjust to Mr. Washington not to acknowledge that in several instances he has opposed movements in the South which were unjust to the Negro; he sent memorials to the Louisiana and Alabama constitutional conventions, he has spoken against lynching, and in other ways has openly or silently set his influence against sinister schemes and unfortunate happenings. Notwithstanding this, it is equally true to assert that on the whole the distinct impression left by Mr. Washington's propaganda is, first, that the South is justified in its present attitude toward the Negro because of the Negro's degradation; secondly, that the prime cause of the Negro's failure to rise more quickly is his wrong education in the past; and, thirdly, that his future rise depends primarily on his own efforts. Each of these propositions is a dangerous halftruth. The supplementary truths must never be lost sight of: first, slavery and race-prejudice are potent if not sufficient causes of the Negro's position; sec-ond, industrial and common-school training were necessarily slow in planning because they had to await the black teachers trained by higher institutions,—it being extremely doubtful if any essentially different development was possible, and certainly a Tuskegee was unthinkable before 1880; and, third, while it is a great truth to say that the Negro must strive and strive mightily to help him-self, it is equally true that unless his striving be not simply seconded, but rather aroused and encouraged, by the initiative of the richer and wiser envi-roning group, he cannot hope for great success.

In his failure to realize and impress this last point, Mr. Washington is especially to be criticised. His doctrine has tended to make the whites, North and South, shift the burden of the Negro problem to the Negro's shoulders and stand aside as critical and rather pessimistic spectators; when in fact the burden belongs to the nation, and the hands of none of us are clean if we bend not our energies to righting these great wrongs.

The South ought to be led, by candid and honest criticism, to assert her better self and do her full duty to the race she has cruelly wronged and is still wronging. The North—her co-partner in guilt—cannot salve her conscience by plaster-ing it with gold. We cannot settle this problem by diplomacy and suaveness, by "policy" alone. If worse comes to worst, can the moral fibre of this country survive the slow throttling and murder of millions of men?

The black men of America have a duty to perform, a duty stern and delicate,—a forward movement to oppose a part of the work of their greatest leader. So far as Mr. Washington preaches Thrift, Patience, and Industrial Training for the masses, we must hold up his hands and strive with him, rejoicing in his honors and glorying in the strength of this Joshua called of God and of man to lead the headless host. But so far as Mr. Washington apologizes for injustice, North or South, does not rightly value the privilege and duty of voting, belittles the emasculating effects of caste distinctions, and opposes the higher training and ambition of our brighter minds,—so far as he, the South, or the Nation, does this,—we must unceasingly and firmly oppose them. By every civilized and peaceful method we must strive for the right which the world accords to men, clinging unwaveringly to those great words which the sons of the Fathers would fain forget: "We hold these truths to be self-evident: That all men are created equal; that they are endowed by their Creator with certain unalienable rights; that among these are life, liberty, and the pursuit of happiness."

BEREA COLLEGE v. COMMONWEALTH OF KENTUCKY.
Supreme Court of the United States
211 U.S. 45; 29 S. Ct. 33; 53 L. Ed. 81; 1908 U.S. LEXIS 1526

Argued April 10, 13, 1908. November 9, 1908, Decided

PRIOR HISTORY:

ERROR TO THE COURT OF APPEALS OF THE STATE OF KENTUCKY.

ON October 8, 1904, the grand jury of Madison County, Kentucky, presented in the Circuit Court of that county an indictment, charging:

"The said Berea College, being a corporation duly incorporated under the laws of the State of Kentucky, and owning, maintaining and operating a college, school and institution of learning, known as 'Berea College,' located in the town of Berea, Madison County, Kentucky, did unlawfully and willfully permit and receive both the white and negro races as pupils for instruction in said college, school and institution of learning."

This indictment was found under an act of March 22, 1904 (acts Kentucky, 1904, chap. 85, p. 181), whose first section reads:

"SEC. 1. That it shall be unlawful for any person, corporation or association of persons to maintain or operate any college, school or institution where persons of the white and negro races are both received as pupils for instruction, and any person or corporation who shall operate or maintain any such college, school or institution shall be fined $1,000, and any person or corporation who may be convicted of violating the provisions of this act shall be fined $100 for each day they may operate said school, college or institution after such conviction."

On a trial the defendant was found guilty and sentenced to pay a fine of one thousand dollars. This judgment was on June 12, 1906, affirmed by the Court of *Appeals of the State (123 Kentucky, 209),* and from that court brought here on writ of error.

MR. JUSTICE BREWER, after making the foregoing statement, delivered the opinion of the court.

There is no dispute as to the facts. That the act does not violate the constitution of Kentucky is settled by the decision of its highest court, and the single question for our consideration is whether it conflicts with the Federal Constitution. The Court of Appeals discussed at some length the general power of the State in respect to the separation of the two races. It also ruled that "the right to teach white and negro children in a private school at the same time and place is not a property right. Besides, appellant as a corporation created by this State has no natural right to teach at all. Its right to teach is such as the State sees fit to give to it. The State may withhold it altogether, or qualify it.

Upon this we remark that when a state court decides a case upon two grounds, one Federal and the other non-Federal, this court will not disturb the judgment if the non-Federal ground, fairly construed, sustains the decision.

Again, the decision by a state court of the extent and limitation of the powers conferred by the State upon one of its own corporations is of a purely local nature. In creating a corporation a State may withhold powers which may be exercised by and cannot be denied to an individual. It is under no obligation to treat both alike. In granting corporate powers the legislature may deem that the best interests of the State would be subserved by some restriction, and the corporation may not plead that in spite of the restriction it has more or greater powers because the citizen has. "The granting of such right or privilege [the right or privilege to be a corporation] rests entirely in the discretion of the State, and, of course, when granted, may be accompanied with such conditions as its legislature may judge most befitting to its interests and policy." The act of 1904 forbids "any person, corporation or association of persons to maintain or operate any college," etc. Such a statute may conflict with the Federal Constitution in denying to individuals powers which they may rightfully exercise, and yet, at the same time, be valid as to a corporation created by the State.

It may be said that the Court of Appeals sustained the validity of this section of the statute, both against individuals and corporations. It ruled that the legislation was within the power of the State, and that the State might rightfully thus restrain all individuals, corporations and associations. But it is unnecessary for us to consider anything more than the question of its validity as applied to corporations.

The statute is clearly separable and may be valid as to one class while invalid as to another. Even if it were conceded that its assertion of power over individuals cannot be sustained, still it must be upheld so far as it restrains corporations.

There is no force in the suggestion that the statute, although clearly separable, must stand or fall as an entirety on the ground the legislature would not have enacted one part unless it could reach all. That the legislature of Kentucky desired to separate the teaching of white and colored children may be conceded, but it by no means follows that it would not have enforced the separation so far as it could do so, even though it could not make it effective under all circumstances. In other words, it is not at all unreasonable to believe that the legislature, although advised beforehand of the constitutional question, might have prohibited all organizations and corporations under its control from teaching white and colored children together, and thus made at least uniform official action. The rule of construction in questions of this nature is stated by Chief Justice Shaw in *Warren v. Mayor of Charlestown, 2 Gray, 84*, quoted approvingly by this court in *Allen v. Louisiana, 103 U.S. 80–84*.

"But if they are so mutually connected with and dependent on each other, as conditions, considerations or compensations for each other as to warrant a belief that the legislature intended them as a whole, and that if all could not be carried into effect, the legislature would not pass the residue independently, and some parts are unconstitutional, all the provisions which are thus dependent, conditional or connected, must fall with them."

See also *Loeb v. Township Trustees, 179 U.S. 472, 490*, in which this court said:

"As one section of a statute may be repugnant to the Constitution without rendering the whole act void, so, one provision of a section may be invalid by reason of its not conforming to the Constitution, while all the other provisions may be subject to no constitutional infirmity. One part may stand, while another will fall, unless the two are so connected or dependent on each other in subject-matter, meaning or purpose, that the good cannot remain without the bad. The point is, not whether the parts are contained in the same section, for, the distribution into sections is purely artificial; but whether [*56] they are essentially and inseparably connected in substance—whether the provisions are so interdependent that one cannot operate without the other."

Further, inasmuch as the Court of Appeals considered the act separable, and while sustaining it as an entirety gave an independent reason which applies only to corporations, it is obvious that it recognized the force of the suggestions we have made. And when a state statute is so interpreted this court should hesitate before it holds that the Supreme Court of the State did not know what was the thought of the legislature in its enactment.

While the terms of the present charter are not given in the record, yet it was admitted on the trial that the defendant was a corporation organized and incorporated under the general statutes of the State of Kentucky, and of course the state courts, as well as this court on appeal, take judicial notice of those statutes. Further, in the brief of counsel for the defendant is given a history of the incorporation proceedings, together with the charters. From that it appears that Berea College was organized under the authority of an act for the incorporation of voluntary associations, approved March 9, 1854 (2 Stanton Rev. Stat. Ky. 553), which act was amended by an act of March 10, 1856 (2 Stanton, 555), and which in terms reserved to the General Assembly "the right to alter or repeal the charter of any associations formed under the provisions of this act, and the act to which this act is an amendment, at any time hereafter." After the constitution of 1891 was adopted by the State of Kentucky, and on June 10, 1899, the college was reincorporated under the provisions of chap. 32, art. 8, Ky. Stat. (Carroll's Ky. Stat. 1903, p. 459), the charter defining its business in these words: "Its object is the education of all persons who may attend its institution of learning at Berea, and, in the language of the original articles, 'to promote the cause of Christ.'" The constitution of 1891 provided in § 3 of the bill of rights that "Every grant of a franchise, privilege or exemption shall remain, subject to revocation, alteration or amendment." Carroll's Ky. Stat. 1903, p. 86. So that the full power of amendment was reserved to the legislature.

It is undoubtedly true that the reserved power to alter or amend is subject to some limitations, and that under the guise of an amendment a new contract may not always be enforcible upon the corporation or the stockholders; but it is settled "that a power reserved to the legislature to alter, amend or repeal a charter authorizes it to make any alteration or amendment of a charter granted subject to it, which will not defeat or substantially impair the object of the grant, or any rights vested under it, and which the legislature may deem necessary to secure either that object or any public right.

Construing the statute, the Court of Appeals held that "if the same school taught the different races at different times, though at the same place or at different places at the same time it would not be unlawful." Now, an amendment to the original charter, which does not destroy the power of the college to furnish education to all persons, but which simply separates them by time or place of instruction, cannot be said to "defeat or substantially impair the object of the grant." The language of the statute is not in terms an amendment, yet its effect is an amendment, and it would be resting too much on mere form to hold that a statute which in effect works a change in the terms of the charter is not to be considered as an amendment, because not so designated. The act itself, being separable, is to be read as though it in one section prohibited any person, in another section any corporation, and in a third any association of persons to do the acts named. Reading the statute as containing a separate prohibition on all corporations, at least, all state corporations, it substantially declares that any authority given by previous charters to instruct the two races at the same time and in the same place is forbidden, and that prohibition being a departure from the terms of the original charter in this case may properly be adjudged an amendment.

Again, it is insisted that the Court of Appeals did not regard the legislation as making an amendment, because another prosecution instituted against the same corporation under the fourth section of the act, which makes it a misdemeanor to teach pupils of the two races in the same institution, even although one race is taught in one branch and another in another branch, provided the two branches are within twenty-five miles of each other, was held could not be sustained, the court saying: "This last section, we think, violates the limitations upon the police power: it is unreasonable and oppressive." But while so ruling it also held that this section could be ignored and that the remainder of the act was complete notwithstanding. Whether the reasoning of the court concerning the fourth section be satisfactory of not is immaterial, for no question of its validity is presented, and the Court of Appeals, while striking it down, sustained the balance of the act. We need concern ourselves only with the inquiry whether the first section can be upheld as coming within the power of a State over its own corporate creatures.

We are of opinion, for reasons stated, that it does come within that power, and on this ground the judgment of the Court of Appeals of Kentucky is Affirmed.

MR. JUSTICE HOLMES and MR. JUSTICE MOODY concur in the judgment.

MR. JUSTICE HARLAN, dissenting.

This prosecution arises under the first section of an act of the General Assembly of Kentucky, approved March 22, 1904. [*59] The purpose and scope of the act is clearly indicated by its title. It is "An act to prohibit white and colored persons from attending the same school." Ky. Acts 1904, p. 181.

The plaintiff in error, Berea College, is an incorporation, organized under the General Laws of Kentucky in 1859. Its original articles of incorporation set forth that the object of the founders was to establish and maintain an institution of learning, "in order to promote the cause of Christ." In 1899 new articles were adopted, which provided that the affairs of the corporation should be conducted by twenty-five persons.

In 1904 the college was charged in a Kentucky state court with having unlawfully and willfully received both white and negro persons as pupils for instruction. A demurrer to the indictment was overruled, and a trial was had which resulted in a verdict of guilty and the imposition of a fine of $1,000 on the college. The trial court refused an instruction asked by the defendant to the effect that the statute was in violation of the Fourteenth Amendment of the Constitution of the United States. A motion in arrest of judgment and for a new trial having been overruled, the case was taken to the highest court of Kentucky, where the judgment of conviction was affirmed, one of the members of the court dissenting.

The state court had before it and determined at the same time (delivering one opinion for both cases) another case against Berea College—which was an indictment based on § 4 of the same statute—under which the college was convicted of the offense of "maintaining and operating a college, school and institution of learning where persons of the white and negro races are both received, and within a distance of twenty-five miles of each other, as pupils for instruction." After observing that there were fundamental limitations upon the police power of the several States which could not be disregarded, the state court held § 4 of the statute to be in violation of those limitations because "unreasonable and oppressive." Treating that particular section as null and void and regarding the other sections as complete in themselves and enforcible, the state court, in the first case (the present case) based on § 1, affirmed, and in the second case based on § 4 of the statute reversed the judgment. It held it to be entirely competent for the State to adopt the policy of the separation of the races, even in private schools, and concluded its opinion in these words: "The right to teach white and negro children in a private school at the same time and place is not a property right." The state court (but without any discussion whatever) added, as if merely incidental to or a make-weight in the decision of the pivotal question, in this case, these words: "Besides, appellant as a corporation created by this State has no natural right to teach at all. Its right to teach is such as the State sees fit to give to it. The State may withhold it altogether or qualify it. *Allgeyer v. Louisiana, 165 U.S. 578.*" It concluded: "We do not think the act is in conflict with the Federal Constitution."

Upon a review of the judgment below this court says that the statute is "clearly separable and may be valid as to one class, while invalid as to another;" that "even if it were conceded that its assertion of power over individuals cannot be sustained, still the statute must be upheld so far as it restrains corporations." "It is unnecessary," this court says, "for us to consider anything more than the question of its validity as applied to corporations. ... We need concern ourselves only with the inquiry whether the first section can be upheld as coming within the power of a State over its own corporate creatures." The judgment of the state court is now affirmed, and thereby left in full force, so far as Kentucky and its courts are concerned, although such judgment rests in part upon the ground that the statute is not, in any particular, in violation of any rights secured by the Federal Constitution. In so ruling, it must necessarily have been assumed by this court that the legislature may have regarded the teaching of white and colored pupils at the same time and in the same school or institution, when maintained by private individuals and associations, as wholly different in its results from such teaching when conducted by the same individuals acting under the authority of or representing a corporation. But, looking at the nature or subject of the legislation it is inconceivable that the legislature consciously regarded the zlature had in mind to prohibit the teaching of the two races in the same private institution, at the same time by whomsoever that institution was conducted. It is a reflection upon the common sense of legislators to suppose that they might have prohibited a private corporation

from teaching by its agents, and yet left individuals and unincorporated associations entirely at liberty, by the same instructors, to teach the two races in the same institution at the same time. It was the teaching of pupils of the two races together, or in the same school, no matter by whom or under whose authority, which the legislature sought to prevent. The manifest purpose was to prevent the association of white and colored persons in the same school. That such was its intention is evident from the title of the act, which, as we have seen, was "to prohibit white and colored persons from attending the same school." Even if the words in the body of the act were doubtful or obscure the title may be looked to in aid of construction.

Undoubtedly, the general rule is that one part of a statute may be stricken down as unconstitutional and another part, distinctly separable and valid, left in force. But that general rule cannot control the decision of this case.

Referring to that rule, this court in *Huntington v. Worthen, 120 U.S. 97, 102*, said that if one provision of a statute be invalid the whole act will fall, where "it is evident the legislature would not have enacted one of them without the other."

***A case very much in point here is that of *Connolly v. Union Sewer Pipe Co., 184 U.S. 540, 565.* Those were actions upon promissory notes, and an open account. The defense was that the notes and the account arose out of business transactions with the Union Sewer Pipe Company, in Ohio corporation doing business in Illinois, and which corporation, it was alleged, was a trust and combination of a class or kind described in the Illinois anti-trust statute. That statute made certain combinations of capital, skill or acts by two or more persons for certain defined purposes illegal in Illinois. The defense was based in part on that statute, and the question was whether the statute was repugnant to the Constitution of the United States, in that, after prescribing penalties for its violation, it provided by a distinct section (§ 9) that its provisions "shall not apply to agricultural products or live stock while in the hands of the producer or raiser." The transactions out of which the notes and account in suit arose had no connection whatever with agriculture or with the business of raising live stock, and yet the question considered and determined— and which the court did not feel at liberty to pass by— was whether the entire statute was not unconstitutional by reason of the fact that the ninth section excepted from its operation agricultural products and live stock while in the lands of the producer or raiser. This court held that section to be repugnant to the Constitution of the

United States, in that it made such a discrimination in favor of agriculturists or live-stock dealers as to be a denial to all others of the equal protection of the laws. The question then arose, whether the other provisions of the statute could not be upheld and enforced by eliminating the ninth section. This court held in the negative, saying: "The principles applicable to such a question are well settled by the adjudications of this court. If different sections of a statute are independent of each other, that which is unconstitutional may be disregarded, and valid sections may stand and be enforced. But if an obnoxious section is of such import that the other sections without it would cause results not contemplated or desired by the legislature, then the entire statute must be held inoperative. ... Looking then at all the sections together, we must hold that the legislature would not have entered upon or continued the policy indicated by the statute unless agriculturists and live-stock dealers were excluded from its operation and thereby protected from prosecution. The result is that the statute must be regarded as an entirety, and in that view it must be adjudged to be unconstitutional as denying the equal protection of the laws to those within its jurisdiction who are not embraced by the ninth section."

The general principle was well stated by Chief Justice Shaw, who, after observing that if certain parts of a statute are wholly independent of each other, one part may be held void and the other enforced, said in *Warren v. Mayor and Aldermen of Charlestown, 2 Gray, 84*: "But if they are so mutually connected with and dependent on each other, as conditions, considerations or compensations for each other as to warrant a belief that the legislature intended them as a whole, and that if all could not be carried into effect, the legislature would not pass the residue independently, and some parts are unconstitutional, all the provisions which are thus dependent, conditional or connected, must fall with them." This statement of the principle was affirmed in *Allen v. Louisiana, 103 U.S. 80, 84*, and again in *Loeb v. Columbia Township Trustees, 179 U.S. 472, 490*, cited by the court. In the latter case the court said: "One part [of a statute] may stand, while another will fall, unless the two are so connected or dependent on each other in subject matter, meaning or purpose, that the good cannot remain without the bad. The point is, not whether the parts are contained in the same section, for, the distribution into sections [*65] is purely artificial; but whether they are essentially and inseparably connected in substance—whether the provisions are so interdependent that one cannot operate

without the other." All the cases are, without exception, in the same direction.

Now, can it for a moment be doubted that the legislature intended all the sections of the statute in question to be looked at, and that the purpose was to forbid the teaching of pupils of the two races together in the same institution, at the same time, whether the teachers represented natural persons or corporations? Can it be said that the legislature would have prohibited such teaching by corporations, and yet consciously permitted the teaching by private individuals or unincorporated associations? Are we to attribute such folly to legislators? Who can say that the legislature would have enacted one provision without the other? If not, then, in determining the intent of the legislature, the provisions of the statute relating to the teaching of the two races together by corporations cannot be separated in its operation [**39] from those in the same section that forbid such teaching by individuals and unincorporated associations. Therefore the court cannot, as I think, properly forbear to consider the validity of the provisions that refer to teachers who do not represent corporations. If those provisions constitute as, in my judgment, they do, an essential part of the legislative scheme or policy, and are invalid, then, under the authorities cited, the whole act must fall. The provision as to corporations may be valid, and yet the other clauses may be so inseparably connected with that provision and the policy underlying it, that the validity of all the clauses necessary to effectuate the legislative intent must be considered. There is no magic in the fact of incorporation which will so transform the act of teaching the two races in the same school at the same time that such teaching can be deemed lawful when conducted by private individuals, but unlawful when conducted by the representatives of corporations.

There is another line of thought. The state court evidently regarded it as necessary to consider the entire act; for it adjudged it to be competent for the State to forbid all teaching of the two races together, in the same institution, at the same time, no matter by whom the teaching was done. The reference at the close of its opinion, in the words above quoted, to the fact that the defendant was a corporation, which could be controlled, as the State saw fit, was, as already suggested, only incidental to the main question determined by the court as to the extent to which the State could control the teaching of the two races in the same institution. The state court upheld the authority of the State, under its general police power, to forbid the association of the two races in the same institution of learning, although it adjudged that there were limitations upon the exercise of that power, and that, under those limitations, § 4 was invalid, because unreasonable and oppressive. If it had regarded the authority of the State over its own corporations as being, in itself, and without reference to any other view, sufficient to sustain the statute, so far as the defendant corporation is concerned, it need only have said that much, and omitted all consideration of the general power of the State to forbid the teaching of the two races together, by anybody, in the same institution at the same time. It need not, in that vies, have made any reference whatever to the twenty-five mile provision in the fourth section as being "unreasonable and oppressive," whether applied to teaching by individuals or by corporations, or held such provision to be void on that special ground.

Some stress is laid upon the fact that when Berea College was incorporated the State reserved the power to alter, amend or repeal its charter. If the State had, in terms, and in virtue of the power reserved, repealed outright the charter of the college, the case might present a different question. But the charter was not repealed. The corporation was left in existence. The statute here in question does not purport to amend the charter of any particular corporation, but assumes to establish a certain rule applicable alike to all individuals, associations or corporations that assume to teach the white and black races together in the same institution. Besides, it should not be assumed that the State intended, under the guise of impliedly amending the charter of a private corporation, to destroy, or that it could destroy, the substantial, essential purposes for which the corporation was created, and yet leave the corporation in existence. The authorities cited by this court, in its opinion, establish the proposition that under the reserved power to amend or alter a charter no amendment or alteration can be made which will "defeat or substantially impair the object of the grant."

In my judgment the court should directly meet and decide the broad question presented by the statute. It should adjudge whether the statute, as a whole, is or is not unconstitutional, in that it makes it a crime against the State to maintain or operate a private institution of learning where white and black pupils are received, at the same time, for instruction. In the view which I have as to my duty I feel obliged to express my opinion as to the validity of the act as a whole. I am of opinion that in its essential parts the statute is an arbitrary invasion of the rights of liberty and property guaranteed by the Fourteenth mendment against hostile state action and is, therefore, void.

The capacity to impart instruction to others is given by the Almighty for beneficent purposes and its use may not be forbidden or interfered with by Government—certainly not, unless such instruction is, in its nature, harmful to the public morals or imperils the public safety. The right to impart instruction, harmless in itself or beneficial to those who receive it, is a substantial right of property—especially, where the services are rendered for compensation. But even if such right be not strictly a property right, it is, beyond question, part of one's liberty as guaranteed against hostile state action by the Constitution of the United States. This court has more than once said that the liberty guaranteed by the Fourteenth Amendment embraces "the right of the citizen to be free in the enjoyment of all his faculties," and "to be free to use them in all lawful ways.". If pupils, of whatever race—certainly, if they be citizens—choose with the consent of their parents or voluntarily to sit together in a private institution of learning while receiving instruction which is not in its nature harmful or dangerous to the public, no government, whether Federal or state, can legally forbid their coming together, or being together temporarily, for such an innocent purpose. If the Commonwealth of Kentucky can make it a crime to teach white and colored children together at the same time, in a private institution of learning, it is difficult to perceive why it may not forbid the assembling of white and colored children in the same Sabbath-school, for the purpose of being instructed in the Word of God, although such teaching may be done under the authority of the church to which the school is attached as well as with the consent of the parents of the children. So, if the state court be right, white and colored children may even be forbidden to sit together in a house of worship or at a communion table in the same Christian church. In the cases supposed there would be the same association of white and colored persons as would occur when pupils of the two races sit together in a private institution of learning for the purpose of receiving instruction in purely secular matters. Will it be said that the cases supposed and the case here in hand are different in that no government, in this country, can lay unholy hands on the religious faith of the people? The answer to this suggestion is that in the eye of the law the right to enjoy one's religious belief, unmolested by any human power, is no more sacred nor more fully or distinctly recognized than is the right to impart and receive instruction not harmful to the public. The denial of either right would be an infringement of the liberty inherent in the freedom secured by the fundamental law. Again, if the views of the highest court of Kentucky be sound, that commonwealth may, without infringing the Constitution of the United States, forbid the association in the same private school of pubils of the Anglo-Saxon and Latin races respectively, or pupils of the Christian and Jewise faiths, respectively. Have we become so inoculated with prejudice of race that an American government, professedly based on the principles of freedom, and charged with the protection of all citizens alike, can make distinctions between such citizens in the matter of their voluntary meeting for innocent purposes simply because of their respective races? Further, if the lower court be right, then a State may make it a crime for white and colored persons to frequent the same market places at the same time, or appear in an assemblage of citizens convened to consider questions of a public or political nature in which all citizens, without regard to race, are equally interested. Many other illustrations might be given to show the mischievous, not to say cruel, character of the statute in question and how inconsistent such legislation is with the great principle of the equality of citizens before the law.

Of course what I have said has no reference to regulations prescribed for public schools, established at the pleasure of the State and maintained at the public expense. No such question is here presented and it need not be now discussed. My observations have reference to the case before the court and only to the provision of the statute making it a crime for any person to impart harmless instruction to white and colored pupils together, at the same time, in the same private institution of learning. That provision is in my opinion made an essential element in the policy of the statute, and if regard be had to the object and purpose of this legislation it cannot be treated as separable nor intended to be separated from the provisions relating to corporations. The whole statute should therefore be held void: otherwise, it will be taken as the law of Kentucky, to be enforced by its courts, that the teaching of white and black pupils, at the same time, even in a private institution, is a crime against that Commonwealth, punishable by find and imprisonment.

In my opinion the judgment should be reversed upon the ground that the statute is in violation of the Constitution of the United States.

MR. JUSTICE DAY also dissents.

McCABE v. ATCHISON, TOPEKA & SANTA FE RAILWAY COMPANY
Supreme Court of the United States (1914)
235 U.S. 151

MR. JUSTICE HUGHES. The legislature of the State of Oklahoma passed ... the 'Separate Coach Law.' It provided that ... nothing contained in the act should be construed to prevent railway companies 'from hauling sleeping cars, dining or chair cars attached to their trains to be used exclusively by either white or negro passengers, separately but not jointly' (§7). ...

On February 15, 1908, just before the time when the statute, by its terms, was to become effective, five negro citizens of the State of Oklahoma ... brought this suit ... to restrain these companies from making any distinction in service on account of race. [The trial court dismissed the suit and the U.S. Court of Appeals affirmed the dismissal.] ...

The conclusions of the court below as stated in its opinion were, in substance:

1. That under the Enabling Act, the State of Oklahoma was admitted to the Union 'on an equal footing with the original States' and with respect to the matter in question had authority to enact such laws, not in conflict with the Federal Constitution, as other States could enact.

2. That it had been decided by this court, so that the question could no longer be considered an open one, that it was not an infraction of the Fourteenth Amendment for a State to require separate, but equal, accommodations for the two races. Plessy v. Ferguson.

3. That the provision of §7, above quoted, relating to sleeping cars, dining cars and chair cars did not offend against the Fourteenth Amendment as these cars were, comparatively speaking, luxuries, and that it was competent for the legislature to take into consideration the limited demand

for such accommodations by the one race, as compared with the demand on the part of the other. ...

In view of the decisions of this court above cited, there is no reason to doubt the correctness of the first, [and] second ... of these conclusions.

With the third, relating to §7 of the statute, we are unable to agree. It is not questioned that the meaning of this clause is that the carriers may provide sleeping cars, dining cars and chair cars exclusively for white persons and provide no similar accommodations for negroes. The reasoning is that there may not be enough persons of African descent seeking these accommodations to warrant the outlay in providing them. Thus, the Attorney General of the State, in the brief filed by him in support of the law, urges that "the plaintiffs must show that their own travel is in such quantity and of such kind as to actually afford the roads the same profits, not per man, but per car, as does the white traffic, or, sufficient profit to justify the furnishing of the facility, and that in such case they are not supplied with separate cars containing the same. This they have not attempted. What vexes the plaintiffs is the limited market value they offer for such accommodations. Defendants are not by law compelled to furnish chair cars, diners nor sleepers, except when the market offered reasonably demands the facility. "And in the brief of counsel for the appellees, it is stated that the members of the legislature "were undoubtedly familiar with the character and extent of travel of persons of African descent in the State of Oklahoma and were of the opinion that there was no substantial demand for Pullman car and dining car service for persons of the African race in the intrastate travel" in that State.

This argument with respect to volume of traffic seems to us to without merit. It makes the constitutional right depend upon the number of persons who may be discriminated against, whereas the essence of the constitutional right is that it is a personal one. Whether or not particular facilities shall be provided may doubtless be conditioned upon there being a reasonable demand therefor, but, if facilities are provided, substantial equality of treatment of persons traveling under like conditions cannot be refused. It is the individual who is entitled to the equal protection of the laws, and if he is denied by a common carrier, acting in the matter under the authority of a state law, a facility or convenience in the course of his journey which under substantially the same circumstances is furnished to another traveler, he may properly complain that his constitutional privilege has been invaded.

There is, however, an insuperable obstacle to the granting of the relief sought by this bill. It was filed, as we have seen, by five persons against five railroad corporations to restrain them from complying with the state statute. The suit had been brought before the law went into effect and this amended bill was filed very shortly after. It contains some general allegations as to discriminations in the supply of facilities and as to the hardships which will ensure. It states that there will be 'a multiplicity of suits,' there being at least 'fifty thousand persons of the negro race in the State of Oklahoma' who will be injured and deprived of their civil rights. But we are dealing here with the case of the complainants, and nothing is shown to entitle them to an injunction. It is an elementary principle that, in order to justify the granting of this extraordinary relief, the complainant's need of it, and the absence of an adequate remedy at law, must clearly appear. The complainant cannot succeed because someone else may be hurt. Nor does it make any difference that other persons, who may be injured are persons of the same race or occupation. It is the fact, clearly established, of injury to the complainant—not to others—which justifies judicial intervention.

We agree with the court below that these allegations are altogether too vague and indefinite to warrant the relief sought by these complainants. It is not alleged that any one of the complainants has ever traveled on any one of the five railroads, or has ever requested transportation on any of them; or that any one of the complainants has ever requested that accommodations be furnished to him in any sleeping cars, dining cars or chair cars; or that any of these five companies has ever notified any one of these complainants that such accommodations would not be furnished to him, when furnished to others, upon reasonable request and payment of the customary charge. Nor is there anything to show that in case any of these complainants offers himself as a passenger on any of these roads and is refused accommodations equal to those afforded to others on a like journey, he will not have an adequate remedy at law. The desire to obtain a sweeping injunction cannot be accepted as a substitute for compliance with the general rule that the complainant must present facts sufficient to show that his individual need requires the remedy for which he asks. The bill is wholly destitute of any sufficient ground for injunction and unless we are to ignore settled principles governing equitable relief, the decree must be affirmed.

PEARSON v. MURRAY
Court of Appeals of Maryland (1936)
182 A. 590

BOND, Chief Judge. The officers and governing board of the University of Maryland appeal from an order ... commanding them to admit a young negro, [Murray], as a student in the law school of the university. ... Murray ... graduated as a bachelor of arts from Amherst College in 1934, and met the standards for admission to the law school in all other respects, but was denied admission on the sole ground of his color. He is twenty-two years of age, and is now, and has been during all his life, a resident of Baltimore City, where the law school is situated. He contests his exclusion as unauthorized by the laws of the state, or, so far as it might be considered authorized, then as a denial of equal rights because of his color, contrary to the requirement of the Fourteenth Amendment of the Constitution of the United States. The appellants reply, first, that by reason of its character and organization the law school is not a governmental agency, required by the amendment to give equal rights to students of both races. Or, if it is held that it is a state agency, it is replied that the admission of negro students is not required because the amendment permits segregation of the races for education, and it is the declared policy and the practice of the state to segregate them in schools, and that although the law school of the university is maintained for white students only, and there is no separate law school maintained for colored students, equal treatment has at the same time been accorded the negroes by statutory provisions for scholarships or aids to enable them to attend law schools outside the state. A further argument in defense is that if equal treatment has not been provided, the remedy must be found in the opening of a school for negroes, and not in their admission to this particular school attended by the whites.

The University of Maryland Law School was a private institution until the year 1920, when ... it was consolidated with the Maryland State College of Agriculture, then an institution of the state government. ...

The consolidation was completed. And from the fact of consolidation with a state agency, under one and the same board of trustees appointed and controlled by the state, it would seem to follow inevitably that the law school maintained is a state agency, or part of one. The one corporation could not be both a public and a private one. It is argued that the school is "in the nature of a private corporation" because it receives the greater part of its support from the students' tuition fees, and therefore its freedom of selection and accommodation of students is not subject to the restriction by the Fourteenth Amendment. But a distinction between agencies which do and those which do not collect fees from individual users of their facilities would not support a distinction between private and public character. It is common practice for unquestionably public corporations to collect pay. Hospitals, and the various municipal corporations or agencies which make charges for utilities supplied, often with a margin of profit over expenses, remain none the less public in character. There is no escape from the conclusion that the school is now a branch or agency of the state government. The state now provides education in the law for its citizens. And in doing so it comes under the constitutional mandates applicable to the actions of the states. ...

As a result of the adoption of the Fourteenth Amendment to the United States Constitution, a state is required to extend to its citizens of the two races substantially equal treatment in the facilities it provides from the public funds. ...

The requirement of equal treatment would seem to be clearly enough one of equal treatment in respect to any one facility or opportunity furnished to citizens, rather than of a balance in state bounty to be struck from the expenditures and provisions for each race generally. We take it to be clear, for instance, that a state could not be rendered free to maintain a law school exclusively for whites by maintaining at equal cost a school of technology for colored students. Expenditures of this state for the education of the latter in schools and colleges have been extensive, but, however they may compare with provisions for the whites, they would not justify the exclusion of colored citizens alone from enjoyment of any one facility furnished by the state. The courts, in all the decisions on application of this constitutional requirement, find exclusion from any one privilege condemned.

Equality of treatment does not require that privileges be provided members of the two races in the same place. The state may choose the method by which equality is maintained. ...

Separation of the races must nevertheless furnish equal treatment. The constitutional requirement cannot be dispensed with in order to maintain a school or schools for whites exclusively. That requirement comes first. And as no separate law school is provided by this state for colored students, the main question in the case is whether the separation can be maintained, and negroes excluded from the present school, by reason of equality of treatment furnished the latter in scholarships for studying outside the state, where law schools are open to negroes. In 1933, an Act of Assembly ... provided that the Regents of the University of Maryland might set aside part of the state appropriation for the Princess Anne Academy, an institution of junior college standing for negro students, now an eastern branch of the university, to establish partial scholarship at-Morgan College in the state, or at institutions outside the state, for negroes qualified to take professional courses not offered them at Princess Anne Academy, but offered for white students in the university. Morgan College has no law school. None of the money necessary was appropriated for distribution under that act. By an Act of 1935 ... a Commission on Higher Education of Negroes was created and directed to administer $10,000 included in the state budget for the years 1935–1936 and 1936–1937, for scholarships of $200 each to negroes, to enable them to attend colleges outside the state, mainly to give the benefit of college, medical, law, and other professional courses to the colored youth of the state for whom no such facilities are available in the state. The allowance of $200 was to defray tuition fees only. This latter act went into effect on June 1, 1935, and it appeared from evidence that by June 18, when this case was tried below, 380 negroes had sought blanks for applying for the scholarships, and 113 applications had been filled in and returned. Only 16 had then sought

opportunities for graduate or professional study, only one of them for study of the law. Applications were to be received during twelve more days. That any one of the many individual applicants would receive one of the 50 or more scholarships was obviously far from assured. For a large percentage of them there was no provision. And if the petitioner should have received one there would have been, as he argues, disadvantages attached.

Howard University, in Washington, District of Columbia, provides the law school for negroes nearest to Baltimore. The yearly tuition fee there is $135, as compared with a fee of $203 in the day school of the University of Maryland, and $153 in its night school. But to attend Howard University the petitioner, living in Baltimore, would be under the necessity of paying the expenses of daily travel to and fro, with some expenses while in Washington, or of removing to Washington to live during his law school education, and to pay the incidental expenses of thus living away from home; whereas in Baltimore, living at home, he would have no traveling expenses, and comparatively small living expenses. Going to any law school in the nearest jurisdiction would, then, involve him in considerable expense even with the aid of one of the scholarships should he chance to receive one. And as the petitioner points out, he could not there have the advantages of study of the law of this state primarily, and of attendance on state courts, where he intends to practice.

The court is clear that this rather slender chance for any one applicant at an opportunity to attend an outside law school, at increased expense, falls short of providing for students of the colored race facilities substantially equal to those furnished to the whites in the law school maintained in Baltimore. The number of colored students affected by the discrimination may be com-paratively small, but it cannot be said to be negligible in Baltimore City, and moreover the number seems excluded as a factor in the problem. In a case on discrimination required by a state between the races in railroad travel, the Supreme Court of the United States has said: "This argument with respect to volume of traffic seems to us to be without merit. It makes the constitutional right depend upon the number of persons who may be discriminated against, whereas the essence of the constitutional right is that it is a personal one. ... It is the individual who is entitled to the equal protection of the laws, and if he is denied by a common carrier, acting in the matter under the authority of a state law, a facility or convenience in the course of his journey which, under substantially the same circumstances, is furnished to another traveler, he may properly complain that his constitutional privilege has been invaded." *McCabe v. Atchison, T. & S. F. R. Co.* Whether with aid in any amount it is sufficient to send the negroes outside the state for like education is a question never passed on by the Supreme Court, and we need not discuss it now.

As has been stated, the method of furnishing the equal facilities required is at the choice of the state, now or at any future time. At present it is maintaining only the one law school, and in the legislative provisions for the scholarships that one school has in effect been declared appropriated to the whites exclusively. The officers and members of the board appear to us to have had a policy declared for them, as they thought. No separate school for colored students has been decided upon and only an inadequate substitute has been provided. Compliance with the Constitution cannot be deferred at the will of the state. Whatever system it adopts for legal education now must furnish equality of treatment now. ... And as in Maryland now the equal treatment can be furnished only in the one existing law school, the petitioner, in our opinion, must be admitted there.

We cannot find the remedy to be that of ordering a separate school for negroes. ... [N]o officers or body of officers are authorized to establish a separate law school, there is no legislative declaration of a purpose to establish one, and the courts could not make the decision for the state and order its officers to establish one. Therefore the erection of a separate school is not here an available alternative remedy. ...

The case, as we find it, then, is that the state has undertaken the function of education in the law, but has omitted students of one race from the only adequate provision made for it, and omitted them solely because of their color. If those students are to be offered equal treatment in the performance of the function, they must, at present, be admitted to the one school provided. And as the officers and regents are the agents of the state entrusted with the conduct of that one school, it follows that they must admit. ...

MISSOURI EX REL. GAINES v. CANADA
Supreme Court of the United States (1938)
305 U.S. 337

The State of Missouri provides separate schools and universities for whites and negroes. At the state university, attended by whites, there is a course in law; at the Lincoln University, attended by negroes, there is as yet none, but it is the duty of the curators of that institution to establish one there whenever in their opinion this shall be necessary and practicable, and pending such development, they are authorized to arrange for legal education of Missouri negroes, and to pay the tuition charges therefor, at law schools in adjacent States where negroes are accepted and where the training is equal to that obtainable at the Missouri State University. Pursuant to the State's policy of separating the races in its educational institutions, the curators of the state university refused to admit a negro as a student in the law school there because of his race; whereupon he sought a mandamus, in the state courts, which was denied.

MR. CHIEF JUSTICE HUGHES. ... In answering petitioner's contention that this discrimination constituted a denial of his constitutional right, the state court has fully recognized the obligation of the State to provide negroes with advantages for higher education substantially equal to the advantages afforded to white students. The State has sought to fulfill that obligation by furnishing equal facilities in separate schools, a method the validity of which has been sustained by our decisions. Plessy v. Ferguson; McCabe v. Atchison, T. & S. F. Ry. Co. Respondents' counsel have appropriately emphasized the special solicitude of the State for the higher education of negroes as shown in the establishment of Lincoln University, a state institution well conducted on a plane with the University of Missouri so far as the offered courses are concerned. It is said that Missouri is a pioneer in that field and is the only State in the Union which has

established a separate university for negroes on the same basis as the state university for white students. But, commendable as is that action, the fact remains that instruction in law for negroes is not now afforded by the State, either at Lincoln University or elsewhere within the State, and that the State excludes negroes from the advantages of the law school it has established at the University of Missouri.

It is manifest that this discrimination, if not relieved by the provisions we shall presently discuss, would constitute a denial of equal protection. That was the conclusion of the Court of Appeals of Maryland in circumstances substantially similar in that aspect. [Pearson] v. Murray. ...

The Supreme Court of Missouri ... has distinguished the decision in Maryland upon the grounds—(1) that in Missouri, but not in Maryland, there is "a legislative declaration of a purpose to establish a law school for negroes at Lincoln University whenever necessary or practical"; and (2) that, "pending the establishment of such a school, adequate provision has been made for the legal education of negro students in recognized schools outside of this State."

As to the first ground, it appears that the policy of establishing a law school at Lincoln University has not yet ripened into an actual establishment, and it cannot be said that a mere declaration of purpose, still unfulfilled, is enough. The provision for legal education at Lincoln is at present entirely lacking. Respondents' counsel urge that if, on the date when petitioner applied for admission to the University of Missouri, he had instead applied to the curators of Lincoln University it would have been their duty to establish a law school. ...

The state court has not held that it would have been the duty of the curators to establish a law school at Lincoln University for the petitioner on his application. Their duty, as the court defined it, would have been either to supply a law school at Lincoln University ... or to furnish him the opportunity to obtain his legal training in another state. ... Thus the law left the curators free to adopt the latter course. ... In the light of its ruling we must regard the question whether the provision for the legal education in other States of negroes resident in Missouri is sufficient to satisfy the constitutional requirement of equal protection, as the pivot upon which this case turns.

The state court stresses the advantages that are afforded by the law schools of the adjacent States,—Kansas, Nebraska, Iowa and Illinois,—which admit non–resident negroes. The court considered that these were schools of high standing where one desiring to practice law in Missouri can get "as sound, comprehensive, valuable legal education" as in the University of Missouri; that the system of education in the former is the same as that in the latter and is designed to give the students a basis for the practice of law in any State where the Anglo–American system of law obtains; that the law school of the University of Missouri does not specialize in Missouri law and that the course of study and the case books used in the five schools are substantially identical. ...

We think that these matters are beside the point. The basic consideration is not as to what sort of opportunities other States provide, or whether they are as good as those in Missouri, but as to what opportunities Missouri itself furnishes to white students and denies to negroes solely upon the ground of color. The admissibility of laws separating the races in the enjoyment of privileges afforded by the State rests wholly upon the equality of the privileges which the laws give to the separated groups within the State. The question here is not of a duty of the State to supply legal training, or of the quality of the training which it does supply, but of its duty when it provides such training to furnish it to the residents of the State upon the basis of an equality of right. By the operation of the laws of Missouri a privilege has been created for white law students which is denied to negroes by reason of their race. The white resident is afforded legal education within the State; the negro resident having the same qualifications is refused it there and must go outside the State to obtain it. That is a denial of the equality of legal right to the enjoyment of the privilege which the State has set up, and the provision for the payment of tuition fees in another State does not remove the discrimination.

The equal protection of the laws is "a pledge of the protection of equal laws." *Yick Wo v. Hopkins.* Manifestly, the obligation of the State to give the protection of equal laws can be performed only where its laws operate, that is, within its own jurisdiction. It is there that the equality of legal right must be maintained. That obligation is imposed by the Constitution upon the States severally as governmental entities,—each responsible for its own laws establishing the rights and duties of persons within its borders. It is an obligation the burden of which cannot be cast by one State upon another, and no State can be excused from performance by what another State may do or fail to do. That separate responsibility of each State within its own sphere is of the essence of statehood maintained under our dual system. It seems to be implicit in respondents' argument that if other States did not provide courses for legal education, it would nevertheless be the constitutional duty of Missouri when it supplied such courses for white students to make equivalent provision for negroes. But that plain duty would exist because it rested upon the State independently of the action of other States. We find it impossible to conclude that what otherwise would be an unconstitutional discrimination, with respect to the legal right to the enjoyment of opportunities within the State, can be justified by requiring resort to opportunities elsewhere. That resort may mitigate the inconvenience of the discrimination but cannot serve to validate it.

Nor can we regard the fact that there is but a limited demand in Missouri for the legal education of negroes as excusing the discrimination in favor of whites. We had occasion to consider a cognate question in the case of *McCabe v. Atchison, T. & S. F. Ry. Co.* There the argument was advanced, in relation to the provision by a carrier of sleeping cars, dining and chair cars, that the limited demand by negroes justified the State in permitting the furnishing of such accommodations exclusively for white persons. We found that argument to be without merit. It made, we said, the constitutional right "depend upon the number of persons who may be discriminated against, whereas the essence of the constitutional right is that it is a personal one. Whether or not particular facilities shall be provided may doubtless be conditioned upon there being a reasonable demand therefor, but, if facilities are provided, substantial equality of treatment of persons traveling under like conditions cannot be refused. It is the individual who is entitled to the equal protection of the laws, and if he is denied by a common carrier, acting in the matter under the authority of a state law, a facility or convenience in the course of his journey which under substantially the same circumstances is furnished to another traveler, he may properly complain that his constitutional privilege has been invaded."

Here, petitioner's right was a personal one. It was as an individual that he was entitled to the equal protection of the laws, and the State was bound to furnish him within its borders facilities for legal education substantially equal to those which the State there afforded for persons of the white race, whether or not other negroes sought the same opportunity. ...

MR. JUSTICE McREYNOLDS, dissenting. ... In *Cumming v. Richmond County Board of Education* this Court through Mr. Justice Harlan declared—"The education of the people in schools maintained by state taxation is a matter belonging to the respective States, and any interference on the part of Federal authority with the management of such schools cannot be justified except in the case of a clear and unmistakable disregard of rights secured by the supreme law of the land."...

For a long time Missouri has acted upon the view that the best interest of her people demands separation of whites and negroes in schools. Under the opinion just announced, I presume she may abandon her law school and thereby disadvantage her white citizens without improving petitioner's opportunities for legal instruction; or she may break down the settled practice concerning separate schools and thereby, as indicated by experience, damnify both races. Whether by some other course it may be possible for her to avoid condemnation is matter for conjecture.

The State has offered to provide the negro petitioner opportunity for study of the law—if perchance that is the thing really desired—by paying his tuition at some nearby school of good standing. This is far from unmistakable disregard of his rights and in the circumstances is enough to satisfy any reasonable demand for specialized training. It appears that never before has a negro applied for admission to the Law School and none has ever asked that Lincoln University provide legal instruction.

The problem presented obviously is a difficult and highly practical one. A fair effort to solve it has been made by offering adequate opportunity for study when sought in good faith. The State should not be unduly hampered through theorization inadequately restrained by experience. ...

SWEATT v. PAINTER
Supreme Court of the United States (1950)
339 U.S. 629

MR. CHIEF JUSTICE VINSON delivered the opinion of the Court. This case and *McLaurin v. Oklahoma State Regents* present different aspects of this general question: To what extent does the Equal Protection Clause of the Fourteenth Amendment limit the power of a state to distinguish between students of different races in professional and graduate education in a state university? ...

In the instant case, petitioner filed an application for admission to the University of Texas Law School for the February, 1946 term. His application was rejected solely because he is a Negro. Petitioner thereupon brought this suit ... against the appropriate school officials ... to compel his admission. At that time, there was no law school in Texas which admitted Negroes.

The state trial court recognized that the action of the State in denying petitioner the opportunity to gain a legal education while granting it to others deprived him of the equal protection of the laws guaranteed by the Fourteenth Amendment. The court did not grant the relief requested, however, but continued the case for six months to allow the State to supply substantially equal facilities. At the expiration of the six months, in December, 1946, the court denied the writ on the showing that the authorized university officials had adopted an order calling for the opening of a law school for Negroes the following February. While petitioner's appeal was pending, such a school was made available, but petitioner refused to register therein. The Texas Court of Civil Appeals set aside the trial court's judgment and ordered the cause "remanded generally to the trial court for further proceedings without prejudice to the rights of any party to this suit."

On remand, a hearing was held on the issue of the equality of the educational facilities at the newly established school as compared with the University of Texas Law School. Finding that the new school offered petitioner "privileges, advantages, and opportunities for the study of law substantially equivalent to those offered by the State to white students at the University of Texas," the trial court denied mandamus. The Court of Civil Appeals affirmed. Petitioner's application for a writ of error was denied by the Texas Supreme Court. We granted certiorari because of the manifest importance of the constitutional issues involved.

The University of Texas Law School, from which petitioner was excluded, was staffed by a faculty of sixteen full-time and three part-time professors, some of whom are nationally recognized authorities in their field. Its student body numbered 850. The library contained over 65,000 volumes. Among the other facilities available to the students were a law review, moot court facilities, scholarship funds, and Order of the Coif affiliation. The school's alumni occupy the most distinguished positions in the private practice of the law and in the public life of the State. It may properly be considered one of the nation's ranking law schools.

The law school for Negroes which was to have opened in February, 1947, would have had no independent faculty or library. The teaching was to be carried on by four members of the University of Texas Law School faculty, who were to maintain their offices at the University of Texas while teaching at both institutions. Few of the 10,000 volumes ordered for the library had arrived; nor was there any fulltime librarian. The school lacked accreditation.

Since the trial of this case, respondents report the opening of a law school at the Texas State University for Negroes. It is apparently on the road to full accreditation. It has a faculty of five full-time professors; a student body of 23; a library of some 16,500 volumes serviced by a full-time staff; a practice court and legal aid association; and one alumnus who has become a member of the Texas Bar.

Whether the University of Texas Law School is compared with the original or the new law school for Negroes, we cannot find substantial equality in the educational opportunities offered white and Negro law students by the State. In terms of number of the faculty, variety of courses and opportunity for specialization, size of the student body, scope of the library, availability of law review and similar activities, the University of Texas Law School is superior. What is more important, the University of Texas Law School possesses to a far greater degree those qualities which are incapable of objective measurement but which make for greatness in a law school. Such qualities, to name but a few, include reputation of the faculty, experience of the administration, position and influence of the alumni, standing in the community, traditions and prestige. It is difficult to believe that one who had a free choice between these law schools would consider the question close.

Moreover, although the law is a highly learned profession, we are well aware that it is an intensely practical one. The law school, the proving ground for legal learning and practice, cannot be effective in isolation from the individuals and institutions with which the law interacts. Few students and no one who has practiced law would choose to study in an academic vacuum, removed from the interplay of ideas and the exchange of views with which the law is concerned. The law school to which Texas is willing to admit petitioner excludes from its student body members of the racial groups which number 85% of the population of the State and include most of the lawyers, witnesses, jurors, judges and other officials with whom petitioner will inevitably be dealing when he becomes a member of the Texas Bar. With such a substantial and significant segment of society excluded, we cannot conclude that the education offered petitioner is substantially equal to that which he would receive if admitted to the University of Texas Law School. ...

We hold that the Equal Protection Clause of the Fourteenth Amendment requires that petitioner be admitted to the University of Texas Law School. ...

MR. CHIEF JUSTICE VINSON. In this case, we are faced with the question whether a state may, after admitting a student to graduate instruction in its state university, afford him different treatment from other students solely because of his race. We decide only this issue.

Appellant is a Negro citizen of Oklahoma. Possessing a Master's Degree, he applied for admission to the University of Oklahoma in order to pursue studies and courses leading to a Doctorate in Education. At that time, his application was denied, solely because of his race. The school authorities were required to exclude him by the Oklahoma statutes, which made it a misdemeanor to maintain or operate, teach or attend a school at which both whites and Negroes are enrolled or taught. Appellant filed a complaint requesting injunctive relief, alleging that the action of the school authorities and the statutes upon which their action was based were unconstitutional and deprived him of the equal protection of the laws. Citing our decisions in *Missouri ex rel. Gaines v. Canada*, ... a statutory three-judge District Court held that the State had a Constitutional duty to provide him with the education he sought as soon as it provided that education for applicants of any other group. It further held that to the extent the Oklahoma statutes denied him admission they were unconstitutional and void. ...

Following this decision, the Oklahoma legislature amended these statutes to permit the admission of Negroes to institutions of higher learning attended by white students, in cases where such institutions offered courses not available in the Negro schools. The amendment provided, however, that in such cases the program of instruction "shall be given at such colleges or institutions of higher education upon a segregated basis." Appellant was thereupon admitted to the University of Oklahoma Graduate School. In apparent conformity with the amendment, his admission was made subject to "such rules and regulations as to segregation as the President of the University shall consider to afford to Mr. G. W. McLaurin substantially equal educational opportunities as are afforded to other persons seeking the same education in the Graduate College," a condition which does not appear to have been withdrawn. Thus he was required to sit apart at a designated desk in an anteroom adjoining the classroom; to sit at a designated desk on the mezzanine floor of the library, but not to use the desks in the regular reading room; and to sit at a designated table and to eat at a different time from the other students in the school cafeteria.

To remove these conditions, appellant filed a motion to modify the order and judgment of the District Court. That court held that such treatment did not violate the provisions of the Fourteenth Amendment and denied the motion. This appeal followed.

In the interval between the decision of the court below and the hearing in this Court, the treatment afforded appellant was altered. For some time, the section of the classroom in which appellant sat was surrounded by a rail on which there was a sign stating, "Reserved For Colored," but these have been removed. He is now assigned to a seat in the classroom in a row specified for colored students; he is assigned to a table in the library on the main floor; and he is permitted to eat at the same time in the cafeteria as other students, although here again he is assigned to a special table.

It is said that the separations imposed by the State in this case are in form merely nominal. McLaurin uses the same classroom, library and cafeteria as students of other races; there is no indication that the seats to which he is assigned in these rooms have any disadvantage of location. He may wait in line in the cafeteria and there stand and talk with his fellow students, but while he eats he must remain apart.

These restrictions were obviously imposed in order to comply, as nearly as could be, with the statutory requirements of Oklahoma. But they signify that the State, in administering the facilities it affords for professional and graduate study, sets McLaurin apart from the other students. The result is that appellant is handicapped in his pursuit of effective graduate instruction. Such restrictions impair and inhibit his ability to study, to engage in discussions and exchange views with other students, and, in general, to learn his profession.

Our society grows increasingly complex, and our need for trained leaders increases correspondingly. Appellant's case represents, perhaps, the epitome of that need, for he is attempting to obtain an advanced degree in education, to become, by definition, a leader and trainer of others. Those who will come under his guidance and influence must be directly affected by the education he receives. Their own education and development will necessarily suffer to the extent that his training is unequal to that of his classmates. State-imposed restrictions which produce such inequalities cannot be sustained.

It may be argued that appellant will be in no better position when these restrictions are removed, for he may still be set apart by his fellow students. This we think irrelevant. There is a vast difference—a Constitutional difference—between restrictions imposed by the state which prohibit the intellectual commingling of students, and the refusal of individuals to commingle where the state presents no such bar. The removal of the state restrictions will not necessarily abate individual and group predilections, prejudices and choices. But at the very least, the state will not be depriving appellant of the opportunity to secure acceptance by his fellow students on his own merits.

We conclude that the conditions under which this appellant is required to receive his education deprive him of his personal and present right to the equal protection of the laws. We hold that under these circumstances the Fourteenth Amendment precludes differences in treatment by the state based upon race. Appellant, having been admitted to a state-supported graduate school, must receive the same treatment at the hands of the state as students of other races.

HENDERSON v. UNITED STATES et al.
Supreme Court of the United States
339 U.S. 816

June 5, 1950, Decided

MR. JUSTICE BURTON delivered the opinion of the Court.

[1]The question here is whether the rules and practices of the Southern Railway Company, which divide each dining car so as to allot ten tables exclusively to white passengers and one table exclusively to Negro passengers, and which call for a curtain or partition between that table and the others, violate § 3 (1) of the Interstate Commerce Act. That section makes it unlawful for a railroad in interstate commerce "to subject any particular person, … to any undue or unreasonable prejudice or disadvantage in any respect whatsoever: …" We hold that those rules and practices do violate the Act.

This issue grows out of an incident which occurred May 17, 1942. On that date the appellant, Elmer W. Henderson, a Negro passenger, was traveling on a first-class ticket on the Southern Railway from Washington, D. C., to Atlanta, Georgia, en route to Birmingham, Alabama, in the course of his duties as an employee of the United States. The train left Washington at 2 p. m. At about 5:30 p. m., while the train was in Virginia,[1] the first call to dinner was announced and he went promptly to the dining car. In accordance with the practice then in effect, the two end tables nearest the kitchen were conditionally reserved for Negroes. At each meal those tables were to be reserved initially for Negroes and, when occupied by Negroes, curtains were to be drawn between them and the rest of the car. If the other tables were occupied before any Negro passengers presented themselves at the diner then those two tables also were to be available for white passengers, and Negroes were not to be seated at them while in use by white passengers.[2] When the appellant reached the diner, the end tables in question were partly occupied by white passengers but at least one seat at them was unoccupied. The dining-car steward declined to seat the appellant in the dining car but offered to serve him, without additional charge, at his Pullman seat. The appellant declined that offer and the steward agreed to send him word when space was available. No word was sent and the appellant was not served, although he twice returned to the diner before it was detached at 9 p. m.

---

[1]No reliance is placed in this case upon any action by any state.

[2]Rule of the Southern Railway Company issued July 3, 1941, and in effect May 17, 1942:

DINING CAR REGULATIONS

"Meals should be served to passengers of different races at separate times. If passengers of one race desire meals while passengers of a different race are being served in the dining car, such meals will be served in the room or seat occupied by the passenger without extra charge. If the dining car is equipped with curtains so that it can be divided into separate compartments, meals may be served to passengers of different races at the same time in the compartments set aside for them." 258 I. C. C. 413, 415, 63 F.Supp. 906, 910.

Joint Circular of the Southern Railway System issued August 6, 1942:

"Effective at once please be governed by the following with respect to the race separation curtains in dining cars:

"Before starting each meal pull the curtains to service position and place a 'Reserved' card on each of the two tables behind the curtains.

"These tables are not to be used by white passengers until all other seats in the car have been taken. Then if no colored passengers present themselves for meals, the curtain should be pushed back, cards removed and white passengers served at those tables.

"After the tables are occupied by white passengers, then should colored passengers present themselves they should be advised that they will be served just as soon as those compartments are vacated.

"'Reserved' cards are being supplied you."

In October, 1942, the appellant filed a complaint with the Interstate Commerce Commission alleging especially that the foregoing conduct violated § 3 (1) of the Interstate Commerce Act.[3] Division 2 of the Commission found that he had been subjected to undue and unreasonable prejudice and disadvantage, but that the occurrence was a casual incident brought about by the bad judgment of an employee. The Commission declined to enter an order as to future practices. A three-judge United States District Court for the District of Maryland, however, held that the railroad's general practice, as evidenced by its instructions of August 6, 1942, was in violation of § 3 (1). Accordingly, on February 18, 1946, it remanded the case for further proceedings. Effective March 1, 1946, the company announced its modified rules which are now in effect. They provide for the reservation of ten tables, of four seats each, exclusively and unconditionally for white passengers and one table, of four seats, exclusively and unconditionally for Negro passengers. Between this table and the others a curtain is drawn during each meal.[4]

On remand, the full Commission, with two members dissenting and one not participating, found that the modified rules do not violate the Interstate Commerce Act and that no order for the future was necessary. The appellant promptly instituted the present proceeding before the District Court, constituted of the same three members as before, seeking to have the Commission's order set aside and a cease and desist order issued. With one member dissenting, the court sustained the modified rules on the ground that the accommodations are adequate to serve the average number of Negro passengers and are "proportionately fair." The case is here on direct appeal. In this Court, the United States filed a brief and argued orally in support of the appellant.

***The right to be free from unreasonable discriminations belongs, under § 3 (1), to each particular person. Where a dining car is available to passengers holding tickets entitling them to use it, each such passenger is equally entitled to its facilities in accordance with reasonable regulations. The denial of dining service to any such passenger by the rules before us subjects him to a prohibited disadvantage. Under the rules only four Negro passengers may be served at one time and then only at the table reserved for Negroes. Other Negroes who present themselves are compelled to await a vacancy at that table, although there may be many vacancies elsewhere in the diner. The railroad thus refuses to extend to those passengers the use of its existing and unoccupied facilities. The rules impose a like deprivation upon white passengers whenever more than 40 of them seek to be served at the same time and the table reserved for Negroes is vacant.

---

[3]"(1) *It shall be unlawful for any common carrier* subject to the provisions of this part *to make, give, or cause any undue or unreasonable preference or advantage to any particular person*, company, firm, corporation, association, locality, port, port district, gateway, transit point, region, district, territory, or any particular description of traffic, *in any respect whatsoever; or to subject any particular person*, company, firm, corporation, association, locality, port, port district, gateway, transit point, region, district, territory, or any particular description of traffic *to any undue or unreasonable prejudice or disadvantage in any respect whatsoever*. . . ." (Emphasis supplied.) 54 Stat. 902, 49 U. S. C. § 3 (1).

The appellant sought an order directing the railroad not only to cease and desist from the specific violations alleged but also to establish in the future, for the complainant and other Negro interstate passengers, equal and just dining-car facilities and such other service and facilities as the Commission might consider reasonable and just, and requiring the railroad to discontinue using curtains around tables reserved for Negroes.

The appellant sought damages, but the Commission found no pecuniary damages and that issue has not been pressed further.

[4]"TRANSPORTATION DEPARTMENT CIRCULAR NO. 142. CANCELLING INSTRUCTIONS ON THIS SUBJECT DATED JULY 3, 1941, AND AUGUST 6, 1942.

"SUBJECT: SEGREGATION OF WHITE AND COLORED PASSENGERS IN DINING CARS.

"To: Passenger Conductors and Dining Car Stewards.

"Consistent with experience in respect to the ratio between the number of white and colored passengers who ordinarily apply for service in available diner space, equal but separate accommodations shall be provided for white and colored passengers by partitioning diners and the allotment of space, in accordance with the rules, as follows:

"(1) That one of the two tables at Station No. 1 located to the left side of the aisle facing the buffet, seating four persons, shall be reserved exclusively for colored passengers, and the other tables in the diner shall be reserved exclusively for white passengers.

"(2) Before starting each meal, draw the partition curtain separating the table in Station No. 1, described above, from the table on that side of the aisle in Station No. 2, the curtain to remain so drawn for the duration of the meal.

"(3) A 'Reserved' card shall be kept in place on the left-hand table in Station No. 1, described above, at all times during the meal except when such table is occupied as provided in these rules.

"(4) These rules become effective March 1, 1946.

We need not multiply instances in which these rules sanction unreasonable discriminations. The curtains, partitions and signs emphasize the artificiality of a difference in treatment which serves only to call attention to a racial classification of passengers holding identical tickets and using the same public dining facility. Cf. *McLaurin* v. *Oklahoma State Regents, ante,* p. 637, decided today. They violate § 3 (1).

[6]Our attention has been directed to nothing which removes these racial allocations from the statutory condemnation of "undue or unreasonable prejudice or disadvantage . ..." It is argued that the limited demand for dining-car facilities by Negro passengers justifies the regulations. But it is no answer to the particular passenger who is denied service at an unoccupied place in a dining car that, on the average, persons like him are served. As was pointed out in *Mitchell* v. *United States,* 313 U. S. 80, 97, "the comparative volume of traffic cannot justify the denial of a fundamental right of equality of treatment, a right specifically safeguarded by the provisions of the Interstate Commerce Act." Cf. *McCabe* v. *Atchison, T. & S. F. R. Co.,* 235 U. S. 151; *Missouri ex rel. Gaines* v. *Canada,* 305 U. S. 337.

That the regulations may impose on white passengers, in proportion to their numbers, disadvantages similar to those imposed on Negro passengers is not an answer to the requirements of § 3 (1). Discriminations that operate to the disadvantage of two groups are not the less to be condemned because their impact is broader than if only one were affected. Cf. *Shelley* v. *Kraemer,* 334 U. S. 1, 22.

Since § 3 (1) of the Interstate Commerce Act invalidates the rules and practices before us, we do not reach the constitutional or other issues suggested.

The judgment of the District Court is reversed and the cause is remanded to that court with directions to set aside the order of the Interstate Commerce Commission which dismissed the original complaint and to remand the case to that Commission for further proceedings in conformity with this opinion.

It is so ordered.

MR. JUSTICE DOUGLAS concurs in the result.

MR. JUSTICE CLARK took no part in the consideration or decision of this case.

BROWN v. BOARD OF EDUCATION OF TOPEKA
[Brown I]
Supreme Court of the United States (1954)
347 U.S. 483

MR. CHIEF JUSTICE WARREN. These cases come to us from the States of Kansas, South Carolina, Virginia, and Delaware. They are premised on different facts and different local conditions, but a common legal question justifies their consideration together in this consolidated opinion.

In each of the cases, minors of the Negro race, through their legal representatives, seek the aid of the courts in obtaining admission to the public schools of their community on a nonsegregated basis. In each instance they had been denied admission to schools attended by white children under laws requiring or permitting segregation according to race. This segregation was alleged to deprive the plaintiffs of the equal protection of the laws under the Fourteenth Amendment. In each of the cases other than the Delaware case, a three-judge federal district court denied relief to the plaintiffs on the so-called "separate but equal" doctrine announced by this Court in *Plessy v. Ferguson.* Under that doctrine, equality of treatment is accorded when the races are provided substantially equal facilities, even though these facilities be separate. In the Delaware case, the Supreme Court of Delaware adhered to that doctrine, but ordered that the plaintiffs be admitted to the white schools because of their superiority to the Negro schools.

The plaintiffs contend that segregated public schools are not "equal" and cannot be made "equal," and that hence they are deprived of the equal protection of the laws. Because of the obvious importance of the question presented, the Court took jurisdiction. Argument was heard in the 1952 Term, and reargument was heard this Term on certain questions propounded by the Court.

Reargument was largely devoted to the circumstances surrounding the adoption of the Fourteenth Amendment in 1868. It covered exhaustively consideration of the Amendment in Congress, ratification by the states, then existing practices in racial segregation, and the views of proponents and opponents of the Amendment. This discussion and our own investigation convince us that, although these sources cast some light, it is not enough to resolve the problem with which we are faced. At best, they are inconclusive. The most avid proponents of the post-War Amendments undoubtedly intended them to remove all legal distinctions among "all persons born or naturalized in the United States." Their opponents, just as certainly, were antagonistic to both the letter and the spirit of the Amendments and wished them to have the most limited effect. What others in Congress and the state legislatures had in mind cannot be determined with any degree of certainty.

An additional reason for the inconclusive nature of the Amendment's history, with respect to segregated schools, is the status of public education at that time. In the South, the movement toward free common schools, supported by general taxation, had not yet taken hold. Education of white children was largely in the hands of private groups. Education of Negroes was almost nonexistent, and practically all of the race were illiterate. In fact, any education of Negroes was forbidden by law in some states. Today, in contrast, many Negroes have achieved outstanding success in the arts and sciences as well as in the business and professional world. It is true that public school education at the time of the Amendment had advanced further in the North, but the effect of the Amendment on Northern States was generally ignored in the congressional debates. Even in the North, the conditions of public education did not approximate those existing today. The curriculum was usually rudimentary; ungraded schools were common in rural areas; the school term was but three months a year in many states; and compulsory school attendance was virtually unknown. As a consequence, it is not surprising that there should be so little in the history of the Fourteenth Amendment relating to its intended effect on public education.

In the first cases in this Court construing the Fourteenth Amendment, decided shortly after its adoption, the Court interpreted it as proscribing all state-imposed discriminations against the Negro race. The doctrine of "separate but equal" did not make its appearance in this Court until 1896 in the case of *Plessy v. Ferguson*, involving not education but transportation. American courts have since labored with the doctrine for over half a century. In this Court, there have been six cases involving the "separate but equal" doctrine in the field of public education. ... In none of these cases was it necessary to re-examine the doctrine to grant relief to the Negro plaintiff. And in *Sweatt v. Painter* the Court expressly reserved decision on the question whether Plessy v. Ferguson should be held inapplicable to public education.

In the instant cases, that question is directly presented. Here, unlike *Sweatt v. Painter*, there are findings below that the Negro and white schools involved have been equalized, or are being equalized, with respect to buildings, curricula, qualifications and salaries of teachers, and other "tangible" factors. Our decision, therefore, cannot turn on merely a comparison of these tangible factors in the Negro and white schools involved in each of the cases. We must look instead to the effect of segregation itself on public education.

In approaching this problem, we cannot turn the clock back to 1868 when the Amendment was adopted, or even to 1896 when *Plessy v. Ferguson* was written. We must consider public education in the light of its full development and its present place in American life throughout the Nation. Only in this way can it be determined if segregation in public schools deprives these plaintiffs of the equal protection of the laws.

Today, education is perhaps the most important function of state and local governments. Compulsory school attendance laws and the great expenditures for education both demonstrate our recognition of the importance of education to our democratic society. It is required in the performance of our most basic public responsibilities, even service in the armed forces. It is the very foundation of good citizenship. Today it is a principal instrument in awakening the child to cultural

values, in preparing him for later professional training, and in helping him to adjust normally to his environment. In these days, it is doubtful that any child may reasonably be expected to succeed in life if he is denied the opportunity of an education. Such an opportunity, where the state has undertaken to provide it, is a right which must be made available to all on equal terms.

We come then to the question presented: Does segregation of children in public schools solely on the basis of race, even though the physical facilities and other "tangible" factors may be equal, deprive the children of the minority group of equal educational opportunities? We believe that it does.

In *Sweatt v. Painter*, in finding that a segregated law school for Negroes could not provide them equal educational opportunities, this Court relied in large part on "those qualities which are incapable of objective measurement but which make for greatness in a law school." *In McLaurin v. Oklahoma State Regents* the Court, in requiring that a Negro admitted to a white graduate school be treated like all other students, again resorted to intangible considerations: "... his ability to study, to engage in discussions and exchange views with other students, and, in general, to learn his profession." Such considerations apply with added force to children in grade and high schools. To separate them from others of similar age and qualifications solely because of their race generates a feeling of inferiority as to their status in the community that may affect their hearts and minds in a way unlikely ever to be undone. The effect of this separation on their educational opportunities was well stated by a finding in the Kansas case by a court which nevertheless felt compelled to rule against the Negro plaintiffs:

> "Segregation of white and colored children in public schools has a detrimental effect upon the colored children. The impact is greater when it has the sanction of the law; for the policy of separating the races is usually interpreted as denoting the inferiority of the negro group. A sense of inferiority affects the motivation of a child to learn. Segregation with the sanction of law, therefore, has a tendency to [retard] the educational and mental development of negro children and to deprive them of some of the benefits they would receive in a racial[ly] integrated school system."

Whatever may have been the extent of psychological knowledge at the time of *Plessy v. Ferguson*, this finding is amply supported by modern authority.[1] Any language in *Plessy v. Ferguson* contrary to this finding is rejected.

We conclude that in the field of public education the doctrine of "separate but equal" has no place. Separate educational facilities are inherently unequal. Therefore, we hold that the plaintiffs and others similarly situated for whom the actions have been brought are, by reason of the segregation complained of, deprived of the equal protection of the laws guaranteed by the Fourteenth Amendment. This disposition makes unnecessary any discussion whether such segregation also violates the Due Process Clause of the Fourteenth Amendment.

Because these are class actions, because of the wide applicability of this decision, and because of the great variety of local conditions, the formulation of decrees in these cases presents problems of considerable complexity. On reargument, the consideration of appropriate relief was necessarily subordinated to the primary question—the constitutionality of segregation in education. We have now announced that such segregation is a denial of the equal protection of the laws. In order that we may have the full assistance of the parties in formulating decrees, the cases will be restored to the docket, and the parties are requested to present further argument on [remedies]. …

---

[1]K.B. Clark, Effect of Prejudice and Discrimination on Personality Development (Midcentury White House Conference on Children and Youth, 1950); Witmer and Kotinsky, Personality in the Making (1952), c. VI; Deutscher and Chein, The Psychological Effects of Enforced Segregation: A Survey of Social Science Opinion, 26 J. Psychol. 259 (1948); Chein, What are the Psychological Effects of Segregation Under Conditions of Equal Facilities?, 3 Int. J. Opinion and Attitude Res. 229 (1949); Brameld, Educational Costs, in Discrimination and National Welfare (MacIver, ed., 1949), 44–48; Frazier, The Negro in the United States (1949), 674–681. And see generally Myrdal, An American Dilemma (1944).

BOLLING v. SHARPE
Supreme Court of the United States (1954)
347 U.S. 497

MR. CHIEF JUSTICE WARREN. This case challenges the validity of segregation in the public schools of the District of Columbia. The petitioners, minors of the Negro race, allege that such segregation deprives them of due process of law under the Fifth Amendment. They were refused admission to a public school attended by white children solely because of their race. They sought the aid of the District Court for the District of Columbia in obtaining admission. That Court dismissed their complaint. The Court granted a writ of certiorari before judgment in the Court of Appeals because of the importance of the constitutional question presented.

We have this day held that the Equal Protection Clause of the Fourteenth Amendment prohibits the states from maintaining racially segregated public schools. The legal problem in the District of Columbia is somewhat different, however. The Fifth Amendment, which is applicable in the District of Columbia, does not contain an equal protection clause as does the Fourteenth Amendment which applies only to the states. But the concepts of equal protection and due process, both stemming from our American ideal of fairness, are not mutually exclusive. The "equal protection of the laws" is a more explicit safeguard of prohibited unfairness than "due process of law," and, therefore, we do not imply that the two are always interchangeable phrases. But, as this Court has recognized, discrimination may be so unjustifiable as to be violative of due process.

Classifications based solely upon race must be scrutinized with particular care, since they are contrary to our traditions and hence constitutionally suspect. As long ago as 1896, this Court declared the principle "that the Constitution of the United States, in its present form, forbids, so far as civil and political rights are concerned, discrimination by the General Government, or by the States, against any citizen because of his race." [*Gibson v. Mississippi*] And in *Buchanan v. Warley* the Court held that a statute which limited the right of a property owner to convey his property to a person of another race was, as an unreasonable discrimination, a denial of due process of law.

Although the Court has not assumed to define "liberty" with any great precision, that term is not confined to mere freedom from bodily restraint. Liberty under law extends to the full range of conduct which the individual is free to pursue, and it cannot be restricted except for a proper governmental objective. Segregation in public education is not reasonably related to any proper governmental objective, and thus it imposes on Negro children of the District of Columbia a burden that constitutes an arbitary deprivation of their liberty in violation of the Due Process Clause.

In view of our decision that the Constitution prohibits the states from maintaining racially segregated public schools, it would be unthinkable that the same Constitution would impose a lesser duty on the Federal Government. We hold that racial segregation in the public schools of the District of Columbia is a denial of the due process of law guaranteed by the Fifth Amendment to the Constitution. ...

BROWN v. BOARD OF EDUCATION
[BROWN II]
Supreme Court of the United States (1955)
349 U.S. 294

MR. CHIEF JUSTICE WARREN. These cases were decided on May 17, 1954. The opinions of that date, declaring the fundamental principle that racial discrimination in public education is unconstitutional, are incorporated herein by reference. All provisions of federal, state, or local law requiring or permitting such discrimination must yield to this principle. There remains for consideration the manner in which relief is to be accorded. ...

Full implementation of these constitutional principles may require solution of varied local school problems. School authorities have the primary responsibility for elucidating, assessing, and solving these problems; courts will have to consider whether the action of school authorities constitutes good faith implementation of the governing constitutional principles. Because of their proximity to local conditions and the possible need for further hearings, the courts which originally heard these cases can best perform this judicial appraisal. Accordingly, we believe it appropriate to remand the cases to those courts.

In fashioning and effectuating the decrees, the courts will be guided by equitable principles. Traditionally, equity has been characterized by a practical flexibility in shaping its remedies and by a facility for adjusting and reconciling public and private needs. These cases call for the exercise of these traditional attributes of equity power. At stake is the personal interest of the plaintiffs in admission to public schools as soon as practicable on a nondiscriminatory basis. To effectuate this interest may call for elimination of a variety of obstacles in making the transition to school systems operated in accordance with the constitutional principles set forth in our May 17, 1954, decision. Courts of equity may properly take into account the public interest in the elimination of such obstacles in a systematic and effective manner. But it should go without saying that the vitality of these constitutional principles cannot be allowed to yield simply because of disagreement with them.

While giving weight to these public and private considerations, the courts will require that the defendants make a prompt and reasonable start toward full compliance with our May 17, 1954, ruling. Once such a start has been made, the courts may find that additional time is necessary to carry out the ruling in an effective manner. The burden rests upon the defendants to establish that such time is necessary in the public interest and is consistent with good faith compliance at the earliest practicable date. To that end, the courts may consider problems related to administration, arising from the physical condition of the school plant, the school transportation system, personnel, revision of school districts and attendance areas into compact units to achieve a system of determining admission to the public schools on a nonracial basis, and revision of local laws and regulations which may be necessary in solving the foregoing problems. They will also consider the adequacy of any plans the defendants may propose to meet these problems and to effectuate a transition to a racially nondiscriminatory school system. During this period of transition, the courts will retain jurisdiction of these cases.

The judgments below ... are accordingly reversed and the cases are remanded to the District Courts to take such proceedings and enter such orders and decrees consistent with this opinion as are necessary and proper to admit to public schools on a racially nondiscriminatory basis with all deliberate speed the parties to these cases. ...

COOPER v. AARON
Supreme Court of the United States
358 U.S. 1; 78 S. Ct. 1401; 3 L. Ed. 2d (1958)

Thurgood Marshall argued the cause for respondents.

MR. JUSTICE WARREN: As this case reaches us it raises questions of the highest importance to the maintenance of our federal system of government. It ... involves a claim by the Governor and Legislature of a State that there is no duty on state officials to obey federal court orders resting on this Court's considered interpretation of the United States Constitution. Specifically it involves actions by the Governor and Legislature of Arkansas upon the premise that they are not bound by our holding in *Brown v. Board of Education.*

On May 17, 1954, this Court decided that enforced racial segregation in the public schools of a State is a denial of the equal protection of the laws enjoined by the Fourteenth Amendment. *Brown v. Board of Education.*

On May 20, 1954, three days after the first *Brown* opinion, the Little Rock District School Board adopted ... a statement of policy entitled "Supreme Court Decision—Segregation in Public Schools."

[The School Board] instructed the Superintendent of Schools to prepare a plan for desegregation, and approved such a plan on May 24, 1955, seven days before the second *Brown* opinion.

While the School Board was thus going forward with its preparation for desegregating the Little Rock school system, other state authorities, in contrast, were actively pursuing a program designed to perpetuate in Arkansas the system of racial segregation which this Court had held violated the Fourteenth Amendment. First came, in November 1956, an amendment to the State Constitution flatly commanding the Arkansas General Assembly to oppose "in every Constitutional manner the Unconstitutional desegregation decisions of May 17, 1954 and May 31, 1955 of the United States Supreme Court." ... Pursuant to this state constitutional command, a law

relieving school children from compulsory attendance at racially mixed schools ... [was] enacted by the General Assembly in February 1957.

The School Board and the Superintendent of Schools nevertheless continued with preparations to carry out the ... desegregation program. Nine Negro children were scheduled for admission in September 1957 to Central High School, which has more than two thousand students.

On September 2, 1957, the day before these Negro students were to enter Central High, the school authorities were met with drastic opposing action on the part of the Governor of Arkansas who dispatched units of the Arkansas National Guard to the Central High School grounds and placed the school "off limits" to colored students. [T]he Governor's action had not been requested by the school authorities, and was entirely unheralded.

The Board's petition ... in this proceeding states: "The effect of that action [of the Governor] was to harden the core of opposition to the Plan and cause many persons who theretofore had reluctantly accepted the Plan to believe there was some power in the State of Arkansas which, when exerted, could nullify the Federal law and permit disobedience of the decree of this [District] Court, and from that date hostility to the Plan was increased and criticism of the officials of the [School] District has become more bitter and unrestrained." The Governor's action caused the School Board to request the Negro students on September 2 not to attend the high school "until the legal dilemma was solved." The next day, September 3, 1957, the Board petitioned the District Court for instructions. ... The court ... ordered the School Board and Superintendent to proceed with ... [the Plan].

On the morning of the next day, September 4, 1957, the Negro children attempted to enter the high school but ... units of the Arkansas National Guard "acting pursuant to the Governor's order, stood shoulder to shoulder at the school grounds and thereby forcibly prevented the 9 Negro students ... from entering," as they continued to do every school day during the following three weeks.

[T]he District Court ... granted a preliminary injunction on September 20, 1957, enjoining the Governor and the officers of the Guard from preventing the attendance of Negro children at Central High School, and from otherwise obstructing or interfering with the orders of the court in connection with the plan. The National Guard was then withdrawn from the school.

The next school day was Monday, September 23, 1957. The Negro children entered the high school that morning under the protection of the Little Rock Police Department and members of the Arkansas State Police. But the officers caused the children to be removed from the school during the morning because they had difficulty controlling a large and demonstrating crowd which had gathered at the high school. On September 25, however, the President of the United States dispatched federal troops to Central High School and admission of the Negro students to the school was thereby effected. Regular army troops continued at the high school until November 27, 1957. They were then replaced by federalized National Guardsmen who remained throughout the balance of the school year. Eight of the Negro students remained in attendance at the school throughout the school year.

We come now to the aspect of the proceedings presently before us. On February 20, 1958, the School Board and the Superintendent of Schools filed a petition in the District Court seeking a postponement of their program for desegregation. Their position in essence was that because of extreme public hostility, which they stated had been engendered largely by the official attitudes and actions of the Governor and the Legislature, the maintenance of a sound educational program at Central High School, with the Negro students in attendance, would be impossible. The Board therefore proposed that the Negro students already admitted to the school be withdrawn and sent to segregated schools, and that all further steps to carry out the Board's desegregation program be postponed for ... two and one-half years.

[T]he District Court granted the relief requested by the Board. Among other things the court found that the past year at Central High School had been attended by conditions of "chaos, bedlam and turmoil"; that there

were "repeated incidents of more or less serious violence directed against the Negro students and their property"; that there was "tension and unrest among the school administrators, the class-room teachers, the pupils, and the latters' parents, which inevitably had an adverse effect upon the educational program"; that a school official was threatened with violence; that a "serious financial burden" had been cast on the School District; that the education of the students had suffered "and under existing conditions will continue to suffer"; that the Board would continue to need "military assistance or its equivalent"; that the local police department would not be able "to detail enough men to afford the necessary protection"; and that the situation was "intolerable."

The Court of Appeals ... reversed the District Court....

[T]he conditions [at Central High School] ... are directly traceable to the actions of legislators and executive officials of the State of Arkansas, taken in their official capacities, which reflect their own determination to resist this Court's decision in the *Brown* case and which have brought about violent resistance to that decision in Arkansas. [T]he School Board itself describes the situation in this language: "The legislative, executive, and judicial departments of the state government opposed the desegregation of Little Rock schools by enacting laws, calling out troops, making statements villifying federal law and federal courts, and failing to utilize state law enforcement agencies and judicial processes to maintain public peace."

The constitutional rights of respondents are not to be sacrificed or yielded to the violence and disorder which have followed upon the actions of the Governor and Legislature. *** Thus law and order are not here to be preserved by depriving the Negro children of their constitutional rights.

The controlling legal principles are plain. The command of the Fourteenth Amendment is that no "State" shall deny to any person within its jurisdiction the equal protection of the laws. "A State acts by its legislative, its executive, or its judicial authorities. ***" In short, the constitutional rights of children not to be discriminated against in school admission on grounds of races or color declared by this Court in the *Brown* case can neither be nullified openly and directly by state legislators or state executive or judicial officers, nor nullified indirectly by them through evasive schemes for segregation whether attempted "ingeniously or ingenuously."

Article VI of the Constitution makes the Constitution the "supreme Law of the Land." In 1803, Chief Justice Marshall ... declared in the notable case of

Marbury v. Madison that "It is emphatically the province and duty of the judicial department to say what the law is." This decision declared the basic principle that the federal judiciary is supreme in the exposition of the law of the Constitution, and that principle has ever since been respected by this Court and the Country as a permanent and indispensable feature of our constitutional system. It follows that the interpretation of the Fourteenth Amendment enunciated by this Court in the *Brown* case is the supreme law of the land, and Art. VI of the Constitution makes it of binding effect on the States "any Thing in the Constitution or Laws of any State to the Contrary notwithstanding." Every state legislator and executive and judicial officer is solemnly committed by oath taken pursuant to Art. VI, cl. 3, "to support this Constitution."

No state legislator or executive or judicial officer can war against the Constitution without violating his undertaking to support it. *** A Governor who asserts a power to nullify a federal court order is similarly restrained. If he had such power, said Chief Justice Hughes, in 1932, ... "it is manifest that the fiat of a state Governor, and not the Constitution of the United States, would be the supreme law of the land; that the restrictions of the Federal Constitution upon the exercise of state power would be but impotent phrases. ..."

It is, of course, quite true that the responsibility for public education is primarily the concern of the States, but it is equally true that such responsibilities, like all other state activity, must be exercised consistently with federal constitutional requirements as they apply to state action. *** State support of segregated schools through any arrangement, management, funds, or property cannot be squared with the [Fourteenth] Amendment's command that no State shall deny to any person within its jurisdiction the equal protection of the laws.

POINDEXTER v. LOUISIANA FINANCIAL ASSISTANCE COMMISSION
U.S. District Court for the Eastern District of Louisiana
275 F. Supp. 833 (1967)

WISDOM, J. This class action by Negro schoolchildren and their parents against the Louisiana Financial Assistance Commission and others attacks the constitutionality of Act 147 of 1962. Under that law the Commission administers a program of tuition grants to pupils attending private schools in Louisiana.

The free lunches and textbooks Louisiana provides for all its school children are the fruits of racially neutral benevolence. Tution grants are not the products of such a policy. They are the fruits of the State's traditional racially biased policy of providing segregated schools for white pupils. Here that policy has pushed the State to the extreme of using public funds to aid private discrimination endangering the public school system and equal educational opportunities for Negroes in Louisiana.

As certainly as "12" is the next number of a series starting 2, 4, 6, 8, 10, Act 147 fitted into the long series of statutes the Louisiana legislature enacted for over a hundred years to maintain segregated schools for white children. After the Supreme Court's 1954 decision in the School Segregation Cases, the legislature rapidly expanded the series. As fast as the courts knocked out one school law, the legislature enacted another. Each of these laws, whether its objective was obvious or nonobvious, was designed to provide a state-supported sanctuary for white children in flight from desegregated public schools.

In 1954, a few months after the Supreme Court decided the first Brown case desegregating public schools, Louisiana amended Article XII, Section 1 of the Constitution of 1921. This amendment expressed the state policy on segregated schools:

"All public elementary and secondary schools in the State of Louisiana shall be operated separately for white and colored children. ***"

The Legislature promptly enacted Acts No. 555 and 556 of 1954. Act 555 carried out the constitutional requirement of separate schools and provided penalties for failing to observe it. *** In February 1956 this Court held that both the amendment to Article XII Section 1 and the two statutes were invalid ...

The Louisiana Legislature immediately enacted a new package of laws. Act 319 of 1956 purported to "freeze" the existing racial status of the public schools in Orleans Parish and to reserve to the legislature the power of racial reclassification of the schools. The Court declared this "legal artifice" unconstitutional on its face.

In 1958 the legislature enacted another bundle of school laws. Professor Charles A. Reynard of Louisiana State University has described these as follows:

Adhering to its steadfast course of circumventing the Supreme Court's decisions forbidding the enforced segregation of the races in public education, the Legislature took steps to provide for the closing of public schools threatened with desegregation and authorized a system of publicly financed private education in lieu thereof.

Act 257 provided in detail for the establishment of educational cooperatives. Act 258 established the first Louisiana system of grants-in-aid for "children attending non-sectartian non-public schools". Its purpose was obvious: The aid was conditioned on there being "no racially separated public school" in the parish. The grant system was to be administered jointly by the State Board of Education and the parish or city school boards.

By 1959 it was apparent to all that the Orleans Parish School Board could not ... carry out the Court's order of February 15, 1956, requiring it to desegregate public schools in New Orleans. *** The Court, on May 16, 1960, entered an order setting forth a plan of desegregation for the Orleans Parish School Board to follow.

The Louisiana Legislature promptly built additional barricades. Act 333 of 1960 prohibited the furnishing of free books, school supplies, school funds or assistance to integrated schools. Act 495 authorized the Governor to close integrated schools. Act 496 purported to "freeze" the racial classification of public schools and reserve to the Legislature the power to change this classification. Act 542 authorized the Governor to close the public schools in case of riots and disorder.

The tempo of resistance increased. July 29, 1960, the Attorney General of Louisiana obtained an injunction in the state courts restraining the Orleans Parish School Board from desegregating its schools. August 17, 1960, the Governor of Louisiana, acting under Act 495 of 1960, took over control of the Orleans public schools. August 27, 1960, a three-judge district court struck down these actions along with Acts 333, 495, 496, and 542 of 1960, Act 555 of 1964, Act 319 of 1956, and Act 256 of 1958.

At this point, the Orleans School Board conferred with the district court. In public session the Board ... announced its intention to comply with the Court's orders.

The Board's compliance brought on five extraordinary sessions of the legislature within four months. Among other actions, the Legislature seized the funds of the Orleans Parish School Board; forbade banks to lend money to this Board; removed as fiscal agent for the state the Bank which honored payroll checks issued by the Orleans Board; ordered a school holiday on November 14, 1960; discharged four of the five Orleans Board members; later repealed the Act creating the Board, then twice created a new School Board for Orleans Parish; and still later discharged the Superintendent, dismissed the Board's attorney, and attempted to require that the State Attorney General be counsel for the Board. The courts declared these and other related acts unconstitutional.

In 1961 the Court of Appeals for the Fifth Circuit affirmed orders requiring the desegregation of public schools in East Baton Rouge and St. Helena Parishes. On the same day the Governor of Louisiana called the Second Extraordinary Session of the Legislature for 1961. *** [Act 2] gave each parish or municipal school board the "option" to close its schools if a majority of the qualified voters in the parish or municipality voted in favor of such action. The school board was then authorized to dispose of its property for such consideration as it deemed appropriate. Act 257 of 1958 had created educational cooperatives which could acquire the property and then operate schools with the state money furnished by the

grant-in-aid program provided for in Act 3 of the Second Extraordinary Session of 1960.

[H]olding the grants in aid unconstitutional, the Court stated: Under Act 3 *** the parish school boards would continue to supervise the "private" schools, under the State Board of Education, by administering the grant-in-aid program of tuition grants payable from state and local funds. ***

This brings us to the 1962 session. First, the legislature repealed outright the state's compulsory school attendance law, Act 128. Act 342 of 1962 appropriated funds for the schools of St. Bernard Parish to compensate for expenses incurred in providing facilities for pupils who were not residents of St. Bernard; most of these were white students who had left the desegregated schools in neighboring Orleans Parish. Act 67 of 1962 purported to restrict the right to sue parish school boards, except by authorization of the Legislature.

This was the background and setting when the Louisiana Legislature enacted the statute under attack in this case.

Thus, for a hundred years, the Louisiana legislature has not deviated from its objective of maintaining segregated schools for white children. Ten years after Brown, declared policy became undeclared policy. Open legislative defiance of desegregation orders shifted to subtle forms of circumvention—although some prominent sponsors of grant-in-aid legislation have been less than subtle in their public expression. But the changes in means reflect no change in legislative ends.

The inevitable effect of the tuition grants was the establishment and maintenance of a state-supported system of segregated schools for white children, making the state a party to organized private discrimination.

The tuition grants authorized under the Act provided the funds indispensable to establishing newly organized private segregated schools for white children. The tuition grants continue to furnish almost all of the funds needed for maintaining these post-Brown schools. *** The tuition grants damage Negroes by draining students, teachers, and funds from the desegregated public school system into a competitive, segregated "quasi-public" school system. The stamp of State approval of "white" schools perpetuates the open humiliation of the Negro implicit in segregated education.

The payment of public funds in any amount through a state commission under authority of a state law is undeniably state action. The question is whether such action in aid of private discrimination violates the equal protection clause.

The criterion is whether the state is so significantly involved in the private discrimination as to render the state action and the private action violative of the equal protection clause.

The constitutional odium of official approval of race discrimination has no necessary relation to the extent of the State's financial support of a discriminatory institution. Any aid to segregated schools that is the product of the State's affirmative, purposeful policy of fostering segregated schools and has the effect of encouraging discrimination is significant state involvement in private discrimination.

Griffin, one of the cases handed down with Brown in 1954, concerned the public schools in Prince Edward County, Virginia. In 1964 the Supreme Court held that the Virginia statute providing tuition grants, when coupled with closing of the public schools, denied Negroes an integrated education. "The same reasoning applies when the grants alone deny Negroes an integrated public education by assisting whites to flee to private schools. It is impossible to set a standard as to the number of whites who may leave before the schools become segregated, but state-encouraged departure of any whites tends to create segregation, and it would seem that any state support of segregation violates the equal protection clause." This conclusion is consistent with the principle expressed in *Cooper v. Aaron* that

State support of segregated schools "through any arrangement, management, funds, or property cannot be squared with the [Fourteenth] Amendment."

The system of private segregated schools the State created and nourishes through Act 147 is in a nascent stage. Its tangible and intangible costs to the State thus far are but a drop in the bucket compared with its future costs—should the courts bless the nourishment the private schools receive from the State. The facts this case presents point in only one direction: Unless this system is destroyed, it will shatter to bits the public school system of Louisiana and kill the hope that now exists for equal educational opportunities for all our citizens, white and black.

We hold that the purpose and natural or reasonable effect of Act 147 of 1962 render it unconstitutional on its face. The law was designed to establish and maintain a system of segregated schools. We hold also that Act 147 of 1962 is unconstitutional in its actual effect. The State has predominantly supplied the financial means necessary to establish and maintain the post-1962 private schools and most of the post-1954 private schools in Louisiana. The State is so significantly involved in the discrimination practiced by the private schools in Louisiana that any financial aid from the State to these schools or newly organized schools in the form of tuition grants or similar benefits violates the equal protection clause of the Fourteenth Amendment.

88 S.Ct. 1689
Supreme Court of the United States
Charles C. GREEN et al. v. COUNTY SCHOOL BOARD OF
NEW KENT COUNTY, VIRGINIA et al.
No. 695.

Argued April 3, 1968. Decided May 27, 1968.

OPINION

Mr. Justice BRENNAN delivered the opinion of the Court.

The question for decision is whether, under all the circumstances here, respondent School Board's adoption of a 'freedom-of-choice' plan which allows a pupil to choose his own public school constitutes adequate compliance with the Board's responsibility 'to achieve a system of determining admission to the public schools on a non-racial basis * * *.' Brown v. Board of Education (Brown II).

Petitioners brought this action in March 1965 seeking injunctive relief against respondent's continued maintenance of an alleged racially segregated school system. New Kent County is a rural county in Eastern Virginia. About one-half of its population of some 4,500 are Negroes. There is no residential segregation in the county; persons of both races reside throughout. The school system has only two schools, the New Kent school on the east side of the county and the George W. Watkins school on the west side. In a memorandum filed May 17, 1966, the District Court found that the 'school system serves approximately 1,300 pupils, of which 740 are Negro and 550 are White. The School Board operates one white combined elementary and high school (New Kent), and one Negro combined elementary and high school (George W. Watkins). There are no attendance zones. Each school serves the entire county.' The record indicates that 21 school buses—11 serving the Watkins school and 10 serving the New Kent school—travel overlapping routes throughout the county to transport pupils to and from the two schools.

The segregated system was initially established and maintained under the compulsion of Virginia constitutional and statutory provisions mandating racial segregation in public education. These provisions were held to violate the Federal Constitution in Davis v. County School Board of Prince Edward County, decided with Brown v. Board of Education of Topeka,(Brown I). The respondent School Board continued the segregated operation of the system after the Brown decisions, presumably on the authority of several statutes enacted by Virginia in resistance to those decisions. Some of these statutes were held to be unconstitutional on their face or as applied. One statute, the Pupil Placement Act, not repealed until 1966, divested local boards of authority to assign children to particular schools and placed that authority in a State Pupil Placement Board. Under that Act children were each year automatically reassigned to the school previously attended unless upon their application the State Board assigned them to another school; students seeking enrollment for the first time were also assigned at the discretion of the State Board. To September 1964, no Negro pupil had applied for admission to the New Kent school under this statute and no white pupil had applied for admission to the Watkins school.

The School Board initially sought dismissal of this suit on the ground that petitioners had failed to apply to the State Board for assignment to New Kent school. However on August 2, 1965, five months after the suit was brought, respondent School Board, in order to remain eligible for federal financial aid, adopted a 'freedom-of-choice' plan for desegregating the schools. Under that plan, each pupil, except those entering the first and eighth grades, may annually choose between the New Kent and Watkins schools and pupils not making a choice are assigned to the school previously attended; first and eighth grade pupils must affirmatively choose a school. After the plan was filed the District Court denied petitioners' prayer for an injunction and granted respondent leave to submit an amendment to the plan with respect to employment and assignment of teachers and staff on a racially nondiscriminatory basis. The amendment was duly filed and on June 28, 1966, the District Court approved the 'freedom-of-choice' plan as so amended. The Court of Appeals for the Fourth Circuit, en banc, affirmed the District Court's approval of the 'freedom-of-choice' provisions of the plan but remanded the case to the District Court for entry of an order regarding faculty 'which is much more specific and more comprehensive' and which would incorporate in addition to a 'minimal, objective time table' some of the faculty provisions of the decree entered by the Court of Appeals for the Fifth Circuit in United States v. Jefferson County Board of Education. Judges Sobeloff and Winter concurred with the remand on the teacher issue but otherwise disagreed, expressing the view 'that the District Court should be directed * * * also to set up procedures for periodically evaluating the effectiveness of the (Board's) 'freedom of choice' (plan) in the elimination of other features of a segregated school system.'

The pattern of separate 'white' and 'Negro' schools in the New Kent County school system established under compulsion of state laws is precisely the pattern of segregation to which Brown I and Brown II were particularly addressed, and which Brown I declared unconstitutionally denied Negro school children equal protection of the laws. Racial identification of the system's schools was complete, extending not just to the composition of student bodies at the two schools but to every facet of school operations—faculty, staff, transportation, extracurricular activities and facilities. In short, the State, acting through the local school board and school officials, organized and operated a dual system, part 'white' and part 'Negro.'

It was such dual systems that 14 years ago Brown I held unconstitutional and a year later Brown II held must be abolished; school boards operating such school systems were required by Brown II 'to effectuate a transition to a racially nondiscriminatory school system.' It is of course true that for the time immediately after Brown II the concern was with making an initial break in a long-established pattern of excluding Negro children from schools attended by white children. The principal focus was on obtaining for those Negro children courageous enough to break with tradition a place in the 'white' schools. See, e.g., Under Brown II that immediate goal was only the first step, however. The transition to a unitary, nonracial system of public education was and is the ultimate end to be brought about; it was because of the 'complexities arising from the transition to a system of public education freed of racial discrimination' that we provided for 'all deliberate speed' in the implementation of the principles of Brown I. Thus we recognized the task would necessarily involve solution of 'varied local school problems.' In referring to the 'personal interest of the plaintiffs in admission to public schools as soon as

practicable on a nondiscriminatory basis,' we also noted that '(t)o effectuate this interest may call for elimination of a variety of obstacles in making the transition * * *.' Yet we emphasized that the constitutional rights of Negro children required school officials to bear the burden of establishing that additional time to carry out the ruling in an effective manner 'is necessary in the public interest and is consistent with good faith compliance at the earliest practicable date.' We charged the district courts in their review of particular situations to consider problems related to administration, arising from the physical condition of the school plant, the school transportation system, personnel, revision of school districts and attendance areas into compact units to achieve a system of determining admission to the public schools on a nonracial basis, and revision of local laws and regulations which may be necessary in solving the foregoing problems. They will also consider the adequacy of any plans the defendants may propose to meet these problems and to effectuate a transition to a racially nondiscriminatory school system.'.

It is against this background that 13 years after Brown II commanded the abolition of dual systems we must measure the effectiveness of respondent School Board's 'freedom-of-choice' plan to achieve that end. The School Board contends that it has fully discharged its obligation by adopting a plan by which every student, regardless of race, may 'freely' choose the school he will attend. The Board attempts to cast the issue in its broadest form by arguing that its 'freedom-of-choice' plan may be faulted only by reading the Fourteenth Amendment as universally requiring 'compulsory integration,' a reading it insists the wording of the Amendment will not support. But that argument ignores the thrust of Brown II. In the light of the command of that case, what is involved here is the question whether the Board has achieved the 'racially nondiscriminatory school system' Brown II held must be effectuated in order to remedy the established unconstitutional deficiencies of its segregated system. In the context of the state-imposed segregated pattern of long standing, the fact that in 1965 the Board opened the doors of the former 'white' school to Negro children and of the 'Negro' school to white children merely begins, not ends, our inquiry whether the Board has taken steps adequate to abolish its dual, segregated system. Brown II was a call for the dismantling of well-entrenched dual systems tempered by an awareness that complex and multifaceted problems would arise which would require time and flexibility for a successful resolution. School boards such as the respondent then operating state-compelled dual systems were nevertheless clearly charged with the affirmative duty to take whatever steps might be necessary to convert to a unitary system in which racial discrimination would be eliminated root and branch. The constitutional rights of Negro school children articulated in Brown I permit no less than this; and it was to this end that Brown II commanded school boards to bend their efforts.

In determining whether respondent School Board met that command by adopting its 'freedom-of-choice' plan, it is relevant that this first step did not come until some 11 years after Brown I was decided and 10 years after Brown II directed the making of a 'prompt and reasonable start.' This deliberate perpetuation of the unconstitutional dual system can only have compounded the harm of such a system. Such delays are no longer tolerable, for 'the governing constitutional principles no longer bear the imprint of newly enunciated doctrine.' Moreover, a plan that at this late date fails to provide meaningful assurance of prompt and effective disestablishment of a dual system is also intolerable. 'The time for mere 'deliberate speed' has run out,' 'the context in which we must interpret and apply this language (of Brown II) to plans for desegregation has been significantly altered.' The burden on a school board today is to come forward with a plan that promises realistically to work, and promises realistically to work now.

The obligation of the district courts, as it always has been, is to assess the effectiveness of a proposed plan in achieving desegregation. There is no universal answer to complex problems of desegregation; there is obviously no one plan that will do the job in every case. The matter must be assessed in light of the circumstances present and the options available in each instance. It is incumbent upon the school board to establish that its proposed plan promises meaningful and immediate progress toward disestablishing state-imposed segregation. It is incumbent upon the district court to weigh that claim in light of the facts at hand and in light of any alternatives which may be shown as feasible and more promising in their effectiveness. Where the court finds the board to be acting in good faith and the proposed plan to have real prospects for dismantling the state-imposed dual system 'at the earliest practicable date,' then the plan may be said to provide effective relief. Of course, the availability to the board of other more promising courses of action may indicate a lack of good faith; and at the least it places a heavy burden upon the board to explain its preference for an apparently less effective method. Moreover, whatever plan is adopted will require evaluation in practice, and the court should retain jurisdiction until it is clear that state-imposed segregation has been completely removed.

We do not hold that 'freedom of choice' can have no place in such a plan. We do not hold that a 'freedom-of-choice' plan might of itself be unconstitutional, although that argument has been urged upon us. Rather, all we decide today is that in desegregating a dual system a plan utilizing 'freedom of choice' is not an end in itself. As Judge Sobeloff has put it,

> "Freedom of choice' is not a sacred talisman; it is only a means to a constitutionally required end—the abolition of the system of segregation and its effects. If the means prove effective, it is acceptable, but if it fails to undo segregation, other means must be used to achieve this end. The school officials have the continuing duty to take whatever action may be necessary to create a 'unitary, nonracial system."

Although the general experience under 'freedom of choice' to date has been such as to indicate its ineffectiveness as a tool of desegregation, there may well be instances in which it can serve as an effective device. Where it offers real promise of aiding a desegregation program to effectuate conversion of a state-imposed dual system to a unitary, non-racial system there might be no objection to allowing such a device to prove itself in operation. On the other hand, if there are reasonably available other ways, such for illustration as zoning, promising speedier and more effective conversion to a unitary, nonracial school system, 'freedom of choice' must be held unacceptable.

The New Kent School Board's 'freedom-of-choice' plan cannot be accepted as a sufficient step to 'effectuate a transition' to a unitary system. In three years of operation not a single white child has chosen to attend Watkins school and although 115 Negro children enrolled in New Kent school in 1967 (up from 35 in 1965 and 111 in 1966) 85% of the Negro children in the system still attend the all-Negro Watkins school. In other words, the school system remains a dual system. Rather than further the dismantling of the dual system, the plan has operated simply to burden children and their parents with a responsibility which Brown II placed squarely on the School Board. The Board must be required to formulate a new plan and, in light of other courses which appear open to the Board, such as zoning, fashion steps which promise realistically to convert promptly to a system without a 'white' school and a 'Negro' school, but just schools.

The judgment of the Court of Appeals is vacated insofar as it affirmed the District Court and the case is remanded to the District Court for further proceedings consistent with this opinion. It is so ordered.

```
┌─────────────────────────────────────────────────────┐
│                  91 S.Ct. 1267                      │
│        Supreme Court of the United States            │
│      James E. SWANN et al., Petitioners,             │
│  v. CHARLOTTE-MECKLENBURG BOARD OF EDUCATION et al.  │
│ CHARLOTTE-MECKLENBURG BOARD OF EDUCATION et al.,     │
│                    Petitioners,                      │
│            v. James E. SWANN et al.                  │
│                 Nos. 281, 349.                       │
│ Argued Oct. 12, 1970. Decided April 20, 1971.        │
│         Rehearing Denied June 7, 1971.               │
└─────────────────────────────────────────────────────┘
```

OPINION

Mr. Chief Justice BURGER delivered the opinion for a unanimous Court.

We granted certiorari in this case to review important issues as to the duties of school authorities and the scope of powers of federal courts under this Court's mandates to eliminate racially separate public schools established and maintained by state action. (Brown I).

This case and those argued with it arose in States having a long history of maintaining two sets of schools in a single school system deliberately operated to carry out a governmental policy to separate pupils in schools solely on the basis of race. That was what Brown v. Board of Education was all about. These cases present us with the problem of defining in more precise terms than heretofore the scope of the duty of school authorities and district courts in implementing Brown I and the mandate to eliminate dual systems and establish unitary systems at once. Meanwhile district courts and courts of appeals have struggled in hundreds of cases with a multitude and variety of problems under this Court's general directive. Understandably, in an area of evolving remedies, those courts had to improvise and experiment without detailed or specific guidelines. This Court, in Brown I, appropriately dealt with the large constitutional principles; other federal courts had to grapple with the flinty, intractable realities of day-to-day implementation of those constitutional commands. Their efforts, of necessity, embraced a process of 'trial and error,' and our effort to formulate guidelines must take into account their experience.

I

The Charlotte-Mecklenburg school system, the 43d largest in the Nation, encompasses the city of Charlotte and surrounding Mecklenburg County, North Carolina. The area is large—550 square miles—spanning roughly 22 miles east-west and 36 miles north-south. During the 1968—1969 school year the system served more than 84,000 pupils in 107 schools. Approximately 71% of the pupils were found to be white and 29% Negro. As of June 1969 there were approximately 24,000 Negro students in the system, of whom 21,000 attended schools within the city of Charlotte. Two-thirds of those 21,000—approximately 14,000 Negro students—attended 21 schools which were either totally Negro or more than 99% Negro.

This situation came about under a desegregation plan approved by the District Court at the commencement of the present litigation in 1965, based upon geographic zoning with a free-transfer provision. The present proceedings were initiated in September 1968 by petitioner Swann's motion for further relief based on and its companion cases. All parties now agree that in 1969 the system fell short of achieving the unitary school system that those cases require.

The District Court held numerous hearings and received voluminous evidence. In addition to finding certain actions of the school board to be discriminatory, the court also found that residential patterns in the city and county resulted in part from federal, state, and local government action other than school board decisions. School board action based on these patterns, for example, by locating schools in Negro residential areas and fixing the size of the schools to accommodate the needs of immediate neighborhoods, resulted in segregated education. These findings were subsequently accepted by the Court of Appeals.

In April 1969 the District Court ordered the school board to come forward with a plan for both faculty and student desegregation. Proposed plans were accepted by the court in June and August 1969 on an interim basis only, and the board was ordered to file a third plan by November 1969. In November the board moved for an extension of time until February 1970, but when that was denied the board submitted a partially completed plan. In December 1969 the District Court held that the board's submission was unacceptable and appointed an expert in education administration, ***

II

Nearly 17 years ago this Court held, in explicit terms, that state-imposed segregation by race in public schools denies equal protection of the laws. At no time has the Court deviated in the slightest degree from that holding or its constitutional underpinnings. None of the parties before us challenges the Court's decision of May 17, 1954, that 'in the field of public education the doctrine of 'separate but equal' has no place. Separate educational facilities are inherently unqual. Therefore, we hold that the plaintiffs and others similarly situated * * * are, by reason of the segregation complained of, deprived of the equal protection of the laws guaranteed by the Fourteenth Amendment. * * *

'Because these are class actions, because of the wide applicability of this decision, and because of the great variety of local conditions, the formulation of decrees in these cases presents problems of considerable complexity.'

*****

Over the 16 years since Brown II, many difficulties were encountered in implementation of the basic constitutional requirement that the State not discriminate between public school children on the basis of their race. Nothing in our national experience prior to 1955 prepared anyone for dealing with changes and adjustments of the magnitude and complexity encountered since then. Deliberate resistance of some to the Court's mandates has impeded the good-faith efforts of others to bring school systems into compliance. The detail and nature of these dilatory tactics have been noted frequently by this Court and other courts.

By the time the Court considered Green v. County School Board, in 1968, very little progress had been made in many areas where dual school systems had historically been maintained by operation of state laws. In Green, the Court was confronted with a record of a freedom-of-choice program that the District Court had found to operate in fact to preserve a dual system more than a decade after Brown II. While acknowledging that a freedom-of-choice concept could be a valid remedial measure in some circumstances, its failure to be effective in Green required that:

'The burden on a school board today is to come forward with a plan that promises realistically to work now * * * until it is clear that state imposed segregation has been completely removed.'

*****

III

The objective today remains to eliminate from the public schools all vestiges of state-imposed segregation. Segregation was the evil struck down by Brown I as contrary to the equal protection guarantees of the Constitution. That was the violation sought to be corrected by the remedial measures of Brown II. That was the basis for the holding in Green that school authorities are 'clearly charged with the affirmative duty to take whatever steps might be necessary to convert to a unitary system in which racial discrimination would be eliminated root and branch.'

If school authorities fail in their affirmative obligations under these holdings, judicial authority may be invoked. Once a right and a violation have been shown, the scope of a district court's equitable powers to remedy past wrongs is broad, for breadth and flexibility are inherent in equitable remedies.

'The essence of equity jurisdiction has been the power of the Chancellor to do equity and to mould each decree to the necessities of the particular case. Flexibility rather than rigidity has distinguished it. The qualities of mercy and practicality have made equity the instrument for nice adjustment and reconciliation between the public interest and private needs as well as between competing private claims.'

This allocation of responsibility once made, the Court attempted from time to time to provide some guidelines for the exercise of the district judge's discretion and for the reviewing function of the courts of appeals. However, a school desegregation case does not differ fundamentally from other cases involving the framing of equitable remedies to repair the denial of a constitutional right. The task is to correct, by a balancing of the individual and collective interests, the condition that offends the Constitution.

In seeking to define even in broad and general terms how far this remedial power extends it is important to remember that judicial powers may be exercised only on the basis of a constitutional violation. Remedial judicial authority does not put judges automatically in the shoes of school authorities whose powers are plenary. Judicial authority enters only when local authority defaults.

School authorities are traditionally charged with broad power to formulate and implement educational policy and might well conclude, for example, that in order to prepare students to live in a pluralistic society each school should have a prescribed ratio of Negro to white students reflecting the proportion for the district as a whole. To do this as an educational policy is within the broad discretionary powers of school authorities; absent a finding of a constitutional violation, however, that would not be within the authority of a federal court. As with any equity case, the nature of the violation determines the scope of the remedy. In default by the school authorities of their obligation to proffer acceptable remedies, a district court has broad power to fashion a remedy that will assure a unitary school system.

****

IV

We turn now to the problem of defining with more particularity the responsibilities of school authorities in desegregating a state-enforced dual school system in light of the Equal Protection Clause. ****

When a system has been dual in these respects, the first remedial responsibility of school authorities is to eliminate invidious racial distinctions. With respect to such matters as transportation, supporting personnel, and extracurricular activities, no more than this may be necessary. Similar corrective action must be taken with regard to the maintenance of buildings and the distribution of equipment. In these areas, normal administrative practice should produce schools of like quality, facilities, and staffs. Something more must be said, however, as to faculty assignment and new school construction.

****

The construction of new schools and the closing of old ones are two of the most important functions of local school authorities and also two of the most complex. They must decide questions of location and capacity in light of population growth, finances, land values, site availability, through an almost endless list of factors to be considered. The result of this will be a decision which, when combined with one technique or another of student assignment, will determine the racial composition of the student body in each school in the system. Over the long run, the consequences of the choices will be far reaching. People gravitate toward school facilities, just as schools are located in response to the needs of people. The location of schools may thus influence the patterns of residential development of a metropolitan area and have important impact on composition of inner-city neighborhoods.

In the past, choices in this respect have been used as a potent weapon for creating or maintaining a state-segregated school system. In addition to the classic pattern of building schools specifically intended for Negro or white students, school authorities have sometimes, since Brown, closed schools which appeared likely to become racially mixed through changes in neighborhood residential patterns. This was sometimes accompanied by building new schools in the areas of white suburban expansion farthest from Negro population centers in order to maintain the separation of the races with a minimum departure from the formal principles of 'neighborhood zoning.' Such a policy does more than simply influence the short-run composition of the student body of a new school. It may well promote segregated residential patterns which, when combined with 'neighborhood zoning,' further lock the school system into the mold of separation of the races. Upon a proper showing a district court may consider this in fashioning a remedy.

In ascertaining the existence of legally imposed school segregation, the existence of a pattern of school construction and abandonment is thus a factor of great weight. In devising remedies where legally imposed segregation has been established, it is the responsibility of local authorities and district courts to see to it that future school construction and abandonment are not used and do not serve to perpetuate or re-establish the dual system. When necessary, district courts should retain jurisdiction to assure that these responsibilities are carried out.

***

V

The central issue in this case is that of student assignment, and there are essentially four problem areas:

(1) to what extent racial balance or racial quotas may be used as an implement in a remedial order to correct a previously segregated system;
(2) whether every all-Negro and all-white school must be eliminated as an indispensable part of a remedial process of desegregation;
(3) what the limits are, if any, on the rearrangement of school districts and attendance zones, as a remedial measure; and
(4) what the limits are, if any, on the use of transportation facilities to correct state-enforced racial school segregation.

***

VI

The Court of Appeals, searching for a term to define the equitable remedial power of the district courts, used the term 'reasonableness.' In Green, supra, this Court used the term 'feasible' and by implication, 'workable,' 'effective,' and 'realistic' in the mandate to develop 'a plan that promises realistically to work, and * * * to work now.' On the facts of this case, we are unable to conclude that the order of the District Court is not reasonable, feasible and workable. However, in seeking to define the scope of remedial power or the limits on remedial power of courts in an area as sensitive as we deal with here, words are poor instruments to convey the sense of basic fairness inherent in equity. Substance, not semantics, must govern, and we have sought to suggest the nature of limitations without frustrating the appropriate scope of equity.

At some point, these school authorities and others like them should have achieved full compliance with this Court's decision in Brown I. The systems would then be 'unitary' in the sense required by our decisions in Green and Alexander.

It does not follow that the communities served by such systems will remain demographically stable, for in a growing, mobile society, few will do so. Neither school authorities nor district courts are constitutionally required to make year-by-year adjustments of the racial composition of student bodies once the affirmative duty to desegregate has been accomplished and racial discrimination through official action is eliminated from the system. This does not mean that federal courts are without power to deal with future problems; but in the absence of a showing that either the school authorities or some other agency of the State has deliberately attempted to fix or alter demographic patterns to affect the racial composition of the schools, further intervention by a district court should not be necessary.

Judgment of Court of Appeals affirmed in part; order of District Court affirmed.

BROWDER v. GAYLE
United States District Court (Alabama) (1956)
142 F. Supp. 707
Affirmed *per curiam*, U.S. Supreme Court (1956)
352 U.S. 903

RIVES, Circuit Judge. ... The purpose of this action is to test the constitutionality of both the statutes of the State of Alabama and the ordinances of the City of Montgomery which require the segregation of the white and colored races on the motor buses of the Montgomery City Lines, Inc., a common carrier of passengers in said City and its police jurisdiction. ...

The Montgomery City Lines, Inc., admits that it has operated, and pursuant to orders of a State Court, continues to operate 'its buses as required by the Statutes and Ordinances set out in the Complaint requiring it to provide equal but separate accommodations for the white and colored races'. Without dispute the evidence is to the effect that, other than being separate, such accommodations are equal. ...

The ultimate question is whether the statutes and ordinances requiring the segregation of the white and colored races on the common carrier motor buses in the City of Montgomery and its police jurisdiction are unconstitutional and invalid. Unless prohibited by the Constitution of the United States, the power to require such segregation is reserved to the States or to the people.—See Tenth Amendment.

In their private affairs, in the conduct of their private businesses, it is clear that the people themselves have the liberty to select their own associates and the persons with whom they will do business, unimpaired by the Fourteenth Amendment. *The Civil Rights Cases.* Indeed, we think that such liberty is guaranteed by the due process clause of that Amendment.

There is, however, a difference, a constitutional difference, between voluntary adherence to custom and the perpetuation and enforcement of that custom by law. The Fourteenth Amendment provides that 'No State shall * * * deprive any person of life, liberty, or property,

without due process of law; nor deny to any person within its jurisdiction the equal protection of the laws.'

Those provisions do not interfere with the police power of the States so long as the state laws operate alike upon all persons and property similarly situated. That Amendment 'merely requires that all persons subjected to such legislation shall be treated alike, under like circumstances and conditions, both in the privileges conferred and in the liabilities imposed.' The equal protection clause requires equality of treatment before the law for all persons without regard to race or color.

In *Plessy v. Ferguson* the Supreme Court held as to intrastate commerce that a Louisiana statute requiring railway companies to provide equal but separate accommodations for the white and colored races was not in conflict with the provisions of the Fourteenth Amendment. That holding was repeatedly followed in later cases.

In *Morgan v. Virginia*, 1964, the Court held that a state statute requiring segregated seats for Negro passengers on interstate buses was an unconstitutional burden of interstate commerce. In *Henderson v. United States*, 1950, the Court held that interstate railroad regulations and practices assigning a separate table in a dining car to Negroes contravened the Interstate Commerce Act. The Court referred to the statutory right as 'a fundamental right of equality of treatment,' and cited cases construing the Fourteenth Amendment, though the Court did not reach the constitutional question. The reasoning applied was similar to that employed in *Shelley v. Kraemer*, where the Court recognized that the underlying philosophy of the Fourteenth Amendment is the equality before the law of each individual.

In the field of college education, beginning in 1938 and continuing to the present time, the Court has first weakened the vitality of, and has then destroyed, the separate but equal concept.

The separate but equal concept had its birth prior to the adoption of the Fourteenth Amendment in the decision of a Massachusetts State court relating to public schools. *Roberts v. City of Boston*, 1849. The doctrine of that case was followed in *Plessy v. Ferguson*. In the School Segregation Cases, *Brown v. Board of Education of Topeka*, and *Bolling v. Sharpe*, the separate but equal doctrine was repudiated in the area where it first developed, i.e., in the field of public education. On the same day the Supreme Court made clear that its ruling was not limited to that field when it remanded 'for consideration in the light of the Segregation Cases * * * and conditions that now prevail' a case involving the rights of Negroes to use the recreational facilities of city parks. *Muir v. Louisville Park Theatrical Association*, 1954.

Later the Fourth Circuit expressly repudiated the separate but equal doctrine as applied to recreational centers. *Dawson v. Mayor and City Council of Baltimore*. Its judgment was affirmed by the Supreme Court. The doctrine has further been repudiated in [Supreme Court] holdings that the cities of Atlanta and of Miami cannot meet the test by furnishing the facilities of their municipal golf courses to Negroes on a segregated basis.

Even a statute can be repealed by implication. A fortiori, a judicial decision, which is simply evidence of the law and not the law itself, may be so impaired by later decisions as no longer to furnish any reliable evidence.

We cannot in good conscience perform our duty as judges by blindly following the precedent of *Plessy v. Ferguson* when our study leaves us in complete agreement with the Fourth Circuit's opinion in *Flemming v. South Carolina Electric & Gas Co.* that the separate but equal doctrine can no longer be safely followed as a correct statement of the law. In fact, we think that *Plessy v. Ferguson* has been impliedly, though not explicitly, over-ruled, and that, under the later decisions, there is now no rational basis upon which the separate but equal doctrine can be validly applied to public carrier transportation within the City of Montgomery and its police jurisdiction. The application of that doctrine cannot be justified as a proper execution of the state police power. ...

SMITH v. ALLWRIGHT
Supreme Court of the United States (1944)
321 U.S. 649

MR. JUSTICE REED. This writ of certiorari brings here for review a claim for damages in the sum of $ 5,000 on the part of petitioner, a Negro citizen of the 48th precinct of Harris County, Texas, for the refusal of respondents, election and associate election judges respectively of that precinct, to give petitioner a ballot or to permit him to cast a ballot in the primary election of July 27, 1940, for the nomination of Democratic candidates for the United States Senate and House of Representatives, and Governor and other state officers. The refusal is alleged to have been solely because of the race and color of the proposed voter.

The actions of respondents are said to violate ... the United States Code in that petitioner was deprived of rights secured by §§ 2 and 4 of Article I and the Fourteenth, Fifteenth and Seventeenth Amendments to the United States Constitution. ...

The State of Texas by its Constitution and statutes provides that every person ... qualified by residence in the district or country "shall be deemed a qualified elector." Primary elections for United States Senators, Congressmen and state officers are provided for by Chapters Twelve and Thirteen of the statutes. Under these chapters, the Democratic party was required to hold the primary which was the occasion of the alleged wrong to petitioner. ... These nominations are to be made by the qualified voters of the party. ...

The Democratic party on May 24,1932, in a state convention adopted the following resolution, which has not since been "amended, abrogated, annulled or avoided":

"Be it resolved that all white citizens of the State of Texas who are qualified to vote under the Constitution and laws of the State shall be eligible to membership in the Democratic party and, as such, entitled to participate in its deliberations."

It was by virtue of this resolution that the respondents refused to permit the petitioner to vote.

Texas is free to conduct her elections and limit her electorate as she may deem wise, save only as her action may be affected by the prohibitions of the United States Constitution or in conflict with powers delegated to and exercised by the National Government. The Fourteenth Amendment forbids a State from making or enforcing any law which abridges the privileges or immunities of citizens of the United States and the Fifteenth Amendment specifically interdicts any denial or abridgement by a State of the right of citizens to vote on account of color. Respondents appeared in the District Court and the Circuit Court of Appeals and defended on the ground that the Democratic party of Texas is a voluntary organization with members banded together for the purpose of selecting individuals of the group representing the common political beliefs as candidates in the general election. As such a voluntary organization, it was claimed, the Democratic party is free to select its own membership and limit to whites participation in the party primary. Such action, the answer asserted, does not violate the Fourteenth, Fifteenth or Seventeenth Amendment as officers of government cannot be chosen at primaries and the Amendments are applicable only to general elections where governmental officers are actually elected. Primaries, it is said, are political party affairs, handled by party, not governmental, officers. ...

We are thus brought to an examination of the qualifications for Democratic primary electors in Texas, to determine whether state action or private action has excluded Negroes from participation. ... Texas requires electors in a primary to pay a poll tax. Every person who does so pay and who has the qualifications of age and residence is an acceptable voter for the primary. ... Texas requires by the law the election of the county officers of a party. These compose the county executive committee. The county chairmen so selected are members of the district executive committee and choose the chairman for the district. Precinct primary election officers are named by the county executive committee. Statutes provide for the election by the voters of precinct delegates to the county convention of a party and the selection of delegates to the district and state conventions by the county convention. The state convention selects the state executive committee. No convention may place in platform or resolution any demand for specific legislation without endorsement of such legislation by the voters in a primary. Texas thus directs the selection of all party officers. ...

The state courts are given exclusive original jurisdiction of contested elections and of mandamus proceedings to compel party officers to perform their statutory duties.

We think that this statutory system for the selection of party nominees for inclusion on the general election ballot makes the party which is required to follow these legislative directions an agency of the State in so far as it determines the participants in a primary election. The party takes its character as a state agency from the duties imposed upon it by state statutes; the duties do not become matters of private law because they are performed by a political party. The plan of the Texas primary follows substantially that of Louisiana, with the exception that in Louisiana the State pays the cost of the primary while Texas assesses the cost against candidates. In numerous instances, the Texas statutes fix or limit the fees to be charged. Whether paid directly by the State or through state requirements, it is state action which compels. When primaries become a part of the machinery for choosing officials, state and national, as they have here, the same tests to determine the character of discrimination or abridgement should be applied to the primary as are applied to the general election. If the State requires a certain electoral procedure, prescribes a general election ballot made up of party nominees so chosen and limits the choice of the electorate in general elections for state offices, practically speaking, to those whose names appear on such a ballot, it endorses, adopts and enforces the discrimination against Negroes, practiced by a party entrusted by Texas law with the determination of the qualifications of participants in the primary. This is state action within the meaning of the Fifteenth Amendment.

The United States is a constitutional democracy. Its organic law grants to all citizens a right to participate in the choice of elected officials without restriction by any State because of race. This grant to the people of the opportunity for choice is not to be nullified by a State through casting its electoral process in a form which permits a private organization to practice racial discrimination in the election. Constitutional rights would be of little value if they could be thus indirectly denied. ...

MR. JUSTICE FRANKFURTER. This litigation challenges the validity, under the United States Constitution, of Local Act No.140, passed by the Legislature of Alabama in 1957, redefining the boundaries of the City of Tuskegee. Petitioners, Negro citizens of Alabama who were, at the time of this redistricting measure, residents of the City of Tuskegee, brought an action in the United States District Court for the Middle District of Alabama for a declaratory judgment that Act 140 is unconstitutional, and for an injunction to restrain the Mayor and officers of Tuskegee and the officials of Macon County, Alabama, from enforcing the Act against them and other Negroes similarly situated. Petitioners' claim is that enforcement of the statute, which alters the shape of Tuskegee from a square to an uncouth twenty-eight-sided figure, will constitute a discrimination against them in violation of the Due Process and Equal Protection Clauses of the Fourteenth Amendment to the Constitution and will deny them the right to vote in defiance of the Fifteenth Amendment. ...

At this stage of the litigation we are not concerned with the truth of the allegations, that is, the ability of petitioners to sustain their allegations by proof. The sole question is whether the allegations entitle them to make good on their claim that they are being denied rights under the United States Constitution. The complaint, charging that Act 140 is a device to disenfranchise Negro citizens, alleges the following facts: Prior to Act 140 the City of Tuskegee was square in shape; the Act transformed it into a strangely irregular twenty-eight-sided figure as indicated in the diagram appended to this opinion. The essential inevitable effect of this redefinition of Tuskegee's boundaries is to remove from the city all save only four or five of its 400 Negro voters while not removing a single white voter or resident. The result of the Act is to deprive the Negro petitioners discriminatorily of the benefits of

residence in Tuskegee, including, inter alia, the right to vote in municipal elections.

These allegations, if proven, would abundantly establish that Act 140 was not an ordinary geographic redistricting measure even within familiar abuses of gerrymandering. If these allegations upon a trial remained uncontradicted or unqualified, the conclusion would be irresistible, tantamount for all practical purposes to a mathematical demonstration, that the legislation is solely concerned with segregating white and colored voters by fencing Negro citizens out of town so as to deprive them of their pre-existing municipal vote. ...

The respondents find [a] barrier to the trial of this case in *Colegrove v. Green.* In that case the Court passed on an Illinois law governing the arrangement of congressional districts within that State. The complaint rested upon the disparity of population between the different districts which rendered the effectiveness of each individual's vote in some districts far less than in others. This disparity came to pass solely through shifts in population between 1901, when Illinois organized its congressional districts, and 1946, when the complaint was lodged. During this entire period elections were held under the districting scheme devised in 1901. The Court affirmed the dismissal of the complaint on the ground that it presented a subject not meet for adjudication. The decisive facts in this case, which at this stage must be taken as proved, are wholly different from the considerations found controlling in *Colegrove.*

That case involved a complaint of discriminatory apportionment of congressional districts. The appellants in *Colegrove* complained only of a dilution of the strength of their votes as a result of legislative inaction over a course of many years. The petitioners here complain that affirmative legislative action deprives them of their votes and the consequent advantages that the ballot affords. When a legislature thus singles out a readily isolated segment of a racial minority for special discriminatory treatment, it violates the Fifteenth Amendment. In no case involving unequal weight in voting distribution that has come before the Court did the decision sanction a differentiation on racial lines whereby approval was given to unequivocal withdrawal of the vote solely from colored citizens. Apart from all else, these considerations lift this controversy out of the so-called "political" arena and into the conventional sphere of constitutional litigation.

In sum, ... a ... statute which is alleged to have worked unconstitutional deprivations of petitioners' rights is not immune to attack simply because the mechanism employed by the legislature is a redefinition of municipal boundaries. According to the allegations here made, the Alabama Legislature has not merely redrawn the Tuskegee city limits with incidental inconvenience to the petitioners; it is more accurate to say that it has deprived the petitioners of the municipal franchise and consequent rights and to that end it has incidentally changed the city's boundaries. While in form this is merely an act redefining metes and bounds, if the allegations are established, the inescapable human effect of this essay in geometry and geography is to despoil colored citizens, and only colored citizens, of their theretofore enjoyed voting rights. That was not *Colegrove v. Green*.

When a State exercises power wholly within the domain of state interest, it is insulated from federal judicial review. But such insulation is not carried over when state power is used as an instrument for circumventing a federally protected right. ... The petitioners are entitled to prove their allegations at trial. ...

HARPER v. VIRGINIA BOARD OF ELECTIONS
Supreme Court of the United States (1966)
383 U.S. 663

MR. JUSTICE DOUGLAS. These are suits by Virginia residents to have declared unconstitutional Virginia's poll tax. [Virginia required annual payment of $1.50 by all persons over the age of 21. Failure to pay stripped a citizen of the right to vote.] ...

We conclude that a State violates the Equal Protection Clause of the Fourteenth Amendment whenever it makes the affluence of the voter or payment of any fee an electoral standard. Voter qualifications have no relation to wealth nor to paying or not paying this or any other tax. Our cases demonstrate that the Equal Protection Clause of the Fourteenth Amendment restrains the States from fixing voter qualifications which invidiously discriminate. ...

Long ago in *Yick Wo v. Hopkins*, the Court referred to "the political franchise of voting" as a "fundamental political right, because preservative of all rights." Recently in *Reynolds v. Sims* we said, "Undoubtedly, the right of suffrage is a fundamental matter in a free and democratic society. Especially since the right to exercise the franchise in a free and unimpaired manner is preservative of other basic civil and political rights, any alleged infringement of the right of citizens to vote must be carefully and meticulously scrutinized." There we were considering charges that voters in one part of the State had greater representation per person in the State Legislature than voters in another part of the State. We concluded:

"A citizen, a qualified voter, is no more nor no less so because he lives in the city or on the farm. This is the clear and strong command of our Constitution's Equal Protection Clause. This is an essential part of the concept of a government of laws and not men. This is at the heart of Lincoln's vision of 'government of the people, by the people, [and] for the people.' The Equal Protection Clause demands no less than substantially equal state legislative representation for all citizens, of all places as well as of all races."

We say the same whether the citizen, otherwise qualified to vote, has $ 1.50 in his pocket or nothing at all, pays the fee or fails to pay it. The principle that denies the State the right to dilute a citizen's vote on account of his economic status or other such factors by analogy bars a system which excludes those unable to pay a fee to vote or who fail to pay.

It is argued that a State may exact fees from citizens for many different kinds of licenses; that if it can demand from all an equal fee for a driver's license, it can demand from all an equal poll tax for voting. But we must remember that the interest of the State, when it comes to voting, is limited to the power to fix qualifications. Wealth, like race, creed, or color, is not germane to one's ability to participate intelligently in the electoral process. Lines drawn on the basis of wealth or property, like those of race (*Korematsu v. United States*), are traditionally disfavored. To introduce wealth or payment of a fee as a measure of a voter's qualification is to introduce a capricious or irrelevant factor. The degree of the discrimination is irrelevant. In this context—that is, as a condition or obtaining a ballot—the requirement of fee paying causes an "invidious" discrimination that runs afoul of the Equal Protection Clause. Levy "by the poll" ... is an old familiar form of taxation; and we say nothing to impair its validity so long as it is not made a condition to the exercise of the franchise. ...

... [T]he Equal Protection Clause is not shackled to the political theory of a particular era. In determining what lines are unconstitutionally discriminatory, we have never been confined to historic notions of equality, any more than we have restricted due process to a fixed catalogue of what was at a given time deemed to be the limits of fundamental rights. Notions of what constitutes equal treatment for purposes of the Equal Protection Clause do change. This Court in 1896 held that laws providing for separate public facilities for white and Negro citizens did not deprive the latter of the equal protection and treatment that the Fourteenth Amendment commands. *Plessy v. Ferguson.* Seven of the eight Justices then sitting subscribed to the Court's opinion, thus joining in expressions of what constituted unequal and discriminatory treatment that sound strange to a contemporary ear. When, in 1954—more than a half-century later—we repudiated the "separate-but-equal" doctrine of *Plessy* as respects public education we stated: "In approaching this problem, we cannot turn the clock back to 1868 when the Amendment was adopted, or even to 1896 when *Plessy v. Ferguson* was written." *Brown v. Board of Education.* ...

Those principles apply here. For to repeat, wealth or fee paying has, in our view, no relation to voting qualifications; the right to vote is too precious, too fundamental to be so burdened or conditioned.

MR. JUSTICE BLACK, dissenting. ... The equal protections cases carefully analyzed boil down to the principle that distinctions drawn and even discriminations imposed by state laws do not violate the Equal Protection Clause so long as these distinctions and discriminations are not "irrational," "irrelevant," "unreasonable," "arbitrary," or "invidious." These vague and indefinite terms do not, of course, provide a precise formula or an automatic mechanism for deciding cases arising under the Equal Protection Clause. The restrictive connotations of these terms, however ..., are a plain recognition of the fact that under a proper interpretation of the Equal Protection Clause States are to have the broadest kind of leeway in areas where they have a general constitutional competence to act. In view of the purpose of the terms to restrain the courts from a wholesale invalidation of state laws under the Equal Protection Clause it would be difficult to say that the poll tax requirement is "irrational" or "arbitrary" or works "invidious discriminations." State poll tax legislation can "reasonably," "rationally" and without an "invidious" or evil purpose to injure anyone be found to rest on a number of state policies including (1) the State's desire to collect its revenue, and (2) its belief that voters who pay a poll tax will be interested in furthering the State's welfare when they vote. Certainly it is rational to believe that people may be more likely to pay taxes if payment is a prerequisite to voting. And if history can be a factor in determining the "rationality" of discrimination in a state law ..., then whatever may be our personal opinion, history is on the side of "rationality" of the State's poll tax policy. Property qualifications existed in the Colonies and were continued by many States after the Constitution was adopted. Although I join the

Court in disliking the policy of the poll tax, this is not in my judgment a justifiable reason for holding this poll tax law unconstitutional. Such a holding on my part would, in my judgment, be an exercise of power which the Constitution does not confer upon me. ...

MR. JUSTICE HARLAN, whom MR. JUSTICE STEWART joins, dissenting. ... My disagreement with the present decision is that in holding the Virginia poll tax violative of the Equal Protection Clause the Court has departed from long-established standards governing the application of that clause.

The Equal Protection Clause prevents States from arbitrarily treating people differently under their laws. Whether any such differing treatment is to be deemed arbitrary depends on whether or not it reflects an appropriate differentiating classification among those affected; the clause has never been thought to require equal treatment of all persons despite differing circumstances. The test evolved by this Court for determining whether an asserted justifying classification exists is whether such a classification can be deemed to be founded on some rational and otherwise constitutionally permissible state policy. This standard reduces to a minimum the likelihood that the federal judiciary will judge state policies in terms of the individual notions and predilections of its own members, and until recently it has been followed in all kinds of "equal protection" cases. ... ... In substance the Court's analysis of the equal protection issue goes no further than to say that the electoral franchise is "precious" and "fundamental," and to conclude that "to introduce wealth or payment of a fee as a measure of a voter's qualifications is to introduce a capricious or irrelevant factor." These are of course captivating phrases, but they are wholly inadequate to satisfy the standard governing adjudication of the equal protection issue: Is there a rational basis for Virginia's poll tax as a voting qualification? I think the answer to that question is undoubtedly "yes."

Property qualifications and poll taxes have been a traditional part of our political structure. In the Colonies the franchise was generally a restricted one. Over the years these and other restrictions were gradually lifted, primarily because popular theories of political representation had changed. Often restrictions were lifted only after wide public debate. The issue of woman suffrage, for example, raised questions of family relationships, of participation in public affairs, of the very nature of the type of society in which Americans wished to live; eventually a consensus was reached, which culminated in the Nineteenth Amendment no more than 45 years ago.

Similarly with property qualifications, it is only by fiat that it can be said, especially in the context of American history, that there can be no rational debate as to their advisability. Most of the early Colonies had them; many of the States have had them during much of their histories; and, whether one agrees or not, arguments have been and still can be made in favor of them. For example, it is certainly a rational argument that payment of some minimal poll tax promotes civic responsibility, weeding out those who do not care enough about public affairs to pay $1.50 or thereabouts a year for the exercise of the franchise. It is also arguable, indeed it was probably accepted as sound political theory by a large percentage of Americans through most of our history, that people with some property have a deeper stake in community affairs, and are consequently more responsible, more educated, more knowledgeble, more worthy of confidence, than those without means, and that the community and Nation would be better managed if the franchise were restricted to such citizens. Nondiscriminatory and fairly applied literacy tests ... find justification on very similar grounds.

These viewpoints, to be sure, ring hollow on most contemporary ears. Their lack of acceptance today is evidenced by the fact that nearly all of the States, left to their own devices, have eliminated property or poll-tax qualifications; by the cognate fact that Congress and three-quarters of the States quickly ratified the Twenty-Fourth Amendment; and by the fact that rules such as the "pauper exclusion" in Virginia law have never been enforced.

Property and poll-tax qualifications, very simply, are not in accord with current egalitarian notions of how a modern democracy should be organized. It is of course entirely fitting that legislatures should modify the law to reflect such changes in popular attitudes. However, it is all wrong, in my view, for the Court to adopt the political doctrines popularly accepted at a particular moment of our history and to declare all others to be irrational and invidious, barring them from the range of choice by reasonably minded people acting through the political process. It was not too long ago that Mr. Justice Holmes felt impelled to remind the Court that the Due Process Clause of the Fourteenth Amendment does not enact the laissez-faire theory of society, *Lochner v. New York*. The times have changed, and perhaps it is appropriate to observe that neither does the Equal Protection Clause of that Amendment rigidly impose upon America an ideology of unrestrained egalitarianism. ...

HUNTER v. ERICKSON
Supreme Court of the United States (1969)
393 U.S. 385

Most ordinances adopted by the City Council of Akron, Ohio become effective thirty days after passage. Section 137 of the City Charter provided a special procedure for ordinances regulating the sale and lease of real property "on the basis of race, color, religion, national origin or ancestry." They became effective only if approved by a majority of the electors voting at a general or special election. The Court finds that Section 137 violates the Equal Protection Clause.

MR. JUSTICE WHITE. The question in this case is whether the City of Akron, Ohio, has denied a Negro citizen, Nellie Hunter, the equal protection of its laws by amending the city charter to prevent the city council from implementing any ordinance dealing with racial, religious, or ancestral discrimination in housing without the approval of the majority of the voters of Akron.

The Akron City Council in 1964 enacted a fair housing ordinance. ... A Commission on Equal Opportunity in Housing was established by the ordinance. ...

Seeking to invoke this machinery ..., Nellie Hunter addressed a complaint to the Commission asserting that a real estate agent had come to show her a list of houses for sale, but that on meeting Mrs. Hunter the agent "stated that she could not show me any of the houses on the list she had prepared for me because all of the owners had specified they did not wish their houses shown to Negroes." Mrs. Hunter's affidavit met with the reply that the fair housing ordinance was unavailable to her because the city charter had been amended to provide:

"Any ordinance enacted by the Council of The City of Akron which regulates the use, sale, advertisement, transfer, listing assignment, lease, sublease or financing of real property of any kind or of any interest therein on the basis of race, color, religion, national origin or ancestry must first be approved by a majority of the electors voting on the question at a regular or general election before said ordinance shall be effective. Any such ordinance in effect at the time of the adoption of this section shall cease to be effective until approved by the electors as provided herein."

... [Hunter] then brought an action in the Ohio courts ... to enforce the fair housing ordinance. ... [T]he trial court held that the fair housing ordinance was rendered ineffective by the charter amendment, and the Supreme Court of Ohio affirmed, holding that the charter amendment was not repugnant to the Equal Protection Clause of the Constitution. ...

[Section 137 is] an explicitly racial classification treating racial housing matters differently from other racial and housing matters. ...

Only laws to end housing discrimination based on "race, color, religion, national origin or ancestry" must run $137's gantlet. It is true that the section draws no distinctions among racial and religious groups. Negroes and whites, Jews and Catholics are all subject to the same requirements if there is housing discrimination against them which they wish to end. But $137 nevertheless disadvantages those who would benefit from laws barring racial, religious, or ancestral discriminations as against those who would bar other discriminations or who would otherwise regulate the real estate market in their favor. The automatic referendum system does not reach housing discrimination on sexual or political grounds, or against those with children or dogs, nor does it affect tenants seeking more heat or better maintenance from landlords, nor those seeking rent control, urban renewal, public housing, or new building codes.

Moreover, although the law on its face treats Negro and white, Jew and gentile in an identical manner, the reality is that the law's impact falls on the minority. The majority needs no protection against discrimination and if it did, a referendum might be bothersome but no more than that. Like the law requiring specification of candidates' race on the ballot, *Anderson v. Martin* (1964), $137 places special burdens on racial minorities within the governmental process. This is no more permissible than denying them the vote, on an equal basis with others. *Gomillion v. Lightfoot. ...*

Because the core of the Fourteenth Amendment is the prevention of meaningful and unjustified official distinctions based on race, racial classifications are "constitutionally suspect," *Bolling v. Sharpe*, and subject to the "most rigid scrutiny," *Korematsu v. United States*. They "bear a far heavier burden of justification" than other classifications.

We are unimpressed with any of Akron's justifications for its discrimination. Characterizing it simply as a public decision to move slowly in the delicate area of race relations emphasizes the impact and burden of $137, but does not justify it. The amendment was unnecessary either to implement a decision to go slowly, or to allow the people of Akron to participate in that decision. Likewise, insisting that a State may distribute legislative power as it desires and that the people may retain for themselves the power over certain subjects may generally be true, but these principles furnish no justification for a legislative structure which otherwise would violate the Fourteenth Amendment. Nor does the implementation of this change through popular referendum immunize it. The sovereignty of the people is itself subject to those constitutional limitations which have been duly adopted and remain unrepealed. Even though Akron might have proceeded by majority vote at town meeting on all its municipal legislation, it has instead chosen a more complex system. Having done so, the State may no more disadvantage any particular group by making it more difficult to enact legislation in its behalf than it may dilute any person's vote or give any group a smaller representation than another of comparable size.

We hold that $137 discriminates against minorities, and constitutes a real, substantial, and invidious denial of the equal protection of the laws. ...

MR. JUSTICE WHITE delivered the opinion of the Court.

The question here is whether Art. I, § 26, of the California Constitution denies "to any person ... the equal protection of the laws" within the meaning of the Fourteenth Amendment of the Constitution of the United States. Section 26 of Art. I, an initiated measure submitted to the people as Proposition 14 in a statewide ballot in 1964, provides in part as follows:

"Neither the State nor any subdivision or agency thereof shall deny, limit or abridge, directly or indirectly, the right of any person, who is willing or desires to sell, lease or rent any part or all of his real property, to decline to sell, lease or rent such property to such person or persons as he, in his absolute discretion, chooses."

The real property covered by § 26 is limited to residential property and contains an exception for state-owned real estate.

The issue arose in two separate actions in the California courts, *Mulkey v. Reitman* and *Prendergast v. Snyder.* In *Reitman*, the Mulkeys, who are husband and wife and respondents here, sued under § 51 and § 52 of the California Civil Code alleging that petitioners had refused to rent them an apartment solely on account of their race. An injunction and damages were demanded. Petitioners moved for summary judgment on the ground that §§ 51 and 52, insofar as they were the basis for the Mulkeys' action, had been rendered null and void by the adoption of Proposition 14 after the filing of the complaint. The trial court granted the motion and respondents took the case to the California Supreme Court.

In the *Prendergast* case, respondents, husband and wife, filed suit in December 1964 seeking to enjoin eviction from their apartment; respondents alleged that the eviction was motivated by racial prejudice and therefore would violate § 51 and § 52 of the Civil Code. Petitioner Snyder cross-complained for a judicial declaration that he was entitled to terminate the month-to-month tenancy even if his action was based on racial considerations. In denying petitioner's motion for summary judgment, the trial court found it unnecessary to consider the validity of Proposition 14 because it concluded that judicial enforcement of an eviction based on racial grounds would in any event violate the Equal Protection Clause of the United States Constitution. The cross-complaint was dismissed with prejudice and petitioner Snyder appealed to the California Supreme Court which considered the case along with *Mulkey v. Reitman.* That court, in reversing the *Reitman* case, held that Art. I, § 26, was invalid as denying the equal protection of the laws guaranteed by the Fourteenth Amendment. For similar reasons, the court affirmed the judgment in the Prendergast case. We granted certiorari because the cases involve an important issue arising under the Fourteenth Amendment.

We affirm the judgments of the California Supreme Court. We first turn to the opinion of that court in Reitman , which quite properly undertook to examine the constitutionality of § 26 in terms of its "immediate objective," its "ultimate effect" and its "historical context and the conditions existing prior to its enactment." Judgments such as these we have frequently undertaken ourselves. But here the California Supreme Court has addressed itself to these matters and we should give careful consideration to its views because they concern the purpose, scope, and operative effect of a provision of the California Constitution.

First, the court considered whether § 26 was concerned at all with private discriminations in residential housing. This involved a review of past efforts by the California Legislature to regulate such discriminations. The Unruh Act, Civ. Code §§ 51–52, on which respondents based their cases, was passed in 1959. The Hawkins Act, formerly Health & Safety Code §§ 35700–35741, followed and prohibited discriminations in publicly assisted housing. In 1961, the legislature enacted proscriptions against restrictive covenants. Finally, in 1963, came the Rumford Fair Housing Act, Health & Safety Code §§ 35700–35744, superseding the Hawkins Act and prohibiting racial discriminations in the sale or rental of any private dwelling containing more than four units. That act was enforceable by the State Fair Employment Practice Commission.

It was against this background that Proposition 14 was enacted. Its immediate design and intent, the California court said, were "to overturn state laws that bore on the right of private sellers and lessors to discriminate," the Unruh and Rumford Acts, and "to forestall future state action that might circumscribe this right." This aim was successfully achieved: the adoption of Proposition 14 "generally nullifies both the Rumford and Unruh Acts as they apply to the housing market," and establishes "a purported constitutional right to privately discriminate on grounds which admittedly would be unavailable under the Fourteenth Amendment *should state action* be involved."

Second, the court conceded that the State was permitted a neutral position with respect to private racial discriminations and that the State was not bound by the Federal Constitution to forbid them. But, because a significant state involvement in private discriminations could amount to unconstitutional state action, the court deemed it necessary to determine whether Proposition 14 invalidly involved the State in racial discriminations in the housing market. Its conclusion was that it did.

***What the court below did was first to reject the notion that the State was required to have a statute prohibiting racial discriminations in housing. Second, it held the intent of § 26 was to authorize private racial discriminations in the housing market, to repeal the Unruh and Rumford Acts and to create a constitutional right to discriminate on racial grounds in the sale and leasing of real property. Hence, the court dealt with § 26 as though it expressly authorized and constitutionalized the private right to discriminate. Third, the court assessed the ultimate impact of § 26 in the California environment and concluded that the section would encourage and significantly involve the State in private racial discrimination contrary to the Fourteenth Amendment.

The California court could very reasonably conclude that § 26 would and did have wider impact than a mere repeal of existing statutes. Section 26 mentioned neither the Unruh nor Rumford Act in so many words. Instead,

it announced the constitutional right of any person to decline to sell or lease his real property to anyone to whom he did not desire to sell or lease. Unruh and Rumford were thereby pro tanto repealed. But the section struck more deeply and more widely. Private discriminations in housing were now not only free from Rumford and Unruh but they also enjoyed a far different status than was true before the passage of those statutes. The right to discriminate, including the right to discriminate on racial grounds, was now embodied in the State's basic charter, immune from legislative, executive, or judicial regulation at any level of the state government. Those practicing racial discriminations need no longer rely solely on their personal choice. They could now invoke express constitutional authority, free from censure or interference of any kind from official sources. All individuals, partnerships, corporations and other legal entities, as well as their agents and representatives, could now discriminate with respect to their residential real property, which is defined as any interest in real property of any kind or quality, "irrespective of how obtained or financed," and seemingly irrespective of the relationship of the State to such interests in real property. Only the State is excluded with respect to property owned by it.

***The assessment of § 26 by the California court is similar to what this Court has done in appraising state statutes or other official actions in other contexts. In *McCabe v. Atchison, Topeka & Santa Fe R. Co.*, the Court dealt with a statute which, as construed by the Court, authorized carriers to provide cars for white persons but not for Negroes. Though dismissal of the complaint on a procedural ground was affirmed, the Court made it clear that such a statute was invalid under the Fourteenth Amendment because a carrier refusing equal service to Negroes would be "acting in the matter under the authority of a state law." This was nothing less than considering a permissive state statute as an authorization to discriminate and as sufficient state action to violate the Fourteenth Amendment in the context of that case.

***Here we are dealing with a provision which does not just repeal an existing law forbidding private racial discriminations. Section 26 was intended to authorize, and does authorize, racial discrimination in the housing market. The right to discriminate is now one of the basic policies of the State. The California Supreme Court believes that the section will significantly encourage and involve the State in private discriminations. We have been presented with no persuasive considerations indicating that these judgments should be overturned.

Affirmed.

JUSTICE BLACKMUN delivered the opinion of the Court.

We are presented here with an extraordinary question: whether an elected local school board may use the Fourteenth Amendment to *defend* its program of busing for integration from attack by the State.

Seattle School District No. 1 (District), which is largely coterminous with the city of Seattle, Wash., is charged by state law with administering 112 schools and educating approximately 54,000 public school students. About 37% of these children are of Negro, Asian, American Indian, or Hispanic ancestry. Because segregated housing patterns in Seattle have created racially imbalanced schools, the District historically has taken steps to alleviate the isolation of minority students; since 1963, it has permitted students to transfer from their neighborhood schools to help cure the District's racial imbalance.

Despite these efforts, the District in 1977 came under increasing pressure to accelerate its program of desegregation. In response, the District's Board of Directors (School Board) enacted a resolution defining "racial imbalance" as "the situation that exists when the combined minority student enrollment in a school exceeds the districtwide combined average by 20 percentage points, provided that the single minority enrollment ... of no school will exceed 50 percent of the student body." The District resolved to eliminate all such imbalance from the Seattle public schools by the beginning of the 1979–1980 academic year.

In September 1977, the District implemented a "magnet" program, designed to alleviate racial isolation by enhancing educational offerings at certain schools, thereby encouraging voluntary student transfers. A "disproportionate amount of the overall movement" inspired by the program was undertaken by Negro students, however, *ibid.*, and racial imbalance in the Seattle

schools was found to have actually increased between the 1970–1971 and 1977–1978 academic years. The District therefore concluded that mandatory reassignment of students was necessary if racial isolation in its schools was to be eliminated. Accordingly, in March 1978, the School Board enacted the so-called "Seattle Plan" for desegregation. The plan, which makes extensive use of busing and mandatory reassignments, desegregates elementary schools by "pairing" and "trading" predominantly minority with predominantly white attendance areas, and by basing student assignments on attendance zones rather than on race. The racial makeup of secondary schools is moderated by "feeding" them from the desegregated elementary schools. The District represents that the plan results in the reassignment of roughly equal numbers of white and minority students, and allows most students to spend roughly half of their academic careers attending a school near their homes.

The desegregation program, implemented in the 1978–1979 academic year, apparently was effective: the District Court found that the Seattle Plan "has substantially reduced the number of racially imbalanced schools in the district and has substantially reduced the percentage of minority students in those schools which remain racially imbalanced."

In late 1977, shortly before the Seattle Plan was formally adopted by the District, a number of Seattle residents who opposed the desegregation strategies being discussed by the School Board formed an organization called the Citizens for Voluntary Integration Committee (Civic). This organization, which the District Court found "was formed because of its founders' opposition to The Seattle Plan," ibid., attempted to enjoin implementation of the Board's mandatory desegregation program through litigation in state court; when these efforts failed, Civic drafted a statewide initiative designed to terminate the use of mandatory busing for purposes of racial integration. This proposal, known as Initiative 350, provided that "no school board ... shall directly or indirectly require any student to attend a school other than the school which is geographically nearest or next nearest the student's place of residence ... and which offers the course of study pursued by such student ...." The initiative then set out, however, a number of broad exceptions to this requirement: a student may be assigned beyond his neighborhood school if he "requires special education, care or guidance," or if "there are health or safety hazards, either natural or manmade, or physical barriers or obstacles ... between the student's place of residence and the nearest or next nearest school," or if "the school nearest or next nearest to his place of residence is unfit or inadequate because of overcrowding, unsafe conditions or lack of physical facilities." Initiative 350 also specifically proscribed use of seven enumerated methods of "[indirect]" student assignment—among them the redefinition of attendance zones, the pairing of schools, and the use of "feeder" schools—that are a part of the Seattle Plan. The initiative envisioned busing for racial purposes in only one circumstance: it did not purport to "prevent any court of competent jurisdiction from adjudicating constitutional issues relating to the public schools."

***On November 8, 1978, two months after the Seattle Plan went into effect, Initiative 350 passed by a substantial margin, drawing almost 66% of the vote statewide. The initiative failed to attract majority support in two state legislative districts, both in Seattle. In the city as a whole, however, the initiative passed with some 61% of the vote. Within the month, the District, together with the Tacoma and Pasco School Districts, initiated this suit against the State in the United States District Court for the Western District of Washington, challenging the constitutionality of Initiative 350 under the Equal Protection Clause of the Fourteenth Amendment. The United States and several community organizations intervened in support of the District; Civic intervened on behalf of the defendants.

***The Equal Protection Clause of the Fourteenth Amendment guarantees racial minorities the right to full participation in the political life of the community. It is beyond dispute, of course, that given racial or ethnic groups may not be denied the franchise, or precluded from entering into the political process in a reliable and meaningful manner. But the Fourteenth Amendment also reaches "a political structure that treats all individuals as equals," *Mobile v. Bolden*, yet more subtly distorts governmental processes in such a way as to place special burdens on the ability of minority groups to achieve beneficial legislation.

*** As Justice Harlan noted while concurring in the Court's opinion in laws structuring political institutions or allocating political power according to "neutral principles"—such as the executive veto, or the typically burdensome requirements for amending state constitutions—are not subject to equal protection attack, though they may "make it more difficult for minorities to achieve favorable legislation." Because such laws make it more difficult for *every* group in the community to enact comparable laws, they "[provide] a just framework within which the diverse political groups in our society may fairly compete." Thus, the political majority may generally restructure the political process to place obstacles in the path of everyone seeking to secure the benefits of governmental action. But a different analysis is required when the State allocates governmental power nonneutrally, by explicitly using the *racial* nature of a decision to determine the decisionmaking process. State action of this kind, the Court said, "places *special* burdens on racial minorities within the governmental process," thereby "making it *more* difficult for certain racial and religious minorities [than for other members of the community] to achieve legislation that is in their interest." Such a structuring of the political process, the Court said, was "no more permissible than [is] denying [members of a racial minority] the vote, on an equal basis with others."

***In our view, Initiative 350 must fall because it does "not [attempt] to allocate governmental power on the basis of any general principle." Instead, it uses the racial nature of an issue to define the governmental decisionmaking structure, and thus imposes substantial and unique burdens on racial minorities.

[o]ur cases suggest that desegregation of the public schools, like the Akron open housing ordinance, at bottom inures primarily to the benefit of the minority, and is designed for that purpose. Education has come to be "a principal instrument in awakening the child to cultural values, in preparing him for later professional training, and in helping him to adjust normally to his environment." When that environment is largely shaped by members of different racial and cultural groups, minority children can achieve their full measure of success only if they learn to function in—and are fully accepted by—the larger community. Attending an ethnically diverse school may help accomplish this goal by preparing minority children "for citizenship in our pluralistic society," while, we may hope, teaching members

of the racial majority "to live in harmony and mutual respect" with children of minority heritage. *Lee v. Nyquist* settles this point, for the Court there accepted the proposition that mandatory desegregation strategies present the type of racial issue implicated by the *Hunter* doctrine.

It is undeniable that busing for integration—particularly when ordered by a federal court—now engenders considerably more controversy than does the sort of fair housing ordinance debated in *Hunter*. But in the absence of a constitutional violation, the desirability and efficacy of school desegregation are matters to be resolved through the political process. For present purposes, it is enough that minorities may consider busing for integration to be "legislation that is in their interest." Given the racial focus of Initiative 350, this suffices to trigger application of the *Hunter* doctrine.

We are also satisfied that the practical effect of Initiative 350 is to work a reallocation of power of the kind condemned in *Hunter*. The initiative removes the authority to address a racial problem—and only a racial problem—from the existing decisionmaking body, in such a way as to burden minority interests. Those favoring the elimination of *de facto* school segregation now must seek relief from the state legislature, or from the statewide electorate. Yet authority over all other student assignment decisions, as well as over most other areas of educational policy, remains vested in the local school board. Indeed, by specifically exempting from Initiative 350's proscriptions most nonracial reasons for assigning students away from their neighborhood schools, the initiative expressly requires those championing school

integration to surmount a considerably higher hurdle than persons seeking comparable legislative action. As in *Hunter*, then, the community's political mechanisms are modified to place effective decisionmaking authority over a racial issue at a different level of government. In a very obvious sense, the initiative thus "disadvantages those who would benefit from laws barring" *de facto* desegregation "as against those who ... would otherwise regulate" student assignment decisions; "the reality is that the law's impact falls on the minority."

***After passage of Initiative 350, authority over all but one of those areas remained in the hands of the local board. By placing power over desegregative busing at the state level, then, Initiative 350 plainly "differentiates between the treatment of problems involving racial matters and that afforded other problems in the same area." The District Court and the Court of Appeals similarly concluded that the initiative restructured the Washington political process, and we see no reason to challenge the determinations of courts familiar with local law.

***In reaching this conclusion, we do not undervalue the magnitude of the State's interest in its system of education. Washington could have reserved to state officials the right to make all decisions in the areas of education and student assignment. It has chosen, however, to use a more elaborate system; having done so, the State is obligated to operate that system within the confines of the Fourteenth Amendment. That, we believe, it has failed to do.

Accordingly, the judgment of the Court of Appeals is *Affirmed*.

MR. JUSTICE REHNQUIST: We are required in this case to decide the constitutionality of Art. VIII, $182, of the Alabama Constitution of 1901, which provides for the disenfranchisement of persons convicted of, among other offenses, "any crime ... involving moral turpitude."

Appellees Carmen Edwards, a black, and Victor Underwood, a white, have been blocked from the voter rolls pursuant to $182 by the Boards of Registrars for Montgomery and Jefferson Counties, respectively, because they each have been convicted of presenting a worthless check. In determining that the misdemeanor of presenting a worthless check is a crime involving moral turpitude, the Registrars relied on opinions of the Alabama Attorney General.

Edwards and Underwood sued the Montgomery and Jefferson Boards of Registrars. ... [They claimed $182 violated the Equal protection Clause because] the misdemeanors encompassed within $182 were intentionally adopted to disenfranchise blacks on account of their race and that their inclusion in $182 has had the intended effect.

The predecessor to $182 was Art. VIII, $3, of the Alabama Constitution of 1875, which denied persons "convicted of treason, embezzlement of public funds, malfeasance in office, larceny, bribery, or other crime punishable by imprisonment in the penitentiary" the right to register, vote or hold public office. These offenses were largely, if not entirely, felonies. The drafters of $182, which was adopted by the 1901 convention, expanded the list of enumerated crimes substantially. ...

The drafters retained the general felony provision— "any crime punishable by imprisonment in the penitentiary"—but also added a new catchall provision covering "any ... crime involving moral turpitude." This latter phrase is not defined, but it was subsequently interpreted by the Alabama Supreme Court to mean an act that is "'immoral in itself, regardless of the fact whether it is punishable by law. The doing of the act itself, and not its prohibition by statute fixes, the moral turpitude.'"

Various minor nonfelony offenses such as presenting a worthless check and petty larceny fall within the sweep of $182, while more serious nonfelony offenses such as second-degree manslaughter, assault on a police officer, mailing pornography, and aiding the escape of a misdemeanant do not because they are neither enumerated in $182 nor considered crimes involving moral turpitude. It is alleged, and the Court of Appeals found, that the crimes selected for inclusion in $182 were believed by the delegates to be more frequently committed by blacks.

Section 182 on its face is racially neutral, applying equally to anyone convicted of one of the enumerated crimes or a crime falling within one of the catchall provisions. Appellee Edwards nonetheless claims that the provision has had a racially discriminatory impact. [T]he Court of Appeals implicitly found the evidence of discriminatory impact indisputable:

"The registrars' expert estimated that by January 1903 section 182 had disfranchised approximately ten times as many blacks as whites. This disparate effect persists today. In Jefferson and Montgomery Counties blacks are by even the most modest estimates at least 1.7 times as likely as whites to suffer disfranchisement under section 182 for the commission of nonprison offenses."

Presented with a neutral state law that produces disproportionate effects along racial lines, the Court of Appeals was correct in applying the approach of Arlington Heights to determine whether the law violates the Equal Protection Clause of the Fourteenth Amendment:

> "[Official] action will not be held unconstitutional solely because it results in a racially disproportionate impact. ... Proof of racially discriminatory intent or purpose is required to show a violation of the Equal Protection Clause." Washington v. Davis.

Once racial discrimination is shown to have been a "substantial" or "motivating" factor behind enactment of the law, the burden shifts to the law's defenders to demonstrate that the law would have been enacted without this factor.

Proving the motivation behind official action is often a problematic undertaking. When we move ... to a body the size of the Alabama Constitutional Convention of 1901, the difficulties in determining the actual motivations of the various legislators that produced a given decision increase.

But [those] ... sort of difficulties ... do not obtain in this case. Although understandably no "eyewitnesses" to the 1901 proceedings testified, testimony and opinions of historians were offered and received without objection. These showed that the Alabama Constitutional Convention of 1901 was part of a movement that swept the post-Reconstruction South to disenfranchise blacks. The delegates to the all-white convention were not secretive about their purpose. John B. Knox, president of the convention, stated in his opening address:

> "And what is it that we want to do? Why it is within the limits imposed by the Federal Constitution, to establish white supremacy in this State."

Indeed, neither the District Court nor appellants seriously dispute the claim that this zeal for white supremacy ran rampant at the convention.

[T]he evidence ... demonstrates conclusively that $182 was enacted with the intent of disenfranchising blacks. We see little purpose in repeating that factual analysis here. At oral argument in this Court appellants' counsel essentially conceded this point, stating: "I would be very blind and naive [to] try to come up and stand before this Court and say that race was not a factor in the enactment of Section 182; that race did not play a part in the decisions of those people who were at the constitutional convention of 1901 and I won't do that."

Appellants contend that the State has a legitimate interest in denying the franchise to those convicted of crimes involving moral turpitude, and that $182 should be sustained on that ground. The Court of Appeals convincingly demonstrated that such a purpose simply was not a motivating factor of the 1901 convention. In addition to the general catchall phrase "crimes involving moral turpitude" the suffrage committee selected such crimes as vagrancy, living in adultery, and wife beating that were thought to be more commonly committed by blacks. ...

[The] original enactment [of $182] was motivated by a desire to discriminate against blacks on account of race and the section continues to this day to have that effect. As such, it violates equal protection under Arlington Heights.

VILLAGE OF ARLINGTON HTS. v. METRO. HOUSING DEVEL. CORP.
Supreme Court of the United States (1976)
429 U.S. 252

MR. JUSTICE POWELL. In 1971 ... Metropolitan Housing Development Corporation (MHDC) applied to the Village of Arlington Heights, Ill., for the rezoning of a 15-acre parcel from single-family to multiple-family classification. Using federal financial assistance, MHDC planned to build 190 clustered townhouse units for low- and moderate-income tenants. The Village denied the rezoning request. MHDC ... brought suit alleg[ing] that the denial was racially discriminatory and that it violated ... the Fourteenth Amendment. ...

Arlington Heights is a suburb of Chicago, located about 26 miles northwest of the downtown Loop area. Most of the land in Arlington Heights is zoned for detached single-family homes, and this is in fact the prevailing land use. The Village experienced substantial growth during the 1960's, but, like other communities in northwest Cook County, its population of racial minority groups remained quite low. According to the 1970 census, only 27 of the Village's 64,000 residents were black.

The Clerics of St. Viator, a religious order (Order), own an 80-acre parcel just east of the center of Arlington Heights. Part of the site is occupied by the Viatorian high school, and part by the Order's three-story novitiate building, which houses dormitories and a Montessori school. Much of the site, however, remains vacant. Since 1959, when the Village first adopted a zoning ordinance, all the land surrounding the Viatorian property has been zoned R-3, a single-family specification with relatively small minimum lot-size requirements. On three sides of the Viatorian land there are single-family homes just across a street; to the east the Viatorian property directly adjoins the backyards of other single-family homes.

The Order decided in 1970 to devote some of its land to low- and moderate-income housing. ... [It contracted to sell 15 acres to MHDC for the purpose of MHDC building such housing, a project called Lincoln Green. The sale was contingent on MHDC being able to have the land rezoned to R-5, multiple-family use.] ...

During the spring of 1971, the Plan Commission considered the proposal at a series of three public meetings, which drew large crowds. Although many of those attending were quite vocal and demonstrative in opposition to Lincoln Green, a number of individuals and representatives of community groups spoke in support of rezoning. Some of the comments, both from opponents and supporters, addressed what was referred to as the "social issue"—the desirability or undesirability of introducing at this location in Arlington Heights low- and moderate-income housing, housing that would probably be racially integrated.

Many of the opponents, however, focused on the zoning aspects of the petition, stressing two arguments. First, the area always had been zoned single-family, and the neighboring citizens had built or purchased there in reliance on that classification. Rezoning threatened to cause a measurable drop in property value for neighboring sites. Second, the Village's apartment policy, adopted by the Village Board in 1962 and amended in 1970, called for R-5 zoning primarily to serve as a buffer between single-family development and land uses thought incompatible, such as commercial or manufacturing districts. Lincoln Green did not meet this requirement, as it adjoined no commercial or manufacturing district.

... [T]he Plan Commission adopted a motion to recommend to the Village's Board of Trustees that it deny the request. ... The Village Board ... denied the rezoning by a 6–1 vote. ...

Our decision last Term in *Washington v. Davis* made it clear that official action will not be held unconstitutional solely because it results in a racially disproportionate impact. ... Proof of racially discriminatory intent or purpose is required to show a violation of the Equal Protection Clause. ...

Davis does not require a plaintiff to prove that the challenged action rested solely on racially discriminatory purposes. Rarely can it be said that a legislature or administrative body operating under a broad mandate made a decision motivated solely by a single concern, or even that a particular purpose was the "dominant" or "primary" one. In fact, it is because Tegislators and administrators are properly concerned with balancing numerous competing considerations that courts refrain from reviewing the merits of their decisions, absent a showing of arbitrariness or irrationality. But racial discrimination is not just another competing consideration. When there is a proof that a discriminatory purpose has been a motivating factor in the decision, this judicial deference is no longer justified. ...

We ... have reviewed the evidence. The impact of the Village's decision does arguably bear more heavily on racial minorities. Minorities constitute 18% of the Chicago area population, and 40% of the income groups said to be eligible for Lincoln Green. But there is little about the sequence of events leading up to the decision that would spark suspicion. The area around the Viatorian property has been zoned R-3 since 1959, the year when Arlington Heights first adopted a zoning map. Single-family homes surround the 80-acre site, and the Village is undeniably committed to single-family homes as its dominant residential land use. The rezoning request progressed according to the usual procedures. The Plan Commission even scheduled two additional hearings, at least in part to accommodate MHDC and permit it to supplement its presentation with answers to questions generated at the first hearing.

The statements by the Plan Commission and Village Board members, as reflected in the official minutes, focused almost exclusively on the zoning aspects of the MHDC petition, and the zoning factors on which they relied are not novel criteria in the Village's rezoning decisions. There is no reason to doubt that there has been reliance by some neighboring property owners on the maintenance of single-family zoning in the vicinity. The Village originally adopted its buffer policy long before MHDC entered the picture and has applied the policy too consistently for us to infer discriminatory purpose from its application in this case. Finally, MHDC called one member of the Village Board to the stand at trial. Nothing in her testimony supports an inference of invidious purpose.

In sum, ... [plaintiffs] simply failed to carry their burden of proving that discriminatory purpose was a motivating factor in the Village's decision. ...

Respondents Harley and Sellers, both Negroes (hereinafter respondents), whose applications to become police officers in the District of Columbia had been rejected, in an action against District of Columbia officials (petitioners) and others, claimed that the Police Department's recruiting procedures, including a written personnel test (Test 21), were racially discriminatory and violated the Due Process Clause of the Fifth Amendment. ... Test 21 is administered generally to prospective Government employees to determine whether applicants have acquired a particular level of verbal skill. Respondents contended that the test bore no relationship to job performance and excluded a disproportionately high number of Negro applicants. ... The District Court, noting the absence of any claim of intentional discrimination, found that respondents' evidence ... warranted the conclusions that (a) the number of black police officers, while substantial, is not proportionate to the city's population mix; (b) a higher percentage of blacks fail the test than whites; and (c) the test has not been validated to establish its reliability for measuring subsequent job performance. While that showing sufficed to shift the burden of proof to the defendants in the action, the court concluded that respondents were not entitled to relief... in view of the facts that 44% of new police recruits were black, a figure proportionate to the blacks on the total force and equal to the number of 20- to 29-year-old blacks in the recruiting area; that the Police Department had affirmatively sought to recruit blacks, many of whom passed the test but failed to report for duty; and that the test was a useful indicator of training school performance (precluding the need to show validation in terms of job performance) and was not designed to, and did not, discriminate against otherwise qualified blacks. ... The Court of Appeals reversed, [invalidating the test solely on the grounds that it disproportionately

excluded minorities and that the Police Department had not proved that the test related to job performance. In effect, the Court of Appeals incorporated into the Fifth and Fourteenth Amendments the Supreme Court's interpretation of Title VII in Griggs v. Duke Power Co. The Supreme Court reverses the Court of Appeals and holds the Constitution not violated without proof of discriminatory intent.]

MR. JUSTICE WHITE. ... The central purpose of the Equal Protection Clause of the Fourteenth Amendment is the prevention of official conduct discriminating on the basis of race. It is also true that the Due Process Clause of the Fifth Amendment contains an equal protection component prohibiting the United States from invidiously discriminating between individuals or groups. *Bolling v. Sharpe.* But our cases have not embraced the proposition that a law or other official act, without regard to whether it reflects a racially discriminatory purpose, is unconstitutional *solely* because it has a racially disproportionate impact.

Almost 100 years ago, *Strauder v. West Virginia* established that the exclusion of Negroes from grand and petit juries in criminal proceedings violated the Equal Protection Clause, but the fact that a particular jury or a series of juries does not statistically reflect the racial composition of the community does not in itself make out an invidious discrimination forbidden by the Clause. ...

The rule is the same in other contexts. *Wright v. Rockefeller* (1964), upheld a New York congressional apportionment statute against claims that district lines had been racially gerrymandered. The challenged districts were made up predominantly of whites or of minority races, and their boundaries were irregularly drawn. The challengers did not prevail because they failed to prove that the New York Legislature "was either motivated by racial considerations or in fact drew the districts on racial lines"; the plaintiffs had not shown that the statute "was the product of a state contrivance to segregate on the basis of race or place of origin." ...

The school desegregation cases have also adhered to the basic equal protection principle that the invidious quality of a law claimed to be racially discriminatory must ultimately be traced to a racially discriminatory purpose. That there are both predominantly black and predominantly white schools in a community is not alone violative of the Equal Protection Clause. The essential element of de jure segregation is "a current condition of segregation resulting from intentional state action." *Keyes v. School Dist. No. 1* (1973). "The differentiating factor between de jure segregation and so called de facto segregation ... is *purpose* or *intent* to segregate." The Court has also recently rejected allegations of racial discrimination based solely on the statistically disproportionate racial impact of various provisions of the Social Security Act because "[t]he acceptance of appellants' constitutional theory would render suspect each difference in treatment among the grant classes, however lacking in racial motivation and however otherwise rational the treatment might be." *Jefferson v. Hackney* (1972).

This is not to say that the necessary discriminatory racial purpose must be express or appear on the face of the statute, or that a law's disproportionate impact is irrelevant in cases involving Constitution-based claims of racial discrimination. A statute, otherwise neutral on its face, must not be applied so as invidiously to discriminate on the basis of race. It is also clear from the cases dealing with racial discrimination in the selection of juries that the systematic exclusion of Negroes is itself such an "unequal application of the law ... as to show intentional discrimination." A prima facie case of discriminatory purpose may be proved as well by the absence of Negroes on a particular jury combined with the failure of the jury commissioners to be informed of eligible Negro jurors in a community, or with racially nonneutral selection procedures. ...

Necessarily, an invidious discriminatory purpose may often be inferred from the totality of the relevant facts, including the fact, if it is true, that the law bears more heavily on one race than another. It is also not infrequently true that the discriminatory impact—in the jury cases for example, the total or seriously disproportionate exclusion of Negroes from jury venires—in may for all practical purposes demonstrate unconstitutionality because in various circumstances the discrimination is very difficult to explain on nonracial grounds. Nevertheless, we have not held that a law, neutral on its face and serving ends otherwise within the power of government to pursue, is invalid under the Equal Protection Clause simply because it may affect a greater proportion of one race than of another. Disproportionate impact is not irrelevant, but it is not the sole touchstone of an invidious racial discrimination forbidden by the Constitution. Standing alone, it does not trigger the rule that racial classifications are to be subjected to the strictest scrutiny and are justifiable only by the weightiest of considerations. ...

As an initial matter, we have difficulty understanding how a law establishing a racially neutral qualification for employment is nevertheless racially discriminatory and denies "any person ... equal protection of the laws" simply because a greater proportion of Negroes fail to qualify than members of other racial or ethnic groups. Had respondents, along with all others who had failed Test 21, whether white or black, brought an action claiming that the test denied each of them equal protection of the laws as compared with those who had passed with high enough scores to qualify them as police recruits, it is most unlikely that their challenge would have been sustained. Test 21, which is administered generally to prospective Government employees, concededly seeks to ascertain whether those who take it have acquired a particular level of verbal skill; and it is untenable that the Constitution prevents the Government from seeking modestly to upgrade the communicative abilities of its employees rather than to be satisfied with some lower level of competence, particularly where the job requires special ability to communicate orally and in writing. Respondents, as Negroes, could no more successfully claim that the test denied them equal protection than could white applicants who also failed. The conclusion would not be different in the face of proof that more Negroes than whites had been disqualified by Test 21. That other Negroes also failed to score well would, alone, not demonstrate that respondents individually were being denied equal protection of the laws by the application of an otherwise valid qualifying test being administered to prospective police recruits.

Nor on the facts of the case before us would the disproportionate impact of Test 21 warrant the conclusion that it is a purposeful device to discriminate against Negroes and hence an infringement of the constitutional rights of respondents as well as other black applicants. ...

A rule that a statute designed to serve neutral ends is nevertheless invalid, absent compelling justification, if in practice it benefits or burdens one race more than another would be far reaching and would raise serious questions about, and perhaps invalidate, a whole range of tax, welfare, public service, regulatory, and licensing statutes that may be more burdensome to the poor and to the average black than to the more affluent white.

Given that rule, such consequences would perhaps be likely to follow. However, in our view, extension of the rule beyond those areas where it is already applicable by reason of statute, such as in the field of public employment, should await legislative prescription. ...

BEAN v. SOUTHWESTERN WASTE MANAGEMENT CORP.
United States District Court for the Southern District of
Texas, Houston Division
482 F. Supp. 673; 1979 U.S. Dist. LEXIS 7827

December 21, 1979

On October 26, 1979, plaintiffs filed their complaint and Motion for Temporary Restraining Order and Preliminary Injunction contesting the decision by the Texas Department of Health to grant Permit No. 1193 to defendant Southwestern Waste Management to operate a Type I solid waste facility in the East Houston-Dyersdale Road area in Harris County. They contend that the decision was, at least in part, motivated by racial discrimination in violation of *42 U.S.C. § 1983* and seek an order revoking the permit. The defendants deny the allegations. ...

The problem is that the plaintiffs have not established a substantial likelihood of success on the merits. The burden on them is to prove discriminatory purpose. *Washington v. Davis, 426 U.S. 229, 96 S. Ct. 2040, 48 L. Ed. 2d 597 (1976); Village of Arlington Heights v. Metropolitan Housing Development Corp., 429 U.S. 252, 97 S. Ct. 555, 50 L. Ed. 2d 450 (1977).* That is, the plaintiffs must show not just that the decision to grant the permit is objectionable or even wrong, but that it is attributable to an intent to discriminate on the basis of race. Statistical proof can rise to the level that it, alone, proves discriminatory intent, as in *Yick Wo v. Hopkins, 118 U.S. 356, 6 S. Ct. 1064, 30 L. Ed. 220 (1886),* and *Gomillion v. Lightfoot, 364 U.S. 339, 81 S. Ct. 125, 5 L. Ed. 2d 110 (1960),* or, this Court would conclude, even in situations less extreme than in those two cases, but the data shown here does not rise to that level. Similarly, statistical proof can be sufficiently supplemented by the types of proof outlined in *Arlington Heights, supra,* to establish purposeful discrimination, but the supplemental proof offered here is not sufficient to do that.

Two different theories of liability have been advanced in this case. The first is that TDH's approval of the permit was part of a pattern or practice by it of discriminating in the placement of solid waste sites. In order to test that theory, one must focus on the sites which TDH has approved and determine the minority population of the areas in which the sites were located on the day that the sites opened. The available statistical data, both city-wide and in the target area, fails to establish a pattern or practice of discrimination by TDH. City-wide, data was produced for the seventeen (17) sites operating with TDH permits as of July 1, 1978. That data shows that 58.8% Of the sites granted permits by TDH were located in census tracts with 25% Or less minority population at the time of their opening and that 82.4% Of the sites granted permits by TDH were located in census tracts with 50% Or less minority population at the time of their opening. In the target area, an area which roughly conforms to the North Forest Independent School District and the newly-created City Council District B and is 70% Minority in population, Plaintiffs' Exhibit 2, two (2) sites were approved by TDH. One, the McCarty Road site, was in a census tract with less than 10% Minority population at the time of its opening. The other, the site being challenged here, is in a census tract with close to 60% Minority population. Even if we also consider the sites approved by TDWR in the target area, which, as discussed earlier, are not really relevant to TDH's intent to discriminate, no pattern or practice of discrimination is revealed. Of all the solid waste sites opened in the target area, 46.2 to 50% Were located in census tracts with less than 25% Minority population at the time they opened. It may be that more particularized data would show that even those sites approved in predominantly Anglo census tracts were actually located in minority neighborhoods, but the data available here does not show that. In addition, there was no supplemental evidence, such as that suggested by *Arlington Heights, supra,* which established a pattern or practice of discrimination on the part of TDH.

The plaintiffs' second theory of liability is that TDH's approval of the permit, in the context of the historical placement of solid waste sites and the events surrounding the application, constituted discrimination. Three sets of data were offered to support this theory. Each set, at first blush, looks compelling. On further analysis, however, each set breaks down. Each fails to approach the standard established by *Yick Wo, supra,* and *Gomillion, supra,* and, even when considered with supplementary proof, *Arlington Heights, supra,* fails to establish a likelihood of success in proving discriminatory intent.

The first set of data focuses on the two (2) solid waste sites to be used by the City of Houston. Both of these sites are located in the target area. This proves discrimination, the plaintiffs argue, because "the target area has the dubious distinction of containing 100% Of the type I municipal land fills that Houston utilizes or will utilize, although it contains only 6.9% Of the entire population of Houston." There are two problems with this argument. First, there are only two sites involved here. That is not a statistically significant number. Second, an examination of the census tracts in the target area in which the sites are located reveals that the East Houston-Dyersdale Road proposed site is in a tract with a 58.4% Minority population, but that the McCarty Road site is in a tract with only an 18.4% Minority population. Thus, the evidence shows that, of the two sites to be used by the City of Houston, one is in a primarily Anglo census tract and one is in a primarily minority census tract. No inference of discrimination can be made from this data.

The second set of data focuses on the total number of solid waste sites located in the target area. The statistical disparity which the plaintiffs point to is that the target area contains 15% Of Houston's solid waste sites, but only 6.9% Of its population. Since the target area has a 70% Minority population, the plaintiffs argue, this statistical disparity must be attributable to race discrimination. To begin with, in the absence of the data on population by race, the statistical disparity is not all that shocking. One would expect solid waste sites to be placed near each other and away from concentrated population areas. Even considering the 70% Minority population of the target area, when one looks at where in the target area these particular sites are located, the inference of racial discrimination dissolves. Half of the solid waste sites in the target area are in census tracts with more than 70% Anglo population. Without some proof that the sites affect an area much larger than the census tract in which they are in, it is very hard to conclude that the placing of a site in the target area evidences purposeful racial discrimination.

The third set of data offered by the plaintiffs focuses on the city as a whole. This data is the most compelling on its surface. It shows that only 17.1% Of the city's solid waste sites are located in the southwest quadrant, where 53.3% Of the Anglos live. Only 15.3% Of the sites are located in the northwest quadrant, where 20.1% Of the Anglos live. Thus, only 32.4% Of the sites are located in the western half of the city, where 73.4% Of the Anglos live. Furthermore, the plaintiffs argue, 67.6% Of the sites are located in the eastern half of the city, where 61.6% Of the minority population lives. This, according to the plaintiffs, shows racial discrimination.

The problem is that, once again, these statistics break down under closer scrutiny. To begin with, the inclusion of TDWR's sites skew the data. A large number of TDWR sites are located around Houston's ship channel, which is in the eastern half of the city. But those sites, the Assistant Attorney General argues persuasively, are located in the eastern half of the city because that is where Houston's industry is, not because that is where Houston's minority population is. Furthermore, closer examination of the data shows that the city's solid waste sites are not so disparately located as they first appear. If we focus on census tracts, rather than on halves or quadrants of the city, we can see with more particularity where the solid waste sites are located. Houston's population is 39.3% Minority and 60.7% Anglo. The plaintiffs argue, and this Court finds persuasive, a definition of "minority census tracts" as those with more than 39.3% Minority population and Anglo census tracts as those with more than 60.7% Anglo population. Using those definitions, Houston consists of 42.5% Minority tracts and 57.5% Anglo tracts. Again using those definitions, 42.3% Of the solid waste sites in the City of Houston are located in minority tracts and 57.7% Are located in Anglo tracts. In addition, if we look at tracts with one or more sites per tract, to account for the fact that some tracts contain more than one solid waste site, 42.2% Are minority tracts and 57.8% Are Anglo tracts. Defendants' Exhibit 30, Plaintiffs' Exhibits 41, 48 and 49. The difference between the racial composition of census tracts in general and the racial composition of census tracts with solid waste sites is, according to the statistics available to the Court, at best, only 0.3%. That is simply not a statistically significant difference. More surprisingly, from the plaintiffs' point of view, to the extent that it is viewed as significant, it tends to indicate that minority census tracts have a tiny bit smaller percentage of solid waste sites than one would proportionately expect.

In support of the proposition that there is a city-wide discrimination against minorities in the placement of solid waste sites, the plaintiffs also argue that the data reveals that, in 1975, eleven solid waste sites were located in census tracts with 100% Minority population and none were located in census tracts with 100% Anglo population. There are problems with this argument, too, however. To begin with, the 1975 data is not entirely reliable. Compared with both the 1970 and the 1979 data, the 1975 data appears to overcount minority population. For example, of the eleven sites mentioned by the plaintiffs, only one had a 100% Minority population in 1979. More importantly, there were, in fact, two sites located in 100% Anglo tracts in 1975. In addition, 18 other sites were located in tracts with a 90% Or greater Anglo population in 1975. Thus, even according to the 1975 data, a large number of sites were located in census tracts with high Anglo populations.

Arlington Heights, supra, 429 U.S. at 267–268, 97 S. Ct. at 564–565, suggested various types of non-statistical proof which can be used to establish purposeful discrimination. The supplementary non-statistical evidence provided by the plaintiffs in the present case raises a number of questions as to why this permit was granted. To begin with, a site proposed for the almost identical location was denied a permit in 1971 by the County Commissioners, who were then responsible for the issuance of such permits. One wonders what happened since that time. The plaintiffs argue that Smiley High School has changed from an Anglo school to one whose student body is predominantly minority. Furthermore, the site is being placed within 1700 feet of Smiley High School, a predominantly black school with no air conditioning, and only somewhat farther from a residential neighborhood. Land use considerations alone would seem to militate against granting this permit. Such evidence seemingly did not dissuade TDH.

If this Court were TDH, it might very well have denied this permit. It simply does not make sense to put a solid waste site so close to a high school, particularly one with no air conditioning. Nor does it make sense to put the land site so close to a residential neighborhood. But I am not TDH and for all I know, TDH may regularly approve of solid waste sites located near schools and residential areas, as illogical as that may seem.

It is not my responsibility to decide whether to grant this site a permit. It is my responsibility to decide whether to grant the plaintiffs a preliminary injunction. From the evidence before me, I can say that the plaintiffs have established that the decision to grant the permit was both unfortunate and insensitive. I cannot say that the plaintiffs have established a substantial likelihood of proving that the decision to grant the permit was motivated by purposeful racial discrimination in violation of *42 U.S.C. § 1983*. This Court is obligated, as all Courts are, to follow the precedent of the United States Supreme Court and the evidence adduced thus far does not meet the magnitude required by *Arlington Heights, supra.*

The failure of the plaintiffs to obtain a preliminary injunction does not, of course, mean that they are foreclosed from obtaining permanent relief. Because of the time pressures involved, extensive pre-trial discovery was impossible in this case. Assuming the case goes forward, discovery could lead to much more solid and persuasive evidence for either side. Ideally, it would resolve a number of the questions which the Court considers unanswered.

Where, for instance, are the solid waste sites located in each census tract? The plaintiffs produced evidence that in census tract 434, a predominantly Anglo tract, the site was located next to a black community named Riceville. If that was true of most sites in predominantly Anglo census tracts, the outcome of this case would be quite different.

How large an area does a solid waste site affect? If it affects an area a great deal smaller than that of a census tract, it becomes particularly important to know where in each census tract the site is located. If it affects an area larger than that of a census tract, then a target area analysis becomes much more persuasive.

How are solid waste site locations selected? It may be that private contractors consider a number of alternative locations and then select one in consultation with city or county officials. If that is so, it has tremendous implications for the search for discriminatory intent. It may be that a relatively limited number of areas can adequately serve as a Type I solid waste site. If that is so, the placement of sites in those areas becomes a lot less suspicious, even if large numbers of minorities live there. Either way, this is information which should be adduced. At this point, the Court still does not know how, why, and by whom the East Houston-Dyersdale Road location was selected.

What factors entered into TDH's decision to grant the permit? The proximity of the site to Smiley High School and a residential neighborhood and the lack of air conditioning facilities at the former were emphasized to the Court. It is still unknown how much, if any, consideration TDH gave to these factors. The racial composition of the neighborhood and the racial distribution of solid waste sites in Houston were primary concerns of the plaintiffs. It remains unclear to what degree TDH was informed of these concerns.

At this juncture, the decision of TDH seems to have been insensitive and illogical. Sitting as the hearing examiner for TDH, based upon the evidence adduced, this Court would have denied the permit. But this Court has a different role to play, and that is to determine whether the plaintiffs have established a substantial likelihood of proving that TDH's decision to issue the permit was motivated by purposeful discrimination in violation of *42 U.S.C. § 1983* as construed by superior courts. That being so, it is hereby ORDERED, ADJUDGED, and DECREED that the plaintiffs' Motion for a Preliminary Injunction be, and the same is, DENIED. For the reasons stated above, the defendants' Motions to Dismiss are also DENIED.

CITY OF MOBILE v. BOLDEN
Supreme Court of the United States (1980)
446 U.S. 55

Mobile, Ala., is governed by a Commission consisting of three members elected at large who jointly exercise all legislative, executive, and administrative power in the city. [Bolden] brought a class action in Federal District Court against the city and the incumbent Commissioners on behalf of all Negro citizens of the city, alleging, inter alia, that the practice of electing the City Commissioners at large unfairly diluted the voting strength of Negroes in violation of the Fourteenth and Fifteenth Amendments. Although finding that Negroes in Mobile "register and vote without hindrance," the District Court nevertheless held that the at-large electoral system violated the Fifteenth Amendment and invidiously discriminated against Negroes in violation of the Equal Protection Clause of the Fourteenth Amendment, and ordered that the Commission be disestablished and replaced by a Mayor and a Council elected from single-member districts. The Court of Appeals affirmed. [The Supreme Court reverses, finding no constitutional violation without proof of intent to discriminate.]

MR. JUSTICE STEWART announced the judgment of the Court and delivered an opinion, in which THE CHIEF JUSTICE, MR. JUSTICE POWELL, and MR. JUSTICE REHNQUIST joined. The city of Mobile, Ala., has since 1911 been governed by a City Commission consisting of three members elected by the voters of the city at large. The question in this case is whether this at-large system of municipal elections violates the rights of Mobile's Negro voters in contravention of federal statutory or constitutional law. ...

The three Commissioners jointly exercise all legislative, executive, and administrative power in the municipality. They are required after election to designate one of their number as Mayor, a largely ceremonial office, but no formal provision is made for allocating specific executive or administrative duties among the three. As required by the state law enacted in 1911, each candidate for the Mobile City Commission runs for election in the city at large for a term of four years in one of three numbered posts, and may be elected only by a majority of the total vote. This is the same basic electoral system that is followed by literally thousands of municipalities and other local governmental units throughout the Nation. ...

The claim that at-large electoral schemes unconstitutionally deny to some persons the equal protection of the laws has been advanced in numerous cases before this Court. That contention has been raised most often with regard to multimember constituencies within a state legislative apportionment system. The constitutional objection to multimember districts ... has been on the lack of representation multimember districts afford various elements of the voting population in a system of representative legislative democracy. "Criticism [of multimember districts] is rooted in their winner-take-all aspects, their tendency to submerge minorities ..., a general preference for legislatures reflecting community interests as closely as possible and disenchantment with political parties and elections as devices to settle policy differences between contending interests." *Whitcomb v. Chavis*.

Despite repeated constitutional attacks upon multimember legislative districts, the Court has consistently held that they are not unconstitutional *per se*. We have recognized, however, that such legislative apportionments could violate the Fourteenth Amendment if their purpose were invidiously to minimize or cancel out the voting potential of racial or ethnic minorities. To prove such a purpose it is not enough to show that the group allegedly discriminated against has not elected representatives in proportion to its numbers. A plaintiff must prove that the disputed plan was "conceived or operated as [a] purposeful [device] to further racial ... discrimination."

This burden of proof is simply one aspect of the basic principle that only if there is purposeful discrimination can there be a violation of the Equal Protection Clause of the Fourteenth Amendment. ...

... [I]t is clear that the evidence in the present case fell far short of showing that the appellants "conceived or operated [a] purposeful [device] to further racial ... discrimination." *Whitcomb v. Chavis.* ...

... The so-called *Zimmer* criteria upon which the District Court and the Court of Appeals relied were most assuredly insufficient to prove an unconstitutionally discriminatory purpose in the present case.

First, the two courts found it highly significant that no Negro had been elected to the Mobile City Commission. From this fact they concluded that the processes leading to nomination and election were not open equally to Negroes. But the District Court's findings of fact, unquestioned on appeal, make clear that Negroes register and vote in Mobile "without hindrance," and that there are no official obstacles in the way of Negroes who wish to become candidates for election to the Commission. Indeed, it was undisputed that the only active "slating" organization in the city is comprised of Negroes. It may be that Negro candidates have been defeated, but that fact alone does not work a constitutional deprivation.

Second, the District Court relied in part on its finding that the persons who were elected to the Commission discriminated against Negroes in municipal employment and in dispensing public services. If that is the case, those discriminated against may be entitled to relief under the Constitution, albeit of a sort quite different from that sought in the present case. The Equal Protection Clause proscribes purposeful discrimination because of race by any unit of state government, whatever the method of its election. But evidence of discrimination by white officials in Mobile is relevant only as the most tenuous and circumstantial evidence of the constitutional invalidity of the electoral system under which they attained their offices.

Third, the District Court and the Court of Appeals supported their conclusion by drawing upon the substantial history of official racial discrimination in Alabama. But past discrimination cannot, in the manner of original sin, condemn governmental action that is not itself unlawful. The ultimate question remains whether a discriminatory intent has been proved in a given case. More distant instances of official discrimination in other cases are of limited help in resolving that question.

Finally, the District Court and the Court of Appeals pointed to the mechanics of the at-large electoral system itself as proof that the votes of Negroes were being invidiously canceled out. But those features of that electoral system, such as the majority vote requirement, tend naturally to disadvantage any voting minority. ... They are far from proof that the at-large electoral scheme represents purposeful discrimination against Negro voters. ...

MR. JUSTICE WHITE, dissenting. ... A plurality of the Court today agrees with the courts below that maintenance of Mobile's at-large system for election of City Commissioners violates the Fourteenth and Fifteenth Amendments only if it is motivated by a racially discriminatory purpose. The plurality ... rejects the inference of purposeful discrimination apparently because each of the factors relied upon by the courts below is alone insufficient to support the inference. ... By viewing each of the factors relied upon below in isolation, and ignoring the fact that racial bloc voting at the polls makes it impossible to elect a black commissioner under the at-large system, the plurality rejects the "totality of the circumstances" approach ... and leaves the courts below adrift on uncharted seas with respect to how to proceed on remand. ...

Contemporary Equal Protection: A Summary

RACE AND THE EQUAL PROTECTION CLAUSE
Law Summary

Race and the equal Protection clause

- Presumptions, Munn *and Lochner*
- *Carolene Products* and Footnote 4
- Equal Protection Analysis

Munn and Lochner

- *Munn v. Illinois*(1877): Court adopts position that in general government is free to regulate and challengers have the burden of establishing that government has exceeded its authority.
- *Lochner v. New York* (1907): Court adopts position that in general people are free of regulation and government has the burden of establishing its authority to regulate.

Foot Note 4:

In United States v. Carolene Products Co. (1938) the Supreme Court reaffirmed its intent to defer to the legislature in economic matters. Presuming that economic legislation rests on "some rational basis within the knowledge or experience of the legislator", the Court indicated its willingness to presume economic legislation constitutional.

- But, in Footnote 4, the Court indicated other areas in which it might not show deference:
  - "when legislation appears on its face to be within a specific prohibition of the Constitution"
  - "legislation which restricts those political processes which can ordinarily be expected to bring about repeal of undesirable legislation"
  - "statutes directed at particular religious, or national, or racial minorities" and when "prejudice against discrete and insular minorities may be a special condition, which tends seriously to curtail the operation of those political processes ordinarily to be relied upon to protect minorities" (all citations omitted).

EQUAL PROTECTION ANALYSIS—RACE

- Used to test the legitimacy of governmental distinctions, i.e., only available when:
  - state (government)action
  - treats some differently than others.
- General Rule:
  - Government actions treating some differently than others are ordinarily; resumed by the courts to be constitutional (i.e., the government is given wide discretion by the courts in governing); the burden of proof is on the challenger to show that the distinction drawn is without rational basis, i.e. is wholly arbitrary or unreasonable. (The "rational basis" or "minimal scrutiny" test.)

- But (the "strict scrutiny" or "maximal scrutiny" test):

  If—a government action which treats some differently than others either:

  1. affects a fundamental constitutional right, or
  2. is predominately motivated by racial considerations,

  Then—the government action is presumed unconstitutional by the courts, and the burden is on the government, if it wishes to carry out the action, to show that the action is

  1. narrowly tailored so as to
  2. achieve a compelling government interest

CHAPTER

THREE

Toward Integration

Themes

- "State" action and the public/private distinction; commerce and the 1964 Civil Rights Act
- Voting rights—vote dilution; majority-minority distracting under the Voting Rights Act: a second-best solution; majority-minority distracting: remedying present discrimination or racial balancing?
- Education—*de jure v. defacto* segregation; dissolving desegregation decrees: how do we know when a system has been put into the position it would have been in absent segregation? Affirmative action in education: precisely what action is permissible, and how will we know it when we see it?
- Employment—disparate treatment and invidious race-conscious employment practices of government and private employers under equal

protection and Title VII; disparate impact and employment practices of private employers under Title VII; affirmative action: What does it mean and what is permissible under equal protection and Title VII?
- Housing—how is it that, while the law in many ways prohibits residential segregation, most American neighborhoods are still highly segregated?
- Speech—to what extent may government punish or suppress hostile or hateful speech based on race?
- Continuing and underlying tensions—state and local v. federal authority; individual v. group rights; legislative v. judicial authority; the debate over affirmative action: what it is and what, if anything, justifies it.

SHELLEY ET UX. v. KRAEMER ET UX.
Supreme Court of the United States
334 U.S. 1; 68 S. Ct. 836; 92 L. Ed. 1161; 1948 U.S. LEXIS 2764;
3 A.L.R.2d 441

January 15-16, 1948, Argued. May 3, 1948, Decided

MR. CHIEF JUSTICE VINSON delivered the opinion of the Court.

These cases present for our consideration questions relating to the validity of court enforcement of private agreements, generally described as restrictive covenants, which have as their purpose the exclusion of persons of designated race or color from the ownership or occupancy of real property. Basic constitutional issues of obvious importance have been raised.

The first of these cases comes to this Court on certiorari to the Supreme Court of Missouri. On February 16, 1911, thirty out of a total of thirty-nine owners of property fronting both sides of Labadie Avenue between Taylor Avenue and Cora Avenue in the city of St. Louis, signed an agreement, which was subsequently recorded, providing in part:

". . . the said property is hereby restricted to the use and occupancy for the term of Fifty (50) years from this date, so that it shall be a condition all the time and whether recited and referred to as [*sic*] not in subsequent conveyances and shall attach to the land as a condition precedent to the sale of the same, that hereafter no part of said property or any portion thereof shall be, for said term of Fifty-years, occupied by any person not of the Caucasian race, it being intended hereby to restrict the use of said property for said period of time against the occupancy as owners or tenants of any portion of said property for resident or other purpose by people of the Negro or Mongolian Race."

The entire district described in the agreement included fifty-seven parcels of land. The thirty owners who signed the agreement held title to forty-seven parcels, including the particular parcel involved in this case. At the time the agreement was signed, five of the parcels in the district were owned by Negroes. One of those had been occupied by Negro families since 1882, nearly thirty years before the restrictive agreement was executed. The trial court

found that owners of seven out of nine homes on the south side of Labadie Avenue, within the restricted district and "in the immediate vicinity" of the premises in question, had failed to sign the restrictive agreement in 1911. At the time this action was brought, four of the premises were occupied by Negroes, and had been so occupied for periods ranging from twenty-three to sixty-three years. A fifth parcel had been occupied by Negroes until a year before this suit was instituted.

On August 11, 1945, pursuant to a contract of sale, petitioners Shelley, who are Negroes, for valuable consideration received from one Fitzgerald a warranty deed to the parcel in question. n1 The trial court found that petitioners had no actual knowledge of the restrictive agreement at the time of the purchase.

On October 9, 1945, respondents, as owners of other property subject to the terms of the restrictive covenant, brought suit in the Circuit Court of the city of St. Louis praying that petitioners Shelley be restrained from taking possession of the property and that judgment be entered divesting title out of petitioners Shelley and revesting title in the immediate grantor or in such other person as the court should direct. The trial court denied the requested relief on the ground that the restrictive agreement, upon which respondents based their action, had never become final and complete because it was the intention of the parties to that agreement that it was not to become effective until signed by all property owners in the district, and signatures of all the owners had never been obtained.

The Supreme Court of Missouri sitting *en banc* reversed and directed the trial court to grant the relief for which respondents had prayed. That court held the agreement effective and concluded that enforcement of its provisions violated no rights guaranteed to petitioners by the Federal Constitution. n2 At the time the court rendered its decision, petitioners were occupying the property in question.

The second of the cases under consideration comes to this Court from the Supreme Court of Michigan. The circumstances presented do not differ materially from the Missouri case. In June, 1934, one Ferguson and his wife, who then owned the property located in the city of Detroit which is involved in this case, executed a contract providing in part:

"This property shall not be used or occupied by any person or persons except those of the Caucasian race."

"It is further agreed that this restriction shall not be effective unless at least eighty percent of the property fronting on both sides of the street in the block where our land is located is subjected to this or a similar restriction."

The agreement provided that the restrictions were to remain in effect until January 1, 1960. The contract was subsequently recorded; and similar agreements were executed with respect to eighty percent of the lots in the block in which the property in question is situated.

By deed dated November 30, 1944, petitioners, who were found by the trial court to be Negroes, acquired title to the property and thereupon entered into its occupancy. On January 30, 1945, respondents, as owners of property subject to the terms of the restrictive agreement, brought suit against petitioners in the Circuit Court of Wayne County. After a hearing, the court entered a decree directing petitioners to move from the property within ninety days. Petitioners were further enjoined and restrained from using or occupying the premises in the future. On appeal, the Supreme Court of Michigan affirmed, deciding adversely to petitioners' contentions that they had been denied rights protected by the Fourteenth Amendment.

Petitioners have placed primary reliance on their contentions, first raised in the state courts, that judicial enforcement of the restrictive agreements in these cases has violated rights guaranteed to petitioners by the Fourteenth Amendment of the Federal Constitution and Acts of Congress passed pursuant to that Amendment. n4 Specifically, petitioners urge that they have been denied the equal protection of the laws, deprived of property without due process of law, and have been denied privileges and immunities of citizens of the United States. We pass to a consideration of those issues.

I

Whether the equal protection clause of the Fourteenth Amendment inhibits judicial enforcement by state courts of restrictive covenants based on race or color is a question which this Court has not heretofore been called upon to consider. Only two cases have been decided by this Court which in any way have involved the enforcement of such agreements. The first of these was the case of *Corrigan v. Buckley, 271 U.S. 323 (1926).* There, suit was brought in the courts of the District of Columbia to enjoin a threatened violation of certain restrictive covenants relating to lands situated in the city of Washington. Relief was granted, and the case was brought here on appeal. It is apparent that that case, which had originated in the federal courts and involved the enforcement of covenants on land located in the District of Columbia, could present no issues under the Fourteenth Amendment; for that Amendment by its terms applies only to the States. Nor was the question of the validity of court enforcement of the restrictive covenants under the Fifth Amendment properly before the Court, as the opinion of this Court specifically recognizes. The only constitutional issue which the appellants had raised in the lower courts, and hence the only constitutional issue before this Court on appeal, was the validity of the covenant agreements as such. This Court concluded that since the inhibitions of the constitutional provisions invoked apply only to governmental action, as contrasted to action of private individuals, there was no showing that the covenants, which were simply agreements between private property owners, were invalid. Accordingly, the appeal was dismissed for want of a substantial question. Nothing in the opinion of this Court, therefore, may properly be regarded as an adjudication on the merits of the constitutional issues presented by these cases, which raise the question of the validity, not of the private agreements as such, but of the judicial enforcement of those agreements.

The second of the cases involving racial restrictive covenants was *Hansberry v. Lee, 311 U.S. 32 (1940).* In that case, petitioners, white property owners, were enjoined by the state courts from violating the terms of a restrictive agreement. The state Supreme Court had held petitioners bound by an earlier judicial determination, in litigation in which petitioners were not parties, upholding the validity of the restrictive agreement, although, in fact, the agreement had not been signed by the number of owners necessary to make it effective under state law. This Court reversed the judgment of the state Supreme Court upon the ground that petitioners had been denied due process of law in being held estopped to challenge the validity of the agreement on the theory, accepted by the state court, that the earlier litigation, in which petitioners did not participate, was in the nature of a class suit. In arriving at its result, this Court did not reach the issues presented by the cases now under consideration.

It is well, at the outset, to scrutinize the terms of the restrictive agreements involved in these cases. In the Missouri case, the covenant declares that no part of the affected property shall be "occupied by any person not of the Caucasian race, it being intended hereby to restrict the use of said property ... against the occupancy as owners or tenants of any portion of said property for resident or other purpose by people of the Negro or Mongolian Race." Not only does the restriction seek to proscribe use and occupancy of the affected properties by members of the excluded class, but as construed by the Missouri courts, the agreement requires that title of any person who uses his property in violation of the restriction shall be divested. The restriction of the covenant in the Michigan case seeks to bar occupancy by persons of the excluded class. It provides that "This property shall not be used or occupied by any person or persons except those of the Caucasian race."

It should be observed that these covenants do not seek to proscribe any particular use of the affected properties. Use of the properties for residential occupancy, as such, is not forbidden. The restrictions of these agreements, rather, are directed toward a designated class of persons and seek to determine who may and who may not own or make use of the properties for residential purposes. The excluded class is defined wholly in terms of race or color; "simply that and nothing more." n6

It cannot be doubted that among the civil rights intended to be protected from discriminatory state action by the Fourteenth Amendment are the rights to acquire, enjoy, own and dispose of property. Equality in the enjoyment of property rights was regarded by the framers of that Amendment as an essential pre-condition to the realization of other basic civil rights and liberties which the Amendment was intended to guarantee. Thus, § 1978 of the Revised Statutes, derived from § 1 of the Civil Rights Act of 1866 which was enacted by Congress while the Fourteenth Amendment was also under consideration, n8 provides:

"All citizens of the United States shall have the same right, in every State and Territory, as is enjoyed by white citizens thereof to inherit, purchase, lease, sell, hold, and convey real and personal property."

This Court has given specific recognition to the same principle. *Buchanan v. Warley, 245 U.S. 60 (1917).*

It is likewise clear that restrictions on the right of occupancy of the sort sought to be created by the private agreements in these cases could not be squared with the requirements of the Fourteenth Amendment if imposed by state statute or local ordinance. We do not understand respondents to urge the contrary. In the case of *Buchanan*

v. Warley, supra, a unanimous Court declared unconstitutional the provisions of a city ordinance which denied to colored persons the right to occupy houses in blocks in which the greater number of houses were occupied by white persons, and imposed similar restrictions on white persons with respect to blocks in which the greater number of houses were occupied by colored persons. During the course of the opinion in that case, this Court stated: "The Fourteenth Amendment and these statutes enacted in furtherance of its purpose operate to qualify and entitle a colored man to acquire property without state legislation discriminating against him solely because of color."

In *Harmon v. Tyler, 273 U.S. 668 (1927),* a unanimous court, on the authority of *Buchanan v. Warley, supra,* declared invalid an ordinance which forbade any Negro to establish a home on any property in a white community or any white person to establish a home in a Negro community, "except on the written consent of a majority of the persons of the opposite race inhabiting such community or portion of the City to be affected."

The precise question before this Court in both the *Buchanan* and *Harmon* cases involved the rights of white sellers to dispose of their properties free from restrictions as to potential purchasers based on considerations of race or color. But that such legislation is also offensive to the rights of those desiring to acquire and occupy property and barred on grounds of race or color is clear, not only from the language of the opinion in *Buchanan v. Warley, supra,* but from this Court's disposition of the case of *Richmond v. Deans, 281 U.S. 704 (1930).* There, a Negro, barred from the occupancy of certain property by the terms of an ordinance similar to that in the *Buchanan* case, sought injunctive relief in the federal courts to enjoin the enforcement of the ordinance on the grounds that its provisions violated the terms of the Fourteenth Amendment. Such relief was granted, and this Court affirmed, finding the citation of *Buchanan v. Warley, supra,* and *Harmon v. Tyler, supra,* sufficient to support its judgment.

But the present cases, unlike those just discussed, do not involve action by state legislatures or city councils. Here the particular patterns of discrimination and the areas in which the restrictions are to operate, are determined, in the first instance, by the terms of agreements among private individuals. Participation of the State consists in the enforcement of the restrictions so defined. The crucial issue with which we are here confronted is whether this distinction removes these cases from the operation of the prohibitory provisions of the Fourteenth Amendment.

Since the decision of this Court in the *Civil Rights Cases, 109 U.S. 3 (1883),* the principle has become firmly embedded in our constitutional law that the action inhibited by the first section of the Fourteenth Amendment is only such action as may fairly be said to be that of the States. That Amendment erects no shield against merely private conduct, however discriminatory or wrongful.

We conclude, therefore, that the restrictive agreements standing alone cannot be regarded as violative of any rights guaranteed to petitioners by the Fourteenth Amendment. So long as the purposes of those agreements are effectuated by voluntary adherence to their terms, it would appear clear that there has been no action by the State and the provisions of the Amendment have not been violated. Cf. *Corrigan v. Buckley, supra.*

But here there was more. These are cases in which the purposes of the agreements were secured only by judicial enforcement by state courts of the restrictive terms of the agreements. The respondents urge that judicial enforcement of private agreements does not amount to state action; or, in any event, the participation of the State is so attenuated in character as not to amount to state action within the meaning of the Fourteenth Amendment. Finally, it is suggested, even if the States in these cases may be deemed to have acted in the constitutional sense, their action did not deprive petitioners of rights guaranteed by the Fourteenth Amendment. We move to a consideration of these matters.

II

That the action of state courts and judicial officers in their official capacities is to be regarded as action of the State within the meaning of the Fourteenth Amendment, is a proposition which has long been established by decisions of this Court. That principle was given expression in the earliest cases involving the construction of the terms of the Fourteenth Amendment. Thus, in *Virginia v. Rives, 100 U.S. 313, 318 (1880),* this Court stated: "It is doubtless true that a State may act through different agencies,—either by its legislative, its executive, or its judicial authorities; and the prohibitions of the amendment extend to all action of the State denying equal protection of the laws, whether it be action by one of these agencies or by another." In *Ex parte Virginia, 100 U.S. 339, 347 (1880),* the Court observed: "A State acts by its legislative, its executive, or its judicial authorities. It can act in no other way." In the *Civil Rights Cases, 109 U.S. 3, 11, 17 (1883),* this Court pointed out that the Amendment makes void "State action of every kind" which is inconsistent with the guaranties therein contained, and

extends to manifestations of "State authority in the shape of laws, customs, or judicial or executive proceedings." Language to like effect is employed no less than eighteen times during the course of that opinion.

Similar expressions, giving specific recognition to the fact that judicial action is to be regarded as action of the State for the purposes of the Fourteenth Amendment, are to be found in numerous cases which have been more recently decided. In *Twining v. New Jersey, 211 U.S. 78, 90–91 (1908),* the Court said: "The judicial act of the highest court of the State, in authoritatively construing and enforcing its laws, is the act of the State." In *Brinkerhoff-Faris Trust & Savings Co. v. Hill, 281 U.S. 673, 680 (1930),* the Court, through Mr. Justice Brandeis, stated: "The federal guaranty of due process extends to state action through its judicial as well as through its legislative, executive or administrative branch of government." Further examples of such declarations in the opinions of this Court are not lacking.

One of the earliest applications of the prohibitions contained in the Fourteenth Amendment to action of state judicial officials occurred in cases in which Negroes had been excluded from jury service in criminal prosecutions by reason of their race or color. These cases demonstrate, also, the early recognition by this Court that state action in violation of the Amendment's provisions is equally repugnant to the constitutional commands whether directed by state statute or taken by a judicial official in the absence of statute. Thus, in *Strauder v. West Virginia, 100 U.S. 303 (1880),* this Court declared invalid a state statute restricting jury service to white persons as amounting to a denial of the equal protection of the laws to the colored defendant in that case. In the same volume of the reports, the Court in *Ex parte Virginia, supra,* held that a similar discrimination imposed by the action of a state judge denied rights protected by the Amendment, despite the fact that the language of the state statute relating to jury service contained no such restrictions.

The action of state courts in imposing penalties or depriving parties of other substantive rights without providing adequate notice and opportunity to defend, has, of course, long been regarded as a denial of the due process of law guaranteed by the Fourteenth Amendment. *Brinkerhoff-Faris Trust & Savings Co. v. Hill, supra.* Cf. *Pennoyer v. Neff, 95 U.S. 714 (1878).* n15

In numerous cases, this Court has reversed criminal convictions in state courts for failure of those courts to provide the essential ingredients of a fair hearing. Thus it has been held that convictions obtained in state courts under the domination of a mob are void. *Moore v. Dempsey, 261 U.S. 86 (1923).*

And see *Frank v. Mangum, 237 U.S. 309 (1915).* Convictions obtained by coerced confessions, by the use of perjured testimony known by the prosecution to be such, or without the effective assistance of counsel, have also been held to be exertions of state authority in conflict with the fundamental rights protected by the Fourteenth Amendment.

But the examples of state judicial action which have been held by this Court to violate the Amendment's commands are not restricted to situations in which the judicial proceedings were found in some manner to be procedurally unfair. It has been recognized that the action of state courts in enforcing a substantive common-law rule formulated by those courts, may result in the denial of rights guaranteed by the Fourteenth Amendment, even though the judicial proceedings in such cases may have been in complete accord with the most rigorous conceptions of procedural due process. n19 Thus, in *American Federation of Labor v. Swing, 312 U.S. 321 (1941),* enforcement by state courts of the common-law policy of the State, which resulted in the restraining of peaceful picketing, was held to be state action of the sort prohibited by the Amendment's guaranties of freedom of discussion. In *Cantwell v. Connecticut, 310 U.S. 296 (1940),* a conviction in a state court of the common-law crime of breach of the peace was, under the circumstances of the case, found to be a violation of the Amendment's commands relating to freedom of religion. In *Bridges v. California, 314 U.S. 252 (1941),* enforcement of the state's common-law rule relating to contempts by publication was held to be state action inconsistent with the prohibitions of the Fourteenth Amendment. n21 And cf. *Chicago, Burlington and Quincy R. Co. v. Chicago, 166 U.S. 226 (1897).*

The short of the matter is that from the time of the adoption of the Fourteenth Amendment until the present, it has been the consistent ruling of this Court that the action of the States to which the Amendment has reference includes action of state courts and state judicial officials. Although, in construing the terms of the Fourteenth Amendment, differences have from time to time been expressed as to whether particular types of state action may be said to offend the Amendment's prohibitory provisions, it has never been suggested that state court action is immunized from the operation of those provisions simply because the act is that of the judicial branch of the state government.

III

Against this background of judicial construction, extending over a period of some three-quarters of a century, we are called upon to consider whether enforcement by state courts of the restrictive agreements in these cases may be deemed to be the acts of those States; and, if so, whether that action has denied these petitioners the equal protection of the laws which the Amendment was intended to insure.

We have no doubt that there has been state action in these cases in the full and complete sense of the phrase. The undisputed facts disclose that petitioners were willing purchasers of properties upon which they desired to establish homes. The owners of the properties were willing sellers; and contracts of sale were accordingly consummated. It is clear that but for the active intervention of the state courts, supported by the full panoply of state power, petitioners would have been free to occupy the properties in question without restraint.

These are not cases, as has been suggested, in which the States have merely abstained from action, leaving private individuals free to impose such discriminations as they see fit. Rather, these are cases in which the States have made available to such individuals the full coercive power of government to deny to petitioners, on the grounds of race or color, the enjoyment of property rights in premises which petitioners are willing and financially able to acquire and which the grantors are willing to sell. The difference between judicial enforcement and non-enforcement of the restrictive covenants is the difference to petitioners between being denied rights of property available to other members of the community and being accorded full enjoyment of those rights on an equal footing.

The enforcement of the restrictive agreements by the state courts in these cases was directed pursuant to the common-law policy of the States as formulated by those courts in earlier decisions. n22 In the Missouri case, enforcement of the covenant was directed in the first instance by the highest court of the State after the trial court had determined the agreement to be invalid for want of the requisite number of signatures. In the Michigan case, the order of enforcement by the trial court was affirmed by the highest state court. The judicial action in each case bears the clear and unmistakable imprimatur of the State. We have noted that previous decisions of this Court have established the proposition that judicial action is not immunized from the operation of the Fourteenth Amendment simply because it is taken pursuant to the state's common-law policy. Nor is the Amendment ineffective simply because the particular pattern of discrimination, which the State has enforced, was defined initially by the terms of a private agreement. State action, as that phrase is understood for the purposes of the Fourteenth Amendment, refers to exertions of state power in all forms. And when the effect of that action is to deny rights subject to the protection of the Fourteenth Amendment, it is the obligation of this Court to enforce the constitutional commands.

We hold that in granting judicial enforcement of the restrictive agreements in these cases, the States have denied petitioners the equal protection of the laws and that, therefore, the action of the state courts cannot stand. We have noted that freedom from discrimination by the States in the enjoyment of property rights was among the basic objectives sought to be effectuated by the framers of the Fourteenth Amendment. That such discrimination has occurred in these cases is clear. Because of the race or color of these petitioners they have been denied rights of ownership or occupancy enjoyed as a matter of course by other citizens of different race or color. The Fourteenth Amendment declares "that all persons, whether colored or white, shall stand equal before the laws of the States, and, in regard to the colored race, for whose protection the amendment was primarily designed, that no discrimination shall be made against them by law because of their color." *Strauder v. West Virginia, supra at 307.* Only recently this Court had occasion to declare that a state law which denied equal enjoyment of property rights to a designated class of citizens of specified race and ancestry, was not a legitimate exercise of the state's police power but violated the guaranty of the equal protection of the laws. *Oyama v. California, 332 U.S. 633 (1948).* Nor may the discriminations imposed by the state courts in these cases be justified as proper exertions of state police power. *Buchanan v. Warley, supra.*

Respondents urge, however, that since the state courts stand ready to enforce restrictive covenants excluding white persons from the ownership or occupancy of property covered by such agreements, enforcement of covenants excluding colored persons may not be deemed a denial of equal protection of the laws to the colored persons who are thereby affected. This contention does not bear scrutiny. The parties have directed our attention to no case in which a court, state or federal, has been called upon to enforce a covenant excluding members of the white majority from ownership or occupancy of real property on grounds of race or color. But there are more fundamental considerations. The rights created by the first section of the Fourteenth Amendment are, by its terms, guaranteed to the individual. The rights established are personal rights. It is, therefore, no answer to these petitioners to say that the courts may also be induced to deny white persons rights of ownership and occupancy on grounds of race or color. Equal protection of the laws is not achieved through indiscriminate imposition of inequalities.

Nor do we find merit in the suggestion that property owners who are parties to these agreements are denied equal protection of the laws if denied access to the courts to enforce the terms of restrictive covenants and to assert property rights which the state courts have held to be created by such agreements. The Constitution confers upon no individual the right to demand action by the State which results in the denial of equal protection of the laws to other individuals. And it would appear beyond question that the power of the State to create and enforce property interests must be exercised within the boundaries defined by the Fourteenth Amendment. Cf. *Marsh v. Alabama, 326 U.S. 501 (1946).*

The problem of defining the scope of the restrictions which the Federal Constitution imposes upon exertions of power by the States has given rise to many of the most persistent and fundamental issues which this Court has been called upon to consider. That problem was foremost in the minds of the framers of the Constitution, and, since that early day, has arisen in a multitude of forms. The task of determining whether the action of a State offends constitutional provisions is one which may not be undertaken lightly. Where, however, it is clear that the action of the State violates the terms of the fundamental charter, it is the obligation of this Court so to declare.

The historical context in which the Fourteenth Amendment became a part of the Constitution should not be forgotten. Whatever else the framers sought to achieve, it is clear that the matter of primary concern was the establishment of equality in the enjoyment of basic civil and political rights and the preservation of those rights from discriminatory action on the part of the States based on considerations of race or color. Seventy-five years ago this Court announced that the provisions of the Amendment are to be construed with this fundamental purpose in mind. Upon full consideration, we have concluded that in these cases the States have acted to deny petitioners the equal protection of the laws guaranteed by the Fourteenth Amendment. Having so decided, we find it unnecessary to consider whether petitioners have also been deprived of property without due process of law or denied privileges and immunities of citizens of the United States.

For the reasons stated, the judgment of the Supreme Court of Missouri and the judgment of the Supreme Court of Michigan must be reversed.

Reversed.

MR. JUSTICE REED, MR. JUSTICE JACKSON, and MR. JUSTICE RUTLEDGE took no part in the consideration or decision of these cases.

LOVING ET UX. v. VIRGINIA
No. 395
Supreme Court of the United States
388 U.S. 1; 87 S. Ct. 1817; 18 L. Ed. 2d 1010; 1967 U.S. LEXIS 1082

April 10, 1967, Argued. June 12, 1967, Decided

JUDGES:

Warren, Black, Douglas, Clark, Harlan, Brennan, Stewart, White, Fortas

OPINION BY:

WARREN

OPINION:

MR. CHIEF JUSTICE WARREN delivered the opinion of the Court.

[1A]This case presents a constitutional question never addressed by this Court: whether a statutory scheme adopted by the State of Virginia to prevent marriages between persons solely on the basis of racial classifications violates the Equal Protection and Due Process Clauses of the Fourteenth Amendment. For reasons which seem to us to reflect the central meaning of those constitutional commands, we conclude that these statutes cannot stand consistently with the Fourteenth Amendment.

In June 1958, two residents of Virginia, Mildred Jeter, a Negro woman, and Richard Loving, a white man, were married in the District of Columbia pursuant to its laws. Shortly after their marriage, the Lovings returned to Virginia and established their marital abode in Caroline County. At the October Term, 1958, of the Circuit Court of Caroline County, a grand jury issued an indictment charging the Lovings with violating Virginia's ban on interracial marriages. On January 6, 1959, the Lovings pleaded guilty to the charge and were sentenced to one year in jail; however, the trial judge suspended the sentence for a period of 25 years on the condition that the Lovings leave the State and not return to Virginia together for 25 years. He stated in an opinion that:

"Almighty God created the races white, black, yellow, malay and red, and he placed them on separate continents.

And but for the interference with his arrangement there would be no cause for such marriages. The fact that he separated the races shows that he did not intend for the races to mix."

After their convictions, the Lovings took up residence in the District of Columbia. On November 6, 1963, they filed a motion in the state trial court to vacate the judgment and set aside the sentence on the ground that the statutes which they had violated were repugnant to the Fourteenth Amendment. ****The Supreme Court of Appeals upheld the constitutionality of the antimiscegenation statutes and, after modifying the sentence, affirmed the convictions. The Lovings appealed this decision, and we noted probable jurisdiction on *December 12, 1966, 385 U.S. 986.*

The two statutes under which appellants were convicted and sentenced are part of a comprehensive statutory scheme aimed at prohibiting and punishing interracial marriages. The Lovings were convicted of violating § 20–58 of the Virginia Code:

"*Leaving State to evade law.*—If any white person and colored person shall go out of this State, for the purpose of being married, and with the intention of returning, and be married out of it, and afterwards return to and reside in it, cohabiting as man and wife, they shall be punished as provided in § 20–59, and the marriage shall be governed by the same law as if it had been solemnized in this State. The fact of their cohabitation here as man and wife shall be evidence of their marriage."

Section 20–59, which defines the penalty for miscegenation, provides:

"*Punishment for marriage.*—If any white person intermarry with a colored person, or any colored person intermarry with a white person, he shall be guilty of a felony and shall be punished by confinement in the penitentiary for not less than one nor more than five years."

Other central provisions in the Virginia statutory scheme are § 20–57, which automatically voids all marriages between "a white person and a colored person" without any judicial proceeding, n3 and §§ 20–54 and 1–14 which, respectively, define "white persons" and "colored persons and Indians" for purposes of the statutory prohibitions. n4 The Lovings have never disputed in the course of this litigation that Mrs. Loving is a "colored person" or that Mr. Loving is a "white person" within the meanings given those terms by the Virginia statutes.

n3 Section 20–57 of the Virginia Code provides:

"*Marriages void without decree.*—All marriages between a white person and a colored person shall be absolutely void without any decree of divorce or other legal process." Va. Code Ann. § 20–57 (1960 Repl. Vol.).

n4 Section 20–54 of the Virginia Code provides:

"*Intermarriage prohibited; meaning of term 'white persons.'*—It shall hereafter be unlawful for any white person in this State to marry any save a white person, or a person with no other admixture of blood than white and American Indian. For the purpose of this chapter, the term 'white person' shall apply only to such person as has no trace whatever of any blood other than Caucasian; but persons who have one-sixteenth or less of the blood of the American Indian and have no other non-Caucasic blood shall be deemed to be white persons. All laws heretofore passed and now in effect regarding the intermarriage of white and colored persons shall apply to marriages prohibited by this chapter." Va. Code Ann. § 20–54 (1960 Repl. Vol.).

The exception for persons with less than one-sixteenth "of the blood of the American Indian" is apparently accounted for, in the words of a tract issued by the Registrar of the State Bureau of Vital Statistics, by "the desire of all to recognize as an integral and honored part of the white race the descendants of John Rolfe and Pocahontas . . . ." Plecker, The New Family and Race Improvement, 17 Va. Health Bull., Extra No. 12, at 25–26 (New Family Series No. 5, 1925), cited in Wadlington, The *Loving* Case: Virginia's Anti-Miscegenation Statute in Historical Perspective, *52 Va. L. Rev. 1189, 1202, n. 93 (1966).*

Section 1–14 of the Virginia Code provides:

"*Colored persons and Indians defined.*—Every person in whom there is ascertainable any Negro blood shall be deemed and taken to be a colored person, and every person not a colored person having one fourth or more of American Indian blood shall be deemed an American Indian; except that members of Indian tribes existing in this Commonwealth having one fourth or more of Indian blood and less than one sixteenth of Negro blood shall be deemed tribal Indians." Va. Code Ann. § 1–14 (1960 Repl. Vol.).

Virginia is now one of 16 States which prohibit and punish marriages on the basis of racial classifications. Penalties for miscegenation arose as an incident to slavery and have been common in Virginia since the colonial period. The present statutory scheme dates from the adoption of the Racial Integrity Act of 1924, passed during the period of extreme nativism which followed the end of the First World War. The central features of this Act, and current Virginia law, are the absolute prohibition of a "white person" marrying other than another "white person," a prohibition against issuing marriage licenses until the issuing official is satisfied that the applicants' statements as to their race are correct, certificates of "racial composition" to be kept by both local and state registrars, and the carrying forward of earlier prohibitions against racial intermarriage.

I

In upholding the constitutionality of these provisions in the decision below, the Supreme Court of Appeals of Virginia referred to its 1955 decision in *Naim v. Naim,* **, as stating the reasons supporting the validity of these laws. In *Naim*, the state court concluded that the State's legitimate purposes were "to preserve the racial integrity of its citizens," and to prevent "the corruption of blood," "a mongrel breed of citizens," and "the obliteration of racial pride," obviously an endorsement of the doctrine of White Supremacy. *** The court also reasoned that marriage has traditionally been subject to state regulation without federal intervention, and, consequently, the regulation of marriage should be left to exclusive state control by the Tenth Amendment.

[2]While the state court is no doubt correct in asserting that marriage is a social relation subject to the State's police power, *** the State does not contend in its argument before this Court that its powers to regulate marriage are unlimited notwithstanding the commands of the

Fourteenth Amendment. Nor could it do so in light of *Meyer v. Nebraska, 262 U.S. 390 (1923)*, and *Skinner v. Oklahoma, 316 U.S. 535 (1942)*. Instead, the State argues that the meaning of the Equal Protection Clause, as illuminated by the statements of the Framers, is only that state penal laws containing an interracial element as part of the definition of the offense must apply equally to whites and Negroes in the sense that members of each race are punished to the same degree. Thus, the State contends that, because its miscegenation statutes punish equally both the white and the Negro participants in an interracial marriage, these statutes, despite their reliance on racial classifications, do not constitute an invidious discrimination based upon race. The second argument advanced by the State assumes the validity of its equal application theory. The argument is that, if the Equal Protection Clause does not outlaw miscegenation statutes because of their reliance on racial classifications, the question of constitutionality would thus become whether there was any rational basis for a State to treat interracial marriages differently from other marriages. On this question, the State argues, the scientific evidence is substantially in doubt and, consequently, this Court should defer to the wisdom of the state legislature in adopting its policy of discouraging interracial marriages.

[3]Because we reject the notion that the mere "equal application" of a statute containing racial classifications is enough to remove the classifications from the Fourteenth Amendment's proscription of all invidious racial discriminations, we do not accept the State's contention that these statutes should be upheld if there is any possible basis for concluding that they serve a rational purpose. The mere fact of equal application does not mean that our analysis of these statutes should follow the approach we have taken in cases involving no racial discrimination where the Equal Protection Clause has been arrayed against a statute discriminating between the kinds of advertising which may be displayed on trucks in New York City, *Railway Express Agency, Inc. v. New York, 336 U.S. 106 (1949)*, or an exemption in Ohio's ad valorem tax for merchandise owned by a nonresident in a storage warehouse, *Allied Stores of Ohio,] Inc. v. Bowers, 358 U.S. 522 (1959)*. In these cases, involving distinctions not drawn according to race, the Court has merely asked whether there is any rational foundation for the discriminations, and has deferred to the wisdom of the state legislatures. In the case at bar, however, we deal with statutes containing racial classifications, and the fact of equal application does not immunize the statute from the very heavy burden of justification which the Fourteenth Amendment has traditionally required of state statutes drawn according to race.

[4]The State argues that statements in the Thirty-ninth Congress about the time of the passage of the Fourteenth Amendment indicate that the Framers did not intend the Amendment to make unconstitutional state miscegenation laws. Many of the statements alluded to by the State concern the debates over the Freedmen's Bureau Bill, which President Johnson vetoed, and the Civil Rights Act of 1866, 14 Stat. 27, enacted over his veto. While these statements have some relevance to the intention of Congress in submitting the Fourteenth Amendment, it must be understood that they pertained to the passage of specific statutes and not to the broader, organic purpose of a constitutional amendment. As for the various statements directly concerning the Fourteenth Amendment, we have said in connection with a related problem, that although these historical sources "cast some light" they are not sufficient to resolve the problem; "[at] best, they are inconclusive. The most avid proponents of the post-War Amendments undoubtedly intended them to remove all legal distinctions among 'all persons born or naturalized in the United States.' Their opponents, just as certainly, were antagonistic to both the letter and the spirit of the Amendments and wished them to have the most limited effect." *Brown v. Board of Education, 347 U.S. 483, 489 (1954)*. See also *Strauder v. West Virginia, 100 U.S. 303, 310 (1880)*. We have rejected the proposition that the debates in the Thirty-ninth Congress or in the state legislatures which ratified the Fourteenth Amendment supported the theory advanced by the State, that the requirement of equal protection of the laws is satisfied by penal laws defining offenses based on racial classifications so long as white and Negro participants in the offense were similarly punished. ***

[6]The State finds support for its "equal application" theory in the decision of the Court in *Pace v. Alabama, 106 U.S. 583 (1883)*. In that case, the Court upheld a conviction under an Alabama statute forbidding adultery or fornication between a white person and a Negro which imposed a greater penalty than that of a statute proscribing similar conduct by members of the same race. The Court reasoned that the statute could not be said to discriminate against Negroes because the punishment for each participant in the offense was the same. However, as recently as the 1964 Term, in rejecting the reasoning of that case, we stated "*Pace* represents a limited view of the Equal Protection Clause which has not withstood analysis in the subsequent decisions of this

Court." *McLaughlin v. Florida, supra, at 188.* As we there demonstrated, the Equal Protection Clause requires the consideration of whether the classifications drawn by any statute constitute an arbitrary and invidious discrimination. The clear and central purpose of the Fourteenth Amendment was to eliminate all official state sources of invidious racial discrimination in the States. ***

[8]There can be no question but that Virginia's miscegenation statutes rest solely upon distinctions drawn according to race. The statutes proscribe generally accepted conduct if engaged in by members of different races. Over the years, this Court has consistently repudiated "distinctions between citizens solely because of their ancestry" as being "odious to a free people whose institutions are founded upon the doctrine of equality." *Hirabayashi v. United States, 320 U.S. 81, 100 (1943).* At the very least, the Equal Protection Clause demands that racial classifications, especially suspect in criminal statutes, be subjected to the "most rigid scrutiny," *Korematsu v. United States, 323 U.S. 214, 216 (1944),* and, if they are ever to be upheld, they must be shown to be necessary to the accomplishment of some permissible state objective, independent of the racial discrimination which it was the object of the Fourteenth Amendment to eliminate. Indeed, two members of this Court have already stated that they "cannot conceive of a valid legislative purpose . . . which makes the color of a person's skin the test of whether his conduct is a criminal offense." *McLaughlin v. Florida, supra, at 198* (STEWART, J., joined by DOUGLAS, J., concurring).

[9]There is patently no legitimate overriding purpose independent of invidious racial discrimination which justifies this classification. The fact that Virginia prohibits only interracial marriages involving white persons demonstrates that the racial classifications must stand on their own justification, as measures designed to maintain White Supremacy. We have consistently denied the constitutionality of measures which restrict the rights of citizens on account of race. There can be no doubt that restricting the freedom to marry solely because of racial classifications violates the central meaning of the Equal Protection Clause.

II

[10]These statutes also deprive the Lovings of liberty without due process of law in violation of the Due Process Clause of the Fourteenth Amendment. The freedom to marry has long been recognized as one of the vital personal rights essential to the orderly pursuit of happiness by free men.

[12]Marriage is one of the "basic civil rights of man," fundamental to our very existence and survival. ***To deny this fundamental freedom on so unsupportable a basis as the racial classifications embodied in these statutes, classifications so directly subversive of the principle of equality at the heart of the Fourteenth Amendment, is surely to deprive all the State's citizens of liberty without due process of law. The Fourteenth Amendment requires that the freedom of choice to marry not be restricted by invidious racial discriminations. Under our Constitution, the freedom to marry, or not marry, a person of another race resides with the individual and cannot be infringed by the State.

These convictions must be reversed.

It is so ordered.

CONCUR BY:

Statutory Prohibitions of Invidious Discrimination: Government (State) and/or Private Action

Vote Dilution and the 1965 Voting Rights Act

VOTING RIGHTS ACT OF 1965
42 U.S.C. §1973

---

§2. (a) No voting qualification or prerequisite to voting or standard, practice, or procedure shall be imposed or applied by any State of political subdivision in a manner which results in a denial or abridgement of the right of any citizen of the United States to vote on account of race or color, or in contravention of the guarantees set forth in section 4(f)(2) [42 USCS §1973b(f)(2)], as provided in subsection (b).

(b) A violation of subsection (a) is established if, based on the totality of circumstances, it is shown that the political processes leading to nomination or election in the State or political subdivision are not equally open to participation by members of a class of citizens protected by subsection (a) in that its members have less opportunity than other members of the electorate to participate in the political process and to elect representatives of their choice. The extent to which members of a protected class have been elected to office in the State or political subdivision is one circumstance which may be considered: Provided, That nothing in this section establishes a right to have members of a protected class elected in numbers equal to their proportion in the population.

HEART OF ATLANTA MOTEL, INC. v. UNITED STATES
Supreme Court of the United States (1964)
379 U.S. 241

MR. JUSTICE CLARK delivered the opinion of the Court. ...

1. The Factual Background and Contentions of the Parties.

The case comes here on admissions and stipulated facts. Appellant owns and operates the Heart of Atlanta Motel which has 216 rooms available to transient guests. The motel is located on Courtland Street, two blocks from downtown Peachtree Street. It is readily accessible to interstate highways 75 and 85 and state highways 23 and 41. Appellant solicits patronage from outside the State of Georgia through various national advertising media, including magazines of national circulation; it maintains over 50 billboards and highway signs within the State, soliciting patronage for the motel; it accepts convention trade from outside Georgia and approximately 75% of its registered guests are from out of State. Prior to passage of the Act the motel had followed a practice of refusing to rent rooms to Negroes, and it alleged that it intended to continue to do so. In an effort to perpetuate that policy this suit was filed.

The appellant contends that Congress ... exceeded its power to regulate commerce under Art. I, §8, cl. 3, of the Constitution ... ; that the Act violates the Fifth Amendment because appellant is deprived of the right to choose its customers and operate its business as it wishes, resulting in a taking of its liberty and property without due process of law and a taking of its property without just compensation; and, finally, that by requiring appellant to rent available rooms to Negroes against its will, Congress is subjecting it to involuntary servitude in contravention of the Thirteenth Amendment. ...

3. Title II of the Act.

This Title is divided into seven sections beginning with §201 (a) which provides that:

> "All persons shall be entitled to the full and equal enjoyment of the goods, services, facilities, privileges, advantages, and accommodations of any place of public accommodation, as defined in this section, without discrimination or segregation on the ground of race, color, religion, or national origin."

There are listed in §201 (b) four classes of business establishments, each of which "serves the public" and "is a place of public accommodation" within the meaning of §201 (a) "if its operations affect commerce, or if discrimination or segregation by it is supported by State action." The covered establishments are: [hotels, motels and lodging places; restaurants; places of entertainment; and all other establishments within which one or more of the above are located]." ...

4. Application of Title II to Heart of Atlanta Motel.

It is admitted that the operation of the motel brings it within the provisions of §201 (a) of the Act and that appellant refused to provide lodging for transient Negroes because of their race or color and that it intends to continue that policy unless restrained.

The sole question posed is, therefore, the constitutionality of the Civil Rights Act of 1964 as applied to these facts. The legislative history of the Act indicates that Congress based the Act on §5 and the Equal Protection Clause of the Fourteenth Amendment as well as its power to regulate interstate commerce. ... [Finding the commerce power adequate, the Court held it was not necessary to consider the other grounds. The Court also held that the *Civil Rights Cases* were not applicable because that Court had not considered whether the 1875 Civil Rights Act might have been upheld under the Commerce Clause.] ...

6.   The Basis of Congressional Action.

While the Act as adopted carried no congressional findings, the record of its passage through each house is replete with evidence of the burdens that discrimination by race or color places upon interstate commerce. This testimony included the fact that our people have become increasingly mobile with millions of people of all races traveling from State to State; that Negroes in particular have been the subject of discrimination in transient accommodations, having to travel great distances to secure the same; that often they have been unable to obtain accommodations and have had to call upon friends to put them up overnight; and that these conditions had become so acute as to require the listing of available lodging for Negroes in a special guidebook which was itself "dramatic testimony to the difficulties" Negroes encounter in travel. These exclusionary practices were found to be nationwide, the Under Secretary of Commerce testifying that there is "no question that this discrimination in the North still exists to a large degree" and in the West and Midwest as well. This testimony indicated a qualitative as well as quantitative effect on interstate travel by Negroes. The former was the obvious impairment of the Negro traveler's pleasure and convenience that resulted when he continually was uncertain of finding lodging. As for the latter, there was evidence that this uncertainty stemming from racial discrimination had the effect of discouraging travel on the part of a substantial portion of the Negro community. This was the conclusion not only of the Under Secretary of Commerce but also of the Administrator of the Federal Aviation Agency who wrote the Chairman of the Senate Commerce Committee that it was his "belief that air commerce is adversely affected by the denial to a substantial segment of the traveling public of adequate and desegregated public accommodations." We shall not burden this opinion with further details since the voluminous testimony presents overwhelming evidence that discrimination by hotels and motels impedes interstate travel.

7.   The Power of Congress Over Interstate Travel.

The power of Congress to deal with these obstructions depends on the meaning of the Commerce Clause. Its meaning was first enunciated 140 years ago by the great Chief Justice John Marshall in *Gibbons v. Ogden* (1824), in these words:

... "It is the power to regulate; that is, to prescribe the rule by which commerce is to be governed. This power, like all others vested in Congress, is complete in itself, may be exercised to its utmost extend, and acknowledges no limitations, other than are prescribed in the constitution. ... If, as has always been understood, the sovereignty of Congress ... is plenary as to those objects [specified in the Constitution], the power over commerce ... is vested in Congress as absolutely as it would be in a single government, having in its constitution the same restrictions on the exercise of the power as are found in the constitution of the United States. The wisdom and the discretion of Congress, their identity with the people, and the influence which their constituents possess at elections, are, in this, as in many other instances, ... the sole restraints on which they have relied, to secure them from its abuse. They are the restraints on which the people must often rely solely, in all representative governments."

In short, the determinative test of the exercise of power by the Congress under the Commerce Clause is simply whether the activity sought to be regulated is "commerce which concerns more States than one" and has a real and substantial relation to the national interest. Let us now turn to this facet of the problem.

That the "intercourse" of which the Chief Justice spoke included the movement of persons through more States than one was settled as early as 1849, in the *Passenger Cases*, where Mr. Justice McLean stated: "That the transportation of passengers is a part of commerce is not now an open question." Again in 1913 Mr. Justice McKenna, speaking for the Court, said: "Commerce among the States, we have said, consists of intercourse and traffic between their citizens, and includes the transportation of persons and property." ...

... In framing Title II of this Act Congress was ... dealing with what it considered a moral problem. But that fact does not detract from the overwhelming evidence of the disruptive effect that racial discrimination has had on commercial intercourse. It was this burden which empowered Congress to enact appropriate legislation, and, given this basis for the exercise of its power, Congress was not restricted by the fact that the particular obstruction to interstate commerce with which it was dealing was also deemed a moral and social wrong.

It is said that the operation of the motel here is of a purely local character. But, assuming this to be true, "if it is interstate commerce that feels the pinch, it does not matter how local the operation which applies the squeeze." As Chief Justice Stone put it in *United States v. Darby*:

> "The power of Congress over interstate commerce is not confined to the regulation of commerce among the states. It extends to those activities intrastate which so affect interstate commerce or the exercise of the power of Congress over it as to make regulation of them appropriate means to the attainment of a legitimate end, the exercise of the granted power of Congress to regulate interstate commerce."

Thus the power of Congress to promote interstate commerce also includes the power to regulate the local incidents thereof, including local activities in both the States of origin and destination, which might have a substantial and harmful effect upon that commerce. One need only examine the evidence which we have discussed above to see that Congress may—as it has—prohibit racial discrimination by motels serving travelers, however "local" their operations may appear.

Not does the Act deprive appellant of liberty or property under the Fifth Amendment. The commerce power invoked here by the Congress is a specific and plenary one authorized by the Constitution itself. The only questions are: (1) whether Congress had a rational basis for finding that racial discrimination by motels affected commerce, and (2) if it had such a basis, whether the means it selected to eliminate that evil are reasonable and appropriate. If they are, appellant has no "right" to select its guests as it sees fit, free from governmental regulation. ...

We find no merit in the remainder or appellant's contentions, including that of "involuntary servitude." As we have seen, 32 States prohibit racial discrimination in public accommodations. These laws but codify the common-law innkeeper rule which long predated the Thirteenth Amendment. It is difficult to believe that the Amendment was intended to abrogate this principle. ...

We, therefore, conclude that the action of the Congress in the adoption of the Act as applied here to a motel which concededly serves interstate travelers is within the power granted it by the Commerce Clause of the Constitution, as interpreted by this Court for 140 years. It may be argued that Congress could have pursued other methods to eliminate the obstructions it found in interstate commerce caused by racial discrimination. But this is a matter of policy that rests entirely with the Congress [and] not with the courts. How obstructions in commerce may be removed—what means are to be employed—is within the sound and exclusive discretion of the Congress. It is subject only to one caveat—that the means chosen by it must be reasonably adapted to the end permitted by the Constitution. We cannot say that its choice here was not so adapted. The Constitution requires no more.

KATZENBACH, ACTING ATTORNEY GENERAL, et al. v. McCLUNG et al.
Supreme Court of the United States
379 U.S. 294

December 14, 1964, Decided

MR. JUSTICE CLARK delivered the opinion of the Court.

This case was argued with *Heart of Atlanta Motel* v. *United States*, decided this date in which we upheld the constitutional validity of Title II of the Civil Rights Act of 1964 against an attack by hotels, motels, and like establishments. This complaint for injunctive relief against appellants attacks the constitutionality of the Act as applied to a restaurant. The case was heard by a three-judge United States District Court and an injunction was issued restraining appellants from enforcing the Act against the restaurant. On direct appeal, we noted probable jurisdiction. We now reverse the judgment.***

2. The Facts

Ollie's Barbecue is a family-owned restaurant in Birmingham, Alabama, specializing in barbecued meats and homemade pies, with a seating capacity of 220 customers. It is located on a state highway 11 blocks from an interstate one and a somewhat greater distance from railroad and bus stations. The restaurant caters to a family and white-collar trade with a take-out service for Negroes. It employs 36 persons, two-thirds of whom are Negroes.

In the 12 months preceding the passage of the Act, the restaurant purchased locally approximately $150,000 worth of food, $69,683 or 46% of which was meat that it bought from a local supplier who had procured it from outside the State. The District Court expressly found that a substantial portion of the food served in the restaurant had moved in interstate commerce. The restaurant has refused to serve Negroes in its dining accommodations since its original opening in 1927, and since July 2, 1964, it has been operating in violation of the Act. The court below concluded that if it were required to serve Negroes it would lose a substantial amount of business.

On the merits, the District Court held that the Act could not be applied under the Fourteenth Amendment because it was conceded that the State of Alabama was not involved in the refusal of the restaurant to serve Negroes. It was also admitted that the Thirteenth Amendment was authority neither for validating nor for invalidating the Act. As to the Commerce Clause, the court found that it was "an express grant of power to Congress to regulate interstate commerce, which consists of the movement of persons, goods or information from one state to another"; and it found that the clause was also a grant of power "to regulate intrastate activities, but only to the extent that action on its part is necessary or appropriate to the effective execution of its expressly granted power to regulate interstate commerce." There must be, it said, a close and substantial relation between local activities and interstate commerce which requires control of the former in the protection of the latter. The court concluded, however, that the Congress, rather than finding facts sufficient to meet this rule, had legislated a conclusive presumption that a restaurant affects interstate commerce if it serves or offers to serve interstate travelers or if a substantial portion of the food which it serves has moved in commerce. This, the court held, it could not do because there was no demonstrable connection between food purchased in interstate commerce and sold in a restaurant and the conclusion of Congress that discrimination in the restaurant would affect that commerce.

The basic holding in *Heart of Atlanta Motel*, answers many of the contentions made by the appellees. There we outlined the overall purpose and operational plan of Title II and found it a valid exercise of the power to regulate interstate commerce insofar as it requires hotels and motels to serve transients without regard to their race or color. In this case we consider its application to restaurants which serve food a substantial portion of which has moved in commerce.

3. The Act As Applied

Section 201 (a) of Title II commands that all persons shall be entitled to the full and equal enjoyment of the goods and services of any place of public accommodation without discrimination or segregation on the ground of race, color, religion, or national origin; and § 201 (b) defines establishments as places of public accommodation if their operations affect commerce or segregation by them is supported by state action. Sections 201 (b)(2) and (c) place any "restaurant … principally engaged in selling food for consumption on the premises" under the Act "if … it serves or offers to serve interstate travelers or a substantial portion of the food which it serves … has moved in commerce."

Ollie's Barbecue admits that it is covered by these provisions of the Act. The Government makes no contention that the discrimination at the restaurant was supported by the State of Alabama. There is no claim that interstate travelers frequented the restaurant. The sole question, therefore, narrows down to whether Title II, as applied to a restaurant annually receiving about $70,000 worth of food which has moved in commerce, is a valid exercise of the power of Congress. The Government has contended that Congress had ample basis upon which to find that racial discrimination at restaurants which receive from out of state a substantial portion of the food served does, in fact, impose commercial burdens of national magnitude upon interstate commerce. The appellees' major argument is directed to this premise. They urge that no such basis existed. It is to that question that we now turn.

4. The Congressional Hearings

As we noted in *Heart of Atlanta Motel* both Houses of Congress conducted prolonged hearings on the Act. And, as we said there, while no formal findings were made, which of course are not necessary, it is well that we make mention of the testimony at these hearings the better to understand the problem before Congress and determine whether the Act is a reasonable and appropriate means toward its solution. The record is replete with testimony of the burdens placed on interstate commerce by racial discrimination in restaurants. A comparison of per capita spending by Negroes in restaurants, theaters, and like establishments indicated less spending, after discounting income differences, in areas where discrimination is widely practiced. This condition, which was

especially aggravated in the South, was attributed in the testimony of the Under Secretary of Commerce to racial segregation. This diminutive spending springing from a refusal to serve Negroes and their total loss as customers has, regardless of the absence of direct evidence, a close connection to interstate commerce. The fewer customers a restaurant enjoys the less food it sells and consequently the less it buys. In addition, the Attorney General testified that this type of discrimination imposed "an artificial restriction on the market" and interfered with the flow of merchandise. In addition, there were many references to discriminatory situations causing wide unrest and having a depressant effect on general business conditions in the respective communities.

Moreover there was an impressive array of testimony that discrimination in restaurants had a direct and highly restrictive effect upon interstate travel by Negroes. This resulted, it was said, because discriminatory practices prevent Negroes from buying prepared food served on the premises while on a trip, except in isolated and unkempt restaurants and under most unsatisfactory and often unpleasant conditions. This obviously discourages travel and obstructs interstate commerce for one can hardly travel without eating. Likewise, it was said, that discrimination deterred professional, as well as skilled, people from moving into areas where such practices occurred and thereby caused industry to be reluctant to establish there.

[7]We believe that this testimony afforded ample basis for the conclusion that established restaurants in such areas sold less interstate goods because of the discrimination, that interstate travel was obstructed directly by it, that business in general suffered and that many new businesses refrained from establishing there as a result of it. Hence the District Court was in error in concluding that there was no connection between discrimination and the movement of interstate commerce. The court's conclusion that such a connection is outside "common experience" flies in the face of stubborn fact.

[8]It goes without saying that, viewed in isolation, the volume of food purchased by Ollie's Barbecue from sources supplied from out of state was insignificant when compared with the total foodstuffs moving in commerce. But, as our late Brother Jackson said for the Court in *Wickard* v. *Filburn*, 317 U.S. 111 (1942):

"That appellee's own contribution to the demand for wheat may be trivial by itself is not enough to remove him from the scope of federal regulation where, as here, his contribution, taken together with that of many others similarly situated, is far from trivial."

We noted in *Heart of Atlanta Motel* that a number of witnesses attested to the fact that racial discrimination was not merely a state or regional problem but was one of nationwide scope. Against this background, we must conclude that while the focus of the legislation was on the individual restaurant's relation to interstate commerce, Congress appropriately considered the importance of that connection with the knowledge that the discrimination was but "representative of many others throughout the country, the total incidence of which if left unchecked may well become far-reaching in its harm to commerce."

[9]With this situation spreading as the record shows, Congress was not required to await the total dislocation of commerce. As was said in *Consolidated Edison Co.* v. *Labor Board*, 305 U.S. 197 (1938):

"But it cannot be maintained that the exertion of federal power must await the disruption of that commerce. Congress was entitled to provide reasonable preventive measures and that was the object of the National Labor Relations Act." At 222.

5. The Power of Congress to Regulate Local Activities

Article I, § 8, cl. 3, confers upon Congress the power "to regulate Commerce … among the several States" and Clause 18 of the same Article grants it the power "to make all Laws which shall be necessary and proper for carrying into Execution the foregoing Powers. …" This grant, as we have pointed out in *Heart of Atlanta Motel* "extends to those activities intrastate which so affect interstate commerce, or the exertion of the power of Congress over it, as to make regulation of them appropriate means to the attainment of a legitimate end, the effective execution of the granted power to regulate interstate commerce.".Much is said about a restaurant business being local but " even if appellee's activity be local and though it may not be regarded as commerce, it may still, whatever its nature, be reached by Congress if it exerts a substantial economic effect on interstate commerce. …" The activities that are beyond the reach of Congress are "those which are completely within a particular State, which do not affect other States, and with which it is not necessary to interfere, for the purpose of executing some of the general powers of the government." This rule is as good today as it was when Chief Justice Marshall laid it down almost a century and a half ago.

This Court has held time and again that this power extends to activities of retail establishments, including restaurants, which directly or indirectly burden or obstruct interstate commerce. We have detailed the cases in *Heart of Atlanta Motel*, and will not repeat them here.

[13]Nor are the cases holding that interstate commerce ends when goods come to rest in the State of destination apposite here. That line of cases has been applied with reference to state taxation or regulation but not in the field of federal regulation.

The appellees contend that Congress has arbitrarily created a conclusive presumption that all restaurants meeting the criteria set out in the Act "affect commerce." Stated another way, they object to the omission of a provision for a case-by-case determination—judicial or administrative—that racial discrimination in a particular restaurant affects commerce.

But Congress' action in framing this Act was not unprecedented. In United *States* v. *Darby*, 312 U.S. 100 (1941), this Court held constitutional the Fair Labor Standards Act of 1938. There Congress determined that the payment of substandard wages to employees engaged in the production of goods for commerce, while not itself commerce, so inhibited it as to be subject to federal regulation. The appellees in that case argued, as do the appellees here, that the Act was invalid because it included no provision for an independent inquiry regarding the effect on commerce of substandard wages in a particular business. But the Court rejected the argument, observing that:

"Sometimes Congress itself has said that a particular activity affects the commerce, as it did in the present Act, the Safety Appliance Act and the Railway Labor Act. In passing on the validity of legislation of the class last mentioned the only function of courts is to determine whether the particular activity regulated or prohibited is within the reach of the federal power."

[14]Here, as there, Congress has determined for itself that refusals of service to Negroes have imposed burdens both upon the interstate flow of food and upon the movement of products generally. Of course, the mere fact that Congress has said when particular activity shall be deemed to affect commerce does not preclude further examination by this Court. But where we find that the legislators, in light of the facts and testimony before them, have a rational basis for finding a chosen regulatory scheme necessary to the protection of commerce, our investigation is at an end. The only remaining question—one answered in the affirmative by the court below—is whether the particular restaurant either serves or offers to serve interstate travelers or serves food a substantial portion of which has moved in interstate commerce.

[6B]The appellees urge that Congress, in passing the Fair Labor Standards Act and the National Labor Relations Act, made specific findings which were embodied in those statutes. Here, of course, Congress has included no formal findings. But their absence is not fatal to the validity of the statute for the evidence presented at the hearings fully indicated the nature and effect of the burdens on commerce which Congress meant to alleviate.

[15]Confronted as we are with the facts laid before Congress, we must conclude that it had a rational basis for finding that racial discrimination in restaurants had a direct and adverse effect on the free flow of interstate commerce. Insofar as the sections of the Act here relevant are concerned, §§ 201 (b)(2) and (c), Congress prohibited discrimination only in those establishments having a close tie to interstate commerce, i. e., those, like the McClungs', serving food that has come from out of the State. We think in so doing that Congress acted well within its power to protect and foster commerce in extending the coverage of Title II only to those restaurants offering to serve interstate travelers or serving food, a substantial portion of which has moved in interstate commerce.

[16]The absence of direct evidence connecting discriminatory restaurant service with the flow of interstate food, a factor on which the appellees place much reliance, is not, given the evidence as to the effect of such practices on other aspects of commerce, a crucial matter.

[17]The power of Congress in this field is broad and sweeping; where it keeps within its sphere and violates no express constitutional limitation it has been the rule of this Court, going back almost to the founding days of the Republic, not to interfere. The Civil Rights Act of 1964, as here applied, we find to be plainly appropriate in the resolution of what the Congress found to be a national commercial problem of the first magnitude. We find it in no violation of any express limitations of the Constitution and we therefore declare it valid.

The judgment is therefore
Reversed.

DURHAM v. RED LAKE FISHING AND HUNTING CLUB, INC.
United States District Court for the Western District of Texas (1987)
666 F. Supp. 954

WALTER S. SMITH, JR., DISTRICT JUDGE. ...

Findings of Fact

Plaintiff, James A. Durham, a black male, brings this cause of action under the civil rights laws dealing with racial discrimination in public accommodations and fair housing. ...

Red Lake Fishing and Hunting Club, Inc. ("Club"), originally organized in 1938, was formally incorporated as a non-profit recreational club under the laws of Texas in 1939. Subsequent to the incorporation, the Club acquired approximately 400 acres of land in Freestone County, Texas. The principal purpose of the Club, as stated in its original charter and its 1979 restated articles of incorporation, was to establish and maintain a fishing, hunting and boating club and to engage in the conservation of wild life and to purchase and own land and bodies of water necessary to accomplish this purpose. The corporation owns all fee title interest in the property, including the lake. A member of the Club is entitled to make improvements to a lot designated for his or her use. The member making the improvement owns such improvements and may sell them to a new member of the Club, or may remove them upon termination of the membership. Currently, Club facilities cover approximately 400 acres with sixteen permanent residents and more than seventy buildings.

Dues are collected yearly from each member to be used for the maintenance of the club facilities and property and the payment of appropriate taxes.

Membership to the Club is limited to eighty members. The procedure for membership includes an application and fee, recommendation by a membership committee, and voting by all members of the Club. Any applicant who receives five or more negative votes will be rejected. The Club has never had a black member.

In the present case Plaintiff James A. Durham agreed to purchase the membership of Club member H. C. Daniel, who is white, in the fall of 1982. Plaintiff would be entitled to use of a specific plot of land and the improvements of such land. H. C. Daniel wrote a letter to the Club requesting a transfer of his membership, share 180, to Plaintiff and highly recommended him for membership. Plaintiff subsequently applied for membership to the Club and was recommended for membership without reservation by the Club's membership committee. Plaintiff was the first black to apply for membership in the Club. On September 14, 1982, a letter was sent by the Secretary of the Club informing members of the dates for voting on the application of James A. Durham. In the letter, Plaintiff was referred to as "the son of Walter Durham of Route 2, Fairfield, Texas." Walter Durham worked for the Club Since the Club's inception in 1938, and was known to be black. After the voting concluded, the counting of the ballots showed that Plaintiff received more than five negative votes and was, therefore, rejected for membership. In January, 1983, Plaintiff resubmitted his application. Again, Plaintiff received more than five negative votes and was rejected for membership. The only justification given by the three board members as to their "no" votes was a concern that Plaintiff would bring too many family members to the Club. There is no limit to the number of guests a member may bring to the Club. Others could not explain why they voted "no." From the Club's inception, only two white applicants have been rejected for membership. The first, Mace Daniel, had violated the Club's rules while visiting as a guest by staying longer than the requisite period and by shooting at and destroying some Club property during target practice. The second, Jim Sanders, was a member of the leadership of the local Jehovah's Witness Church who moved to the area in the late 1960's for the purposes of integrating the racially separate black and white Jehovah's Witnesses Churches. At least five new white members were admitted to the Club during the period in which Plaintiff applied, being admitted with zero negative votes. One white member was admitted with three negative votes.

Conclusions of Law

Discrimination

Courts have consistently held that the Plaintiff establishes a prima facie case ... by proving:

1. That he or she is a member of a racial minority;
2. That he or she applied for and was qualified to rent or purchase certain property or housing;
3. That he or she was rejected; and
4. That the housing or rental property remained available thereafter.

In the present case, Plaintiff James A. Durham is a member of a racial minority, black. Durham applied for and was qualified for H. C. Daniel's membership share number 180, which included use of a specific plot of land on the Club's property and the improvements thereon. Plaintiff was rejected for membership twice and the property remained available thereafter.

Defendant may overcome this prima facie showing of discriminatory intent by articulating some legitimate non-discriminatory reason for the Plaintiff's rejection. *McDonnell Douglas Corp. v. Green.* Three board members of the Club testified that they voted to reject Plaintiff because there was a concern that Plaintiff would bring too many family members as guests to the Club. ... Others who testified that they voted to reject Plaintiff's application could not explain why they voted "no." No evidence was presented that the Club had a limit on the number of guests that a member could bring to the Club. The Club limited its membership to eighty persons, but not the number of guests. Once the Defendant articulates a non-discriminatory reason for the Plaintiff's rejection, the Plaintiff bears the ultimate burden of persuasion as to whether the Plaintiff has been the victim of intentional discrimination. This burden may be met in one of two ways. ... First, a Plaintiff may persuade the Court that the decision to reject was more likely than not motivated by a discriminatory reason. Second, The burden is also satisfied if the Plaintiff shows that the "proffered explanation is

unworthy of credence." The Court finds that the explanation given by the three board members is unworthy of credence and that Plaintiff's rejection was more likely than not motivated by a discriminatory reason. The fact that Plaintiff may bring a large number of family members as guests to the Club may only support further discriminatory intent by the Club since Plaintiff's family members are black. Further, guests are limited as to the number of days allowed in the Club each year which would preclude Plaintiff from having his entire family at the Club at all times.

The Plaintiff may also meet the burden of persuasion by showing direct and indirect evidence as to intent. In the Club's almost fifty year history only two whites have been rejected for membership. One had violated Club policy by staying longer than twenty-eight days as allowed per guest each year and by shooting and destroying Club property during target practice. The other was a member of a Jehovah's Witness Church who was involved in integrating black and white Jehovah's Witness Churches. All other white applicants were accepted. Plaintiff met all of the qualifications for membership and was rejected by a large number of votes. Also, the letter that was sent to each member informing them of the dates for voting on the Plaintiff's application stated that Plaintiff was the son of Walter Durham, who was known by members since he worked for the Club since its inception in 1938. Members would have no problem directly connecting Plaintiff to his race. For the reasons stated above, the Court finds that Plaintiff was denied membership in the Club because of Plaintiff's race, black.

Private Club Exemption

Having found that the Club has discriminated against Plaintiff on the basis of race, the Court must next examine whether the Club falls under the private club exemption as set forth in Title II of the Civil Rights Act of 1964 and codified under 42 U.S.C §2000a. ... Based on the private club exemption, a "truly private club," i.e. one which is genuinely selective in its membership and meets the other tests of *United States v. Jordan*, does have the right to discriminate against potential members based on race; but clearly the only criteria for selection cannot be that one be white. ...

Title 42 U.S.C. §2000a ("Title II") provides that "all persons shall be entitled to the full and equal enjoyment of the goods, services, facilities, privileges, advantages and accommodations of any place of public accommodation." "Public accommodation" is defined . . . as an establishment which operations affect commerce. [Title II] lists an example of a covered establishment as any "place of . . . entertainment." . . . Courts have found places of entertainment to include health and beauty spas, golf clubs, bars and package stores, swimming pools, and athletic clubs. In the present case, the Club's primary purpose is for hunting, fishing and boating. The Court is of the opinion that these recreational activities at the Club place the Club under the definition of "place of entertainment" as applied to Title II. The Club also is a recreational club which affects commerce. For over twenty years the Club was engaged in interstate commerce by entering into oil and gas leases. Oil and gas are substances which move in interstate commerce. Several of the leases were still in effect at the time of Plaintiff's application for membership. During the period that Plaintiff applied for membership, the Club received approximately $ 60,000.00 per year from an oil lease. The Club also affected interstate commerce by allowing various members and guests to bring in boats, camping equipment and guns which had moved in interstate commerce.

The only exception to 42 U.S.C. §2000a is the private club exemption. If the Club is found to be a truly private club, the Club can discriminate. "Private Club" has not been defined by statute or by the Supreme Court. However, various courts have developed standards and specific criteria to make this determination.

In determining whether an establishment is in fact a private club, there is no single test. A number of variables must be examined in the light of the Act's clear purpose of protecting only the genuine privacy of private clubs whose membership is genuinely selective. Each factor should be considered and either "tips the balance for or against private club status."

The District Court in *United States v. Jordan* provided six categories to consider when establishing the existence or lack thereof of a private club. The categories, in order of relative importance, are as follows:

1.   the extent membership is genuinely selective on some reasonable basis;

2.   measure of control the members have over the operations of the establishment;
3.   manner in which the membership corporation was created;
4.   purpose of the membership corporation existing;
5.   formalities which many private clubs observe; and
6.   general characteristics which many private clubs possess.

The core factors [from the list above] which determine whether an establishment "serves the public," or is "a private club or other establishment not in fact open to the public" are the extent to which the membership is genuinely selective on some reasonable basis, and the measure of control the members have over the operations of the establishment.

First, the Club does not follow a very selective membership policy even though it limits membership to eighty members. Only two white applicants have been rejected in the past fifty years, and they both had peculiar circumstances. . . . Although the Club has formal membership requirements, it appears that the club follows "no plan or purpose of exclusiveness." . . . Membership in the Club is limited to eighty members. Each applicant is investigated by the Membership Committee, who then makes a recommendation concerning the applicant. Next, the application is submitted to all the members for voting. It appears that the formal requirements prove that the Club is truly private. However, the Court is persuaded otherwise. Only two past white applicants were denied membership for special reasons, while Plaintiff's application was denied for tenuous reasons at best. . . . "The formalities have little meaning when in fact the Club does not follow a selective membership policy."

Second, the members have little control over the operations of the establishment. . . . The Club also had no control over the roads running through the Club property since Freestone County graded the Club's roads to be used to serve the public. By opening the Club's roads to the public, the Club is no longer private. . . .

The Court finds that the Club is enjoined from denying Plaintiff membership in the Club. The Plaintiff may purchase membership share 180. Plaintiff is also awarded court costs and attorneys fees. . . .

KING v. GREYHOUND LINES, INC.
Court of Appeals of Oregon (1982)
61 Ore. App. 197; 656 P.2d 349

YOUNG, J. : This is an action to recover damages for a violation of the [Oregon] Public Accommodations Act. The trial court, sitting without a jury, found that racial slurs made by defendant's employee during the course of employment did not constitute a violation of the act and entered judgment for defendant. Plaintiff appeals, and we reverse.

We summarize the trial court's findings of fact. Defendant offers transportation services and public accommodations to the general public. On November 30, 1979, plaintiff, a black man, purchased a one-way bus ticket to Long Beach, California, from defendant at its terminal in Portland. On December 13, 1979, plaintiff sought to return the ticket for a refund by tendering it to Cole, defendant's ticket agent at the Portland terminal.

Defendant has a standard refund procedure that requires the employee processing a refund to be satisfied that the person returning the ticket is the original purchaser. When a ticket agent suspects that the person seeking a refund is not the original purchaser, the ticket is routinely forwarded by mail to defendant's regional office, where it is held for 30 days. If no report of loss or theft of the ticket is made during that time, the refund is mailed. To facilitate this procedure, each ticket carries a mark identifying the clerk who sold it. Plaintiff's ticket bore Cole's mark, but Cole did not recognize plaintiff. When asked if he could identify the agent who sold him the ticket, plaintiff incorrectly identified another clerk. Cole declined to issue an immediate cash refund and informed plaintiff of defendant's refund policy. During this transaction, Cole made the following remarks to plaintiff:

"Nigger, where did you get this ticket?"
and
"Now, boy, you get the person who purchased the ticket, and I'll be glad to refund it."

The trial court also found that, while plaintiff had been degraded, humiliated and embarrassed by these racial slurs, he was the victim of prejudice and not the victim of discrimination within the meaning of the statute.

The issue is whether racial insults made by an employee of a place of public accommodation to a customer in the course of serving that customer constitute a "distinction, discrimination or restriction on account of race" in contravention of [the Oregon Public Accommodations Act]. Plaintiff argues that although he was not refused service, the manner in which he was served was discriminatory in that he suffered abuse and inferior service on account of his race. Defendant argues that the act was not intended to make racial slurs actionable.

Although racial insults and verbal harassment made by members of the general public may not be a violation of the act, defendant's proposition overlooks the fact that the verbal abuse in question was made by an employee of a place of public accommodation in the course of serving plaintiff. [The Act] entitles all persons to

"* * * the *full and equal* accommodations, advantages, facilities and privileges of any place of public accommodation without any distinction, discrimination or restriction on account of race * * *." (Emphasis supplied.)

To argue that plaintiff received "full and equal" accommodations even though he suffered racial slurs and animadversions in the course of the transaction is analogous to arguing that separate accommodations may be equal accommodations.

Certainly, if plaintiff was relegated to a certain section of the bus or made to wait until white customers were served, it could not be seriously contended that he received full and equal accommodations. See *Gayle v. Browder*, citing *Brown v. Board of Education*. ...

In short, the statutory prohibition against "distinction, discrimination or restriction" on the basis of race encompasses more than the outright denial of service. It also proscribes serving customers of one race in a manner different from those of another race. As one author noted, after surveying federal and state public accommodation laws:

"The basic violation of the Public Accommodations law is a denial of full and equal services at a covered establishment. Such a denial occurs when there is discriminatory or abusive treatment, service or charges. At present, complaints of insulting or discriminatory treatment intended to discourage certain customers are as common as complaints of outright refusals of entry. Exclusion and unequal treatment which form the core of any public accommodation violation are covered by all statutes."

There is little legislative history describing what is meant by the terms "distinction, discrimination or restriction." Similarly, the few cases construing the act are concerned with what constitutes "a place of public accommodation" and consequently offer little guidance on the issue presented. However, it is clear that the general intent of the legislation when it was enacted in 1953 was to prevent "operators and owners of businesses catering to the general public from subjecting Negroes to oppression and humiliation * * *." To hold that verbal abuse can be a "distinction, discrimination or restriction" on the basis of race is consistent with this broad legislative purpose. Moreover, that interpretation recognizes that the chief harm resulting from the practice of discrimination by establishments serving the general public is not the monetary loss of a commercial transaction or the inconvenience of limited access but, rather, the greater evil of unequal treatment, which is the injury to an individual's sense of self-worth and personal integrity. We hold that defendant violated the act.

The trial court concluded its findings and conclusions as follows:

"In the interest of judicial economy, and without prejudice to the above findings, it is further determined that if there had been an act of unlawful discrimination, plaintiff would be entitled to recover against [defendant] the sums of $500 in general damages and $1,000 as punitive damages. The amount plaintiff would be entitled to recover as reasonable attorney fees, if appropriate, for trial and appeal is left to the appellate court to be determined."

We reverse the judgment in favor of defendant and remand with instructions to enter judgment in favor of plaintiff in accordance with the trial court's determination of general and punitive damages. Plaintiff's reasonable attorney fees at trial shall be determined by the trial court. ...

TITLE VII, CIVIL RIGHTS ACT OF 1964
42 U.S.C. §2000e-2(a)

It shall be an unlawful employment practice for an employer

1. to fail or refuse to hire or to discharge any individual, or otherwise to discriminate against any individual with respect to his compensation, terms, conditions, or privileges of employment, because of such individual's race, color, religion, sex, or national origin; or

2. to limit, segregate, or classify his employees or applicants for employment in any way which would deprive or tend to deprive any individual of employment opportunities or otherwise adversely affect his status as an employee, because of such individual's race, color, religion, sex, or national origin.

RACE DISCRIMINATION IN EMPLOYMENT: TITLE VII: A SUMMARY

RACE DISCRIMINATION IN EMPLOYMENT

- Federal Law
  - Statutory
    - Title VII
    - Other
  - Constitutional
- State Law
- Local Law

Title VII

- Coverage: all public and private employers with fifteen or more employees
- Protected Categories: race, gender, religion, national origin, color
- EEOC and Discrimination Complaints
- Types of Complaints
  - disparate treatment (plaintiff complains of intentional discrimination)
  - disparate impact (the plaintiff complains of conduct which, though not intentionally discriminatory, has the effect of falling more harshly on the members of the protected category than others)

Title VII: Disparate Treatment—The Standard (McDonnell) Cases

- Plaintiff's *prima facie* case: plaintiff bears the burden of establishing a presumption of intentional discrimination

- Defense: the burden then shifts to the defendant to articulate a legitimate business justification defense: defendant denies the discrimination and contends the employment decision was made for a legitimate, non-discriminatory business reason; in this instance the defendant has the burden of articulating and offering evidence of a legitimate reason
- Plaintiff's ultimate burden: if the defendant is successful in articulating and providing evidence of a legitimate, nondiscriminatory business reason, the ultimate burden shifts to the plaintiff to show the offered reason was merely a pretext and that the defendant did in fact deliberately discriminate

Title VII: Disparate Impact

- *Prima facie* burden on plaintiff to show employer's conduct falls more harshly on members of the protected class
- Burden then shifts to the defendant to prove a legitimate business justification, *i.e.,* job validate the employment practice
- Ultimate burden shifts back to the plaintiff to show that less discriminatory practices are available to achieve the employer's goal.

McDONNELL DOUGLAS CORP. v. GREEN
Supreme Court of the United States (1973)
411 U.S. 792

MR. JUSTICE POWELL: … McDonnell Douglas Corp., is an aerospace and aircraft manufacturer headquartered in St. Louis, Missouri, where it employs over 30,000 people. [Green], a black citizen of St. Louis, worked for [McDonnell] as a mechanic and laboratory technician from 1956 until August 28, 1964 when he was laid off in the course of a general reduction in [McDonnell's] work force.

[Green], a long-time activist in the civil rights movement, protested vigorously that his discharge and the general hiring practices of [McDonnell] were racially motivated. As part of this protest, [Green] and other members of the Congress on Racial Equality illegally stalled their cars on the main roads leading to [McDonnell's] plant for the purpose of blocking access to it at the time of the morning shift change. The District Judge described the plan for, and [Green's] participation in, the "stall-in" as follows:

"Five teams, each consisting of four cars would 'tie up' five main access roads into McDonnell at the time of the morning rush hour. The drivers of the cars were instructed to line up next to each other completely blocking the intersections or roads. The drivers were also instructed to stop their cars, turn off the engines, pull the emergency brake, raise all windows, lock the doors, and remain in their cars until the police arrived. The plan was to have the cars remain in position for one hour."

"Acting under the 'stall in' plan, [Green] drove his car onto Brown Road, a McDonnell access road, at approximately 7:00 a.m., at the start of the morning rush hour. [Green] was aware of the traffic problems that would result. He stopped his car with the intent to block traffic. The police arrived shortly and requested [Green] to move his car. He refused to move his car voluntarily. [Green's] car was towed away by

the police, and he was arrested for obstructing traffic. [Green] pleaded guilty to the charge of obstructing traffic and was fined."

On July 2, 1965, a "lock-in" took place wherein a chain and padlock were placed on the front door of a building to prevent the occupants, certain of [McDonnell's] employees, from leaving. Though [Green] apparently knew beforehand of the "lock-in," the full extent of his involvement remains uncertain.

Some three weeks following the "lock-in," on July 25, 1965, [McDonnell] publicly advertised for qualified mechanics, [Green's] trade, and [Green] promptly applied for re-employment. [McDonnell] turned down [Green], basing its rejection on [Green's] participation in the "stall-in" and "lock-in." … [Green filed suit, claiming McDonnell, in violation of Title VII, denied him employment "because of his involvement in civil rights activities" and "because of his race and color."]

The critical issue before us concerns the order and allocation of proof in a private, non-class action challenging employment discrimination. The language of Title VII makes plain the purpose of Congress to assure equality of employment opportunities and to eliminate those discriminatory practices and devices which have fostered racially stratified job environments to the disadvantage of minority citizens. *Griggs. v. Duke Power Co.* As noted in *Griggs*:

"Congress did not intend by Title VII, however, to guarantee a job to every person regardless of qualifications. In short, the Act does not command that any person be hired simply because he was formerly the subject of discrimination, or because he is a member of a minority group. Discriminatory preference for any group, minority or majority, is precisely and only what Congress has proscribed. What is required by

Congress is the removal of artificial, arbitrary, and unnecessary barriers to employment when the barriers operate invidiously to discriminate on the basis of racial or other impermissible classification."

There are societal as well as personal interests on both sides of this equation. The broad, overriding interest, shared by employer, employee, and consumer, is efficient and trustworthy workmanship assured through fair and racially neutral employment and personnel decisions. In the implementation of such decisions, it is abundantly clear that Title VII tolerates no racial discrimination, subtle or otherwise.

In this case [Green] charges that he was denied employment "because of his involvement in civil rights activities" and "because of his race and color." [McDonnell] denied discrimination of any kind, asserting that its failure to re-employ [Green] was based upon and justified by his participation in the unlawful conduct against it. Thus, the issue at the trial on remand is framed by those opposing factual contentions. ...

The complainant in a Title VII trial must carry the initial burden under the statute of establishing a prima facie case of racial discrimination. This may be done by showing (i) that he belongs to a racial minority; (ii) that he applied and was qualified for a job for which the employer was seeking applicants; (iii) that, despite his qualifications, he was rejected; and (iv) that, after his rejection, the position remained open and the employer continued to seek applicants from persons of complainant's qualifications.[1] In the instant case, ... [Green] proved a prima facie case. [McDonnell] sought mechanics, [Green's] trade, and continued to do so after [Green's] rejection. [McDonnell], moreover, does not dispute [Green's] qualifications and acknowledges that his past work performance in petitioner's employ was "satisfactory."

The burden then must shift to the employer to articulate some legitimate, nondiscriminatory reason for the employee's rejection. We need not attempt in the instant case to detail every matter which fairly could be recognized as a reasonable basis for a refusal to hire. Here [McDonnell] has assigned [Green's] participation in unlawful conduct against it as the cause for his rejection. We think that this suffices to discharge [McDonnell's] burden of proof at this stage and to meet [Green's] prima facie case of discrimination. ... [Green] admittedly had taken part in a carefully planned "stall-in," designed to tie up access to and egress from petitioner's plant at a peak traffic hour. Nothing in Title VII compels an employer to absolve and rehire one who has engaged in such deliberate, unlawful activity against it. ...

[McDonnell's] reason for rejection thus suffices to meet the prima facie case, but the inquiry must not end here. While Title VII does not, without more, compel rehiring of [Green], neither does it permit [McDonnell] to use [Green's] conduct as a pretext for the sort of discrimination prohibited by [Title VII]. On remand, [Green] must ... be afforded a fair opportunity to show that [McDonnell's] stated reason for [Green's] rejection was in fact pretext. Especially relevant to such a showing would be evidence that white employees involved in acts against [McDonnell] of comparable seriousness to the "stall-in" were nevertheless retained or rehired. [McDonnell] may justifiably refuse to rehire one who was engaged in unlawful, disruptive acts against it, but only if this criterion is applied alike to members of all races.

Other evidence that may be relevant to any showing of pretext includes facts as to [McDonnell's] treatment of [Green] during his prior term of employment; [McDonnell's] reaction, if any, to [Green's] legitimate civil rights activities; and [McDonnell's] general policy and practice with respect to minority employment. On the latter point, statistics as to [McDonnell's] employment policy and practice may be helpful to a determination of whether [McDonnell's] refusal to rehire [Green] in this case conformed to a general pattern of discrimination against blacks. In short, on the retrial [Green] must be given a full and fair opportunity to demonstrate by competent evidence that the presumptively valid reasons for his rejection were in fact a coverup for a racially discriminatory decision. ...

---

[1]The facts necessarily will vary in Title VII cases, and the specification above of the prima facie proof required from respondent is not necessarily applicable in every respect to differing factual situations.

GRIGGS v. DUKE POWER CO.
Supreme Court of the United States (1971)
401 U.S. 424

MR. CHIEF JUSTICE BURGER: We granted the writ in this case to resolve the question whether an employer is prohibited by the Civil Rights Act of 1964, Title VII, from requiring a high school education or passing of a standardized general intelligence test as a condition of employment in or transfer to jobs when (a) neither standard is shown to be significantly related to successful job performance, (b) both requirements operate to disqualify Negroes at a substantially higher rate than white applicants, and (c) the jobs in question formerly had been filled only by white employees as part of a longstanding practice of giving preference to whites.

... [T]his proceeding was brought by a group of incumbent Negro employees against Duke Power Company. All the petitioners are employed at the Company's Dan River Steam Station, a power generating facility located at Draper, North Carolina. At the time this action was instituted, the Company had 95 employees at the Dan River Station, 14 of whom were Negroes; 13 of these are petitioners here.

The District Court found that prior to July 2, 1965, the effective date of the Civil Rights Act of 1964, the Company openly discriminated on the basis of race in the hiring and assigning of employees at its Dan River plant. The plant was organized into five operating departments: (1) Labor, (2) Coal Handling, (3) Operations, (4) Maintenance, and (5) Laboratory and Test. Negroes were employed only in the Labor Department where the highest paying jobs paid less than the lowest paying jobs in the other four "operating" departments in which only whites were employed. Promotions were normally made within each department on the basis of job seniority. Transferees into a department usually began in the lowest position.

In 1955 the Company instituted a policy of requiring a high school education for initial assignment to any department except Labor, and for transfer from the Coal Handling to any "inside" department (Operations, Maintenance, or Laboratory). When the Company abandoned its policy of restricting Negroes to the Labor Department in 1965, completion of high school also was made a prerequisite to transfer from Labor to any other department. From the time the high school requirement was instituted to the time of trial, however, white employees hired before the time of the high school education requirement continued to perform satisfactorily and achieve promotions in the "operating" departments. Findings on this score are not challenged.

The Company added a further requirement for new employees on July 2, 1965, the date on which Title VII became effective. To qualify for placement in any but the Labor Department it became necessary to register satisfactory scores on two professionally prepared aptitude tests, as well as to have a high school education. Completion of high school alone continued to render employees eligible for transfer to the four desirable departments from which Negroes had been excluded if the incumbent had been employed prior to the time of the new requirement. In September 1965 the Company began to permit incumbent employees who lacked a high school education to qualify for transfer from Labor or Coal Handling to an "inside" job by passing two tests—the Wonderlic Personnel Test, which purports to measure general intelligence, and the Bennett Mechanical Comprehension Test. Neither was directed or intended to measure the ability to learn to perform a particular job or category of jobs. The requisite scores used for both initial hiring and transfer approximated the national median for high school graduates. ...

The objective of Congress in the enactment of Title VH is plain from the language of the statute. It was to achieve equality of employment opportunities and remove barriers that have operated in the past to favor an identifiable group of white employees over other employees. Under the Act, practices, procedures, or tests neutral on their face, and even neutral in terms of intent, cannot be maintained if they operate to "freeze" the status quo of prior discriminatory employment practices.

[O]n the record in the present case, "whites register far better on the Company's alternative requirements" than Negroes. This consequence would appear to be directly traceable to race. Basic intelligence must have the means of articulation to manifest itself fairly in a testing process. Because they are Negroes, petitioners have long received inferior education in segregated schools and this Court expressly recognized these differences in *Gaston County v. United States* (1969). There, because of the inferior education received by Negroes in North Carolina, this Court barred the institution of a literacy test for voter registration on the ground that the test would abridge the right to vote indirectly on account of race. Congress did not intend by Title VII, however, to guarantee a job to every person regardless of qualifications. In short, the Act does not command that any person be hired simply because he was formerly the subject of discrimination, or because he is a member of a minority group. Discriminatory preference for any group, minority or majority, is precisely and only what Congress has proscribed. What is required by Congress is the removal of artificial, arbitrary, and unnecessary barriers to employment when the barriers operate invidiously to discriminate on the basis of racial or other impermissible classification.

... The Act proscribes not-only overt discrimination but also practices that are fair in form, but discriminatory in operation. The touchstone is business necessity. If an employment practice which operates to exclude Negroes cannot be shown to be related to job performance, the practice is prohibited.

On the record before us, neither the high school completion requirement nor the general intelligence test is shown to bear a demonstrable relationship to successful performance of the jobs for which it was used. Both were adopted ... without meaningful study of their relationship to job-performance ability. Rather, a vice president of the Company testified, the requirements were instituted on the Company's judgment that they generally would improve the overall quality of the work force.

The evidence, however, shows that employees who have not completed high school or taken the tests have continued to perform satisfactorily and make progress in departments for which the high school and test criteria are now used. The promotion record of present employees who would not be able to meet the new criteria thus suggests the possibility that the requirements may not be needed even for the limited purpose of preserving the avowed policy of advancement within the Company. In the context of this case, it is unnecessary to reach the question whether testing requirements that take into account capability for the next succeeding position or related future promotion might be utilized upon a showing that such long-range requirements fulfill a genuine business need. In the present case the Company has made no such showing. ...

The Company's lack of discriminatory intent is suggested by special efforts to help the undereducated employees through Company financing of two-thirds the cost of tuition for high school training. But Congress directed the thrust of the Act to the consequences of employment practices, not simply the motivation. More than that, Congress has placed on the employer the burden of showing that any given requirement must have a manifest relationship to the employment in question.

The facts of this case demonstrate the inadequacy of broad and general testing devices as well as the infirmity of using diplomas or degrees as fixed measures of capability. History is filled with examples of men and women who rendered highly effective performance without the conventional badges of accomplishment in terms of certificates, diplomas, or degrees. Diplomas and tests are useful servants, but Congress has mandated the commonsense proposition that they are not to become masters of reality. ...

Nothing in the Act precludes the use of testing or measuring procedures; obviously they are useful. What Congress has forbidden is giving these devices and mechanisms controlling force unless they are demonstrably a reasonable measure of job performance. Congress has not commanded that the less qualified be preferred over the better qualified simply because of minority origins. Far from disparaging job qualifications as such, Congress has made such qualifications the controlling factor, so that race, religion, nationality, and sex become irrelevant. What Congress has commanded is that any tests used must measure the person for the job and not the person in the abstract. ...

CIVIL RIGHTS ACT OF 1866
§ 1982. Property rights of citizens

All citizens of the United States shall have the same right, in every State and Territory, as is enjoyed by white citizens thereof to inherit, purchase, lease, sell, hold, and convey real and personal property.

Civil Rights Act of 1968
Fair Housing Act

§ 3604. Discrimination in the sale or rental of housing.

[I]t shall be unlawful—

a. To refuse to sell or rent after the making of a bona fide offer, or to refuse to negotiate for the sale or rental of, or otherwise make unavailable or deny, a dwelling to any person because of race, color, religion, sex, or national origin.

b. To discriminate against any person in the terms, conditions, or privileges of sale or rental of a dwelling, or int he provision of services or facilities in connections therewith because of race, color, religion, sex, or national origin.

c. To make, print, publish, or cause to be made, printed, or published any notice, statement, or advertisement, with respect to the sale or rental of a dwelling that indicates any preference, limitation, or discrimination based on race, color, religion, sex, or national origin, or an intention to make any such preference, limitation, or discrimination.

d. To represent to any person because of race, color, religion, sex, or national origin that any dwelling is not available for inspection, sale, or rental when such dwelling is in fact so available.

e. For profit, to induce or attempt to induce any person to sell or rent any dwelling by representations regarding the entry or prospective entry into the neighborhood of a person or persons of a particular race, color, religion, sex, or national origin.

MR. JUSTICE STEWART. In this case we are called upon to determine the scope and the constitutionality of an Act of Congress, 42 U. S. C. §1982, which provides that:

"All citizens of the United States shall have the same right, in every State and Territory, as is enjoyed by white citizens thereof to inherit, purchase, lease, sell, hold, and convey real and personal property."

On September 2, 1965, the petitioners filed a complaint in the District Court for the Eastern District of Missouri, alleging the respondents had refused to sell them a home in the Paddock Woods community of St. Louis County for the sole reason that petitioner Joseph Lee Jones is a Negro. Relying in part upon §1982, the petitioners sought injunctive and other relief. The District Court sustained the respondents' motion to dismiss the complaint, and the Court of Appeals for the Eighth Circuit affirmed, concluding that §1982 applies only to state action and does not reach private refusals to sell. We granted certiorari to consider the questions thus presented. For the reasons that follow, we reverse the judgment of the Court of Appeals. We hold that §1982 bars all racial discrimination, private as well as public, in the sale or rental of property, and that the statute, thus construed, is a valid exercise of the power of Congress to enforce the Thirteenth Amendment. ...

We begin with the language of the statute itself. In plain and unambiguous terms, §1982 grants to all citizens, without regard to race or color, "the same right" to purchase and lease property "as is enjoyed by white citizens." ...

On its face, ... §1982 appears to prohibit all discrimination against Negroes in the sale or rental of property—discrimination by private owners as well as discrimination by public authorities. Indeed, even the respondents seem to concede that, if §1982 "means what it says"—to use the words of the respondents' brief—then it must encompass every racially motivated refusal to sell or rent and cannot be confined to officially sanctioned segregation in housing. Stressing what they consider to be the revolutionary implications of so literal a reading of §1982, the respondents argue that Congress cannot possibly have intended any such result. Our examination of the relevant history, however, persuades us that Congress meant exactly what it said. [The Court then examines the legislative history of the statute, rooted in the Civil Rights Act of 1866]. ...

The remaining question is whether Congress has power under the Constitution to do what §1982 purports to do: to prohibit all racial discrimination, private and public, in the sale and rental of property. Our starting point is the Thirteenth Amendment, for it was pursuant to that constitutional provision that Congress originally enacted what is now §1982. The Amendment consists of two parts. Section 1 states:

"Neither slavery nor involuntary servitude, except as a punishment for crime whereof the party shall have been duly convicted, shall exist within the United States, or any place subject to their jurisdiction."

Section 2 provides:

"Congress shall have power to enforce this article by appropriate legislation."

As its text reveals, the Thirteenth Amendment "is not a mere prohibition of State laws establishing or upholding slavery, but an absolute declaration that slavery or involuntary servitude shall not exist in any part of the United States." *Civil Rights Cases*. It has never been doubted, therefore, "that the power vested in Congress to enforce the article by appropriate legislation," *ibid.*, includes the power to enact laws "direct and primary, operating upon the acts of individuals, whether sanctioned by State legislation or not." *Id.*

Thus, the fact that §1982 operates upon the unofficial acts of private individuals, whether or not sanctioned by state law, presents no constitutional problem. If Congress has power under the Thirteenth Amendment to eradicate conditions that prevent Negroes from buying and renting property because of their race or color, then no federal statute calculated to achieve that objective can be thought to exceed the constitutional power of Congress simply because it reaches beyond state action to regulate the conduct of private individuals. The constitutional question in this case, therefore, comes to this: Does the authority of Congress to enforce the Thirteenth Amendment "by appropriate legislation" include the power to eliminate all racial barriers to the acquisition of real and personal property? We think the answer to that question is plainly yes.

"By its own unaided force and effect," the Thirteenth Amendment "abolished slavery, and established universal freedom." *Civil Rights Cases.* Whether or not the Amendment itself did any more than that— a question not involved in this case—it is at least clear that the Enabling Clause of that Amendment empowered Congress to do much more. For that clause clothed "Congress with power to pass all laws necessary and proper for abolishing all badges and incidents of slavery in the United States." *Ibid.* (Emphasis added.) ...

Surely ... Congress has the power under the Thirteenth Amendment rationally to determine what are the badges and the incidents of slavery, and the authority to translate that determination into effective legislation. Nor can we say that the determination Congress has made is an irrational one. For this Court recognized long ago that, whatever else they may have encompassed, the badges and incidents of slavery—its "burdens and disabilities"—included restraints upon "those fundamental rights which are the essence of civil freedom, namely, the same right ... to inherit, purchase, lease, sell and convey property, as is enjoyed by white citizens." *Civil Rights Cases.* Just at the Black Codes, enacted after the Civil War to restrict the free exercise of those rights, were substitutes for the slave system, so the exclusion of Negroes from white communities became a substitute for the Black Codes. And when racial discrimination herds men into ghettos and makes their ability to buy property turn on the color of their skin, then it too is a relic of slavery.

Negro citizens, North and South, who saw in the Thirteenth Amendment a promise of freedom—freedom to "go and come at pleasure" and to "buy and sell when they please"—would be left with "a mere paper guarantee" if Congress were powerless to assure that a dollar in the hands of a Negro will purchase the same thing as a dollar in the hands of a white man. At the very least, the freedom that Congress is empowered to secure under the Thirteenth Amendment includes the freedom to buy whatever a white man can buy, the right to live wherever a white man can live. If Congress cannot say that being a free man means at least this much, then the Thirteenth Amendment made a promise the Nation cannot keep. ...

CUMMINGS, Chief Judge. In 1979 and 1980 William J. Phillips, a successful black businessman, was looking for a new house. He found what he wanted in the Hunter Trails subdivision of Oak Brook, Illinois—a 12,000 square-foot, tri-level home on a large lot. He offered $675,000 for it, and his offer was accepted by the owner, Dennis Broderick, on June 13, 1980. Mr. Phillips deposited $75,000 in earnest money, and a closing date was set for July 21, 1980. In the expectation that they would be able to move into the house as agreed, the Phillipses sold their house in Homewood, Illinois, agreeing to give up possession on July 21, and obtained a mortgage commitment on the new house from Seaway Bank on June 24, 1980.

Between June 24 and July 17, the Phillipses heard nothing about any difficulties with their move. But events were moving rapidly in Hunter Trails. On June 18 fifteen people came to an early morning meeting— officers and directors of the Hunter Trails Community Association and some homeowners—but Mr. Broderick, who had the only first-hand knowledge about the terms of the sale and who was also the vice-president of the Association and a Board member, was not notified of the meeting and did not attend.

One of the covenants that attached to every piece of property in the Hunter Trails subdivision gave the Association a thirty-day right of first refusal on any proposed sale. Accordingly, the Association could have forestalled the Phillipses by buying Broderick's houses for $675,000. The outcome of the June 18 meeting was a decision instead to assign the Association's first refusal right to a syndicate or limited partnership. In the days that followed, no such assignee could be found or formed. The Association therefore turned its attentions to Mrs. Jorie Ford Butler as a potential Purchaser. Mrs. Butler's family had founded Oak Brook and various members of the Butler family still owned property in

Hunter Trails. Mrs. Butler herself had looked at the Broderick house in the early spring of 1980, before the Phillipses saw it, but was not interested in buying it then. When the Association proposal was presented to her in mid-July, however, she agreed to buy the Association's first-refusal option for $10,000 and exercised the option on July 17, agreeing to pay the Brodericks $675,000 for their house. They refused to close the sale on July 19 because she would not indemnify them from possible liability to the Phillipses.

None of these developments were communicated to the Phillips family until July 17, the Thursday before the scheduled Monday closing. By then they were accomplished facts. Predictably, the Phillipses were disappointed, humiliated, and angry. They also had serious practical problems. Having sold their Homewood house, they were forced to live in hotels and with relatives until they found a rental apartment in Hinsdale. They had to put most of their furniture in storage and live out of suitcases. Two of their cars were stolen and other property was lost while they were without a permanent home. And they had to bring a lawsuit to vindicate their right to live in the house they had chosen in Hunter Trails.

That lawsuit was filed on July 22, 1980, under Section 1 of the Civil Rights Act of 1866 (42 U.S.C. §1982) and the Fair Housing Act, 42 U.S.C. §§3601 et seq. The suit sought an immediate injunction to prevent the defendants from concluding the sale of the Broderick house except to the Phillipses, and—on the merits—equitable and declaratory relief, actual and punitive damages, attorneys' fees and costs. After a ten-day trial, Judge Prentice Marshall found for the Phillipses. His final order, entered July 22, 1981, required the house to be sold to them at the agreed price and awarded them actual damages of $52,675 against the Association and Mrs. Butler jointly and severally ... , punitive damages of $100,000 against each of the two defendants, $35,000 in attorneys' fees, and $1,016 in costs. The Phillipses moved into the house shortly thereafter, more than a year after the closing was to have taken place. They and Mrs. Butler entered into a post-judgement settlement and she is no longer a party.

The Association has pursued this appeal. It argues that (1) no discriminatory intent was proved as required under Section 1982, (2) the evidence-did not support the finding that the Association violated the Fair Housing Act, and (3) damages were excessive. Because we find Judge Marshall's decision amply supported in fact and law, we affirm except as to actual damages.

I

The Association's first argument is that intentional racial discrimination was never made out, although it is concededly an essential element of the Phillipses' Section 1982 claim. ...

Judge Marshall ... found numerous indications of unalloyed bigotry. The Association on appeal tries to explain away all of them, forgetting that as a reviewing court we owe great deference to the district judge's factual conclusions and credibility determinations. The following examples are illustrative.

... (2) Judge Marshall found that a number of explicitly racist remarks were made at the [June 18] meeting The Association argues that the ugly atmosphere was dispelled by two Board members' warnings "that the [Phillipses'] race was totally irrelevant to the discussion and that it would be illegal to refuse them the opportunity to purchase the house on the basis of their race." Those Board members themselves admitted that their warnings had little, if any, effect. ... (4) One of the most damning pieces of evidence was a remark by Mr. Steinbock-Sinclair, the Association's attorney, to a business acquaintance the day after the meeting. Mr. Steinbock-Sinclair said that Hunter Trails was an exclusive community that did not include "niggers" and "car wash operators." He vowed to use the subdivision's covenants to make certain that the Phillipses did not get the Broderick house. ...

This Court will not second-guess the district judge on any of these matters. Together they are based on credibility assessments and create a clear picture of intentional racial discrimination by the ... Association.

C.   The applicable legal standard

The Association claims that Judge Marshall used an unprecedented standard, involving both race and occupation, to find discrimination. They point to this passage in the district judge's opinion:

An American Negro car wash operator was not acceptable to the owners in Hunter Trails. Steinbock-Sinclair capsulized the prevailing attitude when he said * * * that Hunter Trails was a community of professionals and was not the place for a "nigger car wash operator."

What the Association neglects to mention is that the district judge was responding to their arguments that Hunter Trails was a racially and occupationally diverse neighborhood. On appeal they sound the same themes: "At least one other black family already lives [in Hunter Trails], as well as several other families of similar racial characteristics,[2] and members of other minority groups," and a broad range of occupations is represented in the subdivision—"builders, grain brokers, engineers, owners of dry cleaning establishments, owners of electronic stores, salesmen of household cookware, and a barber * * *." Neither at trial nor on appeal, however, could the Association demonstrate any overlap between minority race and non-professional occupation. Judge Marshall's statement is simply a recognition that if the Association would approve a white purchaser who owned dry cleaning establishments, but veto a black man who owned a chain of car washes, its decision can only be based on race.

Our conclusion is that the evidence was ample to sustain the judgement in favor of the Phillipses and against the Association under 42 U.S.C. §1982.

II

The Association's second argument is that the evidence was not sufficient to support a finding that the Fair Housing Act was violated. ... To make out their

---

[2]The Association evidently has a restrictive definition of white and an expansive definition of black. Asked at oral argument if any members of the Board of Directors were black, counsel for the Association replied, "One of the members of the Board is a dark-skinned gentleman from South America."

prima facie case under the Fair Housing Act, they had only to show that they were black, that they applied for and were qualified to buy the Broderick house, that they were rejected, and that the Broderick house remained on the market. They clearly made that showing. Then the burden shifted to the defendant to articulate non-racial reasons for its actions. The Association—equally clearly—did not succeed. The Phillipses were as much entitled to their judgment under the Fair Housing Act as under Section 1982.

III

The Association's last line of attack is that the damages awarded by the district court were too generous. The defendant does not contest that portion of the award ($2,675) that represents the Phillipses' out-of-pocket expenses—the cost of the unnecessary move and of storing furniture. The Association does object to the award of $25,000 each to Mr. and Mrs. Phillips for humiliation and embarrassment and to the assessment of $50,000 punitive damages for each plaintiff. We agree that the compensatory damages must be reduced, but we affirm the district judge's award of punitive damages.

A.   Compensatory damages

Injuries like the Phillipses' are by their nature difficult to prove. A reviewing court will not demand more precision than is feasible. ... Furthermore, when a judge functions as the trier of fact, as Judge Marshall did here, his estimate of damages for intangible injuries is subject to the "clearly erroneous" rule. Nonetheless we have the "definite and firm conviction that a mistake has been committed."

The district judge rested his award of damages for mental and emotional distress on the testimony and demeanor of the Phillipses. That is an inadequate basis for an award that is more than twice as much as any other victim of housing discrimination has received for intangible injuries, judging from the parties' submissions and our own research. ...

We have the impression that two factors influenced the district judge. First, the typical housing discrimination case does not involve a $675,000 home. But that is irrelevant to the Phillipses' intangible injuries: the anger and hurt do not correlate with the wealth of the victim or the price of the property. Second, the conduct of the Association was egregious. But that is reflected in the punitive damage assessment. We therefore direct the district court to reduce the compensatory damages to $10,000 for each plaintiff in addition to their actual expenditures of $2,675.

B.   Punitive damages

We do not disturb the punitive damage award. As noted, this is the place where the willfulness of the Association's conduct is appropriately weighed. The record contains ample evidence of intentional disregard of the Phillipses' rights, and the district judge gave careful consideration to the Association's financial position as well. He noted that it had a bank balance of $100,000, cash flow from assessments of $142,000 a year, and the ability to raise money by additional assessments if necessary—a course it would have had to follow if it had exercised its first refusal rights on the Broderick property in a nondiscriminatory way. The Association's arguments—that "the punitive award will take all of the Association's funds and leave nothing to enable it to carry out its obligations to its members" and that "the effect of this award is not merely to punish the Association but to destroy it"—are counterfactual. Undoubtedly the punitive damages will cause the Association some hardship, but that is an essential part of their deterrent function. ...

TONE, District Judge. This action under the Civil Rights Act [of 1866] (42 U.S.C. §1982) raises the issue of whether defendants refused to lease or consent to the sublease of an apartment to two of the plaintiffs because of race. ...

Plaintiff Bonita Nichols, who is white, was the lessee of the subject apartment from defendant Hampton Management Company under a lease that was not to expire until August 31, 1972. When the young woman with whom she shared the apartment moved out because of marriage plans, plaintiff Nichols decided to sublease the apartment. Because the lease required the lessor's consent to a sublease, she reported her decision to Hampton Management's agents in the office of the building, who were defendants Jewel Valerio, desk clerk, and Nora Sudol, assistant manager. Defendant Valerio, in the presence of defendant Sudol, told plaintiff Nichols that a sublease rather than a new lease would have to be executed and that it was the lessee's responsibility to find a sublessee. She also said that plaintiff Nichols should advertise the apartment, find as many applicants as possible, have them fill out applications on forms which were handed to plaintiff Nichols and then bring the completed applications back to the office of the building, where the building agents and plaintiff Nichols would jointly make a selection from those who had applied. The application form stated that it was to be accompanied by a security deposit for one month's rent.

A series of newspaper advertisements placed by plaintiff Nichols in late February, 1972, brought several responses, ... [including] one from plaintiff Valerie Williamson on behalf of herself and plaintiff Joyce Tucker, both single women and both black. All filled out application forms, but plaintiffs Williamson and Tucker were the only applicants to tender a security deposit check with their application. ... [Nichols] ... then called defendant Valerio and ... said plaintiffs would be over that evening to sign the papers. Thereupon defendant Valerio stated that the apartment was rented to someone else, who would move in April 1. Since plaintiff Nichols wanted someone to take over her apartment immediately, she protested, and this litigation ensued. The persons to whom defendants say the apartment has been rented are existing tenants of the building who had been scheduled to move on May 1 into another apartment similar to the one in issue.

The Civil Rights Act of 1866 provides that all citizens have "the same right ... as is enjoyed by white citizens ... to ... lease ... real property." The Civil Rights Act of 1968 makes it unlawful "To refuse to ... rent after the making of a bona fide offer, ... or otherwise make unavailable or deny, a dwelling to any person because of race, color, religion, or national origin." Race need not be the sole reason for the decision to refuse it it is an element in that decision. Finally, a white plaintiff upon whom a discrimination against black persons has an impact may bring an action under the statute.

Plaintiffs Williamson and Tucker made a bona fide offer. Plaintiffs contend that the refusal to accept it was because of race. Defendants contend that the refusal was because Hampton Management has a policy against renting to two single women and also because the incomes of the plaintiff applicants were inadequate to enable them to afford the $265 monthly rent. I find for the plaintiffs.

The conduct of defendants is inconsistent with their present assertion that their refusal was based on a policy against renting to two single women. Defendants rely upon a memorandum in Hampton Management's file dated October 5, 1971, written by a representative of Hampton Management's New York office, which states:

"Please be advised that at no time in the future are we to rent to two girls living in one apartment or two men together or to anybody on welfare. "Such renting reduces the credibility of the building."

215

Defendants Sudol and Valerio gave a reason different from "credibility of the building," whatever that may mean, for the policy as to two single women. They testified that the reason for the policy is the likelihood that one of the women will marry and the other will not want to stay in the apartment alone, with resulting inconvenience to the lessor. I assume a lessor could lawfully adopt and enforce such a policy, if it is enforced without regard to race. But defendants' conduct was inconsistent with any intent to enforce the policy in a non-discriminatory way or indeed to enforce the policy at all except against plaintiffs. Defendant Valerio, when first advised that plaintiff Williamson was single and intended to occupy the apartment with plaintiff Tucker, said the latter would also have to fill out an application. Nothing was said about the alleged policy then or at any time during the discussions among the parties before or at the time of the refusal. Even after the refusal, plaintiff Williamson was told that the applications were "good" and that defendants would keep them on file.

Subsequent to those events, a young white woman named Karen Murphy, who is an employee of the Leadership Council, an organization working in the field of civil rights, went to Hampton Management's offices and stated she was answering a newspaper advertisement of an apartment for rent. She told several representatives of Hampton Management, including defendant Valerio, that she was single and was interested in renting the advertised apartment with a girl friend. She was shown the apartment which the existing tenants who were rerouted to the subject apartment had been scheduled to move into on May 1. Defendant Valerio gave Karen Murphy application forms for herself and her girl friend and asked for a security deposit. It would thus appear that the defendants arranged to rent the subject apartment to the tenants who were planning to move into the other similar apartment, and then began looking for tenants for the other similar apartment and were quite willing to consider the applications of two single white women for that apartment. The fact that Karen Murphy was an employee of the Leadership Council and visited defendants for investigative and evidence-gathering purposes does not impair her credibility as a witness. The only reasonable inference from the evidence, even apart from testimony not heretofore mentioned that defendant Valerio said defendants did not want blacks, is that race and not the supposed policy against renting to two single women was the reason for the refusal to rent.

The contention that defendants were motivated in their refusal by a belief that the incomes of plaintiffs Williamson and Tucker were inadequate to enable them to afford the $265 monthly rent is not plausible. Plaintiff Williamson's salary is $140 per week and plaintiff Tucker's is $724 per month. Together their annual gross incomes exceed $15,000 and are in the highest income category of the multiple-choice question concerning the applicant's income on the Hampton Management rental application form, i.e., "Income in excess of ... $15,000." It is not reasonable to infer that the black plaintiffs' incomes were the reason for the refusal to lease to them. ...

Pursuant to the authority of the Civil Rights Act of 1968, the following relief will be granted:

1. A declaratory judgment will be entered to the effect that plaintiffs Valerie Williamson and Joyce Tucker are entitled to rent the subject apartment.

2. Defendant Hampton Management Company will be directed to tender to those plaintiffs a lease on that apartment or an equivalent apartment in the same building, commencing immediately and expiring on August 31, 1972, at a monthly rental of $265 per month, with the right and privilege of those plaintiffs to renew the lease for such period of time and at such rental as equivalent apartments are offered to white tenants. The defendants will be enjoined from interfering with those plaintiffs' rights to enjoy peaceably the use of the premises during the time the lease and any renewals thereof are in effect.

3. Plaintiff Bonita Nichols will recover the security deposit she made in connection with her lease and have returned to her the check in the amount of $57.50 which she delivered to defendants as a supposed cancellation charge. There is no warrant for such a charge in the lease. Defendant Hampton Management having had the opportunity to receive rental on the apartment without interruption and having lost that opportunity through its own wrongdoing, it would be inequitable to allow it to retain either the Nichols security deposit or the Nichols check. Defendant Hampton Management will also deliver to plaintiff Bonita Nichols evidence of the cancellation of her lease.

4. Plaintiffs Valerie Williamson and Joyce Tucker will each recover from the defendants the sum of $500 as punitive damages.

5. Plaintiffs will recover as attorneys' fees the sum of $750, which is reasonable compensation for preparation of the complaint, trial preparation, three days of trial and related services. ...

Non-Invidious Discrimination (Affirmative Action)

Under Statute

Voting and the 1965 Voting Rights Act

JOHNSON v. DE GRANDY
Supreme Court of the United States (1994)
114 S. Ct. 2647; 129 L. Ed. 2d 775

JUSTICE SOUTER. These consolidated cases are about the meaning of vote dilution and the facts required to show it, when §2 of the Voting Rights Act of 1965 is applied to challenges to single-member legislative districts. We hold that no violation of §2 can be found here, where, in spite of continuing discrimination and racial bloc voting, minority voters form effective voting majorities in a number of districts roughly proportional to the minority voters' respective shares in the voting-age population. ...

[A] group of Hispanic voters including Miguel De Grandy (De Grandy plaintiffs) complained in the United States District Court against the speaker of Florida's House of Representatives, the president of its Senate, the Governor, and other state officials (State). The complainants alleged that the districts from which Florida voters had chosen their state senators and representatives since 1982 were malapportioned, failing to reflect changes in the State's population during the ensuing decade. ...

Several months after the first complaint was filed, on April 10, 1992, the state legislature adopted Senate Joint Resolution 2-G (SJR 2-G), providing the reapportionment plan currently at issue. The plan called for dividing Florida into 40 single-member Senate, and 120 single-member House, districts based on population data from the 1990 census. ...

The ... plaintiffs responded to SJR 2-G by amending their federal complaints to charge the new reapportionment plan with violating §2. They claimed that SJR 2-G "'unlawfully fragments cohesive minority communities and otherwise impermissibly submerges their right to vote and to participate in the electoral process,'" and

they pointed to areas around the State where black or Hispanic populations could have formed a voting majority in a politically cohesive, reasonably compact district (or in more than one), if SJR 2-G had not fragmented each group among several districts or packed it into just a few. ...

... [T]he District Court ... held the plan's provisions for state House districts to be in violation of §2 because "more than [SJR 2-G's] nine Hispanic districts may be drawn without having or creating a regressive effect upon black voters," and it imposed a remedial plan offered by the ... plaintiffs calling for 11 majority-Hispanic House districts. ...

[T]he crux of the State's argument is the power of Hispanics under SJR 2-G to elect candidates of their choice in a number of districts that mirrors their share of the Dade County area's voting-age population (i.e., 9 out of 20 House districts); this power, according to the State, bars any finding that the plan dilutes Hispanic voting strength. The District Court is said to have missed that conclusion by mistaking our precedents to require the plan to maximize the number of Hispanic-controlled districts. ...

The State's argument takes us back to ground covered last Term in ... *Growe* v. *Emison*. In *Growe*, we held that a claim of vote dilution ... requires proof ... [of] three threshold conditions. ... [1] that a minority group be "'sufficiently large and geographically compact to constitute a majority in a single-member district'"; [2] that it be "'politically cohesive'"; and [3] that "'the white majority vote sufficiently as a bloc to enable it ... usually to defeat the minority's preferred candidate'" (quoting *Thornburg* v. *Gingles*). ...

... The dispute in this litigation centers on ... whether, even with all three *Gingles* conditions satisfied, the circumstances in totality support a finding of vote dilution when Hispanics can be expected to elect their chosen representatives in substantial proportion to their percentage of the area's population. ...

We ... part company from the District Court in assessing the totality of circumstances. The District Court found that the three Gingles preconditions were satisfied, and that Hispanics had suffered historically from official discrimination, the social, economic, and political effects of which they generally continued to feel. Without more, and on the apparent assumption that what could have been done to create additional Hispanic super-majority districts should have been done, the District Court found a violation of §2. But the assumption was erroneous, and more is required, as a review of *Gingles* will show.

Thornburg v. *Gingles* prompted this Court's first reading of §2 of the Voting Rights Act after its 1982 amendment. ...

Gingles provided some structure to the statute's "totality of circumstances" test. ... The Court thus summarized the three now-familiar *Gingles* factors (compactness/numerousness, minority cohesion or bloc voting, and majority bloc voting) as "necessary preconditions" for establishing vote dilution. ...

But if *Gingles* so clearly identified the three as generally necessary to prove a §2 claim, it just as clearly declined to hold them sufficient. ... [The Supreme Court then held that the "totality of the circumstances" provision of §2 required a reviewing court to go beyond the evidence from the three *Gingles* factors and consider all other relevant evidence in deciding whether voting dilution did or would occur.] ...

The District Court ... was not critical enough in asking whether a history of persistent discrimination reflected in the larger society and its bloc-voting behavior portended any dilutive effect from a newly proposed districting scheme, whose pertinent features were majority-minority districts in substantial proportion to the minority's share of voting-age population. The court failed to ask whether the totality of facts, including those pointing to proportionality, showed that the new scheme would deny minority voters equal political opportunity.

Treating equal political opportunity as the focus of the enquiry, we do not see how these district lines, apparently providing political effectiveness in proportion to voting-age numbers, deny equal political opportunity. The record establishes that Hispanics constitute 50 percent of

the voting-age population in Dade County and under SJR 2-G would make up super-majorities in 9 of the 18 House districts located primarily within the county. Likewise, if one considers the 20 House districts located at least in part within Dade County, the record indicates that Hispanics would be an effective voting majority in 45 percent of them (i.e., nine), and would constitute 47 percent of the voting-age population in the area. In other words, under SJR 2-G Hispanics in the Dade County area would enjoy substantial proportionality. On this evidence, we think the State's scheme would thwart the historical tendency to exclude Hispanics, not encourage or perpetuate it. Thus in spite of that history and its legacy, including the racial cleavages that characterize Dade County politics today, we see no grounds for holding in this case that SJR 2-G's district lines diluted the votes cast by Hispanic voters. ...

... [T]he State [would have the Court rule] that as a matter of law no dilution occurs whenever the percentage of single-member districts in which minority voters form an effective majority mirrors the minority voters' percentage of the relevant population. Proportionality so defined would thus be a safe harbor for any districting scheme.

The safety would be in derogation of the statutory text and its considered purpose, however, and of the ideal that the Voting Rights Act attempts to foster. An inflexible rule would run counter to the textual command of §2, that the presence or absence of a violation be assessed "based on the totality of circumstances." The need for such "totality" review springs from the demonstrated ingenuity of state and local governments in hobbling minority voting power, a point recognized by Congress when it amended the statute in 1982: "since the adoption of the Voting Rights Act, [some] jurisdictions have substantially moved from direct, overt impediments to the right to vote to more sophisticated devices that dilute minority voting strength," Senate Report 10 (discussing §5). In modifying §2, Congress thus endorsed our view in *White* v. *Regester* that "whether the political processes are 'equally open' depends upon a searching practical evaluation of the 'past and present reality,'" Senate Report 30. In a substantial number of voting jurisdictions, that past reality has included such reprehensible practices as ballot box stuffing, outright violence, discretionary registration, property requirements, the poll tax, and the white primary; and other practices censurable when the object of their use is discriminatory, such as at-large elections, runoff requirements, anti-single-shot devices, gerrymandering, the impeachment of officeholders, the annexation or deannexation of territory, and the creation or elimination of elective offices. Some of those expedients could occur even in a jurisdiction with numerically demonstrable proportionality; the harbor safe for States would thus not be safe for voters. It is, in short, for good reason that we have been, and remain, chary of entertaining a simplification of the sort the State now urges upon us. ...

Even if the State's safe harbor were open only in cases of alleged dilution by the manipulation of district lines, however, it would rest on an unexplored premise of highly suspect validity: that in any given voting jurisdiction (or portion of that jurisdiction under consideration), the rights of some minority voters under §2 may be traded off against the rights of other members of the same minority class. Under the State's view, the most blatant racial gerrymandering in half of a county's single member districts would be irrelevant under §2 if offset by political gerrymandering in the other half, so long as proportionality was the bottom line. ...

Finally, we reject the safe harbor rule because of a tendency the State would itself certainly condemn, a tendency to promote and perpetuate efforts to devise majority-minority districts even in circumstances where they may not be necessary to achieve equal political and electoral opportunity. Because in its simplest form the State's rule would shield from §2 challenge a districting scheme in which the number of majority-minority districts reflected the minority's share of the relevant population, the conclusiveness of the rule might be an irresistible inducement to create such districts. It bears recalling, however, that for all the virtues of majority-minority districts as remedial devices, they rely on

a quintessentially race-conscious calculus aptly described as the "politics of second best". ... If the lesson of *Gingles* is that society's racial and ethnic cleavages sometimes necessitate majority-minority districts to ensure equal political and electoral opportunity, that should not obscure the fact that there are communities in which minority citizens are able to form coalitions with voters from other racial and ethnic groups, having no need to be a majority within a single district in order to elect candidates of their choice. Those candidates may not represent perfection to every minority voter, but minority voters are not immune from the obligation to pull, haul, and trade to find common political ground, the virtue of which is not to be slighted in applying a statute meant to hasten the waning of racism in American politics.

It is enough to say that, while proportionality in the sense used here is obviously an indication that minority voters have an equal opportunity, in spite of racial polarization, "to participate in the political process and to elect representatives of their choice," 42 U.S.C. @ 1973(b), the degree of probative value assigned to proportionality may vary with other facts. No single statistic provides courts with a short-cut to determine whether a set of single-member districts unlawfully dilutes minority voting strength. ...

In sum, the District Court's finding of dilution did not address the statutory standard of unequal political and electoral opportunity, and reflected instead a misconstruction of §2 that equated dilution with failure to maximize the number of reasonably compact majority-minority districts. Because the ultimate finding of dilution in districting for the Florida House was based on a misreading of the governing law, we hold it to be clearly erroneous. ...

TITLE VII: DISPARATE TREATMENT—VOLUNTARY AFFIRMATIVE ACTION CASES

- Defined: employer voluntarily adopts a plan to favor categories of persons previously the victims of discrimination
- The Rule: follows the standard (*McDonnell*) model
  - *prima facie* burden on plaintiff to establish that impermissible criteria used
  - burden then shifts to the defendant to articulate and provide evidence of a legitimate business justification; affirmative action is a legitimate justification
  - burden shifts back to the plaintiff to prove that the affirmative action plan is invalid, *i.e.,* that the plan fails at least one of the following criteria
- Plan offsets actual underrepresentation in traditionally segregated job categories
- plan must be flexible and not authorize blind hiring by the numbers; may authorize membership in the discriminated class as *one* factor to be considered
- cannot unnecessarily trammel the rights of others, nor create an absolute barrier to them
- must be temporary and designed to create a balanced work force

UNITED STEELWORKERS OF AMERICA v. WEBER
Supreme Court of the United States (1979)
443 U.S. 193

MR. JUSTICE BRENNAN: Challenged here is the legality of an affirmative action plan—collectively bargained by an employer and a union—that reserves for black employees 50% of the openings is an in-plant craft-training program until the percentage of black craftworkers in the plant is commensurate with the percentage of blacks in the local labor force. The question for decision is whether Congress, in Tile VII of the Civil Rights Act of 1964, left employers and unions in the private sector free to take such race-conscious steps to eliminate manifest racial imbalances in traditionally segregated job categories. We hold that Title VII does not prohibit such race-conscious affirmative action plans.

I

In 1974, ... United Steelworkers of America (USWA) and ... Kaiser Aluminum & Chemical Corp. (Kaiser) entered into a master collective-bargaining agreement covering terms and conditions of employment at 15 Kaiser plants. The agreement contained, inter alia, an affirmative action plan designed to eliminate conspicuous racial imbalances in Kaiser's then almost exclusively white craftwork forces. Black craft-hiring goals were set for each Kaiser plant equal to the percentage of blacks in the respective local labor forces. To enable plants to meet these goals, on-the-job training programs were established to teach unskilled production workers—black and white—the skills necessary to become craftworkers. The plan reserved for black employees 50% of the openings in these newly created in-plant training programs. ...

During 1974, the first year of the operation of the Kaiser-USWA affirmative action plan, 13 craft trainees were selected from Gramercy's production work force. Of these, seven were black and six white. The most senior black selected into the program had less seniority

than several white production workers whose bids for admission were rejected. Thereafter one of those white production workers, ... Brian Weber ... , instituted this class action in the United States District Court for the Eastern District of Louisiana.

The complaint alleged that the filling of craft trainee positions at the Gramercy plant pursuant to the affirmative action program had resulted in junior black employees' receiving training in preference to senior white employees, thus discriminating against [Weber] and other similarly situated white employees in violation of Title VII. ...

II

We emphasize at the outset the narrowness of our inquiry. Since the Kaiser-USWA plan does not involve state action, this case does not present an alleged violation of the Equal Protection Clause of the Fourteenth Amendment. Further, since the Kaiser-USWA plan was adopted voluntarily, we are not concerned with what Title VII requires or with what a court might order to remedy a past proved violation of the Act. The only question before us is the narrow statutory issue of whether Title VII forbids private employers and unions from voluntarily agreeing upon bona fide affirmative action plans that accord racial preferences in the manner and for the purpose provided in the Kaiser-USWA plan. That question was expressly left open in *McDonald v. Santa Fe Trail Transp. Co.* (1976), which held, in a case not involving affirmative action, that Title VII protects whites as well as blacks from certain forms of racial discrimination.

[Weber] argues that Congress intended in Title VII to prohibit all race-conscious affirmative action plans. [Weber's] argument rests upon a literal interpretation of ... the Act. [The Act] make[s] it unlawful to "discriminate ... because of ... race" in hiring and in the selection of apprentices for training programs. Since, the argument runs, *McDonald v. Santa Fe Trail Transp. Co.* settled that Title VII forbids discrimination against whites as well as blacks, and since the Kaiser-USWA affirmative action plan operates to discriminate against white employees solely because they are white, it follows that the Kaiser-USWA plan violates Title VII.

[Weber's]argument is not without force. But it overlooks the significance of the fact that the Kaiser-USWA plan is an affirmative action plan voluntarily adopted by private parties to eliminate traditional patterns of racial segregation. In this context [Weber's] reliance upon a literal construction of [the Act] and upon *McDonald* is misplaced. It is a "familiar rule, that a thing may be within the letter of the statute and yet not within the statute, because not within its spirit, nor within the intention of its makers." *Holy Trinity Church v. United States* (1892). The prohibition against racial discrimination in ... Title VII must therefore be read against the background of the legislative history of Title VII and the historical context from which the Act arose. Examination of those sources makes clear that an interpretation of the sections that forbade all race-conscious affirmative action would "bring about an end completely at variance with the purpose of the statute" and must be rejected.

Congress' primary concern in enacting the prohibition against racial discrimination in Title VII of the Civil Rights Act of 1964 was with "the plight of the Negro in our economy." Before 1964, blacks were largely relegated to "unskilled and semi-skilled jobs." ... Because of automation the number of such jobs was rapidly decreasing. As a consequence, "the relative position of the Negro worker [was] steadily worsening. In 1947 the nonwhite unemployment rate was only 64 percent higher than the white rate; in 1962 it was 124 percent higher" (remarks of Sen. Humphrey). Congress considered this a serious social problem. As Senator Clark told the Senate:

> "The rate of Negro unemployment has gone up consistently as compared with white unemployment for the past 15 years. This is a social malaise and a social situation which we should not tolerate. That is one of the principal reasons why the bill should pass."

Congress feared that the goals of the Civil Rights Act—the integration of blacks into the mainstream of American society—could not be achieved unless this trend were reversed. And Congress recognized that that would not be possible unless blacks were able to secure jobs "which have a future."... Accordingly, it was clear

to Congress that "[the] crux of the problem [was] to open employment opportunities for Negroes in occupations which have been traditionally closed to them," and it was to this problem that Title VII's prohibition against racial discrimination in employment was primarily addressed.

It plainly appears from the House Report accompanying the Civil Rights Act that Congress did not intend wholly to prohibit private and voluntary affirmative action efforts as one methods of solving this problem. The Report provides:

> "No bill can or should lay claim to eliminating all of the causes and consequences of racial and other types of discrimination against minorities. There is reason to believe, however, that national leadership provided by the enactment of Federal legislation dealing with the most troublesome problems will create an atmosphere conducive to voluntary or local resolution of other forms of discrimination."

Given this legislative history, we cannot agree with [Weber] that Congress intended to prohibit the private sector from taking effective steps to accomplish the goal that Congress designed Title VII to achieve. The very statutory words intended as a spur or catalyst to cause "employers and unions to self-examine and to self-evaluate their employment practices and to endeavor to eliminate, so far as possible, the last vestiges of an unfortunate and ignominious page in this country's history," cannot be interpreted as an absolute prohibition against all private, voluntary, race-conscious affirmative action efforts to hasten the elimination of such vestiges. It would be ironic indeed if a law triggered by a Nation's concern over centuries of racial injustice and intended to improve the lot of those who had "been excluded from the American dream for so long," constituted the first legislative prohibition of all voluntary, private, race-conscious efforts to abolish traditional patterns of racial segregation and hierarchy.

Our conclusion is further reinforced by examination of the language and legislative history of §703 (j) of Title VII. Opponents of Title VII raised two related arguments against the bill. First, they argued that the Act would be interpreted to *require* employers with racially imbalanced work forces to grant preferential treatment to racial minorities in order to integrate. Second, they argued that employers with racially imbalanced work forces would grant preferential treatment to racial minorities, even if not required to do so by the

Act. Had Congress meant to prohibit all race-conscious affirmative action, as respondent urges, it easily could have answered both objections by providing that Title VII would not require of *permit* racially preferential integration efforts. But Congress did not choose such a course. Rather, Congress added §703 (j) which addresses only the first objection. The section provides that nothing contained in Title VII "shall be interpreted to require any employer ... to grant preferential treatment ... to any group because of the race ... of such ... group on account of" a de facto racial imbalance in the employer's work force. The section does not state that "nothing in Title VII shall be interpreted to permit" voluntary affirmative efforts to correct racial imbalances. The natural inference is that Congress chose not to forbid all voluntary race-conscious affirmative action.

The reasons for this choice are evident from the legislative record. Title VII could not have been enacted into law without substantial support from legislators in both Houses who traditionally resisted federal regulation of private business. Those legislators demanded as a price for their support that "management prerogatives, and union freedoms ... be left undisturbed to the greatest extent possible." Section 703 (j) was proposed by Senator Dirksen to allay any fears that the Act might be interpreted in such a way as to upset this compromise. The section was designed to prevent ... Title VII from being interpreted in such a way as to lead to undue "Federal Government interference with private businesses because of some Federal employee's ideas about racial balance or racial imbalance." Clearly, a prohibition against all voluntary, race-conscious, affirmative action efforts would disserve these ends. Such a prohibition would augment the powers of the Federal Government and diminish traditional management prerogatives white at the same time impeding attainment of the ultimate statutory goals. In view of this legislative history and in view of Congress' desire to avoid undue federal regulation of private businesses, use of the word "require" rather than the phrase "require or permit" in §703 (j) fortifies the conclusion that Congress did not intend to limit traditional business freedom to such a degree as to prohibit all voluntary, race-conscious affirmative action plans. ...

III

We need not today define in detail the line of demarcation between permissible and impermissible affirmative action plans. It suffices to hold that the challenged Kaiser-USWA affirmative action plan falls on the permissible side

of the line. The purposes of the plan mirror those of the statute. Both were designed to break down old patterns of racial segregation and hierarchy. Both were structured to "open employment opportunities for Negroes in occupations which have been traditionally closed to them."

At the same time, the plan does not unnecessarily trammel the interests of the white employees. The plan does not require the discharge of white workers and their replacement with new black hirees. Nor does the plan create an absolute bar to the advancement of white employees; half of those trained in the program will be white. Moreover, the plan is a temporary measure; it is not intended to maintain racial balance, but simply to eliminate a manifest racial imbalance. Preferential selection of craft trainees at the Gramercy plant will end as soon as the percentage of black skilled craftworkers in the Gramercy plant approximates the percentage of blacks in the local labor force.

We conclude, therefore, that the adoption of the Kaiser-USWA plan for the Gramercy plant falls within the area of discretion left by Title VII to the private sector voluntarily to adopt affirmative action plans designed to eliminate conspicuous racial imbalance in traditionally segregated job categories. ...

MR. JUSTICE REHNQUIST, dissenting. ... Were Congress to act today specifically to prohibit the type of racial discrimination suffered by Weber, it would be hard pressed to draft language better tailored to the task than that found in §703 (d) of Title VII:

> "It shall be an unlawful employment practice for any employer, labor organization, or joint labor-management committee controlling apprenticeship or other training or retraining, including on-the-job training programs to discriminate against any individual because of his race, color, religion, sex, or national origin in admission to, or employment in, any program established to provide apprenticeship or other training."

... Quite simply, Kaiser's racially discriminatory admission quota is flatly prohibited by the plain language of Title VII. This normally dispositive fact, however, gives the Court only momentary pause. An "interpretation" of the statute upholding Weber's claim would, according to the Court, "'bring about an end completely at variance with the purpose of the statute.'" To support this conclusion, the Court calls upon the "spirit" of the Act, which it divines from passages in Title VII's legislative history indicating that enactment of the statute was prompted by Congress' desire "'to open employment opportunities for Negroes in occupations which [had] been traditionally closed to them.'" But the legislative history invoked by the Court to avoid the plain language of [the Act] simply misses the point. To be sure, the reality of employment discrimination against Negroes provided the primary impetus for passage of Title VII. But this fact by no means supports the proposition that Congress intended to leave employers free to discriminate against white persons. ...

In the opening speech of the formal Senate debate on the bill, Senator Humphrey addressed the main concern of Title VII's opponents, advising that not only does Title VII not require use of racial quotas, it does not permit their use. "The truth," stated the floor leader of the bill, "is that this title forbids discriminating against anyone on account of race. This is the simple and complete truth about title VII." Senator Humphrey continued:

"Contrary to the allegations of some opponents of this title, there is nothing in it that will give any power to the Commission or to any court to require hiring, firing, or promotion of employees in order to meet a racial 'quota' or to achieve a certain racial balance.

"That bugaboo has been brought up a dozen times; but it is nonexistent. In fact, the very opposite is true. Title VII prohibits discrimination. In effect, it says that race, religion and national origin are not to be used as the basis for hiring and firing. Title VII is designed to encourage hiring on the basis of ability and qualifications, not race or religion."

At the close of his speech, Senator Humphrey returned briefly to the subject of employment quotas: "It is claimed that the bill would require racial quotas for all hiring, when in fact it provides that race shall not be a basis for making personnel decisions." ...

To put an end to the dispute, supporters of the civil rights bill drafted and introduced §703 (j). Specifically addressed to the opposition's charge, §703 (j) simply enjoins federal agencies and courts from interpreting Title VII to require an employer to prefer certain racial groups to correct imbalances in his work force. The section says nothing about voluntary preferential treatment of minorities because such racial discrimination is plainly proscribed by [the Act]. Indeed, had Congress intended to except voluntary, race-conscious preferential treatment from the blanket prohibition of racial discrimination ... , it surely could have drafted language better suited to the task than §703 (j). It knew how. Section 703 (i) provides:

"Nothing contained in [Title VII] shall apply to any business or enterprise on or near an Indian reservation with respect to any publicly announced employment practice of such business or enterprise under which a preferential treatment is given to any individual because he is an Indian living on or near a reservation."

JOHNSON v. TRANSPORTATION AGENCY
Supreme Court of the United States (1987)
480 U.S. 616

JUSTICE BRENNAN: ... [The County] Transportation Agency of Santa Clara County, California, unilaterally promulgated an Affirmative Action Plan applicable, inter alia, to promotions of employees. In selecting applicants for the promotional position of road dispatcher, the Agency, pursuant to the Plan, passed over petitioner Paul Johnson, a male employee, and promoted a female employee applicant, Diane Joyce. The question for decision is whether in making the promotion the Agency impermissibly took into account the sex of the applicants in violation of Title VII of the Civil Rights Act of 1964. ... [T]he Agency Plan provides that, in making promotions to positions within a traditionally segregated job classification in which women have been significantly underrepresented, the Agency is authorized to consider as one factor the sex of a qualified applicant. ...

I

The Agency stated that its Plan was intended to achieve "a statistically measurable yearly improvement in hiring, training and promotion of minorities and women throughout the Agency in all major job classifications where they are underrepresented." As a benchmark by which to evaluate progress, the Agency stated that its long-term goal was to attain a work force whose composition reflected the proportion of minorities and women in the area labor force. Thus, for the Skilled Craft category in which the road dispatcher position at issue here was classified, the Agency's aspiration was that eventually about 36% of the jobs would be occupied by women. ...

The Agency's Plan thus set aside no specific number of positions for minorities or women, but authorized the consideration of ethnicity or sex as a factor when evaluating qualified candidates for jobs in which members of such groups were poorly represented. One such job was the road dispatcher position that is the subject of the dispute in this case. ... Nine of the applicants, including Joyce and Johnson, were deemed qualified for the job, and were interviewed by a two-person board. Seven of the applicants scored above 70 on this interview, which meant that they were certified as eligible for selection by the appointing authority. The scores awarded ranged from 70 to 80. Johnson was tied for second with a score of 75, while Joyce ranked next with a score of 73. A second interview was conducted by three Agency supervisors, who ultimately recommended that Johnson be promoted. Prior to the second interview, Joyce had contacted the County's Affirmative Action Office because she feared that her application might not receive disinterested review.[3] The Office in turn contacted the Agency's Affirmative Action Coordinator, whom the Agency's Plan makes responsible for, inter alia, keeping the Director informed of opportunities for the Agency to

---

[3]Joyce testified that she had had disagreements with two of the three members of the second interview panel. One had been her first supervisor when she began work as a road maintenance worker. In performing arduous work in this job, she had not been issued coveralls, although her male co-workers had received them. After ruining her pants, she complained to her supervisor, to no avail. After three other similar incidents, ruining clothes on each occasion, she filed a grievance, and was issued four pairs of coveralls the next day. Joyce had dealt with a second member of the panel for a year and a half in her capacity as chair of the Roads Operations Safety Committee, where she and he "had several differences of opinion on how safety should be implemented." In addition, Joyce testified that she had informed the person responsible for arranging her second interview that she had a disaster preparedness class on a certain day the following week. By this time about 10 days had passed since she had notified this person of her availability, and no date had yet been set for the interview. Within a day or two after this conversation, however, she received a notice setting her interview at a time directly in the middle of her disaster preparedness class. This same panel member had earlier described Joyce as a "rebel-rousing, skirt-wearing person."

accomplish its objectives under the Plan. At the time, the Agency employed no women in any Skilled Craft position, and had never employed a woman as a road dispatcher. The Coordinator recommended to the Director of the Agency, James Graebner, that Joyce be promoted.

Graebner, authorized to choose any of the seven persons deemed eligible, thus had the benefit of suggestions by the second interview panel by the Agency Coordinator in arriving at his decision. After deliberation, Graebner concluded that the promotion should be given to Joyce. As he testified: "I tried to look at the whole picture, the combination of her qualifications and Mr. Johnson's qualifications, their test scores, their expertise, their background, affirmative action matters, things like that. … I believe it was a combination of all those." …

… Johnson filed a complaint … alleging that he had been denied promotion on the basis of sex in violation of Title VII. …

II

As a preliminary matter, we note that petitioner bears the burden of establishing the invalidity of the Agency's Plan. Only last Term, in *Wygant v. Jackson Board of Education* (1986), we held that "[the] ultimate burden remains with the employees to demonstrate the unconstitutionality of an affirmative-action program," and we see no basis for a different rule regarding a plan's alleged violation of Title VII. This case also fits readily within the analytical framework set forth in *McDonnell Douglas Corp. v. Green* (1973). Once a plaintiff establishes a prima facie case that race or sex has been taken into account in an employer's employment decision, the burden shifts to the employer to articulate a nondiscriminatory rationale for its decision. The existence of an affirmative action plan provides such a rationale. If such a plan is articulated as the basis for the employer's decision, the burden shifts to the plaintiff to prove that the employer's justification is pretextual and the plan is invalid. As a practical matter, of course, an employer will generally seek to avoid a charge of pretext by presenting evidence in support of its plan. That does not mean, however, as petitioner suggests, that reliance on an affirmative action plan is to be treated as an affirmative defense requiring the employer to carry the burden of proving the validity of the plan. The burden of proving its invalidity remains on the plaintiff.

The assessment of the legality of the Agency Plan must be guided by our decision in *Weber*. In that case, … [w]e upheld the employer's decision to select less senior black applicants over the white respondent, for

A. we found that taking race into account was consistent with Title VII's objective of "[breaking] down old patterns of racial segregation and hierarchy." …

B. We noted that the plan did not "unnecessarily trammel the interests of the white employees," since it did not require "the discharge of white workers and their replacement with new black hirees."

C. Nor did the plan create "an absolute bar to the advancement of white employees," since half of those trained in the new program were to be white.

D. Finally, we observed that the plan was a temporary measure, not designed to maintain racial balance, but to "eliminate a manifest racial imbalance." …

In reviewing the employment decision at issue in this case, we must first examine whether that decision was made pursuant to a plan prompted by concerns similar to those of the employer in *Weber*. Next, we must determine whether the effect of the Plan on males and nonminorities is comparable to the effect of the plan in that case.

A. The first issue is therefore whether consideration of the sex of applicants for Skilled Craft jobs was justified by the existence of a "manifest imbalance" that reflected underrepresentation of women in "traditionally segregated job categories." …

It is clear that the decision to hire Joyce was made pursuant to an Agency plan that directed that sex or race be taken into account for the purpose of remedying underrepresentation. The Agency Plan acknowledged the "limited opportunities that have existed in the past" for women to find employment in certain job classifications "where women have not been traditionally employed in significant numbers." As a result, observed the Plan, women were concentrated in traditionally female jobs in the Agency, and represented a lower percentage in other job classifications than would be expected if such traditional segregation had not occurred. Specifically, 9 of the 10 Para-Professionals and 110 of the 145 Office and

Clerical Workers were women. By contrast, women were only 2 of the 28 Officials and Administrators, 5 of the 58 Professionals, 12 of the 124 Technicians, none of the Skilled Craft Workers, and 1—who was Joyce—of the 110 Road Maintenance Workers The Plan sought to remedy these imbalances through "hiring, training and promotion of ... women throughout the Agency in all major job classifications where they are underrepresented." ...

The Agency's Plan emphatically did not authorize ... blind hiring [by the numbers]. It expressly directed that numerous factors be taken into account in making hiring decisions, including specifically the qualifications of female applicants for particular jobs. ... [T]he Agency's management ... had been clearly instructed that they were not to hire solely by reference to statistics. ...

... Given the obvious imbalance in the Skilled Craft category, and given the Agency's commitment to eliminating such imbalances, it was plainly not unreasonable for the Agency to determine that it was appropriate to consider as one factor the sex of Ms. Joyce in making its decision. The promotion of Joyce thus satisfies the first requirement enunciated in *Weber*, since it was undertaken to further an affirmative action plan designed to eliminate Agency work force imbalances in traditionally segregated job categories.

B. We next consider whether the Agency Plan unnecessarily trammeled the rights of male employees or created an absolute bar to their advancement. In contrast to the plan in *Weber*, which provided that 50% of the positions in the craft training program were exclusively for blacks, ... the Plan sets aside no positions for women. The Plan expressly states that "[the] 'goals' established for each Division should not be constructed as 'quotas' that must be met." Rather, the Plan merely authorizes that consideration be given to affirmative action concerns when evaluating qualified applicants. As the Agency Director testified, the sex of Joyce was but one of numerous factors he took

into account in arriving at his decision. The Plan thus resembles the "Harvard Plan" approvingly noted by JUSTICE POWELL in *Regents of University of California v. Bakke* (1978), which considers race along with other criteria in determining admission to the college. As JUSTICE POWELL observed: "In such an admissions program, race or ethnic background may be deemed a 'plus' in a particular applicant's file, yet it does not insulate the individual from comparison with all other candidates for the available seats." Similarly, the Agency Plan requires women to compete with all other qualified applicants. No persons are automatically excluded from consideration; all are able to have their qualifications weighed against those of other applicants.

C. In addition, petitioner had no absolute entitlement to the road dispatcher position. Seven of the applicants were classified as qualified and eligible, and the Agency Director was authorized to promote any of the seven. Thus, denial of the promotion unsettled no legitimate, firmly rooted expectation on the part of petitioner. Furthermore, while petitioner in this case was denied a promotion, he retained his employment with the Agency, at the same salary and with the same seniority, and remained eligible for other promotions.

D. Finally, the Agency's Plan was intended to attain a balanced work force, not to maintain one. The Plan contains 10 references to the Agency's desire to "attain" such a balance, but no reference whatsoever to a goal of maintaining it. The Director testified that, while the "broader goal" of affirmative action, defined as "the desire to hire, to promote, to give opportunity and training on an equitable, non-discriminatory basis," is something that is "a permanent part" of "the Agency's operating philosophy," that "broader goal" is divorced, if you will, from specific numbers or percentages.

The Agency acknowledged the difficulties that it would confront in remedying the imbalance in its work force, and it anticipated only gradual increases in the representation of minorities and women. It is thus unsurprising that the Plan contains no explicit end date, for the Agency's flexible, case-by-case approach was not expected to yield success in a brief period of time. Express assurance that a program is only temporary may be necessary if the program actually sets aside positions according to specific numbers. See, e.g., ... *Weber* ... This is necessary both to minimize the effect of the program on other employees, and to ensure that the plan's goals "[are] not being used simply to achieve and maintain ... balance, but rather as a benchmark against which" the employer may measure its progress in eliminating the under-representation of minorities and women. In this case, however, substantial evidence shows that the Agency has sought to take a moderate, gradual approach to eliminating the imbalance in its work force, one which establishes realistic guidance for employment decisions, and which visits minimal intrusion on the legitimate expectations of other employees. Given this fact, as well as the Agency's express commitment to "attain" a balanced work force, there is ample assurance that the Agency does not seek to use its Plan to maintain a permanent racial and sexual balance.

III

We therefore hold that the Agency appropriately took into account as one factor the sex of Diane Joyce in determining that she should be promoted to the road dispatcher position. The decision to do so was made pursuant to an affirmative action plan that represents a moderate, flexible, case-by-case approach to effecting a gradual improvement in the representation of minorities and women in the Agency's work force. Such a plan is fully consistent with Title VII, for it embodies the contribution that voluntary employer action can make in eliminating the vestiges of discrimination in the workplace.

JUSTICE STEVENS, concurring: ... Prior to 1978 the Court construed the Civil Rights Act of 1964 as an absolute blanket prohibition against discrimination which neither required nor permitted discriminatory preferences for any group, minority or majority. The Court unambiguously endorsed the neutral approach, first in the context of gender discrimination and then in the context of racial discrimination against a white

person. As I explained in my separate opinion in *Regents of University of California v. Bakke* and as the Court forcefully stated in *McDonald v. Santa Fe Trail Transportation Co.*, Congress intended "'to eliminate all practices which operate to disadvantage the employment opportunities of any group protected by Title VII, including Caucasians.'" If the Court had adhered to that construction of the Act, petitioner would unquestionably prevail in this case. But it has not done so.

In the *Bakke* case in 1978 and again in *Steelworkers v. Weber*, a majority of the Court interpreted the antidiscriminatory strategy of the statute in a fundamentally different way. The Court held in the *Weber* case that an employer's program designed to increase the number of black craftworkers in an aluminum plant did not violate Title VII. It remains clear that the Act does not require any employer to grant preferential treatment on the basis of race or gender, but since 1978 the Court has unambiguously interpreted the statute to permit the voluntary adoption of special programs to benefit members of the minority groups for whose protection the statute was enacted. ... Thus, ... the only problem for me is whether to adhere to an authoritative construction of the Act that is at odds with my understanding of the actual intent of the authors of the legislation. I conclude without hesitation that I must answer that question in the affirmative. ...

Bakke and *Weber* have been decided and are now an important part of the fabric of our law. This consideration is sufficiently compelling for me to adhere to the basic construction of this legislation that the Court adopted in *Bakke* and in *Weber*. There is an undoubted public interest in "stability and orderly development of the law." ...

JUSTICE SCALIA, dissenting: ... JUSTICE STEVENS' concurring opinion emphasizes the "undoubted public interest in 'stability and orderly development of the law,'" that often requires adherence to an erroneous decision. [H]owever, today's decision is a demonstration not of stability and order but of the instability and unpredictable expansion which the substitution of judicial improvisation for statutory text has produced. For a number of reasons, stare decisis ought not to save *Weber*. ...

In addition to complying with the commands of the statute, abandoning *Weber* would have the desirable side effect of eliminating the requirement of willing suspension of disbelief that is currently a credential for reading our opinions in the affirmative-action field—from *Weber* itself, which demanded belief that the corporate employer adopted the affirmative-action program "voluntarily," rather than under practical compulsion from government contracting agencies; to *Bakke*, ... which demanded belief that the University of California took race into account as merely one of the many diversities to which it felt it was educationally important to expose its medical students; to today's opinion, Which—in the face of a plan obviously designed to force promoting officials to prefer candidates from the favored racial and sexual classes, warning them that their "personal commitment" will be determined by how successfully they "attain" certain numerical goals, and in the face of a particular promotion awarded to the less qualified applicant by an official who "did little or nothing" to inquire into sources "critical" to determining the final candidates' relative qualifications other than their sex—in the face of all this, demands belief that we are dealing here with no more than a program that "merely authorizes that consideration be given to affirmative action concerns when evaluating qualified applicants." Any line of decisions rooted so firmly in naivete must be wrong.

The majority emphasizes, as though it is meaningful, that "No persons are automatically excluded from consideration; all are able to have their qualifications weighed against those of other applicants.": One is reminded of the exchange from Shakespeare's King Henry the Fourth, Part I:

> "GLENDOWER: I can call Spirits from the vasty Deep.
> "HOTSPUR: Why, so can I, or so can any man. But will they come when you do call for them?" Act III, Scene I, lines 53–55.

Johnson was indeed entitled to have his qualifications weighed against those of other applicants—but more to the point, he was virtually assured that, after the weighing, if there was any minimally qualified applicant from one of the favored groups, he would be rejected. ...

Today's decision does more, however, than merely reaffirm *Weber*, and more than merely extend it to public actors. It is impossible not to be aware that the practical effect of our holding is to accomplish de facto what the law—in language even plainer than that ignored in *Weber*—forbids anyone from accomplishing de jure: in many contexts it effectively requires employers, public as well as private, to engage in intentional discrimination on the basic of race or sex. This Court's prior interpretations of Title VII, especially the decision in *Griggs v. Duke Power Co.*, subject employers to a potential Title VII suit whenever there is a noticeable imbalance in the representation of minorities or women in the employer's work force. Even the employer who is confident of ultimately prevailing in such a suit must contemplate the expense and adverse publicity of a trial, because, the extent of the imbalance, and the "job relatedness" of his selection criteria, are questions of fact to be explored through rebuttal and counterrebuttal of a "prima facie case" consisting of no more than the showing that the employer's selection process "selects those from the protected class at a 'significantly' lesser rate than their counterparts." If, however, employers are free to discriminate through affirmative action, without fear of "reverse discrimination" suits by their nonminority or male victims, they are offered a threshold defense against Title VII liability premised on numerical disparities. Thus, after today's decision the failure to engage in reverse discrimination is economic folly, and arguably a breach of duty to shareholders or taxpayers, wherever the cost of anticipated Title VII litigation exceeds the cost of hiring less capable (though still minimally capable) workers. (This situation is more likely to obtain, of course, with respect to the least skilled jobs—perversely creating an incentive to discriminate against precisely those members of the nonfavored groups least likely to have profited from societal discrimination in the past.) It is predictable, moreover, that this incentive will be greatly magnified by economic pressures brought to bear by government contracting agencies upon employers who refuse to discriminate in the fashion we have now approved. A statute designed to establish a color-blind and gender-blind workplace has thus been converted into a powerful engine of racism and sexism, not merely permitting intentional race- and sex-based discrimination, but often making it, through operation of the legal system, practically compelled. ...

MANSMANN, J. In this Title VII matter, we must determine whether the Board of Education of the Township of Piscataway violated that statute when it made race a factor in selecting which of two equally qualified employees to lay off. Specifically, we must decide whether Title VII permits an employer with a racially balanced work force to grant a non-remedial racial preference in order to promote "racial diversity".

In 1975, the Board of Education of the Township of Piscataway, New Jersey, developed an affirmative action policy applicable to employment decisions. In 1983 the Board also adopted a one page "Policy", entitled "Affirmative Action—Employment Practices."

The operative language regarding the means by which affirmative-action goals are to be furthered is identical in the two documents. "In all cases, the most qualified candidate will be recommended for appointment. However, when candidates appear to be of equal qualification, candidates meeting the criteria of the affirmative action program will be recommended." The phrase "candidates meeting the criteria of the affirmative action program" [includes] Blacks. The 1983 document also clarifies that the affirmative action program applies to "every aspect of employment including ... layoffs. ..."

The Board's affirmative action policy did not have "any remedial purpose"; it was not adopted" with the intention of remedying the results of any prior discrimination or identified underrepresentation of minorities within the Piscataway Public School System." At all relevant times, Black teachers were neither "underrepresented" nor "underutilized" in the Piscataway School District work force. Indeed, statistics in 1976 and 1985 showed that the percentage of Black employees in the job category which included teachers exceeded the percentage of Blacks in the available work force.

In May, 1989, the Board accepted a recommendation from the Superintendent of Schools to reduce the teaching staff in the Business Department at Piscataway High School by one. At that time, two of the teachers in the department were of equal seniority, both having begun their employment with the Board on the same day nine years earlier. One of those teachers was plaintiff Sharon Taxman, who is White, and the other was Debra Williams, who is Black. Williams was the only minority teacher among the faculty of the Business Department.

Decisions regarding layoffs by New Jersey school boards are highly circumscribed by state law. ... Thus, local boards lack discretion to choose between employees for layoff, except in the rare instance of a tie in seniority between the two or more employees eligible to fill the last remaining position.

The Board determined that it was facing just such a rare circumstance in deciding between Taxman and Williams. In prior decisions involving the layoff of employees with equal seniority, the Board had broken the tie through "a random process which included drawing numbers out of a container, drawing lots or having a lottery." In none of those instances, however, had the employees involved been of different races.

In light of the unique posture of the layoff decision, Superintendent of Schools Burton Edelchick recommended to the Board that the affirmative action plan be invoked in order to determine which teacher to retain.

While the Board recognized that it was not bound to apply the affirmative action policy; it made a discretionary decision to invoke the policy to break the tie between Williams and Taxman. As a result, the Board "voted to terminate the employment of Sharon Taxman, effective June 30, 1988. ..."

At her deposition, Paula Van Riper, the Board's Vice President at the time of the layoff, described the Board's decision-making process. According to Van Riper, after the Board recognized that Taxman and Williams were of equal seniority, it assessed their classroom performance, evaluations, volunteerism and certifications and determined that they were "two teachers of equal ability" and "equal qualifications."

At his deposition Theodore H. Kruse, the Board's President, explained his vote to apply the affirmative action policy. ...

Asked to articulate the "educational objective" served by retaining Williams rather than Taxman, Kruse stated:

A. In my own personal perspective I believe by retaining Mrs. Williams it was sending a very clear message that we feel that our staff should be culturally diverse, our student population is culturally diverse and there is a distinct advantage to students, to all students, to be made—come into contact with people of different cultures, different background, so that they are more aware, more tolerant, more accepting, more understanding of people of all background.

[T]he United States filed suit under Title VII against the Board in the United States District Court for the District of New Jersey. Taxman intervened. ...

The district court ... granted partial summary judgment to the United States and Taxman, holding the Board liable ... for discrimination on the basis of race.

For a time, the Supreme Court construed [Title VII's] ... language as absolutely prohibiting discrimination in employment, neither requiring nor permitting any preference for any group.

In 1979, however, the Court interpreted the statute's "antidiscriminatory strategy" in a "fundamentally different way", holding in the seminal case of *United Steelworkers v. Weber* that Title VII's prohibition against racial discrimination does not condemn all voluntary race-conscious affirmative action plans.

The Court upheld the Kaiser plan because its purpose "mirrored those of the statute" and it did not "unnecessarily trammel the interests of the [non-minority] employees". ...

We analyze Taxman's claim of employment discrimination under the approach set forth in *McDonnell Douglas v. Green*. Once a plaintiff establishes a prima facie case, the burden of production shifts to the employer to show a legitimate nondiscriminatory reason for the decision; an affirmative action plan may be one such reason. When the employer satisfies this requirement, the burden of production shifts back to the employee to show that the asserted nondiscriminatory reason is a pretext and that the affirmative action plan is invalid.

[T]he parties do not dispute that Taxman has established a prima facie case or that the Board's decision to terminate her was based on its affirmative action policy. The dispositive liability issue, therefore, is the validity of the [affirmative action plan] ... under Title VII.

Having reviewed the analytical framework for assessing the validity of an affirmative action plan as established in *United Steelworkers v. Weber*, we turn to the facts of this case in order to determine whether the racial diversity purpose of the Board's policy mirrors the purposes of the statute.

Title VII was enacted to further two primary goals: to end discrimination on the basis of race, color, religion, sex or national origin, thereby guaranteeing equal opportunity in the workplace, and to remedy the segregation and underrepresentation of minorities that discrimination has caused in our Nation's work force.

[B]ased on our analysis of Title VII's two goals, we are convinced that unless an affirmative action plan has a remedial purpose, it cannot be said to mirror the purposes of the statute, and, therefore, cannot satisfy the first prong of the *Weber* test.

[T]he Board's sole purpose in applying its affirmative action policy in this case was to obtain an educational benefit which it believed would result from a racially diverse faculty. While the benefits flowing from diversity in the educational context are significant indeed, we are constrained to hold ... that inasmuch as "the Board does not even attempt to show that its affirmative action plan was adopted to remedy past discrimination or as the result of a manifest imbalance in the employment of minorities," the Board has failed to satisfy the first prong of the *Weber* test.

We turn next to the second prong of the *Weber* analysis. This second prong requires that we determine whether the Board's policy "unnecessarily trammels ... [nonminority] interests. ..." Under this requirement, too, the Board's policy is deficient.

The affirmative action plans that have met with the Supreme Court's approval under Title VII had objectives, as well as benchmarks which served to evaluate progress, guide the employment decisions at issue and assure the grant of only those minority preferences necessary to further the plans' purpose. *Johnson* (setting forth long-range and short-term objectives to achieve "'a statistically measurable yearly improvement in hiring, training and promotion of minorities and women ... in all major job classifications where they are underrepresented'"); *Weber* (reserving for Black employees 50% of the openings in craft-training programs until the percentage of Black craftworkers reflected the percentage of Blacks in the available labor force). By contrast, the Board's policy, devoid of goals and standards, is governed entirely by the Board's whim. ... Such a policy unnecessarily trammels the interests of nonminority employees.

Moreover, both *Weber* and *Johnson* unequivocally provide that valid affirmative action plans are "temporary" measures that seek to "'attain'", not "maintain" a "permanent racial ... balance." The Board's policy, adopted in 1975, is an established fixture of unlimited duration, to be resurrected from time to time whenever the Board believes that the ration between Blacks and Whites in any Piscataway School is skewed. On this basis alone, the policy contravenes *Weber's* teaching.

Finally, we are convinced that the harm imposed upon a nonminority employee by the loss of his or her job is so substantial and the cost so severe that the Board's goal of racial diversity, even if legitimate under Title VII, may not be pursued in this particular fashion. In *Weber* and *Johnson*, when considering whether nonminorities were unduly encumbered by affirmative action, the Court found it significant that they retained their employment. *Weber* (observing that the plan did not require the discharge of nonminority workers);

Johnson (observing that the nonminority employee who was promoted nonetheless kept his job). We, therefore, adopt the plurality's pronouncement in *Wygant* that "while hiring goals impose a diffuse burden, often foreclosing only one of several opportunities, layoffs impose the entire burden of achieving racial equality on particular individuals, often resulting in serious disruption of their lives. That burden is too intrusive."

Accordingly, we conclude that under the second prong of the *Weber* test, the Board's affirmative action policy violates Title VII. In addition to containing an impermissible purpose, the policy "unnecessarily trammels the interests of the [nonminority] employees."

[W]e will affirm the judgment of the district court.

> What test did the court use to determine whether the Board violated Title VII? What was the purpose of the Board's affirmative action policy? Did that meet the first prong of the test? Why? Did the policy meet the second prong of the test? Why? Do you think the result would have been different if this had been a case in which the affirmative action policy had been used to hire a minority instead of laying off a nonminority employee?

UNITED STATES v. STARRETT CITY ASSOCIATES
United States Court of Appeals for the Second Circuit (1987)
840 F.2d 1096

MINER, Circuit Judge: The United States ... maintained that Starrett's practices of renting apartments in its Brooklyn housing complex solely on the basis of applicants' race or national origin, and of making apartments unavailable to black and Hispanic applicants that are then made available to white applicants, violate [the Fair Housing Act]. ...

Starrett has sought to maintain a racial distribution by apartment of 64% white, 22% black and 8% Hispanic at Starrett City. Id. at 671. Starrett claims that these racial quotas are necessary to prevent the loss of white tenants, which would transform Starrett City into a predominantly [**4] minority complex. Starrett points to the difficulty it has had in attracting an integrated applicant pool from the time Starrett City opened, despite extensive advertising and promotional efforts. Because of these purported difficulties, Starrett adopted a tenanting procedure to promote and maintain the desired racial balance. This procedure has resulted in relatively stable percentages of whites and minorities living at Starrett City between 1975 and the present. ...

Starrett maintained that the tenanting procedures "were adopted at the behest of the state solely to achieve and maintain integration and were not motivated by racial animus." To support their position, [they] submitted the written testimony of three housing experts. They described the "white flight" and "tipping" phenomena, in which white residents migrate out of a community as the community becomes poor and the minority population increases, resulting in the transition to a predominantly minority community. Acknowledging that "'the tipping point for a particular housing development, depending as it does on numerous factors and the uncertainties of human behavior, is difficult to predict with precision,'" one expert stated that the point at which tipping occurs has been estimated at from 1% to 60% minority population, but that the consensus ranged between 10% and 20%. Another expert, who had prepared a report in 1980 on integration at Starrett City for the New York State Division of Housing and Community Renewal, estimated the complex's tipping point at approximately 40% black on a population basis. A third expert, who had been involved in integrated housing ventures since the 1950's, found that a 2:1 white-minority ratio produced successful integration. ...

Discussion

Title VIII of the Civil Rights Act of 1968 ("Fair Housing Act" or "the Act"), was enacted pursuant to Congress' thirteenth amendment powers" to provide, within constitutional limitations, for fair housing throughout the United States." Section 3604 of the statute prohibits discrimination because of race, color or national origin in the sale or rental of housing by, inter alia: (1) refusing to rent or make available any dwelling; (2) offering discriminatory "terms, conditions or privileges" of rental; (3) making, printing or publishing "any notice, statement, or advertisement ... that indicates any preference, limitation, or discrimination based on race, color ... or national origin;" and (4) representing to any person "that any dwelling is not available for ... rental when such dwelling is in fact so available."

Housing practices unlawful under Title VIII include not only those motivated by a racially discriminatory purpose, but also those that disproportionately affect minorities. Section 3604 "is designed to ensure that no one is denied the right to live where they choose for discriminatory reasons." ...

Starrett's allocation of public housing facilities on the basis of racial quotas, by denying an applicant access to a unit otherwise available solely because of race, produces a "discriminatory effect ... [that] could hardly be clearer." ...

Both Starrett and the government cite to the legislative history of the Fair Housing Act in support of their positions. This history consists solely of statements from the floor of Congress. These statements reveal "that at the time that Title VIII was enacted, Congress believed that strict adherence to the antidiscrimination provisions of the Act" would eliminate "racially discriminatory housing practices [and] ultimately would result in residential integration." Thus, Congress saw the antidiscrimination policy as the means to effect the antisegregation-integration policy. While quotas promote Title VIII's integration policy, they contravene its antidiscrimination policy, bringing the dual goals of the Act into conflict. The legislative history provides no further guidance for resolving this conflict.

We therefore look to analogous provisions of federal law enacted to prohibit segregation and discrimination as guides in determining to what extent racial criteria may be used to maintain integration. ... [T]he Supreme Court's analysis of what constitutes permissible race-conscious affirmative action under provisions of federal law with goals similar to those of Title VIII provides a framework for examining the affirmative use of racial quotas under the Fair Housing Act.

Although any racial classification is presumptively discriminatory, see *Personnel Admin. v. Feeney* (1979), a race-conscious affirmative action plan does not necessarily violate federal constitutional or statutory provisions, see, *e.g., United States v. Paradise* (1987) (plurality opinion) (fourteenth amendment); *United Steelworkers v. Weber* (1979) (Title VIII). However, a race-conscious plan cannot be "ageless in [its] reach into the past, and timeless in [its] ability to affect the future." *Wygant v. Jackson Bd. of Educ.* (1986) (plurality opinion). A plan employing racial distinctions must be temporary in nature with a defined goal as its termination point. See, *e.g., Johnson v. Transportation Agency* (1987). ... Moreover, we observe that societal discrimination alone seems "insufficient and over expansive" as the basis for adopting so-called "benign" practices with discriminatory effects "that work against innocent people," in the drastic and burdensome way that rigid racial quotas do. Furthermore, the use of quotas generally should be based on some history of racial discrimination, or imbalance within the entity seeking to employ them. Finally,

measures designed to increase or ensure minority participation, such as "access" quotas, have generally been upheld. However, programs designed to maintain integration by limiting minority participation, such as ceiling quotas, are of doubtful validity ... because they "'single[] out those least well represented in the political process to bear the brunt of a benign program.'"

Starrett's use of ceiling quotas to maintain integration at Starrett City lacks each of these characteristics. First, Starrett City's practices have only the goal of integration maintenance. The quotas already have been in effect for ten years. Appellants predict that their race-conscious tenanting practices must continue for at least fifteen more years, but fail to explain adequately how that approximation was reached. In any event, these practices are far from temporary. Since the goal of integration maintenance is purportedly threatened by the potential for "white flight" on a continuing basis, no definite termination date for Starrett's quotas is perceivable. Second, appellants do not assert, and there is nor evidence to show, the existence of prior racial discrimination or discriminatory imbalance adversely affecting whites within Starrett City or appellants' other complexes. On the contrary, Starrett City was initiated as an integrated complex, and Starrett's avowed purpose for employing race-based tenanting practices is to maintain that initial integration. Finally, Starrett's quotas do not provide minorities with access to Starrett City, but rather act as a ceiling to their access. Thus, the impact of appellants' practices falls squarely on minorities, for whom Title VIII was intended to open up housing opportunities. Starrett claims that its use of quotas serves to keep the numbers of minorities entering Starrett City low enough to avoid setting off a wave of "white flight." Although the "white flight" phenomenon may be a factor "take[n] into account in the integration equation," it cannot serve to justify attempts to maintain integration at Starrett City through inflexible racial quotas that are neither temporary in nature nor used to remedy past racial discrimination or imbalance within the complex. ...

Conclusion

We do not intend to imply that race is always an inappropriate consideration under Title VIII in efforts to promote integrated housing. We hold only that Title VIII does not allow appellants to use rigid racial quotas of indefinite duration to maintain a fixed level of integration at Starrett City by restricting minority access to scarce and desirable rental accommodations otherwise available to them. We therefore affirm the judgement of the district court.

JON O. NEWMAN, Circuit Judge, dissenting: Congress enacted the Fair Housing Act to prohibit racial segregation in housing. Starrett City is one of the most successful examples in the nation of racial integration in housing. I respectfully dissent because I do not believe that Congress intended the Fair Housing Act to prohibit the maintenance of racial integration in private housing. ...

Title VIII bars discriminatory housing practices in order to end segregated housing. Starrett City is not promoting segregated housing. On the contrary, it is maintaining integrated housing. It is surely not within the spirit of the Fair Housing Act to enlist the Act to bar integrated housing. Nor is there any indication that application of the statute toward such a perverse end was within the intent of those who enacted the statute. ...

None of the legislators who enacted Title VIII ever expressed a view on whether they wished to prevent the maintenance of racially balanced housing. Most of those who passed this statute in 1968 probably could not even contemplate a private real estate owner who would deliberately set out to achieve a racially balanced tenant population. Had they thought of such an eventuality, there is not the slightest reason to believe that they would have raised their legislative hands against it. ...

Whether integration of private housing complexes should be maintained through the use of race-conscious rental policies that deny minorities an equal opportunity to rent is a highly controversial issue of social policy. There is a substantial argument against imposing any artificial burdens on minorities in their quest for housing. On the other hand, there is a substantial argument against forcing an integrated housing complex to become segregated, even if current conditions make integration feasible only by means of imposing some extra delay on minority applicants for housing. Officials of the Department of Justice are entitled to urge the former policy. Respected civil rights advocates like the noted psychologist, Dr. Kenneth Clark, are entitled to urge the latter policy, as he has done in an affidavit filed in this suit. That policy choice should be left to the individual decisions of private property owners unless and until Congress or the New York legislature decides for the Nation or for New York that it prefers to outlaw maintenance of integration. I do not believe Congress made that decision in 1968, and it is a substantial question whether it would make such a decision today. Until Congress acts, we should not lend our authority to the result this lawsuit will surely bring about. ...

Affirmative Action and the Constitution: A Summary

AFFIRMATIVE ACTION AND THE CONSTITUTION: A SUMMARY

- Under the Fourteenth Amendment, a government's race conscious affirmative action plan is subject to strict (maximal) scrutiny, i.e. the action is presumed unconstitutional. To save the plan, the government has the burden of proving that:

  - no less damaging alternative is available (*i.e.* the plan is narrowly tailored to just offset the actual discriminatory conduct, and nonracial remedies are unavailing) to serve

- its compelling interest in implementing an affirmative action plan (compelling interest must be demonstrated by showing that the plan only offsets documented past or present discrimination by the governmental unit itself)

MISSOURI v. JENKINS
Supreme Court of the United States (1995)
115 S. Ct. 2038

In 1954, after Brown I, *the Attorney General of Missouri ruled that segregation of public schools in the state was unconstitutional. In 1976, the state abolished its state constitutional provision requiring segregation. In 1977, the Kansas City, Missouri School District (KCMSD), the school board and the children of two school board members sued the State and the Kansas City suburban school districts (SSD's), alleging that the defendants had "caused and perpetuated a system of racial segregation in the schools of the Kansas City metropolitan area." The District Court realigned the KCMSD as a nominal defendant, and certified as a class of plaintiffs present and future students. The court dismissed the suit against the SSD's, but found "that the State and the KCMSD were liable for an intradistrict violation, i.e., they had operated a segregated school system within the KCMSD." Prior to 1954 the defendants had operated a dual (segregated) system, and after that date they had failed in their duty to remove the vestiges of segregation. Specifically, the court found that segregation had caused "a system wide reduction in student achievement in the schools of the KCMSD," and it "identified 25 [of the 68] schools within the KCMSD that had enrollments of 90% or more black students." (The majority of the population living in the district is white.)*

As a result of these findings the District Court entered a series of continuing desegregation decrees, and effectively took superintending control of the schools to assure compliance. Among other things, the decrees required that certain remedial "quality education programs" be funded and maintained, that substantial capital improvements (new and refurbished school buildings) be made, that a system of magnet schools be established, and that teacher and staff salaries be improved. As to the magnet schools, all high schools and middle schools and half of the elementary schools were turned into magnet schools.

By 1995 the KCMSD and the State had spent $220 million on the quality education programs, $540 million on capital improvements, $448 million for the magnet program, and an additional $200 million in salary improvements for all but three of the KCMSD's, 5,000 employees. As a comparison, per pupil costs exclusive of capital expenditures in the SSD's ranged from $2,854 to $5,956; KCMSD's per pupil costs exclusive of capital expenditures are $9,412. The costs of this remedial plan are far beyond the KCMSD's budget, and the brunt of the cost has been borne by the State.

The specific issue in this litigation is the State's assertion that a District Court order to provide additional funding for salary increases and for the quality educational programs is unconstitutional. The State argues that the remedies ordered go beyond the scope of the original injury, and that it has done all it can do to remedy previous wrongs.

The District Court rejected those arguments, noting that student achievement was still "at or below national norms at many grade levels. As the District Court had noted in a 1992 hearing,

"The Court's goal was to integrate the Kansas City, Missouri, School District to the maximum degree possible, and all these other matters were elements to be used to try to integrate the Kansas City, Missouri, schools so the goal is integration. That's the goal. And a high standard of quality education. The magnet schools, the summer school program and all these programs are tied to that goal, and until such time as that goal has been reached, then we have not reached the goal."

The Court of Appeals affirmed the District Court order, but the Supreme Court reverses, concluding that the remedial order goes beyond the scope of the constitutional wrong.

CHIEF JUSTICE REHNQUIST. As this school desegregation litigation enters its 18th year, we are called upon again to review the decisions of the lower courts. In this case, the State of Missouri has challenged the District Court's order of salary increases for virtually all instructional and noninstructional staff within the Kansas City, Missouri, School District (KCMSD) and the District Court's order requiring the State to continue to fund remedial "quality education" programs because student achievement levels were still "at or below national norms at many grade levels." ...

Almost 25 years ago, in *Swann v. Charlotte-Mecklenburg Bd. of Ed.* (1971), we dealt with the authority of a district court to fashion remedies for a school district that had been segregated in law in violation of the Equal Protection Clause of the Fourteenth Amendment. Although recognizing the discretion that must necessarily adhere in a district court in fashioning a remedy, we also recognized the limits on such remedial power:

> "Elimination of racial discrimination in public schools is a large task and one that should not be retarded by efforts to achieve broader purposes lying beyond the jurisdiction of the school authorities. One vehicle can carry only a limited amount of baggage. It would not serve the important objective of *Brown I* to seek to use school desegregation cases for purposes beyond their scope, although desegregation of schools ultimately will have impact on other forms of discrimination."

Three years later, in *Milliken I*, we held that a District Court had exceeded its authority in fashioning interdistrict relief where the surrounding school districts had not themselves been guilty of any constitutional violation. We said that a desegregation remedy "is necessarily designed, as all remedies are, to restore the victims of discriminatory conduct to the position they would have occupied in the absence of such conduct." "Without an interdistrict violation and interdistrict effect, there is no constitutional wrong calling for an interdistrict remedy." We also rejected "the suggestion ... that schools which have a majority of Negro students are not 'desegregated,' whatever the makeup of the school district's population

and however neutrally the district lines have been drawn and administered." ...

Three years later, in *Milliken v. Bradley* (1977) (*Milliken II*), we articulated a three-part framework derived from our prior cases to guide district courts in the exercise of their remedial authority.

> "In the first place, like other equitable remedies, the nature of the desegregation remedy is to be determined by the nature and scope of the constitutional violation. The remedy must therefore be related to 'the condition alleged to offend the Constitution. ...' Second, the decree must indeed be remedial in nature, that is, it must be designed as nearly as possible 'to restore the victims of discriminatory conduct to the position they would have occupied in the absence of such conduct.' Third, the federal courts in devising a remedy must take into account the interests of state and local authorities in managing their own affairs, consistent with the Constitution."

We added that the "principle that the nature and scope of the remedy are to be determined by the violation means simply that federal-court decrees must directly address and relate to the constitutional violation itself." In applying these principles, we have identified "student assignments, ... 'faculty, staff, transportation, extracurricular activities and facilities,'" as the most important indicia of a racially segregated school system.

Because "federal supervision of local school systems was intended as a temporary measure to remedy past discrimination," we also have considered the showing that must be made by a school district operating under a desegregation order for complete or partial relief from that order. In *Freeman*, we stated that

> "among the factors which must inform the sound discretion of the court in ordering partial withdrawal are the following: [1] whether there has been full and satisfactory compliance with the decree in those aspects of the system where supervision is to be withdrawn; [2] whether retention of judicial control is necessary or practicable to achieve compliance with the decree in other facets of the school system; and [3] whether the school district has demonstrated, to the public and to the parents and students of the once disfavored race, its good-faith commitment to the whole of the courts' decree and to those provisions of the law and the Constitution that were the predicate for judicial intervention in the first instance."

The ultimate inquiry is "'whether the [constitutional violator] has complied in good faith with the desegregation decree since it was entered, and whether the vestiges of past discrimination have been eliminated to the extent practicable.'"

Proper analysis of the District Court's orders challenged here, then, must rest upon their serving as proper means to the end of restoring the victims of discriminatory conduct to the position they would have occupied in the absence of that conduct and their eventual restoration of "state and local authorities to the control of a school system that is operating in compliance with the Constitution." We turn to that analysis.

The State argues that the order approving salary increases is beyond the District Court's authority because it was crafted to serve an "interdistrict goal," in spite of the fact that the constitutional violation in this case is "intradistrict" in nature. ...

Here, the District Court has found, and the Court of Appeals has affirmed, that this case involved no interdistrict constitutional violation that would support interdistrict relief. ... Thus, the proper response by the District Court should have been to eliminate to the extent practicable the vestiges of prior *de jure* segregation within the KCMSD: a system-wide reduction in student achievement and the existence of 25 racially identifiable schools with a population of over 90% black students.

The District Court and Court of Appeals, however, have felt that because the KCMSD's enrollment remained 68.3% black, a purely intradistrict remedy would be insufficient. ... But, as noted in *Milliken I*, we have rejected the suggestion "that schools which have a majority of Negro students are not 'desegregated' whatever the racial makeup of the school district's population and however neutrally the district lines have been drawn and administered." ...

Instead of seeking to remove the racial identity of the various schools within the KCMSD, the District Court has set out on a program to create a school district that was equal to or superior to the surrounding SSD's. Its remedy has focused on "desegregative attractiveness," coupled with "suburban comparability." Examination of the District Court's reliance on "desegregative attractiveness" and "suburban comparability" is instructive for our ultimate resolution of the salary-order issue.

The purpose of desegregative attractiveness has been not only to remedy the system-wide reduction in student achievement, but also to attract nonminority students not presently enrolled in the KCMSD. This remedy has included an elaborate program of capital improvements, course enrichment, and extracurricular enhancement not simply in the formerly identifiable black schools, but in schools throughout the district. The District Court's remedial orders have converted every senior high school, every middle school, and one-half of the elementary schools in the KCMSD into "magnet" schools. The District Court's remedial order has all but made the KCMSD itself into a magnet district.

We previously have approved of intradistrict desegregation remedies involving magnet schools. Magnet schools have the advantage of encouraging voluntary movement of students within a school district in a pattern that aids desegregation on a voluntary basis, without requiring extensive busing and redrawing of district boundary lines. As a component in an intradistrict remedy, magnet schools also are attractive because they promote desegregation while limiting the withdrawal of white student enrollment that may result from mandatory student reassignment.

The District Court's remedial plan in this case, however, is not designed solely to redistribute the students within the KCMSD in order to eliminate racially identifiable schools within the KCMSD. Instead, its purpose is to attract nonminority students from outside the KCMSD schools. But this *inter* district goal is beyond the scope of the *intra*district violation identified by the District Court. ...

... A district court seeking to remedy an *intra*district violation that has not "directly caused" significant interdistrict effects, exceeds its remedial authority if it orders a remedy with an interdistrict purpose. This conclusion follows directly from *Milliken II*, ... where we reaffirmed the bedrock principle that "federal-court decrees exceed appropriate limits if they are aimed at eliminating a condition that does not violate the Constitution or does not flow from such a violation." ...

The District Court's pursuit of "desegregative attractiveness" cannot be reconciled with our cases placing limitations on a district court's remedial authority. It is certainly theoretically possible that the greater the expenditure per pupil within the KCMSD, the more likely it is that some unknowable number of nonminority students not presently attending schools in the KCMSD will choose to enroll in those schools. Under this reasoning, however, every increased expenditure, whether it be for teachers, noninstructional employees, books, or buildings, will make the KCMSD in some way more attractive, and thereby perhaps induce nonminority students to enroll in its schools. But this rationale is not susceptible to any objective limitation. ...

... [W]e conclude that the District Court's order of salary increase, which was "grounded in remedying the vestiges of segregation by improving the desegregative attractiveness of the KCMSD," is simply too far removed from an acceptable implementation of a permissible means to remedy previous legally mandated segregation.

Similar considerations lead us to conclude that the District Court's order requiring the State to continue to fund the quality education programs because student achievement levels were still "at or below national norms at many grade levels" cannot be sustained. The State does not seek from this Court a declaration of partial unitary status with respect to the quality education programs. It challenges the requirement of indefinite funding of a quality education program until national norms are met, based on the assumption that while a mandate for significant educational improvement, both in teaching and in facilities, may have been justified originally, its indefinite extension is not.

... In one ... order relied upon by the Court of Appeals, the District Court stated that the KCMSD had not reached anywhere close to its "maximum potential because the District is still at or below national norms at many grade levels."

But this clearly is not the appropriate test to be applied in deciding whether a previously segregated district has achieved partially unitary status. The basic task of the District Court is to decide whether the reduction in achievement by minority students attributable to prior *de jure* segregation has been remedied to the extent practicable. Under our precedents, the State and the KCMSD are "entitled to a rather precise statement of [their] obligations under a desegregation decree." Although the District Court has determined that "segregation has caused a system wide reduction in achievement in the schools of the KCMSD," it never has identified the incremental effect that segregation has had on minority student achievement or the specific goals of the quality education programs.

In reconsidering this order, the District Court should apply our three-part test from *Freeman v. Pitts*. The District Court should consider that the State's role with respect to the quality education programs has been limited to the funding, not the implementation, of those programs. As all the parties agree that improved achievement on test scores is not necessarily required for the State to achieve partial unitary status as to the quality education programs, the District Court should sharply limit, if not dispense with, its reliance on this factor. Just as demographic changes independent of *de jure*

segregation will affect the racial composition of student assignments, so too will numerous external factors beyond the control of the KCMSD and the State affect minority student achievement. So long as these external factors are not the result of segregation, they do not figure in the remedial calculus. Insistence upon academic goals unrelated to the effects of legal segregation unwarrantably postpones the day when the KCMSD will be able to operate on its own. ...

On remand, the District Court must bear in mind that its end purpose is not only "to remedy the violation" to the extent practicable, but also "to restore state and local authorities to the control of a school system that is operating in compliance with the Constitution."

The judgment of the Court of Appeals is reversed.

JUSTICE THOMAS, concurring. It never ceases to amaze me that the courts are so willing to assume that anything that is predominantly black must be inferior. Instead of focusing on remedying the harm done to those black schoolchildren injured by segregation, the District Court here sought to convert the Kansas City, Missouri, School District (KCMSD) into a "magnet district" that would reverse the "white flight" caused by desegregation. In this respect, I join the Court's decision concerning the two remedial issues presented for review. I write separately, however, to add a few thoughts with respect to the overall course of this litigation. In order to evaluate the scope of the remedy, we must understand the scope of the constitutional violation and the nature of the remedial powers of the federal courts.

Two threads in our jurisprudence have produced this unfortunate situation, in which a District Court has taken it upon itself to experiment with the education of the KCMSD's black youth. First, the court has read our cases to support the theory that black students suffer an unspecified psychological harm from segregation that retards their mental and educational development. This approach not only relies upon questionable social science research rather than constitutional principle, but it also rests on an assumption of black inferiority. Second, we have permitted the federal courts to exercise virtually unlimited equitable powers to remedy this alleged constitutional violation. The exercise of this authority has trampled upon principles of federalism and the separation of powers and has freed courts to pursue other agendas unrelated to the narrow purpose of precisely remedying a constitutional harm.

The mere fact that a school is black does not mean that it is the product of a constitutional violation. ...

Without a basis in any real finding of intentional government action, the District Court's imposition of liability upon the State of Missouri improperly rests upon a theory that racial imbalances are unconstitutional. ... In effect, the court found that racial imbalances constituted an ongoing constitutional violation that continued to inflict harm on black students. This position appears to rest upon the idea that any school that is black is inferior, and that blacks cannot succeed without the benefit of the company of whites.

The District Court's willingness to adopt such stereotypes stemmed from a misreading of our earliest school desegregation case. In *Brown v. Board of Education* (*Brown I*), the Court noted several psychological and sociological studies purporting to show that *de jure* segregation harmed black students by generating "a feeling of inferiority" in them. Seizing upon this passage in *Brown I*, the District Court asserted that "forced segregation ruins attitudes and is inherently unequal." The District Court suggested that this inequality continues in full force even after the end of *de jure* segregation:

"The general attitude of inferiority among blacks produces low achievement which ultimately limits employment opportunities and causes poverty. While it may be true that poverty results in low achievement regardless of race, it is undeniable that most poverty-level families are black. The District stipulated that as of 1977 they had not eliminated all the vestiges of the prior dual system. The Court finds the inferior education indigenous of the state-compelled dual school system has lingering effects in the [KCMSD]."

Thus, the District Court seemed to believe that black students in the KCMSD would continue to receive an "inferior education" despite the end of *de jure* segregation, as long as *de facto* segregation persisted. As the District Court later concluded, compensatory educational programs were necessary "as a means of remedying many of the educational problems which go hand in hand with racially isolated minority student populations." Such assumptions and any social science research upon which they rely certainly cannot form the basis upon which we decide matters of constitutional principle.

It is clear that the District Court misunderstood the meaning of *Brown I*. *Brown I* did not say that "racially isolated" schools were inherently inferior; the harm that it identified was tied purely to *de jure* segregation, not

de facto segregation. Indeed, *Brown I* itself did not need to rely upon any psychological or social-science research in order to announce the simple, yet fundamental truth that the Government cannot discriminate among its citizens on the basis of race. As the Court's unanimous opinion indicated: "In the field of public education the doctrine of 'separate but equal' has no place. Separate educational facilities are inherently unequal." At the heart of this interpretation of the Equal Protection Clause lies the principle that the Government must treat citizens as individuals, and not as members of racial, ethnic or religious groups. It is for this reason that we must subject all racial classifications to the strictest of scrutiny, which (aside from two decisions rendered in the midst of wartime, see *Hirabayashi v. United States*, (1943); *Korematsu v. United States*, (1944)) has proven automatically fatal.

Segregation was not unconstitutional because it might have caused psychological feelings of inferiority. Public school systems that separated blacks and provided them with superior educational resources—making blacks "feel" superior to whites sent to lesser schools—would violate the Fourteenth Amendment, whether or not the white students felt stigmatized, just as do school systems in which the positions of the races are reversed. Psychological injury or benefit is irrelevant to the question whether state actors have engaged in intentional discrimination—the critical inquiry for ascertaining violations of the Equal Protection Clause. The judiciary is fully competent to make independent determinations concerning the existence of state action without the unnecessary and misleading assistance of the social sciences.

Regardless of the relative quality of the schools, segregation violated the Constitution because the State classified students based on their race. Of course, segregation additionally harmed black students by relegating them to schools with substandard facilities and resources. But neutral policies, such as local school assignments, do not offend the Constitution when individual private choices concerning work or residence produce schools with high black populations. The Constitution does not prevent individuals from choosing to live together, to work together, or to send their children to school together, so long as the State does not interfere with their choices on the basis of race.

Given that desegregation has not produced the predicted leaps forward in black educational achievement, there is no reason to think that black students cannot learn as well when surrounded by members of their own race as when they are in an integrated environment. Indeed, it may very well be that what has been true for historically black colleges is true for black middle and high schools. Despite their origins in "the shameful history of state-enforced segregation," these institutions can be "'both a source pride to blacks who have attended them and a source of hope to black families who want the benefits of ... learning for their children.'" Because of their "distinctive histories and traditions," black schools can function as the center and symbol of black communities, and provide examples of independent black leadership, success, and achievement.

Thus, even if the District Court had been on firmer ground in identifying a link between the KCMSD's pre-1954 *de jure* segregation and the present "racial isolation" of some of the district's schools, mere *de facto* segregation (unaccompanied by discriminatory inequalities in educational resources) does not constitute a continuing harm after the end of *de jure* segregation. "Racial isolation" itself is not a harm; only state-enforced segregation is. After all, if separation itself is a harm, and if integration therefore is the only way that blacks can receive a proper education, then there must be something inferior about blacks. Under this theory, segregation injures blacks because blacks, when left on their own, cannot achieve. To my way of thinking, that conclusion is the result of a jurisprudence based upon a theory of black inferiority.

This misconception has drawn the courts away from the important goal in desegregation. The point of the Equal Protection Clause is not to enforce strict race-mixing, but to ensure that blacks and whites are treated equally by the State without regard to their skin color. The lower courts should not be swayed by the easy answers of social science, nor should they accept the findings, and the assumptions, of sociology and psychology at the price of constitutional principle.

II ...

The District Court's unwarranted focus on the psychological harm to blacks and on racial imbalances has been only half of the tale. Not only did the court subscribe to a theory of injury that was predicated on black inferiority, it also married this concept of liability to our expansive approach to remedial powers. We have given the federal courts the freedom to use any measure necessary to reverse problems—such as racial isolation or low educational achievement—that have proven stubbornly resistant to government policies. We have not permitted constitutional principles such as federalism or the separation of powers to stand in the way of our drive to reform the schools. Thus, the District Court

here ordered massive expenditures by local and state authorities, without congressional or executive authorization and without any indication that such measures would attract whites back to KCMSD or raise KCMSD test scores. The time has come for us to put the genie back in the bottle.

A. The Constitution extends "that judicial Power of the United States" to "all Cases, in Law and Equity, arising under this Constitution, the Laws of the United States, and Treaties made ... under their Authority." Art. III, §§1, 2. I assume for purposes of this case that the remedial authority of the federal courts is inherent in the "judicial Power," as there is no general equitable remedial power expressly granted by the Constitution or by statute. As with any inherent judicial power, however, we ought to be reluctant to approve its aggressive or extravagant use, and instead we should exercise it in a manner consistent with our history and traditions.

Motivated by our worthy desire to eradicate segregation, however, we have disregarded this principle and given the courts unprecedented authority to shape a remedy in equity. Although at times we have invalidated a decree as beyond the bounds of an equitable remedy, see *Milliken I*, these instances have been far outnumbered by the expansions in the equity power. In *United States v. Montgomery Cty. Bd. of Ed.* (1969), for example, we allowed federal courts to desegregate faculty and staff according to specific mathematical ratios, with the ultimate goal that each school in the system would have roughly the same proportions of white and black faculty. In *Swann v. Charlotte-Mecklenburg Bd. of Ed.* (1971), we permitted federal courts to order busing, to set racial targets for school populations, and to alter attendance zones. And in *Milliken II*, we approved the use of remedial or compensatory education programs paid for by the State.

In upholding these court-ordered measures, we indicated that trial judges had virtually boundless discretion in crafting remedies once they had identified a constitutional violation. ...

It is perhaps understandable that we permitted the lower courts to exercise such sweeping powers. Although we had authorized the federal courts to work toward "a system of determining admission to the public schools on a nonracial basis" in *Brown v. Board of Education* (1955) (*Brown II*), resistance to *Brown I* produced little desegregation by the time we decided *Green v. School Board of New Kent County* [1968]. Our impatience with the pace of desegregation and with the lack of a good-faith effort on the part of school boards led us to approve such extraordinary remedial measures. But such powers should have been temporary and used only to overcome the widespread resistance to the dictates of the Constitution. The judicial overreaching we see before us today perhaps is the price we now pay for our approval of such extraordinary remedies in the past. ...

Our willingness to unleash the federal equitable power has reached areas beyond school desegregation. Federal courts have used "structural injunctions," as they are known, not only to supervise our Nation's schools, but also to manage prisons, mental hospitals, and public housing. Judges have directed or managed the reconstruction of entire institutions and bureaucracies, with little regard for the inherent limitations on their authority.

B. Such extravagant uses of judicial power are at odds with the history and tradition of the equity power and the Framers' design. The available historical records suggest that the Framers did not intend federal equitable remedies to reach as broadly as we have permitted. ...

C. Two clear restraints on the use of the equity power—federalism and the separation of powers—derive from the very form of our Government. Federal courts should pause before using their inherent equitable powers to intrude into the proper sphere of the States. We have long recognized that education is primarily a concern of local authorities. ... A structural reform decree eviscerates a State's discretionary authority over its own program and budgets and forces state officials to reallocate state resources and funds to the desegregation plan at the expense of other citizens, other government programs, and other institutions not represented in court. When District Courts seize complete control over the schools, they strip state and local governments of one of their most important governmental responsibilities, and thus deny their existence as independent governmental entities.

Federal courts do not possess the capabilities of state and local governments in addressing difficult educational problems. ...

The separation of powers imposes additional restraints on the judiciary's exercise of its remedial powers. To be sure, this is not a case of one branch of Government encroaching on the prerogatives of another, but rather of the power of the Federal Government over the States. Nonetheless, what the federal courts cannot do at the federal level they cannot do against the States; in either case, Article III courts are constrained by the inherent constitutional limitations on their powers. There simply are certain things that courts, in order to remain courts, cannot and should not do. There is no difference between courts running school systems or prisons and courts running executive branch agencies.

In this case, not only did the district court exercise the legislative power to tax, it also engaged in budgeting, staffing, and educational decisions, in judgments about the location and aesthetic quality of the schools, and in administrative oversight and monitoring. These functions involve a legislative or executive, rather than a judicial, power. ... Federal judges cannot make the fundamentally political decisions as to which priorities are to receive funds and staff, which educational goals are to be sought, and which values are to be taught. When federal judges undertake such local, day-to-day tasks, they detract from the independence and dignity of the federal courts and intrude into areas in which they have little expertise. ...

D. ... [T]he District Court's remedial orders are in tension with two common-sense principles. First, the District Court retained jurisdiction over the implementation and modification of the remedial decree, instead of terminating its involvement after issuing its remedy. Although briefly mentioned in *Brown II* as a temporary measure to overcome local resistance to desegregation, ("during this period of transition, the courts will retain jurisdiction"), this concept of continuing judicial involvement has permitted the District Courts to revise their remedies constantly in order to reach some broad, abstract, and often elusive goal. Not only does this approach deprive the parties of finality and a clear understanding of their responsibilities, but it also tends to inject the judiciary into the day-to-day management of institutions and local policies—a function that lies outside of our Article III competence. ...

Second, the District Court failed to target its equitable remedies in this case specifically to cure the harm suffered by the victims of segregation. Of course, the initial and most important aspect of any remedy will be to eliminate any invidious racial distinctions in matters such as student assignments, transportation, staff, resource allocation, and activities. This element of most desegregation decrees is fairly straightforward and has not produced many examples of overreaching by the district courts. It is the "compensatory" ingredient in many desegregation plans that has produced many of the difficulties in the case before us.

Having found that segregation "has caused a system wide reduction in student achievement in the schools of the KCMSD," the District Court ordered the series of magnet school plans, educational programs, and capital improvements that the Court criticizes today because of their interdistrict nature. In ordering these programs, the District Court exceeded its authority by benefitting those who were not victims of discriminatory conduct. KCMSD as a whole may have experienced reduced achievement levels, but raising the test scores of the entire district is a goal that is not sufficiently tailored to restoring the victims of segregation to the position they would have occupied absent discrimination. A school district cannot be discriminated against on the basis of its race, because a school district has no race. It goes without saying that only individuals can suffer from discrimination, and only individuals can receive the remedy.

Of course, a district court may see fit to order necessary remedies that have the side effect of benefitting those who were not victims of segregation. But the court cannot order broad remedies that indiscriminately benefit a school district as a whole, rather than the individual students who suffered from discrimination. Not only do such remedies tend to indicate "efforts to achieve broader purposes lying beyond" the scope of the violation, but they also force state and local governments to work toward the benefit of those who have suffered no harm from their actions.

To ensure that district courts do not embark on such broad initiatives in the future, we should demand that remedial decrees be more precisely designed to benefit only those who have been victims of segregation. Race-conscious remedies for discrimination not only must serve a compelling governmental interest (which is met in desegregation cases), but also must be narrowly tailored to further that interest. In the absence of special circumstance, the remedy for *de jure* segregation ordinarily should not include educational programs for students who were not in school (or were even alive) during the period of segregation. Although I do not doubt that all KCMSD students benefit from many of the initiatives ordered by the court below, it is for the democratically accountable state and local officials to decide whether they are to be made available even to those who were never harmed by segregation. ...

JUSTICE SOUTER, with whom JUSTICE STEVENS, JUSTICE GINSBURG, and JUSTICE BREYER join, dissenting. ... On its face, the Court's opinion projects an appealing pragmatism in seeming to cut through the details of many facts by applying a rule of law that can claim both precedential support and intuitive sense, that there is error in imposing an interdistrict remedy to cure a merely intradistrict violation. Since the District Court has consistently described the violation here as solely intradistrict, and since the object of the magnet schools under its plan includes attracting students into the district from other districts, the Court's result seems to follow with the necessity of logic, against which arguments about detail or calls for fair warning may not carry great weight.

The attractiveness of the Court's analysis disappears, however, as soon as we recognize two things. First, the District Court did not mean by an "intradistrict violation" what the Court apparently means by it today. The District Court meant that the violation within the KCMSD had not led to segregation outside of it, and that no other school districts had played a part in the violation. It did not mean that the violation had not produced effects of any sort beyond the district. Indeed, the record that we have indicates that the District Court understood that the violation here did produce effects spanning district borders and leading to greater segregation within the KCMSD, the reversal of which the District Court sought to accomplish by establishing magnet schools.[4] Insofar as the Court assumes that this was not so in fact, there is at least enough in the record to cast serious doubt on its assumption. Second, the Court violates existing case law even on its own apparent view of the facts, that the segregation violation within the KCMSD produced no proven effects, segregative or otherwise, outside it. Assuming this to be true, the Court's decision that the rule against interdistrict remedies for intradistrict violations applies to this case, solely because the remedy here is meant to produce effects outside the district in which the violation occurred, is flatly contrary to established precedent. ...

To the substantial likelihood that the Court proceeds on erroneous assumptions of fact must be added corresponding errors of law. We have most recently summed up the obligation to correct the condition of *de jure* segregation by saying that "the duty of a former *de jure* district is to take 'whatever steps might be necessary to convert to a unitary system in which racial discrimination would be eliminated root and branch.'" Although the fashioning of judicial remedies to this end has been

left, in the first instance, to the equitable discretion of the district courts, in *Milliken I* we established an absolute limitation on this exercise of equitable authority. "Without an interdistrict violation and interdistrict effect, there is no constitutional wrong calling for an interdistrict remedy."

The Court proceeds as if there is no question but that this proscription applies to this case. But the proscription does not apply. We are not dealing here with an interdistrict remedy in the sense that *Milliken I* used the term. In the *Milliken I* litigation, the District Court had ordered 53 surrounding school districts to be consolidated with the Detroit school system, and mandatory busing to be started within the enlarged district, even though the court had not found that any of the suburban districts had acted in violation of the Constitution. ... It was this imposition of remedial measures on more than the one wrongdoing school district that we termed an "interdistrict remedy." ... And it was just this subjection to court order of school districts not shown to have violated the Constitution that we deemed to be in error. ...

We did not hold, however, that any remedy that takes into account conditions outside of the district in which a constitutional violation has been committed is an "interdistrict remedy," and as such improper in the absence of an "interdistrict violation." To the contrary, by emphasizing that remedies in school desegregation cases are grounded in traditional equitable principles, we left open the possibility that a district court might subject a proven constitutional wrongdoer to a remedy with intended effects going beyond the district of the wrongdoer's violation, when such a remedy is necessary to redress the harms flowing from the constitutional violation.

The Court, nonetheless, reads *Milliken I* quite differently. It reads the case as categorically forbidding imposition of a remedy on a guilty district with intended consequences in a neighboring innocent district, unless the constitutional violation yielded segregative effects in that innocent district. ...

Today's decision therefore amounts to a redefinition of the terms of *Milliken I* and consequently to a substantial expansion of its limitation on the permissible remedies for prior segregation. ...

---

[4]This was not the only, or even the principal, purpose of the magnet schools. The District Court found that magnet schools would assist in remedying the deficiencies in student achievement in the KCMSD. Moreover, while the Court repeatedly describes the magnet school program as looking beyond the boundaries of the district, the program is primarily aimed not at drawing back white children whose parents have moved to another district, but rather at drawing back children who attend private schools while living within the geographical confines of the KCMSD, whose population remains majority white. ... As such, a substantial impetus for the District Court's remedy does not consider the world beyond district boundaries at all, and much of the Court's opinion is of little significance to the case before it.

JUSTICE O'CONNOR. ...

In 1989, the Central Federal Lands Highway Division (CFLHD), which is part of the United States Department of Transportation (DOT), awarded the prime contract for a highway construction project in Colorado to Mountain Gravel & Construction Company. Mountain Gravel then solicited bids from subcontractors for the guardrail portion of the contract. Adarand, a Colorado-based highway construction company specializing in guardrail work, submitted the low bid. Gonzales Construction Company also submitted a bid.

The prime contract's terms provide that Mountain Gravel would receive additional compensation if it hired subcontractors certified as small businesses controlled by "socially and economically disadvantaged individuals." Gonzales is certified as such a business; Adarand is not. Mountain Gravel awarded the subcontract to Gonzales, despite Adarand's low bid, and Mountain Gravel's Chief Estimator has submitted an affidavit stating that Mountain Gravel would have accepted Adarand's bid, had it not been for the additional payment it received by hiring Gonzales instead. Federal law requires that a subcontracting clause similar to the one used here must appear in most federal agency contracts, and it also requires the clause to state that "the contractor shall presume that socially and economically disadvantaged individuals include Black Americans, Hispanic Americans, Native Americans, Asian Pacific Americans, and other minorities, or any other individual found to be disadvantaged by the [Small Business] Administration pursuant to section 8(a) of the Small Business Act." Adarand claims that the presumption set forth in that statute discriminates on the basis of race in violation of the Federal Government's Fifth Amendment obligation not to deny anyone equal protection of the laws. ...

After losing the guardrail subcontract to Gonzales, Adarand filed suit against various federal officials ... , claiming that the race-based presumptions involved in the use of subcontracting compensation clauses violate Adarand's right to equal protection. ... The Court of Appeals ... understood our decision in *Fullilove v. Klutznick* to have adopted "a lenient standard, resembling intermediate scrutiny, in assessing" the constitutionality of federal race-based action. Applying that "lenient standard," as further developed in *Metro Broadcasting, Inc. v. FCC*, the Court of Appeals upheld the use of subcontractor compensation clauses. We granted certiorari.

II ...

A. Through the 1940s, this Court had routinely taken the view in non-race-related cases that, "unlike the Fourteenth Amendment, the Fifth contains no equal protection clause and it provides no guaranty against discriminatory legislation by Congress." *Detroit Bank v. United States* (1943). When the Court first faced a Fifth Amendment equal protection challenge to a federal racial classification, it adopted a similar approach, with most unfortunate results. In *Hirabayashi v. United States* (1943), the Court considered a curfew applicable only to persons of Japanese ancestry. The Court observed—correctly—that "distinctions between citizens solely because of their ancestry are by their very nature odious to a free people whose institutions are founded upon the doctrine of equality," and that "racial discriminations are in most circumstances irrelevant and therefore prohibited." But it also cited *Detroit Bank* for the proposition that the Fifth Amendment "restrains only such discriminatory legislation by Congress as amounts to a denial of due process," and upheld the curfew because "circumstances within the knowledge of those charged with the responsibility for maintaining the national defense afforded a rational basis for the decision which they made."

Eighteen months later, the Court again approved wartime measures directed at persons of Japanese ancestry. *Korematsu v. United States* (1944) concerned an order that completely excluded such persons from particular areas. The Court did not address the view, expressed in cases like *Hirabayashi* and *Detroit Bank*, that the Federal Government's obligation to provide equal protection differs significantly from that of the States. Instead, it began by noting that "all legal restrictions which curtail the civil rights of a single racial group are immediately suspect ... [and] courts must subject them to the most rigid scrutiny." That promising dictum might be read to undermine the view that the Federal Government is under a lesser obligation to avoid injurious racial classifications than are the States. ... But in spite of the "most rigid scrutiny" standard it had just set forth, the Court then inexplicably relied on "the principles we announced in the *Hirabayashi* case," to conclude that, although "exclusion from the area in which one's home is located is a far greater deprivation than constant confinement to the home from 8 p.m. to 6 a.m.," the racially discriminatory order was nonetheless within the Federal Government's power.

In *Bolling v. Sharpe* (1954), the Court for the first time explicitly questioned the existence of any difference between the obligations of the Federal Government and the States to avoid racial classifications. *Bolling* did note that "the 'equal protection of the laws' is a more explicit safeguard of prohibited unfairness than 'due process of law.'" But *Bolling* then concluded that, "in view of [the] decision that the Constitution prohibits the states from maintaining racially segregated public schools, it would be unthinkable that the same Constitution would impose a lesser duty on the Federal Government."

Bolling's facts concerned school desegregation, but its reasoning was not so limited. The Court's observations that "distinctions between citizens solely because of their ancestry are by their very nature odious," *Hirabayashi*, and that "all legal restrictions which curtail the civil rights of a single racial group are immediately suspect," *Korematsu*, carry no less force in the context of federal action than in the context of action by the States—indeed, they first appeared in cases concerning action by the Federal Government. *Bolling* relied on those observations and reiterated "'that the Constitution of the United States, in its present form, forbids, so far as civil and political rights are concerned, discrimination by the General Government, or by the States, against any citizen because of his race.'" The Court's application of that general principle to the case before it, and the resulting imposition on the Federal Government of an obligation equivalent to that of the States, followed as a matter of course. ...

B. Most of the cases discussed above involved classifications burdening groups that have suffered discrimination in our society. [Beginning i]n 1978, the Court confronted the question whether race-based governmental action designed to benefit such groups should also be subject to "the most rigid scrutiny." ...

The Court resolved the issue, at least in part, in 1989. *Richmond v. J. A. Croson Co.* (1989) concerned a city's determination that 30% of its contracting work should go to minority-owned businesses. A majority of the Court in *Croson* held that "the standard of review under the Equal Protection Clause is not dependent on the race of those burdened or benefitted by a particular classification," and that the single standard of review for racial classifications should be "strict scrutiny." ...

With *Croson*, the Court finally agreed that the Fourteenth Amendment requires strict scrutiny of all race-based action by state and local governments. But *Croson* of course had no occasion to declare what standard of review the Fifth Amendment requires for such action taken by the Federal Government. ...

Despite lingering uncertainty in the details, however, the Court's cases through *Croson* had established three general propositions with respect to governmental racial classifications. First, skepticism: "'any preference based on racial or ethnic criteria must necessarily receive a most searching examination,'" *Wygant*. Second, consistency: "the standard of review under the Equal Protection Clause is not dependent on the race of those burdened or benefitted by a particular classification," *Croson*, i.e., all racial classifications reviewable under the Equal Protection Clause must be strictly scrutinized. And third, congruence: "equal protection analysis in the Fifth Amendment area is the same as that under the Fourteenth Amendment," *Buckley v. Valeo*. Taken together, these three propositions lead to the conclusion that any person, of whatever race, has the right to demand that any governmental actor subject to the Constitution justify any racial classification subjecting that person the unequal treatment under the strictest judicial scrutiny. ...

A year later, however, the Court took a surprising turn. *Metro Broadcasting, Inc. v. FCC* (1990) involved a Fifth Amendment challenge to two race-based policies of the Federal Communications Commission. In *Metro Broadcasting*, the Court repudiated the long-held notion that "it would be unthinkable that the same Constitution would impose a lesser duty on the Federal Government" than it does on a State to afford equal protection of the laws. It did so by holding that "benign" federal racial classifications need only satisfy intermediate scrutiny, even though *Croson* had recently concluded that such classifications enacted by a State must satisfy strict scrutiny. ...

By adopting intermediate scrutiny as the standard of review for congressionally mandated "benign" racial classifications, *Metro Broadcasting* departed from prior cases in two significant respects. First, it turned its back

on *Croson*'s explanation of why strict scrutiny of all governmental racial classifications is essential:

"Absent searching judicial inquiry into the justification for such race-based measures, there is simply no way of determining what classifications are 'benign' or 'remedial' and what classifications are in fact motivated by illegitimate notions of racial inferiority or simple racial politics. Indeed, the purpose of strict scrutiny is to 'smoke out' illegitimate uses of race by assuring that the legislative body is pursuing a goal important enough to warrant use of a highly suspect tool. The test also ensures that the means chosen 'fit' this compelling goal so closely that there is little or no possibility that the motive for the classification was illegitimate racial prejudice or stereotype." *Croson*.

We adhere to that view today, despite the surface appeal of holding "benign" racial classifications to a lower standard, because "it may not always be clear that a so-called preference is in fact benign."

Second, *Metro Broadcasting* squarely rejected one of the three propositions established by the Court's earlier equal protection cases, namely, congruence between the standards applicable to federal and state racial classifications, and in so doing also undermined the other two—skepticism of all racial classifications, and consistency of treatment irrespective of the race of the burdened or benefitted group. Under *Metro Broadcasting*, certain racial classifications ("benign" ones enacted by the Federal Government) should be treated less skeptically than others; and the race of the benefitted group is critical to the determination of which standard of review to apply. *Metro Broadcasting* was thus a significant departure from much of what had come before it.

The three propositions undermined by *Metro Broadcasting* all derive from the basic principle that the Fifth and Fourteenth Amendments to the Constitution protect persons, not groups. It follows from that principle that all governmental action based on race—a group classification long recognized as "in most circumstances irrelevant and therefore prohibited," *Hirabayashi*—should be subjected to detailed judicial inquiry to ensure that the personal right to equal protection of the laws has not been infringed. These ideas have long been central to this Court's understanding of equal protection, and holding "benign" state and federal racial classifications to different standards does not square with them. "[A] free people whose institutions are founded upon the doctrine of equality," should tolerate no retreat from the principle that government may treat people differently because of their race only for the most compelling reasons. Accordingly, we hold today that all racial classifications, imposed by whatever federal, state, or local governmental actor, must be analyzed by a reviewing court under strict scrutiny. In other words, such classifications are constitutional only if they are narrowly tailored measures that further compelling governmental interests. To the extent that *Metro Broadcasting* is inconsistent with that holding, it is overruled. ...

D.   Our action today makes explicit what Justice Powell thought implicit in the *Fullilove* lead opinion: Federal racial classifications, like those of a State, must serve a compelling governmental interest, and must be narrowly tailored to further that interest. ...

Some have questioned the importance of debating the proper standard of review of race-based legislation. But we agree with JUSTICE STEVENS that, "because racial characteristics so seldom provide a relevant basis for disparate treatment, and because classifications based on race are potentially so harmful to the entire body politic, it is especially important that the reasons for any such classification be clearly identified and unquestionably legitimate," and that "racial classifications are simply too pernicious to permit any but the most exact connection between justification and classification." We think that requiring strict scrutiny is the best way to ensure that courts will consistently give racial classifications that kind of detailed examination, both as to ends and as to means. *Korematsu* demonstrates vividly that even "the most rigid scrutiny" can sometimes fail to detect an illegitimate racial classification. ... Any retreat from the most searching judicial inquiry can only increase the risk of another such error occurring in the future.

Finally, we wish to dispel the notion that strict scrutiny is "strict in theory, but fatal in fact." The unhappy persistence of both the practice and the lingering effects of racial discrimination against minority groups in this country is an unfortunate reality, and government is not disqualified from acting in response to it. As recently as 1987, for example, every Justice of this Court agreed that the Alabama Department of Public Safety's "pervasive, systematic, and obstinate discriminatory conduct" justified a narrowly tailored race-based remedy. When race-based action is necessary to further a compelling interest, such action is within constitutional constraints if it satisfies the "narrow tailoring" test this Court has set out in previous cases.

IV

Because our decision today alters the playing field in some important respects, we think it best to remand the case to the lower courts for further consideration in light of the principles we have announced. The Court of Appeals, following *Metro Broadcasting* and *Fullilove*, analyzed the case in terms of intermediate scrutiny. ... The Court of Appeals did not decide the question whether the interests served by the use of subcontractor compensation clauses are properly described as "compelling." It also did not address the question of narrow tailoring in terms of our strict scrutiny cases, by asking, for example, whether there was "any consideration of the use of race-neutral means to increase minority business participation" in government contracting, *Croson*, or whether the program was appropriately limited such that it "will not last longer than the discriminatory effects it is designed to eliminate," *Fullilove*. ...

Accordingly, the judgment of the Court of Appeals is vacated, and the case is remanded for further proceedings consistent with this opinion. ...

JUSTICE THOMAS, concurring in part and concurring in the judgment. I agree with the majority's conclusion that strict scrutiny applies to all government classifications based on race. I write separately, however, to express my disagreement with the premise underlying JUSTICE STEVENS' and JUSTICE GINSBURG's dissents: that there is a racial paternalism exception to the principle of equal protection. I believe that there is a "moral [and] constitutional equivalence" between laws designed to subjugate a race and those that distribute benefits on the basis of race in order to foster some current notion of equality. Government cannot make us equal; it can only recognize, respect, and protect us as equal before the law.

That these programs may have been motivated, in part, by good intentions cannot provide refuge from the principle that under our Constitution, the government may not make distinctions on the basis of race. As far as the Constitution is concerned, it is irrelevant whether a government's racial classifications are drawn by those who wish to oppress a race or by those who have a sincere desire to help those thought to be disadvantaged. There can be no doubt that the paternalism that appears to lie at the heart of this program is at war with the principle of inherent equality that underlies and infuses our Constitution. See Declaration of Independence ("We hold these truths to be self-evident, that all men are created equal, that they are endowed buy their Creator with certain unalienable Rights, that among these are Life, Liberty, and the pursuit of Happiness").

These programs not only raise grave constitutional questions, they also undermine the moral basis of the equal protection principle. Purchased at the price of immeasurable human suffering, the equal protection principle reflects our Nation's understanding that such classifications ultimately have a destructive impact on the individual and our society. Unquestionably, "invidious [racial] discrimination is an engine of oppression." It is also true that "remedial" racial preferences may reflect "a desire to foster equality in society." But there can be no doubt that racial paternalism and its unintended consequences can be as poisonous and pernicious as any other form of discrimination. So-called "benign" discrimination teaches many that because of chronic and apparently immutable handicaps, minorities cannot compete with them without their patronizing indulgence. Inevitably, such programs engender attitudes of superiority or, alternatively, provoke resentment among those who believe that they have been wronged by the government's use of race. These programs stamp minorities with a badge of inferiority and may cause them to develop dependencies or to adopt an attitude that they are "entitled" to preferences. Indeed, JUSTICE STEVENS once recognized the real harms stemming from seemingly "benign" discrimination. See *Fullilove v. Klutznick* (STEVENS, J., dissenting) (nothing that "remedial" race legislation "is perceived by many as resting on an assumption that those who are granted this special preference are less qualified in some respect that is identified purely by their race"). In my mind, government-sponsored racial discrimination based on benign prejudice is just as noxious as discrimination inspired by malicious prejudice. In each instance, it is racial discrimination, plain and simple.

JUSTICE STEVENS, with whom JUSTICE GINSBURG joins, dissenting. ... The Court's concept of "consistency" assumes that there is no significant difference between a decision by the majority to impose a special burden on the members of a minority race and a decision by the majority to provide a benefit to certain members of that minority notwithstanding its incidental burden on some members of the majority. In my opinion

that assumption is untenable. There is no moral or constitutional equivalence between a policy that is designed to perpetuate a caste system and one that seeks to eradicate racial subordination. Invidious discrimination is an engine of oppression, subjugating a disfavored group to enhance or maintain the power of the majority. Remedial race-based preferences reflect the opposite impulse: a desire to foster equality in society. No sensible conception of the Government's constitutional obligation to "govern impartially" should ignore this distinction. ...

The Court's explanation for treating dissimilar race-based decisions as though they were equally objectionable is a supposed inability to differentiate between "invidious" and "benign" discrimination. But the term "affirmative action" is common and well understood. Its presence in everyday parlance shows that people understand the difference between good intentions and bad. As with any legal concept, some cases may be difficult to classify, but our equal protection jurisprudence has identified a critical difference between state action that imposes burdens on a disfavored few and state action that benefits the few "in spite of" its adverse effects on the many. ...

The Court's concept of "congruence" assumes that there is no significant difference between a decision by the Congress of the United States to adopt an affirmative-action program and such a decision by a State or a municipality. In my opinion that assumption is untenable. It ignores important practical and legal differences between federal and state or local decisionmakers. ...

... In his separate opinion in *Richmond v. J. A. Croson Co.* (1989), JUSTICE SCALIA discussed the basis for this distinction. He observed that "it is one thing to permit racially based conduct by the Federal Government—whose legislative powers concerning matters of race were explicitly enhanced by the Fourteenth Amendment—and quite another to permit it by the precise entities against whose conduct in matters of race that Amendment was specifically directed." Continuing, JUSTICE SCALIA explained why a "sound distinction between federal and state (or local) action based on race rests not only upon the substance of the Civil War Amendments, but upon social reality and governmental theory."

"What the record shows, in other words, is that racial discrimination against any group finds a more ready expression at the state and local than at the federal level. To the children of the Founding Fathers, this should come as no surprise. An acute awareness of the heightened danger of oppression from political factions in small, rather than large, political units dates to the very beginning of our national history." ...

MILLER v. JOHNSON
United States Supreme Court (1995)
63 Law Week 4726

Georgia's congressional districting plan contained three majority-black districts, and was adopted by the State legislature after the Justice Department refused to preclear, under §5 of the Voting Rights Act, two earlier plans that contained only two majority-black districts. Plaintiffs, voters in the new Eleventh District—which joins metropolitan black neighborhoods together with the poor black populace of coastal areas 260 miles away—challenged the District on the ground that it was a racial gerrymander in violation of the Equal Protection Clause. The District Court agreed, holding that evidence of the legislature's purpose, as well as the District's irregular borders, showed that race was the predominant factor in the boundary determination. The Supreme Court affirms.

JUSTICE KENNEDY. ... The Equal Protection Clause of the Fourteenth Amendment provides that no State shall "deny to any person within its jurisdiction the equal protection of the laws." Its central mandate is racial neutrality in governmental decisionmaking. ... Laws classifying citizens on the basis of race cannot be upheld unless they are narrowly tailored to achieving a compelling state interest. ...

II

A. ... *Shaw* recognized a claim "analytically distinct" from a vote dilution claim. Whereas a vote dilution claim alleges that the State has enacted a particular voting scheme as a purposeful device "to minimize or cancel out the voting potential of racial or ethnic minorities," *Mobile v. Bolden*, (1980), an action disadvantaging voters of a particular race, the essence of the equal protection claim recognized in *Shaw* is that the State has used race as a basis for separating voters into districts. Just as the State may not, absent extraordinary justification, segregate citizens on the basis of race in its public parks, buses, golf courses, beaches, and schools, so did we recognize in *Shaw* that it may not separate its citizens into different voting districts on the basis of race. The idea is a simple one: "At the heart of the Constitution's guarantee of equal protection lies the simple command that the Government must treat citizens > as individuals, not "as simply components of a racial, religious, sexual or national class."" When the State assigns voters on the basis of race, it engages in the offensive and demeaning assumption that voters of a particular race, because of their race, "think alike, share the same political interests, and will prefer the same candidates at the polls." Race-based assignments "embody stereotypes that treat individuals as the product of their race, evaluating their thoughts and efforts— their very worth as citizens—according to criterion barred to the Government by history and the Constitution." ...

B. ... Electoral districting is a most difficult subject for legislatures, and so the States must have discretion to exercise the political judgment necessary to balance competing interest. Although race-based decisionmaking is inherently suspect, until a claimant makes showing sufficient to support that allegation the good faith of a state legislature must be presumed. The courts, in assessing the sufficiency of a challenge to a districting plan, must be sensitive to the complex interplay of forces that enter a legislature's redistricting calculus. Redistricting legislatures will, for example, almost always be aware of racial demographics; but it does not follow that race predominates in the redistricting process. ... The distinction between being aware of racial considerations and being motivated by them may be difficult to make. ... The plaintiff's burden is to show, either through circumstantial evidence of a district's shape and demographics or more direct evidence going to legislative purpose, that race was the predominant factor motivating the legislature's decision to place significant number of voters within or without a particular district. To make this showing, a plaintiff must prove that the legislature subordinated traditional race-neutral districting principles, including but not limited to compactness, contiguity, respect for political subdivisions or communities defined by actual shared interests, to racial considerations. ...

In our view, the District Court applied the correct analysis, and its finding that race was the predominant factor motivating the drawing of the Eleventh District was not clearly erroneous. The court found it was "exceedingly obvious" from the shape of the Eleventh District, together with the relevant racial demographics, that the drawing of narrow land bridges to incorporate within the District outlying appendages containing nearly 80% of the district's total black population was a deliberate attempt to bring black populations into the district. Although by comparison with other districts the geometric shape of the Eleventh District may not seem bizarre on its face, when its shape is considered in conjunction with its racial and population densities, the story of racial gerrymandering seen by the District court becomes much clearer. Although this evidence is quite compelling, we need not determine whether it was, standing alone, sufficient to establish a *Shaw* claim that the Eleventh District is unexplainable other than by race. The District Court had before it considerable additional evidence showing that the General Assembly was motivated by a predominant, overriding desire to assign black populations to the Eleventh District and thereby permit the creation of a third majority-black district in the Second.

The court found that "it became obvious," both from the Justice Department's objections letters and the three preclearance rounds in general, "that [the Justice Department] would accept nothing less than abject surrender to its maximization agenda." It further found that the General Assembly acquiesced and as a

consequence was driven by its overriding desire to comply with the Department's maximization demands. ...

Race was, as the District Court found, the predominant, overriding factor explaining the General Assembly's decision to attach to the Eleventh District various appendages containing dense majority-black populations. As a result, Georgia's congressional redistricting plan cannot be upheld unless it satisfies strict scrutiny, our most rigorous and exacting standard of constitutional review. ...

III

To satisfy strict scrutiny, the State must demonstrate that its districting legislation is narrowly tailored to achieve a compelling interest. There is a "significant state interest in eradicating the efforts of past racial discrimination." The State does not argue, however, that it created the Eleventh District to remedy past discrimination, and with good reason: there is little doubt that the State's true interest in designing the Eleventh District was creating a third majority-black district to satisfy the Justice Department's preclearance demands. ...

The Justice Department refused to preclear both of Georgia's first two submitted redistricting plans. The District Court found that the Justice Department had adopted a "black-maximization" policy under §5, and that it was clear from its objection letters that the Department would not grant preclearance until the State ... created a third majority-black district. It is, therefore, safe to say that the congressional plan enacted in the end was required in order to obtain preclearance. It does not follow, however, that the plan was required by the substantive provisions of the Voting Rights Act. We do not accept the contention that the State has a compelling interest in complying with whatever preclearance mandates the Justice Department issues. ...

Our presumptive skepticism of all racial classifications prohibits us as well from accepting on its face the Justice Department's conclusion that racial districting is necessary under the Voting Rights Act. ...

Georgia's drawing of the Eleventh District was not required under the Act because there was no reasonable basis to believe that Georgia's earlier enacted plans violated §5. Wherever a plan is "ameliorative," a term we have used to describe plans increasing the number of majority-minority districts, it "cannot violate §5 unless the new apportionment itself so discriminates on the basis of race or color as to violate the Constitution."

Georgia's first and second proposed plans increased the number of majority-black district from 1 out of 10

(10%) to 2 out of 11 (18.18%). These plans were "ameliorative" and could not have violated §5's non-retrogression principle. ...

... [I]t would appear that Government was driven by its policy of maximizing majority-black districts. Although the Government now disavows having had that policy, and seems to concede its impropriety, the District Court's well-documented factual finding was that the Department did adopt a maximization policy and followed it in objecting to Georgia's first two plans. ...

In utilizing §5 to require States to create majority-minority districts wherever possible, the Department of Justice expanded its authority under the statute beyond what Congress intended and we have upheld.

Section 5 was directed at preventing a particular set of invidious practices which had the effect of "undo[ing] or defeat[ing] the rights recently won by nonwhite voters." As we explained in *Beer v. United States*,

"'Section 5 was a response to a common practice in some jurisdictions of staying one step ahead of the federal courts by passing new discriminatory voting laws an soon as the old ones had been struck down. That practice had been possible because each new law remained in effect until the Justice Department or private plaintiffs were able to sustain the burden of proving that the new law, too, was discriminatory. ... Congress therefore decided, as the supreme Court held it could, "to shift the advantage of time and inertia from the perpetrators of the evil to its victim," by "freezing election procedures in the covered areas unless the changes can be shown to be nondiscriminatory."'"

Based on this historical understanding, we recognized in *Beer* that "the purpose of §5 has always been to insure that no voting-procedure changes would be made that would lead to a retrogression in the position of racial minorities with respect to their effective exercise of the electoral franchise." The Justice Department's maximization policy seems quite far removed from this purpose. ...

The judgment of the District Court is affirmed. ...

JUSTICE STEVENS, dissenting. ... In my view, districting plans violate the Equal Protection Clause when they "Serve no purpose other than to favour one segment—whether racial, ethnic, religious, economic, or political—that may occupy a position of strength at a particular point in time, or to disadvantage a politically weak segment of the community." In contrast, I do not see how a districting plan that favors a politically weak

group can violate equal protection. The Constitution does not mandate any form of proportional representation, but it certainly permits a State to adopt a policy that promotes fair representation of different groups.

JUSTICE GINSBURG, dissenting. ... The Fifteenth Amendment, ratified in 1870, declares that the right to vote "shall not be denied ... by any State on account of race." That declaration, for generations, was often honored in the breach; it was greeted by a near century of "unremitting and ingenious defiance" in several States, including Georgia. After a brief interlude of black suffrage enforced by federal troops but accompanied by rampant violence against blacks, Georgia held a constitutional convention in 1877. Its purpose, according to the convention's leader, was to "'fix it so that the people shall rule and the Negro shall never be heard from.'" In pursuit of this objectives, Georgia enacted a cumulative poll tax, requiring voters to show they had paid past as well as current poll taxes; one historian described this tax as the "most effective bar to Negro suffrage ever devised."

In 1890, the Georgia General Assembly authorized "white primaries"; keeping blacks out of the Democratic primary effectively excluded them from Georgia's political life, for victory in the Democratic primary was tantamount to election. Early in this century, Georgia Governor Hoke Smith persuaded the legislature to pass the "Disenfranchisement Act of 1908"; true to its title, this measure added various property, "good character," and literacy requirements that, as administered, served to keep blacks from voting. The result, as one commentator observed 25 years later, was an "'almost absolute exclusion of the Negro voice in state and federal elections.'"

Faced with a political situation scarcely open to self-correction—disenfranchised blacks had no electoral influence, hence no muscle to lobby the legislature for change—the court intervened. It invalidated white primaries, see *Smith v. Allwright* (1944), and other burdens on minority voting.

It was against this backdrop that the Court, construing the Equal Protection Clause, undertook to ensure that apportionment plans do not dilute minority voting strength. By enacting the Voting Rights Act of 1965, Congress heightened federal judicial involvement in apportionment, and also fashioned a role for the Attorney General. Section 2 creates a federal right of action to challenge vote dilution. Section 5 requires States with a history of discrimination to preclear any changes in voting practices with either a federal court (a three-judge United States District Court for the District of Columbia) or the Attorney General.

These Court decisions and congressional directions significantly reduced voting discrimination against minorities.

In the 1972 election, Georgia gained its first black Member of Congress since Reconstruction, and the 1981 apportionment created the State's first majority-minority district. This voting district, however, was not gained easily. Georgia created it only after the United States District Court for the District of Columbia refused to preclear a predecessor apportionment plan that included no such district—an omission due in part to the influence of Joe Mack Wilson, then Chairman of the Georgia House Reapportionment Committee. As Wilson put it only 14 years ago, "'I don't want to draw nigger districts.'"

II

A.   Before *Shaw v. Reno* this Court invoked the Equal Protection Clause to justify intervention in the quintessentially political task of legislative districting in two circumstances: to enforce the one-person-one-vote requirement, and to prevent dilution of a minority group's voting strength.

In *Shaw*, the Court recognized a third basis for an equal protection challenge to a State's apportionment plan. The Court wrote cautiously, emphasizing that judicial intervention is exceptional. "[S]trict [judicial] scrutiny" is in order, the Court declared, if a district is "so extremely irregular on its face that it rationally can be viewed only as an effort to segregate the races for purposes of voting."

The problem in *Shaw* was not the plan architects' consideration of race as relevant in redistricting. Rather, in the Court's estimation, it was the virtual exclusion of other factors from the calculus. Traditional districting practices were cast aside, the Court concluded, with race alone steering placement of district lines.

B.   The record before us does not show that race similarly overwhelmed traditional districting practices in Georgia. Although the Georgia General Assembly prominently considered race in shaping the Eleventh District, race did not crowd out all other factors, as the Court found it did in North Carolina's delineation of the *Shaw* district.

In contrast to the snake-like North Carolina district inspected in *Shaw*, Georgia's Eleventh District is hardly "bizarre," "extremely irregular," or "irrational on its face." Instead, the Eleventh District's design reflects significant consideration of "traditional districting factors

(such as keeping political subdivisions intact) and the usual political process of compromise and trades for a variety of nonracial reasons." The District covers a core area in central and eastern Georgia, and its total land area of 6,780 square miles is about average for the State. The border of the Eleventh District runs 1,184 miles, in line with Georgia's Second District, which has a 1,243-mile border and the State's Eighth District, with a border running 1,155 miles.

Nor does the Eleventh District disrespect the boundaries of political subdivisions. Of the 22 counties in the District, 14 are intact and 8 are divided. That puts the Eleventh District at about the state average in divided counties. By contrast, of the Sixth District's 5 counties, none are intact, and of the Fourth District's 4 counties, just 1 is intact. Seventy-one percent of the Eleventh District's boundaries track the borders of political subdivisions. Of the State's 11 districts, 5 score worse than the Eleventh District on this criterion, and 5 score better. Eighty-three percent of the Eleventh District's geographic area is composed of intact counties, above average for the State's congressional districts. And notably, the Eleventh District's boundaries largely follow precinct lines. ...

Georgia's Eleventh District, in sum, is not an outlier district shaped without reference to familiar districting techniques. ...

C.   The Court suggests that it was not Georgia's legislature, but the U.S. Department of Justice, that effectively drew the lines, and that Department officers did so with nothing but race in mind. Yet the "Max-Black" plan advanced by the Attorney General was not the plan passed by the Georgia General Assembly. ...

And although the Attorney General refused preclearance to the first two plans approved by Georgia's legislature, the State was not thereby disarmed; Georgia could have demanded relief from the Department's objections by instituting a civil action in the United States District Court for the District of Columbia, with ultimate review in this Court. Instead of pursuing that avenue, the State chose to adopt the plan here in controversy—a plan the State forcefully defends before us. We should respect Georgia's choice by taking its position on brief as genuine.

D. Along with attention to size, shape, and political subdivisions, the Court recognizes as an appropriate districting principle, "respect for … communities defined by actual shared interests." The Court finds no community here, however, because a report in the record showed "fractured political, social, and economic interests within the Eleventh District's black population."

But ethnicity itself can tie people together, as volumes of social science literature have documented—even people with divergent economic interests. For this reason, ethnicity is a significant force in political life. …

To accommodate the reality of ethnic bonds, legislatures have long drawn voting districts along ethnic lines. Our Nation's cities are full of districts identified by their ethnic character—Chinese, Irish, Italian, Jewish, Polish, Russian, for example. … The creation of ethnic districts reflecting felt identity is not ordinarily viewed as offensive or demeaning to those included in the delineation.

III

To separate permissible and impermissible use of race in legislative apportionment, the Court orders strict scrutiny for districting plans "predominantly motivated" by race. No longer can a State avoid judicial oversight by giving—as in this case—genuine and measurable consideration to traditional districting practices. Instead, a federal case can be mounted whenever plaintiffs plausibly allege that other factors carried less weight than race. This invitation to litigate against the State seems to me neither necessary nor proper.

A. The Court derives its test from diverse opinions on the relevance of race in contexts distinctly unlike apportionment. The controlling idea, the Court says, is "'the simple command [at the heart of the Constitution's guarantee of equal protection] that Government must treat citizens as individuals, not as simply components of a racial, religious, sexual or national class.'" But cf. *Strauder v. West Virginia* (1880) (pervading purpose of post-Civil War Amendments was to bar discrimination against once-enslaved race). In adopting districting plans,

however, States do not treat people as individuals. Apportionment schemes, by their very nature, assemble people in groups. States do not assign voters to districts based on merit or achievement, standards States might use in hiring employees or engaging contractors. Rather, legislators classify voters in groups—by economic, geographical, political, or social characteristics—and then "reconcile the competing claims of [these] groups."

That ethnicity defines some of these groups is a political reality. Until now, no constitutional infirmity has been seen in districting Irish or Italian voters together, for example, so long as the delineation does not abandon familiar apportionment practices. If Chinese-Americans and Russian-Americans may seek and secure group recognition in the delineation of voting districts, then African-Americans should not be dissimilarly treated. Otherwise, in the name of equal protection, we would shut out "the very minority group whose history in the United States gave birth to the Equal Protection Clause."

B. Under the Court's approach, judicial review of the same intensity, *i.e.*, strict scrutiny, is in order once it is determined that an apportionment is predominantly motivated by race. It matters not at all, in this new regime, whether the apportionment dilutes or enhances minority voting strength. As very recently observed, however, "[t]here is no moral or constitutional equivalence between a policy that is designed to perpetuate a caste system and one that seeks to eradicate racial subordination."

Special circumstances justify vigilant judicial inspection to protect minority voters—circumstances that do not apply to majority voters. A history of exclusion from state politics left racial minorities without clout to extract provisions for fair representation in the lawmaking forum. … The majority, by definition, encounters no such blockage. White voters in Georgia do not lack means to exert strong pressure on their state legislators. The force of their numbers is itself a powerful determiner of what the legislature will do that does not coincide with perceived majority interests. …

NORTHWEST AUSTIN MUNICIPAL UTILITY DISTRICT NUMBER ONE,
APPELLANT v. ERIC H. HOLDER, JR., ATTORNEY GENERAL, et al.
Supreme Court of the United States
2009 U.S. LEXIS 4539

June 22, 2009, Decided

OPINION BY:

ROBERTS

OPINION

CHIEF JUSTICE ROBERTS delivered the opinion of the Court.

The plaintiff in this case is a small utility district raising a big question—the constitutionality of §5 of the Voting Rights Act. The district has an elected board, and is required by §5 to seek preclearance from federal authorities in Washington, D. C., before it can change anything about those elections. This is required even though there has never been any evidence of racial discrimination in voting in the district.

The district filed suit seeking relief from these preclearance obligations under the "bailout" provision of the Voting Rights Act. That provision allows the release of a "political subdivision" from the preclearance requirements if certain rigorous conditions are met. The court below denied relief, concluding that bailout was unavailable to a political subdivision like the utility district that did not register its own voters. The district appealed, arguing that the Act imposes no such limitation on bailout, and that if it does, the preclearance requirements are unconstitutional.

That constitutional question has attracted ardent briefs from dozens of interested parties, but the importance of the question does not justify our rushing to decide it. Quite the contrary: Our usual practice is to avoid the unnecessary resolution of constitutional questions. We agree that the district is eligible under the Act to seek bailout. We therefore reverse, and do not reach the constitutionality of §5.

I

    A.   The Fifteenth Amendment promises that the "right of citizens of the United States to vote shall not be denied or abridged ... on account of race, color, or previous condition of servitude." In addition to that self-executing right, the Amendment also gives Congress the "power to enforce this article by appropriate legislation.". The first century of congressional enforcement of the Amendment, however, can only be regarded as a failure. Early enforcement Acts were inconsistently applied and repealed with the rise of Jim Crow. Another series of enforcement statutes in the 1950s and 1960s depended on individual lawsuits filed by the Department of Justice. But litigation is slow and expensive, and the States were creative in "contriving new rules" to continue violating the Fifteenth Amendment "in the face of adverse federal court decrees."

Congress responded with the Voting Rights Act. Section 2 of the Act operates nationwide; as it exists today, that provision forbids any "standard, practice, or procedure" that "results in a denial or abridgment of the right of any citizen of the United States to vote on account of race or color." Section 2 is not at issue in this case.

The remainder of the Act constitutes a "scheme of stringent remedies aimed at areas where voting discrimination has been most flagrant.". Rather than continuing to depend on case-by-case litigation, the Act directly pre-empted the most powerful tools of black disenfranchisement in the covered areas. All literacy tests and similar voting qualifications were abolished by §4 of the Act. Although such tests may have been facially neutral, they were easily manipulated to keep blacks from voting. The Act also empowered federal examiners to override state determinations about who was eligible to vote.

These two remedies were bolstered by §5, which suspended all changes in state election procedure until they were submitted to and approved by a three-judge Federal District Court in Washington, D. C., or the Attorney General. Such preclearance is granted only if the change neither "has the purpose nor will have the effect of denying or abridging the right to vote on account of race or color." We have interpreted the requirements of §5 to apply not only to the ballot-access rights guaranteed by §4, but to drawing district lines as well.

To confine these remedies to areas of flagrant disenfranchisement, the Act applied them only to States that had used a forbidden test or device in November 1964, and had less than 50% voter registration or turnout in the 1964 Presidential election. Congress recognized that the coverage formula it had adopted "might bring within its sweep governmental units not guilty of any unlawful discriminatory voting practices." It therefore "afforded such jurisdictions immediately available protection in the form of … [a] 'bailout' suit."

To bail out under the current provision, a jurisdiction must seek a declaratory judgment from a three-judge District Court in Washington, D. C. It must show that for the previous 10 years it has not used any forbidden voting test, has not been subject to any valid objection under §5, and has not been found liable for other voting rights violations; it must also show that it has "engaged in constructive efforts to eliminate intimidation and harassment" of voters, and similar measures. The Attorney General can consent to entry of judgment in favor of bailout if the evidence warrants it, though other interested parties are allowed to intervene in the declaratory judgment action. There are other restrictions: To bail out, a covered jurisdiction must show that every jurisdiction in its territory has complied with all of these requirements. The District Court also retains continuing jurisdiction over a successful bailout suit for 10 years, and may reinstate coverage if any violation is found.

As enacted, §§4 and 5 of the Voting Rights Act were temporary provisions. They were expected to be in effect for only five years. We upheld the temporary Voting Rights Act of 1965 as an appropriate exercise of congressional power in *Katzenbach*, explaining that "[t]he constitutional propriety of the Voting Rights Act of 1965 must be judged with reference to the historical experience which it reflects." We concluded that the problems Congress faced when it passed the Act were so dire that "exceptional conditions [could] justify legislative measures not otherwise appropriate."

Congress reauthorized the Act in 1970 (for 5 years), 1975 (for 7 years), and 1982 (for 25 years). The coverage formula remained the same, based on the use of voting-eligibility tests and the rate of registration and turnout among all voters, but the pertinent dates for assessing these criteria moved from 1964 to include 1968 and eventually 1972. We upheld each of these reauthorizations against constitutional challenges, finding that circumstances continued to justify the provisions. Most recently, in 2006, Congress extended §5 for yet another 25 years. The 2006 Act retained 1972 as the last baseline year for triggering coverage under §5. It is that latest extension that is now before us.

Northwest Austin Municipal Utility District Number One was created in 1987 to deliver city services to residents of a portion of Travis County, Texas. It is governed by a board of five members, elected to staggered terms of four years. The district does not register voters but is responsible for its own elections; for administrative reasons, those elections are run by Travis County. Because the district is located in Texas, it is subject to the obligations of §5, although there is no evidence that it has ever discriminated on the basis of race.

The district filed suit in the District Court for the District of Columbia, seeking relief under the statute's bailout provisions and arguing in the alternative that, if interpreted to render the district ineligible for bailout, §5 was unconstitutional. The three-judge District Court rejected both claims. Under the statute, only a "State or political subdivision" is permitted to seek bailout and the court concluded that the district was not a political subdivision because that term includes only "counties, parishes, and voter-registering subunits," Turning to the district's constitutional challenge, the court concluded that the 25-year extension of §5 was constitutional both because "Congress ... rationally concluded that extending [§]5 was necessary to protect minorities from continued racial discrimination in voting" and because "the 2006 Amendment qualifies as a congruent and proportional response to the continuing problem of racial discrimination in voting." We noted probable jurisdiction and now reverse.

II

The historic accomplishments of the Voting Rights Act are undeniable. When it was first passed, unconstitutional discrimination was rampant and the "registration of voting-age whites ran roughly 50 percentage points or more ahead" of black registration in many covered States. Today, the registration gap between white and black voters is in single digits in the covered States; in some of those States, blacks now register and vote at higher rates than whites. Similar dramatic improvements have occurred for other racial minorities. "[M]any of the first generation barriers to minority voter registration and voter turnout that were in place prior to the [Voting Rights Act] have been eliminated."

At the same time, §5, "which authorizes federal intrusion into sensitive areas of state and local policymaking, imposes substantial 'federalism costs.'" These federalism costs have caused Members of this Court to express serious misgivings about the constitutionality of §5. Section 5 goes beyond the prohibition of the Fifteenth Amendment by suspending *all* changes to state election law—however innocuous—until they have been precleared by federal authorities in Washington, D. C. The preclearance requirement applies broadly and in particular to every political subdivision in a covered State, no matter how small, some of the conditions that we relied upon in upholding this statutory scheme in *Katzenbach* and *City of Rome* have unquestionably improved. Things have changed in the South. Voter turnout and registration rates now approach parity. Blatantly discriminatory evasions of federal decrees are rare. And minority candidates hold office at unprecedented levels.

These improvements are no doubt due in significant part to the Voting Rights Act itself, and stand as a monument to its success. Past success alone, however, is not adequate justification to retain the preclearance requirements. It may be that these improvements are insufficient and that conditions continue to warrant preclearance under the Act. But the Act imposes current burdens and must be justified by current needs.

The Act also differentiates between the States, despite our historic tradition that all the States enjoy "equal sovereignty." Distinctions can be justified in some cases. "The doctrine of the equality of States ... does not bar ... remedies for *local* evils which have subsequently appeared." But a departure from the fundamental principle of equal sovereignty requires a showing that a statute's disparate geographic coverage is sufficiently related to the problem that it targets.

These federalism concerns are underscored by the argument that the preclearance requirements in one State would be unconstitutional in another. Yet considerations of race that would doom a redistricting plan under the Fourteenth Amendment or §2 seem to be what save it under §5"). Additional constitutional concerns are raised in saying that this tension between §§2 and 5 must persist in covered jurisdictions and not elsewhere.

The evil that §5 is meant to address may no longer be concentrated in the jurisdictions singled out for preclearance. The statute's coverage formula is based on data that is now more than 35 years old, and there is considerable evidence that it fails to account for current political conditions. For example, the racial gap in voter registration and turnout is lower in the States originally covered by §5 than it is nationwide. Congress heard warnings from supporters of extending §5 that the evidence in the record did not address "systematic differences between the covered and the non-covered areas of the United States[,] ... and, in fact, the evidence that is in the record suggests that there is more similarity than difference."

The parties do not agree on the standard to apply in deciding whether, in light of the foregoing concerns, Congress exceeded its Fifteenth Amendment enforcement power in extending the preclearance requirements. The district argues that "'[t]here must be a congruence and proportionality between the injury to be prevented or remedied and the means adopted to that end,'"; the Federal Government asserts that it is enough that the legislation be a "'rational means to effectuate the constitutional prohibition,'" That question has been extensively briefed in this case, but we need not resolve it. The

Act's preclearance requirements and its coverage formula raise serious constitutional questions under either test.

In assessing those questions, we are keenly mindful of our institutional role. We fully appreciate that judging the constitutionality of an Act of Congress is "the gravest and most delicate duty that this Court is called on to perform." "The Congress is a coequal branch of government whose Members take the same oath we do to uphold the Constitution of the United States." *Rostker* v. *Goldberg*. The Fifteenth Amendment empowers "Congress," not the Court, to determine in the first instance what legislation is needed to enforce it. Congress amassed a sizable record in support of its decision to extend the preclearance requirements, a record the District Court determined "document[ed] contemporary racial discrimination in covered states." The District Court also found that the record "demonstrat[ed] that section 5 prevents discriminatory voting changes" by "quietly but effectively deterring discriminatory changes."

We will not shrink from our duty "as the bulwar[k] of a limited constitution against legislative encroachments," but "[i]t is a well-established principle governing the prudent exercise of this Court's jurisdiction that normally the Court will not decide a constitutional question if there is some other ground upon which to dispose of the case," Here, the district also raises a statutory claim that it is eligible to bail out under §§4 and 5. ***

The district expressly describes its constitutional challenge to §5 as being "in the alternative" to its statutory argument. The district's counsel confirmed this at oral argument. ("[Question:] [D]o you acknowledge that if we find in your favor on the bailout point we need not reach the constitutional point? [Answer:] I do acknowledge that"). We therefore turn to the district's statutory argument.

III

Section 4(b) of the Voting Rights Act authorizes a bailout suit by a "State or political subdivision." There is no dispute that the district is a political subdivision of the State of Texas in the ordinary sense of the term. The district was created under Texas law with "powers of government" relating to local utilities and natural resources.

The Act, however, also provides a narrower statutory definition in §14(c)(2): "'[P]olitical subdivision' shall mean any county or parish, except that where registration for voting is not conducted under the supervision of a county or parish, the term shall include any other subdivision of a State which conducts registration for voting." The District Court concluded that this definition applied to the bailout provision in §4(a), and that the district did not qualify, since it is not a county or parish and does not conduct its own voter registration.

"Statutory definitions control the meaning of statutory words, of course, in the usual case. But this is an unusual case." Were the scope of §4(a) considered in isolation from the rest of the statute and our prior cases, the District Court's approach might well be correct. But here specific precedent, the structure of the Voting Rights Act, and underlying constitutional concerns compel a broader reading of the bailout provision.

Importantly, we do not write on a blank slate. Our decisions have already established that the statutory definition in §14(c)(2) does not apply to every use of the term "political subdivision" in the Act. We have, for example, concluded that the definition does not apply to the preclearance obligation of §5. According to its text, §5 applies only "[w]henever a [covered] State or political subdivision" enacts or administers a new voting practice. Yet in *Sheffield Bd. of Comm'rs*, we rejected the argument by a Texas city that it was neither a State nor a political subdivision as defined in the Act, and therefore did not need to seek preclearance of a voting change. The dissent agreed with the city, pointing out that the city did not meet the statutory definition of "political subdivision" and therefore could not be covered. The majority, however, relying on the purpose and structure of the Act, concluded that the "definition was intended to operate only for purposes of determining which political units in nondesignated States may be separately designated for coverage under §4(b)."

We reaffirmed this restricted scope of the statutory definition the next Term in *Dougherty County Bd. of Ed.* v. *White*. There, a school board argued that because "it d[id] not meet the definition" of political subdivision in §14(c)(2), it "d[id] not come within the purview of §5." We responded:

"This contention is squarely foreclosed by our decision last Term in [*Sheffield*]. There, we expressly rejected the suggestion that the city of Sheffield was beyond the ambit of §5 because it did not itself register voters and hence was not a political subdivision as the term is defined in §14(c)(2) of the Act. ... [O]nce a State has been designated for coverage, §14(c)(2)'s definition of political subdivision has no operative significance in determining the reach of §5."

According to these decisions, then, the statutory definition of "political subdivision" in §14(c)(2) does not apply to every use of the term "political subdivision" in the Act.

Even the intervenors who oppose the district's bailout concede, for example, that the definition should not apply to §2, which bans racial discrimination in voting by "any State or political subdivision," ("[T]he Supreme Court has held that this definition [in §14(c)(2)] limits the meaning of the phrase 'State or political subdivision' only when it appears in certain parts of the Act, and that it does not confine the phrase as used elsewhere in the Act"). In light of our holdings that the statutory definition does not constrict the scope of preclearance required by §5, the district argues, it only stands to reason that the definition should not constrict the availability of bailout from those preclearance requirements either.

The Government responds that any such argument is foreclosed by our interpretation of the statute in *City of Rome*. There, it argues, we made clear that the discussion of political subdivisions in *Sheffield* was dictum, and "specifically held that a 'city is not a "political subdivision" for purposes of §4(a) bailout.'"

Even if that is what *City of Rome* held, the premises of its statutory holding did not survive later changes in the law. In *City of Rome* we rejected the city's attempt to bail out from coverage under §5, concluding that "political units of a covered jurisdiction cannot independently bring a §4(a) bailout action." We concluded that the statute as then written authorized a bailout suit only by a "State" subject to the coverage formula, or a "political subdivision with respect to which [coverage] determinations have been made as a separate unit," Political subdivisions covered because they were part of a covered State, rather than because of separate coverage determinations, could not separately bail out.***

In 1982, however, Congress expressly repudiated *City of Rome* and instead embraced "piecemeal" bailout. As part of an overhaul of the bailout provision, Congress amended the Voting Rights Act to expressly provide that bailout was also available to "political subdivisions" in a covered State, "though [coverage] determinations were *not* made with respect to such subdivision as a separate unit." In other words, Congress decided that a jurisdiction covered because it was within a covered State need not remain covered for as long as the State did. If the subdivision met the bailout requirements, it could bail out, even if the State could not. In light of these amendments, our logic for denying bailout in *City of Rome* is no longer applicable to the Voting Rights Act—if anything, that logic compels the opposite conclusion.

Bailout and preclearance under §5 are now governed by a principle of symmetry. "Given the Court's decision in *Sheffield* that all political units in a covered State are

to be treated for §5 purposes as though they were 'political subdivisions' of that State, it follows that they should also be treated as such for purposes of §4(a)'s bailout provisions."

The Government contends that this reading of *Sheffield* is mistaken, and that the district is subject to §5 under our decision in *Sheffield* not because it is a "political subdivision" but because it is a "State." That would mean it could bail out only if the whole State could bail out.

The assertion that the district is a State is at least counterintuitive. We acknowledge, however, that there has been much confusion over why *Sheffield* held the city in that case to be covered by the text of §5. But after the 1982 amendments, the Government's position is untenable. If the district is considered the State, and therefore necessarily subject to preclearance so long as Texas is covered, then the same must be true of all other subdivisions of the State, including counties. That would render even counties unable to seek bailout so long as their State was covered. But that is the very restriction the 1982 amendments overturned. Nobody denies that counties in a covered State can seek bailout, as several of them have. Because such piecemeal bailout is now permitted, it cannot be true that §5 treats every governmental unit as the State itself.

The Government's contrary interpretation has helped to render the bailout provision all but a nullity. Since 1982, only 17 jurisdictions—out of the more than 12,000 covered political subdivisions—have successfully bailed out of the Act. It is unlikely that Congress intended the provision to have such limited effect. We therefore hold that all political subdi-visions—not only those described in §14(c)(2)—are eligible to file a bailout suit.

　　　* * *

More than 40 years ago, this Court concluded that "exceptional conditions" prevailing in certain parts of the country justified extraordinary legislation otherwise unfamiliar to our federal system. In part due to the success of that legislation, we are now a very different Nation. Whether conditions continue to justify such legislation is a difficult constitutional question we do not answer today. We conclude instead that the Voting Rights Act permits all political subdivisions, including the district in this case, to seek relief from its preclearance requirements.

The judgment of the District Court is reversed, and the case is remanded for further proceedings consistent with this opinion.

It is so ordered.

February 27, 2013, Argued, June 25, 2013, Decided

OPINION BY

ROBERTS

CHIEF JUSTICE ROBERTS delivered the opinion of the Court.

The Voting Rights Act of 1965 employed extraordinary measures to address an extraordinary problem. Section 5 of the Act required States to obtain federal permission before enacting any law related to voting—a drastic departure from basic principles of federalism. And §4 of the Act applied that requirement only to some States—an equally dramatic departure from the principle that all States enjoy equal sovereignty. This was strong medicine, but Congress determined it was needed to address entrenched racial discrimination in voting, "an insidious and pervasive evil which had been perpetuated in certain parts of our country through unremitting and ingenious defiance of the Constitution." As we explained in upholding the law, "exceptional conditions can justify legislative measures not otherwise appropriate." Reflecting the unprecedented nature of these measures, they were scheduled to expire after five years.

Nearly 50 years later, they are still in effect; indeed, they have been made more stringent, and are now scheduled to last until 2031. There is no denying, however, that the conditions that originally justified these measures no longer characterize voting in the covered jurisdictions. By 2009, "the racial gap in voter registration and turnout [was] lower in the States originally covered by §5 than it [was] nationwide." Since that time, Census Bureau data indicate that African-American voter turnout has come to exceed white voter turnout in five of the six States originally covered by §5, with a gap in the sixth State of less than one half of one percent.

At the same time, voting discrimination still exists; no one doubts that. The question is whether the Act's extraordinary measures, including its disparate treatment of the States, continue to satisfy constitutional requirements. As we put it a short time ago, "the Act imposes current burdens and must be justified by current needs."

***In those jurisdictions, §4 of the Act banned all such tests or devices. Section 5 provided that no change in voting procedures could take effect until it was approved by federal authorities in Washington, D. C.— either the Attorney General or a court of three judges. A jurisdiction could obtain such "preclearance" only by proving that the change had neither "the purpose [nor] the effect of denying or abridging the right to vote on account of race or color."

Sections 4 and 5 were intended to be temporary; they were set to expire after five years. In *South Carolina* v. *Katzenbach*, we upheld the 1965 Act against constitutional challenge, explaining that it was justified to address "voting discrimination where it persists on a pervasive scale."

In 2006, Congress reauthorized the Voting Rights Act for 25 years, again without change to its coverage formula. Section 5 now forbids voting changes with "any discriminatory purpose" as well as voting changes that diminish the ability of citizens, on account of race, color, or language minority status, "to elect their preferred candidates of choice."

***Shelby County is located in Alabama, a covered jurisdiction. It has not sought bailout, as the Attorney General has recently objected to voting changes proposed from within the county. Instead, in 2010, the county sued the Attorney General in Federal District Court in Washington, D. C., seeking a declaratory judgment that sections 4(b) and 5 of the Voting Rights Act are facially unconstitutional, as well as a permanent injunction against their enforcement. The District Court ruled against the county and upheld the Act. The Court of Appeals for the D. C. Circuit affirmed.

***We granted certiorari.

In *Northwest Austin*, we stated that "the Act imposes current burdens and must be justified by current needs." And we concluded that "a departure from the fundamental principle of equal sovereignty requires a showing that a statute's disparate geographic coverage is sufficiently related to the problem that it targets." These basic principles guide our review of the question before us.

The Constitution and laws of the United States are "the supreme Law of the Land." State legislation may not contravene federal law. The Federal Government does not, however, have a general right to review and veto state enactments before they go into effect. **

Outside the strictures of the Supremacy Clause, States retain broad autonomy in structuring their governments and pursuing legislative objectives. Indeed, the Constitution provides that all powers not specifically granted to the Federal Government are reserved to the States or citizens. ***

More specifically, "'the Framers of the Constitution intended the States to keep for themselves, as provided in the Tenth Amendment, the power to regulate elections.'" Of course, the Federal Government retains significant control over federal elections.

***Not only do States retain sovereignty under the Constitution, there is also a "fundamental principle of *equal* sovereignty" among the States.

***The Voting Rights Act sharply departs from these basic principles. It suspends "*all* changes to state election law—however innocuous—until they have been pre-cleared by federal authorities in Washington, D. C." States must beseech the Federal Government for permission to implement laws that they would otherwise have the right to enact and execute on their own, subject of course to any injunction in a §2 action. The Attorney General has 60 days to object to a preclearance request, longer if he requests more information. If a State seeks preclearance from a three-judge court, the process can take years.

And despite the tradition of equal sovereignty, the Act applies to only nine States (and several additional counties). While one State waits months or years and expends funds to implement a validly enacted law, its neighbor can typically put the same law into effect immediately, through the normal legislative process. Even if a noncovered jurisdiction is sued, there are important differences between those proceedings and preclearance proceedings; the preclearance proceeding "not only switches the burden of proof to the supplicant jurisdiction, but also applies substantive standards quite different from those governing the rest of the nation."

***Nearly 50 years later, things have changed dramatically. Shelby County contends that the preclearance requirement, even without regard to its disparate coverage, is now unconstitutional. Its arguments have a good deal of force. In the covered jurisdictions, [v]oter turnout and registration rates now approach parity. Blatantly discriminatory evasions of federal decrees are rare. And minority candidates hold office at unprecedented levels." The tests and devices that blocked access to the ballot have been forbidden nationwide for over 40 years.

Those conclusions are not ours alone. Congress said the same when it reauthorized the Act in 2006, writing that "[s]ignificant progress has been made in eliminating first generation barriers experienced by minority voters, including increased numbers of registered minority voters, minority voter turnout, and minority representation in Congress, State legislatures, and local elected offices." The House Report elaborated that "the number of African-Americans who are registered and who turn out to cast ballots has increased significantly over the last 40 years, particularly since 1982," and noted that "[i]n some circumstances, minorities register to vote and cast ballots at levels that surpass those of white voters." That Report also explained that there have been "significant increases in the number of African-Americans serving in elected offices"; more specifically, there has been approximately a 1,000 percent increase since 1965 in the number of African-American elected officials in the six States originally covered by the Voting Rights Act.

The following chart, compiled from the Senate and House Reports, compares voter registration numbers from 1965 to those from 2004 in the six originally covered States. These are the numbers that were before Congress when it reauthorized the Act in 2006:

	1965			2004		
	White	Black	Gap	White	Black	Gap
Alabama	69.2	19.3	49.9	73.8	72.9	0.9
Georgia	62.[6]	27.4	35.2	63.5	64.2	−0.7
Louisiana	80.5	31.6	48.9	75.1	71.1	4.0
Mississippi	69.9	6.7	63.2	72.3	76.1	−3.8
South Carolina	75.7	37.3	38.4	74.4	71.1	3.3
Virginia	61.1	38.3	22.8	68.2	57.4	10.8

The 2004 figures come from the Census Bureau. Census Bureau data from the most recent election indicate that African-American voter turnout exceeded white voter turnout in five of the six States originally covered by §5, with a gap in the sixth State of less than one half of one percent. See Dept. of Commerce, Census Bureau, Reported Voting and Registration, by Sex, Race and Hispanic Origin, for States (Table 4b). The preclearance statistics are also illuminating. In the first decade after enactment of §5, the Attorney General objected to 14.2 percent of proposed voting changes. In the last decade before reenactment, the Attorney General objected to a mere 0.16 percent.

There is no doubt that these improvements are in large part *because* of the Voting Rights Act. The Act has proved immensely successful at redressing racial discrimination and integrating the voting process. During the "Freedom Summer" of 1964, in Philadelphia, Mississippi, three men were murdered while working in the area to register African-American voters. On "Bloody Sunday" in 1965, in Selma, Alabama, police beat and used tear gas against hundreds marching in support of African-American enfranchisement. Today both of those towns are governed by African-American mayors. Problems remain in these States and others, but there is no denying that, due to the Voting Rights Act, our Nation has made great strides.

Yet the Act has not eased the restrictions in §5 or narrowed the scope of the coverage formula in §4(b) along the way. Those extraordinary and unprecedented features were reauthorized—as if nothing had changed. In fact, the Act's unusual remedies have grown even stronger. When Congress reauthorized the Act in 2006, it did so for another 25 years on top of the previous 40—a far cry from the initial five-year period. Congress also expanded the prohibitions in §5. We had previously interpreted §5 to prohibit only those redistricting plans that would have the purpose or effect of worsening the position of minority groups. In 2006, Congress amended §5 to prohibit laws that could have favored such groups but did not do so because of a discriminatory purpose, even though we had stated that such broadening of §5 coverage would "exacerbate the substantial federalism costs that the preclearance procedure already exacts, perhaps to the extent of raising concerns about §5's constitutionality. In addition, Congress expanded §5 to prohibit any voting law "that has the purpose of or will have the effect of diminishing the ability of any citizens of the United States," on account of race, color, or language minority status, "to elect their preferred candidates of choice." In light of those two amendments, the bar that covered jurisdictions must clear has been raised even as the conditions justifying that requirement have dramatically improved.

***Coverage today is based on decades-old data and eradicated practices. The formula captures States by reference to literacy tests and low voter registration and turnout in the 1960s and early 1970s. But such tests have been banned nationwide for over 40 years. And voter registration and turnout numbers in the covered States have risen dramatically in the years since. Racial disparity in those numbers was compelling evidence justifying the preclearance remedy and the coverage formula. There is no longer such a disparity.

In 1965, the States could be divided into two groups: those with a recent history of voting tests and low voter registration and turnout, and those without those characteristics. Congress based its coverage formula on that distinction. Today the Nation is no longer divided along those lines, yet the Voting Rights Act continues to treat it as if it were.

***But history did not end in 1965. By the time the Act was reauthorized in 2006, there had been 40 more years of it. In assessing the "current need[ ]" for a preclearance system that treats States differently from one another today, that history cannot be ignored. During that time, largely because of the Voting Rights Act, voting tests were abolished, disparities in voter registration and turnout due to race were erased, and African-Americans attained political office in record numbers. And yet the coverage formula that Congress reauthorized in 2006 ignores these developments, keeping the focus on decades-old data relevant to decades-old problems, rather than current data reflecting current needs.

***There is no valid reason to insulate the coverage formula from review merely because it was previously enacted 40 years ago. If Congress had started from scratch in 2006, it plainly could not have enacted the present coverage formula. It would have been irrational for Congress to distinguish between States in such a fundamental way based on 40-year-old data, when today's statistics tell an entirely different story. And it would have been irrational to base coverage on the use of voting tests 40 years ago, when such tests have been illegal since that time. But that is exactly what Congress has done.

***

Striking down an Act of Congress "is the gravest and most delicate duty that this Court is called on to perform." We do not do so lightly. That is why, in 2009, we took care to avoid ruling on the constitutionality of the Voting Rights Act when asked to do so, and instead resolved the case then before us on statutory grounds. But in issuing that decision, we expressed our broader concerns about the constitutionality of the Act. Congress could have updated the coverage formula at that time, but did not do so. Its failure to act leaves us today with no choice but to declare §4(b) unconstitutional. The formula in that section can no longer be used as a basis for subjecting jurisdictions to preclearance.

Our decision in no way affects the permanent, nationwide ban on racial discrimination in voting found in §2. We issue no holding on §5 itself, only on the coverage formula. Congress may draft another formula based on current conditions. Such a formula is an initial prerequisite to a determination that exceptional conditions still exist justifying such an "extraordinary departure from the traditional course of relations between the States and the Federal Government." Our country has changed, and while any racial discrimination in voting is too much, Congress must ensure that the legislation it passes to remedy that problem speaks to current conditions.

The judgment of the Court of Appeals is reversed.

It is so ordered.

ALEXANDER v. PRINCE GEORGE'S COUNTY
U.S. District Court for the District of Maryland
(1995)
901 F. Supp. 986

In 1993, the Prince George's County, Maryland, Fire Department's ("County" or "Department") decided not to hire Marc Alexander as a firefighter.

Since 1984, the Department has used the same procedure to hire firefighters: Applicants are first given a written examination. Those applicants that score 60% or higher on the exam are then orally interviewed. The applicants are then placed in several categories according to their scores. All applicants in the same category were considered to be equally qualified.

Alexander was placed in the top ("Outstanding") category. Several minorities who also placed in that category were hired. Alexander contends that he would have been hired if not for the Department's affirmative action plan (the "Plan").

As part of its hiring process, the Department utilizes its Plan. Based on the County's population, the Plan provides goals for the hiring of minority candidates. It does not require the hiring of a certain number of or unqualified minorities. Its goal was to increase participation by minorities so that within five years the firefighter ranks would more closely represent the entire local labor force.

E.   Strict Scrutiny

It is well-settled that classifications based on race must be evaluated under the strict scrutiny standard. *City of Richmond v. J.A. Croson Co.*, (1989). Under this standard, the classification must be based on a "compelling interest" and the affirmative action plan must be "narrowly tailored." The Supreme Court has recently reminded us that application of strict scrutiny should not be considered fatal to affirmative action plans. *Adarand Constructors, Inc. v. Pena*, (1995).

1. Compelling Interest—To show a compelling interest, the County must show more than

general societal discrimination. [T]he County must demonstrate that its past discrimination has present effects. *Podberesky v. Kirwan*, (1992) Proof of past discrimination generally includes statistical evidence of discrimination and anecdotal evidence.

The Defendants have presented extensive statistical evidence of discrimination. The Department first implemented a minority recruitment program in 1974. At that time, out of 290 firefighters, only approximately eight of its firefighters were minorities, and there were no women in the Department.

One of the major obstacles to the recruitment of minorities was the firefighter examination. This examination ... required knowledge gained through experience as a firefighter. The only individuals with such experience were volunteer firefighters, and the volunteer firefighter organizations in the County were almost exclusively white male. Therefore, as a result, the Department remained almost solely white male.

By end of the 1993, the Department ... was 15% female and 38% minority. The Department's affirmative action goals had not been achieved. The County planned to increase its goals in light of the 1990 census which indicated that the County's labor force was 49.9% female and 57.5% minority.

The Defendants have also presented anecdotal evidence of discrimination in the volunteer fire companies. These companies have traditionally denied memberships to or otherwise discouraged minority and women applicants. For instance, it was commonly known that blacks were not wanted in the companies. Black applicants were sent to the "all black station." Also, black volunteers were hazed more severely than their white counterparts.

Finally, the other volunteers routinely referred to blacks as "niggers."

In addition, women volunteers were subjected to repeated abuse. One woman was told that she couldn't join because she was not a white male property owner. Women were encouraged not to join; they were often called "slut" and "bitch"; most of the stations did not have separate restrooms or sleeping facilities for women; one volunteer reported that a male entered the shower area while she was in the shower, and one volunteer was tied to a pole and sprayed with shaving cream. In short, women "weren't wanted."

Furthermore, although the situation in the Department has greatly improved, there remain lingering effects of the Department's past discrimination. For instance, it is still regarded as a male dominated profession where women are not wanted. Women are still harassed in the Department. Also, the Department has still not met its goals for hiring minorities and women. Additionally, the "good old boy" network still operates to help prevent the hiring of blacks. Thus, the Court finds that there are present effects of the Department's past discrimination.

The Plaintiffs do not deny that there have been racist and discriminatory actions taken against minorities in the past by the volunteer companies. Instead, they argue that the evidence of discrimination must result from the Department's own hiring policies. They maintain that the actions of the volunteer companies are not attributable to the County.

The disparities within the Department, however, are a natural consequence of the Department's hiring policies. For example, the Department's examination ... favored those with volunteer experience. Moreover, the Department did most of its advertising through word of mouth at the volunteer stations. Naturally, women and minorities did not learn about job openings under these circumstances. The Department cannot simply attribute hese blatant discriminatory policies to the volunteer organizations. Therefore, the Court finds that the Department has shown the necessary compelling interest to support an affirmative action plan.

2. Narrowly Tailored—An affirmative action plan must be "narrowly tailored to the achievement of that goal." In determining whether a plan is narrowly tailored, the courts have considered several factors: (1) the efficacy of alternative remedies; (2) the planned duration of the remedy; (3) the relationship between the percentage of minority workers to be employed and the percentage of minority groups in the relevant population; (4) availability of waiver provisions; and (5) the effect of the plan on innocent third parties.

i.   Alternative Remedies—The Plaintiffs argue that alternative steps can be used instead of the Plan. They contend that simply making an effort to recruit minorities will be effective and eliminating the preference for volunteers can alleviate the effects of past discrimination. In short, they maintain that the Plan is not necessary.

The Court is not persuaded by this argument. The alternative remedies (e.g., changing the written test and intensifying minority recruitment) [were] attempted [and] were not effective in achieving the goals of the Plan. Finally, the Department may take affirmative steps to remedy past discrimination rather than simply forbidding discrimination in the future.

ii. Duration—An affirmative action plan will not pass strict scrutiny if it is of unlimited duration. The Plaintiffs argue that the Plan suffers from this weakness. They contend that the County will continue the plan as long as the firefighters do not exactly mirror the County wide population.

The Court is not persuaded by this argument. The Plan is limited in duration and is reviewed annually to see if its goals have been achieved.

iii. Relationship Between Work Force and Population—The Department's Plan is designed to remedy present racial and gender imbalances resulting from past discrimination. [T]he County may use the general labor force as a comparison in choosing its firefighters. The Department, of course, should utilize goals that reflect the current population of the County. Thus, the Court finds that the Plan is narrowly tailored in this regard.

iv. Waiver Provisions—An important attribute of the Plan is its flexibility. The Plan does not require that Department hire a certain number of minorities. For example, in 1993, the County sought to hire five female applicants. However, when five could not be found in the outstanding or well-qualified bands, it chose to hire only four. Accordingly, the Plan does not have the trappings of a quota, and the availability of waivers shows that the Plan is narrowly tailored.

v. Impact on Innocent Third Parties—The Plan does not have a severe impact on innocent third parties. First, it does not bar hiring, and the Department continues to hire many white males. Denial of a possible employment opportunity is less drastic than terminating an existing employee based on race. Moreover, the Plan only gives a preference, not a guarantee of employment, to well-qualified minorities. Finally ... all individuals within a given band are regarded as equally qualified for hire. Therefore, in light of each of these factors, the Court concludes that the Plan is narrowly tailored.

FRANK RICCI, et al., PETITIONERS v. JOHN DESTEFANO et al.
Supreme Court of the United States

2009 U.S. LEXIS 4945 June 29, 2009, Decided *

JUSTICE KENNEDY delivered the opinion of the Court.

In the fire department of New Haven, Connecticut—as in emergency-service agencies throughout the Nation—firefighters prize their promotion to and within the officer ranks. An agency's officers command respect within the department and in the whole community; and, of course, added responsibilities command increased salary and benefits. Aware of the intense competition for promotions, New Haven, like many cities, relies on objective examinations to identify the best qualified candidates.

In 2003, 118 New Haven firefighters took examinations to qualify for promotion to the rank of lieutenant or captain. Promotion examinations in New Haven (or City) were infrequent, so the stakes were high. The results would determine which firefighters would be considered for promotions during the next two years, and the order in which they would be considered. Many firefighters studied for months, at considerable personal and financial cost.

When the examination results showed that white candidates had outperformed minority candidates, the mayor and other local politicians opened a public debate that turned rancorous. Some firefighters argued the tests should be discarded because the results showed the tests to be discriminatory. They threatened a discrimination lawsuit if the City made promotions based on the tests. Other firefighters said the exams were neutral and fair. And they, in turn, threatened a discrimination lawsuit if the City, relying on the statistical racial disparity, ignored the test results and denied promotions to the candidates who had performed well. In the end the City took the side of those who protested the test results. It threw out the examinations.

Certain white and Hispanic firefighters who likely would have been promoted based on their good test performance sued the City and some of its officials.

Theirs is the suit now before us. The suit alleges that, by discarding the test results, the City and the named officials discriminated against the plaintiffs based on their race, in violation of both Title VII of the Civil Rights Act of 1964, and the Equal Protection Clause of the Fourteenth Amendment. The City and the officials defended their actions, arguing that if they had certified the results, they could have faced liability under Title VII for adopting a practice that had a disparate impact on the minority firefighters. The District Court granted summary judgment for the defendants, and the Court of Appeals affirmed.

We conclude that race-based action like the City's in this case is impermissible under Title VII unless the employer can demonstrate a strong basis in evidence that, had it not taken the action, it would have been liable under the disparate-impact statute. The respondents, we further determine, cannot meet that threshold standard. As a result, the City's action in discarding the tests was a violation of Title VII. In light of our ruling under the statutes, we need not reach the question whether respondents' actions may have violated the Equal Protection Clause.

I

This litigation comes to us after the parties' cross-motions for summary judgment, so we set out the facts in some detail. As the District Court noted, although "the parties strenuously dispute the relevance and legal import of, and inferences to be drawn from, many aspects of this case, the underlying facts are largely undisputed."

****

The CSB's decision not to certify the examination results led to this lawsuit. The plaintiffs—who are the petitioners here—are 17 white firefighters and 1 Hispanic firefighter who passed the examinations but were denied a chance at promotions when the CSB refused to certify the test results. They include the named plaintiff, Frank Ricci, who addressed the CSB at multiple meetings.

Petitioners sued the City, Mayor DeStefano, DuBois-Walton, Ude, Burgett, and the two CSB members who voted against certification. Petitioners also named as a defendant Boise Kimber, a New Haven resident who voiced strong] opposition to certifying the results. Those individuals are respondents in this Court. Petitioners filed suit under 42 U.S.C. §§1983 and 1985, alleging that respondents, by arguing or voting against certifying the results, violated and conspired to violate the Equal Protection Clause of the Fourteenth Amendment. Petitioners also filed timely charges of discrimination with the Equal Employment Opportunity Commission (EEOC); upon the EEOC's issuing right-to-sue letters, petitioners amended their complaint to assert that the City violated the disparate-treatment prohibition contained in Title VII of the Civil Rights Act of 1964.

The parties filed cross-motions for summary judgment. Respondents asserted they had a good-faith belief that they would have violated the disparate-impact prohibition in Title VII had they certified the examination results. It follows, they maintained, that they cannot be held liable under Title VII's disparate-treatment provision for attempting to comply with Title VII's disparate-impact bar. Petitioners countered that respondents' good-faith belief was not a valid defense to allegations of disparate treatment and unconstitutional discrimination.

The District Court granted summary judgment for respondents. It described petitioners' argument as "boil[ing] down to the assertion that if [respondents] cannot prove that the disparities on the Lieutenant and Captain exams were due to a particular flaw inherent in those exams, then they should have certified the results because there was no other alternative in place." The District Court concluded that, "[n]otwithstanding the shortcomings in the evidence on existing, effective alternatives, it is not the case that [respondents] *must* certify a test where they cannot pinpoint its deficiency explaining its disparate impact . . . simply because they have not yet formulated a better selection method." It also ruled that respondents' "motivation to avoid making promotions based on a test with a racially disparate impact . . . does not, as a matter of law, constitute discriminatory intent" under Title VII. The District Court rejected petitioners' equal protection claim on the theory that respondents had not acted because of "discriminatory animus" toward petitioners. It concluded that respondents'

actions were not "based on race" because "all applicants took the same test, and the result was the same for all because the test results were discarded and nobody was promoted."

After full briefing and argument by the parties, the Court of Appeals affirmed in a one-paragraph, unpublished summary order; it later withdrew that order, issuing in its place a nearly identical, one-paragraph *per curiam* opinion adopting the District Court's reasoning. Three days later, the Court of Appeals voted 7 to 6 to deny rehearing en banc, over written dissents by Chief Judge Jacobs and Judge Cabranes. This action presents two provisions of Title VII to be interpreted and reconciled, with few, if any, precedents in the courts of appeals discussing the issue. Depending on the resolution of the statutory claim, a fundamental constitutional question could also arise. We found it prudent and appropriate to grant certiorari. We now reverse.

II

Petitioners raise a statutory claim, under the disparate-treatment prohibition of Title VII, and a constitutional claim, under the Equal Protection Clause of the Fourteenth Amendment. A decision for petitioners on their statutory claim would provide the relief sought, so we consider it first.

A. Title VII of the Civil Rights Act of 1964 prohibits employment discrimination on the basis of race, color, religion, sex, or national origin. Title VII prohibits both intentional discrimination (known as "disparate treatment") as well as, in some cases, practices that are not intended to discriminate but in fact have a disproportionately adverse effect on minorities (known as "disparate impact").

As enacted in 1964, Title VII's principal nondiscrimination provision held employers liable only for disparate treatment. That section retains its original wording today. It makes it unlawful for an employer "to fail or refuse to hire or to discharge any individual, or otherwise to discriminate against any individual with respect to his compensation, terms, conditions, or privileges of employment, because of such individual's race, color, religion, sex, or national origin." Disparate-treatment cases present "the most easily understood type of discrimination," and occur where an employer has "treated [a] particular person less favorably than others because of" a protected trait. A disparate-treatment plaintiff must establish "that the defendant had a discriminatory intent or motive" for taking a job-related action.

The Civil Rights Act of 1964 did not include an express prohibition on policies or practices that produce a disparate impact. But in *Griggs* v. *Duke Power Co.* the Court interpreted the Act to prohibit, in some cases, employers' facially neutral practices that, in fact, are "discriminatory in operation." The *Griggs* Court stated that the "touchstone" for disparate-impact liability is the lack of "business necessity": "If an employment practice which operates to exclude [minorities] cannot be shown to be related to job performance, the practice is prohibited." Under those precedents, if an employer met its burden by showing that its practice was job-related, the plaintiff was required to show a legitimate alternative that would have resulted in less discrimination.

Twenty years after *Griggs*, the Civil Rights Act of 1991 was enacted. The Act included a provision codifying the prohibition on disparate-impact discrimination. That provision is now in force along with the disparate-treatment section already noted. Under the disparate-impact statute, a plaintiff establishes a prima facie violation by showing that an employer uses "a particular employment practice that causes a disparate impact on the basis of race, color, religion, sex, or national origin." An employer may defend against liability by demonstrating that the practice is "job related for the position in question and consistent with business necessity." Even if the employer meets that burden, however, a plaintiff may still succeed by showing that the employer refuses to adopt an available alternative employment practice that has less disparate impact and serves the employer's legitimate needs.

B.   Petitioners allege that when the CSB refused to certify the captain and lieutenant exam results based on the race of the successful candidates, it discriminated against them in violation of Title VII's disparate-treatment provision. The City counters that its decision was permissible because the tests "appear[ed] to violate Title VII's disparate-impact provisions."

Our analysis begins with this premise: The City's actions would violate the disparate-treatment prohibition of Title VII absent some valid defense. All the evidence demonstrates that the City chose not to certify the examination results because of the statistical disparity based on race—*i.e.,* how minority candidates had performed when compared to white candidates. As the District Court put it, the City rejected the test results because "too many whites and not enough minorities would be promoted were the lists to be certified." Without some other justification, this express, race-based decisionmaking violates Title VII's command that employers cannot take adverse employment actions because of an individual's race.

The District Court did not adhere to this principle, however. It held that respondents'"motivation to avoid making promotions based on a test with a racially disparate impact ... does not, as a matter of law, constitute discriminatory intent." And the Government makes a similar argument in this Court. It contends that the "structure of Title VII belies any claim that an employer's intent to comply with Title VII's disparate-impact provisions constitutes prohibited discrimination on the basis of race." But both of those statements turn upon the City's objective—avoiding disparate-impact liability—while ignoring the City's conduct in the name of reaching that objective. Whatever the City's ultimate aim—however well intentioned or benevolent it might have seemed—the City made its employment decision because of race. The City rejected the test results solely because the higher scoring candidates were white. The question is not whether that conduct was discriminatory but whether the City had a lawful justification for its race-based action.

We consider, therefore, whether the purpose to avoid disparate-impact liability excuses what otherwise would be prohibited disparate-treatment discrimination. Courts often confront cases in which statutes and principles point in different directions. Our task is to provide guidance to employers and courts for situations when these two prohibitions could be in conflict absent a rule to reconcile them. In providing this guidance our decision must be consistent with the important purpose of Title VII—that the workplace be an environment free of discrimination, where race is not a barrier to opportunity.

With these principles in mind, we turn to the parties' proposed means of reconciling the statutory provisions. Petitioners take a strict approach, arguing that under Title VII, it cannot be permissible for an employer to take race-based adverse employment actions in order to avoid disparate-impact liability— even if the employer knows its practice violates the disparate-impact provision. See Brief for Petitioners 43. Petitioners would have us hold that, under Title VII, avoiding unintentional discrimination cannot justify intentional discrimination. That assertion, however, ignores the fact that, by codifying the disparate-impact provision in 1991, Congress has expressly prohibited both types of discrimination. We must interpret the statute to give effect to both provisions where possible. We cannot accept petitioners' broad and inflexible formulation.

Petitioners next suggest that an employer in fact must be in violation of the disparate-impact provision before it can use compliance as a defense in a disparate-treatment suit. Again, this is overly simplistic and too restrictive of Title VII's purpose. The rule petitioners offer would run counter to what we have recognized as Congress's intent that "voluntary compliance" be "the preferred means of achieving the objectives of Title VII." Forbidding employers to act unless they know, with certainty, that a practice violates the disparate-impact provision would bring compliance efforts to a near standstill. Even in the limited situations when this restricted standard could be met, employers likely would hesitate before taking voluntary action for fear of later being proven wrong in the course of litigation and then held to account for disparate treatment.

At the opposite end of the spectrum, respondents and the Government assert that an employer's good-faith belief that its actions are necessary to comply with Title VII's disparate-impact provision should be enough to justify race-conscious conduct. But the original, foundational prohibition of Title VII bars employers from taking adverse action "because of … race." And when Congress codified the disparate-impact provision in 1991, it made no exception to disparate-treatment liability for actions taken in a good-faith effort to comply with the new, disparate-impact provision in subsection (k). Allowing employers to violate the disparate-treatment prohibition based on a mere good-faith fear of disparate-impact liability would encourage race-based action at the slightest hint of disparate impact. A minimal standard could cause employers to discard the results of lawful and beneficial promotional examinations even where there is little if any evidence of disparate-impact discrimination. That would amount to a *de facto* quota system, in which a "focus on statistics … could put undue pressure on employers to adopt inappropriate prophylactic measures." Even worse, an employer could discard test results (or other employment practices) with the intent of obtaining the employer's preferred racial balance. That operational principle could not be justified, for Title VII is express in disclaiming any interpretation of its requirements as calling for outright racial balancing. The purpose of Title VII "is to promote hiring on the basis of job qualifications, rather than on the basis of race or color."

In searching for a standard that strikes a more appropriate balance, we note that this Court has considered cases similar to this one, albeit in the context of the Equal Protection Clause of the Fourteenth Amendment. The Court has held that certain government actions to remedy past racial discrimination—actions that are themselves based on race—are constitutional only where there is a "'strong basis in evidence'" that the remedial actions were necessary. This suit does not call on us to consider whether the statutory constraints under Title VII must be parallel in all respects to those under the Constitution. That does not mean the constitutional authorities are irrelevant, however. Our cases discussing constitutional principles can provide helpful guidance in this statutory context.

Writing for a plurality in *Wygant* and announcing the strong-basis-in-evidence standard, Justice Powell recognized the tension between eliminating segregation and discrimination on the one hand and doing away with all governmentally imposed discrimination based on race on the other. The plurality stated that those "related constitutional duties are not always harmonious," and that "reconciling them requires ... employers to act with extraordinary care." The plurality required a strong basis in evidence because "[e]videntiary support for the conclusion that remedial action is warranted becomes crucial when the remedial program is challenged in court by nonminority employees." The Court applied the same standard in *Croson*, observing that "an amorphous claim that there has been past discrimination ... cannot justify the use of an unyielding racial quota."

The same interests are at work in the interplay between the disparate-treatment and disparate-impact provisions of Title VII. Congress has imposed liability on employers for unintentional discrimination in order to rid the workplace of "practices that are fair in form, but discriminatory in operation." But it has also prohibited employers from taking adverse employment actions "because of" race. Applying the strong-basis-in-evidence standard to Title VII gives effect to both the disparate-treatment and disparate-impact provisions, allowing violations of one in the name of compliance with the other only in certain, narrow circumstances. The standard leaves ample room for employers' voluntary compliance efforts, which are essential to the statutory scheme and to Congress's efforts to eradicate workplace discrimination. And the standard appropriately constrains employers' discretion in making race-based decisions: It limits that discretion to cases in which there is a strong basis in evidence of disparate-impact liability, but it is not so restrictive that it allows employers to act only when there is a provable, actual violation.

Resolving the statutory conflict in this way allows the disparate-impact prohibition to work in a manner that is consistent with other provisions of Title VII, including the prohibition on adjusting employment-related test scores on the basis of race. Examinations like those administered by the City create legitimate expectations on the part of those who took the tests. As is the case with any promotion exam, some of the firefighters here invested substantial time, money, and personal commitment in preparing for the tests. Employment tests can be an important part of a neutral selection system that safeguards against the very racial animosities Title VII was intended to prevent. Here, however, the firefighters saw their efforts invalidated by the City in sole reliance upon race-based statistics.

If an employer cannot rescore a test based on the candidates' race then it follows *a fortiori* that it may not take the greater step of discarding the test altogether to achieve a more desirable racial distribution of promotion-eligible candidates—absent a strong basis in evidence that the test was deficient and that discarding the results is necessary to avoid violating the disparate-impact provision. Restricting an employer's ability to discard test results (and thereby discriminate against qualified candidates on the basis of their race) also is in keeping with Title VII's express protection of bona fide promotional examinations.

For the foregoing reasons, we adopt the strong-basis-in-evidence standard as a matter of statutory construction to resolve any conflict between the disparate-treatment and disparate-impact provisions of Title VII.

Our statutory holding does not address the constitutionality of the measures taken here in purported compliance with Title VII. We also do not hold that meeting the strong-basis-in-evidence standard would satisfy the Equal Protection Clause in a future case. As we explain below, because respondents have not met their burden under Title VII, we need not decide whether a legitimate fear of disparate impact is ever sufficient to justify discriminatory treatment under the Constitution.

Nor do we question an employer's affirmative efforts to ensure that all groups have a fair opportunity to apply for promotions and to participate in the process by which promotions will be made. But once that process has been established and employers have made clear their selection criteria, they may not then invalidate the test results, thus upsetting an employee's legitimate expectation not to be judged on the basis of race. Doing so, absent a strong basis in evidence of an impermissible disparate impact, amounts to the sort of racial preference that Congress has disclaimed, and is antithetical to the notion of a workplace where individuals are guaranteed equal opportunity regardless of race.

Title VII does not prohibit an employer from considering, before administering a test or practice, how to design that test or practice in order to provide a fair opportunity for all individuals, regardless of their race. And when, during the test-design stage, an employer invites comments to ensure the test is fair, that process can provide a common ground for open discussions toward that end. We hold only that, under Title VII, before an employer can engage in intentional discrimination for the asserted purpose of avoiding or remedying an unintentional disparate impact, the employer must have a strong basis in evidence to believe it will be subject to disparate-impact liability if it fails to take the race-conscious, discriminatory action.

C. The City argues that, even under the strong-basis-in-evidence standard, its decision to discard the examination results was permissible under Title VII. That is incorrect. Even if respondents were motivated as a subjective matter by a desire to avoid committing disparate-impact discrimination, the record makes clear there is no support for the conclusion that respondents had an objective, strong basis in evidence to find the tests inadequate, with some consequent disparate-impact liability in violation of Title VII.

On this basis, we conclude that petitioners have met their obligation to demonstrate that there is "no genuine issue as to any material fact" and that they are "entitled to judgment as a matter of law." On a motion for summary judgment, "facts must be viewed in the light most favorable to the nonmoving party only if there is a 'genuine' dispute as to those facts." "Where the record taken as a whole could not lead a rational trier of fact to find for the nonmoving party, there is no genuine issue for trial." In this Court, the City's only defense is that it acted to comply with Title VII's disparate-impact provision. To succeed on their motion, then, petitioners must demonstrate that there can be no genuine dispute that there was no strong basis in evidence for the City to conclude it would face disparate-impact liability if it certified the examination results.

The racial adverse impact here was significant, and petitioners do not dispute that the City was faced with a prima facie case of disparate-impact liability. On the captain exam, the pass rate for white candidates was 64 percent but was 37.5 percent for both black and Hispanic candidates. On the lieutenant exam, the pass rate for white candidates was 58.1 percent; for black candidates, 31.6 percent; and for Hispanic candidates, 20 percent. The pass rates of minorities, which were approximately one-half the pass rates for white candidates, fall well below the 80-percent standard set by the EEOC to implement the disparate-impact provision of Title VII. Based on how the passing candidates ranked and an application of the "rule of three," certifying the examinations would have meant that the City could not have considered black candidates for any of the then-vacant lieutenant or captain positions.

Based on the degree of adverse impact reflected in the results, respondents were compelled to take a hard look at the examinations to determine whether certifying the results would have had an impermissible disparate impact. The problem for respondents is that a prima facie case of disparate-impact liability—essentially, a threshold showing of a significant statistical disparity, and nothing more—is far from a strong basis in evidence that the City would have been liable under Title VII had it certified the results. That is because the City could be liable for disparate-impact discrimination only if the examinations were not job related and consistent with business necessity, or if there existed an equally valid, less-discriminatory alternative that served the City's needs but that the City refused to adopt. We conclude there is no strong basis in evidence to establish that the test was deficient in either of these respects. We address each of the two points in turn, based on the record developed by the parties through discovery—a record that concentrates in substantial part on the statements various witnesses made to the CSB.

1.　There is no genuine dispute that the examinations were job-related and consistent with business necessity. The City's assertions to the contrary are "blatantly contradicted by the record." The CSB heard statements from Chad Legel (the IOS vice president) as well as city officials outlining the detailed steps IOS took to develop and administer the examinations. IOS devised the written examinations, which were the focus of the CSB's inquiry, after painstaking analyses of the captain and lieutenant positions—analyses in which IOS made sure that minorities were overrepresented. And IOS drew the questions from source material approved by the Department. Of the outside witnesses who appeared before the CSB, only one, Vincent Lewis, had reviewed the examinations in any detail, and he was the only one with any firefighting experience. Lewis stated that the "questions were relevant for both exams." The only other witness who had seen any part of the examinations, Christopher Hornick (a competitor of IOS's), criticized the fact that no one

within the Department had reviewed the tests—a condition imposed by the City to protect the integrity of the exams in light of past alleged security breaches. But Hornick stated that the exams "appea[r] to be ... reasonably good" and recommended that the CSB certify the results.

Arguing that the examinations were not job-related, respondents note some candidates' complaints that certain examination questions were contradictory or did not specifically apply to firefighting practices in New Haven. But Legel told the CSB that IOS had addressed those concerns—that it entertained "a handful" of challenges to the validity of particular examination questions, that it "reviewed those challenges and provided feedback [to the City] as to what we thought the best course of action was," and that he could remember at least one question IOS had thrown out ("offer[ing] credit to everybody for that particular question"). For his part, Hornick said he "suspect[ed] that some of the criticisms ... [leveled] by candidates" were not valid.

The City, moreover, turned a blind eye to evidence that supported the exams' validity. Although the City's contract with IOS contemplated that IOS would prepare a technical report consistent with EEOC guidelines for examination-validity studies, the City made no request for its report. After the January 2004 meeting between Legel and some of the city-official respondents, in which Legel defended the examinations, the City sought no further information from IOS, save its appearance at a CSB meeting to explain how it developed and administered the examinations. IOS stood ready to provide respondents with detailed information to establish the validity of the exams, but respondents did not accept that offer.

2.　Respondents also lacked a strong basis in evidence of an equally valid, less-discriminatory testing alternative that the City, by certifying the examination results, would necessarily have refused to adopt. Respondents raise three arguments to the contrary, but each argument fails. First, respondents refer to testimony before the CSB that a different composite-score calculation—weighting the written and oral examination scores 30/70—would have allowed the City to consider two black candidates for then-open lieutenant positions and one black candidate for then-open captain positions. (The City used a 60/40 weighting as required by its contract with the New Haven firefighters' union.) But respondents have produced no evidence to show that the 60/40 weighting was indeed arbitrary. In fact, because that formula was the result of a union-negotiated collective-bargaining agreement, we presume the parties negotiated that weighting for a rational reason. Nor does the record contain any evidence that the 30/70 weighting would be an equally valid way to determine whether candidates possess the proper mix of job knowledge and situational skills to earn promotions. Changing the weighting formula, moreover, could well have violated Title VII's prohibition of altering test scores on the basis of race. On this record, there is no basis to conclude that a 30/70 weighting was an equally valid alternative the City could have adopted.

Second, respondents argue that the City could have adopted a different interpretation of the "rule of three" that would have produced less discriminatory results. The rule, in the New Haven city charter, requires the City to promote only from "those applicants with the three highest scores" on a promotional examination. A state court has interpreted the charter to prohibit so-called "banding"—the City's previous practice of rounding scores to the nearest whole number and considering all candidates with the same whole-number score as being of one rank. Banding allowed the City to consider three ranks of candidates (with the possibility of multiple candidates filling each rank) for purposes of the rule of three. Respondents claim that employing banding here would have made four black and one Hispanic candidates eligible for then-open lieutenant and captain positions.

A state court's prohibition of banding, as a matter of municipal law under the charter, may not eliminate banding as a valid alternative under Title VII. We need not resolve that point, however. Here, banding was not a valid alternative for this reason: Had the City reviewed the exam results and then adopted banding to make the minority test scores appear higher, it would have violated Title VII's prohibition of adjusting test results on the basis of race. As a matter of law, banding was not an alternative available to

the City when it was considering whether to certify the examination results.

Third, and finally, respondents refer to statements by Hornick in his telephone interview with the CSB regarding alternatives to the written examinations. Hornick stated his "belie[f]" that an "assessment center process," which would have evaluated candidates' behavior in typical job tasks, "would have demonstrated less adverse impact." But Hornick's brief mention of alternative testing methods, standing alone, does not raise a genuine issue of material fact that assessment centers were available to the City at the time of the examinations and that they would have produced less adverse impact. Other statements to the CSB indicated that the Department could not have used assessment centers for the 2003 examinations. And although respondents later argued to the CSB that Hornick had pushed the City to reject the test results, the truth is that the essence of Hornick's remarks supported its certifying the test results. Hornick stated that adverse impact in standardized testing "has been in existence since the beginning of testing," and that the disparity in New Haven's test results was "somewhat higher but generally in the range that we've seen professionally." He told the CSB he was "not suggesting" that IOS "somehow created a test that had adverse impacts that it should not have had." And he suggested that the CSB should "certify the list as it exists."

Especially when it is noted that the strong-basis-in-evidence standard applies, respondents cannot create a genuine issue of fact based on a few stray (and contradictory) statements in the record. And there is no doubt respondents fall short of the mark by relying entirely on isolated statements by Hornick. Hornick had not "stud[ied] the test at length or in detail." And as he told the CSB, he is a "direct competitor" of IOS's. The remainder of his remarks showed that Hornick's primary concern—somewhat to the frustration of CSB members—was marketing his services for the future, not commenting on the results of the tests the City had already administered. Hornick's hinting had its intended effect: The City has since hired him as a consultant. As for the other outside witnesses who spoke to the CSB, Vincent Lewis (the retired fire captain) thought the CSB should certify the test results.

And Janet Helms (the Boston College professor) declined to review the examinations and told the CSB that, as a society, "we need to develop a new way of assessing people." That task was beyond the reach of the CSB, which was concerned with the adequacy of the test results before it.

3. On the record before us, there is no genuine dispute that the City lacked a strong basis in evidence to believe it would face disparate-impact liability if it certified the examination results. In other words, there is no evidence—let alone the required strong basis in evidence—that the tests were flawed because they were not job-related or because other, equally valid and less discriminatory tests were available to the City. Fear of litigation alone cannot justify an employer's reliance on race to the detriment of individuals who passed the examinations and qualified for promotions. The City's discarding the test results was impermissible under Title VII, and summary judgment is appropriate for petitioners on their disparate-treatment claim.

* * *

The record in this litigation documents a process that, at the outset, had the potential to produce a testing procedure that was true to the promise of Title VII: No individual should face workplace discrimination based on race. Respondents thought about promotion qualifications and relevant experience in neutral ways. They were careful to ensure broad racial participation in the design of the test itself and its administration. As we have discussed at length, the process was open and fair.

The problem, of course, is that after the tests were completed, the raw racial results became the predominant rationale for the City's refusal to certify the results. The injury arises in part from the high, and justified, expectations of the candidates who had participated in the testing process on the terms the City had established for the promotional process. Many of the candidates had studied for months, at considerable personal and financial expense, and thus the injury caused by the City's reliance on raw racial statistics at the end of the process was all the more severe. Confronted with arguments both for and against certifying the test results—and threats of a lawsuit either way—the City was required to make a difficult inquiry. But its hearings produced no strong evidence of a disparate-impact violation, and the City was not entitled to disregard the tests based solely on the racial disparity in the results.

Our holding today clarifies how Title VII applies to resolve competing expectations under the disparate-treatment [*61] and disparate-impact provisions. If, after it certifies the test results, the City faces a disparate-impact suit, then in light of our holding today it should be clear that the City would avoid disparate-impact liability based on the strong basis in evidence that, had it not certified the results, it would have been subject to disparate-treatment liability.

Petitioners are entitled to summary judgment on their Title VII claim, and we therefore need not decide the underlying constitutional question. The judgment of the Court of Appeals is reversed, and the cases are remanded for further proceedings consistent with this opinion.

It is so ordered.

PODBERESKY v. KIRWAN
United States Court of Appeals for the Fourth Circuit
(1994)
38 F.3d 147

WIDENER, Circuit Judge: The issue in the case is whether the University of Maryland at College Park may maintain a separate merit scholarship program that it voluntarily established for which only African-American students are eligible. Because we find that the district court erred in finding that the University had sufficient evidence of present effects of past discrimination to justify the program and in finding that the program is narrowly tailored to serve its stated objectives, we reverse ... and we remand for entry of judgment in favor of Podberesky.

... Daniel Podberesky challenges the University of Maryland's Banneker scholarship program, which is a merit- based program for which only African-American students are eligible. The University maintains a separate merit-based scholarship program, the Francis Scott Key program, which is not restricted to African-American students. Podberesky is Hispanic; he was therefore ineligible for consideration under the Banneker Program, although he met the academic and all other requirements for consideration. Podberesky was ineligible for consideration under the Key program because his academic credentials fell just shy of its more rigorous standards.

... The University claimed that four present effects of past discrimination exist at the University: (1) The University has a poor reputation within the African-American community; (2) African-Americans are underrepresented in the student population; (3) African-American students who enroll at the University have low retention and graduation rates; and (4) the atmosphere on campus is perceived as being hostile to African-American students. ...

Because it chose the Banneker Program, which excludes all races from consideration but one, as a remedial measure for its past discrimination against African-Americans, the University stands before us burdened with a presumption that its choice cannot be sustained. ...

We have established a two-step analysis for determining whether a particular race-conscious remedial measure can be sustained under the Constitution: (1) the proponent of the measure must demonstrate a "'strong basis in evidence for its conclusion that remedial action[is] necessary,'" and (2) the remedial measure must be narrowly tailored to meet the remedial goal. ... *Croson* ... makes clear that ... [t]o have a present effect of past discrimination sufficient to justify the program, the ... effects must themselves be examined to see whether they were caused by the past discrimination and whether they are of a type that justifies the program. ...

Turning to the present effects articulated by the University, ... the first effect, a poor reputation in the African-American community, and the fourth effect, a climate on campus that is perceived as being racially hostile, are [not] sufficient, standing alone, to justify the single-race Banneker Program. As the district court's opinion makes clear, any poor reputation the University may have in the African-American community is tied solely to knowledge of the University's discrimination before it admitted African-American students. There is no doubt that many Maryland residents, as well as some citizens in other States, know of the University's past segregation, and that fact cannot be denied. However, mere knowledge of historical fact is not the kind of present effect that can justify a race-exclusive remedy. If it were otherwise, as long as there are people who have access to history books, there will be programs such as this one. Our decisions do not permit such a result.

The hostile-climate effect proffered by the University suffers from another flaw, however. The main support for the University's assertion that the campus climate is hostile to African-American students is contained in a survey of student attitudes and reported results of student focus groups. ... The frequency and regularity of the incidents, as well as claimed instances of backlash to remedial measures, do not necessarily implicate past discrimination on the part of the University, as opposed to present societal discrimination. ...

... [S]ocietal discrimination ... cannot be used as a basis for supporting a race-conscious remedy. There is no doubt that racial tensions still exist in American society, including the campuses of our institutions of higher learning. However, these tensions and attitudes are not a sufficient ground for employing a race-conscious remedy at the University of Maryland.

We next turn to the two effects that rely on statistical data: underrepresentation of African-American students at the University and low retention and graduation rates for African-American students. ...

Even if we assumed that the University had demonstrated that African-Americans were underrepresented at the University and that the higher attrition rate was related to past discrimination, we could not uphold the Banneker Program. It is not narrowly tailored to remedy the underrepresentation and attrition problems. ...

... In determining whether the Banneker Program is narrowly tailored to accomplish its stated objective, we may consider possible race-neutral alternatives and whether the program actually furthers a different objective from the one it is claimed to remedy.

A. Attraction to Only High-Achieving Black Students

The district court found that the Banneker Program ... is employed by the University as an effective recruiting tool that draws high-achieving African-Americans to the University. The district court further noted that the University's "success in curing the vestiges of its past discrimination depends upon it attracting high-achieving African-Americans to the College Park campus." ... [T]he district court did not sufficiently connect the problems the University purports to remedy to the Banneker Program: low retention and graduation rates and underrepresentation. If the purpose of the program was to draw only high-achieving African American students to the University, it could not be sustained. High achievers, whether African-American or not, are not the group against which the University discriminated in the past.

B. Including Non-Residents of Maryland

The district court also erred in giving no weight to Podberesky's argument that the Banneker Program is not narrowly tailored because the scholarships are open to non-Maryland residents.[5] The district court stated that the goals of the program would be served "whether Banneker Scholars are Maryland natives or not." It is at once apparent that the Banneker Program considers all African-American students for merit scholarships at the expense of non-African-American Maryland students.

The University, throughout this case, has taken the position that the pool from which the students eligible to enter UMCP is drawn are from "qualified African-American high school students in Maryland," and "the University expects that the racial composition of its student body will reflect the racial composition of qualified college eligible high school graduates." While all of the prerequisites for membership in the pool were a matter of dispute between the parties, that the University measured its desired number of black students against Maryland high school graduates who are qualified to attend the University is not a matter of dispute. That being true, it is obvious that awarding Banneker Scholarships to non-residents of Maryland is not narrowly tailored to correcting the condition that the University argues, that not enough qualified African-American Maryland residents attend at College Park.

C. Arbitrary Reference Pool

The district court found the program to be narrowly tailored to increasing representation because an increase in the number of high-achieving African-American students would remedy the underrepresentation problem. The district court so found because it reasoned that the Banneker Scholars would serve as mentors and role

---

[5]In 1992, for example, 17 of the 31 Banneker scholarships were awarded to non-residents of Maryland. Podberesky says without refutation that in 1989 a Banneker scholarship was offered to a Jamaican. Thus, the University gives African-American a hemispheric meaning.

models for other African-American students, thereby attracting more African-American students. The Supreme Court has expressly rejected the role-model theory as a basis for implementing a race-conscious remedy, as do we. *Wygant v. Jackson Bd. of Educ.*

Furthermore, ... the district court failed to account for statistics regarding that percentage of otherwise eligible African-American high school graduates who either (1) chose not to go to any college; (2) chose to apply only to out-of-state colleges; (3) chose to postpone application to a four-year institution for reasons relating to economics or otherwise, such as spending a year or so in a community college to save money; or (4) voluntarily limited their applications to Maryland's predominantly African-American institutions. ...

We will not speculate as to what extent these variables might reduce the size of the reference pool, since no definitive information regarding these types of statistics is in the record. We can say with certainty, however, that the failure to account for these, and possibly other, nontrivial variables cannot withstand strict scrutiny. ...

D. Race-Neutral Alternatives

The district court also suggested that an increase in the number of high-achieving African-American students would remedy the low retention and graduation rates for African-American students at the University. Podberesky submitted a 1993 study by two University of Maryland professors which indicates that after the freshman year, in which grades are the principal problem, students leave the University for financial and other reasons.[6] Specifically, students who left the University "tended to be more likely to provide their own expenses, live off campus with long commutes, have a job with long hours, spend few free hours on campus, and have few friends on campus." "Males, minority groups and transfer students show greater attrition because they are more likely to provide their own expenses and have little time for campus activities and friends due to off campus living and work." That study suggests that the best

remedy is "campus job opportunities and convenient, attractive, and economically reasonable campus housing ... available to a greater proportion of students."

The district court rejected Podberesky's argument because it found that, in addition to economic hardship,

> in given cases an absence of commitment to the school because of its poor reputation in the community from which a student comes; the lack of shared experience with family members to help the student through the arduous process of higher education, the absence of African-American members of the faculty to serve as mentors and the existence of a hostile racial atmosphere on campus are other significant contributing factors.

The causes of the low retention rates submitted both by Podberesky and the University and found by the district court have little, if anything, to do with the Banneker Program. To the extent that the district court's opinion can be read as having found a connection between the University's poor reputation and hostile environment and the Banneker Program, it is on either a role model theory or a societal discrimination theory, neither of which can be sustained. In addition, there is no connection between the Banneker Program and shared experience with family members, African-American faculty members, or jobs and housing. Even if there is some connection between the two, the University has not made any attempt to show that it has tried, without success, any race-neutral solutions to the retention problem. Thus, the University's choice of a race-exclusive merit scholarship program as a remedy cannot be sustained.

Because we find that the University has not shown that its programs and quota goals are narrowly tailored, we reverse. ... [O]n remand, the district court will enter its order ... requiring the University to re-examine Podberesky's admission to the Banneker Program as of the date it was made. On such re-examination, the University will be enjoined from ... requir[ing] that the applicant be of the African-American race. ...

---

[6]Students participating in the survey were asked to check a list of factors that were factors in their decisions to leave the University. We note that the students had the opportunity to choose that they "felt discriminated against due to race, gender, religion, or sexual preference."

CHERYL J. HOPWOOD, et al. v. STATE OF TEXAS, et al.
United States Court of Appeals for the Fifth Circuit (1996)
78 F.3d 932

OPINION BY: JERRY E. SMITH

I

A. The University of Texas School of Law is one of the nation's leading law schools, consistently ranking in the top twenty. Accordingly, admission to the law school is fiercely competitive, with over 4,000 applicants a year competing to be among the ... entering class of about 500 students. Many of these applicants have some of the highest grades and test scores in the country.

Numbers are therefore paramount for admission. In the early 1990's, the law school largely based its initial admissions decisions upon an applicant's so-called Texas Index ("TI") number, a composite of undergraduate grade point average ('GPA') and Law School Aptitude Test ("LSAT") score.

Of course, the law school did not rely upon numbers alone. The admissions office necessarily exercised judgment in interpreting the individual scores of applicants. ...

Because of the large number of applicants and potential admissions factors, the TI's administrative usefulness was its ability to sort candidates. For the class entering in 1992 (the admissions group at issue in this case) the law school placed the typical applicant in one of three categories according to his TI scores: "presumptive admit," "presumptive deny," or a middle "discretionary zone." An applicant's TI category determined how extensive a review his application would receive. [Most applicants in the "presumptive admit" category received offers of admission with little review. Most applicants in the "presumptive

deny" category were rejected with little consideration. Applicants in the middle "discretionary zone" received the most extensive review].

Blacks and Mexican Americans were treated differently from other candidates, however. [T]he TI ranges that were used to place them into the three admissions categories were lowered to allow the law school to consider and admit more of them.

These disparate standards greatly affected a candidate's chance of admission. For example, ...-because the presumptive denial score for whites was a TI of 192 or lower, and the presumptive admit TI for minorities was 189 or higher, a minority candidate with a TI of 189 or above almost certainly would be admitted, even though his score was considerably below the level at which a white candidate almost certainly would be rejected.

B. Cheryl Hopwood, Douglas Carvell, Kenneth Elliott, and David Rogers (the "plaintiffs") applied for admission to the 1992 entering law school class. All four were white residents of Texas. ...

The plaintiffs were considered as discretionary zone candidates. [They] had TI's ... at the top end of [the white resident] discretionary zone. [Following a review, all their applications were rejected. However, minority candidates with lower TIs were presumptively admitted.]

II

The plaintiffs sued primarily under the Equal Protection Clause of the Fourteenth Amendment. ... The plaintiffs centra claim is that they were subjected to unconstitutional racial discrimination by the law school's evaluation of their admissions applications.

III

The central purpose of the Equal Protection Clause "is to prevent the States from purposefully discriminating between individuals on the basis of race." It seeks ultimately to render the issue of race irrelevant in governmental decisionmaking.

Accordingly, discrimination based upon race is highly suspect.

[T]he Supreme Court recently has required that any governmental action that expressly distinguishes between persons on the basis of race be held to the most exacting scrutiny.

Under strict scrutiny analysis, we ask two questions: (1) Does the racial classification serve a compelling government interest, and (2) is it narrowly tailored to the achievement of that goal?

With these general principles of equal protection in mind, we turn to the specific issue of whether the law school's consideration of race as a factor in admissions violates the Equal Protection Clause.

A.

1.
* * * *
2.

Here, the plaintiffs argue that diversity is not a compelling governmental interest. …

We agree. …

Indeed, recent Supreme Court precedent shows that the diversity interest will not satisfy strict scrutiny. [T]he Court appears to have decided that there is essentially only one compelling state interest to justify racial classifications: remedying past wrongs.

Within the general principles of the Fourteenth Amendment, the use of race in admissions for diversity in higher education contradicts, rather than furthers, the aims of equal protection. Diversity fosters, rather than minimizes, the use of race. It treats minorities as a group, rather than as individuals. It may further remedial purposes but, just as likely, may promote improper racial stereotypes, thus fueling racial hostility.

The use of race, in and of itself, to choose students simply achieves a student body that looks different. Such a criterion is no more rational on its own terms

than would be choices based upon the physical size or blood type of applicants.

Accordingly, we see the case law as sufficiently established that the use of ethnic give heterogeneity, even as part of the consideration of a number of factors, is unconstitutional.

While the use of race per se is proscribed, state-supported schools may reasonably consider a host of factors—some of which may have some correlation with race—in making admissions decisions. A university may properly favor one applicant over another because of his ability to play the cello, make a downfield tackle, or understand chaos theory. An admissions process may also consider an applicant's home state or relationship to school alumni. Law schools specifically may look at things such as unusual or substantial extracurricular activities in college, which may be atypical factors affecting undergraduate grades. Schools may even consider factors such as whether an applicant's parents attended college or the applicant's economic and social background.

[I]ndividuals, with their own conceptions of life, further diversity of viewpoint. Plaintiff Hopwood is a fair example of an applicant with a unique background. She is the now-thirty-two-year-old wife of a member of the Armed Forces stationed in San Antonio and, more significantly, is raising a severely handicapped child. Her circumstance would bring a different perspective to the law school. The school might consider this an advantage to her in the application process, or it could decide that her family situation would be too much of a burden on her academic performance.

We do not opine on which way the law school should weigh Hopwood's qualifications; we only observe that "diversity" can take many forms. To foster such diversity, state universities and law schools and other governmental entities must scrutinize applicants individually, rather than resorting to the dangerous proxy of race.

B.   We now turn to the district court's determination that "the remedial purpose of the law school's affirmative action program is a compelling government objective."

In contrast to its approach to the diversity rationale, a majority of the Supreme Court has held that a state actor may racially classify where it has a "strong basis in the evidence for its conclusion that remedial action was necessary." Generally, in order to justify an affirmative action program, the State must show there are 'present effects of past discrimination.'"

1. The Supreme Court has "insisted upon some showing of prior discrimination by the governmental unit involved before allowing limited use of racial classifications in order to remedy such discrimination."

   In order for ... a racial preference program at the law school [to be allowed], it must be because of past wrongs at that school.

2. Next, the relevant governmental discriminator must prove that there are present effects of past discrimination of the type that justify the racial classifications at issue ...

   [A]s part of showing that the alleged present effects of past discrimination in fact justify the racial preference program at issue, the law school must show that it adopted the program specifically to remedy the identified present effects of the past discrimination.

   Here, according to the district court: "The evidence presented at trial indicates those effects include [1] the law school's lingering reputation in the minority community, particularly with prospective students, as a "white" school; [2] an underrepresentation of minorities in the student body; and [3] some perception that the law school is a hostile environment for minorities."

   As a legal matter, the district court erred in concluding that the first and third effects it identified, bad reputation and hostile environment, were sufficient to sustain the use of race in the admissions process. The Fourth Circuit examined similar arguments in Podberesky, a recent case that struck down the use of race-based scholarships. The university in that case sought, in part, to justify a separate scholarship program based solely upon race because of the university's "poor reputation within the African-American community" and because "the atmosphere on campus [was] perceived as being hostile to African-American students."

   The Podberesky court rejected the notion that either of these rationales could support the single-race scholarship program. The court reasoned that any poor reputation by the school "is tied solely to knowledge of the University's discrimination before it admitted African-American students." The court found that "mere knowledge of historical fact is not the kind of present effect that can justify a race-exclusive remedy. If it were otherwise, as long as there are people who have access to history books, there will be programs such as this."

We concur in the Fourth Circuit's observation that knowledge of historical fact simply cannot justify current racial classifications.

The Podberesky court rejected the hostile-environment claims by observing that the ... racial tensions were the result of present societal discrimination. There was simply no showing of action by the university that contributed to any racial tension. Similarly, one cannot conclude that the law school's past discrimination has created any current hostile environment for minorities. While the school once did practice de jure discrimination in denying admission to blacks, the Court in Sweatt v. Painter (1950), struck down the law school's program. Any other discrimination by the law school in the 1960's.

By the late 1960's, the school had implemented its first program designed to recruit minorities, and it now engages in an extensive minority recruiting program that includes significant amount of scholarship money. The vast majority on the faculty, staff, and students at the law school had absolutely nothing to do with any discrimination that the law school practiced in the past.

In such a case, one cannot conclude that a hostile environment is the present effect of past discrimination. Any racial tension at the law school is most certainly the results of present societal discrimination and, if anything, is contributed to, rather than alleviated by, the overt and prevalent consideration of race in admissions.

The law school wisely concentrates only on the second effect the district court identified: underrepresentation of minorities because of past discrimination. The law school argues that we should consider the prior discrimination by the State of Texas and its educational system rather than of the law school. The school contends that this prior discrimination by the state had a direct effect on the educational attainment of the pool of minority applicants and that the discriminatory admissions program was implemented partially to discharge the school's duty of eliminating the vestiges of past segregation.

No one disputes that Texas has a history of racial discrimination in education. We have already discussed, however, that the Croson Court unequivocally restricted the proper scope of the remedial interest to the state actor that had previously discriminated. The district court squarely found that "in recent history, there is no evidence of overt officially sanctioned discrimination at the

University of Texas." As a result, past discrimination in education, other than at the law-school, cannot justify the present consideration of race in law school admissions.

In sum, the law school has failed to show a compelling state interest in remedying the present effects of past discrimination sufficient to maintain the use of race in its admissions system. Accordingly, it is unnecessary for us to examine ... [whether] the law school's admissions programs was ... narrowly tailored. ...

In summary, we hold that the University of Texas School of Law may not use race as a factor in deciding which applicants to admit in order to achieve a diverse student body, to combat the perceived effects of a hostile environment at the law school, to alleviate the law school's poor reputation in the minority community, or to eliminate any present effects of past discrimination by actors other than the law school.

Because the law school has proffered these justifications for its use of race in admissions, the plaintiffs have satisfied their burden of showing that they were scrutinized under an unconstitutional admissions system. The plaintiffs are entitled to reapply under an admissions system that invokes none of these serious constitutional infirmities.

DISSENT BY: STEWART

That it is the University of Texas School of Law's admissions policy at issue is a fact whose significance has not been lost on any of us. In 1946, this very school denied admission to Heman Marion Sweatt because he was black, prompting him to sue the University. Sweatt's real difficulties began fifty years before when the United States Supreme Court scripted one of this nation's most evil conceits in Plessy v. Ferguson, (1896), declaring "separate but equal" treatment of black Americans constitutional. Plessy was no more than a license for continued racial discrimination. However, in 1950, the Supreme Court held that excluding Sweatt on account of his race violated the Equal Protection Clause of the Fourteenth Amendment. A year after the Supreme Court ordered that Sweatt be admitted, he left the law school "without graduating after being subjected to racial slurs from students and professors, cross burnings, and tire slashings." Furthermore, "the record reflects that during the 1950s, and into the 1960s, the University of Texas continued to implement discriminatory policies against both black and Mexican-American students." It was not until 1983 that Texas even agreed, after years of threats of federal action, to an acceptable plan to desegregate its higher education system. In 1987 and again in 1994, the Department of Education instructed Texas to maintain its plan. To this day, Texas's higher education system still has not been declared in compliance with Title VI and the Fourteenth Amendment. "The life of the law," Justice Oliver Wendell Holmes observed, "is not logic, but experience." To divorce the time in which it was legally possible for Sweatt to attend the Law School from the reality he experienced there is to ignore the very insidiousness of racial discrimination. It was the vestiges of that discrimination which, far from being destroyed, thrived and drove Sweatt out of the Law School. We act no less callously now. ...

BARBARA GRUTTER, PETITIONER v. LEE BOLLINGER et al.
Supreme Court of the United States

June 23, 2003, Decided

JUSTICE O'CONNOR delivered the opinion of the Court.

This case requires us to decide whether the use of race as a factor in student admissions by the University of Michigan Law School (Law School) is unlawful.

The Law School ranks among the Nation's top law schools. It receives more than 3,500 applications each year for a class of around 350 students. Seeking to "admit a group of students who individually and collectively are among the most capable," the Law School looks for individuals with "substantial promise for success in law school" and "a strong likelihood of succeeding in the practice of law and contributing in diverse ways to the well-being of others." More broadly, the Law School seeks "a mix of students with varying backgrounds and experiences who will respect and learn from each other." In 1992, the dean of the Law School charged a faculty committee with crafting a written admissions policy to implement these goals. In particular, the Law School sought to ensure that its efforts to achieve student body diversity complied with this Court's most recent ruling on the use of race in university admissions. See *Regents of Univ. of Cal. v. Bakke.* Upon the unanimous adoption of the committee's report by the Law School faculty, it became the Law School's official admissions policy.

The hallmark of that policy is its focus on academic ability coupled with a flexible assessment of applicants' talents, experiences, and potential "to contribute to the learning of those around them." The policy requires admissions officials to evaluate each applicant based on all the information available in the file, including a personal statement, letters of recommendation, and an essay describing the ways in which the applicant will contribute to the life and diversity of the Law school. In reviewing an applicant's file, admissions officials must consider the applicant's undergraduate grade point average (GPA) and Law School Admissions Test (LSAT)

score because they are important (if imperfect) predictors of academic success in law school. The policy stresses that "no applicant should be admitted unless we expect that applicant to do well enough to graduate with no serious academic problems."

The policy makes clear, however, that even the highest possible score does not guarantee admission to the Law School. Nor does a low score automatically disqualify an applicant. Rather, the policy requires admissions officials to look beyond grades and test scores to other criteria that are important to the Law School's educational objectives. So-called "'Soft' variables" such as "the enthusiasm of recommenders, the quality of the undergraduate institution, the quality of the applicant's essay, and the areas and difficulty of undergraduate course selection" are all brought to bear in assessing an "applicant's likely contributions to the intellectual and social life of the institution."

The policy aspires to "achieve that diversity which has the potential to enrich everyone's education and thus make a law school class stronger than the sum of its parts." The policy does not restrict the types of diversity contributions eligible for "substantial weight" in the admissions process, but instead recognizes "many possible bases for diversity admissions." The policy does, however, reaffirm the Law School's longstanding commitment to "one particular type of diversity," that is, "racial and ethnic diversity with special reference to the inclusion of students from groups which have been historically discriminated against, like African-Americans, Hispanics and Native Americans, who without this commitment might not be represented in out student body in meaningful numbers." By enrolling a "critical mass' of [underrepresented] minority students," the Law School seeks to "ensure their ability to make unique contributions to the character of the Law School."

The policy does not define diversity "solely in terms of racial and ethnic status." Nor is the policy "insensitive to the competition among all students for admission to the Law School." Rather, the policy seeks to guide admissions officers in "producing classes both diverse and academically outstanding, classes made up of students who promise to continue the tradition of outstanding contribution by Michigan Graduates to the legal profession."

Petitioner Barbara Grutter is a white Michigan resident who applied to the Law School in 1996 with a 3.8 grade point average and 161 LSAT score. The Law School initially placed petitioner on a waiting list, but subsequently rejected her application. In December 1997, petitioner filed suit in the United States District Court for the Eastern District of Michigan against the Law School, the Regents of the University of Michigan, Lee Bollinger (Dean of the Law School from 1987 to 1994, and President of the University of Michigan from 1996 to 2002), Jeffrey Lehman (Dean of the Law School), and Dennis Shields (Director of Admissions at the Law School from 1991 until 1998). Petitioner alleged that respondents discriminated against her on the basis of race in violation of the *Fourteenth Amendment*; Title VI of the Civil Rights Act of 1964, and Rev. Stat. §1977, as amended, *42 U.S.C §1981.*

Petitioner further alleged that her application was rejected because the Law School uses race as a "predominant" factor, giving applicants who belong to certain minority groups "a significantly greater chance of admission than students with similar credentials from disfavored racial groups." Petitioner also alleged that respondents "had no compelling interest to justify their use of race in the admissions process." Petitioner requested compensatory and punitive damages, an order requiring the Law School to offer her admission, and an injunction prohibiting the Law School from continuing to discriminate on the basis of race. Petitioner clearly has standing to bring this lawsuit.

During the 15-day bench trial, the parties introduced extensive evidence concerning the Law School's use of race in the admissions process. Dennis Shields, Director of Admissions when petitioner applied to the Law School, testified that he did not direct his staff to admit a particular percentage or number of minority students, but rather to consider an applicant's race along with all other factors. Shields testified that at the height of the admissions season, he would frequently consult the so-called "daily reports" that kept track of the racial and ethnic composition of the class (along with other information such as residency status and gender). This was done,

Shields testified, to ensure that a critical mass of underrepresented minority students would be reached so as to realize the educational benefits of a diverse student body. Shields stressed, however, that he did not seek to admit any particular number or percentage of underrepresented minority students.

Erica Munzel, who succeeded Shields as Director of Admissions, testified that "'critical mass'" means "'meaningful numbers'" or "'meaningful representation,'" which she understood to mean a number that encourages underrepresented minority students to participate in the classroom and not feel isolated. Munzel stated there is no number, percentage, or range of numbers or percentages that constitute critical mass. Munzel also asserted that she must consider the race of applicants because a critical mass of underrepresented minority students could not be enrolled if admissions decisions were based primarily on undergraduate GPAs and LSAT scores.

The current Dean of the Law School, Jeffrey Lehman, also testified. Like the other Law School witnesses, Lehman did not quantify critical mass in terms of numbers or percentages. He indicated that critical mass means numbers such that underrepresented minority students do not feel isolated or like spokespersons for their race. When asked about the extent to which race is considered in admissions, Lehman testified that it varies from one applicant to another. In some cases, according to Lehman's testimony, an applicant's race may play no role, while in others it may be a "'determinative'" factor.

The District Court heard extensive testimony from Professor Richard Lempert, who chaired the faculty committee that drafted the 1992 policy. Lempert emphasized that the Law School seeks students with diverse interests and backgrounds to enhance classroom discussion and the educational experience both inside and outside the classroom. When asked about the policy's "'commitment to racial and ethnic diversity with special reference to the inclusion of students from groups which have been historically discriminated against,'" Lempert explained that this language did not purport to remedy past discrimination, but rather to include students who may bring to the Law School a perspective different from that of members of groups which have not been the victims of such discrimination. Lempert acknowledged that other groups, such as Asians and Jews, have experienced discrimination, but explained they were not mentioned in the policy because individuals who are members of those groups were already being admitted to the Law School in significant numbers.

Kent Syverud was the final witness to testify about the Law School's use of race in admissions decisions. Syverud was a professor at the Law School when the 1992 admissions policy was adopted and is now Dean of Vanderbilt Law School. In addition to his testimony at trial, Syverud submitted several expert reports on the educational benefits of diversity. Syverud's testimony indicated that when a critical mass of underrepresented minority students is present, racial stereotypes lose their force because nonminority students learn there is no "'minority viewpoint'" but rather a variety of viewpoints among minority students.

In an attempt to quantify the extent to which the Law School actually considers race in making admissions decisions, the parties introduced voluminous evidence at trial. Relying on data obtained from the Law School, petitioner's expert, Dr. Kinley Larntz, generated and analyzed "admissions grids" for the years in question (1995–2000). These grids show the number of applicants and the number of admittees for all combinations of GPAs and LSAT scores. Dr. Larntz made "'cell-by-cell'" comparisons between applicants of different races to determine whether a statistically significant relationship existed between race and admission rates. He concluded that membership in certain minority groups "'is an extremely strong factor in the decision for acceptance,'" and that applicants from these minority groups "'are given an extremely large allowance for admission'" as compared to applicants who are members of nonfavored groups. Dr. Larntz conceded, however, that race is not the predominant factor in the Law School's admissions calculus.

Dr. Stephen Raudenbush, the Law School's expert, focused on the predicted effect of eliminating race as a factor in the Law School's admission process. In Dr. Raudenbush's view, a race-blind admissions system would have a "'very dramatic,'" negative effect on underrepresented minority admissions. He testified that in 2000, 35 percent of underrepresented minority applicants were admitted. Dr. Raudenbush predicted that if race were not considered, only 10 percent of those applicants would have been admitted. Under this scenario, underrepresented minority students would have comprised 4 percent of the entering class in 2000 instead of the actual figure of 14.5 percent.

We granted certiorari to resolve the disagreement among the Courts of Appeals on a question of national importance: Whether diversity is a compelling interest that can justify the narrowly tailored use of race in selecting applicants for admission to public universities. Compare *Hopwood v. Texas*, (holding that diversity is not a compelling state interest), with *Smith v. University of Wash. Law School*, (holding that it is).

Since this Court's splintered decision in *Bakke*, Justice Powell's opinion announcing the judgment of the Court has served as the touchstone for constitutional analysis of race-conscious admissions policies. Public and private universities across the Nation have modeled their own admissions programs on Justice Powell's views on permissible race-conscious policies. We therefore discuss Justice Powell's opinion in some detail.

Justice Powell began by stating that "the guarantee of equal protection cannot mean one thing when applied to one individual and something else when applied to a person of another color. If both are not accorded the same protection, then it is not equal." In Justice Powell's view, when governmental decisions "touch upon an individual's race or ethnic background, he is entitled to a judicial determination that the burden he is asked to bear on that basis is precisely tailored to serve a compelling governmental interest." Under this exacting standard, only one of the interests asserted by the university survived Justice Powell's scrutiny.

First, Justice Powell rejected an interest in "'reducing the historic deficit of traditionally disfavored minorities in medical schools and in the medical profession'" as an unlawful interest in racial balancing. Second, Justice Powell rejected an interest in remedying societal discrimination because such measures would risk placing unnecessary burdens on innocent third parties "who bear no responsibility for whatever harm the beneficiaries of the special admissions programs are thought to have suffered." Third, Justice Powell rejected an interest in "increasing the number of physicians who will practice in communities currently underserved," concluding that even if such an interest could be compelling in some circumstances the program under review was not "geared to promote that goal."

Justice Powell approved the university's use of race to further only one interest: "the attainment of a diverse student body." With the important proviso that "constitutional limitations protecting individual rights may not be disregarded," Justice Powell grounded his analysis in the academic freedom that "long has been viewed as a special concern of the *First Amendment*." Justice Powell emphasized that nothing less than the "'nation's future depends upon leaders trained through wide exposure' to the ideas and mores of students as diverse as this Nation of many peoples." In seeking the "right to select those students who will contribute the most to the 'robust exchange of ideas,'" a university seeks "to achieve a goal that is of paramount importance in the fulfillment of its mission." Both "tradition and experience lend support to the view that the contribution of diversity is substantial."

Justice Powell was, however, careful to emphasize that in his view race "is only one element in a range of factors a university properly may consider in attaining the goal of a heterogeneous student body." For Justice Powell, "it is not an interest in simple ethnic diversity, in which a specified percentage of the student body is in effect guaranteed to be members of selected ethnic groups," that can justify the use of race. Rather, "the diversity that furthers a compelling state interest encompasses a far broader array of qualifications and characteristics of which racial or ethnic origin is but a single though important element."

The *Equal Protection Clause* provides that no State shall "deny to any person within its jurisdiction the equal protection of the laws. Because the *Fourteenth Amendment* "protects *persons*, not *groups*," all "governmental action based on race—a *group* classification long recognized as in most circumstances irrelevant and therefore prohibited—should be subjected to detailed judicial inquiry to ensure that the *personal* right to equal protection of the laws has not been infringed." We are a "free people whose institutions are founded upon the doctrine of equality." It follows from that principle that "government may treat people differently because of their race only for the most compelling reasons."

We have held that all racial classifications imposed by government "must be analyzed by a reviewing court under strict scrutiny." This means that such classifications are constitutional only if they are narrowly tailored to further compelling governmental interests. "Absent searching judicial inquiry into the justification for such race-based measures," we have no way to determine what "classifications are 'benign' or 'remedial' and what classifications are in fact motivated by illegitimate notions of racial inferiority or simple racial politics." we apply strict scrutiny to all racial classifications to "'smoke out' illegitimate uses of race by assuring that [government] is pursuing a goal important enough to warrant use of a highly suspect tool."

Strict scrutiny is not "strict in theory, but fatal in fact." Although all governmental uses of race are subject to strict scrutiny, not all are invalidated by it. As we have explained, "whenever the government treats any person unequally because of his or her race, that person has suffered an injury that falls squarely within the language and spirit of the Constitution's guarantee of equal protection." But that observation "says nothing about the ultimate validity of

any particular law; that determination is the job of the court applying strict scrutiny." When race-based action is necessary to further a compelling governmental interest, such action does not violate the constitutional guarantee of equal protection so long as the narrow-tailoring requirement is also satisfied.

Context matters when reviewing race-based governmental action under the *Equal Protection Clause*. In *Adarand Constructors, Inc. v. Pena*, we made clear that strict scrutiny must take "'relevant differences' into account. Indeed, as we explained, that is its "fundamental purpose." Not every decision influenced by race is equally objectionable and strict scrutiny is designed to provide a framework for carefully examining the importance and the sincerity of the reasons advanced by the governmental decisionmaker for the use of race in that particular context.

With these principles in mind, we turn to the question whether the Law School's use of race is justified by a compelling state interest. Before this Court, as they have throughout this litigation, respondents assert only one justification for their use of race in the admissions process: obtaining "the educational benefits that flow from a diverse student body." In other words, the Law School asks us to recognize, in the context of higher education, a compelling state interest in student body diversity.

We first wish to dispel the notion that the Law School's argument has been foreclosed, either expressly or implicitly, by our affirmative-action cases decided since *Bakke*. It is true that some language in those opinions might be read to suggest that remedying past discrimination is the only permissible justification for race-based governmental action. But we have never held that the only governmental use of race that can survive strict scrutiny is remedying past discrimination. Nor, since *Bakke*, have we directly addressed the use of race in the context of public higher education. Today, we hold that the Law School has a compelling interest in attaining a diverse student body.

The Law School's educational judgment that such diversity is essential to its educational mission is one to which we defer. The Law School's assessment that diversity will, in fact, yield educational benefits is substantiated by respondents and their *amici*. Our scrutiny of the interest asserted by the Law School is no less strict for taking into account complex educational judgements in an area that lies primarily within the expertise of the university. Our holding today is in keeping with our tradition of giving a degree of deference to a university's academic decisions, within constitutionally prescribed limits.

We have long recognized that, given the important purpose of public education and the expansive freedoms of speech and thought associated with the university environment, universities occupy a special niche in our constitutional tradition. In announcing the principle of student body diversity as a compelling state interest, Justice Powell Invoked our cases recognizing a constitutional dimension, grounded in the *First Amendment*, of educational autonomy: "The freedom of a university to make its own judgments as to education includes the selection of its student body." From this premise, Justice Powell reasoned that by claiming "the right to select those students who will contribute the most to the 'robust exchange of ideas,'" a university "seeks to achieve a goal that is of paramount importance in the fulfillment of its mission." Our conclusion that the Law School has a compelling interest in a diverse student body is informed by our view that attaining a diverse student body is at the heart of the Law School's proper institutional mission, and that "good faith" on the part of a university is "presumed" absent "a showing to the contrary."

As part of its goal of "assembling a class that is both exceptionally academically qualified and broadly diverse, " the Law School seeks to "enroll a 'critical mass' of minority students." The Law School's interest is not simply "to assure within its student body some specified percentage of a particular group merely because of its race or ethnic origin." That would amount to outright racial balancing, which is patently unconstitutional. Rather, the Law School's concept of critical mass is defined by reference to the educational benefits that diversity is designed to produce.

These benefits are substantial. As the District Court emphasized, that Law School's admissions policy promotes "cross-racial understanding," helps to break down racial stereotypes, and "enables [students] to better understand persons of different races." These benefits are "important and laudable," because "classroom discussion is livelier, more spirited, and simply more enlightening and interesting" when the students have "the greatest possible variety of backgrounds." The Law School's claim of a compelling interest is further bolstered by its *amici*, who point to the educational benefits that flow from student body diversity. In addition to the expert studies and reports entered into evidence at trial, numerous studies show that student body diversity promotes learning outcomes, and "better prepares students for an increasingly diverse workforce and society, and better prepares them as professionals."

These benefits are not theoretical but real, as major American businesses have made clear that the skills needed in today's increasingly global marketplace can only be developed through exposure to widely diverse people, cultures, ideas, and viewpoints. What is more, high-ranking retired officers and civilian leaders of the United States military assert that, "based on [their] decades of experience," a "highly qualified, racially diverse officers corps ... is essential to the military's ability to fulfill its principle mission to provide national security." The primary sources for the Nation's officer corps are the service academies and the Reserve Officers Training Corps (ROTC), the latter comprising students already admitted to participating colleges and universities. At present, "the military cannot achieve an officer corps that is *both* highly qualified *and* racially diverse unless the service academies and the ROTC used limited race-conscious recruiting and admissions policies." To fulfill its mission, the military "must be selective in admissions for training and education for the officer corps, *and* it must train and educate a highly qualified, racially diverse officer corps in a racially diverse setting." We agree that "it requires only a small step from this analysis to conclude that our country's other most selective institutions must remain both diverse and selective."

We have repeatedly acknowledged the overriding importance of preparing students for work and citizenship, describing education as pivotal to "sustaining our political and cultural heritage" with a fundamental role in maintaining the fabric of society. This Court has long recognized that "education ... is the very foundation of good citizenship." *Brown v. Board of Education*. For this reason, the diffusion of Knowledge and opportunity through public institutions of higher education must be accessible to all individuals regardless of race or ethnicity. The United States, as *amicus curiae*, affirms that "ensuring that public institutions are open and available to all segments of American society, including people of all races and ethnicities, represents a paramount government objective." And, "nowhere is the importance of such openness more acute than in the context of higher education." Effective participation by members of all racial and ethnic groups in the civic life of our Nation is essential if the dream of one Nation indivisible, is to be realized.

Moreover, universities, and in particular, law schools, represent the training ground for a large number of our Nation's leaders. *Sweatt v. Painter*. Individuals with law degrees occupy roughly half the state governorships, more than half the seats in the United States Senate, and more than a third of the seats in the United States House of Representatives. The pattern is even more striking when it comes to highly selective law schools. A handful of these schools accounts for 25 of the 100 United States Senators, 74 United States Courts of Appeals judges, and nearly 200 of the more than 600 United States District Court judges.

In order to cultivate a set of leaders with legitimacy in the eyes of the citizenry, it is necessary that the path to leadership be visibly open to talented and qualified individuals of every race and ethnicity. All members of our heterogeneous society must have confidence in the openness and integrity of the educational institutions that provide this training. As we have recognized, law schools "cannot be effective in isolation from the individuals and institutions with which the law interacts." Access to legal education (and thus the legal profession) must be inclusive of talented and qualified individuals of every race and ethnicity, so that all members of our heterogeneous society may participate in the educational institutions that provide the training and education necessary to succeed in America.

The Law School does not premise its need for critical mass on "any belief that minority students always (or even consistently) express some characteristic minority viewpoint on any issue." To the contrary, diminishing the force of such stereotypes is both a crucial part of the Law School's mission, and one that it cannot accomplish with only token numbers of minority students. Just as growing up in a particular region or having particular professional experiences is likely to affect an individual's views, so too is one's own, unique experience of being a racial minority in a society, like our own, in which race unfortunately still matters. The Law School has determined, based on its experience and expertise, that a "critical mass" of underrepresented minorities is necessary to further its compelling interest in securing the educational benefits of a diverse student body.

Even in the limited circumstance when drawing racial distinctions is permissible to further a compelling state interest, government is still "constrained in how it may pursue that end: The means chosen to accomplish the [government's] asserted purpose must be specifically and narrowly framed to accomplish that purpose." The purpose of the narrow tailoring requirement is to ensure that "the means chosen 'fit' … the compelling goal so closely that there is little or no possibility that the motive for the classification was illegitimate racial prejudice or stereotype."

Since *Bakke*, we have had no occasion to define the contours of the narrow-tailoring inquiry with respect to race-conscious university admissions programs. That inquiry must be calibrated to fit the distinct issues raised by the use of race to achieve student body diversity in public higher education. Contrary to JUSTICE KENNEDY's assertions, we do not "abandon[ ] strict scrutiny." Rather, as we have already explained, *ante*, at 15, we adhere to *Adarand's* teaching that the very purpose of strict scrutiny is to take such "relevant differences into account."

To be narrowly tailored, a race-conscious admissions program cannot use a quota system—it cannot "insulate each category of applicants with certain desired qualifications from competition with all other applicants." Instead, a university may consider race or ethnicity only as a "'plus' in a particular applicant's file," without "insulating the individual from comparison with all other candidates for the available seats." In other words, an admissions program must be "flexible enough to consider all pertinent elements of diversity in light of the particular qualifications of each applicant, and to place them on the same footing for consideration, although not necessarily according them the same weight."

We find that the Law School's admissions program bears the hallmarks of a narrowly tailored plan. As Justice Powell made clear in *Bakke*, truly individualized consideration demands that race be used in a flexible, nonmechanical way. It follows from this mandate that universities cannot establish quotas for members of certain racial groups or put members of those groups on separate admissions tracks. Nor can universities insulate applicants who belong to certain racial or ethnic groups from the competition for admission. *Ibid.* Universities can, however, consider race or ethnicity more flexibly as a "plus" factor in the context of individualized consideration of each and every applicant. *Ibid.*

We are satisfied that the Law School's admissions program, like the Harvard plan described by Justice Powell, does not operate as a quota. Properly understood, a "quota" is a program in which a certain fixed number or proportion of opportunities are "reserved exclusively for certain minority groups." Quotas "'impose a fixed number or percentage which must be attained, or which cannot be exceeded,'" and "insulate the individual from comparison with all other candidates for the available seats." In contrast, "a permissible goal … requires only a good-faith effort … to come within a range demarcated by the goal itself," and permits consideration of race as a "plus" factor in any given case while still ensuring that each candidate "competes with all other qualified applicants," *Johnson v. Transportation Agency, Santa Clara Cty.*

Justice Powell's distinction between the medical school's rigid 16-seat quota and Harvard's flexible use of race as a "plus" factor is instructive. Harvard certainly had minimum *goals* for minority enrollment, even if it had no specific number firmly in mind. What is more, Justice Powell flatly rejected the argument that Harvard's program was "the functional equivalent of a quota" merely because it had some "'plus'" for race, or gave greater "weight" to race than to some other factors, in order to achieve student body diversity.

The Law School's goal of attaining a critical mass of underrepresented minority students does not transform its program into a quota. As the Harvard plan described by Justice Powell recognized, there is of course "some relationship between numbers and achieving the benefits to be derived from a diverse student body, and between numbers and providing a reasonable environment for those students admitted." "Some attention to numbers," without more, does not transform a flexible admissions system into a rigid quota.

That a race-conscious admissions program does not operate as a quota does not, by itself, satisfy the requirement of individualized consideration. When using race as a "plus" factor in university admissions, a university's admissions program must remain flexible enough to ensure that each applicant is evaluated as an individual and not in a way that makes an applicant's race or ethnicity the defining feature of his or her application. The importance of this individualized consideration in the context of a race-conscious admissions program is paramount.

Here, the Law School engages in a highly individualized, holistic review of each applicant's file, giving serious consideration to all the ways an applicant might contribute to a diverse educational environment. The Law School affords this individualized consideration to applicants of all races. There is no policy, either *de jure* or *de facto*, of automatic acceptance or rejection based on any single "soft" variable. Unlike the program at issue in *Gratz v. Bollinger*, the Law School awards no mechanical, predetermined diversity "bonuses" based on race or ethnicity. Like the Harvard plan, the Law School's admissions policy "is flexible enough to consider all pertinent elements of diversity in light of the particular qualifications of each applicant, and to place them on the same footing for consideration, although not necessarily according them the same weight."

We also find that, like the Harvard plan Justice Powell referenced in *Bakke*, the Law School's race-conscious admissions program adequately ensures that all factors that may contribute to student body diversity are meaningfully considered alongside race in admissions decisions. With respect to the use of race itself, all underrepresented minority students admitted by the Law School have been deemed qualified. By virtue of our Nation's struggle with racial inequality, such students are both likely to have experiences of particular importance to the Law School's mission, and less likely to be admitted in meaningful numbers on criteria that ignore those experiences.

The Law School does not, however, limit in any way the broad range of qualities and experiences that may be considered valuable contributions to student body diversity. To the contrary, the 1992 policy makes clear "there are many possible bases for diversity admissions," and provides examples of admittees who have lived or traveled widely abroad, are fluent in several languages, have overcome personal adversity and family hardship, have exceptional records of extensive community service, and have had successful careers in other fields. The Law School seriously considers each "applicant's promise of making a notable contribution to the class by way of a particular strength, attainment, or characteristic— *e.g.*, an unusual intellectual achievement, employment experience, nonacademic performance, or personal background." All applicants have the opportunity to highlight their own potential diversity contributions through the submission of a personal statement, letters of recommendation, and an essay describing the ways in which the applicant will contribute to the life and diversity of the Law School.

What is more, the Law School actually gives substantial weight to diversity factors besides race. The Law School frequently accepts nonminority applicants with grades and test scores lower than underrepresented minority applicants (and other nonminority applicants) who are rejected. This shows that the Law School seriously weights many other diversity factors besides race than can make a real and dispositive difference for nonminority applicants as well. By this flexible approach, the Law School sufficiently takes into account, in practice as well as in theory, a wide variety of characteristics besides race and ethnicity that contribute to a diverse student body. JUSTICE KENNEDY speculates that "race is likely outcome determinative for many members of minority groups" who do not fall within the upper range of LSAT scores and grades. But the same could be said of the Harvard plan discussed approvingly by Justice Powell in *Bakke*, and indeed of any plan that uses race as one of many factors.

Petitioner and the United States argue that the Law School's plan is not narrowly tailored because race-neutral means exist to obtain the educational benefits of student body diversity that the Law School seeks. We disagree. Narrow tailoring does not require exhaustion of every conceivable race-neutral alternative. Nor does it require a university to choose between maintaining a reputation for excellence or fulfilling a commitment to provide educational opportunities to members of all racial groups. Narrow tailoring does, however, require serious, good faith consideration of workable race-neutral alternatives that will achieve the diversity the university seeks.

We agree with the Court of Appeals that the Law School sufficiently considered workable race-neutral alternatives. The District Court took the Law School to task for failing to consider race-neutral alternatives such as "using a lottery system" or "decreasing the emphasis for all applicants on undergraduate GPA and LSAT scores." But these alternatives would require a dramatic sacrifice of diversity, the academic quality of all admitted students, or both.

The Law School's current admissions program considers race as one factor among many, in an effort to assemble a student body that is diverse in ways broader than race. Because a lottery would make that kind of nuanced judgment impossible, it would effectively sacrifice all other educational values, not to mention every other kind of diversity. So too with the suggestion that the Law School simply lower admissions standards for all students, a drastic remedy that would require the Law School to become a much different institution and sacrifice a vital component of its educational mission. The United States advocates "percentage plans," recently adopted by public undergraduate institutions in Texas, Florida, and California to guarantee admission to all students above a certain class-rank threshold in every high school in the State. The United States does not, however, explain how such plans could work for graduate and professional schools. More-over, even assuming such plans are race-neutral, they may preclude the university from conducting the individualized assessments necessary to assemble a student body that is not just racially diverse, but diverse along all the qualities valued by the university. We are satisfied that the Law School adequately considered race-neutral alternatives currently capable of producing a critical mass without forcing the Law School to abandon the academic selectivity that is the cornerstone of its educational mission.

We acknowledge that "there are serious problems of justice connected with the idea of preference itself." Narrow tailoring, therefore, requires that a race-conscious admissions program not unduly harm members of any racial group. Even remedial race-based governmental action generally "remains subject to continuing oversight to assure that it will work the least harm possible to other innocent persons competing for the benefit." To be narrowly tailored, a race-conscious admissions program must not "unduly burden individuals who are not members of the favored racial and ethnic groups."

We are satisfied that the Law School's admissions program does not. Because the Law School considers "all pertinent elements of diversity," it can (and does) select nonminority applicants who have greater potential to enhance student body diversity over underrepresented minority applicants. As Justice Powell recognized in *Bakke*, so long as a race-conscious admissions program uses race as a "plus" factor in the context of individualized consideration, a rejected applicant "will not have been foreclosed from all consideration for that seat simply because he was not the right color or had the wrong surname. ... His qualifications would have been weighed fairly and competitively, and he would have no basis to complain of unequal treatment under the *Fourteenth Amendment*." We agree that, in the context of its individualized inquiry into the possible diversity contributions of all applicants, the Law School's race-conscious admissions program does not unduly harm nonminority applicants.

We are mindful, however, that "[a] core purpose of the *Fourteenth Amendment* was to do away with all governmentally imposed discrimination based on race." Accordingly, race-conscious admissions policies must be limited in time. This requirement reflects that racial classifications, however compelling their goals, are potentially so dangerous that they may be employed no more broadly than the interest demands. Enshrining a permanent justification for racial preference would offend this fundamental equal protection principle. We see no reason to exempt race-conscious admissions programs from the requirement that all governmental use of race must have a logical end point. The Law School, too, concedes that all "race-conscious programs must have reasonable durational limits."

In the context of higher education, the durational requirement can be met by sunset provisions in race-conscious admissions policies and periodic reviews to determine whether racial preferences are still necessary to achieve student body diversity. Universities in California, Florida, and Washington State, where racial preferences in admissions are prohibited by state law, are currently engaged in experimenting with a wide variety of alternative approaches. Universities in other States can and should draw on the most promising aspects of these race-neutral alternatives as they develop.

The requirement that all race-conscious admissions programs have a termination point "assures all citizens that the deviation from the norm of equal treatment of all racial and ethnic groups is a temporary matter, a measure taken in the service of the goal of equality itself." We take the Law School at its word that it would "like nothing better than to find a race-neutral admissions formula" and will terminate its race-conscious admissions program as soon as practicable. It has been 25 years since Justice Powell first approved the use of race to further an interest in student body diversity in the context of public higher education. Since that time, the number of minority applicants with high grades and test scores has indeed increased. We expect that 25 years from now, the use of racial preferences will no longer be necessary to further the interest approved today.

In summary, the *Equal Protection Clause* does not prohibit the Law School's narrowly tailored use of race in admissions decisions to further a compelling interest in obtaining the educational benefits that flow from a diverse student body. Consequently, petitioner's statutory claims based on Title VI and *42 U.S.C. §1981* also fail. The judgment of the Court of Appeals for the Sixth Circuit, accordingly, is affirmed.

JENNIFER GRATZ AND PATRICK HAMACHER, PETITIONERS v. LEE BOLLINGER et al.
SUPREME COURT OF THE UNITED STATES

June 23, 2003, Decided

CHIEF JUSTICE REHNQUIST delivered the opinion of the Court.

We granted certiorari in this case to decide whether "the University of Michigan's use of racial preferences in undergraduate admissions violates the *Equal Protection Clause of the Fourteenth Amendment,* Title VI of the Civil Rights Act of 1964 (*42 U.S.C. §2000d*), or *42 U.S.C. §1981.*" Because we find that the manner in which the University considers the race of applicants in its undergraduate admissions guidelines violates these constitutional and statutory provisions, we reverse that portion of the District Court's decision upholding the guidelines.

Petitioners Jennifer Gratz and Patrick Hamacher both applied for admission to the University of Michigan's (University) College of Literature, Science, and the Arts (LSA) as residents of the State of Michigan. Both petitioners are Caucasian. Gratz, who applied for admission for the fall of 1995, was notified in January of that year that a final decision regarding her admission had been delayed until April. This delay was based upon the University's determination that, although Gratz was "'well qualified,'" she was '"less competitive than the students who has been admitted on first review.'" Gratz was notified in April that the LSA was unable to offer her admission. She enrolled in the University of Michigan at Dearborn, from which she graduated in the spring of 1999.

Hamacher applied for admission to the LSA for the fall of 1997. A final decision as to his application was also postponed because, though his "'academic credentials [were] in the qualified range, they [were] not at the level needed for first review admission.'" Hamacher's application was subsequently denied in April 1997, and he enrolled at Michigan State University.

In October 1997, Gratz and Hamacher filed a lawsuit in the United States District Court for the Eastern District of Michigan against the University of Michigan, the LSA, James Duderstadt, and Lee Bollinger. Petitioners' complaint was a class-action suit alleging "violations and threatened violations of the rights of the plaintiffs and the class they represent to equal protection of the laws under the *Fourteenth Amendment ...,* and for racial discrimination in violation of *42 U.S.C. §§1981, 1983, and 2000d et seq.*" Petitioners sought, *inter alia,* compensatory and punitive damages for past violations, declaratory relief finding that respondents violated petitioners' "rights to nondiscriminatory treatment," an injunction prohibiting respondents from "continuing to discriminate on the basis of race in violation of the *Fourteenth Amendment,*" and an order requiring the LSA to offer Hamacher admission as a transfer student.

The University has changed its admissions guidelines a number of times during the period relevant to this litigation, and we summarize the most significant of these changes briefly. The University's Office of Undergraduate Admissions (OUA) oversees the LSA admissions process. In order to promote consistency in the review of the large number of applications received, the OUA uses written guidelines for each academic year. Admissions counselors make admissions decisions in accordance with these guidelines.

OUA considers a number of factors in making admissions decisions, including high school grades, standardized test scores, high school quality, curriculum strength, geography, alumni relationships, and leadership. OUA also considers race. During all periods relevant to this litigation, the University has considered African-Americans, Hispanics, and Native Americans to be "underrepresented minorities," and it is undisputed that the University admits "virtually every qualified ... applicant" from these groups.

Beginning with the 1998 academic year the OUA dispensed with the Guidelines tables and the SCUGA point system in favor of a "selection index," on which an applicant could score a maximum of 150 points. This index was divided linearly into ranges generally calling for admissions dispositions as follows: 100-150 (admit); 95–99 (admit or postpone); 90-94 (postpone or admit); 75–89 (delay or postpone); 74 and below (delay or reject).

Each applicant received points based on high school grade point average standardized test scores, academic quality of an applicant's high school, strength or weakness of high school curriculum in-state residency, alumni relationship, personal essay, and personal achievement or leadership. Of particular significance here, under a "miscellaneous" category, an applicant was entitled to 20 points based upon his or her membership in an underrepresented racial or ethnic minority group. The University explained that the "'development of the selection index for admissions in 1998 changed only the mechanics, not the substance of how race and ethnicity were considered in admissions.'"

During 1999 and 2000, the OUA used the selection index, under which every applicant from an underrepresented racial or ethnic minority group was awarded 20 points. Starting in 1999, however, the University established an Admissions Review Committee (ARC), to provide an additional level of consideration for some applications. Under the new system, counselors may, in their discretion, "flag" an application for the ARC to review after determining that the applicant (1) is academically prepared to succeed at the University, (2) has achieved a minimum selection index score, and (3) possesses a quality or characteristic important to the University's composition of its freshman class, such as high class rank, unique life experiences, challenges, circumstances, interests or talents, socioeconomic disadvantage, and underrepresented race, ethnicity, or geography. After reviewing "flagged" applications, the ARC determines whether to admit, defer, or deny each applicant.

The parties filed cross-motions for summary judgment with respect to liability. Petitioners asserted that the LSA's use of race as a factor in admissions violates Title VI of the Civil Rights Act of 1964, 78 Stat. 252, *42 U.S.C. §2000d*, and the *Equal Protection Clause of the Fourteenth Amendment*. Respondents relied on Justice Powell's opinion in *Regents of Univ. of Cal. v. Bakke*, to respond to petitioners' arguments. As discussed in greater detail in the Court's opinion in *Grutter v. Bollinger*, Justice Powell, in *Bakke*, expressed the view that the consideration of race as a factor in admissions might in some cases serve a compelling government interest. Respondents contended that the LSA has just such an

interest in the educational benefits that result from having a racially and ethnically diverse student body and that its program is narrowly tailored to serve that interest. Respondent-intervenors asserted that the LSA had a compelling interest in remedying the University's past and current discrimination against minorities.

As they have throughout the course of this litigation, petitioners contend that the University's consideration of race in its undergraduate admissions decisions violates §1 of the *Equal Protection Clause of the Fourteenth Amendment*. We consider first whether petitioners have standing to seek declaratory and injunctive relief, and, finding that they do, we next consider the merits of their claims.

(Discussion of standing omitted)

Petitioners argue, first and foremost, that the University's use of race in undergraduate admissions violates the *Fourteenth Amendment*. Specifically, they contend that this Court has only sanctioned the use of racial classifications to remedy identified discrimination, a justification on which respondents have never relied. Petitioners further argue that "diversity as a basis for employing racial preferences is simply too open-ended, ill-defined, and indefinite to constitute a compelling interest capable of supporting narrowly-tailored means." But for the reasons set forth today in *Grutter v. Bollinger*, the Court has rejected these arguments of petitioners.

Petitioners alternatively argue that even if the University's interest in diversity can constitute a compelling state interest, the District Court erroneously concluded that the University's use of race in its current freshman admissions policy is narrowly tailored to achieve such an interest. Petitioners argue that the guidelines the University began using in 1999 do not "remotely resemble the kind of consideration of race and ethnicity that Justice Powell endorsed in *Bakke*." Respondents reply that the University's current admission program *is* narrowly tailored and avoids the problems of the Medical School of the University of California at Davis program (U.C. Davis) rejected by Justice Powell. They claim that their program "hews closely" to both the admissions program described by Justice Powell as well as the Harvard College admissions program that he endorsed. Specifically, respondents contend that the LSA's policy provides the individualized consideration that "Justice Powell considered a hallmark of a constitutionally appropriate admissions program." For the reasons set out below, we do not agree.

It is by now well established that "all racial classifications reviewable under the *Equal Protection Clause* must be strictly scrutinized." *Adarand Constructors, Inc. v. Pena*.

This "'standard of review ... is not dependent on the race of those burdened or benefited by a particular classification.'" (quoting *Richmond v. J.A. Croson Co..* Thus, "any person, of whatever race, has the right to demand that any governmental actor subject to the Constitution justify and racial classification subjecting that person to unequal treatment under the strictest of judicial scrutiny."

To withstand our strict scrutiny analysis, respondents must demonstrate that the University's use of race in its current admission program employs "narrowly tailored measures that further compelling governmental interests." Because "racial classifications are simply too pernicious to permit any but the most exact connection between justification and classification," our review of whether such requirements have been met must entail "'a most searching examination.'" We find that the University's policy, which automatically distributes 20 points, or one-fifth of the points needed to guarantee admission, to every single "underrepresented minority" applicant solely because of race, is not narrowly tailored to achieve the interest in educational diversity that respondents claim justifies their program.

In *Bakke*, Justice Powell reiterated that "preferring members of any one group for no reason other than race or ethnic origin is discrimination for its own sake." He then explained, however, that in his view it would be permissible for a university to employ an admissions program in which "race or ethnic background may be deemed a 'plus' in a particular applicant's file." ... He explained that such a program might allow for "the file of a particular black applicant [to] be examined for his potential contribution to diversity without the factor of race being decisive when compared, for example, with that of an applicant identified as an Italian-American if the latter is thought to exhibit qualities more likely to promote beneficial educational pluralism." Such a system, in Justice Powell's view, would be "flexible enough to consider all pertinent elements of diversity in light of the particular qualifications of each applicant."

Justice Powell's opinion in *Bakke* emphasized the importance of considering each particular applicant as an individual, assessing all of the qualities that individual possesses, and in turn, evaluating that individual's ability to contribute to the unique setting of higher education. The admissions program Justice Powell described, however, did not contemplate that any single characteristic automatically ensured a specific and identifiable contribution to a university's diversity. Instead, under the approach Justice Powell described,

each characteristic of a particular applicant was to be considered in assessing the applicant's entire application.

The current LSA policy does not provide such individualized consideration. The LSA's policy automatically distributes 20 points to every single applicant from an "underrepresented minority" group, as defined by the University. The only consideration that accompanies this distribution of points is a factual review of an application to determine whether an individual is a member of one of these minority groups. Moreover, unlike Justice Powell's example, where the race of a "particular black applicant" could be considered without being decisive, the LSA's automatic distribution of 20 points has the effect of making "the factor of race. ... decisive" for virtually every minimally qualified underrepresented minority applicant.

Also instructive in our consideration of the LSA's system is the example provided in the description of the Harvard Collage Admission Program, which Justice Powell both discussed in, and attached to, his opinion in *Bakke*. The example was included to "illustrate the kind of significance attached to race" under the Harvard College program. It provided as follows:

"The Admissions Committee, with only a few places left to fill, might find itself forced to choose between A, the child of a successful black physician in an academic community with promise of superior academic performance, and B, a black who grew up in an inner-city ghetto of semi-literate parents whose academic achievement was lower but who had demonstrated energy and leadership as well as an apparently abiding interest in black power. If a good number of black students much like A but few like B had already been admitted, the Committee might prefer B; and vice versa. If C, a white student with extraordinary artistic talent, were also seeking one of the remaining places, his unique quality might give him an edge over both A and B. Thus, the critical criteria are often individual qualities or experience *not dependent upon race but sometimes associated with it.*"

This example further demonstrates the problematic nature of the LSA's admissions system. Even if student C's "extraordinary artistic talent" rivaled that of Monet or Picasso, the applicant would receive, at most, five points under the LSA's system. At the same time, every single underrepresented minority applicant, including students A and B, would automatically receive 20 points for submitting an application. Clearly, the LSA's system does not offer applicants the individualized selection process described in Harvard's example. Instead of considering how the differing backgrounds, experiences, and characteristics of students A, B, and C might benefit the University, admissions counselors reviewing LSA applications would simply award both A and B 20 points because their applications indicate that they are African-American, and student C would receive up to 5 points for his "extraordinary talent."

Respondents emphasize the fact that the LSA has created the possibility of an applicant's file being flagged for individualized consideration by the ARC. We think that the flagging program only emphasizes the flaws of the University's system as a whole when compared to that described by Justice Powell. Again, students A, B, and C illustrate the point. First, student A would never be flagged. This is because, as the University has conceded, the effect of automatically awarding 20 points is that virtually every qualified underrepresented minority applicant is admitted. Student A, an applicant "with promise of superior academic performance," would certainly fit this description. Thus, the result of the automatic distribution of 20 points is that the University would never consider student A's individual background, experiences, and characteristics to assess his individual "potential contribution to diversity," Instead, every applicant like student A would simply be admitted.

It is possible that students B and C would be flagged and considered as individuals. This assumes that student B was not already admitted because of the automatic 20-point distribution, and that student C could muster at least 70 additional points. But the fact that the "review committee can look at the applications individually and ignore the points" once an application is flagged is of little comfort under our strict scrutiny analysis. The record does nor reveal precisely how many applications are flagged for this individualized consideration, but it is undisputed that such consideration is the exception and not the rule in the operation of the LSA's admissions program. Additionally, this individualized review is only provided *after* admissions counselors automatically distribute the University's version of a "plus" that makes race a decisive factor for virtually every minimally qualified underrepresented minority applicant.

Respondents contend that "the volume of applications and the presentation of applicant information make it impractical for [LSA] to use the … admissions system" upheld by the Court today in *Grutter*. But the fact that the implementation of a program capable of providing individualized consideration might present administrative challenges does nor render constitutional an otherwise problematic system. Nothing in Justice Powell's opinion in *Bakke* signaled that a university may employ whatever means it desires to achieve the stated goal of diversity without regard to the limits imposed by our strict scrutiny analysis.

We conclude, therefore, that because the University's use of race in its current freshman admission policy is not narrowly tailored to achieve respondents' asserted compelling interest in diversity, the admissions policy violates the *Equal Protection Clause of the Fourteenth Amendment*. We further find that the admissions policy also violates Title VI and *42 U.S.C.§1981*. Accordingly, we reverse that portion of the District Court's decision granting respondents summary judgment with respect to liability and remand the case for proceedings consistent with this opinion.

┌──┐
│ ABIGAIL NOEL FISHER, PETITIONER v. UNIVERSITY │
│ OF TEXAS AT AUSTIN et al.   │
│ SUPREME COURT OF THE UNITED STATES   │
│ 133 S. Ct. 2411   │
│   │
│   June 24, 2013, Decided │
└──┘

OPINION BY:

KENNEDY

OPINION

JUSTICE KENNEDY delivered the opinion of the Court.

The University of Texas at Austin considers race as one of various factors in its undergraduate admissions process. Race is not itself assigned a numerical value for each applicant, but the University has committed itself to increasing racial minority enrollment on campus. It refers to this goal as a "critical mass." Petitioner, who is Caucasian, sued the University after her application was rejected. She contends that the University's use of race in the admissions process violated the Equal Protection Clause of the Fourteenth Amendment.

The parties asked the Court to review whether the judgment below was consistent with "this Court's decisions interpreting the Equal Protection Clause of the Fourteenth Amendment, including *Grutter* v. *Bollinger.* The Court concludes that the Court of Appeals did not hold the University to the demanding burden of strict scrutiny articulated in *Grutter* and *Regents of Univ. of Cal.* v. *Bakke.* Because the Court of Appeals did not apply the correct standard of strict scrutiny, its decision affirming the District Court's grant of summary judgment to the University was incorrect. That decision is vacated, and the case is remanded for further proceedings.

Located in Austin, Texas, on the most renowned campus of the Texas state university system, the University is one of the leading institutions of higher education in the Nation. Admission is prized and competitive. In 2008, when petitioner sought admission to the University's entering class, she was 1 of 29,501 applicants. From this group 12,843 were admitted, and 6,715 accepted and enrolled. Petitioner was denied admission.

In recent years the University has used three different programs to evaluate candidates for admission. The first is the program it used for some years before 1997, when the University considered two factors: a numerical score reflecting an applicant's test scores and academic performance in high school (Academic Index or AI), and the applicant's race. In 1996, this system was held unconstitutional by the United States Court of Appeals for the Fifth Circuit. It ruled the University's consideration of race violated the Equal Protection Clause because it did not further any compelling government interest. *Hopwood* v. *Texas.*

The second program was adopted to comply with the *Hopwood* decision. The University stopped considering race in admissions and substituted instead a new holistic metric of a candidate's potential contribution to the University, to be used in conjunction with the Academic Index. This "Personal Achievement Index" (PAI) measures a student's leadership and work experience, awards, extracurricular activities, community service, and other special circumstances that give insight into a student's background. These included growing up in a single-parent home, speaking a language other than English at home, significant family responsibilities assumed by the applicant, and the general socioeconomic condition of the student's family. Seeking to address the decline in minority enrollment after *Hopwood,* the University also expanded its outreach programs.

The Texas State Legislature also responded to the *Hopwood* decision. It enacted a measure known as the Top Ten Percent Law. *** the Top Ten Percent Law grants automatic admission to any public state college, including the University, to all students in the top 10% of their class at high schools in Texas that comply with certain standards.

The University's revised admissions process, coupled with the operation of the Top Ten Percent Law, resulted in a more racially diverse environment at the University. Before the admissions program at issue in this case, in the last year under the post-*Hopwood* AI/PAI system that did not consider race, the entering class was 4.5% African-American and 16.9% Hispanic. This is in contrast with the 1996 pre-*Hopwood* and Top Ten Percent regime, when race was explicitly considered, and the University's entering freshman class was 4.1% African-American and 14.5% Hispanic.

Following this Court's decisions in *Grutter* v. *Bollinger* and *Gratz* v. *Bollinger*, the University adopted a third admissions program, the 2004 program in which the University reverted to explicit consideration of race. This is the program here at issue. In *Grutter*, the Court upheld the use of race as one of many "plus factors" in an admissions program that considered the overall individual contribution of each candidate. In *Gratz*, by contrast, the Court held unconstitutional Michigan's undergraduate admissions program, which automatically awarded points to applicants from certain racial minorities.

The University's plan to resume race-conscious admissions was given formal expression in June 2004 in an internal document entitled Proposal to Consider Race and Ethnicity in Admissions. The Proposal relied in substantial part on a study of a subset of undergraduate classes containing between 5 and 24 students. It showed that few of these classes had significant enrollment by members of racial minorities. In addition the Proposal relied on what it called "anecdotal" reports from students regarding their "interaction in the classroom." The Proposal concluded that the University lacked a "critical mass" of minority students and that to remedy the deficiency it was necessary to give explicit consideration to race in the undergraduate admissions program.

To implement the Proposal the University included a student's race as a component of the PAI score, beginning with applicants in the fall of 2004. The University asks students to classify themselves from among five predefined racial categories on the application. Race is not assigned an explicit numerical value, but it is undisputed that race is a meaningful factor.

Once applications have been scored, they are plotted on a grid with the Academic Index on the x-axis and the Personal Achievement Index on the y-axis. On that grid students are assigned to so-called cells based on their individual scores. All students in the cells falling above a certain line are admitted. All students below the line are not. Each college—such as Liberal Arts or Engineering—admits students separately. So a student is considered initially for her first-choice college, then for her second choice, and finally for general admission as an undeclared major.

Petitioner applied for admission to the University's 2008 entering class and was rejected. She sued the University and various University officials in the United States District Court for the Western District of Texas. She alleged that the University's consideration of race in admissions violated the Equal Protection Clause. The parties cross-moved for summary judgment. The District Court granted summary judgment to the University. The United States Court of Appeals for the Fifth Circuit affirmed. It held that *Grutter* required courts to give substantial deference to the University, both in the definition of the compelling interest in diversity's benefits and in deciding whether its specific plan was narrowly tailored to achieve its stated goal. Applying that standard, the court upheld the University's admissions plan.

Over the dissent of seven judges, the Court of Appeals denied petitioner's request for rehearing en banc. Petitioner sought a writ of certiorari. The writ was granted.

Among the Court's cases involving racial classifications in education, there are three decisions that directly address the question of considering racial minority status as a positive or favorable factor in a university's admissions process, with the goal of achieving the educational benefits of a more diverse student body: *Bakke*,; *Gratz*,; and *Grutter*. We take those cases as given for purposes of deciding this case.

***While these are the cases that most specifically address the central issue in this case, additional guidance may be found in the Court's broader equal protection jurisprudence which applies in this context. "Distinctions between citizens solely because of their ancestry are by their very nature odious to a free people," and therefore "are contrary to our traditions and hence constitutionally suspect," "[B]ecause racial characteristics so seldom provide a relevant basis for disparate treatment,'" "the Equal Protection Clause demands that racial classifications ... be subjected to the 'most rigid scrutiny.'"

To implement these canons, judicial review must begin from the position that "any official action that treats a person differently on account of his race or ethnic origin is inherently suspect." Strict scrutiny is a searching examination, and it is the government that bears the burden to prove "'that the reasons for any [racial] classification [are] clearly identified and unquestionably legitimate,'"

II

Grutter made clear that racial "classifications are constitutional only if they are narrowly tailored to further compelling governmental interests." And *Grutter* endorsed Justice Powell's conclusion in *Bakke* that "the attainment of a diverse student body ... is a constitutionally permissible goal for an institution of higher education." Thus, under *Grutter*, strict scrutiny must be applied to any admissions program using racial categories or classifications.

***A university is not permitted to define diversity as "some specified percentage of a particular group merely because of its race or ethnic origin." "That would amount to outright racial balancing, which is patently unconstitutional." "Racial balancing is not transformed from 'patently unconstitutional' to a compelling state interest simply by relabeling it 'racial diversity.'"

Once the University has established that its goal of diversity is consistent with strict scrutiny, however, there must still be a further judicial determination that the admissions process meets strict scrutiny in its implementation. The University must prove that the means chosen by the University to attain diversity are narrowly tailored to that goal. On this point, the University receives no deference. *Grutter* made clear that it is for the courts, not for university administrators, to ensure that "[t]he means chosen to accomplish the [government's] asserted purpose must be specifically and narrowly framed to accomplish that purpose." True, a court can take account of a university's experience and expertise in adopting or rejecting certain admissions processes. But, as the Court said in *Grutter*, it remains at all times the University's obligation to demonstrate, and the Judiciary's obligation to determine, that admissions processes "ensure that each applicant is evaluated as an individual and not in a way that makes an applicant's race or ethnicity the defining feature of his or her application."

Narrow tailoring also requires that the reviewing court verify that it is "necessary" for a university to use race to achieve the educational benefits of diversity. This involves a careful judicial inquiry into whether a university could achieve sufficient diversity without using racial classifications. Although "[n]arrow tailoring does not require exhaustion of every *conceivable* race-neutral alternative," strict scrutiny does require a court to examine with care, and not defer to, a university's "serious, good faith consideration of workable race-neutral alternatives." Consideration by the university is of course necessary, but it is not sufficient to satisfy strict scrutiny: The reviewing court must ultimately be satisfied that no workable race-neutral alternatives would produce the educational benefits of diversity. If "'a non-racial approach ... could promote the substantial interest about as well and at tolerable administrative expense,'" then the university may not consider race. A plaintiff, of course, bears the burden of placing the validity of a university's adoption of an affirmative action plan in issue. But strict scrutiny imposes on the university the ultimate burden of demonstrating, before turning to racial classifications, that available, workable race-neutral alternatives do not suffice.

Rather than perform this searching examination, however, the Court of Appeals held petitioner could challenge only "whether [the University's] decision to reintroduce race as a factor in admissions was made in good faith." And in considering such a challenge, the court would "presume the University acted in good faith" and place on petitioner the burden of rebutting that presumption. The Court of Appeals held that to "second-guess the merits" of this aspect of the University's decision was a task it was "ill-equipped to perform" and that it would attempt only to "ensure that [the University's] decision to adopt a race-conscious admissions policy followed from [a process of] good faith consideration." The Court of Appeals thus concluded that "the narrow-tailoring inquiry—like the compelling-interest inquiry—is undertaken with a degree of deference to the Universit[y]." Because "the efforts of the University have been studied, serious, and of high purpose," the Court of Appeals held that the use of race in the admissions program fell within "a constitutionally protected zone of discretion." .

These expressions of the controlling standard are at odds with *Grutter*'s command that "all racial classifications imposed by government 'must be analyzed by a reviewing court under strict scrutiny.'" In *Grutter*, the Court approved the plan at issue upon concluding that it was not a quota, was sufficiently flexible, was limited in time, and followed "serious, good faith consideration of workable race-neutral alternatives." As noted above, the parties do not challenge, and the Court therefore does not consider, the correctness of that determination.

Grutter did not hold that good faith would forgive an impermissible consideration of race. It must be remembered that "the mere recitation of a 'benign' or legitimate purpose for a racial classification is entitled to little or no weight." Strict scrutiny does not permit a court to accept a school's assertion that its admissions process uses race in a permissible way without a court giving close analysis to the evidence of how the process works in practice.

The higher education dynamic does not change the narrow tailoring analysis of strict scrutiny applicable in other contexts. "[T]he analysis and level of scrutiny applied to determine the validity of [a racial] classification do not vary simply because the objective appears acceptable …. While the validity and importance of the objective may affect the outcome of the analysis, the analysis itself does not change."

The District Court and Court of Appeals confined the strict scrutiny inquiry in too narrow a way by deferring to the University's good faith in its use of racial classifications and affirming the grant of summary judgment on that basis. The Court vacates that judgment, but fairness to the litigants and the courts that heard the case requires that it be remanded so that the admissions process can be considered and judged under a correct analysis. Unlike *Grutter*, which was decided after trial, this case arises from cross-motions for summary judgment. In this case, as in similar cases, in determining whether summary judgment in favor of the University would be appropriate, the Court of Appeals must assess whether the University has offered sufficient evidence that would prove that its admissions program is narrowly tailored to obtain the educational benefits of diversity. Whether this record—and not "simple … assurances of good intention," is sufficient is a question for the Court of Appeals in the first instance.

***

Strict scrutiny must not be "'strict in theory, but fatal in fact,'" But the opposite is also true. Strict scrutiny must not be strict in theory but feeble in fact. In order for judicial review to be meaningful, a university must make a showing that its plan is narrowly tailored to achieve the only interest that this Court has approved in this context: the benefits of a student body diversity that "encompasses a … broa[d] array of qualifications and characteristics of which racial or ethnic origin is but a single though important element." The judgment of the Court of Appeals is vacated, and the case is remanded for further proceedings consistent with this opinion.

OPINION BY:

ROBERTS, SCALIA, THOMAS, ALITO

OPINION

The school districts in these cases voluntarily adopted student assignment plans that rely upon race to determine which public schools certain children may attend. The Seattle school district classifies children as white or nonwhite; the Jefferson County school district as black or "other." In Seattle, this racial classification is used to allocate slots in oversubscribed high schools. In Jefferson County, it is used to make certain elementary school assignments and to rule on transfer requests. In each case, the school district relies upon an individual student's race in assigning that student to a particular school, so that the racial balance at the school falls within a predetermined range based on the racial composition of the school district as a whole. Parents of students denied assignment to particular schools under these plans solely because of their race brought suit, contending that allocating children to different public schools on the basis of race violated the Fourteenth Amendment guarantee of equal protection. The Courts of Appeals below upheld the plans. We granted certiorari, and now reverse.

I

Both cases present the same underlying legal question—whether a public school that had not operated legally segregated schools or has been found to be unitary may choose to classify students by race and rely upon that classification in making school assignments. Although we examine the plans under the same legal framework, the specifics of the two plans, and the circumstances surrounding their adoption, are in some respects quite different.

A

Seattle School District No. 1 operates 10 regular public high schools. In 1998, it adopted the plan at issue in this case for assigning students to these schools. The plan allows incoming ninth graders to choose from among any of the district's high schools, ranking however many schools they wish in order of preference.

Some schools are more popular than others. If too many students list the same school as their first choice, the district employs a series of "tiebreakers" to determine who will fill the open slots at the oversubscribed school. The first tiebreaker selects for admission students who have a sibling currently enrolled in the chosen school. The next tiebreaker depends upon the racial composition of the particular school and the race of the individual student. In the district's public schools approximately 41 percent of enrolled students are white; the remaining 59 percent, comprising all other racial groups, are classified by Seattle for assignment purposes as nonwhite. If an oversubscribed school is not within 10 percentage points of the district's overall white/nonwhite racial balance, it is what the district calls "integration positive," and the district employs a tiebreaker that selects for assignment students whose race "will serve to bring the school into balance." If it is still necessary to select students for the school after using the racial tiebreaker, the next tiebreaker is the geographic proximity of the school to the student's residence.

Seattle has never operated segregated schools—legally separate schools for students of different races—nor has it ever been subject to court-ordered desegregation. It nonetheless employs the racial tiebreaker in an attempt to address the effects of racially identifiable housing patterns on school assignments. Most white students live in the northern part of Seattle, most students of other racial backgrounds in the southern part. Four of Seattle's high schools are located in the north—Ballard, Nathan Hale, Ingraham, and Roosevelt—and five in the south—Rainier Beach, Cleveland, West Seattle, Chief Sealth, and Franklin. One school—Garfield—is more or less in the center of Seattle.

For the 2000-2001 school year, five of these schools were oversubscribed—Ballard, Nathan Hale, Roosevelt, Garfield, and Franklin—so much so that 82 percent of incoming ninth graders ranked one of these schools as their first choice. Three of the oversubscribed schools were "integration positive" because the school's white enrollment the previous school year was greater than 51 percent—Ballard, Nathan Hale, and Roosevelt. Thus, more nonwhite students (107, 27, and 82, respectively) who selected one of these three schools as a top choice received placement at the school than would have been the case had race not been considered, and proximity been the next tiebreaker. Franklin was "integration positive" because its nonwhite enrollment the previous school year was greater than 69 percent; 89 more white students were assigned to Franklin by operation of the racial tiebreaker in the 2000–2001 school year than otherwise would have been. Garfield was the only oversubscribed school whose composition during the 1999–2000 school year was within the racial guidelines, although in previous years Garfield's enrollment had been predominantly nonwhite, and the racial tiebreaker had been used to give preference to white students.

Petitioner Parents Involved in Community Schools (Parents Involved) is a nonprofit corporation comprising the parents of children who have been or may be denied assignment to their chosen high school in the district because of their race. The concerns of Parents Involved are illustrated by Jill Kurfirst, who sought to enroll her ninth-grade son, Andy Meeks, in Ballard High School's special Biotechnology Career Academy. Andy suffered from attention deficit hyperactivity disorder and dyslexia, but had made good progress with hands-on instruction, and his mother and middle school teachers thought that the smaller biotechnology program held the most promise for his continued success. Andy was accepted into this selective program but,

because of the racial tiebreaker, was denied assignment to Ballard High School. Parents Involved commenced this suit in the Western District of Washington, alleging that Seattle's use of race in assignments violated the Equal Protection Clause of the Fourteenth Amendment, and the Washington Civil Rights Act.***

B

Jefferson County Public Schools operates the public school system in metropolitan Louisville, Kentucky. In 1973 a federal court found that Jefferson County had maintained a segregated school system, and in 1975 the District Court entered a desegregation decree. Jefferson County operated under this decree until 2000, when the District Court dissolved the decree after finding that the district had achieved unitary status by eliminating "[t]o the greatest extent practicable" the vestiges of its prior policy of segregation.

In 2001, after the decree had been dissolved, Jefferson County adopted the voluntary student assignment plan at issue in this case. Approximately 34 percent of the district's 97,000 students are black; most of the remaining 66 percent are white. The plan requires all nonmagnet schools to maintain a minimum black enrollment of 15 percent, and a maximum black enrollment of 50 percent.

At the elementary school level, based on his or her address, each student is designated a "resides" school to which students within a specific geographic area are assigned; elementary resides schools are "grouped into clusters in order to facilitate integration." The district assigns students to nonmagnet schools in one of two ways: Parents of kindergartners, first graders, and students new to the district may submit an application indicating a first and second choice among the schools within their cluster; students who do not submit such an application are assigned within the cluster by the district. "Decisions to assign students to schools within each cluster are based on available space within the schools and the racial guidelines in the District's current student assignment plan." If a school has reached the "extremes of the racial guidelines," a student whose race would contribute to the school's racial imbalance will not be assigned there. After assignment, students at all grade levels are permitted to apply to transfer between nonmagnet schools in the district. Transfers may be requested for any number of reasons, and may be denied because of lack of available space or on the basis of the racial guidelines.

When petitioner Crystal Meredith moved into the school district in August 2002, she sought to enroll her son, Joshua McDonald, in kindergarten for the 2002–2003 school year. His resides school was only a mile from his new home, but it had no available space—assignments had been made in May, and the class was full. Jefferson County assigned Joshua to another elementary school in his cluster, Young Elementary. This school was 10 miles from home, and Meredith sought to transfer Joshua to a school in a different cluster, Bloom Elementary, which—like his resides school—was only a mile from home. Space was available at Bloom, and intercluster transfers are allowed, but Joshua's transfer was nonetheless denied because, in the words of Jefferson County, "[t]he transfer would have an adverse effect on desegregation compliance" of Young.

Meredith brought suit in the Western District of Kentucky, alleging violations of the Equal Protection Clause of the Fourteenth Amendment. ***

III

A

It is well established that when the government distributes burdens or benefits on the basis of individual racial classifications, that action is reviewed under strict scrutiny. *Grutter* v. *Bollinger*, Adarand, *supra*. As the Court recently reaffirmed, "'racial classifications are simply too pernicious to permit any but the most exact connection between justification and classification." *Gratz* v. *Bollinger*, (2003). In order to satisfy this searching standard of review, the school districts must demonstrate that the use of individual racial classifications in the assignment plans here under review is "narrowly tailored" to achieve a "compelling" government interest. *Adarand, supra.*

Without attempting in these cases to set forth all the interests a school district might assert, it suffices to note that our prior cases, in evaluating the use of racial classifications in the school context, have recognized two interests that qualify as compelling. The first is the compelling interest of remedying the effects of past intentional discrimination. Yet the Seattle public schools have not shown that they were ever segregated by law, and were not subject to court-ordered desegregation decrees. The Jefferson County public schools were previously segregated by law and were subject to a desegregation decree entered in 1975. In 2000, the District Court that entered that decree dissolved it, finding that Jefferson County had "eliminated the vestiges associated with the former policy of segregation and its pernicious effects," and thus had achieved "unitary" status. Jefferson

County accordingly does not rely upon an interest in remedying the effects of past intentional discrimination in defending its present use of race in assigning students.

Nor could it. We have emphasized that the harm being remedied by mandatory desegregation plans is the harm that is traceable to segregation, and that "the Constitution is not violated by racial imbalance in the schools, without more." Once Jefferson County achieved unitary status, it had remedied the constitutional wrong that allowed race-based assignments. Any continued use of race must be justified on some other basis.

The second government interest we have recognized as compelling for purposes of strict scrutiny is the interest in diversity in higher education upheld in *Grutter*. The specific interest found compelling in *Grutter* was student body diversity "in the context of higher education." The diversity interest was not focused on race alone but encompassed "all factors that may contribute to student body diversity." We described the various types of diversity that the law school sought:

> "[The law school's] policy makes clear there are many possible bases for diversity admissions, and provides examples of admittees who have lived or traveled widely abroad, are fluent in several languages, have overcome personal adversity and family hardship, have exceptional records of extensive community service, and have had successful careers in other fields."

The Court quoted the articulation of diversity from Justice Powell's opinion in *Regents of Univ. of Cal.* v. *Bakke*, noting that "it is not an interest in simple ethnic diversity, in which a specified percentage of the student body is in effect guaranteed to be members of selected ethnic groups, that can justify the use of race." Instead, what was upheld in *Grutter* was consideration of "a far broader array of qualifications and characteristics of which racial or ethnic origin is but a single though important element."

The entire gist of the analysis in *Grutter* was that the admissions program at issue there focused on each applicant as an individual, and not simply as a member of a particular racial group. The classification of applicants by race upheld in *Grutter* was only as part of a "highly individualized, holistic review," As the Court explained, "[t]he importance of this individualized consideration in the context of a race-conscious admissions program is paramount." The point of the narrow tailoring analysis in which the *Grutter* Court engaged was to ensure that the use of racial classifications was indeed part of a broader assessment of diversity, and not simply an effort to achieve racial balance, which the Court explained would be "patently unconstitutional." In the present cases, by contrast, race is not considered as part of a broader effort to achieve "exposure to widely diverse people, cultures, ideas, and viewpoints," *ibid.*; race, for some students, is determinative standing alone. The districts argue that other factors, such as student preferences, affect assignment decisions under their plans, but under each plan when race comes into play, it is decisive by itself. It is not simply one factor weighed with others in reaching a decision, as in *Grutter*; it is *the* factor. Like the University of Michigan undergraduate plan struck down in *Gratz*, the plans here "do not provide for a meaningful individualized review of applicants" but instead rely on racial classifications in a "nonindividualized, mechanical" way.

Even when it comes to race, the plans here employ only a limited notion of diversity, viewing race exclusively in white/nonwhite terms in Seattle and black/"other" terms in Jefferson County. The Seattle "Board Statement Reaffirming Diversity Rationale" speaks of the "inherent educational value" in "[p]roviding students the opportunity to attend schools with diverse student enrollment," But under the Seattle plan, a school with 50 percent Asian-American students and 50 percent white students but no African-American, Native-American, or Latino students would qualify as balanced, while a school with 30 percent Asian-American, 25 percent African-American, 25 percent Latino, and 20 percent white students would not. It is hard to understand how a plan that could allow these results can be viewed as being concerned with achieving enrollment that is "'broadly diverse,"

Prior to *Grutter*, the courts of appeals rejected as unconstitutional attempts to implement race-based assignment plans—such as the plans at issue here—in primary and secondary schools. After *Grutter*, however, the two Courts of Appeals in these cases, and one other, found that race-based assignments were permissible at the elementary and secondary level, largely in reliance on that case.

In upholding the admissions plan in *Grutter*, though, this Court relied upon considerations unique to institutions of higher education, noting that in light of "the expansive freedoms of speech and thought associated with the university environment, universities occupy a special niche in our constitutional tradition." The Court explained that "[c]ontext matters" in applying strict

scrutiny, and repeatedly noted that it was addressing the use of race "in the context of higher education." The Court in *Grutter* expressly articulated key limitations on its holding—defining a specific type of broad-based diversity and noting the unique context of higher education—but these limitations were largely disregarded by the lower courts in extending *Grutter* to uphold race-based assignments in elementary and secondary schools. The present cases are not governed by *Grutter*.

B

Perhaps recognizing that reliance on *Grutter* cannot sustain their plans, both school districts assert additional interests, distinct from the interest upheld in *Grutter*, to justify their race-based assignments. In briefing and argument before this Court, Seattle contends that its use of race helps to reduce racial concentration in schools and to ensure that racially concentrated housing patterns do not prevent nonwhite students from having access to the most desirable schools. Jefferson County has articulated a similar goal, phrasing its interest in terms of educating its students "in a racially integrated environment." Each school district argues that educational and broader socialization benefits flow from a racially diverse learning environment, and each contends that because the diversity they seek is racial diversity—not the broader diversity at issue in *Grutter*—it makes sense to promote that interest directly by relying on race alone.

The parties and their *amici* dispute whether racial diversity in schools in fact has a marked impact on test scores and other objective yardsticks or achieves intangible socialization benefits. The debate is not one we need to resolve, however, because it is clear that the racial classifications employed by the districts are not narrowly tailored to the goal of achieving the educational and social benefits asserted to flow from racial diversity. In design and operation, the plans are directed only to racial balance, pure and simple, an objective this Court has repeatedly condemned as illegitimate.

The plans are tied to each district's specific racial demographics, rather than to any pedagogic concept of the level of diversity needed to obtain the asserted educational benefits. In Seattle, the district seeks white enrollment of between 31 and 51 percent (within 10 percent of "the district white average" of 41 percent), and nonwhite enrollment of between 49 and 69 percent (within 10 percent of "the district minority average" of 59 percent). In Jefferson County, by contrast, the district seeks black enrollment of no less than 15 or more than

50 percent, a range designed to be "equally above and below Black student enrollment systemwide," based on the objective of achieving at "all schools ... an African-American enrollment equivalent to the average district-wide African-American enrollment" of 34 percent. In Seattle, then, the benefits of racial diversity require enrollment of at least 31 percent white students; in Jefferson County, at least 50 percent. There must be at least 15 percent nonwhite students under Jefferson County's plan; in Seattle, more than three times that figure. This comparison makes clear that the racial demographics in each district—whatever they happen to be—drive the required "diversity" numbers. The plans here are not tailored to achieving a degree of diversity necessary to realize the asserted educational benefits; instead the plans are tailored, in the words of Seattle's Manager of Enrollment Planning, Technical Support, and Demographics, to "the goal established by the school board of attaining a level of diversity within the schools that approximates the district's overall demographics."

The districts offer no evidence that the level of racial diversity necessary to achieve the asserted educational benefits happens to coincide with the racial demographics of the respective school districts—or rather the white/nonwhite or black/"other" balance of the districts, since that is the only diversity addressed by the plans. Indeed, in its brief Seattle simply assumes that the educational benefits track the racial breakdown of the district. When asked for "a range of percentage that would be diverse," however, Seattle's expert said it was important to have "sufficient numbers so as to avoid students feeling any kind of specter of exceptionality." The district did not attempt to defend the proposition that anything outside its range posed the "specter of exceptionality." Nor did it demonstrate in any way how the educational and social benefits of racial diversity or avoidance of racial isolation are more likely to be achieved at a school that is 50 percent white and 50 percent Asian-American, which would qualify as diverse under Seattle's plan, than at a school that is 30 percent Asian-American, 25 percent African-American, 25 percent Latino, and 20 percent white, which under Seattle's definition would be racially concentrated.

Similarly, Jefferson County's expert referred to the importance of having "at least 20 percent" minority group representation for the group "to be visible enough to make a difference," and noted that "small isolated minority groups in a school are not likely to have a strong effect on the overall school." The Jefferson County plan, however, is based on a goal of replicating at each school

"an African-American enrollment equivalent to the average district-wide African-American enrollment." Joshua McDonald's requested transfer was denied because his race was listed as "other" rather than black, and allowing the transfer would have had an adverse effect on the racial guideline compliance of Young Elementary, the school he sought to leave. At the time, however, Young Elementary was 46.8 percent black. The transfer might have had an adverse effect on the effort to approach district-wide racial proportionality at Young, but it had nothing to do with preventing either the black or "other" group from becoming "small" or "isolated" at Young.

In fact, in each case the extreme measure of relying on race in assignments is unnecessary to achieve the stated goals, even as defined by the districts. For example, at Franklin High School in Seattle, the racial tiebreaker was applied because nonwhite enrollment exceeded 69 percent, and resulted in an incoming ninth-grade class in 2000-2001 that was 30.3 percent Asian-American, 21.9 percent African-American, 6.8 percent Latino, 0.5 percent Native-American, and 40.5 percent Caucasian. Without the racial tiebreaker, the class would have been 39.6 percent Asian-American, 30.2 percent African-American, 8.3 percent Latino, 1.1 percent Native-American, and 20.8 percent Caucasian. When the actual racial breakdown is considered, enrolling students without regard to their race yields a substantially diverse student body under any definition of diversity.

In *Grutter*, the number of minority students the school sought to admit was an undefined "meaningful number" necessary to achieve a genuinely diverse student body. Although the matter was the subject of disagreement on the Court, the majority concluded that the law school did not count back from its applicant pool to arrive at the "meaningful number" it regarded as necessary to diversify its student body. Here the racial balance the districts seek is a defined range set solely by reference to the demographics of the respective school districts.

This working backward to achieve a particular type of racial balance, rather than working forward from some demonstration of the level of diversity that provides the purported benefits, is a fatal flaw under our existing precedent. We have many times over reaffirmed that "[r]acial balance is not to be achieved for its own sake." *Grutter* itself reiterated that "outright racial balancing" is "patently unconstitutional."

Accepting racial balancing as a compelling state interest would justify the imposition of racial proportionality throughout American society, contrary to our repeated recognition that "[a]t the heart of the Constitution's guarantee of equal protection lies the simple command that the Government must treat citizens as individuals, not as simply components of a racial, religious, sexual or national class." Allowing racial balancing as a compelling end in itself would "effectively assur[e] that race will always be relevant in American life, and that the 'ultimate goal' of 'eliminating entirely from governmental decisionmaking such irrelevant factors as a human being's race' will never be achieved." An interest "linked to nothing other than proportional representation of various races ... would support indefinite use of racial classifications, employed first to obtain the appropriate mixture of racial views and then to ensure that the [program] continues to reflect that mixture."

The validity of our concern that racial balancing has "no logical stopping point," is demonstrated here by the degree to which the districts tie their racial guidelines to their demographics. As the districts' demographics shift, so too will their definition of racial diversity.

The Ninth Circuit below stated that it "share[d] in the hope" expressed in *Grutter* that in 25 years racial preferences would no longer be necessary to further the interest identified in that case. But in Seattle the plans are defended as necessary to address the consequences of racially identifiable housing patterns. The sweep of the mandate claimed by the district is contrary to our rulings that remedying past societal discrimination does not justify race-conscious government action.

The principle that racial balancing is not permitted is one of substance, not semantics. Racial balancing is not transformed from "patently unconstitutional" to a compelling state interest simply by relabeling it "racial diversity." While the school districts use various verbal formulations to describe the interest they seek to promote—racial diversity, avoidance of racial isolation, racial integration—they offer no definition of the interest that suggests it differs from racial balance.

Jefferson County phrases its interest as "racial integration," but integration certainly does not require the sort of racial proportionality reflected in its plan. Even in the context of mandatory desegregation, we have stressed that racial proportionality is not required, and here Jefferson County has already been found to have eliminated the vestiges of its prior segregated school system.

The en banc Ninth Circuit declared that "when a racially diverse school system is the goal (or racial concentration or isolation is the problem), there is no more effective means than a consideration of race to achieve the solution." For the foregoing reasons, this conclusory argument cannot sustain the plans. However closely related race-based assignments may be to achieving racial balance, that itself cannot be the goal, whether labeled "racial diversity" or anything else. To the extent the objective is sufficient diversity so that students see fellow students as individuals rather than solely as members of a racial group, using means that treat students solely as members of a racial group is fundamentally at cross-purposes with that end.

C

The districts assert, as they must, that the way in which they have employed individual racial classifications is necessary to achieve their stated ends. The minimal effect these classifications have on student assignments, however, suggests that other means would be effective. Seattle's racial tiebreaker results, in the end, only in shifting a small number of students between schools. Approximately 307 student assignments were affected by the racial tiebreaker in 2000-2001; the district was able to track the enrollment status of 293 of these students. Of these, 209 were assigned to a school that was one of their choices, 87 of whom were assigned to the same school to which they would have been assigned without the racial tiebreaker. Eighty-four students were assigned to schools that they did not list as a choice, but 29 of those students would have been assigned to their respective school without the racial tiebreaker, and 3 were able to attend one of the oversubscribed schools due to waitlist and capacity adjustments. In over one-third of the assignments affected by the racial tiebreaker, then, the use of race in the end made no difference, and the district could identify only 52 students who were ultimately affected adversely by the racial tiebreaker in that it resulted in assignment to a school they had not listed as a preference and to which they would not otherwise have been assigned.

As the panel majority in *Parents Involved VI* concluded:

"[T]he tiebreaker's annual effect is thus merely to shuffle a few handfuls of different minority students between a few schools—about a dozen additional Latinos into Ballard, a dozen black students into Nathan Hale, perhaps two dozen Asians into Roosevelt, and so on. The District has not met its burden of proving these marginal changes ... outweigh the cost of subjecting hundreds of students to disparate treatment based solely upon the color of their skin."

Similarly, Jefferson County's use of racial classifications has only a minimal effect on the assignment of students. Elementary school students are assigned to their first- or second-choice school 95 percent of the time, and transfers, which account for roughly 5 percent of assignments, are only denied 35 percent of the time—and presumably an even smaller percentage are denied on the basis of the racial guidelines, given that other factors may lead to a denial. Jefferson County estimates that the racial guidelines account for only 3 percent of assignments. As Jefferson County explains, "the racial guidelines have minimal impact in this process, because they 'mostly influence student assignment in subtle and indirect ways.'"

While we do not suggest that *greater* use of race would be preferable, the minimal impact of the districts' racial classifications on school enrollment casts doubt on the necessity of using racial classifications. In *Grutter*, the consideration of race was viewed as indispensable in more than tripling minority representation at the law school—from 4 to 14.5 percent. Here the most Jefferson County itself claims is that "because the guidelines provide a firm definition of the Board's goal of racially integrated schools, they 'provide administrators with the authority to facilitate, negotiate and collaborate with principals and staff to maintain schools within the 15–50% range.'" Classifying and assigning schoolchildren according to a binary conception of race is an extreme approach in light of our precedents and our Nation's history of using race in public schools, and requires more than such an amorphous end to justify it.

The districts have also failed to show that they considered methods other than explicit racial classifications to achieve their stated goals. Narrow tailoring requires "serious, good faith consideration of workable race-neutral alternatives," and yet in Seattle several alternative assignment plans—many of which would not have used express racial classifications—were rejected with little or no consideration. Jefferson County has failed to present any evidence that it considered alternatives, even though the district already claims that its goals are achieved primarily through means other than the racial classifications.

* * *

If the need for the racial classifications embraced by the school districts is unclear, even on the districts' own terms, the costs are undeniable. "[D]istinctions between citizens solely because of their ancestry are by their very nature odious to a free people whose institutions are founded upon the doctrine of equality." Government action dividing us by race is inherently suspect because

such classifications promote "notions of racial inferiority and lead to a politics of racial hostility," "reinforce the belief, held by too many for too much of our history, that individuals should be judged by the color of their skin," and "endorse race-based reasoning and the conception of a Nation divided into racial blocs, thus contributing to an escalation of racial hostility and conflict." As the Court explained in *Rice* v. *Cayetano*, [o]ne of the principal reasons race is treated as a forbidden classification is that it demeans the dignity and worth of a person to be judged by ancestry instead of by his or her own merit and essential qualities."

All this is true enough in the contexts in which these statements were made—government contracting, voting districts, allocation of broadcast licenses, and electing state officers—but when it comes to using race to assign children to schools, history will be heard. In *Brown* v. *Board of Education*, we held that segregation deprived black children of equal educational opportunities regardless of whether school facilities and other tangible factors were equal, because government classification and separation on grounds of race themselves denoted inferiority. It was not the inequality of the facilities but the fact of legally separating children on the basis of race on which the Court relied to find a constitutional violation in 1954. The next Term, we accordingly stated that "full compliance" with *Brown I* required school districts "to achieve a system of determining admission to the public schools *on a nonracial basis.*"

The parties and their *amici* debate which side is more faithful to the heritage of *Brown*, but the position of the plaintiffs in *Brown* was spelled out in their brief and could not have been clearer: "[T]he Fourteenth Amendment prevents states from according differential treatment to American children on the basis of their color or race." What do the racial classifications at issue here do, if not accord differential treatment on the basis of race? As counsel who appeared before this Court for the plaintiffs in *Brown* put it: "We have one fundamental contention which we will seek to develop in the course of this argument, and that contention is that no State has any authority under the equal-protection clause of the Fourteenth Amendment to use race as a factor in affording educational opportunities among its citizens." There is no ambiguity in that statement. And it was that position that prevailed in this Court, which emphasized in its remedial opinion that what was "[a]t stake is the personal interest of the plaintiffs in admission to public schools as soon as practicable *on a nondiscriminatory basis,*" and what was required was "determining admission to the public schools *on a nonracial basis*." What do the racial classifications do in these cases, if not determine admission to a public school on a racial basis?

Before *Brown*, schoolchildren were told where they could and could not go to school based on the color of their skin. The school districts in these cases have not carried the heavy burden of demonstrating that we should allow this once again—even for very different reasons. For schools that never segregated on the basis of race, such as Seattle, or that have removed the vestiges of past segregation, such as Jefferson County, the way "to achieve a system of determining admission to the public schools on a nonracial basis," is to stop assigning students on a racial basis. The way to stop discrimination on the basis of race is to stop discriminating on the basis of race.

The judgments of the Courts of Appeals for the Sixth and Ninth Circuits are reversed, and the cases are remanded for further proceedings.

It is so ordered.

THE COALITION FOR ECONOMIC EQUITY v. PETE WILSON.
United States Court of Appeals for the Ninth Circuit

April 8, 1997

O'SCANNLAIN, Circuit Judge:

We must decide whether a provision of the California Constitution prohibiting public race and gender preferences violates the Equal Protection Clause of the United States Constitution.

On November 5, 1996, the people of the State of California adopted the California Civil Rights Initiative as an amendment to their Constitution. The initiative, which appeared on the ballot as Proposition 209, provides in relevant part that

> the state shall not discriminate against, or grant preferential treatment to, any individual or group on the basis of race, sex, color, ethnicity, or national origin in the operation of public employment, public education, or public contracting.

The California Legislative Analyst's Office portrayed Proposition 209 to the voters as a measure that would eliminate public race-based and gender-based affirmative action programs. The California Ballot Pamphlet explained to voters that:

> A YES vote on [Proposition 209] means: The elimination of those affirmative action programs for women and minorities run by the state or local governments in the areas of public employment, contracting, and education that give "preferential treatment" on the basis of sex, race, color, ethnicity, or national origin.
>
> A NO vote on this measure means State and local government affirmative action programs would remain in effect to the extent they are permitted under the United States Constitution.

The Ballot Pamphlet also included arguments by proponents and opponents of Proposition 209. Proponents urged a "yes" vote, arguing that:

> A generation ago, we did it right. We passed civil rights laws to prohibit discrimination. But special interests hijacked the civil rights movement. Instead of equality, governments imposed quotas, preferences, and set-asides.
>
> And two wrongs don't make a right! Today, students are being rejected from public universities because of their RACE. Job applicants are turned away because their RACE does not meet some "goal" or "timetable." Contracts are awarded to high bidders because they are of the preferred RACE.
>
> That's just plain wrong and unjust. Government should not discriminate. It must not give a job, a university admission, or a contract based on race or sex. Government must judge all people equally, without discrimination!
>
> And, remember, Proposition 209 keep in place all federal and state protections against discrimination!

Opponents of Proposition 209 urged a "no" vote, responding that:

> California law currently allows tutoring, mentoring, outreach, recruitment, and counseling to help ensure equal opportunity for women and minorities. Proposition 209 will eliminate affirmative action programs like these that help achieve equal opportunity for women and minorities in public employment, education and contracting. Instead of reforming affirmative action to make it fair for everyone, Proposition 209 makes the current problem worse.
>
> ...
>
> The initiative's language is so broad and misleading that it eliminates equal opportunity programs including:
>
> – tutoring and mentoring for minority and women students;

– affirmative action that encourages the hiring and promotion of qualified women and minorities;

– outreach and recruitment programs to encourage applicants for government jobs and contracts; and

– programs designed to encourage girls to study and pursue careers in math and science.

Proposition 209 passed by a margin of 54 to 46 percent; of nearly 9 million Californians casting ballots, 4,736,180 voted in favor of the initiative and 3,986,196 voted against it.

On the day after the election, November 6, 1996, several individuals and groups ("plaintiffs") claiming to represent the interests of racial minorities and women filed a complaint in the Northern District of California against several officials and political subdivisions of the State of California ("the State"). The complaint, brought under 42 U.S.C. §1983, alleges that Proposition 209, first, denies racial minorities and women the equal protection of the laws guaranteed by the Fourteenth Amendment, and, second, is void under the Supremacy Clause because it conflicts with Titles VI and VII of the Civil Rights Act of 1964, and Title IX of the Educational Amendments of 1972. As relief, plaintiffs seek a declaration that Proposition 209 is unconstitutional and a permanent injunction enjoining the State from implementing and enforcing it.

With their complaint, plaintiffs filed an application for a temporary restraining order ("TRO") and a preliminary injunction. The district court entered a TRO on November 27, 1996, and granted a preliminary injunction of December 23, 1996. The preliminary injunction enjoins the State, pending trial or final judgment, "from implementing or enforcing Proposition 209 insofar as said amendment to the Constitution of the State of California purports to prohibit or affect affirmative action programs in public employment, public education or public contracting."

The district court provided extensive findings of fact and conclusions of law in support of the injunction. This lawsuit, the court explained, challenges Proposition 209's prohibition against race and gender preferences, not its prohibition against discrimination. Plaintiffs' constitutional challenge is "only to that slice of the initiative that now prohibits governmental entities at every level from taking voluntary action to remediate past and present discrimination through the use of constitutionally permissible race- and gender-conscious affirmative action programs."

The elimination of such programs, the district court found, would reduce opportunities in public contracting and employment for women and minorities. It further would cause enrollment of African-American, Latino, and American Indian students in public colleges to fall, though enrollment of Asian-American students would increase. Finally, the court found that minorities and women, to reinstate race-based or gender-based preferential treatment, would have to re-amend the California Constitution by initiative.

From these findings of fact the district court concluded, first, that plaintiffs have demonstrated a likelihood of success on their equal protection claim. Proposition 209, the court reasoned, has a racial and gender focus which imposes a substantial political burden on the interests of women and minorities. The court held that Hunter v. Erickson, and Washington v. Seattle School District No. 1, prohibit such treatment of racial and gender issues in the political process.

The district court concluded, second, that plaintiffs have also demonstrated a likelihood of success on their pre-emption claims. Title VII, the court reasoned, preserves the discretion of public employers voluntarily to use race and gender preferences. To the extent that Proposition 209 bans such preferences statewide, the court held that Title VII pre-empts it under the Supremacy Clause.

The district court next explained that plaintiffs would suffer irreparable harm if Proposition 209 takes effect. If not enjoined, Proposition 209 immediately would ban existing preference programs in violation of plaintiffs' constitutional rights. The State, in contrast, the court concluded, would suffer little hardship from a preliminary injunction, which merely would suspend implementation of Proposition 209 pending trial.

Finally, the district court believed that a preliminary injunction would serve the public interest. Preserving the pre-election status quo would "harmonize" the public need for "clear guidance with respect to Proposition 209" with "the compelling interest in remedying discrimination that underlies existing constitutionally-permissible state-sponsored affirmative action programs threatened by Proposition 209."

On December 31, 1996, Californians Against Discrimination and Preferences ("CADP"), the defendant/intervenor, applied to the district court for a stay of the preliminary injunction pending appeal. The State joined in the application. CADP and the State also filed notices of appeal to this court on January 3, 1997, and subsequently moved to stay the district court's injunction pending appeal pursuant to *Federal Rule of Appellate Procedure 8*. The district court entered its order declining to stay the injunction on February 7, 1997. On February 10, 1997, we heard oral argument on the application to us for a stay. The parties' arguments for and against a stay pending appeal focused primarily on the merits underlying the preliminary injunction itself. We thus deferred submission of the stay application and expedited submission on the merits, which we now decide.

Before reaching the merits of the preliminary injunction, we pause to consider whether this case even belongs in federal court. No California state court has yet construed the meaning or effect of Proposition 209. Rather, plaintiffs ask a federal tribunal to enjoin flat-out this state constitutional amendment passed by a majority of the voters. The district court remarked that the issue in this case is not "whether one judge can thwart the will of the people; rather, the issue is whether the challenged enactment complies with our Constitution and Bill of Rights."

No doubt the district court is correct. Judges apply the law; they do not sua sponte thwart wills. If Proposition 209 affronts the federal Constitution—the Constitution which the people of the United States themselves ordained and established—the court merely reminds the people that they must govern themselves in accordance with principles of their own choosing. If, however, the court relies on an erroneous legal premise, the decision operates to thwart the will of the people in the most literal sense: What the people of California willed to do is frustrated on the basis of principles that the people of the United States neither ordained nor established. A system which permits one judge to block with the stroke of a pen what 4,736,180 state residents voted to enact as law tests the integrity of our constitutional democracy. These principles of judicial review are no less true today than in the days of *Marbury v. Madison*;

The Supreme Court recently reminded federal judges that we should not even undertake to review the constitutionality of a state law without first asking: "Is this conflict really necessary?" As a general rule, federal courts "ought not to consider the Constitutionality of a state statute in the absence of a controlling interpretation of its meaning and effect by the state courts." Justice Ginsburg emphasized for a unanimous court that "when anticipatory relief is sought in federal court against a state statute, respect for the place of the States in our federal system calls for close consideration of that

core question." "Warnings against premature adjudication of constitutional questions bear heightened attention when a federal court is asked to invalidate a State's law, for the federal tribunal risks friction-generating error when it endeavors to construe a novel state Act not yet reviewed by the State's highest court."

The ink on Proposition 209 was barely dry when plaintiffs filed this lawsuit. For this federal tribunal to tell the people of California that their one-day-old, never-applied-law violates the Constitution, we must have more than a vague inkling of what the law actually does. Plaintiffs challenge Proposition 209 to the extent that it eliminates "affirmative action." A California court that considered Proposition 209's pre-enactment ballot title and ballot label remarked that the term "affirmative action" is an "amorphous, value-laden term," "rarely defined so as to form a common base for intelligent discourse." "Most definitions of the term would include not only the conduct which Proposition 209 would ban, i.e., discrimination and preferential treatment, but also other efforts such as outreach programs."

The district court properly limited its use of the term "affirmative action" to state programs that use race or gender classifications. It enjoined Proposition 209 only to the extent that it eliminates programs that grant preferential treatment to individuals on the basis of their race or gender. The court cited as examples programs that would prefer contractors of a certain race or gender in the evaluation of bids for public contracts, programs that would prefer prospective employees of a certain race or gender for public employment, and programs that would prefer prospective students of a certain race or gender for public education or financial aid. Unlike in Arizonans, the State does not dispute that Proposition 209 operates to eliminate such programs. Quite the contrary, the district court found that Defendant/Appellant Pete Wilson, Governor of California, issued an Executive Order on November 6, 1996, implementing Proposition 209 to do just that.

Without this factual basis, we would not hesitate to remand to the district court for reconsideration of the State's abstention motion in light of *Arizonans*. From the district court's findings, however, we are satisfied, to answer the Supreme Court's question, that "yes—this conflict really is necessary." We may now address the merits.

As a matter of "conventional" equal protection analysis, there is simply no doubt that Proposition 209 is constitutional. The Equal Protection Clause provides that "no State shall ... deny to any person within its jurisdiction the equal protection of the laws." The central purpose of the Equal Protection Clause "is the prevention of official conduct discriminating on the basis of race." *Washington v. Davis,*. The Fourteenth Amendment forbids such conduct on the principle that "distinctions between citizens solely because of their ancestry are by their very nature odious to a free people whose institutions are founded upon the doctrine of equality." Racial distinctions "threaten to stigmatize individuals by reason of their membership in a racial group and to incite racial hostility."

The ultimate goal of the Equal Protection Clause is "to do away with all governmentally imposed discrimination based on race." Therefore, "whenever the government treats any person unequally because of his or her race, that person has suffered an injury that falls squarely within the language and spirit of the Constitution's guarantee of equal protection." *Adarand Constructors v. Pena,*. The Equal Protection Clause also protects against classifications based on gender. "Without equating gender classifications, for all purposes, to classifications based on race or national origin, the Court ... has carefully inspected official action that closes a door or denies opportunity to women (or to men)."

The standard of review under the Equal Protection Clause does not depend on the race or gender of those burdened or benefited by a particular classification. When the government prefers individuals on account of their race or gender, it correspondingly disadvantages individuals who fortuitously belong to another race or to the other gender, "Consistency *does* recognize that any individual suffers an injury when he or she is disadvantaged by the government because of his or her race." Proposition 209 amends the California Constitution simply to prohibit state discrimination against or preferential treatment to any person on account of race or gender. Plaintiffs charge that this ban on unequal treatment denies members of certain races and one gender equal protection of the laws. If merely stating this alleged equal protection violation does not suffice to refute it, the central tenet of the Equal Protection Clause teeters on the brink of incoherence.

The Equal Protection Clause guarantees that the government will not classify individuals on the basis of impermissible criteria. Most laws, of course—perhaps all—classify individuals one way or another. Individuals receive, or correspondingly are denied, governmental benefits on the basis of income, disability, veteran status, age, occupation and countless other grounds. Legislative classifications as a general rule are presumptively valid under the Equal Protection Clause. A legislative classification will deny equal protection only if it is not "rationally related to a legitimate state interest."

The general rule does not apply, however, when a law classifies individuals by race or gender. Any governmental action that classifies persons by race is presumptively unconstitutional and subject to the most exacting judicial scrutiny. To be constitutional, a racial classification, regardless of its purported motivation, must be narrowly tailored to serve a compelling governmental interest, an extraordinary justification. When the government classifies by gender, it must demonstrate that the classification is substantially related to an important governmental interest, requiring an "exceedingly persuasive" justification.

The first step in determining whether a law violates the Equal Protection Clause is to identify the classification that it draws. Proposition 209 provides that the State of California shall not discriminate against, or grant preferential treatment to, any individual or group on the basis of race or gender. Rather than classifying individuals by race or gender, Proposition 209 *prohibits* the State from classifying individuals by race or gender. A law that prohibits the State from classifying individuals by race or gender *a fortiori* does not classify individuals by race or gender. Proposition 209's ban on race and gender preferences, as a matter of law and logic, does not violate the Equal Protection Clause in any conventional sense.

As a matter of "political structure" analysis, however, plaintiffs challenge the level of government at which the State of California has prohibited race and gender preferences. Plaintiffs contend, along with the United States as amicus curiae, that Proposition 209 imposes an unequal "political structure" that denies women and minorities a right to seek preferential treatment from the lowest level of government. The district court agreed, relying on the so-called "*Hunter*" doctrine.

In *Hunter v. Erickson*, the Supreme Court addressed the constitutionality of an amendment to the Charter of the City of Akron, Ohio. Before the charter amendment was enacted, the Akron City Council had authority to pass ordinances regulating the real estate market. Most ordinances became effective thirty days after the Council passed them. The charter amendment operated to prevent the city council from enacting ordinances addressing racial discrimination in housing without majority approval of the Akron voters. The plaintiff, Nellie Hunter, who wanted a fair housing ordinance enforced, claimed that the amendment violated her right to equal protection of the laws.

The Supreme Court found in the charter amendment "an explicitly racial classification treating racial housing matters differently from other racial and housing matters." The law disadvantaged those who would benefit from laws barring racial discrimination in the real estate market as against those who would benefit from other regulations of the real estate market. Absent a compelling state interest, the state "may no more disadvantage any particular group by making it more difficult to enact legislation in its behalf than it may dilute any person's vote or give any group a smaller representation than another of comparable size."

The Court later applied these principles to Washington State's educational decision-making structure in Washington *v. Seattle School District No. 1*. A statewide initiative in Washington barred school boards from assigning students beyond their neighborhood schools. The initiative contained several broad exceptions, which effectively operated to preclude only desegregative busing. Certain school districts challenged the initiative under the Equal Protection Clause.

As in *Hunter*, the Court determined that the initiative effected a racial classification by removing "the authority to address a racial problem—and only a racial problem—from the existing decision-making body, in such a way as to burden minority interests." The initiative had restructured the State's educational decision-making process to differentiate "between the treatment of problems involving racial matters and that afforded other problems in the same area." That differentiation burdened minority interests "by lodging decision-making authority over the question at a new and remote level of government." Absent a compelling state interest, the initiative's unequal reordering of authority of school boards violated the Equal Protection Clause.

The district court applied *Hunter* and *Seattle* to invalidate Proposition 209. Proposition 209, the court found, effected a race and gender classification by singling out race and gender preferences for unique political burdens. The court concluded that race and gender preferences, like antidiscrimination laws and integrative busing, are of special interest to minorities and women. Before Proposition 209 was enacted, the court reasoned, women and minorities could petition local government for preferential treatment. To obtain preferential treatment now, the court concluded, women and minorities must appeal to the statewide electorate, a "new and remote level of government."

The district court next analyzed whether the classifications it gleaned from Proposition 209 withstood "heightened scrutiny." The court concluded that the classifications served no important government interest, let alone a compelling one, thus denying women and minorities equal protection of the laws.

The State contends that the district court's conclusion rests on an erroneous legal premise because Proposition 209, unlike the *Hunter* and *Seattle* initiatives, does not reallocate political authority in a discriminatory manner. CADP contends, additionally, that a majority of the electorate cannot restructure the political process to discriminate against itself. We address the second contention first.

Can a statewide ballot initiative deny equal protection to members of a group that constitutes a majority of the electorate that enacted it? Plaintiffs allege that Proposition 209 places procedural burdens in the path of women and minorities, who together constitute a majority of the California electorate. Is it possible for a majority of voters impermissibly to stack the political deck against itself? The Supreme Court leaves us, quite frankly, a little perplexed as to the answer.

The "political structure" equal protection cases, namely *Hunter* and *Seattle*, addressed the constitutionality of political obstructions that majorities had placed in the way of minorities to achieving protection against unequal treatment. *Hunter*, holding that the Akron amendment denied minorities equal protection of the laws, observed that "the majority needs no protection against discrimination and if it did, a referendum might be bothersome but no more than that." *Seattle* addressed a political structure held "to place special burdens on the ability of minority groups to achieve beneficial legislation." In *Romer v. Evans*, the most recent "political structure" case, Colorado's Amendment 2 left homosexuals to "obtain specific protection against discrimination only by enlisting the citizenry of Colorado." It would seem to make little sense to apply "political structure" equal protection principles where the group alleged to face special political burdens itself constitutes a majority of the electorate.

The difficulty, however, lies in reconciling what seems to be that eminently sensible conclusion with the principle that the Fourteenth Amendment guarantees equal protection to individuals and not to groups. That the Fourteenth Amendment affords individuals, not groups, the right to demand equal protection is a fundamental first principle of "conventional" equal protection jurisprudence. The Equal Protection Clause, after all, prohibits a state from denying "to any *person* within its jurisdiction the equal protection of the laws."

Where a state denies someone a job, an education, or a seat on the bus because of her race or gender, the injury to that individual is clear. The person who wants to work, study, or ride but cannot because she is black or a woman is denied equal protection. Where, as here, a state prohibits race or gender preferences at any level of government, the injury to any specific individual is utterly inscrutable. No one contends that individuals have a constitutional right to preferential treatment solely on the basis of their race or gender. Quite the contrary. What, then, is the personal injury that members of a group suffer when they cannot seek preferential treatment on the basis of their race or gender from local government? This question admits of no easy answer.

Hunter and *Seattle* suggest that the political structures they held unconstitutional imposed individual injuries analogous to "denying [members of a racial minority] the vote, on an equal basis with others." When the electorate votes up or down on a referendum alleged to burden a majority of the voters, it is hard to conceive how members of the majority have been denied the vote. If members of a majority somehow can deny their own right to ask local government for racial preferences, conceivably a statewide referendum *affording* preferential treatment to racial minorities would deny members of the racial majority the right to ask local governments to abolish racial preferences. "Consistency *does* recognize that any individual suffers an injury when he or she is disadvantaged by the government because of his or her race, whatever that race may be."

Thankfully, the absence of any specific findings by the district court in this regard relieves us from having to reconcile "the long line of cases understanding equal protection as a personal right," with *Hunter's* admonition that "the majority needs no protection against discrimination," Our task in this case is merely to determine whether the district court relied on an erroneous legal premise. We accept without questioning the district court's findings that Proposition 209 burdens members of insular minorities within the majority that enacted it who otherwise would seek to obtain race-based and gender-based preferential treatment from local entities. The legal question for us to decide is whether a burden on achieving race-based or gender-based preferential treatment can deny individuals equal protection of the laws.

The Supreme Court has recognized an explicit distinction "between state action that discriminates on the basis of race and state action that addresses, in neutral fashion, race-related matters." The former denies persons against whom the law discriminates equal protection of the laws; the latter does not. Into which category Proposition 209 falls we must now determine.

In *Crawford*, the Supreme Court considered an amendment to the California Constitution that prohibited state courts from mandating pupil assignment or transportation except to remedy a specific equal protection violation. Minority students had alleged that the amendment employed a racial classification that burdened minorities who sought to vindicate state-created rights. The Supreme Court disagreed, holding that the amendment did not employ a racial classification. Unlike the charter amendment in *Hunter*, "the simple repeal or modification of desegregation or antidiscrimination laws, without more, never has been viewed as embodying a presumptively invalid racial classification."

Crawford, thus, on the one hand, dictates that "the Equal Protection Clause is not violated by the mere repeal of race-related legislation or policies that were not required by the Federal Constitution in the first place." *Hunter* and *Seattle*, on the other hand, prohibited states from placing decision-making authority over certain racial issues at higher levels of government.

Plaintiffs attempt to align Proposition 209 with *Hunter* and *Seattle* and distinguish it from *Crawford*. *Crawford*, they argue, addressed an amendment that merely repealed a benefit that the state itself had afforded, not the authority of local subdivisions to afford the same benefit. *Hunter* and *Seattle*, in their view, foreclose the authority of states to withdraw local jurisdiction to enact race and gender preferences unless the state also withdraws local jurisdiction to enact preferences based on any other criteria. Such an extraordinary proposition hardly follows from *Hunter* and *Seattle*.

The *Hunter* doctrine "does not mean, of course, that every attempt to address a racial issue gives rise to an impermissible classification." Rather, for the doctrine to apply at all, the state somehow must reallocate political authority in a discriminatory manner.

States have "extraordinarily wide latitude ... in creating various types of political subdivisions and conferring authority upon them." That a law resolves an issue at a higher level of state government says nothing in and of itself. Every statewide policy has the "procedural" effect of denying someone an inconsistent outcome at the local level. "[A] lawmaking procedure that 'disadvantages' a particular group does not always deny equal protection. Under any such holding, presumably a State would not be able to require referendums on any subject unless referendums were required on all, because they would always disadvantage some group."

Hunter and *Seattle* relied expressly on the states' existing educational and housing decision-making processes to find that they had reallocated authority in a racially discriminatory manner. In *Hunter*, the state obstructed equal housing by removing only racially fair housing prerogatives from the lawmaking procedure for all other housing matters. In *Seattle*, the state obstructed equal education by removing only racially desegregative prerogatives from the lawmaking procedure for all other educational matters.

As the *Seattle* Court explained:

Before adoption of the initiative, the power to determine what programs would most appropriately fill a school district's educational needs—including programs involving student assignment and desegregation—was firmly committed to the local board's discretion. The question whether to provide an integrated learning environment rather than a system of neighborhood schools surely involved a decision of that sort. After passage of Initiative 350, authority over all but one of those areas remained in the hands of the local board. By placing power over desegregative busing at the state level, then, Initiative 350 plainly differentiates between the treatment of problems involving racial matters and that afforded other problems in the same area.

Plaintiffs would have us extrapolate from *Seattle* that a state may never treat race *qua* race differently from any other legal classification. *Seattle* itself, however, declined that invitation.

The *Seattle* majority specifically allayed any concern that is holding rendered the state powerless to address racial issues where localities acted first. Justice Powell had lamented in dissent what a "strange notion" it was, "alien to our system—that local governmental bodies can forever preempt the ability of a State—the sovereign power—to address a matter of compelling concern to the State." He questioned how a statewide repeal of busing created a racial classification when identical action by the local government would not. To him, the decision left "unclear whether the State may set policy in any area of race relations where a local governmental body arguably has done 'more' than the Fourteenth Amendment requires."

The majority responded that the "horribles paraded by the dissent" in footnote 14 were "entirely unrelated to this case." The *Seattle* majority did not question "that the State might have vested all decision-making authority in itself." The State's prerogative in that regard was "irrelevant" in *Seattle*, though, because "the political structure it in fact erected imposed comparative burdens on minority interests. ..." The State, of course, "could have reserved to state officials the right to make all decisions in the areas of education and student assignment." Conversely, the State had "not attempted to reserve to itself exclusive power to deal with racial issues generally." By removing desegregative prerogatives from these general grants of power, the State, as in *Hunter*, differentiated the treatment of racial problems in education from that afforded educational and racial issues generally.

When, in contrast, a state prohibits all its instruments from discriminating against or granting preferential treatment to anyone on the basis of race or gender, it has promulgated a law that addresses in neutral-fashion race-related and gender-related matters. It does not isolate race or gender antidiscrimination laws from any specific area over which the state has delegated authority to a local entity. Nor does it treat race and gender antidiscrimination laws in one area differently from race and gender antidiscrimination laws in another. Rather, it prohibits all race and gender preferences by state entities.

Even a state law that does restructure the political process can only deny equal protection if it burdens an individual's right to equal treatment.

A denial of equal protection entails, at a minimum, a classification that treats individuals unequally. The "political structure" cases do not create some paradoxical exception to this *sine qua non* of any equal protection violation. In *Hunter*, the lawmaking procedure made it more difficult for Nellie Hunter to obtain protection against unequal treatment in the housing market. In *Seattle*, the lawmaking procedure made it more difficult for minority students to obtain protection against unequal treatment in education. In *Romer*, Colorado's Amendment 2 denied homosexuals the ability to obtain "protection against discrimination," thus classifying homosexuals "not to further a proper legislative end but to make them unequal to everyone else."

Plaintiffs challenge Proposition 209 not as an impediment to protection against unequal treatment but as an impediment to receiving preferential treatment. The controlling words, we must remember, are "equal" and "protection." Impediments to preferential treatment do not deny equal protection. It is one thing to say that individuals have equal protection rights against political obstructions to equal treatment; it is quite another to say that individuals have equal protection rights against political obstructions to preferential treatment. While the Constitution protects against obstructions to equal treatment, it erects obstructions to preferential treatment by its own terms.

The alleged "equal protection" burden that Proposition 209 imposes on those who would seek race and gender preferences is a burden that the Constitution itself imposes. The Equal Protection Clause, parked at our most "distant and remote" level of government, singles out racial preferences for severe political burdens— it prohibits them in all but the most compelling circumstances. It is well-settled that "all governmental action based on race—a *group* classification long recognized as in most circumstances irrelevant and therefore prohibited—should be subject to detailed judicial inquiry to ensure that the *personal* right to equal protection of the laws has not been infringed." That is because "there is simply no way of determining what classifications are 'benign' or 'remedial' and what classifications are in fact motivated by illegitimate notions of racial inferiority or simple racial politics." Rather, "any person, of whatever race, has the right to demand that any governmental actor subject to the Constitution justify any racial classification subjecting that person to unequal treatment under the strictest judicial scrutiny." A governmental action that classifies persons on the basis of gender demands and "exceedingly persuasive justification" to survive constitutional scrutiny.

That the Constitution *permits* the rare race-based or gender-based preference hardly implies that the state cannot ban them altogether. States are free to make or not make any constitutionally permissible legislative classification. Nothing in the Constitution suggests the anomalous and bizarre result that preferences based on the most suspect and presumptively unconstitutional classifications— race and gender—must be readily available at the lowest level of government while preferences based on any other presumptively legitimate classification—such as wealth, age or disability—are at the mercy of statewide referenda.

After all, the "goal" of the Fourteenth Amendment, "to which the Nation continues to aspire," is "a political system in which race no longer matters." When the people enact a law that says race somehow matters, they must come forward with a compelling state interest to back it up. Plaintiffs would have us also require the people to come forward with a compelling state interest to justify a state law that says that race cannot matter in public contracting, employment, and education. Plaintiffs' counsel went even one step further at oral argument. He urged that "the people of the State of California are not entitled to make a judgment as to whether compelling state interests have been vindicated. That is for the courts." *Au contraire*! That most certainly *is* for the people of California to decide, *not* the courts. Our authority in this area is limited to deciding whether the interests proffered by the people are sufficient to justify a law that classifies among individuals. If the federal courts were to decide what the interests of the people are in the first place, judicial power would trump self-government as the general rule of our constitutional democracy.

The Constitution permits the people to grant a narrowly tailored racial preference only if they come forward with a compelling interest to back it up. "In the context of a Fourteenth Amendment challenge, courts must bear in mind the difference between what the law permits, and what it requires." To hold that a democratically enacted affirmative action program is constitutionally permissible because the people have demonstrated a compelling state interest is hardly to hold that the program is constitutionally required. The Fourteenth Amendment, lest we lose sight of the forest for the trees, does not require what it barely permits.

A state law that prohibits classifications based on race or gender is a law that addresses in neutral-fashion race-related and gender-related matters. As in *Crawford*, "it would be paradoxical to conclude that by adopting the Equal Protection Clause of the Fourteenth Amendment, the voters of the State thereby had violated it." For these reasons, we are persuaded that the district court relied on an erroneous legal premise when it concluded that plaintiffs have demonstrated a likelihood of success on their equal protection claim.

The district court also concluded that plaintiffs have demonstrated a likelihood of success on their claim that Proposition 209 is invalid under the Supremacy Clause because Title VII of the Civil Rights Act of 1964, preempts it. The district court found Title VII to be "silent" on "the role of voluntary race- and gender-conscious affirmative action" under its schema. It thus turned, pursuant to *Chevron, U.S.A., Inc. v. Natural Resources Defense Council, Inc.*, to an interpretation of the statute by the Equal Employment Opportunity Commission ("EEOC"). An EEOC Guideline states: "Voluntary affirmative action to improve opportunities for minorities and women must be encouraged and protected in order to carry out the Congressional intent embodied in title VII." Applying *Chevron*, the court gave "substantial deference" to this interpretation of the statute.

The district court is correct that federal law may preempt state law to the extent that the state law "stands as an obstacle to the accomplishment and execution of the full purposes and objectives of Congress." The district court apparently overlooked, however, the express preemption provisions of the 1964 Civil Rights Act. "In two sections of the 1964 Civil Rights Act, §§708 and 1104, Congress has indicated that state laws will be preempted only if they actually conflict with federal law."

Section 708 of Title VII provides:

Nothing in this subchapter shall be deemed to exempt or relieve any person from any liability, duty, penalty, or punishment provided by any present of future law of any State or political subdivision of a State, other than any such law which purports to require or permit the doing of any act which would be an unlawful employment practice under this subchapter.

That is all Title VII pre-empts. Proposition 209 does not remotely purport to require the doing of any act which would be an unlawful employment practice under Title VII. Quite the contrary, "discriminatory preference for any group, minority or majority, is precisely and only what Congress has proscribed." *Griggs v. Duke Power Co.*, Title VII, therefore, does not pre-empt Proposition 209.

Section 1104 of Title IX also generally limits the pre-emptive effect of all titles of the Civil Rights Act:

Nothing contained in any title of this Act shall be construed as indicating an intent on the part of Congress to occupy the field in which any such title operates to the exclusion of State laws on the same subject matter, nor shall any provision of this Act be construed as invalidating any provision of State law unless such provision is inconsistent with any of the purposes of this Act, or any provision thereof.

Section 1104's more general pre-emption provisions would operate to pre-empt Proposition 209 only if Proposition 209 were inconsistent with any purpose or

provision of the 1964 Civil Right Act. Title VII's one command regarding race and gender preferences conclusively demonstrates that Proposition 209 is entirely consistent: "Nothing contained in this subchapter shall be interpreted to require any [entity] ... subject to this subchapter to grant preferential treatment to any individual or to any group because of the race, color, religion, sex, or national origin of such individual or group. ..." ("Title VII ... does not demand that an employer give preferential treatment to minorities or women."). Nothing in Title VII suggests that Congress intended to leave government with less latitude under Title VII than private employers. Because Title VII by its plain language does not pre-empt Proposition 209, the district court relied on an erroneous legal premise in concluding that plaintiffs are likely to succeed on the merits of their pre-emption claims.

With no likelihood of success on the merits of their equal protection or pre-emption claims, plaintiffs are not entitled to a preliminary injunction. The district court determined that plaintiffs had demonstrated irreparable harm because Proposition 209 threatened to inflict an immediate and ongoing constitutional injury upon them. That conclusion, for reasons we have explained, rests on an erroneous legal premise. As we explained in *Glick v. McKay*, our review of a constitutional issue is plenary where "the facts are established or of no controlling relevance." Assuming all facts alleged in the complaint and found by the district court to be true, and drawing all reasonable inferences in plaintiffs' favor, we must conclude that, as a matter of law, Proposition 209 does not violate the United States Constitution. With no constitutional injury on the merits as a matter of law, there is no threat of irreparable injury or hardship to tip the balance in plaintiffs' favor.

For the foregoing reasons, we vacate the preliminary injunction, deny the motion to stay the injunction as moot, and remand to district court for further proceedings consistent with this opinion.

Preliminary injunction *VACATED; stay DENIED as moot; REMANDED.*

SCHUETTE v. (BAMN)
SUPREME COURT OF THE UNITED STATES
2014 U.S. LEXIS 2932

October 15, 2013, Argued April 22, 2014, Decided

JUSTICE KENNEDY announced the judgment of the Court and delivered an opinion, in which THE CHIEF JUSTICE and JUSTICE ALITO join.

The Court in this case must determine whether an amendment to the Constitution of the State of Michigan, approved and enacted by its voters, is invalid under the Equal Protection Clause of the Fourteenth Amendment to the Constitution of the United States.

In 2003 the Court reviewed the constitutionality of two admissions systems at the University of Michigan, one for its undergraduate class and one for its law school. The undergraduate admissions plan was addressed in *Gratz* v. *Bollinger,*. The law school admission plan was addressed in *Grutter* v. *Bollinger,* Each admissions process permitted the explicit consideration of an applicant's race. In *Gratz*, the Court invalidated the undergraduate plan as a violation of the Equal Protection Clause. In *Grutter*, the Court found no constitutional flaw in the law school admission plan's more limited use of race-based preferences.

In response to the Court's decision in *Gratz*, the university revised its undergraduate admissions process, but the revision still allowed limited use of race-based preferences. After a statewide debate on the question of racial preferences in the context of governmental decisionmaking, the voters, in 2006, adopted an amendment to the State Constitution prohibiting state and other governmental entities in Michigan from granting certain preferences, including race-based preferences, in a wide range of actions and decisions. Under the terms of the amendment, race-based preferences cannot be part of the admissions process for state universities. That particular prohibition is central to the instant case.

The ballot proposal was called Proposal 2 and, after it passed by a margin of 58 percent to 42 percent, the resulting enactment became Article I, §26, of the Michigan Constitution. As noted, the amendment is in broad terms. Section 26 states, in relevant part, as follows:

"(1) The University of Michigan, Michigan State University, Wayne State University, and any other public college or university, community college, or school district shall not discriminate against, or grant preferential treatment to, any individual or group on the basis of race, sex, color, ethnicity, or national origin in the operation of public employment, public education, or public contracting.

"(2) The state shall not discriminate against, or grant preferential treatment to, any individual or group on the basis of race, sex, color, ethnicity, or national origin in the operation of public employment, public education, or public contracting.

"(3) For the purposes of this section 'state' includes, but is not necessarily limited to, the state itself, any city, county, any public college, university, or community college, school district, or other political subdivision or governmental instrumentality of or within the State of Michigan not included in sub-section 1."

***Before the Court addresses the question presented, it is important to note what this case is not about. It is not about the constitutionality, or the merits, of race-conscious admissions policies in higher education. The consideration of race in admissions presents complex questions, in part addressed last Term in *Fisher* v. *University of Texas at Austin,*. In *Fisher*, the Court did not disturb the principle that the consideration of race in admissions is permissible, provided that certain conditions are met. In this case, as in *Fisher*, that principle is not challenged. The question here concerns not the permissibility of race-conscious admissions policies under the Constitution but whether, and in what manner, voters in the States may choose to prohibit the consideration of racial preferences in governmental decisions, in particular with respect to school admissions.

This Court has noted that some States have decided to prohibit race-conscious admissions policies. In *Grutter*, the Court noted: "Universities in California, Florida, and Washington State, where racial preferences in admissions are prohibited by state law, are currently engaged in experimenting with a wide variety of alternative approaches. Universities in other States can and should draw on the most promising aspects of these race-neutral alternatives as they develop." ***In this way, *Grutter* acknowledged the significance of a dialogue regarding this contested and complex policy question among and within States. There was recognition that our federal structure "permits ' innovation and experimentation" and "enables greater citizen ' involvement in democratic processes." While this case arises in Michigan, the decision by the State's voters reflects in part the national dialogue regarding the wisdom and practicality of race-conscious admissions policies in higher education. See, *e.g., Coalition for Economic Equity* v. *Wilson,*.

In Michigan, the State Constitution invests independent boards of trustees with plenary authority over public universities, including admissions policies. ***Although the members of the boards are elected, some evidence in the record suggests they delegated authority over admissions policy to the faculty. But whether the boards or the faculty set the specific policy, Michigan's public universities did consider race as a factor in admissions decisions before 2006.

In holding §26 invalid in the context of student admissions at state universities, the Court of Appeals relied in primary part on *Seattle, supra*, which it deemed to control the case. But that determination extends *Seattle's* holding in a case presenting quite different issues to reach a conclusion that is mistaken here. Before explaining this further, it is necessary to consider the relevant cases that preceded Seattle and the background against which *Seattle* itself arose.

Though it has not been prominent in the arguments of the parties, this Court's decision in *Reitman* v. *Mulkey,* is a proper beginning point for discussing the controlling decisions. In *Mulkey*, voters amended the California Constitution to prohibit any state legislative interference with an owner's prerogative to decline to sell or rent residential property on any basis. Two different cases gave rise to *Mulkey*. In one a couple could not rent an apartment, and in the other a couple were evicted from their apartment. Those adverse actions were on account of race. In both cases the complaining parties were barred, on account of race, from invoking the protection of California's statutes; and, as a result, they were unable to lease residential property. This Court concluded that the state constitutional provision was a denial of equal protection. *****

The next precedent of relevance, *Hunter* v. *Erickson*, is central to the arguments the respondents make in the instant case. In *Hunter*, the Court for the first time elaborated what the Court of Appeals here styled the "political process" doctrine. There, the Akron City Council found that the citizens of Akron consisted of "'people of different race[s], . . . many of whom live in circumscribed and segregated areas, under sub-standard unhealthful, unsafe, unsanitary and overcrowded conditions, because of discrimination in the sale, lease, rental and financing of housing." To address the problem, Akron enacted a fair housing ordinance to prohibit that sort of discrimination. In response, voters amended the city charter to overturn the ordinance and to require that any additional antidiscrimination housing ordinance be approved by referendum. But most other ordinances "regulating the real property market" were not subject to those threshold requirements. The plaintiff, a black woman in Akron, Ohio, alleged that her real estate agent could not show her certain residences because the owners had specified they would not sell to black persons.

Central to the Court's reasoning in *Hunter* was that the charter amendment was enacted in circumstances where widespread racial discrimination in the sale and rental of housing led to segregated housing, forcing many to live in "'unhealthful, unsafe, unsanitary and overcrowded conditions." The Court stated: "It is against this background that the referendum required by [the charter amendment] must be assessed.". Akron attempted to characterize the charter amendment "simply as a public decision to move slowly in the delicate area of race relations" and as a means "to allow the people of Akron to participate" in the decision. ***The Court found that the city charter amendment, by singling out antidiscrimination ordinances, "places special burden on racial minorities within the governmental process," thus becoming as impermissible as any other government action taken with the invidious intent to injure a racial minority.

***Seattle* is the third case of principal relevance here. There, the school board adopted a mandatory busing program to alleviate racial isolation of minority students in local schools. Voters who opposed the school board's busing plan passed a state initiative that barred busing to desegregate. The Court first determined that, although "white as well as Negro children benefit from" diversity, the school board's plan "inures primarily to the benefit of the minority." The Court next found that "the practical effect" of the state initiative was to "remov[e] the authority to address a racial problem—and only a racial problem—from the existing decisionmaking body, in such a way as to burden minority interests" because advocates of busing "now must seek relief from the state legislature, or from the statewide electorate." The Court therefore found that the initiative had "explicitly us[ed] the racial nature of a decision to determine the decisionmaking process."

Seattle is best understood as a case in which the state action in question (the bar on busing enacted by the State's voters) had the serious risk, if not purpose, of causing specific injuries on account of race, just as had been the case in *Mulkey* and *Hunter*. Although there had been no judicial finding of *de jure* segregation with respect to Seattle's school district, it appears as though school segregation in the district in the 1940's and 1950's may have been the partial result of school board policies that "permitted white students to transfer out of black schools while restricting the transfer of black students into white schools." *Parents Involved in Community Schools* v. *Seattle School Dist. No. 1,*.

***In essence, according to the broad reading of *Seattle*, any state action with a "racial focus" that makes it "more difficult for certain racial minorities than for other groups" to "achieve legislation that is in their interest" is subject to strict scrutiny. It is this reading of *Seattle* that the Court of Appeals found to be controlling here. And that reading must be rejected.

***The expansive reading of *Seattle* has no principled limitation and raises serious questions of compatibility with the Court's settled equal protection jurisprudence. To the extent *Seattle* is read to require the Court to determine and declare which political policies serve the "interest" of a group defined in racial terms, that rationale was unnecessary to the decision in *Seattle*; it has no support in precedent; and it raises serious constitutional concerns. That expansive language does not provide a proper guide for decisions and should not be deemed authoritative or controlling. The rule that the

Court of Appeals elaborated and respondents seek to establish here would contradict central equal protection principles.

In cautioning against "impermissible racial stereotypes," this Court has rejected the assumption that "members of the same racial group—regardless of their age, education, economic status, or the community in which they live—think alike, share the same political interests, and will prefer the same candidates at the polls.*** It cannot be entertained as a serious proposition that all individuals of the same race think alike. Yet that proposition would be a necessary beginning point were the *Seattle* formulation to control, as the Court of Appeals held it did in this case. And if it were deemed necessary to probe how some races define their own interest in political matters, still another beginning point would be to define individuals according to race. But in a society in which those lines are becoming more blurred, the attempt to define race-based categories also raises serious questions of its own. Government action that classifies individuals on the basis of race is inherently suspect and carries the danger of perpetuating the very racial divisions the polity seeks to transcend. Were courts to embark upon this venture not only would it be undertaken with no clear legal standards or accepted sources to guide judicial decision but also it would result in, or at least impose a high risk of, inquiries and categories dependent upon demeaning stereotypes, classifications of questionable constitutionality on their own terms.

Even assuming these initial steps could be taken in a manner consistent with a sound analytic and judicial framework, the court would next be required to determine the policy realms in which certain groups—groups defined by race—have a political interest. That undertaking, again without guidance from any accepted legal standards, would risk, in turn, the creation of incentives for those who support or oppose certain policies to cast the debate in terms of racial advantage or disadvantage. Thus could racial antagonisms and conflict tend to arise in the context of judicial decisions as courts undertook to announce what particular issues of public policy should be classified as advantageous to some group defined by race. This risk is inherent in adopting the *Seattle* formulation.

There would be no apparent limiting standards defining what public policies should be included in what *Seattle* called policies that "inur[e] primarily to the benefit of the minority" and that "minorities …

consider" to be "'in their interest." Those who seek to represent the interests of particular racial groups could attempt to advance those aims by demanding an equal protection ruling that any number of matters be foreclosed from voter review or participation. In a nation in which governmental policies are wide ranging, those who seek to limit voter participation might be tempted, were this Court to adopt the *Seattle* formulation, to urge that a group they choose to define by race or racial stereotypes are advantaged or disadvantaged by any number of laws or decisions. Tax policy, housing subsidies, wage regulations, and even the] naming of public schools, highways, and monuments are just a few examples of what could become a list of subjects that some organizations could insist should be beyond the power of voters to decide, or beyond the power of a legislature to decide when enacting limits on the power of local authorities or other governmental entities to address certain subjects. Racial division would be validated, not discouraged, were the *Seattle* formulation, and the reasoning of the Court of Appeals in this case, to remain in force.

Perhaps, when enacting policies as an exercise of democratic self-government, voters will determine that race-based preferences should be adopted. The constitutional validity of some of those choices regarding racial preferences is not at issue here. The holding in the instant case is simply that the courts may not disempower the voters from choosing which path to follow.

***Here there was no infliction of a specific injury of the kind at issue in *Mulkey* and *Hunter* and in the history of the Seattle schools. Here there is no precedent for extending these cases to restrict the right of Michigan voters to determine that race-based preferences granted by Michigan governmental entities should be ended.

The Court of Appeals for the Ninth Circuit has held that the same amendment, which also barred racial preferences in public education, does not violate the Equal Protection Clause. *Wilson,*. If the Court were to affirm the essential rationale of the Court of Appeals in the instant case, those holdings would be invalidated, or at least would be put in serious question. The Court, by affirming the judgment now before it, in essence would announce a finding that the past 15 years of state public debate on this issue have been improper. The instant case presents the question involved in Coral and Wilson but not involved in *Mulkey, Hunter,* and *Seattle.* That question is not how to address or prevent injury

caused on account of race but whether voters may determine whether a policy of race-based preferences should be continued.

For reasons already discussed, *Mulkey, Hunter,* and *Seattle* are not precedents that stand for the conclusion that Michigan's voters must be disempowered from acting. Those cases were ones in which the political restriction in question was designed to be used, or was likely to be used, to encourage infliction of injury by reason of race. What is at stake here is not whether injury will be inflicted but whether government can be instructed not to follow a course that entails, first, the definition of racial categories and, second, the grant of favored status to persons in some racial categories and not others.

***This case is not about how the debate about racial preferences should be resolved. It is about who may resolve it. There is no authority in the Constitution of the United States or in this Court's precedents for the Judiciary to set aside Michigan laws that commit this policy determination to the voters. Deliberative debate on sensitive issues such as racial preferences all too often may shade into rancor. But that does not justify removing certain court-determined issues from the voters' reach. Democracy does not presume that some subjects are either too divisive or too profound for public debate.

The judgment of the Court of Appeals for the Sixth Circuit is reversed.

It is so ordered.

JUSTICE BREYER, concurring in the judgment.

***[we] do not address the amendment insofar as it forbids the use of race-conscious admissions programs designed to remedy past exclusionary racial discrimination or the direct effects of that discrimination. Application of the amendment in that context would present different questions which may demand different answers. Rather, we here address the amendment only as it applies to, and forbids, programs that, as in *Grutter* v. *Bollinger*, rest upon "one justification": using "race in the admissions process" solely in order to "obtai[n] the educational benefits that flow from a diverse student body,"

Second, dissenting in *Parents Involved in Community Schools* v. *Seattle School Dist. No. 1*, I explained why I believe race-conscious programs of this kind are constitutional, whether implemented by law schools, universities, high schools, or elementary schools. I concluded that the Constitution does not "authorize judges" either to forbid or to require the adoption of diversity-seeking race-conscious "solutions" (of the kind at issue here) to such serious problems as "how best to administer America's schools" to help "create a society that includes all Americans."

I continue to believe that the Constitution permits, though it does not require, the use of the kind of race-conscious programs that are now barred by the Michigan Constitution. The serious educational problems that faced Americans at the time this Court decided *Grutter* endure.

***The Constitution allows local, state, and national communities to adopt narrowly tailored race-conscious programs designed to bring about greater inclusion and diversity. But the Constitution foresees the ballot box, not the courts, as the normal instrument for resolving differences and debates about the merits of these programs. ***In short, the "Constitution creates a democratic political system through which the people themselves must together find answers" to disagreements of this kind.

***In my view, however, neither *Hunter* nor *Seattle* applies here. And the parties do not here suggest that the amendment violates the Equal Protection Clause if not under the *Hunter-Seattle* doctrine.

Hunter and *Seattle* involved efforts to manipulate the political process in a way not here at issue. Both cases involved a restructuring of the political process that changed the political level at which policies were enacted. In *Hunter*, decisionmaking was moved from the elected city council to the local electorate at large. And in *Seattle*, decisionmaking by an elected school board was replaced with decisionmaking by the state legislature and electorate at large.

This case, in contrast, does not involve a reordering of the *political* process; it does not in fact involve the movement of decisionmaking from one political level to another. Rather, here, Michigan law delegated broad policymaking authority to elected university boards, see Mich. Const., Art. VIII, §5, but those boards delegated admissions-related decisionmaking authority to unelected university faculty members and administrators, ***Although the boards unquestionably retained the *power* to set policy regarding race-conscious admissions, in *fact* faculty members and administrators set the race-conscious admissions policies in question. (It is often true that elected bodies—including, for example, school boards, city councils, and state legislatures—have the power to enact policies, but in fact delegate that power to administrators.) Although at limited times the university boards were advised of the content of their race-conscious admissions policies, to my knowledge no board voted to accept or reject any of those policies. Thus, unelected faculty members and administrators, not voters or their elected representatives, adopted the race-conscious admissions programs affected by Michigan's constitutional amendment. The amendment took decisionmaking authority away from these unelected actors and placed it in the hands of the voters.

Why does this matter? For one thing, considered conceptually, the doctrine set forth in *Hunter* and *Seattle* does not easily fit this case. In those cases minorities had participated in the political process and they had won. The majority's subsequent reordering of the political process repealed the minority's successes and made it more difficult for the minority to succeed in the future. The majority thereby diminished the minority's ability to participate meaningfully in the electoral process. But one cannot as easily characterize the movement of the decisionmaking mechanism at issue here—from an administrative process to an electoral process—as diminishing the minority's ability to participate meaningfully in the *political* process. There is no prior electoral process in which the minority participated.

For another thing, to extend the holding of *Hunter* and *Seattle* to reach situations in which decisionmaking authority is moved from an administrative body to a political one would pose significant difficulties. The administrative process encompasses vast numbers of decisionmakers answering numerous policy questions in hosts of different fields. Administrative bodies modify programs in detail, and decisionmaking authority within the administrative process frequently moves around—due to amendments to statutes, new administrative rules, and evolving agency practice. It is thus particularly difficult in this context for judges to determine when a change in the locus of decision-making authority places a comparative structural burden on a racial minority. And to apply *Hunter* and *Seattle* to the administrative process would, by tending to hinder change, risk discouraging experimentation, interfering with efforts to see when and how race-conscious policies work.

Finally, the principle that underlies *Hunter* and *Seattle* runs up against a competing principle, discussed above. This competing principle favors decision-making though the democratic process. Just as this principle strongly supports the right of the people, or their elected representatives, to adopt race-conscious policies for reasons of inclusion, so must it give them the right to vote not to do so.

As I have said, my discussion here is limited to circumstances in which decision-making is moved from an unelected administrative body to a politically responsive one, and in which the targeted race-conscious admissions programs consider race solely in order to obtain the educational benefits of a diverse student body. We need now decide no more than whether the Federal Constitution permits Michigan to apply its constitutional amendment in those circumstances. I would hold that it does. Therefore, I concur in the judgment of the Court.

STATE OF NEW JERSEY v. PEDRO SOTO et al.
SUPERIOR COURT OF NEW JERSEY, LAW DIVISION, GLOUCESTER
COUNTY
324 N.J. Super. 66; 734 A.2d 350; 1996 N.J. Super. LEXIS 544

March 4, 1996

R.E. FRANCIS, J.S.C.

These are consolidated motions to suppress under the equal protection and due process clauses of the Fourteenth Amendment. Seventeen defendants of African ancestry claim that their arrests on the New Jersey Turnpike south of exit 3 between 1988 and 1991 result from discriminatory enforcement of the traffic laws by the New Jersey State Police. After a lengthy hearing, I find defendants have established a prima facie case of selective enforcement which the State has failed to rebut requiring suppression of all contraband and evidence seized.

Defendants base their claim of institutional racism primarily on statistics. During discovery, each side created a database of all stops and arrests by State Police members patroling the Turnpike between exits 1 and 7A out of the Moorestown Station for thirty-five randomly selected days between April 1988 and May 1991 from arrest reports, patrol charts, radio logs and traffic tickets. The databases are essentially the same. Both sides counted 3060 stops which the State found to include 1212 race identified stops (39.6%), the defense 1146 (37.4%).

To establish a standard against which to compare the stop data, the defense conducted a traffic survey and a violator survey. Dr. John Lamberth, Chairman of the Psychology Department at Temple University who I found is qualified as an expert in statistics and social psychology, designed both surveys.

The traffic survey was conducted over twenty-one randomly selected two and one-half hour sessions between June 11 and June 24, 1993 and between 8:00 a.m. and 8:00 p.m. at four sites, two northbound and two southbound, between exits 1 and 3 of the Turnpike. Teams supervised by Fred Last, Esq., of the Office of the Public Defender observed and recorded the number of vehicles that passed them except for large trucks, tractor-trailers, buses and government vehicles, how many contained a "black" occupant and the state of origin of each vehicle. Of the 42,706 vehicles counted, 13.5% had a black occupant. Dr. Lamberth testified that this percentage is consistent with the 1990 Census figures for the eleven states from where almost 90% of the observed vehicles were registered. He said it is also consistent with a study done by the Triangle Group for the U.S. Department of Transportation with which he was familiar.

The violator survey was conducted over ten sessions in four days in July 1993 by Mr. Last traveling between exits 1 and 3 in his vehicle at sixty miles per hour on cruise control after the speedometer had been calibrated and observing and recording the number of vehicles that passed him, the number of vehicles he passed and how many had a black occupant. Mr. Last counted a total of 2096 vehicles other than large trucks, tractortrailers, buses and government vehicles of which 2062 or 98.1% passed him going in excess of sixty miles per hour including 306 with a black occupant equaling about 15% of those vehicles clearly speeding. Multiple violators, that is those violating the speed limit and committing some other moving violation like tailgating, also equaled about 15% black. Dr. Lamberth testified that the difference between the percentage of black violators and the percentage of black travelers from the surveys is statistically insignificant and that there is no evidence traffic patterns changed between the period April 1988 to May 1991 in the databases and June—July 1993 when the surveys were done.

Using 13.5% as the standard or benchmark against which to compare the stop data, Dr. Lamberth found that 127 or 46.2% of the race identified stops between exits 1 and 3 were of blacks constituting and absolute disparity of 32.7%, a comparative disparity of 242% (32.7% divided by 13.5%) and 16.35 standard deviations. By convention, something is considered statistically significant if it would occur by chance fewer than five times in a hundred (over two standard deviations). In case I were to determine that the appropriate stop data for comparison with the standard is the stop data for the entire portion of the Turnpike patrolled by the Moorestown Station in recognition of the fact that the same troopers patrol between exits 3 and 7A as patrol between exits 1 and 3, Dr. Lamberth found that 408 or 35.6% of the race identified stops between exits 1 and 7A were of blacks constituting an absolute disparity of 22.1%, a comparative disparity of 164% and 22.1 standard deviations. He opined it is highly unlikely such statistics could have occurred randomly or by chance.

Defendants also presented the testimony of Dr. Joseph B. Kadane, an eminently qualified statistician. Among his many credentials, Dr. Kadane is a full professor of statistics and social sciences at Carnegie Mellon University, headed the Department of Statistics there between 1972 and 1981 and is a Fellow of the American Statistical Association, having served on its board of directors and a number of its committees and held various editorships on its Journal. Dr. Kadane testified that in his opinion both the traffic and violator surveys were well designed, carefully performed and statistically reliable for analysis. From the surveys and the defense database, he calculated that a black was 4.85 times as likely as a white to be stopped between exits 1 and 3. This calculation led him to "suspect" a racially non-neutral stopping policy. While he noted that the surveys were done in 1993 and compared to data from 1988 to 1991, he was nevertheless satisfied that the comparisons were useable and accurate within a few percent. He was not concerned that the violator survey failed to count cars going less than sixty miles per hour and travelling behind Mr. Last when he started a session. He was concerned, however, with the fact that only 37.4% of the stops in the defense database were race identified. In order to determine if the comparisons were sensitive to the missing racial data, he did calculations performed on the log odds of being stopped. Whether he assumed the probability of having one's race recorded if black and stopped is the same as if white and stopped or two or three times as likely, the log odds were still greater than .99 that blacks were stopped at higher rates than whites on the Turnpike between exits 1 and 3 during the period April 1988 to May 1991. He therefore concluded that the comparisons were not sensitive to the missing racial data.

Supposing that the disproportionate stopping of blacks was related to police discretion, the defense studied the traffic tickets issued by State Police members between exits 1 and 7A on the thirty-five randomly selected days broken down by State Police unit. There are 533 racially identified tickets in the databases issued by either the now disbanded Radar Unit, the Tactical Patrol Unit or general road troopers ("Patrol Unit"). The testimony indicates that the Radar Unit focused mainly on speeders using a radar van and chase cars and exercised limited discretion regarding which vehicles to stop. The Tac-Pac concentrates on traffic problems at specific locations and exercises somewhat more discretion as regards which vehicles to stop. Responsible to provide general law enforcement, the Patrol Unit exercises by far the most discretion among the three units. From Mr. Last's count, Dr. Lamberth computed that 18% of the tickets issued by the Radar Unit were to blacks, 23.8% of the tickets issued by the Tac-Pac were to blacks while 34.2% of the tickets issued by the Patrol Unit were to blacks. South of exit 3, Dr. Lamberth computed that 19.4% of the tickets issued by the Radar Unit were to blacks, 0.0% of the tickets issued by the Tac-Pac were to blacks while 43.8% of the tickets issued by the Patrol Unit were to blacks. In his opinion, the Radar Unit percentages are statistically consistent with the standard established by the violator survey, but the differences between the Radar Unit and the Patrol Unit between both exits 1 and 3 and 1 and 7A are statistically significant or well in excess of two standard deviations.

The State presented the testimony of Dr. Leonard Cupingood to challenge or refute the statistical evidence offered by the defense. I found Dr. Cupingood is qualified to give expert testimony in the field of statistics based on his Ph.D in statistics from Temple and his work experience with the Center for Forensic Economic Studies, a for profit corporation headquartered in Philadelphia. Dr. Cupingood collaborated with Dr. Bernard Siskin, his superior at the Center for Forensic Economic Studies and a former chairman of the Department of Statistics at Temple.

Dr. Cupingood had no genuine criticism of the defense traffic survey. Rather, he centered his criticism of the defense statistical evidence on the violator survey. Throughout his testimony he maintained that the violator survey failed to capture the relevant data which he opined was the racial mix of those speeders most likely to be stopped or the "tail of the distribution." He even recommended the State authorize him to design a study to collect this data, but the State declined. He was unclear, though, how he would design a study to ascertain in a safe way the vehicle going the fastest above the speed limit at a given time at a given location and the race of its occupants without involving the credibility of State Police members. In any event, his supposition that maybe blacks drive faster than whites above the speed limit was repudiated by all State Police members called by the State who were questioned about it. Colonel Clinton Pagano, Trooper Donald Nemeth, Trooper Stephen Baumann and Detective Timothy Grant each testified that blacks drive indistinguishably from whites. Moreover, Dr. Cupingood acknowledged that he knew of no study indicating that blacks drive worse than whites. Nor could he reconcile the notion with the evidence that 37% of the unticketed stops between exits 1 and 7A in his database were black and 63% of those between exits 1 and 3. Dr. James Fyfe, a criminal justice professor at Temple who the defense called in its rebuttal case and who I found is qualified as an expert in police science and police procedures, also testified that there is nothing in the literature or in his personal experience to support the theory that blacks drive differently from whites.

Convinced in his belief that the defense 15% standard or benchmark was open to question, Dr. Cupingood attempted to find the appropriate benchmark to compare with the databases. He did three studies of presumedly race-blind stops: night stops versus day stops; radar stops versus nonradar stops and drinking driving arrests triggered by calls for service.

In his study of night stops versus day stops, he compared the percentage of stops of blacks at night between exits 1 and 7A in the databases with the percentage of stops of blacks during daytime and found that night stops were 37.3% black versus 30.2% for daytime stops. Since he presumed the State Police generally cannot tell race at night, he concluded the higher percentage for night stops of blacks supported a standard well above 15%. His premise that the State Police generally cannot recognize race at night, however, is belied by the evidence. On July 16, 1994 between 9:40 p.m. and 11:00 p.m. Ahmad S. Corbitt, now an assistant deputy public defender, together with Investigator Minor of the Office of the Public Defender drove on the Turnpike at 55 miles per hour for a while and parked perpendicular to the Turnpike at a rest stop for a while to see if they could make out the races of the occupants of the vehicles they observed. Mr. Corbitt testified that the two could identify blacks versus whites about 80% of the time in the moving mode and close to 100% in the stationary mode. Over and above this proof is the fact the databases establish that the State Police only stopped an average of eight black occupied vehicles per night between exits 1 and 7A.

Dr. Cupingood conceded a trooper could probably identify one or two black motorists per night.

Next, in his study of radar stops versus non-radar stops, Dr. Cupingood focused on the race identified tickets where radar was used in the databases and found that 28.5% of them were issued to blacks. Since he assumed that radar is race neutral, he suggested 28.5% might be the correct standard. As Dr. Kadane said in rebuttal, this study is fundamentally flawed because it assumes what is in question or that the people stopped are the best measure of who is eligible to be stopped. If racial prejudice were afoot, the standard would be tainted. In addition, although a radar device is race-blind, the operator may not be. Of far more significance is the defense study comparing the traffic tickets issued by the Radar, Tac-Pac and Patrol Units which shows again that where radar is used by a unit concerned primarily with speeders and acting with little or no discretion like the Radar Unit, the percentage of tickets issued to blacks is consistent with their percentage on the highway.

And lastly in his effort to find the correct standard, Dr. Cupingood considered a DUI study done by Lieutenant Fred Madden, Administrative Officer of the Records and Identification Section of the State Police. Lt. Madden tabulated DUI arrests between July 1988 and June 1991 statewide, statewide excluding the State Police, for Troop D of the State Police which patrols the entire length of the Turnpike, for Moorestown Station of Troop D and for Moorestown Station south of exit 3 broken down by race and between patrol related versus calls for service (i.e. accidents, motorist aids and other—the arrested motorist coming to the attention of the State Police by a tolltaker or civilian). Since Dr. Cupingood believed DUI arrests from calls for service were race neutral, he adopted the percentage of DUI arrests of blacks for the Moorestown Station from calls for service of 23% as a possible standard. Like his radar versus non-radar stop study, his use of the DUI arrest study is fundamentally flawed because he assumed what is in question. Further, he erred in assuming that DUI arrests from calls for service involve no discretion. While the encounters involve no discretion, the arrests surely do.

Statewide (all departments)	12% black
Statewide (excluding State Police)	10.4% black
State Police	16% black
Troop D	23% black
Moorestown Station	34% black
Moorestown Station patrol related	41% black
Moorestown Station patrol related south of exit 3	50% black

He admitted that race/discretion may explain the following widespread statistics in the DUI arrest study:

After hearing the testimony of Kenneth Ruff and Kenneth Wilson, two former troopers called by the defense who were not reappointed at the end of their terms and who said they were trained and coached to make race based "profile" stops to increase their criminal arrests, the State asked Dr. Cupingood to study the race identified stops in his database and see how many possessed the profile characteristics cited by Ruff and Wilson, particularly how many were young (30 or under), black and male. Dr. Cupingood found that only 11.6% of the race identified stops were of young black males and only 6.6% of all stops were of young black males.

The defense then conducted a profile study of its own. It concentrated on the race identified stops of just blacks issued tickets and found that an adult black male was present in 88% of the cases where the gender of all occupants could be determined and that where gender and age could be determined, a black male 30 or younger was present in 63% of the cases. The defense study is more probative because it does concentrate on just stops of blacks issued tickets eliminating misleading comparisons with totals including whites or whites and a 62.6% group of race unknowns. Neither side, of course, could consider whether the blacks stopped and not issued tickets possessed profile characteristics since the databases contain no information about them.

Dr. Cupingood's so-called Mantel-Haentzel analysis ended the statistical evidence. He put forward this calculation of "expected black tickets" in an attempt to disprove the defense study showing the Patrol Unit, the unit with the most discretion, ticketed blacks at a rate not only well above the Radar and Tac-Pac Units, but also well above the standard fixed by the violator survey. The calculation insinuates that the Patrol Unit issued merely 5 excess tickets to blacks beyond what would have been expected. The calculation is worthless. First and foremost, Dr. Cupingood deleted the non-radar tickets which presumably involved a greater exercise of discretion. The role police discretion played in the issuance of tickets to blacks was the object of the defense study. Under the guise of comparing only things similarly situated, he thereupon deleted any radar tickets not issued in one of the four time periods he divided each of the thirty-five randomly selected days into for which there was not at least one race identified radar ticket issued by the Patrol Unit and at least one by the combined Radar, Tac-Pac Unit. He provided no justification for either creating the 140 time periods or combining the tickets of the Radar and Tac-Pac Units. To compound his defective analysis, he pooled the data in each time period into a single number and employed the resultant weighted average of the two units to compute the expected and excess, if any, tickets issued to blacks. By using weighted averages, he once again assumed the answer to the question he purported to address. He assumed the Patrol Unit gave the same number of tickets to blacks as did the Radar, Tac-Pac Unit, rather than test to see if it did. Even after "winnowing" the data, the comparison between the Patrol Unit and the Radar, Tac-Pac Unit is marginally statistically significant. Without winnowing, Dr. Kadane found the comparison of the radar tickets issued by the Patrol Unit to blacks with the radar tickets issued by the Radar, Tac-Pac Unit to blacks constituted 3.78 standard deviations which is distinctly above the 5% standard of statistical significance.

The defense did not rest on its statistical evidence alone. Along with the testimony of former troopers Kenneth Ruff and Kenneth Wilson about having been trained and coached to make race based profile stops but whose testimony is weakened by bias related to their not having been reappointed at the end of their terms, the defense elicited evidence through cross-examination of State witnesses and a rebuttal witness, Dr. James Fyfe, that the State Police hierarchy allowed, condoned, cultivated and tolerated discrimination between 1988 and 1991 in its crusade to rid New Jersey of the scourge of drugs.

Conjointly with the passage of the Comprehensive Drug Reform Act of 1987 and to advance the Attorney General's Statewide Action Plan for Narcotics Enforcement issued in January 1988 which "directed that the enforcement of our criminal drug laws shall be the highest priority law enforcement activity", Colonel Pagano formed the Drug Interdiction Training Unit (DITU) in late 1987 consisting of two supervisors and ten other members, two from each Troop selected for their successful seizure statistics, "… to actually patrol with junior road personnel and provide critical on-the-job training in recognizing potential violators." State Police Plan For Action dated July 7, 1987, at p. 14. According to Colonel Pagano, the DITU program was intended to be one step beyond the existing coach program to impart to newer troopers insight into drug enforcement and the "criminal program" (patrol related arrests) in general. DITU was disbanded in or around July 1992.

No training materials remain regarding the training DITU members themselves received, and few training materials remain regarding the training DITU members provided the newer troopers except for a batch of checklists. Just one impact study was ever prepared regarding the effectiveness of the DITU program rather than periodic impact evaluations and studies as required by S.O.P. F4 dated January 12, 1999, but this one undated report marked D-62 in evidence only provided statistics about the number of investigations conducted, the number of persons involved and the quantity and value of drugs seized without indicating the race of those involved or the number of fruitless investigations broken down by race. In the opinion of Dr. Fyfe, retention of training materials is important for review of the propriety of the training and to discern agency policy, and preparation of periodic impact evaluations and studies is important not only to determine the effectiveness of the program from a numbers standpoint, but more than that to enable administration to monitor and control the quality of the program and its impact on the public, especially a crackdown program like DITU which placed so much emphasis on stopping drug transportation by the use of "consents" to search following traffic stops in order to prevent constitutional excesses.

Despite the paucity of training materials and lack of periodic and complete impact evaluations and studies, a glimpse of the work of DITU emerges from the preserved checklists and the testimony of Sergeants Brian Caffrey and David Cobb. Sergeant Caffrey was the original assistant supervisor of DITU and became the supervisor in 1989. Sergeant Cobb was an original member of DITU and became the assistant supervisor in 1989. Sergeant Caffrey left DITU sometime in 1992, Sergeant Cobb sometime in 1991. Both testified that a major purpose of DITU was to teach trainees tip-offs and techniques about what to look for and do to talk or "dig" their way into a vehicle after, not before, a motor vehicle stop to effectuate patrol related arrests. Both denied teaching or using race as a tip-off either before or after a stop. Nevertheless, Sergeant Caffrey condoned a comment by a DITU trainer during the time he was the supervisor of DITU stating:

"Trooper Fash previously had DITU training, and it showed in the way he worked. He has become a little reluctant to stop cars in lieu [sic] of the Channel 9 News Report. He was told as long as he uses Title 39 he can stop any car he wants. He enjoys DITU and would like to ride again."

As the defense observes in its closing brief, "Why would a trooper who is acting in a racially neutral fashion become reluctant to stop cars as a result of a news story charging that racial minorities were being targeted [by the New Jersey State Police]?" Even A.A.G. Ronald Susswein, Deputy Director of the Division of Criminal Justice, acknowledged that this comment is incomplete because it fails to add the caveat, "as long as he doesn't also use race or ethnicity." Further, Sergeant Caffrey testified that "ethnicity is something to keep in mind" albeit not a tip-off and that he taught attendees at both the annual State Police in-service training session in March 1987 and the special State Police in-service training sessions in July and August 1987 that Hispanics are mainly involved in drug trafficking and showed them the film Operation Pipeline wherein the ethnicity of those arrested, mostly Hispanics, is prominently depicted. Dr. Fyfe criticized Sergeant Caffrey's teaching Hispanics are mainly involved and his showing Operation Pipeline as well as the showing of the Jamaican Posse film wherein only blacks are depicted as drug traffickers at the 1989 annual State Police inservice training session saying trainers should not teach what they do not intend their trainees to act upon. At a minimum, teaching Hispanics are mainly involved in drug trafficking and showing films depicting mostly Hispanics and blacks trafficking in drugs at training sessions worked at cross-purposes with concomitant instruction pointing out that neither race nor ethnicity may be considered in making traffic stops.

Key corroboration for finding the State Police hierarchy allowed and tolerated discrimination came from Colonel Pagano. Colonel Pagano was Superintendent of the State Police from 1975 to February 1990. He testified there was a noisy demand in the 1980s to get drugs off the streets. In accord, Attorney General Cary Edwards and he made drug interdiction the number one priority of law enforcement. He helped formulate the Attorney General's Statewide Action Plan for Narcotics Enforcement and established DITU within the State Police. He kept an eye on DITU through conversations with staff officers and Sergeants Mastella and Caffrey and review of reports generated under the traditional reporting system and D-62 in evidence. He had no thought DITU would engage in constitutional violations. He knew all State Police members were taught that they were guardians of the Constitution and that targeting any race was unconstitutional and poor police practice to boot. He recognized it was his responsibility to see that race was not a factor in who was stopped, searched and arrested. When he became Superintendent, he formed the Internal Affairs Bureau to investigate citizen complaints against State Police members to maintain the integrity of the Division. Substantiated deviations from regulations resulted in sanctions, additional training or counseling.

More telling, however, is what Colonel Pagano said and did, or did not do, in response to the Channel 9 expose entitled "Without Just Cause" which aired in 1989 and which troubled Trooper Fash and what he did not do in response to complaints of profiling from the NAACP and ACLU and these consolidated motions to suppress and similar motions in Warren and Middlesex Counties. He said to Joe Collum of Channel 9 that "[violating rights of motorists was] of serious concern [to him], but no where near the concern that I think we have go to look to in trying to correct some of the problems we find with the criminal element in the State" and "the bottom line is that those stops were not made on the basis of race alone."(emphasis added) Since perhaps these isolated comments were said inadvertently or edited out of context, a truer reflection of his attitude about claims of racism would appear to be his videotaped remarks shown all members of the State Police at roll call in conjunction with the WOR series. Thereon he clearly said that he did not want targeting or discriminatory enforcement and that "when you put on this uniform, you leave your biases and your prejudices behind." But he also said as regarded the charge of a Trenton school principal named Jones that he had been stopped on the Turnpike and threatened, intimidated and assaulted by a trooper, "We know that the teacher assaulted the trooper. He didn't have a driver's license or a registration for his fancy new Mercedes." (emphasis added) And he called Paul McLemore, the first African-American trooper in New Jersey and now a practicing attorney and who spoke of discrimination within the ranks of the State Police, "an ingrate." And he told the members to "keep the heat on" and then assured them:

> "... Here at Division Headquarters we'll make sure that when the wheels start to squeak, we'll do whatever we can to make sure that you're supported out in the field. ... Anything that goes toward implementing the Drug Reform Act is important. And, we'll handle the squeaky wheels here."

He admitted the Internal Affairs Bureau was not designed to investigate general complaints, so he could not refer the general complaints of discrimination to it for scrutiny. Yet he never requested the Analytical Unit to investigate stop data from radio logs, patrol charts and tickets or search and seizure data from arrest reports, operations reports, investigation reports and consent to search forms, not even after the Analytical Unit informed him in a report on arrests by region, race and crime that he had requested from it for his use in the WOR series that "... arrests are not a valid reflection of stops (data relative to stops with respect to race is not compiled)." The databases compiled for these motions attest, of course, to the fact that race identified stop data could have been compiled. He testified he could not launch an investigation into every general complaint because of limited resources and that there was insufficient evidence of discrimination in the Channel 9 series, the NAACP and ACLU complaints and the various motions to suppress for him to spend his "precious" resources. In short, he left the issue of discrimination up to the courts and months of testimony in this and other counties at State expense.

The right to be free from discrimination is firmly supported by the Fourteenth Amendment to the United States Constitution and the protections of Article I, paragraphs 1 and 5 of the New Jersey Constitution of 1947. To be sure, "the eradication of the 'cancer of discrimination' has long been one of our State's highest priorities." *Dixon v. Rutgers, The State University of N.J.*, 110 N.J. 432, 451 541 A.2d 1046 (1988). It is indisputable, therefore, that the police may not stop a motorist based on race or any other invidious classification. See *State v. Kuhn*, 213 N.J. Super. 275, 517 A.2d 162 (1986).

Generally, however, the inquiry for determining the constitutionality of a stop or a search and seizure is limited to "whether the conduct of the law enforcement officer who undertook the [stop or] search was objectively reasonable, without regard to his or her underlying motives or intent." *State v. Bruzzese* 94 N.J. 210, 463 A.2d 320 (1983). Thus, it has been said that the courts will not inquire into motivation of a police officer whose stop of a vehicle was based upon a traffic violation committed in his presence. See *United States v. Smith*, 799 F.2d 704, 708–709 (11th Cir. 1986); *United States v. Hollman*, 541 F.2d 196, 198 (8th Cir. 1976); cf. *United States v. Villamonte-Marquez*, 462 U.S. 579, 103 S. Ct. 2573, 77 L. Ed. 2d 22 (1983). But where objective evidence establishes "that a police agency has embarked upon an officially sanctioned or de facto policy of targeting minorities for investigation and arrest," any evidence seized will be suppressed to deter future insolence in office by those charged with enforcement of the law and to maintain judicial integrity. *State v. Kennedy*, 247 N.J. Super. 21, 588 A.2d 834 (App. Div. 1991).

Statistics may be used to make out a case of targeting minorities for prosecution of traffic offenses provided the comparison is between the racial composition of the motorist population violating the traffic laws and the racial composition of those arrested for traffic infractions on the relevant roadway patrolled by the police agency. *Wards Cove Packing Co. v. Atonio, supra; State v. Kennedy, 247 N.J. Super. at 33–34.* While defendants have the burden of proving "the existence of purposeful discrimination," discriminatory intent may be inferred from statistical proof presenting a stark pattern or an even less extreme pattern in certain limited contexts. *McCleskey v. Kemp, 481 U.S. 279, 107 S. Ct. 1756, 95 L. Ed. 2d 262 (1987). Kennedy, supra,* implies that discriminatory intent may be inferred from statistical proof in a traffic stop context probably because only uniform variables (Title 39 violations) are relevant to the challenged stops and the State has an opportunity to explain the statistical disparity. "[A] selection procedure that is susceptible of abuse ... supports the presumption of discrimination raised by the statistical showing." *Castaneda v. Partida, 430 U.S. 482, 494, 97 S. Ct. 1272, 51 L. Ed. 2d 498 (1977).*

Once defendants expose a prima facie case of selective enforcement, the State generally cannot rebut it by merely calling attention to possible flaws or unmeasured variables in defendants' statistics. Rather, the State must introduce specific evidence showing that either there actually are defects which bias the results or the missing factors, when properly organized and accounted for, eliminate or explain the disparity. *Bazemore v. Friday, 478 U.S. 385, 106 S. Ct. 3000, 92 L. Ed. 2d 315 (1986); EEOC v. General Telephone Co. of Northwest, Inc., 885 F.2d 575 (9th Cir. 1989).* Nor will mere denials or reliance on the good faith of the officers suffice. *Castaneda v. Partida, 430 U.S. at 498 n. 19.*

Here, defendants have proven at least a de facto policy on the part of the State Police out of the Moorestown Station of targeting blacks for investigation and arrest between April 1988 and May 1991 both south of exit 3 and between exists 1 and 7A of the Turnpike. Their surveys satisfy *Wards Cove, supra.* The statistical disparities and standard deviations revealed are indeed stark. The discretion devolved upon general road troopers to stop any car they want as long as Title 39 is used evinces a selection process that is susceptible of abuse. The utter failure of the State Police hierarchy to monitor and control a crackdown program like DITU or investigate the many claims of institutional discrimination manifests its indifference if not acceptance. Against all this, the State submits only denials and the conjecture and flawed studies of Dr. Cupingood.

The eradication of illegal drugs from our State is an obviously worthy goal, but not at the expense of individual rights. As Justice Brandeis so wisely said dissenting in *Olmstead v. United States, 277 U.S. 438, 479, 72 L. Ed. 944, 48 S. Ct. 564 (1928):*

"Experience should teach us to be most on our guard to protect liberty when the government's purposes are beneficent. Men born to freedom are naturally alert to repel invasion of their liberty by evil-minded rulers. The greatest dangers to liberty lurk in insidious encroachment by men of zeal, well-meaning but without understanding."

Motions granted.

HILLS v. GAUTREAUX
Supreme Court of the United States (1976)
425 U.S. 284

MR. JUSTICE STEWART. The United States Department of Housing and Urban Development (HUD) has been judicially found to have violated the Fifth Amendment and the Civil Rights Act of 1964 in connection with the selection of sites for public housing in the city of Chicago. The issue before us is whether the remedial order of the federal trial court may extend beyond Chicago's territorial boundaries. ...

This extended litigation began in 1966 when ... six Negro tenants in or applicants for public housing in Chicago, brought separate actions on behalf of themselves and all other Negro tenants and applicants similarly situated against the Chicago Housing Authority (CHA) and HUD. The complaint ... alleged that between 1950 and 1965 substantially all of the sites for family public housing selected by CHA and approved by the Chicago City Council were "at the time of such selection, and are now," located "within the areas known as the Negro Ghetto." The [tenants] further alleged that CHA deliberately selected the sites to "avoid the placement of Negro families in white neighborhoods" in violation of federal statutes and the Fourteenth Amendment. In a companion suit against HUD the [tenants] claimed that it had "assisted in the carrying on and continues to assist in the carrying on of a racially discriminatory public housing system within the City of Chicago" by providing financial assistance and other support for CHA's discriminatory housing projects.

The District Court ... entered summary judgment against CHA on the ground that it had violated the respondents' constitutional rights by selecting public housing sites and assigning tenants on the basis of race. Uncontradicted evidence submitted to the District Court established that the public housing system operated by CHA was racially segregated, with four overwhelmingly white projects located in white neighborhoods and with 99 1/2% of the remaining family units located in Negro neighborhoods and 99% of those units occupied by Negro tenants. In order to prohibit future violations and to remedy the effects of past unconstitutional practices, the court directed CHA to build its next 700 family units in predominantly white areas of Chicago and thereafter to locate at least 75% of its new family public housing in predominantly white areas inside Chicago or in Cook County. In addition, CHA was ordered to modify its tenant-assignment and site-selection procedures and to use its best efforts to increase the supply of dwelling units as rapidly as possible in conformity with the judgment.

The District Court then ... dismiss[ed] the complaint [against HUD]. ... The United States Court of Appeals for the Seventh Circuit reversed and ordered the District Court to enter summary judgment for the [tenants], holding that HUD had violated both the Fifth Amendment and §601 of the Civil Rights Act of 1964, by knowingly sanctioning and assisting CHA's racially discriminatory public housing program.

On remand, the trial court addressed the difficult problem of providing an effective remedy for the racially segregated public housing system that had been created by the unconstitutional conduct of CHA and HUD. ... The court found that metropolitan area relief was unwarranted because "the wrongs were committed within the limits of Chicago and solely against residents of the City" and there were no allegations that "CHA and HUD discriminated or fostered racial discrimination in the suburbs."

On appeal, the Court of Appeals for the Seventh Circuit, with one judge dissenting, reversed and remanded the case for "the adoption of a comprehensive metropolitan area plan that will not only disestablish

331

the segregated public housing system in the City of Chicago ... but will increase the supply of dwelling units as rapidly as possible." HUD subsequently sought review in this Court of the permissibility ... of "inter-district relief for discrimination in public housing in the absence of a finding of an inter-district violation." We granted certiorari to consider this important question. ...

In *Milliken v. Bradley* this Court considered the proper scope of a federal court's equity decree in the context of a school desegregation case. They respondents in that case had brought an action alleging that the Detroit public school system was segregated on the basis of race as the result of official conduct and sought an order establishing "'a unitary, nonracial school system.'" After finding that constitutional violations committed by the Detroit School Board and state officials had contributed to racial segregation in the Detroit schools, the trial court had proceeded to the formulation of a remedy. Although there had been neither proof of unconstitutional actions on the part of neighboring school districts nor a demonstration that the Detroit violations had produced significant segregative effects in those districts, the court established a desegregation panel and ordered it to prepare a remedial plan consolidating the Detroit school system and 53 independent suburban school districts. ... This Court reversed ..., holding that the multidistrict remedy contemplated by the desegregation order was an erroneous exercise of the equitable authority of the federal courts.

Although the *Milliken* opinion discussed the many practical problems that would be encountered in the consolidation of numerous school districts by judicial decree, the Court's decision rejecting the metropolitan area desegregation order was actually based on fundamental limitations on the remedial powers of the federal courts to restructure the operation of local and state governmental entities. That power is not plenary. It "may be exercised 'only on the basis of a constitutional violation.'" Once a constitutional violation is found, a federal court is required to tailor "the scope of the remedy" to fit "the nature and extent of the constitutional violation." In *Milliken*, there was no finding of unconstitutional action on the part of the suburban school officials and no demonstration that the violations committed in the operation of the Detroit school system had had any significant segregative effects in the suburbs. ... Under these circumstances, the Court held that the interdistrict decree was impermissible because it was not commensurate with the constitutional violation to be repaired.

... As the Court noted [in *Milliken*], school district lines cannot be "casually ignored or treated as a mere administrative convenience" because they separate independent governmental entities responsible for the operation of autonomous public school systems. The Court's holding that there had to be an interdistrict violation or effect before a federal court could order the crossing of district boundary lines reflected the substantive impact of a consolidation remedy on separate and independent school districts. The District Court's desegregation order in *Milliken* was held to be an impermissible remedy not because it envisioned relief against a wrongdoer extending beyond the city in which the violation occurred but because it contemplated a judicial decree restructuring the operation of local governmental entities that were not implicated in any constitutional violation. ...

The question presented in this case concerns only the authority of the District Court to order HUD to take remedial action outside the city limits of Chicago. HUD does not dispute the Court of Appeals' determination that it violated the Fifth Amendment and §601 of the Civil Rights Act of 1964 by knowingly funding CHA's racially discriminatory family public housing program, nor does it question the appropriateness of a remedial order designed to alleviate the effects of past segregative practices by requiring that public housing be developed in areas that will afford respondents an opportunity to reside in desegregated neighborhoods. But HUD contends that the *Milliken* decision bars a remedy affecting its conduct beyond the boundaries of Chicago for two reasons. First, it asserts that such a remedial order would constitute the grant of relief incommensurate with the constitutional violation to be repaired. And, second, it claims that a decree regulating HUD's conduct beyond Chicago's boundaries would inevitably have the effect of "consolidat[ing] for remedial purposes" governmental units not implicated in HUD's and CHA's violations. We address each of these arguments in turn. ...

We reject the contention that, since HUD's constitutional and statutory violations were committed in Chicago, *Milliken* precludes an order against HUD that will affect its conduct in the greater metropolitan area. The critical distinction between HUD and the suburban school districts in *Milliken* is that HUD has been found to have violated the Constitution. ... Our prior decisions counsel that in the event of a constitutional violation "all reasonable methods be available to formulate an effective remedy," and that every effort should be made by a federal court to employ those methods "to achieve the greatest possible degree of [relief], taking into account the practicalities of the situation." ...

Nothing in the *Milliken* decision suggests a *per se* rule that federal courts lack authority to order parties found to have violated the Constitution to undertake remedial efforts beyond the municipal boundaries of the city where the violation occurred. ... [T]he District Court's proposed remedy in *Milliken* was impermissible because of the limits on the federal judicial power to interfere with the operation of state political entities that were not implicated in unconstitutional conduct. Here, unlike the desegregation remedy found erroneous in *Milliken*, a judicial order directing relief beyond the boundary lines of Chicago will not necessarily entail coercion of uninvolved governmental units, because both CHA and HUD have the authority to operate outside the Chicago city limits.

In this case, it is entirely appropriate and consistent with *Milliken* to order CHA and HUD to attempt to create housing alternatives for the respondents in the Chicago suburbs. Here the wrong committed by HUD confined the [tenants] to segregated public housing. The relevant geographic area for purposes of the [tenants'] housing options is the Chicago housing market, not the Chicago city limits. ... An order against HUD and CHA regulating their conduct in the greater metropolitan area will do no more than take into account HUD's expert determination of the area relevant to the [tenants'] housing opportunities and will thus be wholly commensurate with the "nature and extent of the constitutional violation." To foreclose such relief solely because HUD's constitutional violation took place within the city limits of Chicago would transform Milliken's principled limitation on the exercise of federal judicial authority into an arbitrary and mechanical shield for those found to have engaged in unconstitutional conduct. ...

The more substantial question under *Milliken* is whether an order against HUD affecting its conduct beyond Chicago's boundaries would impermissibly interfere with local governments and suburban housing authorities that have not been implicated in HUD's unconstitutional conduct. ...

HUD's position, we think, underestimates the ability of a federal court to formulate a decree that will grant the respondents the constitutional relief of which they may be entitled without overstepping the limits of judicial power established in the Milliken case. HUD's discretion regarding the selection of housing proposals to assist with funding as well as its authority under a recent statute to contract for low-income housing directly with private owners and developers can clearly be directed toward providing relief to the respondents in the greater Chicago metropolitan area without pre-empting the power of local governments by undercutting the role of those governments in the federal housing assistance scheme. ...

The Housing and Community Development Act of 1974 significantly enlarged HUD's role in the creation of housing opportunities. Under the §8 Lower-Income Housing Assistance program, ... HUD may contract directly with private owners to make leased housing units available to eligible lower income persons. As HUD has acknowledged in this case, "local governmental approval is no longer explicitly required as a condition of the program's applicability to a locality." Regulations governing the §8 program permit HUD to select "the geographic area or areas in which the housing is to be constructed," and direct that sites be chosen to "promote greater choice of housing opportunities and avoid undue concentration of assisted persons in areas containing a high proportion of low-income persons." In most cases the Act grants the unit of local government in which the assistance is to be provided the right to comment on the application and, in certain specified circumstances, to preclude the Secretary of HUD from approving the application. Use of the §8 program to expand low-income housing opportunities outside areas of minority concentration would not have a coercive effect on suburban municipalities. For under the program, the local governmental units retain the right to comment on specific assistance proposals, to reject certain proposals that are inconsistent with their approved housing-assistance plans, and to require that zoning and other land-use restrictions be adhered to by builders.

In sum, there is no basis for [HUD's] claim that court-ordered metropolitan area relief in this case would be impermissible as a matter of law under the *Milliken* decision. In contrast to the desegregation order in that case, a metropolitan area relief order directed to HUD would not consolidate or in any way restructure local governmental units. The remedial decree would neither force suburban governments to submit public housing proposals to HUD nor displace the rights and powers accorded local government entities under federal or state housing statutes or existing and-use laws. The order would have the same effect on the suburban governments as a discretionary decision by HUD to use its statutory powers to provide the [tenants] with alternatives to the racially segregated Chicago public housing system created by CHA and HUD.

Since we conclude that a metropolitan are remedy in this case is not impermissible as a matter of law, we … remand […] the case to the District Court "for additional evidence and for further consideration of the issue of metropolitan area relief." Our determination that the District Court has the authority to direct HUD to engage in remedial efforts in the metropolitan are a outside the city limits of Chicago should not be interpreted as requiring a metropolitan area order. The nature and scope of the remedial decree to be entered on remand is a matter for the District Court in the exercise of its equitable discretion, after affording the parties an opportunity to present their views. … Since we conclude that a metropolitan area remedy in this case is not impermissible as a matter of law, we … remand […] the case to the District Court "for additional evidence and for further consideration of the issue of metropolitan area relief." Out determination that the District Court has the authority to direct HUD to engage in remedial efforts in the metropolitan area outside the city limits of Chicago should not be interpreted as requiring a metropolitan area order. The nature and scope of the remedial decree to be entered on remand is a matter for the District Court in the exercise of its equitable discretion, after affording the parties an opportunity to present their views. …

Private Employment

3. Affirmative *Action Policy Arguments*

Following are some policy arguments that are made in support of and in opposition to affirmative action. The list is not exhaustive, is in no particular order and makes no judgment as to truth or validity of any argument. Neither does it attempt to distinguish among the very different definitions of what affirmative action is. What is certain is that you will find people of all colors and ages, and of both genders, identifying with each of the arguments, and not infrequently with one or more arguments from each side of the policy divide, although no one on one side of the divide or the other will accept all of the arguments on that side or even portions of a given argument.

Pro

- a voluntary remedial measure for past discriminatory practices, designed to achieve, but not maintain, racial and gender balance; can be done

without unduly harming others (e.g., taking vested rights from others)
- the benefits of diversity; race and gender bring unique viewpoints
- in a number of situations, particularly but not exclusively in education and in the professions, selection criteria are sufficiently subjective that invidious discrimination can be practiced without detection
- society is racist and male dominated, and affirmative action is the only way of offsetting this; race and gender matter in this society; it is not color blind, and affirmative action is a way of dealing with that reality; differentials in race and gender are not explainable by differences in legitimate qualifications; existing race and gender disparities caused by discrimination, and affirmative action is necessary to remedy that; integration is a desirable social goal and affirmative action is a necessary tool (a desegregation tool) in reaching that end
- affirmative action in its *Griggs* form eliminates irrelevant criteria such as race and gender and permits relevant qualifications to operate
- positive signal to the rest of the world, which is primarily female and people of color
- brings women and minorities into positions previously denied them because of stereotypes; creates role models and positive aspirations; creates opportunities for persons who would otherwise not have had them
- affirmative action may not be the sole remedy to address the disparity among groups, nor even necessarily the primary one, but it can be an effective remedy in concert with others

Con

- past discrimination should be left to the past, and does not justify imposing remedies on present innocents
- ought not remedy discrimination by discrimination; making race or gender a factor violates the ideal of a color blind society; color or gender are made to matter, rather than qualifications for the job; race and gender have become the factors in selection decisions; recognizes rights because of membership in a group, rather than personal qualifications; becomes in effect a quota system

- affirmative action puts unwelcome pressure on its beneficiaries, whose qualifications are then suspect; undermines character and initiative
- pool of qualified minorities may not be proportional to their proportion of the population, contrary to affirmative action presumptions
- let the market make selection decisions; if left alone, it will make efficient decisions
- there is nothing voluntary about the programs; required for employers doing government contracting or institutions receiving government funding
- divisive; engenders opposition, fans hatred, creates tensions
- siphons off just enough anger to make political coalitions for more radical social remedies ineffective

- society is racist and male dominated, and affirmative action will not change that
- violates freedom of association interests; integration may or may not be a viable social goal, but forcing it is not going to contribute to that end
- factors other than race and gender account for statistical disparities among groups work on those factors; the discrimination problems we face are not at root race or gender problems, but class problems: a political economy which by design or by result malapportions power such that the poor are kept poor in order to aid the rich
- race and gender do not bring unique and diverse perspectives; diversity in viewpoint is not race and gender specific.

Hate Speech

DOE v. UNIVERSITY OF MICHIGAN
United States District Court for the Eastern District of Michigan (1989)
721 F. Supp. 852

In 1988 the University of Michigan adopted the Discriminatory Harassment Policy, which subjected persons to discipline for:

Any behavior, verbal or physical, that stigmatizes or victimizes an individual on the basis of race, ethnicity, religion, sex, sexual orientation, creed, national origin, ancestry, age, marital status, handicap or Vietnam-era veteran status, and that

a. Involves an express or implied threat to an individual's academic efforts, employment, participation in University sponsored extra-curricular activities or personal safety; or

b. Has the purpose or reasonably foreseeable effect of interfering with an individual's academic efforts, employment, participation in University sponsored extra-curricular activities or personal safety; or

c. Creates an intimidating, hostile, or demeaning environment for educational pursuits, employment or participation in University sponsored extra-curricular activities.

Shortly after the Policy was adopted, the University issued an Interpretive Guide, a Guide later withdrawn (as "inaccurate") so quietly that few knew it had been withdrawn. The Guide contained examples of punishable behavior:

A flyer containing racist threats distributed in a residence hall.

- Racist graffiti written on the door of an Asian student's study carrel.

- A male student makes remarks in class like "Women just aren't as good in this field as men," thus creating a hostile learning atmosphere for female classmates.

- Students in a residence hall have a floor party and invite everyone on their floor except one person because they think she might be a lesbian.

- A black student is confronted and racially insulted by two white students in a cafeteria.

- Male students leave pornographic pictures and jokes on the desk of a female graduate student.

- Two men demand that their roommate in the residence hall move out and be tested for AIDS.

In addition, the Guide contained a separate section entitled "YOU are a harasser when ..." which contained the following examples of discriminatory conduct:

- You exclude someone from a study group because that person is of a different race, sex, or ethnic origin than you are.

- You tell jokes about gay men and lesbians.

- Your student organization sponsors entertainment that includes a comedian who slurs Hispanics.

- You display a confederate flag on the door of your room in the residence hall.

- You laugh at a joke about someone in your class who stutters.

- You make obscene telephone calls or send racist notes or computer messages.

- You comment in a derogatory way about a particular person or group's physical appearance or sexual orientation, or their cultural origins, or religious beliefs.

Doe is a psychology graduate student. His specialty is the field of biopsychology, which he describes as the interdisciplinary study of the biological bases of individual differences in personality traits and mental abilities. Doe said that certain controversial theories positing biologically-based differences between sexes and races might be perceived as "sexist" and "racist" by some students, and he feared that discussion of such theories might be sanctionable under the Policy. He asserted that his right to freely and openly discuss these theories was impermissibly chilled in violation of the First Amendment's Free Speech Clause, and he requested that the Policy be declared unconstitutional and enjoined on the grounds of vagueness and overbreadth.

COHN, J. ...

V. Vagueness and Overbreadth...

A. Scope of Permissible Regulation

Before inquiring whether the policy is impermissibly vague and overbroad, it would be helpful to first distinguish between verbal conduct and verbal acts that are generally protected by the First Amendment and those that are not. It is the latter class of behavior that the University may legitimately regulate.

Although the line is sometimes difficult to draw with precision, the Court must distinguish at the outset between the First Amendment protection of so-called "pure speech" and mere conduct. As to the latter, it can be safely said that most extreme and blatant forms of discriminatory conduct are not protected by the First Amendment, and indeed are punishable by a variety of state and federal criminal laws and subject to civil actions. Discrimination in employment, education, and government benefits on the basis of race, sex, ethnicity, and religion are prohibited by the constitution and both state and federal statutes. In addition, the state provides criminal penalties and civil remedies for assault and battery, and vandalism and property damage. Federal law imposes civil and criminal sanctions against persons depriving or conspiring to deprive others of rights guaranteed by the United States constitution.

Many forms of sexually abusive and harassing conduct are also sanctionable. These would include abduction, rape, and other forms of criminal sexual conduct. The dissemination of legally obscene materials is also a crime under state law. In addition, a civil remedy exists for women who are subjected to demands for sexual favors by employers as an express or implied quid pro quo for employment benefits. Minorities or women who are exposed to such extreme and pervasive workplace harassment as to create a hostile or offensive working environment are also entitled to civil damages. The First Amendment presents no obstacle to the establishment of internal University sanctions as to any of these categories of conduct, over and above and remedies already supplied by state or federal law. ...

What the University could not do, however, was establish an anti-discrimination policy which had the effect of prohibiting certain speech because it disagreed with ideas or messages sought to be conveyed. As the Supreme Court stated in *West Virginia State Board of Education v. Barnette* (1943):

> If there is any star fixed in our constitutional constellation, it is that no official, high or petty, can prescribe what shall be orthodox in politics, nationalism, religion, or other matters of opinion or force citizens to confess by word or act their faith therein.

Nor could the University proscribe speech simply because it was found to be offensive, even gravely so, by large numbers of people. As the Supreme Court noted in *Street v. New York*:

> It is firmly settled that under our Constitution the public expression of ideas may not be prohibited merely because the ideas are themselves offensive to some of their hearers.

These principles acquire a special significance in the University setting, where the free and unfettered interplay of competing views is essential to the institution's educational mission. With these general rules in mind, the Court can now consider whether the Policy sweeps within its scope speech which is otherwise protected by the First Amendment.

B. Overbreadth

1. Doe claimed that the Policy was invalid because it was facially overbroad. It is fundamental that statutes regulating First Amendment activities must be narrowly drawn to address only the specific evil at hand. ... A law regulating speech will

be deemed overbroad if it sweeps within its ambit a substantial amount of protected speech along with that which it may legitimately regulate.

The Supreme Court has consistently held that statutes punishing speech or conduct solely on the grounds that they are unseemly or offensive are unconstitutionally overbroad. In *Houston v. Hill*, the Supreme Court struck down a City of Houston ordinance which provided that "it shall be unlawful for any person to assault or strike or in any manner oppose, molest, and abuse or interrupt any policeman in the execution of his duty." The Supreme Court also found that the ordinance was overbroad because it forbade citizens from criticizing and insulting police officers, although such conduct was constitutionally protected. The fact that the statute also had a legitimate scope of application in prohibiting conduct which was clearly unprotected by the First Amendment was not enough to save it. ... In *Papish v. University of Missouri* the Supreme Court ordered the reinstatement of a university student expelled for distributing an underground newspaper sporting the headline "Motherfucker acquitted" on the grounds that "the mere dissemination of ideas—no matter how offensive to good taste—on a state university campus may not be shut off in the name alone of conventions of decency." Although the Supreme Court acknowledged that reasonable restrictions on the time, place, and manner of distribution might have been permissible, "the opinions below show clearly that [plaintiff] was dismissed because of the disapproved content of the newspaper." ... These cases stand generally for the proposition that the state may not prohibit broad classes of speech, some of which may indeed be legitimately regulable, if in so doing a substantial amount of constitutionally protected conduct is also prohibited. This was the fundamental infirmity of the Policy.

2. The University repeatedly argued that the Policy did not apply to speech that is protected by the First Amendment. It urged the Court to disregard the Guide as "inaccurate" and look instead to "the manner in which the Policy has been interpreted and applied by those charged with its enforcement." However, as applied by the University over the past year, the Policy was consistently applied to reach protected speech.

On December 7, 1988, a complaint was filed against a graduate student in the School of Social Work alleging that he harassed students based on sexual orientation. ... The basis for the sexual orientation charge was apparently that in a research class, the student openly stated his belief that homosexuality was a disease and that he intended to develop a counseling plan for changing gay clients to straight. He also related to other students that he had been counseling several of his gay patients accordingly. The student apparently had several heated discussions with his classmates over the validity and morality of his theory and program. On January 11, 1989, the Interim Policy Administrator wrote to the student informing him that following an investigation of the complaints, there was sufficient evidence to warrant a formal hearing on the charges of ... sexual orientation harassment. A formal hearing on the charges was held on January 28, 1989. The hearing panel ... refused to convict him of harassment on the basis of sexual orientation. ...

Although the student was not sanctioned over the allegations of sexual orientation harassment, the fact remains that the Policy Administrator—the authoritative voice of the University on these matters—saw no First Amendment problem in forcing the student to a hearing to answer for allegedly harassing statements made in the course of academic discussion and research. Moreover, there is no indication that had the hearing panel convicted rather than acquitted the student, the University would have interceded to protect the interests of academic freedom and freedom of speech.

A second case, which was informally resolved, also demonstrated that the University did not exempt statements made in the course of classroom academic discussions from the sanctions of the policy. On September 28, 1988, a complaint was filed against a student in an entrepreneurship class in the School of Business Administration for reading an allegedly homophobic limerick during a scheduled class public-speaking exercise which ridiculed a well known athlete for his presumed sexual orientation. The Policy Administrator was able to persuade the perpetrator to attend an educational "gay rap" session, write a letter of apology to the Michigan Daily, and apologize to his class and the matter was dropped. No discussion of the possibility that the limerick was protected speech appears in the file or in the Administrator's notes.

A third incident involved a comment made in the orientation session of a preclinical dentistry class. The class was widely regarded as one of the most difficult for second year dentistry students. To allay fears and concerns at the outset, the class was broken up into small sections to informally discuss anticipated problems. During the ensuing discussion, a student stated that "he had heard that minorities had a difficult time in the course and that he had heard that they were not treated fairly." A minority professor teaching the class filed a complaint on the grounds that the comment was unfair and hurt her chances for tenure. Following the filing of the complaint, the student was "counseled" about the existence of the policy and agreed to write a letter apologizing for making the comment without adequately verifying the allegation, which he said he had heard from his roommate, a black former dentistry student.

The manner in which these three complaints were handled demonstrated that the University considered serious comments made in the context of classroom discussion to be sanctionable under the Policy. The innocent intent of the speaker was apparently immaterial to whether a complaint would be pursued. Moreover, the Administrator generally failed to consider whether a comment was protected by the First Amendment before informing the accused student that a complaint had been filed. The Administrator instead attempted to persuade the accused student to accept "voluntary" sanctions. Behind this persuasion was, of course, the subtle threat that failure to accept such sanctions might result in a formal hearing. ... The Administrator's manner of enforcing the Policy was constitutionally indistinguishable from a full blown prosecution. The University could not seriously argue that the policy was never interpreted to reach protected conduct. It is clear that the policy was overbroad both on its face and as applied.

C.   Vagueness

Doe also urges that the policy be struck down on the grounds that it is impermissibly vague. A statute is unconstitutionally vague when "men of common intelligence must necessarily guess at its meaning." A statute must give adequate warning of the conduct which is to be prohibited and must set out explicit standards for those who apply it. ...

Looking at the plain language of the Policy, it was simply impossible to discern any limitation on its scope or any conceptual distinction between protected and unprotected conduct. The structure of the Policy was in two parts; one relates to cause and the other to effect. Both cause and effect must be present to state a prima facie violation of the Policy. The operative words in the cause section required that language must "stigmatize" or "victimize" an individual. However, both of these terms are general and elude precise definition. Moreover, it is clear that the fact that a statement may victimize or stigmatize an individual does not, in and of itself, strip it of protection under the accepted First ... Amendment tests.

The first of the "effects clauses" stated that in order to be sanctionable, the stigmatizing and victimizing statements had to "involve an express or implied threat to an individual's academic efforts, employment, participation in University sponsored extra-curricular activities or personal safety." It is not clear what kind of conduct would constitute a "threat" to an individual's academic efforts. It might refer to an unspecified threat of future retaliation by the speaker. Or it might equally plausibly refer to the threat to a victim's academic success because the stigmatizing and victimizing speech is so inherently distracting. Certainly the former would be unprotected speech. However, it is not clear whether the latter would.

Moving to the second "effect clause," a stigmatizing or victimizing comment is sanctionable if it has the purpose or reasonably foreseeable effect of interfering with an individual's academic efforts, etc. Again, the question is what conduct will be held to "interfere" with an individual's academic efforts. The language of the policy alone gives no inherent guidance. The one interpretive resource the University provided was withdrawn as "inaccurate," an implicit admission that even the University itself was unsure of the precise scope and meaning of the Policy.

... [T]he plain fact [is] that the University never articulated any principled way to distinguish sanctionable from protected speech. Students of common understanding were necessarily forced to guess at whether a comment about a controversial issue would later be found to be sanctionable under the Policy. The terms of the Policy were so vague that its enforcement would violate the due process clause.

VI. Conclusion

... [T]here is nothing in the record to suggest that the University looked at the experience of any other university in developing its approach to the problem of discriminatory harassment. Had it done so, it might have discovered that Yale University, a private institution not subject to the strictures of the First Amendment, faced a similar dilemma pitting its efforts to promote equality against its commitment to free speech. In 1986, a sophomore at Yale was put on probation for two years by a University discipline board for disseminating a malicious flier intended to ridicule the homosexual community. The board eventually reversed the sanction, but only after a second hearing was held at which the student was represented by historian C. Vann Woodward. ... That report concluded that "freedom of expression is a paramount value, more important that civility or rationality." Writing about the case, Professor Woodward observed:

It simply seems unnatural to make a fuss about the rights of a speaker who offends the moral or political convictions passionately held by a majority. The far more natural impulse is to stop the nonsense, shut it up, punish it—anything but defend it. But to give rein to that inclination would be to make the majority the arbiters of truth for all. Furthermore, it would put the universities into the business of censorship.

DAMOND J. KEITH, Circuit Judge. ...

I. Statement of the Case

On May 12, 1991, Dambrot became the head coach of the Central Michigan University men's basketball team. ... This lawsuit arises from events which occurred during the 1992–93 men's basketball season. ...

In January of 1993, Dambrot used the word "nigger" during a locker room session with his players and coaching staff either during the halftime or at the end of a basketball game in which the team lost to Miami University of Ohio. According to Dambrot's testimony, Dambrot told the players they hadn't been playing very hard and then said "Do you mind if I use the N word?" After one or some of the players apparently indicated it was okay, Dambrot said "you know we need to have more niggers on our team. ... Coach McDowell is a nigger, ... Sander Scott who's an academic All-American, a Caucasian, I said Sander Scott is a nigger. He's hard nose, [sic] he's tough, et cetera." He testified he intended to use the term in a "positive and reinforcing" manner. The players often referred to each other using the N-word during games and around campus and in the locker room. Dambrot stated he used the word in the same manner in which the players used the term amongst themselves, "to connote a person who is fearless, mentally strong and tough."

Prior to the January incident, the record shows Dambrot had used the N-word on at least one other occasion. In November, Dambrot apparently addressed the team after a practice and said he wanted the players to 'play like niggers on the court' and wished he had more niggers on the basketball court. He then said he did not want the team to act like niggers in the classroom. When asked why he made these statements Dambrot stated:

Well, that's really a very easy question for me to answer, because we had had an incident early in the year where we had five or six basketball players, some of our bigger kids on our team, in a math class. And our kids were aggressive, tough, you know, a little bit loud, abrasive. And the lady was intimidated, because it was the first year that she ever had taught. And they almost got kicked out of the math class. A matter of fact, Dave Keilitz, myself, Pat Podoll, Doug Nance, who is the faculty rep, and then the head of the department,—I don't remember his name—the math department, met and discussed the situation. And it was my feeling that you can't be aggressive, tough, hard-nosed, abrasive in class, or you're going to get thrown out of classes, especially at a school like Central Michigan where the faculty members don't understand a lot about black people or have many black people in class. And I think our players understood what I meant by, "Don't be niggers in the classroom."

The news Dambrot had used the N-word in the locker room incident became known to persons outside the basketball team. In February 1993, Keilitz interviewed members of the men's basketball team at Dambrot's request. Keilitz reported all the African American players he interviewed said they were not offended by the coach's use of the term. At some point after those interviews, a former member of the men's basketball team, Shannon Norris, complained to the university's affirmative action officer, Angela Haddad, regarding Dambrot's use of the N-word during the November incident. The affirmative action officer confronted Dambrot who admitted using the word but stated he used it in a positive manner. The officer viewed Dambrot's use of the word as a violation of the university's discriminatory harassment policy and recommended Dambrot be disciplined. Dambrot accepted the proposed disciplinary action in lieu of a more formal investigation and was suspended without pay for five days.

News of the locker room incident spread through the campus after Dambrot was suspended. An article in the student newspaper was printed in which Dambrot told his side of the story. The statement was characterized by the district court as "considerably more explanatory and defensive than apologetic in tone." Students staged a demonstration and local, regional and national news media reported accounts of the incident at CMU.

On April 12, 1993, Keilitz, the athletic director, informed Dambrot he would not be retained as head coach for the 1993–94 season. The university stated that it believed Dambrot was no longer capable of effectively leading the men's basketball program.

Dambrot instituted a lawsuit on April 19, 1993, alleging, *inter alia*, he was fired because he used the term "nigger," and the termination violated his First Amendment rights to free speech and academic freedom. Several members of the basketball team joined the lawsuit alleging the university's discriminatory harassment policy was overbroad and vague and violated their First Amendment rights ...

II. Discussion

Defendants appeal the district court's ... holding the CMU discriminatory harassment policy overbroad and void for vagueness violating the First Amendment. Plaintiffs appeal the district court's ... holding CMU's termination of Dambrot did not violate the First Amendment. ... For the following reasons we AFFIRM the district court on each issue.

> A.   The District Court Did Not Err Granting Summary Judgment For Plaintiffs Finding the CMU Discriminatory Harassment Policy Unconstitutional.

... A statute is unconstitutional on its face on overbreadth grounds if there is "a realistic danger that the statute itself will significantly compromise recognized First Amendment protections of parties not before the court ..."

The CMU policy, located in the Plan for Affirmative Action at Central Michigan University, states discriminatory harassment will not be condoned. Racial and ethnic harassment is defined in the policy as

> any intentional, unintentional, physical, verbal, or nonverbal behavior that subjects an individual to an intimidating, hostile or offensive educational, employment or living environment by ... (c) demeaning or slurring individuals through ... written literature

because of their racial or ethnic affiliation; or (d) using symbols, [epithets] or slogans that infer negative connotations about the individual's racial or ethnic affiliation.

The first step in analyzing an overbreadth claim is to "determine whether the regulation reaches a substantial amount of constitutionally protected speech." The language of this policy is sweeping and seemingly drafted to include as much and as many types of conduct as possible. On its face, the policy reaches "a substantial amount of constitutionally protected speech." ...

The next step in analyzing an overbreadth claim is to determine whether the policy is "substantially overbroad and constitutionally invalid under the void for vagueness doctrine."

> Vagueness may take two forms, both of which result in a denial of due process. A vague ordinance denies fair notice of the standard of conduct to which a citizen is held accountable. At the same time an ordinance is void for vagueness if it is unrestricted delegation of power, which in practice leaves the definition of its terms to law enforcement officers, and thereby invites arbitrary, discriminatory and overzealous enforcement.

As the district court notes "in the instant case, both problems—fair notice, and unrestricted delegation— are present." In order to determine what conduct will be considered "negative" or "offensive" by the university, one must make a subjective reference. Though some statements might be seen as universally offensive, different people find different things offensive. The facts of this case demonstrate the necessity of subjective reference in identifying prohibited speech under the policy. Several players testified they were not offended by Dambrot's use of the N-word while student Norris and affirmative action officer Haddad were extremely offended. The CMU policy, as written, does not provide fair notice of what speech will violate the policy. Defining what is offensive is, in fact, wholly delegated to university officials. This "unrestricted delegation of power" gives rise to the second type of vagueness. For these reasons, the CMU policy is also void for vagueness ...

Because the CMU discriminatory harassment policy is overbroad and void for vagueness ..., the CMU discriminatory harassment policy violates the First Amendment of the United States Constitution.

B.   The District Court Did Not Err in Finding Dambrot Was Permissibly Terminated

Dambrot seeks relief from an alleged wrongful termination. ... The district court described Dambrot's argument ... this way: (1) CMU's policy is unconstitutional because it suppresses speech that is protected by the First Amendment; (2) Plaintiff Dambrot was sanctioned pursuant to the policy and eventually terminated from employment as a result of such sanctioning; (3) therefore, plaintiff's termination was violative of the First Amendment. The district court correctly noted while Dambrot's argument has a seductive logic, Dambrot can only demonstrate harm resulted from the application of the invalid policy if his speech was in fact protected. Without a finding that Dambrot's speech is protected under the First Amendment, the application of the policy does not injure Dambrot. Without the demonstration of some harm, Dambrot cannot recover.

The other argument intimated by Dambrot in ... his complaint is that he is protected under the concept of academic freedom. From either perspective, the central issue is whether Dambrot's speech is protected by the First Amendment. We find it is not.

4.   CMU's Termination of Dambrot was Permissible Because Dambrot's Speech Does Not Touch a Matter of Public Concern.

The Supreme Court has held a government employee retains her First Amendment right to comment on matters of public concern without fear of reprisal from the government as employer. *Connick v. Myers*). ...

The *Connick* court describes speech upon matters of public concern as "relating to any matter of political, social, or other concern to the community." "Whether an employee's speech addresses a matter of public concern must be determined by the content, form, and context of a given statement, as revealed by the whole record.". ...

Focusing on the "content, form and context" of Dambrot's use of the word "nigger," this Court can find nothing "relating to any matter of political, social or other concern to the community." Dambrot's locker room speech imparted no socially or politically relevant message to his players. The point of his speech was not related to his use of the N-word but to his desire to have his players play harder. ... Dambrot's use of the N-word was intended to be motivational and was incidental to the message conveyed. ...

The district court constructs an interesting and useful test for assessing under *Connick* the "form and context" of Dambrot's speech.

One way to evaluate the possibility of the "public concern" component in questioned speech is to imagine it being discussed in public. The political compulsion of public employees partially at issue in *Connick*, ... can easily be envisioned as the subject ... of heated disputation, with the contesting points of view hashing it out from soapboxes in the public square. It is considerably more difficult to imagine Coach Dambrot stepping up to the microphone and letting everyone know that his basketball players were expected to be "niggers" during games. Therefore, the facts that Dambrot's speech was given in the particular words chosen, and made in the locker room for his players' private consumption, only add further support to the conclusion that, at least to the "form and context" of it, his speech was not on a matter of public concern.

2.   Dambrot's Speech Does Not Enter the Marketplace of Ideas Or the Realm of Academic Freedom.

Dambrot argues *Connick* is not applicable to his claim but instead the court should recognize his constitutionally protected right to academic freedom because he "was terminated because of the purported 'public outcry' that arose over what he said to his players, when he was instructing them about how they should be playing basketball and about how they should behave in the classroom."

The analysis of what constitutes a matter of public concern and what raises academic freedom concerns is of essentially the same character. In *Swank v. Smart* a police officer was terminated from his employment based on a coworker's report that he picked up a young college student and gave her a ride on the back of his motorcycle. During the ride the officer and the student talked about numerous topics including her coursework, the motorcycle and her former boyfriend. After his dismissal the officer sued the town alleging, inter alia, the termination had violated his free speech rights guaranteed by the First Amendment. The Seventh Circuit held that conversations between the police officer and the young woman did not touch a matter of public concern and merited no First Amendment protection. Judge Posner recognized the purpose of the free-speech clause … is to protect the market in ideas, broadly understood as the public expression of ideas, narratives, concepts, imagery, opinions—scientific, political, or aesthetic—to an audience whom the speaker seeks to inform, edify, or entertain. Casual chitchat between two persons or otherwise confined to a small social group is unrelated, or largely so, to that marketplace, and is not protected. Such conversation is important to its participants but not to the advancement of knowledge, the transformation of taste, political change, cultural expression, and the other objectives, values and consequences of the speech that is protected by the First Amendment.

The principle of academic freedom emphasizes the essentiality of free public expression of ideas. In *Keyishian v. Board of Regents* the Supreme Court recognized the classroom is peculiarly the "marketplace of ideas." The Nation's future depends upon leaders trained through wide exposure to that robust exchange of ideas which discovers truth" out of a multitude of tongues, [rather] than through any kind of authoritative selection."

The linchpin of the inquiry is, thus, for both public concern and academic freedom, the extent to which the speech advances an idea transcending personal interest or opinion which impacts our social and/or political lives.

Compare with the instant case two cases out of the Second Circuit involving the First Amendment rights of two professors from the City University of New York (CUNY). See *Levin v. Harleston* [and] *Jeffries v. Harleston*. In both cases, professors made derogatory remarks about persons of certain racial or ethnic groups and, in both cases, the University took some action which the professor alleged was in retaliation for the exercise of his First Amendment rights. Professor Levin wrote three letters which were published in the *New York Times* and two journals in which he made denigrating comments about the intelligence of African Americans.

The University created a "shadow section" for one of Levin's classes and set up an Ad Hoc Committee to review his fitness to teach. Professor Jeffries made a speech in which he discussed racial bias in the New York public school system and made derogatory comments about Jews. In his case, the University denied Jeffries a three-year term as chairman of the Black Studies department, the post he had held since the department's inception in 1972. In *Levin*, the Second Circuit found Professor Levin's expression of ideas demanded First Amendment protection. In *Jeffries*, the Second Circuit found the speech in question satisfied … the *Connick* test, touching a matter of public concern. The speech and letters advanced viewpoints, however repugnant, which had as their purpose influencing or informing the public debate. Dambrot's speech did not have such a purpose. …

… Assuming but not deciding, Dambrot is subject to the same standards as any teacher in a classroom (as opposed to a locker room setting), Dambrot's speech served to advance no academic message and is solely a method by which he attempted to motivate—or humiliate—his players. In the instant case, the University has a right to terminate Dambrot for recklessly telling these young men to be athletically ardent but academically apathetic in his attempt to boost athletic performance. The University has a right to terminate Dambrot for telling his players that success on the basketball court is not premised on the same principles of discipline, focus and drive that bring success in the classroom. The University has a right to disapprove of the use of the word "nigger" as a motivational tool. … Finally, the University has a right to hold Coach Dambrot to a higher standard of conduct than that of his players. Dambrot's resort to the First Amendment for protection is not well taken.

For the foregoing reasons, Dambrot's speech cannot be fairly characterized as touching a matter of public concern. … Neither does Dambrot's speech raise any academic freedom concerns. …

MARYLAND v. SHELDON
Court of Appeals of Maryland (1993)
629 A.2d 753

MURPHY, J. A Maryland statute requires those who wish to burn crosses or other religious symbols to do two things: (1) secure the permission of the property owner where the burning is to occur and (2) notify the local fire department before engaging in the burning. The issue ... is whether Maryland's "cross burning" law is constitutional.

On October 17, 1991, ... Sheldon ignited a cross on the property of Harry Smith and his family, who are black. Sheldon had not obtained permission to burn the cross on Smith's ... premises, nor had he notified the local fire department of his intentions. ...

... Those who openly burn crosses do so fully cognizant of the controversial racial and religious messages which such acts impart. Historically, the Ku Klux Klan burned crosses to express hostility toward blacks and other groups it disfavored, and it is that idea which contemporary cross burners aim to perpetuate. While the burning of other religious symbols may not carry precisely the same implications, such acts at a minimum signal animosity for members of the religion whose symbol is burned. Because of these well known and painfully apparent connotations of burning religious symbols, there can be no doubt that those who engage in such conduct intend to "convey a particularized message," or that those who witness the conduct will receive the message. ... [Therefore] the burning of a cross or other religious symbols is "speech". ...

We believe the cross burning statute is a content-based regulation of speech, and therefore must be subject to strict scrutiny. The Supreme Court has said:

The principal inquiry in determining content-neutrality ... is whether the government has adopted a regulation of speech because of disagreement with the message it conveys. The government's purpose is the controlling consideration.

The State argues that its purpose in adopting the cross burning statute was to protect property owners from unwanted fires and to safeguard the community from fires generally. The State insists that the cross burning statute "is not intended to impact upon the right of free expression." For two reasons, we disagree.

First, the very definition of content-neutral indicates that the cross burning statute is not [content-neutral]. A content-neutral regulation ... is one which is "justified without reference to the content of the regulated speech." We see no way to justify the cross burning statute without referring to the substance of speech it regulates, because the statute does not protect property owners or the community from unwanted fires any more than the law already protected those groups before the statute's enactment. The General Assembly long ago criminalized the arson of real and personal property, with penalties generally much stiffer than those for cross burning.

Likewise, the Legislature has outlawed trespass on posted property and cultivated land, and trespass remains a common law crime where it amounts to a breach of the peace. The burning of a religious symbol on another's property without permission would certainly constitute trespass and, if the fire spread beyond the burning emblem, perhaps arson. Thus, the cross burning statute adds little in scope to the pre-existing scheme for fire protection created by Maryland's common and statutory law.

Second, the legislative history of the cross burning statute reveals that the State's true purpose in enacting the statute was to express disagreement with the act of burning religious symbols. ... [M]uch testimony and numerous letters ... urged the General Assembly to confront "the increased Klan activity throughout the State," to address "the racist activity of cross burning," and the like. The letters and testimony did not focus at all on the importance of protecting property owners and the community from fires. ...

... [T]he Legislature revisited the cross burning statute ... in 1981. Several delegates ... introduced a bill to make cross burning a felony and to stiffen the punishment. ... According to Delegate Isaiah Dixon, one of the bill's sponsors, the proposed amendment "recognizes ... despicable acts [of cross burning] for what they are: threats of violence and acts of terror and intimidation." Dixon did not mention the prevention of fires. Another speaker ... testified that "the burning of a cross causes considerable fear and conflict and cannot be treated as a simple act of arson." The Baltimore Jewish Council supported the bill "in the hope that a more stringent penalty will discourage those who would perpetrate this senseless and pointless violence." These comments all indicate that the General Assembly regarded the cross burning statute not as a fire prevention measure but as a means of obstructing the message inherent in cross burning. ...

The legislative history of the cross burning statute, as well as the very definition of content-neutrality, clearly establish that the statute is content-based. Ordinarily, then, the next step is to review it with strict scrutiny.

Before we may do so, however, we must accommodate the fact that "even the prohibition against content[-based statutes] that ... the First Amendment requires is not absolute." *R.A.V. v. St. Paul* (1992). In *R.A.V.* ... the Court outlined three exceptions to the usual presumption against the constitutionality of content-based statutes. ... These exceptions hinged on the fact that the Court has long recognized that certain narrow categories of "speech," such as obscenity, defamation, and fighting words, do not enjoy First Amendment protection from regulation. Because the cross burning statute does not fall within any of the *R.A.V.* exceptions to the constitutional presumption against content-based statutes, we now review the statute with strict scrutiny.

To survive strict scrutiny, a law must be "necessary to serve a compelling state interest and ... narrowly drawn to achieve that end." Maryland's cross burning statute cannot survive this scrutiny, because it is not necessary to serve the State's asserted interest. ...

In a complete turnabout from its earlier arguments, the State proclaims that it has "a compelling interest in protecting the community against bias-motivated threats to public safety and order." It argues that the cross burning statute protects the ideal of equal opportunity for all citizens and furthers the "national commitment to the elimination of invidious discrimination." The State thus abandons its prior posture that the statute is a fire protection measure, and essentially concedes that the statute regulates expression to promote social harmony.

To be sure, the State has a compelling interest in protecting the social welfare of all its citizens. Indeed, the promotion of racial and religious tolerance has become not just an interest of Maryland's government but a moral and ethical mission of our entire society, in order both to correct past injustices and to give content to our nation's belief in equality of opportunity. But the Constitution does not allow the unnecessary trammeling of free expression even for the noblest of purposes. ...

In the instant case, Maryland's cross burning law simply cannot be deemed "necessary" to the State's effort to foster racial and religious accord. It is always difficult, of course, to determine what tools will be effective, much less necessary, in the quest for social tolerance. But it is safe to say that the cross burning statute, which merely inconveniences a tiny handful of individuals who would openly burn religious symbols, will not prove indispensable to the endeavor for justice. ...

OPINION BY:

O'CONNOR

In this case we consider whether the Commonwealth of Virginia's statute banning cross burning with "an intent to intimidate a person or group of persons" violates the First Amendment. Va. Code Ann. § 18.2-423 (1996). We conclude that while a State, consistent with the First Amendment, may ban cross burning carried out with the intent to intimidate, the provision in the Virginia statute treating any cross burning as prima facie evidence of intent to intimidate renders the statute unconstitutional in its current form.

I

Respondents Barry Black, Richard Elliott, and Jonathan O'Mara were convicted separately of violating Virginia's cross-burning statute, § 18.2-423. That statute provides:

"It shall be unlawful for any person or persons, with the intent of intimidating any person or group of persons, to burn, or cause to be burned, a cross on the property of another, a highway or other public place. Any person who shall violate any provision of this section shall be guilty of a Class 6 felony.

"Any such burning of a cross shall be prima facie evidence of an intent to intimidate a person or group of persons."

On August 22, 1998, Barry Black led a Ku Klux Klan rally in Carroll County, Virginia. Twenty-five to thirty people attended this gathering, which occurred on private property with the permission of the owner, who was in attendance. The property was located on an open field just off Brushy Fork Road (State Highway 690) in Cana, Virginia.

When the sheriff of Carroll County learned that a Klan rally was occurring in his county, he went to observe it from the side of the road. During the approximately one hour that the sheriff was present, about 40 to 50 cars passed the site, a "few" of which stopped to ask the sheriff what was happening on the property. Eight to ten houses were located in the vicinity of the rally. Rebecca Sechrist, who was related to the owner of the property where the rally took place, "sat and watched to see what [was] going on" from the lawn of her in-laws' house. She looked on as the Klan prepared for the gathering and subsequently conducted the rally itself.

During the rally, Sechrist heard Klan members speak about "what they were" and "what they believed in." The speakers "talked real bad about the blacks and the Mexicans." One speaker told the assembled gathering that "he would love to take a .30/.30 and just randomly shoot the blacks." The speakers also talked about "President Clinton and Hillary Clinton," and about how their tax money "goes to ... the black people." Sechrist testified that this language made her "very ... scared."

At the conclusion of the rally, the crowd circled around a 25- to 30-foot cross. The cross was between 300 and 350 yards away from the road. According to the sheriff, the cross "then all of a sudden ... went up in a flame." As the cross burned, the Klan played Amazing Grace over the loudspeakers. Sechrist stated that the cross burning made her feel "awful" and "terrible."

When the sheriff observed the cross burning, he informed his deputy that they needed to "find out who's responsible and explain to them that they cannot do this in the State of Virginia." The sheriff then went down the driveway, entered the rally, and asked "who was responsible for burning the cross." Black responded, "I guess I am because I'm the head of the rally." The sheriff then told Black, "There's a law in the State of Virginia that you cannot burn a cross and I'll have to place you under arrest for this."

Black was charged with burning a cross with the intent of intimidating a person or group of persons, in violation of § 18.2-423. At his trial, the jury was instructed that "intent to intimidate means the motivation to intentionally put a person or a group of persons in fear of bodily harm. Such fear must arise from the willful conduct of the accused rather than from some mere temperamental timidity of the victim." The trial court also instructed the jury that "the burning of a cross by itself is sufficient evidence from which you may infer the required intent." When Black objected to this last instruction on First Amendment grounds, the prosecutor responded that the instruction was "taken straight out of the [Virginia] Model Instructions." The jury found Black guilty, and fined him $2,500. The Court of Appeals of Virginia affirmed Black's conviction.

On May 2, 1998, respondents Richard Elliott and Jonathan O'Mara, as well as a third individual, attempted to burn a cross on the yard of James Jubilee. Jubilee, an African-American, was Elliott's next-door neighbor in Virginia Beach, Virginia. Four months prior to the incident, Jubilee and his family had moved from California to Virginia Beach. Before the cross burning, Jubilee spoke to Elliott's mother to inquire about shots being fired from behind the Elliott home. Elliott's mother explained to Jubilee that her son shot firearms as a hobby, and that he used the backyard as a firing range.

On the night of May 2, respondents drove a truck onto Jubilee's property, planted a cross, and set it on fire. Their apparent motive was to "get back" at Jubilee for complaining about the shooting in the backyard. Respondents were not affiliated with the Klan. The next morning, as Jubilee was pulling his car out of the driveway, he noticed the partially burned cross approximately 20 feet from his house. After seeing the cross, Jubilee was "very nervous" because he "didn't know what would be the next phase," and because "a cross burned in your yard … tells you that it's just the first round."

Elliott and O'Mara were charged with attempted cross burning and conspiracy to commit cross burning. O'Mara pleaded guilty to both counts, reserving the right to challenge the constitutionality of the cross-burning statute. The judge sentenced O'Mara to 90 days in jail and fined him $2,500. The judge also suspended 45 days of the sentence and $1,000 of the fine.

At Elliott's trial, the judge originally ruled that the jury would be instructed "that the burning of a cross by itself is sufficient evidence from which you may infer the required intent." At trial, however, the court instructed the jury that the Commonwealth must prove that "the defendant intended to commit cross burning," that "the defendant did a direct act toward the commission of the cross burning," and that "the defendant had the intent of intimidating any person

or group of persons." The court did not instruct the jury on the meaning of the word "intimidate," nor on the prima facie evidence provision of § 18.2-423. The jury found Elliott guilty of attempted cross burning and acquitted him of conspiracy to commit cross burning. It sentenced Elliott to 90 days in jail and a $2,500 fine. The Court of Appeals of Virginia affirmed the convictions of both Elliott and O'Mara.

Each respondent appealed to the Supreme Court of Virginia, arguing that § 18.2-423 is facially unconstitutional. The Supreme Court of Virginia consolidated all three cases, and held that the statute is unconstitutional on its face. It held that the Virginia cross-burning statute "is analytically indistinguishable from the ordinance found unconstitutional in *R. A. V.* v. St. Paul. The Virginia statute, the court held, discriminates on the basis of content since it "selectively chooses only cross burning because of its distinctive message." The court also held that the prima facie evidence provision renders the statute overbroad because "the enhanced probability of prosecution under the statute chills the expression of protected speech."

Three justices dissented, concluding that the Virginia cross-burning statute passes constitutional muster because it proscribes only conduct that constitutes a true threat. The justices noted that unlike the ordinance found unconstitutional in *R. A. V.* v. *St. Paul*, the Virginia statute does not just target cross burning "on the basis of race, color, creed, religion or gender." Rather, "the Virginia statute applies to any individual who burns a cross for any reason provided the cross is burned with the intent to intimidate." The dissenters also disagreed with the majority's analysis of the prima facie provision because the inference alone "is clearly insufficient to establish beyond a reasonable doubt that a defendant burned a cross with the intent to intimidate." The dissent noted that the burden of proof still remains on the Commonwealth to prove intent to intimidate. We granted certiorari.

II

Cross burning originated in the 14th century as a means for Scottish tribes to signal each other. See M. Newton & J. Newton, The Ku Klux Klan: An Encyclopedia 145 (1991). Sir Walter Scott used cross burnings for dramatic effect in The Lady of the Lake, where the burning cross signified both a summons and a call to arms. See W. Scott, The Lady of The Lake, canto third. Cross burning in this country, however, long ago became unmoored from its Scottish ancestry. Burning a cross in the United States is inextricably intertwined with the history of the Ku Klux Klan.

The first Ku Klux Klan began in Pulaski, Tennessee, in the spring of 1866. Although the Ku Klux Klan started as a social club, it soon changed into something far different. The Klan fought Reconstruction and the corresponding drive to allow freed blacks to participate in the political process. Soon the Klan imposed "a veritable reign of terror" throughout the South. S. Kennedy, Southern Exposure 31 (1991) (hereinafter Kennedy). The Klan employed tactics such as whipping, threatening to burn people at the stake, and murder. W. Wade, The Fiery Cross: The Ku Klux Klan in America 48–49 (1987) (hereinafter Wade). The Klan's victims included blacks, southern whites who disagreed with the Klan, and "carpetbagger" northern whites.

The activities of the Ku Klux Klan prompted legislative action at the national level. In 1871, "President Grant sent a message to Congress indicating that the Klan's reign of terror in the Southern States had rendered life and property insecure." In response, Congress passed what is now known as the Ku Klux Klan Act. See "An Act to enforce the Provisions of the Fourteenth Amendment to the Constitution of the United States, and for other Purposes,". President Grant used these new powers to suppress the Klan in South Carolina, the effect of which severely curtailed the Klan in other States as well. By the end of Reconstruction in 1877, the first Klan no longer existed.

The genesis of the second Klan began in 1905, with the publication of Thomas Dixon's The Clansmen: An Historical Romance of the Ku Klux Klan. Dixon's book was a sympathetic portrait of the first Klan, depicting the Klan as a group of heroes "saving" the South from blacks and the "horrors" of Reconstruction. Although the first Klan never actually practiced cross burning, Dixon's book depicted the Klan burning crosses to celebrate the execution of former slaves. Cross burning thereby became associated with the first Ku Klux Klan. When D. W. Griffith turned Dixon's book into the movie The Birth of a Nation in 1915, the association between cross burning and the Klan became indelible. In addition to the cross burnings in the movie, a poster advertising the film displayed a hooded Klansman riding a hooded horse, with his left hand holding the reins of the horse and his right hand holding a burning cross above his head. Wade 127. Soon thereafter, in November 1915, the second Klan began.

From the inception of the second Klan, cross burnings have been used to communicate both threats of violence and messages of shared ideology. The first initiation ceremony occurred on Stone Mountain near Atlanta, Georgia. While a 40-foot cross burned on the mountain, the Klan members took their oaths of loyalty. See Kennedy 163. This cross burning was the second recorded instance in the United States. The first known cross burning in the country had occurred a little over one month before the Klan initiation, when a Georgia mob celebrated the lynching of Leo Frank by burning a "gigantic cross" on Stone Mountain that was "visible throughout" Atlanta.

The new Klan's ideology did not differ much from that of the first Klan. As one Klan publication emphasized, "We avow the distinction between [the] races, ... and we shall ever be true to the faithful maintenance of White Supremacy and will strenuously oppose any compromise thereof in any and all things." Violence was also an elemental part of this new Klan. By September 1921, the New York World newspaper documented 152 acts of Klan violence, including 4 murders, 41 floggings, and 27 tar-and-featherings.

Often, the Klan used cross burnings as a tool of intimidation and a threat of impending violence. For example, in 1939 and 1940, the Klan burned crosses in front of synagogues and churches. See Kennedy 175. After one cross burning at a synagogue, a Klan member noted that if the cross burning did not "shut the Jews up, we'll cut a few throats and see what happens." In Miami in 1941, the Klan burned four crosses in front of a proposed housing project, declaring, "We are here to keep niggers out of your town. ... When the law fails you, call on us." And in Alabama in 1942, in "a whirlwind climax to weeks of flogging and terror," the Klan burned crosses in front of a union hall and in front of a union leader's home on the eve of a labor election. These cross burnings embodied threats to people whom the Klan deemed antithetical to its goals. And these threats had special force given the long history of Klan violence.

The Klan continued to use cross burnings to intimidate after World War II. In one incident, an African-American "school teacher who recently moved his family into a block formerly occupied only by whites asked the protection of city police ... after the burning of a cross in his front yard." And after a cross burning in Suffolk, Virginia during the late 1940's, the Virginia Governor stated that he would "not allow any of our people of any race to be subjected to terrorism or intimidation in any form by the Klan or any other organization." These incidents of cross burning, among others, helped prompt Virginia to enact its first version of the cross-burning statute in 1950.

The decision of this Court in Brown v. *Board of Education*, along with the civil rights movement of the 1950's and 1960's, sparked another outbreak of Klan violence. These acts of violence included bombings, beatings, shootings, stabbings, and mutilations. Members of the Klan burned crosses on the lawns of those associated with the civil rights movement, assaulted the Freedom Riders, bombed churches, and murdered blacks as well as whites whom the Klan viewed as sympathetic toward the civil rights movement.

Throughout the history of the Klan, cross burnings have also remained potent symbols of shared group identity and ideology. The burning cross became a symbol of the Klan itself and a central feature of Klan gatherings. According to the Klan constitution (called the kloran), the "fiery cross" was the "emblem of that sincere, unselfish devotedness of all klansmen to the sacred purpose and principles we have espoused." And the Klan has often published its newsletters and magazines under the name The Fiery Cross.

At Klan gatherings across the country, cross burning became the climax of the rally or the initiation. Posters advertising an upcoming Klan rally often featured a Klan member holding a cross. See N. MacLean, Behind the Mask of Chivalry: The Making of the Second Ku Klux Klan 142–143 (1994). Typically, a cross burning would start with a prayer by the "Klavern" minister, followed by the singing of Onward Christian Soldiers. The Klan would then light the cross on fire, as the members raised their left arm toward the burning cross and sang The Old Rugged Cross. Throughout the Klan's history, the Klan continued to use the burning cross in their ritual ceremonies.

For its own members, the cross was a sign of celebration and ceremony. During a joint Nazi-Klan rally in 1940, the proceeding concluded with the wedding of two Klan members who "were married in full Klan regalia beneath a blazing cross." In response to anti-masking bills introduced in state legislatures after World War II, the Klan burned crosses in protest. On March 26, 1960, the Klan engaged in rallies and cross burnings throughout the South in an attempt to recruit 10 million members. See Wade 305. Later in 1960, the Klan became an issue in the third debate between Richard Nixon and John Kennedy, with both candidates renouncing the Klan. After this debate, the Klan reiterated its support for Nixon by burning crosses. And cross burnings featured prominently in Klan rallies when the Klan attempted to move toward more non-violent tactics to stop integration. In short, a burning cross has remained a symbol of Klan ideology and of Klan unity.

To this day, regardless of whether the message is a political one or whether the message is also meant to intimidate, the burning of a cross is a "symbol of hate." And while cross burning sometimes carries no intimidating message, at other times the intimidating message is the *only* message conveyed. For example, when a cross burning is directed at a particular person not affiliated with the Klan, the burning cross often serves as a message of intimidation, designed to inspire in the victim a fear of bodily harm. Moreover, the history of violence associated with the Klan shows that the possibility of injury or death is not just hypothetical. The person who burns a cross directed at a particular person often is making a serious threat, meant to coerce the victim to comply with the Klan's wishes unless the victim is willing to risk the wrath of the Klan. Indeed, as the cases of respondents Elliott and O'Mara indicate, individuals without Klan affiliation who wish to threaten or menace another person sometimes use cross burning because of this association between a burning cross and violence.

In sum, while a burning cross does not inevitably convey a message of intimidation, often the cross burner intends that the recipients of the message fear for their lives. And when a cross burning is used to intimidate, few if any messages are more powerful.

III

A

The First Amendment, applicable to the States through the Fourteenth Amendment, provides that "Congress shall make no law … abridging the freedom of speech." The hallmark of the protection of free speech is to allow "free trade in ideas"—even ideas that the overwhelming majority of people might find distasteful or discomforting. Thus, the First Amendment "ordinarily" denies a State "the power to prohibit dissemination of social, economic and political doctrine which a vast majority of its citizens believes to be false and fraught with evil consequence." The First Amendment affords protection to symbolic or expressive conduct as well as to actual speech.

The protections afforded by the First Amendment, however, are not absolute, and we have long recognized that the government may regulate certain categories of expression consistent with the Constitution. The First Amendment permits "restrictions upon the content of speech in a few limited areas, which are 'of such slight social value as a step to truth that any benefit that may be derived from them is clearly outweighed by the social interest in order and morality."

Thus, for example, a State may punish those words "which by their very utterance inflict injury or tend to incite an immediate breach of the peace." We have consequently held that fighting words—"those personally abusive epithets which, when addressed to the ordinary citizen, are, as a matter of common knowledge, inherently likely to provoke violent reaction"—are generally proscribable under the First Amendment. Furthermore, "the constitutional guarantees of free speech and free press do not permit a State to forbid or proscribe advocacy of the use of force or of law violation except where such advocacy is directed to inciting or producing imminent lawless action and is likely to incite or produce such action." And the First Amendment also permits a State to ban a "true threat."

"True threats" encompass those statements where the speaker means to communicate a serious expression of an intent to commit an act of unlawful violence to a particular individual or group of individuals. The speaker need not actually intend to carry out the threat. Rather, a prohibition on true threats "protects individuals from the fear of violence" and "from the disruption that fear engenders," in addition to protecting people "from the possibility that the threatened violence will occur." Intimidation in the constitutionally proscribable sense of the word is a type of true threat, where a speaker directs a threat to a person or group of persons with the intent of placing the victim in fear of bodily harm or death. Respondents do not contest that some cross burnings fit within this meaning of intimidating speech, and rightly so. As noted in Part II, *supra*, the history of cross burning in this country shows that cross burning is often intimidating, intended to create a pervasive fear in victims that they are a target of violence.

B

The Supreme Court of Virginia ruled that in light of *R. A. V.* v. *City of St. Paul, supra*, even if it is constitutional to ban cross burning in a content-neutral manner, the Virginia cross-burning statute is unconstitutional because it discriminates on the basis of content and viewpoint. It is true, as the Supreme Court of Virginia held, that the burning of a cross is symbolic expression. The reason why the Klan burns a cross at its rallies, or individuals place a burning cross on someone else's lawn, is that the burning cross represents the message that the speaker wishes to communicate. Individuals

burn crosses as opposed to other means of communication because cross burning carries a message in an effective and dramatic manner.

The fact that cross burning is symbolic expression, however, does not resolve the constitutional question. The Supreme Court of Virginia relied upon *R. A. V.* v. *City of St. Paul, supra*, to conclude that once a statute discriminates on the basis of this type of content, the law is unconstitutional. We disagree.

In *R. A. V.*, we held that a local ordinance that banned certain symbolic conduct, including cross burning, when done with the knowledge that such conduct would "'arouse anger, alarm or resentment in others on the basis of race, color, creed, religion or gender'" was unconstitutional. We held that the ordinance did not pass constitutional muster because it discriminated on the basis of content by targeting only those individuals who "provoke violence" on a basis specified in the law. The ordinance did not cover "those who wish to use 'fighting words' in connection with other ideas—to express hostility, for example, on the basis of political affiliation, union membership, or homosexuality." This content-based discrimination was unconstitutional because it allowed the city "to impose special prohibitions on those speakers who express views on disfavored subjects."

We did not hold in *R. A. V.* that the First Amendment prohibits *all* forms of content-based discrimination within a proscribable area of speech. Rather, we specifically stated that some types of content discrimination did not violate the First Amendment:

"When the basis for the content discrimination consists entirely of the very reason the entire class of speech at issue is proscribable, no significant danger of idea or viewpoint discrimination exists. Such a reason, having been adjudged neutral enough to support exclusion of the entire class of speech from First Amendment protection, is also neutral enough to form the basis of distinction within the class."

Indeed, we noted that it would be constitutional to ban only a particular type of threat: "The Federal Government can criminalize only those threats of violence that are directed against the President … since the reasons why threats of violence are outside the First Amendment … have special force when applied to the person of the President." And a State may "choose to prohibit only that obscenity which is the most patently offensive *in its prurience—i.e.,* that which involves the most lascivious displays of sexual activity." Consequently, while the holding of *R. A. V.* does not permit a State to ban only obscenity based on "offensive *political* messages," or "only those threats against the President that mention his policy on aid to inner cities," the First Amendment permits content discrimination "based on the very reasons why the particular class of speech at issue … is proscribable,"

Virginia's statute does not run afoul of the First Amendment insofar as it bans cross burning with intent to intimidate. Unlike the statute at issue in *R. A. V.*, the Virginia statute does not single out for opprobrium only that speech directed toward "one of the specified disfavored topics." It does not matter whether an individual burns a cross with intent to intimidate because of the victim's race, gender, or religion, or because of the victim's "political affiliation, union membership, or homosexuality." Moreover, as a factual matter it is not true that cross burners direct their intimidating conduct solely to racial or religious minorities. Indeed, in the case of Elliott and O'Mara, it is at least unclear whether the respondents burned a cross due to racial animus.

The First Amendment permits Virginia to outlaw cross burnings done with the intent to intimidate because burning a cross is a particularly virulent form of intimidation. Instead of prohibiting all intimidating messages, Virginia may choose to regulate this subset of intimidating messages in light of cross burning's long and pernicious history as a signal of impending violence. Thus, just as a State may regulate only that obscenity which is the most obscene due to its prurient content, so too may a State choose to prohibit only those forms of intimidation that are most likely to inspire fear of bodily harm. A ban on cross burning carried out with the intent to intimidate is fully consistent with our holding in *R. A. V.* and is proscribable under the First Amendment.

IV

The Supreme Court of Virginia ruled in the alternative that Virginia's cross-burning statute was unconstitutionally overbroad due to its provision stating that "any such burning of a cross shall be prima facie evidence of an intent to intimidate a person or group of persons." The Commonwealth added the prima facie provision to the statute in 1968. The court below did not reach whether this provision is severable from the rest of the cross-burning statute under Virginia law. In this Court, as in the Supreme Court of Virginia, respondents do not argue that the prima facie evidence provision is unconstitutional as applied to any one of them. Rather, they contend that the provision is unconstitutional on its face.

The Supreme Court of Virginia has not ruled on the meaning of the prima facie evidence provision. It has,

however, stated that "the act of burning a cross alone, with no evidence of intent to intimidate, will nonetheless suffice for arrest and prosecution and will insulate the Commonwealth from a motion to strike the evidence at the end of its case-in-chief." The jury in the case of Richard Elliott did not receive any instruction on the prima facie evidence provision, and the provision was not an issue in the case of Jonathan O'Mara because he pleaded guilty. The court in Barry Black's case, however, instructed the jury that the provision means: "The burning of a cross, by itself, is sufficient evidence from which you may infer the required intent." This jury instruction is the same as the Model Jury Instruction in the Commonwealth of Virginia.

The prima facie evidence provision, as interpreted by the jury instruction, renders the statute unconstitutional. Because this jury instruction is the Model Jury Instruction, and because the Supreme Court of Virginia had the opportunity to expressly disavow the jury instruction, the jury instruction's construction of the prima facie provision "is a ruling on a question of state law that is as binding on us as though the precise words had been written into" the statute. As construed by the jury instruction, the prima facie provision strips away the very reason why a State may ban cross burning with the intent to intimidate. The prima facie evidence provision permits a jury to convict in every cross-burning case in which defendants exercise their constitutional right not to put on a defense. And even where a defendant like Black presents a defense, the prima facie evidence provision makes it more likely that the jury will find an intent to intimidate regardless of the particular facts of the case. The provision permits the Commonwealth to arrest, prosecute, and convict a person based solely on the fact of cross burning itself.

It is apparent that the provision as so interpreted "'would create an unacceptable risk of the suppression of ideas.'" The act of burning a cross may mean that a person is engaging in constitutionally proscribable intimidation. But that same act may mean only that the person is engaged in core political speech. The prima facie evidence provision in this statute blurs the line between these two meanings of a burning cross. As interpreted by the jury instruction, the provision chills constitutionally protected political speech because of the possibility that a State will prosecute—and potentially convict—somebody engaging only in lawful political speech at the core of what the First Amendment is designed to protect.

As the history of cross burning indicates, a burning cross is not always intended to intimidate. Rather, sometimes the cross burning is a statement of ideology, a symbol of group solidarity. It is a ritual used at Klan gatherings, and it is used to represent the Klan itself. Thus, "burning a cross at a political rally would almost certainly be protected expression." Indeed, occasionally a person who burns a cross does not intend to express either a statement of ideology or intimidation. Cross burnings have appeared in movies such as Mississippi Burning, and in plays such as the stage adaptation of Sir Walter Scott's The Lady of the Lake.

The prima facie provision makes no effort to distinguish among these different types of cross burnings. It does not distinguish between a cross burning done with the purpose of creating anger or resentment and a cross burning done with the purpose of threatening or intimidating a victim. It does not distinguish between a cross burning at a public rally or a cross burning on a neighbor's lawn. It does not treat the cross burning directed at an individual differently from the cross burning directed at a group of like-minded believers. It allows a jury to treat a cross burning on the property of another with the owner's acquiescence in the same manner as a cross burning on the property of another without the owner's permission. To this extent I agree with JUSTICE SOUTER that the prima facie evidence provision can "skew jury deliberations toward conviction in cases where the evidence of intent to intimidate is relatively weak and arguably consistent with a solely ideological reason for burning."

It may be true that a cross burning, even at a political rally, arouses a sense of anger or hatred among the vast majority of citizens who see a burning cross. But this sense of anger or hatred is not sufficient to ban all cross burnings. As Gerald Gunther has stated, "The lesson I have drawn from my childhood in Nazi Germany and my happier adult life in this country is the need to walk the sometimes difficult path of denouncing the bigot's hateful ideas with all my power, yet at the same time challenging any community's attempt to suppress hateful ideas by force of law." The prima facie evidence provision in this case ignores all of the contextual factors that are necessary to decide whether a particular cross burning is intended to intimidate. The First Amendment does not permit such a shortcut.

For these reasons, the prima facie evidence provision, as interpreted through the jury instruction and as applied in Barry Black's case, is unconstitutional on its face. We recognize that the Supreme Court of Virginia has not authoritatively interpreted the meaning of the prima facie evidence provision. Unlike JUSTICE SCALIA, we refuse to speculate on whether *any* interpretation of the prima facie evidence provision would satisfy the First Amendment. Rather, all we hold is that because of the interpretation of the prima facie evidence provision given by the jury instruction, the provision makes the statute facially invalid at this point. We also recognize the theoretical possibility that the court, on remand, could interpret the provision in a manner different from that so far set forth in order to avoid the constitutional objections we have described. We leave open that possibility. We also leave open the possibility that the provision is severable, and if so, whether Elliott and O'Mara could be retried under § 18.2-423.

V

With respect to Barry Black, we agree with the Supreme Court of Virginia that his conviction cannot stand, and we affirm the judgment of the Supreme Court of Virginia. With respect to Elliott and O'Mara, we vacate the judgment of the Supreme Court of Virginia, and remand the case for further proceedings.

It is so ordered.

FLORIDA v. STALDER
Supreme Court of Florida (1994)
630 So. 2d 1072

SHAW, J. We have for review a trial court order declaring ... Florida's Hate Crimes Statute ... unconstitutional. ...

Herbert Cohen went to Richard Stalder's home on April 14, 1991, to retrieve the earrings of a friend. Stalder then assaulted Cohen and maligned his Jewish heritage, according to the police complaint affidavit:

On the above date [Cohen] went [to] the above address [with] his friend, Denise Avard, [she] being a victim of a battery. [Cohen] made contact with [Stalder] and when [Stalder] answered the door, he stated "Hey Jew boy, what do you want?" [Cohen] stated that he was looking for Denise Avard's earrings. According to sworn statements of both [Cohen] and Denise Avard, [Stalder] started to yell statements to the victim about his Jewish descent. At one point [Stalder] pushed [Cohen] and this was witnessed by ... Denise Avard. [Cohen] called the police and [Stalder] went into his house and locked the door and refused to answer the door. According to [Cohen], about two months later the victim was by Denise Avard's house and the [Stalder] drove by in a vehicle and yelled at the victim "Hey Jew boy, I'll see you in court."

On the court date [Cohen] went to court and was confronted by [Stalder], who stated, "Hey Jew boy, suck on my cock." [Cohen] in giving a statement to this officer feels that [Stalder] has a hate for Jewish people and that [Stalder] has a mind set against people who are Jewish. Every time [Cohen] comes in contact with [Stalder] he makes obscene remarks against him and the Jewish religion. The undersigned detective feels that [Cohen] does have the right to believe that [Stalder] hates Jews. Statements from both the witness and victim indicate that the charge of battery could be upgraded to a "hate crime."

The State noted as additional proof of Stalder's commission of a "hate crime" the fact that he denounced Cohen during the initial encounter at Stalder's home as a "Jewish lawyer": "Jew boy, you fat Jewish lawyer get the hell off my property. ..." and "Jewish kike, come on Jewish lawyer ... I'm going to kick your ass. ..."

Stalder was charged with ... simple battery ... for pushing Cohen, and the penalty was [enhanced] from a first-degree misdemeanor to a third-degree felony. ...

... [The enhancement statute] requires penalty enhancement where the commission of any felony or misdemeanor evidences prejudice based on ["]the race, color, ancestry, ethnicity, religion, or national origin of the victim["]. ...

Giving plain meaning to the statute's text and title, the provision punishes all who "evidence," or demonstrate, prejudice in the commission of a crime based on an enumerated characteristic of the victim. The statute has three requirements: 1) The perpetrator must demonstrate prejudice, or bias; 2) the bias must be evidenced in the commission of a crime; and 3) the bias must be based on one or more of the enumerated characteristics of the victim. In assessing the constitutionality of this bias-evidencing crimes statute, we turn to two key United States Supreme Court cases: one dealing with bias-inspired expression; the other addressing bias-motivated crimes.

The United States Supreme Court recently addressed the issue of bias-inspired expression *R.A.V. v. City of St. Paul* (1992). There, a juvenile allegedly burned a cross made of broken chair legs on a African-American family's lawn in the early morning hours of June 21, 1990, and was charged with violating a St. Paul, Minnesota, ordinance that bans use of discriminatory symbols or other bias-inspired expression. ...

The United States Supreme Court ... held the St. Paul ordinance unconstitutional. The Court reasoned thusly: The First Amendment prevents government from banning expressive activity because of disapproval of content or ideas except in certain narrowly defined instances where the category of expression involved is of little social value, such as where the speech constitutes "fighting words." Even with "fighting words," however, a government restriction must operate across the board and may not classify and ban only certain types of "fighting words," for instance only those directed against others based on "race, color, creed, religion or gender." Such a restriction would open the door to government favoritism and protectionism of certain topics and viewpoints and implicit censorship of disfavored ones, as was the case with the St. Paul ordinance. ...

A year after it decided *R.A.V.*, the United States Supreme Court addressed the constitutionality of a state hate crimes statute punishing bias-motivated crimes in *Wisconsin v. Mitchell* (1993). There, a group of African-American youths randomly selected and severely beat a white youth in reaction to a scene in the motion picture "Mississippi Burning" wherein an African-American child was beaten while praying. The defendant, Mitchell, was convicted of aggravated battery and his penalty enhanced under the Wisconsin statute, which provides for penalty enhancement whenever the [defendant] ... ["i]ntentionally selects the person against whom the crime ... is committed ... because of the race, religion, color, disability, sexual orientation, national origin or ancestry of that person["]. ...

The United states Supreme Court upheld Mitchell's enhanced penalty, ruling that because the Wisconsin statute punishes bias-motivated criminal conduct rather than the expression of ideas the First Amendment is not implicated. ...

We conclude that our Florida statute contains elements similar to both the St. Paul ordinance struck down in *R.A.V.* and the Wisconsin statute upheld in *Mitchell*. ... [The statute embraces] two broad classes of offenses. First are those ... offences committed because of prejudice. For instance, A beats B because B is a member of a particular racial group. This class of offense

is virtually identical to the bias-motivated crimes proscribed by the valid Wisconsin statute in *Mitchell*. The targeted activity—the selection of a victim—is an integral part of the underlying crime. As such, the conduct is not protected speech at all, but rather falls outside the First Amendment and may be banned.

Second are those offenses committed for some reason other than prejudice but that nevertheless show bias in their commission. For example, A beats B because of jealousy, but in the course of the battery calls B a racially derogatory term. The targeted conduct here—the expression of bias—is related to the underlying crime in only the most tangential way: The expression and crime share the same temporal framework, nothing more. ...

... [T]his Court is bound "to resolve all doubts as to the validity of [the] statute in favor of its constitutionality, provided the statute may be given a fair construction that is consistent with the federal and state constitutions as well as with the legislative intent."...

Here, our legislature has determined that prejudice resulting in criminal acts against members of particular groups inflicts great individual and societal harm and is thus deserving of enhanced punishment. The legislature's apparent intent is to discourage criminal acts directed against groups that have historically been subjected to prejudicial acts. A reading of [the statute] as embracing only bias-motivated crimes is entirely consistent with this intent. ... [W]e hold that [the statute] applies only to bias-motivated crimes. So read, the statute is constitutional. A bias-motivated crime for purposes of this statute is any crime wherein the perpetrator intentionally selects the victim because of the victim's "race, color, ethnicity, religion, or national origin."

It may seem doubly vile to members of our legal community to denigrate another for being a "Jewish lawyer," as Mr. Stalder allegedly did, but such an act standing alone is every citizen's right—so long as the First Amendment breathes. To assault another solely because he or she is a "Jewish lawyer," on the other hand, is no one's right. When protected speech translates into criminal conduct, even the Free Speech Clause balks. ...

WISCONSIN, PETITIONER v. TODD MITCHELL
Supreme Court of the United States
508 U.S. 476

June 11, 1993, Decided

OPINION BY:

REHNQUIST

OPINION

Respondent Todd Mitchell's sentence for aggravated battery was enhanced because he intentionally selected his victim on account of the victim's race. The question presented in this case is whether this penalty enhancement is prohibited by the First and Fourteenth Amendments. We hold that it is not.

On the evening of October 7, 1989, a group of young black men and boys, including Mitchell, gathered at an apartment complex in Kenosha, Wisconsin. Several members of the group discussed a scene from the motion picture "Mississippi Burning,'" in which a white man beat a young black boy who was praying. The group moved outside and Mitchell asked them: "'Do you all feel hyped up to move on some white people?" Shortly thereafter, a young white boy approached the group on the opposite side of the street where they were standing. As the boy walked by, Mitchell said: "'You all want to fuck somebody up? There goes a white boy; go get him.'" Mitchell counted to three and pointed in the boy's direction. The group ran toward the boy, beat him severely, and stole his tennis shoes. The boy was rendered unconscious and remained in a coma for four days.

After a jury trial in the Circuit Court for Kenosha County, Mitchell was convicted of aggravated battery. That offense ordinarily carries a maximum sentence of two years' imprisonment. But because the jury found that Mitchell had intentionally selected his victim because of the boy's race, the maximum sentence for Mitchell's offense was increased to seven years under § 939.645. That provision enhances the maximum penalty for an offense whenever the defendant "intentionally selects the person against whom the crime ... is committed ... because of the race, religion, color, dis-

ability, sexual orientation, national origin or ancestry of that person . . The Circuit Court sentenced Mitchell to four years' imprisonment for the aggravated battery.

1 At the time of Mitchell's trial, the Wisconsin penalty-enhancement statute provided:

"(1) If a person does all of the following, the penalties for the underlying crime are increased as provided in sub. (2):

"(a) Commits a crime under chs. 939 to 948.

"(b) Intentionally selects the person against whom the crime under par. (a) is committed or selects the property which is damaged or otherwise affected by the crime under par. (a) because of the race, religion, color, disability, sexual orientation, national origin or ancestry of that person or the owner or occupant of that property.

"(2)(a) If the crime committed under sub. (1) is ordinarily a misdemeanor other than a Class A misdemeanor, the revised maximum fine is $10,000 and the revised maximum period of imprisonment is one year in the county jail.

"(b) If the crime committed under sub. (1) is ordinarily a Class A misdemeanor, the penalty increase under this section changes the status of the crime to a felony and the revised maximum fine is $10,000 and the revised maximum period of imprisonment is 2 years.

"(c) If the crime committed under sub. (1) is a felony, the maximum fine prescribed by law for the crime may be increased by not more than $5,000 and the maximum period of imprisonment prescribed by law for the crime may be increased by not more than 5 years.

"(3) This section provides for the enhancement of the penalties applicable for the underlying crime.

The court shall direct that the trier of fact find a special verdict as to all of the issues specified in sub. (1). "(4) This section does not apply to any crime if proof of race, religion, color, disability, sexual orientation, national origin or ancestry is required for a conviction for that crime." [HN4] Wis. Stat. § 939.645 (1989–1990).

Mitchell unsuccessfully sought postconviction relief in the Circuit Court. Then he appealed his conviction and sentence, challenging the constitutionality of Wisconsin's penalty-enhancement provision on First Amendment grounds. The Wisconsin Court of Appeals rejected Mitchell's challenge, but the Wisconsin Supreme Court reversed. The Supreme Court held that the statute "violates the First Amendment directly by punishing what the legislature has deemed to be offensive thought." It rejected the State's contention "that the statute punishes only the 'conduct' of intentional selection of a victim." According to the court, "the statute punishes the 'because of' aspect of the defendant's selection, the *reason* the defendant selected the victim, the *motive* behind the selection." And under *R. A. V.* v. *St. Paul*, "the Wisconsin legislature cannot criminalize bigoted thought with which it disagrees."

The Supreme Court also held that the penalty-enhancement statute was unconstitutionally overbroad. It reasoned that, in order to prove that a defendant intentionally selected his victim because of the victim's protected status, the State would often have to introduce evidence of the defendant's prior speech, such as racial epithets he may have uttered before the commission of the offense. This evidentiary use of protected speech, the court thought, would have a "chilling effect" on those who feared the possibility of prosecution for offenses subject to penalty enhancement. Finally, the court distinguished antidiscrimination laws, which have long been held constitutional, on the ground that the Wisconsin statute punishes the "subjective mental process" of selecting a victim because of his protected status, whereas antidiscrimination laws prohibit "objective acts of discrimination."

We granted certiorari because of the importance of the question presented and the existence of a conflict of authority among state high courts on the constitutionality of statutes similar to Wisconsin's penalty-enhancement provision, We reverse.

Mitchell argues that we are bound by the Wisconsin Supreme Court's conclusion that the statute punishes bigoted thought and not conduct. There is no doubt that we are bound by a state court's construction of a state statute. *Terminiello* v. *Chicago*, (1949). In *Terminiello*, for example, the Illinois courts had defined the term "'breach of the peace,'" in a city ordinance prohibiting disorderly conduct, to include "'stirs the public to anger … or creates a disturbance.'" We held this construction to be binding on us. But here the Wisconsin Supreme Court did not, strictly speaking, construe the Wisconsin statute in the sense of defining the meaning of a particular statutory word or phrase. Rather, it merely characterized the "practical effect" of the statute for First Amendment purposes. ***This assessment does not bind us. Once any ambiguities as to the meaning of the statute are resolved, we may form our own judgment as to its operative effect.

The State argues that the statute does not punish bigoted thought, as the Supreme Court of Wisconsin said, but instead punishes only conduct. While this argument is literally correct, it does not dispose of Mitchell's First Amendment challenge. To be sure, our cases reject the "view that an apparently limitless variety of conduct can be labeled 'speech' whenever the person engaging in the conduct intends thereby to express an idea." Thus, a physical assault is not by any stretch of the imagination expressive conduct protected by the First Amendment.

But the fact remains that under the Wisconsin statute the same criminal conduct may be more heavily punished if the victim is selected because of his race or other protected status than if no such motive obtained. Thus, although the statute punishes criminal conduct, it enhances the maximum penalty for conduct motivated by a discriminatory point of view more severely than the same conduct engaged in for some other reason or for no reason at all. Because the only reason for the enhancement is the defendant's discriminatory motive for selecting his victim, Mitchell argues (and the Wisconsin Supreme Court held) that the statute violates the First Amendment by punishing offenders' bigoted beliefs.

Traditionally, sentencing judges have considered a wide variety of factors in addition to evidence bearing on guilt in determining what sentence to impose on a convicted defendant. The defendant's motive for committing the offense is one important factor. ***Thus, in many States the commission of a murder, or other capital offense, for pecuniary gain is a separate aggravating circumstance under the capital sentencing statute.

But it is equally true that a defendant's abstract beliefs, however obnoxious to most people, may not be taken into consideration by a sentencing judge. *Dawson* v. *Delaware* (1992). In *Dawson*, the State introduced evidence at a capital sentencing hearing that the defendant was a member of a white supremacist prison gang. Because "the evidence proved nothing more than [the defendant's] abstract beliefs," we held that its admission violated the defendant's First Amendment rights. In so holding, however, we emphasized that "the Constitution does not erect a *per se* barrier to the admission of evidence concerning one's beliefs and associations at sentencing simply because those beliefs and associations are protected by the First Amendment." Thus, in *Barclay* v. *Florida*, (1983) (plurality opinion), we allowed the sentencing judge to take into account the defendant's racial animus towards his victim. The evidence in that case showed that the defendant's membership in the Black Liberation Army and desire to provoke a "race war" were related to the murder of a white man for which he was convicted.. Because "the elements of racial hatred in [the] murder" were relevant to several aggravating factors, we held that the trial judge permissibly took this evidence into account in sentencing the defendant to death.

Mitchell suggests that *Dawson* and *Barclay* are inapposite because they did not involve application of a penalty-enhancement provision. But in *Barclay* we held that it was permissible for the sentencing court to consider the defendant's racial animus in determining whether he should be sentenced to death, surely the most severe "enhancement" of all. And the fact that the Wisconsin Legislature has decided, as a general matter, that bias-motivated offenses warrant greater maximum penalties across the board does not alter the result here. For the primary responsibility for fixing criminal penalties lies with the legislature.

Mitchell argues that the Wisconsin penalty-enhancement statute is invalid because it punishes the defendant's discriminatory motive, or reason, for acting. But motive plays the same role under the Wisconsin statute as it does under federal and state antidiscrimination laws, which we have previously upheld against constitutional challenge. Title VII of the Civil Rights Act of 1964, for example, makes it unlawful for an employer to discriminate against an employee "*because of* such individual's race, color, religion, sex, or national origin." In *Hishon*, we rejected the argument that Title VII infringed employers' First Amendment rights. And more recently, in *R. A. V.* v. *St. Paul,*, we cited Title VII as an example of a permissible content-neutral regulation of conduct.

Nothing in our decision last Term in *R. A. V.* compels a different result here. That case involved a First Amendment challenge to a municipal ordinance prohibiting the use of "'fighting words' that insult, or provoke violence, 'on the basis of race, color, creed, religion or gender.'" Because the ordinance only proscribed a class of "fighting words" deemed particularly offensive by the city—*i.e.*, those "that contain … messages of 'bias-motivated' hatred," we held that it violated the rule against content-based discrimination. But whereas the ordinance struck down in *R. A. V.* was explicitly directed at expression (*i.e.*, "speech" or "messages"), the statute in this case is aimed at conduct unprotected by the First Amendment.

Moreover, the Wisconsin statute singles out for enhancement bias-inspired conduct because this conduct is thought to inflict greater individual and societal harm. For example, according to the State and its *amici*, bias-motivated crimes are more likely to provoke retaliatory crimes, inflict distinct emotional harms on their victims, and incite community unrest. The State's desire to redress these perceived harms provides an adequate explanation for its penalty-enhancement provision over and above mere disagreement with offenders' beliefs or biases. As Blackstone said long ago, "it is but reasonable that among crimes of different natures those should be most severely punished, which are the most destructive of the public safety and happiness."

Finally, there remains to be considered Mitchell's argument that the Wisconsin statute is unconstitutionally overbroad because of its "chilling effect" on free speech. Mitchell argues (and the Wisconsin Supreme Court agreed) that the statute is "overbroad" because evidence of the defendant's prior speech or associations may be used to prove that the defendant intentionally selected his victim on account of the victim's protected status. Consequently, the argument goes, the statute impermissibly chills free expression with respect to such matters by those concerned about the possibility of enhanced sentences if they should in the future commit a criminal offense covered by the statute. We find no merit in this contention.

The sort of chill envisioned here is far more attenuated and unlikely than that contemplated in traditional "over-breadth" cases. We must conjure up a vision of a Wisconsin citizen suppressing his unpopular bigoted opinions for fear that if he later commits an offense covered by the statute, these opinions will be offered at trial to establish that he selected his victim on account of the victim's protected status, thus qualifying him for penalty enhancement. To stay within the realm of rationality, we must surely put to one side minor misdemeanor offenses covered by the statute, such as negligent operation of a motor vehicle for it is difficult, if not impossible, to conceive of a situation where such offenses would be racially motivated. We are left, then, with the prospect of a citizen suppressing his bigoted beliefs for fear that evidence of such beliefs will be introduced against him at trial if he commits a more serious offense against person or property. This is simply too speculative a hypothesis to support Mitchell's overbreadth claim.

The First Amendment, moreover, does not prohibit the evidentiary use of speech to establish the elements of a crime or to prove motive or intent. Evidence of a defendant's previous declarations or statements is commonly admitted in criminal trials subject to evidentiary rules dealing with relevancy, reliability, and the like. Nearly half a century ago, in *Haupt* v. *United States*, (1947), we rejected a contention similar to that advanced by Mitchell here. Haupt was tried for the offense of treason, which, as defined by the Constitution (Art. III, § 3), may depend very much on proof of motive. To prove that the acts in question were committed out of "adherence to the enemy " rather than "parental solicitude," the Government introduced evidence of conversations that had taken place long prior to the indictment, some of which consisted of statements showing Haupt's sympathy with Germany and Hitler and hostility towards the United States. We rejected Haupt's argument that this evidence was improperly admitted. While "such testimony is to be scrutinized with care to be certain the statements are not expressions of mere lawful and permissible difference of opinion with our own government or quite proper appreciation of the land of birth," we held that "these statements ... clearly were admissible on the question of intent and adherence to the enemy."

For the foregoing reasons, we hold that Mitchell's First Amendment rights were not violated by the application of the Wisconsin penalty-enhancement provision in sentencing him. The judgment of the Supreme Court of Wisconsin is therefore reversed, and the case is remanded for further proceedings not inconsistent with this opinion.

ROBERT L. YARBROUGH v. STATE OF MISSISSIPPI
Supreme Court of Mississippi
911 So. 2d 951; 2005 Miss. LEXIS 610
September 22, 2005, Decided

OPINION BY: GRAVES

Graves, Justice, for The Court

P1. Robert L. Yarbrough was convicted of the sale of cocaine, in violation of *Miss. Code Ann.***. The trial judge sentenced Yarbrough to a term of eighteen years' imprisonment in the custody of the Mississippi Department of Corrections. Yarbrough timely appealed and charges the trial court with two errors. We affirm.

Facts and Procedural History

P2. On March 11, 2002, Jamie Bozeman, a confidential informant for the Tri-County Narcotics Task Force, met with narcotics agents Don Bartlett and Patrick Evans to arrange an undercover drug buy. After this meeting, Bozeman went to the residence of Robert L. Yarbrough, located in the Linwood community of Neshoba County, and purchased cocaine from him for $160, $40 for a rock of crack cocaine and $ 120 for powdered cocaine. Yarbrough was later arrested and then indicted on November 8, 2002, by the grand jury of Neshoba County for violating *Miss. Code Ann.***

Trial of this matter was scheduled to begin on March 8, 2004. At this time Yarbrough presented a motion to dismiss the indictment, or in the alternative, to continue the case until a jury consisting of a "reasonably sufficient number of members of the black race" could be empaneled. The judge held a brief hearing on the motion but ultimately denied the motion. The State opened its case the following day. Jamie Bozeman testified that he purchased the cocaine from Yarbrough and made an in-court identification of him as the seller. Agent Patrick Ervin also offered testimony as to the drug purchase made by Bozeman. Ervin, in response to a question regarding a pre-buy meeting with Bozeman, stated that "we had talked to Mr. Bozeman about possibly who he could buy illegal drugs from. He mentioned the name of

Robert Yarbrough, which he called him by Peanut, which we knew of him through all our activity that we did here in the city." Yarbrough's counsel objected and moved for a mistrial based on this statement. The judge sustained Yarbrough's objection, instructed the jury to disregard the previous statement, and allowed the trial to continue.

The trial concluded that day, and the jury unanimously found Yarbrough guilty. Two days later, the judge sentenced him to eighteen years' imprisonment with the Mississippi Department of Corrections. Yarbrough's motion for a judgment notwithstanding the verdict (JNOV), or in the alternative, for a new trial, was denied. He then filed his timely notice of appeal. On appeal, Yarbrough alleges that: (1) he was denied a fair trial based on the fact that the jurors did not represent a fair cross-section of the population of Neshoba County, Mississippi; and (2) the trial court erred in refused to grant a mistrial based on the testimony of Patrick Ervin. Finding no error, we affirm.

Discussion

I. Whether Yarbrough was denied a fair trial since the jurors did not represent a fair cross-section of the population of Neshoba County.

The *Sixth Amendment to the United States Constitution* entitles a defendant to a presumption of innocence until he is found guilty by an "impartial jury." Mississippi insures this right through both statutory and case law. *Miss. Code Ann.* *** states:

It is the policy of this state that all persons selected for jury service be selected at random from a fair cross section of the population of the area served by the court, and that all qualified citizens have the opportunity in accordance with this chapter to be considered for jury service in this state and an obligation to serve as jurors when summoned for that purpose. A citizen shall not be excluded from jury service in this state on account of race, color, religion, sex, national origin, or economic status.

This statutory policy has been reinforced by this Court, through its position that "courts must make every reasonable effort to comply with the statutory method of drawing, selecting and serving jurors" to keep the jury system "untainted and beyond suspicion." ***.

Yarbrough argues that, despite these mandates of law, he was denied an impartial jury drawn from a representative cross-section of his community. The motion he presented at trial alleged that less than 2% of the approximately seventy-two people on the six jury panels were members of the black race. His counsel asserted that at least 40% of the residents of Neshoba County were black and that Yarbrough could not "get a fair trial unless he has some black people on the jury, at least in equal proportion to the county." Robert Brooks, an attorney for the State, responded by saying that nine of the forty-four jurors on the four panels before the court were black and that this was a higher percentage of black jurors than Yarbrough alleged. Additionally, Brooks defended the venire by arguing that the proper question was not who is on the panels but rather the methods used for drawing the jurors.

In *Duren v. Missouri, 439 U.S. 357, 99 S. Ct. 664, 58 L. Ed. 2d 579 (1979)*, the United States Supreme Court set forth the test for determining whether there has been a prima facie violation of the fair cross-section requirement. The *Duren* Court ruled a Missouri statute, which exempted all women from jury duty during the process of jury selection if they requested the exemption, unconstitutional because the exemption unnecessarily diluted women from the jury pool, a violation the fair cross-section requirement of the *Sixth Amendment.* **. The test from *Duren* requires a defendant to show: (1) that the group alleged to be excluded is a "distinctive" group in the community; (2) that the representation of this group in venires from which juries are selected is not fair and reasonable in relation to the number of such persons in the community; and (3) that this underrepresentation is due to systematic exclusion of the group in the jury selection process. *Id. at 364*. The *Duren* test has also been adopted by this Court. ***. Yarbrough contends that he has established all three elements necessary to prove a prima facie violation of the fair cross-section requirement, as

articulated in *Duren*. He claims the first element is established because the black population of Neshoba County, the group alleged to be excluded, constitutes a distinctive group within the county. As the State has offered no argument on this point, we find that the State has conceded this element as being established.

Yarbrough also argues that he has established the second element of the *Duren* test because 19.3% of the population in Neshoba County is black yet not one member of the jury in this case was black. The State rebuts this allegation with testimony from the motion hearing. The State correctly notes that the proper test is not how many black people actually serve on the jury but rather whether the method used to draw the venire leads to a fair representation of the black population within Neshoba County.**. Counsel for the State also defended Yarbrough's allegation that blacks composed "less than two percent" of the venire with his assertion that nine of the forty-four panel members (20.5%) before the court were black, a higher percentage than Yarbrough's counsel alleged. We find that Yarbrough has not introduced sufficient evidence to establish the second element of the *Duren* test for a prima facie violation of the fair cross-section requirement.

The third element of the *Duren* test, which Yarbrough claims he can establish, requires him to show that the under-representation of blacks is based on their systematic exclusion from the jury selection process. *See Duren, 439 U.S. at 364*; *Kolberg, 829 So. 2d at 86*. Yarbrough's argument on this element consists primarily of his trial counsel's motion, which stated that "the pattern concerning make up as to race of jurors is more and more becoming a pattern in Neshoba County. Defendant can not obtain a fair and impartial jury and trial under these circumstances ..." unless a sufficient number of black jurors were seated. Yarbrough also cites to Justice Diaz's dissent in *Gathings v. State, 822 So. 2d 266 (Miss. 2002)*, to support his proposition that the impartiality of the jury in this case is questionable, and a new trial necessary, because the number of blacks in the venire is out of proportion to their percentage of the population in Neshoba County. Yarbrough's argument is not consistent with what Justice Diaz actually said in *Gathings*. In *Gathings*, Justice Diaz dissented from the majority opinion because he felt that trial court's decision to allow the jury pool to be drawn from both districts of a two-district county "resulted in the systematic exclusion of African-Americans for every case tried in the second judicial district of Chickasaw

County," which had a much higher African-American population than the first judicial district of the same county. **

In *Duren*, the defendant introduced evidence that the female jurors were being systematically excluded from jury pools because of a state law which allowed women to get out of jury duty for any reason whatsoever. In *Gathings*, the defendant introduced evidence which showed that the inclusion of potential jurors from another judicial district within the county would diminish the pool of potential black jurors from his judicial district. Unlike these two cases, Yarbrough has offered no evidence, either in his motion at trial or on appeal, which alleges the type of systematic exclusion of a distinctive group found in either *Duren* or *Gathings*. In fact, during the hearing on Yarbrough's motion, the prosecution noted that Yarbrough had offered no evidence which suggested racial discrimination in the drawing or selection of jurors. We agree.

The fair cross-section requirement is not violated merely because the all-white jury in Yarbrough's case was not representative of the black community in Neshoba County, because as we noted in *Gathings*, a defendant is "not entitled to a given percentage of jury members of his own race." *Id. at 272.* To prevail on his challenge of the venire, he must prove a prima facie violation of the *Sixth Amendment's* fair cross-section requirement.

We find that Yarbrough has not met his burden. He has failed to prove that the black population of Neshoba County was not fairly or reasonably represented in the venire. Furthermore, he has offered no evidence, only mere assertions, that black citizens of Neshoba County are being systematically excluded from the jury selection process. Therefore, the trial judge did not err in denying Yarbrough's motion for a dismissal of the indictment or his alternative motion for a continuance.** ***

Conviction of sale of cocaine and sentence of eighteen [**18] (18) years in the custody of the Mississppi Department of Corrections, affirmed.

Smith, C.J., Waller and Cobb, P.JJ., Easley, Carlson, Dickinson and Randolph, JJ., Concur Diaz, J., not participating.

OPINION: Johnson, Presiding Judge.

Michelle and Shomari McCastle, who are married, were tried before a jury and convicted of four counts of cruelty to children, based on their alleged abuse of their minor child. They have filed separate appeals from their convictions, n1 but they both assert error in the trial court's denial of their *Batson* motion. Because the appeals arise from the same trial and raise the same issue, we consider them together and conclude that the trial court did err in denying the *Batson* motion.

1. Under *Batson*, a prosecutor may not strike a juror solely because of his race or on the basis of an assumption which arises solely from the juror's race. An evaluation of a *Batson* challenge involves three steps: (1) the party challenging a peremptory strike must make a prima facie showing of racial discrimination; (2) the party that struck the juror must then provide a race-neutral explanation for the strike; and (3) the court must then decide if the party challenging the strike has proven discriminatory intent. n4 On appeal, a trial court's findings are entitled to great deference and will be affirmed unless clearly erroneous.

In the instant case, Michelle McCastle, who is white, and Shomari McCastle, who is black, raised their *Batson* challenge after the prosecutor struck the only two African-American members of the jury pool. The trial court found that there was a prima facie case of racial discrimination and asked the prosecutor to explain the two strikes.

The prosecutor first explained why she struck juror Frederick Douglas. "Mr. Douglas has a son in an interracial marriage. His son is black, as is he. And the defendant in this case is in an interracial marriage. I feel that that might make him have a particular empathy or sympathy for this defense couple, and that is why I struck him."

She then explained that her main reason for striking juror Karlton Richardson was that he was not married

and had no children. She further claimed that she struck him because he did not have significant ties to the community and because of his education level. The trial judge found that the prosecutor's explanations for striking both jurors were race-neutral and he denied the McCastles' *Batson* challenge.

As to juror Richardson, the trial court's denial of the *Batson* motion is not clearly erroneous. This court has previously upheld the denial of a *Batson* challenge where a juror was struck on the basis of being unmarried and childless. And the Supreme Court has found no error in the denial of a *Batson* motion where a juror was struck due to lack of education.

However, as to juror Douglas, the trial court clearly erred in finding that the prosecutor's explanation for striking him was race-neutral. On the contrary, the prosecutor's explanation was, on its face, based on the race of the juror. As the prosecutor plainly stated in her explanation for the strike, Douglas is black, his son is black, and his son is in an interracial marriage. Frankly, we are hard-pressed to understand how the trial judge could have concluded that this explanation was racially neutral.

"A neutral explanation means an explanation based on something other than the race of the juror." Here, the prosecutor's explanation for striking Douglas was not based on something other than his race. Rather, it was plainly premised on Douglas' race, his son's race, the race of his son's wife, as well as the respective races of the McCastles. "We need look no further than the prosecutor's own explanation to determine that a discriminatory purpose was involved in her decision."

(1) Because the prosecutor did not satisfy the second step of the Batson analysis—that of providing a race-neutral explanation which rebuts the McCastles' prima facie showing of racial discrimination—it follows that the trial court clearly erred in ruling that the McCastles had not shown discriminatory intent and in overruling their Batson challenge.

NORRIS v. ALABAMA
Supreme Court of the United States
294 U.S. 587

April 1, 1935, Decided

JUDGES:

Hughes, Van Devanter, Brandeis, Sutherland, Butler, Stone, Roberts, Cardozo; McReynolds did not hear the argument and took no part in the consideration and decision of this case.

OPINION BY:

HUGHES

OPINION

Petitioner, Clarence Norris, is one of nine negro boys who were indicted in March, 1931, in Jackson County, Alabama, for the crime of rape. On being brought to trial in that county, eight were convicted. The Supreme Court of Alabama reversed the conviction of one of these and affirmed that of seven, including Norris. This Court reversed the judgments of conviction upon the ground that the defendants had been denied due process of law in that the trial court had failed in the light of the circumstances disclosed, and of the inability of the defendants at that time to obtain counsel, to make an effective appointment of counsel to aid them in preparing and presenting their defense. *Powell* v. *Alabama*, 287 U.S. 45.

After the remand, a motion for change of venue was granted and the cases were transferred to Morgan County. Norris was brought to trial in November, 1933. At the outset, a motion was made on his behalf to quash the indictment upon the ground of the exclusion of negroes from juries in Jackson County where the indictment was found. A motion was also made to quash the trial *venire* in Morgan County upon the ground of the exclusion of negroes from juries in that county. In relation to each county, the charge was of long continued, systematic and arbitrary exclusion of qualified negro citizens from service on juries, solely because of their race and color, in violation of the Constitution of the United States. The State joined issue on this charge and after

hearing the evidence, which we shall presently review, the trial judge denied both motions, and exception was taken. The trial then proceeded and resulted in the conviction of Norris who was sentenced to death. On appeal, the Supreme Court of the State considered and decided the federal question which Norris had raised, and affirmed the judgment.

[2]*First.* There is no controversy as to the constitutional principle involved. That principle, long since declared, was not challenged, but was expressly recognized, by the Supreme Court of the State. Summing up precisely the effect of earlier decisions, this Court thus stated the principle in *Carter* v. *Texas*, 177 U.S. 442, 447, in relation to exclusion from service on grand juries: "Whenever by any action of a State, whether through its legislature, through its courts, or through its executive or administrative officers, all persons of the African race are excluded, solely because of their race or color, from serving as grand jurors in the criminal prosecution of a person of the African race, the equal protection of the laws is denied to him, contrary to the Fourteenth Amendment of the Constitution of the United States. *Strauder* v. *West Virginia*,; *Neal* v. *Delaware*,; *Gibson* v. *Mississippi*,." This statement was repeated in the same terms in *Rogers* v. *Alabama*, and again in Martin v. Texas,. The principle is equally applicable to a similar exclusion of negroes from service on petit juries. *Strauder* v. *West Virginia, supra*; *Martin* v. *Texas, supra*. And although the state statute defining the qualifications of jurors may be fair on its face, the constitutional provision affords protection against action of the State through its administrative officers in effecting the prohibited discrimination.

[3]The question is of the application of this established principle to the facts disclosed by the record. That the question is one of fact does not relieve us of

the duty to determine whether in truth a federal right has been denied. When a federal right has been specially set up and claimed in a state court, it is our province to inquire not merely whether it was denied in express terms but also whether it was denied in substance and effect. If this requires an examination of evidence, that examination must be made. Otherwise, review by this Court would fail of its purpose in safeguarding constitutional rights. Thus, whenever a conclusion of law of a state court as to a federal right and findings of fact are so intermingled that the latter control the former, it is incumbent upon us to analyze the facts in order that the appropriate enforcement of the federal right may be assured.

[4]Second. The evidence on the motion to quash the indictment. In 1930, the total population of Jackson County, where the indictment was found, was 36,881, of whom 2688 were negroes. The male population over twenty-one years of age numbered 8801, and of these, 666 were negroes.

The qualifications of jurors were thus prescribed by the state statute (Alabama Code, 1923, § 8603): "The jury commission shall place on the jury roll and in the jury box the names of all male citizens of the county who are generally reputed to be honest and intelligent men, and are esteemed in the community for their integrity, good character and sound judgment, but no person must be selected who is under twenty-one or over sixty-five years of age, or, who is an habitual drunkard, or who, being afflicted with a permanent disease or physical weakness is unfit to discharge the duties of a juror, or who cannot read English, or who has ever been convicted of any offense involving moral turpitude. If a person cannot read English and has all the other qualifications prescribed herein and is a freeholder or householder, his name may be placed on the jury roll and in the jury box."

Defendant adduced evidence to support the charge of unconstitutional discrimination in the actual administration of the statute in Jackson County. The testimony, as the state court said, tended to show that "in a long number of years no negro had been called for jury service in that county." It appeared that no negro had served on any grand or petit jury in that county within the memory of witnesses who had lived there all their lives. Testimony to that effect was given by men whose ages ran from fifty to seventy-six years. Their testimony was uncontradicted. It was supported by the testimony of officials. The clerk of the jury commission and the clerk of the circuit court had never known of a negro

serving on a grand jury in Jackson County. The court reporter, who had not missed a session in that county in twenty-four years, and two jury commissioners testified to the same effect. One of the latter, who was a member of the commission which made up the jury roll for the grand jury which found the indictment, testified that he had "never known of a single instance where any negro sat on any grand or petit jury in the entire history of that county."

That testimony in itself made out a *prima facie* case of the denial of the equal protection which the Constitution guarantees. See *Neal* v. *Delaware, supra.* The case thus made was supplemented by direct testimony that specified negroes, thirty or more in number, were qualified for jury service. Among these were negroes who were members of school boards, or trustees, of colored schools, and property owners and householders. It also appeared that negroes from that county had been called for jury service in the federal court. Several of those who were thus described as qualified were witnesses. While there was testimony which cast doubt upon the qualifications of some of the negroes who had been named, and there was also general testimony by the editor of a local newspaper who gave his opinion as to the lack of "sound judgment" of the "good negroes" in Jackson County, we think that the definite testimony as to the actual qualifications of individual negroes, which was not met by any testimony equally direct, showed that there were negroes in Jackson County qualified for jury service.

The question arose whether names of negroes were in fact on the jury roll. The books containing the jury roll for Jackson County for the year 1930–31 were produced. They were produced from the custody of a member of the jury commission which, in 1931, had succeeded the commission which had made up the jury roll from which the grand jury in question had been drawn. On the pages of this roll appeared the names of six negroes. They were entered, respectively, at the end of the precinct lists which were alphabetically arranged. The genuineness of these entries was disputed. It appeared that after the jury roll in question had been made up, and after the new jury commission had taken office, one of the new commissioners directed the new clerk to draw lines after the names which had been placed on the roll by the preceding commission. These lines, on the pages under consideration, were red lines, and the clerk of the old commission testified that they were not put in by him.

The entries made by the new clerk, for the new jury roll, were below these lines.

The names of the six negroes were in each instance written immediately above the red lines. An expert of long experience testified that these names were superimposed upon the red lines, that is, that they were written after the lines had been drawn. The expert was not cross-examined and no testimony was introduced to contradict him.[1] In denying the motion to quash, the trial judge expressed the view that he would not "be authorized to presume that somebody had committed a crime" or to presume that the jury board "had been unfaithful to their duties and allowed the books to be tampered with." His conclusion was that names of negroes were on the jury roll.

We think that the evidence did not justify that conclusion. The Supreme Court of the State did not sustain it. That court observed that the charge that the names of negroes were fraudulently placed on the roll did not involve any member of the jury board, and that the charge "was, by implication at least, laid at the door of the clerk of the board." The court, reaching its decision irrespective of that question, treated that phase of the matter as "wholly immaterial" and hence passed it by "without any expression of opinion thereon."

The state court rested its decision upon the ground that even if it were assumed that there was no name of a negro on the jury roll, it was not established that race or color caused the omission. The court pointed out that the statute fixed a high standard of qualifications for jurors and that the jury commission was vested with a wide discretion. The court adverted to the fact that more white citizens possessing age qualifications had been omitted from the jury roll than the entire negro population of the county, and regarded the testimony as being to the effect that "the matter of race, color, politics, religion or fraternal affiliations" had not been discussed by the commission and had not entered into their consideration, and that no one had been excluded because of race or color.

The testimony showed the practice of the jury commission. One of the commissioners who made up the jury roll in question, and the clerk of that commission, testified as to the manner of its preparation. The other two commissioners of that period did not testify. It was shown that the clerk, under the direction of the commissioners, made up a preliminary list which was based on the registration list of voters, the polling list and the tax list, and apparently also upon the telephone directory. The clerk testified that he made up a list of all male citizens between the ages of twenty-one and sixty-five years without regard to their status or qualifications. The commissioner testified that the designation "col." was placed after the names of those who were colored. In preparing the final jury roll, the preliminary list was checked off as to qualified jurors with the aid of men whom the commissioners called in for that purpose from the different precincts. And the commissioner testified that in the selections for the jury roll no one was "automatically or systematically" excluded, or excluded on account of race or color; that he "did not inquire as to color, that was not discussed."

But, in appraising the action of the commissioners, these statements cannot be divorced from other testimony. As we have seen, there was testimony, not overborne or discredited, that there were in fact negroes in the county qualified for jury service. That testimony was direct and specific. After eliminating those persons as to whom there was some evidence of lack of qualifications, a considerable number of others remained. The fact that the testimony as to these persons, fully identified, was not challenged by evidence appropriately direct, cannot be brushed aside. There is no ground for an assumption that the names of these negroes were not on the preliminary list. The inference to be drawn from the testimony is that they were on that preliminary list, and were designated on that list as the names of negroes, and that they were not placed on the jury roll. There was thus presented a test of the practice of the commissioners. Something more than mere general asseverations was required. Why were these names excluded from the jury roll? Was it because of the lack of statutory qualifications? Were the qualifications of negroes actually and properly considered?

The testimony of the commissioner on this crucial question puts the case in a strong light. That testimony leads to the conclusion that these or other negroes were not excluded on account of age, or lack of esteem in the community for integrity and judgment, or because of disease or want of any other qualification. The commissioner's answer to specific inquiry upon this point was

---

[1]The books containing the jury roll in question were produced on the argument at this bar and were examined by the Court.

that negroes were "never discussed." We give in the margin quotations from his testimony.[2]

We are of the opinion that the evidence required a different result from that reached in the state court. We think that the evidence that for a generation or longer no negro had been called for service on any jury in Jackson County, that there were negroes qualified for jury service, that according to the practice of the jury commission their names would normally appear on the preliminary list of male citizens of the requisite age but that no names of negroes were placed on the jury roll, and the testimony with respect to the lack of appropriate consideration of the qualifications of negroes, established the discrimination which the Constitution forbids. The motion to quash the indictment upon that ground should have been granted.

[5] *Third. The evidence on the motion to quash the trial venire.* The population of Morgan County, where the trial was had, was larger than that of Jackson County, and the proportion of negroes was much greater. The total population of Morgan County in 1930 was 46,176, and of this number 8,311 were negroes.

Within the memory of witnesses, long resident there, no negro had ever served on a jury in that county or had been called for such service. Some of these witnesses were over fifty years of age and had always lived in Morgan County. Their testimony was not contradicted. A clerk of the circuit court, who had resided in the county for thirty years, and who had been in office for over four years, testified that during his official term approximately 2500 persons had been called for jury service and that not one of them was a negro; that he did not recall "ever seeing any single person of the colored race serve on any jury in Morgan County."

There was abundant evidence that there were a large number of negroes in the county who were qualified for jury service. Men of intelligence, some of whom were college graduates, testified to long lists (said to contain nearly 200 names) of such qualified negroes, including many business men, owners of real property and householders. When defendant's counsel proposed to call many additional witnesses in order to adduce further proof of qualifications of negroes for jury service, the trial judge limited the testimony, holding that the evidence was cumulative.

We find no warrant for a conclusion that the names of any of the negroes as to whom this testimony was given, or of any other negroes, were placed on the jury rolls. No such names were identified. The evidence that for many years no negro had been called for jury service itself tended to show the absence of the names of negroes from the jury rolls, and the State made no effort to prove their presence. The trial judge limited the defendant's proof "to the present year, the present jury roll." The sheriff of the county, called as a witness for defendants, scanned the jury roll and after "looking over every single name on that jury roll, from A to Z," was unable to point out "any single negro on it."

For this long-continued, unvarying, and wholesale exclusion of negroes from jury service we find no justification consistent with the constitutional mandate.

---

[2]"Q. Did you ever exclude from the jury rolls any negroes because you found first, he was a man under twenty-one years old or over sixty-five, and he was excluded by reason of his age; secondly because he was a person who wasn't esteemed in the community for being a decent and honorable citizen, for good sound common sense and judgment, did you ever see or hear of them not going to take that negro because he wasn't esteemed in the community for good sense and judgment? A. No, sir.

"Q. Did you ever have occasion to say, I can't take that negro because he is a fellow that has a disease which may affect or does affect, his mentality, did you ever say that to yourself, with reference to any particular negro? A. No, sir, negroes was never discussed.

"Q. Did you ever say to yourself as a jury commissioner in compiling those lists, I am not going to take that negro because he has been convicted before of a crime involving moral turpitude, have you ever excluded a negro on that ground, did you ever find any negro that came within that category, under your personal knowledge in Jackson County? A. I couldn't recall any, no, sir, I don't know.

"Q. Have you ever known of any negro in Jackson County who was excluded by reason of the fact that he could not read English, and that negro at the same time wasn't a free holder or house holder, did you ever say I can't take that negro because he is prohibited under the rules from serving by reason of that provision? A. No, sir.

"Q. Or anybody in your presence? A. It never was discussed.

"Q. You had been a jury commissioner how long? A. I was on it under Bibb Graves administration, 1928, 1929, 1930.

"Q. Three years? A. Yes, sir.

"Q. And you never had occasion to exclude any negro in Jackson County by reason of the disqualifying provisions I have just called to your attention? A. Not to my personal knowledge, no, sir."

We have carefully examined the testimony of the jury commissioners upon which the state court based its decision. One of these commissioners testified in person and the other two submitted brief affidavits. By the state act (Gen. Acts, Ala., 1931, No. 47, p. 55), in force at the time the jury roll in question was made up, the clerk of the jury board was required to obtain the names of all male citizens of the county over twenty-one and under sixty-five years of age, and their occupation, place of residence and place of business. The qualifications of those who were to be placed on the jury roll were the same as those prescribed by the earlier statute which we have already quoted. The member of the jury board, who testified orally, said that a list was made up which included the names of all male citizens of suitable age; that black residents were not excluded from this general list; that in compiling the jury roll he did not consider race or color; that no one was excluded for that reason; and that he had placed on the jury roll the names of persons possessing the qualifications under the statute. The affidavits of the other members of the board contained general statements to the same effect.

We think that this evidence failed to rebut the strong *prima facie* case which defendant had made. That showing as to the long-continued exclusion of negroes from jury service, and as to the many negroes qualified for that service, could not be met by mere generalities. If, in the presence of such testimony as defendant adduced, the mere general assertions by officials of their performance of duty were to be accepted as an adequate justification for the complete exclusion of negroes from jury service, the constitutional provision—adopted with special reference to their protection—would be but a vain and illusory requirement. The general attitude of the jury commissioner is shown by the following extract from his testimony: "I do not know of any negro in Morgan County over twenty-one and under sixty-five who is generally reputed to be honest and intelligent and who is esteemed in the community for his integrity, good character and sound judgment, who is not an habitual drunkard, who isn't afflicted with a permanent disease or physical weakness which would render him unfit to discharge the duties of a juror, and who can read English, and who has never been convicted of a crime involving moral turpitude." In the light of the testimony given by defendant's witnesses, we find it impossible to accept such a sweeping characterization of the lack of qualifications of negroes in Morgan County. It is so sweeping, and so contrary to the evidence as to the many qualified negroes, that it destroys the intended effect of the commissioner's testimony.

In *Neal* v. *Delaware, supra*, decided over fifty years ago, this Court observed that it was a "violent presumption," in which the state court had there indulged, that the uniform exclusion of negroes from juries, during a period of many years, was solely because, in the judgment of the officers, charged with the selection of grand and petit jurors, fairly exercised, "the black race in Delaware were utterly disqualified by want of intelligence, experience, or moral integrity, to sit on juries." Such a presumption at the present time would be no less violent with respect to the exclusion of the negroes of Morgan County. And, upon the proof contained in the record now before us, a conclusion that their continuous and total exclusion from juries was because there were none possessing the requisite qualifications, cannot be sustained.

We are concerned only with the federal question which we have discussed, and in view of the denial of the federal right suitably asserted, the judgment must be reversed and the cause remanded for further proceedings not inconsistent with this opinion.

Reversed.

MR. JUSTICE McREYNOLDS did not hear the argument and took no part in the consideration and decision of this case.

HERNANDEZ v. TEXAS
Supreme Court of the United States
347 U.S. 475

May 3, 1954, Decided

MR. CHIEF JUSTICE WARREN delivered the opinion of the Court.

The petitioner, Pete Hernandez, was indicted for the murder of one Joe Espinosa by a grand jury in Jackson County, Texas. He was convicted and sentenced to life imprisonment. The Texas Court of Criminal Appeals affirmed the judgment of the trial court. Prior to the trial, the petitioner, by his counsel, offered timely motions to quash the indictment and the jury panel. He alleged that persons of Mexican descent were systematically excluded from service as jury commissioners, grand jurors, and petit jurors, although there were such persons fully qualified to serve residing in Jackson County. The petitioner asserted that exclusion of this class deprived him, as a member of the class, of the equal protection of the laws guaranteed by the Fourteenth Amendment of the Constitution. After a hearing, the trial court denied the motions. At the trial, the motions were renewed, further evidence taken, and the motions again denied. An allegation that the trial court erred in denying the motions was the sole basis of petitioner's appeal. In affirming the judgment of the trial court, the Texas Court of Criminal Appeals considered and passed upon the substantial federal question raised by the petitioner. We granted a writ of certiorari to review that decision.

In numerous decisions, this Court has held that it is a denial of the equal protection of the laws to try a defendant of a particular race or color under an indictment issued by a grand jury, or before a petit jury, from which all persons of his race or color have, solely because of that race or color, been excluded by the State, whether acting through its legislature, its courts, or its executive or administrative officers. Although the Court has had little occasion to rule on the question directly, it has been recognized since *Strauder* v. *West Virginia*, that the exclusion of a class of persons from jury service on grounds other than race or color may also deprive a defendant who is a member of that class of the constitutional guarantee of equal protection of the laws. The State of Texas would have us hold that there are only two classes—white and Negro—within the contemplation of the Fourteenth Amendment. The decisions of this Court do not support that view. And, except where the question presented involves the exclusion of persons of Mexican descent from juries, Texas courts have taken a broader view of the scope of the equal protection clause.

Throughout our history differences in race and color have defined easily identifiable groups which have at times required the aid of the courts in securing equal treatment under the laws. But community prejudices are not static, and from time to time other differences from the community norm may define other groups which need the same protection. Whether such a group exists within a community is a question of fact. When the existence of a distinct class is demonstrated, and it is further shown that the laws, as written or as applied, single out that class for different treatment not based on some reasonable classification, the guarantees of the Constitution have been violated. The Fourteenth Amendment is not directed solely against discrimination due to a "two-class theory"—that is, based upon differences between "white" and Negro.

As the petitioner acknowledges, the Texas system of selecting grand and petit jurors by the use of jury commissions is fair on its face and capable of being utilized without discrimination. But as this Court has held, the system is susceptible to abuse and can be employed in a discriminatory manner. The exclusion of otherwise eligible persons from jury service solely because of their ancestry or national origin is discrimination prohibited by the Fourteenth Amendment. The Texas statute makes no such discrimination, but the petitioner alleges that those administering the law do.

The petitioner's initial burden in substantiating his charge of group discrimination was to prove that persons of Mexican descent constitute a separate class in Jackson County, distinct from "whites." One method by which this may be demonstrated is by showing the attitude of the community. Here the testimony of responsible officials and citizens contained the admission that residents of the community distinguished between "white" and "Mexican." The participation of persons of Mexican descent in business and community groups was shown to be slight. Until very recent times, children of Mexican descent were required to attend a segregated school for the first four grades. At least one restaurant in town prominently displayed a sign announcing "No Mexicans Served." On the courthouse grounds at the time of the hearing, there were two men's toilets, one unmarked, and the other marked "Colored Men" and "Hombres Aqui" ("Men Here"). No substantial evidence was offered to rebut the logical inference to be drawn from these facts, and it must be concluded that petitioner succeeded in his proof.

Having established the existence of a class, petitioner was then charged with the burden of proving discrimination. To do so, he relied on the pattern of proof established by *Norris* v. *Alabama*, 294 U.S. 587. In that case, proof that Negroes constituted a substantial segment of the population of the jurisdiction, that some Negroes were qualified to serve as jurors, and that none had been called for jury service over an extended period of time, was held to constitute prima facie proof of the systematic exclusion of Negroes from jury service. This holding, sometimes called the "rule of exclusion," has been applied in other cases, and it is available in supplying proof of discrimination against any delineated class.

The petitioner established that 14% of the population of Jackson County were persons with Mexican or Latin-American surnames, and that 11% of the males over 21 bore such names. The County Tax Assessor testified that 6 or 7 percent of the freeholders on the tax rolls of the County were persons of Mexican descent. The State of Texas stipulated that "for the last twenty-five years there is no record of any person with a Mexican or Latin American name having served on a jury commission, grand jury or petit jury in Jackson County." The parties also stipulated that "there are some male persons of Mexican or Latin American descent in Jackson County who, by virtue of being citizens, householders, or freeholders, and having all other legal prerequisites to jury service, are eligible to serve as members of a jury commission, grand jury and/or petit jury."

The petitioner met the burden of proof imposed in *Norris* v. *Alabama*, *supra*. To rebut the strong prima facie case of the denial of the equal protection of the laws guaranteed by the Constitution thus established, the State offered the testimony of five jury commissioners that they had not discriminated against persons of Mexican or Latin-American descent in selecting jurors. They stated that their only objective had been to select those whom they thought were best qualified. This testimony is not enough to overcome the petitioner's case. As the Court said in *Norris* v. *Alabama*:

> "That showing as to the long-continued exclusion of negroes from jury service, and as to the many negroes qualified for that service, could not be met by mere generalities. If, in the presence of such testimony as defendant adduced, the mere general assertions by officials of their performance of duty were to be accepted as an adequate justification for the complete exclusion of negroes from jury service, the constitutional provision ... would be but a vain and illusory requirement."

The same reasoning is applicable to these facts.

Circumstances or chance may well dictate that no persons in a certain class will serve on a particular jury or during some particular period. But it taxes our credulity to say that mere chance resulted in there being no members of this class among the over six thousand jurors called in the past 25 years. The result bespeaks discrimination, whether or not it was a conscious decision on the part of any individual jury commissioner. The judgment of conviction must be reversed.

To say that this decision revives the rejected contention that the Fourteenth Amendment requires proportional representation of all the component ethnic groups of the community on every jury 16 ignores the facts. The petitioner did not seek proportional representation, nor did he claim a right to have persons of Mexican descent sit on the particular juries which he faced. His only claim is the right to be indicted and tried by juries from which all members of his class are not systematically excluded—juries selected from among all qualified persons regardless of national origin or descent. To this much, he is entitled by the Constitution.

Reversed.

DUREN v. MISSOURI
Supreme Court of the United States
439 U.S. 357

January 9, 1979, Decided

MR. JUSTICE WHITE delivered the opinion of the Court.

In *Taylor* v. *Louisiana*, 419 U.S. 522 (1975), this Court held that systematic exclusion of women during the jury-selection process, resulting in jury pools not "reasonably representative" of the community, denies a criminal defendant his right, under the Sixth and Fourteenth Amendments, to a petit jury selected from a fair cross section of the community. 1 Under the system invalidated in *Taylor*, a woman could not serve on a jury unless she filed a written declaration of her willingness to do so. As a result, although 53% of the persons eligible for jury service were women, less than 1% of the 1,800 persons whose names were drawn from the jury wheel during the year in which appellant Taylor's jury was chosen were female.

At the time of our decision in *Taylor*, no other State provided that women could not serve on a jury unless they volunteered to serve. However, five States, including Missouri, provided an automatic exemption from jury service for any women requesting not to serve. Subsequent to *Taylor* three of these States eliminated this exemption. Only Missouri, respondent in this case, and Tennessee 6 continue to exempt women from jury service upon request. Today we hold that such systematic exclusion of women that results in jury venires averaging less than 15% female violates the Constitution's fair-cross-section requirement.

I

Petitioner Duren was indicted in 1975 in the Circuit Court of Jackson County, Mo., for first-degree murder and first-degree robbery. In a pretrial motion to quash his petit jury panel, and again in a post-conviction motion for a new trial, he contended that his right to trial by a jury chosen from a fair cross section of his community was denied by provisions of Missouri law granting women who so request an automatic exemption from jury service. Both motions were denied.

At hearings on these motions, petitioner established that the jury-selection process in Jackson County begins with the annual mailing of a questionnaire to persons randomly selected from the Jackson County voter registration list. Approximately 70,000 questionnaires were mailed in 1975. The questionnaire contains a list of occupations and other categories which are the basis under Missouri law for either disqualification 9 or exemption from jury service. 11 Included on the questionnaire is a paragraph prominently addressed "TO WOMEN" that states in part:

"Any woman who elects not to serve will fill out this paragraph and mail this questionnaire to the jury commission at once."

A similar paragraph is addressed "TO MEN OVER 65 YEARS OF AGE," who are also statutorily exempt upon request.

The names of those sent questionnaires are placed in the master jury wheel for Jackson County, except for those returning the questionnaire who indicate disqualification or claim an applicable exemption. Summonses are mailed on a weekly basis to prospective jurors randomly drawn from the jury wheel. The summons, like the questionnaire, contains special directions to men over 65 and to women, this time advising them to return the summons by mail if they desire not to serve. The practice also is that even those women who do not return the summons are treated as having claimed exemption if they fail to appear for jury service on the appointed day. Other persons seeking to claim an exemption at this stage must make written or personal application to the court.

Petitioner established that according to the 1970 census, 54% of the adult inhabitants of Jackson County were women. He also showed that for the periods June–October

1975 and January-March 1976, 11,197 persons were summoned and that 2,992 of these, or 26.7%, were women. Of those summoned, 741 women and 4,378 men appeared for service. Thus, 14.5% (741 of 5,119) of the persons on the postsummons weekly venires during the period in which petitioner's jury was chosen were female. In March 1976, when petitioner's trial began, 15.5% of those on the weekly venires were women (110 of 707). Petitioner's jury was selected from a 53-person panel on which there were 5 women; all 12 jurors chosen were men. None of the foregoing statistical evidence was disputed.

In affirming petitioner's conviction, the Missouri Supreme Court questioned two aspects of his statistical presentation. First, it considered the census figures inadequate because they were six years old and might not precisely mirror the percentage of women registered to vote. Second, petitioner had not unequivocally demonstrated the extent to which the low percentage of women appearing for jury service was due to the automatic exemption for women, rather than to sex-neutral exemptions such as that for persons over age 65.

The court went on to hold, however, that even accepting petitioner's statistical proof, "the number of female names in the wheel, those summoned and those appearing were well above acceptable constitutional standards." We granted certiorari, because of concern that the decision below is not consistent with our decision in *Taylor*.

II

We think that in certain crucial respects the Missouri Supreme Court misconceived the nature of the fair-cross-section inquiry set forth in *Taylor*. In holding that "petit juries must be drawn from a source fairly representative of the community," we explained that

"jury wheels, pools of names, panels, or venires from which juries are drawn must not systematically exclude distinctive groups in the community and thereby fail to be reasonably representative thereof."

In order to establish a prima facie violation of the fair-cross-section requirement, the defendant must show (1) that the group alleged to be excluded is a "distinctive" group in the community; (2) that the representation of this group in venires from which juries are selected is not fair and reasonable in relation to the number of such persons in the community; and (3) that

this underrepresentation is due to systematic exclusion of the group in the jury-selection process.

A

With respect to the first part of the prima facie test, *Taylor* without doubt established that women "are sufficiently numerous and distinct from men" so that "if they are systematically eliminated from jury panels, the Sixth Amendment's fair-cross-section requirement cannot be satisfied."

B

The second prong of the prima facie case was established by petitioner's statistical presentation. Initially, the defendant must demonstrate the percentage of the community made up of the group alleged to be underrepresented, for this is the conceptual benchmark for the Sixth Amendment fair-cross-section requirement. In *Taylor*, the State had stipulated that 53% of the population eligible for jury service 21 was female, while petitioner Duren has relied upon a census measurement of the actual percentage of women in the community (54%). In the trial court, the State of Missouri never challenged these data. Although the Missouri Supreme Court speculated that changing population patterns between 1970 and 1976 and unequal voter registration by men and women 22 rendered the census figures a questionable frame of reference, 23 there is no evidence whatsoever in the record to suggest that the 1970 census data significantly distorted the percentage of women in Jackson County at the time of trial. Petitioner's presentation was clearly adequate prima facie evidence of population characteristics for the purpose of making a fair-cross-section violation.

Given petitioner's proof that in the relevant community slightly over half of the adults are women, we must disagree with the conclusion of the court below that jury venires containing approximately 15% women are "reasonably representative" of this community. If the percentage of women appearing on jury pools in Jackson County had precisely mirrored the percentage of women in the population, more than one of every two prospective jurors would have been female. In fact, less than one of every six prospective jurors was female; 85% of the average jury was male. Such a gross discrepancy between the percentage of women in jury venires and the percentage of women in the community requires the conclusion that women were not fairly represented in the source from which petit juries were drawn in Jackson County.

C

Finally, in order to establish a prima facie case, it was necessary for petitioner to show that the underrepresentation of women, generally and on his venire, was due to their systematic exclusion in the jury-selection process. Petitioner's proof met this requirement. His undisputed demonstration that a large discrepancy occurred not just occasionally, but in every weekly venire for a period of nearly a year manifestly indicates that the cause of the underrepresentation was systematic—that is, inherent in the particular jury-selection process utilized.

Petitioner Duren's statistics and other evidence also established when in the selection process the systematic exclusion took place. There was no indication that underrepresentation of women occurred at the first stage of the selection process—the questionnaire canvass of persons randomly selected from the relevant voter registration list. The first sign of a systematic discrepancy is at the next stage—the construction of the jury wheel from which persons are randomly summoned for service. Less than 30% of those summoned were female, demonstrating that a substantially larger number of women answering the questionnaire claimed either ineligibility or exemption from jury service. Moreover, at the summons stage women were not only given another opportunity to claim exemption, but also were presumed to have claimed exemption when they did not respond to the summons. Thus, the percentage of women at the final, venire, stage (14.5%) was much lower than the percentage of women who were summoned for service (26.7%).

The resulting disproportionate and consistent exclusion of women from the jury wheel and at the venire stage was quite obviously due to the *system* by which juries were selected. Petitioner demonstrated that the underrepresentation of women in the final pool of prospective jurors was due to the operation of Missouri's exemption criteria—whether the automatic exemption for women or other statutory exemptions—as implemented in Jackson County. Women were therefore systematically underrepresented within the meaning of *Taylor*.

III

The demonstration of a prima facie fair-cross-section violation by the defendant is not the end of the inquiry into whether a constitutional violation has occurred. We have explained that " States remain free to prescribe relevant qualifications for their jurors and to provide reasonable exemptions so long as it may be fairly said that the jury lists or panels are representative of the community." *Taylor*, 419 U.S., at 538. However, we cautioned that "[the] right to a proper jury cannot be overcome on merely rational grounds,". Rather, it requires that a significant state interest be manifestly and primarily advanced by those aspects of the jury-selection process, such as exemption criteria, that result in the disproportionate exclusion of a distinctive group.

The Supreme Court of Missouri suggested that the low percentage of women on jury venires in Jackson County may have been due to a greater number of women than of men qualifying for or claiming permissible exemptions, such as those for persons over 65, teachers, and government workers. Respondent further argues that petitioner has not proved that the exemption for women had "any effect" on or was responsible for the underrepresentation of women on venires.

However, once the defendant has made a prima facie showing of an infringement of his constitutional right to a jury drawn from a fair cross section of the community, it is the State that bears the burden of justifying this infringement by showing attainment of a fair cross section to be incompatible with a significant state interest. Assuming, *arguendo*, that the exemptions mentioned by the court below would justify failure to achieve a fair community cross section on jury venires, the State must demonstrate that these exemptions caused the underrepresentation complained of. The record contains no such proof, and mere suggestions or assertions to that effect are insufficient.

The other possible cause of the disproportionate exclusion of women on Jackson County jury venires is, of course, the automatic exemption for women. Neither the Missouri Supreme Court nor respondent in its brief has offered any substantial justification for this exemption. In response to questioning at oral argument, counsel for respondent ventured that the only state interest advanced by the exemption is safeguarding the important role played by women in home and family life. But exempting all women because of the preclusive domestic responsibilities of some women is insufficient justification for their disproportionate exclusion on jury venires. What we stated in *Taylor* with respect to the system there challenged under which women could "opt in" for jury service is equally applicable to Missouri's "opt out" exemption:

"It is untenable to suggest these days that it would be a special hardship for each and every woman to perform jury service or that society cannot spare *any* women from their present duties. This may be the case with many, and it may be burdensome to sort out those who should be exempted from those who should serve. But that task is performed in the case of men, and the administrative convenience in dealing with women as a class is insufficient justification for diluting the quality of community judgment represented by the jury in criminal trials.

...

"If it was ever the case that women were unqualified to sit on juries or were so situated that none of them should be required to perform jury service, that time has long since passed."

We recognize that a State may have an important interest in assuring that those members of the family responsible for the care of children are available to do so. An exemption appropriately tailored to this interest would, we think, survive a fair-cross-section challenge. We stress, however, that the constitutional guarantee to a jury drawn from a fair cross section of the community requires that States exercise proper caution in exempting broad categories of persons from jury service. Although most occupational and other reasonable exemptions may inevitably involve some degree of overinclusiveness or underinclusiveness, any category expressly limited to a group in the community of sufficient magnitude and distinctiveness so as to be within the fair-cross-section requirement—such as women—runs the danger of resulting in underrepresentation sufficient to constitute a prima facie violation of that constitutional requirement. We also repeat the observation made in *Taylor* that it is unlikely that reasonable exemptions, such as those based on special hardship, incapacity, or community needs, "would pose substantial threats that the remaining pool of jurors would not be representative of the community."

The judgment of the Missouri Supreme Court is reversed, and the case is remanded for further proceedings not inconsistent with this opinion.

So ordered.

GREGORY WILLIAMS and LEROY WILLIAMS, Plaintiffs, against
NEW YORK CITY HOUSING AUTHORITY, Defendant.
United States District Court for the Southern
District of New York
154 F. Supp. 2d 820

August 1, 2001, Decided; August 1, 2001, Filed

OPINION

ROBERT L. CARTER, District Judge

Defendant **New York** City Housing Authority ("NYCHA") moves pursuant to Rule 12(b)(6), F.R. Civ. P., to dismiss the claim of a hostile work environment contained in plaintiffs Gregory **Williams**' and Leroy **Williams**' complaint. Plaintiffs oppose this motion.

BACKGROUND

In considering a motion to dismiss, the court must accept all of the plaintiffs' allegations as true. Plaintiffs are both African-Americans who were employed at all relevant times as caretakers at the housing project known as Fort Independence Houses. On March 17, 1997, Gregory **Williams** entered the office of his supervisor, Kevin Burns, to turn in a leave of absence form and discuss a paycheck. Gregory **Williams** noticed a **noose** hanging on the wall behind Burns's desk and then left the office without speaking to him.

Gregory **Williams**, and several co-workers, later confirmed that the **noose** remained on display in Burns's office. In the afternoon of the following day, March 18, 1997, Leroy **Williams** entered Burns's office and also noticed the **noose**. The following morning, March 19, 1997, Gregory **Williams** went to Burns's office and asked Burns why the **noose** was hanging on the wall. Burns, visibly uncomfortable in the face of the confrontation, immediately removed the **noose** and stated: "you know I'm not like that," adding, "It was a joke," and "I apologize if it offended you."

On March 25, 1997, Gregory **Williams** filed a formal complaint regarding the **noose** at the NYCHA Office of Equal Opportunity ("OEO"). Leroy **Williams** signed a witness statement the following day to be attached to the complaint. Plaintiffs contend that their complaint was not seriously investigated by the OEO. They also allege that their supervisors began to enforce workplace rules more strictly against the plaintiffs than they had before the complaint was filed and that following their complaint, they were treated differently than other workers. For example, plaintiffs' radios were confiscated while other employees simply were asked not to play theirs.

Plaintiffs filed charges of **employment discrimination** based upon race and retaliation with the United States Equal **Employment** Opportunity Commission (hereinafter "EEOC") on or about November 18, 1997. On December 7, 2000, plaintiff received a "Notice of Right to Sue" from the United States Department of Justice, Civil Rights Division. Thereafter, plaintiffs filed this complaint with the court on March 2, 2001, alleging violations of Title VII of the Civil Rights Act of 1964. The complaint contains two causes of action. First, plaintiffs contend that the defendant subjected them to a hostile work environment. Second, plaintiffs assert that they suffered retaliation for complaining of the allegedly discriminatory treatment. Defendant is seeking dismissal in this motion of the hostile work environment claim.

DISCUSSION

*** To demonstrate a hostile work environment actionable under Title VII, the workplace must be "permeated with 'discriminatory intimidation, ridicule and insult,' that is 'sufficiently severe or pervasive to alter the conditions of the victim's **employment** and create an abusive working environment.'" The United States Supreme Court in *Harris* indicated that there is no precise test for determining whether conduct is severe or pervasive enough to constitute a hostile work environment but indicated that certain guideposts include "the frequency of the discriminatory conduct; its severity; whether it is physically threatening or humiliating, or a mere offensive utterance; and whether it unreasonably interferes with an employee's work performance." The **employment** environment must be abusive both objectively and subjectively.

In addition, plaintiffs must demonstrate "that a specific basis exists for imputing the conduct that created the hostile environment to the employer." Hostile work environments are generally imputed to the employer unless the employer can demonstrate that it took appropriate action to remedy the situation.

In this case, the conduct which demonstrates racial animus was the display of the **noose** in the supervisors' office. The issue therefore is whether this conduct is severe or pervasive enough to alter the conditions of the plaintiffs' **employment.** There is no magical formula in this determination, nor is there a specific minimum "number of incidents below which a plaintiff fails as a matter of law to state a claim." Generally, however, as the conduct in question becomes more severe, fewer occurrences are necessary to create a hostile work environment. Thus, while a single racist remark will usually not support a hostile environment claim, a single physical assault would. These examples, while illustrative of the boundaries of the spectrum of racist conduct, provide little practical guidance in a case, like this, where the conduct falls somewhere between those extremes. The Second Circuit has offered additional guidance, noting that while a single incident must be "extraordinarily severe" to create a hostile work environment, it need not involve actual or threatened physical assault. The courts' failure to enunciate regimented standards is deliberate and is required to ensure adequate flexibility to promote Title VII's broad remedial purpose.

Plaintiffs have satisfied their burden of alleging that the display of the **noose** subjectively altered the conditions of their **employment.** To substantiate their claim, they must also allege facts that, if proven true, would demonstrate that their perception of the workplace was objectively reasonable. The Second Circuit has noted that the placement of a **noose** in the workplace can reasonably be perceived as racially hostile conduct. The question remains, however, whether the conduct in this case was sufficiently pervasive or severe to create a hostile work environment.

Whether the display of the **noose** constitutes pervasive conduct is a complicated issue. This is the only racist act alleged in the complaint. However, the **noose** was prominently displayed for at least three days and presumably was viewed by everyone who entered the supervisors' office. Furthermore, it was only removed after one of the plaintiffs complained. The implication of this is that had the plaintiffs remained silent, it would have been on display indefinitely.

As for the severity of the display of a **noose**, there can be little doubt that such a symbol is significantly more egregious than the utterance of a racist joke. In a case before the Eleventh Circuit, where a plaintiff's state law intentional infliction of emotional distress claim was dismissed, Circuit Judge Fay wrote in dissent:

> Those of us for whom a particular symbol is just that—a symbol—may have difficulty appreciating the very real, very significant fear that such symbols inspire in those to whom they are targeted. No less than the swastika or the Klansman's hood, the **noose** in this context is intended to arouse fear.

Indeed, the **noose** is among the most repugnant of all racist symbols, because it is itself an instrument of violence. It is impossible to appreciate the impact of the display of a **noose** without understanding this nation's opprobrious legacy of violence against African-Americans. One study notes that from 1882, the earliest date for reliable statistics, to 1968, 3,446 African-Americans died at the hands of lynch mobs. Obviously, these figures underestimate the actual number of blacks who were the victims of lynchings because such atrocities were underreported, and southern whites frequently attempted to suppress evidence of mob violence for fear of the enactment of a federal anti-lynching law.

The effect of such violence on the psyche of African-Americans cannot be exaggerated. Sociologists have explained that "lynching was employed to maintain dominance whenever it suited whites to reaffirm their mastery or blacks challenged or seemed about to test the established contours of their subordination." (This observation is especially relevant to this case where the **noose** was displayed not by a co-worker, but by a white supervisor.)

Some have opined that the prevalence of violence against blacks in the South was critical to the migration of African-Americans to the North during the first quarter of the twentieth century. In the words of one migrant, "After twenty years of seeing my people lynched for any offense from spitting on a sidewalk to stealing a mule, I made up my mind that I would turn the prow of my ship toward part of the country where the people at least made a pretense at being civilized."

The lynchings in this nation's past cannot be relegated to the history books. As one essayist noted: "That is [the] rite of colored male passage: having to drag all those lynchings around with them, around their necks: those are their ancestors." The hangman's **noose** remains a potent and threatening symbol for African-Americans, in part because the grim specter of racially motivated violence continues to manifest itself in present day hate crimes. Moreover, persistent inequality in this country resuscitates for modern African-Americans many of the same insecurities felt years ago. It is for this reason that the Civil Rights Act of 1964 was enacted. The courts have a responsibility to be vigilant in enforcing the provisions of this Act to facilitate the eradication of obstacles that currently prevent African-Americans from achieving equality.

Racially motivated physical threats and assaults are the most egregious form of workplace harassment. A review of Second Circuit jurisprudence in this area makes clear that when conduct in the workplace is physically threatening to an individual because of his membership in a protected class, that conduct will almost always create a hostile work environment. The display of a **noose** would fall within this category of intimidating conduct. The fact that a white supervisor was displaying the **noose** obviously intensifies the intimidating effect.

Thus, even though there may not have been a large number of isolated remarks or actions, the severity of the conduct at issue, if proven, would be sufficient to establish a hostile work environment. Obviously, in the end, it is the province of a properly instructed jury to decide whether the conduct in this case was severe or pervasive enough to support plaintiffs' hostile work environment claim. Defendant's contention, however, that the display of a **noose** by a white supervisor in his office could not, as a matter of law, sufficiently "alter the conditions of **employment**" for an African-American employee is naive and untenable.

CONCLUSION

Defendant's motion to dismiss plaintiffs' first cause of action is denied.

IT IS SO ORDERED.

Somerset v. Stewart

Who was James Somerset?

How did James get to England?

What event caused the problem which this case addresses?

What happened when James was captured?

How did James get before the court and Lord Mansfield?

How did James get a lawyer?

What was the issue in the case?

What argument was made on behalf of Charles Stewart, the slave owner?

What argument was made on behalf of James Somerset?

What was the decision of Lord Mansfield?

What were the legal reasons for Judge Mansfield's decision?

What moral reasons did Lord Mansfield give for his decision?

Pattinson v. Whitaker

What happened that caused this case?

What did Pattinson want the court to do for him?

What is a warrant?

What was the issue in the case?

What did the Court decide?

Did the Court accept the slave owner's argument that the Law of Nations wherein nations like Spain and France return property which strays across the border requires the return of the slaves?

Did the court accept the slave owner's argument that the English Common law requires the return of the slaves?

Did the court accept the last argument of the slave owner that since both the United States and England recognize slaves as property and since a treaty binds both countries to protect the rights of each other's citizens to use of their property the slaves must be returned?

Denison v. Tucker

What happened that caused this case?

What did the trial court hold?

What was the issue in the case?

What did the court hold on the issue?

What reasons did the court give for this decision?

What did Judge Woodward conclude from the Treaties between the French and British and then between the British and the United States?

Neal v. Farmer

What event caused this case?

Was it a crime to kill a slave in 1851 and, if so, why wasn't William Neal prosecuted?

What did Nancy Farmer do about William Neal killing her slave?

What was William Neal's claim on appeal to the Georgia Supreme Court?

Why should she have to prove that fact?

What was the issue in the case?

What did the Court hold?

What reasons did the court give for its decision?

Gobu v. Gobu

How did the Plaintiff come to be a slave?

What color was the slave?

What did the plaintiff do when he became an adult?

Where did he get a lawyer?

What was the issue in this case?

What did the court hold?

What was the presumption if your skin was black?

Did the presumption apply to mulattos?

Who has the burden of proof as to whether a mulatto is a slave?

Did the court free the slave? Why?

Adelle v. Beauregard

What were the facts of this case?

What was the issue?

What was the holding of the court?

Why did the court hold the way that it did?

Was the slave freed?

Did the court refer to any precedent for its decision?

WAS that case binding on the Louisiana Court? Why or why not?

Alfred Nichols v. William F. Bell

What were the facts of this case?

How did the court attempt to expand the rule of the Gobu case?

What was the court's problem with extending the rule?

Hudgins v. Wrights

What were the plaintiffs claiming?

The trial court freed the plaintiffs? Why?

Did the trial court give any other reason for freeing the plaintiffs?

When the defendant owner appealed there were two issues facing the court. What were those issues?

What did the appellate court (Judge Tucker) hold on those two issues?

Why did the court rule as it did on issue number one?

Why did the court rule the way it did on issue number 2?

State v. Harden

What were the facts of this case?

What did the defendant claim on appeal?

What was the issue in the case?

What did the court hold?

What did the court say the prosecutor must show to prove that the victim of the crime was free and not slave?

Bulloch v. The Lamar (Georgia 1844)

What were the facts of this case?

What was the issue in the case?

What did the Court hold?

What reasons did the court give for its holding?

What was awarded to the slave's owner?

What was awarded to the relatives of the slaves who were killed?

Gorman v. Campbell (Georgia 1853)

What were the facts of the case?

What was the issue in the case?

What did the court hold?

Would the captain be liable if he had commanded London to help with the logs?

Would the captain be liable if he had just given permission for London to help with the logs?

What were the duties of the Captain under the law?

How far did the captain have to go to protect the slave as property?

Did the Court comment at all about the humanity of protecting the slave?

Ponton v. Wilmington and Weldon RR Co (N.C 1858)

What were the facts of this case?

What was the fellow servant rule?

What was the issue in the case?

What did the court hold?

Why did the court rule that way?

Could the owner of the slave have protected his interests in any way?

State v. Mann

What were the facts of this case?

What instruction had the judge given to the jury?

When Mann appealed what was the issue before the court?

What did the court hold?

Was the court deciding whether Mann could be liable in a Civil Suit?

What relationship did Mann have with the slave?

Could an owner be criminally guilty for an assault on a slave?

What is the only end of slavery?

Did Judge Ruffin believe that the Courts should even get involved in brutality by a master to his slave? Why not?

What did Justice Ruffin say the slaves must be conditioned to believe?

Did Justice Ruffin believe that there were any considerations outside of the court which would protect the slaves?

United States v. Amy

What were the facts of this case?
What was the issue?
What did the Court decide?
Why did court so rule?

The Slave Grace

What were the facts of this case?
What was the issue in the case?
What did the court hold?
What was the rationale for the court's decision?
Why didn't the Somerset case make Grace free? Didn't all slaves chains fall off when they reached England?

Harry v. Decker and Hopkins

What were the facts of the case?
Why couldn't they have been slaves while in Indiana?
What was the issue in the case?
What did the Court hold?
Why did the court free the slaves?

Commonwealth v. Thomas Aves

What were the facts of the case?
What was the issue in the case?
What did the court hold?
Was slavery legal in Massachusetts?
Did the court find any precedent for the proposition that slavery is illegal?
Since slavery was legal in Louisiana shouldn't the Massachusetts's court give comity to that state's law as the Mississippi court did in *Harry v. Decker and Hopkins*? Did it?

Comity would require Massachusetts to give comity to Louisiana's law but the court did not do it. Why not?

What would the slave states especially Louisiana think of this opinion?

Why did the fugitive slave act which requires free states to return slaves escaping from slave states apply and make Massachusetts return the slave?

Scott v. Emerson

What were the facts of the case?

What instructions did the trial court judge give to the jury?

Were the instructions given by the trial court judge correct?

When the master appealed to the Missouri Supreme Court what was the issue?

What did the court decide?

Why?

The Judge writing the majority opinion stated: "We are almost persuaded, that the introduction of slavery amongst us was, in the providence of God, who makes the evil passions of men subservient to His own glory, a means of placing that unhappy race within the pale of civilized nations." What did he mean by that statement?

What did the dissent say?

Pleasants v. Pleasants

What is a will?

What did the will of John Pleasants provide concerning his slaves?

When John Pleasants died were the slaves freed? Why or why not?

Who owned the slaves upon John Pleasant's death?

Did the legislature of Virginia ever allow manumission?

Did the passage of that act affect John Pleasant's former slaves?

What was the issue in the case?

What did the court hold?

What arguments did the heirs who owned the slaves make as to why the will was not valid?

What is the rule against perpetuities?

Why didn't the rule apply in this case?

Bailey v. Poindexter's Ex'or

What were the facts?
What was the issue in the case?
What did the court decide?
What was the court's rationale?
What did the dissenting opinion say?
Why did the court not follow the Pleasant's case and allow the slaves to be free?

Mitchell v. Wells

What were the facts of this case?
What was the issue in the case?
What did the Court hold?
What was the court's rationale?
What did the dissenting opinion say?

Wright v. Deacon

What were the facts?
What was the issue facing the court?
What did the court hold?
What was the court's rationale?

Prigg v. Pennsylvania

What were the facts?
What was the issue?
What did the court hold?
What was the court's rationale?

The Antelope

What were the facts?
What was the issue?
What did the court hold?
What were the reasons for the court's holding?

The Dred Scott Case

Where had we dealt with Dred Scott and why are we dealing with him again?
What was the issue in the case as stated by Justice Taney?
How did Justice Taney hold?
What was Justice Taney's rationale?
Did the fact that some states recognized African Americans as citizens make any difference to Justice Taney?
What other reasons did he give to support his decision?

Could slaves be made citizens by the power of naturalization given to Congress by the Constitution?

In Re: African-American Slave Descendants Litigation. Appeals of: Deadria Farmer-Paellmann

What are the facts of the case?
What was the issue facing the court?
What did the court decide"
What was the court's rationale?
Do you think reparations should be given? Why or why not?

The Civil Rights Cases (Supreme Court 1883)

Congress had passed a law in 1875 which said: That "all persons within the jurisdiction of the United States shall be entitled to the full and equal enjoyment of the accommodations, advantages, facilities, and privileges of inns, public conveyances on land or water, theaters, and other places of public amusement, subject only to the conditions and limitations established by law and applicable alike to citizens of every race and color, regardless of any previous conditions of servitude." Where did Congress think it got the power to pass such a law?
What people were before he Court after having been prosecuted for violating the statute?
What was the claim on appeal?
What was the issue before the court?
What did the court hold?
Did the 14th Amendment give Congress the power to pass this law? Why or why not?
Did the 13th amendment give Congress the power to pass this act?
Did Justice Harlan think that Congress had the power to pass this act under the 13th Amendment? Why or why not?
According to Justice Harlan did the freedom and protection given to African Americans under the 13th Amendment also protect them from discrimination from individuals and corporations? Why or why not?
Did Justice Harlan believe that the 14th Amendment gave Congress the power to pass this act? Why or why not?

Justice Bradley wrote the majority opinion and Justice Harlan was the lone dissenter. Which Justice?
- Was educated in the South?
- Had been a prominent railroad lawyer and Republican activist?
- Owned slaves prior to the Civil War?
- Chewed tobacco?

Plessy v. Ferguson, Supreme Court 1896

What law was passed by Louisiana?

What was the penalty for violating this law?

Who was prosecuted and for what was he prosecuted?

What was the issue in the case?

What was the holding of the court?

Why didn't the majority of the court believe that this law violated the 14th amendment's equal protection clause?

Did Justice Harlan agree? Why or why not?

Berea Collect v. Kentucky

Was this case criminal or civil?

What decision was made in the trial court?

What was the issue before the Supreme Court?

Did the fact that the College was a corporation matter to the court?

What did the Court hold?

What did Justice Harlan say in dissent?

Where did Justice Harlan think the majority decision might lead?

McCabe v. Atchison, Topeka & Santa FE Railway Company, U.S. Sup. Ct. 1914

What law did the Oklahoma Legislature pass which affected African Americans?

Why did they pass such a law?

Who brought suit and what were they asking the court to do?

What was the issue in the case?

What did the court hold?

What did Justice Hughes say about the right to equal treatment even if separate?

Were the comments of Justice Hughes necessary to the holding of the Court?

If the comments Justice Hughes were the law how could the plaintiffs lose?

How could the dicta of this case be used to bring down the separate but equal doctrine?

Pearson v. Murray

What race was Donald G. Murray and where had he gone to undergraduate school?

What did Mr. Murray want to do that caused this lawsuit?

Was he accepted at the University of Maryland law school? Why or why not?

When Mr. Murray sued the State of Maryland what was his theory?

What arguments were made by the State as to why they didn't have to admit Mr. Murray?

What was the issue in the case?

What was the holding of the Court?

What did the Court say was required when a state spends public funds for the citizens of either the white or black race?

Was the requirement of equal treatment met by balancing the funds spent on each race, i.e. spending the same amount of money on each race alone?

Did the State's plan to provide scholarships for Blacks to attend law schools in other states satisfy the 14th Amendment?

What couldn't Murray attend Morgan State, an all black school located in Baltimore?

Why wasn't furnishing a separate law school for Mr. Murray a remedy?

Was it relevant that the only African American who wanted a legal education was Mr. Murray? Why or why not?

What therefore was the remedy which the court gave Mr. Murray?

Missouri Ex Rel. Gaines v. Canada

Who wrote this opinion and what other opinion have we studied by this same justice?

In accordance with the Jim Crow laws had Missouri provided schools for both white and African American people?

Did both schools have a law school?

Had the State of Missouri made any provisions in its law for the legal education of African Americans?

How did the state attempt to distinguish the case of *Pearson v. Murray*

What was the issue in the case?

What was the holding of the Court?

Did the Court think that the fact that these other law schools were excellent was relevant to the issue?

Does the fact that few African Americans in Missouri were seeking a legal education excuse the discrimination? Why or why not?

What did Justice McReynolds say in dissenting?

Sweatt v. Painter

Did Texas provide a law school for African Americans?

When Sweatt sued claiming he was denied equal protection what was the state trial court's ruling?

Did Texas build a law school for African Americans?

How did the law school for African Americans compare to the University of Texas law school?

Did Mr. Sweatt apply to the new law school?

How did the trial court now rule on whether Texas had to let Mr. Sweatt into its law school?

What was the issue in the case?

What did the Supreme Court hold?

In what respects was the law school for Africans inferior to the University of Texas law school?

Which of the foregoing factors could be corrected by the state?

Why did the Court say that exclusion of 85% of the State's population was such an important factor?

McLaurin v. Oklahoma State Regents

What was the law in Oklahoma regarding blacks and whites attending the same school?

Why did Mr. McLaurin apply to the University of Oklahoma?

Was he admitted?

What was the ruling of the Trial Court?

How did the Oklahoma legislature respond to the decision of the Federal Judge?

What were the rules under which Mr. McLaurin was admitted?

What was the issue in the case?

What was the holding of the Court?

Did the court believe that the restrictions interfered with the Plaintiff's ability to learn?

Why was it important that this particular student not suffer from unequal treatment?

What about the argument that even with the restrictions lifted the other students would still discriminate?

Brown v. Board of Education of Topeka

What factual situation was present in this case?

When the plaintiffs sued what did the trial court decide?

What was the argument made by the plaintiffs who were represented by Thurgood Marshall?

What was the issue as stated by the Court?

What did the Court hold?

Did the court find that the circumstances surrounding the adoption of the 14th Amendment shed light on the issue?

Did the court find that the tangible factors (curricula, qualifications and salaries of teachers, buildings) between African American and white schools were equal?

Did the court believe that education in 1954 was different than in 1896 when Plessy was decided?

Why didn't the court believe that it was sufficient if the tangible factors were equal?

What was the court's decision?

What did the Court decide should be the remedy for correcting the unequal schools problem?

Bolling v. Sharpe

What were the facts of the case?

What difference did it make that it occurred in the District of Columbia?

What difference did that fact make to the District Court?

What was the issue in the case?

What did the court hold?

What reasons did the court give for its decision?

Brown v. Board of Education (Brown II)

What was left to be decided about desegregating the public schools after the Brown I decision?

What was the issue in the case?

What did the Court hold?

What did the Court say was to happen if the Schools didn't solve the problem of desegregation?

What law should the District Courts use to guide them?

What other factors should the court consider?

What general directions did the Supreme Court give to the Federal District Courts?

Cooper v. Aaron

What did the School Board of the Little Rock, Arkansas district do as a result of the Brown II decision?

What were other state authorities doing while the School Board was preparing to discriminate?

When the School Board nevertheless attempted to enroll 9 African American students at Central High School what happened?

What was done about the Arkansas Government stopping the enrollment of the African American students at Central High School?

What did the School Board do as a result of the violence caused by attempting to enroll African American students?

What did the District court decide?

What was the issue in the case?

What was the holding of the court?

Why did the court so hold?

Poindexter v. Louisiana Financial Assistance Commission

The State of Louisiana has for over 100 years attempted to keep its schools segregated by a series of laws. Did that stop with the Brown decision?

Did the State of Louisiana support the New Orleans school board in attempting to desegregate the public schools?

What was the issue in this case?

What was the court's holding?

Why did the Court so hold?

Browder v. Gayle

What were the Montgomery City Lines doing and why were they doing it?

What was the issue in the case?

What was the court's holding?

Did the Brown I decision specifically hold that segregation on buses was contrary to the 14th Amendment?

Why did the court hold that segregation on buses was prohibited by the 14th Amendment if Brown I didn't specifically prohibit it?

Smith v. Allwright

What did the Plaintiff want to do in his matter?

Was he allowed to cast a ballot? Why or why not?

Why did the Democratic Party argue that it didn't have to let Plaintiff vote in the primary?

What was the issue in the case?

What was the holding?

What constitutional provisions applied to this case?

What about the argument that the Democratic Party is a private party and not the state?

Gomillion v. Lightfoot

What did the Alabama Legislature do to the city of Tuskegee?

What was the effect of this act?

What was the effect of the redrawing of the City's boundaries?

What was the issue in the case?

What did the court hold?

What about the State's argument that redefining the boundaries of its cities is purely a state function and cannot be regulated by the Federal Government?

Did the Supreme Court's decision mean that the redefining of the city's boundaries was not proper?

Harper v. Virginia Board of Elections

What is a poll tax and what was the plaintiff's complaint about it?

What was the issue in the case?

What did the court hold?

What constitutional right was violated according to the Court?

What about the argument that the poll tax is like a fee for a driver's license which a state can clearly exact from its citizens?

What did the dissenting Justices say?

Hunter v. Erickson

How did ordinances in Akron, Ohio become law?

What ordinance did the City Council of Akron pass?

What was Nellie Hunter's complaint?

Did the City of Akron enforce the Fair Housing law in Nellie's favor?

Did Nellie win in the Ohio State Court?

What was the issue in the United Supreme Court?
What did the Court hold?
Since it discriminates on the basis what test does the court use in analyzing it?

Hunter v. Underwood

What did the Alabama Constitution provide concerning the right to vote?
What is a crime involving "moral turpitude?"
What is wrong with this law? It affects blacks and whites the same doesn't it? What is wrong with that?
Was that the intent?

Village of Arlington Heights v. Metro Housing Devel. Corp.

What kind of a city is Arlington Heights?
How many of the residents of this city were African American?
What did the Clerics of St. Viator own in the city?
What did the Clerics decide to do with some of its land?
What did MHDC try to do in the City?
What happened at the planning commission meeting?
What arguments were raised by the opponents of the rezoning?
What did the planning commission recommend to the Village Council?
What did MHDC do as a result of the denial of the rezoning request?
What was the issue in the case?
What did the court hold?
What principle from *Washington v. Davis* did the court rely upon?
What if racial discrimination was a motivating factor in the Village Council's decision?
Did the Village Council's decision have a racially disproportionate impact?
Did the decision have a discriminatory purpose?
To what evidence did the court look?
Why did the plaintiffs lose?

Washington v. Davis

Who were Harley and Sellers and what did they do?
What test did Harley and Sellers have to pass to become police officers?

Did they pass the test?
When Harley and Sellers sued what did they claim?
Why the Fifth Amendment?
What did the District Court decide?
Were the defendants able to meet that burden and prove to the court that there was no discriminatory intent? How?
What did the Court of Appeals say when the case was appealed to it?
What did that court say?
What was the issue?
What was the holding?
What did the court say about "disproportionate impact" and "discriminatory purpose?"
Is disproportionate impact relevant to the inquiry?
Did the court believe that the use of Test 21 showed purposeful discrimination?
Did the court think that an otherwise neutral act could be invalidated just because it benefits one race more than another?
Could the police department use this test?

Bean v. Southwestern Waste

What were the facts?
What was the claim of the Plaintiffs?
What evidence did they rely upon to support their claim?
Did the court think that such evidence did support Plaintiff's claim?
Did the court's decision mean that the Plaintiffs will definitely lose?

Mobile v. Bolden

What form of City government did Mobile Alabama have?
Was there any problem with African Americans registering to vote and then voting in Mobile?
If they could register and vote why did Bolden sue?
What did the Federal District Court and the U.S. Court of Appeals decide about the method of choosing commissioners?
What was the issue in the case?
What did the court hold?

According to the Supreme Court are governmental schemes like Mobiles always unconstitutional?

Did the court think that Mobile's plan was to discriminate against African Americans? Why or why not?

How had the District Court and the Court of appeals erred in ruling that the plan was unconstitutional?

What was Justice White's argument in dissent?

Shelly v. Kraemer

What were the facts?

What were the issues facing the court?

What law did the court rely upon in deciding this case?

What was the court's decision?

Why did the court so rule?

Loving v. Virginia

What type of case was this one?

What were the facts?

What was the issue?

Why did the State believe that the court should uphold the state statute?

Did the court uphold the state statute?

Why or why not?

Heart of Atlanta Motel, Inc. v. United States, Supreme Court 1964

Where was the Heart of Atlanta Motel located?

Where did the Motel's guests come from?

Did the Motel rent rooms to everyone?

What law did Congress pass in 1964?

What did the law provide in relation to accommodations?

What was a place of accommodation under the new law?

What establishments were covered by the Act?

Why did the Hotel sue?

What were the Hotel's arguments?

What was the issue in the case?

What did the court hold?

Under what provision in the constitution was this law passed?

What is the extent of the Commerce power?

Can purely intrastate activities be regulated under the Commerce clause?

How did the court find that discrimination by a local hotel affected interstate commerce?

What about the argument that the hotel is being deprived of liberty or property under the 5th Amendment?

What did the court say about the argument that the act results in involuntary servitude for the hotel?

Have we seen this same issue before this case?

Why didn't the decision in the Civil Rights Cases control?

Durham v. Red Lake Fishing and Hunting Club, Inc.

How old was the Red Lake club?

What was the club's purpose?

What interest did the Club's members have in the property owned by the club?

How did the Club determine how many members it had?

What happened when the Plaintiff applied for membership in the club?

Had the club ever rejected a member before Mr. Durham?

What was he issue in the case?

What was the holding of the Court?

Under the Civil Rights Act can a truly private club discriminate against African Americans?

What factors are considered in determining whether a club is truly private?

Did this club pass the test?

How was this club engaged in interstate commerce?

Since the club is not private and affects interstate commerce what proofs did plaintiff have to establish in order to present a prima facie case?

When plaintiff proved a prima facie case what defense could the defendant club raise?

What did the court find in regard to the above proofs which each party had to present to win?

What was the decision of the court?

King v. Greyhound Lines

What was Greyhound's policy in regard to ticket refunds?

When Mr. Kings presented a ticket for a refund what was the conclusion of the clerk?

What language did the Greyhound employee use in dealing with Mr. King?

What law did Mr. King sue under?

What was the decision of the trial court judge?

What was the issue?

What did the court hold?

What does a "distinction, discrimination or restriction" on account of race prohibit?

Can verbal abuse be a "distinction, discrimination, or restriction on account of race?

What is the chief harm resulting from such acts? Is it the loss of money?

What was the decision of the court?

McDonnell Douglas Corp v. Green

What did Mr. Green do for a living?

What happened to Mr. Green's job?

What did Mr. Green believe about the company laying him off?

What did Mr. Green and others do to protest the layoffs?

What happened one year later?

Green had worked at the company for 8 prior years and was a good mechanic. Did the company hire him? Why or why not?

What was Mr. Green's theory when he sued McDonnell Douglas?

What did the Civil Rights Act of 1964 say about discrimination in employment?

What was the issue in the case?

What did the Court hold?

What did the court say that the complainant in a Title VII case must prove to present a prima facie case?

If complainant presents a prima facie case what is the employer's burden of proof?

Did McDonnell Douglas Corp meet its burden in this case?

If the employer meets his burden as McDonnell did in this case is that the end of the proofs and the end of the case?

What types of evidence did the court suggest might meet the employee's burden to show a pretext?

What did the court do with the case? Do we know whether Mr. Green ultimately won or lost?

Griggs v. Duke Power Co.

What kind of a company was Duke? Did it discriminate against African Americans before 1965?

Why did the Company stop discriminating openly on July 2, 1965?

What qualifications did the Company requirement for hiring into or transfer into all of the departments in the company except labor?

Did these requirements impact African Americans more than it did whites?

When a group of African American employees sued what was the issue?

What did the Court hold?

What was the objective of Congress in passing Title VII?

Why couldn't practices and tests which were neutral on their face be used?

What did Congress require Employers to do in regard to the employment decision?

What must an employer prove if it wants to use a practice which discriminates against African Americans?

Was it permissible to use general intelligence tests or a high school completion requirement?

What are tests used to determine qualifications for employment supposed to measure?

Was Congress intending to guarantee a job to every person who had been discriminated against regardless of qualifications?

When may testing or measuring devices be used?

Jones Et UX v. Alfred H. Mayer Co.

Who was Joseph Lee Jones and why did he sue the Alfred H. Mayer Co.?

What law was Mr. Jones relying upon?

Why did both the Federal District Court and the Court of Appeals rule against Mr. Jones?

What were the issues in the case?

What did the court hold?

Where did the court think that Congress got the power to pass Section 1982 of the 1866 Civil Rights Act?

What did the Court say about the 13th Amendment acting upon the acts of individuals?

What did the court say about whether section 1982 applies to private as well as public refusals to sell real property?

Phillips v. Hunter Trails Community Association

Who was William J. Phillips and what did he want to buy?

Did Mr. Broderick accept Mr. Phillips offer to purchase his house?

Relying on the purchase agreement what did Mr. Phillips do?

What is a covenant and how did one get in the way of Mr. Phillips purchase of this home?

When the association couldn't raise the money to exercise the right of first refusal what did they do?

Did Mr. Broderick sell the home to Mrs. Butler?

When Broderick didn't close as agreed with Mr. Phillips what happened to Mr. Phillips?

What laws did Mr. Phillips sue under and what relief did he want from the court?

What relief did the District Court give Mr. Phillips?

What was the issue in the case?

What did the Court of Appeals hold?

What evidence supported the trial Judge's decision?

What eveidence did Mr. Phillips present which established a prima facie case for him?

What was the defendant's burden of proof and could they meet it?

Did the Court give any relief to the Defendants?

Williamson v. Hampton Management Company

Who was Bonita Nichols and what kind of a deal did she have with Hampton Management Company?

What did Ms. Nichols want to do when her roommate moved out to get married?

Who were Williamson and Tucker and what happened when they answered the ad for the apartment?

What did Nichols, Williamson, and Tucker do about it?

What did the defendant argue?

What was the issue?

What was the Court's holding?

What rights did the court believe that the 1866 Civil Rights act gave to all citizens who wish to rent or lease property?

What did the court say about the defendant's claim that they didn't rent the apartment to the two women because they were single?

What did the court say about the defendant's claim that they didn't rent the apartment to the two women because their incomes weren't large enough?

What relief did the court give to the plaintiffs?

United Steelworkers of America v. Weber

What kind of an agreement did Kaiser have with the United Steelworkers?

What provision in this agreement was the subject of this lawsuit?

What factual development caused Mr. Weber to start a lawsuit?

What was the issue as stated by the Court?

What did the court hold?

This plan denied equal treatment to white people. Why wasn't it a violation of the 14th Amendment?

Since this plan clearly discriminated against white people why didn't it violate Title VII?

According to Justice Brennan what was the purpose of Title VII?

Why did Justice Brennan believe that Congress intended for private affirmative actions plans to be permitted under Title VII?

Were there any other reasons for believing that Congress intended to allow private affirmative plans in the business world?

Did Justice Brennan put any limitations on such plans?

What did Justice Rehnquist say in his dissent?

Johnson v. Transportation Agency

What kind of a plan did the County promulgate?

What was the purpose of the plan?

Did the plan have a specific goal?

Under the plan what could the County consider in detemining hiring and promotions?

What was done to determine who to promote to the job of a dispatcher?

What was the issue in the case?

What did the court hold?

Why was it permissible to consider sex in determining promotions?

What did it mean that there was an <u>imbalance</u> in the workforce?

Why didn't this plan trammel the rights of male employees?

Why didn't Johnson lose any rights?

Was this plan intended to achieve permanent racial and sexual balance?

Why did Justice Stevens write a concurring opinion?

What did the dissenting opinion think would be the result of the majority's opinion?

Justice Scalia quoted from Shakespeare's King Henry the Fourth, Part I: GLENDOWER: I can call Spirits from the vasty deep. HOTSPUR: Why, so can I, or so can any man. But will they come when you do call for them?

What was the point he was trying to make?

Taxman v. Board of Education of Piscataway

What kind of a plan did the school board adopt?

How did the plan affect hiring and layoff decisions by the School District?

Were African Americans underutilized or underrepresented in the School District?

When the School Board decided to lay off a teacher why didn't it just use seniority to determine whom to lie off?

When affirmative action was not a consideration how had the board decided whom to lay off when there was a tie in seniority?

Why did the School Board choose Debra Williams over Sharon Taxman?

What reason did the School Board President give for hiring Debra Williams?

Who sued? What was the theory?

What was the issue?

What was the holding of the Court?

Did the School Board's affirmative action plan have a remedial purpose? Why does that matter?

What about the goal of achieving cultural diversity?

What affirmative action plans are constitutional?

Why did the Board say that the plan trammeled the rights of nonminority employees?

Who was President of the United States when this case was started in 1989?

Who was President of the United States when this case got to the Court of Appeals in 1995?

Could this case be affected by who was President?

The Supreme Court, however, never decided it. How could that happen? How could they stop it?

United States v. Starrett City Associates

Starrett owns and operates an apartment complex. What plan did they institute which resulted in this lawsuit?

Why did Starrett rent its apartments in this manner?

Did Starrett have any evidence to support its plan?

What was the issue?

What was the holding?

Where did Congress get the power to pass the Fair Housing Act?

What practices are prohibited by the Fair Housing Act?

If any of the above housing practices are engaged in and affect minorities does it matter whether there was intent to discriminate?

What did the Court say about the use of "quotas?"

Why didn't the Court believe the use of quotas was permissible in this case?

What did the dissenting Judge say?

Missouri v. Jenkins

Why was this lawsuit filed back in 1977?

How did the Federal District Court rearrange the parties when the case was begun?

What finding of fact did the trial court make about the schools in Kansas City?

What did the District Court decide to do about such segregation?

Where did the Court get such power?

What did the Court order?

Since the Kansas City schools were poor where did the money come from for the improvements ordered by the court?

What did the Federal District Court order in 1992 and why did he order it?

What did the State of Missouri do?

What did the Court of Appeals hold?

What was the issue?

What did the Court hold?

What did the court say about the scope of the equitable remedies which the trial court could fashion?

What must the School District prove to the Court to get relief from the Court's order?

Why did Justice Rehnquist say that the Trial Court's plan was not permissible?

What did the majority of the Supreme Court do with the case?

What did Justice Thomas say about the effect of segregation on African Americans?

What did Justice Thomas say about the use of equity powers by the Federal District Courts?

What did Justice Thomas say about the Brown Decision?

What was the genie and how did it get out of the bottle?

Did Justice Thomas believe that the power given to the Federal Judges was permitted by the Constitution?

What did the dissenting Justices have to say?

Adarand Contractors, Inc. v. Pena

What was DOT doing?

Which company was hired as the general contractor to build the highway?

When Mountain Town asked for bids from subcontractors to build guardrails along the highway what unique clause in Mountain Town's contract with the government guided the selection of a subcontractor?

Who were considered "socially and economically disadvantaged" individuals?

Which subcontractor submitted the low bid?

Did that subcontractor get the contract? Why or why not?

If it wasn't for the additional payment would Mountain Town have given the contract to Adarand?

When Adarand sued claiming it had been discriminated against what Constitutional Amendment did it say was violated?

Where does the Fifth Amendment say that the Federal Government can't deny anyone equal protection of the laws?

Did Adarand win in the Court of Appeals?

What was the issue in the case?

What did the Court hold?

What did _Richmond v. Croson_ hold?

In Richmond v. Croson (1989) the Supreme Court held that the 14th Amendment requires

strict scrutiny of all race-based action by state and local governments but this case did not apply to the Federal Government.

What had the Supreme Court held in _Metro Broadcasting v. FCC_?

What did the Supreme Court say about the _Metro Broadcasting v. FCC_ decision?

What did Justice O'Connor say that the test would be when a court reviewed racial classifications by the Federal Government?

When Justice O'Connor reversed the case and remanded it back to the Federal District Judge what questions did she direct him/her to ask?

What is "racial paternalism" and what did Justice Thomas say about it?

What did Justice Thomas say that so-called benign racial preferenes teach?

What did the dissenting Justices have to say?

Miller v. Johnson (Supreme Court 1995)

What is a congressional district and how many of such districts which were majority African American did Georgia's redistricting plan have?

Why did the Justice Department have to preclear the State of Georgia's redistricting plan?

Why wouldn't the U.S. Justice Department preclear the Georgia redistricting plan?

Why was the three district plan challenged by a group of voters in Georgia?

What was the issue?

What did the court hold?

What scrutiny test should the court use in reviewing this matter?

What did Georgia have to show to pass the test?

Could Georgia show that there was a compelling governmental interest and that the plan was narrowly tailored?

What did Justice Stevens say in dissent?

What did Justice Ginsburg say in dissent?

Northwest Austin Municipal Utility District v. Holder

What were the facts of the case?

What was the issue facing the Court?

What did the court decide?

Since the Constitutionality of Section 5 of the Voting Rights Act was being challenged why didn't the court Rule on its constitutionality?

Alexander v. Prince George's County

What controversial plan did the County use in hiring firemen?

What was the goal of the plan?

What was the racial and sexual makeup of the fire department in 1974?

In 1993 what was the racial and sexual makeup of the fire department? How was it related to the labor force?

What anecdotal evidence was presented in the case?

Had the situation improved?

Who sued and why?

What was the issue?

What did the Court hold?

What part of the strict scrutiny test did the anecdotal evidence support?

What was the second part of the strict scrutiny test that the defendant had to prove?

Did the court think that the defendant had proved that the plan was narrowly tailored? If so, why?

Frank Ricci v. John Destefano

What were the facts of the case?

What was the issue?

What did the Court decide?

How did this case differ from Alexander v. Prince George's County?

What do you think really motivated the City to throw out the results of the test?

Podberesky v. Kirwan

What types of scholarship programs did the University of Maryland maintain and what were the requirements for each?

Did Mr. Podberesky meet the requirements for either scholarship? Why or why not?

When Mr. Podberesky sued what was his theory?

Why did the University claim that the program was justified?

What did the Federal District Court decide?

When Podberesky appealed to the 4th Circuit Court of Appeals what was the issue before the court?

What did the court hold?

Was curing the present effects of past discrimination a compelling governmental interest that would justify the program?

How does the court determine whether there are "present effects of past discrimination?"

Was it true that the University's reputation in the African-American community was poor and that there was a perceived racially hostile climate on campus?

Did the court feel that such facts were sufficient to make the program compelling?

Was it true that African-American students were underrepresented at the University and that African Americans had low retention and graduation rates?

Why weren't those facts sufficient to justify the program?

Even if there was under representation of African-American students at the University and African Americans had low retention and graduation rates the Banneker Program cannot be upheld because it is not narrowly tailored to remedy the under representation and attrition problems: Why not?

Hopwood v. Texas

The University of Texas used roughly the same formula to determine whom to admit to its law school as other schools use. What is it?

The University of Texas Law School based its admissions on a composite number of undergraduate grade point average and Law School Aptitude Test.

Using that number how many categories did the University create?

Were the scores treated the same for white people and minorities?

What was claimed by some white students including Cheryl Hopwood when they were rejected?

What was the issue?

What did the Court hold?

What did the University argue supported the program?

Did the Court accept that argument?

Did the Court think that there were any things which might have a correlation with race which might be considered in the admission process?

Can the university do anything which is legal to foster diversity according to the court?

Didn't the factors of the schools reputation in the minority community and the perception of it as having a hostile environment for minorities justify the program?

What was the second argument that the University made as to why the program was justified?

Did the Court accept that argument?

Regents v. Bakke

What type of an affirmative action plan did Cal Davis adop?

Why was that plan unconstitutional?

Did Justice Powell suggest any justification for an affirmative action plan?

In what way could Universities administer such a plan?

What University's plan was approved of by Justice Powell?

Grutter v. Bollinger

How many students does Michigan admit to its law school out of the applications it receives?

What does Michigan say it looks for in deciding which students to admit?

When the Dean of the Law School charged a faculty with crafting an admissions policy based upon these goals what case did they claim to follow?

What did the admissions policy require admissions officials to consider in deciding whom to admit to the law school?

Besides the score from the above what does the law school look at in deciding whom to admit?

What type of diversity is the law school committed to achieve?

Why give special treatment to those groups?

Why weren't other groups which have experienced discrimination such as Asians and Jews included in the policy?

How many members of the favored groups did they believe were needed to be meaningful?

How many constitute a "critical mass?"

Describe Barbara Grutter?

What rights did Barbara say the University violated?

Did the law school discriminate against Barbara Grutter based upon her race?

What must Michigan show in order to so discriminate against Barbara?

Why did Justice O'Connor write so much of her opinion discussing Justice Powell's opinion in *Bakke*?

According to Justice O'Connor what reasons given by medical schools for discriminating in favor of minorities in admissions were rejected by Justice Powell?

According to Justice O'Connor what interest of the University did Justice Powell approve?

Why is diversity at universities compelling according to Justice Powell?

What limitations were placed on the selection process by Justice Powell?

What then did the law school want the court to hold?

What did Justice O'Connor say about the argument that only "remedying the present effects of past discrimination" has been held to justify race-based government action?

Did the fact that we were talking about the question in the setting of a University make a difference to the Court?

Where does diversity fit in the selection of a student body?

What did the court think were the benefits of a diverse student body?

Why did the court believe that universities and law schools in particular need to have members of all races?

What was the second issue which the court had to address?

Why didn't Justice O'Connor think that the Michigan plan was a quota?

Why did the court feel the plan was flexible enough to ensure that applicants were evaluated as individuals?

What other types of diversity does the law school claim to consider?

Did the court feel that Michigan considered race neutral alternatives?

What about the requirement that race based preferences must be temporary?

Gratz v. Bollinger

Who were Jennifer Gratz and Patrick Hamacher?

What was their theory when they sued?

What factors did Michigan use during the period of the litigation in deciding whom to accept for admission?

In Michigan's latest plan how much weight was race given?

Since the plan discriminated on the basis of race, what must the University show?

What interest did the University argue justified the program?

Did the Court believe that diversity could be a compelling interest?

Was the program narrowly tailored? Why or why not?

Why didn't the University just use the system approved in the Grutter case?

Did the fact that the Grutter system is impractical sway the court?

Parents v. Seattle

What student assignment plans had the school districts In Seattle and Louisville adopted?

Why did parents in each District sue?

What was the issue as stated by Justice Roberts?

What was the court's holdintg?

Did the plans pass strict scrutiny as remedying the present effects of past discrimination?

Did the plans pass strict scrutiny because they were needed to achieve diversity?

Coalition for Economic Equity v. Wilson

What constitutional amendment did the voters of California approve?

When this law was challenged what was the theory as to why it was unconstitutional?

What was the issue?

What was the court's holding?

When reviewing discrimination by government is one race or gender favored by the courts?

Did the court use the strict scrutiny test in reviewing this law?

How does this law differ from the 14th Amendment itself?

Hills v. Gautreaux, Supreme Court 1976

The Chicago Housing Authority (CHA) and the United States Department of Housing and Urban Development (HUD) received money to build housing in the City of Chicago from 1950 to 1965.

What was the problem?

What did the appeals court order?

What was the issue?

What did the court hold?

Why weren't the suburbs hurt by this ruling?

Doe v. University of Michigan (E.D. Mich. 1989)

The University adopted a Discriminatory Harassment Policy that punished any behavior that stigmatizes or victimizes an individual on the basis of race, etc.

What types of behavior was punished under this policy?

What was the issue?

What did the court hold?

Why was the policy over broad?

Why was the policy vague?

Dambrodt v. Central Michigan University (6th Cir. 1995)

Why was the policy over broad and vague?

Why wasn't the talk to the players protected under the First Amendment's free speech clause?

Maryland v. Sheldon

What statute did the state of Maryland enact to stop cross burning?

What did Mr. Sheldon do that got him charged with a crime?

What did Mr. Sheldon claim on appeal after he was convicted?

What was the issue?

What did the court hold?

What was the State's purpose in passing this statute?

Did the law protect people from unwanted fires?

Is there any speech that does not enjoy first amendment protection?

Under what scrutiny test did the court review the constitutionality of this law? Did this statute pass the test?

Virginia v. Black

What was the Virginia law on Cross Burning?
Who was charged with violating the law and what did they do?
What was the issue before the Supreme Court?
What did the court hold?
How did the court distinguish between the acts of the defendants in burning crosses?
Why did the court make such distinction?

Williams v. New York City Housing

What were the facts this case?
What was the issue facing the court?
What was the holding?
How could the hanging of a noose which was only one incident support a claim of hostile work environment?
Why is the noose one of the most repugnant of all racist symbols?

Florida v. Stalder

What Florida law was being reviewed?
What did Mr. Stalder do?
With what crime was Mr. Stalder charged?
What was the issue?
What was he holding?
What had the Supreme Court held in *Wisconsin v. Mitchell*?
Is it a constitutional right to slander another because of his race?
Is it a constitutional right to assault another because of his race?

New Jersey v. Soto

Who were the Defendants and what was their complaint?
How did they bring their claim to the attention of the New Jersey Trial Court?
What evidence did the defendants present in support of their racial profiling case?
What did that study show?
What claims did the State make as to why the statistical study was not reliable?
How did the defense team refute that argument?
Was there any other evidence that the state troopers were discriminating?
Was there a suggestion as to why the police were profiling African Americans for traffic stops?
What was the issue facing the court?
What did the Court hold?
If a traffic stop and seizure of evidence was objectively reasonable (i.e. defendant was speeding) will the court inquire as to the motivation of the officer for the stop?
When will the court inquire into the motivation of the officers in traffic stops?
Why did the court care about such a policy?
What about the fact that the agency's motivation was a good one, i.e. eradicating illegal drugs from New Jersey?

The Constitution of the United States

Preamble

We, the people of the United States, in order to form a more perfect Union, establish justice, insure domestic tranquility, provide for the common defense, promote the general welfare, and secure the blessings of liberty to ourselves and our posterity, do ordain and establish this Constitution for the United States of America.

Article I

Section 1. Legislative powers; in whom vested

All legislative powers herein granted shall be vested in a Congress of the United States, which shall consist of a Senate and House of Representatives.

Section 2. House of Representatives, how and by whom chosen Qualifications of a Representative. Representatives and direct taxes, how apportioned. Enumeration. Vacancies to be filled. Power of choosing officers, and of impeachment.

1. The House of Representatives shall be composed of members chosen every second year by the people of the several States, and the elector in each State shall have the qualifications requisite for electors of the most numerous branch of the State Legislature.
2. No person shall be a Representative who shall not have attained the age of twenty-five years, and been seven years a citizen of the United States, and who shall not, when elected, be an inhabitant of that State in which he shall be chosen.
3. Representatives [and direct taxes] {Altered by 16th Amendment} shall be apportioned among the several States which may be included within this Union, according to their respective numbers, [which shall be determined by adding the whole number of free persons, including those bound to service for a term of years, and excluding Indians not taxed, three-fifths of all other persons.] {Altered by 14th Amendment} The actual enumeration shall be made within three years after the first meeting of the Congress of the United States, and within every subsequent term of ten years, in such manner as they shall by law direct. The number of Representatives shall not exceed one for every thirty thousand, but each State shall have at least one Representative; and until such enumeration shall be made, the State of New Hampshire shall be entitled to choose three, Massachusetts eight, Rhode Island and Providence Plantations one, Connecticut five, New York six, New Jersey four, Pennsylvania eight, Delaware one, Maryland six, Virginia ten, North Carolina five, South Carolina five, and Georgia three.
4. When vacancies happen in the representation from any State, the Executive Authority thereof shall issue writs of election to fill such vacancies.
5. The House of Representatives shall choose their Speaker and other officers; and shall have the sole power of impeachment.

Section 3. Senators, how and by whom chosen. How classified. State Executive, when to make temporary appointments, in case, etc. Qualifications of a Senator. President of the Senate, his right to vote. President pro tem., and other officers of the Senate, how chosen. Power to try impeachments. When President is tried, Chief Justice to preside. Sentence.

1. The Senate of the United States shall be composed of two Senators from each State, [chosen by the Legislature thereof,] {Altered by 17th Amendment} for six years; and each Senator shall have one vote.

2. Immediately after they shall be assembled in consequence of the first election, they shall be divided as equally as may be into three classes. The seats of the Senators of the first class shall be vacated at the expiration of the second year, of the second class at the expiration of the fourth year, and of the third class at the expiration of the sixth year, so that one-third may be chosen every second year; [and if vacancies happen by resignation, or otherwise, during the recess of the Legislature of any State, the Executive thereof may make temporary appointments until the next meeting of the Legislature, which shall then fill such vacancies.] {Altered by 17th Amendment}

3. No person shall be a Senator who shall not have attained to the age of thirty years, and been nine years a citizen of the United States, and who shall not, when elected, be an inhabitant of that State for which he shall be chosen.

4. The Vice-President of the United States shall be President of the Senate, but shall have no vote, unless they be equally divided.

5. The Senate shall choose their other officers, and also a President pro tempore, in the absence of the Vice President, or when he shall exercise the office of the President of the United States.

6. The Senate shall have the sole power to try all impeachments. When sitting for that purpose, they shall be on oath or affirmation. When the President of the United States is tried, the Chief Justice shall preside: and no person shall be convicted without the concurrence of two-thirds of the members present.

7. Judgement in cases of impeachment shall not extend further than to removal from office, and disqualification to hold and enjoy any office of honor, trust, or profit under the United States: but the party convicted shall nevertheless be liable and subject to indictment, trial, judgement and punishment, according to law.

Section 4. Times, etc., of holding elections, how prescribed. One session in each year.

1. The times, places and manner of holding elections for Senators and Representatives, shall be prescribed in each State by the Legislature thereof; but the Congress may at any time by law make or alter such regulations, except as to the places of choosing Senators.

2. The Congress shall assemble at least once in every year, and such meeting shall be [on the first Monday in December,] {Altered by 20th Amendment} unless they by law appoint a different day.

Section 5. Membership, Quorum, Adjournments, Rules, Power to punish or expel. Journal. Time of adjournments, how limited, etc.

1. Each House shall be the judge of the elections, returns and qualifications of its own members, and a majority of each shall constitute a quorum to do business; but a smaller number may adjourn from day to day, and may be authorized to compel the attendance of absent members, in such manner, and under such penalties as each House may provide.

2. Each House may determine the rules of its proceedings, punish its members for disorderly behavior, and, with the concurrence of two-thirds, expel a member.

3. Each House shall keep a journal of its proceedings, and from time to time publish the same, excepting such parts as may in their judgement require secrecy; and the yeas and nays of the members of either House on any question shall, at the desire of one-fifth of those present, be entered on the journal.

4. Neither House, during the session of Congress, shall, without the consent of the other, adjourn for more than three days, nor to any other place than that in which the two Houses shall be sitting.

Section 6. Compensation, Privileges, Disqualification in certain cases.

1. The Senators and Representatives shall receive a compensation for their services, to be ascertained by law, and paid out of the Treasury of the United States. They shall in all cases, except treason, felony and breach of the peace, be privileged from arrest during their attendance at the session of their respective Houses, and in going to and returning from the same; and for any speech or debate in either House, they shall not be questioned in any other place.

2. No Senator or Representative shall, during the time for which he was elected, be appointed to any civil office under the authority of the United States, which shall have increased during such time; and no person holding any office under the United States, shall be a member of either House during his continuance in office.

Section 7. House to originate all revenue bills. Veto. Bill may be passed by two-thirds of each House, notwithstanding, etc. Bill, not returned in ten days to become a law. Provisions as to orders, concurrent resolutions, etc.

1. All bills for raising revenue shall originate in the House of Representatives; but the Senate may propose or concur with amendments as on other bills.

2. Every bill which shall have passed the House of Representatives and the Senate, shall, before it become a law, be presented to the president of the United States; if he approve, he shall sign it, but if not, he shall return it, with his objections, to that house in which it shall have originated, who shall enter the objections at large on their journal, and proceed to reconsider it. If after such reconsideration, two thirds of that house shall agree to pass the bill, it shall be sent, together with the objections, to the other house, by which it shall likewise be reconsidered, and if approved by two-thirds of that house, it shall become a law. But in all such cases the votes of both houses shall be determined by yeas and nays, and the names of the persons voting for and against the bill shall be entered on the journal of each house respectively. If any bill shall not be returned by the president within ten days (Sundays excepted) after it shall have been presented to him, the same shall be a law, in like manner as if he had signed it, unless the Congress by their adjournment prevent its return, in which case it shall not be a law.

3. Every order, resolution, or vote to which the concurrence of the Senate and House of Representatives may be necessary (except on a question of adjournment) shall be presented to the president of the United States; and before the same shall take effect, shall be approved by him, or, being disapproved by him, shall be re-passed by two-thirds of the Senate and House of Representatives, according to the rules and limitations prescribed in the case of a bill.

Section 8. Powers of Congress

The Congress shall have the power.

1. To lay and collect taxes, duties, imposts and excises, to pay the debts and provide for the common defence and general welfare of the United States; but all duties, imposts and excises shall be uniform throughout the United States:

2. To borrow money on the credit of the United States:

3. To regulate commerce with foreign nations, and among the several states, and with the Indian tribes:

4. To establish an uniform rule of naturalization, and uniform laws on the subject of bankruptcies throughout the United States:

5. To coin money, regulate the value thereof, and of foreign coin, and fix the standard of weights and measures:

6. To provide for the punishment of counterfeiting the securities and current coin of the United States:

7. To establish post-offices and post-roads:

8. To promote the progress of science and useful arts, by securing for limited times to authors and inventors the exclusive right to their respective writings and discoveries:

9. To constitute tribunals inferior to the supreme court:

10. To define and punish piracies and felonies committed on the high seas, and offences against the law of nations:

11. To declare war, grant letters of marque and reprisal, and make rules concerning captures on land and water:

12. To raise and support armies, but no appropriation of money to that use shall be for a longer term than two years:

13. To provide and maintain a navy:

14. To make rules for the government and regulation of the land and naval forces:

15. To provide for calling forth the militia to execute the laws of the union, suppress insurrections and repel invasions:

16. To provide for organizing, arming and disciplining the militia, and for governing such part of them as may be employed in the service of the United States, reserving to the states respectively, the appointment of the officers, and the authority of training the militia according to the discipline prescribed by Congress:

17. To exercise exclusive legislation in all cases whatsoever, over such district (not exceeding ten miles square) as may, by cession of particular states, and the acceptance of Congress, become the seat of the government of the United States, and to exercise like authority over all places purchased by the consent of the legislature of the state in which the same shall be, for the erection of forts, magazines, arsenals, dock-yards, and other needful buildings:

18. To make all laws which shall be necessary and proper for carrying into execution the foregoing powers, and all other powers vested by this constitution in the government of the United States, or in any department or officer thereof.

Section 9. Provision as to migration or importation of certain persons. Habeas Corpus, Bills of attainder, etc. Taxes, how apportioned. No export duty. No commercial preference. Money, how drawn from Treasury, etc. No titular nobility. Officers not to receive presents, etc.

1. The migration or importation of such persons as any of the states now existing shall think proper to admit, shall not be prohibited by the Congress prior to the year 1808, but a tax or duty may be imposed on such importations, not exceeding 10 dollars for each person.

2. The privilege of the writ of habeas corpus shall not be suspended, unless when in cases of rebellion or invasion the public safety may require it.

3. No bill of attainder or ex post facto law shall be passed.

4. [No capitation, or other direct tax shall be laid unless in proportion to the census or enumeration herein before directed to be taken.] {Altered by 16th Amendment}

5. No tax or duty shall be laid on articles exported from any state.

6. No preference shall be given by any regulation of commerce or revenue to the ports of one state over those of another: nor shall vessels bound to, or from one state, be obliged to enter, clear, or pay duties in another.

7. No money shall be drawn from the treasury but in consequence of appropriations made by law; and a regular statement and account of the receipts and expenditures of all public money shall be published from time to time.

8. No title of nobility shall be granted by the United States: And no person holding any office or profit or trust under them, shall, without the consent of the Congress, accept of any present, emolument, office, or title, of any kind whatever, from any king, prince, or foreign state.

Section 10. States prohibited from the exercise of certain powers.

1. No state shall enter into any treaty, alliance, or confederation; grant letters of marque and reprisal; coin money; emit bills of credit; make any thing but gold and silver coin a tender in payment of debts; pass any bill of attainder, ex post facto law, or law impairing the obligation of contracts, or grant any title of nobility.

2. No state shall, without the consent of the Congress, lay any imposts or duties on imports or exports, except what may be absolutely necessary for executing its inspection laws; and the net produce of all duties and imposts, laid by any state on imports or exports, shall be for the use of the treasury of the United States; and all such laws shall be subject to the revision and control of the Congress.

3. No state shall, without the consent of Congress, lay any duty of tonnage, keep troops, or ships of war in time of peace, enter into any agreement or compact with another state, or with a foreign power, or engage in a war, unless actually invaded, or in such imminent danger as will not admit of delay.

Article II

Section 1. President: his term of office. Electors of President; number and how appointed. Electors to vote on same day. Qualification of President. On whom his duties devolve in case of his removal, death, etc. President's compensation. His oath of office.

1. The Executive power shall be vested in a President of the United States of America. He shall hold office during the term of four years, and together with the Vice President, chosen for the same term, be elected as follows

2. [Each State] {Altered by 23rd Amendment} shall appoint, in such manner as the Legislature may direct, a number of electors, equal to the whole number of Senators and Representatives to which the State may be entitled in the Congress: but no Senator or Representative, or person holding an office of trust or profit under the United States, shall be appointed an elector [The electors shall meet in their respective States, and vote by ballot for two persons, of whom one at least shall not be an inhabitant of the same State with themselves. And they shall make a list of all the persons voted for each; which list they shall sign and certify, and transmit sealed to the seat of Government of the United States, directed to the President of the Senate. The President of the Senate shall, in the presence of the Senate and House of Representatives, open all the certificates, and the votes shall then be counted. The person having the greatest number of votes shall be the President, if such number be a majority of the whole number of electors appointed; and if there be more than one who have such majority, and have an equal number of votes, then the House of Representatives shall immediately choose by ballot one of them for President; and if no person have a majority, then from the five highest on the list the said House shall in like manner choose the President. But in choosing the President, the votes shall be taken by States, the representation from each State having one vote; a quorum for this purpose shall consist of a member or members from two-thirds of the States, and a majority of all the States shall be necessary to a choice. In every case, after the choice of the President, the person having the greatest number of votes of the electors shall be the Vice President. But

if there should remain two or more who have equal votes, the Senate shall choose from them by ballot the Vice President.] {Altered by 12th Amendment}

3. The Congress may determine the time of choosing the electors, and the day on which they shall give their votes; which day shall be the same throughout the United States.

4. No person except a natural born citizen, or a citizen of the United States, at the time of the adoption of this Constitution, shall be eligible to the office of President; neither shall any person be eligible to that office who shall not have attained to the age of thirty-five years, and been fourteen years a resident within the United States.

5. [In case of the removal of the President from office, or of his death, resignation, or inability to discharge the powers and duties of the said office, the same shall devolve on the Vice President, and the Congress may by law provide for the case of removal, death, resignation, or inability, both of the President and Vice President, declaring what officer shall then act as President, and such officer shall act accordingly, until the disability be removed, or a President shall be elected.] {Altered by 25th Amendment}

6. The President shall, at stated times, receive for his services, a compensation, which shall neither be increased nor diminished during the period for which he shall have been elected, and he shall not receive within that period any other emolument from the United States, or any of them.

7. Before he enter on the execution of his office, he shall take the following oath or affirmation: "I do solemnly swear (or affirm) that I will faithfully execute the office of the President of the United States, and will to the best of my ability, preserve, protect and defend the Constitution of the United States."

Section 2. President to be Commander-in-Chief. He may require opinions of cabinet officers, etc., may pardon. Treaty-making power. Nomination of certain officers. When President may fill vacancies.

1. The President shall be Commander-in-Chief of the Army and Navy of the United States, and of

the militia of the several States, when called into the actual service of the United States; he may require the opinion, in writing, of the principal officer in each of the executive departments, upon any subject relating to the duties of their respective offices, and he shall have power to grant reprieves and pardons for offenses against against the United States, except in cases of impeachment.

2. He shall have power, by and with the advice and consent of the Senate, to make treaties, provided two-thirds of the Senators present concur; and he shall nominate, and by and with the advice and consent of the Senate, shall appoint ambassadors, other public ministers and consuls, judges of the Supreme Court, and all other officers of the United States, whose appointments are not herein otherwise provided for, and which shall be established by law: but the Congress may by law vest the appointment of such inferior officers, as they think proper, in the President alone, in the courts of law, or in the heads of departments.

3. The President shall have the power to fill up all vacancies that may may happen during the recess of the Senate, by granting commissions, which shall expire at the end of their next session.

Section 3. President shall communicate to Congress. He may convene and adjourn Congress, in case of disagreement, etc. Shall receive ambassadors, execute laws, and commission officers.

He shall from time to time give to the Congress information of the state of the Union, and recommend to their consideration such measures as he shall judge necessary and expedient; he may, on extraordinary occasions, convene both Houses, or either of them, and in case of disagreement between them, with respect to the time of adjournment, he may adjourn them to such time as he shall think proper; he may receive ambassadors, and other public ministers; he shall take care that the laws be faithfully executed, and shall commission all the officers of the United States.

Section 4. All civil offices forfeited for certain crimes.

The President, Vice President, and all civil officers of the United States, shall be removed from office on impeachment for, and conviction of, treason, bribery, or other high crimes and misdemeanors.

Article III

Section 1. Judicial powers. Tenure. Compensation.

The judicial power of the United States, shall be vested in one supreme court, and in such inferior courts as the Congress may, from time to time, ordain and establish. The judges, both of the supreme and inferior courts, shall hold their offices during good behaviour, and shall, at stated times, receive for their services a compensation, which shall not be diminished during their continuance in office.

Section 2. Judicial power; to what cases it extends. Original jurisdiction of Supreme Court Appellate. Trial by Jury, etc. Trial, where

1. The judicial power shall extend to all cases, in law and equity, arising under this constitution, the laws of the United States, and treaties made, or which shall be made under their authority; to all cases affecting ambassadors, other public ministers and consuls; to all cases of admiralty and maritime jurisdiction; to controversies to

which the United States shall be a party; [to controversies between two or more states, between a state and citizens of another state, between citizens of different states, between citizens of the same state, claiming lands under grants of different states, and between a state, or the citizens thereof, and foreign states, citizens or subjects.] {Altered by 11th Amendment}

2. In all cases affecting ambassadors, other public ministers and consuls, and those in which a state shall be a party, the supreme court shall have original jurisdiction. In all the other cases beforementioned, the supreme court shall have appellate jurisdiction, both as to law and fact, with such exceptions, and under such regulations as the Congress shall make.

3. The trial of all crimes, except in cases of impeachment, shall be by jury; and such trial shall be held in the state where the said crimes shall have been committed; but when not committed within any state, the trial shall be at such place or places as the Congress may by law have directed.

Section 3. Treason defined. Proof of. Punishment

1. Treason against the United States shall consist only in levying war against them, or in adhering to their enemies, giving them aid and comfort. No person shall be convicted of treason unless on the testimony of two witnesses to the same overt act, or on confession in open court.
2. The Congress shall have power to declare the punishment of treason, but no attainder of treason shall work corruption of blood, or forfeiture, except during the life of the person attainted.

Article IV

Section 1. Each State to give credit to the public acts, etc. of every other State.

Full faith and credit shall be given in each state to the public acts, records and judicial proceedings of every other state. And the Congress may by general laws prescribe the manner in which such acts, records and proceedings shall be proved, and the effect thereof.

Section 2. Privileges of citizens of each State. Fugitives from Justice to be delivered up. Persons held to service having escaped, to be delivered up.

1. The citizens of each state shall be entitled to all privileges and immunities of citizens in the several states. {See the 14th Amendment}
2. A person charged in any state with treason, felony, or other crime, who shall flee justice, and be found in another state, shall, on demand of the executive authority of the state from which he fled, be delivered up, to be removed to the state having jurisdiction of the crime.
3. [No person held to service or labour in one state, under the laws thereof, escaping into another, shall, in consequence of any law or regulation therein, be discharged from such service or labour, but shall be delivered up on claim of the party to whom such service or labour may be due.] {Altered by 13th Amendment}

Section 3. Admission of new States. Power of Congress over territory and other property.

1. New states may be admitted by the Congress into this union; but no new state shall be formed or erected within the jurisdiction of any other state, nor any state be formed by the junction of two or more states, without the consent of the legislatures of the states concerned, as well as of the Congress.
2. The Congress shall have power to dispose of and make all needful rules and regulations respecting the territory or other property belonging to the United States; and nothing in this constitution shall be so construed as to prejudice any claims of the United States, or of any particular state.

Section 4. Republican form of government guaranteed. Each State to be protected.

The United States shall guarantee to every state in this union, a republican form of government, and shall protect each of them against invasion; and on application of the legislature, or of the executive (when the legislature cannot be convened), against domestic violence.

Article V

Amendments

The Congress, whenever two-thirds of both houses shall deem it necessary, shall propose amendments to this constitution, or on the application of the legislatures of two-thirds of the several states, shall call a convention for proposing amendments, which, in either case, shall be valid to all intents and purposes, as part of this constitution, when ratified by the legislatures of three-fourths of the several states, or by conventions in three-fourths thereof, as the one or the other mode of ratification may be proposed by the Congress: Provided, that no amendment which may be made prior to the year 1808, shall in any manner affect the first and fourth clauses in the ninth section of the first article; and that no state, without its consent, shall be deprived of its equal suffrage in the Senate.

Article VI

1. All debts contracted and engagements entered into, before the adoption of this constitution, shall be as valid against the United States under this constitution, as under the confederation.
2. This constitution, and the laws of the United States which shall be made in pursuance thereof; and all treaties made, or which shall be made, under the authority of the United States shall be the supreme law of the land; and the judges in every state shall be bound thereby, any thing in the constitution or laws of any state to the contrary notwithstanding.
3. The senators and representatives before-mentioned, and the members of the several state legislatures, and all executive and judicial officers, both of the United States and of the several states, shall be bound by oath or affirmation, to support this constitution; but no religious test shall ever be required as a qualification to any office or public trust under the United States.

Article VII

The ratification of the conventions of nine states, shall be sufficient for the establishment of this constitution between the states so ratifying the same.

Amendments to the Constitution

Article I

Congress shall make no law respecting an establishment of religion, or prohibiting the free exercise thereof; or abridging the freedom of speech, or of the press; or the right of the people peaceably to assemble, and to petition the Government for a redress of grievances.

Article II

A well regulated Militia, being necessary to the security of a free State, the right of the people to keep and bear Arms, shall not be infringed.

Article III

No Soldier shall, in time of peace be quartered in any house, without the consent of the Owner, nor in time of war, but in a manner to be prescribed by law.

Article IV

The right of the people to be secure in their persons, houses, papers, and effects, against unreasonable searches and seizures, shall not be violated, and no Warrants shall issue, but upon probable cause, supported by Oath or affirmation, and particularly describing the place to be searched, and the persons or things to be seized.

Article V

No person shall be held to answer for a capital, or otherwise infamous crime, unless on a presentment or indictment of a Grand Jury, except in cases arising in the land or naval forces, or in the Militia, when in actual service in time of War or public danger; nor shall any person be subject for the same offence to be twice put in jeopardy of life or limb; nor shall be compelled in any criminal case to be a witness against himself, nor be deprived of life, liberty, or property, without due process of law; nor shall private property be taken for public use, without just compensation.

Article VI

In all criminal prosecutions, the accused shall enjoy the right to a speedy and public trial, by an impartial jury of the State and district wherein the crime shall have been committed, which district shall have been previously ascertained by law, and to be informed of the nature and cause of the accusation; to be confronted with the witnesses against him; to have compulsory process for obtaining witnesses in his favor, and to have the Assistance of Counsel for his defence.

Article VII

In Suits at common law, where the value in controversy shall exceed twenty dollars, the right of trial by jury shall be preserved, and no fact tried by a jury, shall be otherwise re-examined in any Court of the United States, than according to the rules of the common law.

Article VIII

Excessive bail shall not be required, nor excessive fines imposed, nor cruel and unusual punishments inflicted.

Article IX

The enumeration in the Constitution, of certain rights, shall not be construed to deny or disparage others retained by the people.

Article X

The powers not delegated to the United States by the Constitution, nor prohibited by it to the States, are reserved to the States respectively, or to the people.

Article XI

The Judicial power of the United States shall not be construed to extend to any suit in law or equity, commenced or prosecuted against one of the United States by Citizens of another State, or by Citizens or Subjects of any Foreign State.

Article XII

The Electors shall meet in their respective states, and vote by ballot for President and Vice-President, one of whom, at least, shall not be an inhabitant of the same state with themselves; they shall name in their ballots the person voted for as President, and in distinct ballots the person voted for as Vice-President, and they shall make distinct lists of all persons voted for as President, and of all persons voted for as Vice-President, and of the number of votes for each, which lists they shall sign and certify, and transmit sealed to the seat of the government of the United States, directed to the President of the Senate;—The President of the Senate shall, in the presence of the Senate and House of Representatives, open all the certificates and the votes shall then be counted;—The person having the greatest number of votes for President, shall be the President, if such number be a majority of the whole number of Electors appointed; and if no person have such majority, then from the persons having the highest numbers not exceeding three on the list of those voted for as President, the House of Representatives shall choose immediately, by ballot, the President. But in choosing the President, the votes shall be taken by states, the representation from each state having one vote; a quorum for this purpose shall consist of a member or members from two-thirds of the states, and a majority of all the states shall be necessary to a choice. And if the House of Representatives shall not choose a President whenever the right of choice shall devolve upon them, before the fourth day of March next following, then the Vice-President shall act as President, as in the case of the death or other constitutional disability of the President. *(See Note 14)*—The person having the greatest number of votes as Vice-President, shall be the Vice-President, if such number be a majority of the whole number of Electors appointed, and if no person have a majority, then from the two highest numbers on the list, the Senate shall choose the Vice-President; a quorum for the purpose shall consist of two-thirds of the whole number of Senators, and a majority of the whole number shall be necessary to a choice. But no person constitutionally ineligible to the office of President shall be eligible to that of Vice-President of the United States.

Article XIII

Section 1. Neither slavery nor involuntary servitude, except as a punishment for crime whereof the party shall have been duly convicted, shall exist within the United States, or any place subject to their jurisdiction.

Section 2. Congress shall have power to enforce this article by appropriate legislation.

Article XIV

Section 1. All persons born or naturalized in the United States, and subject to the jurisdiction thereof, are citizens of the United States and of the State wherein they reside. No State shall make or enforce any law which shall abridge the privileges or immunities of citizens of the United States; nor shall any State deprive any person of life, liberty, or property, without due process of law; nor deny to any person within its jurisdiction the equal protection of the laws.

Section 2. Representatives shall be apportioned among the several States according to their respective numbers, counting the whole number of persons in each State, excluding Indians not taxed. But when the right to vote at any election for the choice of electors for President and Vice President of the United States, Representatives in Congress, the Executive and Judicial officers of a State, or the members of the Legislature thereof, is denied to any of the male inhabitants of such State, being twenty-one years of age, *(See Note 15)* and citizens of the United States, or in any way abridged, except for participation in rebellion, or other crime, the basis of representation therein shall be reduced in the proportion which the number of such male citizens shall bear to the whole number of male citizens twenty-one years of age in such State.

Section 3. No person shall be a Senator or Representative in Congress, or elector of President and Vice President, or hold any office, civil or military, under the United States, or under any State, who, having previously taken an oath, as a member of Congress, or as an officer of the United States, or as a member of any State legislature, or as an executive or judicial officer of any State, to support the Constitution of the United States, shall have engaged in insurrection or rebellion against the same, or given aid or comfort to the enemies thereof. But Congress may by a vote of two-thirds of each House, remove such disability.

Section 4. The validity of the public debt of the United States, authorized by law, including debts incurred for payment of pensions and bounties for services in suppressing insurrection or rebellion, shall not be questioned. But neither the United States nor any State shall assume or pay any debt or obligation incurred in aid of insurrection or rebellion against the United States, or any claim for the loss or emancipation of any slave; but all such debts, obligations and claims shall be held illegal and void.

Section 5. The Congress shall have power to enforce, by appropriate legislation, the provisions of this article.

Article XV

Section 1. The right of citizens of the United States to vote shall not be denied or abridged by the United States or by any State on account of race, color, or previous condition of servitude.

Section 2. The Congress shall have power to enforce this article by appropriate legislation.

Article XVI

The Congress shall have power to lay and collect taxes on incomes, from whatever source derived, without apportionment among the several States, and without regard to any census or enumeration.

Article XVII

The Senate of the United States shall be composed of two Senators from each State, elected by the people thereof, for six years; and each Senator shall have one vote. The electors in each State shall have the qualifications requisite for electors of the most numerous branch of the State legislatures.

When vacancies happen in the representation of any State in the Senate, the executive authority of such State shall issue writs of election to fill such vacancies: Provided, That the legislature of any State may empower the executive thereof to make temporary appointments until the people fill the vacancies by election as the legislature may direct.

This amendment shall not be so construed as to affect the election or term of any Senator chosen before it becomes valid as part of the Constitution.

Article XVIII

Section 1. After one year from the ratification of this article the manufacture, sale, or transportation of intoxicating liquors within, the importation thereof into, or the exportation thereof from the United States and all territory subject to the jurisdiction thereof for beverage purposes is hereby prohibited.

Section. 2. The Congress and the several States shall have concurrent power to enforce this article by appropriate legislation.

Section. 3. This article shall be inoperative unless it shall have been ratified as an amendment to the Constitution by the legislatures of the several States, as provided in the Constitution, within seven years from the date of the submission hereof to the States by the Congress.

Article XIX

The right of citizens of the United States to vote shall not be denied or abridged by the United States or by any State on account of sex.

Congress shall have power to enforce this article by appropriate legislation.

Article XX

Section 1. The terms of the President and Vice President shall end at noon on the 20th day of January, and the terms of Senators and Representatives at noon on the 3d day of January, of the years in which such terms would have ended if this article had not been ratified; and the terms of their successors shall then begin.

Section. 2. The Congress shall assemble at least once in every year, and such meeting shall begin at noon on the 3d day of January, unless they shall by law appoint a different day.

Section. 3. If, at the time fixed for the beginning of the term of the President, the President elect shall have died, the Vice President elect shall become President. If a President shall not have been chosen before the time fixed for the beginning of his term, or if the President elect shall have failed to qualify, then the Vice President elect shall act as President until a President shall have qualified; and the Congress may by law provide for the case wherein neither a President elect nor a Vice President elect shall have qualified, declaring who shall then act as President, or the manner in which one who is to act shall be selected, and such person shall act accordingly until a President or Vice President shall have qualified.

Section. 4. The Congress may by law provide for the case of the death of any of the persons from whom the House of Representatives may choose a President whenever the right of choice shall have devolved upon them, and for the case of the death of any of the persons from whom the Senate may choose a Vice President whenever the right of choice shall have devolved upon them.

Section. 5. Sections 1 and 2 shall take effect on the 15th day of October following the ratification of this article.

Section. 6. This article shall be inoperative unless it shall have been ratified as an amendment to the Constitution by the legislatures of three-fourths of the several States within seven years from the date of its submission.

Article XXI

Section 1. The eighteenth article of amendment to the Constitution of the United States is hereby repealed.

Section 2. The transportation or importation into any State, Territory, or possession of the United States for delivery or use therein of intoxicating liquors, in violation of the laws thereof, is hereby prohibited.

Section 3. This article shall be inoperative unless it shall have been ratified as an amendment to the Constitution by conventions in the several States, as provided in the Constitution, within seven years from the date of the submission hereof to the States by the Congress.

Amendment XXII

Section 1. No person shall be elected to the office of the President more than twice, and no person who has held the office of President, or acted as President, for more than two years of a term to which some other person was elected President shall be elected to the office of the President more than once. But this article shall not apply to any person holding the office of President when this article was proposed by the Congress, and shall not prevent any person who may be holding the office of President, or acting as President, during the term within which this article becomes operative from holding the office of President or acting as President during the remainder of such term.

Section 2. This article shall be inoperative unless it shall have been ratified as an amendment to the Constitution by the legislatures of three-fourths of the several states within seven years from the date of its submission to the states by the Congress.

Amendment XXIII

Section 1. The District constituting the seat of government of the United States shall appoint in such manner as the Congress may direct:

A number of electors of President and Vice President equal to the whole number of Senators and Representatives in Congress to which the District would be entitled if it were a state, but in no event more than the least populous state; they shall be in addition to those appointed by the states, but they shall be considered, for the purposes of the election of President and Vice President, to be electors appointed by a state; and they shall meet in the District and perform such duties as provided by the twelfth article of amendment.

Section 2. The Congress shall have power to enforce this article by appropriate legislation.

Amendment XXIV

Section 1. The right of citizens of the United States to vote in any primary or other election for President or Vice President, for electors for President or Vice President, or for Senator or Representative in Congress, shall not be denied or abridged by the United States or any state by reason of failure to pay any poll tax or other tax.

Section 2. The Congress shall have power to enforce this article by appropriate legislation.

Amendment XXV

Section 1. In case of the removal of the President from office or of his death or resignation, the Vice President shall become President.

Section 2. Whenever there is a vacancy in the office of the Vice President, the President shall nominate a Vice President who shall take office upon confirmation by a majority vote of both Houses of Congress.

Section 3. Whenever the President transmits to the President pro tempore of the Senate and the Speaker of the House of Representatives his written declaration that he is unable to discharge the powers and duties of his office, and until he transmits to them a written declaration to the contrary, such powers and duties shall be discharged by the Vice President as Acting President.

Section 4. Whenever the Vice President and a majority of either the principal officers of the executive departments or of such other body as Congress may by law provide, transmit to the President pro tempore of the Senate and the Speaker of the House of Representatives their written declaration that the President is unable to discharge the powers and duties of his office, the Vice President shall immediately assume the powers and duties of the office as Acting President.

Thereafter, when the President transmits to the President pro tempore of the Senate and the Speaker of the House of Representatives his written declaration that no inability exists, he shall resume the powers and duties of his office unless the Vice President and a majority of either the principal officers of the executive department or of such other body as Congress may by law provide, transmit within four days to the President pro tempore of the Senate and the Speaker of the House of Representatives their written declaration that the President is unable to discharge the powers and duties of his office. Thereupon Congress shall decide the issue, assembling within forty-eight hours for that purpose if not in session. If the Congress, within twenty-one days after receipt of the latter written declaration, or, if Congress is not in session, within twenty-one days after Congress is required to assemble, determines by two-thirds vote of both Houses that the President is unable to discharge the powers and duties of his office, the Vice President shall continue to discharge the same as Acting President; otherwise, the President shall resume the powers and duties of his office.

Amendment XXVI

Section 1. The right of citizens of the United States, who are 18 years of age or older, to vote, shall not be denied or abridged by the United States or any state on account of age.

Section 2. The Congress shall have the power to enforce this article by appropriate legislation.

Amendment XXVII

No law varying the compensation for the services of the Senators and Representatives shall take effect until an election of Representatives shall have intervened.

SKILLS
For SUCCESS

with Microsoft®
Excel 2010

COMPREHENSIVE

TOWNSEND | **VAVALIDES** | **HAIN**

Prentice Hall

Boston Columbus Indianapolis New York San Francisco Upper Saddle River
Amsterdam Cape Town Dubai London Madrid Milan Munich Paris Montréal Toronto
Delhi Mexico City São Paulo Sydney Hong Kong Seoul Singapore Taipei Tokyo

Library of Congress Cataloging-in-Publication Data

Townsend, Kris.
  Skills for success with Excel 2010 comprehensive / by Kris Townsend.
     p. cm.
  ISBN 978-0-13-510050-9 (alk. paper)
  1. Microsoft Excel (Computer file).   2. Business—Computer programs.
3. Electronic spreadsheets. I. Title.
HF5548.4.M523T685 2011
005.54—dc22   2010019632

Editor in Chief: *Michael Payne*
AVP/Executive Acquisitions Editor: *Stephanie Wall*
Product Development Manager: *Eileen Bien Calabro*
Editorial Project Manager: *Virginia Guariglia*
Development Editor: *Jeff Riley*
Editorial Assistant: *Nicole Sam*
AVP/Director of Online Programs, Media: *Richard Keaveny*
AVP/Director of Product Development, Media: *Lisa Strite*
Editor—Digital Learning & Assessment: *Paul Gentile*
Product Development Manager, Media: *Cathi Profitko*
Media Project Manager, Editorial: *Alana Coles*
Media Project Manager, Production: *John Cassar*
Director of Marketing: *Kate Valentine*
Senior Marketing Manager: *Tori Olsen Alves*
Marketing Coordinator: *Susan Osterlitz*

Marketing Assistant: *Darshika Vyas*
Senior Managing Editor: *Cynthia Zonneveld*
Associate Managing Editor: *Camille Trentacoste*
Production Project Manager: *Camille Trentacoste*
Senior Operations Supervisor: *Natacha Moore*
Senior Art Director: *Jonathan Boylan*
Art Director: *Anthony Gemmellaro*
Text and Cover Designer: *Anthony Gemmellaro*
Manager, Rights and Permissions: *Hessa Albader*
Supplements Development Editor: *Vonda Keator*
Full-Service Project Management: *MPS Content Services, a Macmillan Company*
Composition: *MPS Content Services, a Macmillan Company*
Printer/Binder: *RR Donnelley/Menasha*
Cover Printer: *Lehigh/Phoenix*
Typeface: *Minion 10.5/12.5*

Credits and acknowledgments borrowed from other sources and reproduced, with permission, in this textbook appear on appropriate page within text.

Microsoft® and Windows® are registered trademarks of the Microsoft Corporation in the U.S.A. and other countries. Screen shots and icons reprinted with permission from the Microsoft Corporation. This book is not sponsored or endorsed by or affiliated with the Microsoft Corporation.

Many of the designations by manufacturers and seller to distinguish their products are claimed as trademarks. Where those designations appear in this book, and the publisher was aware of a trademark claim, the designations have been printed in initial caps or all caps.

Prentice Hall
is an imprint of

www.pearsonhighered.com

10 9 8 7 6 5 4 3
ISBN-10:   0-13-510050-X
ISBN-13: 978-0-13-510050-9

Contents in Brief

Table of Contents

Common Features

Excel

About the Authors

Kris Townsend is an Information Systems instructor at Spokane Falls Community College in Spokane, Washington. Kris earned a bachelor's degree in both Education and Business, and a master's degree in Education. He has also worked as a public school teacher and as a systems analyst. Kris enjoys working with wood, snowboarding, and camping. He commutes to work by bike and enjoys long road rides in the Palouse country south of Spokane.

This book is dedicated to the students at Spokane Falls Community College. Their adventures, joys, and frustrations guide my way.

—Kris Townsend

Philip S. Vavalides is a Professor of Computer Technology at Guilford Technical Community College in North Carolina. He holds a bachelor's degree in Biology, and a Juris Doctorate degree from the University of Tennessee. He has also practiced law. He enjoys golf and traveling.

This book is dedicated to my wife, Teresa, whose support and understanding has been so important, and to my children Elizabeth and Alex, who are constant inspirations.

—Philip S. Vavalides

Catherine Hain is an instructor at Central New Mexico Community College in Albuquerque, New Mexico. She teaches computer applications classes in the Business and Information Technology School, both in the classroom and through the distance learning office. Catherine holds a bachelor's degree in Management and Marketing and a master's degree in Business Administration.

For the love and laughter you bring to my life, this book is dedicated to my husband Tom and to my sisters and brothers: Carol, Jerry, Raymond, Joe, Alice, David, Janet, Jim, Margaret, Richard, and JoAnn.

—Catherine Hain

Contributors

We'd like to thank the following people for their work on Skills for Success:

Instructor Resource Authors

LaDonna Bachand	*Santa Rosa Junior College*	Diane Coyle	*Montgomery County Community College*
Lisa Beach	*Santa Rosa Junior College*	Ranida Harris	*Indiana University Southeast*
Julie Boyles	*Portland Community College*	Belinda Moses	*Wayne County Community College*
Loris Bradshw	*Houston Community College*	Candice Spangler	*Columbia State Community College*

Technical Editors

Tom Lightner	*Missouri State University*	Steve Rubin	*California State University—Monterey Bay*
Joyce Nielsen		Sandy Weber	*Gateway Technical College*
Janet Pickard	*Chattanooga State Tech Community College*	Mara Zebest	
Linda Pogue	*Northwest Arkansas Community College*		

Reviewers

Laura Aagard	*Sierra College*	Tara Cipriano	*Gateway Technical College*
Darrell Abbey	*Cascadia Community College*	Paulette Comet	*Community College of Baltimore County—Catonsville*
John Alcorcha	*MTI College*		
Barry Andrews	*Miami Dade College*	Susana Contreras de Finch	*College of Southern Nevada*
Natalie Andrews	*Miami Dade College*	Gail W. Cope	*Sinclair Community College*
Wilma Andrews	*Virginia Commonwealth University School of Business*	Lennie Coper	*Miami Dade College*
		Chris Corbin	*Miami Dade College*
Bridget Archer	*Oakton Community College*	Janis Cox	*Tri-County Technical College*
Tahir Aziz	*J. Sargeant Reynolds Community College*	Tomi Crawford	*Miami Dade College*
Greg Balinger	*Miami Dade College*	Martin Cronlund	*Anne Arundel Community College*
Terry Bass	*University of Massachusetts, Lowell*	Jennifer Day	*Sinclair Community College*
Lisa Beach	*Santa Rosa Junior College*	Ralph DeArazoza	*Miami Dade College*
Rocky Belcher	*Sinclair Community College*	Carol Decker	*Montgomery College*
Nannette Biby	*Miami Dade College*	Loorna DeDuluc	*Miami Dade College*
David Billings	*Guilford Technical Community College*	Caroline Delcourt	*Black Hawk College*
Brenda K. Britt	*Fayetteville Technical Community College*	Michael Discello	*Pittsburgh Technical Institute*
Alisa Brown	*Pulaski Technical College*	Kevin Duggan	*Midlands Technical Community College*
Eric Cameron	*Passaic Community College*	Barbara Edington	*St. Francis College*
Gene Carbonaro	*Long Beach City College*	Donna Ehrhart	*Genesee Community College*
Trey Cherry	*Edgecombe Community College*	Hilda Wirth Federico	*Jacksonville University*
Kim Childs	*Bethany University*	Tushnelda Fernandez	*Miami Dade College*
Pualine Chohonis	*Miami Dade College*	Arlene Flerchinger	*Chattanooga State Tech Community College*

Hedy Fossenkemper	*Paradise Valley Community College*
Kent Foster	*Withrop University*
Penny Foster-Shiver	*Anne Arundel Community College*
Arlene Franklin	*Bucks County Community College*
George Gabb	*Miami Dade College*
Barbara Garrell	*Delaware County Community College*
Deb Geoghan	*Bucks County Community College*
Jessica Gilmore	*Highline Community College*
Victor Giol	*Miami Dade College*
Melinda Glander	*Northmetro Technical College*
Linda Glassburn	*Cuyahoga Community College, West*
Deb Gross	*Ohio State University*
Rachelle Hall	*Glendale Community College*
Marie Hartlein	*Montgomery County Community College*
Diane Hartman	*Utah Valley State College*
Betsy Headrick	*Chattanooga State*
Patrick Healy	*Northern Virginia Community College—Woodbridge*
Lindsay Henning	*Yavapai College*
Kermelle Hensley	*Columbus Technical College*
Diana Hill	*Chesapeake College*
Rachel Hinton	*Broome Community College*
Mary Carole Hollingsworth	*GA Perimeter*
Stacey Gee Hollins	*St. Louis Community College—Meramec*
Bill Holmes	*Chandler-Gilbert Community College*
Steve Holtz	*University of Minnesota Duluth*
Margaret M. Hvatum	*St. Louis Community College*
Joan Ivey	*Lanier Technical College*
Dr. Dianna D. Johnson	*North Metro Technical College*
Kay Johnston	*Columbia Basin College*
Warren T. Jones, Sr.	*University of Alabama at Birmingham*
Sally Kaskocsak	*Sinclair Community College*
Renuka Kumar	*Community College of Baltimore County*
Kathy McKee	*North Metro Technical College*
Hazel Kates	*Miami Dade College*
Gerald Kearns	*Forsyth Technical Community College*
Charles Kellermann	*Northern Virginia Community College—Woodbridge*
John Kidd	*Tarrant County Community College*
Chris Kinnard	*Miami Dade College*
Kelli Kleindorfer	*American Institute of Business*
Kurt Kominek	*NE State Tech Community College*
Dianne Kotokoff	*Lanier Technical College*
Cynthia Krebs	*Utah Valley University*
Jean Lacoste	*Virgina Polytechnic Institute and State University*
Gene Laughrey	*Northern Oklahoma College*
David LeBron	*Miami Dade College*
Kaiyang Liang	*Miami Dade College*
Linda Lindaman	*Black Hawk College*
Felix Lopez	*Miami Dade College*
Nicki Maines	*Mesa Community College*
Cindy Manning	*Big Sandy Community and Technical College*
Patri Mays	*Paradise Valley Community College*
Norma McKenzie	*El Paso Community College*
Lee McKinley	*GA Perimeter*
Sandy McCormack	*Monroe Community College*
Eric Meyer	*Miami Dade College*
Kathryn Miller	*Big Sandy Community and Technical College, Pike Ville Campus*
Gloria A. Morgan	*Monroe Community College*
Kathy Morris	*University of Alabama, Tuscaloosa*
Linda Moulton	*Montgomery County Community College*
Ryan Murphy	*Sinclair Community College*
Stephanie Murre Wolf	*Moraine Park Technical College*
Jackie Myers	*Sinclair Community College*
Dell Najera	*El Paso Community College, Valle Verde Campus*
Scott Nason	*Rowan Cabarrus Community College*
Paula Neal	*Sinclair Community College*
Bethanne Newman	*Paradise Valley Community College*
Eloise Newsome	*Northern Virginia Community College—Woodbridge*
Karen Nunan	*Northeast State Technical Community College*
Ellen Orr	*Seminole Community College*
Carol Ottaway	*Chemeketa Community College*
Denise Passero	*Fulton-Montgomery Community College*
Americus Pavese	*Community College of Baltimore County*
James Gordon Patterson	*Paradise Valley Community College*
Cindra Phillips	*Clark State CC*
Janet Pickard	*Chattanooga State Tech Community College*
Floyd Pittman	*Miami Dade College*
Melissa Prinzing	*Sierra College*
Pat Rahmlow	*Montgomery County Community College*

Contributors continued

Mary Rasley	*Lehigh Carbon Community College*
Scott Rosen	*Santa Rosa Junior College*
Ann Rowlette	*Liberty University*
Kamaljeet Sanghera	*George Mason University*
June Scott	*County College of Morris*
Janet Sebesy	*Cuyahoga Community College*
Jennifer Sedelmeyer	*Broome Community College*
Kelly SellAnne	*Arundel Community College*
Teresa Sept	*College of Southern Idaho*
Pat Serrano	*Scottsdale Community College*
Amanda Shelton	*J. Sargeant Reynolds Community College*
Gary Sibbits	*St. Louis Community College—Meramec*
Janet Siert	*Ellsworth Community College*
Robert Sindt	*Johnson County Community College*
Karen Smith	*Technical College of the Lowcountry*
Robert Smolenski	*Delaware County Community College*
Robert Sindt	*Johnson County Community College*
Gary R. Smith	*Paradise Valley Community College*
Patricia Snyder	*Midlands Technical College*
Pamela Sorensen	*Santa Rosa Junior College*
Eric Stadnik	*Santa Rosa Junior College*
Mark Stanchfield	*Rochester Community and Technical College*
Diane Stark	*Phoenix College*
Neil Stenlund	*Northern Virginia Community College*
Linda Stoudemayer	*Lamar Institute of Technology*
Pamela Stovall	*Forsyth Technical Community College*
Linda Switzer	*Highline Community College*
Margaret Taylor	*College of Southern Nevada*
Martha Taylor	*Sinclair Community College*
Michael M. Taylor	*Seattle Central Community College*
Roseann Thomas	*Fayetteville Tech Community College*
Ingrid Thompson-Sellers	*GA Perimeter*
Daniel Thomson	*Keiser University*
Astrid Hoy Todd	*Guilford Technical Community College*
Barb Tollinger	*Sinclair Community College*
Cathy Urbanski	*Chandler Gilbert Community College*
Sue Van Boven	*Paradise Valley Community College*
Philip Vavalides	*Guildford Technical Community College*
Pete Vetere	*Montgomery County Community College— West Campus*
Asteria Villegas	*Monroe College*
Michael Walton	*Miami Dade College*
Teri Weston	*Harford Community College*
Julie Wheeler	*Sinclair Community College*
Debbie Wood	*Western Piedmont Community College*
Thomas Yip	*Passaic Community College*
Lindy Young	*Sierra Community College*
Matt Zullo	*Wake Technical Community College*

A Microsoft® Office textbook that recognizes how students learn today–

Skills for Success

with Microsoft® Excel 2010 Comprehensive

- **10 x 8.5 Format** – Easy for students to read and type at the same time by simply propping the book up on the desk in front of their monitor

- **Clearly Outlined Skills** – Each skill is presented in a single two-page spread so that students can easily follow along

- **Numbered Steps and Bulleted Text** – Students don't read long paragraphs or text, but they will read information presented concisely

- **Easy-to-Find Student Data Files** – Visual key shows students how to locate and interact with their data files

Start Here – Students know exactly where to start and what their starting file will look like

Outcome – Shows students up front what their completed project will look like

CHAPTER 1

Getting Started with Windows 7

▸ You use Windows 7 to work with your computer. For example, you start programs, move between windows, and save your work.
▸ In Windows 7, you organize your work by naming files and placing those files into folders that you create.

Your starting screen will look like this:

SKILLS

At the end of this chapter, you will be able to:

- **Skill 1** Personalize the Windows 7 Desktop
- **Skill 2** Add and Remove Gadgets
- **Skill 3** Add Shortcuts
- **Skill 4** Move Between Windows and Customize the Taskbar
- **Skill 5** Resize, Move, and Scroll Windows
- **Skill 6** Use Windows Explorer and Create Folders
- **Skill 7** Move and Rename Folders and Copy Files
- **Skill 8** Move, Rename, and Delete Files
- **Skill 9** Compress Files and Use the Address Bar
- **Skill 10** Describe and Find Files and Folders

MORE SKILLS

- **More Skills 11** Create Backup Copies of Your Work
- **More Skills 12** Use Libraries to Organize Files
- **More Skills 13** Search the Web with Internet Explorer 8
- **More Skills 14** View Pictures from Digital Cameras

2 Getting Started with Windows 7 | **Windows 7 Chapter 1**

Windows 7

Outcome
Using the skills listed to the left will enable you to configure your computer similar to these:

You will save your files as:
Lastname_Firstname_w7_Snip1
Lastname_Firstname_w7_Snip2
Lastname_Firstname_w7_Snip3
Lastname_Firstname_w7_Snip4
Lastname_Firstname_w7_Snips

Windows 7 Chapter 1 | Getting Started with Windows 7 3

Skills List – A visual snapshot of what skills they will complete in the chapter

Sequential Pagination – Saves you and your students time in locating topics and assignments

Skills for Success

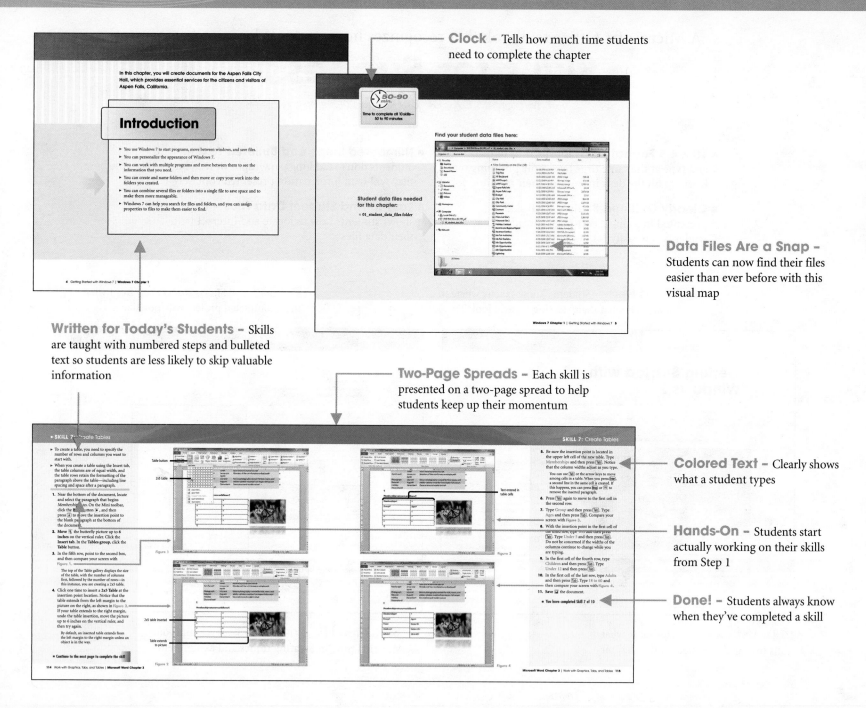

Clock – Tells how much time students need to complete the chapter

Data Files Are a Snap – Students can now find their files easier than ever before with this visual map

Written for Today's Students – Skills are taught with numbered steps and bulleted text so students are less likely to skip valuable information

Two-Page Spreads – Each skill is presented on a two-page spread to help students keep up their momentum

Colored Text – Clearly shows what a student types

Hands-On – Students start actually working on their skills from Step 1

Done! – Students always know when they've completed a skill

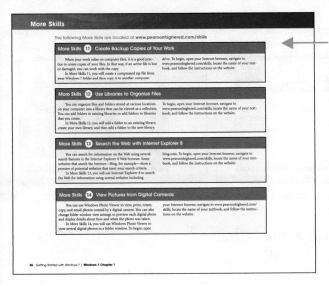

More Skills – Additional skills included online

Online Project – Students practice using Microsoft Help online to help prepare them for using the applications on their own

End-of-Chapter Material – Several levels of assessment so you can assign the material that best fits your students' needs

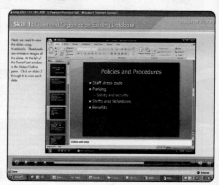

Videos! – Each skill within a chapter comes with a video that includes audio, which demonstrates the skill

NOTE: These videos are only available with *Skills for Success with Office 2010 Volume 1*

Instructor Materials

All Instructor materials available on the IRCD

Instructor's Manual – Teaching tips and additional resources for each chapter

Assignment Sheets – Lists all the assignments for the chapter, you just add in the course information, due dates, and points. Providing these to students ensures they will know what is due and when

Scripted Lectures – Classroom lectures prepared for you

Annotated Solution Files – Coupled with the scoring rubrics, these create a grading and scoring system that makes grading so much easier for you

Power Point Lectures – PowerPoint presentations for each chapter

Prepared Exams – Exams for each chapter

Scoring Rubrics – Can be used either by students to check their work or by you as a quick check-off for the items that need to be corrected

Syllabus Templates – For 8-week, 12-week, and 16-week courses

Test Bank – Includes a variety of test questions for each chapter

Companion Website – Online content such as the More Skills Projects, Online Study Guide, Glossary, and Student Data Files are all at www.pearsonhighered.com/skills

SKILLS For SUCCESS

with Microsoft®
Excel 2010

COMPREHENSIVE

Common Features of Office 2010

▶ The programs in Microsoft Office 2010—Word, Excel, PowerPoint, and Access—share common tools that you use in a consistent, easy-to-learn manner.

▶ Common tasks include opening and saving files, entering and formatting text, and printing your work.

Your starting screen will look like this:

SKILLS

Skills 1-10 Training

At the end of this chapter, you will be able to:

Skill 1 Start Word and Navigate the Word Window

Skill 2 Start Excel and PowerPoint and Work with Multiple Windows

Skill 3 Save Files in New Folders

Skill 4 Print and Save Documents

Skill 5 Open Student Data Files and Save Copies Using Save As

Skill 6 Type and Edit Text

Skill 7 Cut, Copy, and Paste Text

Skill 8 Format Text and Paragraphs

Skill 9 Use the Ribbon

Skill 10 Use Shortcut Menus and Dialog Boxes

MORE SKILLS

More Skills 11 Capture Screens with the Snipping Tool

More Skills 12 Use Microsoft Office Help

More Skills 13 Organize Files

More Skills 14 Save Documents to Windows Live

Outcome

Using the skills listed to the left will enable you
to create documents similar to this:

Visit Aspen Falls!

Aspen Falls overlooks the Pacific Ocean
and is surrounded by many vineyards and
wineries. Ocean recreation is accessed
primarily at Durango County Park. The
Aspen Lake Recreation Area provides year
round fresh water recreation and is the
city's largest park.

Local Attractions

- Wine Country
  - Wine Tasting Tours
  - Wineries
- Wordsworth Fellowship Museum of Art
- Durango County Museum of History
- Convention Center
- Art Galleries
- Glider Tours

Aspen Falls Annual Events

- Annual Starving Artists Sidewalk Sale
- Annual Wine Festival
- Cinco de Mayo
- Vintage Car Show
- Heritage Day Parade
- Harvest Days
- Amateur Bike Races
- Farmer's Market
- Aspen Lake Nature Cruises
- Aspen Falls Triathlon
- Taste of Aspen Falls
- Winter Blues Festival

Contact Your Name for more information.

You will save your files as:

Lastname_Firstname_cf01_Visit1
Lastname_Firstname_cf01_Visit2
Lastname_Firstname_cf01_Visit3

In this chapter, you will create documents for the Aspen Falls City Hall, which provides essential services for the citizens and visitors of Aspen Falls, California.

Common Features of Office 2010

► Microsoft Office is the most common software used to create and share personal and business documents.

► Microsoft Office is a suite of several programs—Word, PowerPoint, Excel, Access, and others—that each have a special purpose.

► Because of the consistent design and layout of Microsoft Office, when you learn to use one Microsoft Office program, you can use most of those skills when working with the other Microsoft Office programs.

► The files you create with Microsoft Office need to be named and saved in locations where they can be easily found when you need them.

Time to complete all
10 skills – 50 to 90 minutes

Find your student data files here:

**Student data files needed
for this chapter:**

- cf01_Visit
- cf01_Visit_Events
- cf01_Visit_River

► The Word 2010 program can be launched by clicking the Start button, and then locating and clicking the *Microsoft Word 2010* command.

► When you start Word, a new blank document displays in which you can type text.

1. In the lower left corner of the desktop, click the **Start** button ⊛.

2. In the lower left corner of the **Start** menu, click the **All Programs** command, and then compare your screen with **Figure 1.**

   The Microsoft Office folder is located in the All Programs folder. If you have several programs installed on your computer, you may need to scroll to see the Microsoft Office folder.

3. Click the **Microsoft Office** folder, and then compare your screen with **Figure 2.**

   Below the Microsoft Office folder, commands that open various Office 2010 programs display.

4. From the **Start** menu, under the **Microsoft Office** folder, click **Microsoft Word 2010**, and then wait a few moments for the Microsoft Word window to display.

5. If necessary, in the upper right corner of the Microsoft Word window, click the Maximize button ▣.

■ **Continue to the next page to complete the skill**

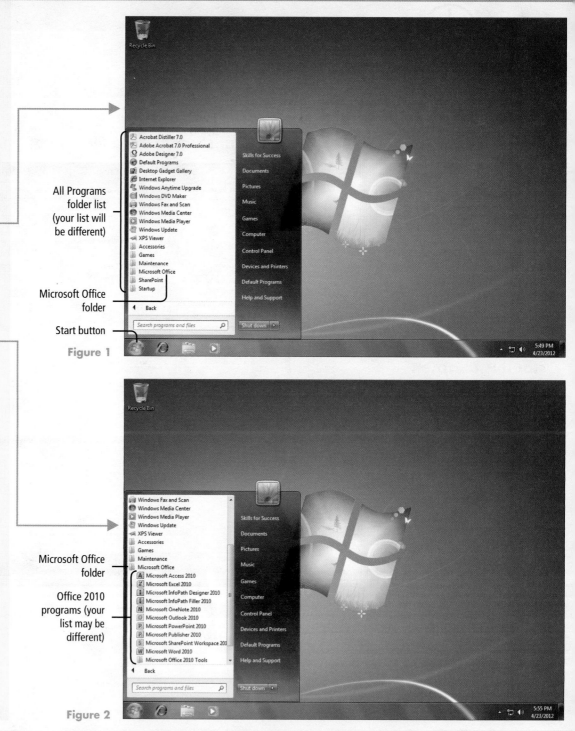

All Programs folder list (your list will be different)

Microsoft Office folder

Start button

Figure 1

Microsoft Office folder

Office 2010 programs (your list may be different)

Figure 2

Ribbon tab names

Home tab

Group names

Paragraph mark and insertion point

Quick Access Toolbar

New blank Word document

Figure 3

Heading 1 thumbnail

Styles group

Show/Hide button selected

Insertion point and paragraph mark

Heading 1 formatting applied

Home tab is active

Figure 4

6. On the Ribbon's **Home tab**, in the **Paragraph group**, click the **Show/Hide** button ¶ until it displays in gold indicating that it is active. Compare your screen with **Figure 3**.

> Above the blank Word document, the Quick Access Toolbar and Ribbon display. At the top of the Ribbon, a row of tab names display. Each Ribbon tab has buttons that you click to perform actions. The buttons are organized into groups that display their names along the bottom of the Ribbon.

> In the document, the *insertion point*— a vertical line that indicates where text will be inserted when you start typing—flashes near the top left corner.

> The Show/Hide button is a *toggle button*— a button used to turn a feature both on and off. The paragraph mark (¶) indicates the end of a paragraph and will not print.

7. In the document, type your first and last names. As you type, notice that the insertion point and paragraph mark move to the right.

8. On the **Home tab**, in the **Styles group**, point to—but do not click—the **Heading 1** thumbnail to show the *Live Preview*—a feature that displays the result of a formatting change if you select it.

9. Click the **Heading 1** thumbnail to apply the formatting change as shown in **Figure 4**. If the Word Navigation Pane displays on the left side of the Word window, click its Close ✖ button.

■ **You have completed Skill 1 of 10**

▶ When you open more than one Office program, each program displays in its own window.

▶ When you want to work with a program in a different window, you need to make it the active window.

1. Click the **Start** button ⊕, and then compare your screen with **Figure 1**.

   Your computer may be configured in such a way that you can open Office programs without opening the All Programs folder. The Office 2010 program commands may display as shortcuts in the Start menu's pinned programs area or the recently used programs area. Your computer's taskbar or desktop may also display icons that start each program.

2. From the **Start** menu, locate and then click **Microsoft Excel 2010**. Depending on your computer, you may need to double-click—not single click—to launch Excel. Compare your screen with **Figure 2**. If necessary, click the Maximize button ▭.

   A new blank worksheet displays in a new window. The first *cell*—the box formed by the intersection of a row and column—is active as indicated by the thick, black border surrounding the cell. When you type in Excel, the text is entered into the active cell.

   The Quick Access Toolbar displays above the spreadsheet. The Excel Ribbon has its own tabs and groups that you use to work with an Excel spreadsheet. Many of these tabs, groups, and buttons are similar to those found in Word.

   On the taskbar, two buttons display—one for Word and one for Excel.

■ **Continue to the next page to complete the skill** ➡

Commands pinned to Start menu

Recently opened Office program

Programs pinned to taskbar

Figure 1

Active cell

New, blank Excel spreadsheet

Excel button

Word button

Figure 2

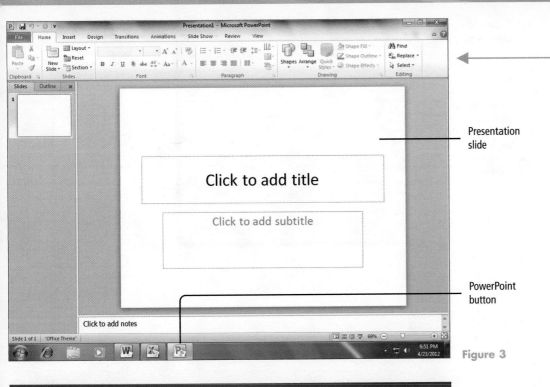

Presentation slide

PowerPoint button

Figure 3

Maximize button replaced the Restore Down button

Text inserted into Excel cells

Current date calculated and displayed

Window restored down (your size and location may be different)

Figure 4

3. From the **Start** menu 🕙, locate and then click **Microsoft PowerPoint 2010**. Compare your screen with **Figure 3**. If necessary, Maximize 🔲 the Presentation1 - Microsoft PowerPoint window.

   A new, blank presentation opens in a new window. The PowerPoint window contains a slide in which you can type text. PowerPoint slides are designed to be displayed as you talk in front of a group of people.

4. In the upper right corner of the **PowerPoint** window, click the **Close** button 🗙.

5. On the taskbar, click the **Word** button to make it the active window. With the insertion point flashing to the right of your name, press Enter, and then type Skills for Success Common Features Chapter

6. In the upper right corner of the **Document1 - Microsoft Word** window, click the **Minimize** button 🔲.

   The Word window no longer displays, but its button is still available on the taskbar.

7. With the Excel window active, in the first cell—cell **A1**—type your first name. Press Tab, and then type your last name.

8. Press Enter, type =TODAY() and then press Enter to calculate the current date and to display it in the cell.

9. In the **Excel** window, click the **Restore Down** button 🔲 and then compare your screen with **Figure 4**.

   The window remains open, but it no longer fills the entire screen. The Maximize button replaced the Restore Down button.

■ **You have completed Skill 2 of 10**

▶ A new document or spreadsheet is stored in the computer's temporary memory (*RAM*) until you save it to your hard drive or USB flash drive.

1. If you are saving your work on a USB flash drive, insert the USB flash drive into the computer now. If the Windows Explorer button 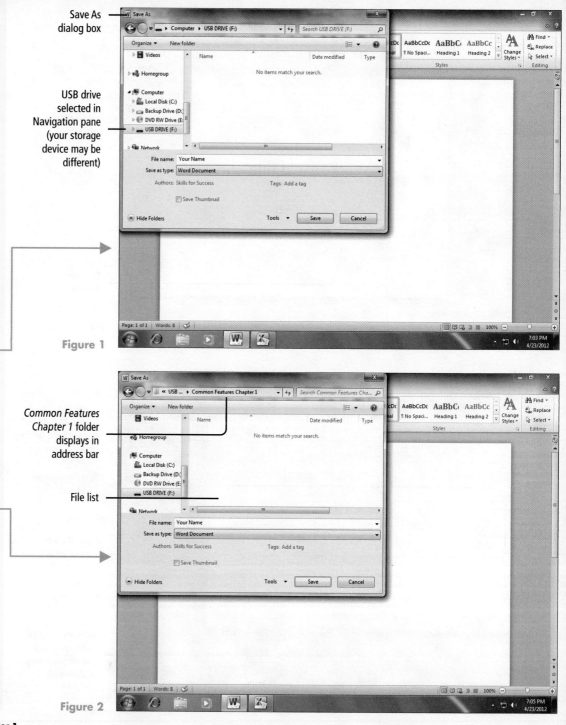 flashes on the taskbar, right-click the button, and then on the Jump List, click Close window.

2. On the taskbar, click the **Word** button to make it the active window. On the **Quick Access Toolbar**, click the **Save** button.

   For new documents, the first time you click the Save button, the Save As dialog box opens so that you can name the file.

3. If you are to save your work on a USB drive, in the Navigation pane scroll down to display the list of drives, and then click your USB flash drive as shown in **Figure 1**. If you are saving your work to another location, in the Navigation pane, locate and then click that folder or drive.

4. On the **Save As** dialog box toolbar, click the **New folder** button, and then immediately type Common Features Chapter 1

5. Press Enter to accept the folder name, and then press Enter again to open the new folder as shown in **Figure 2**.

   The new folder is created and then opened in the Save As dialog box file list.

■ **Continue to the next page to complete the skill**

Save As dialog box

USB drive selected in Navigation pane (your storage device may be different)

Figure 1

Common Features Chapter 1 folder displays in address bar

File list

Figure 2

File name typed in File name box

Figure 3

File names display on title bars

Two saved Office documents

Windows Explorer button

Common Features Chapter 1 folder selected

Figure 4

6. In the **Save As** dialog box, click in the **File name** box one time to highlight all of the existing text.

7. With the text in the **File name** box still highlighted, type Lastname_Firstname_ cf01_Visit1

8. Compare your screen with Figure 3, and then click **Save**.

   After the document is saved, the name of the file displays on the title bar at the top of the window.

9. On the taskbar, click the **Windows Explorer** button 🖿. In the folder window **Navigation** pane, open ▷ the drive on which you are saving your work, and then click the **Common Features Chapter 1** folder. Verify that *Lastname_Firstname_ cf01_Visit1* displays in file list.

10. On the taskbar, click the **Excel** button to make it the active window. On the Excel **Quick Access Toolbar**, click the **Save** button 🖫.

11. In the **Save As** dialog box **Navigation** pane, open ▷ the drive where you are saving your work, and then click the **Common Features Chapter 1** folder to display its file list.

    The Word file may not display because the Save As box typically displays only files created by the program you are using. Here, only Excel files will typically display.

12. Click in the **File name** box, replace the existing value with Lastname_Firstname_ cf01_Visit2 and then click the **Save** button.

13. On the taskbar, click the **Windows Explorer** button, and then compare your screen with Figure 4.

   ▪ **You have completed Skill 3 of 10**

► Before printing, it is a good idea to work in *Page Layout view*—a view where you prepare your document or spreadsheet for printing.

1. On the taskbar, click the **Excel** button, and then click the **Maximize** button.

2. On the Ribbon, click the **View tab**, and then in the **Workbook Views group**, click the **Page Layout** button. Compare your screen with **Figure 1**.

   The worksheet displays the cells, the margins, and the edges of the paper as they will be positioned when you print. The *cell references*—the numbers on the left side and the letters across the top of a spreadsheet that address each cell—will not print.

3. On the Ribbon, click the **Page Layout tab**. In the **Page Setup group**, click the **Margins** button, and then in the **Margins** gallery, click **Wide**.

4. Click the **File tab**, and then on the left side of the Backstage, click **Print**. Compare your screen with **Figure 2**.

   The Print tab has commands that affect your print job and a preview of the printed page. Here, the cell references and *grid lines*—lines between the cells in a table or spreadsheet—do not display because they will not be printed.

5. In the **Print Settings**, under **Printer**, notice the name of the printer. You will need to retrieve your printout from this printer. If your instructor has directed you to print to a different printer, click the Printer arrow, and choose the assigned printer.

■ **Continue to the next page to complete the skill**

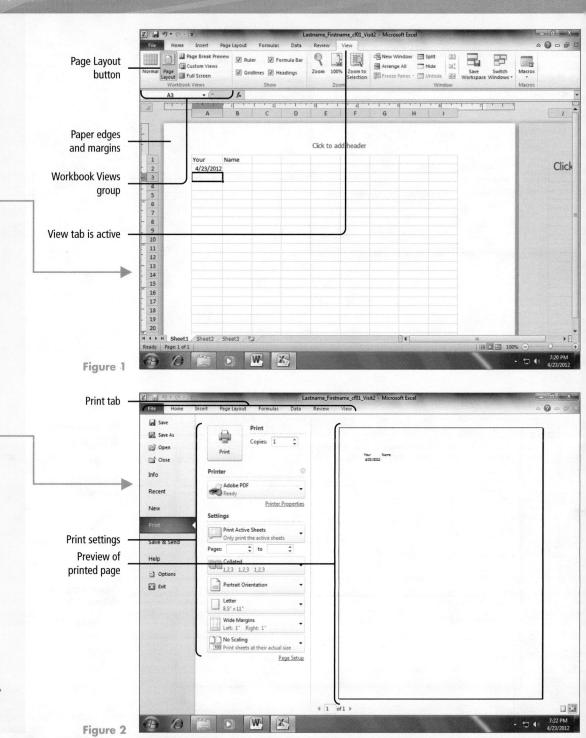

Page Layout button

Paper edges and margins

Workbook Views group

View tab is active

Figure 1

Print tab

Print settings

Preview of printed page

Figure 2

Heading 2 style applied

Figure 3

Message asks if you want to save changes

Figure 4

6. Check with your *Course Assignment Sheet* or *Course Syllabus,* or consult with your instructor to determine whether you are to print your work for this chapter. If you are to print your work, at the top left corner of the Print Settings section, click the Print button. If you printed the spreadsheet, retrieve the printout from the printer.

7. On the **File tab**, click **Save**.

    Because you have already named the file, the Save As dialog box does not display.

8. On the **File tab**, click **Exit** to close the spreadsheet and exit Excel.

9. In the Word document, verify that the insertion point is in the second line of text. If not, on the taskbar, click the Word button to make it the active window.

10. On the **Home tab**, in the **Styles group**, click the **Heading 2** thumbnail. Compare your screen with **Figure 3**.

11. On the **File tab**, click **Print** to display the Print tab. If you are printing your work for this chapter, click the Print button, and then retrieve your printout from the printer.

12. On the **File tab**, click **Exit**, and then compare your screen with **Figure 4**.

    When you close a window with changes that have not yet been saved, a message will remind you to save your work.

13. Read the displayed message, and then click **Save**.

■ **You have completed Skill 4 of 10**

► This book often instructs you to open a student data file so that you do not need to start the project with a blank document.

► The student data files are located on the student CD that came with this book. Your instructor may have provided an alternate location.

► You use Save As to create a copy of the student data file onto your own storage device.

1. If necessary, insert the student CD that came with this text. If the AutoPlay dialog box displays, click Close .

2. Using the skills practiced earlier, start **Microsoft Word 2010**.

3. In the **Document1 - Microsoft Word** window, click the **File tab**, and then click **Open**.

4. In the **Open** dialog box **Navigation** pane, scroll down and then, if necessary, open ▷ Computer. In the list of drives, click the CD/DVD drive to display the contents of the student CD. If your instructor has provided a different location, navigate to that location instead of using the student CD.

5. In the file list, double-click the **01_student_data_files** folder, double-click the **01_common_features** folder, and then double-click the **chapter_01** folder. Compare your screen with **Figure 1**.

6. In the file list, click **cf01_Visit**, and then click the **Open** button. Compare your screen with **Figure 2**.

   If you opened the file from the student CD, the title bar indicates that the document is in **read-only mode**—a mode where you cannot save your changes.

■ **Continue to the next page to complete the skill**

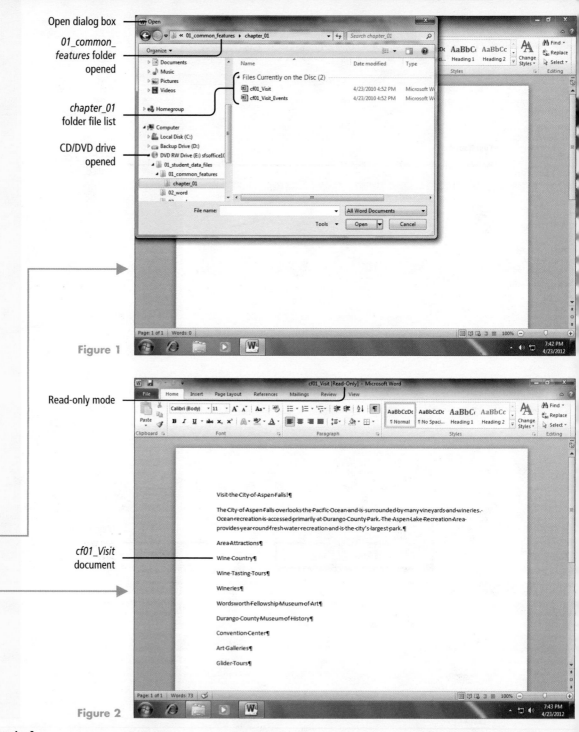

Open dialog box

01_common_ features folder opened

chapter_01 folder file list

CD/DVD drive opened

Figure 1

Read-only mode

cf01_Visit document

Figure 2

Save As dialog box

Common Features Chapter 1 on USB drive (your location may be different)

New file name

Figure 3

Common Features Chapter 1 folder

Three files saved in this project

Figure 4

7. If the document opens in Protected View, click the Enable Editing button.

> **Protected View** is a view applied to documents downloaded from the Internet that allows you to decide if the content is safe before working with the document.

8. Click the **File tab**, and then click **Save As**.

> Because this file has already been saved with a name in a specific location, you need to use Save As to create a copy with a new name and location.

9. In the **Save As** dialog box **Navigation** pane, navigate to the **Common Features Chapter 1** folder that you created previously—open ▷ the drive on which you are saving your work, and then click the **Common Features Chapter 1** folder.

10. In the **File name** box, replace the existing value with Lastname_Firstname_cf01_Visit3 Be sure to use your own first and last names.

11. Compare your screen with **Figure 3**, and then click the **Save** button.

12. On the title bar, notice the new file name displays and *[Read-Only]* no longer displays.

13. On the taskbar, click the **Windows Explorer** button. Verify that the three files you have saved in this chapter display as shown in **Figure 4**.

14. In the Windows Explorer window, navigate to the **student CD**, and then display the **chapter_01** file list.

15. Notice that the original student data file—*cf01_Visit*—is still located in the **chapter_01** folder, and then **Close** ✕ the Windows Explorer window.

■ **You have completed Skill 5 of 10**

► To *edit* is to insert text, delete text, or replace text in an Office document, spreadsheet, or presentation.

► To edit text, you need to position the insertion point at the desired location or select the text you want to replace.

1. With the **Word** document as the active window, in the first line, click to the left of the word *Aspen*. Press Bksp 12 times to delete the words *the City of*. Be sure there is one space between each word as shown in **Figure 1**.

    The Backspace key deletes one letter at a time moving from right to left.

2. In the second line of the document, click to the left of the words *The City of Aspen Falls*. Press Delete 12 times to delete the phrase *The City of*.

    The Delete key deletes one letter at a time moving from left to right.

3. In the line *Area Attractions*, double-click the word *Area* to select it. Type Local and then compare your screen with **Figure 2**.

    When a word is selected, it is replaced by whatever you type next.

■ **Continue to the next page to complete the skill**

Text deleted

Figure 1

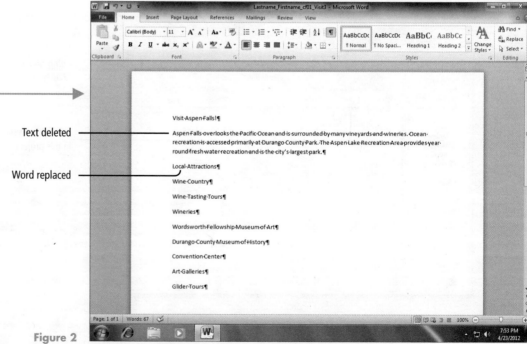

Text deleted

Word replaced

Figure 2

Figure 3

Figure 4

4. Place the pointer approximately 1 inch to the left of the line *Convention Center*. When the ⚐ pointer displays as shown in **Figure 3**, click one time.

    Placing the pointer in the Selection bar and then clicking is a way to select an entire line with a single click. After selecting text, the ***Mini toolbar***—a toolbar with common formatting buttons—may display briefly as you move the mouse.

5. With the entire line still selected, press ⌨Delete to delete the line.

6. On the **Quick Access Toolbar**, click the **Undo** button 🔄 one time. Notice the *Convention Center* line displays again.

    When you perform an incorrect action, clicking the Undo button often returns your document to its previous state.

7. At the end of the last line—*Glider Tours*—click between the last word and the paragraph formatting mark (¶). Press ⌨Enter to insert a new line.

8. With the insertion point in the new line, type Contact Your Name for more information. Be sure to use your first and last names in place of *Your* and *Name*. Compare your screen with **Figure 4**.

9. On the **Quick Access Toolbar**, click **Save** 💾.

    When a document has already been saved with the desired name, click the Save button—the Save As dialog box is not needed.

- **You have completed Skill 6 of 10**

▶ The *copy* command places a copy of the selected text or object in the *Clipboard*—a temporary storage area that holds text or an object that has been cut or copied.

▶ You can move text by moving it to and from the Clipboard or by dragging the text.

1. Click the **File tab**, and then click **Open**. In the **Open** dialog box, if necessary, navigate to the student files and display the contents of the chapter_01 folder. Click **cf01_Visit_Events**, and then click **Open**.

2. On the right side of the Ribbon's **Home tab**, in the **Editing group**, click the **Select** button, and then click **Select All**. Compare your screen with **Figure 1**.

3. With all of the document text selected, on the left side of the **Home tab**, in the **Clipboard group**, click the **Copy** button 📋.

4. In the upper right corner of the Word window, click **Close** ✕. You do not need to save changes—you will not turn in this student data file.

5. In **Lastname_Firstname_cf01_Visit3**, click to place the insertion point to the left of the line that starts *Contact Your Name*.

6. On the **Home tab**, in the **Clipboard group**, point to—but do not click—the **Paste** button. Compare your screen with **Figure 2**.

   The Paste button has two parts—the upper half is the Paste button, and the lower half is the Paste button arrow. When you click the Paste button arrow, a list of paste options display.

■ **Continue to the next page to complete the skill** ➡

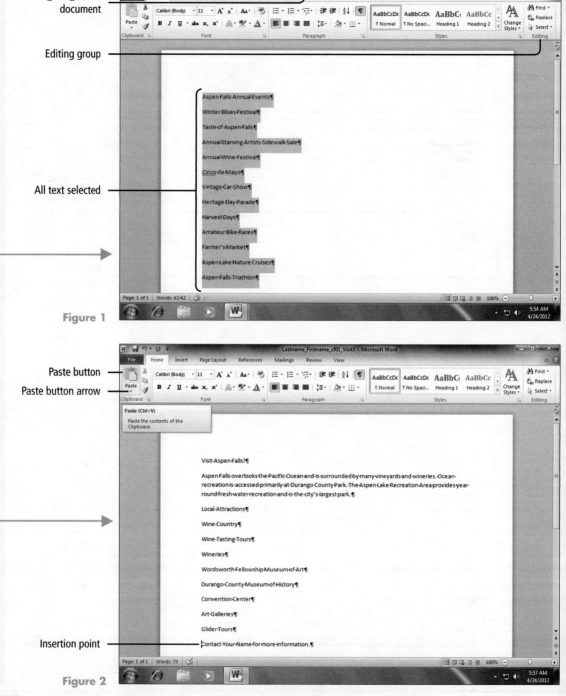

cf01_Visit_Events document

Editing group

All text selected

Figure 1

Paste button
Paste button arrow

Figure 2

7. Click the upper half of the **Paste** button to paste the selected text. Compare your screen with **Figure 3**.

> When you ***paste***, you insert a copy of the text or object stored in the Clipboard and the Paste Options button displays near the pasted text.

8. Press (Esc) to hide the Paste Options button.

9. Scroll up to display the line *Winter Blues Festival.* Place the [I] pointer to the left of the W, and then drag down and to the right to select two lines—*Winter Blues Festival* and *Taste of Aspen Falls.*

> To ***drag*** is to move the mouse while holding down the left mouse button and then to release it at the appropriate time.

10. On the **Home tab**, in the **Clipboard group**, click the **Cut** button .

> The ***cut*** command removes the selected text or object and stores it in the Clipboard.

11. Click to place the insertion point to the left of *Contact Your Name*, and then in the **Clipboard group**, click the **Paste** button to insert the text.

12. Drag to select the text *Taste of Aspen Falls*, including the paragraph mark.

13. With the pointer, drag the selected text to the left of *Winter Blues Festival*. When the pointer displays to the left of *Winter* as shown in **Figure 4**, release the mouse button.

14. On the **Quick Access Toolbar**, click **Save** .

> ■ **You have completed Skill 7 of 10**

Pasted text

Paste Options button

Figure 3

Move pointer and insertion point

Figure 4

▶ To *format* is to change the appearance of the text—for example, changing the text color to red.

▶ Before formatting text, you first need to select the text that will be formatted.

▶ Once text is selected, you can apply formatting using the Ribbon or the Mini toolbar.

1. Scroll to the top of the document, and then click anywhere in the first line, *Visit Aspen Falls*.

2. On the **Home tab**, in the **Styles group**, click the **Heading 1** thumbnail.

When no text is selected, the Heading 1 style is applied to the entire paragraph.

3. Click in the paragraph, *Local Attractions*, and then in the **Styles group**, click the **Heading 2** thumbnail. Click in the paragraph, *Aspen Falls Annual Events*, and then apply the **Heading 2** style. Compare your screen with **Figure 1**.

4. Drag to select the text *Visit Aspen Falls!* Immediately point to—but do not click—the Mini toolbar to display it as shown in **Figure 2**. If necessary, right-click the selected text to display the Mini toolbar.

■ **Continue to the next page to complete the skill**

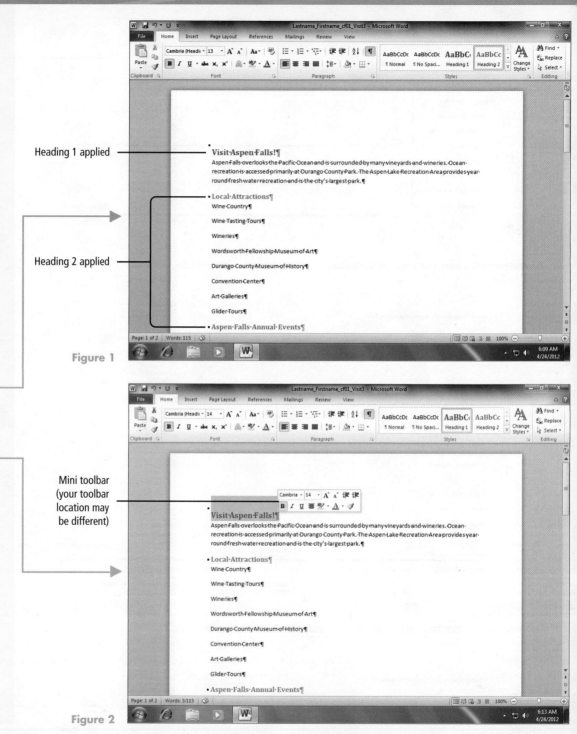

Heading 1 applied

Heading 2 applied

Figure 1

Mini toolbar (your toolbar location may be different)

Figure 2

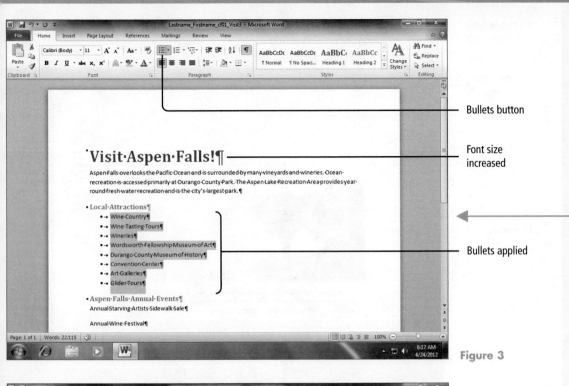

Bullets button

Font size increased

Bullets applied

Figure 3

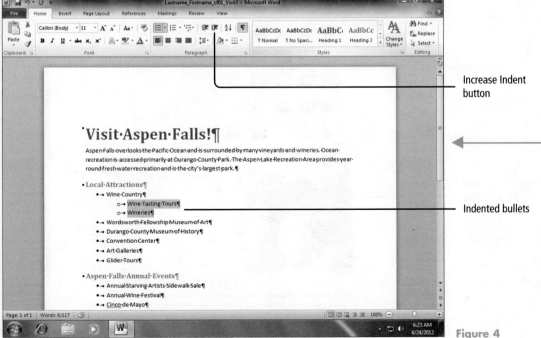

Increase Indent button

Indented bullets

Figure 4

5. On the Mini toolbar, click the **Font Size arrow** ⏷, and then from the list, click **28** to increase the size of the selected text.

6. Place the pointer approximately 1 inch to the left of the line *Wine Country*. When the ⏶ pointer displays, drag straight down. When all the lines between and including *Wine Country* and *Glider Tours* are selected, release the left mouse button.

7. On the Ribbon, in the **Paragraph group**, click the **Bullets** button ⏷, and then compare your screen with **Figure 3**.

8. Click to the left of *Annual Starving Artists Sidewalk Sale*. Scroll down to display the bottom of the page. Press and hold [Shift] while clicking to the right of *Winter Blues Festival* to select all of the text between and including *Annual Starving Artists Sidewalk Sale* and *Winter Blues Festival*.

9. In the **Paragraph group**, click the **Bullets** button ⏷.

10. Scroll to the top of the document. Use either technique just practiced to select *Wine Tasting Tours* and *Wineries*.

11. In the **Paragraph group**, click the **Increase Indent** button ⏷ one time. Compare your screen with **Figure 4**.

12. On the **Quick Access Toolbar**, click **Save** 🖫.

■ **You have completed Skill 8 of 10**

▶ Each Ribbon tab contains commands organized into groups. Some tabs display only when a certain type of object is selected—a graphic, for example.

1. Press and hold Ctrl, and then press Home to place the insertion point at the beginning of the document.

2. On the **Ribbon,** to the right of the **Home tab**, click the **Insert tab**. In the **Illustrations group**, click the **Picture** button.

3. In the **Insert Picture** dialog box, navigate as needed to display the contents of the student files in the **chapter_01** folder. Click **cf01_Visit_River**, and then click the **Insert** button. Compare your screen with **Figure 1**.

   When a picture is selected, the Format tab displays below Picture Tools. On the Format tab, in the Picture Styles group, a *gallery*—a visual display of choices from which you can choose—displays thumbnails. The entire gallery can be seen by clicking the More button to the right and below the first row of thumbnails.

4. On the **Format tab**, in the **Picture Styles group**, click the **More** button ⊡ to display the **Picture Styles** gallery. In the gallery, point to the fourth thumbnail in the first row—**Drop Shadow Rectangle**—to display the ScreenTip as shown in **Figure 2**.

   A *ScreenTip* is informational text that displays when you point to commands or thumbnails on the Ribbon.

5. Click the **Drop Shadow Rectangle** thumbnail to apply the picture style.

■ **Continue to the next page to complete the skill**

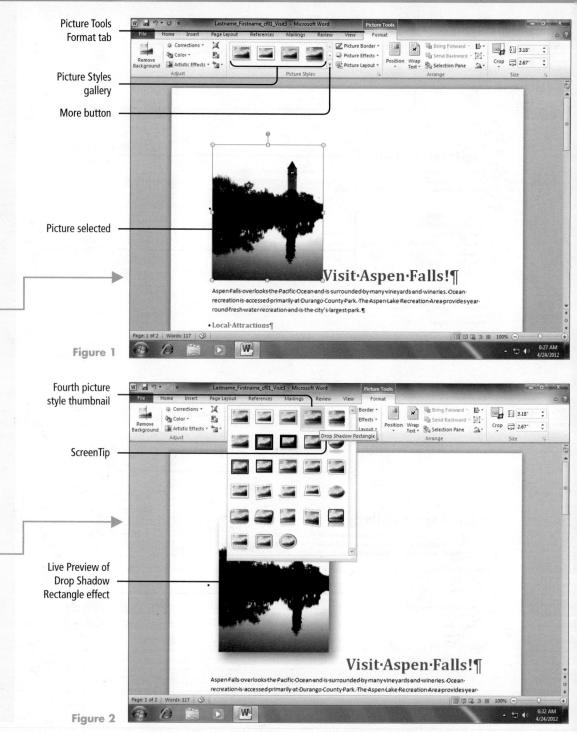

Picture Tools Format tab

Picture Styles gallery

More button

Picture selected

Figure 1

Fourth picture style thumbnail

ScreenTip

Live Preview of Drop Shadow Rectangle effect

Figure 2

Wrap Text button

Picture positioned

Figure 3

6. On the **Format tab**, in the **Arrange group**, click the **Wrap Text** button, and then from the list of choices, click **Square.**

7. Point to the picture, and then with the 📐 pointer, drag the picture to the right side of the page as shown in Figure 3.

8. Click a blank area of the page, and then notice the Picture Tools Format tab no longer displays.

9. On the **Page Layout tab**, in the **Themes group**, click the **Themes** button.

10. In the **Themes** gallery, point to—but do not click—each of the thumbnails to display the Live Preview of each theme. When you are done, click the **Civic** thumbnail.

11. On the **View tab**, in the **Zoom group**, click the **One Page** button to display the entire page on the screen. If necessary, adjust the position of the picture.

12. On the **View tab**, in the **Zoom group**, click the **100%** button.

13. Select the text *Visit Aspen Falls!* without selecting the paragraph mark. Press Alt to display *KeyTips*—keys that you can press to access each Ribbon tab and most commands on each tab. Release Alt, and then press H one time to display the Home tab. Compare your screen with Figure 4.

    With KeyTips displayed on the Home tab, pressing 2 is the same as clicking the Italic button *I*. In this manner, you select Ribbon commands without using the mouse.

14. Press 2 to apply the Italic format to the selected text.

15. **Save** 💾 the document.

■ **You have completed Skill 9 of 10**

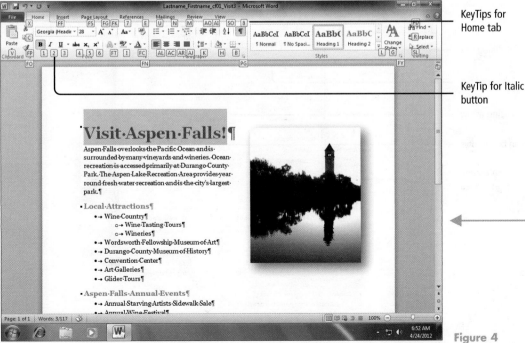

KeyTips for Home tab

KeyTip for Italic button

Figure 4

▶ Commands can be accessed in *dialog boxes*—boxes where you can select multiple settings.

▶ You can also access commands by right-clicking objects in a document.

1. In the paragraph that starts *Aspen Falls overlooks the Pacific Ocean*, **triple-click**—click three times fairly quickly without moving the mouse—to highlight the entire paragraph.

2. On the **Home tab**, in the lower right corner of the **Font group**, point to the **Font Dialog Box Launcher** ⌹ as shown in **Figure 1**.

The ⌹ buttons at the lower right corner of most groups open a dialog box with choices that may not be available on the Ribbon.

3. Click the **Font Dialog Box Launcher** ⌹ to open the Font dialog box.

4. In the **Font** dialog box, click the **Advanced tab**. Click the **Spacing arrow**, and then click **Expanded**.

5. To the right of the **Spacing** box, click the **By spin box up arrow** three times to display *1.3 pt*. Compare your screen with **Figure 2**, and then click **OK** to close the dialog box and apply the changes.

■ **Continue to the next page to complete the skill**

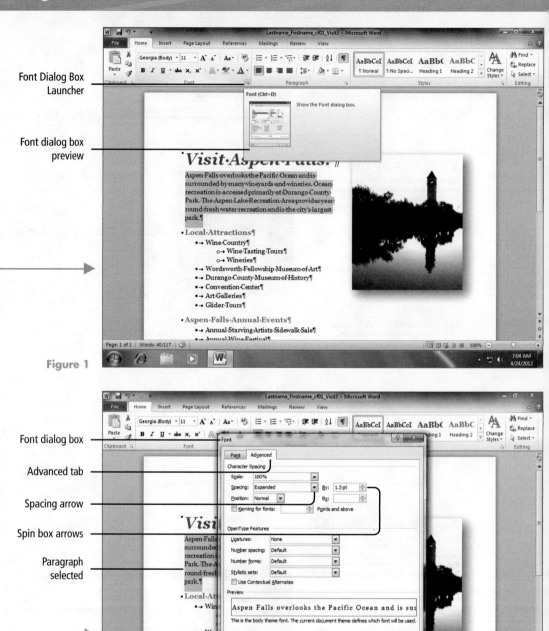

Font Dialog Box Launcher

Font dialog box preview

Figure 1

Font dialog box

Advanced tab

Spacing arrow

Spin box arrows

Paragraph selected

Figure 2

Shortcut menu

Figure 3

6. With the paragraph still selected, *right-click*—click the paragraph with the right mouse button—and then compare your screen with **Figure 3**.

   When you right-click selected text, the Mini toolbar and a shortcut menu display. A *shortcut menu* displays a list of commands related to the type of object that you right-click.

7. From the displayed shortcut menu, click the **Paragraph** command. Alternately, on the Home tab, click the Paragraph Dialog Box Launcher.

8. In the **Paragraph** dialog box, under **Spacing,** click the **Before spin up arrow** three times to display *18 pt*.

9. In the **After** box, highlight the existing value, and then type 15 Compare your screen with **Figure 4**, and then click **OK**.

10. If your instructor asks you to print your work, click the File tab, click Print, and then click the Print button.

11. Click **Save** 🖫, click the **File tab**, and then click **Exit**.

Done! You have completed Skill 10 of 10, and your document is complete!

Paragraph dialog box

Spacing before value changed

Spacing after value typed

Figure 4

The following More Skills are located at **www.pearsonhighered.com/skills**

More Skills Capture Screens with the Snipping Tool

Some of the work that you do in this book cannot be graded without showing your computer screens to the grader. You can use the Snipping Tool to create pictures of your screens. Snip files can be printed or submitted electronically.

In More Skills 11, you will use the Snipping Tool to create a picture of your screen and then copy the picture into a Word document.

To begin, open your web browser, navigate to www.pearsonhighered.com/skills, locate the name of your textbook, and then follow the instructions on the website.

More Skills Use Microsoft Office Help

Microsoft Office 2010 has a Help system in which you can search for articles that show you how to accomplish tasks.

In More Skills 12, you will use the Office 2010 Help system to view an article on how to customize the Help window.

To begin, open your web browser, navigate to www.pearson highered.com/skills, locate the name of your textbook, and then follow the instructions on the website.

More Skills Organize Files

Over time, you may create hundreds of files using Microsoft Office. To find your files when you need them, they need to be well-organized. You can organize your computer files by carefully naming them and by placing them into folders.

In More Skills 13, you will create, delete, and rename folders. You will then copy, delete, and move files into the folders that you created.

To begin, open your web browser, navigate to www.pearsonhighered.com/skills, locate the name of your textbook, and then follow the instructions on the website.

More Skills Save Documents to Windows Live

If your computer is connected to the Internet, you can save your Office documents to a drive available to you free of charge through Windows Live. You can then open the files from other locations such as home, school, or work.

In More Skills 14, you will save a memo to Windows Live.

To begin, open your web browser, navigate to www.pearsonhighered.com/skills, locate the name of your textbook, and then follow the instructions on the website.

Key Terms

Online Help Skills

1. **Start** 🟢 Word. In the upper right corner of the Word window, click the **Help** button 🔘. In the **Help** window, click the **Maximize** 🔲 button.

2. Click in the search box, type Create a document and then click the **Search** button. In the search results, click **Create a document**.

3. Read the article's introduction, and then below **What do you want to do**, click **Start a document from a template**. Compare your screen with Figure 1.

Figure 1

4. Read the Start a document from a template section to see if you can answer the following: What types of documents are available as templates? On the New tab, under Available Templates, what are the two general locations that you can find templates?

Matching

Match each term in the second column with its correct definition in the first column by writing the letter of the term on the blank line in front of the correct definition.

____ **1.** A feature that displays the result of a formatting change if you select it.

____ **2.** A line between the cells in a table or spreadsheet.

____ **3.** A mode where you can open and view a file, but you cannot save your changes.

____ **4.** A view where you prepare your document or spreadsheet for printing.

____ **5.** Quickly click the left mouse button two times without moving the mouse.

____ **6.** To insert text, delete text, or replace text in an Office document, spreadsheet, or presentation.

____ **7.** A command that moves a copy of the selected text or object to the Clipboard.

____ **8.** A command that removes the selected text or object and stores it in the Clipboard.

____ **9.** To change the appearance of the text.

____ **10.** A menu that displays a list of commands related to the type of object that you right-clicked on.

A Copy

B Cut

C Double-click

D Edit

E Format

F Grid line

G Live Preview

H Page Layout

I Read-only

J Shortcut

Multiple Choice

Choose the correct answer.

1. The flashing vertical line that indicates where text will be inserted when you start typing.
   A. Cell reference
   B. Insertion point
   C. KeyTip

2. A button used to turn a feature both on and off.
   A. Contextual button
   B. On/Off button
   C. Toggle button

3. The box formed by the intersection of a row and column.
   A. Cell
   B. Cell reference
   C. Insertion point

4. Until you save a document, it is stored only here.
   A. Clipboard
   B. Live Preview
   C. RAM

5. The combination of a number on the left side and a letter on the top of a spreadsheet that addresses a cell.
   A. Coordinates
   B. Cell reference
   C. Insertion point

6. A temporary storage area that holds text or an object that has been cut or copied.
   A. Clipboard
   B. Dialog box
   C. Live Preview

7. A toolbar with common formatting buttons that displays after you select text.
   A. Gallery toolbar
   B. Mini toolbar
   C. Taskbar toolbar

8. Informational text that displays when you point to commands or thumbnails on the Ribbon.
   A. Live Preview
   B. ScreenTip
   C. Shortcut menu

9. A visual display of choices from which you can choose.
   A. Gallery
   B. Options menu
   C. Shortcut menu

10. An icon that displays on the Ribbon to indicate the key that you can press to access Ribbon commands.
    A. KeyTip
    B. ScreenTip
    C. ToolTip

Topics for Discussion

1. You have briefly worked with three Microsoft Office programs: Word, Excel, and PowerPoint. Based on your experience, describe the overall purpose of each of these programs.

2. Many believe that computers enable offices to go paperless—that is, to share files electronically instead of printing and then distributing them. What are the advantages of sharing files electronically, and in what situations would it be best to print documents?

Create Workbooks with Excel 2010

▶ Microsoft Office Excel 2010 is used worldwide to create workbooks and to analyze data that is organized into columns and rows.

▶ After data is entered into Excel, you can perform calculations on the numerical data and analyze the data to make informed decisions.

Your starting screen will look similar to this:

SKILLS

Skills 1-10 Training

At the end of this chapter, you will be able to:

Skill 1 Create and Save New Workbooks
Skill 2 Enter Worksheet Data and Merge and Center Titles
Skill 3 Construct Addition and Subtraction Formulas
Skill 4 Construct Multiplication and Division Formulas
Skill 5 Adjust Column Widths and Apply Cell Styles
Skill 6 Use the SUM Function
Skill 7 Copy Formulas and Functions Using the Fill Handle
Skill 8 Format, Edit, and Check the Spelling of Data
Skill 9 Create Footers and Change Page Settings
Skill 10 Display and Print Formulas and Scale Worksheets for Printing

MORE SKILLS

More Skills 11 Create New Workbooks from Templates
More Skills 12 Use Range Names in Formulas
More Skills 13 Change Themes
More Skills 14 Manage Document Properties

Outcome

Using the skills listed to the left will enable you to create
a worksheet like this:

Aspen Falls Parks and Recreation							
Bike Rentals at Aspen Lake Recreation Area							
Location	Children	Adult	Total	Difference	Rental Fee		Total Fees
North	139	51	190	88	$	6	$ 1,140
South	108	60	168	48		7	1,176
Central	153	93	246	60		7	1,722
East	175	82	257	93		10	2,570
West	246	170	416	76		7	2,912
Total	**821**	**456**	**1277**				$ **9,520**
Percent of Adult Bikes Rented							
North	26.8%						
South	35.7%						
Central	37.8%						
East	31.9%						
West	40.9%						

Lastname_Firstname_e01_Bikes.xlsx   4/29/2010   Parks and Recreation

**You will save your
workbook as:**

Lastname_Firstname_e01_Bikes

In this chapter, you will create documents for the Aspen Falls City Hall, which provides essential services for the citizens and visitors of Aspen Falls, California.

Introduction

- ▶ Excel is used to perform calculations on numbers. When you make changes to one or more number values, you can immediately see the effect of those changes in totals and charts that rely on those values.

- ▶ An Excel workbook can contain a large amount of data—up to 16,384 columns and 1,048,576 rows.

- ▶ The basic skills you need to work efficiently with Excel include entering and formatting data, and navigating within Excel.

- ▶ When planning your worksheet, think about what information will form the rows and what information will form the columns. Generally, rows are used to list the items and columns to group or describe the items in the list.

Time to complete all
10 skills – 50 to 90 minutes

Find your student data files here:

Student data file needed for this chapter:

■ New blank Excel workbook

▶ Starting Excel displays a new blank *workbook*—a file that you can use to organize various kinds of related information. A workbook contains *worksheets*, also called *spreadsheets*—the primary document that you use in Excel to store and work with data.

▶ The worksheet forms a grid of vertical columns and horizontal rows. The small box where one column and one row meet is a cell.

1. **Start** ⊕ Microsoft Excel 2010. In the lower right, if necessary, click the **Normal** button 🔲. To the right of the button, notice the zoom—magnification level.

   Your zoom level should be 100%, but most figures in this chapter are zoomed to 130%.

2. Verify the cell in the upper left corner is the *active cell*—the cell outlined in black in which data is entered when you begin typing. Notice that columns have alphabetical headings across the top, and rows have numerical headings down the left side, as shown in **Figure 1**.

   When a cell is active, the headings for the column and row in which the cell is located are highlighted. The column letter and row number that identify a cell is the *cell address*, also called the *cell reference*.

3. In cell **A1**, type Aspen Falls Parks and Recreation and then press Enter to store the entry.

4. In cell **A2**, type Bike Rentals at Aspen Lake Area and then press Enter. Compare your screen with **Figure 2**.

■ **Continue to the next page to complete the skill**

Column headings
Cell reference in Name Box
Column A and row 1 headings highlighted
Active cell
Row headings
Zoom level (yours may be 100%)
Normal view button

Figure 1

Worksheet title and subtitle
Active cell is A3

Figure 2

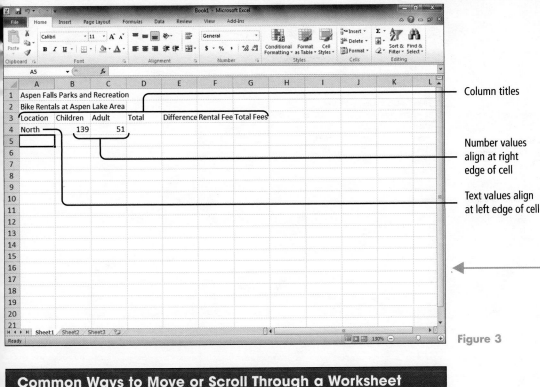

Figure 3

Column titles

Number values align at right edge of cell

Text values align at left edge of cell

Common Ways to Move or Scroll Through a Worksheet

Press	Description
Enter	Move down one row.
Tab	Move one column to the right.
Shift + Tab	Move one column to the left.
↓ ↑ → ←	Move one cell in the direction of the arrow.
Ctrl + Home	Move to cell A1.
Ctrl + End	Move to the lowest row and the column farthest to the right that contains data.

Figure 4

5. Type Location and press Tab to make the cell to the right—**B3**—active.

6. With cell **B3** the active cell, type the following titles, pressing Tab between each title:

Children
Adult
Total
Difference
Rental Fee
Total Fees

Titles above columns help readers understand the data.

To correct typing errors, click a cell and retype the data—the new typing will replace the existing data.

7. Click cell **A4**, type North and then press Tab. Type 139 and press Tab. Type 51 and then press Enter.

Data in a cell is called a *value*. You can have a *text value* (*North*) or a *number value* (*139*). A text value is also referred to as a *label*.

8. Notice that the text values align at the left cell edge, and number values align at the right cell edge, as shown in Figure 3.

9. On the Quick Access Toolbar, click **Save** ⊟. In the **Save As** dialog box, navigate to the location where you are saving your files. Click **New folder**, type Excel Chapter 1 and then press Enter two times. In the **File name** box, using your own name, name the workbook Lastname_ Firstname_e01_Bikes and then press Enter.

Common methods to move between cells in an Excel worksheet are summarized in the table in Figure 4.

■ **You have completed Skill 1 of 10**

► Multiple cells can be selected by dragging so that the selection can be edited, formatted, copied, or moved.

1. In cell **A5**, type Soutth and press Tab. (You will correct the spelling in Skill 8.)

2. In cell **B5**, type 108 and press Tab. In cell **C5**, type 60 and press Enter.

3. In row 6 and row 7, enter the following data:

   Easst   75   32
   West   246   170

4. In cell **A8**, type Total and press Enter. Compare your screen with **Figure 1**.

5. Click cell **B1**, type Worksheet and press Enter. Notice that the text in cell A1 is *truncated*—cut off.

   When text is too long to fit in a cell and the cell to the right of it contains data, the text will be truncated.

6. Click cell **A1**, and then above column D, locate the *formula bar*—a bar below the Ribbon that displays the value contained in the active cell and is used to enter or edit values or formulas. Compare your screen with **Figure 2**.

   Data displayed in a cell is the *displayed value*. Data displayed in the formula bar is the *underlying value*. Displayed values often do not match their underlying values.

7. On the Quick Access Toolbar, click the **Undo** button 🔄 to remove the text in cell B1. Notice that the text in cell A1 now overlaps the cells to the right because those cells are empty.

■ **Continue to the next page to complete the skill**

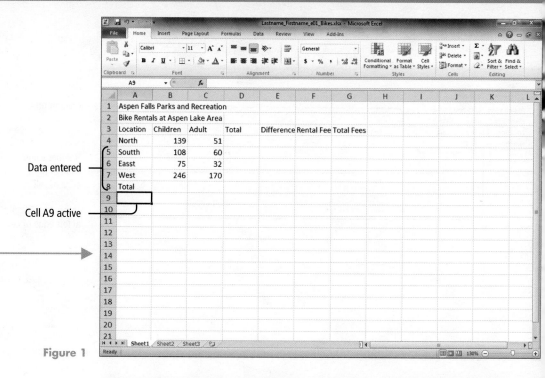

Data entered —

Cell A9 active —

Figure 1

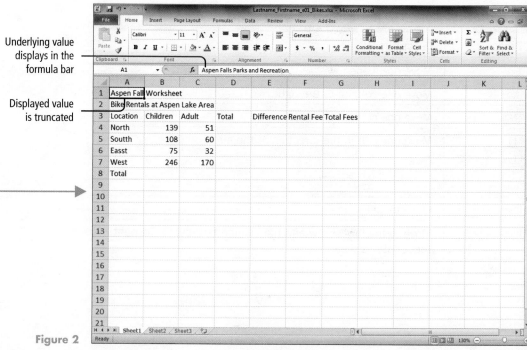

Underlying value displays in the formula bar

Displayed value is truncated

Figure 2

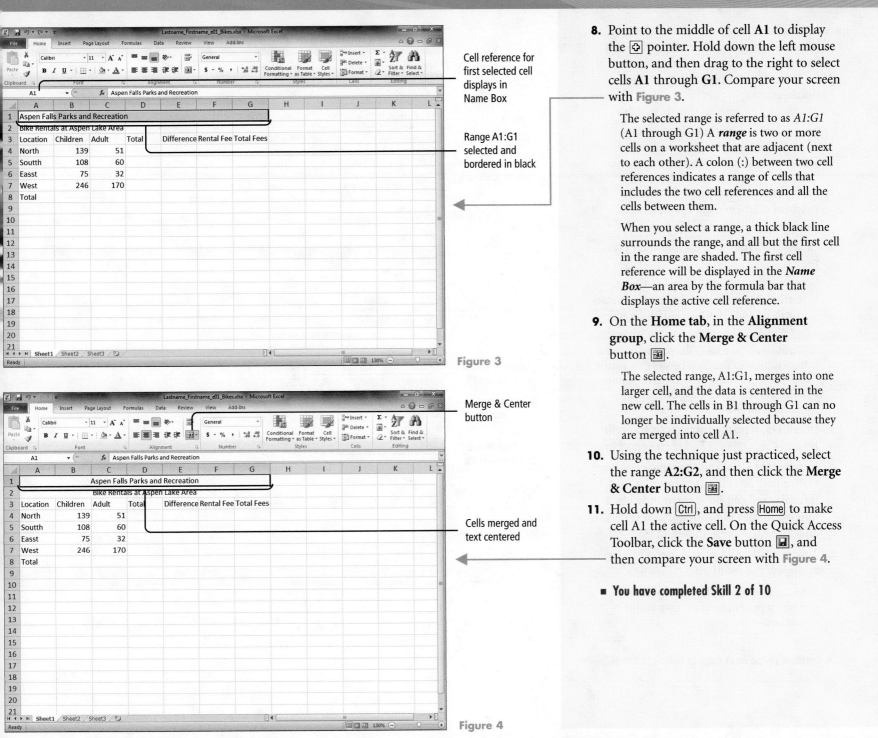

Cell reference for first selected cell displays in Name Box

Range A1:G1 selected and bordered in black

Figure 3

Merge & Center button

Cells merged and text centered

Figure 4

8. Point to the middle of cell **A1** to display the ⊕ pointer. Hold down the left mouse button, and then drag to the right to select cells **A1** through **G1**. Compare your screen with **Figure 3**.

   The selected range is referred to as *A1:G1* (A1 through G1) A *range* is two or more cells on a worksheet that are adjacent (next to each other). A colon (:) between two cell references indicates a range of cells that includes the two cell references and all the cells between them.

   When you select a range, a thick black line surrounds the range, and all but the first cell in the range are shaded. The first cell reference will be displayed in the *Name Box*—an area by the formula bar that displays the active cell reference.

9. On the **Home tab**, in the **Alignment group**, click the **Merge & Center** button ▦.

   The selected range, A1:G1, merges into one larger cell, and the data is centered in the new cell. The cells in B1 through G1 can no longer be individually selected because they are merged into cell A1.

10. Using the technique just practiced, select the range **A2:G2**, and then click the **Merge & Center** button ▦.

11. Hold down Ctrl, and press Home to make cell A1 the active cell. On the Quick Access Toolbar, click the **Save** button ▦, and then compare your screen with **Figure 4**.

■ **You have completed Skill 2 of 10**

► A cell's underlying value can be a text value, a number value, or a formula. A *formula* is an equation that performs mathematical calculations on number values in the worksheet.

► Formulas begin with an equal sign and often include an *arithmetic operator*— a symbol that specifies a mathematical operation such as addition or subtraction.

1. Study the symbols that Excel uses to perform mathematical operations, as summarized in the table in **Figure 1**.

2. In cell **D4**, type =B4+C4 and then press (Enter).

   The total number of bikes rented for the North location equals the sum of the values in cells B4 and C4, which is *190*, the sum of 139 and 51.

   When you type a formula, you might see a brief display of function names that match the first letter you type. This Excel feature, called *Formula AutoComplete*, assists in inserting formulas.

3. In cell **D5**, type the formula to add cells B5 and C5, =B5+C5 and then press (Enter).

4. In cell **D6**, type = and then click cell **B6**. Notice that *B6* is inserted into the formula, and cell **B6** is surrounded by a moving border indicating that it is part of an active formula as shown in **Figure 2**.

5. Type + Click cell **C6**, and then press (Enter) to display the result *107*.

   You can either type formulas or construct them by pointing and clicking in this manner.

■ **Continue to the next page to complete the skill**

Symbols Used in Excel for Arithmetic Operators	
Operator Symbol	**Operation**
+ (plus sign)	Addition
- (minus sign)	Subtraction (also negation)
* (asterisk)	Multiplication
/ (forward slash)	Division
% (percent sign)	Percent
^ (caret)	Exponentiation

Figure 1

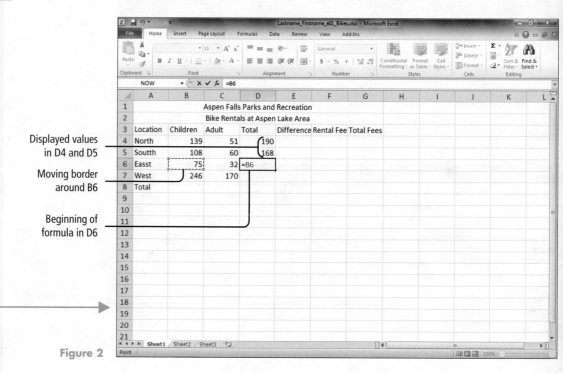

Displayed values in D4 and D5

Moving border around B6

Beginning of formula in D6

Figure 2

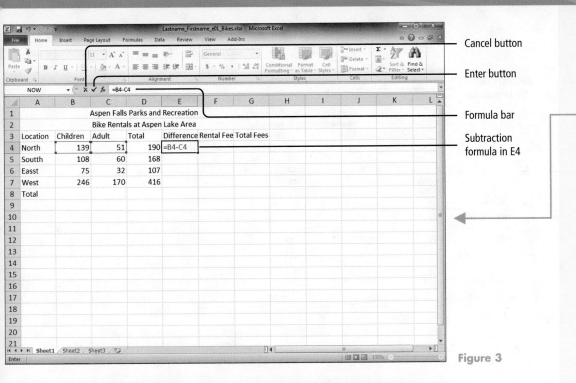

Cancel button

Enter button

Formula bar

Subtraction formula in E4

Figure 3

Data entered

Figure 4

6. In cell **D7**, use point and click to construct a formula that adds cells **B7** and **C7**.

7. In cell **E4**, type =B4-C4 On the **formula bar**, notice that the Cancel and Enter buttons display to the left of the formula as shown in **Figure 3**.

   If you make an error entering a formula, you can click the Cancel button and then start over. Alternately, you can press the [Esc] key.

8. On the **formula bar**, click the **Enter** button ☑ to confirm the entry while keeping cell **E4** the active cell. Notice that the underlying value for cell E4 displays as a formula in the formula bar and the display value, 88, displays in the cell as a result of the formula.

9. In cell **E5**, use point and click to enter the formula =B5-C5 to display the difference for the South location. (You will complete the column E formulas in Skill 7.)

10. Type the following data using the [↓] to move to the next row, and then compare your screen with **Figure 4**.

Cell	Value
F4	6
F5	7
F6	10
F7	7

11. **Save** 🖫 the workbook.

   ■ **You have completed Skill 3 of 10**

► The four most common operators for addition (+), subtraction (-), multiplication (*), and division (/) can be found on the number keypad at the right side of a standard keyboard.

1. In cell **G4**, type =D4*F4—the formula that multiplies the total North bikes rented by its rental fee. On the **formula bar**, click the **Enter** button ✓, and then compare your screen with **Figure 1**.

   The *underlying formula*—the formula as displayed in the formula bar—multiplies the value in cell D4 (*190*)—by the value in cell F4 (*6*) and displays the result in cell G4 (*1140*).

2. In the range **G5:G7**, enter the following formulas:

Cell	Formula
G5	=D5*F5
G6	=D6*F6
G7	=D7*F7

3. In cell **A11**, type Percent of Adult Bikes Rented and then press Enter.

4. Select cells **A11:B11**. On the **Home tab**, in the **Alignment group**, click the **Merge & Center button arrow** 📭, and then on the displayed list, click **Merge Across**. Compare your screen with **Figure 2**.

   Merge Across will merge the selected cells without centering.

■ **Continue to the next page to complete the skill** ➤

Underlying value in the formula bar

Displayed value in G4

Figure 1

Formulas entered into G4:G7

A11:B11 merged with text truncated

Figure 2

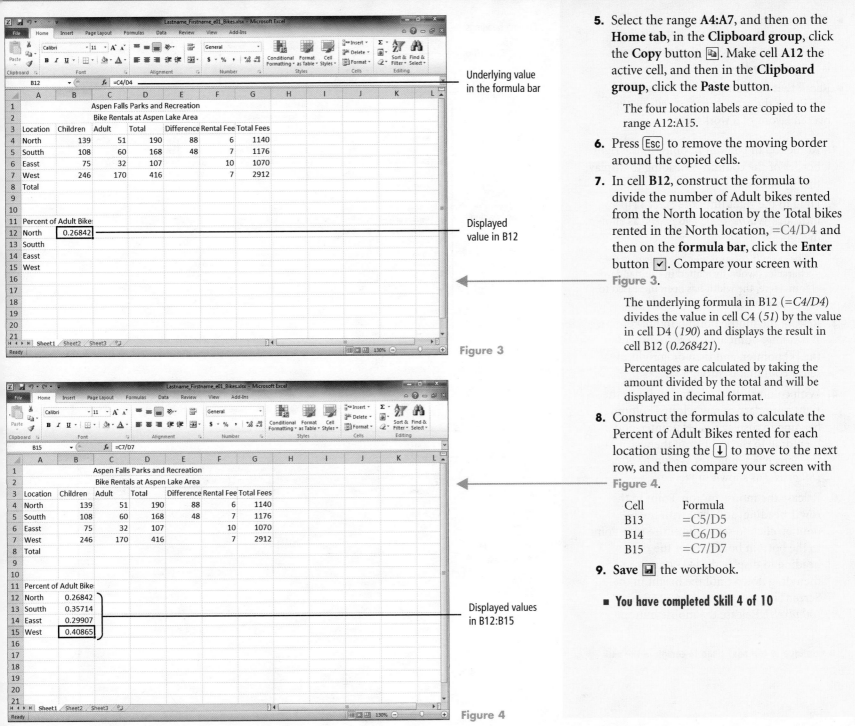

Figure 3

Figure 4

5. Select the range **A4:A7**, and then on the **Home tab**, in the **Clipboard group**, click the **Copy** button. Make cell **A12** the active cell, and then in the **Clipboard group**, click the **Paste** button.

   The four location labels are copied to the range A12:A15.

6. Press [Esc] to remove the moving border around the copied cells.

7. In cell **B12**, construct the formula to divide the number of Adult bikes rented from the North location by the Total bikes rented in the North location, $=C4/D4$ and then on the **formula bar**, click the **Enter** button. Compare your screen with Figure 3.

   The underlying formula in B12 ($=C4/D4$) divides the value in cell C4 (*51*) by the value in cell D4 (*190*) and displays the result in cell B12 (*0.268421*).

   Percentages are calculated by taking the amount divided by the total and will be displayed in decimal format.

8. Construct the formulas to calculate the Percent of Adult Bikes rented for each location using the [↓] to move to the next row, and then compare your screen with Figure 4.

Cell	Formula
B13	$=C5/D5$
B14	$=C6/D6$
B15	$=C7/D7$

9. **Save** the workbook.

■ **You have completed Skill 4 of 10**

► The letter that displays at the top of a column is the *column heading*. The number that displays at the left of a row is the *row heading*.

► Recall that formatting is the process of specifying the appearance of cells or the overall layout of a worksheet.

1. At the top of column **A**, point to the right border of the column **A** heading to display the ⊞ pointer.

2. Drag to the right until the ScreenTip indicates *Width: 13.00 (96 pixels)* as shown in **Figure 1**.

   The default column width will display 8.43 characters when formatted in the standard font. Here, the width has been increased to display more characters.

3. Release the mouse button. In the column **B** heading, point anywhere to display the ↓ pointer, and then drag right to select columns **B** through **G**.

4. With columns **B:G** selected, point to the right boundary of any selected column heading to display the ⊞ pointer, and then drag to the right until the width in the ScreenTip indicates *Width: 12.00 (89 pixels)* as shown in **Figure 2**.

5. Release the mouse button. Point to the row **1** heading, and then with the → pointer, click to select the entire row. Point to the bottom boundary of the row heading to display the ⊞ pointer, and then drag down until the height in the ScreenTip indicates *Height 22.50 (30 pixels)*. Release the mouse button.

■ **Continue to the next page to complete the skill**

Figure 1

Figure 2

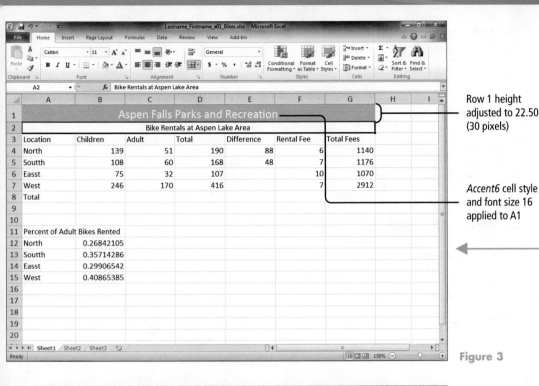

Row 1 height
adjusted to 22.50
(30 pixels)

Accent6 cell style
and font size 16
applied to A1

Figure 3

Italic applied to
cells A3:G3 and
cells A4:A8

40% - Accent6 cell
style applied to A2

Figure 4

6. Click cell **A1**, which is a merged and centered cell. In the **Styles group**, click the **Cell Styles** button. In the **Cell Styles** gallery, under **Titles and Headings**, use Live Preview to view cell **A1** as you point to **Heading 1** and then **Heading 2**.

   A *cell style* is a prebuilt set of formatting characteristics, such as font, font size, font color, cell borders, and cell shading.

7. Under **Themed Cell Styles**, click the **Accent6** style. In the **Font group**, click the **Font Size arrow** [11 ·], and then click **16**. Click cell **A2**, and then compare your screen with **Figure 3**.

8. In cell **A2**, using the technique you just practiced, from the **Cell Styles** gallery, apply the **40% - Accent6** cell style. In the **Font group**, click the **Increase Font Size** button [A] one time to change the font size to **12**.

9. Select the range **A3:G3**. With the [✛] pointer positioned anywhere over the selected range, right-click to display a shortcut menu and the Mini toolbar. On the Mini toolbar, click the **Italic** button [I] to apply italic to the text within each of the selected cells.

10. Select the range **A4:A8**. Display the Mini toolbar, and then apply **Italic** to the selected range. Compare your screen with **Figure 4**.

11. **Save** [💾] the workbook.

■ **You have completed Skill 5 of 10**

► You can create your own formulas, or you can use a *function*—a prewritten Excel formula that takes a value or values, performs an operation, and returns a value or values.

► The Sum button is used to insert common functions into a worksheet.

► When cell references are used in a formula or function, editing the values in those cells results in the formula or function automatically recalculating a new result.

1. Click cell **B8**. In the **Editing group**, click the **Sum** button ∑. Notice that the range **B4:B7** is surrounded by a moving border, and *=SUM(B4:B7)* displays in cell B8 and in the formula bar as shown in **Figure 1**.

   SUM is an Excel function that adds all the numbers in a range of cells. The range in parentheses, *(B4:B7)*, indicates the range of cells on which the SUM function will be performed.

   When the Sum button is used, Excel first looks *above* the selected cell for a suitable range of cells to sum. When no suitable data is detected, Excel then looks to the *left* and proposes a range of cells to sum.

2. Press Enter to display the function result— *568*.

3. Select the range **C8:D8**. On the **Home tab**, in the **Editing group**, click the **Sum** button ∑, and then compare your screen with **Figure 2**.

■ **Continue to the next page to complete the skill**

Sum button

Range of cells to be summed surrounded by moving border

SUM function with range in parentheses

ScreenTip provides additional information about the function

Figure 1

Result of SUM function displays in cells

Figure 2

Underlying SUM function

Displayed value is 6298

Figure 3

B6 and C6 numeric values changed

Total values recalculated

Percent recalculated

Figure 4

4. Click cell **C8**, and then in the formula bar, verify that the SUM function adds the values in the range **C4:C7**.

5. Click cell **D8**, and verify that the SUM function adds the values in the range **D4:D7**.

6. Using the technique just practiced, in cell **G8**, insert the SUM function to add the values in the range **G4:G7**. Select cell **G8**, and then compare your screen with **Figure 3**.

7. In cell **B6**, type 175 Watch the total in cell **B8** update as you press Tab.

    In cell B8, the displayed value changed to 668, but the underlying formula remained the same.

8. In cell **C6**, type 82 and then press Enter to update the values in cells that contain formulas referring to cell C6 as shown in **Figure 4**.

9. **Save** 🔲 the workbook.

■ **You have completed Skill 6 of 10**

► Text, numbers, formulas, and functions can be copied down rows and also across columns to insert formulas and functions quickly.

► When a formula is copied to another cell, Excel adjusts the cell references relative to the new location of the formula.

1. Click cell **E5**.

To use the fill handle, first select the cell that contains the content you want to copy—here the formula =B5-C5.

2. With cell **E5** selected, point to the *fill handle*—the small black square in the lower right corner of the selection—until the ⊞ pointer displays as shown in **Figure 1.**

3. Drag the ⊞ pointer down to cell **E7,** and then release the mouse button.

4. Click cell **E6**, and verify the formula copied from E5 is *=B6-C6.* Click cell **E7,** and verify the copied formula is *=B7-C7* as shown in **Figure 2.**

In each row, Excel copied the formula but adjusted the cell references *relative to* the row number—B5 changed to B6 and then to B7. This adjustment is called a *relative cell reference* because it refers to cells based on their position *in relation to* (relative to) the cell that contains the formula.

■ **Continue to the next page to complete the skill**

⊞ pointer displays over the fill handle of cell E5

Figure 1

B5 changed to *B7* and *C5* changed to *C7*

Figure 2

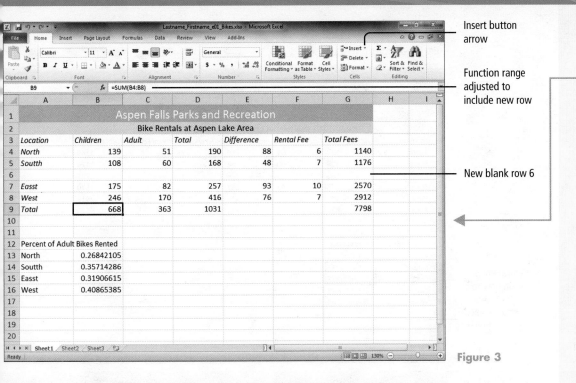

Insert button arrow

Function range adjusted to include new row

New blank row 6

Figure 3

Values in D5:G5 copied to D6:G6

Auto Fill Options button

Number value changes to 8

Figure 4

5. Click cell **A6**. In the **Cells group**, click the **Insert button arrow**, and then click **Insert Sheet Rows**. Click cell **B9**, and then compare your screen with Figure 3.

> The function in cell B9 automatically updates to include the new row.

> When you insert a new row or column, the cell references and the ranges in formulas or in functions adjust to include the new row or column.

6. In cell **A6**, type Central and then press Tab. Notice that the formatting (italic) from cell A7 was applied to the inserted row.

7. In cell **B6**, type 153 and then press Tab to enter the value and update the column total in cell B9 to *821*.

8. In cell **C6**, type 93 and press Tab.

9. Select cells **D5:G5**. Point to the fill handle so that the ⊞ pointer displays, and then drag the ⊞ pointer down one row. Release the mouse button, and notice the Auto Fill Options button ⊞ displays as shown in Figure 4.

> When you copy number values using the fill handle, the numbers automatically increment for each row or column. Here, the number value in cell F5 increased by one when it was copied to cell F6.

10. Click the **Auto Fill Options** button ⊞, and then click **Copy Cells**.

> With the Copy Cells option, number values are literally copied and do not increment. Here, the number value in cell F6 changes to 7.

11. Save 🖫 the workbook.

■ **You have completed Skill 7 of 10**

► Always check spelling after you have finished formatting and editing your worksheet data.

1. Click cell **A15**, and repeat the technique used previously to insert a new row.

2. In cell **A15**, type Central and then press Enter. Click cell **B14**, and then use the fill handle to copy the formula down to cell **B15**. Compare your screen with **Figure 1**.

3. Click cell **A2**. Click in the **formula bar**, and then use the arrow keys to move to the left of the word *Area*. Type Recreation Add a space as needed, and then press Enter.

4. Click cell **F4**, and then with the ⊕ pointer, drag right from cells **F4** to **G4**. Hold down Ctrl, and then click cell **G9**.

    You can select nonadjacent ranges by holding down Ctrl.

5. In the **Styles group**, click the **Cell Styles** button, and then under **Number Format**, click **Currency [0]**.

6. Select the range **B13:B17**. In the **Number group**, click the **Percent Style** button %, and then click the **Increase Decimal** button one time.

    The Increase Decimal and Decrease Decimal buttons do not actually add or remove decimals, but they change how the underlying decimal values *display* in the cells.

7. Select the range **B9:D9**. Hold down Ctrl, and then click cell **G9**. In the **Styles group**, click the **Cell Styles** button. Under **Titles and Headings**, click the **Total** style. Click cell **A10**, and then compare your screen with **Figure 2**.

■ **Continue to the next page to complete the skill**

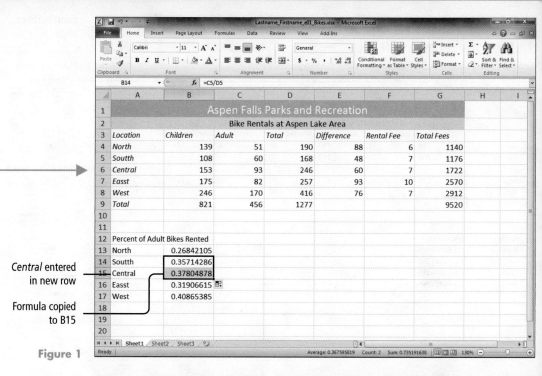

Figure 1

Central entered in new row

Formula copied to B15

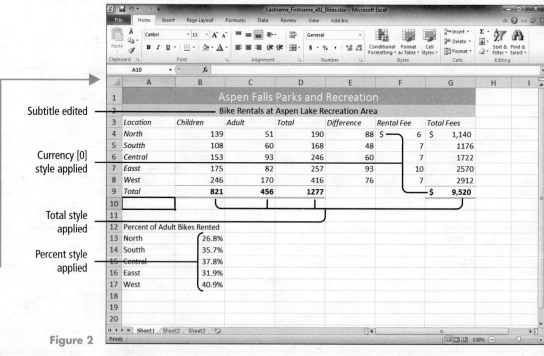

Subtitle edited

Currency [0] style applied

Total style applied

Percent style applied

Figure 2

Spelling dialog box

Word not in Office dictionary

Suggested spelling

Figure 3

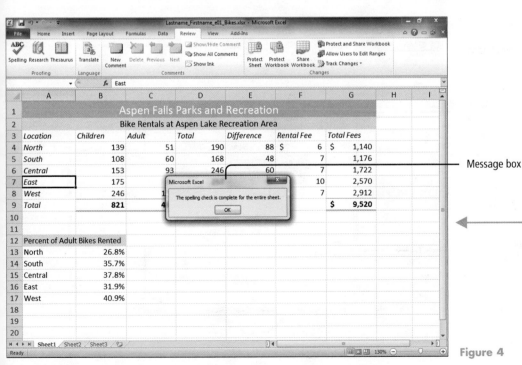

Message box

Figure 4

8. Select the range **G5:G8**. Click the **Cell Styles** button, and then under **Number Format**, click **Comma [0]**. Select cell **A12**. Click the **Cell Styles** button, and then click **40% - Accent6**.

9. Press Ctrl + Home to make cell **A1** active. On the **Review tab**, in the **Proofing group**, click the **Spelling** button.

> The Spelling checker starts with the active cell and moves to the right and down, so making cell A1 the active cell before beginning is useful.

10. In the **Spelling** dialog box, under **Not in Dictionary**, notice the word *Soutth*, as shown in Figure 3.

> This word is not in the Office dictionary; however, words not in the dictionary are not necessarily misspelled. Many proper nouns or less commonly used words are not in the Office dictionary.

11. Under **Suggestions**, verify that the correct spelling, *South*, is selected, and then click the **Change** button to correct the spelling and to move to the next word not in the Office dictionary.

12. Under **Suggestions**, verify that the correct spelling, *East*, is selected, and then click the **Change All** button to correct its spelling in the entire worksheet.

13. Continue to use the Spelling checker to correct any remaining errors. When the message **The spelling check is complete for the entire sheet** displays, as shown in Figure 4, click **OK**.

> When words you use often are not in the Office dictionary, you can click *Add to Dictionary* to add them.

14. Save the workbook.

■ **You have completed Skill 8 of 10**

► In Excel, *Page Layout view* is used to change the page orientation, work with page headers and footers, or set margins for printing.

1. Click the **Insert tab**, and then in the **Text group**, click the **Header & Footer** button to switch to **Page Layout view** and to open the Header area.

2. On the **Design tab**, in the **Navigation group**, click the **Go to Footer** button to move to the Footer area. Click just above the word *Footer* to place the insertion point in the left section of the Footer area. Compare your screen with **Figure 1**.

3. In the **Header & Footer Elements group**, click the **File Name** button to insert the *&[File]* placeholder into the left section of the Footer area.

   Predefined headers and footers insert placeholders with instructions for printing. Here, the *&[File]* placeholder instructs Excel to insert the file name when the worksheet is printed.

4. Click in the middle section of the Footer area, and then click the **Current Date** button. Click the right section of the Footer area, and type Parks and Recreation Click in a cell just above the footer to exit the Footer area.

5. Click the **Page Layout tab**. In the **Sheet Options group**, under **Gridlines**, select the **Print** check box. In the **Page Setup group**, click the **Margins** button, and then below the **Margins** gallery, click **Custom Margins**. In the **Page Setup** dialog box, under **Center on page**, select the **Horizontally** check box, and then compare your screen with **Figure 2**.

■ **Continue to the next page to complete the skill** ▶

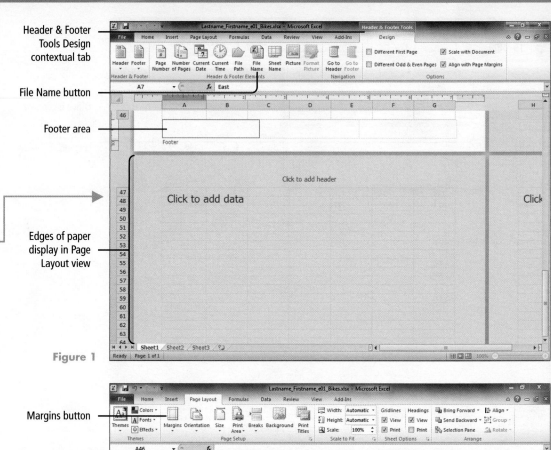

Header & Footer Tools Design contextual tab

File Name button

Footer area

Edges of paper display in Page Layout view

Figure 1

Margins button

Page Setup dialog box

Horizontally check box selected

Figure 2

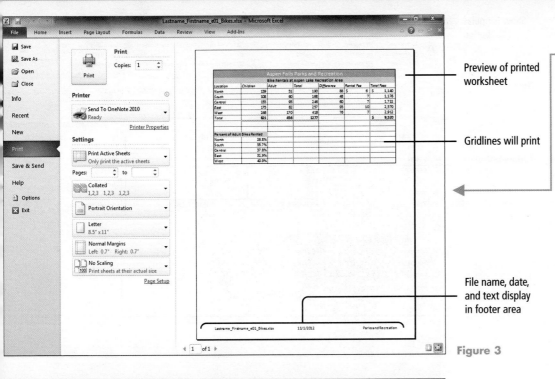

Preview of printed worksheet

Gridlines will print

File name, date, and text display in footer area

Figure 3

Page break—dotted line

Sheet1 renamed

Sheet2 and Sheet3 deleted

Normal button on status bar

Figure 4

6. In the **Page Setup** dialog box, click **Print Preview**, and then compare your screen with **Figure 3**.

In the Backstage, the Print page displays a preview of the worksheet and is used to modify print settings.

7. Click the **Home** tab. On the lower right side of the status bar, click the **Normal** button ▦ to return to Normal view, and then press Ctrl + Home.

Normal view maximizes the number of cells visible on the screen. The page break—the dotted line between columns G and H—indicates where one page ends and a new page begins.

8. At the bottom of your worksheet, click the **Sheet2 sheet tab** to display **Sheet2**. Hold down Ctrl, and then click the **Sheet3 sheet tab**. On the **Home tab**, in the **Cells group**, click the **Delete button arrow**, and then click **Delete Sheet**.

Deleting unused worksheets saves storage space and removes any doubt that additional information is in the workbook. When you delete a worksheet with data, Excel displays a warning so you can cancel the deletion.

9. At the bottom of your worksheet, right-click the **Sheet1 sheet tab**, and then from the shortcut menu, click **Rename**. Type Bike Rentals and then press Enter. Compare your screen with **Figure 4**.

10. **Save** ▦ the workbook. Click the **File tab**, and then click **Print**. If you are directed by your instructor to print, click the Print button.

■ **You have completed Skill 9 of 10**

► Underlying formulas and functions can be displayed and printed.

► When formulas are displayed in cells, the orientation and worksheet scale might need to be changed so that the worksheet prints on a single page.

1. Click the **Formulas tab,** and then in the **Formula Auditing group,** click the **Show Formulas** button to display the underlying formulas in the cells as shown in **Figure 1.**

   Columns often become wider when formulas are displayed. Here, the printed worksheet extends to a second page.

2. Display the **Page Layout tab.** Click the **Page Setup Dialog Box Launcher** ☐. In the **Page Setup** dialog box, click the **Print Preview** button.

   Below the preview of the printed page, *1 of 3* indicates that the worksheet will print on three pages.

3. In the Backstage, on the bottom of the Print page, click the **Next Page** button ▶ two times to view the second and the third pages. Compare your screen with **Figure 2.**

4. On the **Print** page, under **Settings,** click the **Portrait Orientation** button, and then click **Landscape Orientation** so that the orientation will be wider than it is tall.

■ **Continue to the next page to complete the skill**

Show Formulas button

Formulas display in cells

Page break

Figure 1

Page 3 of 3

Figure 2

Page Layout tab

Width button arrow

Height button arrow

Figure 3

5. Click the **Page Layout tab**. In the **Scale to Fit group**, click the **Width button arrow**, and then click **1 page**. Click the **Height button arrow**, and then click **1 page**. The scaling is one page wide by one page tall as shown in **Figure 3**.

Scaling adjusts the size of the printed worksheet to fit on the number of pages that you specify.

6. Click the **File tab**, and then click **Print**. Compare your screen with **Figure 4**.

1 of 1 displays at the bottom middle of the Print page to notify you that the worksheet will now print on one page.

7. If you are directed by your instructor to submit a printout of your formulas, click the **Print** button.

8. Click the **Formulas** tab. In the **Formula Auditing** group, click the **Show Formulas** button.

The values are displayed.

9. Save 🔲 the workbook, and then **Close** Excel.

10. Submit your printouts or file as directed by your instructor.

Done! You have completed Skill 10 of 10 and your document is complete!

Preview of printed worksheet

Formulas display on single page

Landscape orientation applied

Figure 4

The following More Skills are located at **www.pearsonhighered.com/skills**

More Skills Create New Workbooks from Templates

Templates are used to build workbooks without having to start from scratch. You can save one of your own workbooks as a template to use again, or you can download one of many predefined templates from Microsoft Office Online.

In More Skills 11, you will modify a Time Card template downloaded from Microsoft Office Online and then use the template to create a new weekly time card.

To begin, open your web browser, navigate to www.pearsonhighered.com/skills, locate the name of your textbook, and then follow the instructions on the website.

More Skills 12 Use Range Names in Formulas

Instead of using cell references in formulas and functions, you can assign names that refer to the same cell or range. Range names can be easier to remember than cell references, and they can add meaning to formulas, making them easier for you and others to understand.

In More Skills 12, you will open a workbook and practice various ways to name cell ranges. You will then use the names in formulas.

To begin, open your web browser, navigate to www.pearsonhighered.com/skills, locate the name of your textbook, and then follow the instructions on the website.

More Skills 13 Change Themes

Office themes are used to apply a coordinated set of colors, fonts, and graphic effects with a single click. You can use the Office themes, which were developed by graphics professionals, to provide a consistent and polished look and feel for all of your worksheets.

In More Skills 13, you will open a workbook, examine various Office themes, and then change the theme of the worksheet.

To begin, open your web browser, navigate to www.pearsonhighered.com/skills, locate the name of your textbook, and then follow the instructions on the website.

More Skills 14 Manage Document Properties

Document properties are the detailed information about your workbook that can help you identify or organize your files, including the name of the author, the title, and keywords. Some workbook properties are added to the workbook when you create it. You can add others as necessary.

In More Skills 14, you will open a workbook, open the Document Information Panel, and add document properties.

To begin, open your web browser, navigate to www.pearsonhighered.com/skills, locate the name of your textbook, and then follow the instructions on the website.

Key Terms

Online Help Skills

1. Start ● Excel. In the upper right corner of the Excel window, click the Help button ●. In the Help window, click the Maximize ● button.

2. Click in the search box, type insert columns and then click the Search button ●. In the search results, click **Insert or delete cells, rows, and columns**.

3. Read the article's introduction, and then below in this article, click **Insert columns on a worksheet**. Compare your screen with Figure 1.

Figure 1

4. Read the section to see if you can answer the following: Explain how to insert multiple columns and why you might use this feature.

Matching

Match each term in the second column with its correct definition in the first column by writing the letter of the term on the blank line in front of the correct definition.

____ **1.** An Excel file that contains one or more worksheets.

____ **2.** The primary document that you use in Excel to store and work with data, and which is formatted as a pattern of uniformly spaced horizontal and vertical lines.

____ **3.** Another name for a worksheet.

____ **4.** The cell, surrounded by a black border, ready to receive data or be affected by the next Excel command.

____ **5.** The identification of a specific cell by its intersecting column letter and row number.

____ **6.** Data in a cell—text or numbers.

____ **7.** Data in a cell made up of text only.

____ **8.** Data in a cell made up of numbers only.

____ **9.** Another name for a text value.

____ **10.** An Excel window area that displays the address of a selected cell.

A Active cell

B Cell reference

C Label

D Name Box

E Number value

F Spreadsheet

G Text value

H Value

I Workbook

J Worksheet

Multiple Choice

Choose the correct answer.

1. The data displayed in a cell.
   A. Viewed value
   B. Inspected value
   C. Displayed value

2. An equation that performs mathematical calculations on number values.
   A. Method
   B. Formula
   C. System

3. A view that maximizes the number of cells visible on the screen.
   A. Page Layout view
   B. Standard view
   C. Normal view

4. The column letter and row number that identify a cell.
   A. Cell window
   B. Cell address
   C. Cell file name

5. An Excel window area that displays the value contained in the active cell.
   A. Formula bar
   B. Workbook
   C. Name Box

6. Symbols that specify mathematical operations such as addition or subtraction.
   A. Hyperlinks
   B. Bookmarks
   C. Arithmetic operators

7. The number that displays at the left of a row.
   A. Row heading
   B. Row name
   C. Row border

8. A prewritten Excel formula.
   A. A formula
   B. A function
   C. An exponent

9. The small black square in the lower right corner of the active cell.
   A. Border
   B. Fill handle
   C. Edge

10. Page headers and footers can be changed in this view.
    A. Print preview
    B. Page Layout view
    C. Normal view

Topics for Discussion

1. What is the advantage of using cell references instead of actual number values in formulas and functions?

2. What are some things you can do to make your worksheet easier for others to read and understand?

According to the Introduction to this chapter, how do you decide which information to put in columns and which to put in rows?

Skill Check

To complete this project, you will need the following file:

- New blank Excel document

You will save your workbook as:

- Lastname_Firstname_e01_Sales

Figure 1

1. **Start** Excel. In cell **A1**, type Aspen Falls Parks and Recreation and then in cell **A2**, type Concession Sales at Durango County Park In cell **A3**, type Location and then pressing [Tab] after each title, type Food, Drinks, Total Sales, and Difference.

2. In rows **4** through **8**, enter the following data starting in cell **A4**:

Carol's Ice Cream	5794	3448	Joe's Candy	5821	4721
Jerry's Fudge	3950	2520	Alice's Fresh Fruit	9515	8661
Ray's Tacos	7488	7015			

3. In cell **D4**, type =B4+C4 and then in cell **E4**, type =B4-C4 Select the range **D4:E4**. Point to the fill handle, and then drag down through row **8**. Compare your screen with Figure 1.

4. **Save** the workbook in your **Excel Chapter 1** folder with the name Lastname_ Firstname_e01_Sales

5. On the **Insert tab**, in the **Text group**, click the **Header & Footer** button. In the **Navigation group**, click the **Go to Footer** button, and then click in the left footer. In the **Header & Footer Elements group**, click the **File Name** button. Click in a cell just above the footer. On the lower right side of the status bar, click the **Normal** button. Press [Ctrl] + [Home].

6. In cell **A9**, type Totals and then select the range **B9:D9**. On the **Home tab**, in the **Editing group**, click the **Sum** button.

7. Select cell **A7**. In the **Cells group**, click the **Insert button arrow**, and then click **Insert Sheet Rows**. In the new row **7**, type the data David's Biscotti, 7183, and 5492

8. Select the range **D6:E6**, and then use the fill handle to copy the formulas down one row.

9. In cell **A13**, type Drinks as a Percent of Total Sales

10. Select the range **A4:A9**, and then on the **Home tab**, in the **Clipboard group**, click the **Copy** button. Click cell **A14**, and then in the **Clipboard group**, click the **Paste** button. Press [Esc], and then compare your screen with Figure 2.

Figure 2

■ Continue to the next page to complete this Skill Check ▶

Figure 3

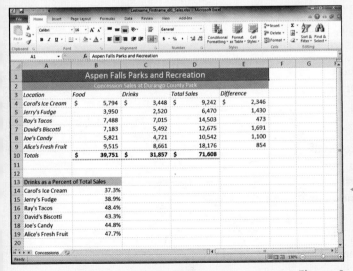

Figure 4

11. In cell **B14**, type =C4/D4 and then on the formula bar, click the **Enter** button. In cell **B14**, use the fill handle to copy the formula down through row **19**. Compare your screen with **Figure 3**.

12. Select the range **A1:E1**, and then on the **Home tab**, in the **Alignment group**, click the **Merge & Center** button. In the **Styles group**, click the **Cell Styles** button, and then click **Accent4**. In the **Font group**, click the **Font Size arrow**, and then click **16**. Select the range **A2:E2**, and then in the **Alignment group**, click the **Merge & Center** button. Click the **Cell Styles** button, and then click **60% - Accent4**.

13. Select columns **A:E**, point to the right boundary of any selected column heading, drag to a column width of *16.00 (117 pixels)*, and then release the mouse button.

14. Select the range **A3:E3**. Hold down ⌈Ctrl⌉, and then select the range **A4:A10**. In the **Font group**, click the **Italic** button.

15. Select range **B4:E4**. Hold down ⌈Ctrl⌉, and then select the range **B10:D10**. In the **Styles group**, click the **Cell Styles** button, and then click **Currency [0]**. Select the range **B10:D10**. Click the **Cell Styles** button, and then click the **Total** style. Select the range **B5:E9**, click the **Cell Styles** button, and then click **Comma [0]**.

16. Select the range **A13:B13**. In the **Alignment group**, click the **Merge & Center button arrow**, and then click **Merge Across**. Click the **Cell Styles** button, and then click **40% - Accent4**.

17. Select the range **B14:B19**. In the **Number group**, click the **Percent Style** button, and then click the **Increase Decimal** button one time.

18. Press ⌈Ctrl⌉ + ⌈Home⌉. On the **Review tab**, in the **Proofing group**, click the **Spelling** button, and then correct any spelling errors.

19. Click the **Sheet2 sheet tab**. Hold down ⌈Ctrl⌉, and then click the **Sheet3 sheet tab**. On the **Home tab**, in the **Cells group**, click the **Delete button arrow**, and then click **Delete Sheet**.

20. Right-click the **Sheet1 sheet tab**, and from the shortcut menu, click **Rename**. Type Concessions and then press ⌈Enter⌉. **Save**, and then compare your screen with **Figure 4**. If asked by your instructor, print the worksheet. If asked by your instructor, display and format the worksheet formulas as described in Skill 10, and then print the worksheet.

21. **Exit** Excel. Submit the printouts or file as directed by your instructor.

Done! You have completed the Skill Check

Assess Your Skills 1

To complete this project, you will need the following file:

- e01_Fees

You will save your workbook as:

- Lastname_Firstname_e01_Fees

1. **Start** Excel. From your student data files, open **e01_Fees**. Save the workbook in your **Excel Chapter 1** folder as Lastname_Firstname_e01_Fees Add the file name to the worksheet's left footer, add the current date to the center footer, and then type **Tax Rates** in the right footer. Return to **Normal** view.

2. For the range **A1:E1**, merge and center and apply the **Accent5** cell style. Increase the font size to **18** points. For the range **A2:E2**, merge and center and apply the **40% - Accent5** cell style. Widen column **A** to 20.00 (145 pixels). For all column and row titles, apply **Italic**.

3. For the range **E5:E13**, insert the **SUM** function to add the three fees for each row. In the range **B14:E14**, insert the **SUM** function to provide totals for each column.

4. Select the nonadjacent ranges **B5:E5** and **B14:E14**. Apply the **Currency [0]** cell style.

5. Select the range **B6:E13**, and then apply the **Comma [0]** cell style. Select the range **B14:E14**, and then apply the **Total** cell style.

6. Insert a new row above row **7**. In cell **A7**, type Silkworth Hiking Area and as the fees for the new location, type 14257 and 9625 and 10925 Use the fill handle to copy the formula in cell **E6** to cell **E7**.

7. **Copy** the location names from the range **A5:A14** to the range **A20:A29**.

8. In cell **B19**, type New Tax Rate In cells **B20** and **B21**, type .03 In cells **B22** and **B23**, type .05 and in cell **B24**, type .06 Use the fill handle to copy the value in cell **B24** down through cell **B29**. Select the range **B20:B29**, and then apply the **Percent Style** number format.

9. In cell **C19**, type New Tax Collections In cell **C20**, enter a formula that calculates the new tax charged by the city by multiplying cell **E5** by cell **B20**. In cell **C20**, use the fill handle to copy the formula down through cell **C29**.

10. Rename the **Sheet1** sheet tab as City Fees and then delete **Sheet2** and **Sheet3**.

11. Use **Page Setup** to center the worksheet **Horizontally**. Set the **Gridlines** to print.

12. Check and correct any spelling errors, ignoring the proper names.

13. Print or submit the workbook electronically as directed by your instructor. If you are instructed to do so, display the worksheet formulas, scale the worksheet to print on one page, and then print.

14. Compare your completed worksheet with Figure 1. **Save** the workbook, and then **Exit** Excel.

Done! You have completed Assess Your Skills 1

Aspen Falls			
Annual Collection of City Fees			

Location	Entrance Fees	Overnight Fees	Parking Fees	Total Fees
Aspen Lakes	$ 16,593	$ 9,385	$ 13,618	$ 39,596
Behrendt Park	14,093	6,965	10,885	31,943
Silkworth Hiking Area	14,257	9,625	10,925	34,807
Hansen Hills	15,182	7,775	13,446	36,403
Terry Park	14,621	5,695	12,437	32,753
Cornish Forest	17,178	7,645	13,971	38,794
Schroder Picnic Area	16,418	-	16,927	33,345
Hamilton Hills Park	13,668	9,253	19,344	42,265
Rodman Biking Path	13,136	-	20,367	33,503
Haack Scuba Center	14,622	-	17,560	32,182
Total	$ 149,768	$ 56,343	$ 149,480	$ 355,591

	New Tax Rate	New Tax Collections	
Aspen Lakes	3%	$ 1,187.88	
Behrendt Park	3%	$ 958.29	
Silkworth Hiking Area	5%	$ 1,740.35	
Hansen Hills	5%	$ 1,820.15	
Terry Park	6%	$ 1,965.18	
Cornish Forest	6%	$ 2,327.64	
Schroder Picnic Area	6%	$ 2,000.70	
Hamilton Hills Park	6%	$ 2,535.90	
Rodman Biking Path	6%	$ 2,010.18	
Haack Scuba Center	6%	$ 1,930.92	

Lastname_Firstname_e01_Fees.xlsx   4/29/2010   Tax Rates

Figure 1

Assessment

Assess Your Skills 3 and 4 can be found at
www.pearsonhighered.com/skills.

Assess Your Skills 2

To complete this project, you will need the following file:

- e01_Visitors

You will save your workbook as:

- **Lastname_Firstname_e01_Visitors**

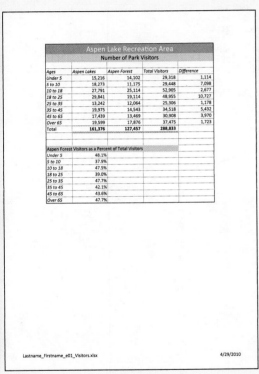

Figure 1

1. **Start** Excel. From the student data files, open **e01_Visitors**. Save the workbook in your **Excel Chapter 1** folder as Lastname_Firstname_e01_Visitors Add the file name to the worksheet's left footer, and then add the Current Date to the right footer. Return to **Normal** view.

2. In cell **D5**, construct a formula to add cells **B5** and **C5**. In cell **E5**, construct a formula to subtract cell **C5** from **B5**. Use the fill handle to copy the formulas in **D5:E5** down through row **11**.

3. In cell **A12**, type Total and then in row **12**, insert the SUM function to total columns **B:D**.

4. Insert a new row above row **7**, and then in the new cell, **A7**, type 10 to 18 In cell **B7**, type 27791 and in cell **C7** type 25114

5. Use the fill handle to copy the formulas in the range **D6:E6** down one row.

6. Merge and center the range **A1:E1**, and then apply the **Accent3** cell style. Increase the font size to **18**. Merge and center the range **A2:E2**, and then apply the **40%-Accent3** cell style. Increase the font size to **14**.

7. Widen column **A** to *10.00 (75 pixels)*, and then widen columns **B:E** to *14.00 (103 pixels)*.

8. For the column and row titles, apply **Italic**. In the range **B5:E13**, apply the **Comma [0]** cell style, and then in range **B13:D13**, apply the **Total** cell style.

9. In cell **A16**, type Aspen Forest Visitors as a Percent of Total Visitors For the range **A16:D16**, apply the **Merge Across** alignment and the **40%-Accent3** cell style.

10. **Copy** the age groups from the range **A5:A12**, and **Paste** them to the range **A17:A24**.

11. In cell **B17**, construct a formula to divide *Aspen Forest* visitors—cell **C5** by *Total Visitors*—cell **D5**. In cell **B17**, apply the **Percent** number style and display one decimal. Use the fill handle to copy the formula down through row **24**.

12. Rename the sheet tab Park Visitors and then delete the worksheets **Sheet2** and **Sheet3**.

13. Check and correct any spelling errors.

14. Use Page Setup to center the page **Horizontally**. Set the **Gridlines** to print, and then **Save** the workbook.

15. Print or submit the workbook electronically as directed by your instructor. If you are instructed to do so, display the worksheet formulas, scale the worksheet to print on one page, and then print.

16. Compare your completed worksheet with Figure 1. **Save** and then **Exit** Excel.

Done! You have completed Assess Your Skills 2

Assess Your Skills Visually

To complete this project, you will need the following file:

- New blank Excel workbook

You will save your workbook as:

- Lastname_Firstname_e01_Boats

Open a new blank workbook, and then **Save** the workbook as Lastname_Firstname_e01_Boats Create the worksheet shown in Figure 1. The width of column A is 14.00 (103 pixels) and the width of columns B:F is 11.00 (82 pixels). Construct formulas that display the results shown in columns D and F, row 11, and the range B15:B21. The title uses the **Accent6** cell style, and the font size is **14**. The subtitle uses the **40%-Accent6** cell style, and the font size is **12**. The title and subtitle should be merged and centered. Using Figure 1 as your guide, apply the **Currency[0]** cell style, the **Comma [0]** cell style, the **Total** cell style, the **Percent** number style, and the **Italic** format. On the range **A14:C14**, use Merge Across and apply the **40%-Accent6** cell style. Rename the Sheet1 sheet tab as Boat Rentals and delete any unused worksheets. Check and correct any spelling errors. Add the file name to the left footer. **Save** the workbook, and then print or submit the file as directed by your instructor.

Done! You have completed Assess Your Skills Visually

Aspen Falls Parks and Recreation						
Hourly Boat Rentals at Aspen Lake Recreation Area						
Location	Canoes	Kayaks	Total Hours	Hourly Fee		Total Fees
North	178	175	353	$	50	$ 17,650
South	251	158	409		60	24,540
Central	112	148	260		75	19,500
Main Entrance	401	370	771		80	61,680
Kid's Corner	491	296	787		40	31,480
East	292	189	481		50	24,050
West	143	193	336		50	16,800
Total	1,868	1,529	3,397			$ 195,700

Canoe Hours as a Percent of Total Hours	
North	50.4%
South	61.4%
Central	43.1%
Main Entrance	52.0%
Kid's Corner	62.4%
East	60.7%
West	42.6%

Lastname_Firstname_e01_Boats.xlsx

Figure 1

Skills in Context

To complete this project, you will need the following file:

- e01_Employees

You will save your workbook as:

- Lastname_Firstname_e01_Employees

Open the workbook **e01_Employees**, and then save the workbook as Lastname_Firstname_e01_Employees The city of Aspen Falls wants to total and compare the number of employees at its recreation areas. Using the skills you practiced in this chapter, insert formulas that calculate the total workers for each park, the total workers in each job category, and the Aspen Lakes employees as a percentage of the total employees. Format the worksheet as appropriate, and adjust column widths as necessary to display all data. Insert the file name in the footer, and check for spelling errors. Save the workbook, and then print or submit the file as directed by your instructor.

Done! You have completed Skills in Context

Skills and You

To complete this project, you will need the following file:

- New blank Excel workbook

You will save your workbook as:

- Lastname_Firstname_e01_My_College

Select six popular courses at your college, for example, *Algebra, Introduction to Computers, Biology, American History*, and so on. Consult your college's course schedule, and note the number of sections for each course that are offered in the Fall term and in the Spring term. Using the skills you have practiced in this chapter, create a worksheet to calculate the total number of sections for each course. SUM the total number of courses for the Fall term and for the Spring term. Below this data, calculate the Fall sections of each course as a percentage of the total courses offered by your school. Add appropriate titles and formatting. Save the workbook as Lastname_Firstname_e01_My_College and then add the file name to the left footer. Delete unused worksheets, check the worksheet for spelling, and then save the workbook. Print or submit the file as directed by your instructor.

Done! You have completed Skills and You

Create Charts

▶ After data is entered into Excel, you can create a visual representation of the data in the form of charts. Excel provides various types of charts that can make your data easier to understand—for example, pie charts show the size of items proportional to the sum of the items.

▶ Charts can be enhanced with effects such as 3-D and soft shadows to create compelling graphical summaries.

Your starting screen will look similar to this:

SKILLS

Skills 1-10 Training

At the end of this chapter, you will be able to:

Skill 1 Open Existing Workbooks and Align Text

Skill 2 Construct and Copy Formulas Containing Absolute Cell References

Skill 3 Format Numbers

Skill 4 Create Column Charts

Skill 5 Format Column Charts

Skill 6 Create Pie Charts and Chart Sheets

Skill 7 Apply 3-D Effects and Rotate Pie Chart Slices

Skill 8 Explode and Color Pie Slices, and Insert Text Boxes

Skill 9 Update Charts and Insert WordArt

Skill 10 Prepare Chart Sheets for Printing

MORE SKILLS

More Skills 11 Insert and Edit Comments

More Skills 12 Change Chart Types

More Skills 13 Copy Excel Data to Word Documents

More Skills 14 Fill Series Data into Worksheet Cells

Outcome

Using the skills listed to the left will enable you to create a worksheet and charts like these:

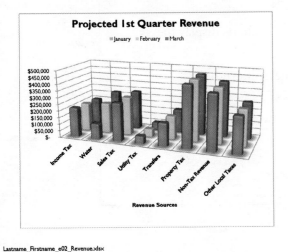

Aspen Falls

Projected 1st Quarter Revenue

Revenue	January	February	March	Quarter Total	Percent of Quarter Revenue
Income Tax	$ 218,000	$ 210,000	$ 205,000	$ 633,000	10.2%
Water	113,000	225,000	275,000	613,000	9.9%
Sales Tax	283,000	285,000	290,000	858,000	13.8%
Utility Tax	56,000	57,000	58,000	171,000	2.8%
Transfers	170,000	172,000	174,000	516,000	8.3%
Property Tax	453,000	455,000	457,000	1,365,000	22.0%
Non-Tax Revenue	405,000	410,000	415,000	1,230,000	19.8%
Other Local Taxes	268,000	270,000	275,000	813,000	13.1%
Total Revenue	$ 1,966,000	$ 2,084,000	$ 2,149,000	$ 6,199,000	

Lastname_Firstname_e02_Revenue.xlsx

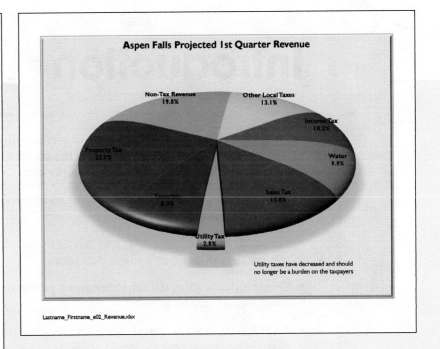

Lastname_Firstname_e02_Revenue.xlsx

You will save your workbook as:

Lastname_Firstname_e02_Revenue

In this chapter, you will create documents for the Aspen Falls City Hall, which provides essential services for the citizens and visitors of Aspen Falls, California.

Introduction

▶ Excel helps you find errors by displaying error values, such as #### when a column is not wide enough to display the content, or #DIV/0! when a formula's divisor is 0 or refers to an empty cell.

▶ Excel provides various number formats so that you can format the worksheet with proper accounting format.

▶ Pie charts illustrate how each part relates to the whole. Pie charts display the relative sizes of items in a single data series.

▶ Column charts show data changes over a period of time or illustrate comparisons among items.

▶ A spreadsheet can be quickly formatted by changing its overall theme or by changing its theme colors, fonts, or effects.

**Time to complete all
10 skills – 50 to 90 minutes**

Find your student data files here:

**Student data file needed
for this chapter:**

■ e02_Revenue

▶ The *Text wrap* format displays text on multiple lines within a cell.

▶ A *document theme*—a set of design elements that provides a unified look for colors, fonts, and graphics—can be applied to a workbook.

1. Start ● Excel. Click the **File tab**, and then click **Open**. In the **Open** dialog box, navigate to your student data files. Select **e02_Revenue**, and then click the **Open** button. Compare your screen with **Figure 1**.

2. Click the **File tab**, and then click **Save As**. Navigate to the location where you are saving your files, create a folder named Excel Chapter 2 and then **Save** the workbook as Lastname_Firstname_e02_Revenue

3. Click the **Insert tab**, and then in the **Text group**, click the **Header & Footer** button. In the **Navigation group**, click the **Go to Footer** button. Click just above the word **Footer**, and then in the **Header & Footer Elements group**, click the **File Name** button. Click a cell above the footer. On the status bar, click the **Normal** button 🔳, and then press Ctrl + Home.

4. In the column heading area, point to the right boundary of column **A** to display the ⊞ pointer, as shown in **Figure 2**.

5. With the ⊞ pointer displayed, double-click to *AutoFit* the column—auto-matically change the column width to accommodate the longest entry.

■ **Continue to the next page to complete the skill** ➡

Cell E2 text is truncated

Column is too narrow to display values

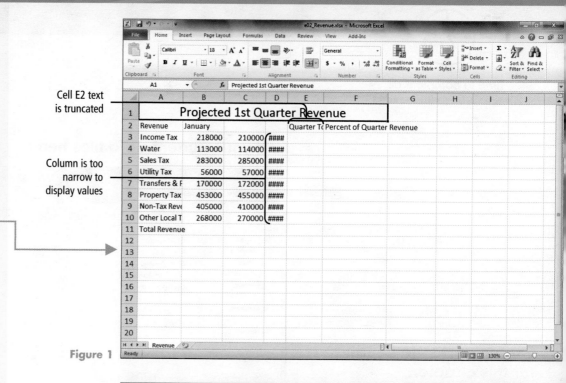

Figure 1

Right column boundary and ⊞ pointer

Figure 2

Figure 3

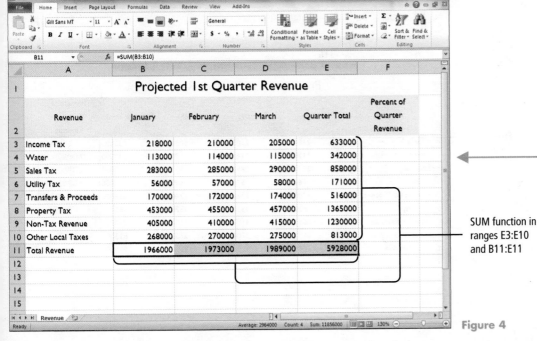

SUM function in ranges E3:E10 and B11:E11

Figure 4

6. In the column heading area, select columns **B:F**. In the **Cells group**, click the **Format** button, and then click **Column Width**. In the **Column Width** dialog box, type 13 and then click **OK**.

7. Click cell **B2**. Point at the fill handle to display the ⊞ pointer, drag right through cell **D2**, and then release the mouse button.

> The headings *February* and *March* display in cells C2 and D2.

8. Select the range **A2:F2**. In the **Alignment group**, click the **Wrap Text** button 📑, the **Middle Align** button ▭, and the **Center** button ▣. Compare your screen with **Figure 3**.

9. On the **Page Layout tab**, in the **Themes group**, click the **Themes** button. Scroll down, and then click **Solstice** to apply the Solstice theme colors, fonts, and effects to the entire workbook.

10. With the range **A2:F2** still selected, on the **Home tab**, in the **Styles group**, click the **Cell Styles** button, and then click **20% - Accent2**.

11. Select the range **A3:A11**, and then in the **Font group**, click the **Italic** button 𝐼.

12. Select the range **E3:E10**, and then in the **Editing group**, click the **Sum** button Σ. Select the range **B11:E11**, and then click the **Sum** button Σ. Compare your screen with **Figure 4**.

13. Save 🖫 the workbook.

■ **You have completed Skill 1 of 10**

▶ Excel uses rules to check for formula errors. When a formula breaks one of the rules, the cell displays an *error indicator*—a green triangle that indicates a possible error in a formula.

▶ In a formula, an *absolute cell reference* is a cell reference that remains the same when it is copied or filled to other cells. To make a cell reference absolute, insert a dollar sign before the row and column reference.

1. Click cell **F3**, and then type =E3/E11 On the **formula bar**, click the **Enter** button ✓ to display *0.106781377*. In the **Number group**, click the **Percent Style** button ％ to display *11%*.

2. Double-click cell **F3** to display the range finder, and then compare your screen with **Figure 1**. ──────

   The *range finder* outlines all of the cells referenced in a formula. It is useful for verifying which cells are used in a formula and for editing formulas. Here, *Income Tax* revenue is divided by *Total Revenue* to determine that Income Tax is 11% of the city's total revenue.

3. Press ⌈Esc⌋ to leave the range finder while keeping cell F3 active. Point to the cell **F3** fill handle, drag down through cell **F10**, and then release the mouse button. Compare your screen with **Figure 2**. ──────

   Error values are messages that display whenever a formula cannot perform the calculations in a formula. The *#DIV/0!* error value displays in a cell whenever the underlying formula attempts to divide by zero.

■ **Continue to the next page to complete the skill**

Underlying formula

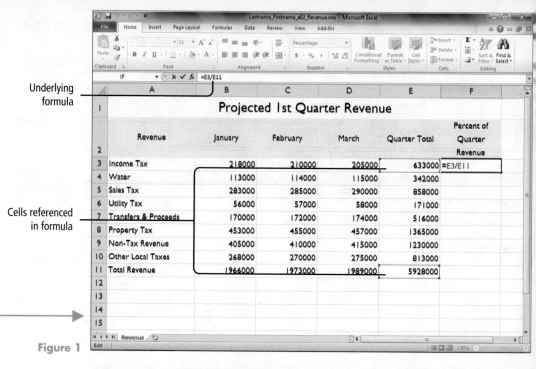

Cells referenced in formula

Figure 1

Error value

Error indicator

Figure 2

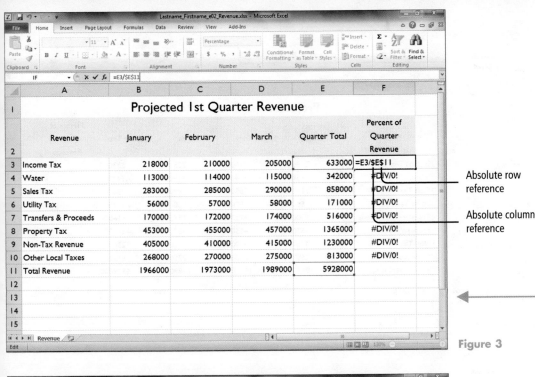

Absolute row reference

Absolute column reference

Figure 3

Relative reference changed from cell E3 to cell E4

Divisor is still $E$11

Figure 4

4. Click cell **F4**. To the left of the cell, point to the displayed **Error Message** button ⬥ to display the ScreenTip—*The formula or function used is dividing by zero or empty cells.*

5. Double-click cell **F4** to display the range finder.

   The formula was copied with a relative cell reference. In the copied formula, the cell reference to cell E4 is correct, but the formula is dividing by the value in cell E12, an empty cell. In this calculation, the divisor must always be cell E11.

6. Press [Esc], and then double-click cell **F3**. Move the insertion point to the end of the formula—to the right of *E11*—and then press [F4] to make the cell reference absolute. Notice that a dollar sign is inserted in front of the column reference *E* and that a dollar sign is inserted in front of the row reference *11*, as shown in **Figure 3**.

7. On the **formula bar**, click the **Enter** button ✔. In cell **F3**, point to the fill handle, and then drag the fill handle to copy the formula down through cell **F10**.

8. Click cell **F4**. Notice that the divisor refers to cell E11, as shown in **Figure 4**.

   The cell reference for the *Water Quarter Total* changed relative to its row; however, the value used as the divisor—*Total Revenue* in cell E11—remained absolute.

9. Press the [↓] repeatedly, and notice that the divisor remains constant—$E$11— while the quotient changes relative to the row.

10. Save 🖫 the workbook.

■ **You have completed Skill 2 of 10**

▶ A *number format* is a specific way that Excel displays numbers. By default, Excel displays the *General format*—a number format that does not display commas or trailing zeros to the right of a decimal point.

▶ The *Accounting number format* applies comma separators where appropriate, inserts a fixed dollar sign aligned at the left edge of the cell, applies two decimal places, and leaves a small amount of space at both the right and left edges of the cell to accommodate parentheses for negative numbers.

▶ The *Comma cell style* adds commas where appropriate and applies the same formatting as the Accounting number format but without a dollar sign.

1. Click cell **B3**, and then on the **Home tab**, in the **Number group**, notice that *General* displays, as shown in **Figure 1**.

2. Select the range **B3:E3**, hold down Ctrl, and then select the range **B11:E11**.

3. With the two nonadjacent ranges selected, on the **Home tab**, in the **Number group**, click the **Accounting Number Format** button $ ·, and then click the **Decrease Decimal** button two times to remove the decimal places. Compare your screen with **Figure 2**.

   Financial worksheets typically display dollar signs only in the first row and in the total row.

■ **Continue to the next page to complete the skill**

General number format

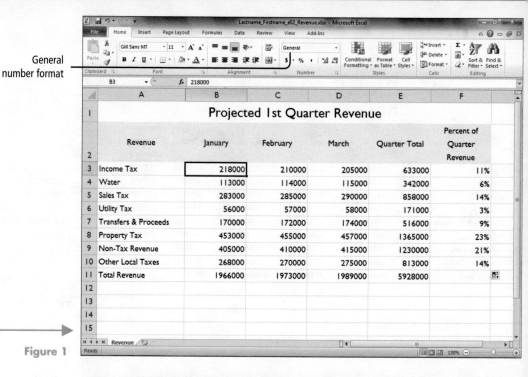

Figure 1

Accounting Number Format button

Decrease Decimal button

Nonadjacent ranges selected and format applied

Figure 2

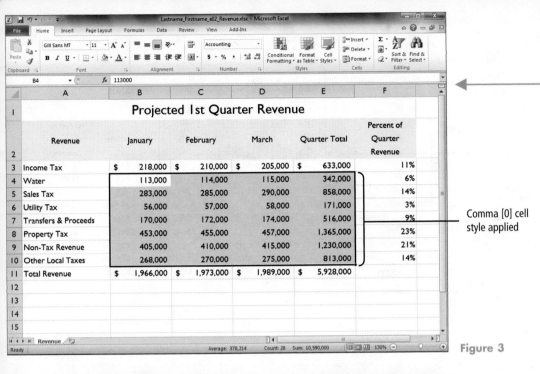

Comma [0] cell style applied

Figure 3

Increase Decimal button

Total cell style format applied

Figure 4

4. Select the range **B4:E10**. In the **Styles group**, click the **Cell Styles** button, and then under **Number Format**, click **Comma[0]**. Compare your screen with Figure 3.

> The Comma[0] cell style inserts commas and rounds the values so that no decimals display.

5. Select the range **F3:F10**. In the **Number group**, click the **Increase Decimal** button one time to add one decimal to the applied Percent style. In the **Alignment group**, click the **Center** button.

6. Select the range **B11:E11**. In the **Styles group**, click the **Cell Styles** button, and then under **Titles and Headings**, click **Total**.

> The *Total cell style* applies a single top border, which indicates that calculations were performed on the numbers above, and a double bottom border, which indicates that the calculations are complete.

7. Right-click cell **A11** to select the cell and to display the Mini toolbar. On the Mini toolbar, click the **Bold** button. Compare your screen with Figure 4.

8. **Save** the workbook.

■ **You have completed Skill 3 of 10**

► A *chart* is a graphic representation of data used to show comparisons, patterns, and trends.

► A *column chart* is useful for illustrating comparisons among related numbers.

1. Select the range **A2:D10**—do *not* include the *Quarter Total* column or the *Total Revenue* row in your selection. On the **Insert tab**, in the **Charts group**, click the **Column** button to display the Chart gallery, as shown in **Figure 1**.

2. In the **Chart** gallery, under **2-D Column**, click the first chart—**Clustered Column**. On the Ribbon, under **Chart Tools**, notice that the Design, Layout, and Format contextual tabs display as shown in **Figure 2**.

   When you insert a chart, borders surround the chart data and an embedded chart is inserted. An *embedded chart* is a chart that is placed on the worksheet containing the data. Embedded charts are beneficial when you want to view or print a chart with its source data.

3. Along the bottom of the chart, locate the names of the revenue categories.

   An *axis* is a line bordering the chart plot area used as a frame of reference for measurement. The *category axis* is the axis that displays the category labels. A *category label* is nonnumeric text that identifies the categories of data. Here, the worksheet's row titles are used for the category labels. For column charts, the category axis is the *x-axis*—the horizontal axis of a chart.

■ **Continue to the next page to complete the skill**

Clustered column chart

Chart gallery

Range A2:D10 selected

Figure 1

Chart Tools contextual tabs display

Borders around chart data

Embedded column chart

Category axis

Figure 2

Figure 3

Figure 4

4. On the left side of the chart, locate the numerical scale, and then on the right side, locate the months displayed in the legend. Compare your screen with Figure 3.

In the worksheet, each cell bordered in blue is referred to as a *data point*—a chart value that originates in a worksheet cell. Each data point is represented in a chart by a *data marker*—a column, a bar, an area, a dot, a pie slice, or another symbol that represents a single data point.

The *value axis* is the axis that displays the worksheet's numeric data. In a column chart, the value axis is the *y-axis*—the vertical axis of a chart.

Data points that are related to one another form a *data series*, and each data series has a unique color or pattern represented in the chart *legend*—a box that identifies the patterns or colors that are assigned to the data series or categories in the chart. Here, each month is a different data series, and the legend shows the color assigned to each month.

5. Point to the upper border of the chart to display the ⌖ pointer, and then move the chart to position its upper left corner in cell **A14**.

6. Scroll down to display row **36**, and then point to the lower right corner of the chart. With the ⌖ pointer, drag to position the lower right corner in the middle of cell **F36**, as shown in Figure 4.

7. Save 🖫 the workbook.

■ **You have completed Skill 4 of 10**

▶ You can customize individual chart elements by using the buttons on the Chart Tools contextual tabs.

▶ You can modify the look of a chart by applying a ***chart layout***—a prebuilt set of chart elements that can include a title, a legend, or labels—or by applying a ***chart style***—a prebuilt chart format that applies an overall visual look to a chart by modifying its graphic effects, colors, and backgrounds.

1. If necessary, click the border of the chart to select the chart. On the **Design tab**, in the **Type group**, click the **Change Chart Type** button. In the displayed **Change Chart Type** dialog box, under **Column**, click **3-D Column**, and then click **OK**.

> The chart is changed from a two-dimensional chart to a three-dimensional chart. **3-D**, which is short for ***three-dimensional***, refers to an image that appears to have all three spatial dimensions—length, width, and depth.

2. In the **Chart Layouts group**, click the **More** button ⬇, and then click **Layout 9** to add the chart title and the axis titles as shown in **Figure 1**.

3. At the top of the chart, click the text *Chart Title*, and type Projected 1st Quarter Revenue Notice the text is inserted in the formula bar. Verify that your text replaced any text, and then press Enter to accept the text.

4. In the **Chart Styles group**, click the **More** button ⬇, and then click **Style 26**. Compare your screen with **Figure 2**.

▪ **Continue to the next page to complete the skill**

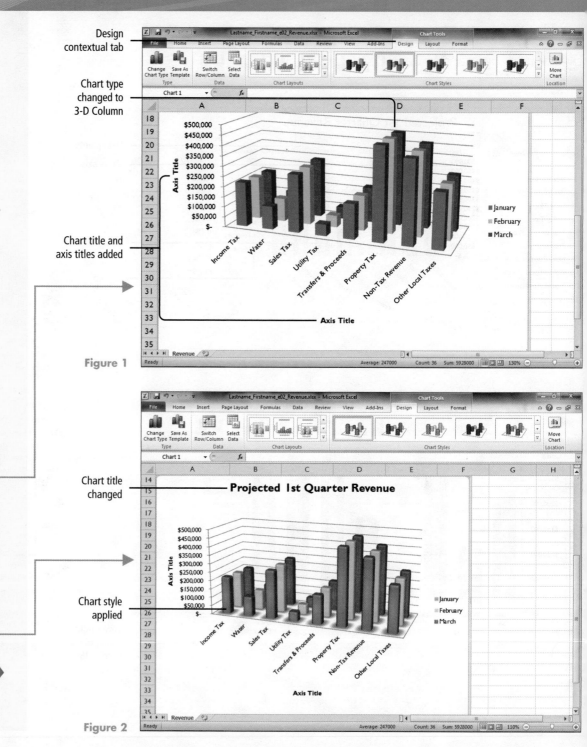

Design contextual tab

Chart type changed to 3-D Column

Chart title and axis titles added

Figure 1

Chart title changed

Chart style applied

Figure 2

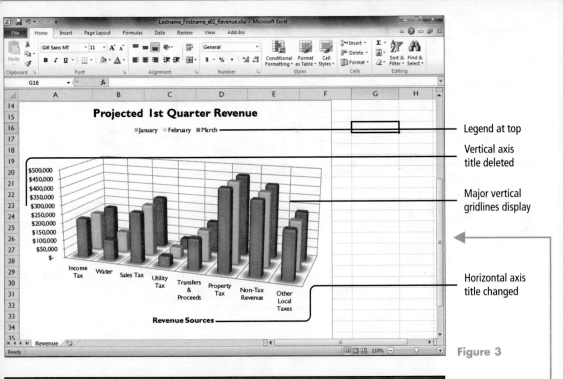

Figure 3

Chart Types Commonly Used in Excel

Chart type	Use to
Column	Illustrate data changes over a period of time or illustrate comparisons among items.
Line	Illustrate trends over time, with time displayed along the horizontal axis and the data point values connected by a line.
Pie	Illustrate the relationship of parts to a whole.
Bar	Illustrate comparisons among individual items.
Area	Emphasize the magnitude of change over time.

Figure 4

5. Below the horizontal axis, click the text *Axis Title*. Type Revenue Sources Verify that your text displays in the formula bar, and then press Enter.

6. In the chart, right-click the *Revenue Sources* axis title to display the shortcut menu and the Mini toolbar. On the Mini toolbar, click the **Font Size** arrow 11 ·, and then click **12**.

7. To the left of the vertical axis, click the text *Axis Title*. Press Delete to delete the vertical axis title.

    The vertical axis title is deleted, and the chart automatically resizes to use the additional space.

8. On the **Layout tab**, in the **Labels group**, click the **Legend** button. From the displayed list, click **Show Legend at Top** to move the legend to the top of the chart.

    When you move chart elements such as the legend, the chart automatically resizes.

9. In the **Axes group**, click the **Gridlines** button. Point to **Primary Vertical Gridlines**, and then click **Major Gridlines** to display vertical grid lines between each category.

10. Click cell **G16** to deselect the chart. **Save** 🖫 the workbook, and then compare your screen with **Figure 3**.

11. Take a moment to examine the various types of charts available in Excel, as summarized in **Figure 4**.

    ■ **You have completed Skill 5 of 10**

▶ A *pie chart* displays the relationship of parts to a whole.

▶ A *chart sheet* is a workbook sheet that contains only a chart and is useful when you want to view a chart separately from the worksheet data.

1. Select the range **A3:A10**. Hold down Ctrl, and then select the range **E3:E10** to select the nonadjacent quarter totals.

2. On the **Insert tab**, in the **Charts group**, click the **Pie** button. Under **3-D Pie**, click the first chart—**Pie in 3-D**.

   The row labels in the range A3:A10 identify the slices of the pie chart. The quarter totals in the range E3:E10 are the data series that determines the size of each pie slice.

3. On the **Design tab**, in the **Location group**, click the **Move Chart** button. In the **Move Chart** dialog box, select the **New sheet** option button. In the **New sheet** box, replace the highlighted text *Chart1* by typing Revenue Chart as shown in **Figure 1**.

4. In the **Move Chart** dialog box, click **OK** to move the pie chart to a chart sheet.

5. On the **Design tab**, in the **Chart Layouts group**, click the **More** button ⊡, and then click **Layout 5**. Compare your screen with **Figure 2**.

   With Chart Layout 5, the chart title displays at the top of the chart, the legend is deleted, and the category names display in each pie slice.

6. Use the technique practiced earlier to change the **Chart Title** to Aspen Falls Projected 1st Quarter Revenue

■ **Continue to the next page to complete the skill**

Move Chart button

Move Chart dialog box

New sheet option button

New sheet name

Figure 1

Chart title added

Chart layout applied

Category names

Chart sheet created

Figure 2

Format
Data Labels
dialog box

Category Name
and Percentage
selected

Inside End
selected

Figure 3

Chart Elements
arrow

Series 1 Data
Labels selected

Data labels
selected

Figure 4

7. On the **Layout tab**, in the **Labels group**, click the **Data Labels** button, and then click **More Data Label Options**.

8. In the **Format Data Labels** dialog box, on the right, under **Label Contains**, verify that the **Category Name** check box is selected, and then select the **Percentage** check box. Clear any other check boxes in this group. Under **Label Position**, select the **Inside End** option button, and then compare your screen with **Figure 3**.

9. In the left side of the **Format Data Labels** dialog box, click **Number**. Under **Category**, click **Percentage**. In the **Decimal places** box, replace the value with 1 and then click **Close**.

10. In the **Current Selection group**, verify that *Series 1 Data Labels* displays as shown in **Figure 4**. If necessary, click the Chart Elements arrow, and then click Series 1 Data Labels.

    You can use the Chart Elements list to select any chart element.

11. Right-click any of the selected data labels to display the Mini toolbar, click the **Bold** button ⊞, and then change the **Font Size** to **12**.

12. On the **Insert tab**, in the **Text group**, click the **Header & Footer** button. In the **Page Setup** dialog box, click the **Custom Footer** button. Verify that the insertion point is in the **Left section** box, and then click the **Insert File Name** button ⊞. Click **OK** two times to insert a footer that will display when the chart sheet is printed.

13. **Save** ⊞ the workbook.

- **You have completed Skill 6 of 10**

► You can modify chart elements by changing the fill color or texture, or by adding an effect such as a shadow, glow, reflection, or bevel.

► You can rotate pie chart slices to present a different visual perspective of the chart.

1. Click the edge of any pie slice to deselect the data labels and to select all of the pie slices—*Series 1*. Compare your screen with **Figure 1**.

2. On the **Format tab**, in the **Shape Styles group**, click the **Shape Effects** button. Point to **Bevel**, and then at the bottom of the Bevel gallery, click **3-D Options**.

3. In the **Format Data Series** dialog box, under **Bevel**, click the **Top** button. In the gallery, under **Bevel**, point to the first thumbnail to display the ScreenTip *Circle*, and then click the **Circle** thumbnail. Click the **Bottom** button, and then click the **Circle** thumbnail.

4. Under **Bevel**, in the four **Width** and **Height** spin boxes, replace the existing value with 512 pt and then compare your screen with **Figure 2**.

5. In the **Format Data Series** dialog box, under **Surface**, click the **Material** button, and then under **Standard**, click the third thumbnail—**Plastic**. In the lower right corner of the dialog box, click the **Close** button.

6. On the **Format tab**, in the **Shape Styles group**, click the **Shape Effects** button, and then point to **Shadow**. At the bottom of the Shadow gallery, under **Perspective**, click the third thumbnail—**Below**.

■ **Continue to the next page to complete the skill**

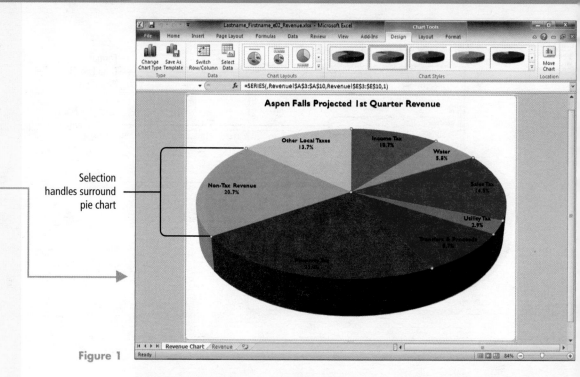

Selection handles surround pie chart

Figure 1

Spin box Widths and Heights set to 512 pt

Material button

Shape effects applied to pie chart

Figure 2

Rotation of X changed to 55

Shadow below chart

Figure 3

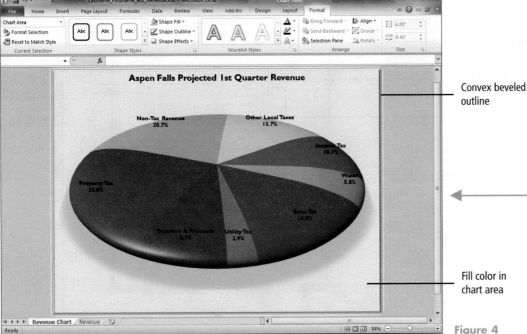

Convex beveled outline

Fill color in chart area

Figure 4

7. Notice the position of the **Utility Tax** slice in the chart. On the **Layout tab**, in the **Background group**, click the **3-D Rotation** button. In the **Format Chart Area** dialog box, under **Rotation**, in the **X** spin box, replace the value with 55 as shown in **Figure 3**.

8. In the **Format Chart Area** dialog box, click the **Close** button.

   The order in which the data series is plotted is determined by the order of the data on the worksheet. The pie chart slices can be rotated up to 360 degrees. Here, the slices were rotated to bring the *Utility Tax* slice to the front of the pie chart.

9. On the **Format tab**, in the **Current Selection group**, verify that the **Chart Elements** box displays the text *Chart Area*. In the **Shape Styles group**, click the **Shape Effects** button, point to **Bevel**, and then under **Bevel**, click the third thumbnail in the second row—**Convex**.

   This effect adds a convex beveled frame around the entire chart.

10. On the **Format tab**, in the **Current Selection group**, click the **Format Selection** button. In the **Format Chart Area** dialog box, select the **Solid fill** option button. Click the **Color button arrow**, and then under **Theme Colors**, click the sixth color in the third row—**Gold, Accent 2, Lighter 60%**. Click the **Close** button, and then compare your screen with **Figure 4**.

11. **Save** 🖫 the workbook.

■ **You have completed Skill 7 of 10**

▶ You can *explode*—pull out one or more slices—of a 3-D pie chart to emphasize a specific slice or slices in a pie chart.

1. Click in the shaded area outside the pie chart to deselect all elements. On the pie chart, click the outer edge of the **Utility Tax** slice once to select the entire pie chart, and then click the **Utility Tax** slice again to select only the one pie slice.

2. Point to the **Utility Tax** slice to display the ⬚ pointer, and then drag the slice away from the center of the pie, as shown in **Figure 1**.

3. Release the mouse button to see the Utility Tax pie slice exploded—pulled away from the pie.

4. With the **Utility Tax** slice still selected, on the **Format tab**, in the **Current Selection group**, click the **Format Selection** button. In the left side of the **Format Data Point** dialog box, click **Fill**. On the right, select the **Solid fill** option button. Click the **Color button arrow**, and then under **Theme Colors**, click the ninth color in the fourth row—**Brown, Accent 5, Lighter 40%**. Compare your screen with **Figure 2**.

5. In the dialog box, click the **Close** button.

6. Click the inner edge of the **Water** pie slice to select only that pie slice. Use the technique just practiced to change the *Water* pie slice solid fill color to the last color in the fourth row—**Indigo, Accent 6, Lighter 40%**. Click the **Close** button.

■ **Continue to the next page to complete the skill**

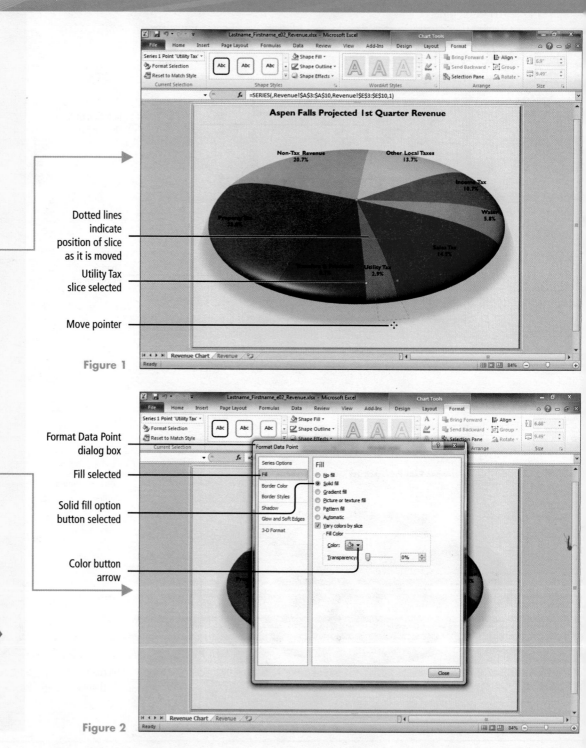

Dotted lines indicate position of slice as it is moved

Utility Tax slice selected

Move pointer

Figure 1

Format Data Point dialog box

Fill selected

Solid fill option button selected

Color button arrow

Figure 2

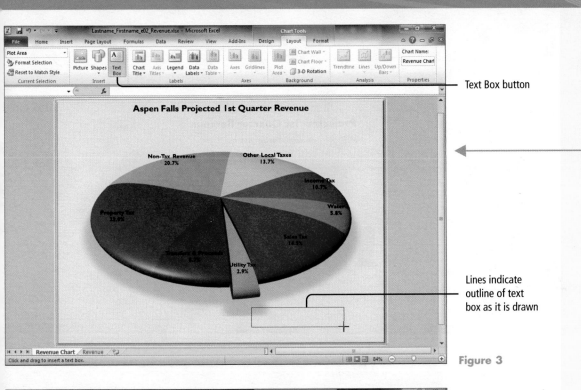

Text Box button

Lines indicate
outline of text
box as it is drawn

Figure 3

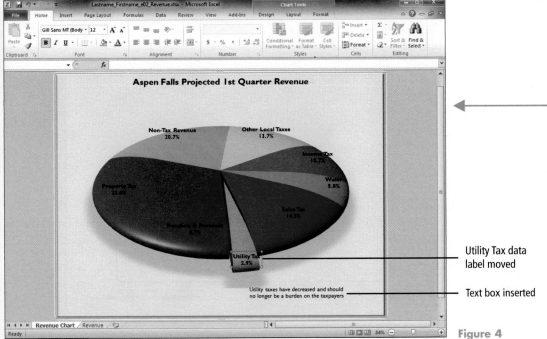

Utility Tax data
label moved

Text box inserted

Figure 4

7. On the **Layout tab**, in the **Insert group**, click the **Text Box** button.

8. Position the displayed ⬇ pointer just under and to the right of the **Utility Tax** pie slice. Hold down the left mouse button, and then drag down and to the right to draw the text box approximately as shown in **Figure 3**.

9. Release the mouse button to insert the text box. With the insertion point blinking inside the text box, type Utility taxes have decreased and should no longer be a burden on the taxpayers

10. Select all the text in the text box, and then right-click the text to display the Mini toolbar. On the Mini toolbar, click the **Font Size arrow** ⌄, and then click **12**. If necessary, resize the text box to display all the text.

11. Click in the Chart Area to deselect the text box. On the chart, click the **Utility Tax** category label once to select all data labels, and then click the **Utility Tax** data label again to select only that one data label. Point to the *Utility Tax* data label's bottom border, and then with the 🔧 pointer, drag the Utility Tax data label to the edge of the exploded slice as shown in **Figure 4**. Adjust the size and position of the data label or text box as needed.

12. **Save** 💾 the workbook.

■ **You have completed Skill 8 of 10**

Microsoft Excel Chapter 2 | Create Charts   **83**

► Recall that a chart's data series and category labels are linked to the source data in the worksheet. When worksheet values are changed, the chart is automatically updated.

► *Sheet tabs* are the labels along the lower border of the workbook window that identify each worksheet or chart sheet.

1. In the sheet tab area at the bottom of the workbook, click the **Revenue** sheet tab to display the worksheet. If necessary, scroll down, and in the column chart, note the height of the Water data markers for February and March.

2. Click cell **C4**, type 225000 and then press Enter to accept the new value. If necessary, scroll down to view the chart. Notice the *Water* value for the month of *February* is updated as shown in **Figure 1.**

    The data marker—the column—representing this data point is updated on the column chart.

3. Click cell **D4**, type 275000 and then press Enter. In cell **F4**, notice the Water revenue now represents 9.9% of the projected 1st Quarter Revenue.

4. Click the **Revenue Chart** sheet tab to display the pie chart and then move the Utility tax data label to the edge of the slice. Verify that in the pie chart, the slice for *Water* displays *9.9%* as shown in **Figure 2.**

    When underlying data is changed, the pie chart percentages and pie slices are automatically recalculated and resized.

■ **Continue to the next page to complete the skill**

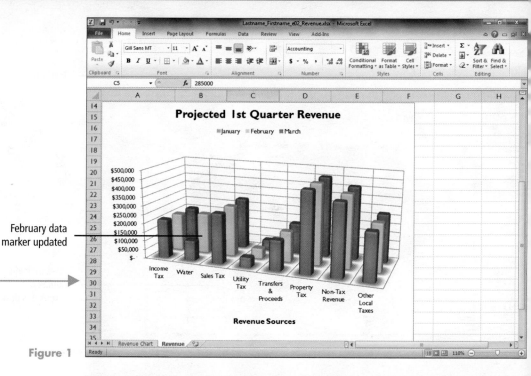

February data marker updated

Figure 1

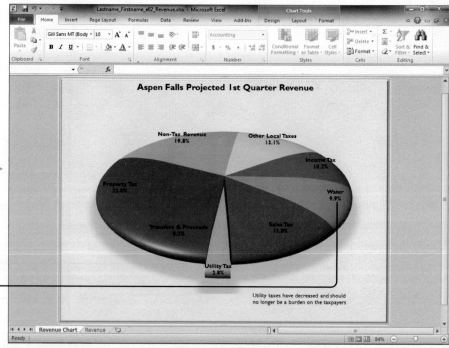

Water data marker updated

Figure 2

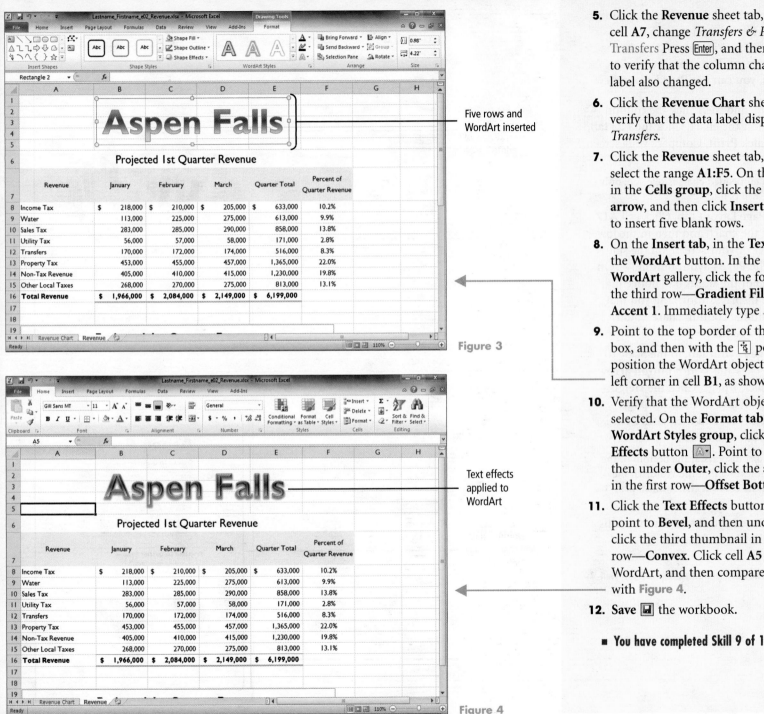

Five rows and WordArt inserted

Figure 3

Text effects applied to WordArt

Figure 4

5. Click the **Revenue** sheet tab, and then in cell **A7**, change *Transfers & Proceeds* to Transfers Press Enter, and then scroll down to verify that the column chart category label also changed.

6. Click the **Revenue Chart** sheet tab, and verify that the data label displays as *Transfers*.

7. Click the **Revenue** sheet tab, and then select the range **A1:F5**. On the **Home tab**, in the **Cells group**, click the **Insert button arrow**, and then click **Insert Sheet Rows** to insert five blank rows.

8. On the **Insert tab**, in the **Text group**, click the **WordArt** button. In the displayed **WordArt** gallery, click the fourth style in the third row—**Gradient Fill - Aqua, Accent 1**. Immediately type Aspen Falls

9. Point to the top border of the WordArt box, and then with the pointer, drag to position the WordArt object in the upper left corner in cell **B1**, as shown in **Figure 3**.

10. Verify that the WordArt object is still selected. On the **Format tab**, in the **WordArt Styles group**, click the **Text Effects** button. Point to **Shadow**, and then under **Outer**, click the second effect in the first row—**Offset Bottom**.

11. Click the **Text Effects** button again, point to **Bevel**, and then under **Bevel**, click the third thumbnail in the second row—**Convex**. Click cell **A5** to deselect the WordArt, and then compare your screen with **Figure 4**.

12. Save the workbook.

■ **You have completed Skill 9 of 10**

► Before you print an Excel worksheet, you can click the File tab and then in the Backstage use the Print tab to preview the printed document. If you need to make adjustments, you can use Page Layout view.

1. Scroll down, and then click the column chart to select the chart. Click the **File tab**, and then click **Print**. Compare your screen with Figure 1.

   When an embedded chart is selected, only the chart will print.

2. Click the **Page Layout tab**. Click cell **A17** to deselect the chart, and then in the lower right corner of your screen, on the status bar, click the **Page Layout** button. On the left side of the status bar, notice that *Page 1 of 2* displays, informing you that the data and the column chart would print on two pages.

3. On the **Page Layout tab**, in the **Scale to Fit group**, click the **Width button arrow**, and then click **1 page**. Click the **Height button arrow**, and then click **1 page**. Click the **File tab**, and then click **Print**. Compare your screen with Figure 2.

   Notice *1 of 1* displays at the bottom of the screen, indicating that the WordArt, the data, and the column chart will all print on one page.

4. Click the **Page Layout tab**. On the status bar, click the **Normal** button.

■ **Continue to the next page to complete the skill**

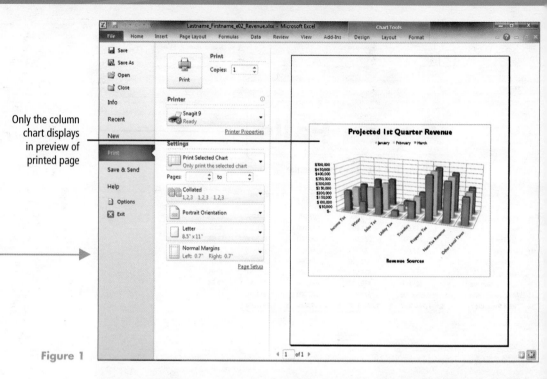

Only the column chart displays in preview of printed page

Figure 1

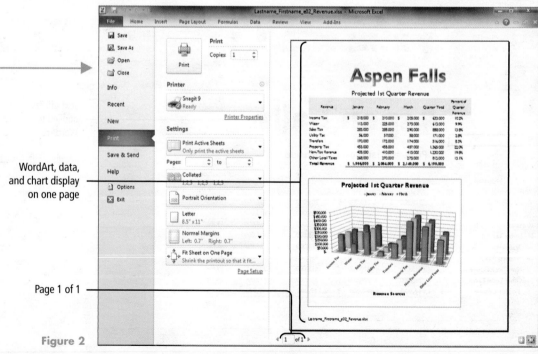

WordArt, data, and chart display on one page

Page 1 of 1

Figure 2

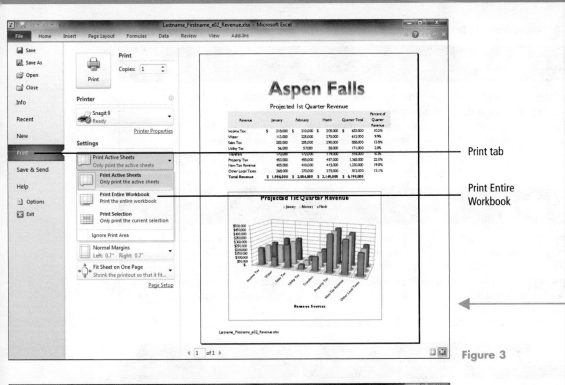

Print tab

Print Entire Workbook

Figure 3

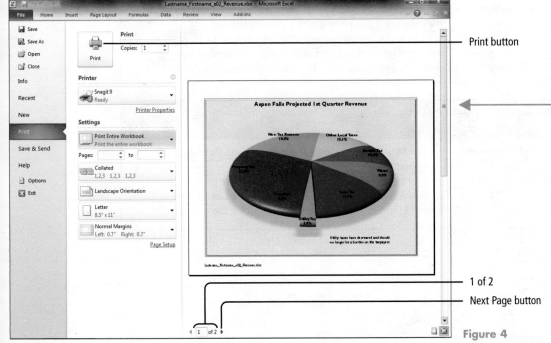

Print button

1 of 2

Next Page button

Figure 4

5. In the **Page Setup group**, click the **Margins** button, and then click **Custom Margins**. In the **Page Setup** dialog box, under **Center on page**, select the **Horizontally** check box, and then click **OK**.

6. Press Ctrl + Home to make cell **A1** the active cell. On the **Review tab**, in the **Proofing group**, click the **Spelling** button, and then check the spelling of the worksheet. When the message *The spelling check is complete for the entire sheet* displays, click **OK**.

7. **Save** 🖫 the workbook.

8. Click the **File tab**, and then click **Print**. Under **Settings**, click the first button as shown in **Figure 3**.

9. On the displayed list, click **Print Entire Workbook**. Notice at the bottom of the screen, *1 of 2* displays, and the chart sheet with the pie chart is the first page, as shown in **Figure 4**.

10. At the bottom of the screen, click the **Next Page** button ▶ to preview the worksheet containing your WordArt, the data, and the column chart. Print the workbook, or submit the file as directed by your instructor. If you are instructed to do so, display and format the worksheet formulas, and then print the formulas.

11. **Close** ⊠ the workbook, and then **Exit** Excel.

Done! You have completed Skill 10 of 10 and your document is complete!

The following More Skills are located at **www.pearsonhighered.com/skills**

More Skills Insert and Edit Comments

You can add comments to cells in a worksheet to provide reminders, to display clarifying information about data within the cells, or to document your work. When you point to a cell that contains a comment, the comment and the name of the person who created the comment display.

In More Skills 11, you will read, create, and edit comments.

To begin, open your web browser, navigate to www.pearsonhighered.com/skills, locate the name of your textbook, and then follow the instructions on the website.

More Skills Change Chart Types

After you create a chart, a different chart type might be easier for the readers of your chart to understand. For example, you can change a column chart to a bar chart. Both a column chart and a bar chart are good choices to illustrate comparisons among items; however, a bar chart might be a better choice when the axis labels are lengthy.

In More Skills 12, you will create a column chart and then change the chart type to a bar chart.

To begin, open your web browser, navigate to www.pearsonhighered.com/skills, locate the name of your textbook, and then follow the instructions on the website.

More Skills Copy Excel Data to Word Documents

You can copy the data and objects created in one application to another application, saving time and providing accuracy because data is entered only one time.

In More Skills 13, you will create a chart in Excel and then copy the chart and paste it into a Word document.

To begin, open your web browser, navigate to www.pearsonhighered.com/skills, locate the name of your textbook, and then follow the instructions on the website.

More Skills Fill Series Data into Worksheet Cells

Instead of entering data manually, you can use the fill handle or the fill command to enter data that follow a pattern or series—for example, hours, days of the week, or numeric sequences such as even numbers.

In More Skills 14, you will use the fill handle and the fill command to enter data in cells.

To begin, open your web browser, navigate to www.pearsonhighered.com/skills, locate the name of your textbook, and then follow the instructions on the website.

Key Terms

Online Help Skills

1. **Start** 🔵 Excel. In the upper right corner of the Excel window, click the **Help** button 🔳. In the Help window, click the **Maximize** 🔳 button.

2. Click in the search box, type create charts and then click the **Search** button 🔳. In the search results, click **Available chart types**.

3. Read the article's introduction, and then below in this article, click **Column charts**. Compare your screen with Figure 1.

Figure 1

4. Read the section and then scroll down and read the section on Pie Charts to see if you can answer the following: A pie chart is more useful than a column chart for showing what type of data?

Matching

Match each term in the second column with its correct definition in the first column by writing the letter of the term on the blank line in front of the correct definition.

____ **1.** A command with which you can display text on multiple lines within a cell.

____ **2.** A cell reference that refers to a cell by its fixed position in a worksheet and that does not change when the formula is copied.

____ **3.** A specific way that Excel displays numbers.

____ **4.** The default format that Excel applies to numbers—whatever you type in the cell will display, with the exception that trailing zeros to the right of a decimal point will not display.

____ **5.** The Excel number format that applies a comma separator where appropriate, inserts a fixed dollar sign aligned at the left edge of the cell, applies two decimal places, and leaves a small amount of space at both the right and left edges of the cell to accommodate parentheses for negative numbers.

____ **6.** A graphic representation of data in a worksheet that shows comparisons, patterns, and trends.

____ **7.** The chart axis that is usually the horizontal axis and contains categories.

____ **8.** The chart axis that is usually the vertical axis and contains data.

____ **9.** To pull out one or more slices of a 3-D pie chart to emphasize a specific slice or slices.

____ **10.** A set of design elements that provides a unified look for colors, fonts, and graphics.

A Absolute cell reference

B Accounting number format

C Category axis

D Chart

E Explode

F General format

G Number format

H Theme

I Text wrap

J Value axis

Multiple Choice

Choose the correct answer.

1. Automatically changing the column width to accommodate the longest column entry is called:
   A. Drag and drop
   B. AutoFit
   C. Auto adjust

2. A green triangle that indicates a possible error in a formula is called:
   A. An error indicator
   B. A message
   C. A Dialog Box Launcher

3. The Excel feature that outlines all of the cells referenced in a formula is the:
   A. Formula finder
   B. Cell finder
   C. Range finder

4. A chart type useful for illustrating comparisons among related numbers is called:
   A. A pie chart
   B. An area chart
   C. A column chart

5. A chart placed on a worksheet with the source data is:
   A. A chart sheet
   B. A column chart
   C. An embedded chart

6. The chart data points related to one another are known as a:
   A. Column
   B. Data series
   C. Chart point

7. The box that identifies the patterns or colors assigned to the data series in a chart is called a:
   A. Legend
   B. Dialog box
   C. Message box

8. A predesigned combination of chart elements is referred to as a:
   A. 3-D chart
   B. Chart layout
   C. Chart

9. The chart type that displays the relationship of parts to a whole is:
   A. A pie chart
   B. An area chart
   C. A column chart

10. A worksheet that contains only a chart is referred to as a:
    A. Worksheet
    B. Chart area
    C. Chart sheet

Topics for Discussion

1. Search some current newspapers and magazines for examples of charts. Which charts catch your eye and why? Do the charts appeal to you because of their color or format? Is something intriguing revealed to you in the chart that you have never considered before? What are some formatting changes that you think make a chart interesting and valuable to a reader?

2. Why is it important to present accounting and financial information in a manner that is attractive and easy to read? What are some of the ways that Excel can help you do so?

Skill Check

To complete this project, you will need the following file:

- e02_Expenses

You will save your workbook as:

- Lastname_Firstname_e02_Expenses

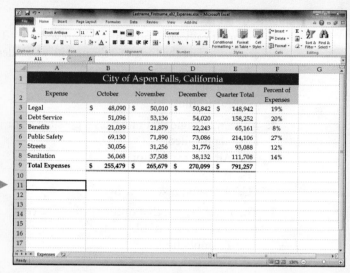

Figure 1

1. **Start** Excel, and open the file **e02_Expenses**. **Save** the file in your **Excel Chapter 2** folder as Lastname_Firstname_e02_Expenses Insert the file name in the left footer and then return to **Normal** view.

2. On the **Page Layout tab**, in the **Themes group**, click the **Themes** button, and then click **Hardcover**.

3. Click cell **B2**, and then use the fill handle to fill the months into the range **C2:D2**. Select the range **A2:F2**. On the **Home tab**, in the **Alignment group**, click the **Wrap Text**, **Middle Align**, and **Center** buttons.

4. Select **E3:E8**, and then in the **Editing** group, click the **SUM** button. In the range **B9:E9**, use the **SUM** function to calculate the *Total Expenses*.

5. In cell **F3**, type =E3/$E$9 and then on the formula bar, click the **Enter** button. Use the fill handle to fill the formula down through cell **F8**. With the range **F3:F8** still selected, in the **Number group**, click the **Percent Style** button. In the **Alignment group**, click the **Center** button.

6. Select the range **B3:E3**, hold down Ctrl, and then select the range **B9:E9**. In the **Number group**, click the **Accounting Number Format** button, and then click the **Decrease Decimal** button two times. Select the range **B4:E8**. In the **Styles group**, click the **Cell Styles** button, and then click **Comma [0]**. Select the range **B9:E9**, click the **Cell Styles** button, and then click **Total**. Click cell **A11**, and then compare your screen with **Figure 1**.

7. Select the range **A2:D8**. On the **Insert tab**, in the **Charts group**, click the **Column** button, and then click **3-D Column**. Move the chart below the data, and then resize the chart to display in approximately the range **A11:F30**. On the **Design tab**, in the **Chart Layouts group**, click **Layout 1**. Click the **Chart Title**, type Expenses and then press Enter. Compare your screen with **Figure 2**.

Figure 2

- Continue to the next page to complete this Skill Check

8. Select the nonadjacent ranges **A3:A8** and **E3:E8**. On the **Insert tab**, in the **Charts group**, click the **Pie** button, and then click **Pie in 3-D**.

9. On the **Design tab**, in the **Location group**, click the **Move Chart** button. In the **Move Chart** dialog box, select the **New sheet** option button, type the sheet name Expenses Chart and then click **OK**.

10. For the pie chart, apply the **Layout 1** chart layout, and then change the **Chart Title** to 4th Quarter Expenses Right-click the chart title, and from the Mini toolbar, change the **Font Size** to **28**.

11. Right-click any of the data labels, and use the Mini toolbar to change the **Font Size** to **14** and to apply the **Bold** format.

12. Click the **Chart Area**. On the **Layout tab**, in the **Current Selection group**, click the **Format Selection** button. In the **Format Chart Area** dialog box, select the **Gradient Fill** option button, and then click **Close**.

13. Click the edge of a pie slice to select all of the slices. On the **Format tab**, in the **Shape Styles group**, click the **Shape Effects** button, point to **Bevel**, and then click **3-D Options**. Click the **Top** button, and then click the **Circle** thumbnail. Click the **Bottom** button, and then click the **Circle** thumbnail. Set the four Bevel **Width** and **Height** spin boxes to 250 pt and then click **Close**. Compare your screen with **Figure 3**.

14. On the **Insert tab**, in the **Text group**, click the **Header & Footer** button. In the **Page Setup** dialog box, click the **Custom Footer** button. Verify that the insertion point is in the Left section, click the **Insert File Name** button, and then click **OK** two times.

15. Click the **Expenses** sheet tab. Select the range **A1:F6**. On the **Home tab**, in the **Cells group**, click the **Insert button arrow**, and then click **Insert Sheet Rows**. On the **Insert tab**, in the **Text group**, click the **WordArt** button, and then in the third row, click the fourth thumbnail—**Gradient Fill - Dark Red, Accent 1**. Immediately type City Expenses and then move the WordArt to the top of the worksheet.

16. Click the **Page Layout tab**. In the **Scale to Fit group**, click the **Width** arrow, and then click **1 page**. In the **Page Setup group**, click the **Margins** button, and then click **Custom Margins**. In the **Page Setup** dialog box, select the **Horizontally** check box, and then click the **Print Preview** button.

17. Compare your screen with **Figure 4**. **Save** the workbook, and then print or submit the file as directed by your instructor.

Done! You have completed the Skill Check

Figure 3

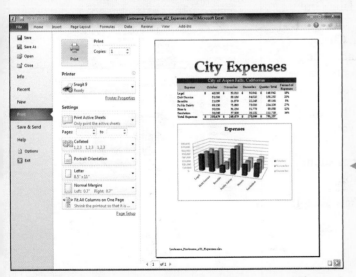

Figure 4

Assess Your Skills 1

To complete this project, you will need the following file:

- e02_Assets

You will save your workbook as:

- Lastname_Firstname_e02_Assets

1. **Start** Excel, and open the file **e02_Assets**. **Save** the workbook in your **Excel Chapter 2** folder as Lastname_Firstname_e02_Assets Add the file name in the worksheet's left footer, and then return to **Normal** view.

2. In the ranges **D4:D10** and **B11:D11**, use the **SUM** function to total the rows and the columns. Select the ranges **B4:D4** and **B11:D11**, apply the **Accounting** number format, and format the range so that no decimals display. For the range **B5:D10**, apply the **Comma [0]** cell style. In the range **B11:D11**, apply the **Total** cell style.

3. Insert a **3-D Clustered Column** chart based on the range **A3:C10**. Move the chart below the data, and then resize the chart to approximately the range **A13:D30**. Apply chart **Style 36**, and then show the legend at the top of the chart. Change the legend font size to **12**.

4. Insert a **Pie in 3-D** chart based on the non-adjacent ranges **A4:A10** and **D4:D10**. Move the pie chart to a chart sheet named Capital Assets Chart and then apply **Layout 1**. Change the chart title to Capital Assets

5. For the data labels, apply **Bold**, and then change the **Font Size** to **14**.

6. Format the **Chart Area** with **Solid fill**, and then change the **Color** to **Red, Accent 2, Lighter 60%**.

7. For all the slices—in Series 1, change the **3-D Rotation** of **X** to **140**, and then explode the **Collections** pie slice. Verify that all data labels display on a pie slice. If necessary, move the Collections pie slice back toward the center of the pie to display the labels on the slices. Display the **3-D Format** settings in the **Format Data Series** dialog box. Change the top bevel to Circle and then change the top bevel width and height to 1000 pt. Change the **Material** setting to **Metal**.

8. For the chart sheet, add a footer with the file name in the left section. Compare your worksheet and chart sheet with **Figure 1**. **Save** the workbook, and then print or submit the file as directed by your instructor.

Done! You have completed Assess Your Skills 1

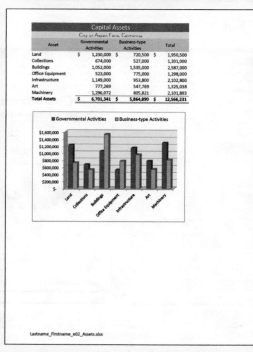

Figure 1

Assessment

Assess Your Skills 3 and 4 can be found at
www.pearsonhighered.com/skills.

Assess Your Skills 2

To complete this project, you will need the following file:

- e02_Debt

You will save your workbook as:

- Lastname_Firstname_e02_Debt

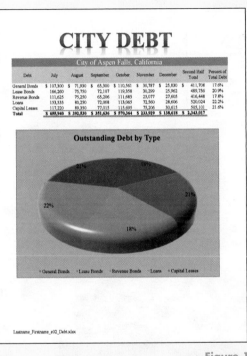

Figure 1

1. **Start** Excel, and open the file **e02_Debt**. **Save** the workbook in your **Excel Chapter 2** folder as Lastname_Firstname_e02_Debt Add the file name in the worksheet's left footer, and then return to **Normal** view.

2. Apply the **Newsprint** theme. In cell **B2**, type July and then Auto Fill the months through cell **G2**.

3. In cell **I3**, calculate the *Percent of Total Debt*. In the formula, use an absolute cell reference when referring to cell **H8**. Copy the formula down through cell **I7**, and then format the results as percentages with one decimal place. Center the results in the cell.

4. Select the ranges **B3:H3** and **B8:H8**, and then apply the **Accounting** number format and display zero decimal places. In the range **B4:H7**, apply the **Comma [0]** cell style, and in the range **B8:H8**, apply the **Total** cell style.

5. Insert a **Pie in 3-D** chart based on the non-adjacent ranges **A3:A7** and **H3:H7**. Move the pie chart below the data, and then resize the chart so that it displays approximately in the range **A11:I38**. Apply **Layout 2**.

6. Change the **Chart Title** to Outstanding Debt by Type and then change the chart title **Font Size** to **20**. Right-click the data labels, and then change the **Font Size** to **14**. Right-click the legend, and then change the **Font Size** to **12**. Display the legend at the bottom of the chart.

7. Format the **Chart Area** to display a **Solid fill** using the ninth color in the third row—**Blue-Gray, Accent 5, Lighter 60%**.

8. Display the **Format Data Series** dialog box. Set a Top **Divot** 3-D Bevel, set the Top **Width** and **Height** to 50 pt and change the **Material** setting to **Soft Edge**.

9. Insert seven sheet rows at the top of the worksheet. Insert a **WordArt**, using the style **Gradient Fill - Blue-Gray, Accent 4, Reflection**. Change the WordArt text to City Debt and then move the WordArt to the top of the worksheet, centering it in the seven blank rows.

10. View the worksheet in **Print Layout** view. Verify that the WordArt, data, and pie chart all print on one page. If necessary, adjust the Scale to Fit to fit all objects on one page.

11. **Save** the workbook, and then print or submit the file as directed by your instructor. Compare your completed workbook with Figure 1.

Done! You have completed Assess Your Skills 2

Assess Your Skills Visually

To complete this project, you will need the following file:

- e02_Net_Assets

You will save your workbook as:

- Lastname_Firstname_e02_Net_Assets

Start Excel, and open the file **e02_Net_Assets**. **Save** the workbook in your **Excel Chapter 2** folder as Lastname_Firstname_e02_Net_Assets Create the worksheet and chart sheet as shown in **Figure 1**. Apply the **Solstice** theme. Auto Fill the months in row 4. Insert totals using the **SUM** function. Calculate the *Percent of Total Net Assets* using an absolute cell reference and then format the values as shown. Create the 3-D pie chart, and move the chart to a chart sheet as shown in the figure. Apply the Layout 1 chart layout and then format the chart title and data labels as shown. Format the 3-D pie chart with the **Circle** bevel 3-D shape effect on both the top and bottom, with all the widths and heights set to 512 pt Use the **Metal** surface, and add a shadow and chart area fill. Explode the *Power* pie slice, and rotate the pie chart as shown. Insert the text box shown in the figure. Insert the file name in the left footer of both sheets. Check the spelling of the worksheet. **Save** the file, and then print or submit it as directed by your instructor.

Done! You have completed Assess Your Skills Visually

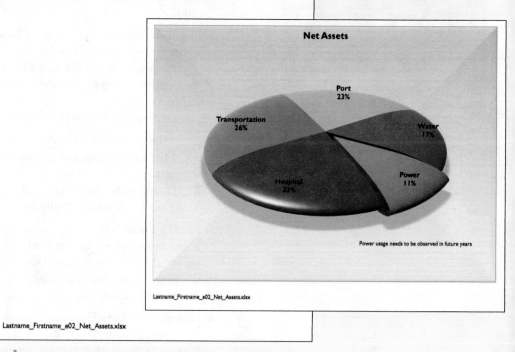

| | | | | | Percent of |
Activity	July	August	September	Total	Total Net Assets
Transportation	$ 268,755	$ 275,082	$ 282,086	$ 825,923	25.9%
Port	242,886	245,688	247,253	735,827	23.1%
Water	175,885	180,256	193,008	549,149	17.2%
Power	117,006	108,832	115,038	340,876	10.7%
Hospital	213,468	250,865	275,066	739,399	23.2%
Total Net Assets	$ 1,018,000	$ 1,060,723	$ 1,112,451	$ 3,191,174	

Aspen Falls / **Net Assets** / **Business-type Activities**

Lastname_Firstname_e02_Net_Assets.xlsx

Lastname_Firstname_e02_Net_Assets.xlsx

Figure 1

Skills in Context

To complete this project, you will need the following file:

- e02_Budget

You will save your workbook as:

- Lastname_Firstname_02_Budget

During the fourth quarter of this year, the Accounting Department developed a summary of the proposed Aspen Falls budget. Open the file **e02_Budget**, and then save the workbook in your **Excel Chapter 2** folder as Lastname_Firstname_e02_Budget Apply a theme of your choice. Compute the totals and the percentage by which each budget item makes up the total budget. Use an absolute cell reference when computing the percentages. Format the values appropriately. Create an embedded column chart that effectively compares the budget data for the three

months in the fourth quarter. Create an attractive pie chart on a separate chart sheet that describes the quarter percentages. Insert blank rows at the top of the worksheet, and then insert a WordArt with the text Proposed Budget Format the WordArt appropriately. Insert the file name in the left footer of both sheets. Save the workbook, and then print or submit the workbook file as directed by your instructor.

Done! You have completed Skills in Context

Skills and You

To complete this project, you will need the following file:

- New blank Excel workbook

You will save your workbook as:

- Lastname_Firstname_e02_Personal_Budget

What items in your monthly budget might you be able to reduce? A pie chart can point out items on which you might be overspending without realizing it. Create a worksheet for a month's worth of your expenses. Total the expenses, and then create a pie chart to show the percentage by which each item makes up your monthly budget. Format the pie chart appropriately. Insert the filename in the left

footer of the worksheet, and then return to **Normal** view. Save the workbook as Lastname_Firstname_e02_Personal_Budget and print or submit the workbook electronically as directed by your instructor.

Done! You have completed Skills and You

Manage Multiple Worksheets

▶ In an Excel workbook, you can insert and move worksheets, or you can group any number of worksheets and then edit or format the data in all of the worksheets at the same time.

▶ Multiple math operators can be used in one formula, and a formula can refer to a cell in another worksheet.

Your starting screen will look similar to this:

SKILLS

myitlab
Skills 1-10 Training

At the end of this chapter, you will be able to:

Skill 1 Work with Sheet Tabs

Skill 2 Enter and Format Dates

Skill 3 Clear Cell Contents and Formats

Skill 4 Move, Copy, Paste, and Paste Options

Skill 5 Work with Grouped Worksheets

Skill 6 Use Multiple Math Operators in a Formula

Skill 7 Format Grouped Worksheets

Skill 8 Insert and Move Worksheets

Skill 9 Construct Formulas That Refer to Cells in Other Worksheets

Skill 10 Create Clustered Bar Charts

MORE SKILLS

More Skills 11 Create Organization Charts

More Skills 12 Create Line Charts

More Skills 13 Set and Clear Print Areas

More Skills 14 Insert Hyperlinks

Outcome

Using the skills listed to the left will enable you to create
a workbook containing worksheets like this:

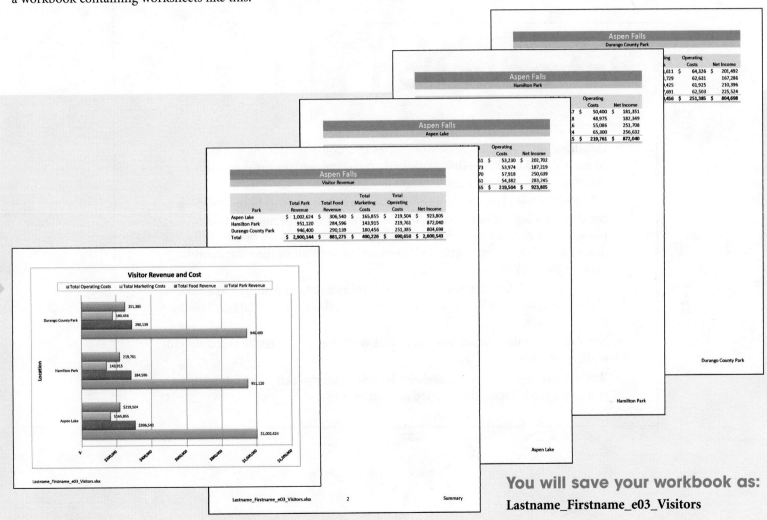

Lastname_Firstname_e03_Visitors.xlsx

You will save your workbook as:

Lastname_Firstname_e03_Visitors

In this chapter, you will create documents for the Aspen Falls City Hall, which provides essential services for the citizens and visitors of Aspen Falls, California.

Introduction

- ▶ Organizations typically create workbooks that contain multiple worksheets. In such a workbook, the first worksheet often summarizes the detailed information in the other worksheets.

- ▶ When you have a large amount of data to organize in a workbook, dividing the data into logical elements such as locations or time periods and then placing each element in a separate worksheet makes sense. In other words, design a *system* of worksheets instead of trying to fit all of the information on a single worksheet.

- ▶ By grouping worksheets, you can edit and format data in multiple worksheets simultaneously. Data that you edit on the active sheet is reflected in all of the selected sheets.

- ▶ You can copy information from one worksheet and then paste it in a different worksheet.

- ▶ You can manage multiple worksheets by color coding each sheet tab so that you can quickly locate the detailed information.

Time to complete all
10 skills – 50 to 90 minutes

Find your student data files here:

**Student data file needed
for this chapter:**

- e03_Visitors

► When a workbook contains more than one worksheet, you can navigate (move) among worksheets by clicking the sheet tabs.

► To view sheet tabs, use the four *tab scrolling buttons*—the buttons to the left of the sheet tabs used to display Excel sheet tabs that are not in view.

1. **Start** ⊕ Excel, and then open **e03_Visitors**. Click the **File tab**, and then click **Save As**. In the **Save As** dialog box, navigate to the location where you are saving your files. Click **New folder**, type Excel Chapter 3 and then press Enter two times. In the **File name** box, using your own name, type Lastname_Firstname_ e03_Visitors and then press Enter.

2. Along the bottom of the Excel window, click the **Sheet2 sheet tab**, and then compare your screen with **Figure 1**.

3. Click the **Sheet1 sheet tab**. In cell **A1**, notice the text *Park 1*.

   The first worksheet becomes the active sheet, and cell A1, which is formatted with a green background, displays *Park 1*.

4. Right-click the **Sheet1 sheet tab**, and then compare your screen with **Figure 2**.

5. From the shortcut menu, click **Rename**. On the **Sheet1 sheet tab**, verify the tab name is selected, and then type Aspen Lake Press Enter.

   You can use up to 31 characters in a sheet tab name. Strive for a short but meaningful name.

■ **Continue to the next page to complete the skill**

Sheet2 tab is active

Sheet tab scrolling buttons

Figure 1

Shortcut menu

Rename command

Sheet1 tab is active

Figure 2

Park 2 displays

Sheet2 tab name selected

Figure 3

6. Double-click the **Sheet2 sheet tab** to make it the active sheet and to select the sheet name, as shown in Figure 3.

7. With the *Sheet2* sheet tab name selected, type Hamilton Park and then press Enter.

8. Using either of the two methods just practiced, rename the **Sheet3 sheet tab** as Durango County Park and then press Enter.

9. Verify that the *Durango County Park* sheet is the active worksheet. On the **Page Layout tab**, in the **Themes group**, click the **Colors** button. Scroll down, and then click **Metro** to change the theme colors for this workbook.

10. On the **Home tab**, in the **Cells group**, click the **Format** button, and then point to **Tab Color** to display the colors associated with the *Metro* theme colors. Click the fourth color in the first row—**Blue-Gray, Text 2**. Alternately, right-click the sheet tab, and then point to Tab Color.

When a worksheet is active, the sheet tab color displays only along the lower edge of the sheet tab. When a worksheet is not active, the entire sheet tab is filled with the selected color.

11. Use the technique just practiced to change the sheet tab color of the **Hamilton Park tab** to the sixth color in the first row—**Pink, Accent 2**.

12. Change the sheet tab color of the **Aspen Lake sheet tab** to the last color in the first row—**Teal, Accent 6**. Compare your screen with Figure 4.

13. **Save** the workbook.

■ **You have completed Skill 1 of 10**

Active sheet displays tab color at lower edge of tab

Sheet tabs named and colored

Figure 4

▶ When you enter a date, it is assigned a *serial number*—a sequential number.

▶ Dates are stored as sequential serial numbers so they can be used in calculations. By default, January 1, 1900 is serial number 1. January 1, 2012 is serial number 40909 because it is 40,908 days after January 1, 1900. Serial numbers make it possible to perform calculations on dates, for example, to find the number of days between two dates by subtracting the older date from the more recent date.

▶ When you type any of the following values into cells, Excel interprets them as dates: *7/4/10, 4-Jul, 4-Jul-10, Jul-10.* When typing in these date formats, the ☐ (hyphen) key and the ☐ (forward slash) key function identically.

▶ You can enter months using the entire name or the first three characters. Years can be entered as two digits or four digits. When you leave the year off, the current year will be inserted.

1. On the **Aspen Lake sheet**, click cell **A14**, and then notice that in the cell the date displays as *1/31*. In the **formula bar**, notice that the underlying value displays as *1/31/2012*, as shown in **Figure 1**.

2. On the **Home tab**, in the **Number group**, click the **Number Format arrow**, as shown in **Figure 2**.

   Here you can select popular date, time, and number formats, or click *More Number Formats* at the bottom of the list to display additional built-in number formats.

■ **Continue to the next page to complete the skill**

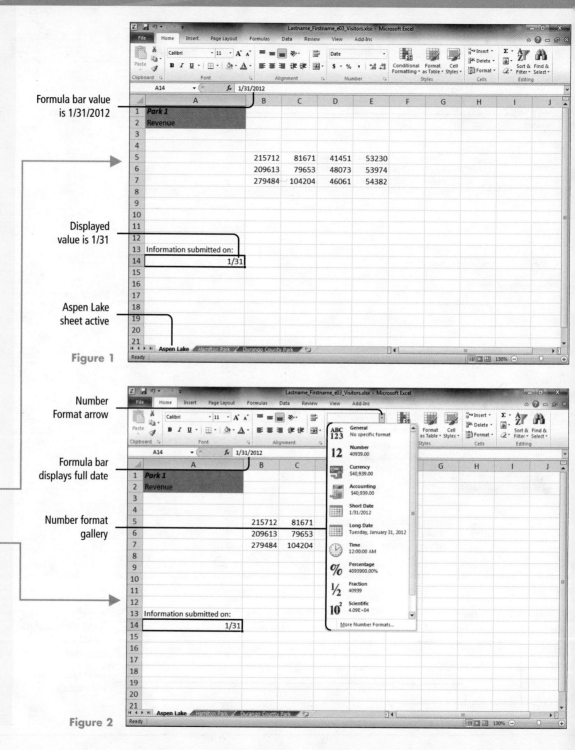

Figure 1

Figure 2

3. At the bottom of the Number Format list, click **More Number Formats**. In the displayed **Format Cells** dialog box, on the **Number tab**, under **Type**, click *Wednesday, March 14, 2001 to show a sample of the selected date format, as shown in Figure 3.

The date *Wednesday, March 14, 2001* will not display in your worksheet. This is a sample of a format that can be applied to your current date.

4. Under **Type**, scroll down, click **March 14, 2001**, and then click **OK**.

The date January 31, 2012 displays in cell A14.

5. Click the **Hamilton Park sheet tab** to make it the active worksheet, and then click cell **A17**. Type 8/11/98 and then on the **formula bar**, click the **Enter** button ☑.

In cell A17, the year changed from *98* to *1998*. When a two-digit year between 30 and 99 is entered, a 20th-century date is assumed.

6. Click the **Durango County Park sheet tab**, and then click cell **A17**. Hold down ⌃Ctrl and press ⌸ ;—the semicolon key. Press ⏎Enter to confirm the entry.

The ⌃Ctrl + ⌸ ; shortcut enters the current date, obtained from your computer, into the selected cell using the default date format. The table in Figure 4 summarizes how Excel interprets various date formats.

7. Save 💾 the workbook.

■ **You have completed Skill 2 of 10**

Number tab selected

Sample of selected format

Date formats

Figure 3

Date Format AutoComplete

Date Typed As	Completed by Excel As
7/4/11	7/4/2011
7-4-98	7/4/1998
7/4 or 7-4	4-Jul (current year assumed)
July 4 or Jul 4	4-Jul (current year assumed)
Jul/4 or Jul-4	4-Jul (current year assumed)
July 4, 1998	4-Jul-98
July 2012	Jul-12
July 1998	Jul-98

Figure 4

► Cells can contain formatting, comments, and *contents*—underlying formulas and data.

► You can clear the contents of a cell, the formatting of a cell, or both.

1. Click the **Aspen Lake sheet tab** to make it the active worksheet, and then click cell **A1**. On the **Home tab**, in the **Editing group**, click the **Clear** button 🖉, and then click **Clear Contents**.

   Alternately, you can press Delete to clear the contents of a cell.

2. Look at cell **A1**, and verify that text has been cleared but that the fill color applied to the cell still displays, as shown in **Figure 1**.

   Deleting the contents of a cell does *not* delete the formatting of the cell.

3. In cell **A1**, type Aspen Lake and then on the **formula bar**, click the **Enter** button ✓.

4. With cell **A1** still selected, in the **Editing group**, click the **Clear** button 🖉, and then click **Clear Formats**. Compare your screen with **Figure 2**.

   Clear Formats deletes the formatting from the cell but does not delete the cell contents.

■ **Continue to the next page to complete the skill** ➡

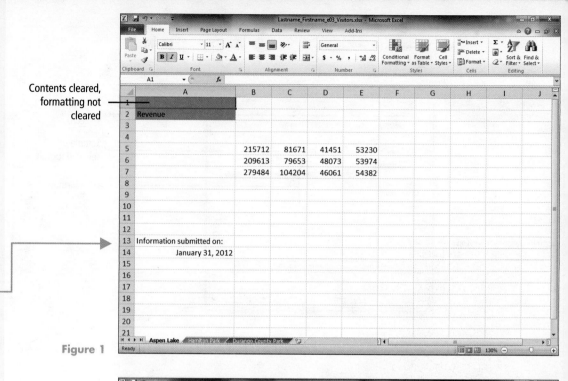

Contents cleared, formatting not cleared

Figure 1

Cell formats cleared, contents not cleared

Figure 2

Contents and formatting cleared

Figure 3

Cell contents and formats cleared

Figure 4

5. Select cell **A2**. On the **Home tab**, in the **Editing group**, click the **Clear** button, and then click **Clear All**. Compare your screen with **Figure 3**.

   Clear All deletes both the cell contents and the formatting.

6. In cell **A14**, use the technique just practiced to clear the formatting from the cell. In the **Number group**, verify that *General* displays as the number format of the cell. Notice that the date format is removed from the cell and that the underlying serial number—a sequential number—displays.

   The date, *January 31, 2012*, displays as 40939—the number of days since the reference date of January 1, 1900.

7. In the **Number group**, click the **Number Format arrow**, click **Long Date**, and then verify that the serial number in cell A14 again displays as a date.

   The long date format is applied to the date—*Tuesday, January 31, 2012*.

8. Display the **Hamilton Park sheet**, and then select the range **A1:A2**. In the **Editing group**, click the **Clear** button, and then click **Clear All**.

9. Display the **Durango County Park sheet**. Select the range **A1:A2**. In the **Editing group**, click the **Clear** button, and then click **Clear All**. Compare your screen with **Figure 4**.

10. Make **Aspen Lake** the active worksheet, and then **Save** the workbook.

■ **You have completed Skill 3 of 10**

► Data from cells and ranges can be copied and then pasted to other cells in the same worksheet, to other worksheets, or to worksheets in another workbook.

► The **Clipboard** is a temporary storage area for text and graphics. When you perform either the Copy command or the Cut command, the selected data is placed in the Clipboard, from which the data is available for pasting.

1. Select the range **A13:A14**. Point to the lower edge of the black border surrounding the selected range until the 📑 pointer displays. Drag downward until the ScreenTip displays *A16:A17*, as shown in **Figure 1**, and then release the mouse button to complete the move.

 Drag and drop is a method of moving objects in which you point to the selection and then drag it to a new location.

2. Click cell **A4**, type Visitor Type and then press Tab. Type the following titles in row **4**, pressing Tab after each title: Park Revenue, Food Revenue, Marketing Costs, Operating Costs, Net Income

3. Select columns **B:F**. In the **Cells group**, click the **Format** button, and then click **Column Width**. In the **Column Width** dialog box, select the displayed number, type 12 and then click **OK**. Compare your screen with **Figure 2**.

4. Select the range **A4:F4**. In the **Styles group**, click the **Cell Styles** button, and then click **20% - Accent6**. In the **Alignment group**, click the **Wrap Text** button 📑 and the **Center** button 📑.

■ Continue to the next page to complete the skill

Black border

Gray border displays where cells will be moved

ScreenTip displays the range A16:A17

Figure 1

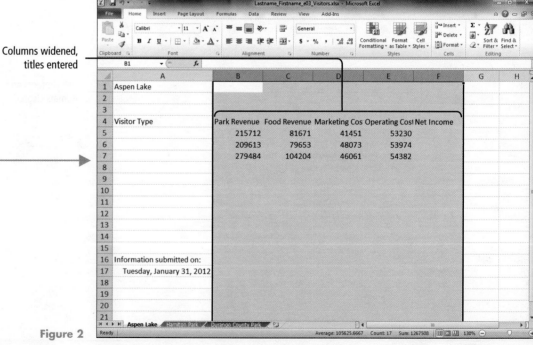

Columns widened, titles entered

Figure 2

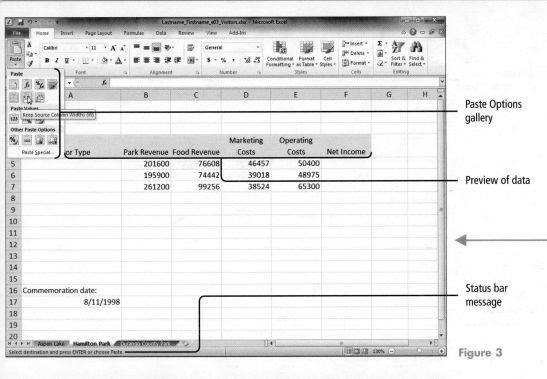

Paste Options gallery

Preview of data

Status bar message

Figure 3

Column widths retained

Column titles and formats pasted

Durango County Park sheet

Figure 4

5. With the range **A4:F4** still selected, in the **Clipboard group**, click the **Copy** button.

   A moving border surrounds the selected range, and a message on the status bar indicates *Select destination and press ENTER or choose Paste*, confirming that your selected range has been copied to the Clipboard.

6. Display the **Hamilton Park sheet**, and then click cell **A4**. In the **Clipboard group**, click the lower half of the **Paste** button to display the **Paste Preview** gallery. Point at the various Paste Options to preview the pasted text, as shown in **Figure 3**.

7. In the **Paste Options** gallery, click the second option in the second row—**Keep Source Column Widths**.

   The column titles are pasted, and the column widths from the source worksheet are retained.

   When pasting a range of cells, you need to select only the cell in the upper left corner of the *paste area*—the target destination for data that has been cut or copied. When an item is pasted, it is not removed from the Clipboard, as indicated by the status bar message.

8. Display the **Durango County Park** worksheet, and then click cell **A4**. Using the technique just practiced, paste the column titles using the Paste Option **Keep Source Column Widths**. Compare your screen with **Figure 4**.

9. Display the **Aspen Lake sheet**, and then **Save** the workbook.

   ■ **You have completed Skill 4 of 10**

▶ You can group any number of worksheets in a workbook. After the worksheets are grouped, you can edit data or format cells in all the grouped worksheets at the same time.

▶ Grouping worksheets is useful when you are creating or modifying a set of worksheets that are similar in purpose and structure.

1. Right-click the **Aspen Lake sheet tab**, and then from the shortcut menu, click **Select All Sheets**.

2. At the top of the screen, on the title bar, verify that *[Group]* displays, as shown in Figure 1.

    All the worksheets are selected, as indicated by *[Group]* on the title bar, and the sheet tab names are underlined in the sheet tab color. An underline on a worksheet tab indicates that the worksheet is active or selected within a group.

3. Click cell **A5**, type Local and then press Enter. In cell **A6**, type Domestic and then press Enter. In cell **A7**, type International and then press Enter.

4. Select the range **A5:A7**. In the **Styles group**, click the **Cell Styles** button, and then under **Titles and Headings**, click **40% - Accent6**.

5. Display the **Hamilton Park sheet**, and verify that the row labels and formats you entered on the **Aspen Lake sheet** display. Compare your screen with Figure 2.

    Data and formats are entered on all grouped worksheets.

▪ **Continue to the next page to complete the skill**

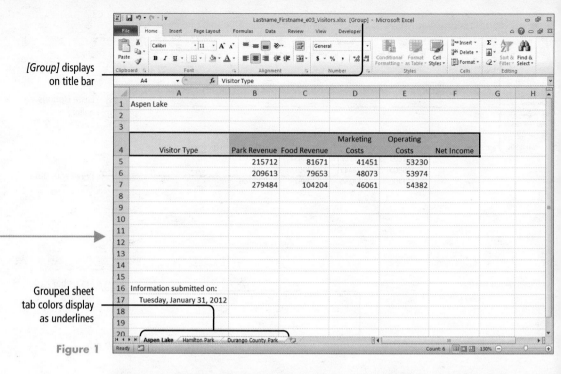

[Group] displays on title bar

Grouped sheet tab colors display as underlines

Figure 1

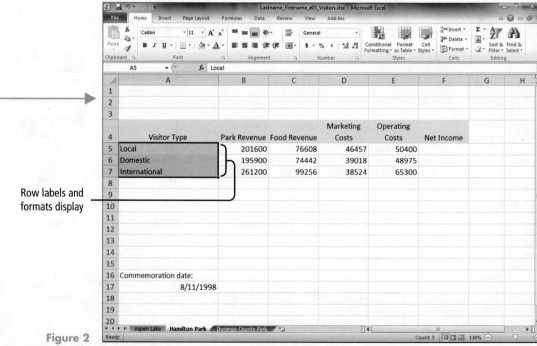

Row labels and formats display

Figure 2

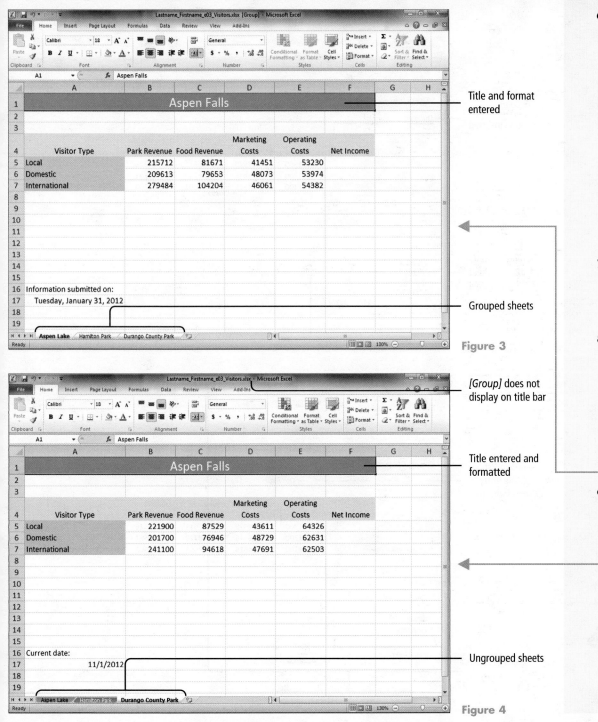

Title and format entered

Grouped sheets

Figure 3

[Group] does not display on title bar

Title entered and formatted

Ungrouped sheets

Figure 4

6. Display the **Durango County Park sheet** to verify that the labels and formats have been entered. In the sheet tab area, verify that both the *Aspen Lake* sheet tab and the *Hamilton Park* sheet tab display a solid color, indicating that they are no longer active in the group. Also verify that at the top of your screen, *[Group]* no longer displays on the title bar.

> Selecting a single sheet cancels a grouping. Because the worksheets were grouped, the text and formatting was entered into all of the selected sheets. In this manner, you can make the same changes to all selected worksheets in a workbook at the same time.

7. Right-click the **Aspen Lake sheet tab**, and then from the shortcut menu, click **Select All Sheets**.

> *[Group]* displays on the title bar.

8. In cell **A1**, press [Delete], type Aspen Falls and then press [Enter]. Select the range **A1:F1**. In the **Alignment group**, click the **Merge & Center** button ⊞. In the **Styles group**, click the **Cell Styles** button, and then click **Accent6**. In the **Font group**, click the **Font Size** button, and then click **18**. Compare your screen with **Figure 3**.

9. Display the **Durango County Park sheet**, and verify that the same changes have been made to this worksheet. **Save** the workbook, and then compare your screen with **Figure 4**.

■ **You have completed Skill 5 of 10**

► When you combine several math operators in a single formula, Excel follows a set of mathematical rules for performing calculations within a formula, called ***operator precedence***. First, expressions within parentheses are calculated. Second, multiplication and division are performed before addition and subtraction.

► When a formula contains operators with the same precedence level, Excel evaluates the operators from left to right. Multiplication and division are considered to be on the same level of precedence. Addition and subtraction are considered to be on the same level of precedence.

1. Display the **Aspen Lake sheet**. Click cell **A2**, type Aspen Lake and then press Enter. Display the **Hamilton Park sheet**. Click cell **A2**, type Hamilton Park and then press Enter. Display the **Durango County Park sheet**. Click cell **A2**, type Durango County Park and then press Enter. Compare your screen with **Figure 1**.

2. Right-click the **Durango County Park sheet tab**, and then click **Select All Sheets**.

3. Select the range **A2:F2**, and then in the **Alignment group**, click the **Merge & Center** button. In the **Styles group**, click the **Cell Styles** button, and then click **40% - Accent6**.

4. Click cell **A13**, type Submitted by: and then press Enter. In cell **A14**, using your first and last names, type Your Name and then press Enter. Compare your screen with **Figure 2**.

■ **Continue to the next page to complete the skill**

Figure 1

Figure 2

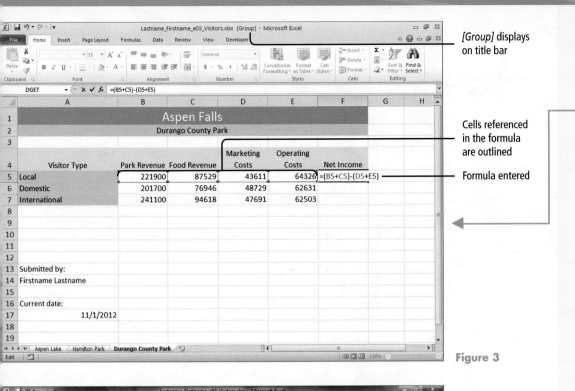

[Group] displays on title bar

Cells referenced in the formula are outlined

Formula entered

Figure 3

Date moved (your date may differ)

Durango County Park worksheet active

Figure 4

5. Verify that *[Group]* still displays on the title bar. If necessary, right-click a sheet tab, and click **Select All Sheets**. Click cell **F5**, enter the formula =(B5+C5)-(D5+E5) and then compare your screen with **Figure 3**.

   The formula *Net Income = Total Revenue – Total Cost* is represented by *(Park Revenue + Food Revenue) – (Marketing Costs + Operating Costs)*. By placing parentheses in the formula, the revenue is first added, the costs are added next, and then the total costs are subtracted from the total revenues. Without the parentheses, the formula would give an incorrect result.

6. On the **formula bar**, click the **Enter** button ☑. Use the **fill handle** to copy the formula down through cell **F7**.

   Recall that because the worksheets are grouped, the formulas have been entered on all three worksheets.

7. Verify that the formula results display in the **Hamilton Park** and **Aspen Lake** sheets.

8. Click the **Durango County Park sheet tab** to make it the active worksheet, and verify that the worksheets are no longer grouped. Click cell **A17**, and then point to the upper edge of the black border surrounding the cell until the ⟰ pointer displays. Drag up to move the cell contents up to cell **A16**. In the message box *Do you want to replace the contents of the destination cells?* click **OK**. Compare your screen with **Figure 4**.

9. **Save** 🖫 the workbook.

   ■ **You have completed Skill 6 of 10**

► When worksheets are grouped, any changes made to a single worksheet are made to each worksheet in the group. For example, if you change the width of a column or add a row, all the worksheets in the group are changed in the same manner.

1. Right-click the **Hamilton Park sheet tab**, and then click **Select All Sheets**.

2. In the row heading area, point to row **7** to display the ➡ pointer. Right-click, and then compare your screen with **Figure 1**.

3. From the shortcut menu, click **Insert** to insert a new blank row above the *International* row. In cell **A7**, type Families and press ⎇Tab⎇.

4. Click the **Aspen Lake sheet tab** to make it the active worksheet and to cancel the grouping of the worksheets. Beginning in cell **B7**, enter the following *Families* data for Aspen Lake:

   297815   41012   30270   57918

5. Click the **Hamilton Park sheet tab**, and then beginning in cell **B7**, enter the following *Families* data for Hamilton Park:

   292420   34290   19916   55086

6. Click the **Durango County Park sheet tab**, and then beginning in cell **B7**, enter the following *Families* data for **Durango County Park**:

   281700   31046   40425   61925

7. Click each of the sheet tabs, and then verify that you entered the values correctly. Click the **Durango County Park sheet tab**, and then compare your screen with **Figure 2**.

■ **Continue to the next page to complete the skill**

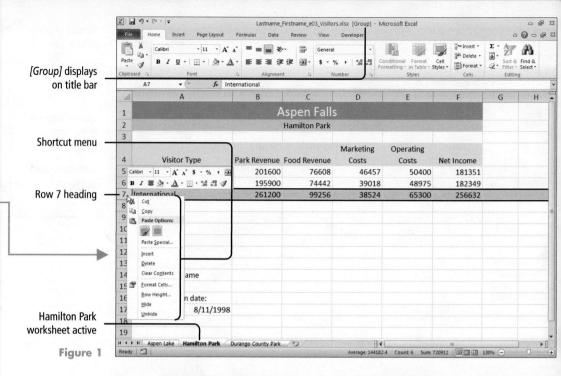

[Group] displays on title bar

Shortcut menu

Row 7 heading

Hamilton Park worksheet active

Figure 1

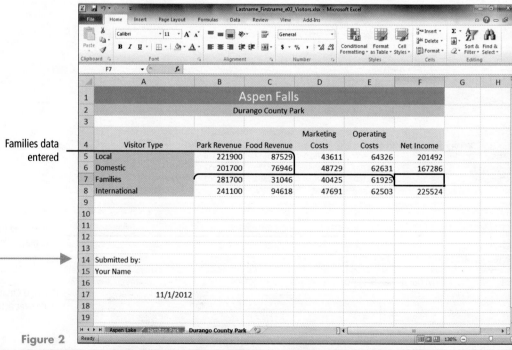

Families data entered

Figure 2

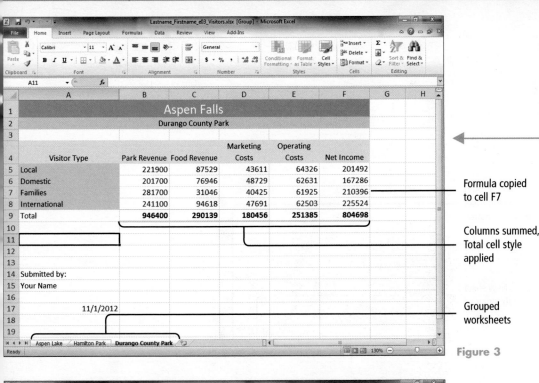

Formula copied
to cell F7

Columns summed,
Total cell style
applied

Grouped
worksheets

Figure 3

Comma [0] applied

Currency [0] applied

Ungrouped
worksheets

Figure 4

8. Right-click the **Durango County Park sheet tab**, and then click **Select All Sheets**. Click cell **F6**, and then use the **fill handle** to copy the formula down to cell **F7**.

9. In cell **A9**, type Total and then press [Enter]. Select the range **B9:F9**. On the **Home tab**, in the **Editing group**, click the **Sum** button [Σ]. With the range still selected, in the **Styles group**, click the **Cell Styles** button, and then click **Total**. Click cell **A11**, and then compare your screen with **Figure 3**.

10. Select the range **B5:F5**, hold down [Ctrl], and then select the range **B9:F9**. In the **Styles group**, click the **Cell Styles** button, and then click **Currency [0]**.

11. Select the range **B6:F8**, click the **Cell Styles** button, and then click **Comma [0]**.

12. Display the **Aspen Lake sheet**, and then verify that the same formulas were entered and the same formatting was applied.

   On the Aspen Lake worksheet, the formula in cell F9 displays as the value *$923,805*.

13. Click the **Hamilton Park sheet tab** to make it the active worksheet, and verify that the formulas and formatting changes were made. Click cell **A11**, and then compare your screen with **Figure 4**.

   On the Hamilton Park worksheet, the formula in cell F9 displays as the value *$872,040*.

14. Click the **Durango County Park sheet tab**, and verify that the formula in cell **F9** displays as the value *$804,698*. **Save** 🖫 the workbook.

   ■ **You have completed Skill 7 of 10**

► To organize a workbook, you can move sheet tabs into any order you desire.

► You can add new worksheets to accommodate new information.

1. To the right of the **Durango County Park sheet tab**, click the **Insert Worksheet** button 🗐.

   A new blank worksheet is inserted with a unique name such as *Sheet1* or *Sheet2*.

2. Double-click the **sheet tab** just inserted, type Summary and then press Enter. Compare your screen with **Figure 1**.

3. In cell **A4**, type Park and then press Tab. In cell **B4**, type Total Park Revenue and then press Tab. In cell **C4**, type Total Food Revenue and then press Tab. In cell **D4**, type Total Marketing Costs and then press Tab. In cell **E4**, type Total Operating Costs and then press Tab. In cell **F4**, type Net Income and then press Enter. Compare your screen with **Figure 2**.

4. Select cell **A1**, and then in the **Cells group**, click the **Format** button, and then click **Column Width**. In the **Column Width** dialog box, type 20 and then click **OK**. Select columns **B:F**, and then using the same technique, widen the columns to *12*.

5. Display the **Aspen Lake sheet**, and click cell **A4**. Click the Copy button 🗐. Display the **Summary sheet**, and then select the range **A4:F4**. Click the **Paste button arrow**. In the **Paste Options** gallery, under **Other Paste Options**, click **Formatting** 🔳.

   The formatting is applied to the range A4:F4.

■ **Continue to the next page to complete the skill**

Insert Worksheet button

New sheet tab renamed

Figure 1

Text truncated

Figure 2

Cell contents pasted

Cell formatting pasted

Figure 3

Caret and paper icon indicate location of moved sheet tab

Figure 4

6. In cell **A5**, type Aspen Lake and then press Enter. In cell **A6**, type Hamilton Park and then in cell **A7**, type Durango County Park

7. Display the **Aspen Lake sheet**, and click cell **A1**. In the **Clipboard group**, click the **Copy** button. Display the **Summary sheet**, and click cell **A1**. In the **Clipboard group**, click the **Paste** button.

   The cell contents, including both the text *Aspen Falls* and the formatting, are pasted.

8. On the **Summary sheet**, in cell **A2**, type Visitor Revenue and press Enter. Display the **Aspen Lake sheet**, and click cell **A2**. Click the **Copy** button. Display the **Summary sheet**, and click cell **A2**. In the **Clipboard group**, click the **Paste button arrow**. In the **Paste Options** gallery, under **Other Paste Options**, click **Formatting**, and then compare your screen with **Figure 3**.

   Only the cell formatting is pasted.

9. Right-click the **Summary sheet tab**, click **Tab Color**, and then click the seventh color in the first row—**Gold, Accent 3**.

10. Point to the **Summary sheet tab**, hold down the left mouse button to display a small black triangle—a caret—and then notice that a small paper icon attaches to the mouse pointer.

11. Drag to the left until the caret and mouse pointer are to the left of the **Aspen Lake tab**, as shown in **Figure 4**.

12. Release the left mouse button to complete the worksheet move.

13. **Save** the workbook.

■ **You have completed Skill 8 of 10**

▶ A *summary sheet* is a worksheet that displays and summarizes totals from other worksheets. A *detail sheet* is a worksheet with cells referred to by summary sheet formulas.

▶ Changes made to the detail sheets that affect their totals will automatically recalculate and display on the summary sheet.

1. On the **Summary sheet**, click cell **B5**. Type = and then click the **Aspen Lake sheet tab**. On the **Aspen Lake sheet**, click cell **B9**, and then press Enter.

   The Summary worksheet displays the value from cell B9 in the Aspen Lake worksheet.

2. Click cell **B5**. In the **formula bar**, notice that the cell reference in the underlying formula includes both a worksheet reference and a cell reference, as shown in **Figure 1**.

   By using a formula of this type, changes made to cell B9 of the *Aspen Lake* worksheet will be automatically updated in this *Summary* worksheet.

3. Click cell **B6**, type = and then click the **Hamilton Park sheet tab**. On the **Hamilton Park sheet**, click cell **B9**, and then press Enter.

4. On the **Summary sheet**, repeat the technique just practiced to place the value in cell **B9** from the **Durango County Park sheet** in cell **B7** of the **Summary sheet**.

5. On the **Summary sheet**, select the range **B5:B7**. Point to the **fill handle**, and then drag to the right to fill the formulas through column **F**. Click cell **F7**, and compare your screen with **Figure 2**.

■ **Continue to the next page to complete the skill**

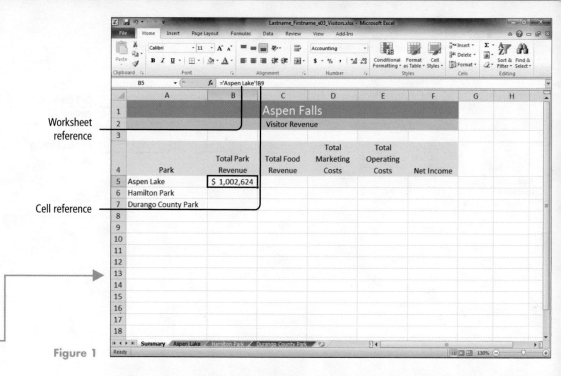

Worksheet reference

Cell reference

Figure 1

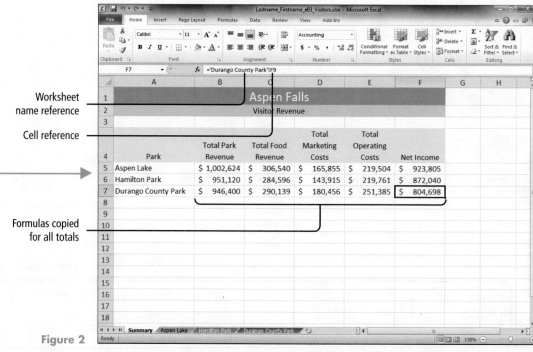

Worksheet name reference

Cell reference

Formulas copied for all totals

Figure 2

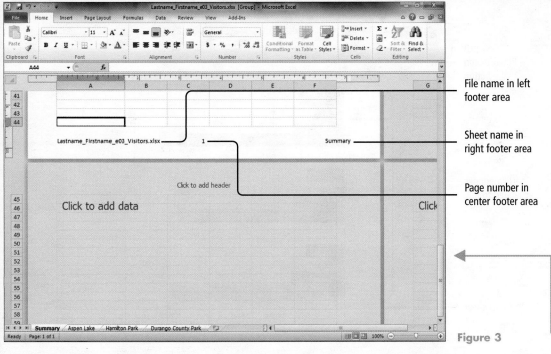

File name in left footer area

Sheet name in right footer area

Page number in center footer area

Figure 3

Page 4 of 4

Next Page button

Durango County Park worksheet footer

Figure 4

6. On the **Summary sheet**, in cell **A8**, type Total and then select the range **B8:F8**. In the **Editing group**, click the **Sum** button Σ, and then apply the **Total** cell style. Select the range **B6:F7**, and then apply the **Comma [0]** cell style.

7. Right-click the **Summary sheet tab**, and then click **Select All Sheets**. On the **Insert tab**, in the **Text group**, click the **Header & Footer** button. Insert the **File Name** in the left footer.

8. Click the **center section** of the footer, and then in the **Header & Footer Elements group**, click the **Page Number** button. Click the right section of the footer, and then in the **Header & Footer Elements group**, click the **Sheet Name** button. Click in a cell just above the footer to exit the **Footer area**, and then compare your screen with **Figure 3**.

9. On the lower right side of the status bar, click the **Normal** button ▦. Hold down Ctrl, and press Home. Click the **File tab**, and then click **Print**. At the bottom of the screen, click the **Next Page** button ▶ three times to view each of the four worksheets, and then compare your screen with **Figure 4**.

   Because the worksheets are grouped, all four worksheets will be previewed and the footer will display in each worksheet.

10. Click the **Home tab**. Right-click the **Summary sheet tab**, and then click **Ungroup Sheets**.

11. Save ▦ the workbook.

■ **You have completed Skill 9 of 10**

▶ A *clustered bar chart* is a chart type that is useful when you want to compare values across categories; bar charts organize categories along the vertical axis and values along the horizontal axis.

1. On the **Summary sheet**, select the range **A4:E7**. On the **Insert tab**, in the **Charts group**, click the **Bar** button, and then under **2-D Bar**, click **Clustered Bar**.

2. On the **Design tab**, in the **Location group**, click the **Move Chart** button. In the **Move Chart** dialog box, select the **New sheet** option button, type Revenue and Cost Chart and then click **OK**.

   The chart is moved to a chart sheet.

3. On the **Design tab**, in the **Data group**, click the **Switch Row/Column** button. Compare your screen with **Figure 1**.

   Because you want to look at revenue and costs by location, displaying the locations on the vertical axis is useful.

4. In the **Chart Layouts group**, click the **More** button ⤓, and then click **Layout 8**. In the **Chart Styles group**, click the **More** button ⤓, and then click **Style 26**.

5. On the **Layout tab**, in the **Axes group**, click the **Axes** button. Point to **Primary Horizontal Axis**, and then click **More Primary Horizontal Axis Options**. On the left side of the **Format Axis** dialog box, click **Alignment**, and then on the right, in the **Custom angle box**, type -40 Click **Close**, and then compare your screen with **Figure 2**.

■ **Continue to the next page to complete the skill** ➤

Switch Row/Column button

Chart categories changed to row names

Chart sheet

Figure 1

Horizontal axis values angled

Chart and axis titles display

Figure 2

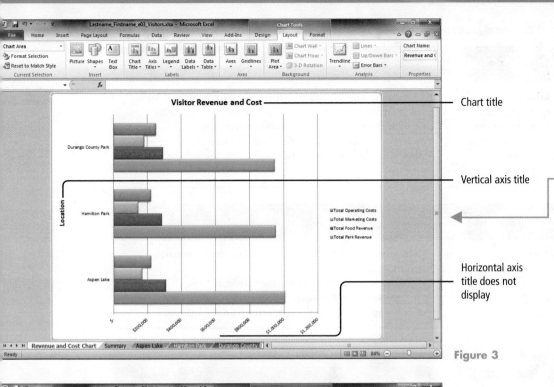

Chart title

Vertical axis title

Horizontal axis title does not display

Figure 3

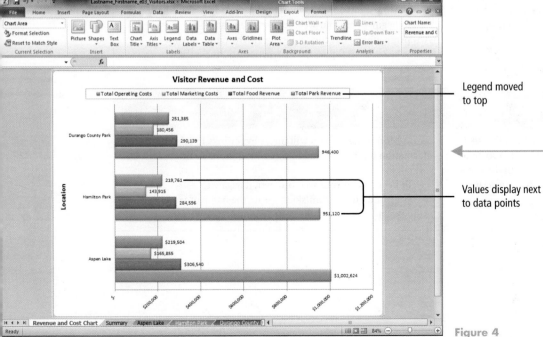

Legend moved to top

Values display next to data points

Figure 4

6. Click the **Chart Title**. Type Visitor Revenue and Cost and then press [Enter].

7. On the left side of the chart, click the vertical **Axis Title**. Type Location and then press [Enter]. Right-click the *Location* title, and then on the Mini toolbar, change the **Font Size** to **14**. At the bottom of the chart, click the horizontal **Axis Title**, press [Delete], and then compare your screen with **Figure 3**.

8. On the **Layout tab**, in the **Labels group**, click the **Legend** button, and then click **More Legend Options**. In the **Format Legend** dialog box, under **Legend Position**, select the **Top** option button. On the left, click **Border Color**, and then on the right, select the **Solid line** option button. Click **Close**. Right-click the legend, and then on the Mini toolbar, change the **Font Size** to **12**.

9. In the **Labels group**, click the **Data Labels** button, and then click **Outside End**. Compare your screen with **Figure 4**.

10. On the **Insert tab**, in the **Text group**, click the **Header & Footer** button. In the **Page Setup** dialog box, click the **Custom Footer** button. Click the **Insert File Name** button 📄, and then click **OK** two times.

11. **Save** the workbook. Print or submit your file as directed by your instructor. To print, click the **File tab**, and then click **Print**. Under Settings, click **Print Active Sheets**, and then click **Print Entire Workbook**. Click the **Print** button. **Exit** Excel.

Done! You have completed Skill 10 of 10 and your document is complete!

More Skills

The following More Skills are located at **www.pearsonhighered.com/skills**

More Skills 11 Create Organization Charts

You can add SmartArt graphics to a worksheet to create timelines, illustrate processes, or show relationships. When you click the SmartArt button on the Ribbon, you can select from among a broad array of graphics, including an organization chart. An organization chart graphically represents the relationships between individuals and groups in an organization.

In More Skills 11, you will insert and modify a SmartArt graphic organization chart.

To begin, open your web browser, navigate to www.pearsonhighered.com/skills, locate the name of your textbook, and then follow the instructions on the website.

More Skills 12 Create Line Charts

Use a line chart when you want to compare more than one set of values over time. Time is displayed along the bottom axis and the data point values are connected with a line. The curves and directions of the lines make trends obvious to the reader.

In More Skills 12, you will create a line chart comparing three sets of values.

To begin, open your web browser, navigate to www.pearsonhighered.com/skills, locate the name of your textbook, and then follow the instructions on the website.

More Skills 13 Set and Clear Print Areas

If you are likely to print the same portion of a particular worksheet over and over again, you can save time by setting a print area.

In More Skills 13, you will set print areas in a worksheet.

To begin, open your web browser, navigate to www.pearsonhighered.com/skills, locate the name of your textbook, and then follow the instructions on the website.

More Skills 14 Insert Hyperlinks

You can insert a hyperlink in a worksheet that can link to a file, a location in a file, a web page on the World Wide Web, or a web page on an organization's intranet. Creating a hyperlink in a workbook is a convenient way to provide quick access to related information.

In More Skills 14, you will insert hyperlinks to related information on the web and to other worksheets in the workbook.

To begin, open your web browser, navigate to www.pearsonhighered.com/skills, locate the name of your textbook, and then follow the instructions on the website.

Key Terms

Online Help Skills

1. **Start** 🔵 **Excel**. In the upper right corner of the Excel window, click the **Help** button 🔘. In the Help window, click the **Maximize** 🔲 button.

2. Click in the search box, type move formula and then click the **Search** button 🔍. In the search results, click **Move or copy a formula**. Compare your screen with **Figure 1**.

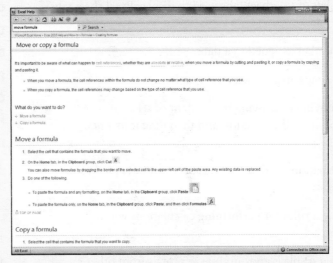

Figure 1

3. Read the article's introduction, and then read the sections **Move a formula** and **Copy a formula** to see if you can answer the following: What can happen to a cell reference when you move or copy a formula?

Matching

Match each term in the second column with its correct definition in the first column by writing the letter of the term on the blank line in front of the correct definition.

____ **1.** The labels along the lower border of the workbook window that identify each worksheet.

____ **2.** Buttons to the left of the sheet tabs used to display Excel sheet tabs that are not in view.

____ **3.** A sequential number assigned to a date.

____ **4.** A temporary storage area for text and graphics.

____ **5.** A method of moving or copying the content of selected cells in which you point to the selection and then drag it to a new location.

____ **6.** The target destination for data that has been cut or copied using the Clipboard.

____ **7.** The mathematical rules for performing calculations within a formula.

____ **8.** A worksheet that displays and summarizes totals from other worksheets in a workbook.

____ **9.** A worksheet that contains the detailed information in a workbook.

____ **10.** A chart type that is useful when you want to compare values across categories; categories are typically organized along the vertical axis, and the values along the horizontal axis.

A Clipboard

B Clustered bar chart

C Detail sheet

D Drag and drop

E Operator precedence

F Paste area

G Serial number

H Sheet tabs

I Summary sheet

J Tab scrolling buttons

Multiple Choice

Choose the correct answer.

1. In an Excel workbook, you can do this.
   A. Insert only one worksheet
   B. Move worksheets
   C. Move only one worksheet

2. Grouped worksheets can be edited and formatted in this way.
   A. All at the same time
   B. Only one worksheet at a time
   C. Only once

3. Deleting the contents of a cell also deletes this.
   A. Only the contents
   B. Only the format
   C. Both contents and format

4. When pasting a range of cells, this cell needs to be selected in the paste area.
   A. Bottom right cell
   B. Center cell
   C. Top left cell

5. When grouping worksheets in a workbook, you can group this number of worksheets.
   A. Only two
   B. Only three
   C. Any number

6. If a workbook contains grouped worksheets, this word will display on the title bar.
   A. [Collection]
   B. [Set]
   C. [Group]

7. When a formula contains operators with the same precedence level, the operators are evaluated in this order.
   A. Left to right
   B. Right to left
   C. From the center out

8. Addition and this mathematical operator are considered to be on the same precedence level.
   A. Multiplication
   B. Division
   C. Subtraction

9. Changes made in a detail worksheet will automatically recalculate and display on this sheet.
   A. Summary
   B. Final
   C. Outline

10. In a chart, the legend can be located here.
    A. The detail sheet
    B. The top of the chart
    C. The summary sheet

Topics for Discussion

1. Think of the various departments and discipline areas at your college. What might be an example of workbooks that would contain data that could be organized into identically structured worksheets and then summarized in a summary sheet? Can you think of any examples specifically for your college athletic department?

2. Illustrate some examples of how a formula's results will be incorrect if parentheses are not used to group calculations in the order they should be performed. Think of averaging three test scores and how you would write the formula to get a correct result.

Skill Check

To complete this workbook, you will need the following file:

- e03_Payroll

You will save your workbook as:

- Lastname_Firstname_e03_Payroll

1. **Start** Excel, and open the file **e03_Payroll**. **Save** the workbook in your **Excel Chapter 3** folder as Lastname_Firstname_e03_Payroll

2. Double-click the **Sheet1 sheet tab**, type Courthouse and then press Enter. Right-click the **Courthouse sheet tab**, click **Tab Color**, and then click **Ice Blue, Accent 5**. Use the same technique to rename **Sheet2** as City Center and then apply the tab color **Gold, Accent 4**. Rename **Sheet3** as Community Center and then apply the tab color **Red, Accent 3**.

3. Right-click a **sheet tab**, and then click **Select All Sheets**. Add the file name in the worksheets left footer, and then add the sheet name in the right footer. Return to **Normal** view.

4. In cell **A4**, type Job Title and then press Tab. In cell **B4**, type Total Gross Pay In cell **C4**, type Income Tax In cell **D4**, type Social Security (FICA) Tax In cell **E4**, type Health Insurance In cell **F4**, type Net Pay

5. Select the range **A4:F4**, and then apply the cell style **40% - Accent3**. In the **Alignment group**, click the **Wrap Text** and the **Center** buttons. Click cell **A10**, and then compare your screen with **Figure 1**. ——————

6. Verify that the worksheets are still grouped. In cell **F5**, type =B5-(C5+D5+E5) and then press Enter to construct the formula to compute the Net Pay as *Total Gross Pay – (Income Tax + Social Security (FICA) Tax + Health Insurance)*. In cell **F5**, use the **fill handle** to copy the formula down through cell **F8**.

7. Select the range **B9:F9**. In the **Editing group**, click the **Sum** button, and then apply the **Total** cell style. Select the nonadjacent ranges **B5:F5** and **B9:F9**, and then apply the **Currency [0]** cell style. In the range **B6:F8**, apply the **Comma [0]** cell style. Right-click a **sheet tab**, and then click **Ungroup Sheets**. Click cell **A10**, and then compare your screen with **Figure 2**. ——————

Figure 1

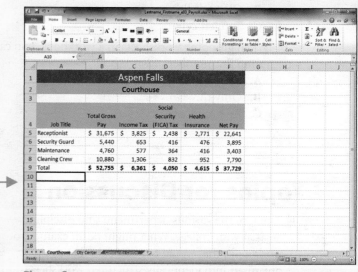

Figure 2

- Continue to the next page to complete this Skill Check

Figure 3

Figure 4

8. Insert a new worksheet. Rename the new sheet tab Summary and then change the **Tab Color** to **Orange, Accent 1**. Move the **Summary sheet** to the first position in the workbook.

9. Display the **Courthouse sheet**, select the range **A1:F4**, and then click **Copy**. Display the **Summary sheet** and then click cell **A1**. Click the **Paste button arrow** and then click **Keep Source Column Widths**. In cell **A2**, type City Payroll and then in cell **A4**, type Location In cell **A5**, type Courthouse In cell **A6**, type City Center In cell **A7**, type Community Center and then in cell **A8**, type Total

10. Click **B5**, type = and then click the **Courthouse sheet tab**. On the **Courthouse sheet**, click cell **B9**, and then press [Enter]. Use the same technique in cells **B6** and **B7** to place the *Total Gross Pay* amounts from the *City Center* and the *Community Center* worksheets on the *Summary* worksheet.

11. On the **Summary sheet**, select the range **B5:B7**, and then use the **fill handle** to copy the formulas to the right through column **F**. Select the range **B8:F8**. In the **Editing group**, click the **Sum** button, and then apply the **Total** cell style. Compare your screen with **Figure 3**.

12. On the **Summary sheet**, select the nonadjacent ranges **A4:A7** and **C4:E7**. On the **Insert tab**, in the **Charts group**, click the **Bar** button, and then click **Clustered Bar**. On the **Design tab**, in the **Location group**, click the **Move Chart** button. Rename the chart sheet Payroll Chart

13. On the **Design tab**, in the **Data group**, click the **Switch Row/Column** button. In the **Chart Styles group**, click the **More** button, and then click **Style 13**. In the **Chart Layouts group**, click **Layout 3**. Click the **Chart Title**, type Payroll Adjustments by Location and then press [Enter]. On the **Layout tab**, in the **Axes group**, click the **Axes** button, point to **Primary Horizontal Axis**, and then click **More Primary Horizontal Axis Options**. On the left, click **Alignment**. In the **Custom angle** box, type -40 and then click **Close**.

14. On the **Insert tab**, in the **Text group**, click the **Header & Footer** button. In the **Page Setup** dialog box, click the **Custom Footer** button, and then in the **Left section**, click the **Insert File Name** button. Click **OK** two times.

15. **Save** the workbook. Group the worksheets. Click the **File tab**, and then click **Print**. Click the **Next Page** button to view the five sheets. Compare your workbook with **Figure 4**. Print or submit the file as directed by your instructor.

Done! You have completed the Skill Check

Assess Your Skills 1

To complete this workbook, you will need the following file:

- e03_Water

You will save your workbook as:

- Lastname_Firstname_e03_Water

1. **Start** Excel, and open the file **e03_Water**. **Save** the workbook in your **Excel Chapter 3** folder as Lastname_Firstname_e03_Water Rename **Sheet1** as October and then apply the sheet tab color **Dark Red, Accent 2**.

2. Group the sheets. In cell **F5**, construct a formula to compute *Net Revenue = (Water Usage * Rate) + (City Sales Tax + Water Tax)*. Copy the formula down. In row **9**, sum the columns. In the range **B9:F9**, apply the **Total** cell style.

3. In the nonadjacent ranges **C5:F5** and **C9:F9**, apply the **Currency** [0] cell style, and then in the ranges **B5:B9** and **C6:F8**, apply the **Comma** [0] cell style.

4. Insert a new worksheet. Rename the new sheet tab Summary and apply the sheet tab color **Orange, Accent1**. Move the new sheet tab to make it the first worksheet in the workbook.

5. Group the sheets. Add the file name in the left footer and the sheet name in the right footer. Return to **Normal View**, and then ungroup the sheets.

6. Copy the range **A1:F4** from any of the other worksheets, and then on the **Summary sheet**, click cell **A1**. Click the **Paste button arrow**, and then click the **Keep Source Column Widths** button. Change the title of cell **A2** to Water Revenue: 4th Quarter and then change the title in cell **A4** to Month In cell **A5**, type

October and then use the fill handle to fill cells **A6** and **A7** with November and December. In cell **A8**, type Total

7. In the *Summary* worksheet, enter a formula in cell **B5** setting the cell equal to cell **B9** in the *October* worksheet. Enter the *Water Usage* total from the *November* and the *December* worksheets in cells **B6** and **B7**. In the *Summary* worksheet, select the range **B5:B7**, and then use the **fill handle** to copy the formulas to the right through column **F**.

8. In row **8**, sum column **B** and the columns **D:F**, and then apply the **Total** cell style to the cells. In the range **D6:F7**, apply the **Comma** [0] cell style. In the ranges **D5:F5** and **D8:F8**, apply the **Currency** [0] cell style.

9. Insert a **Clustered Bar** chart using the non-adjacent ranges **A4:A7** and **D4:E7** as the source data. Move the chart to a chart sheet with the sheet name Tax Chart

10. Apply the **Style 28** chart style, and then apply the **Layout 1** chart layout. For the **Primary Horizontal Axis**, set the **Custom angle** to **-40°**. Change the **Chart Title** to 4th Quarter Taxes

11. On the **chart sheet**, add the file name in the left footer. **Save** the workbook. Compare your completed workbook with **Figure 1**. Print or submit the file as directed by your instructor.

Done! You have completed Assess Your Skills 1

Figure 1

Assessment

Assess Your Skills 3 and 4 can be found at **www.pearsonhighered.com/skills**.

Assess Your Skills 2

To complete this workbook, you will need the following file:

■ e03_Taxes

You will save your workbook as:

■ Lastname_Firstname_e03_Taxes

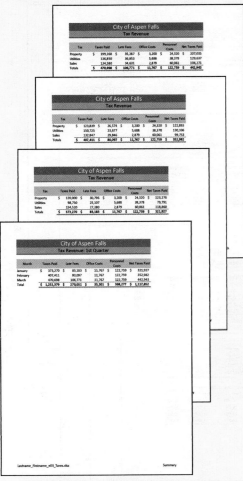

1. **Start** Excel, and open the file **e03_Taxes**. Save the workbook in your **Excel Chapter 3** folder as Lastname_Firstname_e03_Taxes

2. Rename the **Sheet1** sheet tab as January and then apply the sheet tab color **Pink, Text 2**. In cell **A13**, using your first and last names, type Your Name and then in cell **A14** enter the current date.

3. Group the sheets. In cell **F5**, construct a formula to compute *Net Taxes = (Taxes Paid + Late Fees) − (Office Costs + Personnel Costs)*. Copy the formula down, and then in row **8**, sum the columns.

4. In the ranges **B5:F5** and **B8:F8**, apply the **Currency [0]** cell style; in the range **B8:F8**, apply the **Total** cell style; and then in the range **B6:F7**, apply the **Comma [0]** cell style.

5. Insert a new sheet, rename the sheet tab Summary and then change the sheet tab color to **Black, Text 1**. Move the sheet to the first position in the workbook. Copy the range **A1:F4** from another sheet, and then paste the range into the *Summary* sheet using the **Keep Source Column Widths** button.

6. Group the sheets. Add the file name in the left footer and the sheet name in the right footer. Return to **Normal** view, and then ungroup the sheets.

7. On the **Summary sheet**, change the title in cell **A2** to Tax Revenue: 1st Quarter and then change the title in cell **A4** to Month In the

range **A5:A7**, enter the months January, February, and March and in cell **A8**, type Total

8. In cell **B5**, enter a formula setting the cell equal to cell **B8** in the *January* worksheet. Enter the total *Taxes Paid* from the *February* and the *March* worksheets in cells **B6** and **B7** of the **Summary sheet**. In the *Summary* worksheet, copy the range **B5:B7** to the right through column **F**.

9. In the range **B8:F8**, sum the columns, and then apply the **Total** cell style. In the range **B6:F7**, apply the **Comma [0]** cell style.

10. Select the range **A4:E7**, and then from the **Bar Chart** gallery, insert a **Clustered Horizontal Cylinder** chart. Move the chart to a chart sheet with the sheet tab name Tax Chart In the **Data group**, click the **Switch Row/Column** button. Apply the **Layout 1** chart layout and the **Style 26** chart style. Change the chart title to 1st Quarter

11. Show the **Legend** at the top of the chart. For the **Primary Horizontal Axis**, set the **Alignment** to **Custom angle** of **-40°**. Right-click the **Chart Area**, click **Format Chart Area**, and then select the **Gradient fill** option button. Add the file name in the left footer of the chart sheet.

12. **Save** the workbook. Print or submit the file as directed by your instructor. Compare your completed workbook with **Figure 1**.

Done! You have completed Assess Your Skills 2

Figure 1

Assess Your Skills Visually

To complete this workbook, you will need the following file:

- e03_Parking

You will save your workbook as:

- Lastname_Firstname_e03_Parking

Open the file **e03_Parking**, and save the workbook in your **Excel Chapter 3** folder as Lastname_Firstname_e03_Parking Complete the three details sheets as shown in **Figure 1**. To compute the *Net Income*, group the worksheets, and then use the formula *Net Income = (Parking Meters + Parking Tickets) − (Maintenance Cost + Personnel Costs)*. Sum the columns, and then apply appropriate number formats. Create the summary sheet for the 2nd Quarter with the totals from each month and the titles as shown in the figure. Insert a **Clustered Bar chart**, and then move the chart to a chart sheet with the sheet tab name Parking Chart Apply the **Style 27** chart style and the **Layout 1** chart layout. For the chart title, type Parking Revenue and Cost and show the legend at the top. Angle the primary horizontal axis at **-40°**. On all worksheets, add a footer with the file name in the left section and the sheet name in the right section. **Save** the workbook, and then print or submit the workbook electronically as directed by your instructor.

Done! You have completed Assess Your Skills Visually

Figure 1

Skills in Context

To complete this workbook, you will need the following file:

- e03_Center

You will save your workbook as:

- Lastname_Firstname_e03_Center

During each quarter, the city tracked the rental revenue at the City Center. Open the file **e03_Center**, and then save the workbook in your **Excel Chapter 3** folder as Lastname_Firstname_e03_Center For each quarter, compute the net income using the formula *Net Income = Income − (Indirect Costs + Direct Costs)*. Total the columns, and format the numbers appropriately. Create a worksheet named Summary containing the totals for each quarter. Use the same column titles that are on the detail worksheets in the range B4:E4, and change the row titles in the

range A4:A7. Total and format the numbers on the *Summary* worksheet. Insert a clustered bar chart, and move the chart to a chart sheet. Format the chart appropriately. On all sheets, insert the file name in the left footer and the sheet name in the right footer. Save the workbook, and then print or submit the workbook electronically as directed by your instructor.

Done! You have completed Skills in Context

Skills and You

To complete this workbook, you will need the following file:

- New blank Excel workbook

You will save your workbook as:

- Lastname_Firstname_e03_Repairs

How much does it cost your family to own, operate, and maintain more than one vehicle? Recording the cost of owning each vehicle and then comparing the costs might reveal that one or more of your vehicles are costing more in repairs or gasoline than you want to spend. Create a worksheet for each vehicle your family uses. Use months as the row names, and use *Payment*, *Insurance*, *Gasoline*, and *Maintenance and Repairs* as the column names. Record three months of data, and then format the data appropriately. Create a summary sheet for the vehicles. Create a

clustered bar chart, and move the chart to a chart sheet. Switch the rows and columns as necessary so that the vehicles form the vertical axis. You might find that one or more vehicles is using much more gasoline or costing more in repairs and maintenance than you realized. Save the workbook in your **Excel Chapter 3** folder as Lastname_Firstname_e03_Repairs and submit the workbook as directed by your instructor.

Done! You have completed Skills and You

Use Excel Functions and Tables

► The Excel Function Library contains hundreds of special functions that perform complex calculations quickly. Some of the categories in the Function Library include statistical, financial, logical, date and time, and math and trigonometry.

► Excel tables help you manage information by providing many ways to sort, filter, analyze, format, and generate charts from the data in a table.

Your starting screen will look similar to this:

SKILLS

Skills 1-10 Training

At the end of this chapter, you will be able to:

Skill 1 Use the SUM and AVERAGE Functions

Skill 2 Use the MIN and MAX Functions

Skill 3 Move Ranges with Functions, Add Borders, and Rotate Text

Skill 4 Use the IF Function

Skill 5 Apply Conditional Formatting with Custom Formats, Data Bars, and Sparklines

Skill 6 Use Find and Replace and Insert the NOW Function

Skill 7 Freeze and Unfreeze Panes

Skill 8 Create and Sort Excel Tables

Skill 9 Use the Search Filter in Excel Tables

Skill 10 Convert Tables to Ranges, Hide Rows and Columns, and Format Large Worksheets

MORE SKILLS

More Skills 11 Apply Conditional Color Scales with Top and Bottom Rules

More Skills 12 Use the Payment (PMT) Function

More Skills 13 Create PivotTable Reports

More Skills 14 Use Goal Seek

Outcome

Using the skills listed to the left will enable you to create a workbook like this:

You will save your workbook as:

Lastname_Firstname_e04_Fire_Equipment

In this chapter, you will create documents for the Aspen Falls City Hall, which provides essential services for the citizens and visitors of Aspen Falls, California.

Introduction

- ▶ Functions are prewritten formulas that have two parts: the name of the function and the arguments that specify the values or cells to be used by the function.
- ▶ Conditional formatting helps you see important trends and highlight exceptions in your data by applying various formats such as colored gradients, data bars, or icons.
- ▶ You can convert data organized in rows and columns into a Microsoft Office Excel table.
- ▶ Excel tables allow you to add data analysis such as sorting and filtering, summary rows, and calculated columns, and you can format the tables using a large library of table styles.

Time to complete all
10 skills – 50 to 90 minutes

Find your student data files here:

**Student data file needed
for this chapter:**

- e04_Fire_Equipment

► A *function* is a prewritten formula that takes input, performs an operation, and returns a value. Functions are used to simplify and shorten formulas.

► *Statistical functions* are predefined formulas that describe a collection of data—for example, totals, counts, and averages.

► The *AVERAGE function* adds a group of values and then divides the result by the number of values in the group.

1. **Start** ● Excel, and then open **e04_Fire_ Equipment**. Click the **File tab**, and then click **Save As**. In the **Save As** dialog box, navigate to the location where you are saving your files. Click **New folder**, type Excel Chapter 4 and then press (Enter) two times. In the **File name** box, type Lastname_Firstname_e04_Fire_ Equipment and then press (Enter).

2. Click cell **C4**. On the **Home tab**, in the **Editing group**, click the **Sum** button Σ, and then compare your screen with **Figure 1**.

3. With the insertion point in the function parentheses, click cell **A12**, and then press (Ctrl) + (Shift) + (↓) to select the range **A12:A70**. On the formula bar, click the **Enter** button ☑ to display the result *1745*, as shown in **Figure 2**.

   The range in parentheses is the function *argument*—the values that a function uses to perform operations or calculations. The arguments each function uses are specific to that function. Common arguments include numbers, text, cell references, and range names.

■ **Continue to the next page to complete the skill**

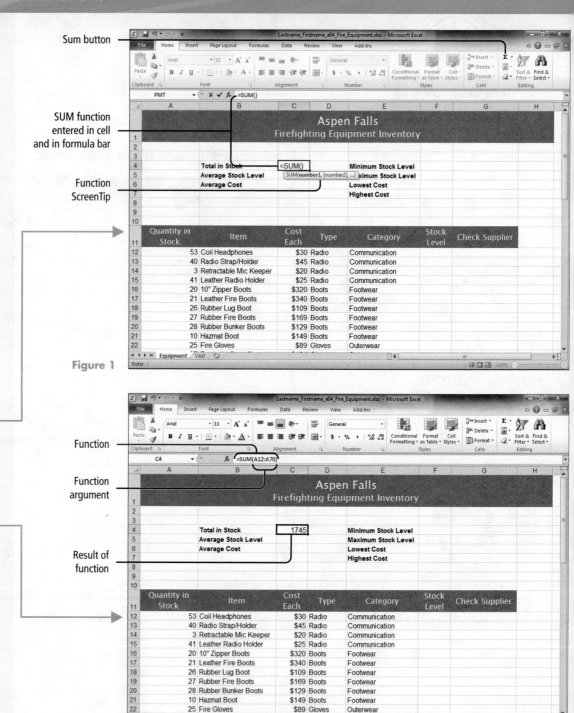

Sum button

SUM function entered in cell and in formula bar

Function ScreenTip

Figure 1

Function

Function argument

Result of function

Figure 2

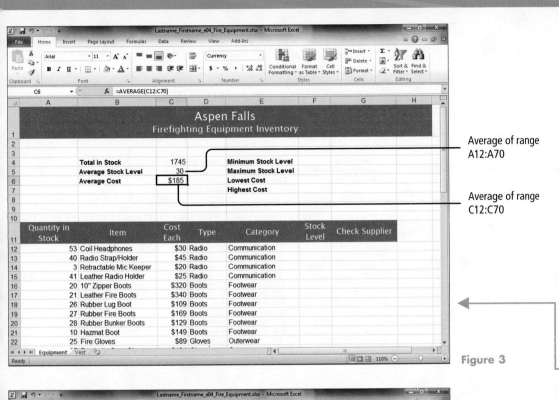

Average of range
A12:A70

Average of range
C12:C70

Figure 3

Sum of range
D5:D16

Average of range
D5:D16

Figure 4

4. Click cell **C5**. In the **Editing group**, click the **Sum button arrow** Σ, and then in the list of functions, click **Average**. In the formula bar and in the cell, notice that Excel proposes to average the value in cell *C4*.

When data is above or to the left of a selected cell, a function will suggest a range. Often, you will need to edit a suggested range.

5. With cell **C4** highlighted in the function argument, select the range **A12:A70**, and then on the formula bar, click the **Enter** button ✓ to display the result *29.5763*. In the **Styles group**, click the **Cell Styles** button, and then click **Comma [0]**.

6. Click cell **C6**. In the **Editing group**, click the **Sum button arrow** Σ, and then in the list, click **Average**. Select the range **C12:C70**, and then click the **Enter** button ✓. Scroll up to display the result *$185*, as shown in **Figure 3**.

7. Click the **Vest** sheet tab, and then click cell **D17**. Using the techniques just practiced, enter the **SUM** function using the argument range **D5:D16**, and then press Enter. In cell **D18**, enter the **AVERAGE** function using the argument range **D5:D16**, and then click the **Enter** button ✓. Verify that cell **D17** is not included in the Average range. Compare your sheet to **Figure 4**.

8. Right-click the sheet tab, and then click **Select All Sheets**. Display the worksheet footers, insert the **File Name** in the left footer and the **Sheet Name** in the right footer. Return to **Normal** view and then press Ctrl + Home.

9. **Save** 🖫 the workbook.

■ **You have completed Skill 1 of 10**

► The *MIN function* returns the smallest value in a range of cells.

► The *MAX function* returns the largest value in a range of cells.

1. Make the **Equipment** sheet the active sheet. Click cell **F4**. In the **Editing group**, click the **Sum button arrow** Σ, and then in the list, click **Min**. With the insertion point blinking in the function, select the range **A12:A70**, and then on the formula bar, click the **Enter** button ✓ to display the result 3.

   The MIN function evaluates all of the values in the range A12:A70 and then returns 3, the lowest value found in the range.

2. Click cell **F5**. In the **Editing group**, click the **Sum button arrow** Σ, and then in the list, click **Max**.

   The function automatically suggests the argument F4 because the cell above contains a value.

3. With cell **F4** selected in the function argument, select the range **A12:A70**, and then on the formula bar, click the **Enter** button ✓ to display the result 90, as shown in **Figure 1**.

   The MAX function evaluates all of the values in the range A12:A70 and then returns the highest value found.

4. Click cell **A12**, type 146 and then press Enter. In cell **A13**, type 2 and then press Enter. Verify that the MIN and MAX functions in cells **F4** and **F5** now display the lowest and highest values in the range **A12:A70**. Verify that the SUM and AVERAGE functions also automatically recalculated, as shown in **Figure 2**.

■ **Continue to the next page to complete the skill**

Result of MIN function

Result of MAX function

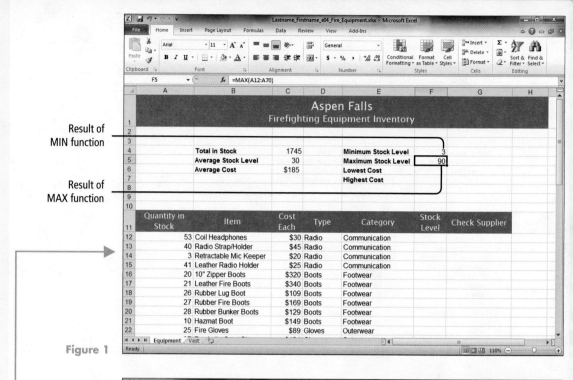

Figure 1

Function results recalculated

Value changed to *146*

Figure 2

MIN function result

MAX function result

Figure 3

MIN function result

MAX function result

Figure 4

5. In cell **F6**, repeat the technique just practiced to insert the **MIN** function using the range **C12:C70** as the argument in the parentheses. Verify that the result is *$11*.

6. In cell **F7**, insert the **MAX** function to return the highest cost in the range **C12:C70**. Verify that the result is *$1,299*. Scroll down to view the worksheet, and verify that the lowest and highest values in column **C** were selected from each of the ranges for the MIN and MAX functions. Compare your screen with Figure 3.

7. Make the **Vest** worksheet the active sheet.

8. In cell **D19**, insert the MIN function to evaluate the lowest monthly cost in the range **D5:D16** as the argument in the parentheses. Do not include the *Total* or *Average Cost* values in the range. Verify that the result is *$160.00*.

9. In cell **D20**, insert the MAX function to evaluate the highest monthly cost in the range **D5:D16** as the argument. Verify that the result is *$325.00*, as shown in Figure 4.

10. Save ▢ the workbook.

■ **You have completed Skill 2 of 10**

► You can move a range of cells containing formulas or functions without changing the cell references in those formulas or functions.

► Borders and shading emphasize a cell or a range of cells, and rotated or angled text draws attention to text on a worksheet.

1. Make the **Equipment** worksheet the active sheet. Select the range **E4:F7**. Point to the top edge of the selected range to display the pointer. Drag the selected range up until the ScreenTip displays the range *E3:F6*, as shown in **Figure 1**, and then release the mouse button to complete the move.

2. Select the range **B4:C6**, and then using the technique you just practiced, move the range to **E7:F9**.

3. On the **Formulas tab**, in the **Formula Auditing group**, click the **Show Formulas** button to display the functions in the cells. Scroll to the right, and then click cell **F2**. Notice that the cell references in the functions did not change, as shown in **Figure 2**.

4. In the **Formula Auditing group**, click the **Show Formulas** button to display the function results in the cells.

5. Select the range **F3:F4**. Hold down ⌐Ctrl⌐, and then select the range **F7:F8**. With the nonadjacent cells selected, on the **Home tab**, in the **Styles group**, click the **Cell Styles** button, and then click **Comma [0]**.

6. Select the range **A11:G11**. On the **Home tab**, in the **Font group**, click the **Border button arrow** ⊞▾, and then click **Thick Bottom Border**.

■ **Continue to the next page to complete the skill**

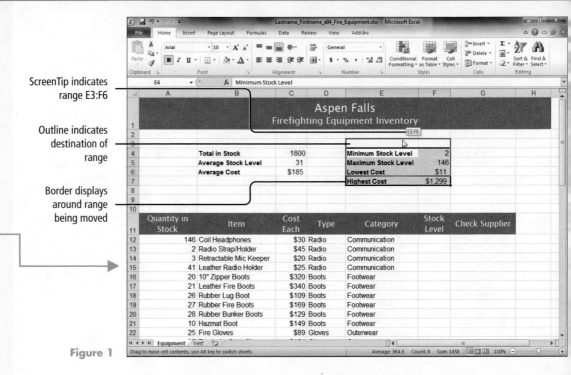

ScreenTip indicates range E3:F6

Outline indicates destination of range

Border displays around range being moved

Figure 1

Cell references remain unchanged

Figure 2

Format Cells dialog box

Outline selected

Selected line style

Color changed

Border preview

Figure 3

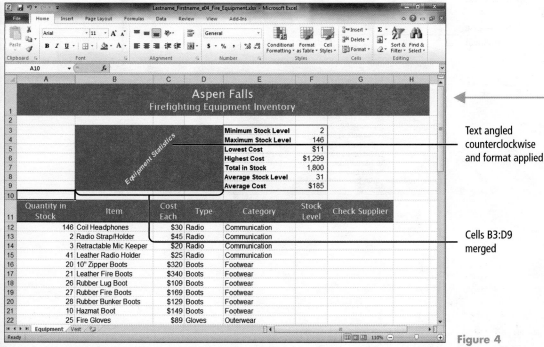

Text angled counterclockwise and format applied

Cells B3:D9 merged

Figure 4

7. Select the range **E3:F9**. In the **Font group**, click the **Border button arrow** ⊞ ▾, and then at the bottom of the gallery, click **More Borders**. In the left of the **Format Cells** dialog box, under **Style**, click the fifth line style in the second column. Click the **Color arrow**, and then click the sixth color in the first row—**Red, Accent 2**. Under **Presets**, click **Outline**, and then compare your screen with **Figure 3**.

   The Format Cells dialog box displays a preview of formatting.

8. At the bottom of the **Format Cells** dialog box, click **OK**. Click cell **B3** to view the border around the range E3:F9.

9. In cell **B3**, type Equipment Statistics and then press [Enter].

10. Select the range **B3:D9**. On the **Home tab**, in the **Alignment group**, click the **Merge & Center** button ▦. In the **Alignment group**, click the **Middle Align** button ▭. In the **Font group**, click the **Fill Color button arrow** ▾, and then click the sixth color in the first row—**Red, Accent 2**. Click the **Font Color button arrow** A ▾, and then click the first color in the first row—**White, Background 1**. Apply the **Bold** and **Italic** format.

11. With the merged cell still selected, in the **Alignment group**, click the **Orientation** button ▨ ▾, and then click **Angle Counterclockwise**. Click cell **A10**, and then compare your screen with **Figure 4**.

12. **Save** 🖫 the workbook.

■ **You have completed Skill 3 of 10**

▶ A *logical test* is any value or expression that can be evaluated as TRUE or FALSE.

▶ A *logical function* applies a logical test to determine whether a specific condition is met. *Criteria* are the conditions specified in the logical test.

▶ The *IF Function* checks whether criteria are met and then returns one value when the condition is TRUE and another value when the condition is FALSE.

1. Click cell **F12**. On the **Formulas tab**, in the **Function Library group**, click the **Logical** button, and then on the list, point to **IF**. Read the ScreenTip, and then click **IF** to display the **Function Arguments** dialog box.

2. With the insertion point in the **Logical_test** box, type A12<10

   The logical test *A12<10* will look at the value in cell A12 and then determine whether the value is less than 10. The expression *<10* includes the < comparison operator, which means *less than*. A *comparison operator* compares two values and returns either TRUE or FALSE. The table in **Figure 1** lists commonly used comparison operators.

3. Press Tab to move the insertion point to the **Value_if_true** box, and then type Order

4. Press Tab to move the insertion point to the **Value_if_false** box, type Level OK and then compare your screen with **Figure 2**.

   Quotation marks display around *Order* and will automatically be inserted around *Level OK* after you click OK. In function arguments, text values are surrounded by quotation marks.

■ **Continue to the next page to complete the skill**

Comparison Operators

Comparison Operator Symbol	Definition
=	Equal to (A1=B1)
>	Greater than (A1>B1)
<	Less than (A1<B1)
>=	Greater than or equal to (A1>=B1)
<=	Less than or equal to (A1<=B1)
<>	Not equal to (A1<>B1)

Figure 1

Logical test argument

Value if true argument with quotation marks indicating text

Value if false argument

Figure 2

Figure 3

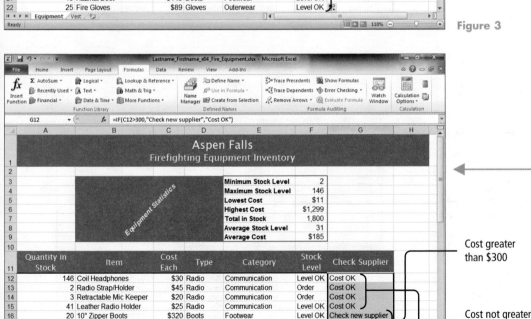

Figure 4

5. Click **OK** to display the result *Level OK* in cell **F12**.

The IF function tests whether cell A12 is less than 10. If this condition were TRUE, *Order* would display. Because cell A12 contains the value *146*, the condition is FALSE, and *Level OK* displays in cell F12.

6. In cell **F12**, point to the fill handle to display the ⊞ pointer, and then double-click to copy the function down through cell **F70**. Click cell **F13**, and then compare your screen with Figure 3.

When a function has multiple arguments, each argument is separated by a comma.

When the function was copied down to cell F13, the cell reference changed from A12 to A13.

7. Click cell **G12**. In the **Function Library group**, click the **Logical** button, and then click **IF**. In the **Logical_test** box, type C12>300 and then press Tab. In the **Value_if_true** box, type Check new supplier and then press Tab. In the **Value_if_false** box, type Cost OK and then click the **OK** button. In cell **G12**, point to the fill handle to display the ⊞ pointer, and then double-click to copy the function down through cell **G70**. Compare your screen with Figure 4.

In each row, the function evaluates the value in column C. When the value in column C is greater than $300, the text *Check new supplier* displays. Otherwise, the text *Cost OK* displays.

8. Save 🖫 the workbook.

■ **You have completed Skill 4 of 10**

▶ *Conditional formatting* is a format, such as cell shading or font color, that is applied to cells when a specified condition is true.

▶ Conditional formatting makes analyzing data easier by emphasizing cell values.

1. Click cell **F12**. Press Ctrl + Shift + ↓ to select the range **F12:F70**.

2. On the **Home tab**, in the **Styles group**, click the **Conditional Formatting** button. On the list, point to **Highlight Cells Rules**, and then click **Text that Contains**. In the **Text That Contains** dialog box, with the insertion point in the first box, type Order as shown in **Figure 1**.

3. In the **Text That Contains** dialog box, click **OK**.

   Within the range F12:F70, cells that contain the text *Order* display with light red fill and dark red text formatting.

4. Using the technique just practiced, select the range **G12:G70**. Click the **Conditional Formatting** button, point to **Highlight Cells Rules**, and then click **Text that Contains**. In the first box, type Check new supplier Click the second box arrow, and on the list, click **Yellow Fill with Dark Yellow Text**. Compare your screen with **Figure 2**.

   The Text That Contains dialog box is used to specify the formatting to apply when the condition is true—here, if the cell contains the text *Check new supplier*. Within the selected range, if a cell contains the text *Check new supplier*, the conditional format is applied.

■ **Continue to the next page to complete the skill**

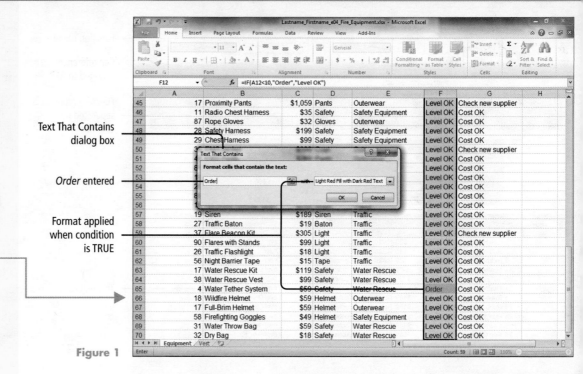

Text That Contains dialog box

Order entered

Format applied when condition is TRUE

Figure 1

Format applied when condition is TRUE

Figure 2

Conditional Formatting button

Orange Data Bar

Live Preview of Orange Data Bar

Figure 3

5. In the **Text That Contains** dialog box, click **OK**.

6. Select the range **A12:A70**. In the **Styles group**, click the **Conditional Formatting** button. On the list, point to **Data Bars**, and then in the gallery, under Gradient Fill, point at **Orange Data Bar**, as shown in **Figure 3**.

A *data bar* provides a visual cue about the value of a cell relative to other cells in a range. Data bars are useful to quickly identify higher and lower numbers within a large group of data, such as very high or very low levels of inventory.

7. Click **Orange Data Bar**, and then click cell **A13**, type 190 and then press Enter.

The data bar in cell A13 is longer than in other cells—a visual indicator that the cell contains a higher value.

8. Make the **Vest** sheet the active sheet. Select the range **C5:C16**. On the **Insert tab**, in the **Sparklines group**, click the **Line** button. In the **Create Sparklines** dialog box, in the **Location Range** box, type B22 and then click **OK**.

9. On the **Design tab**, in the **Show group**, select the **Low Point** check box. In the **Style group**, click the **Sparkline Color** button, and then click **Red, Accent 2**. Click cell **A24**, and then compare your screen with **Figure 4**.

A *sparkline* is a tiny chart used to show data trends.

10. Save the workbook.

■ **You have completed Skill 5 of 10**

Sparkline

Figure 4

► The *Find and Replace* command finds and then replaces a character or string of characters in a worksheet or in a selected range.

► The *NOW function* returns the serial number of the current date and time. Recall from Chapter 3 that a serial number is a sequential number.

1. Make **Equipment** the active sheet. Press Ctrl + Home. On the **Home tab**, in the **Editing group**, click the **Find & Select** button, and then click **Replace**.

2. In the **Find and Replace** dialog box, in the **Find what** box, type Removal and then press Tab. In the **Replace with** box, type Extrication and then compare your screen with **Figure 1**.

3. Click the **Find Next** button, and then verify that cell **B24** is highlighted. In the **Find and Replace** dialog box, click the **Replace** button. Verify that the first occurrence of *Removal* was replaced with *Extrication* and that the second occurrence—in cell **B26**—is automatically located.

   The Replace option will replace a single occurrence of a character or string of characters with the replacement value.

4. Click the **Replace All** button, and then in the message box, notice that **3 replacements** were made, as shown in **Figure 2**.

   The Replace All option replaces all matches of an occurrence of a character or string of characters with the replacement value.

5. Click **OK**, and then click the **Close** button.

6. Press Ctrl + Home.

■ **Continue to the next page to complete the skill**

Find & Select button
Find and Replace dialog box
Find *Removal*
Replace with *Extrication*

Figure 1

Replacements made

Figure 2

Find *Stock*

Replace with *Supply*

All occurrences of *Stock* listed

Figure 3

Description of NOW function

No function arguments

NOW function entered in cell and formula bar

Figure 4

7. In the **Editing group**, click the **Find & Select** button, and then click **Replace**. In the **Find and Replace** dialog box, in the **Find what** box, replace *Removal* with Stock and then press Tab. In the **Replace with** box, replace *Extrication* with Supply and then click the **Find All** button. Resize the **Find and Replace** dialog box as necessary to view the data as shown in **Figure 3**.

   The Find All option finds all occurrences of the search criteria.

8. In the lower portion of the **Find and Replace** dialog box, in the **Cell** column, click **$E$8** to make cell **E8** the active cell, and then click the **Replace** button.

   The word *Stock* in cell E8 is replaced with the word *Supply*.

9. Click the **Replace All** button. Read the message, and then click **OK**. In the **Find and Replace** dialog box, click the **Close** button.

10. Scroll down, click cell **A73**, type Edited by: and then press Enter. In cell **A74**, using your first and last names, type Your Name and then press Enter.

11. On the **Formulas tab**, in the **Function Library group**, click the **Date & Time** button, and then click **NOW**. Read the message, and then compare your screen with **Figure 4**.

   The NOW function takes no arguments, and the result is *volatile*—the date and time will not remain as entered but rather will be updated each time this workbook is opened.

12. Click **OK** to enter the date and time. Save 💾 the workbook.

■ **You have completed Skill 6 of 10**

► The *Freeze Panes* command keeps rows or columns visible when you are scrolling in a worksheet. The frozen rows and columns become separate panes.

► When you freeze panes, you determine the specific rows or columns that you want to remain visible when scrolling. You will likely find it easier to work with large worksheets when you can always view the identifying row or column labels.

1. Press Ctrl + Home, and then scroll down until row **50** displays at the bottom of your window and the column labels are out of view, as shown in **Figure 1**.

   When you scroll in large worksheets, the column and row labels may not be visible, which can make identifying the purpose of each row or column difficult. You may see different rows depending on the zoom level.

2. Press Ctrl + Home, and then click cell **C15**. On the **View tab**, in the **Window group**, click the **Freeze Panes** button, and then click **Freeze Panes**.

   By selecting cell C15, the rows above and the columns to the left of C15 are frozen. A line displays along the upper border of row 15 and on the left border of column C.

3. Click the **Scroll Down** ▾ and **Scroll Right** ▸ arrows to display cell **M80**, and then notice that the top and left panes remain frozen, as shown in **Figure 2**.

■ **Continue to the next page to complete the skill**

Column titles cannot be seen

Row 50 displays at the bottom of the window

Figure 1

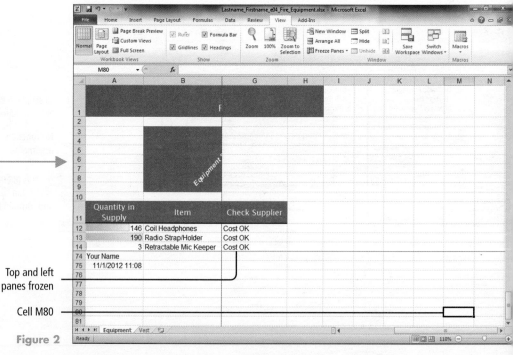

Top and left panes frozen

Cell M80

Figure 2

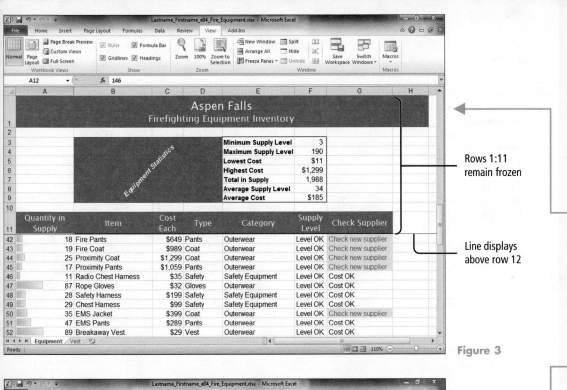

Rows 1:11 remain frozen

Line displays above row 12

Figure 3

Move or Copy dialog box

(move to end) selected

Create a copy selected

Figure 4

4. In the **Window group**, click the **Freeze Panes** button, and then click **Unfreeze Panes**.

   The rows and columns are no longer frozen, and the border no longer displays on row 15 and on column C.

5. Click cell **A12**. In the **Window group**, click the **Freeze Panes** button, and then click **Freeze Panes**.

6. Watch the row numbers below row **11** as you scroll down to row **50**. Compare your screen with **Figure 3**.

   The titles in row 1 through row 11 stay frozen while the remaining rows of data continue to scroll.

7. Right-click the **Equipment** sheet tab, and then from the list, click **Move or Copy**. In the **Move or Copy** dialog box, click (**move to end**), and then select the **Create a copy** check box. Compare your screen with **Figure 4**.

8. In the **Move or Copy** dialog box, click **OK**.

   A copy of the *Equipment* worksheet is created, and the new sheet tab is named *Equipment (2)*.

9. Right-click the **Equipment (2)** sheet tab, click **Rename**, type Sort by Cost and then press Enter. In the **Window group**, click the **Freeze Panes** button, and then click **Unfreeze Panes**. Click the **Equipment** sheet tab, and verify that on this worksheet, the panes are still frozen.

10. Save 🖫 the workbook.

■ **You have completed Skill 7 of 10**

▶ To analyze a group of related data, you can convert a range into an *Excel table*—a series of rows and columns that contain related data. Data in an Excel table are managed independently from the data in other rows and columns in the worksheet.

▶ Data in Excel tables can be sorted in a variety of ways—for example, in ascending order or by color.

1. Click the **Sort by Cost** sheet tab, and then click cell **A11**. On the **Insert tab**, in the **Tables group**, click the **Table** button. In the **Create Table** dialog box, under **Where is the data for your table?** verify that the range =$A$11:$G$70 displays. If necessary, select the *My table has headers* check box, as shown in **Figure 1**.

   The range A11:G70 is automatically selected because there are no blank rows or columns in the range.

2. In the **Create Table** dialog box, click **OK** to convert the range into an Excel table.

   In the Excel table, formatting is applied and the header row displays filter arrows in each column.

3. On the **Design tab**, in the **Table Styles group**, click the **More** button ⊡, and then under **Light**, click **Table Style Light 10**. Click cell **H11**, type Total Cost and then press Enter to automatically include the column in the Excel table.

4. In **H12**, type =A12*C12 and then press Enter to create a *calculated column*—a column in an Excel table that uses a single formula that adjusts for each row—as shown in **Figure 2**.

■ **Continue to the next page to complete the skill**

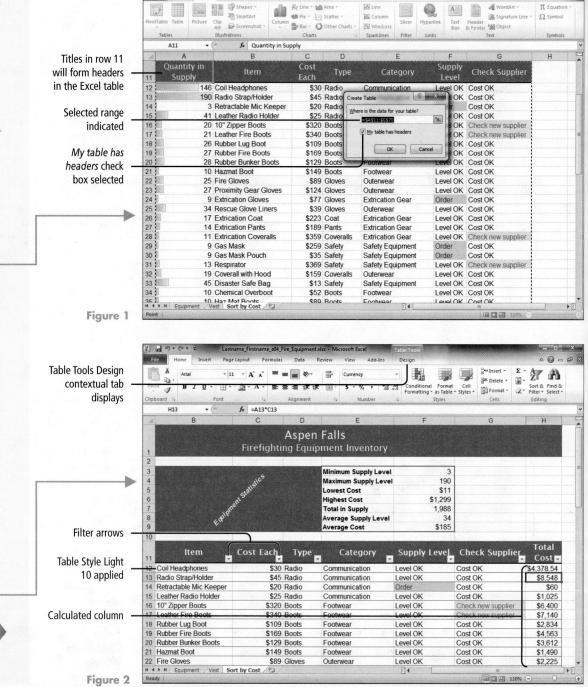

Titles in row 11 will form headers in the Excel table

Selected range indicated

My table has headers check box selected

Figure 1

Table Tools Design contextual tab displays

Filter arrows

Table Style Light 10 applied

Calculated column

Figure 2

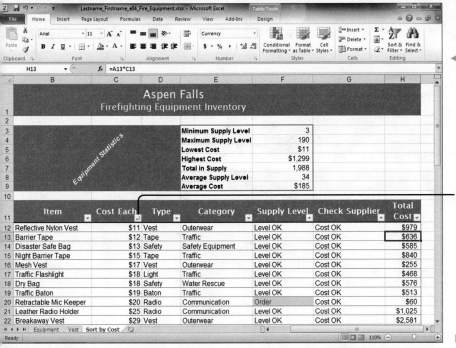

Small up
arrow indicates
ascending
(Smallest to
Largest) sort

Figure 3

Sort by Color

Sort by Cell Color

Pink tile

Figure 4

5. In the header row of the Excel table, click the **Cost Each filter arrow**, and then from the list, click **Sort Smallest to Largest**. Compare your screen with **Figure 3**.

> The rows in the table are sorted by the *Cost Each* values, from the lowest to the highest, as indicated by the up arrow on the column's filter button.

6. In the header row, click the **Total Cost filter arrow**, and then click **Sort Largest to Smallest**.

> The rows in the table are now sorted from the highest to lowest *Total Cost* value, and the small arrow in the Total Cost filter arrow points down, indicating a descending sort. The previous sort on the *Cost Each* column no longer displays.

7. Right-click the **Sort by Cost** sheet tab, and then click **Move or Copy**. In the **Move or Copy** dialog box, click (**move to end**), select the **Create a copy** check box, and then click **OK**.

8. Right-click the **Sort by Cost (2)** sheet tab, click **Rename**, type Supply Level and then press Enter.

9. In the **Supply Level** worksheet, click the **Supply Level filter arrow**, and then point to **Sort by Color**. Notice that the color formats in column **F** display in the list, as shown in **Figure 4**.

> If you have applied manual or conditional formatting to a range of cells, you can sort by these colors.

10. In the **Sort by Color** list, under **Sort by Cell Color**, click the **pink tile** to display the six items that need to be ordered first in the Excel table.

11. Save the workbook.

- **You have completed Skill 8 of 10**

► You can *filter* data to display only the rows of a table that meet specified criteria. Filtering temporarily hides rows that do not meet the criteria.

1. On the **Supply Level** worksheet, click the **Category filter arrow**. From the menu, clear the **(Select All)** check box to clear all the check boxes. Select the **Safety Equipment** check box, and then click **OK**. Compare your screen with **Figure 1**.

   In the *Category* column, only the rows containing *Safety Equipment* display. The rows not meeting this criteria are hidden from view.

2. On the **Design tab**, in the **Table Style Options group**, select the **Total Row** check box.

   The *total row* displays as the last row in an Excel table and provides functions in drop-down lists for each column. Here, *Total* displays in cell A71. In cell H71, the number *$33,816* indicates the SUM of the Total Cost column for the filtered rows.

3. In the Total row, click cell **C71**, and then click the arrow that displays to the right of the selected cell. In the list, click **Average**. Compare your screen with **Figure 2**.

   Excel averages only the visible rows in column C—here, *$150* is the average cost.

4. In the header row, click the **Type filter arrow**. From the menu, clear the **Helmet** and the **Shield** check boxes, and then click **OK**.

   Filters can be applied to more than one column. Here, both the Type and Category columns are filtered.

■ **Continue to the next page to complete the skill**

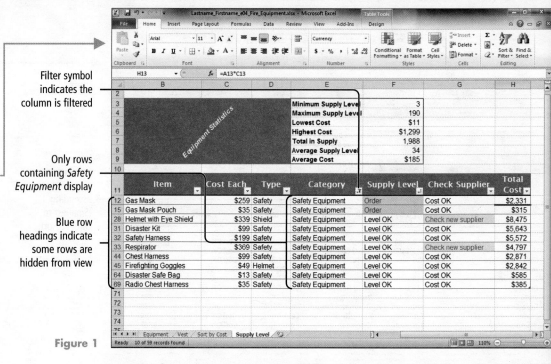

Filter symbol indicates the column is filtered

Only rows containing *Safety Equipment* display

Blue row headings indicate some rows are hidden from view

Figure 1

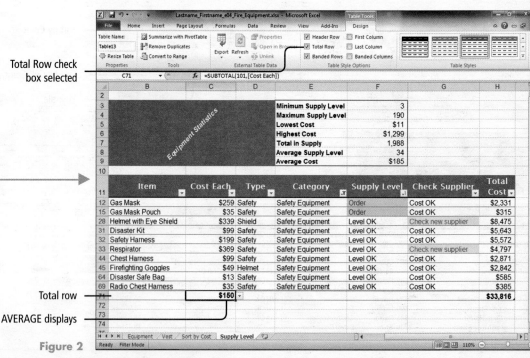

Total Row check box selected

Total row

AVERAGE displays

Figure 2

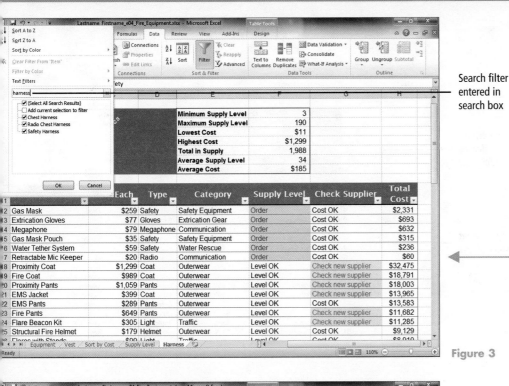

Search filter entered in search box

Figure 3

COUNT function

Figure 4

5. Right-click the **Supply Level** sheet tab, and then using the techniques you just practiced, create a copy of the worksheet and move the sheet to the end. Rename the **Supply Level (2)** sheet tab as Harness

6. With the **Harness** worksheet active, click any cell in the Excel table to make the Excel table active. On the **Data tab**, in the **Sort & Filter group**, click the **Clear** button to clear all the filters and to display all the rows in the Excel table.

   In the Harness worksheet, all the filters are cleared and all the rows in the Excel table redisplay. On the Supply Level worksheet, the filters are still applied.

7. In the header row, click the **Item filter arrow**. From the menu, in the **Search** box, type harness and then compare your screen with **Figure 3**.

8. Click **OK** to display only the three rows containing the text *harness* in the Item column.

9. In the Total row, click cell **C71**. Click the displayed arrow, and then on the list, click **None**. In cell **H71**, repeat the same technique to remove the total from the Total Cost column.

10. Click cell **D71**, click the displayed arrow, and then click **Count**. Compare your screen with **Figure 4**.

    Only the filtered rows are counted. In this manner, you can determine how many items meet a filter criteria.

11. **Save** 🖫 the workbook.

   ■ **You have completed Skill 9 of 10**

► After sorting, filtering, and totaling an Excel table, you can convert the Excel table into a range.

► When a large worksheet is too wide or too long to print on a single page, row and column headings can be printed on each page or the worksheet can be formatted to print on a single page.

1. Right-click the **Harness** sheet tab, create a copy of the sheet at the end of the workbook, and rename the new sheet Inventory

2. Click cell **A11**. On the **Design tab**, in the **Tools group**, click the **Convert to Range** button. Read the message box, click **Yes**, and then compare your screen with **Figure 1**.

   When converting an Excel table into a range, all filters are removed and the heading row no longer displays filter buttons. Any existing sorts and formatting remain.

3. On the status bar, click the **Page Layout** button, and then scroll to the right and down through the worksheet to view the pages. On the **Page Layout tab**, in the **Scale to Fit group**, click the **Width arrow**, and then click **1 page**. Click the **Height arrow**, and then click **1 page**.

4. Click the **Equipment** sheet tab. In the **Scale to Fit group**, click the **Width arrow**, and then click **1 page**. Click the **Height arrow**, and then click **2 pages**.

5. In the **Page Setup group**, click the **Print Titles** button, and then in the **Page Setup** dialog box, under **Print titles**, click in the **Rows to repeat at top** box. Compare your screen with **Figure 2**.

■ **Continue to the next page to complete the skill**

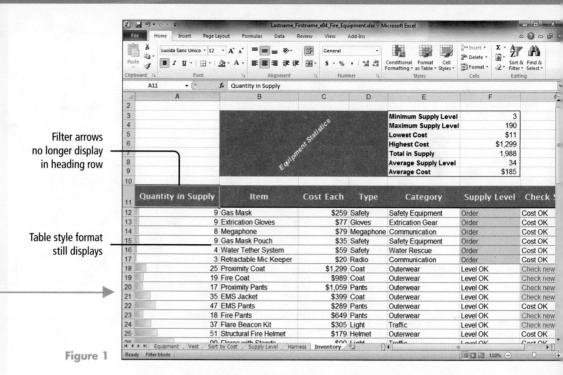

Filter arrows no longer display in heading row

Table style format still displays

Figure 1

Page Setup dialog box

Rows to repeat at top box

Figure 2

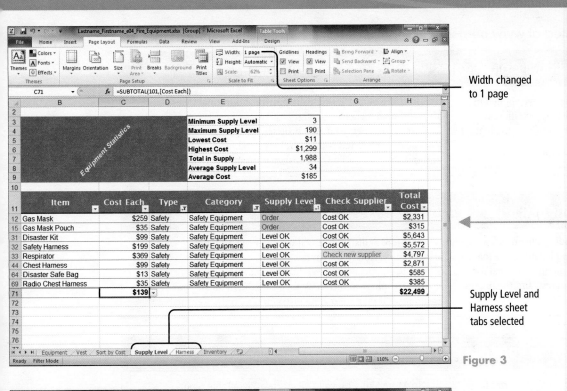

Width changed to 1 page

Supply Level and Harness sheet tabs selected

Figure 3

Columns C and G hidden—*Cost Each* and *Check Supplier* columns

Rows 40:70 hidden

Figure 4

6. In the worksheet, click row **11**. In the **Rows to repeat at top** box, verify that *$11:$11* displays. Click the **Print Preview** button. Click the **Next Page** button to verify that the column labels from row 11 display at the top of page 2.

7. Click the **Page Layout tab**.

8. Click the **Supply Level** sheet tab. Hold down Ctrl, and then click the **Harness** sheet tab. In the **Scale to Fit group**, change the **Width** to **1 page**, as shown in **Figure 3**.

   The scaling is adjusted on both worksheets at the same time.

9. Click the **Sort by Cost** sheet tab. In the **Scale to Fit group**, change the **Width** to **1 page**. Click cell **C13**. On the **Home tab**, in the **Cells group**, click the **Format** button, point to **Hide & Unhide**, and then click **Hide Columns**. Use the same technique to hide column **G**.

10. Select rows **40:70**. In the **Cells group**, click the **Format** button, point to **Hide & Unhide**, and then click **Hide Rows**. Compare your screen with **Figure 4**.

11. Save 🖫 the workbook. Print or submit the file as directed by your instructor. **Close** the workbook, and then **Exit** Excel.

Done! You have completed Skill 10 of 10 and your document is complete!

More Skills

The following More Skills are located at **www.pearsonhighered.com/skills**

More Skills Apply Conditional Color Scales with Top and Bottom Rules

In addition to the conditional formats you have applied in this chapter, you can apply color scales, which apply different colors to the cells, and top/bottom rules, which format the highest or lowest values.

In More Skills 11, you will apply the additional types of conditional formats.

To begin, open your web browser, navigate to www.pearsonhighered.com/skills, locate the name of your textbook, and then follow the instructions on the website.

More Skills Use the Payment (PMT) Function

The PMT function calculates the periodic payment for any loan given the loan amount, interest rate, and length of the loan. When you borrow money from a bank, the amount charged for your use of the borrowed money is called interest, and the interest amount is included in the PMT function.

In More Skills 12, you will use the PMT function to calculate various loan payments.

To begin, open your web browser, navigate to www.pearsonhighered.com/skills, locate the name of your textbook, and then follow the instructions on the website.

More Skills Create PivotTable Reports

A PivotTable report is an interactive way to summarize large amounts of data quickly, to analyze numerical data in depth, and to answer unanticipated questions about your data.

In More Skills 13, you will create a PivotTable report, pivot the data, and then filter the data.

To begin, open your web browser, navigate to www.pearsonhighered.com/skills, locate the name of your textbook, and then follow the instructions on the website.

More Skills Use Goal Seek

Goal Seek is a method to find a specific value for a cell by adjusting the value of another cell. With Goal Seek, you work backward from the desired outcome to find the necessary input to achieve your goal.

In More Skills 14, you will use Goal Seek to determine how much money can be borrowed to achieve a specific monthly payment.

To begin, open your web browser, navigate to www.pearsonhighered.com/skills, locate the name of your textbook, and then follow the instructions on the website.

Key Terms

Online Help Skills

1. Start Excel. In the upper right corner of the Excel window, click the **Help** button. In the **Help** window, click the **Maximize** button.

2. Click in the search box, type sparklines and then click the **Search** button. In the search results, click **Use sparklines to show data trends**. Compare your screen with **Figure 1**.

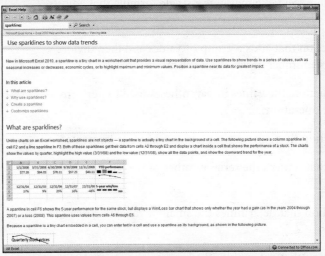

Figure 1

3. Read the article to see if you can answer the following: What are some benefits of using sparklines compared to charts?

Matching

Match each term in the second column with its correct definition in the first column by writing the letter of the term on the blank line in front of the correct definition.

____ **1.** A prewritten formula that performs calculations by using specific values in a particular order or structure.

____ **2.** A column in an Excel table that uses a single formula that adjusts for each row.

____ **3.** The Excel function that adds a group of values and then divides the result by the number of values in the group.

____ **4.** In an Excel function, the values in parentheses used to perform calculations or operations.

____ **5.** A type of function that summarizes a group of measurements.

____ **6.** The function that returns the serial number of the current date and time.

____ **7.** An Excel function that determines the smallest value in a selected range of values.

____ **8.** An Excel function that determines the largest value in a selected range of values.

____ **9.** The type of function that tests for specific conditions and typically uses conditional tests to determine whether specified conditions are TRUE or FALSE.

____ **10.** Conditions that you specify.

A Arguments

B AVERAGE

C Calculated column

D Criteria

E Function

F Logical functions

G MAX

H MIN

I NOW

J Statistical functions

Multiple Choice

Choose the correct answer.

1. This type of test has an outcome of TRUE or FALSE.
   - **A.** Logical
   - **B.** Rational
   - **C.** Normal

2. This function checks whether criteria are met and returns one value if TRUE and another value if FALSE.
   - **A.** BRANCH
   - **B.** TRUE
   - **C.** IF

3. After sorting, filtering, and totaling an Excel table, an Excel table can be converted into this.
   - **A.** Link
   - **B.** Pane
   - **C.** Range

4. This word describes a format, such as cell shading, that is applied to cells when a specified condition is true.
   - **A.** Filtered
   - **B.** Conditional
   - **C.** Calculated

5. This word describes a function that is updated each time the workbook is opened.
   - **A.** Volatile
   - **B.** Changeable
   - **C.** Unstable

6. This command ensures that header rows and columns remain visible when a worksheet is scrolled.
   - **A.** Total Panes
   - **B.** Excel Panes
   - **C.** Freeze Panes

7. This term refers to related data organized in rows and columns that is managed independently from other data in the worksheet.
   - **A.** Pane
   - **B.** Excel table
   - **C.** Window

8. This command displays only the rows of a table that meet specified criteria.
   - **A.** Filter
   - **B.** Standard
   - **C.** Chart

9. This row displays as the last row in an Excel table and provides summary statistics.
   - **A.** Total
   - **B.** Sorted
   - **C.** Changeable

10. These symbols are inserted into logical functions to determine whether a condition is true or false—(<) and (=), for example.
    - **A.** Comparison operators
    - **B.** Mathematical operators
    - **C.** Logical symbols

Topics for Discussion

1. Think about current news stories, including sports stories, and identify one or more in which statistical functions, such as AVERAGE, MIN, or MAX play an important part. For example, when reporting about home prices, the average home price is frequently quoted.

2. Sorting and filtering are two of the most valuable ways to analyze data. If you were presented with an Excel table containing names and addresses, what are some of the ways you might sort or filter the data? If you were presented with an Excel table of a day's cash transactions at your college's cafeteria, what are some ways you could sort, filter, and total?

Skill Check

To complete this project, you will need the following file:

- e04_Surplus

You will save your workbook as:

- Lastname_Firstname_e04_Surplus

1. **Start** Excel, and then open the file **e04_Surplus**. Save the workbook in the **Excel Chapter 4** folder as Lastname_Firstname_e04_Surplus Insert the file name in the worksheet's left footer and the sheet name in the right footer. Return to **Normal** view.

2. Click cell **B4**, and then on the **Home tab**, in the **Editing group**, click the **Sum** button. With the insertion point in the function parentheses, select the range **F9:F48**, and then press [Enter]. With cell **B5** active, in the **Editing group**, click the **Sum button arrow**, and then click **Average**. Select the range **F9:F48**, and then press [Enter]. Using the same range, in cell **B6**, enter the **MAX** function. Compare your screen with **Figure 1**.

3. Select the range **A4:B6**. Point to the right edge of the selected range, and then drag the cells to **D4:E6**. With the range still selected, in the **Font group**, click the **Border button arrow**, and then click **Outside Borders**.

4. In cell **B4**, type Surplus and then merge and center the title in the range **B4:C6**. In the **Alignment group**, click the **Middle Align** button. Click the **Orientation** button, and then click **Angle Counterclockwise**. Click the **Fill Color button arrow**, and then click the color in the fourth row and sixth column— **Blue, Accent 2, Lighter 40%**.

5. Click cell **G9**. On the **Formulas tab**, in the **Function Library group**, click **Logical**, and then click **IF**. In the **Logical_test** box, type E9="Yes" In the **Value_if_true** box, type B9*F9 In the **Value_if_false** box, type 0 and then click **OK**. Copy the function down through cell **G48**, and then on the **Home tab**, in the **Styles group**, click the **Cell Styles** button and apply **Currency [0]** to the range. Compare your screen with **Figure 2**.

Figure 1

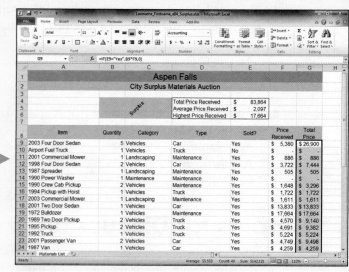

Figure 2

➤ Continue to the next page to complete this Skill Check

6. Select cell **A1**. On the **Home tab**, in the **Editing group**, click the **Find & Select** button, and then click **Replace**. In the **Find what** box, type Sedan In the **Replace with** box, type Car and then click **Replace All**. Click **OK**, and then **Close** the dialog box.

7. Click cell **A9**. On the **View tab**, in the **Window group**, click the **Freeze Panes** button, and then click **Freeze Panes**.

8. Right-click the **Materials List** sheet tab, and then click **Move or Copy**. In the **Move or Copy** dialog box, click (**move to end**), select the **Create a copy** check box, and then click **OK**. Rename the new sheet tab as Price by Car

9. With the *Price by Car* worksheet active, in the **Window group**, click the **Freeze Panes** button, and then click **Unfreeze Panes**. On the **Insert tab**, in the **Tables group**, click the **Table** button. Verify that the **My table has headers** check box is selected, and then click **OK**. On the **Design tab**, in the **Table Styles group**, click the **More** button, and then under **Light**, click **Table Style Light 17**.

10. Click the **Type filter arrow**, and then clear the (**Select All**) check box. Select the **Car** check box, and then click **OK**. Click the **Total Price filter arrow**, and then click **Sort Largest to Smallest**. On the **Design tab**, in the **Table Style Options group**, select the **Total Row** check box. Click cell **B49**, click the arrow that displays, and from the list, click **Sum**.

11. Select the range **F9:F48**. On the **Home tab**, in the **Styles group**, click the **Conditional Formatting** button, point to **Data Bars**, and then click the first choice in the second row—**Orange Data Bar**. Click cell **A9**, and then compare your screen with **Figure 3**.

12. Create a copy of the *Price by Car* worksheet, and then rename the new sheet tab Pickups On the **Data tab**, in the **Sort & Filter group**, click the **Clear** button. Click the **Item filter arrow**. In the **Search** box, type Pickup and then click **OK**.

13. Right-click the sheet tab, and then click **Select All Sheets**. On the **Page Layout tab**, in the **Page Setup group**, click the **Orientation** button, and then click **Landscape**. In the **Scale to Fit group**, change the **Width** to **1 page**.

14. Click the **Materials List** sheet tab, and then in the **Page Setup group**, click the **Print Titles** button. In the **Page Setup** dialog box, click in the **Rows to repeat at top** box, click row **8**, and then press ⏎.

15. **Save** the workbook. Click the **File tab**, and then click the **Print tab**. Under **Settings**, click the button, and then click **Print Entire Workbook**. Compare your workbook with **Figure 4**. Print or submit the file as directed by your instructor. **Close** the workbook. **Exit** Excel.

Done! You have completed the Skill Check

Figure 3

Figure 4

Assess Your Skills 1

To complete this project, you will need the following file:

- e04_Water

You will save your workbook as:

- Lastname_Firstname_e04_Water

1. **Start** Excel, and open the file **e04_Water**. Save the workbook in the **Excel Chapter 4** folder as Lastname_Firstname_e04_Water Insert the file name in the worksheet's left footer and the sheet name in the right footer. Return to **Normal** view.

2. Click cell **F4**. From the **Editing group**, insert the **AVERAGE** function using the range **F12:F41** as the argument. For each cell in the range **F5:F7**, insert the appropriate **Statistical** functions using the values in column **G** as the function arguments.

3. In cell **H12**, insert the **IF** function with the following logical arguments. For the logical test, check whether the **Farm Water** result is greater than the **MCL, TT, or MRDL** value in the same row. If the logical test is true, Yes should display. If the logical test is false, No should display. **Center** the result in the cell, and then copy the function down through cell **H41**.

4. Verify that the range **H12:H41** is selected, and then apply a **Highlight** conditional format that will display any cells that indicate *Yes* formatted with **Light Red Fill with Dark Red Text**.

5. Convert the range **A11:H41** to an Excel table, and then apply the **Table Style Light 16** table style.

6. Create a copy of the *Water* worksheet, and then rename the new sheet tab **Chlorine**. On the *Chlorine* worksheet, filter the table to display only the contaminant Chlorine For the Excel table, display the **Total Row**. In cell **E42**, display the **AVERAGE**, and then in cell **H42**, select **None**. In cell **A42**, change the title to Average

7. Create a copy of the *Chlorine* worksheet, and then rename the new sheet tab Farm Water In the *Farm Water* worksheet, convert the Excel table to a range, and then hide columns **C** and **G**. In cell **A12**, freeze the panes.

8. Click the **Water** sheet tab. In the Excel table, click the **Contaminants filter arrow**, and then click **Sort A to Z**. Select the range **D4:F7**, and then apply a **Thick Box Border**. Click cell **A43**, type High Test Trend and then in cell **A44**, insert the **NOW** function.

9. Select the range **G12:G41**. Using the selected range, insert a **Line Sparkline** in cell **B43**, and then display its **High Point**.

10. Select all the worksheets. Scale both the **Width** and **Height** to **1 page**. Save your workbook. Click the **File tab**, click the **Print tab**, and then compare your workbook with Figure 1. Print or submit the file as directed by your instructor. **Close** the workbook, and then **Exit** Excel.

Done! You have completed Assess Your Skills 1

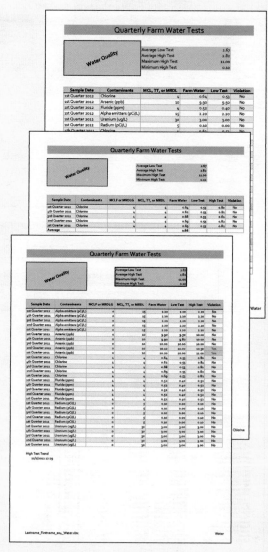

Figure 1

Assess Your Skills 3 and 4 can be found at
www.pearsonhighered.com/skills.

Assess Your Skills 2

To complete this project, you will need the following file:

- e04_Roof

You will save your workbook as:

- Lastname_Firstname_e04_Roof

1. **Start** Excel, and open the file **e04_Roof**. Save the workbook in the **Excel Chapter 4** folder as Lastname_Firstname_e04_Roof Insert the file name in the worksheet's left footer and the sheet name in the right footer. Return to **Normal** view.

2. In the range **B4:B7**, insert the appropriate statistical functions using the appropriate ranges. Move the range **A4:B7** to **D4:E7**.

3. In cell **A4**, type Top Growth and then merge and center the cell across the range **A4:A7**. In the merged cell, apply **Middle Align**, a **Thick Box Border**, the **Fill Color Dark Green, Accent 4, Lighter 60%**, and then change the orientation to **Angle Counterclockwise**.

4. In cell **F10**, insert the **IF** function with the following logical arguments. For the logical test, check whether the **Quantity in Stock** is greater than **20**. If the logical test is true, No should display. If the logical test is false, Reorder should display. **Center** the result in the cell.

5. Copy the function in cell **F10** down through cell **F68**. In the range **F10:F68**, apply a **Highlight** conditional format that will display any cells that indicate *Reorder* formatted with **Light Red Fill**.

6. Find and replace all occurrences of Ground Cover with Herb

7. Convert the range **A9:F68** to an Excel table, and then apply the **Table Style Medium 12** table style. In cell **G9**, type Total Cost and then in cell **G10**, enter the formula to calculate the *Cost Each* multiplied by the *Quantity in Stock*. In columns **A:G**, AutoFit the column width.

8. Scale the page **Width** to **1 page** and the page **Height** to **2 pages**, and then set the titles in row **9** to repeat on each printed page.

9. Create a copy of the worksheet, and then rename the new sheet tab Plants On the *Plants* worksheet, filter the Excel table to display the categories **Bush, Flower,** and **Vegetation**. Sort the table in alphabetical order by **Item**.

10. Display the **Total Row**, and then in **E69**, display the column's **SUM**.

11. **Save** your workbook. Compare your workbook with **Figure 1**. Print or submit the file as directed by your instructor. **Close** the workbook, and then **Exit** Excel.

Done! You have completed Assess Your Skills 2

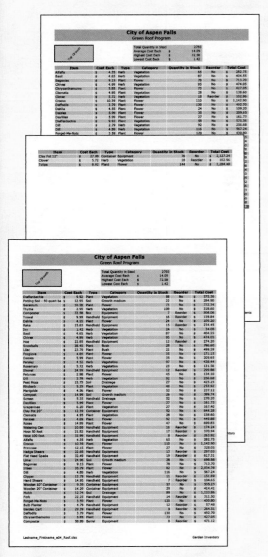

Figure 1

Assess Your Skills Visually

To complete this project, you will need the following file:

- e04_Art

You will save your workbook as:

- Lastname_Firstname_e04_Art

Open the file **e04_Art**, and save the workbook in the **Excel Chapter 4** folder as Lastname_Firstname_e04_Art Add the file name in the worksheet's left footer and the sheet name in the right footer. In the range **E4:E7**, apply appropriate functions to calculate the results shown. In column **F**, use the **IF** logical function indicating *Insure* for art with a value greater than $50,000. Apply conditional formatting to the **Insurance** column, as shown in Figure 1. Create a copy of the worksheet, and rename the new sheet tab Paintings Convert the data to an Excel table, and format with the **Table Style Light 14**. Filter the table to show only the **Painting** category, and sort the table by **Location**. Insert the **Total Row** as shown in Figure 1. **Save** the workbook. Print or submit the file as directed by your instructor.

Done! You have completed Assess Your Skills Visually

Figure 1

Skills in Context

To complete this project, you will need the following file:

- e04_Schools

You will save your workbook as:

- Lastname_Firstname_e04_Schools

Open the file **e04_Schools**, and save the workbook in your **Excel Chapter 4** folder as Lastname_Firstname_e04_Schools Add the file name in the worksheet's left footer. View the worksheet, and decide how best to summarize the data effectively. Add titles and statistical functions similar to those you used in this chapter. In column D, use a logical function to calculate whether a class needs a Teacher Aide—a class needs a Teacher Aide if the class size is greater than 30. Format the data as an Excel table, add a total row, and sort the Excel table from largest to smallest class size. Set the titles in row 12 to repeat on each page. Copy the worksheet, and then in the new worksheet, apply a filter to display the classes that need a teacher aide. Rename the new sheet tab with a worksheet name that describes the filter. Save your workbook, and then print or submit the file as directed by your instructor.

Done! You have completed Skills in Context

Skills and You

To complete this project, you will need the following file:

- **New blank Excel workbook**

You will save your workbook as:

- **Lastname_Firstname_e04_Budget**

Do you ever try to figure out where your money goes? Make a list of major spending categories, such as Housing, Transportation, Food, Clothing, Entertainment, Gifts, Personal Care, and so on. Within each category, make a list of Types. For example, within Clothing, you might have Work Clothes, Leisure Clothes, or Special Occasion Clothes. Next, for a one-week or a one-month period, keep an exact record of every financial transaction you make. In an Excel worksheet, use a new row for every transaction. Record the amount and a description of the transaction, and assign a type and a category. Use Excel's table feature to sort and filter your information to see how much you are spending for specific types of expenses. Save your workbook as Lastname_Firstname_e04_Budget and submit the workbook as directed by your instructor.

Done! You have completed Skills and You

CHAPTER 5

Format Cells and Worksheets

▶ In a workbook, you can format the cells to change the way that data is displayed without changing the underlying values of the data. Formatting the background and border of a cell often improves the appearance of the worksheet.

▶ Worksheets are formatted to provide a consistent or a unique look to an organization's documents.

Your starting screen will look like this:

SKILLS **myitlab** Skills 1-10 Training

At the end of this chapter, you will be able to:

Skill 1 Insert Symbols and Create Custom Number Formats

Skill 2 Format Cells with the Format Painter

Skill 3 Apply Icon Sets as Conditional Formatting

Skill 4 Use Formulas to Write Multiple Conditional Formatting Rules

Skill 5 Insert and Delete Rows, Columns, and Cells

Skill 6 Change Cell Backgrounds and Modify Borders

Skill 7 Create and Apply Custom Cell Styles

Skill 8 Customize, Save, and Apply Themes

Skill 9 Add Watermarks and Modify Background Colors

Skill 10 Hide Gridlines and Column and Row Headings

MORE SKILLS

More Skills 11 Copy Styles Between Workbooks

More Skills 12 Draw Borders

More Skills 13 Convert Comma-Separated Text into Columns

More Skills 14 Create Screen Clippings

Outcome

Using the skills listed to the left will enable you to create
worksheets like this:

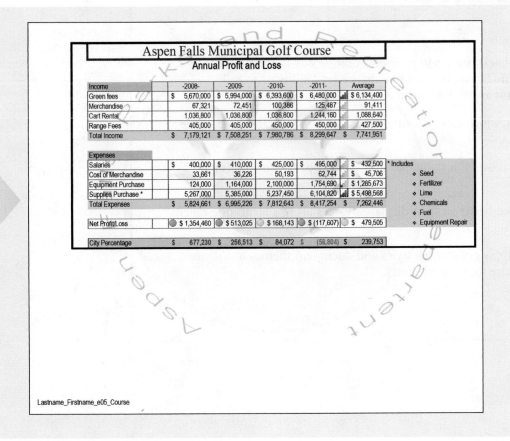

Lastname_Firstname_e05_Course

**You will save this
workbook as:**

Lastname_Firstname_e05_Course

In this chapter, you will create documents for the Aspen Falls City Hall, which provides essential services for the citizens and visitors of Aspen Falls, California.

Introduction

▶ You can modify cell backgrounds to provide a unique way to identify spreadsheets. Cell borders can be used to enhance readability or to call attention to important areas of a worksheet.

▶ You can use symbols, which can be formatted as text, to create the appearance of a bulleted list.

▶ The Format Painter allows you to quickly and easily copy the formatting in one cell to another cell.

▶ Cells can be formatted based on their displayed values using a technique called conditional formatting.

▶ You can create and apply custom cell styles and document themes to maintain a consistent appearance for all worksheets.

Time to complete all
10 skills – 50 to 90 minutes

Find your student data files here:

Student data files needed
for this chapter:

- e05_Course

- e05_Course_Logo

▶ A symbol can be used to create the appearance of a *bulleted list*—a list of items that are preceded by symbols.

▶ A *symbol* is a character such as the copyright symbol © or a bullet character that is not found on common keyboards.

▶ Once a symbol is inserted into a cell, the cell contents can be formatted as text.

1. **Start** ⊕ Excel and then open **e05_Course**. On the Ribbon, click the **File tab**, and then click **Save As**. In the **Save As** dialog box, navigate to the location where you are saving your files. Click **New folder**, type Excel Chapter 5 and then press [Enter] two times. In the **File name** box, using your own name, name the file Lastname_Firstname_e05_Course and then press [Enter]. Add the file name in the worksheet's left footer.

2. Return to **Normal** view. Select cell **K17**. On the Ribbon, click the **Insert tab**. In the **Symbols group**, click the **Symbol** button. Compare your screen with **Figure 1**.

3. In the **Symbol** dialog box, click the **Font arrow**, and then click **Wingdings**.

   Wingdings is a font that displays *character graphics*—small graphic characters based on text characters that can be formatted as text.

4. In the displayed gallery of symbols, use the vertical scroll bar to locate and select the diamond-shaped symbol with four smaller diamonds ❖, as shown in Figure 2.

5. Click the **Insert** button and then click the **Close** button to close the dialog box. Notice that the symbol is inserted into cell **K17**.

■ **Continue to the next page to complete the skill**

Symbol button

Figure 1

Wingdings font selected

Diamond shape selected

Figure 2

Custom formatting

Custom selected

Figure 3

Common Custom Formatting Characters

Character	Description
#	Specifies a placeholder for a digit.
0	Specifies a placeholder for any digit. When the value is less than zero, a 0 will be displayed.
.	Specifies the location of a decimal point.
,	Specifies the location where a comma will be displayed.
[color]	Specifies the color used to display negative numbers.
mm	Displays the month with a leading zero.
dd	Displays the day with a leading zero.
yy	Displays the year using two digits.

Figure 4

6. With cell **K17** still selected, point to the fill handle, and then with the ⊞ pointer, drag down through cell **K22**.

7. With the range **K17:K22** selected, display the **Home tab**, and then in the **Alignment group**, click the **Align Right** button ≣.

   Aligning the symbols on the right creates the appearance of a bulleted list.

8. With the range **K17:K22** still selected, change the **Font Size** to **8** points.

9. Select the range **E5:H5**, and then on the **Home tab**, click the **Number Dialog Box Launcher** ⊡.

10. In the **Format Cells** dialog box, on the **Number tab**, under **Category**, click **Custom**. In the **Type** box, replace the existing value with -yyyy- Be sure to include the hyphen characters (-), as shown in **Figure 3**.

    Custom formatting allows you to format text and numbers. Here, the four characters indicate the numbers used to create a four-digit year, and the hyphen characters will be inserted before and after the number. Common formatting characters are summarized in the table shown in **Figure 4**.

11. Click **OK**. Notice the custom number format is applied to the range.

12. Select the range **E10:H10** and then click the **Smart Tag** arrow ◈. Click **Ignore Error**.

    An error appears in these cells because row 5, which might need to be included in the calculations, is a row of labels and is omitted.

13. Save ⊟ your work.

■ **You have completed Skill 1 of 10**

► The **Format Painter** is a tool used to copy formatting from one place to another.

► In Excel, the Format Painter is used to copy text formats, number formats, borders, and cell shading.

1. Select cell **E5**, and then on the **Home tab**, in the **Alignment group**, click the **Center** button.

2. In the **Clipboard group**, click the **Format Painter**. With the pointer, drag across the range **F5:I5** and then release the mouse button. Notice the formatting in cell **E5** is applied to the range and the Format Painter is no longer active, as shown in **Figure 1**.

3. Select cell **E6**. On the **Home tab**, in the **Number group**, click the **Accounting Number Format** button $ and then click the **Decrease Decimal** button two times.

4. In the **Clipboard group**, click the **Format Painter** button. With the pointer, drag through the range **F6:I6**.

   The number formatting in cell E6 is applied across the range. A series of # signs appears, indicating that the column is too narrow to display the numeric values.

5. Select columns **E:I**. In the **Cells group**, click the **Format** button and then click **AutoFit Column Width**. Compare your screen with **Figure 2**.

   Setting the columns to AutoFit the width will let them expand to display each cell's numeric values.

■ **Continue to the next page to complete the skill**

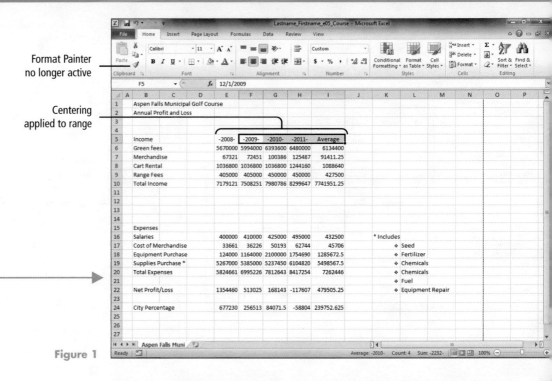

Format Painter no longer active

Centering applied to range

Figure 1

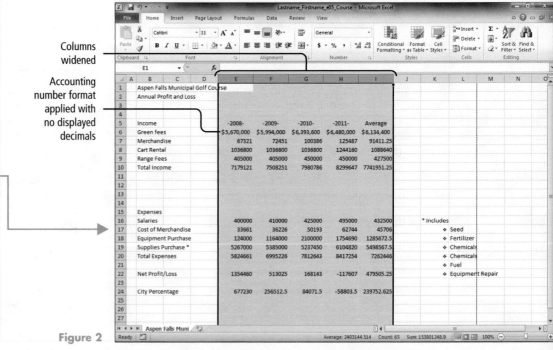

Columns widened

Accounting number format applied with no displayed decimals

Figure 2

Format Painter still active

Formatting applied to several ranges

Figure 3

Comma [0] format applied to two ranges

Figure 4

6. Select cell **E6**, and then in the **Clipboard group**, double-click the **Format Painter** button ☑. With the 🖌 pointer, drag through range **E10:I10**. Notice that **Format Painter** is still active.

7. With the 🖌 pointer, drag through the following ranges: **E16:I16, E20:I20, E22:I22**, and then **E24:I24**. Compare your screen with **Figure 3**.

   In this manner, double-clicking Format Painter enables you to apply formatting to several worksheet areas without clicking the Format Painter each time.

8. Press Esc to release Format Painter.

9. Select the range **E7:I9**. In the **Styles group**, click the **Cell Styles** button and then click **Comma [0]**.

10. Using one of the techniques just practiced, use **Format Painter** to apply the formatting in cell **E7** to the range **E17:I19** and then compare your screen with **Figure 4**.

11. If necessary, press Esc to release Format Painter. **Save** 💾 your work.

■ **You have completed Skill 2 of 10**

► A *conditional format* is a format that changes the appearance of a cell or range when one or more conditions are true.

► *Icon Sets* classify a range of data into three to five categories and display small graphics in each cell depending on that cell's value.

► The style or color of the icon set represents the relative value of the cell compared to other cells in the range.

1. Select the range **I6:I9**. On the **Home tab**, in the **Styles group**, click the **Conditional Formatting** button. In the displayed list, point to **Icon Sets** and then compare your screen with **Figure 1**.

   There are a number of predefined icon sets that are available.

2. In the displayed gallery, under **Ratings**, click **5 Ratings**—the second choice in the right column. **AutoFit** column **I**.

   Icon Sets display different icons depending on the relative values of each cell in the range. Here, the icon in cell I6 reflects that the cell's value is substantially larger than the other values in the range.

3. Select cell **I6** and then click the **Format Painter** button. With the pointer, drag through the range **I16:I19** and then compare your screen with **Figure 2**.

   This action applies the icon set conditional formatting to the expenses averages so that their formatting matches the income formatting.

■ **Continue to the next page to complete the skill**

Icon Sets gallery

Figure 1

5 Ratings icon set

Conditional Formatting copied to range

Figure 2

Figure 3

Figure 4

4. Select the range **E22:I22** and then click the **Conditional Formatting** button. Click **New Rule**.

5. In the **New Formatting Rule** dialog box, under **Edit the Rule Description**, click the **Format Style arrow** and then click **Icon Sets**.

6. Under **Icon**, click the **Type arrow** for the green icon and then click **Number**. In **Value** box for the green icon, type 500000

7. Under **Icon**, click the **Type arrow** for the yellow icon and then click **Number**. Compare your screen with **Figure 3**.

Notice that when you click Number, the yellow icon Value box is set to zero (0).

8. Click **OK**. AutoFit columns **E:I** and then compare your screen with **Figure 4**.

In the range, the cells greater than $500,000 display a green icon. The cells between $0 and $500,000 display a yellow icon. The cells that reflect a loss—that is, they are less than $0—display a red icon.

9. **Save** 🖫 your work.

■ **You have completed Skill 3 of 10**

▶ You can enter formulas as conditional formatting rules so that cells display formatting based on the results of those rules.

1. Select cell **E24**. In the **Styles group**, click **Conditional Formatting** and then click **New Rule**.

2. In the **New Formatting Rule** dialog box, under **Select a Rule Type**, click **Use a formula to determine which cells to format**. Compare your screen with **Figure 1**.

3. Under **Edit the Rule Description**, in the **Format values where this formula is true** box, type =E24>250000 Compare your screen with **Figure 2**.

   This rule applies the desired formatting only when the value in cell E24 is greater than $250,000—the desired minimum profit.

4. Under **Edit the Rule Description**, click the **Format** button.

5. In the **Format Cells** dialog box, on the **Font tab**, under **Font style**, click **Bold**.

6. Click the **Color arrow**. In the displayed gallery, under **Theme Colors**, click the seventh color in the sixth row—**Olive Green, Accent 3, Darker 50%**.

■ **Continue to the next page to complete the skill**

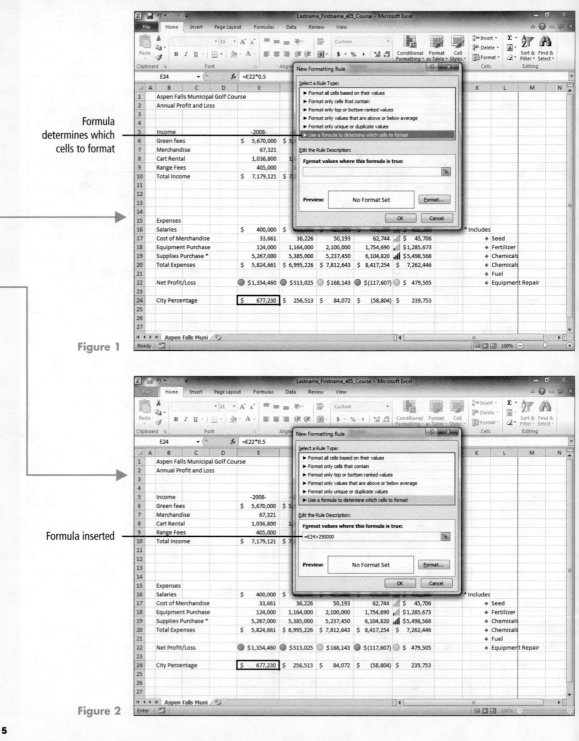

Formula determines which cells to format

Figure 1

Formula inserted

Figure 2

Preview of conditional formatting

Figure 3

Formatted cells

Red color

Conditional formatting applied to E24:I24

Figure 4

7. Click **OK** and then in the **New Formatting Rule** dialog box, click **OK**.

> Here, the cell value is greater than $250,000 and the text is dark green and bold.

8. Click the **Conditional Formatting** button and then click **Manage Rules**. In the **Conditional Formatting Rules Manager** dialog box, click the **New Rule** button.

9. In the **New Formatting Rule** dialog box, under **Select a Rule Type**, click **Use a formula to determine which cells to format**. Under **Edit the Rule Description**, in the **Format values where this formula is true** box, type =E24<0

10. Click the **Format** button. In the **Format Cells** dialog box, on the **Font tab**, under **Font style**, click **Bold**. Click the **Color arrow**. In the displayed gallery, under **Standard Colors**, click the second color— **Red**. Click **OK** and then compare your screen with **Figure 3**.

> The Preview box displays how the cell will be formatted when its value is less than zero.

11. Click **OK** two times. Use **Format Painter** to copy the formatting in cell **E24** to the range **F24:I24**. Click cell **A1** and then compare your screen with **Figure 4**.

12. Save 💾 the workbook.

■ **You have completed Skill 4 of 10**

▶ Rows and columns can be inserted into or deleted from a worksheet as needed.

▶ When you delete cells—but not an entire row or column—you need to specify which direction the remaining cells in the sheet will move.

1. In the row headings, point to **3**, and then with the ⊡ pointer, click to select the entire row. On the **Home tab**, in the **Cells group**, click the **Delete button arrow**. Click **Delete Sheet Rows** and then compare your screen with **Figure 1**. Alternatively, right-click the row and then from the displayed shortcut menu, click **Delete**.

2. Repeat this technique to delete rows **10** through **12**.

3. Select the range **K15:L15**. In the **Cells group**, click the **Delete button arrow** and then click **Delete Cells**.

4. In the **Delete** dialog box, under **Delete**, verify that the **Shift cells up** option button is selected. Compare your screen with **Figure 2**.

5. Click **OK** to close the **Delete** dialog box. With the range **K15:L15** selected, in the **Cells group**, click the **Insert button arrow** and then click **Insert Cells**.

■ **Continue to the next page to complete the skill**

Row deleted

Figure 1

Delete dialog box

Shift cells up selected

Figure 2

Shift cells down selected

Figure 3

Column widths changed

Figure 4

6. In the **Insert** dialog box, under **Insert**, verify that the **Shift cells down** option button is selected. Compare your screen with **Figure 3**. Click **OK**.

Two cells are inserted and the remaining cells are shifted down one row.

7. Select cell **K14**. With the ⊞ pointer, drag the cell's fill handle down to cell **K15** to copy the symbol. Select cell **L15**, type Lime and then press Enter.

8. Select column **D**, press and hold Ctrl, and then click column **J**. In the **Cells group**, click the **Delete** button.

9. Select the range **B1:H1** and then in the **Alignment group**, click the **Merge & Center** button ☲. Select the range **B2:H2** and then click the **Merge & Center** button ☲.

10. Click the **Select All** button ☐. In the **Cells group**, click the **Format arrow** and then click **AutoFit Column Width**.

When the entire worksheet is selected, AutoFit is applied to worksheet columns.

11. Select column **A**, press and hold Ctrl, and then click column **C**. In the **Cells group**, click the **Format** button and then click **Column Width**. In the **Column Width** dialog box, type 4 and then click **OK**. Compare your screen with **Figure 4**.

12. **Save** 🖫 the workbook.

■ **You have completed Skill 5 of 10**

► Recall that a *cell fill color*—also known as a *background color*—is the shading assigned to a cell.

► A *cell border*—decorative lines that can be applied to worksheet cells—is added to differentiate, emphasize, or group cells.

1. Click cell **B4,** press and hold Ctrl, and then click cell **B11**. Compare your screen with **Figure 1.**

2. On the **Home tab**, in the **Font group**, click the **Fill Color button arrow** ![fill color icon]. In the displayed gallery, under **Theme Colors**, click the third color in the third row—**Tan, Background 2, Darker 25%**. Select cell **A1**, and compare your screen with **Figure 2.**

   The darker tan color calls attention to the *Income* and *Expenses* headers of the worksheet.

3. Select the range **B9:H9**, press and hold Ctrl, and then select the range **B16:H16**.

4. In the **Font group**, click the **Fill Color button arrow** ![fill color icon]. In the displayed gallery, under **Theme Colors**, click the third color in the second row—**Tan, Background 2, Darker 10%**.

■ **Continue to the next page to complete the skill**

Nonadjacent cells selected

Figure 1

Fill color applied

Figure 2

Fill color changed

Figure 3

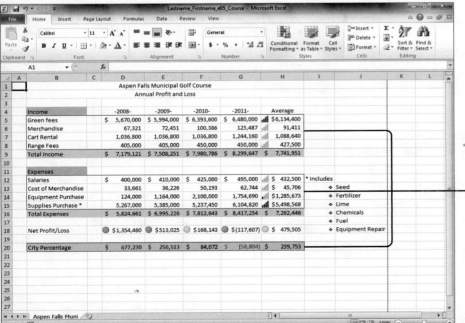

Borders applied

Figure 4

5. Select the range **B20:H20**. Using the skills just practiced, change the **Fill Color** to **Olive Green, Accent 3, Lighter 40%**—the seventh color in the fourth row. Select cell **A1**, and compare your screen with **Figure 3**.

6. Select the nonadjacent ranges **B5:H8** and **B12:H15**. In the **Font group**, click the **Border button arrow** ⊞▾ and then click **More Borders**.

7. In the **Format Cells** dialog box, on the **Border tab**, under **Style**, click the last line style in the left column. Click the **Color arrow** and then under **Theme Colors**, click the third color in the fifth row— **Tan, Background 2, Darker 75%**.

8. Under **Presets**, click the **Outline** button and then click **OK**.

9. Select the range **B20:H20**. In the **Font group**, click the **Border button arrow** ⊞▾ and then click **More Borders**.

10. On the **Border tab**, under **Style**, be sure that the last line style in the left column is selected. Click the **Color arrow** and then in the displayed gallery, click the third color in the fifth row—**Tan, Background 2, Darker 75%**.

11. Under **Presets**, click the **Outline** button and then click **OK**. Click cell **A1** and then compare your screen with **Figure 4**.

12. Save 💾 the workbook.

■ **You have completed Skill 6 of 10**

► A *style* is a group of formatting choices that can be applied in a single step.

► Excel has several prebuilt cell styles, and you can also create and save your own styles.

► Styles are saved in the workbook where they are created.

1. On the **Home tab**, in the **Styles group**, click the **Cell Styles** button. At the bottom of the **Cell Styles** gallery, click **New Cell Style** and then compare your screen with **Figure 1**.

2. In the **Style** dialog box, in the **Style Name** box, type Aspen Falls Golf and then click the **Format** button.

3. In the **Format Cells** dialog box, click the **Number tab** and then under **Category**, click **Text**.

   The *Text format* treats the cell value as text even when the cell contains numbers.

4. Click the **Alignment tab**. Under **Text Alignment**, click the **Horizontal arrow** and then click **Center**. Click the **Vertical arrow**, click **Center**, and then compare your screen with **Figure 2**.

5. Click the **Font tab** and then under **Font**, click **Times New Roman**. Under **Size**, click **20**.

6. Click the **Color button arrow** and then in the displayed gallery, under **Theme Colors**, click the third color in the fifth row—**Tan, Background 2, Darker 75%**.

■ **Continue to the next page to complete the skill**

Style dialog box

Figure 1

Alignment tab

Horizontal and Vertical alignment set to Center

Figure 2

Border formatting preview

Figure 3

Custom style applied

Figure 4

7. Click the **Border tab**. Under **Style**, click the next to last line style in the right column. Click the **Color arrow** and then in the displayed gallery, click the third color in the fifth row—**Tan, Background 2, Darker 75%**. Under **Presets**, click the **Outline** button. Compare your screen with Figure 3.

8. Click **OK** to close the **Format Cells** dialog box. In the **Style** dialog box, click **OK** to close the dialog box and to save the new *Aspen Falls Golf* style.

9. Select cell **B1**. In the **Styles group**, click **Cell Styles**, and under **Custom**, click **Aspen....** Notice the custom cell style formatting is applied to the range.

10. Select cell **B2**. In the **Font group**, click the **Font Size arrow** and then click **16**. Select cell **A1** and compare your screen with Figure 4.

11. **Save** 🖫 the workbook.

   The custom cell style is saved with the worksheet and can be applied as often as needed within the current worksheet.

■ **You have completed Skill 7 of 10**

► Recall that a document theme is a set of colors, fonts, lines, and fill effects that can be applied to entire worksheets or to individual cells.

► Microsoft Office applications, including Word, Excel, Access, and PowerPoint, share the same themes.

► Themes can be customized by changing the colors, fonts, and effects assigned to them. Care should be taken to choose color combinations that look professional.

1. On the Ribbon, click the **Page Layout tab**. In the **Themes group**, click the **Fonts** button and then compare your screen with **Figure 1**.

2. In the displayed gallery, click **Create New Theme Fonts**.

3. In the **Create New Theme Fonts** dialog box, click the **Heading font arrow**, scroll down the displayed list, and then click **Century Gothic**.

   When the new theme is applied, all heading cell styles that have not been customized will display in the Century Gothic font.

4. Click the **Body font arrow**, scroll up the displayed list, and then click **Arial Narrow**.

   The default font face and size for Excel 2010 is Calibri, size 11. When you change the body font, you change the default font for the workbook. Here, the default font has been changed to Arial Narrow.

   Under Sample, a sample of the selected font choices displays for the heading and body font styles.

5. In the **Name** box, delete the existing text and then type Aspen Falls Golf Fonts Compare your screen with **Figure 2**.

■ **Continue to the next page to complete the skill**

Built-in fonts themes

Create New Theme Fonts

Figure 1

Heading font changed

Body font changed

Theme fonts name

Sample fonts

Figure 2

Body font is
Arial Narrow

Figure 3

Page Setup
dialog box

Margin widths
changed

Horizontally
centered selected

Figure 4

6. Click **Save** to save the custom fonts theme. If necessary autofit the column width, and then compare your screen with **Figure 3**.

   In the worksheet, the body fonts are formatted as Arial Narrow. The heading fonts do not change because those cells are individually formatted, which overrides the theme fonts.

7. On the **Page Layout tab**, in the **Themes group**, click the **Fonts** button. Verify that the *Aspen Falls Golf Fonts* theme displays at the top of the displayed gallery, and then click a blank cell to close the gallery.

8. In the **Page Setup group**, click the **Margins** button and then in the displayed gallery, click **Custom Margins**.

9. In the **Page Setup** dialog box, in the **Left** box, select *0.7* and then type .5 In the **Right** box, select *0.7* and then type .5

   Customizing the margins is a useful way to include all of your data when the page is slightly wider than the default margin of 0.7 inches.

10. Under **Center on page**, select the **Horizontally** check box and then compare your screen with **Figure 4**.

    This setting will center the spreadsheet on the printed page horizontally so that it is presented in a professional fashion.

11. Click **OK** and then **Save** 🖫 the workbook.

    ■ **You have completed Skill 8 of 10**

► Background colors can be applied to ranges of cells to add interest to a worksheet.

► A *watermark* is a graphic inserted into a workbook background. Watermarks are typically inserted into the header.

1. Display the **Insert tab** and then in the **Text group**, click the **Header & Footer** button.

2. Be sure the insertion point is in the center header, as shown in **Figure 1**.

3. On the **Design tab**, in the **Header & Footer Elements group**, click the **Picture** button.

4. In the **Insert Picture** dialog box, navigate to your student data files, select **e05_Course_Logo**, and then click **Insert**. Notice *&[Picture]* displays in the header.

5. Click cell **A1** to close the **Header & Footer** and to display the watermark as shown in **Figure 2**.

   You can use any picture as a watermark. By adding an image to the header, it is displayed behind the data on the spreadsheet instead of on top of the data. This allows a background image to act as a watermark.

6. Click the **View tab** and then in the **Workbook Views group**, click **Normal**. Notice the watermark does not display in **Normal** view.

7. Select the range **C4:H4** and then display the **Home tab**. In the **Font group**, click the **Fill Color button arrow** . In the displayed gallery, under **Theme Colors**, click the third color in the first row— **Tan, Background 2**.

■ **Continue to the next page to complete the skill**

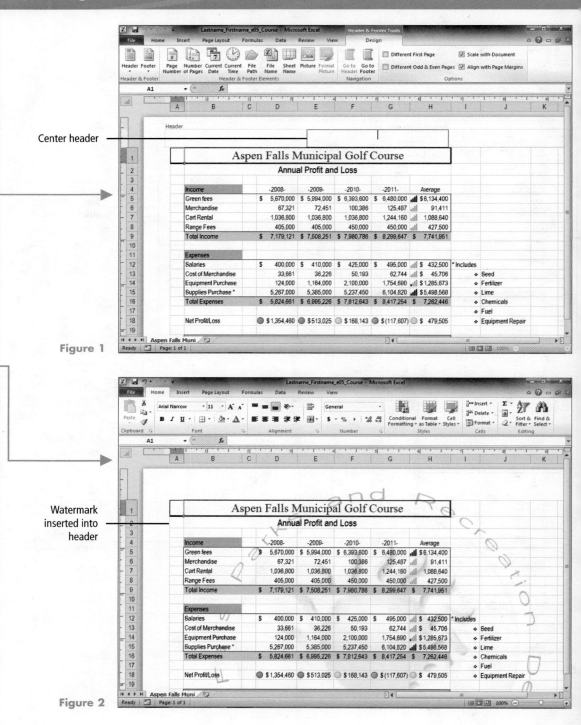

Center header

Figure 1

Watermark inserted into header

Figure 2

Line style

Outline and Inside borders applied

Color changed

Figure 3

8. With the range **C4:H4** still selected, in the **Font group**, click the **Borders button arrow** and then click **More Borders**.

9. In the **Format Cells** dialog box, under **Style**, be sure the last line in the left column is selected. Click the **Color arrow** and then under **Theme Colors**, click the sixth color in the fifth row—**Red, Accent 2, Darker 25%**. Under **Presets**, click the **Outline** button and then click the **Inside** button.

10. Compare your screen with **Figure 3** and then click **OK**.

11. Select the range **B18:H18**. In the **Font group**, click the **Borders button arrow** and then click **More Borders**. In the **Format Cells** dialog box, under **Style**, be sure the last line style in the left column is selected. Click the **Color arrow** and then under **Theme Colors**, click the sixth color in the fifth row—**Red, Accent 2, Darker 25%**. Under **Presets**, click the **Outline** button and then click the **Inside** button. Click **OK**.

12. Select the range **I12:J18** and then in the **Font group**, click the **Fill Color button arrow**. In the displayed gallery, under **Theme Colors**, click the seventh color in the third row—**Olive Green, Accent 3, Lighter 60%**. Click cell **A1** and then compare your screen with **Figure 4**.

13. **Save** the workbook.

■ **You have completed Skill 9 of 10**

Borders applied

Fill color applied

Figure 4

► *Gridlines* are the lines that run between the cells in a worksheet.

► Gridlines are useful when working with the spreadsheet, but they can be hidden after the worksheet is completed.

1. Display the **Page Layout tab** and then in the **Sheet Options group**, under **Gridlines**, clear the **View** check box.

2. Select the range **B5:H8**, press and hold Ctrl, and then select the range **B12:H15**.

3. On the **Home tab**, in the **Font group**, click the **Font Dialog Box Launcher** . In the **Format Cells** dialog box, click the **Border tab**. Compare your screen with **Figure 1**.

4. In the **Format Cells** dialog box, under **Style**, be sure that the last line style on the left is selected. Click the **Color arrow** and then under **Theme Colors**, make sure the third color in the fifth row—**Tan, Background 2, Darker 75%**—is selected.

5. Under **Presets**, click the **Inside** button, click the **Outline** button, and then click **OK**. Select cell **A1** and compare your screen with **Figure 2**.

6. Select the range **A1:J20** and then in the **Font group**, click the **Font Dialog Box Launcher** . In the **Format Cells** dialog box, click the **Border tab**.

■ **Continue to the next page to complete the skill**

Format Cells dialog box

Border tab

Gridlines do not display

Figure 1

Formatting applied

Figure 2

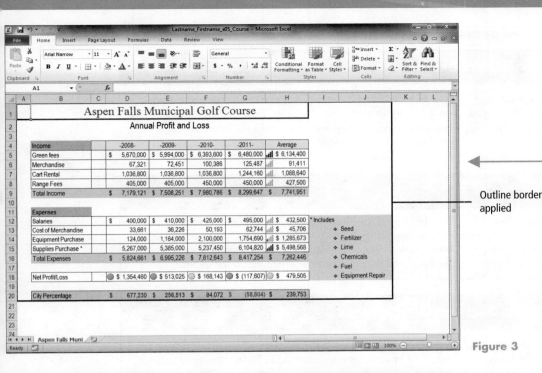

Outline border
applied

Figure 3

Print preview

Figure 4

7. In the **Format Cells** dialog box, under **Style**, click the next-to-last line style in the right column. Click the **Color arrow** and then under **Theme Colors**, click the third color in the sixth row—**Tan, Background 2, Darker 90%**.

8. Under **Presets**, click the **Outline** button and then click **OK**. Click cell **A1** and then compare your screen with Figure 3.

9. Display the **Page Layout tab** and then in the **Sheet Options group**, under **Headings**, clear the **View** check box.

10. Display the **File tab** and then click **Print**. Compare your screen with Figure 4.

11. If you are printing your work for this project, print the worksheet.

12. Click **Save** and then submit the file as directed by your instructor.

Done! You have completed Skill 10 of 10 and your workbook is complete!

More Skills

The following More Skills are located at **www.pearsonhighered.com/skills**

More Skills 11 Copy Styles Between Workbooks

Custom styles are saved only in the workbook in which they are created. When you have styles saved in another workbook, you can copy them into your current workbook.

In More Skills 11, you will copy cell styles from one workbook to another workbook. To begin, open your web browser, navigate to www.pearsonhighered.com/skills, locate the name of your textbook, and then follow the instructions on the website.

More Skills 12 Draw Borders

You can apply preset borders to a cell, but it is often beneficial to draw custom borders so that the worksheet looks exactly as you intend when you create it. Custom borders are drawn using the Draw Border group, which is found in the Borders gallery.

In More Skills 12, you will open a workbook and draw custom borders. To begin, open your web browser, navigate to www.pearsonhighered.com/skills, locate the name of your textbook, and then follow the instructions on the website.

More Skills 13 Convert Comma-Separated Text into Columns

Tabular data often comes from text files that do not have columns. Here, each column is separated by commas. In Excel, when a cell contains values separated by commas, use the Convert Text to Columns Wizard to convert the text into columns.

In More Skills 13, you will open a worksheet and convert text separated by commas into columns. To begin, open your web browser, navigate to www.pearsonhighered.com/skills, locate the name of your textbook, and then follow the instructions on the website.

More Skills 14 Create Screen Clippings

Screen clippings can be inserted directly into an Excel worksheet without using an external image-capturing program. The Screen Clipping tool captures an image from your computer and inserts it directly into Excel, where it can be manipulated and saved.

In More Skills 14, you will open a workbook and a website, and then using the Screen Clipping tool, you will capture a portion of the webpage, insert it into the worksheet, and recolor the image. To begin, open your web browser, navigate to www.pearsonhighered.com/skills, locate the name of your textbook, and then follow the instructions on the website.

Key Terms

Online Help Skills

1. **Start** ⊕ Excel. In the upper right corner of the Excel window, click the **Help** button ⊡. In the **Help** window, click the **Maximize** ⊡ button.

2. Click in the search box, type conditional formatting and then click the **Search** button ⊡. In the search results, click **Add, change, find, or clear conditional formats**.

3. Read the article's introduction, and then below **In this article**, click **Use a formula to determine which cells to format**. Compare your screen with Figure 1.

Figure 1

4. Read the section to see if you can answer the following: What type of formula can be used to specify conditional formatting criteria? What types of cell references are automatically inserted when using conditional formatting?

Matching

Match each term in the second column with its correct definition in the first column by writing the letter of the term on the blank line in front of the correct definition.

____ **1.** Decorative lines that can be applied to worksheet cells.

____ **2.** A set of colors, fonts, lines, and fill effects.

____ **3.** A list of items that are preceded by symbols.

____ **4.** A conditional formatting tool used to classify data into three to five categories that allows you to see the value of a cell in relation to other cells.

____ **5.** Changes the appearance of a cell range based on a condition.

____ **6.** A command that copies formatting from one place and applies it to another.

____ **7.** The color of the worksheet itself.

____ **8.** The background color of a cell.

____ **9.** Lines that run horizontally and vertically across a worksheet.

____ **10.** Formatting options applied to a cell.

A Gridlines

B Format Painter

C Borders

D Background color

E Icon Set

F Conditional formatting

G Bulleted list

H Cell fill color

I Theme

J Style

Multiple Choice

Write the correct answer in the space provided.

1. Seeing multiple pound signs— ##### —in a cell, indicates this about the column width.
   - **A.** Too Wide
   - **B.** Too Narrow
   - **C.** Too Short

2. This technique changes the appearance of a cell range based on the underlying cell values.
   - **A.** Conditional formatting
   - **B.** Cell formatting
   - **C.** Functional formatting

3. This is a conditional formatting tool used to classify data into three to five categories that uses images to allow you to see the value of a cell in relation to other cells.
   - **A.** Cell rule
   - **B.** Color Scale
   - **C.** Icon Set

4. You must specify which direction to move the surrounding cells whenever you perform this operation on a worksheet.
   - **A.** Formatted
   - **B.** Inserted
   - **C.** Copied

5. This is where custom styles are saved.
   - **A.** Application
   - **B.** Workbook
   - **C.** Computer

6. This is a set of colors, fonts, lines, and fill effects that can be applied to entire worksheets.
   - **A.** Format
   - **B.** Style
   - **C.** Theme

7. This is a graphic that is inserted into a document background.
   - **A.** Background
   - **B.** Logo
   - **C.** Watermark

8. These are the lines that run horizontally and vertically across a worksheet.
   - **A.** Rulers
   - **B.** Gridlines
   - **C.** Alignment marks

9. Once a character graphic is inserted into a cell, it can be formatted like this element of a workbook.
   - **A.** Text
   - **B.** An image
   - **C.** A style

10. This is a saved and named set of formatting options applied to a cell.
    - **A.** Format
    - **B.** Style
    - **C.** Theme

Topics for Discussion

1. You have added conditional formatting that displays icon sets, data bars, and color scales. Do you think these special formats add to or detract from the data's meaning? Why?

2. In this chapter, you placed borders and shading in cells and then hid the gridlines and column and row headings. Compare this format with one that displays only gridlines and headings but does not display borders and shading. Which format do you think is easiest for others to read? Why?

Skill Check

To complete this project, you will need the following files:

- e05_Golf
- e05_Golf_Logo

You will save your file as:

- Lastname_Firstname_e05_Golf

1. **Start** Excel and open the student data file **e05_Golf**. **Save** the file in your **Excel Chapter 5** folder with the name Lastname_Firstname_e05_Golf

2. Select column **A**. In the **Cells group**, click **Insert**. Right-click column **A** and then click **Column Width**. In the **Column Width** box, type 4 and then click **OK**.

3. Select cell **D21** and on the **Home tab**, in the **Number group**, click the **Format Cells Dialog Box Launcher**. Display the **Number tab** and under **Category**, click **Custom**. Under **Type**, type $## and then click **OK**. Use the **Format Painter** and copy the format from cell **D21** to cell **D22**. Compare your screen with **Figure 1**.

4. Select cell **H5**. In the **Clipboard group**, click **Format Painter** and then copy the format in cell **H5** through the range **C18:F18**.

5. Select the range **B4:H18**. In the **Font group**, click the **Fill Color button arrow** and then under **Theme Colors**, click the seventh color in the second row—**Olive Green, Accent 3, Lighter 80%**. In the **Font group**, click the **Border button arrow** and then click **Thick Box Border**. Click the **Border button arrow** and then click **More Borders**. Under **Style**, click the last line style in the left column. Click the **Color arrow** and then under **Theme Colors**, click the third color in the fifth row—**Tan, Background 2, Darker 75%**. Click the **Inside** button and then click **OK**.

6. Select row **17** and then in the **Cells group**, click **Insert**. Compare your screen with **Figure 2**.

7. Select the range **C19:F19**. Click **Conditional Formatting**, point to **Icon Sets**, and then click **More Rules**. In the **New Formatting Rule** dialog box, under **Edit the Rule Description**, click the **Icon Style arrow**, click **3 Symbols (Circled)**, and then click **OK**.

Figure 1

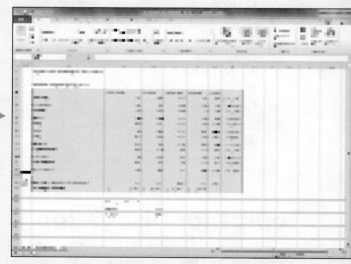

Figure 2

■ **Continue to the next page to complete this Skill Check**

Figure 3

Figure 4

8. Select the range **H5:H16**. In the **Styles group**, click **Conditional Formatting** and point to **Icon Sets**. Under **Ratings**, click **5 Ratings**—the last set in the right column.

9. Select columns **C:H**. In the **Cells group**, click **Format** and then click **AutoFit Column Width**.

10. Select cell **B22**. On the **Insert tab**, click **Symbol**. In the **Symbol** dialog box, click the **Font arrow** and then click **Wingdings**. Locate and then click the **diamond symbol** (◆). Click **Insert** and then click **Close**. Press Enter and then select cell **B22**. Change the **Font Size** to 8. Apply the **Align Right** style. Use the fill handle to copy cell **B22** to cell **B23**.

11. Select cell **A1**. On the **Home tab**, in the **Styles group**, click **Cell Styles** and then click **New Cell Style**. In the **Style name** box, type Aspen Golf Rounds

12. Click **Format**. In the Format Cells dialog box, click the **Number tab** and then, under **Category**, click **Text**. Click the **Alignment tab**. Under **Text Alignment**, click the **Horizontal arrow** and then click **Center Across Selection**. Click the **Vertical arrow** and then click **Center**. Click the **Font tab**. Under **Font**, click **Comic Sans MS**. Under **Font style**, click **Bold**. Under **Size**, click **20**. Click the **Color arrow** and then under **Theme Colors**, click the third color in the fifth row—**Tan, Background 2, Darker 75%**. Click **OK** two times.

13. Select the range **B1:H1**. In the **Cells group**, click **Cell Styles** and then under **Custom**, click **Aspe . . . .**

14. Select row **2** and then in the **Cells group**, click **Delete**. Select the range **C3:H15** and then in the **Alignment group**, click **Center**. Select cell **A1** and then compare your screen with **Figure 3**.

15. Display the **Page Layout tab**. In the **Themes group**, click **Fonts** and then click **Create New Theme Fonts**.

16. In the **Create New Theme Fonts** dialog box, click the **Body font arrow** and then click **Arial Narrow**. In the **Name** box, type Aspen Falls Golf Rounds and then click **Save**.

17. On the **Insert tab**, in the **Text group**, click **Header & Footer**. In the **Header &Footer Elements group**, click **Picture**. Locate and click **e05_Golf_Logo** and then click **Insert**. Add the file name in the worksheet's left footer. Click cell **A1**.

18. Display the **Page Layout tab**. In the **Sheet Options group**, under **Gridlines**, clear the **View** check box. Under **Headings**, clear the **View** check box.

19. Display the **File tab** and then click **Print**. Compare your screen with **Figure 4**.

20. Return to **Normal** view. **Save** the workbook and submit it as directed.

Done! You have completed the Skill Check

Assess Your Skills 1

To complete this project, you will need the following files:

- e05_Fuel
- e05_Fuel_Logo

You will save your file as:

- Lastname_Firstname_e05_Fuel

1. **Start** Excel and open the student data file **e05_Fuel**. Save the file in your **Excel Chapter 5** folder as Lastname_Firstname_e05_Fuel Select the range **A1:D17** and apply a **Red, Accent 2, Lighter 80% Fill** color. Insert a new column **A** and then resize the column to **4**. Resize column **F** to **4**.

2. Use **Format Painter** to copy the format in cell **C5** to the range **C17:E17**. Apply the **Comma[0]** style to the range **C6:E16**.

3. Select cell **E5** and create a new conditional format rule with the following condition: =E5<0 When the condition is true, display the cell text as **Bold** and **Red**. Use **Format Painter** to apply the formatting in cell **E5** to the range **E6:E16**.

4. In the range **E5:E16**, apply the **3 Arrows (Colored)** icon set. Customize the icon set to display a green arrow when the cell value is greater than 100 and a red arrow when the value is less than 0.

5. Create a new **Cell Style** named Aspen Fuel For the style, set the **Horizontal** alignment to **Center Across Selection**. Set the **Font** to **Arial**, size **18**. Set the font color to **Dark Blue, Text 2**. On the **Fill** tab, under **Background Color** click *No Color*. Apply the **Aspen Fuel** style to the range **B1:E1**.

6. Select the range **A1:F18** and apply a **Thick Box Border**. Select the range **B4:E17**, apply a thick line outline border with the **Purple, Accent 4, Darker 50%** color. Apply a **thin** line **inside** border, **Purple, Accent 4, Darker 50%**. **AutoFit** columns **B:E**.

7. Create a new **Theme font**. Name the new theme font Aspen Falls Fuel Apply **Comic Sans MS** for the **Heading font** and **Arial** for the **Body font**.

8. Apply the **Heading 4** cell style to the range **C4:E4** and to cell **B17**.

9. Display the headers and in the middle header, insert a watermark using the file **e05_Fuel_Logo**. Insert the file name in the left section of the footer. Switch to **Normal** view and select cell **A1**.

10. **Save** the file and submit it to your instructor as directed. Compare your completed workbook with **Figure 1**.

Done! You have completed Assess Your Skills 1

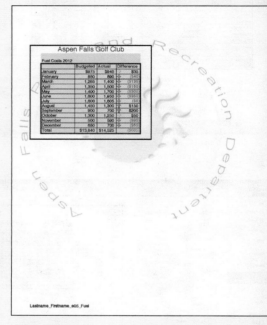

Figure 1

Assess Your Skills 2

To complete this project, you will need the following file:

- e05_Income

You will save your file as:

- Lastname_Firstname_e05_Income

Aspen Falls Golf Club			
Range Income 2012			
	Budgeted	Actual	Difference
January-2012	$ 1,200	$ 1,490	$ 290
February-2012	1,400	1,350	(50)
March-2012	1,600	1,400	(200)
April-2012	1,200	1,135	(65)
May-2012	1,000	840	(160)
June-2012	1,000	890	(110)
July-2012	800	670	(130)
August-2012	1,000	1,300	300
September-2012	1,200	1,435	235
October-2012	1,600	1,900	300
November-2012	1,200	1,395	195
December-2012	800	855	55
Total	14000	14660	660

◆ Unacceptable

Lastname_Firstname_e05_Income

Figure 1

1. **Start** Excel and open the student data file **e05_Income**. Save the file in your **Excel Chapter 5** folder as Lastname_Firstname_ e05_Income Insert the file name in the left footer. Select cell **A4** and create a new **Cell Style** named Aspen Falls Date For the style, apply the custom number format mmmm-yyyy Select the range **A4:A15** and apply the **Aspen Falls Date** style.

2. Use **Format Painter** to copy the format from cell **B4** to the ranges **C4:D4** and **B16:D16**. Apply the **Comma [0]** cell style to the range **B5:D15**.

3. Select the range **D4:D15** and then apply the **3 Traffic Lights (Rimmed)** icon set conditional format.

4. Select the range **A3:D16** and apply an **Orange, Accent 6, Lighter 80%** fill color to the range. Insert a new column **A** and then resize the column to **6**. Resize columns **F** and **G** to **6**.

5. Create a new **Cell Style** named Aspen Golf Range with the following formatting: **Center Across Selection**, **Arial**, size **16**, and a font color of **Red, Accent 2 Darker 50%**. For the new style, apply a thick **Red, Accent 2, Darker 50%** border along the **bottom** edge of the cell only. Select the range **B2:E2** and apply the **Aspen Golf Range** style.

6. Insert a new row **1** and then resize the row to **20**

7. Create a new **Cell Style** named Aspen Falls Dollar Format the style with a **double border Dark Blue, Text 2** to the **top** of the cell only. Format the two sides with a thin line **Dark Blue, Text 2** border. Set the **Fill** color to **Aqua, Accent 5, Lighter 60%**— the ninth color in the second row. Select the range **B17:E17** and apply the **Aspen Falls Dollar** cell style. **AutoFit** columns **B:E**.

8. Select the range **A1:G19** and apply the **Thick Box Border**. Select the range **B2:E17** and apply a **Dark Blue, Text 2, thick Outline** border. Select the range **B4:E16** and apply a **Dark Blue, Text 2 thin inside** border.

9. Click cell **B18**, insert the Wingdings four diamond symbol (◆), apply the **Align Right** style, and then change the **Font size** to **8**. Select cell **C18** and type Unacceptable

10. In cell **F5**, insert the following IF function: =IF(E5<=0, "v"," ") Use the fill handle to copy the function across the range **F6:F16**.

11. **Save** the file and submit it as directed. Compare your completed workbook with Figure 1.

Done! You have completed Assess Your Skills 2

Assess Your Skills Visually

To complete this project, you will need the following file:

- e05_ Scorecard

You will save your file as:

- Lastname_Firstname_e05_Scorecard

Start Excel and open the student data file **e05_Scorecard**. Save the file in your **Excel Chapter 5** folder with the name Lastname_Firstname_e05_Scorecard Format the worksheet as shown in Figure 1. Format, merge, and center the worksheet title—**Comic Sans MS, size14. Rows 2, 3,** and **17** and **columns A** and **M** use **Tan, Background 2, Darker 10%** fill color. Apply a thick box border around the range **A2:M17** and the range **B4:L16**. Apply a thin inside border to the range **B4:L16**. Apply the **Red – Yellow – Green Color Scale** conditional formatting to the range **C9:K12**. Apply the **4 Arrows (Colored)** conditional formatting to the range **L9:L12**. Apply a background color to the entire worksheet or to the individual cells as appropriate. The background is **Tan, Background 2, Darker 10%**. The fill color over the scoring area (**B9:L14**) is **Olive Green, Accent 3, Lighter 80%**. Insert the file name in the footer and then print or submit electronically as directed.

Done! You have completed Assess Your Skills Visually

DownRiver Golf Club											
Holes	1	2	3	4	5	6	7	8	9		
Black Tees	510	400	430	165	355	450	405	190	520	3425	
Blue Tees	500	360	405	135	330	405	375	160	455	3125	
White Tees	475	335	360	115	300	380	340	135	420	2860	
Red Tees	410	275	300	100	270	315	325	110	375	2480	
John	6	6	6	4	4	7	5	3	8	49	
Robert	5	3	4	3	4	6	6	3	5	39	
David	5	4	4	3	5	5	6	3	5	40	
Ralph	8	6	7	5	5	7	5	6	7	56	
Par	5	4	4	3	4	4	4	3	5	36	
Handicap	7	15	5	11	9	3	13	17	1		

Lastname_Firstname_e05_Scorecard

Figure 1

Skills in Context

To complete this project, you will need the following file:

- e05_DownRiver

You will save your file as:

- **Lastname_Firstname_e05_DownRiver**

The Aspen Falls Golf Club is trying to project staffing needs for future years. Open the student data file **e05_DownRiver** and then save it in your chapter folder as Lastname_Firstname_e05_DownRiver Create a new style and then apply the style to all worksheet headings. Apply formatting that makes the headings stand out from the worksheet. Create a separate style that formats the numbers as appropriate. For the worksheet totals, apply

conditional formatting so that the golf course managers can easily tell which months are the busiest. Create a new font style that changes the body text to a font of your choice. Add the file name in the left footer. Save your workbook and then print or submit it electronically as directed.

Done! You have completed Skills in Context

Skills and You

To complete this project, you will need the following file:

- e05_Skills

You will save your file as:

- **Lastname_Firstname_e05_Skills**

Using the skills you have practiced in this chapter, modify the **e05_Skills** file to display the grades that you have earned in a college course or other data as appropriate. Apply a conditional

formatting icon set that shows whether each individual grade exceeds, meets, or is below your desired grade.

Done! You have completed Skills and You

Work with Advanced Functions and Formulas

▶ Excel functions are used to perform complex operations easily—for example, you can manipulate text and calculate the future value of assets.

▶ Excel analysis tools are used to perform what-if analysis and to determine which variables need to be changed in order to meet your goals.

Your starting screen will look similar to this:

SKILLS

Skills 1-10 Training

At the end of this chapter, you will be able to:

Skill 1 Modify Text Using Text Functions

Skill 2 Use Paste Options to Change Underlying Values

Skill 3 Write Nested IF Functions

Skill 4 Look Up Data Using Lookup Functions

Skill 5 Apply Logical Functions

Skill 6 Use COUNTA and COUNTIF Functions

Skill 7 Use the Scenario Manager to Perform What-If Analysis

Skill 8 Calculate Future Value

Skill 9 Use Goal Seek

Skill 10 Calculate Conditional Sums

MORE SKILLS

More Skills 11 Query Tables Using Criteria Ranges

More Skills 12 Use Solver

More Skills 13 Delete Duplicate Records

More Skills 14 Use External Data Links to Update Data

Outcome

Using the skills listed to the left will enable
you to create worksheets like this:

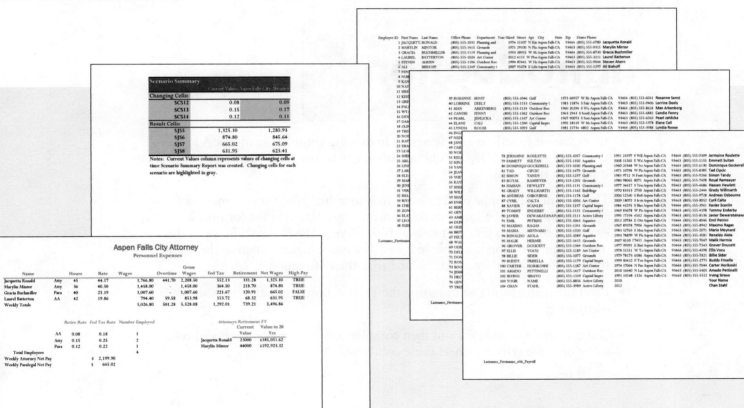

In this chapter, you will create documents for the Aspen Falls City Hall, which provides essential services for the citizens and visitors of Aspen Falls, California.

Introduction

▶ IF statement functions can be nested to develop complex formulas. A lookup table using the VLOOKUP function often can be used in place of nested IF statement functions.

▶ The IF function can be used to evaluate a formula. When the formula is evaluated as true, the function displays one answer; when the formula is evaluated as false, a different answer is displayed. The IF function is not the only logical function available in Excel. The other logical functions become more useful when they are combined with the IF function.

▶ Excel calculates future values using the FV function, when the interest rate is constant.

▶ You can create conditions and then complete calculations on ranges of cells, using only the cells that meet those conditions.

**Time to complete all
10 skills – 50 to 75 minutes**

**Files needed for this
chapter:**

- e06_Payroll

Find your data files here:

► The *CONCATENATE* function is a text function used to join the text in two cells into one cell.

► The *PROPER* function converts text to initial case—the first letter of each word is capitalized.

1. **Start** 🅔 Excel, and then open **e06_Payroll**. On the Ribbon, click the **File tab**, and then click **Save As**. In the **Save As** dialog box, navigate to the location where you are saving your files. Click **New folder**, type Excel Chapter 6 and then press [Enter] two times. In the **File name** box, using your own name, name the file Lastname_Firstname_e06_Payroll and then press [Enter].

2. Select cell **A1**, and then display the **Page Layout** tab. In the **Page Setup** group, click **Orientation**, and then click **Landscape**. Display the **View** tab. In the **Workbook Views** group, click **Normal**.

3. Display the **Employees** worksheet tab, and select cell **M2**.

4. Display the **Formulas** tab, and in the **Function Library** group, click **Text**, and then click **CONCATENATE**. Compare with **Figure 1**.

5. In the **Function Arguments** dialog box, place the insertion point in the **Text1** box, and then click cell **B2**. Press [Tab] to move the insertion point to the **Text2** box.

6. In the **Text2** box, press the [Spacebar], and then press [Tab] to move to the **Text3** box. Notice the quotation marks inserted around the blank space in the **Text2** box.

7. With the insertion point in the **Text3** box, click cell **C2**. Compare with **Figure 2**.

■ **Continue to the next page to complete the skill**

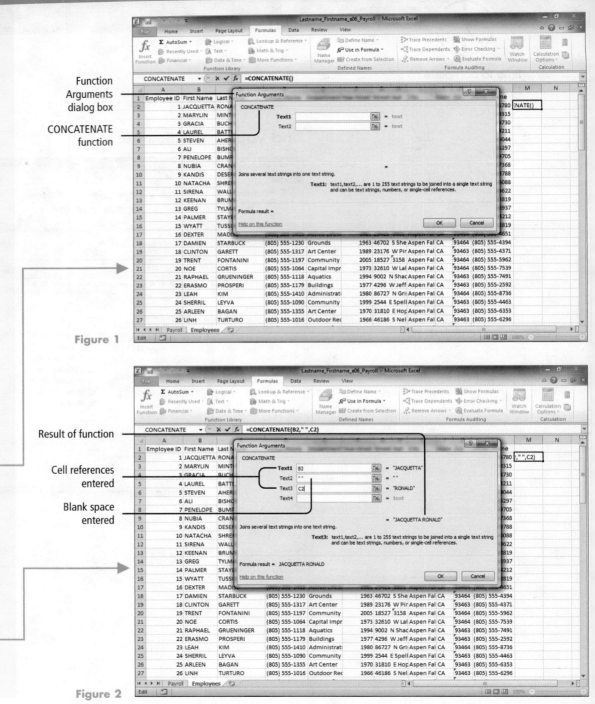

Function Arguments dialog box

CONCATENATE function

Figure 1

Result of function

Cell references entered

Blank space entered

Figure 2

Nested formula

Title case values
displayed in cell

Figure 3

Formula copied
to entire column

Figure 4

8. Click **OK** to close the dialog box. Notice the displayed value in cell **M2**.

   The CONCATENATE function combined the First Name and Last Name values into a single *string*—any sequence of letters and numbers in a field. For readability, a blank space was inserted between the two fields.

9. With cell **M2** selected, click in the formula bar, and then position the insertion point between the = sign and the word *CONCATENATE*.

10. Type PROPER(making sure to include the parenthesis after PROPER, and then press End to move the insertion point to the end of the expression in the formula bar. Add a closing parenthesis character [ )], and then press Enter. Select cell **M2**, and compare your screen with **Figure 3**.

    A *nested function* is a function placed inside another function. The CONCATENATE function is nested within the PROPER function. Here, the text is first concatenated, and then the PROPER function converts the result to title case.

11. With cell **M2** still selected, point to the **fill handle**, and then with the + pointer, drag down to cell **M105**. Press Ctrl + Home, and compare your screen with **Figure 4**.

12. Save 🖫 the workbook.

   ▪ **You have completed Skill 1 of 10**

► When you copy a cell or a group of cells and paste them into a new location, you also paste the formatting of the original cell.

► Paste Special enables you to change the formatting or underlying values of a cell when you paste the cell contents to a new location.

1. If necessary, display the **Employees** worksheet, and scroll to the top of the worksheet.

2. Select the range **M2:M5**. Display the **Home** tab, and in the **Clipboard** group, click **Copy** 📋.

3. Display the **Payroll** worksheet tab, and select cell **A5**.

4. In the **Clipboard** group, click the **Paste** button. Point to the displayed error message button 🔷▾, and read the displayed message as shown in **Figure 1**.

   The error indicator, error value—#REF!—and error message all indicate a problem with the function in the pasted cells. Recall that the underlying value of the cells just copied and pasted contain functions that concatenate text and convert it to title case. In the location just pasted, these functions now refer to the wrong cells. Common error values are summarized in the table in **Figure 2**.

■ **Continue to the next page to complete the skill**

Error indicator
Error message button
#REF! error value
Paste Options button

Figure 1

Common Excel Error Values

Error Message	Error
#DIV/0!	Indicates that a number is being divided by zero.
#N/A	When using a Lookup function, this displays if there is no match.
#NAME?	Refers to formula text that Excel does not recognize in a formula.
#REF!	Indicates that the referenced cells do not contain any data.
#VALUE	Indicates that a formula contains the wrong type of data—for example, text instead of numbers.

Figure 2

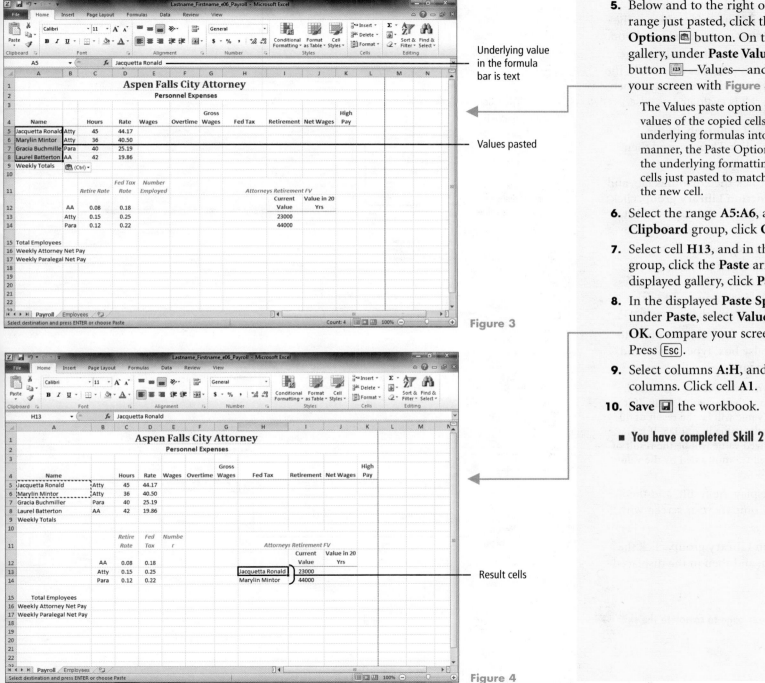

Underlying value in the formula bar is text

Values pasted

Figure 3

Result cells

Figure 4

5. Below and to the right of the selected range just pasted, click the **Paste Options** button. On the displayed gallery, under **Paste Values**, click the first button—Values—and then compare your screen with **Figure 3**.

The Values paste option pastes the displayed values of the copied cells instead of their underlying formulas into the cell. In this manner, the Paste Options button changes the underlying formatting or values of the cells just pasted to match the formatting in the new cell.

6. Select the range **A5:A6**, and then in the **Clipboard** group, click **Copy**.

7. Select cell **H13**, and in the **Clipboard** group, click the **Paste** arrow. On the displayed gallery, click **Paste Special**.

8. In the displayed **Paste Special** dialog box, under **Paste**, select **Values**, and then click **OK**. Compare your screen with **Figure 4**. Press Esc.

9. Select columns **A:H**, and **AutoFit** the columns. Click cell **A1**.

10. **Save** the workbook.

■ **You have completed Skill 2 of 10**

▶ The IF function is used to evaluate the contents of a cell to determine whether the value in the cell meets a specified condition.

▶ When the formula in a cell is evaluated as true, the IF function provides one result; the IF function provides a different result when the formula in a cell is evaluated as false.

1. Display the **Page Layout** tab. In the **Themes** group, click **Themes**, and then click **Equity**.

2. Select cell **E5**. Click the **Formulas** tab, and then in the **Function Library** group, click the **Logical** button. In the displayed list, click **IF**.

3. In the **Function Arguments** dialog box, with the insertion point in the **Logical_test** box, type C5>=40 and press `Tab` to move the insertion point to the **Value_if_true** box, and then type 40*D5

4. Press `Tab` to move the insertion point to the **Value_if_false** box, type C5*D5 and then compare your screen with **Figure 1**.

   The IF function tests whether the value in cell C5 is greater than or equal to 40. If it is, the displayed value will be the result of 40 multiplied by the value in cell D5. If it is not, the displayed value will be the result of the value in cell C5 multiplied by the value in cell D5.

5. Click **OK** to display the result, and then select cell **F5**. Compare your screen with **Figure 2**.

6. In the **Function Library** group, click the **Logical** button, and then in the displayed list, click **IF**.

■ **Continue to the next page to complete the skill**

IF function
Values to display if true or false
Current displayed value

Figure 1

Result of IF function

Figure 2

Nested IF function

Collapsed Function Arguments box

Figure 3

Gross wages calculated

Figure 4

7. In the **Function Arguments** dialog box, with the insertion point in the **Logical_ test** box, type C5<=40 and press Tab to move the insertion point to the **Value_ if_true** box. Type "0"

> If the employee works 40 hours or less, a 0 displays in the Overtime column.

8. Press Tab to move the insertion point to the **Value_if_false** box. Click the **Collapse Dialog** button 🔲, and in the **Function Arguments** box, type IF(C5<=44, (C5-40)*D5*1.5, (C5-40)*D5*2) and compare your screen with **Figure 3**.

> If the employee works more than 40 hours, this formula will calculate the overtime pay. Employees who work between 40 and 44 hours are paid 1.5 times their hourly rates for any hours over 40. If an employee works more than 44 hours, she is paid 2 times her hourly rate for all hours worked over 40.

9. Click the **Expand Dialog** button 🔲, and then click **OK**. Verify that *441.70* displays in cell **F5**.

> Since the value in cell C5 is equal to 45, the employee is entitled to twice his usual pay rate for the extra hours. The value in cell F5 (441.70) is equal to the rate of 44.17 times 5 hours, times 2. It is more than 44 hours, so the employee is paid twice the usual rate for those hours worked.

10. Select cell **G5**, type =E5+F5 and then press Enter. **AutoFit** the column. Compare your screen with **Figure 4**.

> The regular wages are added to the overtime wages to determine the gross wages.

11. **Save** 🔲 the workbook.

■ **You have completed Skill 3 of 10**

► *Lookup functions* are used to find values that are stored in *lookup tables*—data organized into rows and columns in a way that values can be easily retrieved.

► The VLOOKUP function finds values in a table where categories are organized by columns. The function searches down the table's first vertical column.

1. Select cell **H5**, and display the **Formulas** tab. In the **Function Library** group, click the **Lookup & Reference** button, and then click **VLOOKUP**.

2. With the insertion point in the **Lookup_value** box of the displayed **Function Arguments** dialog box, type B5. Press [Tab] to move the insertion point to the **Table_array** box. Compare your screen with **Figure 1**.

3. In the **Table_array** box, click the **Collapse Dialog** button 📧, drag through the range **B12:D14**, and then press [F4]. Click the **Expand Dialog Box** button 📧, and compare your screen with **Figure 2**.

Recall that when you press [F4], you create an absolute cell reference. Here, the lookup table is the range B12:D14. Referring to the lookup table using absolute cell references enables you to copy the cell reference to other cells without altering the cell references to the lookup table.

■ **Continue to the next page to complete the skill**

Figure 1

Figure 2

Lookup value reference

Data table reference

Column with desired data

Current result

Figure 3

Retirement and Net Wages calculated

Figure 4

4. Press `Tab` to move the insertion point to the **Col_index_num** box, and type 3 Compare your screen with **Figure 3**.

   Here, the VLOOKUP function searches the data table (B12:D14) for the value in cell B5. When it finds the value, it returns the value in the data table's third column (Col_index_num). To work reliably, the first column in a vertical data table must be sorted alphabetically.

5. Click **OK** to close the dialog box. In the **formula bar**, place the insertion point at the end of the formula, type *G5 and then press `Tab`. Verify that *552.13* displays—the result of Gross Wages times the tax rate for *Atty* found in the data table.

6. With cell **I5** selected, in the **Function Library** group, click the **Lookup & Reference** button, and then click **VLOOKUP**. With the insertion point in the **Lookup_value** box, type B5 and then press `Tab`. Click the **Table_array Collapse Dialog** button, and then drag through range B12:D14. Press `F4`, and then click the **Expand Dialog Box** button. Press `Tab`. In the **Col_index_num** box, type 2 and click **OK**.

7. With cell **I5** selected, in the formula bar, add *G5 at the end of the formula. Press `Tab`.

8. In cell **J5**, type =G5-H5-I5 and then press `Enter`. Compare your screen with **Figure 4**.

   Net Wages, which equals Gross Wages less taxes and retirement, is calculated in cell J5.

9. **Save** the workbook.

■ **You have completed Skill 4 of 10**

► *Logical functions* are used to create formulas to test whether a condition is true or false.

► Logical functions are typically nested in other functions to display one value when they are true and another value when they are false.

1. Select cell **K5**, and then on the **Formulas** tab, in the **Function Library** group, click the **Logical** button. On the displayed list, click **OR** and compare your screen with **Figure 1.**

   The OR function evaluates two or more conditions. When either condition is TRUE, the result will be TRUE.

2. In the displayed **Function Arguments** dialog box, in the **Logical1** box, type D5>=27 Notice that this condition is TRUE.

3. Press Tab, and then in the **Logical2** box, type C5>40 Compare your screen with **Figure 2.**

4. Click **OK**. In cell **K5**, notice the displayed value is *TRUE*, indicating that Jacquetta Ronald is a highly paid employee.

■ **Continue to the next page to complete the skill**

OR Function Arguments dialoge box

Function description

Figure 1

Two conditions entered

Current conditions are TRUE

Figure 2

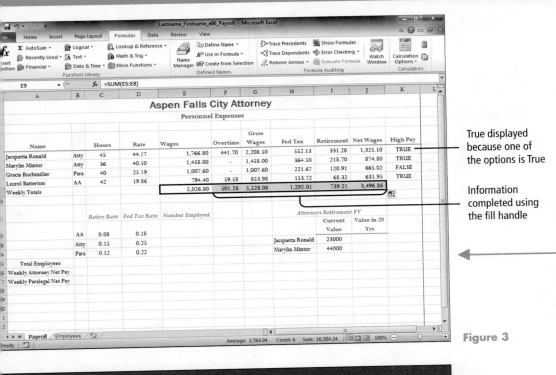

True displayed because one of the options is True

Information completed using the fill handle

Figure 3

5. Select the range **E5:K5**, and then use the fill handle to drag down to **Row 8**.

Notice that the value in K6 is *TRUE*. Marylin Mintor worked only 36 hours, which means the OR function evaluated that part of the equation as *FALSE*, but since she is paid more than $27 per hour, that part of the function was evaluated as *TRUE*. With the OR function, when either part is true, the value returned is *TRUE*. Notice that cell K7 is *FALSE* because Gracia Buchmiller is paid less than $27 per hour and did not work more than 40 hours. So both parts of the function were evaluated as false.

6. Select cell **E9**, and then in the **Function Library** group, click **AutoSum**, and press Enter.

7. Select cell **E9**, and then with the + pointer, drag the fill handle through the range **E9:J9** to display the column totals. Compare your screen with **Figure 3**.

You can combine logical functions with each other or with many other functions to create a formula that is carefully designed to display the required information. Logical functions are summarized in the table in **Figure 4**.

8. Save 💾 the workbook.

■ **You have completed Skill 5 of 10**

Common Excel Logical Functions

Function	Description
AND	Displays TRUE when all of the conditions are true.
IF	Performs a test to determine when one of the specified conditions is true.
IFERROR	Displays a message of your choice when there is an error in the formula. When there is not an error, it displays the result of the formula.
NOT	Evaluates the opposite of a condition. For example, $NOT < 5$ returns TRUE when the condition is not less than five.
OR	Displays TRUE if any one of the conditions is TRUE.

Figure 4

► The **COUNTA** function counts the number of cells containing values that you specify. When no values are specified, it counts the number of cells in a range that are not blank.

► The **COUNTIF** function counts the number of cells in the range that meet a specified condition. The condition might be a number, an expression, or text. When using COUNTIF, you specify the criterion that determines which cells in a range should be counted.

1. Select cell **E15**, and on the **Formulas** tab, in the **Function Library** group, click **More Functions**. In the displayed list, point to **Statistical**, and then click **COUNTA**. Compare your screen with **Figure 1**.

   COUNTA is a *statistical function*—a function that describes a collection of data such as totals, counts, and averages. COUNTA counts the number of values in a range.

2. In the **Function Arguments** dialog box, place the insertion point in the **Value1** box, and replace the existing text with . **B5:B8** Compare your screen with **Figure 2** and then click **OK**.

   In the formula, the range in parentheses is referred to as a function criterion.

3. Select cell **E12**. In the **Function Library** group, click the **More Functions** button, point to **Statistical**, and then click **COUNTIF**.

   COUNTIF is a statistical function that counts the number of cells that match the specified criteria.

■ **Continue to the next page to complete the skill**

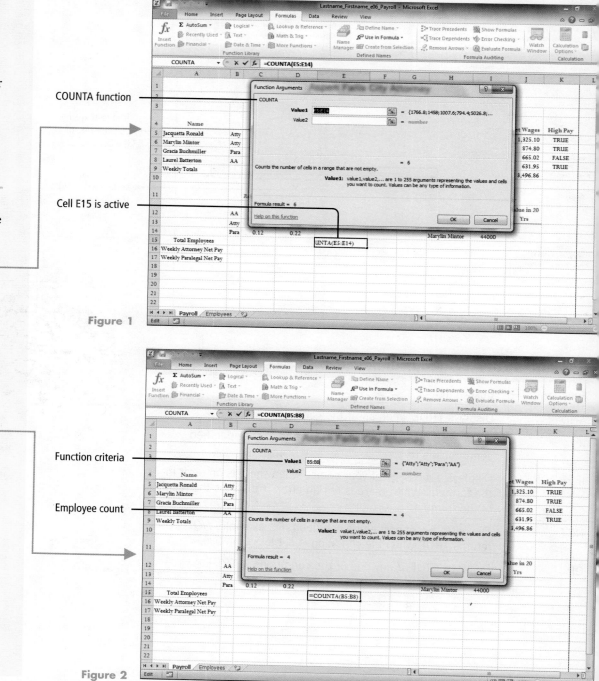

COUNTA function

Cell E15 is active

Figure 1

Function criteria

Employee count

Figure 2

Figure 3

Figure 4

4. In the **Function Arguments** dialog box, place the insertion point in the **Range** box, drag through the range **B5:B8**, and then press Tab.

5. In the **Criteria** box, type AA and then press Tab. Notice that Excel adds quotation marks around *AA* since it is a text value. Compare your screen with **Figure 3**, and click **OK**.

   The COUNTIF function counts the number of *AA* values in the range B5:B8 and returns the result of one (1), which is displayed in the Function Arguments dialog box as a preview.

6. Select cell **E13**. In the **Function Library** group, click the **Recently Used** button, and then click **COUNTIF**. With the insertion point in the **Range** box, drag through the range **B5:B8**, and then press Tab to move the insertion point to the **Criteria** box. In the **Criteria** box, type Atty and then click **OK**.

7. Select cell **E14**. In the **Function Library** group, click the **Recently Used** button, and then click **COUNTIF**. With the insertion point in the **Range** box, drag through the range **B5:B8**, and then press Tab to move the insertion point to the **Criteria** box. With the insertion point in the **Criteria** box, type B14 and then click **OK**. Compare your screen with **Figure 4**.

8. **Save** 💾 the workbook.

■ **You have completed Skill 6 of 10**

► The *what-if analysis* tools can save several sets of values so that you can quickly view the various results.

► Each set of values saved by the what-if analysis tools is called a *scenario*. Use Scenario Manager to save different groups of values, and then switch to those values to view the results.

1. Select the range **C12:C14**, and then display the **Data** tab. In the **Data Tools** group, click the **What-If Analysis** button, and then click **Scenario Manager**.

   Before creating a scenario, you should select the cells that will change. In this exercise, the Retirement Rate values will be changed to show how the changes will affect the payroll.

2. In the **Scenario Manager** dialog box, click **Add**. Compare your screen with **Figure 1**.

   The Add Scenario dialog box asks you to specify a name for the scenario.

3. In the **Add Scenario** dialog box, in the **Scenario name** box, type Aspen Falls City Attorney and press [Tab].

4. In the **Changing cells** box, verify that **C12:C14** is displayed, and then press [Tab]. Compare your screen with **Figure 2**.

   Since you selected the range C12:C14 before starting Scenario Manager, the Changing cells box was filled in automatically.

■ **Continue to the next page to complete the skill**

Figure 1

Figure 2

Figure 3

Figure 4

Scenario Values dialog box

Original changing cell values

Scenario Summary

Current changing cell values

Original result values

5. In the **Comment** box, replace the existing text with Analyzes tax rate changes.

The comment helps you recall the purpose of the scenario.

6. Click **OK**, and then compare your screen with **Figure 3**.

The Scenario Values dialog box displays the current values in the range C12:C14.

7. In the **Scenario Values** dialog box, in box **1**, type .09 Press Tab, and in box **2**, type .17 Press Tab, and then in box **3**, type .11 Click **OK**.

These are the new values that will be used to calculate the final net wages each week.

8. In the **Scenario Manager** dialog box, click **Summary**. In the **Scenario Summary** dialog box, in the **Result Cell** box, type J5:J8 Click **OK**.

9. Display the **Scenario Summary** worksheet tab, and then compare your screen with **Figure 4**.

The Scenario Summary worksheet displays the current values in the ranges C12:C14 and J5:J8 in column D. Column **E** displays what happens to the values in the range J5:J8 when you change the values in the range C12:C14. Some of the values in the range C12:C14 were increased, putting more money into retirement each week and reducing Net Wages, while other values were decreased, increasing Net Wages.

10. Display the **Payroll** worksheet tab. Notice that none of the values in the range **C12:C14** was changed on the original worksheet.

11. Save 🖫 the workbook.

■ **You have completed Skill 7 of 10**

► The *future value* of an asset, such as an investment or a car, is its value at the end of a period of time.

► The future value of an asset can be calculated when constant payments are made over time and the interest rate remains fixed.

1. On the **Payroll** worksheet tab, select cell **J13**.

2. Display the **Formulas** tab, and then in the **Function Library** group, click the **Financial** button. Scroll down the displayed list, and click **FV**. Compare your screen with **Figure 1**.

   In the Function Arguments dialog box, the FV function requires three arguments: the interest rate for each payment, the total number of payments, and the payment amount. When you are calculating the future value of an investment, the present value of the investment can also be entered here.

3. In the displayed **Function Arguments** dialog box, in the **Rate** box, type 4.5%/12 and then press Tab. Compare your screen with **Figure 2**.

   In this exercise, the annual interest rate of 4.5% is divided by 12 to calculate the interest rate for each monthly payment.

■ **Continue to the next page to complete the skill**

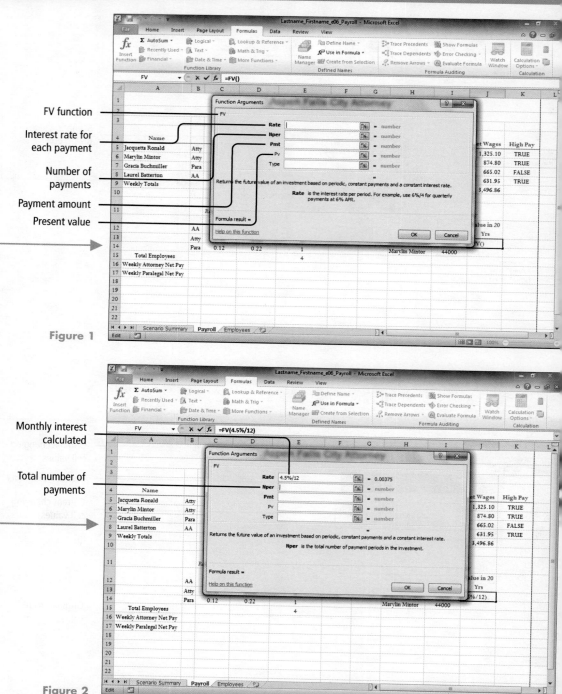

FV function

Interest rate for each payment

Number of payments

Payment amount

Present value

Figure 1

Monthly interest calculated

Total number of payments

Figure 2

Figure 3

4. In the **Nper** box, type $12*20$ and then press `Tab` to move to the **Pmt** box.

The monthly payments to the Attorney Retirement account will be made for 20 years. The total number of payments—Nper— equals 20 multiplied by 12.

5. In the **Pmt** box, type I5 and then press `Tab` to move to the **PV** box.

6. With the insertion point in the **PV** box, type I13 and compare your screen with **Figure 3**.

The present value of the investment is the current value that is in Jacquetta Ronald's retirement account.

7. Click **OK** to close the dialog box.

8. With cell **J13** selected, place the insertion point in the **formula bar** between the = symbol and **FV**. Type – Move the insertion point to the end of the formula, and then press `Enter`.

9. Select cell **J13**. Drag the cell's fill handle down to cell **J14**, and then **AutoFit** column **J**.

Common financial functions are summarized in the table in **Figure 4**.

10. **Save** 🖫 the workbook.

■ **You have completed Skill 8 of 10**

Monthly payment

Calculated balance of retirement account

Common Financial Functions

Function	Purpose
PV	The value of an investment or a loan at the beginning of its term.
PMT	The amount of money being paid to reduce a loan value or increase the value of an asset.
RATE	The interest earned by an investment or the interest paid for a loan.
FV	The value of an investment or asset at some point in the future.
NPER	The total number of payments made over the term of a loan or the total number of contributions made to an investment.

Figure 4

► Recall that during a what-if analysis, you change values in cells referenced by formulas to see how the new values affect results. When you know what the result should be but are unsure what changes will produce the desired result, you can use Goal Seek to calculate the required change.

► Goal Seek requires that the cell representing your goal contains a formula. Goal Seek can then change one cell referenced by that formula to produce the desired goal.

1. On the **Payroll** worksheet tab, select cell **G9**.

2. Display the **Data** tab, and in the **Data Tools** group, click **What-If Analysis**, and then click **Goal Seek**. Compare your screen with **Figure 1**.

   In the displayed Goal Seek dialog box, the Set cell box is the cell that represents the desired goal. Here, a goal will be set for the total gross wages displayed in cell G9.

3. Click in the **To value** box, type 6000 and then press Tab.

   Here, the goal is to increase gross wages to $6,000.

4. With the insertion point in the **By changing cell** box, click cell **D5**. Compare your screen with **Figure 2**.

   The cell to be changed to reach the goal is set in the By changing cell box. Goal Seek will change the pay rate for Jacquetta Ronald to achieve the goal of $6,000 in weekly gross wages.

■ **Continue to the next page to complete the skill**

Goal Seek dialog box

Cell representing desired goal

Figure 1

Cell to be changed

Desired value

Figure 2

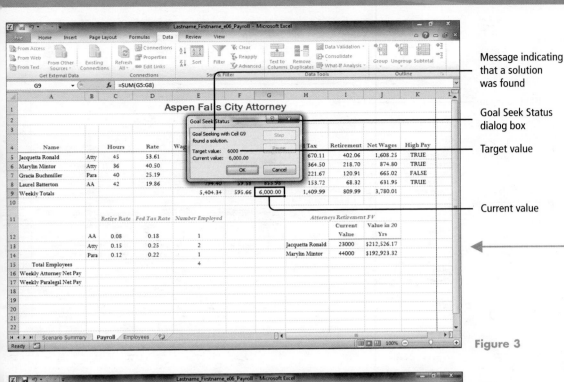

Message indicating that a solution was found

Goal Seek Status dialog box

Target value

Current value

Figure 3

5. Click **OK**, and then compare your screen with **Figure 3**. Do not close the dialog box.

The displayed Goal Seek Status dialog box indicates that a solution was found. The pay rate for Jacquetta Ronald was increased to 53.61. The desired outcome is displayed in cell G9.

6. With the Goal Seek Status dialog box still open, click **Start** 🔵, click **All Programs**, and then open the **Accessories** folder. Click **Snipping Tool**, click the **New** button arrow, and then click **Full-screen Snip**.

7. Click the **Save Snip** button 🔲. In the **Save As** dialog box, navigate to your **Excel Chapter 6** folder, **Save** the file as Lastname_Firstname_e06_Payroll_Snip and then **Close** ✖ the Snipping Tool window.

8. In the **Goal Seek Status** box, click **Cancel**, and then compare your screen with **Figure 4**.

The figures in the workbook return to the original values.

9. Save 🔲 the workbook.

■ **You have completed Skill 9 of 10**

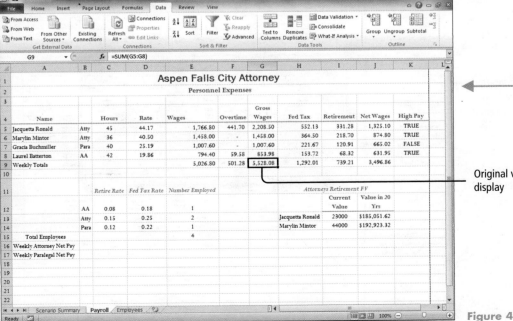

Original value display

Figure 4

▶ You use the *SUMIF* function when you want to calculate the total of a range, but you want to add only the cells that meet a specified condition.

1. On the **Payroll** worksheet tab, select cell **D16**.

2. Display the **Formulas** tab, and then in the **Function Library** group, click the **Math & Trig** button. Scroll down the displayed list, and then click **SUMIF**. Compare your screen with **Figure 1**.

3. In the **Function Arguments** dialog box, with the insertion point in the **Range** box, type B5:B8 and then press Tab.

   In the SUMIF function, the Range argument defines the range to be tested by the criteria. The Range argument might contain the values to be added. In this exercise, the Range argument lists the job categories that should be checked.

4. In the **Criteria** box, type Atty and then press Tab.

   The criteria is the value that should be evaluated. Here, only the cells where the job category equals *Atty* will be added.

5. With the insertion point in the **Sum_Range** box, type J5:J8 and then compare your screen with **Figure 2**.

   The Sum_Range is the range containing the cells to be added together. In this exercise, the values in the Net Wages column will be added only when the job category is *Atty*.

▪ **Continue to the next page to complete the skill**

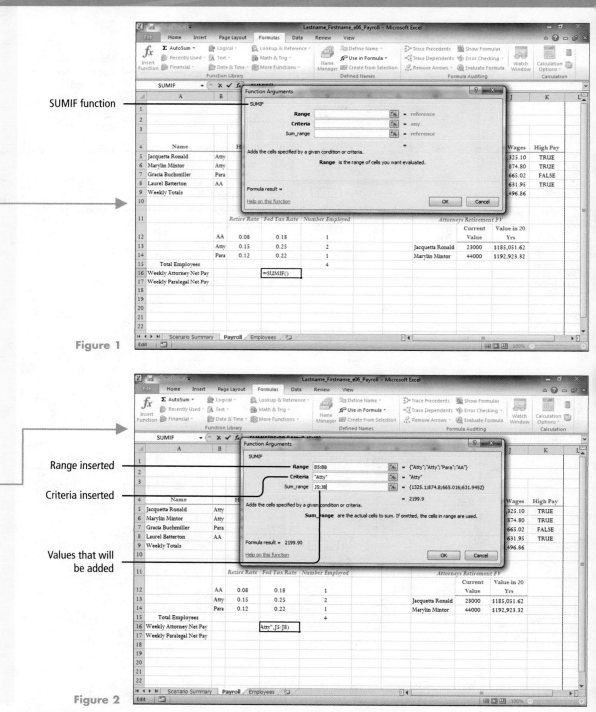

SUMIF function

Figure 1

Range inserted

Criteria inserted

Values that will be added

Figure 2

SUMIF arguments entered

Figure 3

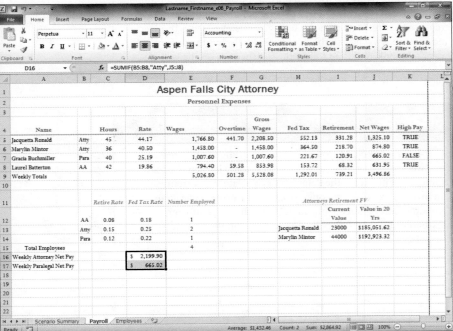

Figure 4

6. Click **OK** to close the Function Arguments dialog box. In cell **D16**, verify that *2199.90* displays.

7. Select cell **D17**, and then in the **Function Library** group, click the **Math & Trig** button, and then click **SUMIF**.

8. In the **Function Arguments** dialog box, in the **Range** box, type B5:B8 and then press Tab. In the **Criteria** box, type Para and then press Tab. In the **Sum_range** box, type J5:J8 and then compare your screen with **Figure 3**.

9. Click **OK**, and then notice that the value of cell **D17** is *665.02*.

10. Select the range **D16:D17**, and display the **Home** tab. In the **Number** group, click **Accounting Number Format** [$ ▾], and then **AutoFit** column **D** as needed to accommodate the values. Compare your screen with **Figure 4**.

11. Select the **Payroll** worksheet tab, right-click, and then click **Select All Sheets**. Add the file name in the worksheets' left footers. Select cell **A1**, and return to **Normal** view. Ungroup the worksheets.

12. **Save** [icon] the workbook. Print or submit electronically the file and the snip as directed by your instructor.

Done! You have completed Skill 10 of 10 and your workbook is complete!

The following More Skills are located at **www.pearsonhighered.com/skills**

 More Skills **11** **Query Tables Using Criteria Ranges**

Spreadsheets can contain hundreds to tens of thousands of records. When spreadsheets become this large, you often need to filter the data so that you can work with it. You can query tabular data using a criteria range to display the information you seek.

In More Skills 11, you will create a criteria range and then use it to create a custom filter that locates the data and displays the desired data. To begin, open your web browser, navigate to www.pearsonhighered.com/skills, locate the name of your textbook, and then follow the instructions on the website.

 More Skills **12** **Use Solver**

You can use the Solver tool to change multiple values to achieve a desired goal. Solver can also find a solution within limitations that you set—such as a maximum value a cell can be changed to, for example. Before using Solver, you must install it as an Excel Add-In.

In More Skills 12, you will install the Solver Add-In and then use Solver to determine the rate to change to reach a desired retirement savings amount. To begin, open your web browser, navigate to www.pearsonhighered.com/skills, locate the name of your textbook, and then follow the instructions on the website.

 More Skills **13** **Delete Duplicate Records**

Excel workbooks that contain large amounts of tabular data might have rows with duplicate values. Duplicated rows can cause errors that lead to inaccurate information. You can search for and remove duplicates using the Remove Duplicates tool.

In More Skills 13, you will open a spreadsheet with a number of duplicated records. You will use the Remove Duplicates tool to remove the duplicate records. To begin, open your web browser, navigate to www.pearsonhighered.com/skills, locate the name of your textbook, and then follow the instructions on the website.

 More Skills **14** **Use External Data Links to Update Data**

You can automatically connect to External Databases on the Internet to update workbook data. You can then use the data as if it had been entered directly into the workbook.

In More Skills 14, you will open a workbook and create a link to a web-based database of stock prices. You will then use the values obtained from the database to calculate the current value of an investment. To begin, open your web browser, navigate to www.pearsonhighered.com/skills, locate the name of your textbook, and then follow the instructions on the website.

Key Terms

Online Help Skills

1. **Start** ⊙ Excel. In the upper right corner of the Excel window, click the **Help** button ⊙. In the **Help** window, click the **Maximize** ⊡ button.

2. Click in the search box, type scenario manager and then click the **Search** button ⊙. In the search results, click **Introduction to what-if analysis**.

3. Read the article's introduction, and then below **In this article**, click Use **Goal Seek to find out how to get a desired result**. Compare your screen with **Figure 1**.

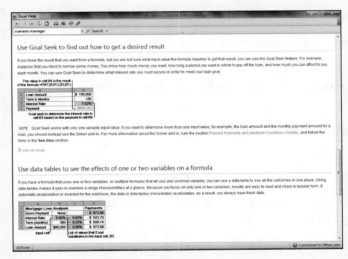

Figure 1

4. Read the section to see if you can answer the following: When should you use the goal seek tool and when should you use the solver add in?

Matching

Match each term in the second column with its correct definition in the first column by writing the letter of the term on the blank line in front of the correct definition.

____ **1.** A text function that is used to join text or text from separate columns together.

____ **2.** A text function that converts text to initial case.

____ **3.** A function placed inside another function.

____ **4.** A function that is used to find values that are stored in a table in a spreadsheet.

____ **5.** A function that displays TRUE only when all of the conditions are TRUE.

____ **6.** A function that adds a range of cells using only the cells that meet specified criteria.

____ **7.** A function that describes a collection of data.

____ **8.** A function used to create a formula that always has a result of either TRUE or FALSE.

____ **9.** A set of saved values that can be placed in cells whenever one is selected.

____ **10.** The function used to calculate the value of an investment or asset at some point in the future.

A AND

B CONCATENATE

C FV

D Logical function

E Lookup function

F Nested function

G PROPER

H Scenario

I Statistical function

J SUMIF

Multiple Choice

Write the correct answer in the space provided.

1. This function is used to convert text to initial case.
   - A. CONCATENATE
   - B. PROPER
   - C. SUBSTITUTE

2. This case is the format style that is displayed when you change text so that the first letter of each word is capitalized.
   - A. Initial
   - B. Proper
   - C. Title

3. These types of functions are used to create formulas that always have a result of either TRUE or FALSE.
   - A. Logical
   - B. Informational
   - C. Statistical

4. This is a function that is used to join text and text from separate cells.
   - A. LINK
   - B. CONCATENATE
   - C. JOIN

5. This is the value of an asset at the end of a period of time.
   - A. Future value
   - B. Earnings
   - C. Investment value

6. Use this option to change the formatting or underlying values of cells as they are pasted.
   - A. Paste
   - B. Paste Special
   - C. Copy

7. This function is used to count the number of cells in a range that meet a certain criteria.
   - A. COUNTA
   - B. SUM
   - C. COUNTIF

8. This type of function used to describe groups of data—sums, averages, and counts.
   - A. Logical
   - B. Lookup
   - C. Statistical

9. Use this tool to change cells to see how those changes affect a desired outcome.
   - A. Goal Seek analysis
   - B. What-if analysis
   - C. Data table

10. This function is used when you want to calculate the total of a range but you want to add only the cells that meet a specified condition.
    - A. SUM
    - B. SUMIF
    - C. TOTAL

Topics for Discussion

1. A manufacturing company must raise the cost of an item to cover an increase in production costs. Yet the company does not want the profit margin to dip below a certain percentage. How could the manufacturing company use Excel to predict the profit that they would make on this item?

2. A trucking company has a large fleet of vehicles. The company maintains detailed reports of maintenance costs. Each type of vehicle uses a fixed amount of oil and transmission fluid each time the vehicle is serviced. How could an Excel spreadsheet be structured so that by entering a vehicle ID number, the cost for fluids would be automatically entered into the worksheet?

Skill Check

To complete this workbook, you will need the following file:

- e06_Utilities

You will save your file as:

- Lastname_Firstname_e06_Utilities

1. **Start** Excel, and then open the student data file **e06_Utilities**. Save the file in your **Excel Chapter 6** folder with the name Lastname_Firstname_e06_Utilities

2. Display the **Customers** worksheet tab. Select cell **E2**. Display the **Formulas** tab. In the **Function Library** group, click **Text**, and then click **CONCATENATE**. In the **Text1** box, type C2 In the **Text2** box, add a space. In the **Text3** box, type D2 Click **OK**.

3. In the **Formula bar**, place the insertion point between = and *CONCATENATE*, and type PROPER(At the end of the formula, add a closing parenthesis. Press [Enter]. Select cell **E2**. Fill the formula down through cell **E16**.

4. Copy the range **E2:E11**. Display the **Region 1** worksheet tab. Select cell **A4**. Display the **Home** tab. In the **Clipboard** group, click the **Paste** arrow, and then click **Paste Values**. **AutoFit** column **A**.

5. Select cell **E4**. On the **Formulas** tab, in the **Function Library** group, click **Lookup & Reference**, and then click **VLOOKUP**. In the **Lookup_Value** box, type C4 In the **Table_array** box, type $J$4:$K$6 In the **Col_index_num** box, type 2 and then click **OK**. At the end of the formula, type *C4 Press [Enter]. Compare with **Figure 1**.

6. Select cell **F4**. Insert a **VLOOKUP** function. In the **Lookup_Value** box, type D4 In the **Table_array** box, type $J$10:$K$12 In the **Col_index_num** box, type 2 and then click **OK**. At the end of the formula, type *D4 Press [Enter].

7. Select cell **G4**. In the **Function Library** group, click **Logical**. Click **IF**. In the **Logical_test** box, type C4>=1000 In the **Value_if_true** box, type 0 In the **Value_if_false** box, click the **Collapse Dialog** button. In the **Function Arguments** box, type IF(C4<750,E4*.1,E4*.05) Click the **Expand Dialog** button, and then click **OK**. Compare your screen with **Figure 2**.

Figure 1

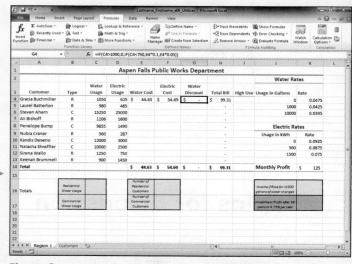

Figure 2

- Continue to the next page to complete this Skill Check

8. Select the range **E4:H4**. Fill the formula down to **E13:H13**.

9. Click cell **I4**, and display the **Formulas** tab. In the **Function Library** group, click **Logical**, and then click **AND**. In the **Logical1** box, type E4>50 In the **Logical2** box, type F4>120 Click **OK**.

10. Fill down the formula in cell **I4** through cell **I13**.

11. Select cell **C16**. In the **Function Library** group, click **Math & Trig**, and then click **SUMIF**. In the **Range** box, type B4:B13 In the **Criteria box**, type R In the **Sum_range** box, type C4:C13 and then click **OK**.

12. Select cell **C17**. In the **Function Library** group, click **Math & Trig**, and then click **SUMIF**. In the **Range** box, type B4:B13 In the **Criteria box**, type C In the **Sum_range** box, type C4:C13 and then click **OK**.

13. Select cell **F16**. In the **Function Library** group, click **More Functions**, point to **Statistical**, and then click **COUNTIF**. With the insertion point in the **Range** box, drag through the range **B4:B13**, and then press (Tab). In the **Criteria** box, type R and then click **OK**.

14. Select cell **F17**. In the **Function Library** group, click **More Functions**, point to **Statistical**, and then click **COUNTIF**. In the Range box, type B4:B13 In the **Criteria** box, type C Click **OK**.

15. Select cell **K17**. In the **Function Library** group, click **Financial**, and then click **FV**. In the **Rate** box, type 6.75%/12 In the **Nper** box, type 12*10 In the **Pmt** box, type −K14 and then click **OK**. Compare your screen with **Figure 3**.

16. Copy cell **H14**, and then select cell **K16**. Display the **Home** tab. In the **Clipboard** group, click the **Paste** arrow. Under **Paste Values**, click **Values & Number Formatting**.

17. Display the **Data** tab. In the **Data Tools** group, click **What-If Analysis**, and then click **Goal Seek**. In the **Set cell** box, type K17 In the **To value** box, type 22500 In the **By changing cell** box, type K14 and then click **OK**. Click **OK** again.

18. In the **Data Tools** group, click **What-If Analysis**, and then click **Scenario Manager**. In the **Scenario Manager** dialog box, click **Add**.

19. In the **Scenario Name** box, type Utilities In the **Changing cells** box, type K4,K12 Click **OK**.

20. In the **1:** box, type .06 In the **2:** box, type .08 and then click **OK**.

21. Click **Summary**, and then click **OK**. Compare your screen with **Figure 4**. Add the file name in all of the worksheets' left footers. Select cell **A1**. Ungroup the worksheets, and return to **Normal** view. Display the **Region 1** worksheet tab. **Save** the workbook, and submit it as directed.

Done! You have completed the Skill Check

Figure 3

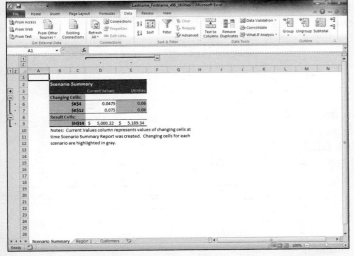

Figure 4

Assess Your Skills 1

To complete this workbook, you will need the following file:

- e06_Investments

You will save your file as:

- Lastname_Firstname_e06_Investments

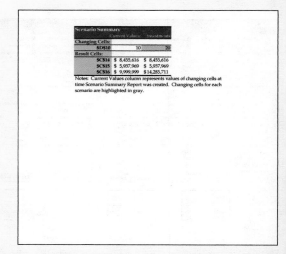

1. **Start** Excel, and then open the student data file **e06_Investments**. Save the file in your **Excel Chapter 6** folder as Lastname_Firstname_e06_Investments

2. In cell **E6**, enter a future value (FV) function with the following arguments: Rate should be **C6**, Nper should be **D6**, the Pmt should be left blank, and the PV should be **-B6**. In cell **E6**, apply the **Accounting Number Format** with 0 decimals displayed. Copy the function down through cell **E10**. In the range **B6:B10** and **E7:E10**, apply the **Comma [0]** cell style.

3. In cell **I14**, insert the **CONCATENATE** function to combine the following: **G14**, a space character, and then **H14**. In the function just inserted, nest the **PROPER** function so that title case is applied to the text. Copy the function down through cell **I17**.

4. In cell **H6**, insert the **VLOOKUP** function using **G6** for the **Lookup_value**, $F$14:$I$17 for the **Table_array**, and 4 for the **Col_index_num**, and then click **OK**. Copy the function down through cell **H10**. **AutoFit** column **H**.

5. In cell **B14**, insert the **COUNTIF** function, and use $F$6:$F$10 as the **Range** and Roads as the **Criteria**. Click **OK**. Use the same function in **B15:B16**, substituting the appropriate **Criteria**.

6. In cell **C14**, insert the **SUMIF** function using $F$6:$F$10 as the **Range**, Roads as the **Criteria**, and $E$6:$E$10 as the **Sum_range**. Click **OK**. Use the same function in the range **C15:C16**, substituting the appropriate **Criteria**.

7. Use **Goal Seek** to set cell **E10** to 9999999 by changing cell **C10**. Verify that the value returned for cell **C10** is 3.63%.

8. From the **Data** tab, start the **What-If Analysis Scenario Manager**. **Add** a scenario named Investments Set cell **D10** as the **Changing cells**. Click **OK**. In the **Scenario Values** dialog box, type 20. Click **OK**. Click **Summary**, and then click **OK**.

9. On the **Bonds** worksheet tab, **AutoFit** columns **A:I**.

10. On the Bonds worksheet tab, in cell **I6**, insert the **Logical** function **AND** using C6<=0.04 as **Logical1** and D6<=15 as **Logical2** Click **OK**. Copy the function down through cell **I10**. Compare your screen with **Figure 1**.

11. Add the file name in the left section of the footers of both worksheets. Select cell **A1**. Display the **Bonds** worksheet tab. Return to **Normal** view. **Save** the file, and then submit it as directed.

Done! You have completed Assess Your Skills 1

Figure 1

Assess Your Skills 2

To complete this workbook, you will need the following file:

- e06_Rec_Members

You will save your file as:

- Lastname_Firstname_e06_Rec_Members

Aspen Falls
Recreation Department - Membership Report

New Recreation Memberships

Type	Members as of 1/1	Dues	Initiation	Initiations FV	Total Initiation Fees
Golf	45	$ 7,470	$ 72,000	$1,659.99	$74,699.56
Pool	30	2,100	36,000	1,245	37,350
Tennis	27	2,430	27,000	1,037	28,012
Total		**12,000**	**135,000**	**3,942**	**140,062**

Type	Dues	Initiation Assessment *	Monthly Amount		Membership type
Golf	$ 166.00	$ 1,600.00	$ 133.33	1	Golf
Pool	$ 70.00	$ 1,200.00	$ 100.00	2	Tennis
Tennis	$ 90.00	$ 1,000.00	$ 83.33	3	Pool

* Paid over 12 months with 8% interest

Figure 1

1. **Start** Excel, and then open the student data file **e06_Rec_Members**. Save the file in your **Excel Chapter 6** folder as Lastname_Firstname_e06_Rec_Members

2. Display the **Members** worksheet tab. **Copy** column D. Use the **Paste Options** button to **Paste** the **Values and number formats** to column E. Delete column D. Select cell **C2**, and from the **Formulas** tab, insert the **Text** function **CONCATENATE**. Use A2 for **Text1**, press the Spacebar for **Text2**, and then use B2 for **Text3**. Click **OK**. Add the **PROPER** function to the result. Copy the function in cell **C2** down through cell **C103**. **AutoFit** the width of column **C**.

3. Display the **Report** worksheet tab. Select cell **B6**. Use the **COUNTIF** function with Members!$D$2:$D$103 as the **Range** and 1 as the **Criteria**. Click **OK**. Use the same function in cells **B7:B8** using 2 and 3 as the **Criteria**.

4. Select cell **C6** and insert the formula =IF(A6="Golf",$B$6*$B$12,(IF(A6="Pool", $B$7*$B$13,$B$8*$B$14)) Copy the function down through cell **C8**. Format the range **C6:F6** with **Accounting Number Format** with 0 decimals.

5. Select cell **D6**, and then from the **Formulas** tab, insert the **Lookup & Reference** function **VLOOKUP**. For the arguments, use A6 for the **Lookup_value**, $A$12:$D$14 for the **Table_array**, and 3 for the **Col_index_num**. Click **OK**. Multiply the function by cell **B6**. Copy the function down through cell **D8**.

6. Select cell **E6**, and then from the **Formulas** tab, insert the **Financial** function **FV**. For the arguments, use 8%/12 for the **Rate**, 12 for the **Nper**, and -D12 for **Pmt**. Copy the function down through cell **E8**.

7. Select cell **F6**, and then enter a formula to multiply cell **B6** by cell **E6**. Copy the formula down through cell **F8**.

8. Sum columns **C:F** in row **9**. Apply the **Total** cell style to row **9**.

9. Format the range **C7:F9** with the **Comma [0]** cell style.

10. From the **Data** tab, start the **What-If Analysis Goal Seek**. For the **Set cell** argument, use C9 for the **To value** argument, type 12000 and for the **By changing cell** argument, use B12. Click **OK**. The value retuned for B12 is **166.00** Click **OK**. Compare your screen with **Figure 1**.

11. Add the file name in the left section of the footers of both worksheets. Return to **Normal** view, and then select cell **A1**. Display the **Report** worksheet tab. **Save** the file, and then submit it as directed.

Done! You have completed Assess Your Skills 2

Assess Your Skills Visually

To complete this workbook, you will need the following file:

- e06_Public_Safety

You will save your file as:

- Lastname_Firstname_e06_Public_Safety

Start Excel, open the student data file **e06_Public_Safety_Fuel**, and then using your own name, **Save** it as Lastname_Firstname_e06_Public_Safety

In the range **E5:E11**, use the **VLOOKUP** function to determine the fuel costs per gallon for June. The cost is determined by the prices in the lookup table in the range **A14:D16** and the **Fuel Type** assigned to each vehicle. The **Fuel Cost Per Mile** in the range **F5:F11** is calculated by dividing **Fuel Costs Per Gallon** by **Miles Per Gallon**. In the range **G5:G11**, calculate the monthly costs for each vehicle. In cell **I5**, calculate how much each vehicle is under or over budget. In row **12**, insert the appropriate statistical function as reflected in **Figure 1**. Add the file name in the worksheet's left footer. **Save** the workbook, and then submit it as directed.

Done! You have completed Assess Your Skills Visually

Aspen Falls Public Safety
June Fuel Expense

Vehicle	Fuel Type	Miles Per Gallon	Miles Driven	Fuel Cost per Gallon	Fuel Cost Per Mile	Monthly Cost	Budget	Under/Over
P-08-01	Gas	14	4,534	3.499	0.250	1,133.18	1,200.00	66.82
P-08-12	Gas	12.9	5,892	3.499	0.271	1,598.15	1,500.00	(98.15)
S-09-11	Diesel	15	6,834	2.897	0.193	1,319.87	1,500.00	180.13
P-10-4	Gas	12	8,955	3.499	0.292	2,611.13	2,400.00	(211.13)
F-01-3	Diesel	8	1,250	2.897	0.362	452.66	400.00	(52.66)
F-05-32	Gas	8.7	950	3.499	0.402	382.07	250.00	(132.07)
EM-11-11	Diesel	6.3	3,492	2.897	0.460	1,605.77	1,600.00	(5.77)
Monthly Totals		10.99	31,907	3.24	0.32	9,102.82	8,850.00	(252.82)

Fuel Prices per Gallon	May	June	July
Diesel	3.312	2.897	2.499
Gas	3.295	3.499	2.999

Figure 1

Skills in Context

To complete this workbook, you will need the following file:

- e06_Brokerage

You will save your file as:

- Lastname_Firstname_e06_Brokerage

Start **Excel**, and then open the student data file **e06_Brokerage**. Using your own name, **Save** it as Lastname_Firstname_e06_Brokerage

In the **Names** worksheet of the student data file **e06_Brokerage**, use a function in the range **D2:D11** that combines the text in the **Symbol1** and **Symbol2** columns to display a four-character symbol. Copy the range **D2:D11**, and use **Paste Options** to paste only the values into the range **F5:F14** of the **Values** worksheet.

In the range **E5:E14**, calculate the future value of the investments in 20 years assuming monthly payments are made every month and the return is fixed as specified in the worksheet. Add the file name in the left section of the footer, and then submit the file as directed by your instructor.

Done! You have completed Skills in Context

Skills and You

To complete this workbook, you will need the following file:

- New blank Excel workbook

You will save your file as:

- Lastname_Firstname_e06_Skills

Using the skills you have practiced in this chapter, create a spreadsheet that calculates the future value of a savings account. You should assume that the bank pays interest at a fixed rate for the life of the account and that the same amount is deposited into the account each month. Insert the file name in the left section of the footer, and then submit the file as directed by your instructor.

Done! You have completed Skills and You

CHAPTER 7

Work with Data and Audit Formulas

▶ Data can be imported into Excel from a variety of file formats and then analyzed and manipulated in Excel.

▶ When errors occur in a formula, Excel provides tools to locate and fix the source of the error.

Your starting screen will look similar to this:

SKILLS

Skills 1-10 Training

At the end of this chapter, you will be able to:

Skill 1 Import Data from Text Files

Skill 2 Sort Data and Apply Advanced AutoFilters

Skill 3 Sort Data Based on Conditional Formatting

Skill 4 Use the Subtotal Tool to Summarize Data

Skill 5 Trace and Evaluate Formulas

Skill 6 Audit Formulas Using Cell Watch

Skill 7 Create One-Variable Data Tables

Skill 8 Create Two-Variable Data Tables

Skill 9 Create Custom Table Quick Styles

Skill 10 Convert Tables to Ranges

MORE SKILLS

More Skills 11 Create Amortization Tables

More Skills 12 Use the ROUND Function

More Skills 13 Use Information Functions

More Skills 14 Sort Tables Based on Multiple Criteria

Outcome

Using the skills listed to the left will enable you to create worksheets like these:

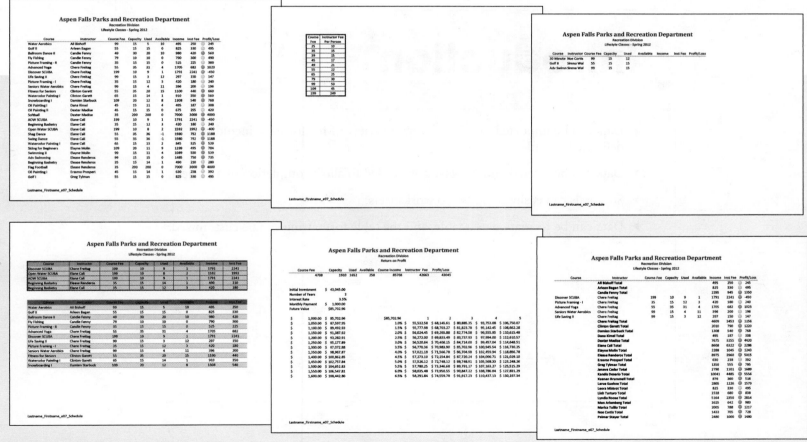

You will save your files as:

Lastname_Firstname_e07_Schedule   Lastname_Firstname_e07_Schedule_Eval   Lastname_Firstname_e07_Schedule_Watch

In this chapter, you will create workbooks for the Aspen Falls City Hall, which provides essential services for the citizens and visitors of Aspen Falls, California.

Introduction

- ▶ Data can be imported into Excel from a variety of file formats, including delimited text files.

- ▶ Data can be filtered and displayed as needed to allow completion of a project.

- ▶ Subtotals can easily be added to worksheets.

- ▶ Data can be formatted as a table, and the table formatting can be customized.

Time to complete all
10 skills – 50 to 75 minutes

Find your student data files here:

Student data files needed
for this chapter:

- e07_Schedule
- e07_Schedule_Classes

► Data can be imported into a workbook from a ***delimited text file***—a file where the data in each column is separated by an identifying character such as a comma, a space, or a Tab character.

1. **Start** 🌐 Excel, and then open **e07_ Schedule**. On the Ribbon, click the **File** tab, and then click **Save As**. In the **Save As** dialog box, navigate to the location where you are saving your files. Click **New folder**, type Excel Chapter 7 and then press Enter two times. In the **File name** box, using your own name, name the file Lastname_Firstname_e07_Schedule and then press Enter.

2. Start 🌐 Word, and then open the text file **e07_Schedule_Classes**. You might need to change the file type to **All Files** to locate the file.

3. On the **Home** tab, in the **Paragraph** group, click the **Show/Hide** button ¶ until it is shaded gold, as shown in **Figure 1.**

   The data in the text file, which can be opened in Microsoft Word, is organized into rows and columns by using a Tab character. A Tab character, indicated by an arrow, has been inserted to indicate each new column. The paragraph character at the end of each row indicates where a new row begins. In this manner, tabular data can be represented in a ***text file***—a file that stores only the text characters but not the formatting, tab stops, or tables.

4. **Close** Word. If prompted to save changes to the file, click **Don't Save**.

5. In the **Schedule** worksheet, click cell **A6**, and then display the **Data** tab. In the **Get External Data** group, click the **From Text** button. Compare your screen with **Figure 2.**

■ **Continue to the next page to complete the skill**

Show/Hide button shaded gold

Paragraph character

Tab character

Figure 1

Figure 2

Tab delimiter selected

Data preview shows text arranged in columns

Figure 3

Columns widened

Imported data

Figure 4

6. In the **Import Text File** dialog box, navigate to your student data files. Select **e07_Schedule_Classes**, and then click the **Import** button.

7. In the first step of the **Text Import Wizard**, under **Original data type**, verify that the **Delimited** option button is selected.

8. Click **Next**. In the second step of the wizard, under **Delimiters**, verify that the **Tab** check box is selected. Compare your screen with **Figure 3**.

   Under Data preview, the data is arranged into columns. The wizard uses the tab delimiter to determine when to place each value in the text file into a new column.

9. Click **Finish**. In the **Import Data** dialog box, verify that the **Existing worksheet** option button is selected, and that the box displays the text *=$A$6*.

   The data will be imported into the Schedule worksheet beginning in cell A6.

10. Click **OK**. Select columns **A:I**, and then **AutoFit** the column width. Click cell **A1**.

11. View the **Schedule** worksheet. Notice that the data from the file has been imported into the Schedule worksheet and placed into rows and columns as shown in **Figure 4**.

12. **Save** 💾 the workbook.

■ **You have completed Skill 1 of 10**

► You can sort data by text, numbers, or dates, or by a custom list that includes colors and icon sets.

► Like preset filters, custom filters can be written using your own criteria, and then combined with other filters to apply multiple criteria.

1. Select cell **A6**, and then display the **Data** tab. In the **Sort & Filter** group, click **Filter**.

2. Select cell **B5** and then click the arrow. From the displayed filter galley, point to **Text Filters**, and then click **Custom Filter**.

3. On the **Custom AutoFilter** dialog box, under **Instructor**, verify that the first box reads **equals**. Click the second **Instructor** box arrow, scroll down, and then click **Noe Cortis**.

4. Select the **Or** option button. Click the first **Or** box arrow, and then click **equals**. Click the second **Or** box arrow, scroll down, and then click **Sirena Wallo**. Compare your screen with **Figure 1**.

   OR is a logical operator that returns true if either one of the criteria is true. The custom filter will display only the rows where either *Noe Cortis* or *Sirena Wallo* is the instructor.

5. Click **OK**, and then **AutoFit** the width of columns **A:I**. Click cell **A1**.

6. In cell **C5**, click the filter arrow and then from the displayed filter gallery, point to **Number Filters**, and then click **Greater Than or Equal To**. In the **Custom AutoFilter** dialog box, in the second **Course Fee** box, type 55 Click **OK**, and then compare your screen with **Figure 2**.

■ Continue to the next page to complete the skill

Custom AutoFilter dialog box

Figure 1

Course Fee greater than or equal to 55

Instructor column filtered

Figure 2

Row numbers remain unchanged

Figure 3

Calculated values filled into columns F:I

Figure 4

7. Select the range **A1:I59**, and on the **Home** tab, in the **Clipboard** group, click **Copy**. Compare your screen with **Figure 3**.

> When copying filtered records, only the displayed rows are copied. The moving dotted lines indicate that the range A1:I59 will be copied. Only the three filtered rows are copied to the Clipboard.

8. Display the **Filtered** worksheet tab, and then select cell **A1**. Display the **Home** tab, and then in the **Clipboard** group, click **Paste**.

> The pasted rows are renumbered and are no longer filtered.

9. Click the **Schedule** worksheet tab, press (Esc), and then display the **Data** tab. In the **Sort & Filter** group, click the **Filter** button to remove the custom filter.

10. Click cell **F6**, type =D6-E6 and then press (Tab). In cell **G6**, type =C6*E6 and then press (Tab).

11. Select cell **H6**, and display the **Formulas** tab. In the **Function Library** group, click **Lookup & Reference**, and then click **VLOOKUP**. In the **Function Arguments** dialog box, in the **Lookup_value** box, type C6 Place the insertion point in the **Table_array** box, and then type Lookup!$B$4:$C$14 In the **Col_index_num** box, type 2 Click **OK**. In the **formula bar**, type *E6 at the end of the formula. Press (Enter).

12. Click cell **I6**, type =G6-H6 and then press (Enter).

13. Select the range **F6:I6**, and then fill the range down through **Row 75**. Compare your screen with **Figure 4**.

14. Save the workbook.

■ **You have completed Skill 2 of 10**

► Data can be sorted based on the conditional formatting applied to each cell in a column. For example, when icon sets are applied to a column, you can sort the column by the icon set applied to each cell instead of the underlying numeric values in those cells.

1. On the **Schedule** worksheet tab, select the range **I6:I75**.

2. Display the **Home** tab, and then in the **Styles** group, click **Conditional Formatting**. Point to **Icon Sets**, and then click **More Rules**.

3. In the **New Formatting Rule** dialog box, under **Edit the Rule Description**, click the first **Type** box arrow, and then click **Number**. In the **Value** box for the green icon, type 500 Click the **Type** box arrow for the yellow icon, and then click **Number**. In the yellow icon **Value** box, verify that *0* displays. Compare your screen with **Figure 1**, and then click **OK**.

There is no option to change the third icon because all of the possible options are taken into consideration by changing the first two values.

4. With the range **I6:I75** still selected, display the **Data** tab, and in the **Sort & Filter** group, click the **Sort** button. Read the **Sort Warning** message. Verify that the **Expand the selection** option button is selected, and then click **Sort**. Compare your screen with **Figure 2**. ─────

Expanding the selection will ensure that the row data does not become separated. If the selection is not expanded, only the selected column is sorted.

■ **Continue to the next page to complete the skill** ▶

New formatting rules to be applied

Figure 1

Sort dialog box

Figure 2

Three classes with a loss display first

Figure 3

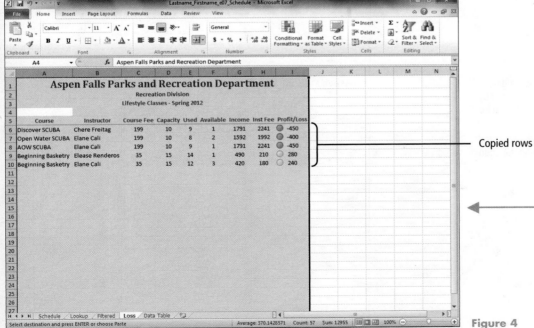

Copied rows

Figure 4

5. In the **Sort** dialog box, under **Column**, click the **Sort by** arrow, and then click **Profit/Loss**.

    The rows will be sorted based on the values in the Profit/Loss column.

6. Click the **Sort On** arrow, and then on the displayed list, click **Cell Icon**. In the **Order** box, verify that the red icon displays. In the last box, verify that **On Top** is displayed, and then click **OK**. Verify that three cells with the red icon display in the first three rows. Compare your screen with **Figure 3**.

    The cells with the red icons are now at the top of the list. These cells indicate classes that have lost money.

7. Select the range **A1:I10**. Display the **Home** tab, and then in the **Clipboard** group, click the **Copy** button.

    The worksheet titles and the first five rows of data are copied to the Clipboard.

8. Display the **Loss** worksheet tab, and then select cell **A1**. In the **Clipboard** group, click the **Paste** button. Select columns **A:I**, and then **AutoFit** the column widths. Compare your screen with **Figure 4**.

9. Display the **Schedule** worksheet tab, and then press [Esc]. Click cell **A1**. **Save** the workbook.

- **You have completed Skill 3 of 10**

▶ When tabular data is sorted, the data is grouped by the column being sorted.

▶ When data is grouped, the Excel Subtotal tool can be used to display summary statistics—sums and counts, for example—for each group.

1. Display the **Schedule** worksheet tab, and then select cell **B6**. On the **Data** tab, in the **Sort & Filter** group, click the **Sort A to Z** button [↓]. Compare your screen with **Figure 1**.

The rows are now grouped by Instructor. When sorted in this manner, the Subtotal tool can provide subtotals for each instructor.

2. Select cell **A6**, and then in the **Outline** group, click **Subtotal**.

In the Subtotal dialog box, you specify which column contains the grouped data, which summary function to use, and which columns to apply the summary function to.

3. In the **Subtotal** dialog box, click the **At each change in** arrow, and then click **Instructor**. Verify that the **Use function** box displays *Sum*, and then under **Add subtotal to**, scroll and click as necessary to select the **Income**, the **Inst Fee**, and the **Profit/Loss** check boxes. Compare your screen with **Figure 2**.

Subtotals will be displayed for each instructor and will include the Course Income, the Instructor Fees, and the Profit/Loss columns.

■ **Continue to the next page to complete the skill**

Rows grouped by Instructor

Figure 1

Column data is grouped by Instructor

Assigned summary function

Selected columns to subtotal

Figure 2

Figure 3

Figure 4

4. Click **OK**, and then compare your screen with **Figure 3**.

The table is organized as an outline with three levels, and the Outline pane displays. For each instructor, the specified columns display subtotals. For example, the *Course Income* for Candie Fenny's three classes, as shown in cell G13, is *2295*.

5. In the **Outline** pane, click the **Outline Level 2** ② button.

Displaying outline level 2 collapses the outline so that only the Subtotal rows display.

6. In the **Outline** pane, click the **Expand** button ⊞ to the left of row **19** to display all of the rows for Chere Freitag.

Using this method, the Subtotal outline can be collapsed and expanded.

7. Right-click the **Schedule** worksheet tab, and then in the displayed shortcut menu, click **Move or Copy**. In the **Move or Copy** dialog box, under **Before sheet**, click **(move to end)**, select the **Create a copy** check box, and then click **OK**.

8. Right-click the **Schedule (2)** worksheet tab, and select **Rename**. On the worksheet tab, replace the text with Subtotal Press Enter, and then compare your screen with **Figure 4**.

9. Click the **Schedule** worksheet tab, and then in the **Outline** group, click the **Subtotal** button. In the **Subtotal** dialog box, click **Remove All**.

10. Click cell **A6**, and then on the **Data** tab, in the **Sort & Filter** group, click the **Sort A to Z** button ↓.

11. **Save** 💾 the workbook.

■ **You have completed Skill 4 of 10**

► A *precedent* is any cell value that is referred to in a formula and a function. A *dependent* is any cell value that depends on the value in a given cell.

► Tracing the precedents or dependents of a given cell helps you evaluate worksheet formulas and is useful when you need to determine the cause of an error.

1. On the **Schedule** worksheet, select cell **G6**, and then type =A6*C6*E6 Press Enter.

   The #VALUE! error value indicates that the wrong type of data is being used in the formula. The error displays in cells G6 and I6 because cell A6 contains a text value. Excel cannot perform mathematical calculations when one of the values being multiplied is formatted as text.

2. Select cell **G6**. On the **Formulas** tab, in the **Formula Auditing** group, click the **Trace Precedents** button. In the **Formula Auditing** group, click the **Trace Dependents** button, and then compare your screen with **Figure 1**.

   The precedents are indicated by a blue line with blue dots indicating the cells used in the formula. The dependents are indicated by a red line.

3. With cell **G6** still selected, in the **Formula Auditing** group, click the **Evaluate Formula** button. In the **Evaluate Formula** dialog box, click **Step In**. Compare your screen with **Figure 2**.

   The Evaluate Formula dialog box is used to evaluate each part of a formula in a step-by-step process. The underlying formula in cell G6 displays and cell A6 is highlighted to indicate that it is the cell being evaluated in this step.

■ **Continue to the next page to complete the skill**

Trace Precedents and Trace Dependents buttons

Trace precedents line

Trace dependents line

Figure 1

Underlying formula

A6 being evaluated in current step

Figure 2

Underline
indicates steps
evaluated

Figure 3

Error value displays
in place of A6

Figure 4

4. Notice that cell **A6** contains a text value, *30 Minute Meals*, and then click the **Step Out** button. Click **Step In**, and notice that cell **C6** contains a numeric value, *99*, and then click **Step Out**. Compare your screen with **Figure 3**.

The Evaluation box indicates the steps evaluated to this point by displaying actual values and underlining each part of the formula that has been evaluated. Here *"30 Minute Meals"*99* has been evaluated. In this manner, each step in a formula can be analyzed.

5. Click the **Evaluate** button, and then compare your screen with **Figure 4**.

The Evaluation box displays an error value in place of the information that was previously displayed. The error value helps you locate the exact cell causing the error value.

6. If necessary, drag the **Evaluate Formula** dialog box down so that both trace lines display.

7. Using the skills you previously practiced, create a full-screen snip. **Save** 🖫 the snip in your **Excel Chapter 7** folder as Lastname_Firstname_e07_Schedule_Eval and then **Close** ⊠ the **Snipping Tool** window.

8. In the **Evaluate Formula** dialog box, click **Close**. In the **Formula Auditing** group, click the **Remove Arrows** button to remove the trace lines.

9. In cell **G6**, type =C6*E6 and then press Enter. **Save** 🖫 the workbook.

■ **You have completed Skill 5 of 10**

► The *Watch Window toolbar* displays cells and the formulas in those cells when they are not visible on the screen.

► The Watch Window toolbar does not change when you scroll in the worksheet, and you can move or dock it as needed.

1. On the **Schedule** worksheet, select cell **H6**. On the **Formulas** tab, in the **Formula Auditing** group, click the **Watch Window** button.

2. In the **Watch Window** toolbar, click **Add Watch**, and then compare your screen with **Figure 1**.

3. In the **Add Watch** dialog box, verify that the value =*Schedule$H$6* displays, and then click **Add**.

4. Select cell **I21**, click **Add Watch**, and then click **Add**. If necessary, resize the Watch Window toolbar to display all of the **VLOOKUP** formula as shown in **Figure 2**.

   The underlying formulas for the two cells are added to the Watch Window toolbar display. In this manner, multiple cells can be added to the Watch Window.

■ **Continue to the next page to complete the skill**

Selected cell

Watch Window toolbar

Add Watch dialog box

Figure 1

Two cells added to Watch Window toolbar

Entire LOOKUP formula displays

Figure 2

Figure 3

Figure 4

New cell values in Schedule worksheet

Changed values in lookup table

Watch Window toolbar

Updated cell values

5. Display the **Lookup** worksheet. Move the **Watch Window** toolbar so that the upper left corner is in cell **E3**. In the Watch Window, notice that the Value column for cell H6 displays *540*.

6. Select cell **C12**, and type **50** In the **Watch Window** toolbar, watch the **Value** for cell **H6**, and then press Enter. Notice the value changes from *540* to *600*.

   The Watch Window toolbar enables you to view changes in cells that are not currently displayed in the worksheet.

7. In cell **C8**, replace the existing value with **21** and then press Enter. Notice that the **Value** of cell **I21** on the **Watch Window** toolbar changes from *1470* to *1372* as shown in **Figure 3**.

8. Display the **Schedule** worksheet. Verify that the value in cell **H6** is *600* and that the value in cell **I21** is *1372*, as shown in **Figure 4**. If necessary, move the Watch Window toolbar as shown in the figure.

9. Using the skills you previously practiced, create a full-screen snip. **Save** 🔲 the snip in your **Excel Chapter 7** folder as Lastname_Firstname_e07_Schedule_ Watch and then **Close** ❎ the **Snipping Tool** window.

10. **Close** ☒ the **Watch Window** toolbar, and then **Save** 🔲 the workbook.

■ **You have completed Skill 6 of 10**

▶ In Excel, a **_data table_** is a range of cells that is set up to show how changing one or two values in a formula will affect the results of the formula.

▶ Data tables are used to perform what-if analysis and can contain one or two variables. A **_one-variable data table_** changes one value in a formula using input from either a row or a column.

1. Display the **Data Table** worksheet, and then select cell **B9**. Type =G6 and then press [Enter].

2. In cell **B10**, type 3 and then press [Enter]. In cell **B11**, type 3.5% Press [Enter]. In cell **B12**, type 1000 Press [Enter], and then compare your screen with **Figure 1.** ────────

   These values reflect an investment earning 3.5% interest per year. The initial investment is the class profit of $43,045, and monthly payments of $1,000 will be added for 3 years.

3. Select cell **B13**, and then on the **Formulas** tab in the **Function Library** group, click **Financial**, and then click **FV**.

4. In the **Rate** box, type B11/12 In the **Nper** box, type B10*12 In the **Pmt** box, type -B12 In the **Pv** box, type -B9 and then click **OK**. Compare your screen with **Figure 2.** ────────

   The result of the future value function indicates that the initial investment will grow to $85,702.96 if the investment earns 3.5% and monthly payments of $1,000 are made. Recall that both the initial amount invested and the payment amount should be negative values because the money is an outflow—money being paid out to the investment.

■ **Continue to the next page to complete the skill**

Values typed

Figure 1

Future value of the investment calculated

Figure 2

Figure 3

$B$12 entered as data table variable

Figure 4

Column input cells

Data table calculates possible future values based on monthly payment

5. Select cell **B15**, type =B13 and then press Enter.

   A data table must be built from an underlying formula. Here, the results of the future value formula in cell B13 will be the data table's underlying function.

6. Select the range **A15:B27**. On the **Data** tab, in the **Data Tools** group, click the **What-If Analysis** button, and then click **Data Table**.

7. In the **Data Table** dialog box, click the **Column input cell** box, and then click cell **B12**. Notice that Excel automatically converts the value to an absolute cell reference, as shown in **Figure 3**.

   The Monthly Payment value in cell B12 represents the variable that will be changed using the values in the first column of the data table.

8. Click **OK**. Select cell **B9**, press and hold Ctrl, and then select the range **B15:B27**. Display the **Home** tab, and then in the **Number** group, click the **Accounting Number Format** button $ ·. Click cell **D15**, and then compare your screen with **Figure 4**.

   For each row in this data table, the payment value used in the FV function (B12) was changed to the corresponding value in column A. For example, in cell B17, the future value of the investment with a payment of *$1,100* would be *$89,492.93*.

9. **Save** 💾 the workbook.

■ **You have completed Skill 7 of 10**

► A *two-variable data table* uses two inputs—one from a column and one from a row.

► Two-variable data tables display the results across a range of cells.

1. On the **Data Table** worksheet tab, select cell **E15**, type =B13 and then press [Enter].

   Cell E15 will be the underlying formula for a two-variable data table.

2. In cell **E16**, type 1.0% and then press [Enter]. In cell **E17**, type 1.5% and then press [Enter].

3. Select the range **E16:E17**, and then on the **Home** tab, in the **Number** group, click the **Decrease Decimal** button [⬚] one time. With the range **E16:E17** still selected, drag the **fill handle** down through cell **E27**. Compare your screen with **Figure 1**.

   In the range E16:E27, the values will be the different interest rates used as the column input in a data table.

4. In cell **F15**, type 1 and then press [Tab]. In cell **G15**, type 2 Select the range **F15:G15**, and then drag the **fill handle** to the right through cell **J15**. Compare your screen with **Figure 2**.

   The range F15:J15 will display the number of years used as the row input in the data table.

■ **Continue to the next page to complete the skill**

Interest rates entered into column E

Figure 1

Year values entered into row 15

Figure 2

Number of years
entered as
Row input cell

Interest rate
entered as
Column input cell

Figure 3

5. Select the range **E15:J27**, and then display the **Data** tab. In the **Data Tools** group, click **What-If Analysis**, and then click **Data Table**.

   The Data Table dialog box displays. There are boxes to add two variables. The Row input cell is equal to the number of years. The Column input cell is equal to the interest rate.

6. In the **Data Table** dialog box, with the insertion point in the **Row input cell** box, click cell **B10**—the number of years the investment payments will be made. Press Tab.

7. With the insertion point in the **Column input cell** box, click cell **B11**—the interest rate earned by the investment. Compare your screen with **Figure 3**, and then click **OK**.

8. Select the range **F16:J27**, and then display the **Home** tab. In the **Number** group, click the **Accounting Number Format** $ button. Select cell **A1**, and compare your screen with **Figure 4**.

   A data table displays the results of its underlying function using two different variables. Here, the future value of the investment is calculated using the different interest rates in column E and the different years in row 15. For example, the future value of the investment after four years at 5.0% interest is $105,568.33.

9. **Save** the workbook.

- **You have completed Skill 8 of 10**

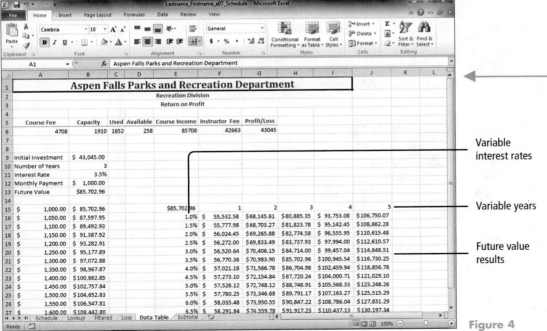

Variable
interest rates

Variable years

Future value
results

Figure 4

► A *table quick style* is a collection of table formatting options that can be applied to a range with a single click.

► Quick styles are displayed in a gallery with a small sample image of the style called a *thumbnail*.

1. Display the **Loss** worksheet tab, and select the range **A5:I10**. Display the **Home** tab. In the **Styles** group, click **Format as Table**, and then in the displayed gallery, click **New Table Style**.

2. In the **New Table Quick Style** dialog box, in the **Name** box, type Aspen Falls Lifestyle Classes Compare your screen with **Figure 1**.

    You use the New Table Quick Styles dialog box to create custom table quick styles that you name and format yourself.

3. In the **New Table Quick Style** dialog box, under **Table Element**, click **Whole Table**, and then click the **Format** button.

4. In the **Format Cells** dialog box, click the **Border** tab. In the **Line Style** box, click the next to last style in the right column. Click the **Color** arrow, and then under **Theme colors**, click the fourth color in the first row—**Dark Blue, Text 2**. Under **Presets**, click **Outline**. Compare your screen with **Figure 2**.

■ **Continue to the next page to complete the skill**

Quick Style name entered

Figure 1

Thick, blue outside border preview

Figure 2

Sample background color

Figure 3

Range converted to an Excel table

Custom table quick style applied

Figure 4

5. In the **Line Style** box, click the last style in the left column, and then under **Presets**, click **Inside**.

   A thin, blue inside border is applied.

6. Click the **Fill** tab, and then under **Background Color**, click the first color in the third row. Compare your screen with **Figure 3**.

   Under Sample, a fill color has been applied to the whole table.

7. Click **OK**. In the displayed **New Table Quick Style** dialog box, under **Table Element**, click **Header Row**, and then click the **Format** button.

8. In the **Format Cells** dialog box, on the **Fill** tab, under **Background Color**, click the first color in the fifth row, and then click **OK**.

9. In the **New Table Quick Style** dialog box, click **OK**.

10. With the range **A5:I10** selected, display the **Home** tab. In the **Styles** group, click **Format as Table**. In the displayed gallery, under **Custom**, point to the thumbnail, and then notice that the name of the custom table quick style just created displays. Click the *Aspen Falls Lifestyle Classes* thumbnail to apply the quick style.

11. In the **Format As Table** dialog box, verify that the **Where is the data for your table** box reads =$A$5:$I$10. Verify the **My table has headers** check box is selected, and then click **OK**. Select cell **A1**, and then compare your screen with **Figure 4**.

   The custom table quick style is applied to the specified range, and the range is converted into an Excel table. Darker shading has been applied to the header row.

12. **Save** 🖫 the workbook.

   ■ **You have completed Skill 9 of 10**

► When a table is converted to a range, the table functions are removed and the formatting remains.

► Tables can be expanded or decreased using the Resize Table tool.

1. On the **Schedule** worksheet, click cell **B6**. Display the **Data** tab, and then in the **Sort & Filter** group, click **Sort A to Z** [↓].

2. Select the range **A5:I18**, display the **Home** tab, and then in the **Clipboard** group, click **Copy** [🗐].

3. Display the **Loss** worksheet, and select cell **A13**. In the **Clipboard** group, click **Paste**, and then compare your screen with **Figure 1**.

4. On the **Loss** worksheet, select the range **A13:I26**, if necessary, and then display the **Home** tab. In the **Styles** group, click **Format as Table**. In the displayed gallery, under **Medium**, click the third style in the first row—**Table Style Medium 3**. Compare your screen with **Figure 2**.

5. On the **Format As Table** dialog box, verify that the **My table has headers** check box is selected, and then click **OK**.

   The range is formatted as an Excel table with filter and sort buttons in the header row.

■ **Continue to the next page to complete the skill**

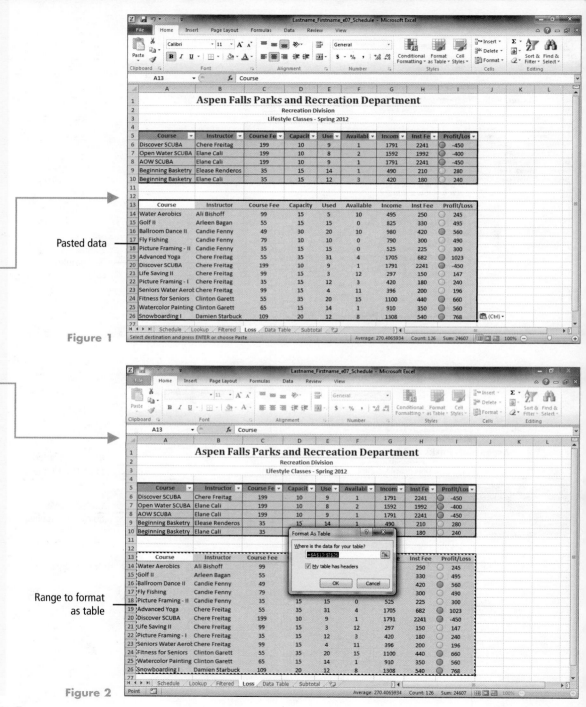

Pasted data

Figure 1

Range to format as table

Figure 2

Header row

Range formatted as a table

Filtered data

Figure 3

Formatting remains

Data converted to a range

Figure 4

6. Select columns **A:I**, and then **AutoFit** the contents.

7. Click the cell **B13** filter arrow. In the displayed gallery, clear the **Select All** check box, and then select the *Arleen Bagan* and *Clinton Garett* check boxes. Click **OK**. Select cell **A1**, and then compare your screen with **Figure 3**.

8. Select the range **A13: I25**. On the **Design** tab, in the **Tools** group, click **Convert to Range**. Read the displayed message, and then click **Yes**. Select cell **A12**, and then compare your screen with **Figure 4**.

   The table is converted to a range. The filter that had been applied is removed. The formatting of the table remains, and the range is no longer an Excel table.

9. Display the **Schedule** worksheet, and then click cell **A1**. Right-click the **Schedule** worksheet tab, and then click **Select All Sheets**. Insert the file name in the left footer. Return to **Normal** view, and then click cell **A1**. Right-click the **Schedule** worksheet tab, and then click **Ungroup Sheets**.

10. Save 🖫 the workbook, and then print or submit it—and the snips made previously—as directed by your instructor.

Done! You have completed Skill 10 of 10 and your workbook is complete!

More Skills

The following More Skills are located at **www.pearsonhighered.com/skills**

More Skills Create Amortization Tables

An amortization table is a useful tool that allows you to keep track of payments that are being made on an investment. A well-designed amortization table will display the amount of principal and interest that are paid each month along with the remaining balance on the principal.

In More Skills 11, you will create an amortization table showing the payments on a 72-month loan with an initial principal amount of $45,000 and an interest rate of 5.65%.

To begin, open your web browser, navigate to www.pearsonhighered.com/skills, locate the name of your textbook, and then follow the instructions on the website.

More Skills Use the ROUND Function

You use the ROUND function to round a number to a specified number of decimal places. This function is often used to display numbers as whole numbers instead of showing the decimal places.

In More Skills 12, you will open a workbook and then use the ROUND, ROUNDUP, and ROUNDDOWN functions to change the way numbers are displayed so that numbers with large numbers of digits to the right of the decimal point are easier to read.

To begin, open your web browser, navigate to www.pearsonhighered.com/skills, locate the name of your textbook, and then follow the instructions on the website.

More Skills Use Information Functions

Excel has a collection of functions that are used to provide you with information about the data that is contained within a workbook. The ISODD and ISERROR functions evaluate data and provide True or False results.

In More Skills 13, you will use both the ISODD and ISERROR functions to calculate values that are used to calculate another value.

To begin, open your web browser, navigate to www.pearsonhighered.com/skills, locate the name of your textbook, and then follow the instructions on the website.

More Skills Sort Tables Based on Multiple Criteria

In Excel, you can sort a table based on as many criteria as needed. The criteria can be values, cell colors, or icons.

In More Skills 14, you will sort a table based on multiple criteria.

To begin, open your web browser, navigate to www.pearsonhighered.com/skills, locate the name of your textbook, and then follow the instructions on the website.

Key Terms

Online Help Skills

1. **Start** 🌐 Excel. In the upper right corner of the Excel window, click the **Help** button 🔘. In the **Help** window, click the **Maximize** 🔲 button.

2. Click in the search box, type data tables and then click the **Search** button 🔍. In the search results, click **Calculate multiple results by using a data table**.

3. Read the article's introduction, and then below **In this article**, click **Overview**. Compare your screen with **Figure 1**.

Figure 1

4. Read the section to see if you can answer the following: How many different what-if analysis tools are available in Excel? Which what-if analysis tool should you use if you want to analyze more than two variables?

Matching

Match each term in the second column with its correct definition in the first column by writing the letter of the term on the blank line in front of the correct definition.

____ **1.** A file that stores only the text characters but not the formatting, tab stops, or tables.

____ **2.** A logical operator that returns true if either one of the criteria is true.

____ **3.** A tool that displays summary statistics for grouped data in an outline format.

____ **4.** An error value indicating that the wrong type of data is being used in the formula.

____ **5.** A process that analyzes a function by stepping in and out of each part of the function.

____ **6.** A toolbar that provides information about selected cells when those cells are not currently displayed on the screen.

____ **7.** A range of calculations based on a single underlying formula that uses either rows or columns as inputs.

____ **8.** The Data Table command can be found by clicking this button.

____ **9.** A data table type that takes input from a row and input from a column.

____ **10.** Table quick styles that you create and name display in the gallery under this category.

A #VALUE

B Custom

C Data table

D Evaluation

E OR

F Subtotal

G Text file

H Two-variable

I Watch Window

J What-If Analysis

Multiple Choice

Write the correct answer in the space provided.

1. This refers to a file where the data in each field is separated by the Tab character.
   A. delimited
   B. plain
   C. comma-separated

2. This command displays only rows that meet a specified condition.
   A. arranger
   B. sorter
   C. filter

3. This is a name for a cell value that is referred to by a function in another cell.
   A. dependent
   B. precedent
   C. variable

4. When a cell value depends on the value in a given cell is known as this type of cell.
   A. dependent
   B. precedent
   C. variable

5. This toolbar is used to watch cells and the formulas in those cells when they are not visible on the screen.
   A. Watch Window
   B. Status Bar
   C. Formula Bar

6. This refers to a range of cells that are set up like a table and is used to show how changing one or two values in a formula will affect the result of those formulas.
   A. data table
   B. range
   C. table

7. These types of data tables are created using two different variables.
   A. one-variable
   B. two-variable
   C. complex-variable

8. This is a collection of formatting options that can be applied with a single click.
   A. style template
   B. quick style
   C. table style

9. This is a small sample image of a style.
   A. thumbnail
   B. live preview
   C. preview

10. When you refer to a group of cells is called this term.
    A. style
    B. range
    C. gallery

Topics for Discussion

1. What kind of information do you think a small business or organization would have in a text file or a database that would need to be imported into a spreadsheet?

2. Why would you use the filter and sort tools when you work with spreadsheets?

Skill Check

To complete this workbook, you will need the following files:

- e07_Concessions_Report
- e07_Concessions_Orders

You will save your files as:

- Lastname_Firstname_e07_Concessions_Report
- Lastname_Firstname_e07_Concessions_Error
- Lastname_Firstname_e07_Concessions_Watch
- Lastname_Firstname_e07_Concessions_Filtered

1. **Start** Excel, and then open the student data file **e07_Concessions_Report**. Save the file in your **Excel Chapter 7** folder with the name Lastname_Firstname_e07_Concessions_Report Group the worksheets, and add the file name in the left section of the footer. Ungroup the sheets, and return to **Normal** view.

2. On the **Report** worksheet tab, select cell **A6**. Display the **Data** tab. In the **Get External Data** group, click **From Text**. In the **Import Text File** dialog box, locate **e07_Concessions_Orders**, and then click **Import**. In the **Text Import Wizard**, click **Finish**, and then in the **Import Data** dialog box, click **OK**. **AutoFit** columns **A:F** and then compare your screen with **Figure 1**. ⎯⎯⎯

3. Select cell **B6**, and then on the **Data** tab, click **Sort A to Z**. If necessary, in the **Sort Warning** dialog box, verify that the **Expand the selection** option button is selected, and then click **Sort**.

4. Select cell **E7**, and display the **Formulas** tab. Click **Trace Precedents**, and then click **Trace Dependents**. Click **Evaluate Formula**. Click **Evaluate**, and then click **Step In**. Click **Step Out**, and then click **Evaluate**.

5. Create a full-screen snip, **Save** it in your **Excel Chapter 7** folder as Lastname_Firstname_e07_Concessions_Error and then close the Snipping Tool window. Compare your screen with **Figure 2**. In the **Evaluate Formula** dialog box, click **Close**. Click **Remove Arrows**, select cell **E7**, and then type 0 and press (Enter).

6. Select cell **E28**, and then in the **Formula Auditing** group, click **Watch Window**. Click **Add Watch**, and then click **Add**. Add cell **E13** to the Watch Window. Select cell **D13**, type 52 and then press (Enter). Create a full-screen snip, **Save** it in your **Excel Chapter 7** folder as Lastname_Firstname_e07_Concessions_Watch and then close the Snipping Tool window. Close the **Watch Window**.

Figure 1

Figure 2

■ Continue to the next page to complete this Skill Check

7. Display the **Data** tab. In the **Sort & Filter** group, click **Filter**. Click the cell **B5** filter arrow, point to **Text Filters**, and then click **Contains**. Under **Item**, click the second box arrow, and then click **Assorted Snack Crackers**. Select the **Or** option button, and then under **Or**, click the first box arrow, and then click **Contains**. Click the second box arrow, and then click **Hot Dogs (Dozen)**. Click **OK**.

8. In the **Sort & Filter** group, click **Sort**. Under **Columns**, click **Sort by**, and then click **Amount to Order**. Under **Sort On**, click **Values**. Under **Order**, click **Largest to Smallest**, and then click **OK**. Compare your screen with **Figure 3**.

9. Create a full-screen snip, **Save** it in your **Excel Chapter 7** folder as Lastname_Firstname_e07_Concessions_Filtered and then close the Snipping Tool window.

10. Click **Filter** to remove the AutoFilter. Select cell **B5** and click **Sort A to Z**, and then in the **Outline** group, click **Subtotal**. Under **At each change in**, click the arrow, and then select **Item**. Under **Add Subtotal to**, select the **Amount to Order** check box (if necessary), and then click **OK**. Click the **Outline Level 2**.

Figure 3

11. Display the **DataTable** worksheet. Select the range **A17:B23**. Click **What-If Analysis**, and then click **Data Table**. On the **Data Table** dialog box, in the **Column input cell** box, type D14 Click **OK**. Select the range **D17:H23**. Click **What-If Analysis**, and then click **Data Table**. On the **Data Table** dialog box, in the **Row input cell** box, type D13 In the **Column input cell** box, type D14 Click **OK**. AutoFit columns **A:H**.

12. Select the range **A5:D12**. On the **Home** tab, click **Format as Table**. Click **New Table Style**. In the **Name** box, type Aspen Falls Rec Under **Table Element**, select **Whole Table**. Click **Format**. Click the **Border** tab. Under **Style**, click the last style in the left column. Click the **Color** arrow. Under **Theme colors**, click the sixth color in the first row. Click **Outline**, and then click **Inside**. Click the **Fill** tab. Click the sixth color in the second row, and then click **OK**. Click **Header Row**, and then click **Format**. On the **Fill** tab, click the third color in the third row. Click **OK** two times.

13. Click **Format as Table**, and then under **Custom**, click the quick style. In the dialog box, click **OK**.

14. On the **Design** tab, in the **Tools** group, click **Convert to Range**. Click **Yes**. Click cell **A1**, and then compare your screen with **Figure 4**.

15. **Save** the workbook, and then print or submit it—and the snips you made previously—as directed by your instructor

Figure 4

Done! You have completed the Skill Check

Assess Your Skills 1

To complete this workbook, you will need the following files:

- e07_Recreation_Investments
- e07_Recreation_Report

You will save your files as:

- Lastname_Firstname_e07_Recreation_Report
- Lastname_Firstname_e07_Recreation_Savings
- Lastname_Firstname_e07_Recreation_Formula
- Lastname_Firstname_e07_Recreation_Watch

1. **Start** Excel, and open the student data file **e07_Recreation_Report**. Save the file in your **Excel Chapter 7** folder with the name Lastname_Firstname_e07_Recreation_Report Select cell **A7**, and then using all the wizard defaults, import the data in the delimited text file **e07_Recreation_Investments**. **AutoFit** columns **A:E**. Add the file name in the left section of the footer.

2. Sort the range **A7:E19** by **Interest Rate** by sorting on the **Cell Icon**. Set the **Order** so that the green icon is on top.

3. Filter the range **A6:E19** so that only the rows where the **Account Type** is **Savings** display. For the range, add a **Number Filter** so that the interest rate must be greater than 2.88%.

4. Create a full-screen snip, **Save** it in your **Excel Chapter 7** folder as Lastname_Firstname_e07_Recreation_Savings and then close the Snipping Tool window.

5. Remove all filters, and then sort the range **A7:E19** in ascending order by **Facility**. Add subtotals to provide a sum for the **Balance** column at each change in **Facility**.

6. Display the **Trace Precedents** line for cell **E7**. For cell **E7**, use the **Evaluate Formula** dialog box to step through the process. Click **Step In** and **Step Out** one time each, and then click **Evaluate**. Move the **Evaluate Formulas** dialog box so that the **Precedent** line displays, and then create a full-screen snip. **Save** it in your **Excel Chapter 7** folder as Lastname_Firstname_e07_Recreation_Formula and then close the Snipping Tool window. Close the **Evaluate Formula** dialog box. Click **Remove Arrows**.

7. Add cell **E16** to the **Watch Window** toolbar. Move the Watch Window so that row 16 is visible. Select cell **D16**, type 4.25 and then press (Tab). Create a full-screen snip, **Save** it in your **Excel Chapter 7** folder as Lastname_Firstname_e07_Recreation_Watch and then close the Snipping Tool window. **Close** the **Watch Window**.

8. Select the range **A6:E24**, and then create a new table quick style. **Name** the style Capital For the **Whole Table**, apply the following **Outline** and **Inside** borders: select the last line style in the left column. For the color, apply the sixth color in the top row. On the **Fill** tab, click the first color in the third row. Close all open dialog boxes, and then apply the new quick style to the range. Click **Yes** on the message box. Click cell A1, and then compare your screen with **Figure 1**.

9. **Save** the workbook, and then print or submit it—and the snips you made previously—electronically as directed by your instructor.

Done! You have completed Assess Your Skills 1

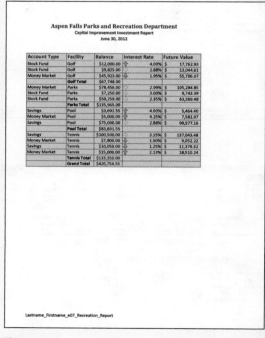

Account Type	Facility	Balance	Interest Rate	Future Value
Stock Fund	Golf	$12,000.00	4.00%	$ 17,762.93
Stock Fund	Golf	$9,825.00	2.88%	$ 13,044.61
Money Market	Golf	$45,923.00	1.95%	$ 55,706.07
Golf Total		$67,748.00		
Money Market	Parks	$78,456.00	2.99%	$ 105,284.85
Stock Fund	Parks	$7,250.00	3.00%	$ 9,743.39
Stock Fund	Parks	$50,259.00	2.35%	$ 63,369.48
Parks Total		$135,965.00		
Savings	Pool	$3,691.55	4.00%	$ 5,464.40
Money Market	Pool	$5,000.00	4.25%	$ 7,581.07
Savings	Pool	$75,000.00	2.88%	$ 99,577.16
Pool Total		$83,691.55		
Savings	Tennis	$100,500.00	3.15%	$ 137,043.48
Money Market	Tennis	$7,800.00	1.50%	$ 9,052.22
Savings	Tennis	$10,050.00	1.25%	$ 11,379.32
Money Market	Tennis	$15,000.00	2.13%	$ 18,510.24
Tennis Total		$133,350.00		
Grand Total		$420,754.55		

Aspen Falls Parks and Recreation Department
Capital Improvement Investment Report
June 30, 2012

Lastname_Firstname_e07_Recreation_Report

Figure 1

Assess Your Skills 2

To complete this workbook, you will need the following file:

- e07_Endowment

You will save your files as:

- Lastname_Firstname_e07_Endowment
- Lastname_Firstname_e07_Endowment_Snip

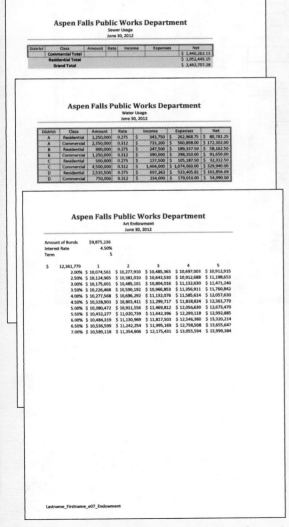

Figure 1

1. **Start** Excel, and then open the student data file **e07_Endowment**. Save the file in your **Excel Chapter 7** folder with the name Lastname_Firstname_e07_Endowment Group all of the worksheets, and then add the file name in the left section of the footer. Return to **Normal** view, and then ungroup the sheets.

2. In cell **A9** of the **Endowment** worksheet, insert the **FV** function. Type B6/12 for the **Rate**, B7*12 for the **Nper**, and -B5 for the **Pv**. Format cell **A9** with the **Currency [0]** cell style.

3. For the range **A9:F20**, create a two-variable data table that uses the term for the row input and the interest rate for the column input. Apply the **Currency [0]** style to the range **B10:F20**, and **AutoFit** columns **A:F**.

4. Display the **Usage** worksheet. Create a new table quick style with the **Name** Water Bonds Assign the following **Inside** border for the **Whole table**: apply the last line style in the left column, and apply the **Red, Accent 2 Color**. Use the same color and the next-to-last line in the right column for the outline border. On the **Fill** tab, click the first color in the third row, and then click **OK**. For the **Water Bonds** table quick style, assign the fourth color in the second row of the **Fill** tab to the table's **Header Row**.

5. Select the range **A5:G13**, and apply the **Water Bonds** custom table quick style.

6. For the range **A5:G13**, apply a custom **Number Filter** so that only the rows where the **Income** value is **greater than or equal to $247,500** and **is less than or equal to $390,000** display.

7. Create a full-screen snip, **Save** it in your **Excel Chapter 7** folder as Lastname_Firstname_e07_Endowment_Snip and then close the Snipping Tool window.

8. Remove all filters. Convert the table **A5:G13** to a range.

9. Display the **Table** worksheet tab. Select cell **B6**, and then click **Sort A to Z**. Use the **Subtotal** command to sum the **Net** column for each change in **Class**. **AutoFit** columns **A:G**. Collapse the subtotals to level 2.

10. Compare your worksheet with Figure 1. **Save** the workbook, and then print or submit it—and the snips you made previously—electronically as directed by your instructor.

Done! You have completed Assess Your Skills 2

Assess Your Skills Visually

To complete this workbook, you will need the following files:

- e07_Equipment_Inventory
- e07_Equipment_Fire

You will save your file as:

- **Lastname_Firstname_e07_Equipment_Inventory**

Start Excel, and then open the student data file **e07_Equipment_Inventory**. Save the file in your **Excel Chapter 7** folder with the name Lastname_Firstname_e07_Equipment_Inventory Import the data from **e07_Equipment_Fire**, and then create a custom table quick style named Inventory with borders and shading similar to the table shown in **Figure 1**. Apply the table quick style to the table, and then convert the table to a range. Use the Subtotal tool to organize and summarize the data as shown in **Figure 1**. **Save** the workbook, and then print the file or submit the file as directed by your instructor.

Done! You have completed Assess Your Skills Visually

Figure 1

Skills in Context

To complete this workbook, you will need the following file:

- e07_Health_Care

You will save your file as:

- Lastname_Firstname_e07_Health_Care

Aspen Falls tracks employee health care claims on a yearly basis in an effort to reduce costs and promote employee well-being. **Start** Excel, and then open the student data file **e07_Health_Care**. Save the file in your **Excel Chapter 7** folder with the name Lastname_Firstname_e07_Health_Care Format the range **A5:F107** as a table using **Table Style Medium 4**. Remove all external connections. Using the trace and evaluation tools, locate and fix the four errors in the table. **Sort** the table by **Code**, and Convert the table to a range to retain the formatting. Subtotal both the **Fee** and **Co-Pay** columns. Collapse the subtotals to **Level 2**, and then **AutoFit** columns **A:F**. **Save** the workbook with the filter applied, and then print the file or submit the file as directed by your instructor.

Done! You have completed Skills in Context

Skills and You

To complete this workbook, you will need the following file:

- New blank Excel workbook

You will save your file as:

- e07_Skills_and_You_Your_Name

Using the skills you have practiced in this chapter, create a spreadsheet that tracks your personal budget. It will include at least one income item and 12 expense items that you pay each month. The entries should be categorized using the following categories: income, housing, fuel, insurance, utilities, food, and clothing.

Include data for at least three months. Sort all of the entries by category, subtotal the amounts by category, and then create a year-end report.

Done! You have completed Skills and You

Insert and Format Graphics and Shapes

► You can improve the appearance of an Excel workbook by adding images and graphics.

► You can insert shapes to call attention to important areas on a worksheet.

Your starting screen will look similar to this:

SKILLS

Skills 1-10 Training

At the end of this chapter, you will be able to:

Skill 1 Insert Graphics into Headers

Skill 2 Resize, Crop, and Compress Images

Skill 3 Insert, Modify, and Remove Backgrounds from Clip Art

Skill 4 Recolor Graphics and Apply Artistic Effects

Skill 5 Create SmartArt Organization Charts

Skill 6 Apply Quick Styles and Resize SmartArt

Skill 7 Resize and Position SmartArt Shapes

Skill 8 Format Individual SmartArt Shapes

Skill 9 Insert and Format Shapes

Skill 10 Group and Resize Shapes

MORE SKILLS

More Skills 11 Add Alternate Text to Graphics

More Skills 12 Add Graphics to SmartArt Shapes

More Skills 13 Convert Graphics to SmartArt Shapes and Use the Selection and Visibility Pane

More Skills 14 Insert PowerPoint Slides into Worksheets

Outcome

Using the skills listed to the left will enable you to create worksheets like these:

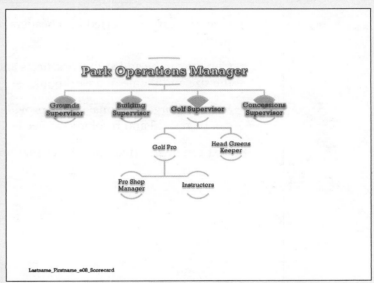

You will save this workbook as:

Lastname_Firstname_e08_Scorecard

In this chapter, you will create workbooks for the Aspen Falls City Hall, which provides essential services for the citizens and visitors of Aspen Falls, California.

Introduction

- ▶ Graphics can be inserted into headers so that they display on every page of the worksheet.

- ▶ Clip art can be added to worksheets and then recolored and resized to match the size and theme of a workbook.

- ▶ SmartArt organizational charts provide a graphical view of information. They can be resized and recolored as needed.

- ▶ Text can be inserted into shapes that point to important areas of a worksheet.

**Time to complete all
10 skills – 50 to 75 minutes**

Find your data files here:

Files needed for this chapter:

- e08_Scorecard
- e08_Scorecard_Logo

► You can insert digital images that are stored on your computer or available online into a worksheet.

► Pictures can be inserted in any of the Header area sections. For example, you can call attention to your company by inserting its logo in the worksheet header.

1. **Start** Excel, and then open **e08_Scorecard**. Click the **File** tab, and then click **Save As**. In the **Save As** dialog box, navigate to the location where you are saving your files. Click **New folder**, type Excel Chapter 8 and then press Enter two times. In the **File** name box, using your own name, name the file Lastname_Firstname_e08_Scorecard

2. Display the **Insert** tab, and then in the **Text** group, click **Header & Footer**. Compare your screen with **Figure 1**.

   The workbook switches to Page Layout view with the Header area active. The Header & Footer Tools contextual tab displays the Design tab. You use the commands on the Design tab to modify content and objects in the header and footer.

3. Click in the left Header area section, and then on the **Design** tab, in the **Header & Footer Elements** group, click **Picture**. In the **Insert Picture** dialog box, navigate to the location where your student data files are stored, and then select **e08_Scorecard_Logo**.

4. In the **Insert Picture** dialog box, click **Insert**. Compare your screen with **Figure 2**.

   When the image is first inserted, a place-holder—&[Picture]—appears instead of the picture. The placeholder indicates that a picture will appear in the header but does not provide a preview of the image.

■ **Continue to the next page to complete the skill**

Picture

Header

Figure 1

Picture placeholder

Figure 2

ScreenTip

Distorted picture in Header area

Vertical ruler

Figure 3

Top margin adjusted

Figure 4

5. Click in the middle Header area section to display the picture.

    When a header area section is not active, the picture displays instead of the &[Picture] placeholder. Here, a small portion of the image displays.

6. Click cell **A15** to close the Header area.

    With the Header area no longer active, the image fills the entire header area. Because the worksheet is wider than the original image, the image distorts as it stretches to fill the entire width of the header.

7. Click the **View** tab, and then in the **Show** group, verify that the **Ruler** check box is selected. On the left edge of the worksheet, point to the top of row 1, at the right edge of the vertical ruler, to display the ⬍ pointer and the ScreenTip with the text *Top Margin: 0.75 Inches*, as shown in **Figure 3**.

8. With the ⬍ pointer still displayed, drag down until the ScreenTip displays *Top Margin: 1.35 Inches*. Release the left mouse button, and then compare your screen with **Figure 4**.

9. Group both worksheets, and then add the file name in the left footer. **Ungroup** the worksheets, and then **Save** 🖫 the workbook.

■ **You have completed Skill 1 of 10**

► Images can be resized and cropped. To *crop* is to remove unwanted areas along the edges of a graphic or picture.

► Photographs taken with digital cameras are often very large. To *compress* an image is to change the way the image is stored, which reduces the size of the file.

1. With the worksheet in Page Layout view, click the left Header section to select the picture placeholder. On the **Design** tab, in the **Header & Footer Elements** group, click **Format Picture**.

2. In the **Format Picture** dialog box, be sure the **Size** tab displays. Under **Scale**, clear the **Lock aspect ratio** check box, and then clear the **Relative to original picture size** box. Compare your screen with **Figure 1**.

> The *aspect ratio* is the ratio of the width and height of an image expressed as its width divided by its height. Locking the aspect ratio of an image keeps the height and width in the same proportion to each other when the image is resized. The *Relative to original picture size* option changes the image size based on a percentage of the original picture size.

3. Under **Size and rotate**, click the **Height** down spin arrow to display *0.99"*.

4. In the **Width** box, select the existing value, and then type .97 Compare your screen with **Figure 2**.

> The image will be approximately 1 inch tall and 1 inch wide to fit in the upper left corner of the worksheet. The original image dimensions display at the bottom of the dialog box.

■ **Continue to the next page to complete the skill** ➤

Lock aspect ratio check box cleared

Relative to original picture size check box cleared

Figure 1

Height and Width values changed

Figure 2

5. In the **Format Picture** dialog box, display the **Picture** tab, and then under **Crop from**, replace the value in the **Left** box with .25 Replace the value in the **Right** box with .25 Compare your screen with **Figure 3**.

> One-quarter inch of the picture's left and right edges will be cropped.

6. Under **Image Control**, move the **Brightness** slider to the right so that the **Brightness** box displays *60%*. Move the **Contrast** slider to the left so that the **Contrast** box displays *25%*.

> *Contrast* is the difference between light and dark areas. Decreasing the contrast and increasing the brightness creates a washout effect.

7. Click the **Compress** button, and then in the **Compress Pictures** dialog box, under **Change resolution**, click the **Web/Screen** option button. Verify that the remaining settings are selected as shown in **Figure 4**.

> *Resolution* refers to the number of dots per square inch—also known as *dpi*. The Web/Screen resolution saves space by changing the dpi to 96, which reduces the amount of information needed to display the picture. When a picture is cropped, the cropped areas are not actually removed unless the picture is compressed using the compression option Delete cropped areas of pictures.

8. Click **OK**, read the message, and then click **Apply**. In the **Format Picture** dialog box, click **OK**, and then click cell **A16** to display the picture in the Heading area.

9. Switch to **Normal** view, and press Ctrl + Home. **Save** 💾 the workbook.

■ **You have completed Skill 2 of 10**

Left and Right crop values changed

Figure 3

Web/Screen resolution option selected

Delete cropped areas of pictures option selected

Figure 4

▶ *Clip art* is a set of images, drawings, photographs, videos, and sounds included with Microsoft Office or accessed from Microsoft Office Online.

▶ After you insert clip art into a workbook, you can format, move, and resize the clip art. You can also remove backgrounds.

1. In the **Scores** worksheet, select cell **D19**. On the **Insert** tab, in the **Illustrations** group, click **Clip Art**. In the Clip Art task pane, verify that the Include Office.com check box is selected, and then replace any text in the **Search for** box with golf Click the **Results should be** arrow, and then, in the displayed list, clear the **All media types** check box, and select only the **Photographs** check box. Compare your screen with **Figure 1**.

2. In the **Clip Art** task pane, click **Go**. Locate the picture shown in **Figure 2**—a golf ball on a tee with a club behind it. Point to the image, click the arrow on the image, and then click **Insert**. If that image is not available, insert the file **e08_Scorecard_ Club** into cell D19.

3. With the picture selected, on the **Format** tab, in the **Size** group, change the **Height** to *2"*.

    Because the aspect ratio is locked, the width is also changed to approximately 3 inches.

4. Drag the picture so that the upper left corner is in cell **A15**. Compare your screen with **Figure 2**.

■ **Continue to the next page to complete the skill**

Search for box

Media types

Figure 1

Clip art image inserted, sized, and positioned

Figure 2

Height adjusted

Figure 3

Clip art resized and positioned

Background removed

Figure 4

5. Select cell **J17**, and then in the **Clip Art** task pane, locate the picture shown in **Figure 3**—a golf bag with clubs. If that image is not available, insert the file **e08_ Scorecard_Bag**. Click the picture one time to insert it into the worksheet. **Close** ☒ the **Clip Art** task pane.

6. On the **Format** tab, in the **Size** group, change the **Height** to 2″. Drag the picture so that the upper right corner is in cell **K15**. Compare your screen with **Figure 3**.

7. With the second picture still selected, on the **Format** tab, in the **Adjust** group, click **Remove Background**. Using the middle sizing handle on the left side, drag so that the left edge of the selection is in the middle of column I, next to the left edge of the golf bag. With the ⊞ pointer, drag the middle-top sizing handle up to the top of the image.

8. Click the **Background Removal** tab, and then in the **Close** group, click **Keep Changes** to remove the background so that only the golf bag and clubs display.

9. Select cell **G15**. Compare your screen with **Figure 4**.

10. **Save** 🖫 the workbook.

▪ **You have completed Skill 3 of 10**

► Clip art can be recolored to match the theme colors in your worksheet.

► *Artistic Effects* are changes that can be applied to images to make them more visually appealing.

1. Select the image of the golf ball on the tee. On the **Format** tab, in the **Adjust** group, click the **Color** button to display the Recolor gallery, as shown in **Figure 1**.

   The Recolor gallery displays color variations commonly applied to photographs, such as *grayscale*—a range of shades of gray—and *sepia*—a range of shades of brown.

2. Under **Recolor**, click the first color in the second row—**Dark Blue, Text color 2 Dark**—to apply a blue tint to the image.

3. In the **Picture Styles** group, click the **More** button ⌄, and then in the gallery, click the 22nd style—**Bevel Perspective**.

4. In the **Adjust** group, click **Artistic Effects**, and then click the second option in the third row—**Watercolor Sponge**. Compare your screen with **Figure 2**.

5. Select the image on the right—the bag of clubs. In the **Picture Styles** group, click the **More** button ⌄, and then in the gallery, click the 28th style—**Metal Oval** picture style. In the **Adjust** group, click **Artistic Effects**, and then click the second option in the first row—**Marker**.

■ **Continue to the next page to complete the skill**

Recolor gallery

Dark Blue, Text color 2 Dark

Figure 1

Bevel perspective style applied

Figure 2

Picture shape changed and corrections applied

Figure 3

Crop button

Left side cropped

Figure 4

6. With the golf bag image still selected, in the **Adjust** group, click the **Corrections** button. Under **Sharpen and Soften**, click the last option—**Sharpen 50%**. Click the **Corrections** button, and then under **Brightness and Contrast**, click the second option in the fourth row—**Brightness: -20% Contrast +20%**. Compare your screen with **Figure 3**.

7. With the right picture still selected, in the **Size** group, click the **Crop** button to select the image with cropping handles.

8. With the ⊞ pointer, point to the left-middle crop handle. When the ⊞ pointer displays, drag to the right until the left edge of the picture is near the left edge of the golf bag. In the **Size** group, click the **Crop** button to turn off the **Crop** tool, and then compare your screen with **Figure 4**.

9. With the right picture still selected, hold down Ctrl, and then click the picture on the left. Release Ctrl, and then, in the **Adjust** group, click **Compress Pictures** ⊠.

10. In the **Compress Pictures** dialog box, verify that both **Apply only to this picture** and the **Delete cropped areas of pictures** check boxes are selected, and then under **Target output**, select the **Print** option button. Click **OK**.

    You may not notice any change to the pictures on the screen. The resolution has been decreased, and the cropped area has been removed, reducing the file size when the worksheet is saved.

11. **Save** 🖫 the workbook.

■ **You have completed Skill 4 of 10**

► A *SmartArt* graphic is a visual representation of information that is used to communicate a message.

► An *organization chart* is a SmartArt layout used to show relationships in an organization hierarchically.

1. Display the **Organization** worksheet, and then on the **Insert** tab, in the **Illustrations** group, click the **SmartArt** button. Compare your screen with **Figure 1**.

   The left side of the Choose a SmartArt Graphic dialog box displays the different layout categories. The center section displays the layouts for the selected category, and the right section describes the selected layout.

2. At the left side of the **Choose a SmartArt Graphic** dialog box, click **Hierarchy**. In the center section, click the **Half Circle Organization Chart**, as shown in **Figure 2**.

   If the example shape does not have the layout or number of shapes you want, you can modify it after you insert it into the worksheet.

3. Read the description in the right section of the dialog box, and then click **OK**.

■ **Continue to the next page to complete the skill**

Available layouts

Layout categories

Description of selected layout

Figure 1

Example of selected layout

Half Circle Organization Chart layout selected

Hierarchy category selected

Figure 2

Text pane

First bullet text entered

Figure 3

Added shapes and inserted text

Figure 4

4. On the **Design** tab, in the **Create Graphic** group, click the **Text Pane** button as needed to display the Text pane.

> The Text pane can be used to enter and edit the text that displays in each SmartArt shape. Each bullet in the Text pane corresponds to a shape in the SmartArt graphic.

5. With the insertion point in the first bullet in the **Text pane**, type Park Operations Manager

6. Press Del two times to delete the next two bullets. Compare your screen with **Figure 3**.

> Deleting bullets in the Text pane deletes the corresponding SmartArt shapes.

7. In the **Text pane**, click the first empty placeholder—[**Text**]—and then type Grounds Supervisor Click the next [**Text**] placeholder, and then type Building Supervisor

8. Press Enter to create a new bullet and shape, and then type Golf Supervisor

9. Press Enter, and then press Tab to indent the new bullet point and create a subordinate shape in the organization chart.

10. Type Golf Pro and press Enter. Type Head Greens Keeper Press Enter, and then type Concessions Manager Compare your screen with **Figure 4**.

> As you enter text and create or delete shapes, the font size adjusts to accommodate the longest entry.

11. On the **Design** tab, in the **Create Graphic** group, click the **Text Pane** button to close the Task pane.

12. Save 🖫 the workbook.

- **You have completed Skill 5 of 10**

► *Quick Styles* are prebuilt sets of formatting options that can be applied to a document or an object.

► SmartArt graphics are moved by dragging their borders, and they are resized by dragging their resizing handles.

1. Display the **Page Layout** tab, and then in the **Themes** group, click the **Themes** button. In the Themes gallery, under Built-In, click **Foundry** to apply the colors, fonts, and effects of the Foundry theme to the workbook.

2. If necessary, click to the left of the *Park Operations Manager* shape to select the entire SmartArt graphic. Verify that none of the individual SmartArt shapes are selected.

   When a shape is selected instead of the entire SmartArt graphic, the changes are applied only to the selected shape(s).

3. On the **Design** tab, in the **SmartArt Styles** group, click the **More** □ button. Compare your screen with **Figure 1**.

   The SmartArt Styles gallery displays thumbnails of each Quick Style formatted with the selected theme.

4. In the gallery, under **3-D**, click the second style—**Inset**.

5. In the **SmartArt Styles** group, click the **Change Colors** button. Under **Colorful**, click the second thumbnail—**Colorful Range - Accent Colors 2 to 3**.

6. Display the **Format** tab, and then in the **WordArt Styles** group, click the **Text Fill** button. In the gallery, under **Theme Colors**, click the last color in the fourth row—**Rose, Accent 6, Darker 50%**—to change each shape's text color as shown **Figure 2**.

■ **Continue to the next page to complete the skill** ►

Thumbnail

SmartArt Quick Styles gallery

Foundry theme applied

Figure 1

Text color changed

SmartArt Style applied

Figure 2

SmartArt resize handle

Shape selection border

SmartArt border

Text pane button

Figure 3

7. Click the **Park Operations Manager** shape, and then take a moment to familiarize yourself with the various SmartArt selection tools shown in **Figure 3**.

   The border and resizing handles around the Park Operations Manager shape indicate that the shape is selected. The resizing handles on the SmartArt border display as three dots. The button near the left-middle resizing handle opens and closes the Text pane.

8. Point to any area on the **SmartArt** border that is not a resizing handle. With the pointer, drag the SmartArt so that the upper left corner is in the middle of cell **A1**.

9. On the **SmartArt** shape border, point to the lower right resize handle, and then with the pointer, drag down and to the right so that the lower right corner is in the middle of cell **K26**. Notice that the shapes automatically resize to fill the larger area, as shown in **Figure 4**.

10. **Save** the workbook.

■ **You have completed Skill 6 of 10**

SmartArt moved and resized

Figure 4

► The individual shapes in a SmartArt graphic can be resized independent of each other.

► The layout of an organization chart can be changed—for example, assistants can display along a horizontal line instead of vertically.

1. Click the **Park Operations Manager** text box shape to select it. Point to the right-middle resizing handle. With the ⟷ pointer, drag to the right until the border is approximately aligned with the right side of column **I**. Compare your screen with **Figure 1**.

   The shape automatically centers as you adjust its width, and the font size increases to fill the larger area.

2. Click the **Golf Supervisor** shape to select it. On the **Design** tab, in the **Create Graphic** group, click the **Layout** button, and then click **Standard**. Compare your screen with **Figure 2**.

   The standard layout displays assistants in a horizontal line. Here, the standard layout emphasizes that the three Golf Supervisor assistants are on the same level within the organization's hierarchy.

■ **Continue to the next page to complete the skill**

Shape moved and sized

Figure 1

Standard layout applied

Figure 2

Figure 3

Figure 4

3. Click the **Golf Pro** shape to select it. In the **Create Graphic** group, click the **Add Shape** button arrow. In the list, click **Add Assistant**. With the new shape selected, type Pro Shop Manager Compare your screen with **Figure 3**.

> In this manner, you can add shapes without using the Text pane.

4. Select the **Golf Pro** shape, and then repeat the technique just practiced to add an assistant shape with the text Instructors

5. In the **Create Graphic** group, click the **Right to Left** button to reverse the shape order from left to right. Click the **Right to Left** button to toggle back to the original order.

6. Select the **Concessions Manager** shape, and then in the **Create Graphic** group, click the **Promote** button to promote the assistant shape to a higher level.

7. In the **Concessions Manager** shape, select the word *Manager*, and then type Supervisor Compare your screen with **Figure 4**.

8. **Save** 🖫 the workbook.

■ **You have completed Skill 7 of 10**

Assistant shape added

Assistant shape promoted and text edited

► You can change the style and color of an entire SmartArt graphic or an individual shape.

► You can modify a shape by applying Shape styles, and you can modify the shape's text by applying WordArt styles.

1. In the SmartArt graphic, triple-click the text *Park Operations Manager* to select the shape's text. On the **Format** tab, in the **WordArt Styles** group, click the first thumbnail—**Fill - Tan, Text 2, Outline - Background 2**. Click cell **L1**, and compare your screen with **Figure 1**.

   When a single shape is selected, the changes are applied only to the selected shape.

2. Click the **Grounds Supervisor** shape— not the text—to select it. Press and hold Ctrl, and then click just above the text *Building Supervisor*. Continue in this manner to add the **Golf Supervisor** and **Concessions Supervisor** shapes to the selection.

3. With the four shapes selected, on the **Format** tab, in the **Shape Styles** group, click the **Shape Fill** button. Under **Theme Colors**, click the last color in the second row—**Rose, Accent 6, Darker 10%**.

   The *Shape fill* is the background color of a shape.

4. Using the technique just practiced, select the text boxes—not the entire shape—in the four supervisor shapes, and then in the **WordArt Styles** group, click **Text Effects**. Point to **Glow**, and then under **Glow Variations**, click the last thumbnail in the last row. Compare your screen with **Figure 2**.

■ **Continue to the next page to complete the skill** ▶

WordArt style modified

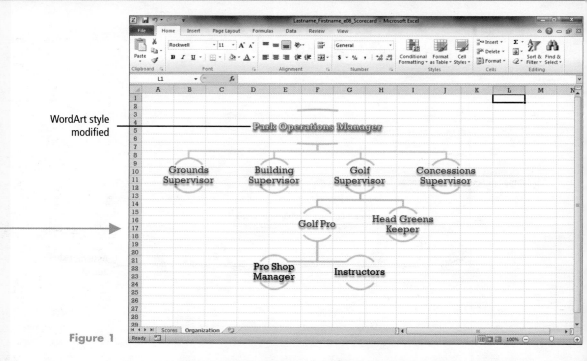

Figure 1

Supervisor shapes modified

Figure 2

Assistant shapes modified

Figure 3

Font sizes changed

Figure 4

5. Repeat the technique just practiced to select the following text boxes: **Golf Pro**, **Head Greens Keeper**, **Pro Shop Manager**, and **Instructors**. With the four shapes selected, in the **WordArt Styles** group, click the **Text Fill** button, and then under **Theme Colors**, click the fourth color in the first row—**Olive Green, Text 2**.

6. With the four shapes still selected, from the **WordArt Styles** group, click the **Text Effects** button. In the gallery, point to **Bevel**, and then under **Bevel**, click the first shape—**Circle**. Compare your screen with **Figure 3**.

7. Select the text in the **Park Operations Manager** text box. On the **Home** tab, in the **Font** group, click the **Font Size** arrow, and then click **28**.

8. Select the **Grounds Supervisor**, **Building Supervisor**, **Golf Supervisor**, and **Concessions Supervisor** text boxes, and change the **Font Size** to **16** points.

9. Repeat the techniques just practiced to change the font size of the four shapes in the bottom two rows of the hierarchy to **14** points. Compare your screen with **Figure 4**.

10. Select cell **L1**, and then **Save** ⊟ the workbook.

■ **You have completed Skill 8 of 10**

► Shapes can be used to call attention to important parts of a worksheet.

► You can add text to most shapes or place a text box over the shapes as a way of adding comments to a worksheet.

1. Display the **Scores** worksheet, and then display the **Insert** tab. In the **Illustrations** group, click the **Shapes** button, and then compare your screen with **Figure 1.**

> The Shapes gallery displays the available shapes organized by type. The Recently Used Shapes section displays the shapes that have been recently used.

2. In the **Shapes** gallery, under **Callouts**, click the third shape—**Oval Callout**. With the ⊞ pointer, drag from cell **E17** down and to the right to cell **H26**, and then release the mouse button.

3. Click in cell **A16** to deselect the callout shape. You should have a callout shape that is approximately 2 inches tall and 2 inches wide, as shown in **Figure 2.**

> The oval callout is formatted with the colors, fonts, and effects of the current theme—Foundry.

4. Select the shape just inserted, and then on the **Format** tab, in the **Insert Shapes** group, click the **Text Box** button.

> A **text box** is a rectangular object that is placed on a worksheet; it can contain text that is typed by the user.

■ **Continue to the next page to complete the skill**

Recently Used Shapes (your list may vary)

Shapes gallery

Oval Callout shape

Figure 1

Callout shape inserted

Figure 2

Text box in front of callout shape

Figure 3

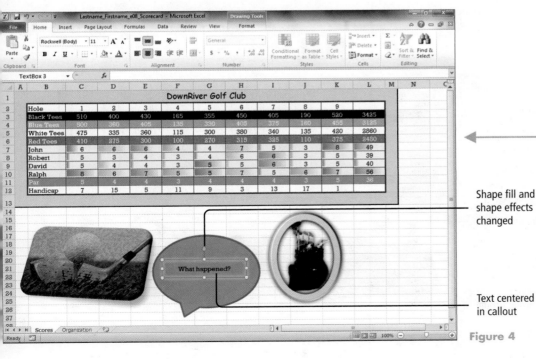

Shape fill and shape effects changed

Text centered in callout

Figure 4

5. Place the pointer in the callout shape approximately over cell **F18**, and then drag down and to the right. When pointer is over cell **H21**, release the mouse button. You should have a text box approximately 1 inch tall and 1.5 inches wide, as shown in **Figure 3**.

   The text box is placed in front of the callout shape. The text box can be formatted and moved independently of the callout shape.

6. With the insertion point in the text box, type What happened?

7. With the text box selected, on the **Format** tab, in the **Shape Styles** group, click **Shape Fill**. In the gallery, under **Standard Colors**, click **No Fill**.

   When no fill color is selected, the text box becomes transparent and the objects or cells behind the text box display.

8. In the **Shape Styles** group, click **Shape Effects**. In the gallery, point to **Glow**, and then under **Glow Variations**, click the second thumbnail in the second row—**Light Green, 8 pt glow, Accent color 2**.

9. Display the **Home** tab, and then in the **Alignment** group, click the **Middle Align** button, and then click the **Center** button.

10. Using **Figure 4** as your guide, point to the text box border, and then position the text box as shown. If necessary, use the resize handles to adjust the size of the text box so that the text is on one line.

11. **Save** the workbook.

   ■ **You have completed Skill 9 of 10**

▶ Shapes are resized and formatted using the same techniques that are used to resize and format other graphics, such as pictures and clip art.

▶ Callout shapes have pointers that can be moved so that they point to the data you want to call attention to.

1. If necessary, select the text box with the text *What happened?* by clicking the border of the text box. Press and hold Ctrl while clicking the Oval Callout shape. With both objects selected, on the **Format** tab, in the **Arrange** group, click the **Group** button, and then click **Group**.

> To *group* is to merge separate objects into one object that can be resized as a single object.

2. Point to the selected shape's lower-middle sizing handle, and then with the ⬍ pointer, drag upward until the sizing handle is in cell **G22**. Release the mouse button, and then compare your screen with **Figure 1**.

> When shapes are grouped, all the shapes are resized as a single object.

3. With the grouped shape selected, click one time inside the Oval Callout shape, and then take a moment to familiarize yourself with the selection handles described in **Figure 2**.

> Individual objects within a group can be selected. Here, the grouped object is selected, as indicated by the dotted border with sizing handles. The Oval Callout shape is also selected, as indicated by the solid border and sizing handles. The yellow diamond is the sizing handle for the callout pointer.

■ **Continue to the next page to complete the skill** ▶

Figure 1

Figure 2

Callout pointer moved

Shape style applied

Figure 3

Text box shape changed and resized

Figure 4

4. Point to the callout pointer selection handle—the yellow diamond—and then with the pointer, drag upward until the sizing handle is pointing to the value in cell **C10**, and then release the mouse button.

5. On the **Format** tab, in the **Shape Styles** group, click the **More** ⊡ button to display the **Shape Styles** gallery. Click the sixth effect in the fourth row—**Subtle Effect - Tan, Accent 5**. Compare your screen with **Figure 3**.

6. Click the text box to select it, and then display the **Format** tab. In the **Insert Shapes** group, click the **Edit Shape** button ⌁. Point to **Change Shape**, and in the gallery, under **Basic Shapes**, click the first shape in the first row—**Oval**.

    Rectangular text box shapes can be changed to any shape in the Shapes gallery.

7. Using the sizing handles on the text box, increase the size of the text box to accommodate the text, as shown in **Figure 4**.

8. Select cell **A1**, **Save** 🖬 the workbook, and then print or submit the file as directed by your instructor.

Done! You have completed Skill 10 of 10 and your worksheets are complete!

The following More Skills are located at **www.pearsonhighered.com/skills**

More Skills Add Alternate Text to Graphics

When you create a workbook that includes images, you might need to add alternate text so that users who are using a screen reader will be provided with a description of the image.

In More Skills 11, you will add a title and a description to the Aspen Falls logo. To begin, open your web browser, navigate to www.pearsonhighered.com/skills, locate the name of your textbook, and then follow the instructions on the website.

More Skills Add Graphics to SmartArt Shapes

Several SmartArt layouts are designed to use images and text. These layouts have shapes in which you insert pictures from files and corresponding shapes in which you type your text.

In More Skills 12, you will open a workbook and create a SmartArt graphic that contains images. To begin, open your web browser, navigate to www.pearsonhighered.com/skills, locate the name of your textbook, and then follow the instructions on the website.

More Skills Convert Graphics to SmartArt Shapes and Use the Selection and Visibility Pane

Any graphic can be converted to a SmartArt image, allowing you to customize your SmartArt. An image converted to a SmartArt graphic may have a number of components. The Selection Pane allows you to separate the parts so that they are easier to manipulate.

In More Skills 13, you will convert a graphic to a SmartArt shape and use the Selection and Visibility pane to hide parts of the image. To begin, open your web browser, navigate to www.pearsonhighered.com/skills, locate the name of your textbook, and then follow the instructions on the website.

More Skills Insert PowerPoint Slides into Worksheets

When you need to reference a slide in a PowerPoint presentation, you can add the slide into a worksheet. You can insert and display one slide or multiple slides from a PowerPoint presentation directly into a workbook.

In More Skills 14, you will insert a PowerPoint slide into a worksheet. To begin, open your web browser, navigate to www.pearsonhighered.com/skills, locate the name of your textbook, and then follow the instructions on the website.

Key Terms

Online Help Skills

1. **Start** ⊕ Excel. In the upper right corner of the Excel window, click the **Help** button ◉. In the **Help** window, click the **Maximize** ▭ button.

2. Click in the search box, type graphics and then click the **Search** button 🔎. In the search results, click **Learn more about SmartArt graphics**.

3. Read the article's introduction, and then below **In this article**, click **What to consider when choosing a layout**. Compare your screen with Figure 1.

Figure 1

4. Read the section to see if you can answer the following: What are three factors that you should consider when choosing a SmartArt graphic's layout? What can you do to improve the appearance of a SmartArt graphic?

Matching

Match each term in the second column with its correct definition in the first column by writing the letter of the term on the blank line in front of the correct definition.

____ **1.** The ratio of the width and height of an image expressed as its width divided by its height.

____ **2.** The amount of difference between light and dark areas in a graphic.

____ **3.** The number of dots per square inch.

____ **4.** To reduce the size of a file by changing the way the images are stored.

____ **5.** Images that are included with Microsoft Office or obtained from other sources that can be inserted into workbooks.

____ **6.** A range of shades of brown.

____ **7.** A visual representation of information that you can use to communicate a message or an idea.

____ **8.** A prebuilt set of formatting options.

____ **9.** In a SmartArt graphic, the pane in which shapes can be inserted and deleted.

____ **10.** To merge separate objects into one object that can be resized as a single object.

A Aspect

B Clip art

C Compress

D Contrast

E Group

F Quick Style

G Resolution

H Sepia

I SmartArt

J Text

Multiple Choice

Choose the correct answer.

1. This is a placeholder in a header that contains an image.
   - A. &[File]
   - B. &[Picture]
   - C. &[Time]

2. This term describes changes that can be applied to images to make them more visually appealing.
   - A. Artistic Effects
   - B. Cropping
   - C. Compressing

3. To apply a 3-D bevel effect to a picture, click this button.
   - A. Artistic Effects
   - B. Fill Effects
   - C. Picture Effects

4. This term refers to a range of gray tones in an image.
   - A. Grayscale
   - B. Gradients
   - C. Hues

5. To change the background color of the shape, click this button.
   - A. Base color
   - B. Shape fill
   - C. Shading

6. This type of tab appears only when needed.
   - A. Design tabs
   - B. Formatting tabs
   - C. Contextual tabs

7. This kind of chart shows relationships in an organization hierarchically.
   - A. Organizational chart
   - B. Hierarchical chart
   - C. Relational chart

8. These are the different shapes and structures provided as built-in SmartArt graphics.
   - A. Views
   - B. Designs
   - C. Layouts

9. This term refers to a rectangular object that is placed on a worksheet that can contain text that is added by the user.
   - A. Text box
   - B. Shape holder
   - C. Image box

10. Shapes can be formatted using the same techniques used to format these.
    - A. Other graphics
    - B. Text
    - C. Charts

Topics for Discussion

1. You have seen a workbook in which clip art has been inserted. Discuss situations in which this technique enhances the worksheet's message and situations in which this technique detracts from the worksheet's message.

2. Use the Choose a SmartArt Graphic dialog box to explore the various types of layouts. Which layouts do you think would best complement the types of information typically found in an Excel worksheet? Why?

Skill Check

To complete this workbook, you will need the following files:

- e08_Portfolio
- e08_Portfolio_Bank
- e08_Portfolio_Skyline

You will save your file as:

- Lastname_Firstname_e08_Portfolio

1. **Start** Excel, and then open the student data file **e08_Portfolio**. **Save** the file in your **Excel Chapter 8** folder with the name Lastname_Firstname_e08_Portfolio Add the file name in the left footer of both worksheets.

2. With the **Bonds** worksheet active, display the **Insert** tab. In the **Text** group, click **Header & Footer**, and then click the left section of the Header. In the **Header & Footer Elements** group, click **Picture**. Navigate to your student data files, select **e08_Portfolio_Skyline**, and then click **Insert**.

3. On the **Design** tab, click **Format Picture**. Display the **Picture** tab, and then under **Crop from**, change the **Left** value to .25 and the **Right** value to .25 Change the **Top** and **Bottom** values to .25 **Under Image Control**, drag the **Brightness** slider to *40%*, and then drag the **Contrast** slider to *25%*.

4. Click **Compress**, and then click **OK**. Click **Apply**, and then click **OK**. Click cell **A2**, and then compare your screen with **Figure 1**.

5. Switch to **Normal** view. Select cell **B14**, and then on the **Insert** tab, click **Clip Art**. Verify that the Include Office.com content check box is selected, and then in the **Search for** box, type atm Under **Results should be**, verify that only **Photographs** is selected. Click **Go**. Locate an image of a hand inserting a card into an ATM machine, and click to insert the image. If that image is not available, insert the file **e08_Portfolio_Bank** from your student data files.

6. In the **Size** group, change the **Height** box value to 1.0 and press Enter. Close the **Clip Art** task pane.

7. With the image selected, on the **Format** tab, click **Remove Background**. Use the sizing handles to adjust the area so that the hand and debit card are included but nothing else, and then on the **Background Removal** tab, click **Keep Changes**. Compare your screen with **Figure 2**.

Figure 1

Figure 2

■ Continue to the next page to complete this Skill Check ▷

8. In the **Adjust** group, click **Color**, and then under **Recolor**, click the fourth color in the second row—**Aqua, Accent color 3 Dark**. Click **Artistic Effects**, and then click the second option in the fourth row—**Texturizer**. Click **Corrections**, and then under **Brightness and Contrast**, click the fifth selection in the first row—**Brightness: +40% Contrast: −40%**.

9. Display the **Organization** worksheet. On the **Insert** tab, in the **Illustrations** group, click **SmartArt**. Click **Hierarchy**, and then click the first layout in the first row—**Organization Chart**. Click **OK**. Return to **Normal** view.

10. Display the **Text Pane**, if necessary. In the first bullet, type President Press Delete two times to delete the next two bullets. In the second bullet, type VP Operations In the third bullet, type VP Administration **Close** the Text pane.

11. Select the **SmartArt** object. On the **Design** tab, in the **SmartArt Styles** group, click the **More** button. Under **3-D**, click the third style—**Cartoon**.

12. Select all three shapes in the SmartArt graphic. On the **Format** tab, in the **Shape Styles** group, click **More**, and then click the second shape in the sixth row—**Intense Effect – Tan, Accent 1**. Click **Shape Effects**, point to **Preset**, and then under **Presets**, click the third shape in the second row—**Preset 7**.

13. Select the **SmartArt** object, and then on the **Format** tab, click the Size button. In the **Height** box, type 2.5 In the **Width** box, type 6.5 Drag the **SmartArt Graphic** so that the upper left corner is in cell **B2**.

14. Select the *VP Administration* shape. Drag the right-middle sizing handle to the middle of **Column J**.

15. Select all of the shapes in the graphic, and then on the **Design** tab, in the **SmartArt Styles** group, click **Change Colors**. Under **Accent 3**, click the first thumbnail—**Colored Outline - Accent 3**.

16. On the **Format** tab, in the **WordArt Styles** group, click the **More** button, and then click the fifth color in the fourth row—**Gradient Fill – Blue, Accent 4, Reflection**. Compare your screen with **Figure 3**.

17. Display the **Bonds** worksheet. On the **Insert** tab, click **Shapes**, and then under **Block Arrows**, click the second shape in the first row—**Left Arrow**. Drag from cell **D6** to cell **F9** to insert the shape.

18. On the **Format** tab, click **Text Box**. Drag from cell **E8** to cell **F9**. In the text box, type Too High Click **Shape Fill**, and then under **Standard Colors**, click **No Fill**. Select the arrow shape, press and hold Ctrl, and then click the text box. On the **Format** tab, in the **Arrange** group, click the **Group** button, and then click **Group**. Compare your screen with **Figure 4**.

19. **Save** the workbook, and then print or submit as directed.

Done! You have completed the Skill Check

Figure 3

Figure 4

Assess Your Skills 1

To complete this workbook, you will need the following files:

- e08_Fuel
- e08_Fuel_City

You will save your file as:

- Lastname_Firstname_e08_Fuel

---

1. **Start** Excel, and then open the student data file **e08_Fuel**. Save the file in your **Excel Chapter 8** folder with the name Lastname_Firstname_e08_Fuel Add the file name in the worksheet's left footer. Insert the image file **e08_Fuel_City** in the left section of the header.

2. Resize the header image to a width of *1.5* and a height of *1.5*. Crop 1 inch from both the left and right edges of the picture, and then set the **Brightness** to *40%* and the **Contrast** to *25%*.

3. Compress the picture with the options to delete the cropped areas and the resolution set to **Web/Screen**.

4. Switch to **Normal** view. Use the **Clip Art** task pane to search for photographs related to fuel Locate and select an image of a gas nozzle going into the filler on the car, and then insert it into the worksheet. If that image is not available, insert the file **e08_Fuel_Filler** from the student data disk. Resize the photograph so that the height is *1.0*. Move the picture so that the upper left corner is in cell **G13**. Close the Clip Art task pane.

5. Remove the background so that only the nozzle remains. Change the color of the photograph using the third color in the second row of the **Recolor** gallery—**Red, Accent color 2 Dark**. Apply the **Pencil Sketch** Artistic Effect.

6. Insert a **Rounded Rectangular Callout** shape—the second shape in the first row under callouts—in the range **C18:G21**. Move the callout pointer so that it points to cell **C16**. Change the fill color of the callout to **Blue, Accent 1, Lighter 40%**, and then apply the **Preset 2** shape effect.

7. Insert a text box in front of the callout in the range **C19:F21**. Add the text Too High! and then change the fill of the text box to **No Fill**. Apply the **Red, Accent 2, Darker 25%** shape outline to the text box.

8. **Center** and **Middle** align the text in the text box, and then apply the **Red, Accent 2, Darker 25%** font color. Click cell **A20**, and then compare your screen with **Figure 1**.

9. **Save** the workbook, and then print or submit the file as directed by your instructor.

Done! You have completed Assess Your Skills 1

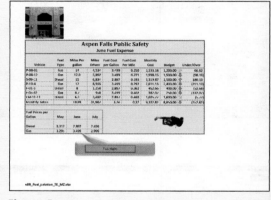

Figure 1

Assess Your Skills 2

To complete this workbook, you will need the following file:

- New blank Excel workbook

You will save your file as:

- Lastname_Firstname_e08_Structure

Figure 1

1. **Start** Excel, and then create a new blank Excel workbook. **Save** the file in your **Excel Chapter 8** folder with the name Lastname_Firstname_e08_Structure Delete **Sheet2** and **Sheet3**, and then rename **Sheet1** Management Add the file name in the worksheet's left footer, and then set the page orientation to **Landscape**.

2. Insert the **Hierarchy Organization Chart** SmartArt shape. In the first shape, type City Manager Add the following subordinates to *City Manager:* Assistant City Manager and Public Information Specialist and Human Resources Below *Human Resources*, add the following assistants: Human Resources Director and Benefits Specialist and Risk Management Add or delete shapes as needed. **Close** the Text pane.

3. Set the SmartArt height to *4* inches and the width to *5* inches. Move the **SmartArt Graphic** so that the upper left corner is in cell **B2**. Apply the **Intense Effect** SmartArt style, and then change the SmartArt colors to **Colorful – Accent Colors**.

4. Select the SmartArt graphic, and then apply the **Fill - Red, Accent 2, Matte Bevel** WordArt style to all text in the shape.

5. In the range **I12:L16**, insert a **Left Arrow** shape. In the range **J14:L16**, insert a text box in front of the left arrow shape. In the text box, type Should this be under HR? Set the fill for the text box to **No Fill**. Expand the left arrow shape and the text box so that all of the text fits on a single line. **Group** the left arrow shape and the text box. For the text box, apply the **No Outline** shape outline and the **Yellow** font color. Center the text in the text box, and then align it to the middle.

6. Search **Clip Art** using the search term city Locate and insert the photograph of a city skyline. If that image is not available, insert the file **e08_Structure_Building** from the student data disk. On the Format Picture dialog box, unselect the Lock aspect ratio check box, and then resize the image to 2 inches by 2 inches, and position the upper left corner in cell **H2**. Change the image color to **Sepia**. Compress the image using the **Screen** Target output option. Apply the **Beveled Oval, Black** effect picture style to the picture.

7. Compare your screen with **Figure 1**. **Save** the workbook, and then print or submit the file as directed by your instructor.

Done! You have completed Assess Your Skills 2

Assess Your Skills Visually

To complete this workbook, you will need the following files:

- New blank Excel workbook
- e08_Aspen_Logo

You will save your file as:

- Lastname_Firstname_e08_Aspen

Start Excel, and create a new blank workbook. Save the file in your **Excel Chapter 8** folder with the name Lastname_Firstname_e08_Aspen Add the file name in the left footer. Set the page orientation to **Landscape.** Create the worksheet shown in **Figure 1**. The header graphic file is **e08_Aspen_Logo** and has been resized to 1 inch by 1 inch. Create the **Name and Title Organization Chart** SmartArt as shown. The SmartArt style is **Inset**. The color is **Colorful Range – Accent Colors 3 to 4**. The SmartArt graphic is sized 4 inches high by 6 inches wide. The font size for *Mayor* and *City Manager* is 24 points. The font size for the other titles is 12 points. The font size for all of the names is 10 points. Insert the **Left Arrow** shape, and then place a text box in front of the arrow as shown. The text in the text box is Add Photo and has its fill color removed. The arrow uses the **Colored Fill – Blue, Accent 1** shape style.

Save the workbook, and then print or submit the file as directed by your instructor.

Done! You have completed Assess Your Skills Visually

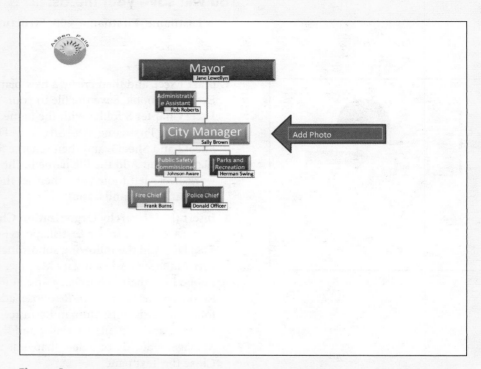

Figure 1

Skills in Context

To complete this workbook, you will need the following file:

- e08_Org_Chart

You will save your file as:

- **Lastname_Firstname_e08_Org_Chart**

Start Excel, and open the student data file **e08_Org_Chart**. Save the file in your **Excel Chapter 8** folder with the name Lastname_Firstname_e08_Org_Chart Add the file name to the left section of the footer. Using the data on the **Organization** worksheet, create an organizational chart using a SmartArt graphic. Each shape is indicated by one line of text in the data, and the level in the hierarchy is indicated by the indent level of each line. When the SmartArt is completed, delete the original text, and then position and size the SmartArt to fill the screen without scrolling. Be sure the graphic prints on a single page. Format the SmartArt as appropriate using the techniques practiced in this chapter. Print or submit the file as directed by your instructor.

Done! You have completed Skills in Context

Skills and You

To complete this workbook, you will need the following file:

- **New blank Excel workbook**

You will save your file as:

- **Lastname_Firstname_e08_Family_Tree**

Using the skills you have practiced in this chapter, create a SmartArt graphic that includes at least three generations of your family tree. Position and size the SmartArt to fill the screen without scrolling. Format the SmartArt as appropriate using the techniques practiced in this chapter. Print or submit the file as directed by your instructor.

Done! You have completed Skills and You

Import Data, Create PivotTable Reports and PivotChart Reports

▶ PivotTable reports are used to dynamically summarize and analyze large amounts of data.

▶ PivotTable report data can be graphically summarized using PivotChart reports.

Your starting screen will look similar to this:

SKILLS

Skills 1-10 Training

At the end of this chapter, you will be able to:

Outcome

Using the skills listed to the left will enable you to create worksheets like these:

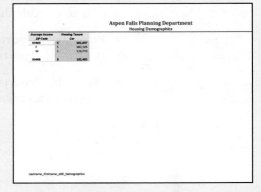

You will save your files as:

Lastname_Firstname_e09_Demographics
Lastname_Firstname_e09_Slicer

In this chapter, you will create workbooks for the Aspen Falls City Hall, which provides essential services for the citizens and visitors of Aspen Falls, California.

Introduction

- ▶ PivotTable reports allow you to summarize a large set of data in a table format.

- ▶ You can use PivotTable and PivotChart reports to place category data in both rows and columns to produce a variety of results in the value fields.

- ▶ PivotTable reports allow you to perform different types of calculations on the data to provide different types of results in the value fields.

- ▶ PivotChart reports graphically display the results that are calculated in PivotTable reports.

- ▶ PivotTable reports and PivotChart reports can be filtered to show only the data that meets criteria you specify.

**Time to complete all
10 skills – 50 to 75 minutes**

Find your data files here:

Files needed for this chapter:

- **New blank Excel workbook**
- **e09_Demographics**

► You can import data stored in an Access database into Excel worksheets.

► When data is imported from Access into Excel, it is displayed in an Excel table.

1. Start ⊕ **Access**, and then open **e09_Demographics**. If the **Security Warning** bar displays, click **Enable Content**. In the Navigation Pane, double-click **Data: Table** to open the table. Compare your screen with **Figure 1**.

   Access tables organize data into rows and columns where each row is a *record*— a collection of related information that displays in a single row of a database table. In this Access table, the *ID* column stores a number that uniquely identifies each record.

2. Exit **Access**. If prompted to save the table design changes, click No.

3. Start ⊕ Excel to create a new blank workbook. Click the **File** tab, and then click **Save As**. In the **Save As** dialog box, navigate to the location where you are saving your files. Click **New folder**, type Excel Chapter 9 and then press [Enter] two times. In the **File name** box, using your own name, name the file Lastname_Firstname_e09_Demographics and then click **Save**.

4. In cell **A1**, type Aspen Falls Planning Department and press [Enter]. Select the range **A1:I1**, and then click **Merge and Center** ⊞. Apply the **Title** cell style to the range.

5. Select cell **A2**, type Housing Demographics and press [Enter]. Select the range **A2:I2**, click **Merge and Center** ⊞, and then apply the **Heading 1** cell style to the range. Press [Enter] and compare your screen with **Figure 2**.

■ **Continue to the next page to complete the skill**

Navigation Pane
Unique identifiers

Table datasheet

Figure 1

Figure 2

Figure 3

Figure 4

6. Select cell **A4**, and then display the **Data** tab. In the **Get External Data** group, click the **From Access** button.

7. In the **Select Data Source** dialog box, navigate to the student data files for this chapter, select **e09_Demographics**, and then click **Open**.

8. In the **Import Data** dialog box, verify that the **Table** option button is selected. In the **Existing worksheet** box, verify that the value displayed is =$A$4. Compare your screen with **Figure 3**.

> The import process will place the data from the Access table into the workbook starting in cell A4.

9. Click **OK** to import the data.

> The Access data is imported as an Excel table with column labels in the range A4:I4.

10. Scroll down and verify that rows **5** through **1004** contain data, and then press Ctrl + Home to return to cell **A1**.

> The table stores demographic data from a survey of 1000 Aspen Falls citizens.

11. Rename the **Sheet1** worksheet as Survey Data

12. Right-click the **Sheet2** worksheet tab, and then in the displayed shortcut menu, click **Delete**. Delete **Sheet3**, and then compare your screen with **Figure 4**.

13. **Save** the workbook.

- **You have completed Skill 1 of 10**

Table option

Data will be placed starting in cell A4

► A ***PivotTable report*** is an interactive way to summarize, explore, and analyze data.

► PivotTable reports group, filter, and sort large amounts of data so that you can quickly create different views of the same data.

1. Select cell **A5**. On the **Insert** tab, in the **Tables** group, click the **PivotTable** button arrow, and then click **PivotTable**. Compare your screen with **Figure 1**.

   The Table/Range value is *Table_e09_ Demographics.accdb*—the named range assigned to the data imported from the Access database. A PivotTable report can be placed in a new worksheet or in an existing worksheet. By default, the New Worksheet option is selected.

2. In the **Create PivotTable** dialog box, click **OK** to create a new worksheet with a PivotTable report and to display the PivotTable Field List task pane.

3. Display the **Survey Data** worksheet, select the range **A1:A2**, and then on the **Home** tab, click the **Copy** button. Display the **Sheet4** worksheet, select cell **A1**, and then click the **Paste** button. Rename the **Sheet4** worksheet tab to Survey PivotTable

4. Click cell **A3** to display the PivotTable Field List. On the **Options** tab, in the **PivotTable** group, change the value in the box under **PivotTable Name** to Survey Press Enter, and then compare your screen with **Figure 2**.

■ **Continue to the next page to complete the skill**

Create PivotTable dialog box

Named range assigned to imported data

New Worksheet selected

Figure 1

PivotTable Name

PivotTable Field List task pane

Survey PivotTable worksheet

Figure 2

Figure 3

Figure 4

ZIP Code field

Housing Tenure field

Column Labels box

Values box

5. In the **PivotTable Field List** task pane, under **Choose fields to add to report**, select the **ZIP Code** and **Housing Tenure** check boxes, and then compare your screen with Figure 3.

In a data table, *fields*—categories of data—are organized into columns. In a PivotTable report, fields can be organized in either rows or columns. *Row labels* are the fields used to categorize the data by rows. In this PivotTable report, the *ZIP Code* field displays in rows and will group the data in the PivotTable report.

6. In the **PivotTable Field List**, under **Choose fields to add to report**, select the **ID** check box.

The *Sum of ID* values are *PivotTable values*—the fields for which summary statistics are calculated.

7. In the **Drag fields between areas below** section, in the **Row Labels** box, point to **Housing Tenure**, and then with the pointer, drag the field into the **Column Labels** box.

8. In the **Values** box, select **Sum of ID**, and then on the **Options** tab, in the **Active Field** group, click **Field Settings**. In the **Value Field Settings** dialog box, under **Summarize value field by**, click **Count**, and then click **OK**.

9. Select cell **A4**, replace the existing text with ZIP Code and then press Enter. Select cell **B3**, replace the existing text with Housing Tenure and then press Enter. Compare your screen with Figure 4.

10. Save the workbook.

■ **You have completed Skill 2 of 10**

▶ You can quickly change how the data is presented in PivotTable reports.

▶ The PivotTable Field List is used to change fields from rows to columns, to add or remove fields, and to change the fields used to calculate values.

1. In the **Survey PivotTable** worksheet, click cell **A5**.

   Selecting a cell in a PivotTable report displays the PivotTable Field List. Alternately, you can click the Field List button in the Show group of the Options tab.

2. In the **PivotTable Field List** task pane, under **Choose fields to add to report**, select the **Gender** check box, and then compare your screen with **Figure 1**.

   The Gender field is added to the Row Labels section of the PivotTable Field List. The values section displays the number of households within each ZIP Code, grouped by gender.

3. In the **PivotTable Field List**, drag **Gender** from the **Row Labels** box to the **Column Labels** box. Compare your screen with **Figure 2**.

   The PivotTable report has been changed so that the number of households headed by each gender is displayed in a separate column for each housing tenure.

■ **Continue to the next page to complete the skill**

Gender added

Figure 1

Gender moved to Column Labels box

Figure 2

Commute added
to Row Labels

Figure 3

Walkers in
93464

Bus riders in
93468

Figure 4

4. In the **PivotTable Field List** task pane, under **Choose fields to add to report**, drag the **Commute** field into the **Row Labels** box, and then compare your screen with **Figure 3**.

   Within each ZIP Code and Housing Tenure, the PivotTable displays how many individuals own their homes and how many rent their homes, how many households are headed by males and how many are headed by females, and how each household commutes to work. In this manner, PivotTable reports can change how the data is summarized.

5. In the **PivotTable Field List** task pane, under **Drag fields between areas below**, drag the **Gender** field from the **Column Labels** box to the **Row Labels** box. Notice the changes to the PivotTable.

6. Drag the **Commute** field from the **Row Labels** box to the **Column Labels** box. Notice the changes to the PivotTable.

7. In the **Column Labels** box, click the **Housing Tenure** arrow, and then from the displayed list, click **Remove Field**. Compare your screen with **Figure 4**.

   This pivot shows the way that each household commutes to work from each ZIP Code area. The pivot also shows the total males and females that are designated as the heads of households within each ZIP Code.

8. **Save** 🖫 the workbook.

■ **You have completed Skill 3 of 10**

► By default, PivotTable reports summarize fields by calculating a total for each group. Other summary statistics, including count, average, minimum, or maximum, can also be calculated.

► PivotTable reports are formatted by applying PivotTable styles.

1. In the **PivotTable Field List** task pane, under **Choose fields to add to report**, select the **Household Income** check box. Select cell **C5**, and then on the **Options** tab, in the **Active Field** group, click **Field Settings**. Compare your screen with **Figure 1**.

2. In the **Value Field Settings** dialog box, under **Summarize value field by**, click **Average**.

3. Click the **Number Format** button. In the **Format Cells** dialog box, under **Category**, click **Accounting**. In the **Decimal places** box, change the value to **0**, and then click **OK**.

4. In the **Value Field Settings** dialog box, in the **Custom Name** box, type Average Income Compare your screen with **Figure 2**, and then click **OK**.

   In this manner, you can customize values fields to calculate different summary statistics and display different number formats.

5. In the **PivotTable Field List**, under **Drag fields between areas below** in the **Values** box, click the **Count of ID** arrow, and then click **Remove Field**.

■ **Continue to the next page to complete the skill**

Field Settings button

Value Field Settings dialog box

Figure 1

Average Income custom name

Average selected

Number Format button

Figure 2

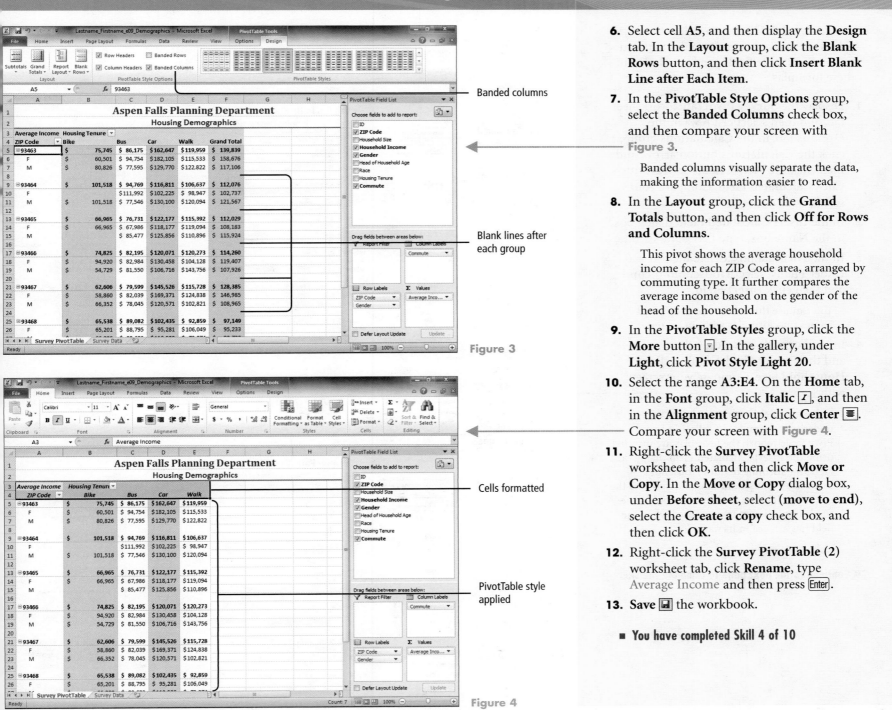

Banded columns

Blank lines after each group

Figure 3

Cells formatted

PivotTable style applied

Figure 4

6. Select cell **A5**, and then display the **Design** tab. In the **Layout** group, click the **Blank Rows** button, and then click **Insert Blank Line after Each Item**.

7. In the **PivotTable Style Options** group, select the **Banded Columns** check box, and then compare your screen with **Figure 3**.

Banded columns visually separate the data, making the information easier to read.

8. In the **Layout** group, click the **Grand Totals** button, and then click **Off for Rows and Columns**.

This pivot shows the average household income for each ZIP Code area, arranged by commuting type. It further compares the average income based on the gender of the head of the household.

9. In the **PivotTable Styles** group, click the **More** button ⊡. In the gallery, under **Light**, click **Pivot Style Light 20**.

10. Select the range **A3:E4**. On the **Home** tab, in the **Font** group, click **Italic** ⓘ, and then in the **Alignment** group, click **Center** ⓔ. Compare your screen with **Figure 4**.

11. Right-click the **Survey PivotTable** worksheet tab, and then click **Move or Copy**. In the **Move or Copy** dialog box, under **Before sheet**, select (**move to end**), select the **Create a copy** check box, and then click **OK**.

12. Right-click the **Survey PivotTable (2)** worksheet tab, click **Rename**, type Average Income and then press ⏎.

13. **Save** 🖫 the workbook.

■ **You have completed Skill 4 of 10**

► A *calculated field* is a data field whose values are derived from formulas that you create. PivotTable fields can be included in these formulas.

1. Display the **Survey PivotTable** worksheet tab, and then select cell **A5**. On the **Options** tab, in the **Calculations** group, click the **Calculations** button arrow, and then click the **Fields, Items & Sets** button. Click **Calculated Field**. Compare your screen with **Figure 1**.

2. In the **Insert Calculated Field** dialog box, in the **Name** box, type PerCapita Income

3. In the **Formula** box, delete the text *= 0*. Under **Fields**, select **Household Income**, and then click **Insert Field**.

   You can use this method to insert field names into formulas without typing.

4. In the **Formula** box, add a slash (/), and then under **Fields**, double-click **Household Size**. Compare your screen with **Figure 2**.

   Calculated fields work much like the underlying formulas in cells, but in a PivotTable report, the formulas are inserted using the Insert Calculated Field dialog box. Here, the formula divides Household Income by Household Size to determine the per capita income of each household. The single quotation marks are used when the field has a space in its name.

■ **Continue to the next page to complete the skill**

Insert Calculated Field dialog box

Figure 1

Calculated field name

Formula inserted

Figure 2

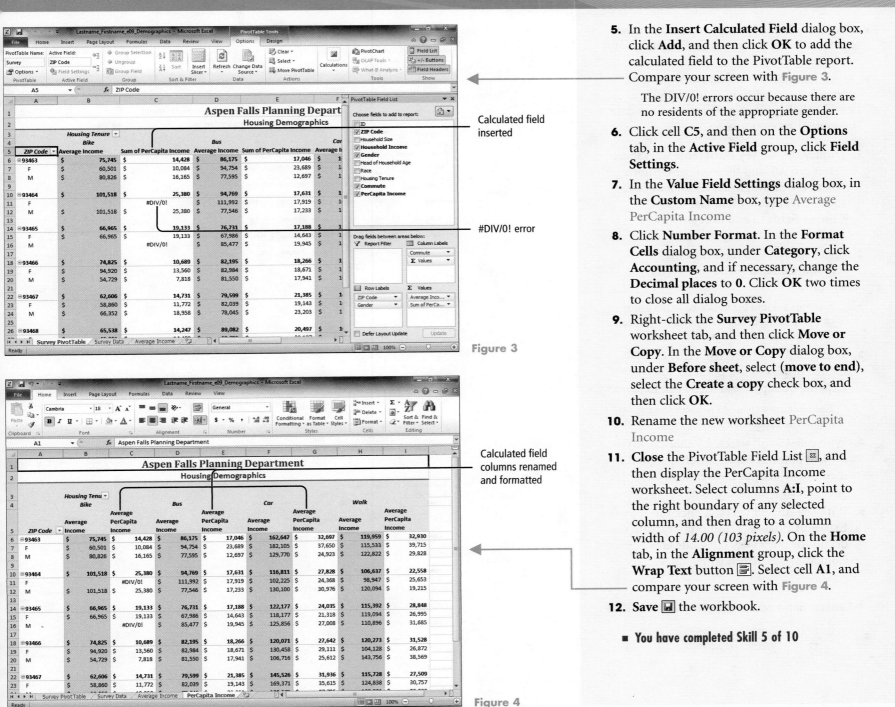

Calculated field inserted

#DIV/0! error

Figure 3

Calculated field columns renamed and formatted

Figure 4

5. In the **Insert Calculated Field** dialog box, click **Add**, and then click **OK** to add the calculated field to the PivotTable report. Compare your screen with **Figure 3**.

> The DIV/0! errors occur because there are no residents of the appropriate gender.

6. Click cell **C5**, and then on the **Options** tab, in the **Active Field** group, click **Field Settings**.

7. In the **Value Field Settings** dialog box, in the **Custom Name** box, type Average PerCapita Income

8. Click **Number Format**. In the **Format Cells** dialog box, under **Category**, click **Accounting**, and if necessary, change the **Decimal places** to **0**. Click **OK** two times to close all dialog boxes.

9. Right-click the **Survey PivotTable** worksheet tab, and then click **Move or Copy**. In the **Move or Copy** dialog box, under **Before sheet**, select (**move to end**), select the **Create a copy** check box, and then click **OK**.

10. Rename the new worksheet PerCapita Income

11. **Close** the PivotTable Field List ⊠, and then display the PerCapita Income worksheet. Select columns **A:I**, point to the right boundary of any selected column, and then drag to a column width of *14.00 (103 pixels)*. On the **Home** tab, in the **Alignment** group, click the **Wrap Text** button 📷. Select cell **A1**, and compare your screen with **Figure 4**.

12. **Save** 📘 the workbook.

■ **You have completed Skill 5 of 10**

► PivotTable Report groups can be collapsed or expanded to show or hide the details for each group.

► Recall that *filtering* displays only the data that satisfies conditions you specify. In a PivotTable Report, AutoFilter can filter data by rows or by columns.

1. Display the **Survey PivotTable** worksheet. Select cell **A5**, and then on the **Options** tab, in the **Show** group, click **Field List**. In the **PivotTable Field List**, under **Choose fields to add to report**, clear the **PerCapita Income** check box.

2. Select cell **A5**, and then click the **Expand/Collapse** ⊟ button to collapse the row.

   A minus symbol ⊟ indicates that a group can be collapsed. A plus ⊞ symbol indicates that a group can be expanded.

3. With cell **A5** still selected, right-click. On the displayed list, point to **Expand/Collapse**, and then click **Expand**.

   The rows are expanded to show the full details for the category.

4. With cell **A5** still selected, right-click. On the list, point to **Expand/Collapse**, and then click **Collapse Entire Field**. Compare your screen with **Figure 1**.

5. With cell **A5** still selected, click the **Expand/Collapse** ⊞ button to expand the details for the 93463 ZIP Code area. Compare your screen with **Figure 2**.

■ **Continue to the next page to complete the skill**

Expand/Collapse button

Figure 1

Expanded category

Collapsed category

Figure 2

Column filter to be applied

Figure 3

Rows filtered and expanded

Figure 4

6. Select cell **B3**, and then click the **Housing Tenure** filter arrow ⌄. In the AutoFilter list, clear the **Select All** check box, and then select the **Car** check box. Compare your screen with **Figure 3**, and then click **OK**.

   The filter displays only the column where the commuting method is by car.

7. Select cell **A4**, and then click the **ZIP Code** filter arrow ⌄. In the displayed AutoFilter list, clear the (**Select All**) check box, select the **93463** and **93468** check boxes, and then click **OK**. Compare your screen with **Figure 4**.

   The filter is applied to the PivotTable rows so that only the summary data for the selected ZIP Codes displays.

8. Right-click the **Survey PivotTable** worksheet tab, and then click **Move or Copy**. In the **Move or Copy** dialog box, under **Before sheet**, click (**move to end**). Select the **Create a copy** check box, and then click **OK**.

9. Rename the new worksheet Filtered Survey

10. Display the **Survey PivotTable** worksheet. Click the **ZIP Code** filter 🔽, select the (**Select All**) check box, and then click **OK**. Select the **Housing Tenure** filter, select the (**Select All**) check box, and then click **OK**

11. Select cell **A5**, and then right-click. On the displayed menu, point to **Expand/Collapse**, and then click **Expand Entire Field**.

12. Select cell **A1**, and then **Save** 💾 the workbook.

■ **You have completed Skill 6 of 10**

▶ *Slicer* is a tool that is used to filter data in PivotTable views.

▶ Slicers filter data based on distinct values in columns.

1. Select cell **A5**, display the **Options** tab, and then in the **Sort & Filter** group, click **Insert Slicer**.

2. In the **Insert Slicers** dialog box, select the **Commute** check box, and then select the **Race** check box. Click **OK**.

   Two slicers are created. One filters the data based on the race of the commuters; the other filters the data based on the method of commuting.

3. Select the **Race** slicer. Using the mouse, move the slicer so that the upper left corner is in cell **D3**. Move the **Commute** slicer so that the upper left corner is in cell **D18**. Compare your screen with **Figure 1**.

4. In the Race slicer, click **African American**.

   The data in the PivotTable Report is now filtered to show only the results when the commuter is African American.

5. In the **Commute** slicer, click **Walk**. Compare your screen with **Figure 2**.

   The data in the PivotTable report is filtered so that only the information that pertains to African American commuters who walk to work is displayed. Notice that each slicer has only a single blue bar, indicating the option that has been selected. The options in the slicer that are not selected are displayed with a white background.

■ **Continue to the next page to complete the skill** ▶

Race slicer

Commute slicer

Figure 1

Housing Tenure filtered by Race and Commute

Figure 2

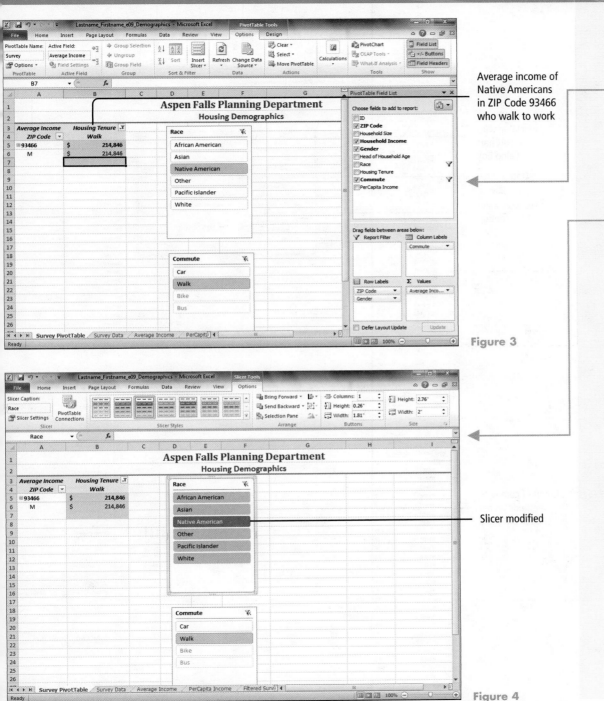

Average income of Native Americans in ZIP Code 93466 who walk to work

Figure 3

Slicer modified

Figure 4

6. In the **Race** slicer, click **Native American**. Notice that the PivotTable report changes to display only Native American commuters who walk to work. Compare your screen with **Figure 3**.

   The sliced PivotTable report shows that the only Native Americans who walk to work live in the 93466 ZIP Code.

7. Click the **Race** slicer. Display the **Options** tab, and then in the **Slicer Styles** group, click **More**, and then click **Slicer Style Dark 2**. Compare your screen with **Figure 4**.

8. With the **Survey PivotTable** worksheet tab displayed, click **Start**, click **All Programs**, and then open the **Accessories** folder. Click **Snipping Tool**, click the **New** button arrow, and then click **Full-screen Snip**. **Save** the snip in your **Excel Chapter 9** folder as Lastname_Firstname_e09_Slicer and then Close the **Snipping Tool** window.

9. In the **Race** slicer, click the **Filter** icon to remove the **Race** filter. Notice that the values in the cells change. In the **Commute** slicer, click the **Filter** icon to remove the filter.

10. Right-click in the title bar of the **Race** slicer, and then click **Remove Race**. Right-click in the title bar of the **Commute** slicer, and then click **Remove Commute**.

11. **Save** the workbook.

- **You have completed Skill 7 of 10**

► A *PivotChart report* is a dynamic visual representation of data. For example, you can assign any field to the value axis or category axis and then apply filters.

► The data source for a PivotChart can be an external file, such as a table in a database file.

1. Display the **Survey Data** worksheet tab, and then display the **Insert** tab. In the **Tables** group, click the **PivotTable** button arrow, and then click **PivotChart**.

2. In the **Create PivotTable with PivotChart** dialog box, select the **Use an external data source** option button. Click the **Choose Connection** button, and then in the **Existing Connections** dialog box, under **Connection Files on this Computer**, select **e09_Demographics Data**, and click **Open**.

3. In the **Create PivotTable with PivotChart** dialog box, verify that the **New Worksheet** option is selected. Compare your screen with **Figure 1**, and then click **OK**.

   A PivotTable with a PivotChart is created. When the PivotChart is selected, the PivotTable Field List displays the Legend Fields and Axis Fields boxes.

4. In the **PivotTable Field List**, under **Choose fields to add to report**, select the **ID**, **Commute**, and **ZIP Code** check boxes.

5. Click cell **B1**. On the **Options** tab, in the **Active Field** group, click **Field Settings**. In the **Value Field Settings** dialog box, click **Count**, and then click **OK**. Compare your screen with **Figure 2**.

■ Continue to the next page to complete the skill ➤

Create PivotTable with PivotChart dialog box

Data source

New Worksheet option

Figure 1

Count of commute methods within each ZIP Code

Figure 2

(All) check box cleared

Single commuting method selected

Select Multiple Items check box

Figure 3

6. Click the **PivotChart** report to select it. In the **PivotTable Field List**, under **Drag fields between areas below**, click **Commute**, and then drag it from the **Axis Fields** box into the **Report Filter** box.

7. Select cell **B1**, click the filter arrow ▼, and then in the **AutoFilter** list, select the **Select Multiple Items** check box. Clear the **(All)** check box, and then select the **Bus** check box. Compare your screen with **Figure 3**, and then click **OK**.

   The chart displays the number of people who commute by bus, grouped by ZIP Code.

8. Click the **PivotChart** report to select it. In the **PivotTable Field List**, drag **Housing Tenure** into the **Legend Fields** box.

   When you know what type of field you need, you can drag it directly into the desired box and it will automatically be selected in the PivotTable Field List.

9. In cell **B3**, click the **Column Labels** filter arrow ▼, and then in the displayed **AutoFilter** list, clear the **Owner** check box. Click **OK**, and then compare your screen with **Figure 4**.

10. Move the **PivotChart** so that the upper left corner is located in **A13**, and then Rename the **Sheet8** worksheet tab as Filtered Chart

11. Select cell **A1**, and then **Save** 💾 the workbook.

   ■ **You have completed Skill 8 of 10**

Renters who commute by bus from each ZIP Code

Figure 4

▶ A PivotChart report can be created from an existing PivotTable report.

▶ A PivotChart report can be placed on the same worksheet that contains the PivotTable report or moved to its own worksheet.

1. Display the **Survey PivotTable** worksheet, and then click cell **A5** to select the PivotTable.

2. On the **Options** tab, in the **Tools** group, click the **PivotChart** button.

3. In the **Insert Chart** dialog box, in the left pane, verify that **Column** is selected. With the first chart—**Clustered Column**—selected, click **OK**. Compare your screen with **Figure 1**.

   A clustered column chart is inserted on top of the PivotTable report.

4. In the **PivotChart report**, click the **Commute** arrow, and then clear the **(Select All)** check box. Select the **Car** check box, and click **OK**. Compare your screen with **Figure 2**.

   Filtering the chart reduces the amount of information displayed and emphasizes the remaining data.

■ **Continue to the next page to complete the skill**

Clustered column chart

Figure 1

Filter applied

Chart data filtered

Figure 2

Figure 3

Figure 4

5. In the **PivotChart** report, click the **Gender** arrow, and then clear the **F** check box. Click **OK**, and then compare your screen with **Figure 3**.

6. On the **Analyze** tab, in the **Show/Hide** group, click **Field List** to hide the **PivotTable Field List**. In the **Show/Hide** group, click the **Field Buttons** arrow, and then click **Hide All**.

7. Move the chart so that the upper left corner is in **D4**.

8. On the **Layout** tab, in the **Labels** group, click **Legend**, and then click **Show Legend at Bottom**.

9. On the **Design** tab, in the **Chart Styles** group, click the **More** button ▾. In the displayed gallery, click the second style in the fourth row—**Style 26**. Compare your screen with **Figure 4**.

10. **Save** 🖫 the workbook.

■ **You have completed Skill 9 of 10**

▶ Many elements of PivotCharts can be formatted like other charts.

1. Display the **Filtered Chart** worksheet tab, and then click the **PivotChart Report** to select it.

2. On the **Format** tab, in the **Current Selection** group, click the box arrow 🔽, and then click **Chart Area** to verify that the entire chart is selected.

3. In the **Shape Styles** group, click the **More** button 🔽. In the displayed **Shape Styles** gallery, click the last thumbnail in the fourth row—**Subtle Effect – Orange, Accent 6**. Compare your screen with **Figure 1**.

4. In the **Current Selection** group, click the box arrow, and then click **Plot Area**. In the **Current Selection** group, click **Format Selection**.

5. In the **Format Plot Area** dialog box, under **Fill**, select the **Solid fill** option button. Click the **Color** button arrow, and then in the color gallery, under **Theme Colors**, click the third color in the third row— **Tan, Background 2, Darker 25%**.

6. In the left pane, click **Border Color**, and then under **Border Color**, click the **Solid line** option button. Click the **Color** button arrow, and then under **Theme Colors**, click the fourth color in the first row— **Dark Blue, Text 2**.

7. In the left pane, click **Border Styles**. Under **Border Styles**, click the **Width** up arrow five times, until the value reads *2 pt*. Click **Close**, and then compare your screen with **Figure 2**.

   Notice that the Plot area turns a tan color and is surrounded by a dark blue border.

■ **Continue to the next page to complete the skill**

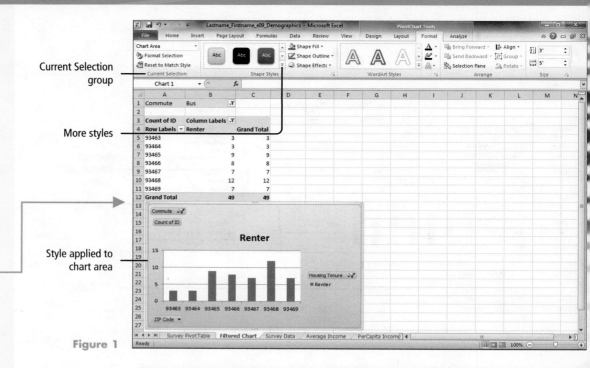

Current Selection group

More styles

Style applied to chart area

Figure 1

Plot area formatted

Figure 2

Legend formatted

Figure 3

Vertical axis formatted

Figure 4

8. In the **Current Selection** group, click the box arrow, and then click **Legend**. On the **Home** tab, change the **Font size** to **12**, and then change the **Font Color** to the fourth color in the last row—**Dark Blue, Text 2, Darker 50%**.

9. On the **Format** tab, in the **WordArt Styles** group, click the **Text Effects** button. Point to **Shadow**, and then under **Outer**, click the first shape—**Offset Diagonal Bottom Right**. Compare your screen with **Figure 3**.

10. In the **Current Selection** group, click the box arrow, and then click **Vertical (Value) Axis**. Click the **Format Selection** button.

11. In the **Format Axis** dialog box, under **Axis Options** and to the right of **Major unit**, click the **Fixed** option button. In the **Major unit** box, replace the value with **3.0**.

12. Click **Line Color**, and then under **Line Color**, click the **Solid line** option button. Click the **Color** button arrow, and then under **Theme Colors**, click the fourth color—**Dark Blue, Text 2**. Click **Close**. Click **D1**, and then compare your screen with **Figure 4**.

13. Group the worksheets, add the file name in the left footer, and then select cell A1 and return to **Normal** view. On the **Page Layout** tab, in the **Page Setup** group, set each worksheet to print in **Landscape** orientation. **Ungroup** the worksheets.

14. Save the workbook. Print or submit it—and the snip you made previously—as directed by your instructor.

Done! You have completed Skill 10 of 10 and your workbook is complete!

The following More Skills are located at **www.pearsonhighered.com/skills**

More Skills 11 Import Word 2010 Tables

Tables that are created in Word 2010 can be imported into Excel. You can then manipulate the data, just as if the table had been created as an Excel table.

In More Skills 11, you will copy a table created in Word 2010 into Excel 2010 and then format the table in Excel. To begin, open your web browser, navigate to www.pearsonhighered.com/skills, locate the name of your textbook, and then follow the instructions on the website.

More Skills 12 Create Web Queries and Clear Hyperlinks

Financial data is often found on the web. You can import this data into an Excel spreadsheet so that it is available to you when you are not connected to the Internet. When you import that data, a hyperlink to the source website is created that will automatically update when the file is opened. You can clear the hyperlink so that it no longer exists in the workbook.

In More Skills 12, you will import a table from a web page and then format the table in Excel. To begin, open your web browser, navigate to www.pearsonhighered.com/skills, locate the name of your textbook, and then follow the instructions on the website.

More Skills 13 Change PivotChart Report Types and Print PivotChart Reports

Data tables display the data used to create PivotChart reports. Including the data provides information in another format to assist you in analyzing your results.

In More Skills 13, you will create a PivotChart report and then display the underlying data table with the chart. Next you will format the chart in an attractive fashion. To begin, open your web browser, navigate to ww.pearsonhighered.com/skills, locate the name of your textbook, and then follow the instructions on the website

More Skills 14 Use Paste Special

Paste Special is used to change the format or data type of the values being pasted. For example, you can transpose rows into columns or paste the value of a cell instead of pasting the formula that underlies the value. You can also use the Paste Special command to perform some mathematical calculations.

In More Skills 14, you will copy data and use Paste Special to paste links to cells, copy formatting, add the values in cells, and paste values without pasting formulas. To begin, open your web browser, navigate to www.pearsonhighered.com/skills, locate the name of your textbook, and then follow the instructions on the website.

Key Terms

Online Help Skills

1. **Start** ⊕ Excel. In the upper right corner of the Excel window, click the **Help** button ⊚. In the **Help** window, click the **Maximize** ☐ button.

2. Click in the search box, type pivot tables and then slick the **Search** button ⊠. In the search results, click **Overview of PivotTable and PivotChart reports**.

3. Read the article's introduction, and then below **In this article**, click **Ways to work with a PivotTable** report. Compare your screen with **Figure 1**.

Figure 1

4. Read the section to see if you can answer the following: What are three ways to work with a PivotTable report? What are three ways to explore the data in a PivotTable report?

Matching

Match each term in the second column with its correct definition in the first column by writing the letter of the term on the blank line in front of the correct definition.

____ **1.** An interactive way to summarize, explore, and analyze data.

____ **2.** Categories of data organized into columns.

____ **3.** Located in the first column of a PivotTable report, these identify each category.

____ **4.** Located along the top row of a PivotTable report, these identify categories.

____ **5.** The default function used to summarize PivotTable values.

____ **6.** A new column or row with values from a formula you write.

____ **7.** Indicates that a group can be collapsed.

____ **8.** The technique used to display a portion of the data in a PivotTable or PivotChart report.

____ **9.** An interactive, visual representation of external data or PivotTable data.

____ **10.** A data set used to create a PivotTable or PivotChart report.

A Calculated field

B Column labels

C Data source

D Field

E Filtering

F Minus symbol

G PivotChart report

H PivotTable report

I Row labels

J SUM

Multiple Choice

Choose the correct answer.

1. Data can be imported into Excel from this source.
   - A. An Access database
   - B. A Word document
   - C. A PowerPoint presentation

2. Large amounts of data can be summarized using this tool.
   - A. An Access database
   - B. A PivotTable report
   - C. A PowerPoint presentation

3. In a PivotTable report, the intersection of rows and columns displays fields in this way.
   - A. Reports
   - B. Records
   - C. Values

4. In a PivotTable report, the top row and first column display fields in this way.
   - A. Records
   - B. Categories
   - C. Values

5. In the Create PivotTable dialog box, you specify this for the data.
   - A. Source
   - B. Records
   - C. Values

6. In a data table, fields are organized in this way.
   - A. Columns
   - B. Records
   - C. Rows

7. This is used to change fields from rows to columns, to add or remove fields, and to change the fields used to calculate values.
   - A. Configure dialog box
   - B. Data tab
   - C. PivotTable Field List

8. Calculated fields work much like these items.
   - A. Formulas
   - B. Solutions
   - C. Values

9. To expand a collapsed group, click this.
   - A. Minus symbol
   - B. Plus symbol
   - C. Expand All button

10. In addition to an external file, this can be the data source for a PivotChart report.
    - A. PowerPoint presentation
    - B. Excel chart
    - C. PivotTable report

Topics for Discussion

1. What are the advantages and disadvantages of using PivotTable or PivotChart reports to find meaning from large sets of data?

2. PivotTable and PivotChart reports are designed to be fluid—constantly changing as you work with the data. What problems might this cause, and what techniques could be used to avoid them?

Skill Check

To complete this workbook, you will need the following files:

- **New blank Excel workbook**
- **e09_Population**

You will save your file as:

- **Lastname_Firstname_e09_Population**

1. **Start** Excel to create a new blank workbook. Save the workbook in your **Excel Chapter 9** folder with the name Lastname_Firstname_e09_Population

2. On the **Sheet1** worksheet tab, select cell **A1**. On the **Data** tab, in the **Get External Data** group, click **From Access**. In the **Select Data Source** dialog box, navigate to e09_Population, and then click **Open**. In the **Import Data** dialog box, click **OK**.

3. Rename **Sheet1** as Population Data and then delete **Sheet2** and **Sheet3**. Compare your screen with **Figure 1**.

Figure 1

4. With cell **A1** selected, on the **Insert** tab, in the **Tables** group, click **PivotTable**. In the **Create PivotTable** dialog box, click **OK** to create a PivotTable report in a new worksheet.

5. On the **Options** tab, in the **PivotTable** group, in the **PivotTable Name** box, type Households In the **PivotTable Field List**, select **Household Size, Household Income, Race,** and **Housing Tenure**. Move **Sum of Household Size** from the **Values** box to the **Row Labels** box. Move the **Race** field to the **Column Labels** box.

6. Select cell **A3**, and then on the **Options** tab, in the **Active Field** group, click **Field Settings**. In the **Value Field Settings** dialog box, select **Average**. Click the **Number Format** button, and then change the number format to **Accounting** with **0** decimal places. Click **OK** two times.

7. Change the text in cell **A4** to Household Size and then rename **Sheet4** as Population PivotTable Click cell **A5**, and compare your screen with **Figure 2**.

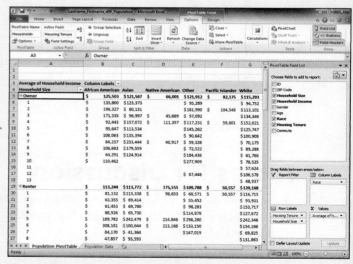

Figure 2

8. On the **Design** tab, in the **Layout** group, click **Blank Rows**, and then click **Insert Blank Line after Each Item**.

9. In the **PivotTable Styles** group, click the **More** button. Under **Medium**, click the third style in the first row—**Pivot Style Medium 3**.

10. Select cell **A5**, and then click the **Expand/Collapse** button. Repeat for cell **A7**.

▪ Continue to the next page to complete this Skill Check ▶

Figure 3

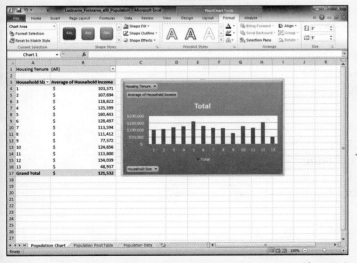

Figure 4

11. Select cell **B3**, and in the **Formula Bar**, type Race and press Enter. Select cell **B3**, and then click the arrow. Select only the **African American** check box, and then click **OK**.

12. On the **Options** tab, click the **Calculations** button, and then click **Fields, Items, & Sets**. Click **Calculated Field**. In the **Name** box, type PerCapita In the **Formula** box, delete the text. Under **Fields**, double-click **Household Income**, type a slash (/), and then double-click **Household Size**. Compare your screen with **Figure 3**. Click **Add**. Click **OK**.

13. In the **PivotTable Field List**, under the **Values** box, click the **Sum of PerCapita** arrow, and then click **Value Field Settings**. Click **Average**. Format the field as **Accounting [0]**, and then click **OK**.

14. In the **Sort & Filter** group, click **Insert Slicer**, select **ZIP Code**, and then click **OK**. Click **93466**.

15. Select cell **A1**. On the **Insert** tab, in the **Tables** group, click the **PivotTable** button arrow, and then click **PivotChart**. In the **Create PivotTable with PivotChart** dialog box, select the **Use an external data source** option button. Click **Choose Connection**, and then in the **Existing Connections** dialog box, select **e09_Population**, and click **Open**. Select the **New Worksheet** option button. Click **OK**. Rename **Sheet5** as Population Chart

16. In the **PivotTable Field List**, select **Household Income, Household Size**, and **Housing Tenure**. Move **Housing Tenure** into the **Report Filter** box, and then move **Sum of Household Size** into the **Axis Fields** box.

17. Select cell **B3**, and then on the **Options** tab, in the **Active Field** group, click **Field Settings**. In the **Value Field Settings** dialog box, click **Average**, and then set the **Number Format** to *Accounting* with *0* decimal places. Click **OK** two times. In the **Show** group, click **Field List**. Select cell **A3**, and in the Formula bar replace the type Household Size

18. Select the **PivotChart report**. Move the upper left corner to cell **C3**. On the **Layout** tab, in the **Labels** group, click **Legend**, and then click **Show Legend at Bottom**. On the **Design** tab, in the **Chart Styles** group, click the **More** button, and then click **Style 4**. On the **Format** tab, in the **Shape Styles** group, click the **More** button, and then click the sixth style in the sixth row—**Intense Effect – Aqua, Accent 5**. Compare your screen with **Figure 4**.

19. Select all of the worksheets, and add the file name in the left footer. Change the **Orientation** to **Landscape**. Click cell **A1**. Switch to **Normal** view. Ungroup the worksheets. Click **Save**, and then print or submit electronically as directed by your instructor. **Exit** Excel.

Done! You have completed the Skill Check

Assess Your Skills 1

To complete this workbook, you will need the following files:

- ■ **New blank Excel workbook**
- ■ **e09_Vendors**

You will save your file as:

- ■ **Lastname_Firstname_e09_Vendors**

1. **Start Excel** to create a new blank Excel workbook. Save the workbook in your **Excel Chapter 9** folder with the name Lastname_Firstname_e09_Vendors

2. Import the Access table from the file **e09_Vendors** into cell **A1**. Rename **Sheet1** as Vendors Data Delete **Sheet2** and **Sheet3**.

3. Using the Excel table—**Table_e09_ Vendors**—as the data source, insert a PivotTable report into a new worksheet. Rename **Sheet4** as Vendors PivotTable and then name the PivotTable Vendors

4. For the PivotTable, add **Vendor** as a column label, and then add **Date** and **Invoice #** as row labels. In the **Row Labels** box, position **Date** above **Invoice #**.

5. Add **Amount** as a value field that calculates sums formatted as **Accounting** with 2 decimal places displayed.

6. On the **Design** tab, in the **Layout** group, insert a blank line after each item. Change the PivotTable style to **Pivot Style Medium 5**—the fifth style in the first row under **Medium**.

7. Insert a calculated field named Tax To create the formula, multiply the **Amount** field by .03

8. Set the width of columns **A:K** to **12.00**.

9. Select cell **A6**, and collapse the entire field.

10. Insert a **Slicer**, and select **Vendor**. Display only the data from **Aspen Falls Meats**. Move the **Slicer** so that the data is visible.

11. In cell **B5**, type Invoice Amount In cell **C5**, type Tax Due and press `Tab`. Display the **Design** tab, and using the **Layout** group, display **Grand Totals** for **Columns Only**. Move the Slicer to cell **D3**.

12. Insert a **PivotChart** into a new worksheet using the table in the **Vendors Data** worksheet as the data source.

13. Add **Vendor** as an axis field, and then add **Tax** and **Amount** as value fields. Place **Tax** above **Amount** in the list. Filter the **Axis** field to display only the **Catering of the Falls** vendor. Add **Date** as a filter, and then use the filter to display only invoices **1/31/2012, 2/28/2012,** and **3/31/2012.**

14. Change the chart style to **Style 42**, and then display the legend at the top of the chart. Format the **Sum of Amount** values and **Sum of Tax** values as **Accounting** with 2 decimal places. Close the **PivotTable Field List**. Resize the chart so that it fits in **A8:D24**.

15. Add the file name in the left footer of each worksheet. Select cell **A1**, and return to **Normal** view. Compare your worksheets with **Figure 1**. Click **Save**, and then print or submit electronically as directed by your instructor. **Exit** Excel.

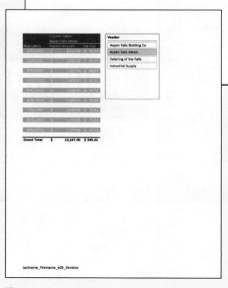

Done! You have completed Assess Your Skills 1

Figure 1

Assess Your Skills 2

To complete this workbook, you will need the following file:

- e09_Invoices

You will save your file as:

- Lastname_Firstname_e09_Invoices

1. **Start** Excel, and open the student data file **e09_Invoices**. Save the workbook in your **Excel Chapter 9** folder with the name Lastname_Firstname_e09_Invoices

2. Using the Excel table in the range **A1:D65** as the data source, insert a PivotTable report into a new worksheet. Rename the new worksheet as Aspen Falls Bottling and then name the PivotTable Aspen Falls Bottling

3. Add the **Vendor** as a **Report Filter**. Add **Invoice Number** and **Description** as **Row Labels**. Place **Invoice Number** above **Description**. Add **Amount** as a value.

4. Add a calculated field named Discount that multiplies the **Amount** field by .03 Format the field as **Accounting** with **2** decimal places.

5. Add another calculated field named Amount Due that subtracts the **Discount** field from the **Amount** field. Format the field as **Accounting** with **2** decimal places.

6. Use a **Slicer** to display **Vendors** with the value **Aspen Falls Bottling Co**. Collapse the entire field. Insert a blank line after each item. Move the upper left corner of the **Slicer** to cell **A17**.

7. Using the **Data** worksheet as the data source, insert a **Clustered Column PivotChart** in a new sheet named AFB Invoice PivotChart Add the following as value fields, in this order: **Discount, Amount,** and **Amount Due**. Add **Invoice Number** and then

Description as axis fields. Add **Vendor** as a **Report Filter**. Close the **PivotTable Field List**, and then display the legend at the bottom of the chart.

8. Filter the chart to show only the values from the **Aspen Falls Bottling Co** vendor. Hide columns **A:D**. Change the **Orientation** to **Landscape**. Resize the chart by dragging the lower right corner of the chart down to cell **Q25**.

9. Change the chart type to a **Clustered Bar** chart, and then apply the **Style 26** Chart Style.

10. Format the **Plot Area** with a solid fill background using the fourth color in the fourth row—**Dark Blue, Text 2, Lighter 40%**.

11. Format the **Chart Area** with a solid fill background using the tenth color in the third row—**Orange, Accent 6, Lighter 60%**.

12. Insert a **Chart Title** above the chart with the text AFB Invoices Change the title font color to the fourth color in the first row—**Dark Blue, Text 2**—and then change the **Font Size** to **28**. Select cell **E1**.

13. Add the file name to the left footer of all of the worksheets. Set the orientation of all pages to landscape. Compare your worksheets with **Figure 1**. Click **Save**, and then print or submit electronically as directed by your instructor. **Exit** Excel.

Done! You have completed Assess Your Skills 2

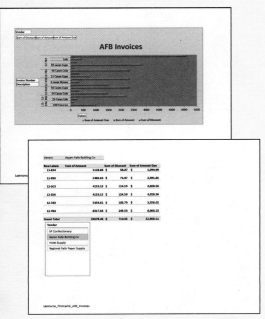

Figure 1

Assess Your Skills Visually

To complete this workbook, you will need the following files:

- New blank Excel workbook
- e09_Concessions

You will save your file as:

- Lastname_Firstname_e09_Concessions

Open a new blank Excel workbook, and then import **e09_Concessions** into cell **A1**. Save the file with the name Lastname_Firstname_e09_ Concessions Use the imported data to create the **PivotTable** and **PivotChart** report shown in Figure 1. When changing the names in cell **C5** and cell **D5**, add a blank space after the text that appears. The **Discount** values are calculated by multiplying the **Cost** field by **0.1**. The **Final Cost** is calculated by subtracting the **Discount** field from the **Cost** field. Apply the **Style 42** chart style, and display the legend as shown in Figure 1. Add the title, and then size and position the chart as shown in Figure 1. Delete the **Sheet2** worksheet tab and the **Sheet3** worksheet tab. Rename the **Sheet1** worksheet tab Sales and the **Sheet4** worksheet tab Sales Chart Add the file name in the footer on both sheets. Set the **Orientation** for both sheets to **Landscape**. Print or submit electronically as directed by your instructor.

Done! You have completed Assess Your Skills Visually

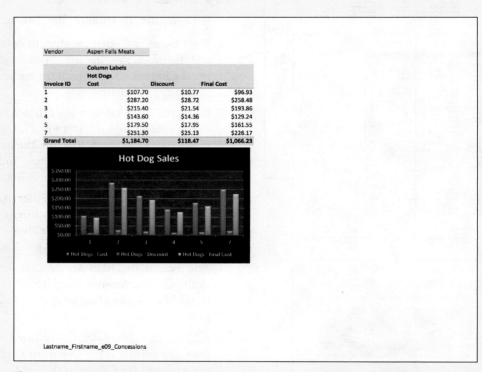

Figure 1

Skills in Context

To complete this workbook, you will need the following file:

- e09_Water_Usage

You will save your file as:

- Lastname_Firstname_e09_Water_Usage

The Aspen Falls Public Works Department provides water to the city. In an effort to meet the needs of the citizens, the department monitors water usage by ZIP Code and month to ensure sufficient water is available where and when it is needed. The water used by each household for the months April, May, and June 2012 is recorded in **e09_Water_Usage**. Create a PivotTable report and a PivotChart report that answers the following question: How does average water usage vary by ZIP Code for the months of April, May, and June?

Done! You have completed Skills in Context

Skills and You

To complete this workbook, you will need the following file:

- e09_Grades

You will save your file as:

- Lastname_Firstname_e09_Grades

Using **e09_Grades** as a template, create a workbook that tracks your grades for each of your classes. Add your own information. Create a **PivotTable** report and a **PivotChart** report that summarizes your scores for each course. Save the file as Lastname_ Firstname_e09_Grades and submit it as directed.

Done! You have completed Skills and You

CHAPTER **10**

Share Workbooks
and Create Macros

▶ When you collaborate with others to build a worksheet, each team member can add comments and you can track each change made. You can also protect the worksheet so that only certain types of changes are allowed.

▶ You can create macros to automate common tasks.

Your starting screen will look like this:

Outcome

Using the skills listed to the left will enable you to create worksheets like these:

You will save your files as:

Lastname_Firstname_e10_Police1

Lastname_Firstname_e10_Police2

Lastname_Firstname_e10_Police1_Web

Lastname_Firstname_e10_Police1_Macro

In this chapter, you will create workbooks for the Aspen Falls City Hall, which provides essential services for the citizens and visitors of Aspen Falls, California.

Introduction

- ► When sharing a workbook, you can track each member's changes so that you can accept or reject those changes later.

- ► You can write validation rules so that only certain types of data can be entered, and you can protect the workbook so that only the cells you specify can be changed.

- ► Before sharing a workbook as a web page, you can search for and remove personal information from the workbook.

- ► Macros can perform a series of tasks with a single click.

Time to complete all
10 skills – 50 to 75 minutes

Find your data files here:

**File needed for
this chapter:**

- e10_Police1

▶ Reviewer *comments* are descriptive text that you can add to cells without modifying the data in the worksheet. When collaborating on a project, reviewers can use comments to make suggestions.

▶ You can personalize your copy of Excel by changing the settings in the Excel Options dialog box.

1. **Start** 🔵 Excel, and open **e10_Police1**. Display the **File** tab, and then click **Save As**. In the **Save As** dialog box, navigate to the location where you are saving your files. Click **New folder**, type Excel Chapter 10 and then press ⏎ two times. In the **File name** box, using your own name, name the file Lastname_Firstname_ e10_Police1 and then press ⏎. Add the file name in the worksheet's left footer. Click cell **A1**, and return to **Normal** view.

2. Display the **File** tab, and then click **Options**. Compare your screen with **Figure 1**.

   The left side of the Excel Options dialog box displays 10 option categories. By default, the General category is selected. The 10 option categories are summarized in the table shown in **Figure 2**.

3. In the **Excel Options** dialog box, under **Personalize your copy of Microsoft Office**, note the current value in the **User name** box so that you can restore it later. Change the **User name** to your own first and last name, and then click **OK**.

   The Excel user name identifies the author of comments as the comments are added to the spreadsheet.

■ **Continue to the next page to complete the skill**

Excel Options dialog box

Option categories

Current user name (yours will be different)

Figure 1

Excel Options Window

Section	Purpose
General	Provides access to the most commonly used settings.
Formulas	Provides options for how formulas are calculated and how errors are checked.
Proofing	Provides options for how spelling and grammar are checked.
Save	Provides options for how workbooks are saved.
Language	Provides options for setting Office Language Preferences.
Advanced	Provides access to 13 subcategories of options.
Customize Ribbon	Provides a way to customize the Ribbon.
Quick Access Toolbar	Provides a way to customize the Quick Access Toolbar.
Add-Ins	Provides a way to manage Excel Add-ins.
Trust Center	Provides options for managing privacy and security.

Figure 2

Show All Comments

Comments displayed

Figure 3

Three comments added

Comment box positioned

Figure 4

4. On the **Employees** worksheet, point to cell **F2** so that the comment from Richard Mack displays.

   Cells with comments display a ***comment indicator***—a small red triangle in the upper right corner of a cell.

5. Display the **Review** tab, and then in the **Comments** group, click **Show All Comments**. Compare your screen with **Figure 3**.

   Showing all comments allows you to read all of the comments at one time.

6. Select cell **B13**. In the **Comments** group, click **New Comment**.

7. In the comment box, type Is this supposed to be 9/1/1999?

8. With the comment attached to cell **B13** still selected, point to the comment box border, and then with the 🖑 pointer, drag so that the upper left corner of the comment box is in the middle of cell **A20**.

9. Select cell **E9**, and then click **New Comment**. In the comment box, type Is this the correct salary for Gracia? I thought it was $24,950.

10. With the comment attached to cell **E9** still selected, point to the comment box border, and then with the 🖑 pointer, drag so that the upper left corner of the comment box is in the middle of cell **H13**.

11. Select cell **C12**, and click **New Comment**. In the comment box, type Promote John to Major? Compare your screen with **Figure 4**.

12. Click cell **A1**, and then in the **Comments** group, click **Show All Comments** to hide the comments from view.

13. Save 🖫 the workbook.

■ **You have completed Skill 1 of 10**

► ***Data validation rules*** place restrictions on the types of data that can be entered in cells.

1. Select the range **B3:B19**. Display the **Data** tab, and in the **Data Tools** group, click the **Data Validation** button.

2. In the **Data Validation** dialog box, on the **Settings** tab, click the **Allow** arrow, and then click **Date**. Click the **Data** arrow, click **greater than**, and then in the **Start date** box, type 1/1/1950 Compare your screen with **Figure 1**.

3. In the **Data Validation** dialog box, display the **Input Message** tab, and then in the **Title** box, type Hire Date In the **Input message** box, type Hire date cannot be before 1950

   An ***input message*** is a data validation message that informs the data entry operator about the types of data that can be entered into the cell.

4. Display the **Error Alert** tab. In the **Title** box, type Invalid Hire Date In the **Error message** box, type The hire date must be after 1/1/1950. Click **OK**. Select cell **A1**.

5. In the **Data Tools** group, click the **Data Validation** button arrow, and then click **Circle Invalid Data**. Click cell **A20**, and then compare your screen with **Figure 2**.

   When a data rule has been applied to a cell, Excel can indicate invalid data by circling the cell when its value does not match the rule.

■ **Continue to the next page to complete the skill**

Data Validation dialog box

Validation rule allows dates greater than 1/1/1950

Figure 1

Invalid data circled

Figure 2

Validation rule allows decimal numbers between two values

Figure 3

Data validation error message

Message box title

Figure 4

6. Select cell **B4**, and verify that the Input message displays.

7. Select the range **E3:E19**, and then click the **Data Validation** button. In the **Data Validation** dialog box, display the **Settings** tab. Click the **Allow** arrow, and then click **Decimal**. With the **Data** box set to **between**, in the **Minimum** box, type 19500.00 In the **Maximum** box, type 99500.00 and then compare your screen with **Figure 3**.

   This validation rule specifies that decimal numbers between the minimum and the maximum should be entered.

8. In the **Data Validation** dialog box, display the **Error Alert** tab. Click the **Style** arrow, and then click **Warning**. In the **Title** box, type Salary Alert In the **Error message** box, type Salary should be more than $19,500 and less than $99,500. Click **OK**.

9. Click cell **B3**, type 3/1/1949 and then press Enter. Compare your screen with **Figure 4**.

10. Click **Retry**, type 1/6/2010 and then press Enter. Change cell **B7** to 8/20/2009

11. In cell **E4**, change the salary to 395000 and then press Enter.

   When the Error style is set to *Warning*, you are given the option to proceed when the data is invalid.

12. In the **Salary Alert** error message, click **No**. In cell **E4**, change the salary to 39500 and then press Enter.

13. Save ⊟ the workbook.

■ **You have completed Skill 2 of 10**

► When you are collaborating with others, you can see each reviewer's changes by enabling *change tracking*—a feature that tracks all the changes made to a worksheet.

1. Select cell **A1**. On the **Review** tab, in the **Changes** group, click **Track Changes**, and then click **Highlight Changes**. Compare your screen with **Figure 1**.

   To track changes, the workbook must be a *shared workbook*—a workbook where multiple users on a network can make changes to the workbook at the same time.

2. In the **Highlight Changes** dialog box, select the **Track changes while editing** check box to track changes and share the workbook. Select the **Who** check box. Compare your screen with **Figure 2**.

3. Click **OK**. Read the displayed message, and then click **OK**.

   The Excel title bar displays the text *[Shared]* to indicate that the workbook is currently being shared with others.

4. Display the **File** tab, and then click **Save As**. Save the workbook in your **Excel Chapter 10** folder as Lastname_ Firstname_e10_Police2

5. Display the **File** tab, and then click **Options**. In the **Excel Options** dialog box, change the **User name** to Thelma Perkins and then click **OK**.

   You will now be editing the spreadsheet as Thelma Perkins.

■ **Continue to the next page to complete the skill** ➤

Figure 1

Figure 2

Blue triangle and blue border

Details of the change

Figure 3

Formatted cells

Figure 4

6. Select cell **C6**, type Chief and then press Enter. Click cell **A1**, and then point to cell **C6** to display the comment box, as shown in **Figure 3**.

When a change is tracked, a blue line appears around the changed cell, and a blue triangle appears in the upper left corner of the cell. When you point to the cell, details about the change display. The date and time of the change, and the original values display.

7. Select cell **B15**, type 9/1/2009 and press Enter. Continue in this manner to make the following changes:

   Cell **B17**   6/1/2007

   Cell **E8**   45595

   Cell **E16**   92500

8. Select the range **G4:G19**, and apply the **Comma [0]** cell style. Select cell **A1**, and then compare your screen with **Figure 4**.

   Notice that there are no blue lines around the range G4:G19. Only changes that affect the cell data are tracked. The formatting changes applied to the range were not tracked.

9. **Save** 💾 the workbook.

■ **You have completed Skill 3 of 10**

► Excel maintains a record of tracked changes in the *change history*—a log that records each data change, who made the change, and when the data was changed.

► When changes are tracked, you can accept or reject each change.

1. Display the **Review** tab, and in the **Changes** group, click **Track Changes**, and then click **Highlight Changes**. In the **Highlight Changes** dialog box, select the **List changes on a new sheet** check box. Compare your screen with **Figure 1**.

2. Click **OK**, and then compare your screen with **Figure 2**.

   A temporary worksheet—*History*—is added to the workbook. The History worksheet displays the entire change history. All of the changes made by Thelma Perkins are listed.

3. With the **History** worksheet tab displayed, click **Start** ⊙, click **All Programs**, and then open the **Accessories** folder. Click **Snipping Tool**, click the **New** button arrow, and then click **Full-screen Snip**. Save ⊟ the snip in your **Excel Chapter 10** folder as Lastname_Firstname_e10_ Police2_Changes_Snip and then **Close** ⊠ the **Snipping Tool** window. If you are printing your work for this project, print the **History** worksheet.

   The History worksheet is dynamic and will not automatically display when the worksheet is opened again.

4. **Save** ⊟ the workbook.

   Notice that the History worksheet disappears.

■ **Continue to the next page to complete the skill**

List changes on a new sheet selected

Figure 1

History worksheet is added and displayed

Figure 2

Figure 3

Figure 4

Cell C6 selected

Accept or Reject Changes dialog box

Accept and Reject buttons

Accept or Reject Changes dialog box

Accept All button

5. On the **Review** tab, click **Track Changes**, and then click **Accept/Reject Changes**.

6. In the **Select Changes to Accept or Reject** dialog box, verify that the **When** box displays **Not yet reviewed**, and then click **OK**. Compare your screen with **Figure 3**.

The Accept or Reject Changes dialog box selects changed cells one at a time so that you can accept or reject each change. Cell C6 is selected, and the details of the change display in the dialog box.

7. In the dialog box, click **Reject** to restore the original value in cell **C6**. Read the change details for change 2 of 5—cell **B15**—and then click **Accept** to accept the change and override the original value.

8. Read the change details for change 3 of 5—cell **B17**—and then click **Accept**. Compare your screen with **Figure 4**.

9. Click **Accept All** to accept all the remaining changes.

10. Save 💾 and then **Close** the workbook.

■ **You have completed Skill 4 of 10**

▶ *Compare and merge* is a process that combines the changes from multiple copies of a workbook into a single copy.

▶ To use compare and merge, the Compare and Merge button must be added to the Quick Access Toolbar.

1. Open **Lastname_Firstname_e10_Police1**. Using the skills previously practiced, open the **Excel Options** dialog box, and change the **User name** to your own first and last name.

2. In the **Excel Options** dialog box, in the left pane, click **Quick Access Toolbar**.

3. Under **Customize the Quick Access Toolbar**, click the **Customize Quick Access Toolbar** arrow, and then click **For Lastname_Firstname_e10_Police1.xlsx**.

4. Click the **Choose commands from** arrow, and then click **Commands Not in the Ribbon**.

5. Scroll down the displayed list, click **Compare and Merge Workbooks**, and then click **Add**. Compare your screen with **Figure 1**.

6. Click **OK** to close the **Excel Options** dialog box. Compare your screen with **Figure 2**.

    Notice that the Compare and Merge command is added to the Quick Access Toolbar.

7. From the **Quick Access Toolbar**, click the **Compare and Merge Workbooks** button. Read the displayed message, and then click **OK**.

■ **Continue to the next page to complete the skill**

Commands Not in the Ribbon selected

Quick Access Toolbar

Current workbook selected

Compare and Merge Workbooks command added

Figure 1

Compare and Merge Documents button

Figure 2

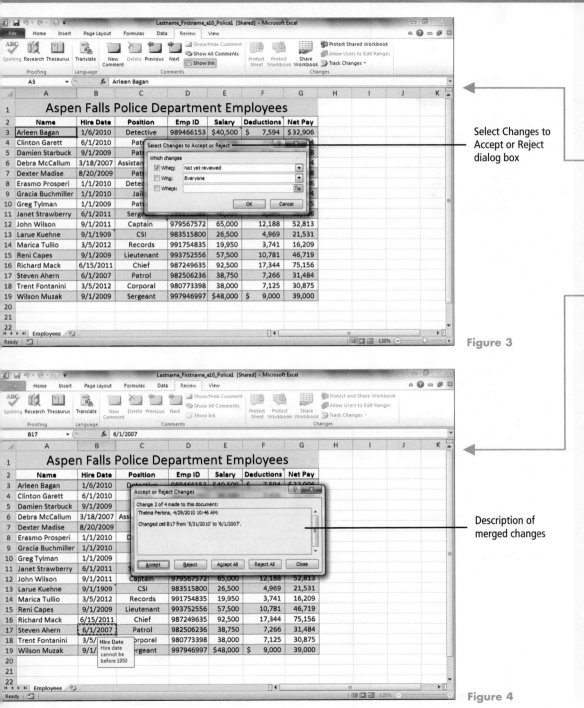

Select Changes to Accept or Reject dialog box

Figure 3

Description of merged changes

Figure 4

8. In the **Select Files to Merge Into Current Workbook** dialog box, open your **Excel Chapter 10** folder, click **Lastname_Firstname_e10_Police2**, and then click **OK**.

9. Select cell **A3**. On the **Review** tab, click **Track Changes**, and then click **Accept/Reject Changes**. Compare your screen with **Figure 3**.

10. Verify that the **When** box reads *Not yet reviewed*. Select the **Who** check box, and then verify that the **Who** box reads *Everyone*.

11. Click **OK**. Review the information in the **Accept or Reject Changes** dialog box, and then click **Accept**. Compare your screen with **Figure 4**.

12. In the **Accept or Reject Changes** dialog box, click **Accept All**.

13. Click **Track Changes**, and then click **Highlight Changes**. In the **Highlight Changes** dialog box, clear the **Track changes while editing** check box, and then click **OK**.

14. Read the message, click **Yes**, and then **Save** 🖫 the workbook.

■ **You have completed Skill 5 of 10**

► *Document properties* are details that describe a workbook file. For example, the author name, company name, or comments may be stored in the document properties.

► Before sharing a workbook, you should search for and remove any personal information that may be stored in the file.

---

1. Display the **File** tab, and compare your screen with **Figure 1**.

   The Document Information Panel displays the file's *metadata*—information that describes the data in an Excel file. Here, the metadata has personally identifiable information, such as a name in the Author property.

2. In the **Info** group, click the **Check for Issues** button, and then click **Inspect Document**.

3. In the **Document Inspector**, clear the **Comments and Annotations** check box, and compare your screen with **Figure 2**.

   The Document Inspector searches comments, metadata, headers, footers, and other elements that may be hidden from view.

■ **Continue to the next page to complete the skill**

Document Information Panel

Check for Issues button

Author property

Figure 1

Document Inspector

Check box cleared

Figure 2

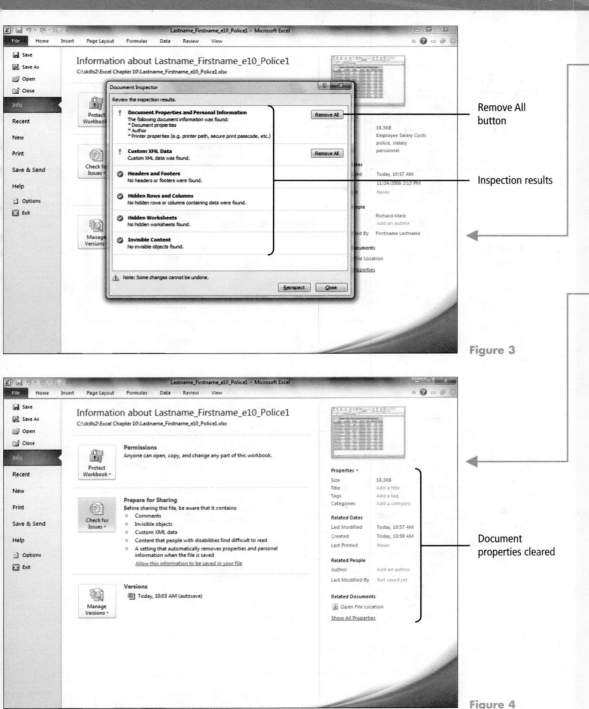

Remove All button

Inspection results

Figure 3

Document properties cleared

Figure 4

4. In the **Document Inspector** dialog box, click **Inspect**. Wait a few moments, and then compare your screen with **Figure 3**.

   The Document Inspector searches the workbook and displays the results. If an item is found, the Remove All button displays. Document properties and personal information were found in the workbook.

5. To the right of **Document Properties and Personal Information**, click the **Remove All** button, and then click **Close**.

6. In the **Document Information Panel**, notice that under **Related People**, the **Author** has been cleared. Only the information about who last modified the workbook remains. Compare your screen with **Figure 4**.

7. In the **Document Information Panel**, click **Add an author**. In the **Author** box, type your first and last name, and then press Enter. On the **Check Names** dialog box, click **Cancel**.

8. **Save** 🖫 the workbook.

   ■ **You have completed Skill 6 of 10**

► *HTML*—Hypertext Markup Language—is used to mark up text files so that they can be viewed on the Internet.

► You can save all or part of a spreadsheet as an HTML web page.

► HTML text files are typically given an *.htm* or *.html* file extension so that they can be viewed in a web browser.

1. Display the **File** tab, and then click **Save As**.

2. In the **Save As** dialog box, click the **Save as type** arrow, and then in the displayed list of file types, click **Web Page**.

3. In the **Save As** dialog box, navigate to your **Excel Chapter 10** folder, and then in the **File name** box, type Lastname_Firstname_ e10_Police1_Web Compare your screen with **Figure 1**.

4. In the **Save As** dialog box, click the **Change Title** button.

5. In the **Enter Text** dialog box, under **Page title**, type Police Pay Compare your screen with **Figure 2**, and then click **OK**.

■ **Continue to the next page to complete the skill**

Excel Chapter 10 folder

Web Page file type selected

Figure 1

Enter Text dialog box

Figure 2

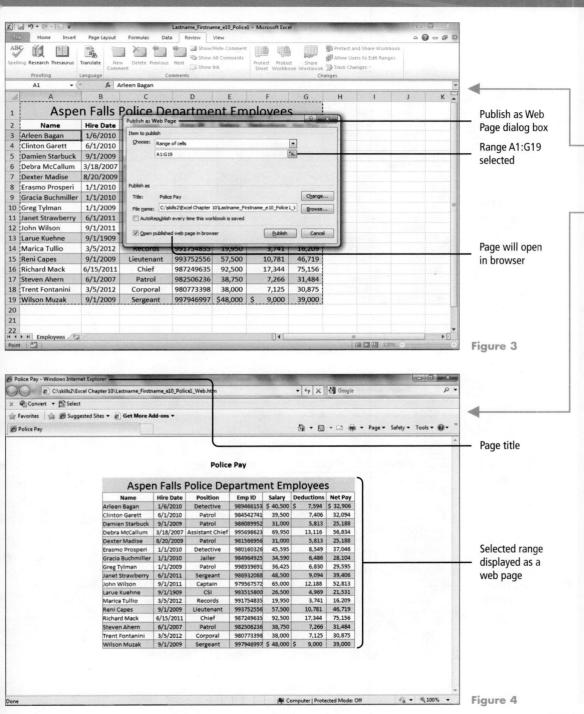

Figure 3

Figure 4

6. In the **Save as** dialog box, click **Publish**.

7. In the **Publish as Web Page** dialog box, click the **Choose** arrow, and then click **Range of cells**. In the second **Choose** box, type A1:G19 Under **Publish as**, verify that the **Open published web page in browser** check box is selected. Compare your screen with **Figure 3**.

8. Click **Publish**, and then wait a few moments for the page to display in your computer's default web browser. Compare your screen with **Figure 4**.

    The page title displays in the browser's title bar.

9. If you are printing this project, print the web page.

10. **Close** ⊠ your web browser, and then **Save** 🔲 the workbook.

■ **You have completed Skill 7 of 10**

Publish as Web Page dialog box

Range A1:G19 selected

Page will open in browser

Page title

Selected range displayed as a web page

► Protecting a worksheet prevents unauthorized individuals from making changes.

► To allow revisions to parts of a protected workbook, you must first unlock the cells you want to change.

1. On the **Employees** worksheet tab, select the range **A3:E19**. On the **Home** tab, in the **Cells** group, click the **Format** arrow, and then in the displayed list, notice that **Lock Cell** is toggled on, as indicated by the gold color around the icon. Compare your screen with **Figure 1**.

> All cells are locked by default, but the lock is not enforced until worksheet protection is enabled.

2. In the **Format** menu, click **Protect Sheet**.

3. In the **Protect Sheet** dialog box, in the **Password to unprotect sheet** box, type Success!

4. Under **Allow all users of this worksheet to**, select the **Format cells** check box. Compare your screen with **Figure 2**, and then click **OK**.

> When protecting workbooks, use a *strong password*—a password that contains a combination of uppercase and lowercase letters, numbers, and symbols. In this exercise, the selected protection options will allow individuals to select cells and format cells. No changes to formulas or cell data will be allowed.

5. In the **Confirm Password** dialog box, type Success! and then click **OK**.

■ **Continue to the next page to complete the skill**

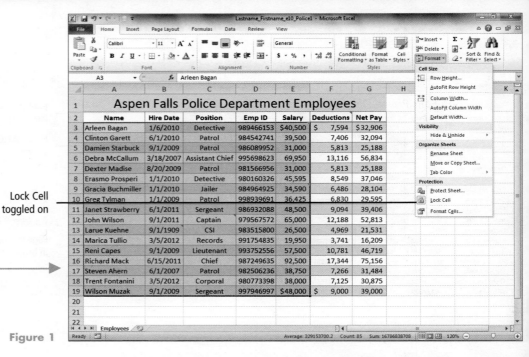

Lock Cell toggled on

Figure 1

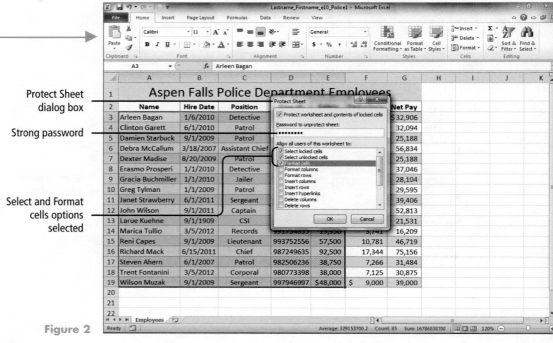

Protect Sheet dialog box

Strong password

Select and Format cells options selected

Figure 2

Figure 3

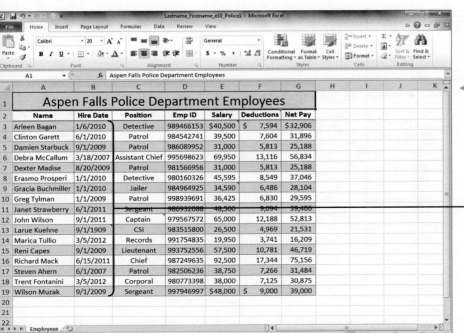

Figure 4

6. Select cell **F4**, attempt to type 8232 and then compare your screen with **Figure 3**.

   The message informs you that the cell is protected and cannot be changed until protection is removed.

7. Click **OK** to close the message. On the **Home** tab, in the **Cells** group, click **Format**, and then click **Unprotect Sheet**. In the **Unprotect Sheet** box, type Success! and then click **OK**.

8. Select the range **F3:F19**. In the **Cells** group, click **Format**, and then click **Lock Cell** to toggle the lock off of the selected range.

9. Select the range **A3:G19**. Use the techniques just practiced to toggle on protection for the range using the password Success!

10. Click cell **E4**, and attempt to change the value. Read the message, and then click **OK**.

11. Click cell **F4**, and then in Formula bar, select the existing text, and type =E4*0.1925 to change the formula. Press Enter.

    When a cell's lock is toggled off, you can make changes to the cell when protection is on.

12. Select the range **B3:B19**, and then in the **Alignment** group, click the **Align Text Left** button. Select cell **A1**, and then compare your screen with **Figure 4**.

    Because formatting changes were allowed in the Protect Sheet dialog box, the formatting change was accepted.

13. **Save** and then **Close** the workbook.

■ **You have completed Skill 8 of 10**

▶ A *macro* is a stored set of instructions that automate common tasks.

▶ The macro recorder creates a macro by recording the steps you perform in a routine activity. The recorded steps are then performed whenever the macro is run.

1. Open **e10_Police1** from your student data files. Display the **File** tab, and click **Save As**. Navigate to your **Excel Chapter 10** folder, and then in the **Save As** dialog box, click the **Save as type** arrow. In the list of file types, click **Excel Macro-Enabled Workbook**. In the **File name** box, using your own name, name the file Lastname_Firstname_e10_Police1_Macro and then press Enter.

2. Display the **File** tab, and then click **Options**. In the **Excel Options** dialog box, click **Customize Ribbon**. Under **Main Tabs**, select the **Developer** check box. Compare your screen with **Figure 1**, and then click **OK**.

3. Select cell **A1**, and then on the **Developer** tab, in the **Code** group, click **Record Macro**.

4. In the **Record Macro** dialog box, in the **Macro name** box, type InsertInfo In the **Shortcut key** box, and type m In the **Description** box, type Inserts the name and date in cells A1:A2 Compare your screen with **Figure 2**, and then click **OK**.

5. On the **Home** tab, in the **Cells** group, click the **Insert** button two times.

■ **Continue to the next page to complete the skill**

Developer check box

Figure 1

Record Macro dialog box

Macro name

Shortcut key

Description

Figure 2

Trust Center

Macro Settings

Figure 3

Name and date
inserted by macro

Figure 4

6. In cell **A1**, type your first and last name, and then press [Enter]. In cell **A2**, type =NOW() and then press [Enter].

7. Select the range **A1:A2**, and then change the font size to **8**. Click the **Font Color** button arrow, and then under **Standard Colors**, click **Dark Blue**.

8. On the **Developer** tab, in the **Code** group, click **Stop Recording**.

9. In the **Code** group, click **Macro Security**. In the **Trust Center** dialog box, select the **Disable all macros with notification** option. Compare your screen with **Figure 3**, and then click **OK**.

> The security setting will not allow a macro to execute without asking your permission to do so. Since macros are sometimes used to spread *malware*—software that is designed to harm a computer—you should enable only macros that are from trusted sources.

10. Delete rows **1** and **2**. Click **Save** 🖫, and then **Close** the workbook.

11. Open **Lastname_Firstname_e10_ Police1_Macro**. In the **Message Bar**, click **Enable Content**.

> When you open a workbook with a macro, the Security bar informs you when the workbook contains a macro. You can then choose to enable or disable the macro.

12. Select cell **A1**, and then on the **Developer** tab, in the **Code** group, click **Macros**. In the **Macro** dialog box, select **InsertInfo**, and then click **Run**. Compare your screen with **Figure 4**.

13. Delete rows **1** and **2**, and then select cell **A1**. Press [Ctrl] + [M] to verify that the macro runs when the assigned shortcut key is pressed. Click **Save** 🖫.

■ **You have completed Skill 9 of 10**

► *Visual Basic for Applications (VBA)* is a high-level programming language that can be used to write and modify macros.

► VBA macros are written in the Visual Basic Editor (VBE).

1. Display the **Developer** tab, and then in the **Code** group, click **Visual Basic**.

2. In the **Visual Basic Editor**, from the **Insert** menu, click **Module**. Compare your screen with **Figure 1**. ────────

    The *Code window*—the window in which VBA code is written—for Module2 displays.

3. In the **Code** window, type the following sub and comments. Be sure the last two lines begin with a single quotation mark as shown:

```
Sub InsertFileName()
'Created by Your Name
'Inserts the file name in the footer
```

    A *sub* is a group of instructions that is a subset of a program.

    The sub named *InsertFileName* has two comments, which display in green. Programming *comments* are statements that document what the code does.

4. After the last comment, press [Enter], and then type the following statements on two lines as indicated:

```
ActiveSheet.PageSetup.LeftFooter = "&F"
ActiveWindow.View=xlNormalView
```

5. Compare your screen with **Figure 2**. ────────

    The sub has two comments and two *programming statements*—instructions stored in a subroutine. The two statements insert the filename in the left footer and then return the spreadsheet to Normal view. In VBA, all subs end with *End Sub*.

■ **Continue to the next page to complete the skill**

Visual Basic Editor

Module2 Code window

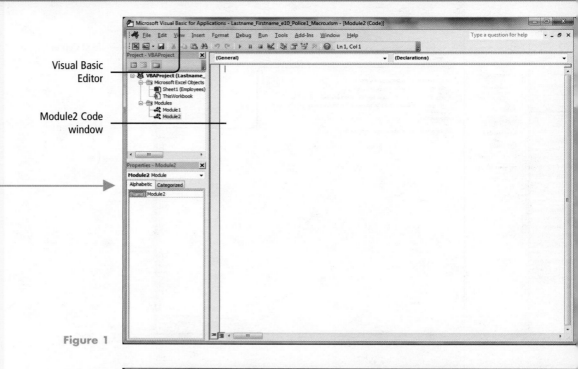

Figure 1

Two comments

Two statements

End Sub

Figure 2

VBA macro

Recorded macro

Figure 3

File name
inserted in footer

Lastname_Firstname_e10_Police1_Macro

Figure 4

6. From the **File** menu, click **Close and Return to Microsoft Excel**.

7. On the **Developer** tab, in the **Code** group, click **Macros**. Compare your screen with Figure 3.

   The Macro dialog box displays two macros, the recorded macro and the VBA macro.

8. In the **Macro** dialog box, select **InsertFileName**, and then click **Run**. If an error message displays, click the **Debug** button, and then on the **VBE Standard** toolbar, click the **Reset** button. In the displayed **Code** window, carefully check your typing, and then return to Excel.

9. On the **View** tab, in the **Workbook Views** group, click the **Page Layout** button. Scroll to display the footer, and compare your screen with Figure 4.

   The VBA macro inserted the file name in the footer.

10. Return to **Normal** view, and then click cell **A1**.

11. Display the **File** tab, and click **Options**. Click **Customize Ribbon**, and then clear the check box to display the **Developer** tab. In the left pane, click **General**, and then restore the Excel user name to the value you recorded in Skill 1. Click **OK** to accept the changes and close the dialog box.

12. **Save** 🖫 the workbook, and then print or submit it—and the snip you made previously—along with the other workbooks as directed by your instructor.

13. **Exit** Excel.

Done! You have completed Skill 10 of 10 and your workbook is complete!

The following More Skills are located at **www.pearsonhighered.com/skills**

More Skills Hide Cells

At times, you may need to show the result of a calculation without showing the formula used to reach the result, such as when the information in the formula is an industry secret. The Hide Cells feature in Excel allows you to hide the formulas of specified cells.

In More Skills 11, you will hide cells, preventing their underlying formulas from being displayed. To begin, open your web browser, navigate to www.pearsonhighered.com/skills, locate the name of your textbook, and then follow the instructions on the website.

More Skills Modify the Ribbon

As you use Excel 2010, you will discover that you begin to use the same tools regularly. Excel allows you to modify the Ribbon by creating a custom tab that contains any commands that suit your needs.

In More Skills 12, you will modify the Ribbon by creating a custom tab and adding commands to the tab. To begin, open your web browser, navigate to www.pearsonhighered.com/skills, locate the name of your textbook, and then follow the instructions on the website.

More Skills Save a Workbook as a PDF File

Users can view Excel files even if they don't have Excel installed on their computers. First, however, the Excel file must be saved in an alternate format, such as Portable Document Format (PDF).

In More Skills 13, you will save an Excel workbook in PDF format. To begin, open your web browser, navigate to www.pearsonhighered.com/skills, locate the name of your textbook, and then follow the instructions on the website.

More Skills Add a Macro Button to the Quick Access Toolbar

When you have created a macro that you use regularly, you can add a shortcut to the Quick Access Toolbar that allows you to run the macro without having to display the Developer tab on the Ribbon.

In More Skills 14, you will create a macro and then add a custom command to the Quick Access Toolbar to run the macro. To begin, open your web browser, navigate to www.pearsonhighered.com/skills, locate the name of your textbook, and then follow the instructions on the website.

Key Terms

Online Help Skills

1. Start ⊕ Excel. In the upper right corner of the Excel window, click the **Help** button ⓘ. In the Help window, click the Maximize ▭ button.

2. Click in the search box, type track changes and then click the **Search** button 🔍. In the search results, click **Track changes in a shared workbook**.

3. Read the article's introduction, and then below **In this article**, click **Changes that Excel does not track or highlight**. Compare your screen with Figure 1.

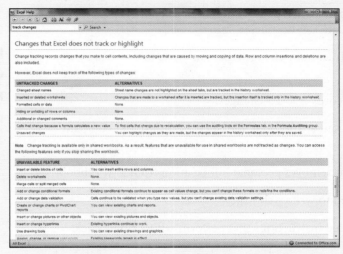

Figure 1

4. Read the section to see if you can answer the following: What are three changes that Excel does not track? What are three features of Excel that cannot be used when you share a workbook?

Matching

Match each term in the second column with its correct definition in the first column by writing the letter of the term on the blank line in front of the correct definition.

____ **1.** Descriptive text added to cells that does not modify the data in the worksheet.

____ **2.** A rule that restricts the type of data that can be entered into a cell.

____ **3.** A box that displays when data is entered in a cell that specifies what types of data can be entered into the cell.

____ **4.** A feature that tracks any changes that are made to the data in a worksheet.

____ **5.** The log that records tracked changes.

____ **6.** Information about a workbook file, such as author and company name.

____ **7.** The feature that removes personal information from a workbook.

____ **8.** A language used to write web pages.

____ **9.** A group of stored instructions that perform with a single click.

____ **10.** A high-level programming language that can be used to write and modify macros.

A Change history

B Change tracking

C Comments

D Data validation

E Document Inspector

F Document properties

G HTML

H Input message

I Macro

J Visual Basic for Applications

Multiple Choice

Choose the correct answer.

1. To assign tracked changes and comments to individual reviewers, Excel uses this file property.
   A. User name
   B. File owner
   C. File creator

2. A triangle of this color, displayed in the top-right corner of a cell, is a comment indicator.
   A. Blue
   B. Green
   C. Red

3. A triangle of this color, in the top-left corner of a cell, indicates a changed cell.
   A. Blue
   B. Green
   C. Red

4. This term refers to a workbook in which multiple users on a network can make changes at the same time.
   A. Common
   B. Shared
   C. Master

5. This process combines the changes from multiple copies of a workbook into a single copy.
   A. Compare
   B. Merge
   C. Compare and merge

6. This term is another way of referring to document properties.
   A. Metadata
   B. File information
   C. File data

7. This word describes a password that contains a combination of uppercase and lowercase letters, numbers, and symbols.
   A. Combination
   B. Strong
   C. Standard

8. VBA code is written in this window.
   A. VBE
   B. Module
   C. Code

9. These lines in the programming code document what the code does.
   A. Programming comments
   B. File notes
   C. Instructions

10. These statements are instructions stored in a subroutine.
    A. Informational
    B. Comment
    C. Programming

Topics for Discussion

1. What types of common tasks might a business worker want to automate by recording the steps in those tasks in a macro?

2. In a worksheet that you plan to give to others to use, what types of cells should be locked and what types should be unlocked?

Skill Check

To complete this workbook, you will need the following file:

- e10_Gas1

You will save your files as:

- Lastname_Firstname_e10_Gas1
- Lastname_Firstname_e10_Gas1_Macro
- Lastname_Firstname_e10_Gas2
- Lastname_Firstname_e10_Gas1_Web

1. **Start** Excel, and then open the student data file **e10_Gas1**. Save the file in your **Excel Chapter 10** folder with the name Lastname_Firstname_e10_Gas1.

2. Display the **File** tab, and then click **Options**. Note the **User name**. In the **User name** box, type your own name. Click **OK**.

3. Select cell **B14**. On the **Review** tab, click **New Comment**, and then type This is too high. Select cell **A1**, and then toggle the **Show All Comments** button off.

4. Select the range **B7:B23**. On the **Data** tab, click **Data Validation**, and then in the **Data Validation** dialog box, click the **Allow** arrow, and then click **Decimal**. In the **Minimum** box, type 25 In the **Maximum** box, type 31

5. Display the **Error Alert** tab, and then in the **Title** box, type Pressure In the **Error message** box, type Invalid Pressure and then click **OK**. Click the **Data Validation** arrow, and then click **Circle Invalid Data**. Compare your screen with **Figure 1**.

Figure 1

6. On the **Review** tab, in the **Changes** group, click **Track Changes**. Click **Highlight Changes**, and then select the **Track changes while editing** check box. Click **OK** two times. Use **Save As** to save the workbook in your **Excel Chapter 10** folder with the name Lastname_Firstname_e10_Gas2

7. Change the **User name** to Diane Payne and then make the following changes:

   Cell **A23**   4/17   Cell **B23**   25.3498

8. On the **Review** tab, click **Track Changes**. Click **Accept/Reject Changes**. Click **OK** two times. Click **Accept All**. **Save** and then **Close** the workbook.

9. Open **Lastname_Firstname_e10_Gas1**. Change the user name to your name. Display the **File** tab, and click **Options**. In the left pane, click **Quick Access Toolbar**. Click the **Customize Quick Access Toolbar** arrow, and then click **Lastname_Firstname_e10_Gas1.xlsx**. Compare your screen with **Figure 2**.

Figure 2

10. Click the **Choose commands from** arrow, and then click **Commands Not in the Ribbon**. Click **Compare and Merge Workbooks**, click **Add**, and then click **OK**.

■ Continue to the next page to complete this Skill Check

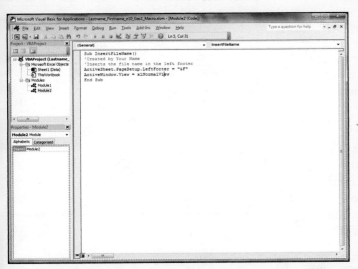

11. On the **Quick Access Toolbar**, click **Compare and Merge Workbooks**, and then click **OK**. Click **Lastname_Firstname_e10_Gas2**, and then click **OK**. On the **Review** tab, click **Track Changes**. Click **Accept/Reject Changes**. Click **OK**, and then click **Accept All**.

12. Click **Track Changes**. Click **Highlight Changes**. Clear the **Track changes while editing** check box, click **OK**, and then click **Yes**. **Save** the workbook.

13. Display the **File** tab, and click **Check for Issues**. Click **Inspect Document**. Clear the **Comments and Annotations** check box, and then click **Inspect**. Click the **Remove All** button beside **Document Properties and Personal Information**. **Close** the Document Inspector.

14. Select cell **A1**. Click **Save As**, and in the **File name** box, type Lastname_Firstname_e10_Gas1_Web Click the **Save as type** arrow, and then click **Web Page**. Navigate to your **Excel Chapter 10** folder, and then click **Publish** two times. Compare your screen with **Figure 3**, and then **Close** the web browser.

15. On the **Home** tab, in the **Cells** group, click **Format**. Click **Protect Sheet**. In the **Password to unprotect sheet** box, type Success! Click **OK**, and then type Success! and click **OK**. **Save** and then **Close** the workbook.

16. Open **e10_Gas1**. Save the file as a **Excel Macro-Enabled Workbook** in your **Excel Chapter 10** folder as Lastname_Firstname_e10_Gas1_Macro Hide all comments.

17. Display the **File** tab, and then click **Options**. Click **Customize Ribbon**. Select the **Developer** check box. Click **OK**. Select cell **A1**, and then on the **Developer** tab, click **Record Macro**. In the **Macro name** box, type InsertInfo Click **OK**. Right-click **Row 1**, and then click **Insert**. In cell **A1**, type your name. Click cell **A2**. Click **Stop Recording**.

18. On the **Developer** tab, click **Visual Basic**. In the VBE window, from the **Insert** menu, click **Module**. In the **Code** window, type the following, and then compare your screen with **Figure 4**:

```
Sub InsertFileName()
'Created by Your Name
'Inserts the file name in the left footer
ActiveSheet.PageSetup.LeftFooter = "&F"
ActiveWindow.View = xlNormalView
```

19. Click **File**, and then click **Close and Return to Microsoft Excel**. In the **Code** group, click **Macros**, click **InsertFileName**, and then click **Run**.

20. If necessary, restore the Excel user name and hide the **Developer** tab. **Save** the workbook. Print or submit the files electronically as directed by your instructor. **Exit** Excel.

Figure 3

Figure 4

Done! You have completed the Skill Check

Assess Your Skills 1

To complete this workbook, you will need the following file:

- e10_Bonds1

You will save your files as:

- Lastname_Firstname_e10_Bonds1
- Lastname_Firstname_e10_Bonds2
- Lastname_Firstname_e10_Bonds1_Web
- Lastname_Firstname_e10_Bonds1_Macro

1. **Start** Excel, and then open the student data file **e10_Bonds1**. Save the file in your **Excel Chapter 10** folder with the name Lastname_Firstname_e10_Bonds1 Change the user name to Cyril Shore

2. In cell **C7**, insert the following comment: Can this be resold? Hide all of the comments.

3. In the range **C6:C9**, write a data validation rule that requires a decimal value that is less than or equal to .04 Create an input message titled Interest Rate that displays The interest rate should not exceed 4.00% Create a **Warning Style** error alert with the title Excessive Interest Rate and the message Interest rate is too high!

4. Turn on **Track Changes**. Save the workbook as Lastname_Firstname_e10_Bonds2 Change the **User name** to *Your name*. Change cell **C7** to 3.75% Change cell **F9** to Clubhouse

5. Accept all changes. **Save** and then **Close** the workbook.

6. Open **Lastname_Firstname_e10_Bonds1**. Add the **Compare and Merge Workbooks** command to the Quick Access Toolbar. Merge **Lastname_Firstname_e10_Bonds2** with the open document. Accept all changes. Stop sharing the workbook.

7. Use the **Document Inspector** to remove all document properties except the comments.

8. Publish the entire workbook as an HTML web page file named Lastname_Firstname_e10_Bonds1_Web Title the page Aspen Falls Bonds **Save** and then **Close** the workbook.

9. Open **e10_Bonds1**. Save the file in your **Excel Chapter 10** folder as an **Excel Macro-Enabled Workbook** named Lastname_Firstname_e10_Bonds1_Macro

10. If necessary, display the **Developer** tab. Record a macro named FileInformation While recording, complete the following four tasks, and then stop recording: in the right header section, add the **Number of Pages**; in the center header section, type your name. Select cell **A1**, and then return to **Normal** View.

11. Delete the header text, and then run the macro to verify that it runs correctly.

12. In the sub, use the code from Skill 10 as your guide to type a VBA statement that inserts the file name in the left footer. Insert another VBA statement that returns the spreadsheet to Normal view. **Close** the **Visual Basic Editor**, and then run the macro.

13. If necessary, restore the Excel user name and hide the **Developer** tab. **Save** the workbook. Print or submit the files electronically as directed by your instructor. **Exit** Excel.

Done! You have completed Assess Your Skills 1

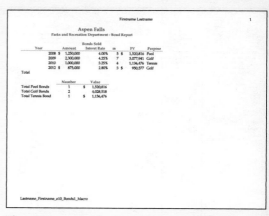

Figure 1

Assess Your Skills 2

To complete this workbook, you will need the following file:

- e10_Loan1

You will save your files as:

- **Lastname_Firstname_e10_Loan1**
- **Lastname_Firstname_e10_Loan2**
- **Lastname_Firstname_e10_Loan1_Macro**
- **Lastname_Firstname_e10_Loan1_Web**

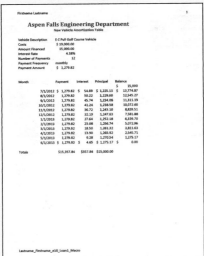

Figure 1

1. **Start** Excel, and then open the student data file **e10_Loan1**. Save the file in your **Excel Chapter 10** folder with the name Lastname_Firstname_e10_Loan1

2. Change the user name to Leah Kim Insert a comment in cell **B7** that reads Can we get a better rate? Hide all of the comments.

3. In cell **B8**, write a data validation rule that requires a decimal value that is less than or equal to 36 Create an input message titled Loan Term that displays Loan term cannot exceed 36 months Create a **Warning Style** error alert with the title Excessive Term and the message The loan term should not exceed 36 months.

4. Turn on **Track Changes**. Save the workbook as Lastname_Firstname_e10_Loan2 Change cell **B7** to 7.75 Change cell **B8** to 42 In the warning box, click **Yes**. **Reject** the change in cell **B7**. **Accept** the change in cell **B8**. **Save** and then **Close** the workbook.

5. Open **Lastname_Firstname_e10_Loan1**. Add the **Compare and Merge Workbooks** command to the Quick Access Toolbar. Merge **Lastname_Firstname_e10_Loan2** with the open workbook. **Accept** all changes. Stop sharing the workbook.

6. Use the **Document Inspector** to remove all of the document properties except the comments.

7. Publish the workbook as a web page. Save the file with the name Lastname_Firstname_e10_Loan1_ Web

8. Unlock the range **B5:B8**, and then protect the worksheet using Success! as the password. **Save** and **Close** the workbook.

9. Open **e10_Loan1**. Save the file from last pass as an **Excel Macro-Enabled Workbook** named Lastname_Firstname_e10_Loan1_Macro

10. Display the **Developer** tab. Open the **Visual Basic Editor**. Insert a new module. In the **Code** window, type the following sub and comments:

    Sub AddFooter ()
    'Created by Your Name
    'Adds the file name to the left footer

11. In the sub, use the code from Skill 10 as your guide to type a VBA statement that inserts the file name in the left footer. Insert another VBA statement that returns the spreadsheet to Normal view. Close the Visual Basic Editor. Run the macro.

12. If necessary, restore the Excel user name. **Save** the workbook. Print or submit the files electronically as directed by your instructor. **Exit** Excel.

Done! You have completed Assess Your Skills 2

Assess Your Skills Visually

To complete this workbook, you will need the following file:

- e10_Pay

You will save your files as:

- **Lastname_Firstname_e10_Pay**
- **Lastname_Firstname_e10_Pay_Snip**

Start Excel, and open the student data file **e10_Pay**. Save the file in your **Excel Chapter 10** folder with the name Lastname_Firstname_e10_Pay Apply the validation rules necessary to mark the circled invalid data as shown in Figure 1. In column C, the number of hours cannot exceed 50. In column D, the rate of pay must be between $19.00 and $44.00. The text length in column B must be four characters. When you are done, circle the invalid data to match the figure. Using the skills you previously practiced, create a full-screen snip. **Save** the snip in your **Excel Chapter 10** folder as Lastname_Firstname_e10_Pay_Snip and then **Close** the **Snipping Tool** window. **Save** the file, and then print or submit the files electronically as directed by your instructor.

Done! You have completed Assess Your Skills Visually

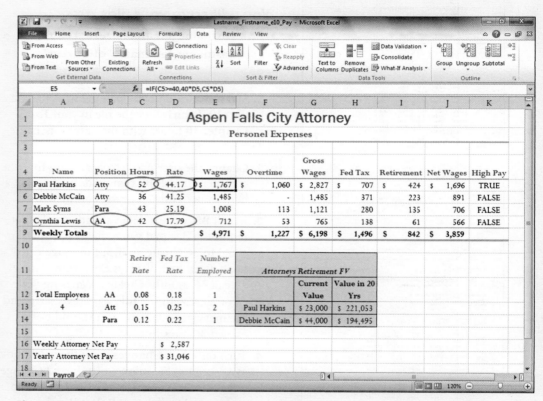

Figure 1

Skills in Context

To complete this workbook, you will need the following file:

- e10_Class

You will save your file as:

- Lastname_Firstname_e10_Class

Start Excel, and then open the student data file **e10_Class**. Save the file in your **Excel Chapter 10** folder as a macro-enabled workbook with the name Lastname_Firstname_e10_Class Record a macro named InsertData that inserts the file name in the left footer, the current date and the number of pages in the middle footer, and your name in the right footer. Assign a shortcut key of Ctrl + M to the macro. **Save** the workbook, and then print or submit the file electronically as directed by your instructor.

Done! You have completed Skills in Context

Skills and You

To complete this workbook, you will need the following file:

- New blank Excel workbook

You will save your file as:

- Lastname_Firstname_e10_Private

Using the skills you have practiced in this chapter, on your home or work computer, create a blank new worksheet. Use the Document Information Panel to view all of the document properties, and then use the Document Inspector to remove all the personal information from the workbook. Save the file and then submit as directed by your instructor.

Done! You have completed Skills and You

Glossary

3-D Short for three-dimensional.

Absolute cell reference A cell reference that remains the same when it is copied or filled to other cells. An absolute cell reference takes the form $A$1.

Accounting number format A number format that applies comma separators where appropriate, inserts a fixed U.S. dollar sign aligned at the left edge of the cell, applies two decimal places, and leaves a small amount of space at both the right and left edges of the cell to accommodate parentheses for negative numbers.

Active cell The cell outlined in black in which data is entered when you begin typing.

Alternate Text Hidden text that is added to images so that persons who are visually impaired will be provided with a description of the image if they are using a screen reader.

Amortization tables Tables that are used to track loan payments for the life of a loan.

Area chart A chart type that emphasizes the magnitude of change over time.

Argument The values that a function uses to perform operations or calculations. The type of argument a function uses is specific to the function. Common arguments include numbers, text, cell references, and names.

Arithmetic operator A symbol that specifies a mathematical operation such as addition or subtraction.

Artistic Effects Changes that can be applied to images to make them more visually appealing.

Aspect ratio The ratio of the width and height of an image expressed as its width divided by its height.

AutoFit Automatically changes the column width to accommodate the longest entry.

AVERAGE function A function that adds a group of values and then divides the result by the number of values in the group.

Axis A line bordering the chart plot area used as a frame of reference for measurement.

Background color The shading assigned to a cell.

Bar chart A chart type that illustrates comparisons among individual items.

Bulleted list A list of items that are preceded by symbols.

Calculated column An Excel table feature that uses a single formula that adjusts for each row and automatically expands to include additional rows so that the formula is immediately extended to those rows.

Calculated field A new data field whose values come from a custom calculation.

Category axis The axis that displays the category labels.

Category label A label that identifies the categories of data in a chart.

Cell The box formed by the intersection of a row and column.

Cell address The column letter and row number that identify a cell; also called the cell reference.

Cell border Decorative lines that can be applied to worksheet cells.

Cell fill color The shading assigned to a cell—also known as a background color.

Cell reference The column letter and row number that identify a cell; also called a cell address.

Cell style A prebuilt set of formatting characteristics, such as font, font size, font color, cell borders, and cell shading.

Change history A log that records each data change, who made the change, and when the data was changed.

Change tracking A feature that details the changes made to a worksheet.

Character graphic A small graphic character that is based on text characters that can be formatted as text.

Chart A graphic representation of data used to show comparisons, patterns, and trends.

Chart layout A prebuilt set of chart elements that can include a title, legend, and labels.

Chart sheet A workbook sheet that contains only a chart and is useful when you want to view a chart separately from the worksheet data.

Chart style A prebuilt chart format that applies an overall visual look to a chart by modifying its graphic effects, colors, and backgrounds.

Clip art Images that are included with Microsoft Office or obtained from other sources that can be inserted into workbooks.

Clipboard A temporary storage area that holds text or an object that has been cut or copied.

Clustered bar chart A chart type useful for comparing values across categories; bar charts organize categories along the vertical axis and values along the horizontal axis.

Code window The window in which VBA code is written.

Color scales Visual guides that help the user understand data distribution and variation.

Column chart A chart type useful for illustrating comparisons among related categories.

Column heading The letter that displays at the top of a column.

Comma cell style A cell style that adds commas where appropriate and applies the same formatting as the Accounting number format but without a dollar sign.

Comma-separated values Text that uses commas to separate each column of text.

Comment A note that is attached to a cell, separate from other cell content.

Comment (programming) Statement that explains what the code does.

Comment (reviewer) Descriptive text that can be added to cells without modifying the data in the worksheet.

Comment indicator A small red triangle in the upper right corner of a cell that indicates a comment is attached to the cell.

Compare and merge A process that combines the changes from multiple copies of a workbook into a single copy.

Comparison operator An operator used to compare two values; for example, = (equal to) and < (less than).

Compress Change the way the image is stored, which reduces the size of the file.

CONCATENATE A text function used to join text in two cells into one cell.

Conditional formatting A type of formatting that applies formatting only to values that meet the conditions that you specify.

Contents Underlying formulas and data in a cell.

Contrast The difference between light and dark areas in an image.

Copy A command that places a copy of the selected text or object in the Clipboard.

COUNTA A function that counts the number of cells containing the values that you specify. When no values are specified, it counts the number of cells in a range that are not blank.

COUNTIF A function that counts the number of cells in a range that meet a specified condition. The condition might be a number, an expression, or text.

Criteria Conditions specified to limit choices.

Crop Remove unwanted areas along the edges of a graphic or picture.

Cut A command that removes the selected text or object and stores it in the Clipboard.

Data bar Provides a visual cue to the reader about the value of a cell relative to other cells. The length of the data bar represents the value in the cell.

Data marker A column, bar, area, dot, pie slice, or other symbol that represents a single data point.

Data point A chart value that originates in an Excel worksheet cell, a Word table cell, or an Access field.

Data series In a chart, data points that are related to one another.

Data table A range of cells that is set up to show how changing one or two values in a formula will affect the result of the formulas.

Data validation rules Rules that place restrictions on the types of data that can be entered in cells.

Delimited text file A file where the data in each field is separated by the Tab character.

Delimiter A character used to separate columns of text in a data table.

Dependent Any cell value that depends on the value in a given cell.

Detail sheet A worksheet with cells referred to by summary sheet formulas.

Dialog box A box where you can select multiple settings.

Displayed value Data displayed in a cell.

Document Information Panel A panel that displays above the worksheet window in which properties or property information is added, viewed, or updated.

Document properties Information about a document that can help you identify or organize your files, such as the name of the document author, the file name, and keywords.

Document theme A set of design elements that provides a unified look for colors, fonts, and graphics.

Dpi Dots per square inch.

Drag To move the mouse while holding down the left mouse button and then to release it at the appropriate time.

Drag and drop A method of moving objects, in which a selection is pointed to and then dragged to a new location.

Edit To insert text, delete text, or replace text in an Office document, spreadsheet, or presentation.

Embedded chart A chart that is placed on the worksheet containing the data. An embedded chart is beneficial when you want to view or print a chart with its source data.

Error indicator A green triangle that indicates a possible error in a formula.

Error value A message that displays whenever a formula cannot perform the calculations in the formula.

Excel add-in A tool that adds features and commands, extending Excel's capabilities as if the tool's capabilities were part of Excel.

Excel table A series of rows and columns that contain related data that is managed independently from the data in other rows and columns on the worksheet.

Explode Pulling out one or more slices of a 3-D pie chart to emphasize a specific slice or slices.

Field In a PivotTable, summarizes multiple rows of information from the source data.

Fill handle The small black square in the lower right corner of the selection.

Filter A feature that hides Excel rows or Access records that do not meet certain criteria.

Find and Replace A command that enables you to find and then replace a character or string of characters in a worksheet or in a selected range.

Format Painter A tool used to copy formatting from one place to another.

Format To change the appearance of the text, such as changing the text color to red.

Formula An equation that performs mathematical calculations on number values in the workshee

Formula AutoComplete A feature that assists in inserting functions.

Formula bar A bar below the Ribbon that displays the value contained in the active cell and is used to enter or edit values or formulas.

Freeze Panes A command used to keep rows or columns visible when scrolling in a worksheet. The frozen rows and columns become separate panes.

Function A prewritten Excel formula that takes a value or values, performs an operation, and returns a value or values.

Future value (Fv) In a loan, the value at the end of the time periods, or the cash balance you want to attain after the last loan payment is made. The future value for a loan is usually zero.

Gallery A visual display of choices from which you can choose.

General format The default number format that does not display commas or trailing zeros to the right of a decimal point.

Goal Seek A what-if analysis tool that finds a specific value for a cell by adjusting the value of another cell.

Grayscale A range of shades of gray.

Grid line A line between the cells in a table or spreadsheet.

Group Merge separate objects into one object that can be resized as a single object.

HTML (Hypertext Markup Language) A language used to mark up text files so that they can be viewed on the Internet.

Hyperlink Text or other object that displays another document, a location within a document, or a web page on the Internet.

Icon Set A type of conditional formatting that classifies a range of data into three to five categories and displays small graphics in each cell depending on that cell's value.

IF function A function that checks whether criteria is met and then returns one value when the condition is TRUE and another value when the condition is FALSE.

Information function An Excel function that provides information about the cell contents.

Input message A data validation message that informs the data entry operator about the types of data that can be entered into the cell.

Insertion point A vertical line that indicates where text will be inserted when you start typing.

Interest The charge for borrowing money; generally a percentage of the amount borrowed.

KeyTip An icon that displays in the Ribbon to indicate the key that you can press to access Ribbon commands.

Label Text data in a cell; also called a text value.

Legend A box that identifies the patterns or colors that are assigned to the data series or categories in the chart.

Line chart A chart type that illustrates trends over time, with time displayed along the x-axis and the data point values connected by a line.

Live Preview A feature that displays the result of a formatting change if you select it.

Logical function A function that applies a logical test to determine whether a specific condition is met.

Logical function A function used to create a formula that always has a result of either TRUE or FALSE.

Logical test Any value or expression that can be evaluated as TRUE or FALSE.

Lookup function A type of function that is used to find values that are stored in a table in a spreadsheet.

Lookup table Data that is organized into rows and columns so that values can be easily retrieved.

Macro A stored set of instructions that automates common tasks.

Malware Software that is designed to harm a computer.

MAX function A function that returns the largest value in a range of cells.

Metadata Information that describes the data in an Excel file.

MIN function A function that returns the smallest value in a range of cells.

Mini toolbar A toolbar with common formatting buttons that displays after you highlight text.

Name A word that represents a cell or a range of cells that can be used as a cell or range reference. Names used in formulas and functions clarify the meaning of the formula and assist in navigating large worksheets.

Name Box An area by the formula bar that displays the active cell reference.

Nested function A function that is placed inside another function.

Normal view A view that maximizes the number of cells visible on the screen.

NOW function A function that returns the serial number of the current date and time.

Number format A specific way that Excel displays numbers.

Number value Numeric data in a cell.

One-variable data table A data table that changes one value in a formula using input from either a row or a column.

Operator precedence The mathematical rules for performing calculations within a formula.

OR A logical operator that returns true if either of one criteria is true.

Organization chart A chart that graphically represents the hierarchy of relationships between individuals and groups in an organization.

Page Layout view A view where you prepare your document or spreadsheet for printing.

Paste To insert a copy of the text or an object stored in the Clipboard.

Paste area The target destination for data that has been cut or copied.

Pie chart A chart type that illustrates the relationship of parts to a whole.

PivotChart report A dynamic visual representation of data.

PivotTable report An interactive, cross-tabulated Excel report that summarizes and analyzes data—such as database records—from various sources, including ones that are external to Excel.

PivotTable values The fields for which summary statistics are calculated.

PMT function Calculates the payment for a loan based on constant payments and a constant interest rate.

Precedent Any cell value that is referred to in a formula and function.

Present value (Pv) The initial amount of the loan; the total amount that a series of future payments is worth today.

Principal The initial amount of the loan; the total amount that a series of future payments is worth today. Also called the present value (Pv) of a loan.

Programming statements Instructions stored in a subroutine.

PROPER A function that converts text to initial case—the first letter of each word is capitalized.

Protected View A view applied to documents downloaded from the Internet that allows you to decide if the content is safe before working with the document.

Quick Styles Prebuilt sets of formatting options that can be applied to a document or an object.

RAM The computer's temporary memory.

Range Two or more cells on a worksheet that are adjacent.

Range finder An Excel feature that outlines all of the cells referenced in a formula. It is useful for verifying which cells are used in a formula and for editing formulas.

Rate The percentage that is paid for the use of borrowed money.

Read-only mode A mode where you cannot save your changes.

Record A collection of related information that displays in a single row of a database table.

Relative cell reference Refers to cells based on their position in relation to (relative to) the cell that contains the formula.

Resolution Refers to the number of dots per square inch—also known as dpi.

Right-click Click the paragraph with the right mouse button.

Row heading The number that displays at the left of a row.

Row label Used to categorize the data by rows.

Scenario A set of values that Excel can save and automatically substitute in cells.

Screen clipping A picture of a portion of your computer screen that you insert into your worksheet.

Screen shot A picture of your computer screen, a window, or a selected region saved as a file that can be printed or shared electronically.

ScreenTip Informational text that displays when you point to commands or thumbnails in the Ribbon.

Sepia A range of shades of brown.

Serial number A sequential number.

Series A group of numbers, text, dates, or time periods that come one after another in succession—for example, the months January, February, March.

Shape fill The background color of the shape.

Shared workbook A workbook in which multiple users on a network can make changes to the workbook at the same time.

Sheet tab A label along the lower border of the workbook window that identifies each worksheet or chart sheet.

Shortcut menu A list of commands related to the type of object that you right-click.

Slicer A tool that is used to filter data in PivotTable views.

SmartArt A visual representation of information that is used to communicate a message.

Snip A screen capture created with the Snipping Tool.

Source data The data used to create a PivotTable report.

Sparkline A tiny chart used to show data trends.

Spreadsheet The primary document that you use in Excel to store and work with data; also called a worksheet.

Statistical function A predefined formula that describes a collection of data—for example, totals, counts, and averages.

String Any sequence of letters and numbers in a field.

Strong password A password that contains a combination of uppercase and lowercase letters, numbers, and symbols.

Style A group of formatting choices that can be applied in a single step.

Sub (VBA) A group of instructions that is a subset of a program.

SUM An Excel function that adds all the numbers in a range of cells.

SUMIF A function that is used to calculate the total of a range using only cells that meet a specified condition.

Summary sheet A worksheet that displays and summarizes totals from other worksheets.

Symbol A character such as the copyright symbol © or a bullet character that is not found on common keyboards.

Tab scrolling buttons The buttons to the left of the sheet tabs used to display Excel sheet tabs that are not in view.

Table quick style A collection of table formatting options that can be applied to a range with a single click.

Template A prebuilt workbook used as a pattern for creating new workbooks. You use a template to build a workbook without having to start from a blank workbook.

Text box A rectangular object that is placed on a worksheet that can contain text that is typed by the user.

Text file A file that stores only the text characters but not the formatting, Tab stops, or tables.

Text format A formatting rule that treats the cell value as text even when the cell contains numbers.

Text value Character data in a cell; also called a label.

Text wrap A format that displays text on multiple lines within a cell.

Theme A set of unified design elements that provides a unique look for your presentation, using colors, fonts, and graphics.

Three-color scale A color scale that compares a range of cells by using a gradation of three colors; the shades represent higher, middle, or lower values.

Three-dimensional Refers to an image that appears to have all three spatial dimensions—length, width, and depth.

Thumbnail A small sample image of a style.

Toggle button A button used to turn a feature both on and off.

Top/Bottom Rules Enables the user to apply conditional formatting to the highest or lowest values in a range of cells.

Total cell style A cell style that applies a single top border, which indicates that calculations were performed on the numbers above, and a double bottom border, which indicates that the calculations are complete.

Total row A row that displays as the last row in an Excel table and provides functions in drop-down lists for each column.

Triple-click Click three times fairly quickly without moving the mouse.

Truncated Cut off.

Two-color scale A color scale that compares a range of cells by using a gradation of two colors; the shade of the color represents higher or lower values.

Two-variable data table A data table that uses two inputs—one from a column and one from a row.

Underlying formula The formula as displayed in the formula bar.

Underlying value Data displayed in the formula bar.

Value Data in a cell.

Value axis The axis that displays the worksheet's numeric data.

Visual Basic for Applications (VBA) A high-level programming language used to write and modify macros.

Volatile The result of a function will not remain as entered but will be updated each time the workbook is opened.

Watch Window toolbar A toolbar that is used to watch cells and the formulas in those cells when they are not visible on the screen.

Watermark A graphic inserted into a workbook background, usually in the header.

Web queries Requests that are sent to web pages to retrieve and display data in Excel workbooks.

What-if analysis Tools that change the values in cells to show how those changes affect the outcome of other formulas on the worksheet.

Windows Live A free online storage that can be used to save and open your files from any computer connected to the Internet.

Windows Live ID A unique name and password—a Hotmail or Windows Live e-mail user name and password, for example.

Windows Live network A group of people whom you have invited to share files or to chat using Instant Messenger.

Workbook A file that you can use to organize various kinds of related information.

Worksheet The primary document you use in Excel to store and work with data; also called a spreadsheet.

X-axis Another name for the horizontal axis of a chart.

Y-axis Another name for the vertical axis of a chart.

Index

The internet icon represents Index entries found within More Skills on the Companion Website: www.pearsonhighered.com/skills

Skills for Success with Excel 2010 | Index **375**

SINGLE PC LICENSE AGREEMENT AND LIMITED WARRANTY

READ THIS LICENSE CAREFULLY BEFORE OPENING THIS PACKAGE. BY OPENING THIS PACKAGE, YOU ARE AGREEING TO THE TERMS AND CONDITIONS OF THIS LICENSE. IF YOU DO NOT AGREE, DO NOT OPEN THE PACKAGE. PROMPTLY RETURN THE UNOPENED PACKAGE AND ALL ACCOMPANYING ITEMS TO THE PLACE YOU OBTAINED THEM. *THESE TERMS APPLY TO ALL LICENSED SOFTWARE ON THE DISK EXCEPT THAT THE TERMS FOR USE OF ANY SHAREWARE OR FREEWARE ON THE DISKETTES ARE AS SET FORTH IN THE ELECTRONIC LICENSE LOCATED ON THE DISK:*

1. GRANT OF LICENSE and OWNERSHIP: The enclosed computer programs ("Software") are licensed, not sold, to you by Prentice-Hall, Inc. ("We" or the "Company") and in consideration of your purchase or adoption of the accompanying Company textbooks and/or other materials, and your agreement to these terms. We reserve any rights not granted to you. You own only the disk(s) but we and/or our licensors own the Software itself. This license allows you to use and display your copy of the Software on a single computer (i.e., with a single CPU) at a single location for academic use only, so long as you comply with the terms of this Agreement. You may make one copy for back up, or transfer your copy to another CPU, provided that the Software is usable on only one computer.

2. RESTRICTIONS: You may not transfer or distribute the Software or documentation to anyone else. Except for backup, you may not copy the documentation or the Software. You may not network the Software or otherwise use it on more than one computer or computer terminal at the same time. You may not reverse engineer, disassemble, decompile, modify, adapt, translate, or create derivative works based on the Software or the Documentation. You may be held legally responsible for any copying or copyright infringement which is caused by your failure to abide by the terms of these restrictions.

3. TERMINATION: This license is effective until terminated. This license will terminate automatically without notice from the Company if you fail to comply with any provisions or limitations of this license. Upon termination, you shall destroy the Documentation and all copies of the Software. All provisions of this Agreement as to limitation and disclaimer of warranties, limitation of liability, remedies or damages, and our ownership rights shall survive termination.

4. DISCLAIMER OF WARRANTY: THE COMPANY AND ITS LICENSORS MAKE NO WARRANTIES ABOUT THE SOFTWARE, WHICH IS PROVIDED "AS-IS." IF THE DISK IS DEFECTIVE IN MATERIALS OR WORKMANSHIP, YOUR ONLY REMEDY IS TO RETURN IT TO THE COMPANY WITHIN 30 DAYS FOR REPLACEMENT UNLESS THE COMPANY DETERMINES IN GOOD FAITH THAT THE DISK HAS BEEN MISUSED OR IMPROPERLY INSTALLED, REPAIRED, ALTERED OR DAMAGED. THE COMPANY DISCLAIMS ALL WARRANTIES, EXPRESS OR IMPLIED, INCLUDING WITHOUT LIMITATION, THE IMPLIED WARRANTIES OF MERCHANTABILITY AND FITNESS FOR A PARTICULAR PURPOSE. THE COMPANY DOES NOT WARRANT, GUARANTEE OR MAKE ANY REPRESENTATION REGARDING THE ACCURACY, RELIABILITY, CURRENTNESS, USE, OR RESULTS OF USE, OF THE SOFTWARE.

5. LIMITATION OF REMEDIES AND DAMAGES: IN NO EVENT, SHALL THE COMPANY OR ITS EMPLOYEES, AGENTS, LICENSORS OR CONTRACTORS BE LIABLE FOR ANY INCIDENTAL, INDIRECT, SPECIAL OR CONSEQUENTIAL DAMAGES ARISING OUT OF OR IN CONNECTION WITH THIS LICENSE OR THE SOFTWARE, INCLUDING, WITHOUT LIMITATION, LOSS OF USE, LOSS OF DATA, LOSS OF INCOME OR PROFIT, OR OTHER LOSSES SUSTAINED AS A RESULT OF INJURY TO ANY PERSON, OR LOSS OF OR DAMAGE TO PROPERTY, OR CLAIMS OF THIRD PARTIES, EVEN IF THE COMPANY OR AN AUTHORIZED REPRESENTATIVE OF THE COMPANY HAS BEEN ADVISED OF THE POSSIBILITY OF SUCH DAMAGES. SOME JURISDICTIONS DO NOT ALLOW THE LIMITATION OF DAMAGES IN CERTAIN CIRCUMSTANCES, SO THE ABOVE LIMITATIONS MAY NOT ALWAYS APPLY.

6. GENERAL: THIS AGREEMENT SHALL BE CONSTRUED IN ACCORDANCE WITH THE LAWS OF THE UNITED STATES OF AMERICA AND THE STATE OF NEW YORK, APPLICABLE TO CONTRACTS MADE IN NEW YORK, AND SHALL BENEFIT THE COMPANY, ITS AFFILIATES AND ASSIGNEES. This Agreement is the complete and exclusive statement of the agreement between you and the Company and supersedes all proposals, prior agreements, oral or written, and any other communications between you and the company or any of its representatives relating to the subject matter. If you are a U.S. Government user, this Software is licensed with "restricted rights" as set forth in subparagraphs (a)-(d) of the Commercial Computer-Restricted Rights clause at FAR 52.227-19 or in subparagraphs (c)(1)(ii) of the Rights in Technical Data and Computer Software clause at DFARS 252.227-7013, and similar clauses, as applicable.

Should you have any questions concerning this agreement or if you wish to contact the Company for any reason, please contact in writing:

Multimedia Production
Higher Education Division
Prentice-Hall, Inc.
1 Lake Street
Upper Saddle River NJ 07458